S 1958124

Twentieth-Century Literary Criticism

Topics Volume

Guide to Gale Literary Criticism Series

For criticism on	Consult these Gale series
Authors now living or who died after December 31, 1999	**CONTEMPORARY LITERARY CRITICISM (CLC)**
Authors who died between 1900 and 1999	**TWENTIETH-CENTURY LITERARY CRITICISM (TCLC)**
Authors who died between 1800 and 1899	**NINETEENTH-CENTURY LITERATURE CRITICISM (NCLC)**
Authors who died between 1400 and 1799	**LITERATURE CRITICISM FROM 1400 TO 1800 (LC)** **SHAKESPEAREAN CRITICISM (SC)**
Authors who died before 1400	**CLASSICAL AND MEDIEVAL LITERATURE CRITICISM (CMLC)**
Authors of books for children and young adults	**CHILDREN'S LITERATURE REVIEW (CLR)**
Dramatists	**DRAMA CRITICISM (DC)**
Poets	**POETRY CRITICISM (PC)**
Short story writers	**SHORT STORY CRITICISM (SSC)**
Black writers of the past two hundred years	**BLACK LITERATURE CRITICISM (BLC)** **BLACK LITERATURE CRITICISM SUPPLEMENT (BLCS)**
Hispanic writers of the late nineteenth and twentieth centuries	**HISPANIC LITERATURE CRITICISM (HLC)** **HISPANIC LITERATURE CRITICISM SUPPLEMENT (HLCS)**
Native North American writers and orators of the eighteenth, nineteenth, and twentieth centuries	**NATIVE NORTH AMERICAN LITERATURE (NNAL)**
Major authors from the Renaissance to the present	**WORLD LITERATURE CRITICISM, 1500 TO THE PRESENT (WLC)** **WORLD LITERATURE CRITICISM SUPPLEMENT (WLCS)**

Volume 122

Twentieth-Century Literary Criticism

Topics Volume

Criticism of Various Topics in Twentieth-Century Literature, including Literary and Critical Movements, Prominent Themes and Genres, Anniversary Celebrations, and Surveys of National Literatures

Janet Witalec
Project Editor

Detroit • New York • San Diego • San Francisco • Cleveland • New Haven, Conn. • Waterville, Maine • London • Munich

Twentieth-Century Literary Criticism, Vol. 122

Project Editor
Janet Witalec

Editorial
Jenny Cromie, Scott Darga, Kathy D. Darrow, Julie Keppen, Ellen McGeagh, Linda Pavlovski

Research
Nicodemus Ford, Sarah Genik, Tamara C. Nott, Tracie A. Richardson

Permissions
Shalice Shah-Caldwell

Product Design
Michael Logusz

Composition and Electronic Capture
Carolyn Roney

Manufacturing
Stacy L. Melson

© 2002 by Gale. Gale is an imprint of The Gale Group, Inc., a division of Thomson Learning, Inc.

Gale and Design™ and Thomson Learning™ are trademarks used herein under license.

For more information, contact
The Gale Group, Inc.
27500 Drake Rd.
Farmington Hills, MI 48331-3535
Or you can visit our internet site at
http://www.gale.com

ALL RIGHTS RESERVED
No part of this work covered by the copyright herein may be reproduced or used in any form or by any means—graphic, electronic, or mechanical, including photocopying, recording, taping, Web distribution, or information storage retrieval systems—without the written permission of the publisher.

This publication is a creative work fully protected by all applicable copyright laws, as well as by misappropriation, trade secret, unfair competition, and other applicable laws. The authors and editors of this work have added value to the underlying factual material herein through one or more of the following: unique and original selection, coordination, expression, arrangement, and classification of the information.

For permission to use material from the product, submit your request via the Web at http://www.gale-edit.com/permissions, or you may download our Permissions Request form and submit your request by fax or mail to:

Permisssions Department
The Gale Group, Inc.
27500 Drake Rd.
Farmington Hills, MI 48331-3535
Permissions Hotline:
248-699-8006 or 800-877-4253, ext. 8006
Fax 248-699-8074 or 800-762-4058

Since this page cannot legibly accommodate all copyright notices, the acknowledgments constitute an extension of the copyright notice.

While every effort has been made to secure permission to reprint material and to ensure the reliability of the information presented in this publication, the Gale Group neither guarantees the accuracy of the data contained herein nor assumes any responsibility for errors, omissions or discrepancies. Gale accepts no payment for listing; and inclusion in the publication of any organization, agency, institution, publication, service, or individual does not imply endorsement of the editors or publisher. Errors brought to the attention of the publisher and verified to the satisfaction of the publisher will be corrected in future editions.

LIBRARY OF CONGRESS CATALOG CARD NUMBER 76-46132

ISBN 0-7876-5936-3
ISSN 0276-8178

Printed in the United States of America
10 9 8 7 6 5 4 3 2 1

Contents

Preface vii

Acknowledgments xi

Literary Criticism Series Advisory Board xiii

Exile in Literature
Introduction 1
Representative Works 1
Overviews and General Studies 2
Exile in Fiction 33
German Literature in Exile 92
Further Reading 129

Literary Prizes
Introduction 130
Representative Works 130
Overviews and General Studies 131
The Nobel Prize in Literature 135
The Pulitzer Prize 183
Further Reading 203

Modern French Literature
Introduction 205
Representative Works 206
Overviews and General Studies 207
French Theater 243
Gender Issues and French Women Writers 277
Ideology and Politics 315
Modern French Poetry 324
Resistance Literature 341
Further Reading 359

Literary Criticism Series Cumulative Author Index 361

Literary Criticism Series Cumulative Topic Index 449

TCLC Cumulative Nationality Index 459

Preface

Since its inception more than fifteen years ago, *Twentieth-Century Literary Criticism* (*TCLC*) has been purchased and used by nearly 10,000 school, public, and college or university libraries. *TCLC* has covered more than 500 authors, representing 58 nationalities and over 25,000 titles. No other reference source has surveyed the critical response to twentieth-century authors and literature as thoroughly as *TCLC*. In the words of one reviewer, "there is nothing comparable available." *TCLC* "is a gold mine of information—dates, pseudonyms, biographical information, and criticism from books and periodicals—which many librarians would have difficulty assembling on their own."

Scope of the Series

TCLC is designed to serve as an introduction to authors who died between 1900 and 1999 and to the most significant interpretations of these author's works. Volumes published from 1978 through 1999 included authors who died between 1900 and 1960. The great poets, novelists, short story writers, playwrights, and philosophers of the period are frequently studied in high school and college literature courses. In organizing and reprinting the vast amount of critical material written on these authors, *TCLC* helps students develop valuable insight into literary history, promotes a better understanding of the texts, and sparks ideas for papers and assignments. Each entry in *TCLC* presents a comprehensive survey on an author's career or an individual work of literature and provides the user with a multiplicity of interpretations and assessments. Such variety allows students to pursue their own interests; furthermore, it fosters an awareness that literature is dynamic and responsive to many different opinions.

Every fourth volume of *TCLC* is devoted to literary topics. These topics widen the focus of the series from the individual authors to such broader subjects as literary movements, prominent themes in twentieth-century literature, literary reaction to political and historical events, significant eras in literary history, prominent literary anniversaries, and the literatures of cultures that are often overlooked by English-speaking readers.

TCLC is designed as a companion series to Gale's *Contemporary Literary Criticism*, (*CLC*) which reprints commentary on authors who died after 1999. Because of the different time periods under consideration, there is no duplication of material between *CLC* and *TCLC*.

Organization of the Book

A *TCLC* entry consists of the following elements:

- The **Author Heading** cites the name under which the author most commonly wrote, followed by birth and death dates. Also located here are any name variations under which an author wrote, including transliterated forms for authors whose native languages use nonroman alphabets. If the author wrote consistently under a pseudonym, the pseudonym will be listed in the author heading and the author's actual name given in parenthesis on the first line of the biographical and critical information. Uncertain birth or death dates are indicated by question marks. Single-work entries are preceded by a heading that consists of the most common form of the title in English translation (if applicable) and the original date of composition.

- A **Portrait of the Author** is included when available.

- The **Introduction** contains background information that introduces the reader to the author, work, or topic that is the subject of the entry.

- The list of **Principal Works** is ordered chronologically by date of first publication and lists the most important works by the author. The genre and publication date of each work is given. In the case of foreign authors whose works have been translated into English, the English-language version of the title follows in brackets. Unless otherwise indicated, dramas are dated by first performance, not first publication.

- Reprinted **Criticism** is arranged chronologically in each entry to provide a useful perspective on changes in critical evaluation over time. The critic's name and the date of composition or publication of the critical work are given at the beginning of each piece of criticism. Unsigned criticism is preceded by the title of the source in which it appeared. All titles by the author featured in the text are printed in boldface type. Footnotes are reprinted at the end of each essay or excerpt. In the case of excerpted criticism, only those footnotes that pertain to the excerpted texts are included.

- A complete **Bibliographical Citation** of the original essay or book precedes each piece of criticism.

- Critical essays are prefaced by brief **Annotations** explicating each piece.

- An annotated bibliography of **Further Reading** appears at the end of each entry and suggests resources for additional study. In some cases, significant essays for which the editors could not obtain reprint rights are included here. Boxed material following the further reading list provides references to other biographical and critical sources on the author in series published by Gale.

Indexes

A **Cumulative Author Index** lists all of the authors that appear in a wide variety of reference sources published by the Gale Group, including *TCLC*. A complete list of these sources is found facing the first page of the Author Index. The index also includes birth and death dates and cross references between pseudonyms and actual names.

A **Cumulative Nationality Index** lists all authors featured in *TCLC* by nationality, followed by the number of the *TCLC* volume in which their entry appears.

A **Cumulative Topic Index** lists the literary themes and topics treated in the series as well as in *Classical and Medieval Literature Criticism, Literature Criticism from 1400 to 1800, Nineteenth-Century Literature Criticism,* and the *Contemporary Literary Criticism* Yearbook, which was discontinued in 1998.

An alphabetical **Title Index** accompanies each volume of *TCLC*. Listings of titles by authors covered in the given volume are followed by the author's name and the corresponding page numbers where the titles are discussed. English translations of foreign titles and variations of titles are cross-referenced to the title under which a work was originally published. Titles of novels, dramas, nonfiction books, and poetry, short story, or essay collections are printed in italics, while individual poems, short stories, and essays are printed in roman type within quotation marks.

In response to numerous suggestions from librarians, Gale also produces an annual paperbound edition of the *TCLC* cumulative title index. This annual cumulation, which alphabetically lists all titles reviewed in the series, is available to all customers. Additional copies of this index are available upon request. Librarians and patrons will welcome this separate index; it saves shelf space, is easy to use, and is recyclable upon receipt of the next edition.

Citing *Twentieth-Century Literary Criticism*

When writing papers, students who quote directly from any volume in the Literary Criticism Series may use the following general format to footnote reprinted criticism. The first example pertains to material drawn from periodicals, the second to material reprinted from books.

George Orwell, "Reflections on Gandhi," *Partisan Review* 6 (Winter 1949): 85-92; reprinted in *Twentieth-Century Literary Criticism,* vol. 59, ed. Jennifer Gariepy (Detroit: The Gale Group, 1995), 40-3.

William H. Slavick, "Going to School to DuBose Heyward," *The Harlem Renaissance Re-examined,* ed. Victor A. Kramer (AMS, 1987), 65- 91; reprinted in *Twentieth-Century Literary Criticism,* vol. 59, ed. Jennifer Gariepy (Detroit: The Gale Group, 1995), 94-105.

Suggestions are Welcome

Readers who wish to suggest new features, topics, or authors to appear in future volumes, or who have other suggestions or comments are cordially invited to call, write, or fax the Project Editor:

Project Editor, Literary Criticism Series
The Gale Group
27500 Drake Road
Farmington Hills, MI 48331-3535
1-800-347-4253 (GALE)
Fax: 248-699-8054

Acknowledgments

The editors wish to thank the copyright holders of the excerpted criticism included in this volume and the permissions managers of many book and magazine publishing companies for assisting us in securing reproduction rights. We are also grateful to the staffs of the Detroit Public Library, the Library of Congress, the University of Detroit Mercy Library, Wayne State University Purdy/Kresge Library Complex, and the University of Michigan Libraries for making their resources available to us. Following is a list of the copyright holders who have granted us permission to reproduce material in this volume of *TCLC*. Every effort has been made to trace copyright, but if omissions have been made, please let us know.

COPYRIGHTED MATERIAL IN *TCLC*, VOLUME 122, WAS REPRODUCED FROM THE FOLLOWING PERIODICALS:

The Horn Book Magazine, v. lxxvii, May-June, 2001. © 2001 Horn Book Inc. Reproduced by permission.—*Journal of European Studies,* v. 15, June, 1985. © 1985 Science History Publications Ltd. Reproduced by permission.—*Modern Language Review,* v. 96, January, 2001. © Modern Humanities Research Association 2001. Reproduced by permission.—*Publishers Weekly,* v. 232, December 18, 1987. Copyright 1987 by Reed Publishing USA. Reproduced by permission.—*Victorians Institute Journal,* v. 28, 2000. Reproduced by permission.—*World Literature Today,* v. 55, Summer, 1981; v. 62, Spring, 1988.. Copyright 1981, 1988 by the University of Oklahoma Press. Both reproduced by permission.

COPYRIGHTED MATERIAL IN *TCLC*, VOLUME 122, WAS REPRODUCED FROM THE FOLLOWING BOOKS:

Adler, Thomas P. From *Mirror on the Stage: The Pulitzers Plays as an Approach to American Drama.* Purdue University Press, 1987. Copyright © 1987 by Purdue Research Foundation. All rights reserved. Reproduced by permission.—Atack, Margaret. From *Literature and the French Resistance: Cultural Politics and Narrative Forms, 1940-1950.* Manchester University Press, 1989. © Margaret Atack 1989. Reproduced by permission of the author.—Balakian, Anna. From *Writing In a Modern Temper: Essay on French Literature and Thought in Honor of Henri Peyre.* Edited by Mary Ann Caws. ANMA Libri, 1984. © 1984 by ANMA Libri & Co. All rights reserved. Reproduced by permission of the publisher and the Literary Estate of Anna Balakian.—Berghaus, Gunter. From *Theatre and Film in Exile: German Artists in Great Britain, 1933-1945.* Edited by Gunter Berghaus. Berg Publishers, 1989. © Gunter Berghaus 1989. Reproduced by permission.—Birkett, Jennifer and James Kearns. From *A Guide to French Literature: From Early Modern to Postmodern.* St. Martin's Press, 1997. Copyright © 1997 by Jennifer Birkett and James Kearns. All rights reserved. Reproduced by permission of Palgrave Macmillan.—Bishop, Michael. From *The Contemporary Poetry of France: Eight Studies.* Rodopi, 1985. © Editions Rodopi B. V. Reproduced by permission.—Bradby, David. From *Modern French Drama 1940-1980.* Cambridge University Press, 1984. © Cambridge University Press 1984. Reproduced by permission of the publisher and the author.—Fallaize, Elizabeth. From *Contemporary French Fiction by Women: Feminist Perspectives.* Edited by Margaret Atack and Phil Powrie. Manchester University Press, 1990. © Manchester University Press 1990. Chapter © Elizabeth Fallaize 1990. Reproduced by permission of the author.—Feldman, Burton. From *The Nobel Prize: A History of Genius, Controversy, and Prestige.* Arcade Publishing, 2000. Copyright © 2000 by Burton Feldman. Reproduced by permission.—Guerin, Jeanyves. From *Myths and Realities of Contemporary French Theater: Comparative Views.* Edited by Patricia M. Hopkins and Wendell M. Aycock. Texas Tech Press, 1985. Reproduced by permission.—Gunther, Ralph. From *Giants in Their Field: An Introduction to the Nobel Prizes in Literature.* Scripta Humanistica, 1993. © Ralph Gunther 1993. Reproduced by permission.—Gurko, Leo. From *Joseph Conrad: Giant in Exile.* The Macmillan Company, 1962. © Leo Gurko 1962. All rights reserved. Reproduced by permission of Scribner, an imprint of Simon & Schuster Adult Publishing Group.—Gurr, Andrew. From *Writers in Exile: The Identity of Home in Modern Literature.* The Harvester Press, 1981. © Andrew Gurr, 1981. Reproduced by permission of the author.—Higgins, Ian. From *Anthology of Second World War French Poetry.* Edited by Ian Higgins. Methuen Educational Ltd., 1982. © 1982 Ian Higgins. All rights reserved. Reproduced by permission of the author.—Houlding, Elizabeth. From *Gender and Fascism in Modern France.* Edited by Melanie Hawthorne and Richard J. Golsan. University Press of New England, 1997. © 1997 by Trustees of Dartmouth College. All rights reserved. Reproduced by permission.—Kamla, Thomas A. From *Confrontation with Exile: Studies in the German Novel.* Herbert Lang Bern, 1975. © Peter Lang Gmbh 1975. Reproduced by permission of the author.—Kennedy, J. Gerald. From *Imagining Paris: Exile, Writing, and American Identity.* Yale University Press, 1993. Copyright © 1993 Yale University.

All rights reserved. Reproduced by permission.—King, Adele. From *French Women Novelists: Defining a Female Style.* Macmillan Press Ltd., 1989. © Adele King 1989. All rights reserved. Reproduced by permission of Palgrave Macmillan.—Knapp, Bettina L. From *Exile and the Writer: Exoteric and Esoteric Experiences: A Jungian Approach.* The Pennsylvania State University Press, 1991. Copyright © 1991 The Pennsylvania State University. All rights reserved. Reproduced by permission of the author.—Knapp, Bettina L. From *French Theatre, 1918-1939.* Macmillan Publishers Ltd., 1985. © Bettina L. Knapp 1985. All rights reserved. Reproduced by permission of Palgrave Macmillan.—Krispyn, Egbert. From *Anti-Nazi Writers in Exile.* The University of Georgia Press, 1978. Copyright © 1978 by the University of Georgia Press. All rights reserved. Reproduced by permission.—Milbauer, Asher Z. From *Transcending Exile: Conrad, Nabokov, I.. B. Singer.* University Presses of Florida, 1985. Copyright © 1985 by the Board of Regents of the State of Florida. Reproduced by permission.—Pfeiler, Wm. K. From *German Literature in Exile: The Concern of the Poets.* The University of Nebraska Press, 1957. Copyright 1957 by The University of Nebraska. © renewed 1985 by the University of Nebraska Press. Reproduced by permission.—Schenck, Celeste M. From *Women's Writing in Exile.* Edited by Mary Lynn Broe and Angela Ingram. The University of North Carolina Press, 1989. © 1989 The University of North Carolina Press. All rights reserved. Reproduced by permission.—Stuckey, W. J. From *The Pulitzer Prize Novels: A Critical Backward Look.* Second edition. University of Oklahoma Press, 1981. Copyright © 1981 by the University of Oklahoma Press. Reproduced by permission.

Literary Criticism Series Advisory Board

The members of the Gale Group Literary Criticism Series Advisory Board—reference librarians and subject specialists from public, academic, and school library systems—represent a cross-section of our customer base and offer a variety of informed perspectives on both the presentation and content of our literature criticism products. Advisory board members assess and define such quality issues as the relevance, currency, and usefulness of the author coverage, critical content, and literary topics included in our series; evaluate the layout, presentation, and general quality of our printed volumes; provide feedback on the criteria used for selecting authors and topics covered in our series; provide suggestions for potential enhancements to our series; identify any gaps in our coverage of authors or literary topics, recommending authors or topics for inclusion; analyze the appropriateness of our content and presentation for various user audiences, such as high school students, undergraduates, graduate students, librarians, and educators; and offer feedback on any proposed changes/enhancements to our series. We wish to thank the following advisors for their advice throughout the year.

Dr. Toby Burrows
Principal Librarian
The Scholars' Centre
University of Western Australia Library

David M. Durant
Reference Librarian, Joyner Library
East Carolina University

Steven R. Harris
English Literature Librarian
University of Tennessee

Mary Jane Marden
Literature and General Reference Librarian
St. Petersburg Jr. College

Mark Schumacher
Jackson Library
University of North Carolina at Greensboro

Gwen Scott-Miller
Fiction Department Manager
Seattle Public Library

Exile in Literature

INTRODUCTION

The theme of exile has engaged the imagination of many writers in the course of literary history, either because they experienced having to leave their native country for political reasons, or because they felt a disaffection with their society and consciously chose to live elsewhere. In fiction, as in life, there are many kinds of exile, as individual as the people experiencing and writing about it.

Martin Tucker, Celeste M. Schrenck, and Edward W. Said, among many other scholars, have written about the general characteristics and implications of exile. Schenck focuses on the special displacement experienced by women writers in exile, while Said emphasizes the personal and literary repercussions of exile—in his own case, as a writer from Palestine. Discussing the generation of American expatriate writers who lived in Paris in the 1920s, J. Gerald Kennedy comments on some of the reasons why, for them, Paris "inescapably reflects the creation of an exilic self." Many scholars have also dealt with the theme of exile in fictional works, linking a writer's treatment of that theme with the writer's own situation. For example, Samuel Lyndon Gladden has discussed Oscar Wilde's writings following the completion of his prison sentence and move to France; Leo Gurko has written about Joseph Conrad's experience as a Pole living in England and writing in English; and Kennedy has focused on F. Scott Fitzgerald's *Tender Is the Night* (1934) as it reflects Fitzgerald's temporary self-exile in France.

Sometimes historical circumstances dictate that a number of a nation's leading intellectuals and writers leave in order to seek personal as well as artistic freedom. Such was the case in Germany just before and during World War II, for example, when many liberals and anti-Nazi writers left the country in protest, creating a parallel body of German literature written outside of Germany during that period. Wm. K. Pfeiler, Thomas A. Kamla, and Egbert Krispyn have analyzed the general historical climate that led to the German writers' exodus and have highlighted some specific cases, like those of Konrad Merz, Thomas Mann, and Arthur Koestler. Günter Berghaus has written about the community of German writers and artists living in Great Britain during the war years and beyond, noting their contribution to intellectual life in their new environment.

REPRESENTATIVE WORKS

Djuna Barnes
Nightwood (novel) 1936

Samuel Beckett
Molloy (novel) 1951
En Attendant Godot [*Waiting for Godot*] (drama) 1953

Béla Belász
The Theory of the Drama (criticism) 1922

Joseph Conrad
Lord Jim (novel) 1900

e. e. cummings
The Enormous Room (prose narrative) 1922

F. Scott Fitzgerald
Tender Is the Night (novel) 1934

Joris-Karl Huysmans
Á rebours [*Against the Grain*] (novel) 1884

James Joyce
Dubliners (short stories) 1914
A Portrait of the Artist as a Young Man (novel) 1914-15
Exiles (drama) 1919
Ulysses (novel) 1922
Finnegans Wake (novel) 1939

Arthur Koestler
Spanish Testament (autobiography) 1937
Scum of the Earth (autobiography) 1941

Thomas Mann
Die Geschichten Jaakobs [*Joseph and His Brothers*] (novel) 1934
Lotte in Weimar [*The Beloved Returns*] (novel) 1939

Konrad Merz
Ein mensch fällt aus Deutschland (novel) 1936

Czesław Miłosz
Ziemia Ulro [*Land of Ulro*] (poetry) 1977

Vladimir Nabokov
The Real Life of Sebastian Knight (novel) 1939

Anäis Nin
The Diaries of Anäis Nin (diary) 1966-80

Saint-John Perse
Eloges [*Eloges and Other Poems*] (poetry) 1911
Anabase [*Anabasis*] (poetry) 1924

Isaac Bashevis Singer
Shosha (novel) 1978

Oscar Wilde
Sebastian Melmoth (prose) 1904

Stefan Zweig
The World of Yesterday (autobiography) 1943

OVERVIEWS AND GENERAL STUDIES

Celeste M. Schenck (essay date 1989)

SOURCE: Schenck, Celeste M. "Exiled by Genre: Modernism, Canonicity, and the Politics of Exclusion." In *Women's Writing in Exile,* edited by Mary Lynn Broe and Angela Ingram, pp. 225-50. Chapel Hill: University of North Carolina Press, 1989.

[*In the following essay, Schenck discusses the poetry of female modernists in terms of their state of being exiled from the political, cultural, and social mainstream.*]

When I first mapped out an essay on what I'd like to call modernist women's exiles, I envisioned an article on the exchanges between gender and genre, raised exponentially to include geography in the case of those triply exiled expatriate women poets. The task has been more difficult than I imagined for two reasons: first, my perfectly sonorous third—gender, genre, geography—collapsed under pressure of a less concordant trio—race, class, and sexual preference; second, because Gilbert and Gubar's observation that "verse genres have been even more thoroughly male than fictional ones" (*Madwoman,* 68), with its corollary that women writers able to make themselves at home in the house of prose were exiles when it came to poetic genres, simply did not hold up as a theory in a period that willingly consigned poetic forms into the hands of genteel poetesses, keeping the "new poetry" safe for the experimenters, the form-breakers, and the vers-librists—that is, the men.

It may seem old that I take up the banner of genre at a moment when Modernists were doing all they could to dislodge it as an evaluatory criterion of poetry, but in fact the debate raged in periodicals of the day in a manner I find chillingly gendered. In a 1914 polemic against that "decorative straight-jacket, rhymed verse," a *Little Review* essayist asks us: "Suppose I were a Bluebeard who had enticed a young girl into my dim chamber of poetic-thought. Suppose I took the little knife of rhyme and coolly sliced off one of her ears, two or three of her fingers, and finished by clawing out a generous handful of her shimmering, myriad-tinted hair, with the hands of meter" (Bodenheim, 22). Although the butchered victim in this fantasy is poetry, the hostility generated by rhymed verse extends metonymically to her largely female practitioners. For example, John Crowe Ransom, in "The Poet as Woman," an essay in condescending praise of Edna St. Vincent Millay, quibbles with her choice of the indeterminate word *comfort,* shortened to keep meter. Accusing Millay of obedience to "the mechanical determinism of metrical necessity," he turns the Procrustean metaphor back on her by ending his essay with an image of female dismemberment, once again, ostensibly, of poetry: "Procrustes, let us say with absurd simplicity, finds the good word *comforter* too long for the bed. So he lops off her feet" (110).[1]

But in the foregoing examples I have only described the woman poet's Charybdis. She is equally censured, often out of the other corner of the male critic's mouth, for being inadequately formal, that is, ill-suited to mastery of poetic genres by temperament and education. In the same essay quoted above, Ransom calls Millay "not a good conventional or formalist poet . . . because she allows the forms to bother her and to push her into absurdities. I imagine there are few women poets of whom this is not so, and it would be because they are not strict enough and expert enough to manage forms,—in their default of the disciplines under which men are trained" (103). William Archer says, apparently in praise of Alice Meynell:

> Few poetesses of the past have shown a very highly developed faculty for strict poetical form. I am not aware that the works of any woman in any modern language are reckoned among the consummate models of metrical style . . . ladies as a rule seem to have aimed at a certain careless grace rather than a strenuous complexity or accuracy of metrical structure . . . Mrs. Meynell is one of the rare exceptions to this rule. Within a carefully limited range, her form is unimpeachable.
>
> (Quoted in Schlack, 112)

It is little wonder, given the prescriptive nature of Archer's praise, that Meynell wrote a poem called "The Laws of Verse" in which she invites the erotic embrace of a controlling prosody and rhyme.

> Dear laws, come to my breast!
> Take all my frame, and make your close arms meet
> Around me; and so ruled, so warmed, so pressed,
> I breathe, aware; I feel my wild heart beat.
>
> (*Poems,* 173)

The double bind of the woman poet, as I redefine it for the female Modernist, her simultaneous exile *from* and *to* poetic form, almost makes comprehensible Edith Sitwell's defensive *ars poetica* in this peevish letter to Maurice Bowra:

> Women's poetry, with the exception of Sappho . . . and . . . "Goblin Market" and a few deep and concentrated, but fearfully incompetent poems of Emily Dickinson, is *simply awful*—incompetent, floppy, whining,

arch, trivial, self-pitying,—and any woman learning to write, if she is going to be any good at all, would, until she had made a technique for herself (and one has to forge it for oneself, there is no help to be got) write in as hard and glittering a manner as possible, and with as strange images as possible—strange, but believed in. Anything to avoid that ghastly wallowing.

(Letters, 116)

The ample quotation from Sitwell is intended to illustrate that this debate over genre not only installed itself along gender lines, inscribing itself in a familiar binary opposition between male Modernists and female poetesses, but cut across gender lines to enforce differences among women poets. In an essay titled "Some Observations on Women's Poetry," for example, Sitwell praises Rossetti's *Goblin Market*—"the perfect poem written by a woman" (59)—and censures Barret Browning's *Aurora Leigh*—"Mrs. Browning used a technique and a manner which is only suitable to a man," that is, she avoids versification and the control it implies. The result, according to Sitwell, is a kind of ill health in Barrett Browning's poetry that is emblemized by the vision of her "horsehair sofa": "She is always prostrated and never in fine fighting trim—the pink of condition for a poet" (59). The issue for Sitwell, who, like Meynell, feels "we cannot dispense with our rules," is to achieve a glittering hardness that will compensate for the sickliness/softness of what Sitwell would call, excepting Sappho, Rossetti, and herself, "women's poetry." In drawing out the implications and undertext of Sitwell's judgment on Barrett Browning, I mean to expose the bind she is caught in. She is committed *both* to a separate tradition of women's poetry—"it is of a different kind altogether, needing different subjects and a different technique" (59)—*and* to outdoing male poets in fashioning a poetics that is anything but wallowing and soft. Her recourse to form, then, was both prescribed and understandably defensive.

Why might women poets be especially susceptible to the (contradictory) criticisms of being too strong/too weak, too rigid/too flabby, too hard/too soft?[2] Theodore Roszak, in an early discussion of the sexual politics of Modernism, "The Hard and the Soft," points to the sexual imagery in the discourse of the period more generally, to its obsession with male impotence, sterility, and fears of castration in the face of female strength; that is, he views the contrast of a male and female Modernism in terms of the familiar opposition of his title. Gilbert and Gubar destabilize this binary scheme at the end of their "Tradition and the Female Talent" by suggesting that the "female half of the dialogue is considerably more complicated than the male" because women writers respond to male anxiety with guilt of their own rather than with the heightened competency men fear (204). I would suggest, framing the problem in Sherry Ortner's now famous anthropological terms, that women are always subjected to competing stereotypes: they are both "beneath" culture—too mired in nature to master the codes or poetic forms—and (notably in and after the Victorian period) "upholders of" culture—hence, rigid, conservative, form-bound, repressive of spontaneity and experimentation. The whole idea of the "genteel" against which Modernism defined itself seems to be inextricably bound to these contradictory, even schizophrenic, notions of femininity. One wonders, for example, which of the two Max Beerbohm is censuring in his faint praise of Virginia Woolf's writing for its likeness to her father's: "If he had been a 'Georgian' and a woman, just so would he have written" (quoted in Gilbert and Gubar, "Tradition," 183). If gentility in poetry carries the disparaging connotation of soft and female, or worse, not male enough, it can also bear the opposite meaning of conservative and rigid, rhymed, and therefore masculine and hard. Given the impossibility of separating the two valences of the term, it is no wonder that women poets found themselves divided in the debate over genre.

Not only, then, must we contextualize the notion of poetic form during the period known as Modernism—conventional form, although alive and well in genteel Georgian verse, was the *bête noire* of the Modernist movement in poetry, and therefore, although devalued, comparatively open to women poets. I will also ask that we attend to the differences between the female voices of rear-guard and avant-garde modernism. If we listen to the more traditional meters of Anna Wickham, Charlotte Mew, Sylvia Townsend Warner, Alice Meynell, and even Edith Sitwell (not to mention the some five hundred British women who wrote strong war poetry during the years around 1914) as attentively as we now hear the daring verbal experiments of H.D., Stein, and increasingly Mina Loy, we must renounce, I believe salutarily, any hope for a unitary, global theory of female poetic modernism.[3]

My polemic must be taken in the context of the ongoing project of Modernism's revisionary history, that is, the critique of the ideology of Modernism from the vantage point of all the new politics—Marxist, feminist, neohistoricist. I could not argue for a reconsideration of Modernism's foreclosed archives, except after and in light of Georg Lukács's essay on Modernist ideology in *The Meaning of Contemporary Realism,* Lillian Robinson's and Lise Vogel's 1971 polemic *against* the detachment of culture from history in Modernist art and *for* the study of race, class, and sex as factors of exclusion, and, finally, feminist critical salvaging of H.D., Stein, and Loy from the overwhelmingly masculine domination of the period. Without the work of Susan Stanford Friedman, Rachel DuPlessis, and Cyrena Pondrom on H.D., Catharine Stimpson, Marianne DeKoven, and Shari Benstock on Stein, and Carolyn Burke, Virginia Kouidis, and Roger Conover on Mina Loy, it would not be possible for me to argue for further opening of the canon to women poets. After all, H.D. had to be carried out of the burning city on the shoulders of her literary daughters if Robert Graves's dismissive censure of her is to be considered typical: "The only excuse to be made for those who once found H.D. 'incomprehensible' is that her work was so thin, so poor, that its emptiness seemed 'perfection,' its insipidity to be concealing a 'secret,' its superficiality so 'glacial' that it created a false 'classical atmosphere.' She was never able, in her temporary immortality, to reach a real climax in any of her poems. . . . All that they told was a story of feeble personal indecision; and her immortality came to an end so soon that her bluff was never called" (Riding and Graves, 122-23).[4]

But my business is not with the now safely restored H.D., or with Stein, or with Hugh Kenner's canonized Six, on which Modernist board only the sanitized Miss Moore sits as representative female (49-61),[5] nor even with what Virginia Kouidis calls, making a place for Mina Loy, the "Stein—Pound—Williams—Moore current of modernism" (24). In fact, the hard question I would like to pose is whether we feminist critics, in privileging those female poets who broke form with the boys (even if, as it turned out, they broke form *for* the boys), have reproduced the preferences of dominant critical discourse and extended the hegemony of an exclusive, in this case antigeneric, prejudice which consigned most women poets to debased use of tired forms. Shouldn't the canonizing of Stein and H.D., like that of Dickinson at the behest of the elegant deconstructors, give us pause, if it is accomplished at the expense of striking poets like Wickham and Mew, Wylie and Meynell, from the Modernist register? Furthermore, linking poetic practice to politics, might our collusion with the aesthetic Aryanism of the Modernist canon and its inevitable tendency to produce elite readers, even when we open that canon to women, amount to an enforcement of its exclusionary politics? Sonia Saldívar-Hull's reading of Stein in another essay in this volume poignantly forces us to confront a Chicana reader's alienation before Stein's racism and classism. How shall we choose to address those moments when Stein—formally and politically—has more in common with William or Henry James, Picasso, or for that matter Jacques Derrida, than with Ma Rainey[6] or Melanctha? Will the motley multiple determinants of literary modernism—gender, genre, geography, class, race, and sexual preference—finally force us to abandon a specious and essential, although for a time useful, difference between male and female Modernism?

My project here will be to isolate a few instances that roughen up the history of literary Modernism and present a paradox: if, as both Lukács and feminist critics have demonstrated, the radical poetics of Modernism often masks a deeply conservative politics, might it also possibly be true that the seemingly genteel, conservative poetics of women poets whose obscurity even feminists have overlooked might pitch a more radical politics than we had considered possible? I wish, in short, to question the equation both conservative Modernists and radical theorists have made between radical form and radical politics—even a critical theorist like Julia Kristeva might coconspire in a Modernist hegemony that fetishizes formal experiment. The situation of marginalized modernists such as Wickham, Mew, Townsend Warner, Meynell, and Sitwell has much to tell us not only about the dispersive underside of the Modernist monolith but also about the politics of canonicity and even about inadvertent feminist adherence to a politically suspect hierarchy of genre.

"Exile Begins as an Apprehension Visited in Secret"

The female affinity for fixed forms has been explained variously—in terms of the woman poet's reproduction of the struggle against cultural containment, of her need to "rein in her strong, unruly feelings" by recourse to formal strictures like the straitjacket of rhyme mentioned above (Fried, 2), finally of formal counter to very real social and sexual marginality. Marianne DeKoven explains female reticence to engage in experimental writing by arguing that "women writers, until, literally, now [with Stein], have been struggling to gain the position which male writers have been free to see as false" (*Different Language*, xx). Elaine Marks, Susan Gubar, and Elyse Blankley all note the coincidence of Renée Vivien's exotic sexuality with her self-exile into rhymed Alexandrines in an expatriate tongue of a century before, and others suggest that her incarceration in sentimental, imitative verse parallels her bodily anorexia or her imprisonment within the "doomed lesbian" image of the nineteenth century (Faderman, 268). Similarly, Louis Kannenstine, in a massive dismissal of all of Djuna Barnes's early verse, considers that her "conventional use of metre and rhymes was perhaps intended to provide a neutral ground to counter the strain" of her sexual preference (23). I would argue that recourse to convention does not always constitute a desire for constriction—Debra Fried's stunning reading of Millay's sonnets, for example, demonstrates that the freeing-by-binding trope might very well prove more explanatory of male than female formal experiment. Although certain of the vague pastorals sandwiched between stories in Barnes's *A Book* might have merited Kannenstine's disdain, the rhymed, "matched accentual lines" (Field, 70) of *A Book of Repulsive Women* do not in my view function as a safety valve or counter to the transgressiveness of the subject matter, nor are they the result of pure "stylistic excess" (Kannenstine, 32). Mina Loy's formal experiments with "Pig Cupid," "rooting erotic garbage"—sans commas, sans rhyme—seem tame next to the sexual radicalism of Barnes's unnervingly regular, rhymed syllabic verse:

> Someday beneath some hard
> Capricious star,
> Spreading its light a little
> Over far,
> We'll know you for the woman
> That you are,
> See you sagging down with bulging
> Hair to sip,
> The dappled damp from some vague
> Under lip,
> Your soft saliva, loosed
> With orgy, drip.
>
> ("From Fifth Avenue Up," 1-2)

In short, an alternate sexual politics is surprisingly announced in the *Repulsive Women* "rhythms"—a politics that would both impose exile and profit by it, a politics that would defiantly set itself up in the conformity of rhyme and meter, a politics that would challenge the heterosexism and homophobia of the dominant Modernist discourse in perfectly rhymed verse. Still, Barnes would shortly, largely as a result of her prose, achieve canonicity among the avant-garde, and her place in the feminist canon will be assured by the publication of Mary Lynn Broe's forthcoming revaluation of Barnes, *Silence and Power*.

Whereas Barnes's lesbian eroticism may no longer provoke surprise, it does startle to find the following lines in Charlotte Mew's "On the Road to the Sea": "We passed each other, turned and stopped for half an hour, then went our way, / I who make other women smile did not make you" (29). The achieved smile by the end of the poem is associated with dying climactically: "Reeling,—with all the cannons at your ear." In "The Fête" female sexuality receives equally delicate but nonetheless explicit treatment:

> At first you scarcely saw her face,
>   You knew the maddening feet were there,
> What called was that half-hidden, white unrest
> To which now and then she pressed
>   Her finger-tips; but as she slackened pace
> And turned and looked at you it grew quite bare:
> There was not anything you did not dare:—
>
> (Warner, 6-7)

"Absence," perhaps more than any other Mew poem, evokes both delight in female sexuality and conflict over its homoerotic expression. As anatomically suggestive of female anatomy as Sappho's imagery, Mew's adumbration of hooded female pleasures safe from the destructive beat of masculine hooves eases the traditional sapphic concern for a lost maidenhead, trampled by shepherds until only a purple stain remains upon the ground.

> In sheltered beds, the heart of every rose
>   Serenely sleeps to-night. As shut as those
> Your guarded heart; as safe as they from the beat, beat
> Of hooves that tread dropped roses in the street.
>
> (Warner, 47)

But the cost to the post-speaker of answering the call of her female lover's eyes is conveyed in an arresting image of silencing at the hands of Christ:

> But call, call, and though Christ stands
>   Still with scarred hands
> Over my mouth, I must answer. So,
>   I will come—He shall let me go!

Even more unsettling is the morbid but fascinating exploration of enveloping female eroticism in "The Forest Road" (Warner, 20-22), a poem pronounced pathological by a contemporary physician. It is, no less than Shelley's *Alastor*, a quest for what the speaker thinks is other and learns is in fact same. By the close of each, a binding love tryst gives over to death, as the poet-speaker confronts his/her own soul in the figure of the other. But whereas Shelley's poet's pursuit of an elusive maiden brings him to the grave, "The Forest Road" explores the contours of a female symbiosis that reads simultaneously as ecstasy and death. The poet knows she "could go free" if only she could separate from the other's enlacing hair: "I must unloose this hair that sleeps and dreams / About my face, and clings like the brown weed / To drowned, delivered things." Trying to quiet her female other, to "hush these hands that are half-awake / Groping for me in sleep," at the last she cannot separate from her. The image of double suicide that closes the poem marks a mutual female climax as well: as the "dear and wild heart" of the one has been broken in its breast of "quivering snow / With two red stains on it," the other determines to "strike and tear / Mine out, and scatter it to yours." In spite of its exploration of the dangers of giving in to the "poor, desolate, desperate hands" of the other, the poem ends ecstatically: "I hear my soul, singing among the trees!" Although Mew's biographers agree that her love for women remained to the end of her days a locus of conflict and psychic pain, her appreciation of female sexuality, in both benign and threatening manifestations, is at the heart of her best poetry.

The violence of "The Forest Road" is balanced by the delicate evocation of autoerotic pleasure in Mew's magnificent "Madeleine in Church." These lines fairly exult in the capacity for female self-enjoyment apart from the determining sexual presence of an other.

> I could hardly bear
> The dreams upon the eyes of white geraniums in the dusk,
>   The thick, close voice of musk,
>   The jessamine music on the thin night air,
> Or, sometimes, my own hands about me anywhere—
> The sight of my own face (for it was lovely then) even the
>   scent of my own hair,
> Oh, there was nothing, nothing that did not sweep to the high seat
>   Of laughing gods, and then blow down and beat
> My soul into the highway dust, as hoofs do the dropped roses
>   of the street.
>   I think my body was my soul,
>   And when we are made thus
>   Who shall control
> Our hands, our eyes, the wandering passion of our feet
>
> (Warner, 23).

This long poem of over two hundred lines, Mew's best poem, is composed of both varying rhyme schemes and stanza structures; each movement of this dramatic monologue is accompanied and marked by elaborate formal variation. In this section in particular, the incantatory rhythms and the sexual content of the lines invite enormous variation in length and emphasis, whereas other, less dreamlike and more conversational sections call for greater regularity in meter and line length. As a whole, "Madeleine in Church" should be seen as the culmination of a genre, a revision of the Victorian Fallen Woman poem, which Mew appropriates to champion rather than punish female sexuality, a revision informed as much by her own sexual conflicts as by her impatience with traditional mythologies of the "pécheresse" (Mizejewski, 283, 301): Mew gives her modern magdalen both a voice—of which the canon, preferring to describe her, had deprived her—and entitlement to full sexual enjoyment, autoerotic, heterosexual, or lesbian.

Although Virginia Woolf once wrote to Vita Sackville-West that she had just met "Charlotte Mew, (the greatest living poetess),"[7] critics have only begun to revalue the corpus that Mew's contemporaries, Woolf and Thomas Hardy among them, and even some followers, most notably Marianne Moore, so admired. Val Warner's 1981 reissue of Mew's *Collected Poems,* accompanied by her complete prose, and Penelope Fitzgerald's tasteful but forcibly limited biography, *Charlotte Mew and Her Friends,* praised by Brad Leithauser in a kind but still somewhat patronizing review essay on Mew in the *New York Review of Books* (called "Small Wonder"), have brought her work back to light. Although a number of critics, most notably Leithauser, have singled Mew out for her "indigenous originality" (25), her distinctive voice, they tend to censure her at the same time for her small, unoracular formalism—"her pitch is refined and her scale is modest" (31). When they do attribute to her some "nervy bravado," they do so for the Hardyesque roughed-up rhythms, the ventriloquistic experiments with dialect, the perseverance of repeated rhyme which Marianne Moore would later make famous and acceptable (Leithauser, 26). In fact, "Madeleine in Church" is anything but regular in rhythm, anything but conventional in line length and stanza form—its enormous formal variety marks its dramatic and sophisticated shifts in tone. Additionally, in their haste to excuse her "measured and unspectacular" production aside the form-shattering norms set by a masculinist Modernism, these critics fail to read beyond what they see as rhythmical familiarity and rhyme to a strikingly unconventional content (Leithauser, 25). But the sexual radicalism of this untypically formal corpus has been overlooked even by feminist critics attuned to Mew's revisionary impulses. Even Linda Mizejewski's sensitive reading of the Fallen Woman poems stops at Mew's poetic protest against heterosexual inscription into femininity. Beyond Mew's personal and idiosyncratic voice, beyond even her occasional generic daring, is an elected erotic politics belied by the shape of the poems.

Not just the experimental female modernists, then, but a good number of those faithful to meter and rhyme as well wrote a poetry of marked sexual preference: Anna Wickham, married mother of four, who developed a passionate attachment to Natalie Barney late in her life, freely admitting to her "biting lust" (*Writings,* 46); Charlotte Mew, pictured in her *Collected Poems* in full cross-dress, a would-be lover of novelist May Sinclair; Sylvia Townsend Warner, who copublished *Whether a Dove or a Seagull* with her lover, effacing the distinction of authorship from the face of the poems in a perfect emblem of their symbiosis (Marcus, 59); and even Edith Sitwell, probably asexual but certainly galvanized by her intense relationship with her governess, Helen Rootham. Each shares a politics with the more critically fashionable Barnes, coding in what we have learned to call conventional poetry the secret exile of sexual preference.

"ONE STEPS ABOARD; / THE BOAT SLOWLY / ABANDONS THE PORT / AND NOTHING HAS CHANGED"

Anna Wickham, like her contemporary Charlotte Mew, has lapsed into obscurity for reasons that have everything to do with the form of her verse and the manner of her dress—Harold Acton, for example, found her poetry as unfashionable as her person (Smith, 2). Unlike Mina Loy, whose elegance after four babies was continually remarked, Wickham was large and haphazard in appearance (gypsylike if the critics were feeling kind). She once deliberately wore a wool jumper to an affair at which Edith Sitwell was sure to show up in gold brocade. Charlotte Mew always wore a tweed topcoat over her often frankly masculine dress and sported a "felt pork-pie hat put on very straight" (Monro, viii). Wickham was prolific (nearly fourteen hundred poems in twenty years) where Mew was spare (her first book came out in 1916, when she was nearly fifty), yet both wrote overtly feminist poetry that was highly recognized in its day. Thomas Hardy called Charlotte Mew "far and away the best living woman poet—who will be read when others are forgotten" (quoted in Fitzgerald, 174), and Anna Wickham had by 1932 an international reputation—anthologies of the day printed more of her poems than those of Walter de la Mare, Robert Graves, and in some volumes, even William Butler Yeats (Smith, 23). Neither Wickham nor Mew had anything like a formal education and no formal study of poetry, although Wickham's father apparently made her promise to become a poet. Mew destroyed everything that might constitute a record of her life except for the few pieces that make up her *Collected Poems* and some stories, and most of Wickham's papers and letters were lost during the 1943 bombing of her Hampstead home. Both Wickham and Mew questioned the church, but whereas Wickham's revisionary supplication of the feminized deity poignantly redresses banishment—"In nameless, shapeless God found I my rest, / Though for my solace I build God a breast"—Mew's resignation, in "Madeleine in Church," is complete—"I do not envy Him His victories, His arms are full of broken things" (Warner, 26). Finally, both Wickham and Mew committed suicide. The indignity of Mew's death by the ingestion of disinfectant was matched only by the carelessness of her obituary: "Charlotte New, said to be a writer" (Monro, xii). Wickham's fate is as banal: The London *Picture Post* did a feature on her in 1946 called "The Poet Landlady" (Smith, 28).

A closer look at the life's work of the colorful Wickham, a free-spirited, half-working-class Australian émigrée, who began her career as an opera singer and then divided her life between London and Paris, might cause us to agree with Stanley Kunitz that the neglect of Anna Wickham is "one of the great mysteries of contemporary literature" (quoted in Wickham, *Writings,* front blurb, n.p.). A pacifist who nonetheless supported the Great War effort, a deprived and unhappy wife who remained faithful to her husband during the entire course of their tumultuous relationship until his death, an acquaintance of Pound, Barnes, D. H. Lawrence, and Dylan Thomas who was as comfortable in a London pub as she was on the fashionable Left Bank, a staunch feminist and supporter of women's rights who harbored a masochistic sexuality founded in motherlack and Catholic education, Wickham was an exciting mass of contradictions of which her poetry is the record. Her Australian childhood offered freedoms unknown to Englishwomen and seems to have stamped Wickham with a robust sense of sexual entitlement, a view of social inequity, and an authentic personal voice, all of which set her apart from other women poets of that period. For all the exhilaration of her Australian exile, however, the return to England and her sensitivity to inequities of class heightened her sense of herself as an outsider. The social rivalry between her mother's and father's families finds its way into poems like "Descent of Dorelia" and "The Little Old House." And her own marriage into a family of aristocratic birth initiated her into the oppression of the female spirit in Victorian bourgeois culture. The rhyme scheme and alternating meter of the following poem sets off rather than contains the rage of "Nervous Prostration":

> I married a man of the Croydon class
> When I was twenty-two.
> And I vex him, and he bores me
> Till we don't know what to do!
> It isn't good form in the Croydon class
> To say you love your wife,
> So I spend my days with the tradesmen's books
> And pray for the end of life. . . .
>
> I married a man of the Croydon class
> When I was twenty-two.
> And I vex him, and he bores me
> Till we don't know what to do!
> And as I sit in his ordered house,
> I feel I must sob or shriek,
> To force a man of the Croydon class
> To live, or to love, or to speak!
>
> (210)

There is defiance in the emphasis of the rhyme scheme and not a little irony in its metrical regularity. The poem is closer to folk balladry than to the genteel metrics of the Croydon class; we might even term it deliberately lowbred, even doggerel, a formal as well as political spoof on bourgeois values. This poem, "Dedication of the Cook," "The Angry Woman," "Definition," "The Wife," "All Men to Women," "Divorce," and "The Song of the Low-Caste Wife" criticize prevailing domestic politics, especially in their analysis of sexual difference within the culture that Wickham, marginalized by caste and country as well as gender, could see clearly as triple outsider. Wickham's formal conventionality is often the very vehicle of her poetic politics: her forced rhymes are meant to be funny and irreverent and to set off the political conflicts of which her poetry is made; they should not merely be read as unsophisticated concessions to the popular conventions of the day. "Meditation at Kew," outlining a poignant but humorous utopian program for marital reform, is the poetic version of her 1938 feminist manifesto, *The League for the Protection of the Imagination of Women. Slogan: World's Management by Entertainment* (Smith, 27).

> Alas! for all the pretty women who marry dull men,
> Go into the suburbs and never come out again,
> Who lose their pretty faces and dim their pretty eyes,
> Because no one has skill or courage to organize.
>
> What do pretty women suffer when they marry?
> They bear a boy who is like Uncle Harry,
> A girl who is like Aunt Eliza, and not new,
> These old dull races must breed true.
>
> I would enclose a common in the sun,
> And let the young wives out to laugh and run;
> I would steal their dull clothes and go away,
> And leave the pretty naked things to play.
>
> (45)

Wickham's poems range from feminist pieces on marital relations and on the conflict between mothering and writing, to analyses of the domination of one class by another as in "Laura Grey," "Comments of Kate the Cook," "The Butler and the Gentleman," "Daughter of the Horse-Leech," and "Woman to a Philosopher." "Song of the Low-Caste Wife," unlike "Meditation at Kew," is rythmically uneven and unrhymed, but it is no less than revolutionary in its analysis of the healthful dilution of the bloodline, its dramatization of the rift between herself and the women of her husband's family and class, its claim for "new myths" on the brains of "new men" mothered by underclass women, its valorization of lust and energy, change and growth, over "old glories" and "dead beauty."

> What have you given me for my strong sons?
> O scion of kings!
> In new veins the blood of old kings runs cold.
> Your people thinking of old victories, lose the lust of conquest,
> Your men guard what they have,
> Your women nurse their silver pots,
> Dead beauty mocks hot blood!
> What shall these women conceive of their chill loves
> But still more pots?
>
> But I have conceived of you new men;
> Boys brave from the breast,
> Running and striving like no children of your house
> And with their brave new brains
> Making new myths.
>
> My people were without while yours were kings,
> They sang the song of exile in low places
> And in the stress of growth knew pain.
> The unprepared world pressed hard upon them,
> Women bent beneath burdens, while cold struck babes,
> But they arose strong from the fight,
> Hungry from their oppression.
>
> And I am full of lust,
> Which is not stayed with your old glories.
> Give me for all old things that greatest glory.
> A little growth.
>
> (165)

"The Angry Wife" is similarly unremarkable in its formal aspects but trenchant in its analysis of motherhood as both experience and institution. The poem first describes marriage in political terms—"If sex is a criterion for power, and never strength / What do we gain by union?" (202)—and then protests the institutional version of parenting which issues from that sexual politics, necessitating the (male) child's revolt against the mother.

> I am not mother to abstract Childhood, but to my son,
> And how can I serve my son, but to be much myself.
>
> My motherhood must boast some qualities,
> For as motherhood is diverse
> So shall men be many charactered
> And show variety, as this world needs. . . .
>
> Why should dull custom make my son my enemy
> So that the privilege of his manhood is to leave my house?
>
> (203)

"The Fired Pot" is a representative Wickham poem, combining personally registered awareness of the suffering of others with her characteristic directness about her own experience. In this poem, as in "The Song of the Low-Caste Wife," she claims a right to her own sexual desire; here, as in that poem as well, lust is a motivating energy that propels action and promotes change. In the monotonous life of the town she describes, it is, even when unconsummated, a mode of survival.

> In our town, people live in rows.
> The only irregular thing in a street is the steeple;
> And where that points to, God only knows,
> And not the poor disciplined people!
>
> And I have watched the women growing old,
> Passionate about pins, and pence, and soap,
> Till the heart within my wedded breast grew cold,
> And I lost hope.
>
> But a young soldier came to our town,
> He spoke his mind most candidly.
> He asked me quickly to lie down,
> And that was very good for me.
> For though I gave him no embrace—
> Remembering my duty—
> He altered the expression of my face,
> And gave me back my beauty.
>
> (47)

The reference to duty here is probably to the bounden husband to whom Wickham professed lifelong fidelity, but a humorous interpretation of those lines would not be uncharacteristic of her. She may in fact be referring to the wartime decree, under the Defense of the Realm Act, that it was a penal offense to communicate a venereal disease to a soldier.[8]

Finally, in "The Mill," the concord of heart at one with specific, palpably felt environment is expressed by means of a regularized rhyme scheme, the purposive flowing of alternating rhyme into matched concluding couplets.

> I hid beneath the covers of the bed,
> And dreamed my eyes were lovers
> On a hill that was my head.
> They looked down over the loveliest country I have seen,
> Great fields of red-brown earth hedged round with green.
> In these enclosures I could see
> The high perfection of fertility,
> I knew there were sweet waters near to feed the land,
> I heard the churning of a mill on my right hand,
> I woke to breathlessness with a quick start,
> And found my mill the beating of your heart.
>
> (48)

I do not mean to suggest that the enormously uneven Wickham corpus remains undiscovered as a pretext of literary Modernism. Mew must be admitted to the canon as an overlooked treasure of the period, while Wickham remains important for reasons other than either experimentalism or formalism in verse. I would, however, like to see the personal and material specificity of "The Mill" have its history among our modernisms, reflecting—alongside Eliot's phlegmatic portrayals of deceptive lovers, Joyce's spoofs on the magazine romanticism of the day, Loy's send-ups of the masculine sexual principle, and Barnes's decadent New Woman poems—its own particular vision, neither ironized nor sentimental, of the way we loved then.

"No one comes after you / in this rain."

When Wickham writes at the head of her extraordinary autobiography: "I am a woman artist and the story of my failure should be known" (52), she compels the rereading I urge upon us here, not only to account for her disappearance from the annals of Modernism but also to understand the politics of our collusion as feminist critics in that exile. Wickham's poems of class consciousness are a salutary addition to a Modernist canon insufficiently concerned with the differentials of class and ethnicity. And next to Mina Loy's explorations of the decadent "Café du Néant" we will want to place Charlotte Mew's poems of France, among them "Pécheresse" and "Le Sacré-Coeur," "Monsieur qui Passe," and the Madeleine poem mentioned above, all of which analyze the uses to which female sexuality is put: "*Une jolie fille à vendre, très cher,* / A thing of gaiety, a thing of sorrow, / Bought to-night, possessed, and tossed / Back to the mart again tomorrow" (Warner, 31). Mew also wrote a handful of war poems during the years 1915-19, which are among the most iconoclastic and feminist of that period: rhymed, metered, and divided conventionally into stanzas, "The Cenotaph" and "May 1915" are pacifist hymns that re-member the "young, piteous, murdered face[s]" of the war dead by giving voice to grieving women, those "watchers by lonely hearths" who "from the thrust of an inward sword have more slowly bled" (Warner, 35).

Similarly, our analysis of Stein's linguistic iconoclasm should not eclipse Sitwell's accentual and rhythmic experiments. She set herself against the Georgian tradition of the day and counted herself among those Modernist poets who sought a reflection of the disintegration of Europe in their disruption of conventional form, although literary history has not preserved her inclusion. For all the ornamentation of her verse and person, the idiosyncratic nursery vocabulary of the early poems, and the lapidary persistence of her imagery, Sitwell also wrote some of the best poems we have about World War II. "Gold Coast Customs," "Still Falls the Rain," and "A Mother to Her Dead Child" (*Collected Poems*, 237-52, 272, 286), representatively, reach beyond the Chinoiserie for which she has been limitingly known, beyond the occasion of the poems themselves—the devastating air raids of 1940—to broad cultural criticism for which she has been inadequately recognized.

Our work must also include greater attention to comparison among women writers, especially across the Modernist barrier of form. We must, for example, continue to read H.D. in context of other women poets, not merely as that Pound-fashioned founder of Imagism resultingly isolated from less "fashionable" women poets. Alice Meynell's revisionary maternal theology, for example, admittedly conventional in its formal expression, bears comparison with H.D.'s feminized mythologies: Meynell's "Aenigma Christi" revises the mother-and-male-child configuration by centering upon the mother—"Yet I saw the whole / Eternal, infinite Christ within the one / Small mirror of her soul" (*Poems*, 195)—in much the way that H.D. encircles Mary at the end of *Trilogy*. Similarly, Meynell engaged head-on with the experience of World War I in her "Parentage" and "A Father of Women: Ad Sororem E.B." by aligning destruction with the patriarchal fathers and refiguring the place of the feminine in a reconstructed cultural ideology in much the way that H.D. maternally salvages the postwar wasteland in *Trilogy*. Although Meynell was of aristocratic birth, a devout, converted Catholic, and a happily married mother of eight, and H.D., by contrast, lived an expatriate life on the margins of conventional sexual and professional choices, both were ardent feminists with uncannily similar strategies for revising inherited mythologies. Our failure to read H.D. and Meynell together for the possibilities comparison offers enforces a masculinist Modernist prejudice against the practice of all but experimental form.

The differences among women modernists, particularly as established across the divide of poetic form, encourage us to think of genre, not as a pure, hypostasized, aesthetic category, but instead as a highly textured, overdetermined site of political contention, a literary space constructed often ex post facto from the conflicting materials of critical, political, racial, and sexual bias. A function of gender and geography, of class as well as critical consciousness, of exile at times imposed and at others elected, poetic genre not only divides male from female authors in the period we have come to call Modernism. I will argue in closing that, as a conflictual site, genre itself might serve as that Archimedean point of contradiction and comparison Myra Jehlen imagined in her "Paradox of Feminist Criticism,"

that necessary ground we stand so as to question our own assumptions. But Jehlen's scheme now requires revision: it is no longer the contrast between men's and women's writing that will save us from critical solipsism but the "radical comparativism" among women writers which we have just begun to practice, a comparativism alert to the politics of exile and exclusion that still underwrites canonicity.

Notes

I use the expression *politics of exclusion* to stand for a complex process by which women poets are exiled from canonical representation by both traditional critics and feminists. The term was first used, but differently, by Gayatri Spivak (276), to describe "moments on the edges or borders" of critical theories at which the "ideological trace" remains of their need to exclude the other to preserve identity or sameness. This essay was first presented at a 1986 MLA Division Meeting on Twentieth-Century English Literature, "Women Writers in Exile III: The Female Diaspora—(Dis)Placement and Difference." I thank Jane Marcus for inviting me to write on this topic and for her scrupulous attention to an early draft, and Susan Stanford Friedman, Lisa Ruddick, Rachel Blau DuPlessis, and the editors of this collection for valuable suggestions on subsequent versions. Shari Benstock and Susan Hastings generously shared personal copies of primary materials from European collections.

The three section heads are taken from a Michèle Murray poem, "Internal Emigrations," a meditation on the various forms the experience of expatriation takes—racial, sexual, cultural, and geographical.

1. See Gilbert and Gubar, "Tradition and the Female Talent," for similar examples of sadistic imagery in short stories by male Modernist writers.

2. I am grateful to Lisa Ruddick for encouraging me to deepen my analysis of this point and for suggesting the anthropological reading of the woman (modernist) poet's bind.

3. My polemic throughout this essay is the dismantling of a monolithic Modernism defined by its iconoclastic irreverence for convention and form, a difference that has contributed to the marginalization of women poets during the period and even division among them, a difference I have taken care to signal by substituting the plural and uncapitalized "modernisms" for "Modernism" as a marker of such omissions and exclusions. It is my contention, shared by Susan Stanford Friedman in her unpublished essay, "Forbidden Fruits of Lesbian Experimentation," that the "presumed chasm between experimental and realist writing is misleading for the study of women's writing" (2). I also suggest that although a certain stylistic designation is lost if we open up Modernism to anything written between 1910 and 1940, we lose in at least equal measure if we restrict that literary critical marker of periodization to experimental writing

alone. We lose, in short, all the other modernisms against which a single strain of white, male, international Modernism has achieved such relief.

4. Riding has since repudiated collaborative solidarity with Graves's position on "woman." See her response to John Wain's review of volume 1 of Richard Perceval Graves's (Robert Graves's nephew) study of the poet ("Taking His Measure," 59-60).

5. Marianne Moore and Elizabeth Bishop are the only women poets to be embraced unreservedly by the male Modernist establishment in a token stroke of inclusion that isolates them from other women poets. As a counter to Kenner's canonization of Miss Moore for her muscularity of style, her minimalism, her daring verbal experimentalism, in short, her "hardness" as a poet, I would direct the reader to Bonnie Costello's repositioning of Moore as a modernist. Rescuing her from Eliot's, Jarrell's, Blackmur's, and Ransom's approval of her "ladylikeness," Costello regenders Moore as a *woman* poet. Adrienne Rich, too, notes that "the woman poet most admired at the time (by men) was Marianne Moore, who was maidenly, elegant, intellectual, discreet" ("Re-Vision," in *Lies*, 39). Equally dangerous to women writers of this period is their reverse idealization—for their "ladyhood," or ethereal softness—in such articles as Earl Rovit's patronizing "Our Lady-Poets of the Twenties," published in 1980 and seemingly in ignorance of feminist criticism on Teasdale, Millay, Moore, and others. It is precisely this marginalization which Sitwell resists in the passages I quote above.

6. My allusion here is to the compelling peroration of Catharine Stimpson in a paper read at MLA (New York, 1986) on Stein and Moore. After establishing the links between them in a comparative move which I worry was meant to lend Stein credibility and status by comparison with the already credentialed Modernist Moore, Stimpson pays final, exhortative lip service to Stein's contemporary Ma Rainey, whose "laughter" and "songs" on another continent "also engendered Modernism." In fact, Stimpson's has been admittedly a "Tale of Three"—Stein, Moore, and the father whose gaze they both returned, Henry James. I worry similarly that the three panels organized by the 1986 Division of Late Nineteenth and Early Twentieth Century American Literature— "(En)Gendering Modernism: Gertrude Stein, H.D., Marianne Moore"; "Intertextual Modernism: H.D., Marianne Moore, and Gertrude Stein"; and "Disrupting Difference(s): Getrude Stein and Marianne Moore"—may inadvertently erect a complementary Modernist canon to the one already in place: retroactively gendered but inadequately flexible generically as to include Ma Rainey's exuberantly uncanonical blues rhythms and Mew's and Wickham's unexpectedly unconventional politics. My concern for the way an alternative canon might be positioned and co-opted does not displace my recognition of the difficulty feminist critics faced in getting Stein and H.D. into the canon in the first place.

I do not mean here to establish a simple equation between left wing politics and less experimental formal stances. Although not all Modernist experiments in form are uniformly tied to right wing sentiments, most that *are* happen to be male. For Woolf and H.D., however, most notably, the notion of breaking sentence and sequence was a way of rupturing political assumptions of great pertinacity and of making a radical criticism of power and status. I do not mean to imply, by asking that we review the work of less experimental poets of the period, that such leftward critiques remain the exclusive province of non-experimenters, but rather to include within our feminist rewriting of periodization poets who were not compelled, stylistically speaking, to "make it new." It is not that the sentence-breaking, female-authored works of that period necessarily collude with a reactionary politics, but that restriction of feminist critical interest to experimentalists may inadvertently work to reify Modernism as a term.

7. Woolf presumably met Mew at the bedside of Hardy's wife, Florence (*Diary*, 2:319 and n. 9; *Letters*, 2:140), and therefore we might conclude that the opinion of Mew's reputation, added parenthetically, might be that of Hardy, approved by Woolf herself. Earlier in the *Letters*, however, Woolf writes to R. C. Trevelyan that she has "got Charlotte Mews book" [*The Farmer's Bride*]. "I think her very good and interesting and unlike anyone else" (2:419).

8. I am grateful to Angela Ingram for sharing this insight.

Works Cited

Barnes, Djuna. "From Fifth Avenue Up." In *A Book of Repulsive Women*. Guido Bruno Chapbooks 2, 6, November 1915, pp. 1-2.

———. *Ladies Almanack*. 1928. Facs. ed. New York: Harper & Row, 1972.

Benstock, Shari. "Beyond the Reaches of Feminist Criticism: A Letter from Paris." *Tulsa Studies in Women's Literature* 3 (Spring-Fall 1984): 5-27.

———. *Women of the Left Bank: Paris, 1900-1940*. Austin: University of Texas Press, 1986.

Blankley, Elyse. "Return to Mytilène: Renée Vivien and the City of Women." In *Women Writers and the City*, edited by Susan Merrill Squier, 45-67. Knoxville: University of Tennessee Press, 1984.

Bodenheim, Maxwell. "The Decorative Straight-Jacket: Rhymed Verse." *Little Review* 1 (December 1914): 22-23.

Burke, Carolyn. "'Accidental Aloofness': Barnes, Loy and Modernism." In *Silence and Power: A Reevaluation of Djuna Barnes*, edited by Mary Lynn Broe. Carbondale: Southern Illinois University Press, forthcoming.

———. "Becoming Mina Loy." *Women's Studies* 7 (1980): 137-50.

———. "Gertrude Stein, the Cone Sisters, and the Puzzle of Female Friendship." In *Writing and Sexual Difference*, edited by Elizabeth Abel, 221-42. Chicago: University of Chicago Press, 1982.

———. "The New Poetry and the New Woman: Mina Loy." In *Coming To Light: American Women Poets in the Twentieth Century*, edited by Diane Middlebrook and Marilyn Yalom, 37-57. Ann Arbor: University of Michigan Press, 1985.

———. "Without Commas: Gertrude Stein and Mina Loy." *Poetics Journal* 4 (1984): 43-52.

Conover, Roger, ed. and Intro. *The Last Lunar Baedeker*. Highlands, N.C.: Jargon, 1982.

Costello, Bonnie. "The 'Feminine' Language of Marianne Moore." In *Women and Language in Literature and Society*, edited by Sally McConnell-Ginet, Ruth Borker, and Nelly Furman, 222-38. New York: Praeger, 1980.

DeKoven, Marianne. *A Different Language: Gertrude Stein's Experimental Language*. Madison: University of Wisconsin Press, 1983.

———. "Gertrude Stein and Modern Painting: Beyond Literary Cubism." *Contemporary Literature* 22 (1981): 81-95.

DuPlessis, Rachel. "Romantic Thralldom and 'Subtle Genealogies' in H.D." In *Writing Beyond the Ending: Narrative Strategies of Twentieth-Century Women Writers*. Bloomington: Indiana University Press, 1985.

Faderman, Lillian. *Surpassing the Love of Men: Romantic Friendship and Love between Women from the Renaissance to the Present*. New York: William Morris, 1981.

Field, Andrew. *Djuna: The Life and Times of Djuna Barnes*. New York: Putnam's, 1983.

Fifer, Elizabeth. "Is Flesh Advisable? The Interior Theater of Gertrude Stein." *Signs* 4 (Spring 1979): 472-83.

Fitzgerald, Penelope. *Charlotte Mew and Her Friends*. London: Collins, 1984.

Fried, Debra. "Andromeda Unbound: Gender and Genre in Millay's Sonnets." *Twentieth Century Literature* 32 (Spring 1986): 1-22.

Friedman, Susan Stanford. "Forbidden Fruits of Lesbian Experimentation." Paper presented at the Modern Language Association, Chicago, Illinois, December 1985.

———. *Psyche Reborn: The Emergence of H.D.* Bloomington: Indiana University Press, 1981.

Gilbert, Sandra. "Soldier's Heart: Literary Men, Literary Women, and the Great War." *Signs* 8 (Winter 1982): 422-50.

Gilbert, Sandra, and Susan Gubar. *The Madwoman in the Attic: The Woman Writer and the Nineteenth-Century Literary Imagination*. New Haven: Yale University Press, 1979.

———. "Tradition and the Female Talent." In *The Poetics of Gender*, edited by Nancy K. Miller, 183-207. New York: Columbia University Press, 1986.

Glück, Louise. "Hyacinth." In *The Triumph of Achilles*, 14-15. New York: Ecco, 1985.

Gubar, Susan. "Sapphistries." *Signs* 10 (Autumn 1984): 43-62.

Hastings, Susan. "Two of the Weird Sisters: The Eccentricities of Gertrude Stein and Edith Sitwell." *Tulsa Studies in Women's Literature* 4 (Spring 1985): 101-22.

Jehlen, Myra. "Archimedes and the Paradox of Feminist Criticism." In *Feminist Theory: A Critique of Ideology*, edited by Nannerl O. Keohane, Michelle Rosaldo, and Barbara Gelpi, 189-216. Chicago: University of Chicago Press, 1981.

Kammer, Jeanne. "The Art of Silence and the Forms of Women's Poetry." In *Shakespeare's Sisters: Feminist Essays on Women Poets*, edited by Sandra Gilbert and Susan Gubar, 153-64. Bloomington: Indiana University Press, 1979.

Kannenstine, Louis. *The Art of Djuna Barnes: Duality and Damnation*. New York: New York University Press, 1977.

Kenner, Hugh. "The Making of the Modernist Canon." *Chicago Review* 34 (1984): 49-61.

Kouidis, Virginia. *Mina Loy: American Modernist Poet*. Baton Rouge: Louisiana State University Press, 1980.

Leithauser, Brad. "Small Wonder." Review of Fitzgerald's *Charlotte Mew and Her Friends*. *New York Review of Books*, January 15, 1987, pp. 25-31.

Lukács, Georg. "The Ideology of Modernism." *The Meaning of Contemporary Realism*. Translated by John Mander and Necke Mander. London: Merlin, 1963.

Marcus, Jane. "The Asylums of Antaeus: Women, War and Madness: Is There a Feminist Fetishism?" In *The Differences Within: Feminism and Critical Theory*, edited by Elizabeth Meese and Alice Parker, 49-81. Amsterdam: John Benjamins, 1989.

Marks, Elaine. "Lesbian Intertextuality." In *Homosexualities and French Literature: Cultural Contexts/Critical Texts*, edited by George Stambolian and Elaine Marks, 353-77. Ithaca: Cornell University Press, 1979.

Meynell, Alice. *The Poems of Alice Meynell*. London: Oxford University Press, 1940.

Mizejewski, Linda. "Charlotte Mew and the Unrepentant Magdalene: A Myth in Transition." *Tulsa Studies in Literature and Language* 26 (Fall 1984): 282-302.

Monro, Alida. "Charlotte Mew—A Memoir." In *Collected Poems of Charlotte Mew*. London: Duckworth, 1953.

Morse, Samuel French. "The Rediscovery of Mina Loy and the Avant-Garde." *Wisconsin Studies in Contemporary Literature* 2 (Spring-Summer 1961): 12-19.

Murray, Michèle. "Internal Emigrations." *Women's Studies* 7 (1980): 210-11.

Perloff, Marjorie. "Poetry as Word-System: The Art of Gertrude Stein." *American Poetry Review* 8 (1979): 33-43.

Pondrom, Cyrena. "H.D. and the Origins of Modernism." *Sagetrieb* 4 (Spring 1985): 75-100.

Ransom, John Crowe. "The Poet as Woman." In *The World's Body.* Baton Rouge: Louisiana State University Press, 1938.

Reilly, Catherine, ed. *Scars upon My Heart: Women's Poetry and Verse of the First World War.* London: Virago, 1981.

Rich, Adrienne. *On Lies, Secrets and Silence: Selected Prose, 1966-1978.* New York: Norton, 1979.

Riding, Laura. "Taking His Measure." *New York Review of Books,* September 24, 1987, pp. 59-60.

———, and Robert Graves. *A Survey of Modernist Poetry.* Garden City, N.Y.: Doubleday, Doran, 1928.

Robinson, Lillian, and Lise Vogel. "Modernism and History." *New Literary History* 3 (Autumn 1971): 177-99.

Roszak, Theodore. "The Hard and the Soft." In *Masculine/Feminine: Readings in Sexual Mythology and the Liberation of Women,* edited by Betty Roszak and Theodore Roszak, 87-104. New York: Harper, 1969.

Rovit, Earl. "Our Lady-Poets of the Twenties." *Southern Review* 16 (January 1980): 65-85.

Saldívar-Hull, Sonia. "Wrestling Your Ally: Stein, Racism, and Feminist Critical Practice," in this volume.

Salter, Elizabeth, and Allanah Harper. *Edith Sitwell: Fire of the Mind.* New York: Vanguard, 1976.

Schlack, Beverly Ann. "The 'Poetess of Poets': Alice Meynell Rediscovered." *Women's Studies* 7 (1980): 111-26.

Sitwell, Edith. *Collected Poems.* London: Macmillan, 1957.

———. "Modernist Poets." *Echanges* 2 (June 1930): 78.

———. "Some Observations on Women's Poetry: A Defense of the Theory That Male Technique Is Entirely Unsuitable to the Poetry of Women." *Vogue* (London) 65 (March 1925): 59.

———. "To Maurice Bowra, January 24, 1944." In *Selected Letters,* edited by John Lehmann and Derek Parker, 116-17. London: Macmillan, 1970.

Smith, R. D. Introduction. *The Writings of Anna Wickham.* London: Virago, 1984.

Spivak, Gayatri Chakravorty. "The Politics of Interpretations." *Critical Inquiry* 9 (September 1982): 259-78.

Stimpson, Catharine. "Gertrice/Altrude: Stein, Toklas, and the Paradox of the Happy Marriage." In *Mothering the Mind: Twelve Studies of Writers and Their Silent Partners,* edited by Ruth Perry and Martine Brownley, 123-39. New York: Holmes and Meier, 1984.

———. "The Mind, the Body, and Gertrude Stein." *Critical Inquiry* 3 (1977): 491-506.

———. "The Somagrams of Gertrude Stein." *Poetics Today* 6 (1985): 67-80.

———. "Women Writers and the Avant-Garde." Paper presented at the Modern Language Association, New York, New York, December 1986.

Warner, Val. Introduction. *Charlotte Mew: Collected Poems and Prose.* Manchester: Carcanet (Virago), 1981.

Wickham, Anna. *The Writings of Anna Wickham.* Edited and Introduction by R. D. Smith. London: Virago, 1984.

Woolf, Virginia. *The Diary of Virginia Woolf.* Edited by Anne Olivier Bell assisted by Andrew McNeillie. Vol. 2. New York: Harcourt Brace Jovanovich, 1978.

———. *The Letters of Virginia Woolf.* Edited by Nigel Nicolson and Joanne Trautmann. Vols. 1 and 2. London: Hogarth, 1976, 1977.

Martin Tucker (essay date 1991)

SOURCE: Tucker, Martin. An introduction to *Literary Exile in the Twentieth Century: An Analysis and Biographical Dictionary,* edited by Martin Tucker, pp. xiii-xxiv. New York: Greenwood Press, 1991.

[*In the following excerpt, Tucker attempts to define the concept of exile in historical, cultural, and literary terms, comparing various exiles' notions about the theme.*]

Because the awareness of exile has recently grown to such an extent—witnessed by the many studies of it published in the past fifty years and by university courses specifically centered on the definition and experience of exile—the term has become a generalized one. Exile as a concept and as an experience is never vague, but it is a complex of emotional reactions and residues of feelings. Its complex nature, based on a simple fact of rejection or isolation, has caused sympathetic observers and speculative commentators to apply its characteristics in varying ways and means. It is best, at this point, to go beyond the beginning to define terms.

Exile is not a new phenomenon: it is as old as the first home one has left in the prime of consciousness. Its growing incidence, and the psychic states attendant upon the awareness of the loss it renders, is, however, a contemporary phenomenon. Exile, or the consciousness of it, has become a dominant part of the modern age and in some cases has acted as a nurturing stimulus to creative expression of its impact.

Historically, exile has always been awesome, drawing on mythic sources to sustain its power, whether those powers stem from religious, psychological, geographic, political, or social and communal pressures. By its nature exile posits the awareness of loss. In this volume psychic loss as exemplified in works of literature generated either by forced or voluntary physical separation is considered the basic content of exile. But as in all vital content, the experience of it is rendered in different forms and produced by different agents in different fashion. Exile is invidious, but the stages of its mutabilities are protean.

In the past the use of the word *exile* was generally restricted to the incidence of forced physical separation, to a decree of banishment by an external force, whether that force were governmental, churchly, communal, or authoritarian in some other guise. A form of expulsion associated with national, communal, and religious roots, the term rarely has been applied to such mundane expulsions as those from a school, fraternal group, or community organization. The feelings generated by expulsion—those of separation, isolation, alienation, loss, confusion, desire to rejoin the group or its converse, unrelenting rancor against the expelling body—are similar, and they delineate what some commentators call the exilic behavorial response. It is assumed that loss of one's country or religion or family is of a profounder nature than loss of one's school or club, but in a psychological perspective and context the matter is debatable. That which makes one feel exiled is the form and shape of exile; its affect is its own demonstration of the fact of an incontrovertible feeling. In this study, exile is viewed as the experience of rejection from one's native land; all other incidences of exile as they spring from this loss of literal land may follow, but inclusion in these pages demands the loss or rejection of country as a primary, native consideration. Thus, internal exiles and dissidents and writers in prison for their ideas—all forms of another body of exile, which some critics put under the umbrella term *internal exile*—are not listed here. If the internal exile in turn becomes a victim banished from his native land, he or she is included in this survey. On a few occasions, when the banishment is to another part of the country or geographic area that is *different* in feel and culture from the lost land, the act is recorded in these pages as one of exile.

This study, however, treats more than the literal exile. Exile, even by denotative signification, covers in its blanket sweep the voluntary exile, that is, one who chooses to absent himself from his country and often in consequence his home and family. The word, which comes from the Latin root *to jump,* carries with it the notion of flight, as one must jump from somewhere, and the *where* in a jump must come from above in order for descent to be made. Both in the classical and in Joyce's modern version, the figure of Daedalus is an exilic one, who must fly by the nets that constrain him from wandering, as well as through the nets of wandering to home; both the Greek Daedalus (and his son Icarus) and the Joycean Dedalus must jump into flight in order to conclude their period of exile.

Daedalus is but one example of exile; in the classical version he is motivated into it by a whimsical emperor who wants his crafty mazeman by his side, but the crafty inventor in his turn finds escape through flight. An earlier Egyptian example of exile may be found in the legend of Osiris and Isis. When the king Osiris was assassinated by his brother, the assassin ordered that the coffin bearing his brother's body be taken beyond the country's borders; even death in this tale is put out to exile. After the discovery that the jewelled coffin bearing Osiris's body had been brought back to his native land by Osiris's loyal wife, Isis, and hidden in a swamp, the brotherly assassin went mad with rage and cut his brother's dead body into fourteen parts. Such is the power of allegial presence; such is the desire to disperse and thus exile any presence of a powerful memory.

Other examples abound from the classical past: Sappho on Lesbos, Ariadne on Naxos, Oedipus on Colonnus; from Roman history: Ovid and Seneca banished by their emperors; from the medieval and Renaissance periods: Dante, who wrote his masterpiece in exile, and Shakespeare, whose works exhibit a context of exile's enduring presence. Compare, for example, the most tender banishment, that of Romeo, but also the bitter spite of Timon, who spits on his countrymen; Coriolanus, who rejects the Rome that has rejected him; Antony, who gives up a world of honor for bondage in Egypt in the arms of Cleopatra; the Moor Othello, yearning for his native land even as he performs his yeoman service for the Venetian Republic; and most profoundly, Lear, banished from castle, family, and all in which he has vainly believed before he becomes a new citizen unto himself again, shorn of everything but his awakening and longed-for death.

Conceivably the sense of wandering, nostalgia, yearning for its own sake that would produce oxymorons of pleasurable pain began at the end of the eighteenth century when reason was discovered to be less than visionary and a rational worldview insufficient to meet the demands of a sensuous soul. *Weltschmerz,* however, is not a German prerogative, and its coinage is a period piece; its phenomenal appearance in the nineteenth century, along with the rooted veils of the Romantic movement, bears intense witness to the exilic contagion that spread over Europe in that century.

Some observers see as the primal exile that of the expulsion of Adam and Eve from the Garden, or in its psychological parallel, that of the child wrenched from the womb of utter self-centeredness. The theme and position of exile dominate religion and religious lore—Moses and the flight from Egypt to the Promised Land; Jesus and the exile to martyrdom as the son of God; Muhammed and the Hegira to Mecca; Buddha and Tao on their pilgrimages to vision.

In this study such concepts of extranational exile as those mentioned above are surveyed in the personal experiences of writers who have departed their country because of religious, social, communal, sexual, political, and personal pressures. Some of these flights into exile have been voluntary, if by voluntary is meant that no specific authoritarian force or decree was employed in the isolate action of exit. Voluntary exit is, however, as much a form of exile as an involuntary move, if what follows it is the pattern of exilic behavior. Thus an expatriate may be viewed as a variant form of exile, if what drives him from his native land to a foreign one is a sense of aloneness, psychic separation, and the despair of nonbelonging. Expatriation is of course a happier state than exile; for the expatriate, if nothing else, is a willing exile who can take his baggage of home supplies with him; he does not have to take flight at a moment's notice, and he can return at whatever point he wishes, unlike the banished victim of exile who must wait for a new order in his land.

What both the exile and the expatriate feel in common is this apprehension of being cast out from their group. Though expatriates do not wander like the exile Cain with the brand of memory goading them, they are never at home till they travel beyond their home communities. The expatriate has been included in this survey as a representative example of the modern phenomenon of the choice of a foreign land over one's own. That choice represents, if not literal exile, the evidence of psychological exile and separation from community.

Literary terms have their semester of fashion as do any other quotients of living language. In the twentieth century, the image of the suitcase is intimately associated with the modern refugee—once the suitcase has been taken away, or the refugee no longer worries where his suitcase sits, he is transformed from a refugee into some other being; he acquires a new name, whether for the better or the worse. An exile then may also be defined as a refugee without a suitcase, one who has found a place after much wandering, and one who begins the equally tortuous routes of wandering through memory and yearning.

One critic, Leszek Kolakowski (in the *Times Literary Supplement,* October 11, 1985), separates the refugee from the exile in terms of personal action. The refugee is one who flees (suitcase or no) to a new border; the exile is one whom his group expels or banishes. In Kolakowski's view the exile is acted upon, while the refugee, shabby as his material condition may be, has engaged in a heroic retreat from the tyranny of the majority and keeps as an option a later battle with his oppressors. Kolakowski places the exile in such a mode of transport as physical deportation or banishment, while the refugee is a fugitive who has made good his escape from persecution and a possible death sentence from his enemies. He is in effect living in self-exile.

Kolakowski sees in the distinction not so much an operating terminology as a means of insight into psychological states and conditions of being. The refugee may harbor guilt for having fled and survived, while those left behind, or those who chose on their own to remain, may have suffered imprisonment or death. Conversely, the exile, if he or she survives, may feel freed from all lingering responsibility to his or her national and local state, and for his or her physical and psychological state, having borne the consequences meted to him or her. The exile in such a case becomes a stoic creature accepting the tragedy of history.

Distinction must also be made between exile and émigré, émigré and emigrant. One is an active choice, the other is a passive reaction, though decision and action are taken in the tension of reaction. Émigré activity follows a flight by choice, a decision taken on to avoid a feared harm or wrong and/or an expulsion by decree of the sociopolitical unit, whether it be a group of people, a religious community, or a local/national government. An émigré, in this scheme, flees to avoid harassment, torture, imprisonment, or worse apprehensions; the method of operation is a matter of varying circumstance and opportunity. An exile, by contrast, is more passive; choice is determined by a decree of banishment from a group above. Continuing this scheme, the emigrant is one who leaves not out of fear but out of the apprehension of a larger, better opportunity elsewhere. Yet, while each distinction is clear in the abstract of definition, every concrete case is murky in its peculiarities. Exclusivity of label, in effect, includes profound deviations from the exclusivity of the label; the exilic complex is never a simple sentence of biography. For example, émigrés and exiles arrive in a foreign land as a result of the same circumstances and attitudes; they feel the same pangs of loss. Even emigrants, who consciously and without ostensible fear of physical harm have chosen to leave, suffer the guilt of the survivor; they sometimes desire to return to that land they thought they had put into a past tense. Again, it is more pertinent to refer to each case, circumstance by circumstance, in order to understand and to draw configurations of the exilic complex.

Paul Tabori, in his pioneering study *The Anatomy of Exile* (London, 1972), a book now sadly out of print, lists several terms that together make up the exilic experience but singly represent different aspects of it. These differences are subtle, sometimes protean, but always *felt*. It is essential to keep such differences in mind when reading the various entries on individual writers in this book, but it is impossible to label a writer definitively by these intellectual categories, simply because a writer's work reflects many moving experiences—that is, the writer's material is transmitted by his or her *being* into a *been* that subsumes differences before they are analyzed. Few of us are pure in any case (although we can be "purified" in case studies for analytic purposes). Our experiences reveal an amalgam of virtues and ideals, decadence and failures, and occasionally premeditated crimes against personhood and community. The reader in using this study will find that a writer's exilic experience is described in biographic/historic terms and his or her work examined in literary/critical ones; on further study the student may discover that distinguishing referents can be applied to the writer so that his or her uniqueness can be summed up by a specialized term. The decision of the editor to use such terms sparingly in the biocritical entries is based on a simple precept: it is better to be reportorial in commentary before approaching critical encapsulation.

Yet the dangers of such an approach are also apparent. Exile, defined as national allegial loss or psychic-centered void, is so broad a concept that a whole age can be swallowed in it without the distinctions (the teeth) that aid understanding (digestion). To avoid enveloping fumes of critical haze, the following flags have been set up as markers for communities of exile.

Political. Writers who have been forced to leave or who have fled their native land to avoid feared arrest and/or harassment by ruling local or national authorities. Among the state conflicts of the twentieth century that have resulted in political exile of writers are the rise of Hitler in Germany and later the German military action in Europe; the Spanish Civil War; the change of national boundaries after World War I; World War II; the Russian Revolutions of 1905 and 1917; the military dictatorships of Latin America, whether on the Right or Left; the Socialist Revolutions in China and the ensuing Cultural Revolution in the four decades since the 1950s; Red Scares in the United States and Canada following World War I and during the era of Senator Joseph McCarthy's anti-communist campaign in the 1950s; the repressive regimes in East and West Europe; the abuse in many areas of the world of individual rights and political persuasions; the Armenian Genocide, in which some 2,000,000 people of one faith were slaughtered or starved; and the revolutions in Iran, Cuba, Kenya, Iraq, and elsewhere, which both freed and later imprisoned outspoken, independent critics.

Religious. Writers who have been forced to leave, or who have fled before their feared arrest, harassment, and/or ostracism because of conflicts in their religious beliefs with those of their local and national community. Among such conflicts are the Holocaust, with its record of extermination of 6,000,000 Jews; persecution in socialist and communist revolutionary states in which atheism is proclaimed as the national and single religion; civil war, in Africa and Ireland over religious beliefs; Iran, where a zealous and theocratic state punishes non-believers in fundamental Islam; and Israeli and Arab wars of hatred and the ensuing stones of the heart.

Cultural. Writers who have left their country because they desired a freer state of being, whether in politics, religious observance, or social and/or sexual mores. Generally, this work lists expatriates as examples of this kind of exile. The American expatriate movement in Paris in the post-World War I decade is seen as a form of voluntary cultural exile. (The expatriates would probably say they gained a new culture rather than lost an old one, since they did not view their departure from their country as any significantly cultural sacrifice.) Under this rubric would also be found colonial writers who chose to emigrate to the large metropolis, to the supposed center or dominant focal place of culture. Frantz Fanon's concept of the colonial victim manipulated by imperialistic forces, and his struggle for freedom from its cultural yoke, serves as an example of cultural exile both for the colonized writer who takes flight to the imperial center and for the writer who moves into another domain. Among these colonial writers are Katherine Mansfield, V. S. Naipaul, Sam Selvon, Ngugi wa Thiong'o, Randolph Stow, Doris Lessing, and Jean Rhys.

Personal/Social. Writers who have chosen separation from their social groups or communities for a number of reasons other than the specific ones listed here. What distinguishes them is their sense of isolation.

Sexual. Writers who have left their country for greater freedom in their sexual expression and/or for a sense of acceptance in a less hostile world. Some of these writers have felt more like exiles in their home communities than in their adopted land. Most of these writers have not been banished or expelled and possibly not even harassed for their sexual behavior or for their writings, but they consider themselves nevertheless victims of repressive milieus. Many of these writers have also felt alienated from their social communities in political, cultural, and economic matters as well. See the group entry "Gay and Lesbian Writers in Exile" as well as individual entries on Gore Vidal, Frederick Rolfe (Baron Corvo), Robin Maugham, and Alfred Chester, among others.

Legal and Criminal. Some writers have chosen exile and/or emigration for reason of tax abatement, finance, or flight from criminal prosecution. Although such writers are not exiles in that they have not fled or left their country for any reason beyond the mundanely personal one of saving money or ameliorating their financial or legal situations, they often suffer the consequences of exile. Their works bear the stamp of loneliness and yearning for a return home, or they are a broad, often satirical, canvas of memories and observations. Those writers who have fled their country either as criminals or as fugitives from criminal prosecution bear the burden of a home lost to them with a heavy reparation as the condition of return. Among such writers may be mentioned Eldridge Cleaver and Louis-Ferdinand Céline.

It should be emphasized again that these "markers" are guideposts and directional signals for clarification in a complex of observations. No one category may be fully satisfactory for an encapsulation of a writer's work in exile; religious persecution in Hitlerite Germany, for example, was a political event as well as an antireligious act. Indeed all religious persecution is political in consequence, if not also in origin, and all cultural harassment is equally an abuse of political freedom, as no culture exists in a societal vacuum. Lists of writers are provided under each of the above categories in the appendices at the end of this book, but individual entries of specific writers should be studied for a less terminal understanding of categorical exile.

Unfortunately, the most virulent form of exile in the modern period is the obvious one—forced emigration because of political, religious, and communal harassment. The diasporas continue in modern times; once started, the stones of the heart they induce cannot be rolled back but must in some way be shattered into the powder of transcendent adaptation. The reverberations of the Jewish exile from the Holy Land thousands of years ago continue, both in the current loyalty to a Zionist state and in the awareness of Jewish people in various countries of their differentness from the majority of their community; in the black experience, both in return-to-Africa movements and in the striving for more viable worlds and landscapes of different and equal crops of human activity and responsibility; in the Holocaust, with its afflictions of the knowledge of horror and evil, which lie dormant but tensed for awakening in the capacious breasts of humans; in the revolutions in the name of greater religious or social good that have displaced hundreds of thousands, in some cases millions, of nonbelievers in those later adherences that evolve from the newly established systems of revolutionary activity. In the twentieth century the list is frighteningly fulsome.

Although other centuries have played host to persecution and exile, it is apparent that exile is more than a passing current in the modern era: it is one of its most dominant literary fortresses and a stasis of the time. The critic Terry Eagleton has asserted that among the eight major writers of the first half of the twentieth century, only one, D. H. Lawrence, is a nonémigré. (See Eagleton's book *Exiles and Emigres: Studies in Modern Literature,* 1970.) Eagleton's point may be strengthened by my assertion that D. H. Lawrence is a preeminent example of an exile, a wanderer whose roots were in no land but that of his visionary world of pantisocracy and who traveled, restlessly, for thirty years after World War I to find a place he could call home. Lawrence chose Taos, New Mexico, with its mix of ancient North American and Renaissance Spanish culture as his "favorite" place; his ashes are buried there, brought by his widow Frieda. The exile thus came home to a foreign place more natural to his nature than the England that lay behind his novels, short stories, and plays.

Exile may also be perceived as a concomitant of the Western postempirical age, with its cause rooted in a political system rather than in such aberrations of history as the Holocaust and the Armenian genocide. The critic Andrew Gurr posits that exile is integral to empire, and that the colonized victim who becomes a writer exploits his empirical servitude and imposed menial status into a nurturing material of literary exploitation and substance. Gurr's thesis of exile as a constructive force for the colonized writer may be compared to Edmund Wilson's earlier premise (in turn indebted to Sigmund Freud) that the artist works from a wound that shoots its own arrows of artistic strength and stimulation. Gurr proposes the consideration that the colonized writer, growing up in a place distant from the metropolis of the empire, or its ruling center, makes a conscious, and subconscious, decision to flee from his origins and to build a new home on foreign shores. The colonized writer is already a victim of alienation; in his new surroundings in the metropolis he gains strength from his memory of what he has fled, and he uses material of early life for the substance of his work. The pattern is suggestive of that of James Joyce, who, adopting the creed of silence, exile, and cunning, wandered through Europe but never forsook the land of his birth and in the process immortalized Ireland, the Catholic church, and his family in every one of his fictions. The colonized writer's pattern, then, is that of flight at an early age, reconstruction during the next decade of his origins through revision of memory, followed by an artistic flowering. By their reliance on concrete details of memory of home, these writers are saved from the self-pity, isolation, and alienation an impersonal and often amorphous metropolitan society imposes on its inhabitants.

The most significant ironies in Gurr's thesis are that the artist, if he is successful in his constructs—that is, if he achieves the creations of his vision—will emerge without any home or history. For in creating his own myths about his native land he will have rendered the historical constructs of them anachronistic. This pattern again is similar to the one Joyce exemplifies—Joyce's Ireland is not a reportorial land naturalistically described, but a modernist communion with Celtic myth and history filtered through the unique Joycean vat of ironic glories and comic quiddities. Not merely for literary declaration did Joyce parallel Ireland with Homer's Greece, but for a deeper rationale—the need of the psychic exile to make contact with a cosmology and an era that would return him to his local place in a universality of time, and in the process transform history into both legend and a new period literature.

The converse of the exile who refuses repatriation is the one who returns to the homeland he has left earlier. He returns to the rocks and sturdy trees of his origin to find he no longer bears the same spacial relationship to those physical manifestations he has sheltered in his dreams during his long years of exile; he no longer is a perennial season, becoming green again each spring like the trees in their appointed (for him preappointed) places. Such a return is at least as unbearably painful as the concomitant knowledge that time passes all human things into a great wash of record. For such a writer-observer, the knowledge of such experience is likely to lead again to the preference of memory over revisitation. The harbor of memory eliminates the inconveniences of new sailings, protecting berthrights from trauma. In some exilic works, the shelter of dream visions overcomes historical realities, but the dreams are of an imposed past overwhelming the tension of a personal and future mood. Such dreams represent an allegiance to shadows that will not dim their lights.

Such exiles, full of the certitude of uncertainty, construct order over the chaos they feel by re-creating in their literary renderings a world turned static; their memorialized perspective provides a reassuring system of time's notation for their traumatized dynamic. This operation of activity cuts reality down to the size of entropy in a long run of time, but in the immediacy of therapy it realizes a profundity of vitality. Judgment on whether the look-back opens the course into the future, or whether such gleanings are the symptoms of cantankerous despair, lies with each individual reader. One reader will find in Vladimir

Nabokov or in James Joyce a linguistic wordplay that dramatizes the profound game of freedom and represents a player's fight against a world armed with clubs that smash niceties of language in their uniform regulations. Others will see in Nabokov's and Joyce's work a profusion of puns, anagrams, and eccentricities of extraordinary variety and craft but without much redeeming social grace or communal utility.

Judgment of the work of literary exiles may thus be seen as inextricably connected with the persona of these works, if by persona is meant the totality of the writer's content, form, style, personal vision, and intimate baggage of technique by which the gift of personality is made. All writers of course use their experience in some way as the premise of their art and as a conclusion to the transmutation of it. What lies, or tells the truth, in the middle of it is the alchemy that changes their biographical experience into something universally new and by so doing creates a felt experience for readers and viewers coming into contact with it. By its nature art is both a birth and a reconstruction of existent material; it is a new body flying in space traveled for the first time every time it is traveled by the high flyer, the Daedalus-like reader who becomes one with the Daedalus creator. What is new if literature is to be made anew is the material presentation of the writer, but the material itself has been present and available since consciousness began. What happens when the fabric is—or fabrics are—suddenly, violently or irremediably torn away becomes the matter of exile. The reader will have noticed the use of dualisms in the previous sentence; this awareness of duality for anyone pursuing the quest of the meaning of exile becomes endemic, since an exile immediately has two selves. He is from *there,* but he is *here* now. Where then is he at base? Once having left a place, he has literally reshaped it by a wrenching of its steady habitual appointments. Even if he goes back to the original place, it cannot be the same. For indeed he has changed, by the fact and means of leaving. And if the place has literally stayed the same, then it has atrophied by remaining unchanged and thus decaying, while other constants have moved and replenished their shape. James Joyce knew this fact of time, this irreversible presence facing every exile's choice of departure and return. He could not go back to Dublin because to do so would destroy his memory of it, his grasp of the truth of its *place* which he was stealing into his art. Only by distance was he able to come home. Only by separation was he able to stay a true Catholic in the capital sense of the word, and only by using the confines of a relatively small world capital was he able to remain catholic in his range of material.

Joyce's transplantation and his protective devices to keep the seeds of his plant and flowering art warm are one way of dealing with exile. Joyce chose exile—or rather he recognized its nature, which a less discerning eye, the conventional citizen of Dublin, avoided through the eager aid of their willing ignorance. Other writers have chosen or been forced to accept other ways of transplanting themselves and thus their creativity, and other methods of keeping alive their roots in an alien land. I. B. Singer came to the United States because he had to flee his native land or suffer the deadly horrors of the Holocaust. He chose never to desert his native language—but which was his native language? Polish, the language of the country in which he was born? Yiddish, the international language of the group by which he achieves his profoundest identity? or English, specifically the version of the English language spoken by Jews in the United States, a land in which Singer has lived for more than forty years. For Singer, the choice has been Yiddish, from first to last, with only an occasional aside in English. For Singer, his style, his view, his meaning has been *Yiddishkeit,* the sheltering community (and possibly ghetto) of Jewishness, the sense of or rather attempt at making sense of a world gone awry. Singer's transplantation may be seen in his current living habits—is he an exile in Miami from New York? The question, deceptively comic at first (one hopes), is ironic because it is the root question in any discussion of exile. In deciding how to identify a person's *place*—that is, the spirit of the place of a person—the observer is deciding how to place him in the context of profoundest identity. There is a second step to this process, and that is the process of transcending exile, of integrating past into present, of discovering that roots have grown anew without severance of old vines. The critic and scholar Asher Milbauer has written on this phenomenon of transcendence of exile, using three literary exiles—Joseph Conrad, Vladimir Nabokov, and Isaac Bashevis Singer—to justify his assertion. Milbauer's analyses illuminate the pattern by which literary exiles go beyond their past into a future that does not deny the validity of the past while assigning it a less dominant territory than its former hegemony. I would suggest in addition that transcendence works in a multitude of ways: for some, the bridges of memory become routes to another path of life; for others, transcendence burns its own bridges of memory, creating a new life without seeds to till anew; for still others, transcendence loses its power because belief in it may be or become less potent than the routine of hopeless habit. In sum, there is a point for some writers at which memory refuses to seed its distinctive parochial boundaries and demands a recognition of isolate identity. Thus the exiled writer achieves again another instance of duality—he has a new identity, a new tradition of which he is a part, a tradition that has helped to shape him but allows him distance as well.

Language, which makes possible a writer and whose "foreignness" makes possible the destruction of that same writer, is another measure of both psychic, rooted exile and literal exile. Indeed, language may be the ultimate measure of psychic exile, for the exilic sense of separation springs from the fall of communication between foreign writer and local/national community. When a writer's language is not comprehended, he is as isolated spiritually as he is physically in an alien land. When he begins to understand the foreign tongue of the land in which he resides, his exile is lessened, for the intelligible world has joined him to a new confederacy. When a writer begins to write in the adopted language of his new country, he may well be stating that he has reached the end of his exile, that he is now associating himself with a new identity, a *word* no longer foreign to him. In this sense, a writer transcends exile once he adopts the home of a new language. Joseph Conrad and Nabokov exemplify this moment of literary conversion, while, representing an alternative view, I. B. Singer has steadfastly refused to divorce himself from Yiddish. In Conrad's case the issue is layered in the fact that Conrad did not write for publication, with rare exceptions, in any language but English; at the earliest stage of his literary career, he chose English as his medium. Although Conrad did not change his literary language in midstream, he did arrive at English as a third linguistic way. His background was Polish, and he spoke fluent French before he chose English as his writer's voice. Conrad's pattern represents the reverse of the usual exilic experience; his was an act of selfmotivated declaration rather than a practical reaction to circumstance. Nabokov's case differs from Conrad's in that he began the composition of his novel *The Real Life of Sebastian Knight* in 1939 in English, fully conscious of forsaking one language (in which he had achieved public distinction) for another. It is pertinent that in *Sebastian Knight* Nabokov explores the question of identity and puts his protagonist through a series of unveilings that allows the character to clothe himself in the new trappings of an emigrant. At the same time Nabokov continued his Russian literary studies and translated work from the Russian into English.

Yet while language is a measure of the distance spanned in the circles of isolation and community, it is a fluid measure. Many writers do not simply exchange languages. More often they become bilingual or trilingual and write in a language that suits their particular context. It may be argued that such a stance proves the validity of the proposed thesis of language as a measure of exile and the isolation erased from it as on a palimpsest of new allegiance. For if a writer retains his native language and learns no other while living in a new land, he is likely to become one kind of exile and remain one kind of foreigner; if he adopts a new language he is likely to become a naturalized citizen of his adopted language-country, though his naturalness with it will come in questing stages; if he learns many languages and uses each in his planned turn of events, then he is more likely to become another kind of exile, perhaps a transcendent of it if he integrates his employment of languages into a unified personal vision rather than a dichotomous, partite set of specific goals. Examples may clarify the issue, although they cannot resolve it: Joyce knew many languages but chose to write in only one; Stefan Heym writes alternately in two, English and German, and lives in one state of Germany which until 1989 banned his work while the other state of Germany read it eagerly; Joseph Brodsky has written in two languages and seems determined to employ English as his language from this point on; Thomas Mann, although he lived for a long time in the United States and expressed his gratitude to his place of haven (even when he departed from it in fear of what he conceived as its political hysteria), did not forsake the German language and relied on translators to spread the word in his fictions; Samuel Beckett, an Irishman resident in France, wrote in French for many years and only later in life wrote in English (a reverse from his earlier habit of writing first in English and then translating into French); Ngugi wa Thiong'o and Chinua Achebe, who once wrote in English and who now write in their African languages (Kikuyu and Ibo), either before or after writing their creations in English, in their attempts to reach and educate a local audience and to reach and educate in a different way the Western and Eastern worlds; and Jerzy Kosinski, who writes only in English, having made a conscious choice to identify himself with the new society he chose to enter a generation ago.

Life is never a losing matter, even in the gain of loss and sorrow. Accretion of experience is what shapes our present and future and makes possible our understanding of the past. In this sense memory is a revisionist movement, forcing us to see yesterday in present light. The duality of perspective is shared by others besides the exile, but the impact of the lensing experience may provide a greater illumination to the exile's consciousness than to others.

Exile is a living tissue that grows in stages and degrees. We are exiled from the womb in the psychological apparatus of growing up. We have been exiled from the Garden of Eden. We leave things behind and cannot go back to them at many moments in our lives, and there are moments we cannot revisit; moments pass even when we are silent and hold our breaths in the fierce wish to hug a moment forever to our breasts. Such examples are universal and common to mankind, but rarely studied as exile. The more usual forms have been mentioned earlier: the historical, the political, the religious, the social and cultural, the sexual. Exile has been studied as a time capsule—a hurtling from the space of time as well as from the land.

I believe that now, at the end of the twentieth century, exile may be seen as one of the most deeply rooted characteristics of the modern era. Exile, which by definition makes one feel always the other, has become a widely traveled terrain of our times. It represents one of the modern era's significant communities of experience.

J. Gerald Kennedy (essay date 1993)

SOURCE: Kennedy, J. Gerald. "Place, Self, and Writing: Toward a Poetics of Exile." In *Imagining Paris: Exile, Writing, and American Identity,* pp. 1-37. New Haven: Yale University Press, 1993.

[*In the following excerpt, Kennedy analyzes how Paris became for such writers as e.e. cummings, Ernest Hemingway, and Anaïs Nin a place that "inescapably reflects the creation of an exilic self."*]

Shortly after returning from a prison camp in France, E. E. Cummings composed *The Enormous Room* (1922), an experimental novel recounting his ordeal as a Norton Harjes ambulance driver arrested (with his friend Slater Brown) on suspicion of German sympathy and incarcerated by French authorities. From his confinement with a motley assortment of men, Cummings created an exuberant, heterogeneous narrative mixing French with English, traditional allegory with naturalistic detail, and verbal portraiture with stream-of-consciousness impressionism. As implied by the title, the broad subject of this autobiographical account is the experience of place; the camp at La Ferté Macé and the "enormous room"—a dark, oblong enclosure "unmistakably ecclesiastical in feeling"—comprise Cummings' minimal world.[1] In this dismal compound, as he vents his scorn for French officialdom, the writer forms memorable friendships with fellow prisoners and thus recovers a faith in human goodness. His experience transforms the enormous room from a chamber of horror echoing with "weird cries, oaths, laughter" (42) into a scene of community filled with "a new and beautiful darkness" (233).

Oddly enough, however, the place which most clearly reflects the inner change in Cummings is Paris. He passes through the city twice: once on his way to the prison, when the idea of his arrest still seems preposterous, and then again after his discharge, en route to America. The earlier scene indeed depicts an ecstatic return to the city where Cummings and Brown had enjoyed a five-week revel before going to the Western Front. As the crowded night train approaches a station, the idea of Paris explodes into consciousness; the city's very name becomes a magical incantation: "Some permissionaires cried 'Paris.' The woman across from me said 'Paris, Paris.' A great shout came up from every insane drowsy brain that had travelled with us—a fierce and beautiful cry, which went the length of the train. . . . Paris where one forgets, Paris which is Pleasure, Paris in whom our souls live, Paris the beautiful, Paris enfin" (30). In a chapter significantly titled "A Pilgrim's Progress," Cummings enters a Celestial City which promises to satisfy all human longings. Richard S. Kennedy observes that "when the train reaches Paris, it is a holy place: the people on the streets are 'divine,' a motherly woman sells [Cummings] coffee, a 'sacredly delicious' brew."[2] Yet we know that Cummings is merely in transit; unlike Bunyan's pilgrim, his ultimate destination is "La Misere," the place of misery.

When the dazed Cummings finally obtains his release from prison, he can barely comprehend an order to report to the American Embassy in Paris. After four months in a dark pen, he feels disoriented: "Where in Hell am I? What is Paris—a place, a somewhere, a city, life, to live: infinitive. . . . Paris. Life. Liberté. La Liberté. 'La Liberté'—I almost shouted in agony" (237). From the mud and filth of La Ferté Macé, Paris is simply an idea of survival and freedom. By the time Cummings reaches the city, however, he finds quite a different place:

> The streets. Les rues de Paris. I walked past Notre Dame. I bought tobacco. Jews are peddling things with American trademarks on them, because in a day or two it's Christmas I suppose. Jesus it is cold. Dirty snow. Huddling people. La guerre. Always la guerre. And chill. Goes through these big mittens. Tomorrow I shall be on the ocean. . . . Les rues sont tristes. Perhaps there's no Christmas, perhaps the French government has forbidden Christmas. Clerk at Norton Harjes seemed astonished to see me. O God it is cold in Paris. Everyone looks hard under lamplight, because it's winter I suppose. Everyone hurried. Everyone hard. Everyone cold. Everyone huddling. Everyone alive; alive: alive.
>
> (240-41)

After his stint in prison (where he has heard about the horrors of war from other inmates), Cummings sees the city as a site not of beauty or pleasure but of suffering. The air is cold, the snow dirty, the streets sad, the faces hard; even Cummings' style seems austere. The city has been transformed by winter and "la guerre." The authorities who threw him into prison may even cancel Christmas, but thanks to the brotherhood he has discovered at La Misère, Cummings now experiences place as a focus of community; in winter Paris is bearable because everyone is "alive." That perspective, so different from his earlier, effusive vision of "Paris the beautiful," marks a crucial change in Cummings himself, whose experience of hardship now enables him to set aside his illusions of Paris, to recognize its wartime sadness and to value its defiant vitality.

Three decades later, in *I: Six Nonlectures* (1953), Cummings looked back upon Paris (to which he had returned in the twenties as a painter-poet) not as an aggregate of buildings and monuments but as a place manifesting "the humanness of humanity": "Everywhere I sensed a miraculous presence, not of mere children and women and men, but of living beings; and the fact that I could scarcely understand their language seemed irrelevant, since the truth of our momentarily mutual aliveness created an imperishable communion." From the perspective of his sixtieth year he sees Paris as the meeting place of two realms, the sacred and the secular. He recalls an image from his "Post Impressions" of the twenties:

> Paris; this April sunset completely utters
> utters serenely silently a cathedral
> before whose upward lean magnificent face
> the streets turn young with rain.[3]

These lines, he asserts, demonstrate the happy coexistence of the material and the ethereal; he claims to have celebrated in Paris "an immediate reconciling of spirit and flesh, now and forever, heaven and earth." In retrospect, Cummings translates the city of exile into a symbol of his own contradictory desires: "Paris was for me precisely and complexly this homogeneous duality: this accepting transcendence; this living and dying more than death or life."[4]

What do these separate representations of *la ville lumière* suggest about the nature of place? What do they imply about the way human beings conceptualize places and form attachments to them? In the progression of responses sketched above—from the novel to the poem to the late philosophical "nonlecture"—we see that Paris changes: not the actual city (although the novel implies a change of seasons) but the city of words constructed by Cummings. Through these brief passages, we witness the evolution of an imaginary city while regarding its transformation as a sign of the changes which Cummings (or his persona) has undergone. The phrases which constitute this imaginary city are mimetic, but what they "represent" are the psychic and emotional conditions under which he has contemplated Paris or his own mental image of Paris. These fugitive references, supposedly to a real city, thus mirror certain changes in the writer's own consciousness and sensibility. In this respect they suggest the potential function of place in every textual representation of self; more broadly, they imply that identity itself inheres in the relation which the self assumes to its surroundings (material and human). We see in Cummings' novel that he makes sense of his wartime ordeal through a contemplation of two sites: the "enormous room" at La Misère—which becomes a microcosm of Europe and an emblem of the human community—and the city of Paris, which in its contrasting aspects discloses his own growth. Recounting his transformative experiences, Cummings reveals the orienting function of place; he can tell his story only through the reconstruction of those sites. For him, as for other American writers, Paris was a scene of metamorphosis; the city's image, inscribed in the expatriate text, inescapably reflects the creation of an exilic self.

To pose the question of place is to revive an issue which criticism apparently disposed of decades ago with the concept of "setting." Yet as Leonard Lutwack has recently remarked, we still lack "a theory of the formal use of place in literature." Though all narrative action unfolds in space and time, criticism has concerned itself almost exclusively with temporality; we have barely begun to consider the textual implications of place. Lutwack proposes that all literary projections of locale express "symbolic purposes even though in their descriptiveness they may be rooted in fact."[5] This figurality derives from both archetypal associations (mountains connote vision, spirituality, and so on) and particular implications of place generated by a given work (the vulgarity of Yonville, for example, in *Madame Bovary*). Lutwack asserts that "the most elemental orientation of a reader to a narrative text is through its evocation of places" (37). Here he refers to "those aspects of the actual environment" forming the world inhabited by fictive characters; he claims that correlations between real and fictional topography determine the reader's preliminary assumptions about narrative form and mode.

If Lutwack establishes the importance of place in literature and the diversity of its treatment, however, his distinction between the "actual environment" and an imaginative landscape bears reexamination. A real environment becomes intelligible—and comparable—only after it enters into language as an instance of place; yet as geographical theorists have suggested, all conceptions of place are inherently and inescapably subjective. According to Yi-Fu Tuan, "place" is a "concretion of value," space endowed with value; Edward Relph speaks of places as "focuses of intention."[6] For both, the notion of place implies the projection of human sensibility upon the natural or built environment. Hence one cannot compare an "actual" place with its literary representation, since there is literally no "place" apart from an interpreting consciousness. The only possible comparison for the critic is thus between a personal, readerly concept of place (perhaps informed by knowledge of an existent site) and a textual, writerly image. This distinction forces a rethinking of the status of literary topography, for the salient difference lies not in the relation between real and fictive environments but between textual scenes and the symbolic experiences of place which they inscribe. In the case of Cummings' novel, Paris is first synonymous with beauty and pleasure, then with life and liberty, and finally with the persistence of humanity in the face of war. What matters is not the discrepancy between his version of the city and that of the Baedeker guide but rather the connection between his city of words and the internalized place to which it refers. Perhaps every textual construction of place implies just such a mapping or symbolic re-presentation of an interior terrain.

In everyday conversation, the word *place* designates a portion of the physical world, detaches it from its surroundings, and tacitly attributes a distinctiveness: "Vienna is a place I want to visit." The uniqueness or difference assumed by such a statement resides not in the material configuration of streets, buildings, trees, or rivers but in an *idea* of place already embedded in consciousness and shaped by cultural forces (art, literature, advertising, journalism), as well as personal fantasy. The same place may, as we know, hold radically different meanings for different persons: on a visit to London, the traveler who loses her passport and gets food poisoning will have a significantly different sense of the city than someone who falls in love in Hyde Park. Relph shows how the identity of a place derives from three intertwined yet irreducible elements—"physical features or appearance, observable activities and functions, and meanings or symbols." Some of these components seem fixed, objective, and independent of subjective judgment; yet even so empirical a criterion as the "appearance" of a place implies its contemplation from a certain vantage point or through a particular representation. We can distinguish between a popularly held image (Rome, the eternal city) and an individual perception of place, but both are ultimately human constructions; the supposed "identity" of a place may be little more than the dominant popular image. A person's sense of place emerges from a fusion of perceptions occurring on several levels—a process which inevitably remains conditional and arbitrary. Such an operation hinges, according to Relph, on one's existential relation to place, which may be characterized by some form of "insideness" or "outsideness."[7] The extent of one's psychic involvement in or identification with a given place affects—and is affected by—the symbolic meanings associated with that site. "Outsideness" connotes the persistent sense of exclusion from or disregard for one's material surroundings.

From the converse perspective of "insideness," place becomes (as Tuan says) a "calm center of established values," a symbolic constant amid change and movement; he thus ascribes a groundedness, a sense of orientation and identity to the root concept of meaningful space. Here place connotes security and belonging, as in the expression "my place," a synonym for home.[8]

Feelings of "insideness" and "outsideness" occur as more or less conscious responses to milieu; but we can also experience place as space which has penetrated to the level of the unconscious. Pierre Sansot appositely remarks: "To the rather embarrassing question 'What is the essence of a place?' one must often substitute another question: 'What can one dream about it?'" To dream of place is to experience the intrusion of landscape into the deepest recesses of the psyche and to recognize the inevitably symbolic structure which our perceptions of the environment assume. But dreams typically manifest a topography quite different from conscious perceptions. Our residual, waking remembrance of dreamscapes may, for example, call to mind a place in childhood, a scene of trauma or pleasure, without providing any specific visual correlation; we recognize through pure intuition the site of an essential though repressed episode. This phenomenon of intuitive recognition suggests that one's sense of place is determined less by specific geographical features than by experiential associations. It also implies, however, that the assimilation of experience in the unconscious—the processing of everyday life—depends in some way upon these spatial and topical attachments. Beyond their conscious symbolic or functional importance, places thus invade the unconscious and acquire oneiric potency. According to Gaston Bachelard, the most powerful psychospatial image is the house in which we were raised, which is "physically inscribed in us" and "imbued with dream values which remain after the house is gone."[9] The house of childhood recurs in the unconscious as a phantasmic repository of early impressions and sensations, ordinarily as the embodiment of at-homeness.

Summing up the multiple implications of place for what Heidegger might call our being-in-the-world, Relph argues that

> the essence of place lies in the largely unselfconscious intentionality that defines places as profound centers of human existence. There is for virtually everyone a deep association with and consciousness of the places where we were born and grew up, where we live now, or where we have had particularly moving experiences. This association seems to constitute a vital source of both individual and cultural identity and security, a point of departure from which we orient ourselves in the world.[10]

This process of orientation, of situating ourselves in space and coming to know the surrounding environment, seems indispensable to the recognition of the self as a self. The elements of place to which we are most responsive (consciously or unconsciously) comprise the physical signs of our deepest intentions and desires. Gabriel Marcel once observed that "an individual is not distinct from his place; he is that place." His contention is not that geography determines personality (otherwise all natives of a region would be indistinguishable) but that we find or know ourselves principally through the attachments we form to a place.

Similarly, we organize our experiences with other people through associations with place; to recall an acquaintance is to visualize scenes and contexts in which we have known that individual. This is precisely the psychic connection between identity and setting evoked when we try to "place" someone who looks vaguely familiar: we recollect a college lecture hall and instantly recognize an old classmate. The identification occurs not through a rational calculation of time or chronology but by recalling some physical scene which condenses past experience as a nexus of associations. Roger M. Downs and David Stea make the intriguing suggestion that we can have no awareness of past events in our lives "without a sense of the place in which they happened."[11] They contend that we reconstruct the past largely through the imagery of place and imply that memory is less the retrieval of bygone time than a recovery of symbolic space.

Despite its title (which underscores the passage of time), Proust's *A la recherche du temps perdu* demonstrates this point: in the first volume, *Du côté de chez Swann,* the narrator recovers an earlier self by evoking the village of Combray, a place associated with childhood visits to his aunt's house. Through the lapse of time, his image of the town had become dim and unreal: "These Combray streets exist in so remote a corner of my memory, painted in colors so different from those in which the world is decked for me today, that in fact one and all of them, and the church which towered above them on the Square, seem to me now more unsubstantial than the projections of my magic-lantern."[12] Conjured up by the taste of lime tea and *petites madeleines,* however, the memory of that lost world returns: the church of Sainte-Hilaire, Tante Léonie's house, the streets and lanes of the village, the "two ways" (the Méséglise and Guermantes), the ruined castle, and all of the other images of Combray which compose its particularity. For Proust the village is that network of associations within which he locates himself as a subject. Yet he also knows that the place of memory bears little relation to contemporary Combray, where even the landscape has changed; he recalls promenades along the rue des Perchamps, "a street for which one might search in vain through the Combray of today, for the public school [which in the actual village of Illiers has been renamed the Lycée Marcel Proust] now rises upon its site" (213).

The remembered sites which hold the key to our being thus have a shadowy, precarious existence:

> The places that we have known belong now only to the little world of space on which we map them for our own convenience. None of them was ever more than a thin slice, held between the contiguous impressions

that composed our life at that time; remembrance of a particular form is but regret for a particular moment; and houses, roads, avenues are as fugitive, alas, as the years.

(551)

Despite their evanescent nature, however, places known in the past remain with us like certain tastes and smells, ready to be summoned into consciousness and to unfold a profusion of meaning; according to Proust these places form part of the "vast structure of recollection" (58) through which we order and interpret our past lives. He uses the metaphor of Japanese cutouts that expand in a bowl of water from tiny crumbs to recognizable shapes of "flowers or houses or people" to suggest how a single image or impression may evoke a detailed recollection of place. Throughout his later experiences in Balbec and Paris, Proust's narrator draws upon memories of Combray as a point of reference and a source of coherence. The quintessential episode associated with Combray—his mother's refusal to bestow the goodnight kiss—indeed holds the key to Marcel's subsequent preoccupation with the paradoxes of desire.

A shorter modernist text, Hemingway's "Snows of Kilimanjaro," enables us to examine with perhaps greater efficiency this complicated relation between place and memory. Here, a dying writer on safari in Africa visualizes a series of mental scenes—the rail station at Karagatch, the Alpine village of Schruns, a trout stream in the Black Forest—each of which evokes certain moments or phases of consciousness. Set against the immediate environment of the African plain, these flashbacks imply a process of re-collection, a psychic review *in extremis* of experiences which have shaped a life. In effect, the narrative enacts the gesture of autobiography, the effort to locate in past experience those episodes in which the self has defined itself through its responses to the world. As the writer, Harry, recalls these sites of being, he acknowledges the function of place in remembrance; each separate locale, evoked by sensory images, epitomizes an entire episode. More poignantly, these scenes signify stories which will go untold, for Harry recognizes that "he would never write the things that he had saved to write until he knew enough to write them well."[13] Hemingway here manifests more than self-pity: Harry's remorse betrays a profound attachment to places where he has glimpsed basic truths. These sites mark moments in which he has been fully alive to the world, and in the chagrin of lost opportunity, the writer virtually equates place with writing. The "things that he had saved to write" all reside within recollections of physical scenes: the ranch out West, his grandfather's log house on a hill above the lake, the streets of Constantinople, the working-class neighborhood in Paris.

In the italicized passages which comprise Harry's reveries, Hemingway implies that in some fundamental way, we do not inhabit places so much as they inhabit us. Each of the physical scenes, linked (in Relph's phrase) with "particularly moving experiences," persists in memory and dream as a psychic landmark. The writer's life is obviously more than the sum of those places in which he has lived, but the difference between one place and another makes possible the recollection of that life and in effect determines the very structure of remembrance. Wyoming, Paris, and Constantinople constitute more than settings in which meaningful events have unfolded; they designate separate spheres of being, each marked by specific impressions, desires, and contingencies. As Harry recalls these scenes, he implicitly takes the measure of his existence, trying to discern in memory some scheme or pattern which will account for the cruel irony of his death in Africa by gangrenous infection. But in depicting this "recherche du temps perdu," Hemingway reflects less on time than on the primacy of place in the writer's conception of self. If memory is the crux of identity, images of place determine the act of remembrance. Late in his career Hemingway wrote: "We live by accidents of terrain, you know. And terrain is what remains in the dreaming part of your mind."[14] In "The Snows of Kilimanjaro," the dying writer surveys that inner terrain, the symbolic landscape of his life, to understand who he is and what he has been; like Tolstoy's Ivan Ilych, Harry confronts the enigma of self in the imminence of annihilation. Each of the places in which he has lived holds a clue to the essential identity threatened by the absolute displacement of death.

As if to preserve these memories of place (and hence the remembering self) from oblivion, the writer at one point considers dictating his recollections to Helen, the wife at his bedside. He recalls one site so integral to his self-conception, however, that it cannot be thus transcribed:

> *You could dictate* [*the fishing trip to the Black Forest*]. *but you could not dictate the Place Contrescarpe where the flower sellers dyed their flowers in the street and the dye ran over the paving where the autobus started and the old men and the women, always drunk on wine and bad marc; and the children with their noses running in the cold; the smell of dirty sweat and poverty and drunkenness at the Café des Amateurs and the whores at the Bal Musette they lived above.*

(69)

The significance of the Left Bank setting is not immediately clear. The flashback follows two previous allusions to Paris in dialogue with Helen; Paris also figures in a recollection of the writer's encounter with the Dadaists of Montparnasse, evoked by the image of an *"American poet with . . . a stupid look on his potato face"* (identified in manuscript as Malcolm Cowley) talking in a café *"with a Roumanian who said his name was Tristan Tzara"* (66). Through these references Hemingway draws an implicit contrast between the elegant Parisian haunts Harry has known with his wealthy second wife and the more modest environs associated with a previous marriage and the beginnings of his career.

But why is the author unable to dictate a description of the quarter around the place de la Contrescarpe? Why does that sketch seem possible only if he writes it himself? In two sentences Hemingway discloses the psychic importance of this place for Harry's conception of himself:

> *In that poverty, and in that quarter across the street from a Boucherie Chevaline and a wine co-operative he had written the start of all he was to do. There never was another part of Paris that he loved like that, the sprawling trees, the old white plastered houses painted brown below, the long green of the autobus in the round square, the purple flower dye upon the paving, the sudden drop down the hill of the rue Cardinal Lemoine to the River, and the other way the narrow crowded world of the rue Mouffetard.*
>
> (70)

This section of Paris—the very milieu where Hemingway served his apprenticeship in 1922-23—thus becomes associated with the life of writing and with a period of ambition and hard work prior to the dissipation of Harry's middle years. Throughout the passage, he recalls with disdain the drunken locals, contrasting their *ivresse* with his own industry and recollecting the room he rented in the hotel where Verlaine died: *"He had a room on the top floor of that hotel that cost him sixty francs a month where he did his writing, and from it he could see the roofs and chimney pots and all the hills of Paris."* While the view from his apartment is restricted (*"you could only see the wood and coal man's place"*), the writing room significantly affords a panorama; by this vertical ascent, a secular, urban mode of transcendence, the writer claims a position of symbolic dominion. Seen in its totality, the confusing maze of Paris reveals its ultimate form and organization. From this loft, in a hotel which once housed a famous poet, Harry knows where he is and who he is. The old neighborhood, recollected in vivid colors, becomes associated with the formation of this writing self; it is appropriately only through an act of writing that he can recover the immediacy of that place which, in its remembered details, yields his original identity as an author.

But that task remains uncompleted, and Harry's lingering regret is that *"he had never written about Paris. Not the Paris that he cared about"* (71). Hemingway here discloses a nostalgia for the lost world of his own youth. By the mid-1930s he had realized the importance to his development of those lucky years on the Left Bank; yet not until the late fifties, as he struggled against infirmity and despair, did he compose (in *A Moveable Feast*) his memoirs of "the Paris that he cared about." The dying protagonist of "Snows" receives no second chance to preserve the story of a life lived in and shaped by memorable places. Instead, like the doomed hero of Borges' "Secret Miracle," he must content himself with the cerebral projection of never-to-be-completed writing. In the end, his memories reveal the psychic fusion of topography and experience, as desire resolves into the forms and features of place. Hemingway's story culminates in a vision of Kilimanjaro, which in the spatial dynamic of the narrative marks an apotheosis of place, the geographical concretion of the longing for artistic transcendence figured in Harry's climb to the top-floor room. In this final fantasy, the dying writer reinscribes the dream of a younger self, confirming again the symbolic status of landscape in the conceptualizing of a life story.

Although Hemingway's story enables us to consider the role of place in the structure of remembrance, we must look elsewhere for insight into the daily process by which one internalizes surroundings and thus orients and defines the self. Downs and Stea call this phenomenon "cognitive mapping" and define it as "a series of psychological transformations by which an individual acquires, codes, stores, recalls, and decodes information about the relative locations and attributes of phenomena in his everyday spatial environment."[15] That is, cognitive mapping describes the assimilation of sensory information about the places we inhabit or traverse not as raw impressions but as a "code" of meaningful signs which collectively produce a mental map. This cartography enables us to function by providing a sense of distance and relation and by schematizing our experiential world in terms of valued or significant sites. Social scientists have examined spatial behavior dependent on cognitive mapping: giving directions, taking shortcuts, determining shopping routes, or even choosing one's place of residence. They have acknowledged, moreover, that beyond the conduct of daily business, this topographical orientation seems vital to personal survival in a complex environment; without this internalized map we would literally be unable to find our way home.[16]

But cognitive mapping surely affects more than spatial behavior. We have already seen in Proust and Hemingway how encoded landscape figures in the operation of memory; other literary texts suggest that place enters importantly into the day-to-day construction of the self. Of particular relevance here is the autobiographical form most attentive to everyday life: the journal or diary. In her *Early Diary,* the French-born American writer Anaïs Nin records her agonizing return to Paris in late 1924. Before leaving the United States she had mused: "The New Yorker dreams of Paris while the Parisian wonders about New York. And we go through life without definitely realizing any place. They all remain unreal for us."[17] Yet her experience proved otherwise; after moving to Paris with her husband, Hugh Guiler, Nin became obsessed with the reality of the city, which for nearly three years seemed to determine the course of her existence. Her profound ambivalence toward Paris forms a key to her diary during this period and mirrors an ongoing psychological conflict.

Perhaps because she recalled the Paris of her childhood, Nin returned full of illusions. Her first weeks there established a pattern of sharply vacillating emotion: one day the air was sweet, and Nin felt "the pleasure of being in Paris" (81); a few days later "Paris was gloomy," and she wished that she had never come back (84). But she nevertheless began to reorient herself, walking with Hugh through the Tuileries . . . , beside the river, and along the grand boulevards. Recurrent references in the diary indicate sites of personal significance: the place des Vosges, the Louvre, Notre Dame, the Luxembourg Gardens, and the bookstalls along the Seine. For a few months in 1925 Nin lived on the Right Bank near the Etoile and enjoyed promenades along the fashionable boulevard Haussmann; the couple subsequently took a Left Bank apartment on the rue Schoelcher in Montparnasse. Nin took a skeptical view of this quarter (then teeming with expatriate artists) and preferred little side streets—like the rue Vavin—to the broad boulevard du Montparnasse. When urban crowds aroused her disgust, Nin alternately sought out quiet parks or remained ensconced in the apartment. But despite a reclusive tendency, she also loved walking and became familiar with the streets of the city's central arrondissements. Her perambulations reflect a seemingly deliberate effort to absorb the geography of the city—as if absolute spatial orientation might somehow reconcile her to the invisible Paris which oppressed her.

Much as she tried to understand the city, though, Nin felt a revulsion toward it and confided in her diary: "This Parisian life, I am convinced now, is a constant source of irritation to me" (142). We can identify three separate sources of dis-ease which undermined "the pleasure of being in Paris." The first was the "intolerable pain" inflicted upon the modest young wife by the spectacle of "impurities"—public displays of sensuality or vulgarity. Prior to the awakening which plunged her into sexual adventures as well as the composition of erotica, Nin discovered in Parisian culture a bawdiness which tainted her perception of the physical city:

> Paris is like a giant park, riotous in coloring, festive in its fountains and flowers, glorious in its monuments. When I stand at the top of the Champs-Elysées, with its chestnut trees in flower, its undulations of shining cars, its white spaciousness, I feel as if I were biting into a utopian fruit, something velvety and lustrous and rich and vivid.
>
> But the worms are gnawing it. A repugnant phrase in a book, a coarse breath of the theatre, a look from sacrilegious eyes, the smell of something foul and abysmal, . . . and the fruit turns bitter in my mouth. I stand in the same place, but shivering, nauseated.
>
> My reaction to sensuality causes me infinite pain.
>
> (142-43)

Nin's reaction was complicated by her relationship to her philandering father—who personified "intelligent, insidious, cultured Paris"—and to her husband Hugh, the "humorous banker" whose character would be corrupted, she worried, by the "poisoned life" of the city. Reading between the lines, we see that Nin also feared the transformation of her own nature—specifically, the loss of those constraints which protected her from the seductive influence of Paris. Like Lambert Strether in James's *Ambassadors* (a novel she greatly admired), Nin felt strangely intrigued and repelled by the complicated amours of the French.

A second source of unhappiness was the climate of Paris. Weather seems to have determined both her mood and her perception of the city; with keen self-awareness she observed: "I react with the exactitude of a barometer to the atmosphere" (95). On 2 January 1925 she confessed: "Tonight I hate Paris. The wind is blowing heavy rain-drops about; the streets are wet and muddy; the automobile horns, more discordant and insistent than ever" (82). Nin's attentiveness to climate illustrates the influence of weather on the experience of place. Rain and gloomy skies triggered her most despairing characterizations of Paris:

> Hateful gray days—short and dark and oppressing, wrapped in mists, with a pale, powerless sun appearing occasionally through them like a mockery. You see the copper circle, but its rays cannot reach you—the fog swallows them and cuts up the warmth halfway. And to me it is even sadder to see the sun and not to feel it, to be reminded that on other worlds it shines so deliciously. . . . I want to go *anywhere,* but away from loathsome Paris.
>
> (243)

Yet pleasant weather could transform the city: "Paris on a sunny day is such a different thing!" (84). Sometimes atmospheric conditions enabled her to recover a romantic perspective: "Today, in the dense fog, I saw Paris like a magic city. The shadowy people, the muffled sounds, the fantastic air that hung over the most common *voitures à bras,* over the vague and featureless heads of the vendors. The Seine has completely disappeared. I walked over a bridge that spanned two clouds" (89). But such moments came infrequently. Throughout the diary, Nin traced a curious relationship to Paris in which she had seemingly surrendered her will: the city in its various seasonal and meteorological aspects controlled her emotional life.

Finally, Nin felt oppressed by the weight of French literary tradition. Unlike most Americans in Paris, she enjoyed fluency in French; she read the literary journals, attended lectures at the Sorbonne, and retained from childhood a reverence for the *grands hommes* of French letters. Nin registered the ordeal of finding her literary identity in the shadow of such brilliance; she conceived herself as the victim of "a Monster, . . . the perpetual presence of Letters" in Paris which "swallows your individuality." Sensing that she had become paralyzed, she wrote in the dramatic entry of 11 April 1926: "Paris kills my writing. I have been oppressed and belittled and silenced in Paris. As soon as I leave it, I feel free again, vivid, enthusiastic, fervent, creative. . . . I have been spiritually crucified in Paris" (189). Nin here acknowledges the intimidating—and patently masculine—authority of French tradition as enshrined at the Sorbonne, the Panthéon, and the Académie Française. She felt that her survival depended upon relocating, finding a milieu in which writing would be possible: "All I need now," she wrote, "is a chance to develop in a place where I am allowed to breathe" (191).

For a time Nin imagined that a room above the rooftops might enable her to come to terms with the city she described as "hell on earth" (198). After seeing a movie with aerial views of the capital, she felt a need to "get a sweeping sight of the whole" for she had seen "only parts of Paris at a time" (99-100). She thought that a panoramic view would disclose "the beauty of the whole" which—in her experience—was often "lost in the sourness of the details." Nin couched in aesthetic terms her own desire for an elevated perspective: to scan the horizon, note landmarks, and absorb the spatial configuration is to conduct an essential remapping, to place oneself above a landscape thus rendered coherent, picturesque, and benign. By surmounting Paris literally she hoped to conquer the effects of the oppressive, internalized city. This desire for "a sweeping sight of the whole" led to the discovery in May 1926 of a top-floor servant's room on the rue Schoelcher, which the couple rented as "a Secret Refuge, a workroom." Nin called it "the High Place" and recognized its psychic importance: "On this little terrace, seeing Paris from such a high plane, nothing can affect us" (205). Although not quite a room of her own, the loft offered "peace and books and sunshine" (224) as well as superb views of Montmartre and Sacré Coeur. But Nin found the loneliness "intolerable"; four months after renting the top-floor room, she acknowledged a "fear of the High Place, where I am alone with my ideas, alone with my hate of Paris" (233).

Unable to relieve her anguish by positioning herself above the city, Nin tried yet another strategy of adjustment. In December 1926 she vowed: "I shall try to turn my hate of Paris into writing and make it harmless" (248). Hugh had suggested that she consolidate her journal entries under the title "Two Years in Paris," and she initially undertook an analysis of Montparnasse: "I am going to study my quarter, my neighbors, and their life." She examined the bohemianism of the Rotonde and the Dôme . . . , concluding that the great cafés were "fake in spirit," crowded with "men and women who make sport of art" (252). But Nin wanted to take a wider view of Paris; in a passage framed as the opening of her book, she offered a striking parallel:

> Night and day the gargoyles of Notre Dame look down upon Paris with a sinister expression, with derision, mockery, amusement, with hate, fear, disgust. For two years I looked down into Paris, and tried to understand why the gargoyles had such expressions.
>
> It seemed strange that they should be able to look in such a manner at the lovely river, the graceful bridges, the ancient palaces, the gardens, the majestic avenues, the flowers, the quays and the old books, the bird market, the lovers, the students. What do they see beneath these attractive surfaces? Why do they frown perpetually and mock eternally? What monstrous secrets made their eyes bulge out, twisted their mouths, filled their heads with wrinkles and grimaces?
>
> I know now.
>
> (253)

Observing a disparity between the city's "attractive surfaces" and its "monstrous secrets," Nin conducts a further remapping of the visible Paris in order to disclose an invisible world. The avenues, bridges, and palaces merely point toward an unspeakable abyss. But while this passage seems initially to reinscribe Nin's misery, we should note that by bringing Paris into her own discourse she has achieved a conceptual breakthrough implied by the final claim "I know now." Precisely *what* she knows remains unspecified, but the comparison of her vantage point with that of the gargoyles seems revealing. For Nin has found at the geographical and symbolic center of Paris, literally amid the stones of its most fabled monument, a figure for her own relation to the city. She has in effect metaphorized her alienation from Paris in the gargoyle's sardonic gaze; she has articulated her displacement through a recognizable sign of place. . . .

Nin's "Two Years in Paris" apparently never reached completion. But the project seems to have marked a turning point in her relation to the city. In early 1927, she listed an achievement of the preceding year: "I faced and accepted Paris as a test of my courage" (258). A visit to America that summer placed her life in France in a new perspective; recounting for a friend her experiences in Paris, Nin confessed: "I found myself drawing an intensely interesting picture, full of color, movement, rhythm, meaning and beauty. And unexpectedly, I was struck by the conviction that the life in New York could not hold me, that I longed to return to Paris" (283). Into the quarrel with Paris she had of course projected other struggles: with loneliness and depression, with the burden of household duties, with doubt about her talent, with worries about her "perfect" marriage, with suppressed desires and disturbing temptations. But her relentless contemplation of the city—"the lovely river, the graceful bridges, the ancient palaces, the gardens, the majestic avenues, the flowers, and the quays and the old books"—finally culminated in a reconciliation to place, renewed purpose in her writing, and a growing acceptance of her sensuality.

Nin's diary displays, to be sure, many other facets of her emotional and intellectual life. But her encounter with the city reflects with remarkable precision the course of that life and illuminates its essential unfolding. Because the diary provides only a selective condensation of daily thoughts and activities, however, we cannot reconstruct Nin's response to Paris in its full complexity; what remains is at best a partial, residual image of the city she had internalized, suggesting certain reference points in a private, symbolic cartography. But the diary nevertheless testifies to the function of such mapping in realizing a sense of self; if Nin's vision of the Champs-Elysées in 1925 exposes an initial uncertainty and vulnerability, her identification with the gargoyles of Notre Dame in late 1926 manifests a perspective that is at once more cynical and more secure. As she absorbed the topographical subtleties of Paris and demystified its monstrous presence, she gained a more confident sense of her literary identity. By August 1927 Nin had returned to the High Place to work, and at year's end she reported in her diary: "Every day I feel surer of myself, my desires soar higher, I feel power in myself, conviction."[18]

Beyond their autobiographical interest, Nin's many allusions to Paris raise the question of how cognitive mapping affects textual versions of place. Downs and Stea have noted that mapping consists of two basic stages, encoding and decoding. That is, the mind converts perceptions of place into images that are symbolic, schematic, and functional.[19] Theoretically this mental grid helps us resolve spatial questions—which route is most direct? which is most scenic?—and implicitly directs our movement toward centers of value or interest. But does *writing* about place entail the same encoding and decoding? Or does the textual representation of place reverse the process of mapping by depositing reformulated signs of spatial experience? Insofar as Nin's diary sheds light on this problem, allusions to her apartment, the Luxembourg Gardens, the Louvre, the Seine, and other locales may describe important nodes of an internal map; but her attention to these sites also forms part of a deliberate strategy of self-presentation. Despite its apparent status as a truthful, uncensored record, Nin's diary (like all diaries) betrays a self-conscious selection and manipulation of details to produce an ultimately fictive image.[20] It yields a portrait of the writing self constructed from the diverse signs by which personality inscribes itself—especially from those reencoded signs of place which encompass and epitomize the struggle for identity. In Nin's diary, the gargoyles of Notre Dame figure crucially in her fabulation and illustrate the textual encoding of the city by which the self discovers and defines itself.

Not all prose forms, of course, entail the representation of place. Nor does place invariably indicate a writer's effort to articulate an image of self. Certain genres, such as travel narratives or landscape sketches, emphasize topography to assert the charm or distinctiveness of particular sites. The writer's attachment to place may color the account but remains incidental to the task of delineation. Other types of prose (the reflective essay, for example) incorporate physical scenes chiefly when locus figures as an explicit object of contemplation. In short stories and novels, however, place often plays an integral role in narrative conception as the matrix of action. Indeed, we speak of plot as what "takes place," what assumes localized form, in fiction. The French expression *avoir lieu* captures this same sense of an action or incident which literally must "have a place" in order to happen at all.

Localization is, however, scarcely a uniform principle of fiction; some writers, curiously indifferent to geography, have seemed content to embed plot in obscure or generalized settings. Lutwack notes that after Fielding locates the story of *Tom Jones* in Somersetshire and depicts the house of Squire Allworthy in pastoral terms, "place ceases to function in the novel."[21] For the most part, Poe's tales of effect employ vague, unlocatable European settings to lend remoteness to events and underscore their ambiguity. In Kafka's fiction, the physical scene also remains ambiguous, a dreamscape which metaphorizes the protagonist's anxieties but which in its surreal figurality resists facile biographical association. Recently the more realistic stories of Raymond Carver have inscribed a postmodern placelessness—a flat, undifferentiated suburban scene marked by anomie and emptiness.

But fiction more often embodies a purposive image of place, as we see in evocations of locale by Hawthorne, Flaubert, and Hardy.[22] In this century, both Anderson's *Winesburg, Ohio* and Faulkner's *Absalom! Absalom!* have appeared with maps tracing the configuration of imaginary towns and thus called attention to spatial relations within these fictive worlds. Faulkner's representation of Yoknapatawpha County indeed remains an unparalleled instance of the literary concretion of place. Modern fiction presents other notable instances of what Bachelard has called "topophilia": Joyce's obsessive attention to the geography of his native city in *Dubliners, Portrait of the Artist as a Young Man,* and *Ulysses*; Virginia Woolf's material evocation of place (her parents' summer house in Cornwall) in the brilliant "Time Passes" section of *To the Lighthouse*; Thomas Wolfe's meticulous rendering of his mother's boarding house and the streets of Asheville in *Look Homeward, Angel.*

These last three examples suggest a possible correlation in fiction between an elaboration of place and an autobiographical project. I do not mean to suggest that all novels which emphasize locale should be read as autobiography; it seems more plausible to assume that a writer's fixation with place may signal the *desire* of autobiography: the longing to reconstruct—albeit in fictive terms—the relation between an authorial self and a world of located experience. As we have seen, this is precisely the gap bridged in Hemingway's "Snows of Kilimanjaro." Autobiographies like Nabokov's *Speak, Memory* and Soyinka's *Aké: The Years of Childhood* reinforce the impression that place may be crucial to autobiography; both writers reconstruct their early years through evocations of specific, almost magical sites associated with indelible, formative experiences. Indeed, in theoretical terms it is difficult to imagine the recounting of a life story apart from the tangible, physical scenes where important episodes have occurred. As Plato observed in the *Timaeus,* place is a veritable matrix of energies, the "nurturing container" of experience. Summing up Plato's ideas on *chora* (place), E. V. Walter writes: "People and things in a place participate in one another's natures. Place is a location of mutual immanence, a unity of effective presences abiding together." Chora is more than mere position, more than a constellation of material forms or structures: it is "the active receptacle of shapes, powers, feelings, and meanings, organizing the qualities within it, energizing experience."[23] It would thus seem imperative for a writer constructing a narrative of lived experience to acknowledge the receptacle which gives that experience definition and sustenance.

Yet autobiography as a form exhibits as much variety in treatment of place as fiction; although numerous critical discussions examine time in autobiography, place remains an apparently incidental issue.[24] Whether the autobiographer acknowledges the influence of certain locations or, conversely, ignores locale seems finally to hinge upon the life itself, upon the degree of the writer's attachment to indigenous or customary scenes. Milton's Satan insisted that "the mind is its own place," and for writers ensconced in their own mental worlds, the physical environment may indeed remain an irrelevant background. But for writers attentive to lived, sensory experience, place proves (as Plato insisted) a nurturing medium, a source of both thought and identity.

Insofar as all writers of fiction and autobiography display differing attachments to place and different patterns of habitation and movement, one might conceive a range of possible spatial attachments. There are, at one end of the scale, writers whose work is rooted in the life and landscape of a specific region and whose projections of place imply a groundedness, a sense of belonging. Eudora Welty serves here as the representative figure; her *Place in Fiction* acknowledges the determinative role of locale in narrative:

> Place in fiction is the named, identifiable, concrete, exact and exacting, and therefore credible, gathering-spot of all that has been felt, is about to be experienced, in the novel's progress. Location pertains to feeling; feeling profoundly pertains to place; place in history partakes of feeling, as feeling about history partakes of place. Every story would be another story, and unrecognizable as art, if it took up its characters and plot and happened somewhere else.[25]

Then there are those diverse writers for whom place is a matter of happenstance or preference, simply the present locus of activity. Their fiction tends to register the commonalities of contemporary culture rather than regional peculiarities. Some attachment to roots may remain, but these writers inhabit a changing, megalopolitan scene which has little meaning *as place* in their writing, however realistic its portrayal. Among current American writers, John Updike and Anne Tyler may perhaps be said to possess such an orientation. Perceptibly more dislocated are those writers of internal exile whose attachments to place have been complicated by feelings of alienation, marginalization, or exclusion. Their identification with a given locale may be as intense as that of the regionalist but is accompanied by a complex, ironic detachment. In quite different ways, Flannery O'Connor and Ralph Ellison may be seen as figures of domestic exile, projecting into their fiction a contradictory, often hostile relation to place. Finally, at the other end of the spectrum, we locate those writers whose careers have been marked by prolonged absence or even permanent exile from homeland. Their passage from familiar, native grounds to an alien scene poses in the sharpest terms the difference between one place and another and produces the perspective of displacement. Conrad, Joyce, and Mann all drew upon that perspective to reconstruct the geography of their own experience.[26]

Reductive as this scheme may be, it helps to explain the singular importance of expatriate writings for a study of place. It might be argued that, among all forms of prose discourse, narratives of exile (including novels, short stories, autobiographies, and diaries) seem most likely to incorporate reflections on the problem of place and the relation of place to writing. Near the end of a career marked by his own relentless search for what his protagonist Nick Adams called "the good place," Hemingway speculated in *A Moveable Feast* that "transplanting" might be as necessary for the writer as for other growing things, insofar as relocation produced a new perspective from which a previous haunt might be written about. His theory is revealing: like many a modernist, Hemingway regarded displacement as an elective strategy of replenishment, a way of shifting one's angle of vision. Unlike such precursors as Ovid or Dante, who were banished for political reasons, the modern literary expatriate has (with certain exceptions) often experienced exile as a quest for a more productive milieu. In his determination to "fly the nets" of language, religion, and country, Joyce's Stephen Dedalus may be seen as the exemplary exiled modernist, though of course Joyce himself made a career of self-exile in Trieste, Zurich, and Paris. Gertrude Stein observed pointedly that in the twentieth century writers needed two countries because the creative life depended upon that detachment or ungrounding only available in a foreign place.[27] Stein's claim resonates with Henry Miller's declaration in *Tropic of Cancer*: "I'm not an American any more, nor a New Yorker, and even less a European, or a Parisian. . . . I'm a neutral."[28] What Stein and Miller identify is the expatriate's oddly indeterminate status of being imaginatively neither *here* nor *there*. Moving from the place where one "belongs" to an unreal second country implies a deliberate renunciation of origins and the assumption of an ambiguous position between "outsideness" and "insideness."

Yet as Hemingway realized, this deliberate dislocation can become a mode of vision. Lloyd S. Kramer has observed that the situation of exile produces a heightened consciousness of the physical and social environment; more significantly, Kramer adds, "the experience of living among alien people, languages, and institutions can alter the individual's sense of self . . . [provoking] important changes in self-perception and consciousness."[29] The writing which emerges from this experience tends to reflect both an intensified awareness of place and an instinctive preoccupation with the identity of the alienated self. In an essay on the expatriate "avant-garde autobiography," William Boelhower claims that this type of narrative embodies "the larger crisis of *habitare* that characterizes the modernist condition." In this form of discourse, "the avant-garde autobiographer, in his attempt to create a coherent grammar of the self out of the spatial vocabulary of the metropolis, ends up with a loosely bound inventory of fragmented forms."[30] That is, the city of exile offers a source of signs from which the author constructs a provisional expatriate identity.

In this sense the modern expatriate writer also reenacts an ancient human predicament, the dilemma of the ungrounded self. Reconsidering Freud's reading of Sophocles' Oedipus cycle, E. V. Walter shows how the psychoanalyst abstracted the mythic hero from his environment to underscore the "universal drives of infantile mental life." But Freud thus overlooked (and quite literally displaced) an important dimension of the tragic myth, the relation of sacred or portentous sites to the mystery of identity: "Taken together, *Oedipus the King* and *Oedipus at Colonus* go beyond psychological insight to grounded insight. They present the drama of place and the crisis of the placeless self. Together, they probe the riddle of alienation and explore the relation between the self and its place."[31] This dilemma continues to inscribe itself in Western cultural attitudes. Whatever differences may be seen in the experiences of the aforementioned expatriates, each to some extent participated in and wrote about the crisis of the displaced self—a crisis which, to be sure, has certain modernist aspects but which in the search for identity and grounding traces an archetypal struggle.

Although expatriation remains a problematic concept, often loosely invoked to claim dubious commonalities, we can nevertheless recognize that a lengthy stay in an alien place must produce certain changes in the way one feels, thinks, sees, and writes. In the difference between the immediate scene of exile, the "unreal" site of expatriation (as Stein would have it), and those real, remembered scenes of homeland, one confronts the anxiety of the ungrounded self. No mere homesickness, this condition exposes a radical uncertainty about one's relation to "home" and to the self one has been. In *Invisible Cities,* Italo Calvino depicts the situation of the wandering expatriate in paradoxical terms: "Arriving at each new city, the traveler finds again a past of his that he did not know he had: the foreignness of what you no longer are or no longer possess lies in wait for you in foreign, unpossessed places."[32] The experience of exile reveals a different, foreign self while disclosing the stranger whom one no longer resembles. As it calls identity into question, expatriation forces a rethinking of the relation between place and self.

To dwell in another country also opens the expatriate to awareness of another kind of exile, the homelessness that may be traced in Western, Judeo-Christian culture to the loss of Eden. Perhaps our longing for and attachment to earthly places derives from an ineradicable collective memory of that forfeited paradise. Heidegger suggests that a consciousness of this plight may ironically provide the basis for dwelling: "As soon as man *gives thought* to his homelessness, it is a misery no longer. Rightly considered and kept well in mind, it is the sole summons that *calls* mortals into their dwelling."[33] If a sense of homelessness indeed leads to dwelling, then exile must be seen as an enabling exercise, an ironic means of inserting the self into the world so as to "bring dwelling to the fullness of its nature." In effect, expatriation creates a space for being, thinking, and writing by rupturing those relations to place which obscure the nature of our homelessness. In exile, the longing of the self for place reveals itself as pure nostalgia—as a futile yearning for *nostos* (home), for a ground of being. This is the desire identified by Plato and later expressed by Hemingway and Nin, the desire to discover the "good place" or the "high place" wherein the ungrounded self might at last escape homelessness and find bliss. But exile also makes literal one's existential displacement, and it is this consciousness which impels the writer's effort to construct a city of words which may be inhabited by a textual self.

Just as exile foregrounds the problem of place by posing an implicit contrast between new surroundings and old, it also produces a fresh perspective on cultural differences. Kramer points out that "extended contact with a foreign *mentalité* helps [exiles] to recognize the unconscious social or ideological hierarchies that create order and meaning in their native culture but pass unnoticed by people who never leave home. The 'normal' (or normative) values of the home country become more relative: simply *one* way of explaining reality or social experience rather than *the* way."[34] This vantage point "on the margin of two cultures" also works the other way, enabling the emigré to see revealing features of daily life in a foreign country which might escape the notice of the native. For the writer, exile thus provides an immediate spectacle that yields material for reflection and composition as it supplies a new perspective from which to contemplate the distant homeland.

While the tradition of literary exile extends back to the classical period, the condition of expatriation has become so pervasive in the twentieth century that, according to Andrew Gurr, we should regard exile itself as "the essential characteristic of the modern writer."[35] By definition a separation from a familiar and significant native landscape, exile presupposes no particular destination. Yet displaced writers of the modern age have in fact converged mainly upon a half-dozen great cities, presumably finding in them the cosmopolitan density of experience and urban energy conducive to the production of modern literature.[36] Among these centers of emigré activity, Paris has since the mid-nineteenth century claimed preeminence as a city of exile. We may summarize those key cultural factors which made it a haven for expatriates, taking note of a few earlier writers who sojourned in Paris and began to explore the vantage point of modern literary exile.

As Kramer and others have demonstrated, the conditions of Parisian life during the nineteenth century made the city powerfully attractive to a large population of exiled artists, writers, and intellectuals. Under the relaxed regime of Louis-Philippe (1830-48), France enjoyed "more freedom for publishing and political activity" than any country in "southern or central Europe"; Paris consequently became a "refuge for displaced radicals" escaping repressive conditions in Italy, Germany, Poland, and Russia.[37] The so-called "bourgeois monarchy" of Louis-Philippe also produced material prosperity and cultural dynamism; the rise of bourgeois capitalism inspired a lively counter-culture known as Bohemia, an underworld populated by students, artists, and intellectuals linked mainly by their desire to scandalize the bourgeoisie and to repudiate its materialism.[38] Though caricatured in Murger's *Scènes de la Vie Bohème* (1851), Bohemia developed a romantic allure as a site of rebellious creativity; it defined a climate hospitable to the marginalized artist-exile by rejecting social distinctions and setting itself in opposition to elitist (and xenophobic) high culture. Paris also attracted exiles as the "capital of the nineteenth century," placing on display the most advanced forms and styles of what Walter Benjamin has called "commodity fetishism." Through such projects as the construction of the arcades in the 1830s, the staging of world exhibitions, and the modernization of Parisian streets under Baron Haussmann, "Paris was confirmed in its position as the capital of luxury and fashion" and presented a "dreamworld" of progress which fascinated even the politically disaffected.[39]

The figure whose career most fully embodies the tensions of nineteenth-century French culture and who serves ironically as a prototype of the exiled writer is the Parisian Charles Baudelaire. His brooding sense of isolation, his cultivation of the contradictory roles of dandy and bohemian, his identification with the *poète maudit* Edgar Allan Poe, his obsession with the crowd and the city streets, his diabolism, and his participation in "the cult of multiplied sensation" all defined aspects of Baudelaire's estrangement from middle-class life. In the poems grouped as *Tableaux parisiens* and in the prose-poems titled *Le Spleen de Paris* (now available in English as *The Parisian Prowler*), he uncovered the grim, fantastic world of the streets, using his sense of self-exile from the Paris of bourgeois splendor as a lens through which to observe the grotesque low-life types—beggars, degenerates, freaks—whose misery appalled and fascinated him. An inveterate *flâneur* (stroller), Baudelaire metaphorized Paris now as an "ant-like city, full of dreams," now as a "terrifying landscape," now as a "gloomy old man doomed to toil." Benjamin contends that "the Paris of his poems is a sunken city, and more submarine than subterranean," a city upon which Baudelaire cast "the allegorist's gaze" while accentuating "the modern" in his poetry.[40] Contemplating a Parisian underclass of victims, misfits, and outcasts, he constructed a model of metropolitan exploration which would influence not only later French *symbolistes* (especially Jules LaForgue) but also such international exiles as Rilke and Eliot, who came to Paris and briefly adopted what Benjamin calls "the gaze of the *flâneur*."

So many notable exiles lived and worked in Paris during the century preceding the expatriate invasion of the 1920s that a separate book would be necessary to do justice to the topic. Kramer's fine study treats three exemplary figures—Heine, Marx, and Mickiewicz—who experienced self-discovery and developed new perspectives on modernity while living in France under the "bourgeois monarchy." Yet he does not mention another important literary expatriate, Turgenev, who during the revolutionary epoch of 1847-50 composed in Paris the majority of the pieces included in *A Sportsman's Sketches* (1852), the collection of stories about Russian peasant life which helped to bring about the abolition of serfdom in 1861.[41] Exile apparently enabled Turgenev to see more clearly the distinctive features of the rural subculture he sought to represent. After returning to Russia and suffering internal exile—banishment to a remote provincial town—Turgenev resumed a pattern of periodic visits to France in the late 1850s, primarily to be close to his love, Pauline Viardot. From 1871-83 he lived more or less continuously in Paris, establishing literary connections with Flaubert, Zola, Sand, Daudet, and the brothers Goncourt; during this prolonged exile he wrote *The Torrents of Spring,* a novel which a half century later provided an American expatriate, Ernest Hemingway, with the title for a parody.

Through his participation in Flaubert's salon, Turgenev made the acquaintance of another international exile, Henry James, who spent a crucial year in Paris (1875-76) before establishing residence in England. As a correspondent for the *New York Tribune,* James reported on developments in Parisian culture, with emphasis on literary and theatrical fashions. In his first dispatch, he reflected on the American obsession with Paris, the inevitability of recurrent visits, and the effect of leaving and returning upon the perception of place: "No American, certainly, since Americans were, has come to Paris but once, and it is when he returns, hungrily, inevitably, fatally, that his sense of Parisian things becomes supremely acute."[42] James found his own "sense of Parisian things" so intense that he shortly began to write a novel dramatizing an American encounter with the city and its vast social complexity. In *The American* (1876) he analyzed the dazzling effect of culture, tradition, and manners upon a crass but good-hearted entrepreneur from the West who falls in love with a French noblewoman in the waning years of the Second Empire. The famous opening scene, set in the Salon Carré of the Louvre, epitomizes that craving for cultural refinement which in the case of Christopher Newman nearly becomes a destructive obsession. Perhaps fearing his own susceptibility to the charms of Paris, James retreated to England but retained throughout his career (as Edwin Sill Fussell has shown) a veritable preoccupation with France and its capital, as well as with French language and literature.[43]

With the suppression of the Commune of 1871 and the rise of the Third Republic, the buoyant Parisian cultural scene produced, as Roger Shattuck has shown, a lively avant-garde movement which, like the earlier Bohemian movement, flaunted the sort of creative freedom enticing to international exiles of art.[44] During the "banquet years" celebrated by Shattuck, August Strindberg returned to France, determined to win fame. The Swedish playwright had visited Paris twice before, but in August 1894 he returned for a longer stay. Already celebrated as the author of such naturalistic dramas as *The Father* and *Miss Julie,* Strindberg considered Paris as his "intellectual Mecca" and hoped to promote the French translation and production of his works. But he also feared a loss of identity in the great, indifferent city; and the sudden departure of his wife Frida in October 1894 effectively signalled the failure of his second marriage. Beyond these anxieties he also suffered increasingly from bizarre hallucinations and delusions, including recurrent paranoia. As if to insulate himself from neglect as an expatriate dramatist, he pursued a fugitive career as a scientist, conducting experiments to determine the chemical composition of iodine and to extract gold from sulphur.

The record of Strindberg's strange two years in Paris appears in *Inferno,* the somewhat exaggerated memoir he composed in Sweden in 1897. The account traces the development of his mania partly through adventures in the streets of Paris; his chance discoveries, clairvoyant experiences, and occult intuitions curiously anticipate the narratives of French surrealists like Breton, Aragon, and Soupault three decades later. One evening, for example, Strindberg takes a walk in a gloomy *quartier* on the Right Bank:

> I crossed the Canal St. Martin, black as a grave, a most suitable place for drowning oneself in. I stopped at the corner of the rue Alibert. Why Alibert? Who was he? Wasn't the graphite that the analytical chemist had found in my sample of sulphur called Alibert graphite? What did that imply? It was odd, but I could not rid my mind of the impression that there was something inexplicable about this.[45]

His stroll becomes progressively nightmarish: "Suspicious-looking persons brushed past me," he reports, "shouting out coarse words as they did so." He stumbles into a blind alley "that seemed to be the abode of human trash, vice, and crime" before finding his way to the Porte Saint-Martin. On another occasion, he notices in the Montparnasse cemetery a monument to "Orfila, Chemist and Toxicologist"; a week later on the rue d'Assas, he comes upon the Hôtel Orfila. Assuming this to be a mystical sign, Strindberg takes a room there in February 1896, but the place becomes his "purgatory" as weird, unnerving experiences recur. In the hotel vestibule he notices a letter addressed to a person with the surname of his estranged wife; the letter has come, coincidentally, from the very Austrian village where his wife and child are living. Later he hears someone playing a familiar song on the piano and suspects that a former disciple has followed him from Berlin to Paris to kill him. Finally, in July, he interprets odd noises in adjacent rooms as evidence of a plot by one or more strangers to pass an electric current through him. Horrified, Strindberg flees the Orfila and shortly thereafter leaves France to seek treatment for his delusions.

Unlike Turgenev, who during his first long stay in Paris wrote about the Russian countryside, Strindberg exploited the estrangement of exile to describe uncanny aspects of Parisian life. Both perspectives, however, figure in Rainer Maria Rilke's *The Notebooks of Malte Laurids Brigge,* a work which begins (like Strindberg's *Inferno*) with a slightly fictionalized memoir of the writer's first sojourn in Paris but ends with haunting childhood memories of family and homeland. As Naomi Segal points out, the *Notebooks* thus involve a subtle fusion of past and present, remembrance and perception: "We must ask ourselves whether this strange, often grim childhood produced an adult destined to receive Paris in precisely this way, or whether the stimuli of Paris induced him to remember certain things in a certain way."[46] Rilke arrived in Paris in late August 1902 and stayed for six months, principally to write a book about his hero, the sculptor Auguste Rodin. But the young poet from Prague also felt the influence of Baudelaire and composed a number of poems about the city generally reminiscent of the *Tableaux parisiens.*

His most complex response to the city came in the *Notebooks,* however, where he registered what Segal calls "the ubiquity and anonymity of urban death." His persona and alter-ego Brigge defines his principal task as "learning to see" and quickly begins to notice the horrors of the metropolis. In a key paragraph he reflects on his progress as a writer and considers the effects of his exile:

> I am in Paris; those who learn this are glad, most of them envy me. They are right. It is a great city; great and full of strange temptations. As concerns myself, I must admit that I have in certain respects succumbed to them. I believe there is no other way of saying it. I have succumbed to these temptations, and this has brought about certain changes, if not in my character, at least in my outlook on the world, and, in any case, in my life. An entirely different conception of all things has developed in me under these influences; certain differences have appeared that separate me from other men, more than anything heretofore. A world transformed. A new life filled with new meanings. For the moment I find it a little hard because everything is too new. I am a beginner in my own circumstances.[47]

Brigge realizes that his experiences in the city have produced a "new life" and a different understanding of the world; his stay has also clarified what it is that separates him from others. This sense of alienation appears to motivate the reflections on his childhood which fill the last half of the *Notebooks.* Though he visited Paris many times, Rilke discovered during his first sojourn there the peculiarly stimulating effect of solitude in the city of exile.

These few figures—Turgenev, James, Strindberg, and Rilke—represent a much larger contingent of expatriate writers who established at least temporary residence in Paris during the period stretching from about 1850 until the outbreak of the Great War. Discussions of such diverse figures as Knut Hamson, Oscar Wilde, and Edith Wharton might enlarge or modify the emerging model of exilic experience. But the cases briefly outlined above at least indicate certain potential consequences of displacement and identify a basic tension between the new, different, and perhaps disorienting conditions of an unfamiliar foreign scene and the remembered features of an abandoned native scene, now made strange by the perspective of exile. Kramer writes of the three subjects of his study: "All felt themselves to be alienated from the French culture in which they lived, alienated from their native countries, and also alienated from the general development of nineteenth-century European capitalist society."[48] Although later exiles seem to have been generally less troubled by capitalism, the experience of living in an alien culture did (as I will suggest later) complicate some responses to the changes associated with modernity.

Reduced to elemental terms, the situation of exile produces a revealing contrast between one place and another, a contrast which implicitly poses the question of which qualities or features determine the distinctive identity of a place. But this question leads us back to an earlier, more basic question: what is a place? Does place exist "out there" in a purely objective form susceptible to empirical analysis, or does it lie within the human mind, as a set of internalized images always already contained and determined by language? In a recent discussion of this problem, J. Nicholas Entrikin describes the "betweenness of place," arguing for a concept of liminality which sees place as a shifting function of reciprocal but contradictory realities.[49] He thus sees place as a construct caught between the subjective and the objective. This formulation recalls an idea advanced by Henri Bergson, who in *Time and Free Will* commented on the interpenetration of subject and object while analyzing the relation between time and memory:

> Every day I perceive the same houses, and as I know that they are the same objects, I always call them by the same name and I fancy that they always look the same to me. But if I recur, at the end of a sufficiently long period, to the impression which I experienced during the first few years, I am surprised at the remarkable, inexplicable, and indeed inexpressible change which has taken place. It seems that these objects, continually perceived by me and constantly impressing themselves on my mind, have ended by borrowing from me something of my own conscious existence; like myself they have lived, and like myself they have grown old.[50]

Bergson's sense that these houses have been "impressing themselves" on his consciousness and "borrowing" from it at the same time provides a revealing gloss on many of the representations of Paris to be examined in subsequent chapters. It also suggests that the problem of place is caught up in the phenomenology of subject-object relations and perhaps belongs to that intermediate reality which Bergson calls the "image"—that construction halfway between an idea and a thing, determined by objective reality but registered only through perception—or additionally through inscription. For the writing of place, the textual construction of a perceived environment, gives at least a tentative account of the interplay between the inner and outer realities which merge to produce our sense of where we are.

This notion of place remains crucial, for as Entrikin reminds us, "place serves as an important component of our sense of identity as subjects."[51] No experience intensifies our consciousness of this fact more than immersion in a foreign environment, which exposes not only our complex dependence upon knowledge of topography, climate, language, and culture (among the most obvious determinants of place) but also reveals the considerable extent to which we are creatures of place, deriving our most basic sense of self from the relation which we have formed with the place or chora in which we have our being. The experience of expatriation often discloses an alternate self, responsive to the differences which constitute the foreignness of another place.

Precisely this dilemma of identity accounts for the dramatic power of James's late novel *The Ambassadors*. His American protagonist, Lambert Strether, comes to Paris with the delicate mission of retrieving the errant son of wealthy Mrs. Newsome. But Strether recognizes first in the prodigal behavior of Chad Newsome and then in his own fascination with Chad's lover, Madame de Vionnet, the potential transformation of perspective and sensibility which the expatriate may undergo in Paris. To his astonishment, Strether finds his notions of New England propriety undermined by what Chad calls "the charm of life over here"; the struggle between Strether's sense of duty to Mrs. Newsome and his attraction to the European sophistication of Madame de Vionnet persists to the final page in his quandary about remaining abroad and marrying Maria Gostrey.[52] James's novel also poses the special problem of American expatriation in Europe, a return to the Old World from which the New has obtained much of its cultural identity. Strether's conflict of values is inherently a crisis of self-conception, and in the following chapters we shall explore other versions of this predicament. Exile affords the opportunity for change, growth, and insight as well as the possibility of alienation, confusion, and corruption. The terms of this crisis are different for Stein, Hemingway, Miller, Fitzgerald, and Barnes, but their representations of Paris enable us to trace the implications of each writer's attachment to the city of exile.

Notes

1. E. E. Cummings, *The Enormous Room*, ed. George James Firmage (1922; reprint, New York: Liveright, 1978), 50. Subsequent parenthetical page references to the novel correspond to this edition.

2. Cummings, *The Enormous Room*, xiv.

3. E. E. Cummings, *Complete Poems, 1913-1962* (San Diego: Harcourt Brace Jovanovich), 93.

4. E. E. Cummings, *I: Six Nonlectures* (Cambridge: Harvard University Press, 1953), 53.

5. Leonard Lutwack, *The Role of Place in Literature* (Syracuse: Syracuse University Press, 1984), 12, 31. Subsequent page references to this work will be noted parenthetically.

6. Yi-Fu Tuan, *Space and Place: The Perspective of Experience* (Minneapolis: University of Minnesota Press, 1977), 6, 12; Edward Relph, *Place and Placelessness* (London: Plon, 1976), 43.

7. Relph, *Place and Placelessness*, 50-56, 61.

8. Tuan, *Space and Place*, 54. The expression "knowing one's place" appeals to just this sense of being where one belongs, though it also figures in the discourse of repression to exclude individuals or groups from a guarded, symbolically important place.

9. Pierre Sansot, *Poétique de la ville* (Paris: Editions Klinksieck, 1969), 23; Gaston Bachelard, *The Poetics of Space*, trans. Maria Jolas (Boston: Beacon Press, 1969), 14, 17.

10. Relph, *Place and Placelessness*, 43.

11. Roger M. Downs and David Stea, *Maps in Minds: Reflections on Cognitive Mapping* (New York: Harper and Row, 1977), 27.

12. Marcel Proust, *Swann's Way,* trans. C. K. Scott Moncrieff (New York: Modern Library, 1956), 59. Subsequent references to this edition will be noted parenthetically.

13. Ernest Hemingway, *The Short Stories of Ernest Hemingway* (New York: Scribner's, 1939), 54. Subsequent parenthetical page references to the story correspond to this edition.

14. Ernest Hemingway, *Across the River and into the Trees* (New York: Scribner's, 1950), 123.

15. Downs and Stea, "Cognitive Maps and Spatial Behavior: Process and Products," in Roger M. Downs and David Stea, eds., *Image and Environment: Cognitive Mapping and Spatial Behavior* (Chicago: Aldine, 1973), 9.

16. Kevin Lynch describes victims of brain injury who "cannot find their own rooms again after leaving them, and must wander helplessly until conducted home, or until by chance they stumble upon some familiar detail." See Lynch, "Some References to Orientation," in Downs and Stea, eds., *Image and Environment,* 301.

17. *The Early Diary of Anaïs Nin,* vol. 3 (San Diego: Harcourt Brace Jovanovich, 1983), 40. Subsequent citations from the *Early Diary* refer to this edition. The question of Nin's national identity is complicated by the fact that her father was of Spanish and her mother of French-Danish descent; both parents were born in Cuba. Nin moved to New York with her mother in 1914 at the outbreak of the Great War.

18. *The Early Diary of Anaïs Nin,* vol. 4 (San Diego: Harcourt Brace Jovanovich, 1985), 42.

19. Downs and Stea, *Maps in Minds,* 78. Kevin Lynch also develops a theory of "imageability"—the "quality in a physical object which gives it a high probability of evoking a strong image in any given observer." See his *Image of the City* (Cambridge: M.I.T. Press, 1960), 9.

20. Those volumes of the diary (from 1934 on) which Nin herself prepared for publication reflect careful revision and purging of indiscreet entries. So, for instance, the published diary deletes references to her sexual liaisons with Henry Miller and others. The recent appearance of *Henry and June* (1987), eidted by Rupert Pole, makes available some of this previously suppressed material.

21. Lutwack, *The Role of Place in Literature,* 21.

22. A fine recent study of British and French fiction reinforces the importance of place as a repository of meaning and demonstrates new interest in this aspect of narrative. See Gillian Tindall, *Countries of the Mind: The Meaning of Place to Writers* (London: Hogarth, 1991).

23. E. V. Walter, *Placeways: A Theory of the Human Environment* (Chapel Hill: University of North Carolina Press, 1988), 121, 205.

24. See, e.g., the bibliography appended to *Autobiography: Essays Theoretical and Critical,* ed. James Olney (Princeton: Princeton University Press, 1980), 343-52. Six of the fifteen contributors to this important collection address the problem of time in autobiographical narrative; none, however, deal substantively with the problem of place.

25. Eudora Welty, *Place in Fiction* (New York: House of Books, 1957), 11.

26. See Harry Levin, "Literature and Exile," *The Listener* (15 October 1959): 613-17. My thanks to Lewis P. Simpson for bringing this essay to my attention and for sharing his work-in-progress on Robert Penn Warren as a figure of internal exile.

27. Gertrude Stein, *Paris, France* (New York: Scribner's, 1940), 2.

28. Henry Miller, *Tropic of Cancer* (1934; reprint New York: Grove Press, 1961), 153.

29. Lloyd S. Kramer, *Threshold of a New World: Intellectuals and the Exile Experience in Paris, 1830-1848* (Ithaca: Cornell University Press, 1988), 9.

30. William Boelhower, "Avant-Garde Autobiography: Deconstructing the Modernist Habitat," in *Literary Anthropology,* ed. Fernando Poyatos (Amsterdam: John Benjamins: 1988), 274, 276. Thanks to Paul Smith for bringing this essay to my attention.

31. Walter, *Placeways,* 98, 99.

32. Italo Calvino, *Invisible Cities,* trans. William Weaver (San Diego: Harcourt Brace Jovanovich, 1974), 28-29.

33. Martin Heidegger, *Poetry, Language, Thought,* trans. Albert Hofstadter (New York: Harper and Row, 1971), 161.

34. Kramer, *Threshold of a New World,* 10.

35. Andrew Gurr, *Writers in Exile* (Sussex: Harvester, 1981), 14.

36. See Malcolm Bradbury's suggestive essay "The Cities of Modernism," in *Modernism 1890-1930,* ed. Malcolm Bradbury and James McFarlane (London: Penguin, 1976), 96-104.

37. Kramer, *Threshold of a New World,* 18, 20-21.

38. Jerrold Siegel, *Bohemian Paris: Culture, Politics, and the Boundaries of Bourgeois Life, 1830-1930* (New York: Viking, 1986), 7-13. The Bohemians were, as Siegel suggests (51), often products of middle-class culture who harbored contradictory attitudes toward wealth and comfort.

39. Walter Benjamin, *Charles Baudelaire: A Lyric Poet in the Era of High Capitalism,* trans. Harry Zohn (London: Verso, 1983), 166, 176.

40. Benjamin, *Charles Baudelaire*, 171.

41. Leonard Shapiro remarks that it is "quite certain that the future Emperor Alexander II was influenced by the *Sketches* in his final decision to put through the emancipation of the serfs, and Turgenev regarded this as his main achievement in life." See Shapiro, *Turgenev: His Life and Times* (New York: Random House, 1978), 66.

42. *Parisian Sketches: Letters to the New York Tribune 1875-76,* ed. Leon Edel and Ilse Dusoir Lind (London: Rupert Hart-Davis, 1958), 3.

43. See Edwin Sill Fussell, *The French Side of Henry James* (New York: Columbia University Press, 1990).

44. Roger Shattuck, *The Banquet Years: The Origins of the Avant-Garde in France, 1885 to World War I* (New York: Vintage, 1968).

45. August Strindberg, *Inferno and From an Occult Diary,* trans. Mary Sandbach (New York: Penguin, 1979), 111.

46. Naomi Segal, "Rilke's Paris—'cité pleine de rêves,'" in *Unreal City: Urban Experience in Modern European Literature and Art,* eds. Edward Timms and David Kelley (New York: St. Martin's, 1985), 103.

47. Rainer Maria Rilke, *The Notebooks of Malte Laurids Brigge,* trans. M. D. Herder Norton (New York: Norton, 1964), 67.

48. Kramer, *Threshold of a New World,* 230.

49. J. Nicholas Entrikin, *The Betweenness of Place: Towards a Geography of Modernity* (Baltimore: Johns Hopkins, 1991).

50. Henri Bergson, *Time and Free Will: An Essay on the Immediate Data of Consciousness,* trans. F. L. Pogson (1910; reprint, New York: Harper and Row, 1960), 129.

51. Entrikin, *The Betweenness of Place,* 13.

52. See especially Fussell's *French Side of Henry James,* 177-214, and Michael Seidel, *Exile and the Narrative Imagination* (New Haven: Yale University Press, 1986), 131-63, for discussions which foreground the problem of place and the displacement of exile.

EXILE IN FICTION

Leo Gurko (essay date 1962)

SOURCE: Gurko, Leo. "The Reluctant Underground." In *Joseph Conrad: Giant in Exile*, pp. 7-20. New York: Macmillan 1962.

[*In the following excerpt, Gurko explores some of Joseph Conrad's writings in the context of his exile from Poland.*]

The tragedy of Poland was not only geographic, but psychological. It was bad enough that fate had ringed her with powerful enemies. Worse still was that the same fate did not equip her to discharge effectively the role demanded by a malevolent geography.

For nearly two centuries Poland has been forced, against her own nature and traditions, into a conspiratorial underground, a role she has played with notable unsuccess. Poland was traditionally divided between a small nobility and a numerous peasantry. The nobles were given to stiff-necked patriotism, complicated etiquette, and grandiloquent gestures. The peasants, largely illiterate, were equally patriotic, aggressively obstinate, and subject to spasmodic fits of bigotry. It was a society made for parade-ground wars, headlong cavalry charges, and a relatively simple, straightforward diplomacy. Instead, it was forced into undercover activities, subtle Machiavellisms, elaborate pretenses of obedience masking a violent passion for independence. Partitioned originally among three great powers, forced to swallow two hated foreign languages, Poland oscillated throughout the nineteenth century between sudden bloody outbursts of rebellious ardor and relapses into sullen passivity bordering on the comatose. There was a touch of disaster and futility to all her enterprises in bondage, quite in keeping with the split between her temperament and lot.

"You seem to forget that I am a Pole," Conrad wrote to Garnett in October, 1907. "You forget that we have been used to go to battle without illusions. It's you Britishers that 'go in to win' only. We have been 'going in' these last hundred years repeatedly, to be knocked on the head only . . ."[1] Conrad's despair about Poland—an emotion endemic to the country—was, in his particular case, heightened by the unhappy experiences of his father, Apollo Korzeniowski, as an unsuccessful conspirator against the Russian occupation.

His father's melancholy private history encapsulates the chronicle of Poland. He was filled with ardor, élan, a capacity to entertain only one political idea at a time, a naïve zeal for the use of short-term methods to achieve long-range objectives, and a rigid inability to live life on any terms but his own. Under normal circumstances, he would have had a career as a scholar or a man of letters. But he lived in an unsettled time, which brought to the surface the restless, unstable sides of his character, and in the end turned even his virtues into faults. The failure of Conrad's father as a rebel personifies the failure of Poland in the same role. Man and country failed for the same reasons. They were both naïve, simple, feudal, brave, filled with chivalrous notions of gallantry and exaggerated heroism when the times called for cunning, concealment, prudence, and sophistication.

Conrad's father was a man of brilliant but unsettled parts. As a student he had pursued oriental languages without finishing. When he lost his own family property through unwise investments, he took to managing the estates of others, also unsuccessfully. But he cut an arresting figure in provincial society, becoming known and feared for a witty, sarcastic tongue. He had literary ambitions, wrote plays and poems of no great distinction, but skillfully translated Hugo, Shakespeare, and Alfred de Vigny into Polish. Highly temperamental and bitterly romantic, he fell in love with Evelina Bobrowska and waited eight long unhappy years for her disapproving father to die and her reluctant mother to give an uneasy consent to their marriage.

The antagonism between the Bobrowskis and Korzeniowskis reflected still another conflict in the history of Poland. Each represented a different aspect of the Polish gentry. The Korzeniowskis were fire-eaters, hotheads, romantic idealists, willing, even eager to die for Poland, impatient of the long view, and allergic to cautious planning. The Bobrowskis were just as patriotic and longed just as much for independence, but they were sober, restrained, willing to get along as best they could with the occupying power while working quietly for a goal they recognized, realistically, to be distant. They disapproved of Evelina's marrying a Korzeniowski, and the later disasters confirmed their opinion.

After their marriage, Conrad's parents lived in the country on a large estate Apollo was managing near the Ukrainian town of Berdichev. There, on December 3, 1857, their son and only child was born. He was named Józef Teodor Konrad Nalecz Korzeniowski.[2] At home the boy was always called by the third of his names, Konrad, which he was later to adopt as his English surname. In his merchant seaman days he was to sign himself in various ship's registers and in letters as Conrad Korzeniowski, Konrad Korzeniowski, K. N. Korzeniowski, and J. Conrad Korzeniowski. He seems to have enjoyed these variants on his name, which in themselves suggest the radical metamorphoses in his life.

In 1861, when Conrad was three, his father repaired to Warsaw in pursuit of a formal literary career. Instead, he became involved with a patriotic group planning a revolt against Russia. Characteristically, he attached himself to the radical wing advocating instant action, was arrested before firing a shot or distributing a proclamation, and was sent into exile. When the next great Polish uprising finally did erupt, in 1863, Apollo Korzeniowski was many hundreds of miles away, in the Vologda region of northern Russia.

His legitimate and justifiable literary ambitions had led him from the relative quiet of the countryside to the great capital, where the temptations of politics operating upon an already aroused patriotic sensibility caught him up in dangerous events for which he was unsuited by nature. Like Poland, he was the tragic victim of a split between his capacities and the pressures imposed upon them. Thirty years later this split was to become one of Conrad's great and recurrent themes.

Apollo's attachment to his wife and son moved him to agree to their company in the harshness of exile. At the camp in Vologda, the inmates were given numbers: Apollo became no. 21, his wife no. 22, Conrad no. 23. Evelina was already in delicate health, and the rigors of their existence hastened her death, which occurred in 1865, when Conrad was seven. After the shock of his wife's passing, Apollo was allowed by the authorities to move to southern Russia where, gazing at the Black Sea, his young son got his first glimpse of boundless water. Eventually, broken in health by the ravages of tuberculosis and no longer considered dangerous, Korzeniowski was allowed to return home. His last months were spent in Cracow, a city noted for its churches and mausoleums, memorializing its medieval past, a city of the glorious and epic dead. On his death in 1869 he was given a great public funeral, befitting a man who sacrificed himself, however foolishly, for the national cause, and three years later his son received the freedom of the city as a last tribute to his father, now enshrined in the myth of Poland.

What Russia must have looked like to the small boy is uncertain, though there are powerful descriptions of the endless empty countryside in *Under Western Eyes* and in an unfinished early story, *The Sisters*. What his father seemed like to him is more evident. Conrad had spent his fourth to eleventh year almost exclusively in the company of his father. More than thirty years later Conrad was to recall him in a letter to Garnett:

> A man of great sensibilities; of exalted and dreamy temperament; with a terrible gift of irony and of gloomy disposition; withal of strong religious feeling degenerating after the loss of his wife into mysticism touched with despair. His aspect was distinguished; his conversation very fascinating; but his face in repose sombre lighted all over when he smiled. I remember him well.[3]

This restless man, at war with himself, unable to reconcile conflicting impulses and to come to terms with the world around him, is the one constant figure in his son's novels. The identity and impact of his mother are more shadowy, but she may well have inspired the figure of Mrs. Gould, one of Conrad's most loving and attractive women, who slowly withers in *Nostromo* as her husband sinks in the swamp of his high-minded, unattainable, and finally corrupting ideal. Evelina, the first name of Conrad's mother, is not unlike Mrs. Gould's Emilia, and the similarity in their life situation is striking.

Conrad's early childhood, isolated in an enemy country, cut off from young companions, thrown into the exclusive company of two parents dying visibly before his eyes, exposed him to abnormal tension. In the impressionable years before he came to speculate and philosophize about the nature of things, Conrad intimately absorbed the attitude of his parents: his father's rebellious lashing out against oppression, his mother's uncomplaining acceptance and endurance.

He was eleven when his father died. He was turned over to the guardianship of his maternal uncle, Tadeusz Bobrowski, and now came in contact with still a third personality. Uncle Tadeusz was a believer in order, reason, and balance, and was willing to pay a price for them by swallowing a little of his nationalistic pride. Inside the Russian occupation he adjusted himself to political realities while maintaining his identity as a Pole. Was it possible to live like a civilized man and still maintain political and patriotic honor? To this delicate question his answer was Yes, and it served as a rule of thumb by which he sought to guide his nephew. Since he felt that an honorable and civilized life was possible in occupied Poland, he would later oppose Conrad's wish to leave. But once Conrad had detached himself from the Polish community, he urged him to embrace another, since civilization involved belonging to a community and was conceivable only in terms of work, duty, and professionalism. First, Conrad was to go to France, and then, England. It was his uncle who would urge British citizenship upon the hesitating young man. He had opposed his going to sea, but once Conrad went, encouraged him to perform his tasks as well as possible and climb in this unexpected profession as high as his talents would allow. He had distrusted his brother-in-law for attempting the impossible, and wished to control the impulsiveness and quixoticism he found in Conrad. Uncle Tadeusz was a great advocate of the possible. Whatever could be done should be done; what should be done acquired value only within the framework of organized society, which alone guaranteed the doctrine of humane realism he sought to inculcate in the boy turned over to his care.

One of Conrad's childhood companions, Jadwiga Kalucka, remembered him at eleven as a lively, merry boy of extraordinary intelligence. He spent holidays with her family in Lwow. He wrote comedies, organized amateur theatricals, quoted from Adam Mickiewicz, the Polish epic poet, demonstrated prodigally the literary training he had received from his father, and was altogether the life of the household.[4] Literature and a literary sensibility were quite plainly intimate parts of his earliest experience. During his early years of close companionship with his father, Conrad had enjoyed hearing him read aloud from his translations of French and English writers. The boy himself had occasionally stolen into his father's study and read from the galley proofs.

After his father's death, the five years Conrad spent going to school in Cracow seemed tame indeed. They consisted of a routine of uninspired studies. Like all educated Poles of the nineteenth century, he learned to speak French as a matter of course. But except for geography, everything was academic and cut-and-dried, and aroused in the boy only an irritated and rebellious boredom. And even geography, he remembered many years afterward, was taught by "mere bored professors . . . who were not only middle-aged but looked to me as if they had never been young. And their geography was very much like themselves, a bloodless thing with a dry skin covering a repulsive armature of uninteresting bones."[5] A passion for "the geography of open spaces and wide horizons" had already been aroused by the memoirs of Mungo Park and Captain Cook, which he had come upon in private.

The traditional system of loyalties that most boys accept automatically appeared not to have taken deep hold of Conrad. He did not believe in the superiority or expertise of his teachers; they frankly bored him. Although he always remained on affectionate terms with his relatives, as a family unit they failed to inspire him with awe. He was born a Roman Catholic and brought up in an orthodox way, yet religion never seems to have moved him deeply; he was to grow up a nonbeliever. As to Poland, for all his natural feelings of patriotism and national pride, the last thing in the world he wanted to do was join its underground.

The years in Cracow were punctuated by a romantic attachment to an equally youthful cousin named Tekla that offended the family's sense of propriety, and were climaxed by the crisis over his decision to leave Poland (then completely landlocked) for the sea. His study of geography had roused in him an interest in places far from home. Mungo Park's Africa, the Pacific regions of Captain Cook appeared to him magical. And when he was not reading books of travel and exploration, he was losing himself in the sea stories of Hugo, Marryat, and Fenimore Cooper, and the first tenuous thought of becoming a sailor himself took root in his mind.

Once there, this strange ambition flourished vigorously and was not to be dislodged. His uncle did everything in his power to stifle it, without success. Arguments, family conferences, exhortations to nationalism, efforts at passing off the impulse as a passing phase of romantic adolescence were all unavailing. In the summer of 1873, when Conrad was fifteen, a university student was engaged to take him on a walking tour of Switzerland and northern Italy with the express purpose of talking the boy out of his folly.[6] But a glimpse of the Adriatic at Venice seems to have canceled out the tutor's most eloquent arguments. Even his uncle, to whom he was strongly attached, could not deflect Conrad. In the end, with cautious, regretful wisdom, Bobrowski let the boy go. It was typical of his sober realism that he did not allow him to depart unprovided for, but arranged a monthly allowance and gave him letters of introduction to connections in Marseilles.

To the end of his days Conrad remembered the pressure upon him to remain. "Stupid obstinacy" and "fantastic caprice" were among the milder epithets applied. In the struggle to leave he was without allies, and was even unable to summon reasons for his folly. They were not verbalized or analyzed, but deeply and temperamentally felt. He was vehemently assured on all sides that what he wanted to do was wrong. Jarring though this was, it had no effect on his resolve to do it. But his sense of anguish, amounting perhaps to a complex of guilt, remained with him throughout life and created in him a perpetual desire to justify his action. In *A Personal Record* he recalls the shocked opposition to it in tones whose dryness does not conceal the surviving tension.

> I don't mean to say that a whole country had been convulsed by my desire to go to sea. But for a boy between fifteen and sixteen, sensitive enough, in all con-

science, the commotion of his little world had seemed a very considerable thing indeed. So considerable that, absurdly enough, the echoes of it linger to this day. I catch myself in hours of solitude and retrospect meeting arguments and charges made thirty-five years ago by voices now forever still; finding things to say that an assailed boy could not have found, simply because of the mysteriousness of his impulses to himself. I understood no more than the people who called upon me to explain myself. There was no precedent. I verily believe mine was the only case of a boy of my nationality and antecedents taking a, so to speak, standing jump out of his racial surroundings and associations.

(pp. 120-121)

The pressure exerted to keep him from taking the jump left its mark. He was given to ironic outbursts, reminiscent of his father, followed by moody silences when he was altogether withdrawn.

His passion to go to sea, vague at first, grew steadily more powerful, and was linked in an equally powerful way with a personal need to break out of the dark tunnel of Poland. Since the remote places which made their appeal to him in geography and fiction were invariably reached by water, the sea became the imaginative means of exit from the prison of land. He longed as much as any Pole for his country's independence, but did not believe it would come. He had seen his father and mother swallowed up by Poland's oppressive situation, learned of the melancholy death of his father's two brothers in misadventures that were partly political in character, and was constantly reminded of the heroic sacrifices made by his patriotic ancestors for the Polish cause. These reminders filled him with pride, but also with futility. Polish patriotism was marked by valor and self-sacrifice; yet it seemed always to end in failure and death. He belonged to a country doomed by history to be crushed. The impulse to free himself of these burdensome traditions, to get out from under the weight of this tragic destiny, flared up in him. If his father had rebelled against Russia because he found life in occupied Poland intolerable, Conrad was to rebel against Poland for exactly the same reason. It was the revolt of a youth against iron circumstance which he felt could not be altered, neither by him nor by his compatriots.

His father's tragedy, which Conrad was as resolutely determined to avoid as his nation's, was that of a man cast by circumstance into a role he was unfit to play. Later, Conrad realized that it was not only circumstance but something in his father's own nature that had compelled him to play it. The same tragic fate affected the country; it, too, was thrust into an underground role with a psychic apparatus equipped to function only in the open. This was in due course the tragedy of *Lord Jim* in the celebrated novel written by Conrad twenty-five years after his exit from the reluctant underground of Poland. Jim, too, was wedded to an ideal of conduct that the resources of his nature were unequipped to realize—the inward division that Conrad projects with an imaginative energy that goes back to his own earliest experience.

The state of the father and the nation was mirrored, also, in the ancient south Polish city where Conrad lived and attended school from 1869 to 1874. Cracow, torn between a glorious past and a drab present, offered still another portrait of a divided self to the impressionable boy. One of his younger contemporaries, J. H. Retinger, grew up in the same town, which he described in a book of reminiscences.

. . . its hundred churches, each of them a reliquary of some past splendor, an unending procession of architectural glory—and the drabness of everyday life. Cracow the most beautiful of ancient towns—and the most uninspiring. . . .

In opposition to the past, the present in Cracow did not supply any spiritual food for youthful, adventurous imagination—there was, indeed, a complete lack of faith in it. . . . The greatest festivities of the town were celebrations in honor of men dead a long time ago, of those who had toiled and suffered for Poland. Festivities of mourning!

In my childish imagination the part of Cracow which was not a temple or museum, was a cemetery![7]

From this magnificently preserved cemetery Conrad was resolved to escape. As a microcosm of Poland, Cracow reinforced his earliest impressions of his country's fate. His father's feverish, futile, desperate life had come to an end there, and in memorializing him, in placing a stamp of heroic legend upon him, the city fathers were dramatizing his dissociation from the living present. Conrad's experiences during his first sixteen years were remarkably consistent. They built up in his mind an image of existence which was not only to inform his books but to drive him irresistibly into exile.

One of the more fascinating and persistent theories about Conrad postulates a feeling of guilt at deserting Poland in her hour of greatest need, at the time in her history when she was most ground down under the heel of powerful oppressors. Gustav Morf first advanced this idea in *The Polish Heritage of Joseph Conrad*. Morf explores all the novels, *Lord Jim* in particular, as subconscious efforts by Conrad to purge himself of the burden of betrayal which he assumed that fateful October day in 1874 when he boarded the train for France. Jim deserts the *Patna* (Poland) with its cargo of sleeping pilgrims (the Poles faithful to their belief in independence), and jumps into the "everlasting black hole" of the lifeboat (exactly like Conrad's "jump out of his racial associations"). He has been urged to abandon ship by the rascally German captain (Germany was one of Poland's traditional enemies). The *Patna*, however, did not go down; by some miracle she stayed afloat. Some time later she was rescued and towed into port by a French gunboat (France was Poland's traditional friend and ally). Jim tries to exorcise his guilt by standing trial and by justifying his actions to Marlow (Conrad addressing himself to his readers, for, according to Morf, his art is an attempt to work out his deeply buried anxieties symbolically, and thus rid himself of them). A subtle variation on this approach to *Lord Jim* is suggested by the émigré Polish writer Czeslaw Milosz: with a slight change of the ship's name *Patna* to *Patria,* the whole drama of national loyalties emerges.[8]

The approach is ingenious, and lends a note of authentic fascination to the reading of the novel. But is it true? It would perhaps be more persuasive if we were sure that the feelings Conrad carried with him on "deserting" Poland required exorcism. There is no real evidence that they did. He was disturbed by the opposition of his family, but though very young and utterly alone he followed his own intent unswervingly and never, in any of his later writings or letters, gave any indication that he regretted his decision. On several later occasions, his uncle, hoping this would win him back, urged him to write travel pieces for Polish magazines; he never showed the slightest interest in doing so. As a young man he returned to Poland to see his uncle, and in 1914, twenty years after his uncle's death, took his English wife and two sons back for a stay that was cut short by the war. These visits were undertaken as perfectly matter-of-fact vacation trips and were scarcely the actions of a man consumed in the deepest part of his self with a sense of treason.

Yet Conrad was visibly upset by Polish attacks upon him after his career as an English writer had begun. Was he indeed a betrayer who had put even his talent to the service of another country? The accusation may have wounded him because it was true. The reverse is equally plausible. It may have wounded him because it was false. Painful falsehoods can rend us as deeply as painful truths; it is sentimental to ascribe to the second a more penetrative power than the first. At any rate, his own private relations with Poland remained friendly. He was gratified when his books were first translated into his native language, the more so because the translator was his cousin. And in many an essay and declaration he espoused the cause of Polish independence, and expressed his pleased surprise when this actually came about after the First World War.

Yet if the theory of guilt is not valid in the personal sense, it has validity in an imaginative sense. The entire syndrome of guilt and treason took sharp hold of Conrad's mind when he was exposed to it as a boy. It became for him a constant of human experience not because he accepted the accusations of treason launched against himself, but because he was intimately involved in them. Against his will he was appointed a central actor in the drama of betrayal, without accepting or giving inner consent to the role of betrayer forced upon him by his accusers. Thus the whole issue penetrated his imagination far more than it did his conscience.

It is therefore conceivable that he called Jim's ship the *Patna* because the name began with the same consonant as Poland and had the same number of syllables. If so, the suggestion of the country behind the ship derived less from Conrad's need to exorcise private ghosts than from an imaginative capacity to derive parallels and find analogies to a situation which he understood very well and regarded as a fixed point of the human condition. To pursue Morf's line is to accept the book as the victim of the man, where it deserves to be accepted as a demonstration of his insight and aesthetic power. We see clearly in Conrad's case how his life experiences fed his imagination and nourished his art, how in the writing of his books, as he observes in the Preface to *The Nigger of the "Narcissus,"* "the artist descends within himself, and in that lonely region of stress and strife, if he be deserving and fortunate, he finds the terms of his appeal" (pp. xi-xii). To the degree that his stories remain victimized by the specific circumstances of his life, to that degree they remain unconquered by the imagination, and serve mainly as indexes and guides to the biography of one man rather than as universal statements. To read *Lord Jim* as a compendium of clues to Conrad's personal feelings is to shrink its range of discourse and turn literature generally into a treasure hunt for disguised personal references, which in any given instance may or may not be there.[9]

One other aspect of Conrad's life in Poland remains to be mentioned, the impact of Shakespeare upon him. When still a boy, he had read a number of the plays in his father's translations. Centuries of research have failed to reveal that Shakespeare had a "philosophy," in the sense that Dante or Tolstoy had one. It is hard to say with certainty that in his work he had opinions or assumed attitudes, as Dickens did. What Conrad in his extremely impressionable early years derived from Shakespeare was none of these; even if they existed in articulated form, it is doubtful that they would have meant anything to him between the ages of seven and twelve. What he did derive, rather, were examples and situations: bold men hurling themselves into large endeavors, or sensitive figures like Hamlet being trapped into misfortune and disaster. There was the constant Shakespearian spectacle of the miscast man forced into circumstances that go athwart his nature: not simply Hamlet alone, but Othello, driven to endure the devious modes of jealousy though his character is tuned to straightforwardness and candor; Brutus forced to assassination and war though essentially of a quiet, reflective disposition; Hotspur the victim of an age where his purely medieval pride and honor were out of place; Romeo and Juliet committed to stealth and subterfuge while their youthful ardor can flourish only in the open.

Conrad's father was also a miscast man, belonging to a country trapped into a miscast role. To Conrad the plays of Shakespeare were violent, dramatic demonstrations of the same pattern, made all the more eloquent by their richness of action and the phenomenal vitality of their language. These belied the sad ends of the heroes, kept the tragedies from being depressing, and made bearable the idea that life was often too much for the men who lived it. The human lot may be described as a hard and limited one, but if a writer asserts it with enough imagination and gusto, it has a way of shedding its limitations. Shakespeare asserted it with all the imagination and gusto of the Renaissance. To the boy caught within the enclosed world of Russia and Russian Poland in the 1860's the plays supplied whatever élan, whatever impulse to self-fulfillment that he may not have secured from Marryat, Hugo, and Mungo Park.

When Conrad boarded the express on October 26, 1874, for Marseilles,[10] he was still six weeks short of his seventeenth birthday, but he brought with him the emotional baggage of a grown man. The harshness of his experiences had clouded his youthful spirit, but had not crushed it. It deepened the strain of melancholy in him, the melancholy that was later to erupt so frequently into fits of prolonged depression when a sense of his own emptiness, if not of the emptiness of the world, would overwhelm him. He had already learned to protect his inner self by the mask of manners, another of the legacies from Poland. The Polish gentry had wrapped itself for centuries in a thick veneer of etiquette. An elaborate courtliness of gesture and speech had survived virtually unchanged from medieval times and retained a defiantly feudal air into the present. It served as a wall to keep out inquiring eyes, behind which the privacy of emotion could be freely cultivated. Manners coated Conrad like a suit of armor, and would one day harden into a formidable reserve, an impenetrably aristocratic air that would bloom like an exotic continental plant during his years in rural England.

A precocious sense of tragedy, an exultant if vague desire for the adventure and excitement of some widening experience outside the claustrophobia of his native country, an encrustation of polished etiquette, and a facility in two languages, Polish and French, were the main items in the assorted paraphernalia Conrad took with him on the train to France.

Notes

1. *Letters from Joseph Conrad, 1895-1924,* ed. by Edward Garnett (Indianapolis, 1928), p. 209. All future references to this volume will be abbreviated to Garnett.
2. The name Korzeniowski derived from *korzén,* the Polish word for root.
3. January 20, 1900, Garnett, p. 167.
4. "Conradiana VI," *Poland,* August, 1927.
5. "Geography and Some Explorers," *Last Essays,* p. 12.
6. Joseph Conrad, *A Personal Record,* p. 43.
7. *Conrad and His Contemporaries* (New York, 1943), pp. 19-20.
8. "Joseph Conrad in Polish Eyes," *The Atlantic Monthly,* November, 1957, p. 226.
9. Elsewhere, Morf's comments retain their interest while growing more conjectural and farfetched. He regards Almayer as a composite symbol of Conrad's paternal grandfather and two paternal uncles who lost their fortunes and lives speculating, gambling, and drinking. He spots Conrad himself among the crew of the *Narcissus* in the person of the Finn. This sailor is a foreigner betrayed by his accent, has a dreaming temperament, and comes from a country under Russian rule. Finally, Morf regards Conrad's reversion in his last writings to southern France as a veiled return to Poland, since the two regions have "a strong temperamental affinity." Though one of the earliest books on Conrad, Morf's opus remains, for all its wild-eyed speculations and occasional nonsense, one of the more fascinating.
10. "I got into the train as a man gets into a dream," was the way in which he remembered the incident forty years later (Letter to Harriet Capes, July 22, 1914, Yale).

Andrew Gurr (essay date 1981)

SOURCE: Gurr, Andrew. "A Foot in Both Jungles: Katherine Mansfield." In *Writers in Exile: The Identity of Home in Modern Literature,* pp. 33-64. Sussex, England: Harvester Press, 1981.

[*In the following excerpt, Gurr comments on Katherine Mansfield's attitude toward her being, in effect, an exile in England from her native New Zealand.*]

1. THE LITTLE COLONIAL

The exiled artist is like the rag which is tied in the middle of the rope used in a tug of war. He marks the still point between two straining forces. From one direction he is pulled by the sense of his own individuality which helped to make him an artist, the distinctive voice ready to tell its audience what they are not yet conscious of. From the other direction comes the tug of the unknown, the blank fear of the exile who has lost that sense of identity which comes from the feeling of belonging in a community. By reacting against this community the artist knows his individuality. By exiling himself he loses it. If the two pulls are equal the rope under the rag will quiver but get nowhere. The artist likewise will strain in one direction, towards the realisation of his individual vision, but find it impossible to move to it because of the counter-pull towards the communal identity which has shaped that individuality and without which he has no identity, or therefore individuality, of any kind. The result is fear, and stasis.

Katherine Mansfield acknowledged this two-way strain. In a review she wrote in 1920, about a book by another New Zealander, she notes sympathetically her fellow-colonial's struggle to write. The impulse to compose and to realise one's self in words is so often nullified, Mansfield declares, by timidity, the insistent need for the security which comes from modelling oneself on somebody else. And yet standing out from chapters of imitative prose, she observes, "there is a sentence, there is a paragraph, a whole page or two, which starts in the mind of the reviewer the thrilling thought that this book was written because the author wanted to write."¹ But such self-realisation easily drowns in a sea of timidity. "One would imagine that round the corner there was a little band of jeering, sneering, superior persons ready to leap up and laugh if the cut of the newcomer's jacket is not of the strangeness they consider admissible." The true personal voice lacks the confidence to be itself in a crowd of strangers. Her image is of a new boy at school, or a colonial under the long noses of fashionable society. "In the name of the new novel, the new sketch, the new story, if they are really there, let us defy them."

This lament sets out the fundamental values by which Katherine Mansfield lived. The artist has an individual voice which is distinctive, uniquely the artist's. His or her duty as an artist is to use it. Fashionable accents and the weight of received opinion are dangerous because they destroy that individuality if the fear they inspire overcomes the artist's determination to be himself. Fear is a natural condition for the artist because of his isolation, his individuality. Defiance, overcoming the timidity which grows out of isolation, is the obligation the artist owes to his individuality. It follows from this, too, that the cost of being oneself, of artistic freedom, is isolation.

One of the rewards of reading Katherine Mansfield is a sense of the unity of her work. Her personality emerges naturally from the style of her writing. Whether this is because she wrote mainly in the form of the short story—a form whose ancestry in the folk tale and whose brevity emphasise the narrator's voice and personality—or because of the accessibility of her intimate writings, all the letters and journals published posthumously by her husband, the result is a clear aura of her personality in all she wrote. The same narrator, the same marvellous command of exact description and delicate nuance, present the same acutely discerning vision in her private writing and her fiction alike. So the life and the work, both in the end products of the impulse to flight, must be taken together.

2. The Life of an Exile

Katherine Mansfield was an identity, the colonial writer in London, assumed by the girl born as Kathleen Mansfield Beauchamp in 1888. Her birthplace was Wellington, in New Zealand—in a distant province, as she and all her fellow-countrymen thought themselves to be, a remote colony of Britain. Culture was what arrived, packaged, on the mail steamer after six or eight weeks of unavoidable delay. With greater comfort than in the British climate and with no very special sense of an exotic setting, Wellingtonians at the turn of the century lived their lives in accordance with an idealised model filtered through distance and inaccessibility.

Because it was idealised, and because of the predominantly mercantile ethos of the people who idealised it, the culture of provincial Wellington was emphatically, insistently, bourgeois-respectable. Although the country was still largely dominated by pioneers—Wellington was less than fifty years old when Kathleen Beauchamp was born there—its values were not frontier values. It was, on the whole, suburban England which was transplanted to Wellington. Even its politics were local government politics. The transplant was too young to have evolved any very sturdy growth of its own. Cultural values, which usually evolve more slowly than material or political changes, were almost wholly imitative of London.

It was natural therefore that Kathleen Beauchamp and her sisters, as the daughters of one of Wellington's leading merchants, should finish their education at a school for young ladies in London. She spent three years of her adolescence, from fifteen to seventeen, at Queen's College in Harley Street. There she read a lot, not very conscientiously, but with a keen appetite for the most modern cultural delicacies. These were chiefly Wilde and the Decadents, and they stimulated in her the kind of tastes which provincial Wellington was never going to satisfy. Predictably, therefore, within two years of her return with her family to New Zealand, she had prevailed on her apprehensive father to release her for some real adventures as a young adult back in London.

He had good reason to be apprehensive. It was much more her strength (all her sisters agree on her egocentricity) than his judgement which got her away. He could see that the intensity of her appetites and the sharpness of her vision might make her a self-destroying rebel against his bourgeois values. "Isn't it terrible to love anything so much?" she asked herself in her journal before leaving Wellington. "I do not care at all for men, but *London*—it is life."² So (following the metaphor of colonial transplantation) she bundled her roots around her and planted herself back at the source, in London. She adopted Wilde's principles: art and life were inseparable, life must be crammed with experiences to feed art, and the artist must be free both to receive experience and to record it. "Art is absolutely self-development", she declared.³ In provincial Wellington the development of the artistic self was constrained. Deracination was accordingly a condition of art.

She left New Zealand thinking of herself as an expatriate, not an exile. To her father she made it clear that she wanted to return to England to become a writer. The early stories he helped her to get published in the Australian *Native Companion* convinced him of her talent. What he must have sensed, but feared to admit, was her own precondition for writing, the experience of life which would fertilise her art. Experience as a precondition for art was the dogma she had learned from Wilde. The artist might adopt fictive roles and names, but the experience which art recorded had to be real. A later writer has observed that by the age of fourteen most writers have enough experience for a lifetime of art. But Katherine/Kathleen was a girl, in a society which put up even more nets against female freedom than Joyce's Stephen Dedalus was trapped by, and she spent several years struggling in the nets before she could feel the truth of that simple assertion.

In the next four years she got the experience which turned her from an expatriate into an exile. As her friend of the time, Beatrice Campbell, rather sniffily described it many years afterwards,

> With some idea of gaining "experience", she got herself involved in about as much suffering as any young writer ever faced up to. A broken and meaningless marriage, unhappy love affairs, poverty, two pregnancies of illegitimate children of which one ended in a miscarriage and one in an abortion . . .[4]

If her devotion to the cultural metropolis was not enough in itself to cut her off from her New Zealand roots, the life of those years certainly was. She acted out many roles in this period—the allowance from her father was not enough to finance all her experiences, and she used many ways of getting money, including a chorus line in repertory in northern England, and entertaining at parties in London drawing rooms. Role-playing and attitudinising were the only means she had of getting through her experiences in a society she felt increasingly to be alien.

During these years she never belonged to Bohemia, unless it was on the fringe of Orage's *New Age* coffee shop coterie. For two years she wrote regularly for *The New Age*, chiefly under the feminist banner of Orage's fellow editor Beatrice Hastings. But she was too separate from any community, too bare in her sensibilities, to feel she belonged. She blundered from crisis to crisis, plunging in (for instance into her one-day marriage) and then running away as far as her finances would allow. Not until she met Middleton Murry early in 1912 did she stop running. He, because he was passive and did not hurt her, and because he was undemanding, provided her with what she most needed, an artistic platform, a place where she could freely do what she still wanted above all things. His role was to give her a point of rest where she could stop and put her experiences into place in her mind. He gave her at last the freedom to write. From this time on she stopped playing with names and different roles and firmly became Katherine Mansfield the writer.

For more than a year the two of them lived for their work, editing Murry's magazine *Rhythm* (called for its last three issues *The Blue Review*), writing for it and financing it. By the time it collapsed, leaving Murry a bankrupt and sucking away her allowance, their relationship was a working (in both senses of the word) partnership, a bond. Their lifestyle, living for their art, satisfied her highest priority, and the intimacy of two eased some of her day-to-day discomforts. Murry was cool, slow, not phlegmatic but certainly not irascible, fairly painless to live with and a stabilising point for her literary ambitions. For nearly eight years their relationship was the mainstay of that insecure mainmast her emotional life. In 1918 she wrote to him from Bandol, "the more I think the more astounded I am at the immense division between you and me and—everybody else alive."[5] But she was then in the south of France for her health, and twelve days after this declaration she began to cough up the blood which confirmed the existence of tuberculosis. This, as much as the physical separation it forced on them, sent her off on her own again.

When the tuberculosis was confirmed she began an increasingly frantic search for recovery, for any escape from the terror of death which possessed her life. It separated her from Murry, even though they still lived together for years at a time—ironically she began to cough blood only two months before they were freed from her first marriage and she could become Mrs Murry. It was beginning to separate them by the time they did get married, in May 1918. From then on her vision was less and less the unit of two against the world. She became more and more isolated by her sickness. (Several hotels refused to take her in; she got a bed once in Switzerland only by claiming, she declared, the wrong symptoms: a weak heart and lungs "of Spanish leather".)[6] She was free to write but not to live. In 1920 she wrote to Ann Estelle Rice that, lovingly nursed though she was by her elderly cousin in Menton, "I pine for *my own people,* my own wandering tribe."[7] She wrote to Murry in the same month "It is a great strain to live away from one's own tribe, with people who, however dear they are, are not ARTISTS."[8] Wryly using a different metaphor, more appropriate than the lost people of Israel to her residence in a Catholic household and her enforced solitude, she told Dorothy Brett, "We belong to the Order of Artists, and it's a strict order."[9] By 1920 Murry was no longer her community. Her freedom as a writer was now complete. She no longer depended even on the order of two against the world for her security. Her finest work came in the years that followed the achievement of this isolation.

Insecurity dogged her whole life. She saw it as the chief constraint on the artistic freedom which was always her proclaimed goal. "If you are without fear you are free', she wrote in 1921 to her brother-in-law, the aspirant painter Richard Murry. "Writers . . . are self-conscious to such a pitch now-a-days that their feeling for life seems to be absolutely stopped—arrested."[10] She never herself had the unselfconscious security of belonging anywhere, even to her wandering Order, and she valued the sense of belonging and the security which belonging somewhere gave accordingly. Her ultimate home was far away, in place and time, though her father always kept her supplied with enough money to subsist on. Her finances were one of the securities she did have. They were kept independent of Murry's and she fought hard to hold them that way.

Her insecurity was in England, and was largely social. The South African exile Beatrice Hastings was her mentor for a while. Later the Irish Beatrice Campbell became her confidante. She has said in retrospect that she and Katherine were relaxed together "rather as if we were both exiles and did not 'belong' in London."[11] In the early years with Murry their closest friends were exiles—the Russian Koteliansky, Lawrence the internal emigré with German Frieda, the American Anne Estelle Rice, the Campbells. In his autobiography *Between Two Worlds* Murry tells anecdotes which illustrate the social insecurity which he shared with Katherine and Lawrence.[12] In his own journal he says, "We were all socially outsiders, quite without the social and domestic tradition of which the Bloomsburies, Aldous Huxley, and expatriate—*plus royaliste que le roi*—Eliot inherited."[13] The feeling seems to have been mutual. Virginia Woolf always saw Murry as the leader of what she called the underworld, and after her first evening with Katherine she described her in a letter to her sister as stinking like a civet cat which had taken to prostitution, a simile presumably inspired by Katherine's unsubtle perfume. Ida Baker, Katherine's most lasting friend, who called for her at the end of the evening, was described equally acidly as "another of those females on the border land of propriety and naturally inhabiting the underworld."[14] They were guests in Bloomsbury, but there was no warmth in the welcome.

In his biography of Virginia Woolf Quentin Bell writes that she used the term underworld "with malicious intent and certainly with a kind of snobbery, sometimes with a purely social meaning, but also to classify those who were not so much creative artists as critics and commentators—people who could write a clever essay or a smart review; people who were more interested in reputations than in talents."[15] In fact her initially snobbish social reaction to Katherine Mansfield was diluted even at the first encounter. "She is so intelligent and inscrutable that she repays friendship", was her conclusion. What they had in common in the end overran the social hostility. Virginia Woolf records a meeting in the summer of 1920 which began coolly, but "then we talked about solitude and I found her expressing my feelings as I never hear them expressed . . . A queer effect she produces of someone apart, entirely self-centred; altogether concentrated upon her 'art': almost fierce to me about it."[16] But this affinity was a late and isolated occurrence. For most of her writing career Mansfield was inextricably tied in Bloomsbury eyes to Murry, and Murry was never welcome. As Bell again records, "The perpetual president and oracle of the Underworld was John Middleton Murry, for he added another ingredient—a high moral tone, a pretentious philosophy borrowed in part from his friend D. H. Lawrence—which allowed the game to be played under the cover of deep, manly, visceral feelings and virtuous protestations."[17] So long as Katherine Mansfield clung to Murry as the one tree on her island, so long would Bloomsbury see her as an outcast, a colonial.

She herself knew all this, and at times hated England for it. Although she went to stay with Ottoline Morrell at Garsington and to evenings at the Woolfs', her letters to them are always strained and unspontaneous. To Virginia Woolf in April 1919, for instance, she wrote in an English falsetto, "You write so *damned* well, so *devilish* well."[18] To Murry she wrote of loathing the English. About to visit Garsington she reassures him that she feels quite strong enough to face them. "I feel I could get into the very middle of a Bloomsbury tangi and remain untouched."[19] The Maori word (a *tangi* is a communal feast, the antithesis of isolation) stresses her feeling of alienation. Later she took Bloomsbury as the focus of her anger against that section of English culture which tried to ignore the war and the way it transformed everything.

She felt less alienated in France. Bandol in particular, during her first stay there, before the war changed it, gave her a feeling of security like home. "Oh God, this place is as fair as New Zealand to me", she wrote to Murry, "as apart, as secret, as much a place where you and I are alone and untroubled."[20] Being in England was an imprisonment, and she felt while she was there as unsafe as a criminal. Several letters written in the summer of 1921 from Switzerland speak of her sense of being cut off from life as a result of being "*on the island*".[21] The "little band of jeering, sneering, superior persons" that she wrote of in her review of 1920, the Bloomsbury *tangi,* was never far from her mind while she lived in England. Isolated, in France or Switzerland, or in her private memories, she was free to be unselfconscious. Writing to Dorothy Brett from Hampstead, shortly before the decision was again taken to travel to the sun for her health, she confessed, "I have to keep as solitary as I can, to have nobody *depending* and to *depend* as little as I can."[22] Not even Murry was a protection by then. And in the same letter, defending her solitude as the price of her freedom, she added, "Were I perfectly sincere I'd have to confess that I was always acting a part in my old palmy days. And now I've thrown the palm away." In England, conscious of her exclusion, she could either live a pretence or retreat into isolation.

Katherine Mansfield wrote a number of fine, delicate stories about the relationship between Murry and herself and about their English life. To the insect-on-a-pin scrutiny of the triangle, her French lover Francis Carco, Murry and herself in "Je ne parle pas français" of February 1918 she added the portrait of the man living abroad for the sake of his invalid wife in "The Man without a Temperament" in January 1920. The period in 1917 when the two of them had separate establishments lies behind "Psychology", while "The Escape" (1920) is a superb portrait of a strained, destructive relationship, the woman as compulsive bitch and the man as tortured evader:

> And she bent her spiteful, smiling eyes upon him, regardless of the driver. "I'll go myself. I'll walk back and find it, and trust you not to follow. For"—knowing the driver did not understand, she spoke softly, gently—"if I don't escape from you for a minute I shall go mad."
>
> She stepped out of the carriage. "My bag." He handed it to her.
>
> "Madame prefers . . ."
>
> But the driver had already swung down from his seat, and was seated on the parapet reading a small newspaper. The horses stood with hanging heads. It was still. The man in the carriage stretched himself out, folded his arms. He felt the sun beat on his knees. His head was sunk on his breast. "Hish, hish," sounded from the sea. The wind sighed in the valley and was quiet. He felt himself, lying there, a hollow man, a parched, withered man, as it were, of ashes. And the sea sounded, "Hish hish."

To these stories of strain she added others from her English experience, catching moments of infidelity, epiphanies of English life ("Bliss", "Revelations"). Others were written with the same incisive anger that informs the earlier stories she wrote for *The New Age*. There is a surge of feminism behind "The Little Governess" (1915) and "Mr Reginald Peacock's Day" (1917), and a warmer kind of derision in the stories of human weakness such as "Marriage à la mode" or the extended joke "Feuille d'Album". Taken as a whole, however, they vary in quality much more than the New Zealand stories. One of the English stories in particular may help to explain why.

All the English or European stories share the economic precision of phrase which is one of the characteristics of her style. The last section of "Life of Ma Parker", for instance, opens with a pair of similes which compose a marvellously exact and compact word-picture:

> It was cold in the street. There was a wind like ice. People went flitting by, very fast; the men walked like scissors; the women trod like cats.

The short sentences hurry along with the urgent rhythm of the street scene. The strong, evocative similes make the atmosphere thus created visual. And the similes do not stand out as a casual vividness. The mature stories are all perfectly integrated structures—difficult to quote from without the feeling that the passage has been crudely ripped out of its context. In this passage, for instance, the men like scissors and the women like cats are at the same time visual images and menacing ideas, the dangerous, hostile creatures of the chilly world Ma Parker walks out into. In fact the paragraph continues directly from the similes into Ma Parker's response to the cold world of scissors and cats:

> . . . And nobody knew—nobody cared. Even if she broke down, if at last, after all these years, she were to cry, she'd find herself in the lock-up as like as not.

A superb pair of similes, deployed with an exact regard for their place in the story as a whole. And yet this paragraph, the opening of the final section of "Life of Ma Parker", is to my mind one of the most awkward passages in all of Katherine Mansfield's mature writing. It is bad for reasons which I think relate directly to her position as an exile in the England of which she is writing. Integrated though the similes are into the associative design of the whole their evocativeness has to appear as Ma Parker's own verbalisation of her grief. And it does not work. The vision—scissors and cats in the cold street—is Ma Parker's but the words are the author's. Ma Parker is too alien, too different a creature from her author to share her language. The technique of sliding from an authorial voice imperceptibly into the mind of the beholder was a normal device in Katherine Mansfield's short stories, one of the advances she made for the short story form. In the opening of "At the Bay" it works immaculately.

> Very early morning. The sun was not yet risen, and the whole of Crescent Bay was hidden under a white sea-mist. The big bush-covered hills at the back were smothered. You could not see where they ended and the paddocks and bungalows began. The sandy road was gone and the paddocks and bungalows the other side of it; there were no white dunes covered with reddish grass beyond them; there was nothing to mark which was beach and where was the sea. A heavy dew had fallen. The grass was blue. Big drops hung on the bushes and just did not fall; the silvery, fluffy toi-toi was limp on its long stalks, and all the marigolds and the pinks in the bungalow gardens were bowed to the earth with wetness. Drenched were the cold fuchsias, round pearls of dew lay on the flat nasturtium leaves. It looked as though the sea had beaten up softly in the darkness, as though one immense wave had come rippling, rippling—how far? Perhaps if you had waked up in the middle of the night you might have seen a big fish flicking in at the window and gone again . . .

The morning landscape and mood are evoked by a seamless transition from word-painting to the child's vision from her bedroom overlooking the bay. No such seamless transition is possible with Ma Parker because to her author she is an alien.

The story of Ma Parker is of course a rather special case in the Katherine Mansfield canon. Interior monologue was by no means an essential technique, and some of the best of the English stories do very well without it. And yet the best of the English stories are the ones which venture the shortest distance from her own intimate experience: "The Man without a Temperament", "The Daughters of the Late Colonel", "Bliss". The finest of them all, "The Daughters of the Late Colonel", was readily recognised and acknowledged by its model Ida Baker as "that gentle caricature of her cousin Sylvia Payne and me".[23] It was actually written in Ida's company, and Ida made the tea for a celebration when it was finished. Apart from that one rather anomalous achievement, Katherine Mansfield wrote her best about intimately known subjects held at a distance. "The Man without a Temperament" and "Je ne parle pas français" she wrote while she was in France and Murry was in London. England was too oppressive, her isolation from it was never sufficiently complete for the elevation and detachment in which she wrote at her best. The isolation she needed was a freedom from the social pressures which the metropolis laid on her. Even Murry became oppressive in time.

The part Murry played in the growth of her isolation is complex. The process was gradual, and her shift from relying on him as the other half of the twosome facing a hostile world towards withdrawal into self-consuming solitude is marked only crudely by such milestones as the first diagnosis of her disease. In 1919 her journal records two versions of an experience when the geraniums in her Hampstead garden seemed to be shouting "Impudence!" at the colonial.

> I am the little Colonial walking in the London garden patch—allowed to look, perhaps, but not to linger. If I lie on the grass they positively shout at me: "Look at her, lying on *our* grass, pretending she lives here, pre-

tending this is her garden, and that tall back of the house, with the windows open and the coloured curtains lifting, is her house. She is a stranger—an alien. She is nothing but a little girl sitting on the Tinakori hills and dreaming: 'I went to London and married an Englishman, and we lived in a tall grave house with red geraniums and white daisies in the garden at the back.' *Im*-pudence!"

It was a small epiphany which she felt was worth working over.

The entries were followed by a note about a talk between Murry and his brother Richard in which they speculated about the need for a sense of place. She registers her own rejection of England, and adds "They were of one nation, I of another, as we sat talking. I felt R. offered himself to his brother, in my stead."[24] The world of two babes in the wood was not evident that night. Alienation has no visible stigmata, but this note records a wound which Murry did not have in common with his wife. She was apart from him by then not only in her social insecurity (they were then living in Hampstead, and he was editing *The Athenaeum*), but in her consciousness of the world he would never share, her New Zealand memories. There is a touch of self-pity and perhaps of self-dramatisation in both the note about the geraniums and the note about different nations, but it affirms that she knew that she was withdrawing, and where.

During the five years of her final illness, when she was struggling with tuberculosis and the physical isolation it so often imposed on her, she frequently referred in her notebooks and letters to her fellow consumptives Chekhov and Keats. They were the saints she worshipped in her Order of Artists, and their experiences gave her comfort in her solitude. But she had other, unique company through that time, company guaranteed by and guaranteeing her solitude, her remembered childhood.

Notes

1. *Novels and Novelists by Katherine Mansfield*, ed. J. Middleton Murry, London, 1930, p.220. First published 9.7.1920.
2. *The Journal of Katherine Mansfield*, p.21. Entry dated 21.10.1907.
3. *Ibid*, p.37. Entry dated May 1908.
4. Beatrice Campbell, Lady Glenavy, "*Today we will only Gossip*", London, 1964, p.56.
5. *Katherine Mansfield's Letters to John Middleton Murry 1913-1922*, ed. J. Middleton Murry, London, 1951, p. 156. Letter dated 7.2.1918.
6. *The Journal of Katherine Mansfield*, p.249.
7. *The Letters of Katherine Mansfield*, ed. J. Middleton Murry, 2 vols, London, 1928, II, p.24.
8. *Letters to John Middleton Murry*, p.503. Dated March 1920.
9. *The Letters of Katherine Mansfield*, II, p.23. Dated 26.3.1920.
10. *Ibid*, II, p.27. Dated 9.8.1921.
11. "*Today we will only Gossip*", p.69.
12. *Between Two Worlds. An Autobiography*, London, 1935, pp.289-92.
13. Quoted by F.A. Lea, *The Life of John Middleton Murry*, London, 1959, p.110.
14. Quentin Bell, *Virginia Woolf. A Biography*, 2 vols. London, 1972, II, p.45.
15. *Ibid*, II, p.50.
16. *Ibid*, II, pp.70-1.
17. *Ibid*, II, p.50.
18. *The Letters of Katherine Mansfield*, I, p.227. Dated April 1919.
19. *Letters to John Middleton Murry*, p.275. Dated 1.6.1918.
20. *Ibid*, p.78. Dated 29.12.1915.
21. *The Letters of Katherine Mansfield*, II, p.124. Dated July 1921.
22. *Ibid*, I, p.231. Dated 10.6.1919.
23. Ida Baker, *Katherine Mansfield. The Memories of L.M.*, London, 1971, p.153.
24. *The Journal of Katherine Mansfield*, p.158.

Asher Z. Milbauer (essay date 1985)

SOURCE: Milbauer, Asher Z. "I. B. Singer: The Convergence of Art and Faith." In *Transcending Exile: Conrad, Nabokov, I. B. Singer*, pp. 73-120. Miami: Florida International University Press, 1985.

[*In the excerpt below, Milbauer focuses on Isaac Bashevis Singer's novel* Shosha *as a vehicle for the writer's commenting both on his own destiny as an exile and on the collective destiny of the Jewish people.*]

Binele, I won't abandon you. I swear by the soul of your mother.

I. B. Singer, "The Lecture"

I will make it so you will live forever.

I. B. Singer, *Shosha*

In 1967, in the December issue of *Playboy* magazine, I. B. Singer published one of his best short stories, "The Lecture." This short piece, included later in the collection *The Seance and Other Stories*, can rightfully stand as an epigraph for the Yiddish writer's entire literary production. The theme of an exiled writer's efforts to relate his own past experience (as well as that of the entire Jewish nation) to the life of the present is a constant ingredient of both his novels and stories. "The Lecture" is a paradigm of it all.

The plot of the short story is as straightforward and uncomplicated as that of the majority of Singer's writings. But this simplicity will not deceive an attentive reader; it adds dimension and strength to the sincerity, agony, tragedy, and deep pain embedded in each word, sentence, and paragraph. I begin with this story not only because of its representative character in Singer's work, but because it bears a remarkable and revealing resemblance to Nabokov's novel *Pnin*, both in theme and in plot.

In the opening scenes of both the story and the novel, we encounter the main protagonists, N. and Pnin, two intellectuals, two exiled authors, who are on their way to deliver lectures to audiences who represent a vanished but still haunting past. (Nabokov would have been delighted at the coincidence that both he and Singer's character share the same initial letter in their names.) Letting the reader penetrate the minds of Pnin and N., the writers reveal an initially startling similarity in the patterns of their thinking as well as in the nature of the problems that obsess them. Both Pnin and N. are worried about their money, their passports, and their manuscripts, which, needless to say, get lost on their way to exotic, faraway places. Both find it necessary to describe in detail their journey on the train, meticulously pointing out all the complications that befall them. They share identical feelings of isolation and alienation from their fellow travelers. But, most important, the two exiled writers are constantly brooding about their past experiences, which they thought they would be able to leave behind them when forced to leave Eastern Europe. Both Pnin and N. return often in their reminiscences to the Holocaust and Stalin's purges—the two catastrophes that have so radically changed the course of events in the twentieth century. Both direct as well as indirect encounters with these events played a major role in turning the two writers into exiles. It is not just a mere coincidence, therefore, that both should respond similarly to the European cataclysms that had disrupted their personal lives and altered the destinies of their people.

Singer and Nabokov use identical techniques to convey the sense of tragedy, a permanent companion to exiled intellectuals, over the loss of a world that is no more. Scenes of the present invariably evoke Pnin's and N.'s reminiscences. Frequently, both in the story and in the novel, the distinctions between past and present are blurred, and it remains the reader's task, in order to gain a better insight into the texts, to distinguish the two planes of existence that are so intricately intertwined and often indiscernible. But, as I hope to show, it is even more important for the two protagonists to be able not only to disentangle their experiences but also to balance past and present, thus establishing an equilibrium that will ensure their intellectual survival.

While waiting to board his train, N. feels alienated from his fellow travelers: "It was as if they knew nothing of the existence of world problems or eternal questions, as though they had never heard of death, sickness, war, poverty, betrayal, or even such troubles as missing a train, losing a ticket, or being robbed."[1] In this condensed statement, Singer makes a veiled reference to a horrible past that means nothing to N.'s new countrymen, Americans.

N.'s lecture is to deal with the future of Yiddish as a language. He is going to argue for optimism about the survival of this language, despite the fact that the Holocaust reduced by several million the number of its speakers. As a result of the Holocaust, Yiddish has, paradoxically, turned into a holy language, *lashon hakodesh*, thus taking the place of Hebrew, which became the everyday language in the state of Israel. Although N.'s predictions are going to be optimistic, he has doubts about his presentation; the closer the train brings him to his destination the deeper his doubts become. His mental changes are paralleled by the physical changes on the train. The feelings of comfort and the relaxing heat of the compartment give way to restlessness and the discomforting cold. When the train suddenly breaks down and the freezing winter temperatures begin to penetrate its every corner, the narrator's thoughts turn more often to his past, to Poland, to the people he will never see again. The sense of isolation becomes more acute; the only means he has to warm himself is the bottle of cognac that he was wise enough to bring with him from New York.

It is past midnight when the train finally pulls into the depot. The station is abandoned and covered by a white carpet of deep snow. The cold is miserable; N. is on the verge of despair. But suddenly he notices two figures, whom he instinctively approaches. The two women, mother and daughter, are the only ones who waited for the renowned Yiddish writer to arrive. Hardly have they exchanged greetings, when the mother, a "lame woman," is already talking about dreadful and traumatic experiences in the displaced persons' camps, relating in frightful detail the fate of her family. The younger woman, Binele, who is herself survivor of Auschwitz, tries to calm her mother. But the daughter's admonitions are of no avail—nothing can silence her mother, who was so impatiently waiting for the great Yiddish author precisely in order to pour her heart out. Her behavior implies that she places high hopes on N., since only a true artist is able to perceive and fully comprehend the grief which has never ceased to torture her.

Survivors, Singer suggests, cannot be quiet, and even when they are, their silence sometimes assumes more meaning than volumes written by the most eloquent writers. N. knows that it is his duty to listen and to absorb everything this tragic figure, this miraculously saved remnant of the past, has to relate to him and, through him, to the entire world. The blood-chilling stories do nothing to relieve his feelings of cold. The frost becomes nearly unbearable to him. This sensation of cold is intensified when N. enters the tiny, run-down house of the two survivors where he is to spend the night. As if the cold were not enough to make him miserable, N. suddenly becomes aware that he has lost his manuscript; he is not even sure whether he still has his citizenship papers; he feels as if he is getting pneumonia. Suddenly he becomes conscious of painfully familiar odors that assail him from all the corners of the little house that evoke images from the past better forgotten. N. does not even try to fight them off; like Pnin, he cannot forget the unforgettable; he cannot and probably does not want to run away from the impressions that the old woman's Holocaust stories make on him.

Failing to overcome insomnia, unable to warm up even under three layers of blankets, N. tries consciously to get the feeling of what it meant to live through the Nazi atrocities: "Well, let me imagine that I remained under Hitler in wartime. Let me get some taste of that, too" (pp. 76-77). And as if to answer his call for a complete identification with the survivors, fate plays a foul trick on the narrator; in the middle of the night the old woman suddenly dies. Terror strikes N. when he hears the heartbreaking, horror-filled lamentations of the daughter. *Now,* indeed, he seems to comprehend fully what it means to be a victim, misunderstood, forgotten, ignored by the entire world. A neighbor, when solicited for help, is quite indifferent to what has just happened one floor below his apartment. Not only does he fail to grasp the tragedy of the situation, but, in addition, he cannot or does not want to understand English. Singer here suggests that the present circumstances are analogous to those in the past; then there was no common language between the victim and the outside world, a world that did nothing to prevent the destruction of almost a whole nation.

This event in the present gives rise to N.'s thoughts about the past: "My years in America seemed to have been swept away by that one night and I was taken back, as though by magic, to my worst days in Poland, to the bitterest crisis of my life" (p. 81). The present is inseparable from the past. The death of this survivor indicates to the narrator, and to Singer as well, that a true artist cannot keep silent about the events of the past, that it is his moral duty to relate the Holocaust experience to those who care to know. This is the legacy that N. inherits from the old woman. At once, looking at the tattoed number on Binele's wrist, he proudly accepts the bittersweet burden of the rememberer. At the deathbed of yet another Nazi victim, N. gives his solemn oath to the six million Jewish people, who cannot, unfortunately, be among his readers and listeners: "'Binele, I won't abandon you. I swear by the soul of your mother'" (p. 83). And only at this moment does the cold finally let up and the snow begin to melt. The artist, thus, becomes the only true intermediary between the past and present.

I. B. Singer did not break the promise made by his double to Binele and her mother. He knew that the delayed death of a miraculously saved soul was an unequivocal message to a Yiddish writer, an outcry not to forget, a plea to commemorate through art not only the tragic events of the past but also the endurance and the vital powers of the Jewish people. Singer's novel *Shosha* can be justly regarded as his protagonist's fulfillment of the commitment he made at the deathbed of Binele's mother. N.'s pledge to never forget resounds in Aaron Gredinger's oath to Shosha to remember her forever, not to "forget anything," and to "make it so that [she'll] live forever."[2]

Prior to being published as a full-length novel in 1978, *Shosha* was serialized in the New York—based Yiddish newspaper, *The Forward,* under the title *Soul Expeditions.* (Why the book's title was changed will become clear later.) The name Shosha is familiar to most of Singer's readers: he has devoted an entire chapter to this "image" of his past in his compilation of children's stories *A Day of Pleasure*; he also mentions her several times in his memoir, *In My Father's Court.* His insistence on having this character reappear time and again in his literary works should put Singer's reader on alert. Fortunately, Singer is not writing a detective novel, and he has no intention of keeping the reader in suspense in regard to Shosha's frequent appearances in his fiction. In the novel, Betty, one of Aaron's numerous mistresses, asks him what he sees in Shosha that he should be so drawn to her. His answer is curt and defeatingly sincere: he sees in Shosha himself, that is, his past, which, as becomes clear later, is inseparable from his present existence.

Shosha is not a simple novel. One can wholeheartedly sympathize with Aaron's agonies when writing his play, *The Lubomir Maiden,* which, according to his own admission, contained a "magical theme—like the Torah, it seemed to possess seventy different faces" (p. 58). *Shosha* too is a multifaceted book, a large canvas, that betrays the author's ambition to incorporate into it the many elements scattered through all his novels and stories, as well as to add new dimenions to his literary activity. *Shosha* summarizes what he has done in his entire literary career; in other words, the novel is yet another fictionalized memoir of Isaac Bashevis Singer. Like Nabokov's *Mary, Shosha* is a novel about the birth of an artist.

Biography and fiction are nearly indistinguishable in *Shosha.* Edward Alexander, in his full-length book, *I. B. Singer,* points out that *Shosha* is Singer's first novel published in English that is written as a first-person narrative.[3] This fact, coupled with the reader's awareness of the publication of *A Young Man in Search of Love,* a nonfictional Singer memoir issued almost simultaneously with *Shosha,* adds to the impression that *Shosha* is a fictional autobiography. Indeed, when one compares the memoir and the novel, one cannot help noticing how much of what is in the memoir finds its way into the novel.

Both the book and the memoir address themselves to questions invariably posed by young, aspiring artists. What is the purpose of literature? What should one write about? How is one to translate into writing the creative powers one possesses? The list of inquiries can go on endlessly; these questions are ageless. But what makes the complexities of the problems raised by Singer's doubles even more pointed is the reader's singular awareness of the historical circumstances under which a Singerian artist has to function.

Most of the events in *Shosha* take place in the nineteen twenties and thirties, that is, the years between the two world wars. The place is Poland; the main characters are Jews. Hasidism, a Jewish mystical movement founded in Poland in about 1750 in opposition to rationalism and ritual laxity, and the movement of Haskalah or Enlightenment become the two poles of thinking within the Jewish population of Poland. There are those who advocate the traditional way of life, that is, the way of life to which Polish Jews were accustomed during the eight centuries of exile in that country. On the other hand, there emerges an ever-growing segment of mostly young people who want to leave the ghettos and whose search for a new identity places them in extreme opposition to their upbringing. They want worldliness, assimilation, enlightenment.

To be sure, neither of these groups is homogeneous in its demands and visions of the future. Even the Hasidim, proponents of the traditional, are not like their fathers who established the tradition. Bashele, Shosha's mother, sums it up this way: "'There are no such Jews anymore. Even Hasidim dress like dandies today—cutaway gaberdines, polished boots'" (p. 78). The divergences among the enlightened Jews are no less noticeable. For some, Soviet Russia and its socioeconomic structure is the only model to follow; Stalin is often portrayed as a savior of the world from the evils that beset it. Others advocate total assimilation, announcing thus the inconsequentiality of the two thousand years of Jewish life in the Diaspora. Yet another group calls upon the Jews to return to the Holy Land and build a state that will express the new Jewish identity and consciousness.

But all of these impassioned theories of change and newness are overshadowed by constant feelings of doubt and ambivalence. Somewhere deep in their minds and hearts, these people are conscious of the futility of their efforts to escape their heritage. Aaron's pointed observation aptly expresses the essence of the state of mind of those around him: "We are running away and Mount Sinai runs after us. This chase has made us sick and mad" (p. 255). The significance of this statement is heightened when one rememebers that the sinister shadow of Nazi Germany has by this time covered nearly all Europe. In consequence of this, Polish Jewry feels that it is gradually becoming entrapped between the forces of Polish Panslavic anti-Semitism and Hitler's destructive force that threatens its annihilation.

It is in these times and under such circumstances that Aaron Greidinger firmly decides to become a writer and devote his life to art. Like Singer, the son of an Orthodox rabbi, Aaron "was brought up on three dead languages—Hebrew, Aramaic, Yiddish . . . and a culture that developed in Babylon: the Talmud" (p. 1). In this very first sentence of the novel, Singer points out the two problems that are inseparable companions of any transplanted writer, namely, language and exile. The influence of his home, deeply steeped in tradition, is apparent in all Singer's writings. Aaron's home is identical to Singer's. From an early age the boy had a strong urge to write. He once confided to Shosha, who lived in the same apartment house on Krochmalna Street, that he "was writing a book" (p. 7). As a teenager, Aaron was a voracious reader; his reading had to be done in secret because his father would not tolerate any writing outside of the realm of the Pentateuch, the Talmud, and the Mishna. Aaron, though, indulged in worldly books, written by such (to his father) sinister figures as Dostoyevsky, Spinoza, Schopenhauer. The young man was searching for the answer to the eternal question of how one can remain a Jew and be worldly at the same time.

Both Singer and his double, Aaron, were very much involved in the intellectual Yiddish milieu of Warsaw. As a member of the writers' club, Aaron had a chance to meet with older as well as younger aspiring artists, all of whom were posing similar questions. These encounters, though primarily futile, taught Aaron one thing: he should be different, he should be above the gossip and trivialities in which his pseudointellectual colleagues indulged. They, he understood, could not become the models after whom he might fashion himself. Aaron felt that he was not tailored to write works that would advance political slogans or adhere to the principles of "socialist realism" then in vogue among writers with procommunist inclinations. Neither was the young man overanxious to cram his future books with messages that might suit the needs of the hour. This is not to say that he did not understand the dangers of Nazism and the urgency to stand up against it; he was aware of the calls of politically conscious critics to expose Hitlerism as well as their insistence on writing plays on the "need of resistance by the Jewish masses, not dramas that brought back superstition of the Middle Ages" (p. 115). Literature, according to Aaron, should be above politics; to mix the two was not his inclination, not yet. On the other hand, this son of a rabbi was not willing to conform to the views of the hedonists and escapists who argued that the only things Jews wanted to see in the books of contemporary authors were trash and sex.

Caught in the middle of this controversy, Aaron remains creatively impotent, chastising himself for wasting his time and indulging in daydreaming and sexual escapades. He often thinks of suicide. Yet despite his self-destructive urges, Aaron never abandons his desire to define to himself, as well as to others, his role as an artist. "What kind of writer was I," he frequently asks himself. "I hadn't published a single book . . . I . . . imagined I had written a work that would startle the world. But what could startle the world? No crime, no misery, no sexual perversion, no madness. Twenty million people had perished in the Great War, and here the world was preparing for another conflagration. What could I write about that wasn't already known? A new style? Every experiment with words quickly turned into a collection of mannerisms" (p. 25). This statement not only illuminates the workings of an artist's mind; it also makes the reader understand Aaron's ahistorical view of history. On another occasion, he reinforces this view by defining the history of the world as a long chain of wars, a version of Pnin's assertion that the history of mankind is the history of pain.

Indeed, what could a writer like Aaron write about if history (and consequently suffering) repeats itself with such a morbid regularity? He was conscious of and well versed in the history of the Jews; he could not fail to see that their prospects at present were grim, to say the least. Nevertheless, his mind was set—he had to write even though it might mean the repetition of old truths and old ideas.

The people with whom Aaron surrounded himself were not helpful. Most of them were resigned to their deaths. Morris Feitelzohn, Aaron's self-appointed mentor and patron who chose the exile of Poland over the exile of America and who preached hedonism as the only escape from the burdens of the past and the futility of the present, was of no assistance to Aaron. His cynicism had no appeal to the young man who vehemently rejected the older man's advice to give the Jews what they wanted most—"sex, Torah, Revolution." Betty, the cosmopolitan actress who crosses and recrosses the Atlantic in search of her identity, uses a double-edged sword in her relationship with Aaron, whose mistress she eventually becomes. On the one hand, she encourages him to write and shows genuine feeling for the young man; on the other hand, she distorts and destroys the play he is writing for her, which is the result of numerous sleepless nights and hard creative labor. She is unable to understand that her constant prattle about suicide as well as her insatiable sexual desires tend to stifle rather than revive the young man's artistic urges. And then there is Celia, a middle-aged woman, surrounded by riches and art objects, pampered by her immature husband, used by Feitelzohn, her idol and lover. Celia's entire time is spent either in a dimly lit, cozy living room or in the embraces of her entertainers, Aaron among them, brooding ceaselessly over death and suicide. What could she offer Aaron? Inspiration?—probably not. Her body?—it did not differ much from others that he had known. Solace?—in death, maybe.

Even more destructive to Aaron's writing career were the predictions of these characters about the future of the Jews in Poland. Betty and Celia, Feitelzohn and Haiml, Sam and Tekla are constantly warning the young writer that total annihilation of the Polish Jewry is on its way. Their predictions of the Holocaust indicate the homogeneity of thought among representatives of different strata of Polish society. Here is Morris: "'Tsutsik, don't stay in Poland. A holocaust is coming here that will be worse than in Chmielnitsky's time. If you can get a visa—even a tourist visa—escape!'" (p. 151). (These are the words of a self-appointed priest of the hedonist temple.) Haiml, Celia's husband who preaches the doctrines of Poale Zion, according to which Jews have to forget about the thousands of years in exile and go to Palestine, also urges Aaron to leave, though he himself behaves contrary to the principles he is so wholeheartedly embracing. "'If you have a chance to escape from here, don't wait,'" he admonishes Aaron. "'We're caught between Hitler and Stalin. Whichever invades the country will bring a cataclysm'" (p. 64).

Aaron feels the need to justify his immobility and inertia. He witnesses Hitler's occupation of one country after another: he is bitter about the Allies assuming a "wait and see" position; he clearly perceives that all these developments leave the Jews of Poland without any hope. "But running away," he asserts, "and leaving at bay those who were dear to me was not in my nature" (p. 120). Given his resolution, not even the businesslike exhortations of Sam Dreiman can be of any avail to him. "'Things will not end well in Poland,'" Sam predicts. "'That beast Hitler will soon come with his Nazis. There'll be a great war. Americans will lend a hand and they'll do what they did in the last war, but before that the Nazis will attack the Jews and there'll be nothing but grief for you here'" (pp. 155-56).

After reading these warnings, the paradox embedded in them is clear: these people clearly perceived the grief Hitler's inevitable occupation would bring, yet they didn't leave in time to prevent their own destruction.

Celia provides at least a partial answer to this paradox. She is also among those who embody ambivalent attitudes toward Aaron. On the one hand, she urges Aaron to escape and avoid committing "literary suicide," but she herself is determined to die in Poland rather than attempt a new start as an exile in still another country: "'I keep myself going only with the force of inertia, or call it what you will. I don't want to go to a foreign land and lie sick in some hotel room or hospital. I want to die in my own room. I don't want to rest in a strange cemetery'" (p. 244-45). Exile is what most frightens these people; they are tired of being wandering Jews. Betty, the actress constantly on the run, speaks for all of them when she says that "the sad truth is that for me there isn't *one* place in the world where I feel at home" (p. 132). And yet, these homeless people beg Aaron to escape. Consciously or subconsciously, all of them believe in Aaron's artistic genius. They urge him to write because by writing he will survive and atone for the sins that resulted in their exile. The frequent, and only slightly camouflaged admissions of the sinful existence they lead testify to their awareness that they are following in the path of their forefathers, committing the very idolatry that caused the expulsion of the Jews from the land of Israel. Writing is seen by them as a means to transcend alienation and estrangement from tradition. On the other hand, these people, who have resigned themselves to death, need someone to record and take account of their lives. They desire a rememberer who will through his writings make future generations more aware of the Jewish Polish milieu and of the fate they already anticipate at the hands of the Nazis. Celia and Haiml, Aaron and Dora, Morris and Betty—all of them are conscious of abandoning the true path of Judaism, committing thus the sin that brought upon them the curse of exile. Aaron is an artist, a writer, whom they choose as their intermediary between righteousness and evil, between the past and the present. They never doubt his literary genius; they believe that he will not fail to perform the holy duty with which they have entrusted him—to intercede for them and to commemorate their lives in his writings.

But Aaron does not flee, not yet. Before he escapes he must know exactly what he is leaving behind; he has to have a precise, nearly scientific knowledge of the society he abandons. Superficial knowledge of the past cannot satisfy the young man; he must get to its core, learn its nature, understand its inner workings. He has to touch it, to smell it, to see it as it is and as it was for hundreds of years. At this point in his life Shosha, the ageless, physically deformed, blonde, blue-eyed girl with a short nose and thin lips—the girl who spoke the pure Yiddish of Krochmalna Street and who, as Aaron puts it, "in her own fashion denied death" (p. 91)—begins to work miracles on the artist. None of Aaron's enlightened friends can explain why Aaron is so drawn to Shosha; later, when he decides to marry the cripple, all of them are shocked because they see his action as a denial of common sense, and a fatal obstacle to leaving Poland. Aaron is hard put to explain this step; all he can say to his stubborn interrogators is that Shosha "is a girl from my childhood. We were neighbors at No. 10 Krochmalna Street. Later I went away and for many years" (p. 136). Aaron fails to finish the sentence, and it remains the reader's task to complete it by closely following the development of the events of the novel.

Shosha, as later becomes clear, represents to the young artist the coherence and integrity of the Jewish people and their past. Even while absent from Krochmalna Street, Aaron did not forget this girl; the memories of her were deeply embedded in his mind, only to surface later and drastically change his behavior and actions. He often dreamed of Shosha, and in his dreams the two were invariably together joined by a miraculous bond.

Prior to achieving the oneness with Shosha that brings him the peace of mind necessary for his creative powers to return, Aaron has to undergo a crisis of self-doubt and resignation. But once he decides to be reunited with his childhood sweetheart, with his past, it is easier for him to shake off the destructive influences of his friends and mistresses. He abandons Dora because of her reluctance to give up her utopian communist views; Aaron cannot identify with totalitarian regimes. He is not just against communism but against all other "isms" as well. He finally finds the strength to reject Betty and Celia and to be free from the intrigues and slime into which they dragged him. Feitelzohn's theories do not appeal to him any more; he sees clearly that Morris created them solely to escape reality rather than to admit the meaninglessness of his existence. Aaron is beginning to understand that he "has thrown away four thousand years of Jewishness and exchanged it for meaningless literature, Yiddishism, Feitelzohnism" (p. 257). It also takes the sharp razor blade of an anti-Semitic Polish barber held at his throat as well as the prophetic voice of his dead father, speaking to him in the most crucial moment of his life, to rouse him from lethargy and move him to transform his life.

Leaving the barber shop, where he is mistaken for a gentile and therefore privileged to hear the most hideous anti-Semitic pronouncements, Aaron is shaking with fear, disgust, and shame. "I began to race," he recalls, "not knowing in what direction I was going. *No, I wouldn't stay in Poland! I'd leave at any price!* (p. 164). Having made this decision, though not knowing yet what direction to take, Aaron now fully understands the admonitions of his father whose tradition he had denied, the admonitions earlier conveyed to him in a sudden vision of the old man accompanied by the thunderous voice of the righteous:

> "Run!" a voice cried within me. "You'll sink into a slime from which you'll never be able to get out. They'll drag you into the abyss!" . . . "Don't shame me, your mother and your holy ancestors! All your deeds are noted in heaven." . . . "Heathen! Betrayer of Israel! See what happens when you deny the Almighty! 'You shall utterly detest it and you shall utterly abhor it, for it is a cursed thing.'"
>
> (p. 158)

And run Aaron does, with his first stop at Bashele's apartment on Krochmalna Street, where the pure and virginal Shosha was patiently waiting for him.

Only when he is back on the street where he grew up, reunited with his past, does Aaron begin to attain some spiritual calm and tranquility. Only when he becomes one with Shosha, Singer seems to imply, do his creative powers return to him and enable him to write a novel that miraculously integrates the feuding Jewish camps, the traditional and the enlightened. Singer's intentions are clear at this point: literature and art can perform miracles where other intellectual institutions fail.[4]

Clearly Shosha inspires Aaron; she resurrects for him a past that the two once so happily shared. However, Shosha also threatens to endanger the writer's further creative existence. She provides a temporary, though necessary respite by recreating his past. It is true that awareness of the past is a required condition for Aaron's creative powers to be sustained. But to ignore and blot out the present will jeopardize his intellectual survival. He has to learn how to balance the two.

With Shosha's generous help, Aaron finally acquires the exact and so persistently sought knowledge of his past. Not only has he learned how to avoid being paralyzed by it, he has also learned how to benefit from the past's life-giving powers. Now, reunited with Shosha and having paid tribute to his past by his literary endeavors in the Polish exile, Aaron can run and fight for his survival without feelings of guilt for betraying those dear to him.

The Victorian epilogue of the novel provides additional information about its main characters. Aaron Greidinger, the now acclaimed and distinguished American Yiddish author, is brought by Singer to visit the land of Israel, where, thirteen years after leaving Poland, he meets Haiml, the only survivor of his days of youth. It is through his account to Haiml that we learn about Shosha's death as well as about Aaron's exodus from Poland. The two, together with other refugees, were nearly out of the country when Shosha suddenly fell to the ground and died. Her death had a twofold effect on Aaron: it caused him much grief, but at the same time, it made his road to freedom much easier. In the literal sense, Aaron did not succeed. But, paradoxically, he became the beneficiary of Shosha's death. He inherited from her the knowledge that otherwise would have been lost to himself and therefore to his readers. Shosha presented Aaron with a store of memories that enrich the experiences of his present life and enable him to memorialize the past of the Jewish people of Eastern Europe and their lives in his many novels and stories. His works will always be a reminder of a world that is no more.

Notes

1. I. B. Singer, "The Lecture," in *The Seance and Other Stories,* p. 66. Subsequent references to this edition will appear in the text.

2. I. B. Singer, *Shosha,* p. 7. Subsequent references to this edition will appear in the text.

3. Edward Alexander, *Isaac Bashevis Singer,* p. 113.

4. The idea of an artist's omnipotence as a peacemaker in times of crises caused by exile has been explored by Singer on earlier occasions as well. The story "The Yearning Heifer" is typical in this respect. Only through the generous efforts of a Jewish writer is peace restored among the members of a troubled family, which finds itself transplanted to an isolated farm somewhere in New York State. A young writer's presence in their home makes the members of the family forget their troubles and cope with their exiled situation.

Bettina L. Knapp (essay date 1991)

SOURCE: Knapp, Bettina L. "Huysmans's *Against the Grain*: The Willed Exile of the Introverted Decadent." In *Exile and the Writer: Exoteric and Esoteric Experiences—A Jungian Approach,* pp. 75-92. University Park: University of Pennsylvania Press, 1991.

[*In the following excerpt, Knapp discusses Joris-Karl Huysmans' controversial novel* Against the Grain, *suggesting that des Esseintes's self-imposed exile attests to his being deprived of love in childhood, resulting in his present inability to love.*]

Willed exile and the deepest condition of introversion was the way chosen by Duke Jean des Esseintes in Joris-Karl Huysmans's[1] extraordinary novel *Against the Grain* (1884). Inability to face reality, uncontrollable ennui, and hatred fo a society he saw as superficial, banal, vulgar, and materialistic: all motivated des Esseintes's withdrawal from the world and seclusion in a country home not far from Paris. Alienated from his fellow beings, Huysmans's antihero hoped that by cutting himself from the intellectual, spiritual, and philosophical morass of contemporary society he would be left untainted and free to indulge his every wish.

To this end, he regulated his life in such a way as to keep his mind and senses forever active in the creation of his own world of fantasy and artifice. His dehumanized existence revolved around the acquisition of rare and exotic objects: furnishings, paintings, books, flowers, foods, liqueurs.

The duke's exile, then, was based on neither a need for increased consciousness or understanding nor a desire to attain higher spiritual values. It was designed to cultivate sensual highs, states he would then analyze with the finesse and perspicuity of a scientist. His home, transformed into a virtual hothouse, resembled a laboratory for experimentation, offering him the visceral pleasures of the synesthetic experience. The resulting reveries and dreams, revolving for the most part around sexual encounters, including voyeurism, sadomasochism, homosexuality, and extreme misogyny, indicated a condition of severe psychological disequilibrium, unalleviated and in fact accentuated by exile and escapism.

Arthur Symons called *Against the Grain* "the breviary of Decadence." Indeed, it was just that. The word *decadent* (from the Latin, *cadere,* to fall, to decline), is an exact description of Huysmans's hyperaesthetic, misanthropic, morbid antihero. It has been claimed that des Esseintes's comportment and inclinations were modeled on those of the effete Baron de Montesquiou-Fezensac and on Ludwig II of Bavaria, as well as on the author himself. Mention must also be made in this regard of Edmond de Goncourt's protagonist in *Faustin* (1882), a work that had much impressed Huysmans. Above all, Baudelaire and Poe were Huysmans's mentors. Like them, des Esseintes was morose by temperament, and a dandy who longed to bathe in an ideal world of eternal beauty and artifice. Unlike these writers, however, he was not a creative type; his yearnings were focused solely on the most efficacious gratification of his senses.

Neurologists and psychiatrists have ascribed des Esseintes's pathologically passive and morbid nature to *erethism,* a malady causing abnormal irritability of the nerves and hyperresponsiveness to stimulation. Inordinate acuteness of the sense of hearing (*hyperacusis*), of touch (*hyperesthesia*), and of smell (*hyperosmia*) encouraged him purposefully and systematically to excite his senses, allowing these to impact as powerfully as possible on his psyche and body.

Exile/Escapism

The Duke des Esseintes, the last descendent of an illustrious, noble, and inbred French family that had received its education from the Jesuits, lost his parents when he was seventeen. Never having received their love, he had always lived a lonely and detached existence. Thin and handsome, with steely blue eyes and overrefined aristocratic manners, he was deeply disdainful and resentful of his restrictive upbringing. That he opted for a life of debauchery and indulged in all types of excessive and unhealthy sexual experiences undermined his health and accounted for a turning-inward. Having sold the Château de Lourps, his ancestral manor, he moved to a villa in the outskirts of Paris, at Fontenay-aux-Roses, where he took up residence with only two human presences: the elderly couple who had cared for his mother.

The world of artifice into which des Esseintes exiled himself could, in some ways, be likened to that of a religious ascetic. Like the Trappists, for example, when des Esseintes gave up enslavement to society he opted for another rule: obedience to a dogma. His daily routine, like that of a monk, followed certain disciplines: he slept by day and remained awake at night; his meals followed certain culinary specifications; and silence was maintained at all times in his home. However, unlike the religious ascetic, who lives on a spiritual level, des Esseintes deluded himself that he sought solitude because of his hatred for the vulgar, his contempt for the mediocre, his hostility toward bourgeois entrepreneurs, and ignorant masses.

The evils this post-Romantic young man attributed to the outer world were, psychologically, a projection or a mirror image of his own empty and arid inner world. Unable to create or to give of himself and incapable of sounding out those factors which troubled him, he spent his time cultivating the exotic, preternatural, and involuted world of his fantasies.

Unbeknown to des Esseintes, exile was really a strategy: the elimination of the world of people and its replacement by a world of things. This strategy was instrumental in further dehumanizing an already severely alienated young man. His extreme cerebralness was focused on finding ways to take him out of himself by transcending empirical reality. Just as monks were constantly occupied with prayers or litanies, des Esseintes was obsessively concerned with the most effective way to ascend to supernatural spheres through ritualistic uses of objects.

The duke's approach to the world of things also had sexual implications; it was a means of sublimating his erotic impulses. Like fetishes, objects upon which certain values are projected, des Esseintes endowed paintings, rugs, plants, or even a bejeweled turtle with dynamic energy; this energy in turn activated his subliminal world. The redirection of his libido (psychic energy) from his unconscious to the outer world impregnated objects with certain virtues and powers. In des Esseintes's case, such excitation titillated his senses, thus arousing him sexually. The *abaissement du niveau mental* and the concomitant rise in emotional level put an end, at least momentarily, to his underlying fears of castration and impotence. So effective a healing technique did des Esseintes consider the world of things, that he looked upon objects as having medicinal value. The aged couple who were his only companions, in keeping with the hospital environment he had created for himself, were dispensers of drugs.

Des Esseintes's belief that seclusion would help him find release from his paralyzing and fearsome ennui was, of course, an illusion. Seclusion was an escape mechanism his superficial and undeveloped psyche considered a panacea. Such a view, however, is not unusual. Indeed, it is characteristic of some unformed and immature *puer aeternus* types who have never evolved or strengthened their ego (center of consciousness). Like the *puer aeternus,* des Esseintes wandered about from one experience to another, yielding to bouts of despair, despondency, and helplessness. Incapable of dealing with the problems at hand, of facing and struggling through the difficulties marring his life, he sought answers in the world of objects and the erotic fantasies, dreams, and hallucinations triggered by them.

House/Womb/Tomb/Unconscious

What does the house signify that des Esseintes chose not only to withdraw into it but to furnish it in keeping with his aesthetic sense? A mother symbol, it represents a containing, protective womb, and it is also tomblike. Like the mother, it is empowered with both positive and negative attributes: if the house is creative, nourishing, and fertilizing, it encourages growth; if it imprisons mind and psyche, it has the power to destroy life, to encourage rot and decay.

Psychologically, the house may also be looked upon as a symbol for the unconscious. Closed, hidden, filled with shadowy and mysterious elements, it is the setting within which des Esseintes performs his insalubrious rituals. Governed by subjective factors, he relies on what the outer object, the *thing,* constellates in his subliminal sphere. His already weakened ego is further devitalized, precipitating a condition of morbid subjectification.

Books

Books, particularly those of Classical Latin writers, hold des Esseintes in thrall. His choice of authors and works reveals a correspondence between his inner climate and the one depicted in the particular work he is reading. As a mirror image or reflection of his unconscious, specific volumes may be viewed as mediators between invisible and visible worlds, encouraging cogitation. Let us note that the Latin word for mirror is *speculum,* the implication being that this object encourages speculation, contemplation, understanding.

The emphasis the duke places on books, and his boundless knowledge of literature in general and Latin texts in particular, indicates his highly developed thinking faculty. Everything in the outer world is related to or associated with the intellect through the *logos* principle, which connects, structures, abstracts, and conceptualizes all facts. Des Esseintes, therefore, feels comfortable theorizing on everything from mathematical problems to colors to perfumes, and he does so with the exactingness of a scientist. His meditations, focusing on harmonious gradations and degradations of tones, colorations, and ideas, act as catalysts, ushering him into a dreamworld. Thus is he able to continue to escape ever more deeply into his world of delusion and phantasmagoria.

As suggestive powers, books encourage him to displace himself via reverie or dream without ever leaving his chair. As a thinking/sensation type, he can experience with ease distant lands, mountains, ports, continually varying sounds, textures, odors, and sights. The libido he concentrates on the book (or any object) is so intense that it leads to its overvaluation. Moreover, his apperception of a volume encourages an introjection of his own inner state: a transfer of an unconscious content onto the object. The aesthetic enjoyment he derives from a book, and the rationalization that he believes is an objectification of his sense of pleasure, is in fact, an indication of his poor adaptation to life in general and to the volume—object/stimulus—in particular (Jung, *Collected Works,* 6:309, 360).

Because he is an introverted thinking/sensation type, his senses are conditioned to his thoughts. This determines the type of book he will enjoy, and indeed the works des Esseintes likes most are those that release the strongest sensations within him. Understandably, then, certain books have a strong erotic hold and act as a kind of instinctual or vital function.

The Latin writers he identifies as "decadent," whose works line one wall of his orange and blue study, are des Esseintes's favorites. For him, the "decadent" period is positive, in sharp contrast to the negative characteristics the Sorbonne professors attach to it. Vergil's *Aeneid,* written in the so-called great period, he finds derivative: a mass of borrowings from Homer and others. Nor do Theocritus, Ennius, and Lucretius hold any interest for him. Cicero and Caesar are "dry" and "constipated." Seneca, Suetonius, Tacitus, Juvenal, Quintilian, Pliny, Plautus, and Titus Livius incite no emotional reaction in him whatsoever.

The duke's favorite work is the *Satyricon* of Petronius. This author's vivid, sardonic, and intensely accurate vision of the vices and luxuries of imperial Rome is written objectively and without concern for humanity, like "decadent" novels, which contain no criticism of sociopolitical regimes and no attempt to reform noxious conditions. No better example of this genre can be found than *Satyricon,* which analyzes in the most delicate and perspicacious ways the mores of a period.

Petronius spares the reader no details, des Esseintes maintains, in his stagings of sodomy and lubricity, analyzing these with the finesse of a jeweler, while also omitting all moral commentaries. The duke's visceral reactions to *Satyricon,* as well as to other works of the period, such as the *Metamorphoses,* of Apuleius, are overt. He openly enjoys the erotic stimulation aroused by his readings and visualizations of happenings revolving around sadomasochistic pantomimes, voyeurism, enactments of lustful and perverse relationships, and debaucheries of all types. He visualizes the details like film clips, pondering one image after another: naked women on the prowl, men and women peeking at lovemaking in bedrooms through doors slightly ajar. Such mental voyeurism allows him to be the passive recipient in his own fantasy world. *Satyricon* opens him up to the bejeweled domain of exciting erotic and masturbational sensations.

Jewels and Stones

As a thinking/sensation type, des Esseintes is aroused by the continuously changing colorations of stones, depending upon their cut, shape, and the intensity or dullness of the light rays shining upon them. For him, they are living and active entities, just like books. Stones, like the duke's steely eyes and unfeeling heart, are hard and compassionless. The thirty-year-old nervous, hollow-cheeked bachelor experiences the luster, texture, and shape of stones in his house of dreams as yet another way of escaping. He bypasses the banal empirical world, penetrating an earthly paradise of his own manufacture.

The search for rare and exotic objects to furnish his solitude is uppermost in the duke's mind. Artifice, as opposed to objects emanating from the natural world, is what he most prizes. The many pages Huysmans devotes to descriptions of heteroclite jewels—their shapes, textures, and tints ranging from electric to cobalt blues, multiple nuances of indigos, blacks, greys, turquoises, salmons, roses, cinnabars, viscous reds, violets in all of their shadowy intensities—are not only marvels in themselves, but also disclose the author's empathy for his antihero's intensely sensual nature.

That stone is durable and less subject to the laws of birth and decay is a truism. As used by des Esseintes, however, the stone does not represent continuity, any more than does a mood or thought. Like fleeting luminosities or scintillae that shine when the lighting is right, the powers of stones are ephemeral, tenuous, and fragmented, concrete manifestations of des Esseintes's split psyche, when fantasies emerge, either beauteously prismatic or in horrific and deformed images. The thinking/sensation type cannot assimilate such ephemera into his psyche (Franz and Hillman).

The gem merchant, the only visitor allowed in des Esseintes's home, brings with him a most singular object: a living turtle with a shell that is painted brilliant gold and encrusted with rare stones. Des Esseintes has ordered it for a very special purpose. It is to be placed on his Oriental rug of yellow and purple tonalities, where the sparkling brilliance of its bejeweled carapace will create a sharp contrast, thereby lending the rug just the antique look he wants.

The turtle, from the Greek word *Tartaros,* a part of Hades sectioned off for punishment of the wicked, is complex in its symbology. The Egyptians looked upon the turtle as a chthonian entity, a fearsome power because it emerged clandestinely from beneath the waters or earth. To ward off any harm the turtle might inflict, such phrases as "May

Ra live and may the turtle die" were formulated by this ancient people. As representative of the dark or shadowy aspects of the underworld, the turtle represented a negative factor in many cultures. Its domelike carapace, identified at times with a cosmos, house, or cranium, was frequently an unwelcome sight. However, because its four paws were firmly planted upon the earth, the turtle has also been associated with solidity, stability, longevity, and a material rather than a spiritual approach to life. An engraving in a fifteenth-century allegory, *The Hypnerotomachia Poliphili*, depicts a woman holding a pair of outspread wings in one hand and a turtle in the other, contrasting spiritual and material domains (Fisher, 195).

Other attributes of the turtle explain the duke's choice of this animal. Because of its carapace, the turtle has a containing quality about it, and accordingly, is identified with woman and lubricity. In that its head and feet have the ability to protrude or withdraw, a phallocentric image is suggested. Interestingly enough, this androgynous animal, depicted in *The Chimeras* by Gustave Moreau, one of the duke's favorite painters, is featured with a woman's head; in his *Orpheus*, it stands for everything that is disquieting and negative. With respect to des Esseintes's psychology, the turtle signals dark, shadowy, regressive, and inverted powers within him. Its slowness represents stagnation; its involuted and obscure nature suggest confusion; its grounded condition enslaves it to matter alone.

Des Esseintes had chosen a cluster of flowers in Japanese arrangement for the turtle's lapidary decoration. The petals, leaves, stems, and border were to be set in brilliant and tastefully colored gems. Any jewels that might appeal to the upper bourgeoisie or to the masses, such as diamonds, emeralds, rubies, and the like, were anathema to the duke. His eyes were fixed on exotic stones: beryls, peridots, olivines, micas, cat's-eyes, cymophanes, and others. He would have these blended according to their tones, thus highlighting their inner flame and enhancing their effects upon each other. The uniqueness of the art object, which combined the natural with the artificial, made des Esseintes "perfectly happy."

In addition to the immense pleasure brought him by the bejeweled turtle, he indulged his senses in yet another manner: by taking advantage of his *hyperechema*: the exaggeration of auditory sensations. With this in mind, he had built what he called a *mouth organ*: a closet filled with the rarest liqueurs, each bottle lying horizontally and each having its own silver spigot. By pressing a button hidden behind the closet's paneling, he controlled the spigot he wanted as well as the combinations and amounts of liqueurs to be decanted into his glass. Even more fascinating was the fact that each liqueur corresponded for him to the sound of an instrument: kummel was an oboe; mint and anisette were both flutes; kirsch was a trumpet. Certain virtually scientifically blended mélanges triggered his taste buds to such an extent that they would in turn heighten his auditory nerves, thus enabling him to hear entire symphonies, concertos, quartets, quintets, trios, chorales, pastorals, romances, whatever he programmed for himself.

Des Esseintes's synesthetic experience was so complete that he could hear complicated melodies in major and minor keys, as well as intricate rhythmic patterns, in terms of what he called mint solos, rum duets, and the like. Once his taste buds had been activated, his hearing became intensely acute, as did his olfactory sense; his thought patterns followed suit, triggering all types of melodies and revivifying memories from a distant past.

The synesthetic experience, as practiced by T. E. Hoffmann, Baudelaire, and other creative persons, is defined as a fusion of the senses, allowing the visual to be heard, smelled, touched, and tasted; the heard to be seen, touched, tasted, and smelled; and so on with all the senses. Synesthesia has been described as a great awakening, a psychic happening within the unconscious. In des Esseintes's case it affected his whole nervous system, with sometimes soothing but mostly shattering results.

The simultaneity of sense impressions during the synesthetic experience took des Esseintes into the timeless dimensions of reverie and of hallucination. During periods of heightened awareness, he succeeded in escaping his prosaic present and savoring the beauty and refinement of the fleeting sensation. On certain occasions, he was ushered into an incredible world of fantasy, ranging from the most exquisite to the most gruesome of privileged moments. One such reverie, brought on after the bejeweled turtle's arrival and following a synesthetic experience resulting from his use of the "mouth organ," re-created an excruciatingly painful experience that had taken place three years previously: a toothache that had caused des Esseintes to awaken in the middle of the night. The pain was so acute that after waiting until seven in the morning, he ran out in search of a dentist. Stopping at the first dentist's premises he saw, he ran up a flight of filthy stairs. Although nauseated by the dirt and bloody spittle he saw around him, his torment was so great that he let the dentist push his index finger into his mouth, then take an instrument, and, with nothing to alleviate the pain, extract the decayed tooth. Strangely enough, after it was all over, des Esseintes felt "happy, younger by ten years."

That the reverie focused on the extraction of a tooth is symptomatic to a great extent of the duke's psychological condition. In that teeth cut and dismember food, thereby paving the way for its ingestion into the stomach to enrich and strengthen the body, these entities are associated with the aggressiveness needed both to persevere in and preserve life. Because des Esseintes's tooth had split, rotted, and caused him lacerating pain that only extraction could remedy, one may view his reverie as a premonitory happening: his extreme introversion and reclusion was leading to a disintegration of his own ability to nourish himself, and was an important factor in depleting his vital energy. No longer was he able to defend himself from inner decay; no longer could he assimilate or cope with anything from the outside world. The extraction of the tooth indicated the necessity of ending the self-imposed exile that encouraged his introverted way of life.

Following des Esseintes's reverie, he happened to look down at the rug where the turtle had been placed to notice that it was no longer moving. After palpating it, he realized it was dead. Accustomed to a simple life of obscurity, the turtle did not have the stamina to bear the dazzling array of jewels embedded in its coat. It was so out of tune with itself that it could no longer function.

The synesthetic experience, the reverie focusing on the extraction of the tooth, and the death of the turtle indicate a disequilibrium within des Esseintes's psyche. Slowly and methodically, he was poisoning himself. Extreme seclusion and introversion were suffocating his very life. He had become a man imprisoned in his own mind. The ending of all communication with the outer world had cut off all flow of new air into his world. Thus did his ideas and the sensations to which they gave rise atrophy. Depleted and solipsistic, des Esseintes's world had become fungal and parasitic, feeding exclusively on itself. The psyche had offered him a premonitory *sign*: "extraction" from his hermetic life-style was the only alternative to death.

THE ART OBJECT

Des Esseintes was not yet ready to give up an existence that seemingly gratified all of his wishes. In the world of art, as in other domains, he veered away from any painting that might appeal to the masses or to the bourgeoisie. What haunted and mesmerized him were "subtle, exquisite" canvases "bathing in an ancient dream" and in utter corruption. Scenes of this type worked on his nerves and, by intensifying their perceptiveness, were instrumental in plunging him into unknown dimensions and bringing on the nightmares that were henceforth to plague his existence.

Des Esseintes was enraptured by one artist above all others: Gustave Moreau. He responded erotically to the depraved and seductive details and colorations in Moreau's painting *Salomé*. Its palace/cathedral with its crystalized mosaics and brilliant semiprecious stones, its architecture combining Muslim and Byzantine styles, mesmerized him. Most exciting to him, however, was Salomé's "solemn, almost august" stance as she began her lecherous dance. Her sensuality was strikingly enhanced for the duke by the "odor of the perverse perfumes" that emanated from her body through the shapes, rhythms, and textures embedded in the canvas itself.

Because des Esseintes viewed Salomé as an eternal and universal figure capable of transcending centuries—"superhuman" as "indestructible Lewdness" and "cursed Beauty"—she takes on archetypal stature. She is the Terrible Earth Mother, that feminine principle who demands the head of the Christian martyr as punishment for thwarting her desires. Destroying everything that lies in her path to sexual fulfillment, she becomes the agent of the enormous energy buried within the archetype. For the ascetic Christian, in this case John the Baptist, she is an abomination. For the materialistic Herod, whose weakly structured ego is under the complete dominion of his wife, Herodias, she is the incarnation of sensuality.

The more powerful the denunciation of Salomé in the Gospels, the more formidable does this erotic archetypal force become, and the more she seeks to transform John the Baptist into an object to manipulate, dominate, and conquer. As depicted dancing in Moreau's canvas, her feet touch the Great Earth Mother, drawing from it sustenance and power. Having completed her lustful dance, she is served John's head on a silver shield. Seizing it, she kisses it, trembles, delighting as she looks deeply upon its eyes, tongue, hair; her fervor remains unappeased even as she kisses the martyr's mouth. Unguided by any moral credo, Salomé lives out the most primitive level of her instinctual world while salivating for her prey. Huysmans writes:

> In the works of Gustave Moreau . . . des Esseintes realized at last the weird and superhuman Salomé he had dreamed of. No longer was she merely the dancing girl who extorts a cry of lust and concupiscence from an old man by the lascivious contortions of her body . . . she was now revealed in a sense as the symbolic incarnation of indestructible Lust, the goddess of immortal Hysteria, of cursed Beauty supreme above all other beauties . . . the monstrous Beast [of the Apocalypse], indifferent, irresponsible, insensible, poisoning, like Helen of Troy . . . everything that approaches her, everything that sees her, everything she touches.
>
> (Muehsam, 409)

So enraptured is des Esseintes by Salomé's sadistic play and so dependent is he upon her ability to arouse his whole erotic world that this archetypal figure has come to represent for him a grave psychological dancer. Men, exploited by her, become her votaries, passive recipients of her needs and desires, never aggressive or energetic in their own rights. Salomé has intrigued men of the cloth as well as creative spirits ever since Christian times, as attested to by the Gospels and many Patristic texts. Writers such as Flaubert and Wilde, artists such as Beardsley and Moreau, composers such as Richard Strauss: all were inspired by this awesome archetypal figure.

Psychologically, Salomé represents the castrating female who entices and then destroys the male while initiating him into her arcane and libidinous world. Like the prostitute, she is a woman degraded, who unconsciously chastises herself every time she performs a service for the man. By the same token, when the man buys her services, he is experiencing similar feelings of shame and debasement. It is not he who is of import to her, but what he can offer in material gifts. Without gold or lucre of some sort, he is valueless; hence each is an object and not a subject for the other. Both, therefore, experience schizoid attitudes; neither is able to relate to the other or to him/herself.

Des Esseintes—like Moreau, who drew Salomé over a hundred times in settings of sumptuous palaces, mosques, cathedrals, and Hindu temples—was haunted by her image. The intensity of his sensual reactions to Moreau's paintings of Salomé discloses his penchant for the harlot in general, and her in particular, as she swirls and swoops, rotates and pivots.

Other paintings by Moreau also electrified, vivified, and disquieted des Esseintes: for example, *The Apparition,* featuring Herod's palace, which now resembled the Alhambra, and an almost nude Salomé after the decapitation. Des Esseintes, the voyeur, seemed especially stimulated sexually by the gory details he ferreted out in this canvas: John the Baptist's flaming, gleaming, shining head, the tints radiating from its coagulated blood ranging from deep purple to lighter tonalities depending upon their placement near the beard and hair. The duke's identification with the old king, who "remained crushed, destroyed, overcome with vertigo," as this "dangerous idol" danced in all of her eroticism, had a hypnotic effect upon him.

Some of Moreau's paintings preyed on des Esseintes's mind in the same way as did some of Baudelaire's poems. Both in their own way were "symbols of perversity," of "superhuman loves," of divine depravity. Moreau's canvases, unlike those of other painters whose works had been influenced by past masters, "derived from no one," des Esseintes believed. Moreau had neither ancestors nor would he have any descendents.

Other works of art also hung on the duke's walls: the fantastic, lugubrious, and terrifying *Religious Persecutions* by the engraver Jan Luyken; Rodolphe Bresdin's landscapes bristling with their terrifying trees (*The Comedy of Death, The Good Samaritan*); El Greco's sketch of a Christ with its exaggerated lines and "ferocious colors"; Odilon Redon's horrific heads, his fearful humanized spiders, his stagnant livid heavens, monstrous flora and fauna, fearsome faces with their immense crazed eyes. The duke's taste in paintings was drawn to all that was freakish, abnormal, and distorted.

The archetypal images delineated in such paintings not only twisted and triturated the duke's optical and auditory nerves, but activated all of his senses, forcing them into the deepest of subliminal realms. Battling in his psyche were the Divine Christ (all Light, all Purity, all Good), versus Salomé (the Beast of the Apocalypse, the Terrible Earth Mother, the Evil and Sordid Harlot). In that both figures, psychologically speaking, are archetypal in nature, the power they exerted in des Esseintes's collective unconscious (that suprapersonal and nonindividual layer within the psyche) was inordinate.

The duke's erethism, accounting for his abnormal responsiveness to stimulation, was becoming acute, creating havoc with his psyche as well as with his digestive system. Rather than inspiring serenity and wholeness, his protracted contemplations of paintings, engravings, and drawings, particularly those revolving around the Salomé archetype, had a psychologically dismembering effect. Certain sexual proclivities, such as voyeurism, sadomasochism, and homosexuality, which des Esseintes had lived out during his years of excesses in Paris, had again taken hold in his world of reverie and dream, indicating the destructive nature and effect of these visualizations.

Homosexuality

That des Esseintes is fascinated by the Salomé archetype, which is identified, psychologically, with the *vagina dentata,* indicates the power this devouring female has over him. In myths and legends, this kind of woman not only devours her lover emotionally, but tears his psyche to pieces by pulling and tugging at it with her demands. Unless the young male succeeds in breaking or at least loosening the stranglehold this Negative Earth Mother has on his psyche, he cannot hope to free himself from her, not will he ever experience ego consciousness or evolve psychologically. Throughout the centuries, the men associated with dragons and snakes, such as Saint Patrick, Saint George, and Saint Michael, to mention but a few, have succeeded in destroying the *vagina dentata* women in their mythical battles, thus disentangling themselves from the tentacles of the man-eating feminine principle.

Des Esseintes's extreme passivity and solipsistic nature have never entered into conflict with the *vagina dentata* power. Instead, he has allowed his psyche to be aroused and dominated by Salomé's energy and force. Because of des Esseintes's inability to relate to either men or women, and therefore to himself, his *eros* cannot connect or empathize with or even understand others, and is so repressed as to be virtually nonexistent. He frequently regresses in his reveries and dreams to childhood images and incidents revolving around homosexual and bisexual episodes. One icy evening, for example, seated in front of a warm hearthfire, he recalls an experience he had a few years earlier, when he met a street urchin, probably about sixteen years old, so pale and thin as to be almost girllike. "Sucking on a cigarette" that would not draw, he approached des Esseintes for a light. After giving him one of his finest aromatic cigarettes, des Esseintes began chatting with the boy and then invited him for a drink, followed by a visit to an elegant brothel. Because it was the young man's first time, des Esseintes took pleasure in the lad's naiveté, gaucheries, and the mocking he received at the hands of the prostitutes. Significant as well was des Esseintes's goal of turning the young man into a thief. He reasoned that by indoctrinating him into a world of sexual pleasures, he would become accustomed to these joys, and that the moment des Esseintes stopped giving him the funds necessary to support his habit, the lad would steal to maintain it.

Although the duke's confusion as to gender identification, frequently evident in the *puer aeternus* type, is apparent in the above episode, what is particularly arresting is the fact that the lad is a mirror image of des Esseintes as he used to be at that age. He projects upon him (and the exquisite pleasure he derives from using the lad as a sex object in the brothel is increased by alluding to his feminine and virginal nature) a symbolic way of violating, of deflowering him. Whatever sadism is involved, it calls into activity the other half of the dynamic: masochism. Des Esseintes wants to experience the rejection and humiliation of the sophisticated ladies and the chastisement of society by becoming a criminal. Let us note that sadomasochism has frequently been identified with a death wish.

Flowers and Plants

Des Esseintes's attention now focuses on the acquisition of rare and exotic species of flowers and plants. His personification of these brings a completely new dimension into his search for sensual gratification.

Flowers played an important role in antiquity. Certain gods, such as the handsome Tammuz, Attis, Adonis, Hyacinth, and Narcissus, were identified with their ephemeral natures: they died young, never developing into full manhood. Psychologically, they were prevented from doing so by the mother figure (symbolized frequently by the dragon or snake): the *vagina dentata,* a castrating force.

The aforementioned gods, also associated with the *puer aeternus,* lived through the woman (or the male partner) and were unable to grow firm roots into the soil (the world). They existed in a state of perpetual psychological incest with the mother or with what she symbolized for them. It is she whom they loved, feared, or sought to destroy. As appendages of the mother and, like an evanescent force or dream, they lived ephemerally, as does the flower (Neumann, *Origins and History of Consciousness,* 44).

In that flowers and plants are associated with the *vagina dentata* type, it is understandable that des Esseintes should be drawn to them. They are usually chosen for the home because of their beauty and sweetness of aroma, but the duke's tropical varieties are chosen for just the opposite reasons. The more bizarre, grotesque, terrifying, and destructive they are, the more he is attracted to them.

Used by him for ritualistic purposes, these Negative Earth Mother archetypes are animate in every sense of the word. Their branches, like venomous and constrictive snakes, are ready to coil and strangle any male approaching them. Their petals or "skin" are scarred, hairy, encrusted with scabs and blotched like ulcerated canker sores, rot, and gangrene. The leaves are engraved with furrows ("false veins") and are covered with syphilitic and leprous pustules.

Moreover, many of the "vegetal ghouls" inhabiting the duke's home are carnivorous: there are Insect Eaters from the Antilles, Droserae of the peat-bogs "garnished with their glandular hairs," and Cephalothi "capable of digesting, absorbing real meats." Some flowers and plants with their tumorlike/tuberlike excrescences remind des Esseintes of the severely ill; others, endowed with long metallic leaves curling way down, he associates with umbilical cords. The very language used to describe these hideously scaled and deformed varieties suggests the visceral quality of his emphatic relationship with them.

The more macabre, grotesque, and spine-chilling these symbols of destructive feminine forces are, the more they arouse the duke's lust and passion. That des Esseintes's thinking also comes into play with regard to flowers and plants is evident in the scientific accuracy with which he enumerates and describes them. Nor can such verbal imagery be outdone even by such artists as Bresdin, with his hideous trees and plantings (*The Comedy of Death* and *The Holy Family*), or Redon, and his gruesomely fearsome faces (*The Cactus Man,* or *Marsh Flower, Eyes in the Forest*), which des Esseintes admires.

The second step in des Esseintes's ritualistic use of flowers and plants occurs in the olfactory domain. His exaggerated sense of smell (*hyperosmia*) has the power of bringing on hallucinations and dreams. Perfumes and other aromas are able to lead him into ever-profounder levels of introversion. Like primitive man and his magical ceremonies and sacrifices using incense of all types, des Esseintes sets his mind to work thinking up new ways of using things to enliven his autoerotic world.

As the air in the room inhabited by the flowers and plants becomes increasingly rarefied, their aromatic qualities exert an anesthetic effect. Like a narcotic (from the Greek, *narke,* numbness), they dull des Esseintes's rationality, while also encouraging his eyes to wander onto "the horrible tiger markings" of the Caladium, which he identifies with syphilis. Indeed, looking at them all, he remarks, "Everything is syphilis." His reverie then takes root as he sees all of humanity attacked by this ancient and eternal virus. Exhumed in fossils, having been passed on from father to son, it is still active today "in all of its splendor, on the colored leaves of the plants!" Premonitory signs of some future cosmic cataclysm, they are to be viewed as rumblings of the giant battle to be waged between perversity and purity.

The intensity of des Esseintes's archetypal vision, the stifling heat of the room, and the mélange of aromas emanating from the flora has a soporific effect upon him. Lying down on his bed, he falls asleep moments later—not a restful slumber, for des Esseintes becomes a prey to a nightmare. Among its many terrifying incidents, one finds him riding on horseback at dusk in an alley when, suddenly, a human form appears before him. His blood congeals. He feels nailed to the ground.

> This ambiguous sexless face was green; and opened onto violet eyelids; terribly cold, clear, blue eyes; and pimples surrounding the mouth; extraordinarily thin arms, skeletal arms, nude up to the elbows, trembling with fever, emerging from tattered sleeves; and emaciated thighs shivering in overly large cauldronlike boots.

The dread vision in question is that of Syphilis. As she (it) presses hard against him, des Esseintes breaks away, runs as swiftly as possible, only to see this "lamentable and grotesque" creature forever before him no matter what direction he takes. At one point she begins to cry; she tells des Esseintes she has lost her teeth, then taking some clay pipes from her apron, breaks them and plunges the shards into the holes in her gums. No sooner is this done than he warns her they will fall out and they do. His new attempt to flee leads to exhaustion. He shuts his eyes, again attempting to block out this diseased presence, whereupon he realizes that no matter what he does he can never evade or avoid "the horrific stare of Syphilis." Neither walls, nor barriers, nor flight can shut the Flower-Virus out of his world. She is always there in multiple forms and with outstretched arms ready to encircle and strangle him. Indeed, she is now doing just that, as she mutates into a ferocious Nidularium with bladelike leaves that cut him severely. As blood flows and des Esseintes, now insane with fear, makes a superhuman effort to disengage himself, he awakens to realize that it is "only" a dream.

That des Esseintes associates destructive, though alluring, flowers and plants with the feminine principle and with Syphilis is a commentary on his fear and hatred of women. As castrators, these Flower-Women are *vagina dentata* types waiting to work their wiles on the unsuspecting male. In des Esseintes's dream, the narcotic effect of the Nidularium's aroma forces his defense to drop, making him all the more vulnerable. As he attempts to extricate himself from the grasp of this Flower-Woman, the blood oozing from the cut symbolizes castration, a loss of energy, and a wounding of the psyche. Unconsciously, women, for des Esseintes, are viewed as practitioners of sacred feminine rituals who wreak havoc upon young, innocent males. As they unleash their pent-up emotions, until then lying buried beneath a mask of voluptuous and enticing sensuality, they wound the young men for life.

That des Esseintes should identity women with flowers, plants, and disease also suggests a regressive approach to life. Vegetative imagery also abounds in Poe's "The Fall of the House of Usher" (1839), a work Huysmans admired immensely. Fungi and rotting or moldy plants delineate a comatose condition or severe mental illness. Since vegetation feeds directly on inorganic matter, it is looked upon as being connected with the chemical somatic process. To express this condition, Huysmans, like Poe, introduces plant life into his narrative, and in its most rudimentary and negative form, thereby underscoring the retrograde and miasmic elements involved.

The Sex Change

Recurring nightmares work on des Esseintes's already taut nerves. As his olfactory, visual, tactile, and auditory senses became increasingly acute, so, too, does his sense of taste, as previously noted. When he sucks on *sarcanthus,* violet candy, its strange properties, described as "a drop of feminine essence," evoke an even more revealing reverie from his distant bawdy past.

The image of Miss Urania appears full-blown in his mind's eye. He resees her as she was in the past: an American circus acrobat of renown, with muscles like steel and arms like cast iron, who succeeded in arousing him sexually because as he peered at her she seemed to be undergoing a sex change. Her serpentine wiles, airs, affectations, and all those "sickening womanly sentimental ways" suddenly vanished, to be replaced by a highly developed, strong, agile, and powerful male. Concomitant with Miss Urania's sex change, des Esseintes felt himself becoming more feminine and overpowered by a desire to possess this woman/male. Needless to say, disappointment followed the consummation of the sex act. Instead of relaxing in the powerful and brutal arms of a Hercules, he was faced with woman in all of her "stupidity" and "puritanical" reserve. Worse, his reactions to her "glacial fondlings" made him increasingly impotent.

Such *intersexuality,* a shifting from one sex to another, indicates confusion and a lack of sexual identity, resulting often from a fear of castration. The derivation of Miss Urania's name in itself suggests the nature of the emotional distress: *Uranus,* the primordial Greek God of heaven, unwilling to allow his children to be born to the light of day for fear they would overthrow him, concealed them in the depths of the earth. His wife, the Great Earth Mother, encouraged them to rebel against him. The youngest, Cronus, waiting until Uranus was asleep, grasped his father's genitals with his left hand and castrated him with the flint sickle his mother had given him.

Symbolically, castration by the Great Earth Mother suggests the destruction of all creativity, aggressivity, and direction in life. In that *puer aeternus* types, such as des Esseintes, are her slaves and votaries, they are owned by her and involuntarily sacrificed to her. Psychologically, we may say that the duke's adolescent ego (sense of identity), has been drowned by the unconscious, which is tantamount to the ego's dismemberment. The phenomenon of castration, although implicit in previous images, is most overt in the Flower-Woman-Syphilis and Miss Urania sequences.

Since the fear of matriarchal castration has so deflated and degraded des Esseintes's ego, he loses all sense of reality with regard to his own body and sexuality. His regressing libido reactivates parental images, reestablishing an infantile relationship with them (Jung, *Collected Works,* 5:204). In des Esseintes's case, the devouring Great Mother is held accountable for the amputation of his ego, to be equated with the loss of his penis (Neumann, *Origins and History of Consciousness,* 117). Is it any wonder that his exile from society increases his already powerful feelings of alienation and cuts him off from any connection with life?

Although other visions of beguiling and powerful *vagina dentata* types point to des Esseintes's castration complex, an encounter of another kind, reveals his homosexual bent. One day, years earlier, near the Invalides, he had met a young schoolboy whose slim torso and thighs attracted him. What he looked upon with the greatest of pleasure, however, were the youngster's cherry lips. A liaison followed, and he confesses that he had never known such "perils of the flesh" nor felt more "painfully satisfied."

Des Esseintes's hallucinatory reveries and dreams and his synesthetic experiences are draining his strength, leaving him devastated and distressed to the extreme. Suffering from double vision, dizziness, and continuous nausea, he finds himself unable to digest any food. His intensely nervous state is followed by high fevers and chills. A doctor is called. After examining des Esseintes he tells him that he has to leave "this solitude," for it is a question "of life or death." The reader is not told exactly what happens to him, but it is assumed that he reenters the venal city of Paris, for he does not seem cut out to lead any other kind of life, certainly not that of a Trappist.

Exile and introversion might have been a salutary way for des Esseintes had he analyzed his acts objectively and assimilated his fantasies consciously. Because they were used exclusively to cultivate his eroticosexual pulsations, to encourage hallucinatory reveries, and to fill the void which was his life, exile and willed introversion endangered his already weakened ego to the point of virtual dismemberment.

Throughout his months of exile, des Esseintes lived out the fate of the *puer aeternus*. As a personification of the infantile or inferior side of his character, he was fated to remain the undeveloped and callow youth about whom he fantasized in his sadomasochistic, transsexual, and homosexual encounters. That he experienced (temporary) satisfaction only with Miss Urania and in the consummation of the homosexual act suggests that it was only through the male that he could come into contact with the feminine aspect of himself, which he lived out through projection.

The scenes of voyeurism depicted in his reveries revolving around certain paintings and episodes in *Satyricon* allowed him to experience lascivious acts vicariously. His constant yearning for what he lacked, sexual consummation and the concomitant feelings of fulfillment and serenity, did not indicate a need for love or for the sexual act (as such yearning is commonly thought to indicate) but rather showed an inability to love. Had des Esseintes experienced real love from his parents during his early years, he might have related to others and to himself, understood and responded to the feelings called into play. Deprivation, however, had denied him the possibility of bestowing love upon others by giving of himself in a relationship.

Note

1. J.-K. Huysmans, *A Rebours*. 116. Shortly after Huysman's birth in 1848 in Paris, his father became ill and his mother spent long years caring for him. When his father died in 1856, Huysmans was deeply depressed. He considered his mother's remarriage (to a Protestant) an act of betrayal to his father's memory. The birth of his half-sisters increased his sense of neglect and the rancor he felt against his mother. After passing his *baccalauréat,* he held a job at the Ministry of the Interior, did a stint in the army, and then began writing. His mentor was Zola, to whom he dedicated his novel *The Vatard Sisters* (1879) and *Down Stream* (1882); morose and misogynistic works followed. Only the world of art offered him some semblance of contentment and feelings of relatedness. *Against the Grain* was followed by *Down There* (1891), *En Route* (1895), *The Cathedral* (1898), and *The Oblate* (1903), his last works dealing with his search for holiness and need for penitence. He became deeply religious and spent some days among the Trappist monks.

J. Gerald Kennedy (essay date 1993)

SOURCE: Kennedy, J. Gerald. "Modernism as Exile: Fitzgerald, Barnes, and the Unreal City." In *Imagining Paris: Exile, Writing, and American Identity,* pp. 185-242. New Haven: Yale University Press, 1993.

[*In the following excerpt, Kennedy discusses F. Scott Fitzgerald's* Tender Is the Night *in light of some American writers' attempts to go into voluntary exile in Paris in order to refresh their cultural perceptions.*]

Gertrude Stein remarked that modernist writers and artists of her time had converged on the capital of France because "Paris was where the twentieth century was." The city not only incorporated within its diverse cultural life the most distinctive projects and features of modernism, but (as her claim implies) it had also become a geographical sign of the modern. Other European cities—notably Vienna, Berlin, and London—had harbored important avant-garde coteries during the two decades bracketing the turn of the century, but by 1910, Paris had achieved preeminence as a site of modernist production. Stein suggests that she became an exile in order to position herself at the center of a historical phenomenon—as if the temporal (the twentieth century) had suddenly assumed a spatial form which might be located and occupied. The conflation of time and space in Stein's observation itself reflects a distinctively modern tendency to problematize categories of thought and perception. New ways of conceptualizing time, space, form, distance, speed, and direction emerged, as Stephen Kern has shown, from revolutionary developments in art, philosophy, science, and technology during the years between 1880-1918. Kern demonstrates how these changes radically altered the general meaning of the past, present, and future as frames of experiential reference. His analysis also redefines aspects of modern consciousness in ways which seem especially apposite to the problem of exile, and his account of the interplay between material culture on the one hand and intellectual and aesthetic life on the other offers a fresh perspective on the narrative construction of identity and experience in the city where (as Stein believed) the twentieth century first revealed its distinctive qualities.[1]

To be sure, every age witnesses changes and marks transitions; even in apparently quiescent phases, culture on some level remains astir, dynamic. There is, moreover, another sense in which every period seems modern in relation to an earlier time; each era defines itself by its innovations, by its distinctive crises, and by its repudiations of outworn conventions, philosophies, and practices. Yet no previous "modern" age had ever brought such precipitous and sweeping change to everyday life and to human understanding. Within a few years, new technologies of communication and transportation changed the pace of daily activity, widened the horizons of personal consciousness, broke down geographical barriers, and made these changes instantly perceptible to a mass culture linked by electronic media. Writers variously expressed a recognition of unprecedented, fundamental transformations: Henry Adams believed that the year 1900 marked the onset of a new historical epoch; Virginia Woolf speculated with mock precision that "on or about December, 1910, human nature changed"; Charles Peguy declared in 1913 that "the world has changed less since Jesus Christ than it has in the last thirty years." Diverse as such claims may be, the peculiar urge to specify a date for the advent of the modern age reflects an awareness of new conditions of being, coinciding (very roughly) with the turn of the twentieth century. Whatever the discrepancy between the estimates of Adams, Woolf, and Peguy, their efforts to designate the exact moment at which the Western world entered into this phase testifies both to a consciousness of historical liminality—a sense of living (and writing) on the threshold of a new era—and to a recognition that this epoch had arrived abruptly rather than gradually, through cataclysm rather than through evolution.

The various inventions and technologies which helped to produce new forms of modern consciousness had, as Kern notes, manifold effects on literary and artistic expression. For example, the establishment of World Standard Time in the 1890s, the "universal diffusion of pocket watches" about 1900, and the introduction in 1916 of electric clocks all served to intensify the distinction between public time and inner, subjective time—the very distinction upon which Henri Bergson had developed his theories of duration. Thus, as Kern points out, Proust's *A la Recherche du temps perdu* and Joyce's *Ulysses* both entail deliberate though contrasting explorations of the psychological experience of time (16-18). Likewise the telephone enabled journalists of the late 1890s to report events unfolding almost as the paper rolled off the presses. This mind-boggling simultaneity of experience also occurred on the level of personal communication as long distance lines made possible direct conversations with far-flung acquaintances. Obviously, the consciousness of other peoples and cultures did not itself arise from the technological advances of the late nineteenth century; but the capacity to converse with those far away endowed the remote with a presence and tangibility it had never before possessed. As Kern speculates, this new consciousness of events unfolding at the same instant in different places probably influenced both Joyce's representation of a "temporally thickened present" in *Ulysses* and Stein's effort to expand the present moment with verbs in the continuous present and with successive reiterations of opening lines (85-86).

Concurrent developments in transportation had a comparable effect on the perception of space and place. In the 1890s the popularization of the bicycle and the subsequent introduction of the automobile stimulated leisure travel and altered basic conceptions of speed and distance, dramatically extending what might be called the proximate landscape while fostering an expanded sense of geographical contiguity. Motorized trams, subways, and elevators accelerated personal movement within urban spaces; high-speed passenger steamers plied the Atlantic in record time, and airplanes flew over topographical and national boundaries, dissolving notions of remoteness and separation while producing a new consciousness of global relations. Reflecting on the emerging "technology of speed," Octave Uzanne commented in 1912 that "the rapid movement which sweeps us in space and piles up a variety of impressions and images in a short time gives life a plenitude and a unique intensity" (128). After the Great War (which saw fearsome applications of the new technology), these forms of transportation produced a tremendous vogue for international travel which helped to spawn both the American expatriate movement and the great exodus of writers from Great Britain during the twenties and thirties. The ease and relative swiftness of international travel contributed to the notion of place as a commodity of tourism and as an arbitrary locus of experience. When Hemingway's Robert Cohn proposes to Jake Barnes that they abandon Paris for South America, he typifies the modern notion of travel as an easy collapsing of great distance to obtain (like some consumer product) a fresh view or a new range of possibilities. As a result of what Paul Fussell terms the "unceasing kinesis" of postwar travelers, the "travel sense of place" soon yielded to "the touristic phenomenon of placelessness," the perception of the external scene as an unreal spectacle.[2]

The various types of transportation and communication which emerged in the modern period thus produced new ways of conceiving and experiencing time and space. Rapid, incessant travel and immediate electronic contact with distant places and cultures broke down provincial perspectives and helped to generate a cosmopolitan consciousness which transcended national themes and issues. Malcolm Bradbury and James McFarlane argue that "the essence of Modernism is its international character," and this confluence of sensibilities promoted the formation of a synthetic culture infused with the sense of its absolute modernity. The inescapable multiplicity of twentieth-century experience—its inherently pluralistic, multicultural nature—seemed to substantiate Ortega y Gasset's concept of perspectivism which held, as Kern reminds us, that "there are as many realities as points of view" (151). Cubism provided a visual corroboration of sorts, breaking objects into geometrical shapes viewed, seemingly, from several perspectives at once. The idioms of modern painting from Impressionism to Fauvism and Cubism also suggested a corollary consequence of multiplicity: the dismantling of representation as the unitary function of visual art and the liberation of painting from a rational system of proportionality.

Everywhere the proliferation of theories and viewpoints bore out the realization that knowledge itself had become relative and problematic; one could no longer assume the existence of essential, objective truths behind surface phenomena. Alan Bullock has noted that "between 1895 and 1915 the whole picture of the physical universe, which had appeared not only the most impressive but also the most secure achievement of scientific thought, was brought in question and the first bold attempts made to replace it with a new model."[3] This intellectual upheaval caused a general disorientation in which the conditions of everyday life became suddenly defamiliarized by the collapse of assumptions once thought to be secure. McFarlane describes three discrete stages in what might be called the reformulation of reality under modernism:

> Initially, the emphasis is on fragmentation, on the breaking up and the progressive disintegration of those meticulously constructed "systems" and "types" and "absolutes" that lived on from the earlier years of the [nineteenth] century, on the destruction of belief in large general laws to which all life and conduct could be claimed to be subject. As a second stage . . . there came a re-structuring of parts, a re-relating of the fragmented concepts, a re-ordering of linguistic entities to match what was felt to be the new order of reality. . . . Finally, in its ultimate stages, thought seemed to undergo something analogous to a change of state: a dissolving, a blending, a merging of things held to be forever mutually exclusive. A sense of flux, a notion of continuum, the running together of things in ways often contrary to the dictates of simple common sense (though familiar enough in dream) alone seemed able to help in the understanding of certain bewildering and otherwise inexplicable phenomena of contemporary life.[4]

From a formalist perspective, these phases roughly correspond to the tendencies of modernist art which Roger Shattuck has identified as fragmentation, juxtaposition, and superposition.[5] But beyond such aesthetic implications, the stages outlined above suggest important correlations with expatriate experience and indeed permit us to regard modernism itself as a kind of exile.

In the first phase of modernism—a disintegration of intellectual systems and laws governing "life and conduct"—we see a loss of orienting structures comparable to the exile's renunciation of the functional security of homeland: the familiar geography, language, and customs which enable one to negotiate more or less unconsciously the routines of everyday life. The phase of restructuring, the assimilation of a "new order of reality," likewise corresponds to the experience of immersion in an alien culture and the metabolizing of differences at virtually every level of consciousness, beginning with the problem of renaming reality itself in the dominant language of the country of exile. In the third stage of modernism, marked by a strange dissolving of differences, a merging of conceptual opposites, and a dreamlike confusion of categories, we find an analogy to the bemusement of the expatriate for whom the foreign has become familiar while remaining paradoxically unreal. This third stage recalls Stein's comment that writers needed a second country that was "not real" yet "really there." Modernism effects displacement through "future shock" (in Alvin Toffler's phrase) when the rate of change in a customary environment exceeds one's capacity to assimilate change. Thus, insofar as exile marks a rupture with the past, a loss of the familiar, a relocation amid alien surroundings, and a persistent sense of estrangement, it thus provides a suggestive model for the experience of modernism.

In its dizzying third phase, this reformulation of reality produces disorientation both through the appearance of new forms and conditions and through the collapse of previous barriers, boundaries, and oppositions. McFarlane observes that under modernism, human nature could no longer be contained or explained by "vast and exhaustive inventories of naturalistic detail arranged and sorted under prescriptive heads" but instead revealed itself to be "elusive, indeterminate, multiple, often implausible, infinitely various and essentially irreducible."[6] Perhaps the most basic human distinction to be challenged and "demolished" by modernist thought was that between subject and object, between "man the observer and nature the observed." Just as Virginia Woolf wrote of Mrs. Ramsay (in *To the Lighthouse*) that she "became the thing she looked at," so other modernist writers explored the suddenly ambiguous relation between self and other, sometimes figured as a convergence of the internal and the external. As McFarlane notes, the philosopher Ernst Mach insisted on "an intimate interpenetration between things inner and things outer" in which the terms "within" and "without" no longer marked an absolute breach. In psychoanalysis as well as in quantum physics, entities once conceived as opposites— love and hate, matter and energy—proved to be interrelated, even indistinguishable. Influenced by Nietzsche, much of Western thought—certainly the domain of metaphysics—underwent a skeptical reexamination of its suppositions. Kern describes a corollary "breakdown of old forms" which "leveled hierarchies" and undermined a range of conceptual dichotomies: "solid/porous, opaque/transparent, inside/outside, public/private, city/country, noble/common, countryman/foreigner, framed/open, actor/audience, ego/object, space/time" (209-10). The crisis of modernity perhaps arose less from the fragmentation of reality into discrete phenomena than from the erasing of those distinctions which seemed to hold in place the conventional order of things. With some urgency Yeats asked, "How can we tell the dancer from the dance?" This blurring of traditional oppositions—social, moral, physical, and psychological—pervaded the culture of modernism and informed its most distinctive literary texts.

In one such work, *The Waste Land,* Eliot evokes a teeming "Unreal City" in which life and death have become indistinguishable; he thereby calls attention to the undeniably urban nature of modernism itself. The various transformations of culture bracketed by this concept of course first manifested themselves within the great cities of Vienna, London, Berlin, New York, and Paris. Reminding us of the metropolitan character of "experimental modernism," Malcolm Bradbury points out that with vast, heterogeneous populations, cities inevitably became "places of friction, change and new consciousness."[7] This multiplicity attracted a new kind of artist or writer seeking to escape regional influences, to absorb the diversity of cosmopolitan life, and through self-conscious displacement to achieve a more intimate involvement with art or writing. Raymond Williams has sketched the way in which the cities of modernism thus fostered a poetics of exile:

> The key cultural factor of the modernist shift is the character of the metropolis . . . in its direct effects on form. The most important general element . . . is the fact of immigration to the metropolis, and it cannot too often be emphasized how many of the major innovators were, in this precise sense, immigrants. At the level of theme, this underlies, in an obvious way, the elements of strangeness and distance, indeed of alienation, which so regularly form part of the repertory. But the decisive aesthetic effect is at a deeper level. Liberated or breaking from their national or provincial cultures, placed in quite new relations to those other native languages or native visual traditions, encountering meanwhile a novel and dynamic common environment from which many of the older forms were obviously distant, the artists and writers and thinkers of this phase found the only community available to them: a community of the medium; of their own practices.[8]

Attempting to free themselves from the influence of familiar, native settings, writers and artists underwent dislocation to achieve a new relation to their work and to the verbal or visual language of its composition. The city of exile combined for them the strangeness of the foreign and the unreality of the modern, producing an alienation from the immediate environment while at the same time endowing it with the sort of imaginary power which only the unreal can possess. Works from the mid-thirties by Scott Fitzgerald and Djuna Barnes convey the unreality of Paris from this perspective of modernist displacement.

Whatever its residue of personal calamity, Fitzgerald's *Tender Is the Night* (1934) stands as a tortured record of the psychic and cultural confusions of modernism. As Matthew J. Bruccoli has shown, this novel underwent twelve drafts in three separate versions, emerging over a period of nine frantic years spent mostly abroad.[9] In its portrayal of Dick Diver's disintegration and his wife Nicole's recovery from mental illness, the narrative also captures the reckless unreality of the twenties, a condition metaphorized throughout by allusions to movie-making and acting as the construction of illusion. Chaotic in its stylistic excesses, its bizarre episodes, its shifts of perspective, and its lapses of chronology, the novel betrays distraction even as it displays hard-won insight into the contradictions of desire and the ironies of American optimism.

Most revealingly, the work depicts the situation of modernist exile as a struggle against deracination and historical discontinuity; Diver's collapse results both from the loss of his American roots (symbolized by his father's death) and from the destruction of fundamental certainties by the violence of the Great War. The novel finally suggests that expatriates of the twenties faced the double jeopardy of spatial and temporal dislocation.

Fitzgerald's biographers have provided an ample account of the author's four visits to Europe from 1921 to 1931. We know, for example, that his first extended stay (from mid-1924 through the end of 1926) grew out of a need to free himself from the Long Island social circuit—from what James Mellow has called "continuous and extensive weekend partying" and from resultant debt and emotional exhaustion.[10] Afflicted by a sense of his own "deterioration," Fitzgerald sailed for France with his wife and daughter to test his friend Edmund Wilson's theory that the cultural density of France made that country a more propitious place to complete his new novel, *The Great Gatsby*. "We were going to the Old World to find a new rhythm for our lives," Fitzgerald wrote, "with a true conviction that we had left our old selves behind forever." But if he believed that one could become a different person in another country, he nevertheless avoided the sort of cultural immersion that some of his contemporaries sought. André LeVot notes that Fitzgerald had

> very little communication with the French writers of the period and does not seem to have taken any interest in the literary movements (Dada, Surrealism) of the time. Unlike Hemingway, who shared for a while the life of the poor, his relationships with the French were those of a rich tourist who spoke the language badly and dealt mostly with paid employees—taxi-drivers, restaurant and bar waiters, servants, and nurses and policemen when things were getting out of hand.[11]

As a Minnesotan educated at an Eastern prep school and then at Princeton, Fitzgerald remained curiously indifferent to those aspects of daily life in France which intrigued Stein, Hemingway, and Miller. Part of this indifference may be attributed to the drinking which especially during 1925—the summer of "1000 parties and no work"—left him oblivious to a great deal of what was happening around him. Another factor was his essentially bourgeois conventionality; as Wilson had observed in 1921, he was "so saturated with twentieth century America, bad as well as good, . . . so used to hotels, plumbing, drugstores, aesthetic ideals and vast commercial prosperity" that he could not readily appreciate the ancient and foreign.[12] While Fitzgerald later assured Wilson that he had "gotten to like France," what he liked most was his relative affluence (in 1925 a dollar bought twenty-two francs), the availability of liquor (while America endured Prohibition), and the presence of lively American friends like Gerald and Sara Murphy.

The three later sojourns nevertheless produced inexorable changes in the Fitzgeralds. Their first extended stay witnessed Zelda's 1924 affair with a French aviator, Scott's completion of *Gatsby,* his acquaintance with Hemingway, his preliminary work on the book to become *Tender Is the Night,* and his developing obsession with the Murphys, the original models for Dick and Nicole Diver. During this visit, the Fitzgeralds made merry in St. Raphaël, Rome, Capri, Cap d'Antibes, Juan-les-Pins, and for much of 1925 in a luxury flat (14, rue Tilsitt) near the Arc de Triomphe in Paris. During a five-month visit to France in 1928, they occupied an apartment (58, rue de Vaugirard) opposite the Luxembourg Gardens; Zelda studied ballet, Scott met James Joyce, and the Fitzgeralds plunged into social activities which included evenings at the sapphic salon of Natalie Clifford Barney (20, rue Jacob). Scott's work on the new novel sputtered, and "desolate" side trips to the battlefields at Verdun and Rheims did not relieve a domestic discontent rooted in his drinking, Zelda's compulsive dancing, and mutual suspicions of homosexuality.[13] The third excursion (March 1929-September 1931) began with a sodden summer in Cannes and culminated in Zelda's mental collapse in Paris in early 1930. While she received treatment for schizophrenia at a Swiss clinic above Lake Geneva, Fitzgerald weathered her confinement mostly in nearby towns, shuttling to Paris periodically to visit his daughter.[14] In such places as Vevey, Caux, and Lausanne, he grappled with despair over Zelda's illness and with his own concomitant guilt and self-pity.

He also worked on several short stories, including two which indicate progress toward the still-unfinished novel. In the first of these, "One Trip Abroad," Fitzgerald traces the effect of prolonged expatriation on a young, affluent American couple, the Kellys. The story unfolds over several years; in the first scene, set in Algeria, Fitzgerald contrasts the couple's innocence with the jaded attitude of an older couple named Miles. Mrs. Miles acknowledges what Fussell has called the "touristic phenomenon of placelessness" when she comments: "Every place is the same. . . . The only thing that matters is who's there. New scenery is fine for half an hour, but after that you want your own kind to see. That's why some places have a certain vogue, and then the vogue changes and people move somewhere else. The place itself never really matters." For such exiles, foreign settings are meaningless backdrops for social transactions, and soon Nelson and Nicole Kelly likewise succumb to the movement and merriment of an existence as unreal as it is enervating. After a Parisian scene in which they have been duped into hosting an expensive riverboat party on the Seine, Fitzgerald shows them at Lake Geneva, trying to recover their health as they confront in yet another young couple the mirror image of their own debauchery. To underscore the danger of placelessness, Fitzgerald remarks: "This is the story of a trip abroad, and the geographical element must not be slighted. Having visited North Africa, Italy, the Riviera, Paris and points in between, it was not surprising that the Kellys should go to Switzerland. Switzerland is a country where very few things begin, but many things end."[15] He thus locates in the itinerary of their travels a symptom of some underlying malaise.

As Fitzgerald came to recognize, the glamorous lifestyle of the expatriate leisure class concealed certain insidious risks, including not only the loss of innocence and optimism but also the danger of a pointless, ungrounded existence which might finally threaten both sanity and selfhood. In "One Trip Abroad" we see him moving toward *Tender Is the Night* through an analysis of expatriate corruption figured as symbolic geography. Meditating on the causes of Zelda's breakdown and his own dissipation, he came increasingly to associate expatriation with a compulsive yet random quest for absolute freedom and pleasure, for a life based on hedonistic impulse, facilitated by wealth, and conducted without regard for those local customs or cultural differences which might by comparison afford insight into one's own values and practices.

In a subsequent story, "Babylon Revisited," he offers closer analysis of this rootless existence, exposing both its inherent unreality and its potentially tragic toll. Set in Paris shortly after the stock market crash, the story depicts the dilemma of Charlie Wales, who wishes to escape the memory of past dissolution but who must return to the site of those escapades to reclaim his daughter Honoria, who has been raised since his wife's death by his sister-in-law, Marion, and her husband, Lincoln. Transparently the story thus portrays Charlie's effort to recover his honor; yet he cannot quite shake the dissolute past personified by his tipsy friends Duncan and Lorraine, who disrupt a crucial meeting with Marion and scuttle his negotiations. Noting that Charlie invites trouble by leaving Marion's address for Duncan at the Ritz, Roy R. Male points out the protagonist's ambivalence: "He *still* wants both worlds," the world of family and respectability and the world of irresponsible pleasure.[16] Fitzgerald compresses the fantastic quality of the "crazy years" in the story of Helen Wales' death, which—following a hysterical outburst at the Hotel Florida where she has just "kissed young Webb at the table"—results from her wandering about Paris in a snowstorm, "too confused to find a taxi." For his part, Charlie is one of those negligent revelers "who locked their wives out in the snow, because the snow of twenty-nine wasn't real snow."[17]

As a sketch for *Tender Is the Night,* "Babylon Revisited" anticipates the fate of Dick Diver, who (like Charlie) loses his wife and family, "everything [he] wanted." Indeed Fitzgerald would repeat almost verbatim in the novel his summary of Charlie Wales's misfortune: "He wasn't young any more, with a lot of nice thoughts and dreams to have by himself" (633). Perhaps more importantly, the story sheds light on the disjointed Parisian section comprising the last half of book one in the novel. Returning to Paris, Charlie now sees the city as an alien place and laments, "I spoiled this city for myself" (618). He finds the Ritz "strange and portentous" and remarks that the bar is no longer American, having "gone back into France" (616). His taxi ride also betrays a basic topographical confusion; in a passage echoed in the novel Charlie travels from the Right Bank to the Left: "The Place de la Concorde moved by in pink majesty; they crossed the logical Seine, and

Charlie felt the sudden provincial quality of the Left Bank" (617). Yet in the next sentence he directs the driver back to the avenue de l'Opéra—to the Right Bank from which he has just come—before again rolling "on to the Left Bank." Whether intended or inadvertent, this zigzag route contributes to the sense of Charlie's ambivalence and disorientation. For him the bars and cabarets of Montmartre seem menacing: "Zelli's was closed, the bleak and sinister cheap hotels surrounding it were dark. . . . the Café of Heaven and the Café of Hell still yawned—even devoured, as he watched, the meager contents of a tourist bus" (620). Unlike the crazy years, when wealth insulated him from the foreign, Charlie now perceives himself as a stranger in a strange land. But the effect of strangeness conceals the irony that he now sees Paris more or less as it is, not as it appeared during the alcoholic binges of the twenties.[18]

By representing the city as a "Babylon," a scene of riotous living and emotional betrayal, Fitzgerald anticipates key elements of the Paris section in *Tender Is the Night*. Charlie Wales looks back on a dizzying epoch just reaching its peak when Dick and Nicole Diver arrive in Paris in 1925. Projecting a more intricate sense of time and place, the novel effects a distorted but revealing image of the city. Indeed, insofar as this section depicts a pivotal phase in the career of Dick Diver, it also reflects the crisis of modernity itself and suggests that the city, in its fantastic unreality, embodies the terms and conditions of this immense upheaval. The improbable events which transpire in Paris typify the irrationality, violence, and uncertainty which in part define the climate of modernism. As Bruce L. Grenberg has argued, the city here represented by Fitzgerald constitutes "the image and substance of modern, postwar life-in-death."[19]

Although the novel contains only a few formal traits which might be associated with modernism—such as the cinematic foreshortening of time in book two—the story of the Divers and their relationship to Rosemary Hoyt incorporates many signs of modernist culture and its discontents which cohere in the image of Paris.[20] Among these, the most evident is the psychoanalytic matrix within which Fitzgerald frames the narrative. Via Yale, Oxford, and Johns Hopkins, Dick Diver has trained as a psychoanalyst in Vienna, presumably under "the great Freud" himself (115). At one point Doctor Dohmler gives Nicole "a little Freud to read," and though Dick does not cite specific Freudian texts, concepts associated with psychoanalysis (such as hysteria, schizophrenia, transference, and repression) traverse the novel and inform its crucial scenes. For example, the so-called "father complex" evoked by the title of Rosemary's film "Daddy's Girl" clarifies the incestuous coupling between Nicole and Devereux Warren and elucidates her subsequent attraction to Dick, an authority figure whom she addresses in letters as "captain." Similarly, when Collis Clay alludes to the "heavy stuff going on" (88) between Rosemary and a Yale man aboard a train, he constructs a primal scene which for Dick becomes a virtual fixation. Glimpses of clinical work call attention to the etiology of neuroses and suggest the curious ways in which childhood relationships with parents affect later emotional and sexual experience. The case of Señor Pardo y Ciudad Real and his intractably homosexual son (243-45) marks one such demonstration. But Fitzgerald's psychoanalytic perspective achieves a larger purpose than simply documenting the subculture of a Swiss psychiatric clinic; he suggests that the exploration of the unconscious in modernism has radically problematized identity and sexuality by calling into question the boundaries which had previously circumscribed both self and gender.

As a consequence, *Tender Is the Night* presents personality as an unstable and indeterminate nexus of tendencies. The novel relentlessly questions the distinction between self and other, and even as Nicole receives treatment for a "split" personality, Fitzgerald implies that all personalities are multiple and that people tend to "become" the persons with whom they associate. In the stream-of-consciousness section which cinematically telescopes Nicole's transformation, she thinks: "When I talk I say to myself that I am probably Dick. Already I have even been my son, remembering how wise and slow he is. Sometimes I am Doctor Dohmler and one time I may even be an aspect of you, Tommy Barban" (162). Lest we construe this as evidence of her derangement, the narrator himself later tells us that "somehow Dick and Nicole had become one and equal, not opposite and complementary; she was Dick too, the drought in the marrow of his bones. He could not watch her disintegrations without participating in them" (190-91). As the preceding sentence implies, Nicole is not alone in her psychic assimilations; Dick too possesses a composite personality and feels "condemned to carry with him the egos of certain people, early met and early loved, and to be only as complete as they were complete themselves" (245). When Nicole's lover Tommy Barban calls her "a little complicated after all," her ironic reply sums up Fitzgerald's implicit theory of personality: "No, I'm not really—I'm just a—I'm just a whole lot of different simple people" (292). In a novel informed by an obsessive attention to psychoanalytic patterns of relationship—to conflicted ties between fathers and daughters, fathers and sons, or mothers and daughters—Fitzgerald suggests that unconscious incorporation makes it impossible to say precisely where one's own personality ends and others begin.

Through various strategies he also represents the distinction between male and female as relative rather than absolute, fluid rather than fixed; as in *The Garden of Eden* (a work surely influenced by Fitzgerald's novel) androgynous metamorphosis surfaces repeatedly, and scenes of gender ambivalence mirror the broader sexual confusion of the culture of modernism. Early in the novel, Rosemary witnesses an odd episode on the beach in which Dick goes into his dressing tent and emerges wearing only a pair of "transparent black lace drawers" which Nicole has handed him. Albert McKisco's quip—"Well if that isn't a pansy's trick!"—crudely associates Dick's stunt with homosexuality, perhaps to taunt the homophiles, Campion and Dunphry, who witness the display. Yet the joke (Nicole has lined the panties with flesh-colored cloth) literally invites closer examination. Dick's gratuitous exhibitionism, really a transvestite performance, signals not only his own tendency to assume conventionally female functions but also the pattern of gender reversal which runs through the novel. One notable transposition has occurred prior to the opening of the novel: Fitzgerald had initially conceived of the Rosemary Hoyt character, the young American with the overbearing mother, as a boy named Francis Melarky.[21] Traces of this sex change remain in Mrs. Spears' advice to Rosemary about pursuing a relationship with Dick: "Whatever happens it can't spoil you because economically you're a boy, not a girl" (40). Mrs. Spears' own name too obviously implies the phallic authority which she assumes in her daughter's life. Conversely Dick plays a maternal role with respect to Nicole, who continues "her dry suckling at his lean chest" (279). Later, in a symbolic metaphor, she severs the umbilical cord which links her to Dick, deciding to "cut the cord forever" (302). Her presenting the black lace panties to Dick in the opening scene may thus be seen as a prefiguration of the sexual transformation which she must effect in him to free herself from the dominating father.[22]

But sexual reversal may also be associated, as McKisco insinuates, with homosexuality. Thus Fitzgerald tells us that Luis Campion affects a "disinterested motherliness" (34) and that the son of Señor Pardo y Ciudad Real flaunts his inversion as "the Queen of Chili," whereas Mary North and Lady Caroline Sibly-Biers dress as French sailors to pick up two girls. These instances of deviance belong to a larger pattern of aberration which includes Mr. Warren's incest and Dick's late problem with nympholepsy in which "he was in love with every pretty woman he saw" (201). Fitzgerald tells us that in Rome, an angry crowd mistakes Dick for "a native of Frascati [who] had raped and slain a five-year-old child" (234). Through such details he hints at the ubiquity of perversion in a novel marked by sexual turmoil, ambiguous erotic relations, and indefinite gender roles. In this sexual economy, desire itself seems inevitably displaced, deflected, or deformed.

Linked to his emphasis on psychoanalysis, Fitzgerald's treatment of the Great War also posits a modernist perspective in *Tender Is the Night*. With the exception of a battlefield visit which colors the events of the Paris section, the war emerges almost entirely through oblique, fugitive references. Fitzgerald sums up the doctor's war experience in two meager sentences: "After he took his degree, he received his orders to join a neurological unit forming at Bar-sur-Aube. In France, to his disgust, the work was executive rather than practical" (117-18). Yet the conflict remains for Dick an obsession manifesting itself in dreams; on one occasion he awakens from "a long dream of war" which Fitzgerald summarizes: "His dream had begun in sombre majesty; navy blue uniforms crossed a dark plaza behind bands playing the second movement of Prokofieff's 'Love of Three Oranges.' Presently there were fire engines, symbols of disaster, and a ghastly uprising of the mutilated in a dressing station." Analyzing his own dream, Dick arrives at a "half-ironic" diagnosis: "Non-combattant's shell-shock" (180). This dream of uniformed men juxtaposed against the "ghastly" image of *mutilés de guerre* resonates with his later experience of waking to find passing beneath his window "a long column of men in uniform" who were "going to lay wreaths on the tombs of the dead" (200). Through such brief and seemingly incidental touches, Fitzgerald establishes the idea that although Dick did not see action at the front, he—like others of his generation—has been traumatized by the horrific carnage. The story of Dick and Nicole unfolds specifically within "the broken universe of the war's ending" (245), and Grenberg contends that the novel even implies a "precise" analogy between Nicole's illness and American involvement in the conflict.[23] Be that as it may, Fitzgerald's broad implication is that as a consequence of the Great War, the Divers move within a sphere of pervasive disillusionment and pent-up violence. Noting the postwar tendency among combat veterans toward escapist fantasy, historian Modris Eksteins makes a comment strikingly relevant to the world of *Tender Is the Night*: "What was true of the soldiers was true with somewhat less immediacy and poignancy of civilians. The crowded nightclubs, the frenzied dancing, the striking upsurge of gambling, alcoholism, and suicide, the obsession with flight, with moving pictures, and with film stars evinced on a popular level these same tendencies, a drift toward irrationalism."[24]

The various eruptions of violence or insanity which mark the novel thus contribute to its modernist, postwar *vraisemblance*. Fitzgerald also represents the culture of modernism through his attention to new conceptions of time and space. For example, the Bergsonian notion of personal or subjective time forms the implicit basis of a comparison between Dick and Nicole: "For him time stood still and then every few years accelerated in a rush, like the quick rewind of a film, but for Nicole the years slipped away by clock and calendar and birthday" (180). The reference to the rewinding of a film as a metaphor for time implicitly recalls the tropes which Bergson used to describe the uncoiling or unwinding of time in "real duration."[25] In another passage, Fitzgerald alludes to a new, modern mode of keeping time when he describes Dick sitting "in the big room a long time listening to the buzz of the electric clock, listening to time" (171). Like Proust's *A la recherche du temps perdu,* Woolf's *To the Lighthouse,* and Faulkner's *Sound and the Fury, Tender Is the Night* reflects a peculiarly modernist concern for the psychological experience of time; as critics have often observed, the narrative structure calls attention to the effects of time by bracketing the story between two beach scenes, set five years apart, which dramatize basic changes in the principal characters. According to Alan Trachtenberg, the disintegration of Dick Diver results in part from his "dislocated sense of historical time."[26]

In a less obvious way, the novel also embodies certain modernist attitudes about space and place. Fitzgerald depicts the Gare St. Lazare, for example, as a locus of metamorphosis for homebound Americans: "Standing in the station, with Paris in back of them, it seemed as if they were vicariously leaning a little over the ocean, already undergoing a sea-change, a shifting about of atoms to form the essential molecule of a new people" (83). This comment resonates with his later observation that "on the long-roofed steamship piers one is in a country that is no longer here and not yet there" (205). That is, international postwar tourism effects a displacement by problematizing the very concept of place. To some extent, Dick suffers from that sense of "placelessness" expressed by Mrs. Miles in "One Trip Abroad." In Rome, when Dick visits the house where Keats died, Fitzgerald notes that "he cared only about people; he was scarcely conscious of places except for their weather, until they had been invested with color by tangible events" (220). Elsewhere the author implies that an indifference to place may reflect a specifically American tourist mentality; he observes about Rosemary and her mother that "after lunch they were both overwhelmed by the sudden flatness that comes over American travellers in quiet foreign places. No stimuli worked upon them, no voices called them from without, no fragments of their own thoughts came suddenly from the minds of others, and missing the clamor of Empire they felt that life was not continuing here" (13). Their inability to respond to "quiet foreign places" reveals not only a crass preference for excitement ("the clamor of Empire") but also an indifference—endemic to the moneyed expatriate—to the physical realities of daily life in ordinary European towns and cities.[27]

In the incessant movement of his major characters, Fitzgerald implies the superficiality of their grounding in the world. When Dick flies to Munich, he gazes down on the landscape from an implicitly abstract, modernist perspective which yields delight: "It was simple looking at the earth from far off, simple as playing grim games with dolls and soldiers" (195). As this glancing allusion to soldiers implies, Fitzgerald sees the Great War itself as a product of the technology of power which has placed Dick far above the countryside he surveys with detachment. From a certain height, human beings shrink to nothingness, communities become indistinguishable, and geography assumes a fantastic unreality which bears no relationship to an earthbound sense of scale and distance. Dick's gaze from the airplane in fact epitomizes Fitzgerald's treatment of place in *Tender Is the Night,* which is not so much realized as sur-realized by the experience of displacement.

Nowhere is this tendency more apparent than in the bewildering Paris section of the novel, which arguably marks a decisive turn in the Divers' marriage, in Dick's loss of professional discipline, and in Nicole's reliance upon Dick as a source of emotional protection. Yet these crucial developments unfold within the context of scenes that seem disconnected, hallucinatory, and even incoherent. When the action shifts to Paris, Fitzgerald discloses through a chaotic sequence of events the impulsive, irrational forces at large there. The two shootings which punctuate this section seem grotesque and initially reveal little except the presence of racial and sexual hostilities beneath the dreamlike surface of life in the capital of modernism. Ostensibly the Divers have come to Paris with Rosemary to see the alcoholic Abe North off to America. During five momentous days which blur together through a surfeit of movement and scene-shifting, we witness a developing romance between Dick and Rosemary, played out against an increasingly fantastic urban backdrop. In this treatment, the palpable unreality of place objectifies the confusion and ambivalence felt most keenly by Dick; the kaleidoscopic settings represent Paris as a locus of volatile change and cultural multiplicity.

In an opening scene in a Right Bank restaurant, Fitzgerald alludes to the touristic dislocation of his characters: "They had been two days in Paris but actually they were still under the beach umbrella" (52). For the Divers, the Norths, and Rosemary, actual surroundings scarcely matter; place is the immaterial context for social pleasure. At Voisin's (261, rue St.-Honoré), the group seems mainly concerned with distancing themselves from other Americans: Dick amuses them by pointing out American men lacking "repose," while Fitzgerald observes that "their own party was overwhelmingly American and sometimes scarcely American at all" (52), thus raising the problem of American identity which becomes associated with their various destinies. But the crux of this chapter lies in a conversation between the Divers, overheard by Rosemary from a telephone booth:

"—So you love me?"

"Oh, *do* I!"

It was Nicole—Rosemary hesitated in the door of the booth then she heard Dick say:

"I want you terribly—let's go to the hotel now." Nicole gave a little gasping sigh. For a moment the words conveyed nothing at all to Rosemary—but the tone did. The vast secretiveness of it vibrated to herself.

"I want you."

"I'll be at the hotel at four."

(53-54)

While revealing the Divers' passion for each other, the dialogue enables Rosemary to imagine an "assignation" which she soon wishes to reenact with Dick, just as Collis Clay's story of Rosemary on the train later excites Dick's longing for her. Through these reciprocal moments of voyeuristic arousal, Fitzgerald advances the tacitly Freudian theory that desire originates in a primal scene which evokes rivalry and which persists through a mimetic doubling which, among other results, generates the symbolic repetition apparent throughout *Tender Is the Night.* For Dick and Rosemary, the formation of their mutual sexual fantasies significantly begins in Paris, a city linked increasingly with the eruption of forbidden impulses.

After a brief shopping trip with Rosemary in which Nicole indulges in material excess, Fitzgerald transports his characters from Paris to a French battlefield near Amiens. Between the villages of Thiepval and Beaumont Hamel, where in 1914 the British had engaged the Germans in the bloody Battle of the Somme, Dick explains to Rosemary (though apparently not to Nicole) the human cost of the campaign; "his throat straining with sadness," he expounds the notion that it was "a love battle" fought to preserve nineteenth-century nationalistic values. Melodramatically Dick announces: "All my beautiful lovely safe world blew itself up here with a great gust of high explosive love" (57). Little does he guess the personal, prophetic implications of his reference to the "explosive" potentialities of love. Partly confession, partly romantic posturing, Dick's remark expresses a conventional sentiment about the loss of traditional certainties, but he also portrays himself as a victim of the war's violence. His battlefield commentary reflects a sympathetic identification with the "Wurtemburgers, Prussian Guards, Chasseurs Alpins, Manchester mill hands and old Etonians" who "pursue their eternal dissolution under the warm rain"; yet it also betrays an awareness of his effect on the tearful Rosemary, who tells him, "You know everything" (57). If Dick's historical consciousness enables him to grasp the significance of the battle, however, his sense of place seems pretentious, markedly less genuine than that of Abe North, who has at least seen combat. At the end of the chapter Fitzgerald confides that to impress Rosemary, Dick has used a battlefield guidebook to make "a quick study of the whole affair, simplifying it always until it bore a faint resemblance to one of his own parties" (59). The gentle derision implies that Dick has exploited the sentimental possibilities of place to launch his own "love battle" for Rosemary's affections.[28]

His tactic meets with quick success: following their return to Paris, Nicole retires to the hotel while Dick, Rosemary, and the Norths visit an exposition and then sip champagne at a houseboat café, enjoying the picturesque view: "The river shimmered with lights from the bridges and cradled many cold moons" (60). Shortly after learning that Dick is a medical doctor—like her own deceased father—Rosemary attempts to seduce him. Despite his infatuation Dick resists, but the effort exposes his vulnerability: "He was suddenly confused, . . . and for a moment his usual grace, the tensile strength of his balance, was absent" (65). At the battlefield Dick had waxed eloquent about the "tremendous sureties" destroyed by the war; now in his private life he confronts for the first time a wavering sense of appropriate conduct. Rosemary's charms have aroused in him an unconscious need to become the lover of yet another eighteen-year-old girl with a father complex, to reenact with Rosemary his romance six years earlier with Nicole. On this night he fights the temptation, but after a few more days in the unreal city he will be ready to yield to desire.

Fitzgerald stretches out the next day over three chapters, depicting events which intensify the strangeness of the Parisian scene and expose the unconscious urges at work on the principal characters. When Rosemary and Nicole meet in the morning for "a series of fittings," the author implies a developing rivalry: in the taxi Rosemary "looked at Nicole, matching herself against her" (67). The twinning implied here finds a geographical correlative, as Rosemary and Nicole discover that as girls they have both lived on the rue des Saints-Peres, the street of the Holy Fathers, an address hinting at the father-fixation which they share. After a luncheon at the Norths' apartment on the rue Guynemer (where the Murphys lived in 1928), Dick, Nicole, Rosemary, Abe, and Mary meet young Collis Clay at Franco-American Films in Passy for a screening of *Daddy's Girl*. Here and elsewhere in *Tender Is the Night*, Fitzgerald's representation of the film industry, the cult of stardom, and the phantasm of cinema itself bears witness to that "flight from reality" which Eksteins associates with the twenties. Dazzled by Rosemary's Hollywood aura, Dick begins to see her as a glamorous incarnation of modernity itself.[29] If his clinical training exposes the crude psychoanalytic meaning of her film role—which involves "a father complex so apparent that he winced for all psychologists at the vicious sentimentality" (69)—the screening also quickens a desire to be "united" with Rosemary like the father in the film.

After the Norths and Nicole leave to run errands, Dick and Rosemary attend a tea party on the Left Bank. This hallucinatory episode offers a glimpse of the lesbian community there and plunges Rosemary into the confusion of sexual ambiguity. Again the street name carries a suggestive connotation: the women's salon is located on the rue Monsieur. Through a bit of creative geography, Fitzgerald hints at the dissolving of sexual difference which occurs at this address.[30] At the moment of entering the house, Rosemary feels that she has entered a new age:

> Once inside the door there was nothing of the past, nor of any present that Rosemary knew. The outer shell, the masonry, seemed rather to enclose the future so that it was an electric shock, a definite nervous experience, perverted as a breakfast of oatmeal and hashish, to cross that threshold, if it could be so called, into the long hall of blue steel, silver-gilt, and the myriad facets of many oddly bevelled mirrors.
>
> (71)

Perceiving the unreality of the place, Rosemary has the momentary sensation of being on a motion-picture set. The physical setting creates the impression of crossing a boundary or threshold into a realm of sensation in which "oddly bevelled mirrors" fragment reality into multiple, incongruous images—in effect, into the perspective of modernism. Fitzgerald depicts an interior room which conveys the idea of ambiguous change: "no one knew what this room meant because it was evolving into something else, becoming everything a room was not" (71-72). Rosemary faces a crowd composed mostly of women and notices a striking trio sitting on a bench: "They were all tall and slender with small heads groomed like manikins' heads, and as they talked the heads waved gracefully about above their dark tailored suits, rather like long-stemmed flowers and rather like cobras' hoods" (72). These stylish yet venomous lesbians are gossiping about the Divers, and as Rosemary masks her indignation she finds herself talking to "a neat, slick girl with a lovely boy's face" who begins to "play up" and beg for a date. Confused by the odd ambience and by sexual advances from a girl who looks like a boy, Rosemary quickly departs with Dick, "moving over the brief threshold of the future to the sudden past of the stone façade without" (74). In a scene which anticipates Djuna Barnes' *Nightwood*, Fitzgerald represents a lesbian subculture which in its appropriation of bourgeois conventions embodies the subversive force of modernism itself.[31]

Another kind of unreality typifies the moveable feast which Dick stages later that night, presumably for Rosemary's benefit. The party involves "a quick Odyssey over Paris" in a caravan featuring a jeweled car owned by the shah of Persia. The Norths, the Divers, and Rosemary attract an international group which includes "the heir to a Scandinavian throne." Fitzgerald reprots that "people joined them as if by magic, accompanied them as specialists, almost guides, through a phase of the evening" (76). Dick's organization of events, his "technic of moving many varied types" into position, as if he were commanding "an infantry battalion," delights Rosemary, who compares the evening to a Hollywood party. At the Ritz bar, the Americans dupe the waiters into singing war songs for Abe North, who impersonates General Pershing. The revelers insist that the general "brooks no delay. Every man, every gun is at his service" (78). The reconnoitering of Paris, the use of "guides," Dick's marshaling of his "battalion," and the evocation of Pershing all suggest that the party in some obscure way unfolds as a parodic military exercise in which Dick and his friends turn their recent, melancholy visit to Thiepval and Beaumont Hamel into madcap escapism. Their hilarity obliquely implies the emotional and psychological burden which the war has imposed.

On another level the pace and extravagance of the party, together with the associations of royalty, underscore Fitzgerald's familiar claim that the rich are different because they lead unimaginably fabulous lives. For Dick and his cohorts, Paris provides an ideal space for the staging of fantasies: it offers a visual spectacle which for a certain amount of money can be requisitioned as image or illusion. The denouement of the party illustrates this point: after Dick and Nicole have returned to their hotel, Rosemary finds herself atop a market wagon filled with "thousands of carrots," rolling along with the Norths, Collis Clay, and two improbable nouveau riche types, "a manufacturer of dolls' voices from Newark and . . . a big splendidly dressed oil Indian named George T. Horseprotection" (79). Fitzgerald's giddy expatriates have commandeered a farm wagon en route to market, not to indulge in agricultural nostalgia but precisely to flaunt their privileged status as rich Americans and their class difference from the wagon's owner. The economic reality expressed by the fresh produce never impinges on Rosemary's fantasy: "The earth in the carrot beards was fragrant and sweet in the darkness, and Rosemary was so high up in the load that she could hardly see the others. . . . Their voices came from far off, as if they were having experiences different from hers, different and far away" (79). The external scene seems a mere extension of her desire, and when she notices at dawn's early light a truck transporting "a huge horsechestnut tree in full bloom bound for the Champs-Elysées," she sees it as a "lovely person," identifies herself with it, and imagines that "everything all at once seemed gorgeous" (79). Paris has on this evening become the narcissistic reflection of her all-American loveliness.

The following morning, though, a darker fantasy envelops Fitzgerald's characters. At the Gare St. Lazare . . . , a dissipated Abe waits "under the fouled glass dome" for the boat train which will take him back to the United States. His sullen demeanor betrays his "will to die" (83), and as events later confirm, he will indeed disappear "into the dark maw of violence," beaten to death in an American speakeasy.[32] On this occasion, however, violence erupts in Paris; just as the train is pulling out, a young American woman, Maria Wallis, pulls a revolver from her purse and shoots a man on the platform. Signaling a theme of mounting importance, Fitzgerald notes that the victim, an Englishman, has been shot "through his identification card" (84). The attack seems unmotivated, and we never discover what "dark matter" precipitated it; yet we may infer that a relationship has gone horribly awry. The shooting has a temporary, estranging effect even upon the would-be lovers, Dick and Rosemary: "For a moment each seemed unreal to the other." Through rhetorical hints, Fitzgerald indicates that Dick experiences "a loss of control" and feels "panic" while Rosemary suffers from "a totality of shock." The scene at the station has "ended the time in Paris" and stunned Fitzgerald's characters:

> The shots had entered into all their lives: echoes of violence followed them out onto the pavement where two porters held a post-mortem beside them as they waited for a taxi.
>
> "Tu as vu le revolver? Il était très petit, vraie perle—un jouet."
>
> "Mais, assez puissant!" said the other porter sagely. "Tu as vu sa chemise? Assez de sang pour se croire à la guerre."

(85-86)

Once again the author invokes the memory of the war, here to suggest an implicit connection between the shooting at the Gare St. Lazare and the bloodshed of 1914-18. A contagion of violence has infected the world, and its eruption at the train station—at a precarious moment in the intimate relations between Dick, Nicole, and Rosemary—displays the deadly force of "high-explosive love."

At an alfresco luncheon "across from the Luxembourg Gardens," the three subsequently try to forget the morning's horrors. But Rosemary develops menstrual cramps, Dick feels "profoundly unhappy," and even Nicole exhibits testiness. They dine in an atmosphere of tension and mounting suspicion; Dick privately wonders, "What did Nocole think?" The afternoon takes a Freudian turn, however, after the departure of Rosemary and Nicole; Collis

Clay happens along, shares some wine with Dick, and casually relates the story of Rosemary and a Yale man on the train to Chicago. "Seems they locked the door and pulled down the blinds," Clay says, "and I guess there was some heavy stuff going on when the conductor came for the tickets and knocked on the door." The story has an immediate, unnerving effect on Dick:

> With every detail imagined, with even envy for the pair's community of misfortune in the vestibule, Dick felt a change taking place within him. Only the image of a third person, even a vanished one, entering into his relation with Rosemary was needed to throw him off his balance and send him through waves of pain, misery, desire, desperation. The vividly pictured hand on Rosemary's cheek, the quicker breath, the white excitement of the event viewed from outside, the inviolable secret warmth within.
>
> —Do you mind if I pull down the curtain?
>
> —Please do. It's too light in here.
>
> (88)

Through successive reiterations of the last lines, Fitzgerald implies the obsessive force of the story as a primal scene. When Dick later drops by his bank to cash a check, his manner implies agitation; he tries to calculate which clerk "would guess least of the unhappy predicament in which he found himself and, also, which one would be least likely to talk" (89). Even if he is withdrawing funds to finance an affair, it is hard to imagine how a bank clerk could surmise the specific nature of Dick's "predicament." As he sorts through his mail, finding a letter for Rosemary, a distressing question flashes through his consciousness: "Do you mind if I pull down the curtain?" In the wake of the shooting, the story of her presumed deflowering has shattered Dick's composure, triggering desire as well as prospective guilt.

At this juncture Fitzgerald uses Parisian topography to signal Dick's disorientation. Instinctively pursuing Rosemary, he hires a taxi to take him to her studio in Passy. "Go to the Muette," he tells the driver. "I'll direct you from there." Yet Dick does not give directions: "He was rendered so uncertain by the events of the last forty-eight hours that he was not even sure what he wanted to do" (91). He gets out at La Muette, a park near the Bois du Boulogne, and brandishing his briefcase and walking stick—signs of his precarious respectability—he walks along "swayed and driven as an animal." Soon he finds himself in the midst of a "melancholy neighborhood," surrounded by strangely portentous signs: "'Vêtements Ecclésiastiques,' 'Déclaration de Décès' and 'Pompes Funèbres.' Life and Death" (91). Clerical clothing, death notices, funerals: Dick, the minister's son from Buffalo, perceives in these signs a reflection of his fateful errancy.[33] "He knew that what he was now doing marked a turning point in his life," Fitzgerald remarks. "It was out of line with everything that had preceded it—even out of line with what effect he might hope to produce upon Rosemary." His behavior represents, instead, the "projection of some submerged reality"; Dick, the psychologist, has surrendered to the irrational, to the unconscious urges which have been exposed and activated by the unreal city in which his dreamlike experience unfolds.

For three-quarters of an hour, Dick paces the rue des Saintes-Anges, an invented street which ironically evokes the image of Rosemary as one of Dick's "holy angels."[34] At this acknowledged "turning point," Fitzgerald stages a puzzling confrontation in which an American war veteran with a "sinister smile" accosts Dick on the sidewalk. Though his "menacing eyes" seem to bespeak criminal intent, the stranger boasts that he has "made plenty money" in Paris selling newspapers to American tourists; he carries a cartoon depicting "Americans pouring from the gangplank of a liner freighted with gold" (93). The fellow obviously typifies that swarm of American opportunists which inundated Paris in the twenties; Fitzgerald here suggests a vast qualitative difference between the two compatriots.[35] Yet late in the novel, he undercuts this contrast: on the Riviera, at yet another turning point, Dick again meets the same American "of sinister aspect," recognizing him by the clipping with "cartooned millions of Americans pouring from liners with bags of gold" (309). While the man is still hawking newspapers to rich tourists, Dick himself has now become an antithetical caricature of the American moneybags—a ruined and depleted expatriate about to return to the United States.

As he languishes in Passy, Dick has already yielded to that complex "submerged reality" which will effect his deterioration. At a corner café, his telephone call to Rosemary (who is back at the hotel) reveals his "extraordinary condition"; when he asks if she is alone, the primal scene again flashes through his mind (94). Under its spell, he has only one desire: to be alone with her, to pull down the curtain himself as a prelude to lovemaking. As they talk, Dick imagines her room and remembers the "dust of powder over her tan," surrendering to the fantasy constructed by his own longing. When he emerges from the café, still carrying the accoutrements of class and profession, his disorientation seems complete: "In a minute he was out in the street marching along toward the Muette, *or away from it,* his small brief-case still in his hand, his gold-headed stick held at a sword-like angle" (94, my emphasis). With his stick poised for action, announcing his sexual readiness, Dick's topographical confusion betrays a concomitant loss of moral direction. Ironically, he makes his way back to the hotel only to discover that Rosemary, feeling "not very well" at the onset of her period, has elected to dine alone.

The last nightmarish day in Paris begins, appropriately, in confusion, as Nicole awakens to find Dick's bed empty (a sign of his unrest) and a police officer at the door looking for one "Mr. Afghan North." Though Nicole declares that Abe has "gone to America," she learns that he is indeed still in Paris; the officer explains that North has been robbed by a Negro and must identify a suspect. "Mystified" by the account, Nicole sends the officer away; she brusquely slams down the receiver when the hotel office calls to ask whether she will speak to a Negro named "Crawshow," whose friend Mr. Freeman has been mistakenly put in prison. The situation becomes more muddled when Abe later explains to Dick that he has "launched a race riot" and that he intends to "get Freeman out of jail" (98). Abe's predicament offers further evidence of his dissolution, leading Nicole to wonder why "so many smart men go to pieces nowadays" and to ask Dick pointedly: "Why is it just Americans who dissipate?" Abe's disintegration of course prefigures Dick's decline; and both in effect herald the crash of the American stock market in 1929. But Nicole's question goes to the very heart of Fitzgerald's critique of American identity and implies the existence of a self-destructive contradiction at its very core.

At lunch downstairs, the three find themselves surrounded by "families of Americans staring around at families of Americans"; a waiter identifies them as "gold-star muzzers"—mothers of the American war dead. Again an incidental detail evokes a remembrance of combat casualties; slipping into a reverie Dick recalls not only the Great War but also the Civil War: "Momentarily, he sat again on his father's knee, riding with Moseby while the old loyalties and devotions fought on around him" (101). The presence of the Gold Star mothers puts Dick in touch with "an older America" and briefly stirs his faith in the nineteenth-century ideals of his father. But Dick is caught between two sets of values, one belonging to an idealistic past and the other to a crass, acquisitive present; in Fitzgerald's mythography he embodies the contradictory essence of the American self. If the Gold Star mothers represent an old-fashioned gallantry, Nicole and Rosemary epitomize "the whole new world in which he believed"—the world of pleasure, wealth, glamour, and power. Ironically as he dines in the company of "sobered women who had come to mourn for their dead," an overwhelming question stirs his brain: "Do you mind if I pull down the curtain?" (101). Here Fitzgerald again hints at the potent connection between death and desire, helping us to understand how the slaughter of 1914-18 might have triggered what he elsewhere called the "precocious intimacies" of the twenties.[36]

After an uneventful chapter which depicts Abe North in the Ritz bar, drinking to forget the "nightmare" in which he has become involved, Fitzgerald resumes Dick's libidinal quest, noting the early stages of his psychic fragmentation: "Dick moved on through the rain, demoniac and frightened, the passions of many men inside him and nothing simple that he could see" (104). Troubled by the events of the previous twenty-four hours, Rosemary, too, has been "playing around with chaos," yet when Dick enters her room, the sexual consummation of their romance seems imminent. They are not exactly in love with each other; rather, they are in love with the illusions each has created about the other. Rosemary presses her lips "to the beautiful cold image she had created" and then in a moment of rare insight tells Dick, "Oh, we're such *actors*—you and I" (105), perhaps suspecting the psychoanalytic truth that each is acting out a rehearsed, fantasized scene with the other. But a knock at the door interrupts their tryst and plunges them both into the racial nightmare excited by Abe North.

Incongruities multiply when North introduces "a very frightened, concerned colored man," a "Mr. Peterson of Stockholm" (105), who has witnessed "the early morning dispute in Montparnasse" (106). This is the very man earlier identified as "a Negro from Copenhagen" in Abe's report of "a race riot in Montmartre" (98). Peterson has falsely accused one black man who was not even present at the time of the robbery; when those charges were dropped, the police then wrongly arrested "the prominent Negro restaurateur, Freeman." A third black man, the actual "culprit," has surfaced to explain that he had grabbed a "fifty-franc note to pay for drinks that Abe had ordered." The net effect of this wild account is that "Abe had succeeded in the space of an hour in entangling himself in the personal lives, consciences, and emotions of one Afro-European and three Afro-Americans inhabiting the French Latin quarter" (106). Fearing retribution from Freeman, the "Afro-European" Peterson begs Dick for help and then withdraws to the hall to let Abe plead his case. When Rosemary returns to her room moments later, looking for her wristwatch, she discovers "a dead Negro . . . stretched upon her bed" (109).

This unlikely sequence of events, which most critics have ascribed to Fitzgerald's thematic overreaching in *Tender Is the Night*, raises a number of disconcerting issues.[37] The principal difficulty concerns the relation of Peterson's murder to the intrigue involving Dick, Nicole, and Rosemary. This problem seems linked, moreover, to the larger question of Fitzgerald's construction of racial and ethnic difference. In the elegant milieu of the Divers, Abe North has committed an expatriate social blunder by "entangling himself" with black people, by crating the situation of "unfamiliar Negro faces bobbing up in unexpected places and around unexpected corners, and insistent Negro voices on the phone" (106). These intrusions of the black into the privileged space of the (white) American expatriate are made to seem both offensive and threatening. Dick fails to "appreciate the mess that Peterson's in," because he regards the whole affair as "some nigger scrap" (110); a dispute between two blacks can have no claim to his attention. He tries to stereotype Peterson as "a small, respectable Negro, on the suave model that heels the Republican party in the border states" (106). Yet as a Scandinavian black, Peterson represents an ethnic anomaly, perhaps even an affront to some unspoken notion of Nordic purity. (One recalls Tom Buchanan in *The Great Gatsby* spouting racist theory.) For Dick, Peterson is a nuisance not simply because he has attached himself to Abe North but also because he represents the potential collapse of those social barriers which have long kept the darker races in their supposed "places."[38]

Thus when Rosemary finds Peterson's bloody corpse in her bed, Dick acts quickly to remove the body, to reinscribe the boundaries of racial difference, and thus to restore order. He knows that the discovery of a black man, even a dead one, in the bed of the white, putatively virginal "Daddy's girl" would generate a scandal disastrous to Rosemary's career. But the bizarre coincidence of Peterson's being found precisely in that place where Dick had hoped to be raises a more complicated issue, compelling us to ask what it means when a black man displaces a white at the site of erotic fantasy. Does it disclose a fear of sexual encroachment by the dark-skinned Other? Does it imply that Rosemary's status as a cultural goddess is assured by a system of patriarchal domination which requires the sacrifice of the black? Fitzgerald offers no explanations, and it seems highly unlikely that he even considered such theoretical implications. But with an instinct for suggestive "grotesquerie," he places Peterson in Rosemary's bed so that the black man's blood saturates her coverlet and blanket, effecting another intriguing substitution—here, for the menstrual (if not hymenal) stain which might have resulted from her intercourse with Dick.

The stained coverlet and blanket of course produce another, more perplexing substitution. Dick disposes of the bedding by handing it to Nicole, who carries it to the bathroom where she suffers a mental relapse at the sight of the blood. Releasing a torrent of "verbal inhumanity," she accuses Dick of intruding on her privacy with his bloody bedspread, thereby alluding to yet another primal scene, that of her father's incestuous violation. Because the bedding which precipitates this breakdown actually comes from the bed of "Daddy's girl," Nicole's outburst obviously reinforces the symbolic parallel between her situation and Rosemary's. But what does Nicole's loss of virginity have to do with the bloody death of Jules Peterson, the Afro-European? Perhaps the clue lies in Peterson's role as a "small manufacturer of shoe polish," driven into exile because he refused to divulge his formula in Stockholm. If Devereux Warren is the prototype of the successful white capitalist, Peterson represents the emerging black entrepreneur bidding to compete for wealth and power. As the dark rival of the white capitalist, Peterson has been driven from Scandinavia; as the black counterpart of Devereux Warren, he also functions as a scapegoat, undergoing an absolute reversal of Warren's fate in what René Girard would call an act of "sacrificial substitution." Innocent of any impropriety with Rosemary, he sheds his *own* blood in the bed of Daddy's girl, suffering the death that Warren "didn't have the nerve" to inflict upon himself. Far from causing psychological damage to Rosemary, Peterson by his death frees her from Dick's paternal attachment; after the crime, she moves to another hotel and leaves Paris without saying good-bye to the Divers. Patently a sacrificial figure, Peterson also restores at least a semblance of devotion to the marriage of Dick and Nicole; by his blood they are redeemed, temporarily at least, from suspicion and enmity.

The histrionic scene which unfolds in the Divers' bathroom caps a sequence of confrontations and discoveries which occur in Paris and which associate the city with a dreamlike or hallucinatory unreality. These uncanny scenes expose unconscious desires and anxieties, fantasies of power or sexual conquest, and nightmares of violence or powerlessness. Through such episodes as the lesbian party on the rue Monsieur, the "fabulous" mobile fête, the shooting at the Gare St. Lazare, Dick's disorientation in Passy, and the assassination of Jules Peterson, as well as through the evocation of three secret sexual scenes, Fitzgerald exposes the social and psychological chaos beneath the seemingly ordered surface of everyday life. The recurrent intrusion of the unconscious manifests those forces which are commonly repressed or denied: the irrational urges and volatile tensions masked by legal constraints and hierarchical social practices. Fitzgerald allows us to glimpse, in the Paris section, an impending explosion; Nicole's breakdown in the hotel bathroom seems emblematic insofar as it represents the return of the repressed, the eruption of chaos. Three times Dick tells her, "Control yourself." Yet what the bloody bedspread has summoned forth is precisely the irrepressible and uncontrollable. In the Freudian scheme of the novel, this scene acknowledges the power of the unconscious, and throughout the Paris section, a relaxed morality allows the unconscious to manifest itself repeatedly.

Within the novel's historical framework, this moment also discloses on the social level a ubiquitous violence. The bloody result of a "race riot," Peterson's death implies the presence of a rage which rarely obtrudes upon the comfortable world of the Divers. Yet Fitzgerald means by this and other details to uncover a seething, revolutionary fury loosed upon the dying Western world. His references to Russians displaced by the Bolsheviks or to ethnic types (like George T. Horseprotection) who appear in unlikely places all point toward a vast social upheaval, implicitly disconcerting to the Dick Divers whose sense of personal security is grounded in a notion of "the exact relation that existed between the classes." *Tender Is the Night* calls attention to the breakdown of class differences and expresses alarm at the transgression of social boundaries. Jules Peterson personifies the social transformations associated with the modern age, with what Fitzgerald (following Spengler) assumes to be the decline of the West. The shoe polish manufacturer defies the stereotype of Nordic racial purity, threatens the hegemony of white capital, and at last violates the sanctum of the all-American white goddess. He embodies the principle of social chaos which figures to disrupt the caste system to which Dick Diver subscribes.

The Paris section occupies roughly one-fifth of *Tender Is the Night*; yet it marks a pivotal phase, a point of crisis, for the Divers. If their respective destinies form a crisscrossed plot through the reciprocal stories of Nicole's recovery and Dick's collapse, the vectors of change intersect in Paris. Clearly, by pursuing Rosemary, Dick commits himself to a project as compulsive as it is destructive; his yearning for "Daddy's girl" soon becomes a generalized obsession for young women which undermines his professional discipline.[39] As we see in the bathroom scene, Nicole likewise suffers a crisis in Paris. Whereas her hysteria on the Riviera had not been so serious, "the collapse in Paris was another matter, adding significance to the first one. It prophesied possibly a new cycle, a new pousse of the malady" (168). In her bathroom ravings, Nicole seems to confuse Dick with her father, telling him, "I'll wear [the bloody spread] for you—I'm not ashamed, though it was such a pity" (112). This breakdown of the distinction between the wounding, biological father and the nurturing, symbolic father implies an erosion of Nicole's trust. The week in Paris changes her relationship to Dick and injects an element of doubt which paradoxically opens the way to her eventual self-reliance.

Judged by locodescriptive criteria, Fitzgerald's representation of Paris in *Tender Is the Night* seems comparatively superficial. The author did not possess that attentiveness to the inner life of the city which excited Miller; he never shared Hemingway's fetish for geographical precision. Jean Méral characterizes the Paris of Fitzgerald's novel as "a vague limbo in which characters hang suspended." In only two incidents—the party on the rue Monsieur and the shooting at the Gare St. Lazare—do tangible places assume interpretive significance. The third-person Frances Melarky version of the novel included a wild scene with the Norths, George T. Horseprotection, and the manufacturer of dolls' voices carousing at a Montmartre night spot called the Georgia Cabin.[40] But in the published version, that episode becomes a mere allusion to Montmartre by Abe North. The novel offers glimpses of Voisin's restaurant, the Ritz bar, the Hotel Roi George (the Georges V), the Muette quarter of Passy, the Luxembourg Gardens, the rue de Rivoli, and the Champs-Elysées. Expressing a French perspective, Méral insists that these backgrounds possess "the unreality of a theater set."[41] But that is exactly Fitzgerald's point: the city is fundamentally a locus of the imaginary. For Dick and his expatriate cohorts, Paris is a theater of dreams, a scene of fantasy and excess which becomes a terrifying site of violent change.

Fear and loathing also pervade the Parisian setting of Djuna Barnes's *Nightwood* (1936), a novel which propels us into an even stranger and denser atmosphere of unreality. For all of its Gothic flourishes and Elizabethan sonorities, the narrative projects an unmistakably modernist vision of exile as it juxtaposes the problem of gender against the dilemma of American identity. In this formulation, nocturnal Paris objectifies the libidinal confusion of the novel's personae, who move in seemingly random fashion as if caught in a circular dream of longing and betrayal. Their various journeys home (or to places once conceived to be home) help to illuminate the experience of exile, yet *Nightwood* resists the operations which would reduce it to paraphrase. Its modernity resides in its representation of ambiguous, undecidable relations and in its insistence upon the enigmatic duality of the human animal. Barnes raises the latter issue repeatedly by collapsing the distinction between the human and the bestial. Andrew Field has commented on the clash in Barnes's writing between "contrary forces of bestiality and rectitude," a conflict which produces odd tensions and perplexing contrasts.[42] Yet despite its singularities, the novel nevertheless affords a suggestive comparison with *Tender Is the Night* as a reconstruction of American disorientation in Paris in the late twenties.

After establishing herself in New York as a free-lance journalist linked to the bohemian community of Greenwich Village, Barnes began to find newspaper features a limited genre; she left for France in 1920 under an informal agreement with *McCall's* to act as a European correspondent.[43] In her 1922 essay "Vagaries Malicieux," she recounted her first trip abroad (at age twenty-eight) on a boat jammed with "disappointed teachers from the Middle West, who sat on deck eating gift fruit sarcastically." Arriving at the Gare St. Lazare, Barnes confronted the foreignness of Paris and what sounded to her like the gabble of the French language. "It took me several days to get over the sensation of dangerous make-believe," she confessed, expressing the essential dislocation of the exile. From her hotel on the rue Jacob, Barnes visited the church of St. Germain des Prés, met James Joyce at Deux Magots, and admired "the chic of Paris, the beauty of its women, the magic of its very existence." Yet she refused to romanticize the city, informing a Frenchman that "the multiplication of Paris had been its destruction." She feared that "too many people had reported Paris,—it had the fame of a too beautiful woman." Dismissing such touristic sites as Napoleon's tomb, the Luxembourg Gardens, and the Folies-Bergère, she conceded a liking for men's walking styles and women's cosmetics, for cafés, for religious paintings ("dwindled Christs and Madonnas"), and for churches. She also liked the Cluny museum where amid its medieval treasures she sought an effigy of the mythical Thaïs. "I was told," she confesses, "that in one museum or other, there lay the body of the most beautiful woman,—brief of flesh and of legend immortal, and . . . I had come to Paris more on her account than she on mine, and herein lay my pleasure and my pain."[44] As this remark implies, Barnes had come to Paris in part to search for female beauty and to explore her lesbian inclinations, confronting the pleasure and pain of her attraction to women.

Apart from three relatively brief visits to America, Barnes lived in Paris continuously from 1920 until 1932. During those dozen years she published numerous magazine and newspaper articles; a score of short stories (collected in three different volumes); a parodic illustrated survey of lesbianism in Paris (*The Ladies' Almanack*); and a baroque, mock-epic novel (*Ryder*), which served roughly the same function in Barnes's career that *The Making of Americans* did in Stein's: to throw off the patriarchal influence of her American past through a disguised version of family history.[45] Paris provided the requisite distance from which Barnes could satirize the bucolic childhood world of Storm-King mountain near Cornwall-on-Hudson, a world dominated in the novel by the polygamist-patriarch, Wendell Ryder, a figure palpably inspired by Wald Barnes. Field suggests that in *Ryder* Barnes grappled with the dominance of her father, whose unorthodox notion of an extended family apparently induced him to offer his teenage daughter as a sexual "gift" to his brother-in-law, with the collusion of Djuna's grandmother, Zadel Barnes Gustafson.[46] Whether or not Barnes suffered precisely this fate, she detested her father, assumed thereafter a loosely feminist view of gender relations, and struggled throughout much of her adult life with a deeply conflicted sense of affectional preference. After a three-year heterosexual affair with a New York journalist named Courtenay Lemon, Barnes lived during the twenties in Paris (at 9, rue St.-Romain) with Thelma Wood, an American sculptor and silverpoint artist. In a famous remark Barnes later declared: "I'm not a lesbian. I just loved Thelma." Biographical evidence partly supports her claim: the liaison with Thelma Wood was Barnes's only significant love affair with a woman; by contrast, she had many briefer, intimate relationships with men.[47] Yet as she hints in "Vagaries Malicieux" and elsewhere in her writing, she felt irresistibly attracted to certain women and stirred by desires which she was reluctant to name or to acknowledge publicly.

Nowhere did Barnes articulate more brilliantly the contradictions of her own situation as an American exile of uncertain sexual affinity than in *Nightwood* (1936). Composed mostly in England in the aftermath of her break with Thelma, the novel rewrites that troubled romance as a "haunted" relationship between two radically dissimilar women, Nora Flood and Robin Vote, who are separated by a meddlesome intruder, the "squatter" Jenny Petherbridge. Yet Barnes's text goes far beyond a roman à clef: to this trio of American women the author links Felix Volkbein, an Austro-Italian Jew obsessed by the idea of aristocracy and consumed by the need to beget and protect the son who will carry on his spurious nobility. As a commentator on the dark universe inhabited by these characters, Barnes retrieves from *Ryder* Dr. Matthew O'Connor, the homosexual obstetrician, who emerges in *Nightwood* as a garrulous poseur, a transvestite whose raging, impossible desire is to be a mother.

As several critics have remarked, O'Connor's role resembles that of Eliot's Tiresias insofar as he witnesses the sexual rivalry provoked by Robin Vote and though male displays an empathetic understanding of female experience. The parallel seems deliberate; Barnes admired *The Waste Land*, later acceded to Eliot's editorial ideas about cutting the novel, and welcomed his suggestion for its eventual title. As Donna Gerstenberger has noted, *Nightwood* "stakes out the same territory as Eliot's poem, which is that of a civilization (particularly Western European) in decay, an aristocracy in disarray, a people estranged from a sense of identity." But she goes further, arguing that Barnes's novel is "a more radically experimental work than *The Waste Land*."[48] Initially this last claim seems extravagant: *Nightwood* followed Eliot's poem by fourteen years (as it did another influential text, Joyce's *Ulysses*). More than a decade of subsequent literary experimentation—much of it conducted in the little magazines published in Paris and elsewhere—helped Barnes to achieve the modernist effects of her second novel.[49] In some respects her novel seems, moreover, scarcely innovative: Barnes divides the narrative into separate chapters which form a chronological progression; the characters' lives connect intelligibly; an effaced, seemingly omniscient narrator tells much of the story; certain motifs (such as animal imagery, or the gesture of "bowing down") give the story a modicum of formal unity.

Yet there can be no question about the novel's status as an innovative modernist text. Despite the role of Barnes's narrator, Karen Kaivola rightly remarks that "many voices speak in *Nightwood,* undermining the authority of any one position and producing a contradictory and heterogeneous discourse composed of an amalgam of styles." Judith Lee perceives the novel as "distinctively modern . . . in its consideration of what our concepts of masculine and feminine imply," while Jane Marcus discusses *Nightwood* as "the representative modernist text, a prose poem of abstraction, tracing the political unconscious of the rise of fascism."[50] While all of these claims have validity, Gerstenberger locates the quintessential, modernist feature which distinguishes *Nightwood* from *The Waste Land*: "It is a novel that rages against the imprisoning structures of the language and narratives of the 'day,' which create a history built on the oppositions of night/day, past/present, reason, madness, 'normal'/'abnormal,' truth/falsehood, gender, and origins (both historical and textual). It is a book that relentlessly undermines grounds for categorization. The ideal and the real, the beautiful and the ugly, subject and object become irrelevant distinctions."[51] Her observation resonates with a claim by Jane Marcus, that "*Nightwood* is about merging, dissolution, and, above all, hybridization—mixed metaphors, mixed levels of discourse from the lofty to the low, mixed 'languages' from medical practice, circus argot, church dogma, and homosexual slang."[52] That is, Barnes's novel relentlessly subverts those "rational" distinctions and differences which, until the advent of modernism, held in place traditional notions of moral and social order and conventional ways of defining the self.

Precisely in the way that it challenges the concept of identity, *Nightwood* exposes a crisis symptomatic of modernism and justifies Barnes's attention to the experience of exile. In some sense all of her expatriate characters suffer from a profound uncertainty about who they are, where they "belong," and what they desire. Apart from portions of the first chapter set in Vienna and Berlin and some brief American scenes, the drama of their various anxieties takes place—significantly—in what Marcus calls "the night world of lesbian, homosexual, and transvestite Paris." In the chapter entitled "Watchman, What of the Night?" Barnes suggests that the nocturnal world over which O'Connor presides is figuratively the region of the irrational, the unconscious, and the bestial. The doctor himself explains that "the very constitution of twilight is a fabulous reconstruction of fear, fear bottom-out and wrong side up" (80). Fantastic metamorphoses occur in this shadow world where the self becomes another. Nora tells O'Connor, "Now I see that the night does something to a person's identity, even when asleep" (81). More radically the doctor describes an "unknown land" where the dreamer, in the company of anonymous "merrymakers," commits unspeakable acts "in a house without an address, in a street in no town, citizened with people with no names to deny them" (88). In the Freudian logic of the narrative, these phantom conspirators are always projections of the dreamer: "Their very lack of identity makes them ourselves." The night world thus dissolves the difference between subject and object, making the other a double of self even as that self remains anonymous and unknowable; it is the place where, as Karen Kaivola says, "one most directly encounters the instability and contradictions of identity."[53]

Nightwood thus projects the condition of uncertainty as the distinguishing sign of modernist experience. "There are only confusions," O'Connor tells Nora, "confusions and defeated anxieties" (22). In her fictional analysis of the turmoil of modernism, Barnes returns insistently to the question of identity, tying the ontological perplexities of her characters to the enigma of self. This question arises at a dinner party in Berlin when the Duchess of Broadback asks Felix Volkbein, "Am I what I say? Are you? Is the doctor?" (25). Later, Felix formulates what appears to be the author's skeptical conclusion when he observes that "the more we learn of a person, the less we know" (111). More pointedly O'Connor frames the issue as an exclamation, a cry of exasperation, rather than a query: "Who is anybody!" (154). Yet this elemental uncertainty marks the speculative crux of *Nightwood*; Barnes engages the problem at several levels and contemplates not only the fate of identity under modernism but also the general dilemma of the exiled self and the specific vicissitudes of the American exile, male and female. Her exploration of the problematic aspects of modernist identity emphasizes three constituent features, indicated by one's relation to gender, to memory, and to place, respectively. By linking the stories of her principal characters, Barnes suggests ways in which these conditions of being impinge upon the sense of self. Ultimately she examines three kinds of dissociation which destabilize personal identity. Paris provides the essential context for this study, insofar as its nocturnal unreality evokes those compulsions and fears which expose the inherent confusions of modernism.

Within what James B. Scott calls "the inverted and introspective world of *Nightwood*," gender and the ambiguities of desire pose the most formidable problem for Barnes's characters.[54] Her representation of "deviance" can scarcely be summarized, for each figure incorporates an idiosyncratic notion of gender and acts out a different search for love; indeed, her characters represent an array of alternative sexualities, implied by specific preferences, fetishes, and fantasies. Yet this novel so manifestly about gender and sexuality has little to do with eroticism.[55] Barnes glosses over the impregnation of Robin by Felix and depicts only fleeting scenes of passion between women, such as the groping of Jenny and Robin in the carriage, which prompts O'Connor to voice what may have been the author's own cynical view of desire: "Love, that terrible thing!" (75). In some sense, all of her characters are prisoners of the flesh, alienated from their own bodies and their own sexualities. The recurrent animal imagery connects the carnal with the bestial, suggesting Barnes's underlying perception of lust as horror.

But her characters suffer as well from other forms of alienation. Effectively cut off from the past and from history itself, they are exiled in the modernist moment; the marginality of these misfits excludes them from what Julie L. Abraham calls "the history of the official record."[56] Moreover, each has an ironic relation to memory which complicates the construction of identity and the articulation of a gendered role. As in *Tender Is the Night*, a psychoanalytic matrix focuses attention in *Nightwood* upon repetition mechanisms which betray repressed material. But Barnes's characters are typically unable to reconstruct the past in ways which free them from its effects; they remain only obscurely aware of prior events which might explain present confusions. They seem likewise displaced geographically and circulate in the city of exile in ways which which suggest the ironies of their dislocation. That is, their patterns of movement and association within the Parisian milieu provide an index to their alienation from themselves.

Felix Volkbein, who clings to the title of Baron "to dazzle his own estrangement," suffers because he has no real past and no meaningful attachment to his native Vienna except as a locus of illusion. Orphaned from birth, his passion for history springs from an anxiety about his antecedents—a problem represented by the portraits said to be of his grandparents, which in fact depict two "ancient actors" whose likenesses his father Guido purchased to provide "an alibi for the blood" (7). Guido has in fact concealed his Jewish heritage with a fraudulent Austrian pedigree; this ambiguous fiction of nobility, passed on to Felix by his aunt, comprises all that the son understands of his origins. Tormented by insecurity, he launches a patriarchal project: "He wished a son who would feel as he felt about the 'great past'" (38). At age forty Felix plans to validate his dubious claim to aristocracy through descendants; he hopes to define the paternal line by extending it. His need for self-legitimation thus leads him to France, where he seeks the wife destined to bear "sons who would recognize and honour the past" (45).

Judging Paris to be the center of European social elegance, Felix thus arrives in 1920 "bowing, searching, with quick pendulous movements, for the correct thing to which to pay tribute: the right street, the right café, the right building, the right vista" (9). He delights in the "old and documented splendour" of the Musée Carnavalet and finds lodging in rooms hallowed because "a Bourbon had been carried from them to death" (9). But the location of this apartment remains unspecified, suggesting his attachment to a dream of history rather than to a tangible place. We see Felix only fleetingly in the sixth arrondissement: "fate and entanglement" lead him to the Hôtel Récamier, where (with O'Connor) he first gazes upon the literally unconscious American, Robin Vote. Carrying two volumes of "the life of the Bourbons," he next meets Robin on the rue Bonaparte (a wry historical irony) and walks with her in the "bare chilly" Luxembourg Gardens, describing his banking position with Crédit Lyonnais. They visit unnamed museums and "an antique shop facing the Seine"; their perfunctory courtship ends—in a subplot reminiscent of Henry James—in marriage between the European and the American.

Yet here Barnes dismantles the international romance: after an abortive wedding journey to Vienna which bores Robin and disillusions Felix (who finds how slight his connections to that city really are), they return to Paris to take up the chore of producing an heir.[57] The heterosexual contact is a trial for both: "He came and took her by the arm and lifted her toward him. She put her hand against his chest and pushed him, she looked frightened, she opened her mouth but no words came. He stepped back, he tried to speak, but they moved aside from each other saying nothing" (47). Felix must overcome his own "lack of desire" (8) and his "unaccountable apprehension" of sensuality (42) to sire an heir, while Robin responds to his advances by cursing. She expresses her aversion to marriage and maternity by leaving Paris after the birth of her sickly son.

What then does the sad case of Felix Volkbein reveal? Lacking any memory of a significant past, Felix suffers from a confusion of identity which impels his scheme to beget a son. This contradictory project, undertaken despite his own sexual reticence with a woman uncertain of her gender, produces the ultimate expression of his alienation, a boy "too estranged to be argued with" whose existence entails the "demolition of [Felix's] own life" (108). Realizing that young Guido will never justify his own nobility, Felix appeals to the church to accept his son into a sacred order. The irony of this strategy lies in the recognition that Felix attempts to relieve his alienation by delivering his son into Christendom. But from the outset Barnes indicates that Felix, a veritable Wandering Jew, will never solve the problem of his exile and displacement: "No matter where and when you meet him you feel that he has come from some place—no matter from what place he has come—some country that he has devoured rather than resided in, some secret land that he has been nourished on but cannot inherit, for the Jew seems to be everywhere from nowhere" (7). Detached from history, bereft of a homeland, and obscurely alienated from his own sexuality, Felix suffers the classic ruptures of modernity. Clinging pathetically to traces of the Bourbon monarchy in Paris, he tries to assert the difference of his nobility in a period marked by the dissolving of such archaic distinctions.[58]

Explaining his attraction to Robin Vote, Felix declares his preference for an American wife because "with an American anything can be done" (39). In some way she epitomizes American democracy, for her surname alludes to the Nineteenth Amendment, which belatedly extended the ballot to American women. Her ambiguous, indefinite personality makes her (in the eyes of Felix) the mother of all possibilities. She indeed tries "to make everyone happy" (155), yet she remains distracted and desperate, the victim of ineradicable difficulties with gender, memory, and place. Barnes characterizes her as a "born somnabule, who lives in two worlds" (35), and of all the characters in *Nightwood*, Robin seems caught most precariously between the human order and the bestial, "a wild thing caught in a woman's skin" (146). As implied by her androgynous first name, her sexuality partakes of both genders; recurrently associated with white trousers, she is "a tall girl with the body of a boy" (46). Profoundly conflicted, she seems at once unsexed and promiscuous, devoid of desire yet wanton in behavior. In Paris she seeks out bars and churches, moving between the profane and the sacred; she shuttles between France and America, between heterosexuality and lesbianism. She moves from Felix to Nora, then to Jenny, then briefly to a girl named Sylvia. To all she remains a riddle; even the possessive Jenny admits: "I don't understand her at all, though I must say I understand her better than other people" (115).

Barnes displays this confusion most tellingly in Robin's peculiar fugue-like travel and compulsive cruising of the Parisian night world. When Felix begins to force his patriarchal, heterosexual will upon her, she reacts in singular fashion: "Robin prepared herself for her child with her only power: a stubborn cataleptic calm, conceiving herself pregnant before she was; and, strangely aware of some lost land in herself, she took to going out; wandering the countryside; to train travel, to other cities, alone and engrossed" (45). *Nightwood* projects her crisis of gender and identity in specifically geographical terms, as the search for a "lost land" within herself, perhaps some dreamed-of female utopia or simply the surrendered terrain of her privacy. When she returns to Paris, Robin takes "the Catholic vow" and attempts to find a literal sanctuary: "Many churches saw her: *St. Julien le Pauvre,* the church of *St. Germain des Prés, Ste. Clothilde.* . . . She strayed into the *rue Picpus,* into the gardens of the convent of *L'Adoration Perpetuelle*" (46). Her anxiety returns after the birth of Guido: "Robin took to wandering again, to intermittent travel from which she came back hours, days later, disinterested" (48). Then her search—a differently motivated, female version of Felix's quest for "the right street, the right café, the right building"—leads to her incessant prowling in bars and cafés among "people of every sort" (49). After visiting the United States, Robin returns to Paris with Nora and gradually resumes her roving ways; in the cafés she moves from "table to table, from drink to drink, from person to person," into the "night life" of the city. (59). Much later, she goes back to America with Jenny Petherbridge but again strays: "She began to haunt the terminals, taking trains into different parts of the country, wandering without design, going into many out-of-the-way churches, sitting in the darkest corner or standing against the wall" (167).

From the outset, Nora senses in Robin a profound disorientation and worries, after setting up housekeeping with her new companion, that "if she disarranged anything

Robin might become confused—might lose the scent of home" (56). Barnes points out that even people on the street recognize Robin's displacement: "It was this characteristic that saved her from being asked too sharply 'where' she was going; pedestrians who had it on the point of their tongues, seeing her rapt and confused, turned instead to look at each other" (60). Through their intimacy Nora realizes that "Robin had come from a world to which she would return" (58); she sings songs of a secret unknown life, "snatches of harmony as tell-tale as the possessions of a traveller from a foreign land." Yet Robin's actual provenance remains unidentified; though she has (according to Felix) a certain "'odour of memory,' like a person who has come from some place that we have forgotten and would give our life to recall" (118), she has no remembrance of that place of origin. Nowhere does she reflect explicitly upon her past; it seems not to exist. O'Connor observes that "she has difficulty in remembering herself" (121) and Nora suggests a connection between amnesia and errantry: "Robin can go anywhere, do anything . . . because she forgets" (152). This gap between present and past, so characteristic of modernism, estranges Robin Vote from any sense of American identity and leaves her exiled within a Parisian scene which fails to provide the refuge that she seeks. Hinting at this lack, Robin keeps "repeating in one way or another her wish for a home" (55). Her relentless, unconscious travels through the cities of Europe and America bring her no closer, however, to that "lost land" which stirs her nostalgia.

Her radical displacement and loss of memory seem linked ultimately to the gender confusion which complicates her emotional life. We know that Robin's indefinite sexuality and ambivalent desire make her a puzzle to others; Nora speculates that she "wants to be loved and left alone, all at the same time" (155). Robin indeed desires both "love and anonymity" (55), relationship and separateness, and the strange pattern of her compulsive wandering may be the acting out of this uncertainty. For we see that in each instance, her journeys coincide with new emotional encumbrances; they manifest her bid for the freedom of solitude. More poignantly, they perhaps reflect her effort to solve the dilemma of gender by avoiding the scene of desire.

Just as Robin's anguish arises from the undecidability of her sexual orientation, her repetition of symbolic infanticide expresses the very ambivalence which impels her wandering. Robin's first violent gesture occurs just after the birth of Guido: "One night, Felix, having come in unheard, found her standing in the centre of the floor holding the child high in her hand as if she were about to dash it down, but she brought it down gently" (48). Explaining her desperation to Felix, she exclaims furiously, "I didn't want him!" (49). She later repeats this gesture to different effect with Nora, who tells O'Connor: "Sometimes, if she got tight by evening, I would find her in the middle of the room in boy's clothes, rocking from foot to foot, holding the doll she had given us—"our child"—high above her head, as if she would cast it down, with a fury on her face" (147). To hurt Nora, Robin eventually smashes the doll, hurling it to the floor and "crushing her heel into it" until the china head has been reduced to dust. Marcus sees this violence as a reaction to Nora's love, said to be "possessive, patriarchal in its insistence on monogamy and control of the beloved."[59] But this reading conflates the original scene of threatened violence with its truly violent sequel, reducing Robin's act simply to a female resistance to male oppression. Through the "boy's clothes" that Robin wears, Barnes indicates, however, that the smashing of the doll has a different meaning than her threat to Guido. O'Connor speculates that "the last doll, given to age, is the girl who should have been a boy, and the boy who should have been a girl." He sees the doll as a sign of the gender trouble which causes its destruction. But his subsequent comment exposes the crux of Robin's problem: "The doll and the immature have something right about them, the doll because it resembles but does not contain life, and the third sex because it contains life but resembles the doll" (148). By suggesting a resemblance between the homosexual or lesbian and the doll, Barnes points to the paradox of the "third sex": that it both "contains life" and precludes procreation; that its members are alive but unable to reproduce. Nora later remarks that when a woman gives a doll to a woman, "it is the life they cannot have" (142). What Robin destroys is a figure of lesbian sterility, and the repetition of her gesture implies the despair of her bisexual androgyny: because she is both male and female, she can be neither homosexual nor heterosexual. Her tormenting ambivalence, projected in her wandering between intimacy and anonymity, makes Robin in some sense a victim of modernism and its erasure of difference.

The other androgyne of *Nightwood* presents quite a different version of the problem of modernist identity. Ironically Matthew O'Connor idealizes the maternal role which Robin rejects. The fantastic doctor tells Nora: "No matter what I may be doing, in my heart is the wish for children and knitting. God, I never asked better than to boil some good man's potatoes and toss up a child for him every nine months by the calendar" (91). This "womb envy" perhaps explains his blatant transvestism; when Nora comes to learn about the night, she finds him surrounded by cosmetics and lingerie: "From the half-open drawers of this chiffonier hung laces, ribands, stockings, ladies' underclothing and an abdominal brace, which gave the impression that the feminine finery had suffered venery" (78-79). With his cheeks "heavily rouged" and his "lashes painted," the doctor lies in bed wearing "a woman's flannel nightgown." This spectacle of cross-dressing, a travesty of the "feminine," reinscribes sexual difference only to imply that conventional markers of gender (rouge, stockings, painted lashes) are superficial, arbitrary, and potentially ludicrous.[60]

The doctor's transvestism forms but part of his complicated, ambiguous sexuality. As his monologues indicate, he possesses an extensive knowledge of homosexual Paris; he haunts the pissoirs and boasts that he can tell a man's arrondissement and quarter by the "size and excellence" of his sexual equipment. In matters anatomical he insists upon a geographical determinism: "Sea level and atmospheric pressure and topography make all the difference in the world!" (92). For O'Connor the "best port" for such trade is the place de la Bastille, though he himself inhabits the quarter around the Eglise St. Sulpice, lives on the rue Servandoni, and patronizes the Café de la Mairie du VIe. When Robin awakens in the Hôtel Récamier, she cannot quite identify the doctor: "She had seen him somewhere. But, as one may trade ten years at a certain shop and be unable to place the shopkeeper if he is met in the street or in the *promenoir* of a theatre, the shop being a portion of his identity, she struggled to place him now that he had moved out of his frame" (36-37). The doctor's "frame," the place St. Sulpice, indeed forms "a portion of his identity"; he has been seen there "buying holy pictures and *petit Jésus* in the *boutique* displaying vestments and flowering candles" (29). Barnes's designation of this neighborhood with its ecclesiastical shops as "the doctor's 'city'" helps to account for the tension between O'Connor's homosexual lubricity and his tirades against modern love and its maculate forms. The full extent of O'Connor's conflict with his own sexuality becomes apparent in the chapter "Go Down, Matthew," which (as its title suggests) functions as a prophetic utterance, a jeremiad against this "bloody time" (165).

In the café a defrocked priest extracts from O'Connor a clue to his contradictory sexuality. Asked if he has ever been married, the doctor claims that he has but adds, "What if the girl *was* the wife of my brother and the children my brother's children?" He subsequently demands, "Who's to say that I'm not my brother's wife's husband and that his children were not fathered in my lap?" (159-60). These allusions to incest, which might otherwise be dismissed as characteristic prattle, echo his self-incriminating question to Jenny and Robin: "What manner of man is it that has to adopt his brother's children to make a mother of himself, and sleeps with his brother's wife to get him a future—it's enough to bring down the black curse of Kerry" (73). This implied sexual transgression may explain both O'Connor's self-loathing and his homosexual orientation: he associates heterosexuality with the violation of a taboo.

Such a view reduces his gender confusion to an intelligible psychosexual complaint. But clearly the problem is more complicated, as we see when O'Connor (commenting on Nora's preference for "a girl who resembles a boy") delivers his most challenging analysis of sexual difference and desire:

> What is this love we have for the invert, boy or girl? It was they who were spoken of in every romance that we ever read. The girl lost, what is she but the Prince found? The Prince on the white horse that we have always been seeking. And the pretty lad who is a girl, what but the prince-princess in point lace—neither one and half the other, the painting on the fan! We love them for that reason. We were impaled in our childhood upon them as they rode through our primers, the sweetest lie of all, now come to be in boy or girl, for in the girl it is the prince, and in the boy it is the girl that makes the prince a prince—and not a man. They go far back in our lost distance where what we never had stands waiting; it was inevitable that we should come upon them for our miscalculated longing has created them.
>
> (136-37)

Barnes here reformulates the fairy-tale romance to show that its conventional grounding in heterosexual difference implies an equivalence between the "girl lost" and the "Prince found." In O'Connor's tortuous reading, the powerful fascination of the Prince lies precisely in his incorporation of the feminine. The doctor's critique effaces sexual difference to suggest that the androgynous Prince arouses "the prince" in the girl and "the girl" in the boy, producing by this transposition a longing for the same-sex figure in the romantic paradigm.[61]

This modernist version of the fairy-tale romance helps to explain the rampant sexual confusion of *Nightwood* and the particular difficulty of O'Connor, who persistently refers to himself as a "girl" and fancies that long ago he has been female: "In the old days I was possibly a girl in Marseilles thumping the dock with a sailor, and perhaps it's that memory that haunts me" (90-91). The doctor's alienation from his own sexuality becomes obvious in the darkness of the Eglise St. Merri when, weeping in anguish, he holds his penis (Tiny O'Toole) and asks, "What is this thing, Lord?" (132). For all of his theorizing with Felix and Nora, O'Connor is unable to fathom the mystery of himself and can only sigh: "C'est le plaisir qui me bouleverse" (it is pleasure which undoes me).[62] Like Robin, he vacillates between the night world of homosexual Paris and the churches within which he seeks to reconcile his male anatomy with his female longings. However, unlike Robin, who expresses gender ambivalence through evasions of sexuality, the doctor flaunts both his homosexuality and his transvestism. Though he inhabits the St. Sulpice quarter, his true domain is the "Town of Darkness" and the "unknown land" of night (81, 87); within this unreal, nocturnal world he acts out his estrangement from the world of everyday reality. The doctor articulates his fundamental displacement by insisting that "he's been everywhere at the wrong time and has now become anonymous" (82). Alienated from his American roots (the Barbary Coast of Pacific Street, San Francisco), from a past made unthinkable by incest, and from the sexual mistake of his male body, he lives out his exile in the shadow of St. Sulpice, apocalyptically warning fellow patrons of the Café de la Mairie du VI: "It's all over, everything's over, and nobody knows it but me. . . . Now, . . . the end—mark my words—now *nothing, but wrath and weeping*" (165-66).

In contrast to the grotesque afflictions of the doctor, the confusions of Nora Flood seem more plausible, perhaps because insofar as *Nightwood* carries autobiographical resonances, Nora most closely resembles Barnes herself.[63] Nora's significant connections with an American past and a native landscape appear in the chapter "Night Watch," where we learn of her estate near New York—a house "couched in the centre of a mass of tangled grass and weeds," a burial ground, and a "decaying chapel." In her home Nora hosts a strange salon "for poets, radicals, beggars, artists, and people in love; for Catholics, Protestants, Brahmins, dabblers in black magic and medicine" (50). At these "incredible meetings" of "paupers" and misfits, the mood is retrospective: "one felt that early American history was being re-enacted." In this singular ambience,

> the Drummer Boy, Fort Sumter, Lincoln, Booth, all somehow came to mind; Whigs and Tories were in the air; bunting and its stripes and stars, the swarm increasing slowly and accurately on the hive of blue; Boston tea tragedies, carbines, and the sound of a boy's wild calling; Puritan feet, long upright in the grave, striking the earth again, walking up and out of their custom; the calk of prayers thrust in the heart. And in the midst of this, Nora.
>
> (51)

Whereas Robin Vote recalls American democracy and women's suffrage, Nora becomes more broadly identified with the land and its settlers. She somehow personifies the idea of the "Westerner," conjures up images of "covered wagons," and has "the face of all people who love the people" (50-51). Thus rooted in a specific place and involved in American history, Nora seems an unlikely exile.

But when she meets Robin at the Denckman circus in New York in 1923, her orientation begins to change. Significantly Robin's first words to Nora at the circus initiate escape: "Let's get out of here." Outside, Robin's destination seems uncertain: "She looked about her distractedly. 'I don't want to be here.' But it was all she said; she did not explain where she wished to be" (55). Although this remark indeed signals the dislocation from which Robin can never escape, Nora with characteristic generosity assumes the impossible task of providing shelter, first in her home and then abroad. Their European travels take them "from Munich, Vienna and Budapest into Paris," where Nora buys an apartment—chosen by Robin—in the rue du Cherche-Midi.[64] The courtyard contains a symbolic figure, "a tall granite woman bending forward with lifted head," her hand "held over the pelvic round as if to warn a child who goes incautiously." The apartment amounts to a physical emblem of their relationship: "Every object in the garden, every item in the house, every word they spoke, attested to their mutual love, the combining of their humours" (55). After the onset of Robin's straying, however, this "museum of their encounter" becomes a source of suffering and "punishment" for Nora. While Robin wanders the cafés at night, Nora either stays home or stalks the streets "looking for what she's afraid to find," searching for "traces of Robin" yet "avoiding the quarter where she knew her to be, where by her own movements the waiters, the people on the terraces, might know that she had a part in Robin's life" (61).

Nora's relationship to Robin thus determines her movements and evasions in Paris. But the meaning of Nora's exile from America emerges only through the cryptic dream which recurs one night while she waits for Robin to return from her nocturnal adventures. This intricate dream re-presents Nora's American past, the house of her childhood, and a confusing encounter with her grandmother. Nora sees herself upstairs in her grandmother's room, which though full of furnishings seems empty, as "bereft as the nest of a bird which will not return." On the wall are "portraits of her uncle Llewellyn, who died in the Civil War," linking the place both to family history and to nineteenth-century America. From this room Nora looks down into an interior space, sees Robin, and calls out: "From round about her in anguish Nora heard her own voice saying, 'Come up, this is Grandmother's room,' yet knowing it was impossible because the room was taboo" (62). As Nora cries out, Robin seems to recede from her, and the room becomes suddenly strange and haunted: "This chamber that had never been her grandmother's, which was, on the contrary, the absolute opposite of any known room her grandmother had ever moved or lived in, was nevertheless saturated with the lost presence of her grandmother, who seemed in the continual process of leaving it." This bent, spectral figure recalls to the dreaming Nora an earlier incarnation of her grandmother, whom she had run into "at the corner of the house—the grandmother who, for some unknown reason, was dressed as a man, wearing a billycock and a corked mustache, ridiculous and plump in tight trousers and a red waistcoat, her arms spread saying with a leer of love, 'My little sweetheart.'" Nora subconsciously links the image of her grandmother disguised as a man with "something being done to Robin, Robin disfigured and eternalized by the hieroglyphics of sleep and pain" (63).

As improbable as any sequence in Kafka, this dream bears witness to a complex estrangement. It stages the conditions of Nora's exile from her own past and from the proprieties of her American childhood through the bizarre transformation by which her cross-dressed grandmother seems to express some form of sexual danger. While she is in the upstairs room, in the place of the grandmother, Nora makes an overture to the woman whom she loves; but she instantly recalls the "taboo" which places the room off limits and proscribes lesbian lovemaking.[65] Though she feels an attraction to Robin as the symbolic counterpart of her grandmother, whom she "loved more than anyone" (148), such a relationship literally has no place within the American setting: Robin, in the floor below, seems increasingly remote. In her apparition as a male, the grandmother subsequently acts out the confusion of gender and the deformation of desire, producing an image which may express the grandmother's experience of denial within marriage or (alternatively) the threat posed by Robin's androgyny or by her vulnerability to a disfiguring desire.

Ironically, as Nora awakens from this dream, she sees Robin outside her window in the embrace of Jenny Petherbridge. This moment marks a decisive turn, for as Barnes reports, "It was not long after this that Nora and Robin separated; a little later Jenny and Robin sailed for

America" (77). Nora thus finds herself alone in Paris, an exile for love yet deserted by her lover. Devastated by loss, she expresses her alienation through travel which seems aimless: "I sought Robin in Marseilles, in Tangier, in Naples, to understand her, to do away with my terror" (156). She also consults O'Connor, hoping to learn from him something about the unconscious urges which have led Robin away from her into the night world. Noting that "the day and the night are two travels," the doctor explains that while the French accept creatureliness and "filthiness," thinking of the day and night "as one continually," the American, obsessed by cleanliness, "separates the two for fear of indignities" (85). By this line of reflection, O'Connor means to suggest that Nora's own puritanical tendencies have alienated Robin. Later, Nora herself recalls a night in Montparnasse when Robin has reproached her: "'You are a devil! You make everything dirty!' (I had tried to take someone's hands off her. They always put hands on her when she was drunk.) 'You make me feel dirty and tired and old!'" (143). Ironically, though Nora has left America (presumably) to find the cultural freedom in which to pursue her unconventional relationship with Robin, the moral instincts of her American past obtrude to complicate her life in exile.

But Nora's problem goes beyond the puritanical inhibitions which she has carried to France. In a subsequent conversation with O'Connor, she tries to comprehend her continuing fixation upon Robin—her compulsive fascination with "a girl who resembles a boy" (136). Increasingly she understands the narcissistic aspect of this attraction: "A man is another person—a woman is yourself, caught as you turn in panic; on her mouth you kiss your own" (143). She later asks O'Connor: "Have you ever loved someone and it became yourself?" (152). Nora's discovery of her own narcissism exposes a paradox, however, for while she recognizes that her desire for Robin lies in the fact that she is not male and that in kissing this woman Nora kisses herself, still Robin "resembles a boy" and thus on some level represents to Nora the possibility of kissing and loving a male or, more radically, of becoming a male so that she can love a woman without encountering in her own guilt the resistance of patriarchal law. In Robin's androgyny, that is, Nora confronts the unresolved problem of her own unconscious sexual ambivalence. Through O'Connor's revelations of the bestial night world, she also glimpses the fearful aspect of her American rectitude: "There's something evil in me that loves evil and degradation—purity's black backside!" (135). These insights reveal Nora's estrangement from her prior American identity and suggest the emergence of an exilic self more attentive to the ambiguities which mark her relation to gender, memory, and place.

Out of these stories of obsession and displacement, Barnes constructs her haunting, dissonant novel. While Felix Volkbein embodies, almost prophetically, the fate of the Jew as the outcast of European modernism, O'Connor, Robin, Nora, and even the contemptible Jenny Petherbridge—about whom it is said that "the places [she] moults in are her only distinction" (97)—reflect the peculiar confusions of the American who is both exiled from homeland and marginalized in Paris as a denizen of the homosexual/lesbian night world. Although *Nightwood* closes with an American homecoming which reunites Robin and Nora in the deserted chapel, Barnes avoids romanticizing the exile's return, projecting it instead as a revolting event: into the night the distraught Nora runs "crusing and crying," only to find Robin "in her boy's trousers" in the throes of bestial frenzy, apparently attempting to mate with Nora's dog. In this scene, the "confusions and defeated anxieties" of *Nightwood* reach a grotesque climax; long alienated from her body, emptied of memory, and dislocated geographically, the anonymous Robin has at last become estranged from her own humanity, abandoning herself to animal instinct. In an age profoundly influenced by Freud's privileging of the id and his foregrounding of sexuality as the crucial determinant of psychic adjustment, Robin's "obscene" barking perhaps serves as Barnes's sardonic reminder that the unconscious, that locus of unspeakable urges, is not a pretty site.

During the early 1930s, Fitzgerald and Barnes both worked under heavy emotional burdens to complete novels which indirectly summarized their responses to the experience of exile and to the culture of modernism. Away from France, both portrayed characters caught up in and to some extent corrupted by the decadence of Paris (and Europe generally) in the late twenties and early thirties. Neither writer presumed to analyze the crisis of values which ensued in the decade after the Great War; rather, both took for granted an undercurrent of cynicism and despair, a revolution in sexual attitudes and practices, a pervasive sense of drift, and a widespread rootlessness, borne of the recognition that one could not go home again because there was no place of retreat from the violent, alluring transformations of modernism itself. Their respective novels portray a period of experiential perplexity, marked by the breakdown of those conceptual oppositions which seemed to give structure and certainty to everyday life.

Within this cultural matrix, Fitzgerald and Barnes saw Paris as a physical emblem of unreality; both portrayed the city through incongruous images reminiscent of dreams and nightmares, thereby reinforcing the psychological—and at times patently Freudian—implications of the stories they told. Though neither writer had much interest in geography for the sake of verisimilitude, both found the context of Paris in the twenties, particularly the city at night, conducive to the representation of *les années folles,* the crazy years. In the titles of their respective novels, these authors alluded to a nocturnal world at times seductive but more often chaotic or irrational. *Tender Is the Night* and *Nightwood* project an oneiric unreality through seemingly random movement, bizarre encounters, and disconcerting settings. For Fitzgerald, the house on the rue Monsieur which generates an "electric-like shock" with its unusual decor and "oddly bevelled mirrors" typifies his dreamlike distortion of Parisian places. Barnes likewise depicts an unreal scene when Nora looks out on the garden "in the faint light of dawn" to see "a double shadow falling from the statue, as if it were multiplying" (64). In *Nightwood,* as in *Tender Is the Night,* the strangeness of Paris conveys the alienation and confusion of characters who are themselves displaced and thus psychically detached from the city of exile.

The sense of place in these novels may be contrasted with the hallucinatory versions of Paris by French surrealist authors of the twenties and thirties. In narratives by Aragon, Breton, Soupault, Desnos, and Péret, the effect of strangeness emerges not from the perceived unreality of the material environment but conversely from an intimate knowledge of its particularity. For example, Aragon's *Paysan de Paris* transforms the Parc des Buttes-Chaumont into a fantastic site partly through a summary of inscriptions on an obelisk containing a directory of the nineteenth arrondissement.[66] This meticulous scrutiny of banal municipal "facts," in the context of a nighttime quest for mystical illumination, has the effect of defamiliarizing the obelisk and exposing its oddities—including the disclosure that the project was concocted by a traveling salesman. Similarly in *Nadja,* Breton exhibits his knowledge of Parisian places while recalling encounters with the visionary title character; in the place Dauphine, which Breton calls "one of the most profoundly secluded places I know of, one of the worst wastelands in Paris," a distracted Nadja seems to see a crowd of dead people massing in the darkness.[67] The dull, "wasteland" aspect of the place Dauphine contributes to the sinister impression which the narrative thus evokes. In Soupault's *Dernières Nuits de Paris* the narrator remarks that "places and environment have a profound influence on memory and imagination," and for several years the peculiarities of Paris obsessed the surrealists. Despite their disdain for certain aspects of French society and politics, they consistently manifested what Relph would call the perspective of "insideness" in their projections of a city rife with esoteric metaphors and signs.[68]

Their method of defamiliarizing a place understood in intimate detail helps to clarify the exilic perspective of "outsideness" in Fitzgerald and Barnes. By projecting a strangeness upon an obscure and sometimes incomprehensible cityscape, both writers suggest the anxieties of central characters afflicted by problems of American identity. Unfamiliar or threatening aspects of the Parisian scene objectify their intensely personal dilemmas. The surrealists represent the city mindful of its complex cultural meanings (which their works often subvert or challenge), whereas Barnes, Fitzgerald, and their American contemporaries inevitably write from the outside, even when they affect—as Hemingway does—what Relph aptly calls "vicarious insideness."[69] Allowing for obvious differences of style and content, we can see that both *Tender Is the Night* and *Nightwood* portray the experience of exile as a crisis in which the expatriate, opened to new desires in a seemingly unreal place, discovers internal contradictions and tensions. Paris thus figures as a fantastic scene of conflict and possibility, presenting those dilemmas of choice through which the self constructs and defines itself.

This is perhaps only an exaggerated version of the situation recreated in the narratives of Stein, Hemingway, and Miller. For them, Paris was the indispensable "world elsewhere" (to appropriate Richard Poirier's phrase), a city foreign enough in architecture, customs, and language to seem on some level exotic and thus to grant them a freedom from the constraints and inhibitions of American life as well as from the failures, real or imagined, of an American past. (It is worth noting that all of the writers discussed here had reached vocational impasses in America.) Paris granted the American a certain anonymity, a release from old routines and responsibilities, even an exemption from the duty to be one's old self. It presented the expatriate with the opportunity for metamorphosis, for the reformulation of ambitions, habits, and inclinations; the city thus nurtured an exilic identity, a different way of conceiving one's connections to place and populace. Paris also provided the conditions for writing, its very indifference to the foreigner ensuring the privacy essential to creative work. Finally, the strangeness of the French-speaking milieu produced a heightened consciousness of language itself and the tenuous relation between words and things which can be altered by crossing a linguistic border.

For these American writers, the city of exile thus remained to some extent alien and illegible. Amid the novelties of the modernist era, they gazed upon the same physical surroundings and social transformations observed by their French contemporaries. But they did so from a position of exteriority, tending to regard the city on some level as an illusory spectacle. Displaced from a native setting which though forsaken continued to determine their perception of difference, these writers developed attachments to Paris reflecting various levels of geographical understanding, cultural awareness, and linguistic competence. None, however, became entirely assimilated; none lost altogether that residual habit of mind which, for want of a more precise term, might be called "American." Repeatedly encountering those differences which set Paris and France apart from remembered American scenes, Stein, Hemingway, Miller, Fitzgerald, and Barnes all composed works which directly or indirectly contemplated the relationship between place and identity. These writers faced a common predicament: far from the homeland which once formed the ground of being, they found themselves in a great foreign city which remained ultimately elusive or inscrutable despite the local knowledge each had acquired. In texts as diverse as their own experiences, they portrayed the dilemma of the expatriate self, projecting imaginary versions of Paris which in their differing particulars suggest each writer's accommodation to the possibilities and risks of modernist displacement. Insistently, these narratives of exile also evoked the nagging question of American identity, because the encounter with cultural difference typically exposed—as it did for James's Lambert Strether—the presence of an obstinate American self. Reflecting upon his return from Europe in "American Letter," Archibald MacLeish examined his simultaneous longing for "a land far off, alien" and his bone-deep ties to a country that is "neither a place nor a blood name." Summing up these contradictions he observed: "It is a strange thing to be an American." Nowhere was that strangeness more keenly felt or more brilliantly translated into modernist texts than in the Paris of writing.

Notes

1. Stephen Kern, *The Culture of Time and Space: 1880-1918* (Cambridge: Harvard University Press, 1983). Subsequent references to Kern's study will be given parenthetically.

2. The standard accounts of these movements appear in Malcolm Cowley, *Exile's Return,* and Paul Fussell, *Abroad: British Literary Traveling Between the Wars* (New York: Oxford University Press, 1980), in which the comment on placelessness appears (70).

3. Alan Bullock, "The Double Image," in *Modernism, 1890-1930,* ed. Malcolm Bradbury and James McFarlane (New York: Viking Penguin, 1976), 66.

4. James McFarlane, "The Mind of Modernism," in *Modernism, 1890-1930,* 80-81.

5. See Roger Shattuck, *The Banquet Years: The Origins of the Avant-Garde in France, 1885 to World War I* (New York: Vintage, 1958), 340-45.

6. McFarlane, "The Mind of Modernism," 81.

7. Malcolm Bradbury, "The Cities of Modernism," in *Modernism 1890-1930,* 98-99.

8. Raymond Williams, "The Metropolis and the Emergence of Modernism," in *Unreal City: Urban Experience in Modern European Literature and Art,* ed. Edward Timms and David Kelley (New York: St. Martin's, 1985), 21.

9. See Matthew J. Bruccoli, *The Composition of "Tender Is the Night"* (Pittsburgh: University of Pittsburgh Press, 1963). Bruccoli provides an indispensable reconstruction and analysis of the various manuscript and typescript versions.

10. James Mellow, *Invented Lives: F. Scott and Zelda Fitzgerald* (Boston: Houghton Mifflin, 1984), 168.

11. André LeVot, "Fitzgerald in Paris," *Fitzgerald/Hemingway Annual 1973,* ed. Matthew J. Bruccoli and C. E. Frazer Clark, Jr. (Washington: Microcard Editions, 1974), 49-50.

12. Edmund Wilson, letter to F. Scott Fitzgerald, 5 July 1921, *Letters on Literature and Politics, 1912-1972,* ed. Elena Wilson (New York: Farrar, Straus & Giroux, 1977), 63.

13. See André LeVot, *F. Scott Fitzgerald: A Biography,* trans. William Byron (Garden City, N.Y.: Doubleday, 1983), 235-37.

14. Scottie, a Parisian schoolgirl, was left in the custody of a nursemaid. In addition to his trips to Paris, Fitzgerald also made a hasty journey to the United States in early 1931 to attend his father's funeral in Maryland.

15. *The Short Stories of F. Scott Fitzgerald,* ed. Matthew J. Bruccoli (New York: Scribner's, 1989), 580, 594.

16. Roy R. Male, "'Babylon Revisited': A Story of the Exile's Return," in *Modern Critical Views: F. Scott Fitzgerald,* ed. Harold Bloom (New York: Chelsea House, 1985), 94.

17. *The Short Stories of F. Scott Fitzgerald,* 633. Subsequent parenthetical page references to "Babylon Revisited" correspond to this edition.

18. For an analysis of parallels between "Babylon Revisited" and *Tender Is the Night,* as well as a discussion of two other Fitzgerald stories thematically related to the novel ("Two Wrongs" and "The Rough Crossing"), see Richard D. Lehan, "*Tender Is the Night,*" in "*Tender Is the Night*: Essays in Criticism," ed. Marvin J. LaHood (Bloomington: Indiana University Press, 1969), 61-85.

19. Bruce L. Grenberg, "Fitzgerald's 'Figured Curtain': Personality and History in *Tender Is the Night,*" in *Critical Essays on F. Scott Fitzgerald's "Tender Is the Night,"* ed. Milton R. Stern (Boston: G. K. Hall, 1986), 221.

20. See F. Scott Fitzgerald, *Tender Is the Night* (New York: Scribner's, 1934), 159-62, for his emulation of cinematic montage. Subsequent parenthetical page references to the novel correspond to this edition.

21. From 1925-30, Fitzgerald worked on the Melarky version, which hinged on a young Hollywood technician's hatred of his mother and on his attraction to a glamorous expatriate couple, Seth and Dinah Roreback (or Piper). Bruccoli insists that "nothing of Francis' personality clings to Rosemary," who is a "completely feminine creature." See Bruccoli, *The Composition of "Tender Is the Night,"* 95-96.

22. Commenting on Dick Diver's own ambivalent sexual impulses, James E. Miller, Jr. notes the "strange element in Nicole's relationship to him," presaged by a passage in one of her early letters to him: "I have only gotten to like boys who are rather sissies. Are you a sissy?" See Miller, "*Tender Is the Night,*" in "*Tender Is the Night*": Essays in Criticism, 98.

23. Grenberg, "Fitzgerald's 'Figured Curtain,'" 213-15.

24. Modris Eksteins, *Rites of Spring: The Great War and the Birth of the Modern Age* (Boston: Houghton Mifflin, 1989), 293.

25. See Kern, *The Culture of Time and Space,* 25.

26. Alan Trachtenberg, "The Journey Back: Myth and History in *Tender Is the Night,*" in *Critical Essays on "Tender Is the Night,"* 172. The problem of time also created nagging doubts for Fitzgerald about the proper arrangement of the novel—whether (as in the original version) to use a long flashback in book two to recount Dick's career and his romance with Nicole, or whether to tell the story chronologically, as in Malcolm Cowley's 1951 revised version.

27. Fitzgerald referred to a similar American deracination in his notebooks: "In England, property begot a strong sense of place, but Americans, restless and with shallow roots, needed fins and wings." See *The Notebooks of F. Scott Fitzgerald,* ed. Matthew J. Bruccoli (New York: Harcourt Brace Jovanovich, 1978), 35.

28. Fitzgerald indulges here in subtle sentimentality; as Grenberg points out, the "red-haired girl from Tennessee" looking for the grave of her brother marks an anachronism: the American army did not fight at the Somme; the U.S. did not enter the war until 1917.

29. See Eksteins, *Rites of Spring,* 257-58. Grenberg sees Dick's "infatuation with Rosemary" as a symptom of his brief "love affair with modernity." See Grenberg, "Fitzgerald's 'Figured Curtain,'" 225.

30. Noting that the same setting was used in Fitzgerald's 1929 short story "The Swimmers," André LeVot points out Fitzgerald's topographical "mistake": although the house is said to be "hewn from the frame of Cardinal de Retz's palace," the seventeenth-century prelate never lived on the rue Monsieur, a street created in the eighteenth century. See LeVot, "Fitzgerald in Paris," 65.

31. In an early version of the novel, Francis takes a romantic interest in a young woman named Wanda Brested, who is associated with a lesbian coterie. In one scene, Francis finds Wanda in the company of three other girls with mannequins' heads. See the facsimile edition of the Melarky-narrator version, Matthew J. Bruccoli, ed., *F. Scott Fitzgerald Manuscripts, Tender Is the Night,* vol. 2 (New York: Garland, 1990), 164.

32. Fitzgerald speaks of this wave of American violence in "Echoes of the Jazz Age," in *The Crack Up,* ed. Edmund Wilson (New York: New Directions, 1945), 20.

33. The same signs and shop windows appear in the opening paragraphs of the 1929 short story "The Swimmers."

34. There was no such street in the fashionable sixteenth arrondissement near Passy, but there was a passage St.-Ange (masculine) near the Porte de St. Ouen in a working-class neighborhood in the seventeenth arrondissement. By placing the Films Par Excellence studio at 341, rue des Saintes-Anges, Fitzgerald makes the angels feminine and plural, again implying the doubling of Dick's relationship to Nicole in his attachment to Rosemary.

35. In 1931 Fitzgerald superciliously noted the influx of American ethnic types in Paris about 1928: "There was something sinister about the crazy boatloads." See "Echoes of the Jazz Age," 20.

36. See Fitzgerald, "Echoes of the Jazz Age," 15-17.

37. Typical of extant criticism is Mary E. Burton's remark that "the inclusion of the Negro murder remains mysterious." She speculates that since earlier versions of the novel included a homicide, Fitzgerald "felt impelled to include a murder somehow—perhaps quickly to bring the reader up against the unreality and 'enchanted' quality of the Divers' lives by a shocking intrusion of reality from the passions and problems of another class and race." See Mary E. Burton, "The Counter-Transference of Doctor Diver," *Journal of English Literary History* 38 (1971): 469.

38. This same anxiety recurs later when Dick worries about the bathwater his children have shared with the Indian stepchildren of Mary North Minghetti. Mary's Asian husband is said to be "not quite light enough to travel in a Pullman south of Mason-Dixon" (258). My own understanding of the race problem in this novel has been enriched by the work of Felipe Smith, who argues persuasively that the author's symbolic treatment of race in *Tender Is the Night* "amounts to an elaboration of the racial holocaust he had hinted at in *The Beautiful and the Damned* and *The Great Gatsby.*" See Felipe Smith, "The Dark Side of Paradise: Race and Ethnicity in the Novels of F. Scott Fitzgerald," Ph.D. diss., Louisiana State University, 1988, 207.

39. At a Swiss ski resort about five months after the Parisian episode, Dick becomes briefly fixated upon a "special girl" at the table behind him (174); subsequently Fitzgerald reports: "He was in love with every pretty woman he saw now, their forms at a distance, their shadows on a wall" (201).

40. See *F. Scott Fitzgerald Manuscripts, Tender Is the Night,* vol. 4, part 2, 251-55.

41. Jean Méral, *Paris in American Literature,* trans. Laurette Long (Chapel Hill: University of North Carolina Press, 1989), 162, 176.

42. Andrew Field, *Djuna: The Life and Times of Djuna Barnes* (New York: G. P. Putnam, 1983), 29.

43. As Field points out, Barnes's earliest contribution to *McCall's* did not appear until 1925; she may also have had an arrangement with *Vanity Fair,* where her articles, poems, plays, and satires began to appear in 1922. See *Djuna,* 104, 129. Throughout his eccentric book, Field rarely provides specific documentation for such biographical details; yet his is the only full-length study of Barnes' life currently available.

44. Djuna Barnes, "Vagaries Malicieux," *The Double Dealer* 3 (1922): 249, 251, 256, 258.

45. Barnes's short stories from this period appeared in *A Book* (1923), *A Night Among the Horses* (1929), and *Spillway* (1962).

46. See Field, *Djuna,* 43. Some of the evidence for the impromptu marriage rests on literary inference. In the original version of *Nightwood* (titled *Bow Down*) and in *The Antiphon* (1958), Barnes's late verse drama, there are scenes suggesting that the author

experienced the "wedding" as a rape. See also Mary Lynn Broe, "My Art Belongs to Daddy," in *Women's Writing in Exile*, ed. Mary Lynn Broe and Angela Ingram (Chapel Hill: University of North Carolina Press, 1989), 42-43, 69-73.

47. For the remark about Thelma Wood, see Field, *Djuna*, 101. Barnes had friendships with a number of lesbian women, including Mary Pyne in New York and Natalie Clifford Barney in Paris. But there was apparently no cohabitation or sustained intimacy. Such matters are, of course, crudely speculative; they arise here only because Barnes's sexual ambivalence figures crucially in *Nightwood*.

48. Donna Gerstenberger, "The Radical Narrative of Djuna Barnes's *Nightwood*," in *Breaking the Sequence: Women's Experimental Fiction*, ed. Ellen G. Friedman and Miriam Fuchs (Princeton: Princeton University Press, 1989), 130.

49. Carolyn Burke points out that "*Ulysses* and *Finnegan's Wake*, which she followed closely as *Work in Progress*, confirmed Barnes in her own idiosyncratic modernism." See Carolyn Burke, "'Accidental Aloofness': Barnes, Loy, and Modernism," in *Silence and Power: A Reevaluation of Djuna Barnes*, ed. Mary Lynn Broe (Carbondale: Southern Illinois University Press, 1991), 73. To date, the most authoritative study of the little magazines is Hugh Ford's *Published in Paris: American and British Writers, Printers, and Publishers in Paris, 1920-1930* (New York: Macmillan, 1975).

50. See Karen Kaivola, *All Contraries Confounded: The Lyrical Fiction of Virginia Woolf, Djuna Barnes, and Marguerite Duras* (Iowa City: University of Iowa Press, 1991), 63; Judith Lee, "*Nightwood*: 'The Sweetest Lie,'" in *Silence and Power*, 207; Jane Marcus, "Laughing at Leviticus: *Nightwood* as Woman's Circus Epic," in *Silence and Power*, 231.

51. Gerstenberger, "The Radical Narrative of Djuna Barnes's *Nightwood*," 130.

52. Marcus, "Laughing at Leviticus," 223.

53. Kaivola, *All Contraries Confounded*, 94.

54. James B. Scott, "Reminiscences," in *Silence and Power*, 344.

55. Studies of the original, uncut manuscript suggest that Eliot may have excised some provocative material. But on the basis of the published text alone, we can infer that Barnes was not much inclined toward erotic relations; what matters, at least for the women in *Nightwood*, is the difference between solitude and companionship.

56. Julie L. Abraham, "'Woman, Remember You': Djuna Barnes and History," in *Silence and Power*, 257. Attributing a prescience to Barnes, Jane Marcus goes further, seeing the "lesbians, blacks, circus people, Jews, [and] transvestites" of *Nightwood* as a prophetic grouping of "soon-to-be-exterminated human types," in "Laughing at Leviticus," 231.

57. Felix betrays the limits of his own memory when he shows Robin historical sites: "He tried to explain to her what Vienna had been before the war; what it must have been before he was born; yet his memory was confused and hazy, and he found himself repeating what he had read" (43).

58. Our last glimpse of Felix finds him back in Vienna, bowing madly and pathetically to a man he assumes to be the Grand Duke Alexander of Russia (123).

59. Marcus, "Laughing at Leviticus," 234.

60. Benstock points out that this transvestism "calls attention to woman's role as *ornament* in society." See *Women of the Left Bank*, 258.

61. Insisting that the "prince-princess" personifies not androgyny but narcissism, Judith Lee construes "the myth of romantic love" as "the sweetest lie" to support a circular argument that "male and female are inherently and inevitably incompatible." See "*Nightwood*: 'The Sweetest Lie,'" 209, 212.

62. Marcus speculates plausibly that O'Connor is a parodic version of Dr. Freud and that his "womb envy is so strong that it parodies Freudian penis envy mercilessly." See "Laughing at Leviticus," 233.

63. In a reminiscence, Hank O'Neal reports that Barnes identified the model for Nora as Henrietta Metcalf. See *Silence and Power*, 351.

64. Barnes doubtless chose the rue du Cherche-Midi because it was around the corner from the apartment she shared with Thelma Wood at 9, rue St.-Romain.

65. Mary Lynn Broe underscores the patently lesbian intimacy between Barnes and her grandmother, Zadel Gustafson Barnes, in "My Art Belongs to Daddy," in *Women's Writing in Exile*, 42. We may expect further elaboration of this issue in the forthcoming volume of Barnes' letters, *Cold Comfort*, being edited by Mary Lynn Broe and Frances McCullough.

66. Louis Aragon, *Nightwalker (Le Paysan de Paris)*, trans. Frederick Brown (1926; Englewood Cliffs, N.J.: Prentice-Hall, 1970), 133.

67. André Breton, *Nadja*, trans. Richard Howard (1928; New York: Grove Press, 1960), 80, 83.

68. Philippe Soupault, *Last Nights of Paris*, trans. William Carlos Williams (1928; New York: Macaulay, 1929), 53, 73, 129. Marie-Claire Bancquart speaks of the veritable "cult of Paris" developed by surrealists for whom the city was a site of quest and initiation as well as a source of metaphors and signs. See Bancquart, *Paris des Surréalistes*, 186, 189, 199.

69. Relph, *Place and Placelessness*, 52-53.

Samuel Lyndon Gladden (essay date 2000)

SOURCE: Gladden, Samuel Lyndon. "'Sebastian Melmoth': Wilde's Parisian Exile as the Spectacle of Sexual, Textual Revolution." *Victorians Institute Journal* 28 (2000): 39-63.

[*In the following essay, Gladden analyzes Oscar Wilde's journal, written under the pseudonym Sebastian Melmoth, in terms of his thoughts about being exiled from England after serving his prison term.*]

> Many men on their release carry their prison about with them into the air, and hide it as a secret disgrace in their hearts, and at length, like poor poisoned things, creep into some hole and die. It is wretched that they should have to do so, and it is wrong, terribly wrong, of society that it should force them to do so. . . . For I have come, not from obscurity into the momentary notoriety of crime, but from a sort of eternity of fame to a sort of eternity of infamy, and sometimes seem to myself to have shown, if indeed it required showing, that between the famous and the infamous there is but one step, if as much as one.
>
> —Oscar Wilde, *De Profundis*

> Every one is born a king, and most people die in exile, like most kings.
>
> —Oscar Wilde, *A Woman of No Importance*

> Exile, n. One who serves his country by residing abroad.
>
> —Ambrose Bierce, *The Devil's Dictionary*

In recent years, much scholarship has been devoted to a reevaluation of Oscar Wilde, arguably the most famous—and certainly the most infamous—of all late nineteenth-century British writers; such scholarship, in particular Ed Cohen's groundbreaking study of fin-de-siècle constructions of masculinity in *Talk on the Wilde Side,* has demonstrated the centrality of the figure of Wilde to late nineteenth-century British culture and to emerging debates over the pathology of sexuality and disease or, to use an appropriate but unfortunately ubiquitous Deconstructionist metaphor, dis-ease. However, comparatively little substantive criticism has been written about Wilde's brief life following his release from Reading Gaol on 18 May 1897, a period Wilde spent traveling throughout Europe until his journey culminated in Paris at the rather run-down Hôtel D'Alsace, a decidedly unglamorous locale which, ironically, witnessed the death of Wilde, the nineteenth century's most famous Æsthete.

Wilde's oft-repeated "deathbed" remark, "Either the curtains go, or I do," reminds us of the writer's lifelong association with æstheticism, his appreciation for beauty. In truth, Wilde's remark preceded his death by about a month,[1] when he did indeed disparage the decor of his embarrassingly thrifty rooms in the Hôtel D'Alsace, rooms whose ambiance dramatically lowered the standards to which Wilde had become accustomed long before his sudden fall from success and his imprisonment in Reading Gaol, where he served two years hard labor as punishment for acts of "gross indecency." Wilde's clever remark nevertheless figures as an important paratext for the final phase of his life, for his anxiety over the decor of his last room metonymizes the whole history of Wilde's retreat into exile following his release from prison in 1897. Rather than following other critics in dismissing Wilde's final years as completely devoid of artistic or personal meaning, I want instead to chart the ways in which Wilde's Parisian exile demonstrates a revolutionary impulse even amidst the dramatic decline of the writer's tragically abbreviated life; specifically, I want to unravel the threads of meaning woven throughout Wilde's exilic pseudonym, "Sebastian Melmoth," in order to demonstrate how that name functions as a code for the revolutionary.[2]

Following his release from prison, Wilde left England for Europe, settling finally in Paris, that prototypical nineteenth-century site of Revolutionary excess, where, like a criminal, he adopted an assumed name, an alias: "Sebastian Melmoth." Even before leaving prison, Wilde remarked on his investment in the processes of naming; lamenting in *De Profundis* the shame his actions brought upon his family and his country, Wilde anticipates his decision to contrive an alias and to abandon the country, clearly in an effort to leave behind the name and the nation he has already so besmirched:

> [My mother] and my father had bequeathed me a name they had made noble and honoured, not merely in literature, art, archæology, and science, but in the public history of my own country, in its evolution as a nation. I had disgraced that name eternally. I had made it a low byword among low people. I had dragged it through the very mire. I had given it to brutes that they might make it brutal, and to fools that they might turn it into a synonym for folly. What I suffered then, and still suffer, is not for pen to write or paper to record.
>
> (27-28)

The passage effectively announces Wilde's disinclination to review the history of his disgrace and shame; more importantly, the passage anticipates Wilde's decision to abandon both the name and the nation that witnessed his decline. In assuming an alias and in moving away from England, Wilde's desire not to record the history of his downfall will, he hopes, be realized, and indeed, in France, "Sebastian Melmoth" would find what Oscar Wilde lost in England—freedom, contentment, and some measure of self-respect.

More generally, the significance of Wilde's alias resonates on the broader levels of politics, history, art, and identity formation. "Sebastian Melmoth" imbricates two nineteenth-century manifestations of revolution by conjoining a code for an emerging identity, the homosexual (suggested by the name "Sebastian"), and shorthand for a style of writing, the Gothic (suggested by the name "Melmoth," the title character of the 1820 Gothic novel *Melmoth the Wanderer,* an enormously popular work penned by Wilde's great uncle, Charles Robert Maturin). Wilde's alias calls to mind both the textual strategy that marked early nineteenth-century responses to the French Revolution and the notorious lifestyle that galvanized fin-de-siècle discourse as the site and the sight—the space and the spectacle—of an erotic revolution that threatened to return the world to the chaos of another Great Terror. As we shall see, Wilde's fin-de-siècle self-exile conflates a revolutionary identity and a revolutionary literary style, so that in retreating into infamy, Wilde-as-"Sebastian Melmoth" embodies a complex hybrid of nineteenth-century manifestations of subversion, dissent, and chaos—in short, the seeds of revolution.[3]

From the earliest days of his fame, Wilde had been recognized—marked—as a symbolic figure for a literary or artistic style as well as for the lifestyle of the Decadent. Max Nordau's 1892 tome on the decay of modern society, *Degeneration*, pointed specifically to Wilde as the emblem for this anti-social, unhealthy movement:

> [t]he ego-mania of decadentism, its love of the artificial, its aversion to nature, and to all forms of activity and movement, its megalomaniacal contempt for men and its exaggeration of the importance of art, have found their English representative among the 'Æsthetes,' the chief of whom is Oscar Wilde.
>
> (317)

Wilde, Nordau argues, "despises nature," is "a 'cultivator of the Ego,'" and revels in "inactivity," "contemplation," "immorality, sin and crime" (320-321).

Wilde's elevation—or decline—to the level of symbol was not lost on the writer, who self-consciously represented himself as such upon the publication of *The Ballad of Reading Gaol*, a meditation on public humiliation, notoriety, shame, and redemption, which Wilde wrote while in prison and for which he substituted his prison-cell identity, "c.3.3," in place of his own name on the title page (Ellmann 559). Astonished when the poem sold 5099 copies—barely three months after its first printing—Wilde agreed to insert his own name in brackets next to "c.3.3" to claim authorship directly (560). By this time, of course, such a gloss was hardly necessary, for the poem's readers knew that Wilde and "c.3.3"—name and number, identity and symbol—were one and the same. The frontispiece to the 1924 Methuen and Company edition of the *Ballad*, a woodcut by Frans Masereel, neatly comments on Wilde's status as symbol: the author's face—his image—is obfuscated by a black text-box, a dark cell, which contains Wilde's cell-block identity, reminding the reader that in falling into infamy, Wilde "shifted" from author (one who produces text) to text itself (that which is to be read), from one who composes or controls meaning (subject) to one who is mastered by the disciplining eyes of others (object).

Wilde's self-representation-as-symbol percolates throughout *De Profundis*, his lengthy prison-house letter to Lord Alfred Douglas, as well: Wilde recognizes his status as ". . . a man who stood in symbolic relations to the art and culture of my age. I had realised this for myself at the very dawn of my manhood, and had forced my age to realise it afterwards" (36). Among the letter's most heart-wrenching passages is Wilde's account of his transfer to prison, during which his protracted stay on a railway platform exposed him to the taunts and jeers of passersby:

> Everything about my tragedy has been hideous, mean, repellent, lacking in style. . . . On November 13th, 1895, I was brought down here from London. From two o'clock till half-past two on that day I had to stand on the centre platform of Clapham Junction in convict dress, and handcuffed, for the world to look at. . . . Of all possible objects I was the most grotesque. When people saw me they laughed. Each train as it came up swelled the audience. Nothing could exceed their amusement. That was, of course, before they knew who I was. As soon as they had been informed they laughed still more. For half an hour I stood there in the grey November rain surrounded by a jeering mob.
>
> (103)

Wilde's status as spectacle found no reprieve inside the prison walls, either; writing in the 31 July 1895 edition of the *Echo de Paris*, Ange Goldemar describes glimpsing the disgraced Wilde through a window and, recognizing that figure's shame, feeling compelled to turn away from the image:

> The door closes. It's Wilde. His first gesture is to stretch out his arms; then he takes off his cap. He is barely recognizable. Not that he has lost so much weight—his frame is still hefty, his shoulders broad. . . . His face seems to give the appearance of health, despite the yellowish tinge which has replaced the rosiness of before. The change is all in his head, hideously shaved, almost bald in an awful prison tonsure that reduces Wilde's head to insignificant dimensions, dull, doll-like, expressionless. . . . Several of us [left] the observation post behind the barred window, so overcome were we by the spectacle.
>
> (trans. and qtd. in Erber 574-575)

Clearly, Wilde had become, as he recognizes at the close of *De Profundis*, "[l']enfant de mon siècle" (119), an exhausted, fallen, beleaguered embodiment of an age drained by what Karl Beckson characterizes as "the damnation of Decadence" (32). In another passage from *De Profundis* that echoes the language of Nordau's *Degeneration*, Wilde casts his own body as a corporeal manifestation of the degenerate text, lamenting that

> . . . I am quite conscious of the fact that when the end does come I shall return an unwelcome visitant to a world that does not want me; a *revenant*, as the French say, and one whose face is grey with long imprisonment and crooked with pain. Horrible as are the dead when they rise from their tombs, the living who come out from tombs are more horrible still. Of all this I am only too conscious.
>
> (6)

In private conversation, Wilde observed that he could not possibly outlive the fin-de-siècle culture he had come to symbolize: three months before his death, Wilde remarked that "[i]f another century began, and I [were] still alive, . . . it would really be more than the English could stand" (qtd. in Coakley 215). But the twentieth century nonetheless kept alive Wilde's spirit—or his demon, as many might have disparaged it—as a symbolic embodiment of the outcast, the "other." Much like the Spaniard of *Melmoth the Wanderer*, upon whose presence "[a]ll order is broken, all discipline subverted" (Maturin 162), "[i]ntellectual, artistic and erotic life in the years leading up to World War I was lived in the shadow of the Oscar Wilde debacle," writes historian Ian Young, for "[t]he persecution of Wilde served to frighten and mute intellectual and sexual heretics for decades" (264). Wilde's symbolic life extends even beyond the death of the writer's physical body, too; in the late twentieth century, pop-culture references to Wilde still conjured the specter of homosexuality, whether in covert affiliations with "the love that dare not speak its name" or as an epithet of derision.[4]

Wilde's meteoric rise and fall collapses any clear distinction between the categories of public and private, as well as the corollary categories of production (of the text) and pleasure (of the Decadent). Recalling what he characterizes as "the Romantic '90s," Wilde's friend Richard Le Gallienne situates the author as a symbolic figure for the Decadent age, a latter-day Caliban whose response to his own horrifyingly primitive image remains endlessly conflicted: Le Gallienne writes, "[h]e is, beyond comparison, the incarnation of the spirit of the '90s. . . . Out of the 1890s chaos [Wilde] emerged [as] an astonishing, imprudent microcosm. In him[,] the period might see its own face in a glass" (156, 157). Sixteen years after Wilde's death, another of the writer's contemporaries, John Cowper Powys, agreed with Le Gallienne's assessment, writing of Wilde that "[h]is influence is everywhere, like an odour, like an atmosphere, like a diffused flame. We cannot escape from him" (417). Powys' assessment is, admittedly, a complicated and ambivalent one, for even as he seems to pay homage to the figure of Wilde, the image he constructs of an age attempting to "flee" from Wilde's influence suggests a lingering anxiety over the author's symbolic place in British culture, his ambiguous status as both hero and villain, both angel and devil.

A good deal of Wilde's later correspondence addresses the problems of self-representation, the traps of symbolic status. In an April 1898 letter written in response to a poem by Henry D. Davray, Wilde considers the role and meaning of the outcast, and he carefully distinguishes the outcast from the more general category of the underprivileged by aligning the outcast with figures of notoriety—of, one could suggest, rampant publicity; in exemplifying the outcast, Wilde names Lord Byron, another literary giant whose notorious reputation chased him into exile, as well (*Letters* 729). Just one month before, Wilde wrote to Robbie Ross about his situation in exile, musing cynically on his status as an outcast, particularly as it had emerged in English press attacks on his work and lifestyle: citing W. E. Henley's hostile review of *The Ballad of Reading Gaol*, Wilde writes that, "I am quite obliged to [Henley] for playing the rôle of *Advocatus Diaboli* so well. Without it my beatification as a saint would have been impossible, but I shall now live as the Infamous St. Oscar of Oxford, Poet and Martyr" (720). Just a few days later, however, Wilde's ambivalence about his status as a symbolic figure—a wounded hero, a martyr—emerges in a letter to George Ives: considering the unprecedented success of the *Ballad*, Wilde writes, "I have no doubt we [exiles] shall win, but the road is long, and red with monstrous martyrdoms" (721). One of the martyrdoms about which Wilde might have been thinking was the death of John Keats, whom Wilde eulogized in a sonnet entitled "The Grave of Keats" by memorializing the poet as "[t]he youngest of the Martyrs" and by comparing the long-suffering Keats to St. Sebastian, a figure Wilde sets as Keats' equal in beauty and his predecessor in an untimely death (42).[5]

We see in Wilde's own words, then, his understanding of his status as a symbolic figure as well as his struggle to come to terms with his new role as a particular type of martyr, an exile, one who has been pushed "out" of British culture even as his absence—his emptiness, his reduction to pure symbol, his devaluation to the status of nothing—assumes a central place in British culture as the image of the "other," that figure whose very difference threatens to undermine the bases of mainstream British society. Perhaps in response to this recognition, Wilde begins traveling and corresponding under a name of his own invention, thereby creating for himself a new identity. Wilde's letters connect his motivation for taking on an alias with his desire to travel and to correspond undetected, to "pass" in European culture as something other than its "other," despite the fact that he understood himself to be a spectacle no less recognizable to—and no less sought after by—English tourists than the Eiffel Tower (Ellmann 586). Thus failing in its intended value as a shield around the notoriously symbolic figure, Wilde's alias operates instead as a screen upon which an entire constellation of differences is projected, a map according to which a variety of fin-de-siècle anxieties may be cartographized. Just as Wilde exemplified the corporeal manifestation of otherness, of, to borrow Beckson's phrase, "the damnation of Decadence" (32), so too did his alias emerge as a textual manifestation of the very forces for which he had been excoriated. Specifically, these may be described as the forces of revolution, both sexual and textual, private and public.[6]

While residing at the Hôtel d'Alsace in Paris, Wilde composed a letter to Louis Wilkinson on 4 January 1900 which closed with Wilde's response to Wilkinson's query about his assumed name. Wilde explains:

> You asked me about "Melmoth:" of course I have not changed my name: in Paris I am as well known as in London: it would be childish. But to prevent postmen having fits I sometimes have my letters inscribed with the name of a curious novel by my grand-uncle, Maturin: a novel that was part of the romantic revival of the early century, and though imperfect, a pioneer. . . .
>
> (*Letters* 813)

Wilde's explanation rings with *double-entendre,* primarily with the description of Maturin's novel as "curious," a term which by the late 1890s had entered English *parlance* as slang, or code, for homosexual (Holder 53) or, to use a term Wilde himself might have invoked, for "Uranian"; secondarily, Wilde's characterization of the novel as "a pioneer" must also be read symbolically, for surely Wilde was a pioneer as well, not only in the sense that he was the first generally recognized Uranian, but also in that in leaving his homeland and making a place for himself in Paris, Wilde, like a pioneer, was staking out new territory to claim a space for himself in a seemingly distant and exotic land. In another letter, Wilde describes Maturin's novel as "an extinct volcano" (Coakley 209-210), again suggesting a slip between impotence and power, between uselessness and productivity—the very sort of ambivalence his alias encodes and the very sort of balance his exilic life epitomizes.[7]

William A. Cohen observes that at least since the onslaught of the trials of 1895, for Wilde, ". . . posing had become a particularly literary question, since Wilde was understood [by those in the court] to represent himself—that is, to pose—in his literary persona" (216). Of course, such a claim is proven in the records of Wilde's trials, where the author's works were placed in evidence to support the Marquis of Queensberry's charge, notoriously misspelled on the calling card that set off the explosion of the trials, that Wilde was "posing [as a] Somdomite [*sic*]." For Wilde, "posing" named a complicated activity that included both corporeal and textual embodiments, both private life, or pleasures, and public presence, or reputation, conflations which remind us of the ways in which the focus of gossip—its specifically demonized *object*—figures both corporeally and textually, since, after all, gossip textualizes corporeality.[8] The phenomena linking the narratives—the histories, the tales—of Melmoth and Wilde are remarkable: Melmoth's imprisonment in a maniac's cell predicts Wilde's own incarceration; Melmoth's suffering under the omnipotence of the Inquisition finds form in Wilde's courtroom examination and exposure; and Melmoth's assumption of false identities is followed by corporeal decline culminating in death, as Wilde's. That Melmoth epitomizes the figure of the Wandering Jew is strikingly appropriate, for, like the Wandering Jew, Wilde-in-exile is a text-to-be-read, a story-to-be-told, and even in his attempts to shield himself in the textual anonymity of an alias, Wilde remained nonetheless a recognized and symbolic—a *readable*—figure: like the exilic Wilde, Melmoth is marked by "an indelible stain, like original sin itself" (Baldick xii), and he becomes "an existence made up largely of report, reputation, and expectant surmise" (xvi), a figure whose strongest presence takes the form of absence and whose "direct presence, corrosive as it is, is not necessary to [the] dissolution of stable identities" (xvi). While the pose of "Sebastian Melmoth" may have succeeded at the level of the textual, it failed at the level of the corporeal, never effectively covering over the spectacle of Wilde himself, never shielding the sometimes-reluctant celebrity from public view, for Europeans in general never failed to recognize the defamed celebrity in exile. In short, Wilde-as-Sebastian Melmoth-as-Wandering Jew suggests the author's centrality to a nineteenth-century literary trope, for the wandering narrator figures prominently from the earliest examples of the Gothic mode, epitomized by Maturin's *Melmoth the Wanderer,* throughout the Romantic and Victorian ages and right up to Wilde's own *Picture of Dorian Gray,* in which the need to tell the secret becomes the undoing not so much of the teller of the tale as of its listeners, its would-be gossips.

The Gothic, a form of writing for which the name "Melmoth" serves as a kind of talisman, has itself been recognized as the textual embodiment of a revolutionary force. In his study, *Seven Gothic Dramas,* Jeffrey N. Cox argues that not only is the Gothic "a particular response to the literary, theatrical, and political pressures of the age of revolution," but that what Cox describes as the "second phase" of the Gothic is exemplified in the works of Maturin, where Gothicism functions less in the spirit of entertainment than in the interest of political protest (4, 58). In short, Cox regards the Gothic as a deliberately subtle attempt to work out and to spectacularize both the ideological and the aesthetic problems that plague the late eighteenth and early nineteenth centuries (12). In the same vein, Judith Halberstam argues that the designation "'Gothic' describes a discursive strategy which produces monsters as a kind of temporary but influential response to social, political, and sexual problems" ("Technologies of Monstrosity" 339). More specifically, Cox argues that "the Gothic setting and plot . . . could be read as embodying the rhythms of the [French] Revolution and its liberation of enclosed spaces from the powers of the past" (18). In the end, Cox insists, the first interest of the Gothic is the celebration of the potential of Revolution; the second, the vindication of the villain-as-hero (30-31).[9]

Cox situates the Gothic as a liminal form, as "a meeting point between high and low culture" (4). Matthew C. Brennan agrees that the Gothic "undermines boundaries" (3), that the mode of writing might best be described as "an aesthetics of nightmare, . . . of crossed or open boundaries" (6). Halberstam draws these boundaries more specifically, finding in the Gothic a tension and a constant threat of the breakdown "between good and evil, health and perversity, crime and punishment, truth and deception, [and] inside and outside," all of which "dissolve and threaten the integrity of the narrative itself," not to mention the stability of the culture out of which the Gothic text emerges (*Skin Shows* 2). As a liminal site, the Gothic functions as the space against which, as Halberstam recognizes, "deviant subjectivities" are produced "opposite which the normal, the healthy, and the pure can be known" (2). The Gothic thus functions *contra* hegemony in order to produce—to embody—the "other" against whom society defines itself, the threat which must be disciplined, if not eradicated, for the maintenance of hegemony to continue uninterrupted.

The particular threat of the Gothic lies in what Cox characterizes as that form's propensity for "seduction," one of the many threats embedded within the Gothic's "theater of shock, surprise, . . . and terror" (13), a sensational mixture that threatens to "[uncover] the desires repressed by modern culture" (7): Brennan, quoting William Patrick Day, agrees with Cox's assessment, adding that the Gothic "addressed 'those parts of the nineteenth-century reader's inner life that were disordered and fragmented'" (5). Eve Kosofsky Sedgwick locates the seductive potential of the Gothic in its celebration of the trope of "the 'unspeakable'" (94), which she situates in *Melmoth the Wanderer* at the site of the text itself: throughout Maturin's Gothic tale, Melmoth is cursed, doomed to suffer until he can find another to listen to his story and to assume his heavy burden of guilt and shame; but time and again, as Sedgwick observes, Melmoth's very narrative becomes "unspeakable" as "[t]he manuscripts crumble . . . or are 'wholly illegible,' the speaker is strangled by the unutterable word, or the proposition is preterited as 'one so full of horror and impiety, that, even to listen to it, is scarce less a crime than to comply with it'" (94, Maturin qtd. in Sedgwick). In Wilde's day, of course, the "unspeakable" would have included—ironically, would have *spoken of*—"the love that dare not speak its name," so that Wilde-as-Gothic-Monster or Wilde-as-Melmoth or Wilde-as-text embodies the unspeakable—*viz.* homosexuality, an antihegemonic engagement which, as Sedgwick compellingly demonstrates, finds form in the Gothic (90-92), so that once again we see the collusion of sexuality and textuality in a deviant form (the Gothic in general and Wilde in particular), which hegemony recognizes and excoriates—casts out—as dangerous, as revolutionary.

Because the Gothic explodes the ideological forces that lead to repression and entrapment, because the Gothic makes explicit the link between political and erotic freedom (Cox 25), and because the Gothic explores border-crossings, repressed desires, and the specter of homoeroticism, so too might the Gothic serve as a meta-narrative for Wilde's very public fall, his punishment, and, finally, his move into exile, an experiential space that may be characterized as Gothic given its status as a space outside of—in exile from—conventional morality (14). In Wilde's exilic surname, then, we find a textual embodiment for this revolutionary mode of writing, a code whose narrative suggests Wilde's deliberate celebration, rather than his ambivalent erasure, of his own "curious" stature—his "villainous" nature, his infamous "crimes."

Just as Wilde's exilic surname textualizes political revolution, his exilic Christian name, "Sebastian," celebrates, rather than declaims, sexual revolution—Wilde's own profligate past. Most scholars agree that Wilde adopted the name "Sebastian" from the Christian martyr, whose appeal to Wilde was three-fold: first, Saint Sebastian represents a protracted triumph over earthly defeat, or punishment; second, Saint Sebastian affords the viewer a homoerotic pleasure, for he is generally represented as a comely and semi-nude youth; third, Saint Sebastian's arrow-pierced—multiply penetrated—body corporealizes the spectacle of gay male pleasure even as it anticipates Wilde's own body-to-be-clothed in a standard-issue prison uniform, which, scored with arrows, textualizes Wilde's body as a criminal site.[10] But in addition to these associations, I want to argue that Wilde's exilic Christian name embeds a variety of meanings beyond the most obvious, which I have described. For in addition to serving as a corporeally inscribed code for the forces of good and evil, or victory and defeat, the name "Sebastian" suggests a kind of border-crossing of its own, just as Wilde's move into exile transports him across the borders of nations. As Jan B. Gordon has argued, "[b]y using 'Sebastian' as a prefix, Wilde was perhaps attempting to combine the Hebraic questor without a home with the Hellenic saint, in [a state of] equipoise . . ." ("'Decadent Spaces'" 56). In Gordon's reading, the name "Sebastian" evokes the condition of liminality, within which a variety of apparent oppositions may be resolved. The image of the martyr is thus mediated by the image of the hero, complicating the apparent status of "Sebastian" as victor or vanquished and thereby repeating—textualizing—the paradoxical space the exilic Wilde himself had come to occupy. Such a mediation reinscribes the formulation of Wilde-as-liminal-as-Gothic, and it calls to mind Wilde's sonnet on "The Grave of Keats," in which the ephebic poet is glorified and, in such a state of glory, aligned with the similarly young, similarly beautiful, and similarly tragic Saint Sebastian.

Yet another meaning lies latent in the name "Sebastian," one which, I believe, is perhaps more *apropos* of Wilde's exilic attitude toward his own identity as a criminal or villain, as his culture's other. A number of scholars have recuperated Wilde's exile as, at least in part, a mitigated victory, for in exile we find Wilde beyond the constraints of English law and order, and, at least to some degree, removed from the gaze—the prying eyes, the gossipy nature—of Englishmen in general. While a great many critics dismiss Wilde's exile as a period of loss or failure (see note 2), many others regard Wilde's exile as a personal and ideological victory, as the triumph of queer pleasure. Jonathan Dollimore argues that Wilde's aesthetic avoids *Angst* and, quite to the contrary, activates a flight into *jouissance* (73), but Dollimore's abstraction is perhaps better qualified by the more concrete memoirs and accounts of Wilde's contemporaries and biographers. Rupert Croft-Cooke characterizes Wilde's final years as offering "fulfillment of another kind. There were no more attempts to write, or even think about writing; friendship with Bosie was without passion or strain, and [Wilde] lounged about the boulevards and amused himself with young male prostitutes and wrote supremely entertaining letters about them to [Robbie] Ross and Reggie Turner" (238). Croft-Cooke includes these letters among many written during Wilde's final years which, "for the most part," suggest the image of "a cheerful man chuckling over the absurdities of life about him and his own misfortunes; . . . a comic artist turning every grotesque or whimsical incident to a laugh . . ." (279). In fact, Wilde wrote to Robbie Ross from Paris that "[l]ater on in life, humour goes, but laughter is the primaeval attitude towards life—a mode of approach that survives only in artists and criminals" (*Letters* 767), and in a letter to W. Morton Fullerton, he characterized the humor of nonsense as "a form of art the French are rich in, but the English sadly to [*sic*] seek" (804).

H. Montgomery Hyde's assessment of Wilde's final years concurs with Croft-Cooke's; he notes that "[t]he return of freedom gave [Wilde] back the sense of humour . . ." (*Oscar Wilde: The Aftermath* 209), and while Wilde may have been "disgusted at the implication that he would be welcomed back [to England] for his 'airy mood and spirit,' but only if a conversion of his sexual preference could be extorted from him" (Schmidgall 341), Hyde recounts moments in which Wilde managed to turn his controversial sexuality—such as his experiments at a (heterosexual) brothel in Dieppe—into marks of his own queer victory: "'The first in these ten years,' [Wilde] said to Dowson in a low voice, 'and it will be the last. It was like cold mutton!' And then, raising his voice so that the crowd could hear, he added, 'But tell it in England, for it will entirely restore my character!'" (*Oscar Wilde: A Biography* 373). Once in Paris, Wilde flaunted the very vices for which England had placed him under lock and key: writing to Ross, Wilde comments that "[i]t is very unfair people being horrid to me about Bosie and Naples. A patriot put in prison for loving his country loves his country, and a poet in prison for loving boys loves boys. To have altered my life would have been to have admitted that Uranian love is ignoble. I hold it to be noble—more noble than other forms" (*Letters* 705). Chris Baldick offers evidence to suggest that Wilde's mitigated victory in exile repeats his ancestor Maturin's:

> Having helped a few years earlier to prepare a biographical introduction to an edition of his great-uncle's novel, Wilde knew the history and reputation of the Revd Charles Robert Maturin, Anglican curate of St. Peter's in Dublin, novelist, playwright, eccentric, and failure: Maturin had died in poverty in 1824, his literary efforts frowned upon by his ecclesiastical superiors in Dublin, slighted by most of the critics in Edinburgh, and laughed off the stage in London. In Paris, however, his reputation had flourished posthumously.
>
> (vii)

Perhaps Wilde's own exilic flourishing is best exemplified in the sexual relationships he enjoyed after being released from prison: in addition to a brief though ultimately unhappy reunion with Lord Alfred Douglas, Wilde enjoyed the company of a variety of young men in the years between his release from prison and his death in Paris in 1900.[11] Wilde's exile, though certainly compromised by poverty, personal struggles, and professional humiliation, nonetheless afforded him the pleasure of the spectacle of revolution—of the attenuated triumph, of the subversive victory of Wilde-as-"Sebastian Melmoth."

The name "Sebastian," I argue, textualizes the "deviant"—specifically, the homosexual—pleasures that marked Wilde's exile, for the name functions as a code for the emerging identity of the Uranian, that creature who, under the contemporary designation "invert," had been pathologized as a chaotic amalgamation—a blur, a border-crossing—of male and female. Surely Wilde must have recognized the gender-blurring associated with the name "Sebastian" in Shakespeare's *Twelfth Night,* in which the character Sebastian is, at one point, mistaken for Viola, who herself has donned male disguise. More locally, Wilde's appropriation of the name as an in-the-know gay code reappears in his one-time friend André Raffalovich's conversion to Catholicism and admission into the lay order under the name "Brother Sebastian" (Rosario 162), an appellation Wilde would certainly have recognized as paying homage—intentionally or not—perhaps to Wilde's exile and certainly to Raffalovich's own gay past as well as to his ongoing amorous relationship with John Gray, the beautiful young poet who, many have argued, provided the model for Wilde's own Dorian. Richard Ellmann notes (although perhaps pejoratively), that Sebastian has, traditionally, been "the favorite saint among homosexuals" (71n), and Camille Paglia describes Sebastian as the image in which "[h]omoerotic iconicism goes full circle" (112). Ellmann also reproduces Guido Reni's highly eroticized painting of the arrow-pierced body of that saint, which he describes as one of Wilde's favorite works. Ian Young comments on the significance of Wilde's appropriation of the name "Sebastian" as well, arguing provocatively that "[t]he sadomasochistic image [of the martyred saint] is intensified . . . by his traditional depiction as suffering a kind of ecstasy as he is penetrated by a gang of men—Roman soldiers with arrows. Here is male beauty, oppressed, penetrated, and transformed, a perfect icon for the homosexual in Christian culture, who is so often characterized as suffering, nobly or ignobly, and dying young" (16). "Sebastian" thus designates Wilde as a martyr, in the tradition of the Christian saint and, later, Keats; as a metaphor for Wilde-as-prisoner; as a gay icon, in the image of the comely, nearly nude, penetrated youth; and, finally, as a corporeal manifestation for a play across the lines of gender, a blur between "manhood" and "womanhood," a pleasure in the repose of inversion.

Lorraine Janzen Kooistra has argued that "[b]order-crossing was absolutely necessary to Wilde, whose sexual orientation gave him a marginal, not to say criminal and subversive, subject position. . . . Wilde believed that the creative artist must cross gender borders, representational borders, truth borders and law and order borders, in order to realize fully his personality in his art" (140-141). Wilde's ultimate physical location, Paris, is perhaps as significant as his alias in making sense of the writer's symbolic status in the final period of his life. Baldick's observation about the significance of the name "Melmoth" to fin-de-siècle Parisian culture underscores the argument I have suggested regarding Wilde's motives for leaving England for the continent and, finally, for settling in Paris: ". . . as Wilde well knew, the name of Melmoth still echoed in France, as it did no longer in Ireland or England, with the notoriety of high Romantic despair and damnation; it was the badge of the eternal outcast, of his grandiose self-hatred, and of his withering scorn for heaven and earth" (vii). Wilde's removal to Paris, one might argue, follows his choice of alias, for in a letter to Ada Leverson, Wilde encouraged her to address him by his alias, and he pointed out that the name was to be preceded by the French designation "Monsieur" rather than followed by the English "Esquire" (Hyde 368). Wilde thus contextualizes his alias as a specifically French identity, a move we should not find surprising given his response to English prudery following the banning of *Salome* in 1894: enraged, Wilde gave vent to his expatriate fantasies in a Parisian newspaper, pontificating that "'[m]y resolution is deliberately taken. Since it is impossible to have a work of art performed in England, I shall transfer myself to another fatherland [France], of which I have been long enamoured'" (qtd. in Holland 86).[12]

Elsewhere in his letters, Wilde's sense of alienation from England emerges time and again: writing to Ross in January 1898, he describes Oxford as "that sweet grey city that nurtured me," but in which he has "of disciples 'but few or none'" (*Letters* 752). In his essay "The Soul of Man Under Socialism," Wilde expresses his disaffiliation with English prudery by observing that individualism, which Dollimore describes as the recognition and respect of cultural and personal differences (9), is antithetical to what Wilde characterizes as that "immoral idea of uniformity of type and conformity to rule which is so prevalent everywhere, and is perhaps most obnoxious in England" (1041). Elsewhere in the same essay, Wilde writes that "Art is Individualism and Individualism is a disturbing and disintegrating force. Therein lies its immense value" (1030). For Wilde, England must have seemed hostile toward him on at least two counts: for his Decadent works and for his "Uranian" habits—two forces, one textual, the other sexual, which together posed a double threat to the British sense of normalcy.

Hyde characterizes the Decadent period as ". . . the culmination in England of the movement which had developed in France with the concept of personality in the Revolution a century before and which had reached the height of a collective expression on the other side of the English Channel in the glorification of Napoleon" ("Introduction" xi). Hyde's contextualization of Decadence as an originally French phenomenon imported to England through the spirit of Revolutionary fervor reminds us of the always-political nature of Decadence itself, of its enduring links to the social and political turmoil that gripped France in the age of Revolution. Hyde's complicated formulation embeds a wide range of translations, or crossings, and all of these, I believe, find embodiment in the figure of Oscar Wilde.

Wilde's turn to France seems an appropriate response to his excoriation by an English public who, before the spectacle of Wilde's fall, loved and adored the writer as if he were one of their own; that is, at his height, Wilde's popularity seemed to erase the difference—specifically, his Irishness—that set him apart from mainstream English culture, but after his fall, Wilde was attacked and rejected on the basis of a whole spectrum of differences—now including much more serious charges, of course, than mere Irishness. While the term "Natural Enemies" had long been used in British newspapers as shorthand for an ongoing English/French tension (Abrams 940n8), in the case of Wilde, that tension finds literal embodiment, and thus Wilde's body continues to function as a nexus for the textual and the corporeal. In its account of Wilde's trial on 6 April 1895, for example, *The Daily Telegraph* fueled anti-French sentiment in its demonization of the besieged Wilde: "Everybody can see and read for himself, every honest and wholesome-minded Englishman must grieve to notice how largely this French and Pagan plague has filtered into the healthy fields of British life" (qtd. in Goodman 76).[13] In moving into exile and, finally, in settling in Paris, Wilde returns to the prototypical nineteenth-century site of Revolution, for that city's name continued to resound throughout the age with the ring of political upheaval and erotic license.

Wilde's *The Importance of Being Earnest,* a comedy that was enjoying great success at the time of the writer's arrest, comments on the "proper" English excoriation of all things French: Lady Bracknell, that play's primary voice of traditional British values, responds in horror when she is told that Bunbury, the symbolic figure whose always-absent body metonymizes a range of decadent pleasures—among them deceit, treachery, and, Christopher Craft has argued, homosexuality[14]—has died or, to quote Algernon Moncrieff exactly, has been ". . . quite exploded," Lady Bracknell exclaims, "Exploded! Was he the victim of some revolutionary outrage?" (act 3). While Algernon admits that Bunbury's demise resulted not so much from corporeal as from textual explosion—he was, Algernon says, "found out," or *read*—earlier in the play another Bunbury's death is more specifically located: arriving in the country, Jack Worthing announces that his brother Ernest (a figure who, for Jack, fulfills the same purpose as does Bunbury for Algernon) has ". . . died abroad; in Paris, in fact" (act 2). When Jack adds that Ernest ". . . expressed a desire to be buried in Paris," the Reverend Chasuble, another of the play's voices of traditional British morality, shakes his head and retorts, "In Paris!. . . . I fear that hardly points to any very serious state of mind at the last" (act 2). Nearer the beginning of the play, Lady Bracknell sets the tone for the symbolic meaning of Paris as the site of the wicked, or, as her attitude suggests, the anti-British, when she remarks to Jack that what we might call his luggage-lineage sets him outside of British culture, rendering him an embodiment of the other: "To be born, or at any rate, bred in a handbag, whether it had handles or not, seems to me to display a contempt for the ordinary decencies of family life that reminds one of the excesses of the French Revolution. And I presume you know what that unfortunate movement led to?" (act 1). Lady Bracknell's final question is a rhetorical one; its answer, implicit in the speech itself, is that the French Revolution led to the breakdown of the family and, by extension, to the breakdown of all social order—the very sort of threat posed by Wilde's so-called "gross indecency." Wilde's characters thus espouse a typically British attitude toward the city that Wilde came to call home in his last days: throughout the play (whose initial run, as it happens, neatly bracketed the months that witnessed Wilde's fall from the heights of fame to the depths of notoriety), Paris emerges as the place of excess, the site of indecency; in short, the city functions symbolically as the space of the other, as a haven for the outcast.

Wilde once celebrated France as "manag[ing] . . . better" the split, the distance between public and private lives ("The Soul of Man Under Socialism" 1034), thus situating the country which in his final years he came to call home as a safe haven for the object of gossip, as a land that respects the boundaries between the personality one exercises in public and the pleasures one enjoys in private. In France, Wilde-as-"Sebastian Melmoth" embodied the conditions of excess that framed the nineteenth century—the excesses of the French Revolution and their textual embodiment in the form of the Gothic, and the excesses of fin-de-siècle decadence and their corporeal embodiment in the figure of Wilde himself. As the site of revolution moves throughout the century from one odd tendency to another, at first textual and finally sexual, Wilde's retreating figure—retreating both in its disinclination to respond to the wrongs perpetrated against it, and retreating in its decided move *out* of England and into Paris—looms as the spectacle of nineteenth-century revolutionary potential. At once sexual and textual, "Sebastian Melmoth" functions not as a shield of anonymity but as a badge of defiance, a sign that announces Wilde's self-identification as his culture's "other," a self-inflicted mark of Cain that articulates Wilde's allegiance to a sexuality and a textuality his fellow Englishmen excoriated as the sites of revolutionary excess.

During the recitation of his tale to Maturin's Melmoth, the Spaniard remarks with some ironic pleasure on his status as an outsider: "Doors were clapped to wherever I was heard to approach; and three or four would stand whispering near where I walked, and clear their throats, and exchange signs, and pass *audibly* to the most trifling topics in my hearing, as if to intimate, while they affected to conceal it, that their last topic had been *me*. I laughed at this internally" (101). Wilde's experience in exile strikes a parallel chord: Croft-Cooke observes that though "[l]ife in Paris suited Wilde[, who] had always regarded the city as a refuge and a playground . . ." (257), the writer's exile proved a mixture of victory and defeat, pleasure and pain, optimism and regret. In exile, "Sebastian Melmoth" continued to inhabit that anxious space of the blur in which either/or gives way to both/and, that dizzying space of revolution in which rule and order are suspended as the "other" is tossed back and forth from objectivity to subjectivity, from containment to freedom, from discipline to pleasure. Somewhere in this mix, I like to think, Wilde-as-Sebastian Melmoth savored the spectacle of his protracted triumph over the culture that sought to exclude him.

Notes

1. In fact, Wilde's remark was no "deathbed" declaration at all: Ellmann reports that Wilde uttered the clever quip to Claire de Pratz on 29 October 1900, a full month before his demise. Wilde's exact words were as follows: "'My wallpaper and I are fighting a duel to the death. One or the other of us has to go'" (qtd. in Ellmann 581).

2. A great many critics dismiss Wilde's exile as a period of aesthetic and ideological loss or, even worse, as a personal failure. Among these, the following are the most representative. Frank Harris, Wilde's friend and sometime-companion during the writer's final years, remembers how Wilde's rooms "affected [him] unpleasantly," those "ordinary, mean, little French rooms, furnished without taste"; "[w]hat struck me was the disorder everywhere; . . . [t]he sense of order and neatness which he used to have in his rooms at Tite Street was utterly lacking. He was not living here, intent on making the best of things; he was merely existing without plan or purpose" (307). Near the end of his memoir, Harris admits that "the truth [about Wilde] is still more appalling," and he goes on to catalogue the symptoms of Wilde's plunge into decline, including physical illness and excessive drinking (316). Sadly, Harris's disgust resounds throughout the one-sentence paragraph that follows his account of Wilde's death: "[e]ven the bedding had to be burned" (316). Philippe Jullian draws on the recollections of Wilde's friend Vincent O'Sullivan to remark that, in his final years, Wilde habitually "[passed] a trembling hand over his face *as if to brush aside a nightmare*" (391, emphasis added); according to O'Sullivan, Wilde once admitted to him that "'I died in prison'" (qtd. in Jullian 392). Wilde's grandson, Merlin Holland, follows Frank Harris's lead in his book-length homage to his grandfather, *The Wilde Album*: he writes, "[w]ith little left to live for, Oscar's last two and a half years were a long slide to the grave. He spent them wandering aimlessly around Europe, poor but not penniless, alone but not without friends" (180). Nancy Erber, quoting the novelist Lucien Muhlfeld, suggests that "'. . . after his trial and his stint of "hard labour" . . . Paris took no notice of the man it had taken up'" (586). Richard Ellmann says of Wilde's exile that "Wilde's place in the world was now fixed for good—no longer at its center, but always on its outskirts" (554). While many might argue that the outskirts mark the space of perversion, the domain of subversive pleasure and power, Ellmann invokes the term pejoratively, as the final chapters of his biography make clear. Stephen Calloway and David Colvin comment that Wilde's death brought to an end the dark period of exile—"the most devastating and heartbreaking of all the states of the soul" (101)—"during which [Wilde's] mental decline had been almost as marked as his physical" (6); "[b]y stages, Wilde became a tragic figure. . . . Looking shabby, his former pride in his dress and toilette gone for ever, Oscar slipped into the habit of importuning old friends, and even perfect strangers; even his sole remaining asset, his talk,

became worn and threadbare, and like Brummell before him, he cut a sorry figure" (103). A 1995 publication commemorating the centenary of the Wilde trials, *Reading Wilde, Querying Spaces,* opens with an introduction whose first paragraph concludes that "[c]onvicted of practicing 'indecent acts,' the notorious writer spent the next two years kept to hard labor in prison, dying barely two and a half years after his release" (iv). Michael S. Foldy begins his account of *The Trials of Oscar Wilde* by commenting that "[t]he three years between his release from prison in 1897 and his death in 1900 were spent living in poverty, shame, and, most sadly of all perhaps, unproductivity" (ix); "[e]ven though he was eventually able to leave England behind, Wilde was never able to escape his notoriety or to reclaim the secrecy his private life had previously afforded him" (128).

3. Wilde, as history and Hawthorne show, was not alone in his appropriation of renaming as a strategy for personal and political re-alignment. Melanie C. Hawthorne recounts the Wilde family's decision, following the writer's disgrace, to flee ". . . into exile in Europe to avoid the unwanted publicity generated by the trial" and to adopt the name "Holland," a pseudonym "unrelated to the Dutch origin of the Wildes" yet nonetheless "obviously [preserving], even [embodying], the trace of the very criminal identity that the family wished to escape. Holland is home to Dutchmen, [so-called] queer and unpatriotic men like Wilde and [J.T.] Grien," director of the Independent Theater Society, whose planned production of *Salome* in 1918 led to a court case against Grien, Maud Allan, and others, raising the specter of Wilde as a still-potent symbol of deviance almost 20 years after his death (176). "By taking their place of origin as . . . patronymic, [the family] preserves [their] affiliations in the very act of repudiating them" (176) in exactly the way that "Sebastian Melmoth" preserves Wilde's revolutionary commitments even as it seems to suggest his desire to escape from the burdens of his name.

4. Specifically, I am thinking of the appropriation of the name and image of Wilde in two instances: first, by the British pop singer Morrissey, who has used such symbology for the last decade and a half to signify his investment in what Lord Alfred Douglas and, later, Wilde, referred to as "the love that dare not speak its name"; second, by a moment in the 1995 American film *Clueless,* in which a homosexual newcomer is "outed" by a heterosexual classmate's string of epithets, which include the fascinating phrase "Oscar-Wilde-reading. . . ." Richard A. Spears notes that in the twentieth century, the term "Oscar" functioned as a euphemism for what mainstream culture still considered a "deviant" identity and action: as a noun, the term names "a homosexual male"; as a verb ("oscarizing"), it describes the act of "commit[ting] pederasty" (284).

5. Wilde and Keats may also be connected in terms of their deaths: though Keats's demise resulted from consumption, or tuberculosis, and Wilde's, depending upon which account one consults, from either a botched ear infection or tertiary syphilis, both deaths symbolically manifest the vituperance of outraged critics on the body of the embattled artist, thus registering textual invective as corporeal decline. Keats, as Byron famously remarked, was so weak that he was, in effect, killed by criticism: to Percy Bysshe Shelley, he wrote that "I am very sorry to hear what you say of Keats—is it *actually* true? I did not think criticism had been so killing" (601), and to John Murray he confided that ". . . I did not approve of Keats's poetry, or principles of poetry, or of his abuse of Pope;. . . . [h]owever, he who would die of an article in a review would probably have died of something else equally trivial" (661). Wilde, too, symbolically succumbed to public outrage, admitting to Vincent O'Sullivan that "'Lucien hanged himself, Julian died on the scaffold, and I died in prison'" (qtd. in Jullian 392). Both Wilde and Keats suffered death at the level of the textual, when their works came under heavy attack from conservative readers and critics who launched arsenals of criticism against them; ultimately, such "fatal" offensives led to their downfalls, symbolically hastening their real, physical deaths.

6. For readings of the press coverage of the Wilde trials in terms of the textualization of the corporeal—the discussion and depiction of Wilde's body-as-narrative—see Cohen and Goodman, *passim.*

7. The letter, though quoted in Coakley, is inadequately documented, and its correspondent remains unidentified.

8. Jan B. Gordon defines gossip as "the (often) studied resistance to *prop*riety—the ownership of discourse marginalized to be self-same or identical" (*Gossip and Subversion* xii); "[g]ossip, speech that is trafficked as opposed to being held in reserve, would obviously assume values antithetical to those of Western liberalism's vulnerable 'inner voice': repetition rather than a self-identical 'sincerity'; the loss of a private self; an enforced conformity with institutional demands; an instrumental posture toward the self; and a dissonance which subverts self-knowledge" (300). Patricia Ann Meyer Spacks devotes an entire study to the discussion of the mechanisms of gossip; see her book, *Gossip.*

9. A more recent book by David Punter, *Gothic Pathologies: The Text, The Body and The Law,* situates the Gothic as the locus of a variety of strategies of transgression, all of which work against and must be contained by culturally sanctioned apparatuses, such as the law.

10. Wilde plays on the multiple significations of his arrow-scored prison uniform in another passage from

De Profundis: "[o]ther miserable men when they are thrown into prison, if they are robbed of the beauty of the world are at least safe in some measure from the world's most deadly slings, most awful arrows. They can hide in the darkness of their cells and of their very disgrace make a mode of sanctuary. The world having had its will goes its way, and they are left to suffer undisturbed. With me it has been different. Sorrow after sorrow has come beating at the prison doors in search of me; they have opened the gates wide and let them in" (33). Wilde's lament invokes the physical image of the prison uniform and raises the image of the (prisoner's) body to the level of the (prisoner's) experience, textualizing the corporeal by way of the figure of speech "slings and arrows," always understood to be verbal—textual—taunts that attack at the level of the corporeal, but here also including the very condition of the (prisoner's) body itself, which registers those arrows as *actual arrows,* as the sight and the site—in short, as the spectacle—of excoriation.

11. For accounts of Wilde's exilic escapades, see Wilde, *Letters* 563-844; Harris, *Oscar Wilde* 264-322; Croft-Cooke 238-282; Jullian 358-398; Ellmann 527-589; and Schmidgall 331-344.

12. In writing to Lord Alfred Douglas from prison, Wilde, though clearly cognizant of the bleak prospect the future held for his return to the pleasures of old, nonetheless looks forward to his move away from England as an opportunity for a kind of purification: "The sea, as Euripides says in one of his plays about Iphigeneia, washes away the stains and wounds of the world" (*De Profundis* 115).

13. In "The Soul of Man Under Socialism," Wilde considers the current vogue for the term "unhealthy" in criticism of the arts, and he concludes that "[i]n fact, the popular novel that the public call healthy is always a thoroughly unhealthy production; and what the public call an unhealthy novel is always a beautiful and healthy work of art" (1033).

14. See Craft's "Alias Bunbury: Desire and Termination in *The Importance of Being Earnest*" for a reading of the play's central device of "bunburying" as, among other things, "a pragmatics of gay misrepresentation, a nuanced and motile doublespeak, driven both by pleasure and, as Gide puts it, 'by the need of self-protection'" (28).

Works Cited

Baldick, Chris. "Introduction." *Melmoth the Wanderer,* by Charles Robert Maturin. 1820. Ed. Douglas Grant. New York: Oxford UP, 1989.

Beckson, Karl. *London in the 1890s: A Cultural History.* New York: W. W. Norton, 1992.

Bierce, Ambrose. *The Devil's Dictionary.* 1911. New York: Dover Publications, Inc., 1993.

Brennan, Matthew C. *The Gothic Psyche: Disintegration and Growth in Nineteenth-Century English Literature.* Columbia: Camden House, 1997.

Byron, George Gordon. *Byron: A Self-Portrait in His Own Words.* Ed. Peter Quennell. 1950. New York: Oxford UP, 1990.

Calloway, Stephen, and David Colvin. *Oscar Wilde: An Exquisite Life.* New York: Barnes and Noble Books, 1998.

Coakley, Davis. *Oscar Wilde: The Importance of Being Irish.* 1994. Dublin: Town House, 1995.

Cohen, Ed. *Talk on the Wilde Side: Toward a Genealogy of a Discourse on Male Sexuality.* New York: Routledge, 1993.

Cohen, William A. "Indeterminate Wilde." *Sex Scandal: The Private Parts of Victorian Fiction.* Durham: Duke UP, 1996. 191-236.

Clueless. Dir. Amy Heckerling. Perf. Alicia Silverstone. Paramount Pictures, 1995.

Cox, Jeffrey N. "Introduction." *Seven Gothic Dramas 1789-1825.* Athens: Ohio UP, 1992. 1-77.

Craft, Christopher. "Alias Bunbury: Desire and Termination in *The Importance of Being Earnest.*" *Representations* 31 (Summer 1990): 47-68.

Croft-Cooke, Rupert. *The Unrecorded Life of Oscar Wilde.* New York: David McKay Company, 1972.

Dollimore, Jonathan. *Sexual Dissidence: Augustine to Wilde, Freud to Foucault.* Oxford: Clarendon Press, 1991.

Ellmann, Richard. *Oscar Wilde.* New York: Knopf, 1988.

Erber, Nancy. "The French Trials of Oscar Wilde." *Journal of the History of Sexuality* 6 (April 1996): 549-588.

Foldy, Michael S. *The Trials of Oscar Wilde: Deviance, Morality, and Late-Victorian Society.* New Haven: Yale UP, 1997.

Goodman, Jonathan. *The Oscar Wilde File.* London: Allison and Busby, 1988.

Gordon, Jan B. "'Decadent Spaces': Notes for a Phenomenology of the *Fin de Siècle.*" *Decadence and the 1890s.* Ed. Ian Fletcher. London: Edward Arnold, 1979. 31-58.

———. *Gossip and Subversion in Nineteenth-Century British Fiction: Echo's Economies.* New York: St. Martin's Press, Inc., 1996.

Halberstam, Judith. *Skin Shows: Gothic Horror and the Technology of Monsters.* Durham: Duke UP, 1995.

———. "Technologies of Monstrosity: Bram Stoker's *Dracula.*" *Victorian Studies* 36 (Spring 1993): 333-352.

Harris, Frank. "Oscar Wilde." *Contemporary Portraits.* New York: Mitchell Kennerly, 1915. 97-126.

———. *Oscar Wilde.* 1916. Intro. Merlin Holland. New York: Carroll and Graf Publishers, Inc., 1997.

Hawthorne, Melanie C. "'Comment Peut-on Être Homosexuel?': Multinational (In)Corporation and the Frenchness of *Salomè*." *Perennial Decay: On the Aesthetics and Politics of Decadence*. Ed. Liz Constable, Dennis Denisoff, and Matthew Potolsky. Philadelphia: U Pennsylvania P, 1999. 159-182.

Holder, R. W. *A Dictionary of American and British Euphemisms: The Language of Evasion, Hypocrisy, Prudery and Deceit*. Bath: Bath UP, 1987.

Holland, Merlin. *The Wilde Album*. New York: Henry Holt and Company, 1997.

Holland, Vyvyan. *Oscar Wilde*. 1960, 1966. London: Thames and Hudson, 1988.

Hyde, H. Montgomery. "Introduction." *The Romantic '90s*, by Richard Le Gallienne. 1926, 1951. London: Robin Clark Limited, 1993. vii-xxx.

———. *Oscar Wilde: The Aftermath*. New York: Farrar, Straus, and Company, 1963.

———. *Oscar Wilde: A Biography*. New York: Farrar, Straus and Giroux, 1975.

Jullian, Philippe. *Oscar Wilde*. 1968. Trans. Violet Wyndham. London: Constable, 1969.

Kooistra, Lorraine Janzen. *The Artist as Critic: Bitextuality in Fin-de-Siècle Illustrated Books*. Brookfield, Vermont: Ashgate, 1995.

Le Gallienne, Richard. *The Romantic '90s*. 1926, 1951. Intro. H. Montgomery Hyde. London: Robin Clark Limited, 1993.

Maturin, Charles Robert. *Melmoth the Wanderer*. 1820. Intro. Chris Baldrick. Ed. Douglas Grant. The World's Classics. New York: Oxford UP, 1989.

Nordau, Max. *Degeneration*. 1892. Intro. George L. Mosse. New York: D. Appleton, 1895. Lincoln: U of Nebraska P, 1993.

Paglia, Camille. *Sexual Personæ: Art and Decadence from Nefertiti to Emily Dickinson*. 1990. New York: Vintage Books, 1991.

Powys, John Cowper. *Suspended Judgments: Essays on Books and Sensations*. New York: G. Arnold Shaw, 1916.

Punter, David. *Gothic Pathologies: The Text, The Body and The Law*. New York: St. Martin's Press, 1998.

Reading Wilde, Querying Spaces: An Exhibition Commemorating the 100th Anniversary of the Trials of Oscar Wilde. New York: New York University, 1995.

Rosario, Vernon A. III. "Pointy Penises, Fashion Crimes, and Hysterical Mollies." *Homosexuality in Modern France*. Ed. Jeffrey Merrick and Bryant T. Ragan, Jr. New York: Oxford UP, 1996. 146-176.

Sedgwick, Eve Kosofsky. *Between Men: English Literature and Male Homosocial Desire*. New York: Columbia UP, 1985.

Spacks, Patricia Ann Meyer. *Gossip*. New York: Alfred A. Knopf, 1985.

Spears, Richard A. *Slang and Euphemism: A Dictionary of Oaths, Curses, Insults, Sexual Slang and Metaphor, Racial Slurs, Drug Talk, Homosexual Lingo, and Related Matters*. Middle Village: Jonathan David Publishers, Inc., 1981.

Wilde, Oscar. *A Woman of No Importance*. 1893. *The Works of Oscar Wilde*. Leicester: Galley Press, 1987. 416-466.

———. *De Profundis*. 1905. 2nd ed. Ed. Robert Ross. New York: G. P. Putnam's Sons, 1909.

———. "The Grave of Keats" 1877. *The Works of Oscar Wilde*. Leicester: Galley Press, 1987. 756.

———. *The Importance of Being Earnest*. 1895, 1899. *The Norton Anthology of English Literature*. Vol. 2. 6th ed. Gen. ed. M. H. Abrams. New York: W. W. Norton, 1993. 1629-1667.

———. *The Letters of Oscar Wilde*. Ed. Rupert Hart-Davis. New York: Harcourt, Brace & World, 1962.

———. "The Soul of Man Under Socialism." 1891. *The Works of Oscar Wilde*. Leicester: Galley Press, 1987. 1018-1043.

Young, Ian. *The Stonewall Experiment: A Gay Psychohistory*. London: Cassell, 1995.

GERMAN LITERATURE IN EXILE

Wm. K. Pfeiler (essay date 1957)

SOURCE: Pfeiler, Wm. K. "German Literature outside the Third Reich." In *German Literature in Exile: The Concern of the Poets,* pp. 3-23. Lincoln: University of Nebraska Press, 1957.

[*In the following excerpt, Pfeiler examines the circumstances that led to the creation of a German literature in exile and comments on some of its main characteristics and figures.*]

The unprecedented political upheaval following Hitler's assumption of power, specifically after the Reichstag fire in February, 1933, manifested itself to Germany's neighbors dramatically by the early exodus of tens of thousands of people who, for "racial" reasons or political nonconformity, thought it wise to leave the realm of the Third Reich, where freedom and lives were endangered. The steady flow of fugitives never stopped; they were called *emigrants* or *émigrés* if their goal was permanent settlement abroad and if "legal" sanction for going abroad was given by the Nazi authorities; *refugees* or *exiles,* if their ultimate hope was a return to the fatherland after the restoration of a German *Rechtsstaat*. For both types the term *exile* came into common use.[1] The flight reached its peak after the annexation of Austria and the pogroms of November, 1938. Despite the misery and wretchedness awaiting the large majority of exiles—only comparatively few individuals were able to transfer substantial values to the lands of their refuge—they were fortunate when one considers the fate of those who by choice or necessity stayed behind and who later had to die by untold numbers in the process of planned extermination.

At first, only Germany's neighboring countries were "invaded" by the stream of fugitives; later practically no part of the globe failed to get its share of the victims of Nazi persecution. Between 1933 and 1941 perhaps from 450,000 to half a million people left Germany and Austria, an exit still being possible then, and of these about twenty percent fled, not for racial but definitely for political reasons. The great majority of the refugees were of Jewish origin; about eight to ten percent of the total number were not.

In this mass flight from Germany, the intellectuals of various professions constituted a historically unprecedented high percentage in the host of expatriates. As to the representatives of literature, never before in history had the élite of the cultural life of a nation departed on such a scale. It left the homeland almost depleted of its internationally recognized cultural stock. To the world it looked as if a whole literary generation had withdrawn almost in a body. Hardly any writers of world-wide reputation were left.[2] Although handicapped in their profession more than expelled people in any other occupation—for their tools were the words of their native tongue in an environment alien in language, tradition and custom and often bitterly hostile—many exiled writers persisted in their work with such a tenacious devotion and remarkable success that it would elicit universal admiration if the world knew of it. Even in the Germany of today, which vigorously endeavors to make good the past and to catch up with the twelve long years lost, the knowledge of this so-called *Emigrantenliteratur* is spotty, often superficial and vitiated by emotionally rooted prejudices.[3]

An immense German literature came into being abroad, regrettably *unübersehbar* now because of the failure to create biographic and bibliographic centers that could have recorded systematically the names of exiled German authors and their works. It has become almost impossible to obtain a complete bibliography of the German literature created abroad in the years of Nazi rule, a job nevertheless now undertaken by W. Sternfeld in London under the sponsorship of the *Deutsche Bibliothek* and its director, Hanns W. Eppelsheimer. However, it must be recognized that early some remarkable bibliographic efforts were made, for which present and future researchers will be indebted. Since 1937 Kurt Pinthus had tried in vain to have various institutions start systematic collections of titles and data about exiled authors. He and F. C. Weiskopf for many years gathered important bibliographical data which to some extent were made accessible in the latter's readable survey of the German literature that had been written "under foreign skies."[4]

Walter A. Berendsohn in Stockholm started early to gather primary material for his introduction to the German *Emigrantenliteratur*, stressing especially its militant-humanist character.[5] Richard Drews and Alfred Kantorowicz published biographies with selections of writings of authors who had been suppressed in Germany for twelve years and whose works had been "banned and burned."[6] In his "Literature as History," Paul E. Lüth also devoted some space to the literature in exile.[7] It is a hopeful sign for the slowly growing attention paid to the neglected field of German exile literature when a book of general reference like the *Deutschland-Jahrbuch* includes an article on emigrated authors which—while it has to be brief and compact—gives fair recognition to their work. It gives sympathetic emphasis to the fact that the literary achievements of the exile belong legitimately to German Literature proper.[8]

Such a view, of course, was at the time totally unacceptable to the Nazi guardians of the German *Schrifttum*, and even though these may—or may not—have entered well-merited oblivion, the question of whether the *Emigrantenliteratur* "belongs" is by no means universally answered in the affirmative.[9]

Speaking of a German Literature in Exile, one may ask: How is this literature to be defined? What is meant by it? The answer could be simply this: German literature in general is the body of writing in the German language; it is differentiated by the character of its creators, who, by native endowment, tradition, environment and numerous other factors, some not always easily comprehended in rational terms, give substantial expression to their reactions to the world about or within them. Literature in Exile is a part of the German Literature and is, above all, a *formale Kategorie*. It is the literature created by authors who were forced or chose to leave their native land and who continued their work in German no matter where they might find themselves. Of course, the writing done in exile assumed features which reflected the specific circumstances of their existence. But it is part and parcel of German literature as a whole. The domicile of a writer is not and never was a decisive, qualitative criterion concerning his belonging to a certain literature.

While this statement may have the naive charm of simplicity, it should not be taken as more than it claims to be. The character of exile literature, as that of any literature, is complex and has given rise to lively theoretical discussions. As Thomas Mann pointed out early, the boundary line between "emigrated" and "non-emigrated" literature cannot be drawn easily, but it certainly does not coincide with territorial boundaries.[10]

Attempts to come to definitional terms about the literature in exile started early. In line with the objective of this study, to give in an expository fashion a picture of the currents and problems of the German literature abroad, some of the efforts toward analyzing and clarifying it may be recounted.[11]

In 1934, the Dutch writer Menno ter Braak, in an article *"Emigranten-Literatur,"* called to task exiled writers and critics, who in their indulgence in *adoration mutuelle,* failed in what the objective of a true literature in exile should be.[12] He denied that there was anything "essential" in practically any literature, and doubted that literature per se expresses "values of life"; it rather presents a distortion of them, owing to the process of artistic shaping. In many respects, German literature before Hitler's reign had been a concern of the *literati* only, and the impression was now that the emigrants simply "continue their business." The new situation was, if different at all, noticeable only in the choice of *Motive.* Yet these were not decisive criteria in a valid appraisal of literature. A rousing indignation as, for instance, that of Ernst Toller was more welcome than "smooth literature." Writers regard their own work rather naively, in that they take their disguises, their gestures, their "airs" as essence, and thus no surprise should be registered when the writers who had been driven out of their land now developed *Kritiklosigkeit* into a complex. In the necessity of defending himself against degrading calumny, against the Nazi idiocy that palmed itself off as mysticism, the writer necessarily resorted to defensive armor and weapons, and this well-understandable fact made him supersensitive to any criticisms toward himself and his colleagues in a similar position. Hence the mutual gushing praise observed in the reviews of works of emigrants. But the *Emigrantenliteratur* should be more than a perpetuation of the old modes and attitudes. The refugee writer should get a firmer grasp of his European mission and not permit the domineering influences that were generated by the fight against the false mysticism of the blood-and-soil idolatry. Criticism should have as its standard the genius of great personalities, not the smooth skill of the literary craftsman.

The article stirred up a vigorous response. Erich Andermann, in his refutation of the charges, arrived at some formulations which seem to have validity beyond the discussion at the time.[13] The implicit premise of ter Braak that the grievous experience of the refugee writers should have had a stimulating rather than a paralyzing effect was unacceptable, aside from the fact that there was no such intellectual-spiritual (*geistige*) entity as *Emigrantenliteratur.* The common experience of exile, to which its participants were led by far from uniform reasons, created at best a "community of fate" and nothing more. To challenge this heterogeneous group to a fulfillment of a European mission would first require a specific clarification of this term. Meanwhile, what else could reasonably be expected from the writers other than the continuation of the work begun at home? A certain leniency in criticism of their books was imperative under the extreme jeopardy of publishing in foreign lands. At home, adverse judgments could be absorbed and, indeed, with profit, because of the vast audience an author potentially enjoyed there; however, any adverse criticism in exile might mean the death knell not only for an author's work but for his very physical existence.

Ludwig Marcuse, one of the most prolific and vigorous writers of the exile, now professor at the University of Southern California, also rejected the reference to an *Emigrantenliteratur* because, as a generic concept, it was void of a "deeper, factual justification."[14] He called this literature the sum of all books by authors writing in German who either *could* or *would* not work at home under Hitler's rule. There was no correlation between the commonly shared fact of living in exile and literary communality. He rightly raised the question: Why should a writer outside of Germany not continue his earlier work in the same spirit and manner as he had done before? It speaks for his intellectual solidness and integrity when he does so. The fact was that the world view of the exiled writer stood the acid test of uprooting and transposition, while, on the other hand, the attitude of many authors remaining at home in Germany had to undergo radical changes if they wanted to stay in good health.

Another reaction to ter Braak came from Hans Sahl.[15] He went beyond Andermann's assertion that the writer's task was to cultivate the German language and be the guardian of the true German spirit. Sahl asked for more lucid and more obligating challenges; he insisted that categories other than the aesthetic ought to be used to determine the value of existence of a literature; it could be reduced to a common denominator just as little as the whole of the emigration from Nazi rule. He felt certain that this exile literature would bring forth what any literature would: the good, the trifling and the bad and, yes, maybe even something truly great. This, however, was not the salient point. The decisive question to be asked was: Is a sense, a meaning, being found for or given to the phenomenon of emigration? Certain works published had already attempted to give an answer to this question. The expatriated German literature would overcome the geographic distance from its native soil by proximity of the spirit; and it would assist in the building of a new Germany by everywhere securing cadres of her true representatives.

In challenging the free writers to tasks clearly outside the concept of an art per se, Sahl touched upon a theme that, as will be seen, was to engage considerable attention of writers and critics during the years of exile. Book after book, as well as significant articles in periodicals, appeared in German, a fact which gave substance to the claim that the center of the German cultural sphere might not necessarily be any longer found inside the territorial boundaries of Germany but had shifted outside the borders of the Reich.

The first general survey of the "free German book" was published in January, 1935, less than two years after the beginning of the exile.[16] Far from complete, and with emphasis on Soviet orientation, the *Almanach* was the result of the cooperation of sixteen publishers; it offered the view of a rich and vigorously unfolding literature in its summary of titles and the compact, if not always reliable, synopsis of the books.

About two years later, in November, 1936, the *Schutzverband deutscher Schriftsteller in Paris,* the protective association of German writers—which had aimed to establish a tradition of commemorating the ignominious day of Nazi book-burning on May 10, 1933, by founding exactly a year after this date the German "Freedom-Library"—provided the first concrete evidence of a vast German literature abroad by sponsoring in Paris a remarkable exhibition *Das freie deutsche Buch.*[17] Extensive bibliographies of publications followed year after year at a pace that soon made it extremely difficult to keep track of all the literary work done. Had there been adequate finances to subsidize the collecting and administering of this literature of the unhampered German mind as had been advocated by Kantorowicz, Pinthus and others, there would be a much better chance to study what is now "gone with wind."[18]

The first two noteworthy attempts for a general comprehension of this, by now, great body of literature in terms of serious categories and interpretative literary history appeared about five years after the exile began in 1933.

Odd Eidem, a young Norwegian writer who, from the start, had followed the events with sympathetic concern, wrote a study which, in a mainly sociologically determined approach, found the common denominator of the *Emigrantenliteratur* in the "universal unfortunate political fate" of its representatives.[19] He saw a militant literature emerging as the mouthpiece of an enslaved and silenced Germany, a literature that would become the standard-bearer in the fight for freedom. As such, it concerned even non-Germans to a high degree.

The primary objective of Eidem's study was to describe this fight. After briefly outlining the collapse of the Weimar Republic, the taking over of power by the Nazis and the initial effects on the cultural life of the nation, Eidem submitted to the reader not only a generally sympathetic picture of the fate of the exiled authors, but he also desired to have their situation and struggle comprehended in terms of history. In this manner, he presented the *Emigrantenliteratur* as a historical phenomenon.[20] While wholly aware of the heterogeneity of the exile literature (always referred to as *Emigrantenliteratur*), Eidem arrived at some semblance of order by giving special consideration to three distinct groups. The chapter on Jewish nationalism pointed out that the Jewish people constituted the largest component among the exiles; their writings were mainly of a polemic and confessional character. The national-conscious Jews could clearly be recognized as a separate group, an assertion against which the critic Werner Türk pointed to the indubitable fact that, for example, Arnold Zweig and Alfred Döblin not only were Jewish ideologists but also very definitely, and "above all," German authors.[21] In another chapter, Eidem dealt with the socialist writers of the emigration. Since the "essential" part of German refugees consisted of persons who had left for political reasons, the socialist writers gave more adequate expression to the general mentality of the German emigration. Their characteristic trait was optimism, despite the extraordinarily heartbreaking conditions under which they had to do their writing.

The non-socialist, individualistic authors were discussed by Eidem in a chapter entitled "The Emigrant Writer and History." These lacked the firm intellectual-spiritual (*geistig*) basis which the writers of the other two groups could claim. The individualists had turned to history in order to find parallels for the contemporary situation.[22] Biographies and historical novels were therefore preponderantly their domain. It might be of interest to note that Eidem included in his list of exiled writers some Austrians, who did not have to go into banishment until a few months later.

The preliminary character of Eidem's mainly sociological appraisal was recognized by the critics; it was frankly conceded even by the author himself when, for example, he named Lion Feuchtwanger as one who would fit into each of his three classes of writers. However, Eidem's pioneering essay was the first serious and informative introduction to the intellectual and political currents and points of view prevalent within the literature of the German refugees. Its drawback was that the author's eagerness to give a view of contemporary German history in vividly presented book summaries resulted in an unevenness of presentation not commensurate with the importance of the individual writers and the specific literary merits of their works.[23]

The literary situation in Germany before 1933 as he saw it was the starting point of Alfred Döblin's almost debonair survey of the German literature in exile, an essay that claimed as its core a "dialogue between politics and art."[24] From what is called a "historical point of view," Döblin perceived three great contemporary "classes" in German literature since 1900: first there were the feudalists, the agrarian and expansive-bourgeois conservatives whose gaze was turned backward and who were inclined toward "classicism." Then we would find the humanists with liberal, progressive and conciliatory middle-class tendencies. Finally, the intellectual-revolutionary group would come into view, alert to the present but with accents often quite contradictory. There were either political and non-political rationalists or mystics beholden to no definite political creed. This group especially represented the younger generation.

Such, then, was the situation in 1933. When, at that time, German Literature broke apart, the question was: Did this happen along lines predetermined according to the above grouping of the literary forces? The answer of Döblin was: in part, yes. The conservatives found in Nazism much to their liking. To be sure, the Caliban manners of the new masters thoroughly startled them, and Nazi reality had little in common with their own dreams of a new Reich shaped according to the romantic ideas of a Richard Wagner. Yet most of the "conservatives," if "racially" in the clear, stayed home.

Harder hit were the humanists. Their nature revolted against totalitarianism and dictatorship; to them *Gleichschaltung,* coordination, seemed, of course, out of the question. But was this so with all of them? Quite a few were scions of the well-to-do middle class who liked their comfort—and would not the realm of ideas and ideals always be free? So many remained at home and learned to hold their tongues, for they long since had become incapable of straightforward, honest hatred and hostility anyway. Those who did not succumb were pushed out or left on their own, branded by the Nazis as liberals, reactionaries and *Judenknechte.* In consequence, many of the authors of the cultured middle class were found abroad.

The class of intellectual revolutionaries was sharply torn asunder. There were those who shared with the conservatives the contempt for the liberal and humanist ideas that had "grown stale"; again, others had a certain affinity toward the mystic and the irrational. The rightist radicals among the *Geistesrevolutionäre* swung, for a while at least, into the Nazi orbit. However, the exodus of leftists occurred in great numbers.

The result of the break-up of German literature in 1933 was, then, that inside the Third Reich the conservatives and feudalists, rightist radicals and a few, very few, cryptohumanists carried on, even though they were under constant pressure. Abroad were found, besides a few splinter elements of group one, the block of the humanists and the greater part of the intellectual revolutionaries. The question of "aryan or non-aryan" was, of course, an important factor not to be forgotten.

After its severance from the Reich, the German literature abroad was by no means a torso. No matter how indigent and handicapped in innumerable ways the authors might have been, they continued to develop and grow in their craft. They were not necessarily "leftist" when they insisted on working "as they pleased." Freedom was indispensable for creative literary work; if it was denied, true art had to die. Literature in exile was free, yet Döblin contended that this fact in itself gave but a modicum of encouragement. Like cultures of bacteria, the writers had been transplanted into a different, and highly dubious, new "nutrient solution." Free German-writing authors had only parts of Switzerland and Russia for an immediate clientele, in addition to sporadic readers in Holland, Scandinavia and the U.S.A. But there was more to the exile than this material shrinkage of an audience. A writer in his native country absorbed, according to Döblin, consciously or unconsciously, the thousand impacts and vibrations of his fellow countrymen, which induced in him an ever-changing field of tension and would call forth an energy that made him grow and prosper in his art. How different the situation in exile! A total change in the environment brought almost complete social isolation, and even the close circle of his friends and "fellows in fate" was of little help because they, too, were involved in the same compulsive process of desperately trying to come to terms with a new world.

If this sad plight would now lead an observer, continued Döblin, to expect with apprehension a creeping anemia of the German literature abroad, his alarm would be groundless. In vain would future historians look for signs of weakness as a mark of this literature. Each in his individual way, most writers in exile went about their task with courage, with loyalty to themselves and their calling. Exile was more than a crushing blow of fate; it was the acid test for a man to prove his mettle. As the banishment dragged on and on, as it turned more and more into a long and wearisome march through waste and desert lands, the character was steeled and the work continued, even if it meant the critical tapping of irreplaceable reserves. The suffering, the strength and greatness of this literature thrown out of its native land was worthy of songs of high praise. It was, Döblin stated, German literature, not just a "literature of emigrants."

This literature now became subject to attacks from various quarters, not to mention the absolute and vicious hostility of the Nazis. The primarily politically minded people levelled the charge against it that its preoccupation with historic topics of past ages and of various climes ignored the burning issues of the day, and that it thus turned into a kind of escape from reality. The answer that literature might very well deal with peoples and epochs of the past and yet in doing so report passionately on the burning issues of the present was brushed aside; the imperious demand was made that literature in general, and especially this one of the exile, should not deal with aesthetic or psychological questions of a private nature, but stress political and social values above all. The response of Döblin was that the writers produced and did whatever was in their might and talent; they continued, each one individually, as they had done at home, spinning the thread of their work. The deepest misery in exile could not change the basic facts of their existence which were the indispensable presuppositions and conditions for all art and literature. They worked at long range; they were concerned with man and the world in their totality; and they had to follow their own creative impulses. The "practical man" and the "political man" may counter: You writers own a weapon greatest force, the living word. Do not use it in artful play while the world seems doomed to perish; use it to give direction and aim to the forces that will heal the world, else your art may go hang.

The confrontation of these views is, or course, a simplification and, at the same time, is overlaborated in its formulation. An artist, a writer, truly could not and should not cultivate "private" concerns to the exclusion of considerations of vital communal interest. He has, indeed, to put up with some curtailment of the self-sovereignty as an artist and examine his position. But fundamentally this was the artist's—Döblin's—answer:

Each artist, each writer, carries the community in which he lives along into his deepest solitude. Through language, judgments, images and concepts the community has a share in the artist's creative process. The writer is by no means struck dumb when in his solitude. He carries on innumerable 'conversations' all around, merging with them his inspiration."²⁵ Isolation or communal contact was therefore not a question for an author, but the problem was, what kind of society has generated the directive force even into his most private sphere.

Many German writers, in contrast to French authors, had carried only wretched miniature editions of their society into their solitude, showing a very low degree of communality spirit, *Gesellschaftlichkeit*. There were determining predelections for the abstract and morally arrogant (and stupid) contempt for the everyday life, the *Alltag*; instead, "eternal problems" were the exclusive concern; the interest in the fullness of human life for which Goethe once had raised his voice had gone by the board. A short circuit into mysticism often took place, a *Kurzschluss in die Mystik*.

The secularization of German literature, a process somewhat parallel to the gradual lowering of political barriers, had been infinitely slow. But pushing too hard in this direction had led to another short circuit, that one into the ephemeral problems of the day and into party politics, a danger to which French and English literature also had begun to succumb. Tolstoy and Gorki, Flaubert and Keller were able through their work to stir up a sense of social awareness because their hearts gave truth and completeness to their stories, not party platforms and a desire to accommodate politicians. It was ridiculous and provoking to Döblin when theoreticians, critics and writers solicited in exile the creation of antifascist works. The writers ought to be left strictly alone in their work. They were *The German Literature* abroad, and they should not tolerate indoctrination by politicians. It was they who continued the free German literature and they had to be on guard not to fall prey to compulsory neuroses. Cliques of the German political parties, irresponsible and detestable, had tried in exile to elbow their way into literary criticism. For their own selfish purposes they began to classify "friendly" and "hostile" authors, and they also singled out those to be ruined by the "silent treatment.²⁶

The sensible attitude, so Döblin continued, would be to encourage free German writers to aim at a closer attachment to society and to have them develop a spirit of communality, *Gemeinschaft*. An author would find far deeper satisfaction if he would enter the complex web of human relations, rather than explore his own private sphere to the point of exhaustion. But no political program could animate the working toward such a goal, only the slow-working impact of personal experience. Political formulae and manifestos are intellectual abstractions; in the field of art they amount at best to labels and slogans and nothing more.

The world was a world of horror, and even if the authors could not help but be incorrigible glorifiers and lovers of life and would never give up that which they knew was its depth and magic, more than heretofore they would have to deal with the "tiger face" of the world, whose features were composed of evil, harshness and war. Insignificant as he may have felt, the writer had to put greater trust in the "gentle and great" power of art and the creative word, and be convinced that he was the guardian of a fire through which the "tiger" had to be tamed and conquered. His field was the world and not just the drawing rooms of the—after all not so—mighty ones. While he himself kept aloof from politics and the struggles for power, inasmuch as they are manifested in society as well as in private lives, he had to recognize the forces at work and react to them positively through his creative art.

In concluding the theoretical discussion of the literature in exile, Döblin wanted to make it clear that his negative criticism was mainly aimed at the contempt of "reality" and of "the human community"; he wanted to score the clinging to bloodless phantoms and abstractions that posed as *Mystik* but were, in fact, only indications of hollowness, disillusionment and degeneration. Religion, genuine *Mystik,* was part of the creative basis of a new humanity, and literature was to share in the great process of recovery and restitution in the degree to which it penetrated into the ancient core of life from whence radiated all the forces of creation.

In the second part of Döblin's book, about forty writers pass in review, among them, naturally, the best known. Brief samples of some of their works illustrate the points Döblin wanted to make. His comments are presented in a style that is as compact as it is elegant and fluent, if not without caprice. The impression left by Döblin is that the body of literature created by the German writers abroad was true German literature in its proper sense; it was not a questionable branch to be stigmatized by derogatory overtones which, intended or not, would brand it inferior and illegitimate.²⁷

A vigorous brief against classifying the work of authors in exile as a "literature of emigrants" was presented by Hermann Kesten in the same year in which Döblin's study appeared.²⁸ Point by point he examined and rejected the arguments in favor of using qualifying terms for the literature produced abroad, although he recognized that Hitler's murderous persecution of the free spirit resulted from the start in a "double-entry bookkeeping" concerning literature. A Chinese wall arose between the censored and the free book. Numerically the greater part of writers, of course, remained in the Third Reich, but nowhere do quantitative terms mean less than in the realm of the spirit. A very significant group of authors went into exile or returned to their homelands: Switzerland, Austria, Czechoslovakia. A magnificent and prospering literature turned its back for a while on a dishonored motherland. Yet there did not run a truly deep schism between the Nazi-corralled literature and the *Emigrantenliteratur*.²⁹ Neither exile nor membership in the Reich's official chamber of writers separated *die "beiden deutschsprachigen Literaturen"* (sic), the two German-language literatures. Along with writers of genius and character, scoundrels and amateurs also went into exile, and within the Reich remained upright patriots and charming talents beside "chained dogs" and lick-spittles. The dividing line between the living free German literature and the National-Socialist *Gräberliteratur,* the literature of the tombs, ran straight through the Reich and through the exile as it did through those free countries where German was the mother tongue or one of the mother tongues.

No German *Emigrationsliteratur* existed, according to Kesten, in the sense in which this word was often employed, either in a hateful attitude or with a benevolent intent. Nobody had succeeded in postulating one single valid and unifying principle by which the term "literature of emigrants" could be justified. For what, besides the German language, had the writers of the emigration in common? Certainly not German citizenship nor the place of domicile. Or should, perhaps, the fact that their works were banned in Germany unite them? Hermann Hesse was still published there, and Thomas Mann was until recently; they were humanists both and deadly enemies of Nazism, but Otto Strasser, whose work clearly revealed fascist tendencies, was banned also. Were perhaps the inner and external factors of exile a common denominator? The great divergencies in the fate of many proved this argument illusionary. The firmly stated conclusion of Kesten was that no common character for the *Emigrationsliteratur* existed, just as there was none for the literature in the Reich. The fact of exile or the banishment of his works did not create a literary postulate and criterion for judging a writer. The exile left traces as did any experience, but no single experience was sufficient in itself to have art and literature named after or classified by it, nor was any experience significant enough to require it.

In a review of Döblin's study especially aimed at what he considered the questionable and faulty application of sociological principles, Ferdinand Lion shared with Kesten the thesis that style and form immanent to the artistic creation had to provide the evaluating criteria; they afforded the drawing of much sharper lines of demarcation than a social grouping into feudalists, humanists and revolutionaries—if a classification of literature was possible at all in the desire for getting a grasp of the creative spirit in terms of rational comprehension. Contrary to Kesten, however, Lion "cannot get rid of a feeling that one deals with a compact body that is fighting and feels *solidarisch.*"[30] In literature, the decision about a new intellectual-spiritual German existence, and hence a new definitional category, could be made only when a "new style" would make an appearance. Caution was advisable for the history of the European Mind abounds in quickly succeeding theses, antitheses and syntheses of styles which, in fact, mark the caesuras of the Mind's "real revolutions." The magic formula of such a "new style" might be created even by someone who was still in the camp of the opposition, maybe now living within the Reich, but whom to welcome into exile would be an honor. Lion acknowledged by inference the oneness of German literature in its essence, although he was aware that there was a body of literature outside the Reich even if a common denominator for it was lacking.

The eloquent and often violent objections to the term *Emigrantenliteratur,* based on theoretic, aesthetic, political and historical arguments, may have had a much simpler fundamental cause. In torrents of slander and abuse, Goebbels tried to hammer this term into the minds of the German people as a concomitant to venomous hate, treachery and revulsion. Vicious persecution was directed against the free German literature wherever the organs and agencies of Nazism had a chance, not only inside but also outside the Reich. No wonder the exiles resented this term with such deadly enmity; they could not help but hear it with a sense of shame and deepest indignation. Furthermore, German literature in exile, with its achievements and free cultural tradition that stemmed from many roots, could not be qualified so narrowly as to be just a "literature of emigrants."

In view of these facts, Berendsohn and others had a losing battle on their hands in favoring the concept of a German "literature of emigrants." Berendsohn's definition and interpretation which aimed at dispelling the detestable connotations of the term and having it turned into a badge of honor may have been made in the same spirit as the Dutch adopted the term *gueux* against their Spanish oppressors, but it never seemed to have found general acceptance.[31] Aside from serious theoretical objections, the resentment against this designation was too bitter. Prejudice and aversions against *Emigranten* still do exist in some quarters in Germany even today; it is not uncommon to see *Emigrantendeutsch* and *Emigrantenliteratur* used there as terms of derogation. It explains why, if for no other reasons, Berendsohn's advocacy of the term *Emigrantenliteratur* might be without success.

Theoretical discussions about whether there was a German literature abroad and what it should be called subsided during the war years and the time immediately after. But when conditions became somewhat more settled, interest began to develop, if only slightly, in the work of exiled German authors. The year 1933 was recognized as not having a specific qualitative meaning in literature, although it was the date when Nazism got into power and when a far-reaching relocation of writers got under way. But their creativity and production had suffered no really fatal break in continuity.[32]

Oskar Maria Graf concluded a cogent analysis of the situation in exile and its specific problems for a German writer with a pointed warning against accepting the concept of a divided German literature: "Whoever tries—no matter whether in malice or in blindness—to break up today our much-harassed, great literature, which is now but slowly recovering, into an emigrated part and into one that stayed at home, yes, or even into a Western and an Eastern half, he commits as dastardly a crime as did Hitler and his helpers. He betrays the wholeness of our spirit and of our people. Our literature, the noblest and the unique medium for our common understanding, is as indivisible as the language that joins together all of us."[33]

While "German Literature in Exile" cannot be considered an entity per se and while it is part and parcel of the greater German Literature, it seems justified as a factual term of simple, convenient reference. But it is more. As the national currents of literature in Europe around 1880 began to form a mainstream of greater European significance within which German literature, however, retained characteristic features of its own—in no small measure the result of the political happenings of the time—so it was with the literature in exile after 1933. This literature continued, outside the Reich, the development that was already in progress before under the all-covering term German Literature. It was inside Hitler's realm where the break was almost complete with a rich and chaotic, contradictory and paradoxical, spiritual-intellectual creative field of force which German Literature had encompassed. Impulses welling from deepest indignation about a cruel persecution, re-enforced by political passions and understandable "group hatred," even led to assertions that the exile literature was *the* German Literature of the day; such a conclusion, however, is simply not borne out by facts. Many upright and competent authors and, of course, poets remained in Germany and, despite the loathsome rush with which opportunist writers after the war claimed "hibernation" into *innere Emigration* (inward emigration), this term stands for a reality, often deeply tragic. The men and women of the "emigration within" represent "rightfully an essential part of the German intellectual-spiritual (*geistig*) life" during the years of the Nazi regime.[34]

Art and literature signify peculiar ways of creative man's coming to terms with the world about and in him. The exile, with everything this word suggests, exerted influences, scarcely perceptible in some, greatly in the case of others. The exiled writer was attacked when he continued his work "as usual," and was berated as well when, self-conscious and under compulsion, he tried to break with the past and plow new fields. The awareness of his existence in a given environment peculiar to him is the start for any writer and artist. His experiences give and modify the direction to his aims and they furnish the substance for his formative genius. The creative mind can never be wholly fathomed nor fully understood, yet certain facts are clear. The writer-artist must be intelligent in his own line; he must have a power of discrimination and judgment. Experiences move him more than ordinary people; yet in a way he is detached and objective about them. This power of detachment is vital. The experienced event can be quite trifling in itself, or it may be a series of stirring happenings, almost anything. Some inner awareness registers the events, thoughts, feelings and actions; there is perhaps a flash of recognition and empathy, and then all may sink down for a while below the threshold of consciousness. This "sinking down" is of crucial importance, for far below—in "the abyss of the soul"—a mysterious process is going on which may cause the matter to come up again in a new guise, so that the original emotional-intellectual experience is juxtaposed with other material, and the whole fused into something "new." What was an isolated instance or a fragment of outer or inner experiences becomes now "part of a whole." With slowly growing momentum, insight spreads. Along with this, a coldly critical faculty takes over, aware of everything pertinent or extraneous to the project on hand, which is: to translate the inner world through words into an objective creation. The vision within is unerringly right for the artist, and it is only when some veil or curtain of "foreign" origin comes between him and the deep well of his awareness that he may fail and become a fraud; he is a fraud when he *tries* to be an artist. What comes out may be poetry or drama or an epic creation; it can be anything. In the process of artistic creative action, two acts occur simultaneously: the material wells up as from a volcano, and it may often stimulate a search for elements of affinity not yet grasped, but at the same time, organization, sorting and ruthless rejection also take place. Many a writer has failed in this work of self-criticism because he found equally good whatever the inner volcano poured forth. Some with only little creative fire are able to manipulate with great skill their limited talent to the point of perfection. The real genius has the great fire burning inside together with a coldly critical eye for whatever comes forth, and no mercy is shown toward his own work if it fails to meet his standards.

Keeping these facts of the creative process in mind, it is obvious that the exile had to leave its mark on the writer. While it might be right and fitting not to speak of a divided German literature, the de facto situation must be recognized. Kesten and others who reject, and rightly so, the concept of *Emigrantenliteratur* must refer to this body of literature somehow. They do so by using, as a way out, the term in quotation marks. But they do use it, and have to, if some kind of reference is to be made at all to the work done in exile.

But the designation *Literature of Emigrants* will not do for the reasons stated; to speak of the *Literature in Exile*, however, seems justified. If it fails to suggest a common intellectual-spiritual denominator and cannot stand as a concept for a homogeneous literary substance, one may ask: When did German Literature ever exact such definitional basis? What have Mörike and Heine, Schnitzler and Kafka, Albrecht Schaeffer and Döblin, Stefan George and Arno Holz, Thomas Mann and Herman Stehr, Barlach and Zuckmayer, and countless others in common which permits speaking of them as belonging to *one* literature? The language, indeed! But even here how different the style and diction, the imagery and point of view and values, the *Gehalt und Gestalt*. Why then not speak of a literature in exile? It did exist, although without a common unifying principle. In fact, one may ask: When has such a vigorous principle been in effect in any literature?

The concept of a German literature in exile as used in this study refers to a specific body of writing and as such is first of all a term of reference. It embraces works of high and low quality; it is the creation of a host of writers of most divergent genius, talents, tendencies and beliefs. Their fate as writers in exile, when viewed in the light of history, was not as unique as it might seem at first. The portent of exile could almost be called a professional hazard for many masters of the pen. A long and proud record from the days of the Greeks and Romans up to modern times tells the story of authors whom tyranny had driven from their native soil and forced onto the "battlefield of exile."[35]

A frequently heard charge against the German Literature in Exile since 1933 is that it could not claim authenticity because of its removal from the "mother soil" and its being cut off from the "eternal spring of folkdom." In variations, the indictment runs like this: You emigrants claim to be the guardians of German culture, yet you live far away from the land whose language you speak. You can cultivate this language in but narrow circles; your work is overshadowed by the bitterness of the fact that your presence is barely tolerated by your hosts; you have been torn from your native soil which sustained you, and now the contact with the living community which furnished the substance of your being is severed; through the telescope of emigration you see what happens at home only in dim outlines, and the years abroad will ever more confuse your view of your compatriots and their lives in Germany.

On close examination these arguments are as hollow as they are superficially intriguing. History tells how in all ages strong personalities had found exile, while rich in tension and bitter disappointments, a challenge for creative and abiding work. Some of the great masterpieces of the world's literature were produced in exile: the *Septuagint,* the *Koran,* Dante's *Divina Commedia,* the pedagogic works of Comenius, great works of Lord Byron and Victor Hugo, to name just a few. So far as German Literature is concerned, from Ulrich von Hutten onward, the exiled writer was by no means an exceptional figure. The hackneyed arguments against the quality of the literature in exile fall flat in view of the existence of a body of writing that is as strong, vigorous and sometimes great as it was free. There never ceased to be a deep feeling of oneness and understanding with the people at home that lived under the swastika. There was a correct, precise knowledge and a keen awareness of what was going on at home; a constant alert guard was mounted from many vantage points of observation throughout the years of exile, which to many writers meant just a temporary shelter. They "carried Germany within" wherever they went, to quote a statement by Thomas Mann. *Coelum non animum mutant qui transmare currunt* is as true today as it was in the days of Horace (Ep. I, 11, 27). The exile meant an uprooting from customs and environment and lifelong associations, but the minds that left Germany suffered no severance from the rich intellectual-spiritual substance of her cultural history. In an essay on the history of political emigration, Arthur Rosenberg concluded that by far the largest part of the "thinking and intellectually creative Germany" was found in exile, and that this part had as the true basis for its work the community of the people at home. Each volume of poetry, each novel or political book that the exile brought forth with such vigor, intensity and effectiveness was one proof more that the abiding cultural-political forces were not aligned with the Nazi world at home; they were underground there. "The heart and mind, the eye and the pen" did not stop at the Reich's boundaries; in writing, the authors in exile always had the beloved homeland and its people in mind, and the results of their labor were works of lasting artistic merit and humanist-political enlightenment.[36]

The German literature in exile can justly claim to be German Literature, and while its freedom was the conspicuous great asset, other aspects of it should not be overlooked. To quote again a shrewd observer like Hermann Kesten, he says: "The break-up of German Literature by tyranny and exile muddled up all shades of literary fashions and schools and falsified the artistic rank. Added to this must be the peculiar tendencies toward a stagnation of attitudes found in the sealed-off group of emigrants who, so to speak, put their judgments, dispositions, quarrels and prejudices on ice. . . ."[37] This was indeed true to a high degree, and it is recognized. There were many discussions of the advantages, as well as of the limitations, of the writer in exile. Soul-searching and self-examination were favored practices among the many conscientious ones, but there was also inflexibility of spirit and stubborn dogmatism. Exaggerated recognition was claimed on the ground of the praiseworthy antifascist spirit of a work, regardless of literary merits. So the picture of the literature in exile is far from uniformly positive. Top performance was as rare in exile as it is everywhere. True artists may have both talent, perhaps genius, *and* ethical integrity, that is to say, character. But this is not necessarily so, and the history of the literature in exile gives evidence of this fact.[38]

However, arrogance and boastfulness were rare among the more significant writers. In a speech at the opening of the book exhibition of the organization of free German writers in Paris, Heinrich Mann said—and the tragic overtones are saddening indeed—"Perhaps these works give witness of an exile that might be forgotten soon, and they will be just the traces of an era which otherwise will leave no other mark—we must be prepared to face the fact that the tomorrow will not know of us any more." Having conceded this, H. Mann, with the unconquerable fortitude that was his, went on to express the hope that nevertheless, one day, the *Hingabe an Ideen,* the devotion of the exile writers to ideas, might yet be recognized, for it was from these very ideas that a better future world could arise.[39]

O. M. Graf saw in the exile an intensified challenge to return to that "readiness to take in the world" which had always marked the true German spirit; it meant to a writer "proving his mettle to himself." Graf's evaluation of the situation is representative of that of many exiled German writers. Exile demanded being on constant guard and squaring one's own intellectual and emotional endowment with whatever seemingly alien elements rushed into the writer's sphere, thus creating crises often more hazardous and dangerous to the writer than the daily battle for material existence.

Those refugees who were most deeply rooted in what might be called specifically German culture were in greatest danger of turning small and petty in their outlook. They were not only incapable of absorbing intelligently the foreign elements about them—they fought tooth and nail against an unprejudiced appraisal of their new surroundings. Only with difficulty did they realize how much such a stubborn rejection of their new world made them appear nationalistic, arrogant and overbearing fools, nor did they perceive how this attitude made them sink ever deeper into utter forsakenness and mental desolation, a status in which no positive answer would come forth any longer to any question.

The crisis usually began with an acute, indescribable nostalgia, with a longing for all that once had given stimulus and energy and faith for work. It ended with "going to the dogs," and it was not until then that the exile became an *emigrant* in the saddest meaning of the word. Now they belonged nowhere, not even into their "own time."

Graf pointed to the high number of suicides in exile. Few of these were disappointed for political reasons. Neither lack of recognition or literary success nor material want was always the decisive factor. Tucholski, Toller, Stefan Zweig and, of late, the tragic figure of Klaus Mann never suffered from these. What brought about the breakdown in some was a human factor tied indissolubly to artistic creative impulses. They were *German* writers; they were the "prisoners of their own language"; their thinking had been formed and shaped by it. The transfer to other modes of thought was far from simple, and some writers would need decades to grasp fully the "fluidity of reasoning" in the inflections and nuances of another language. Many were tormented by paralyzing doubts as to whether "their word" continued to be heard and hit the mark; to make sure, Klaus Mann and others resolved "the flight into another tongue." To be translated into other languages, even successfully, was small consolation for a Toller and a Stefan Zweig. It did not help their enervating impatience and sense of frustration which they finally carried to the point where voluntary death seemed the only choice left.[40]

Isolation in one form or another was the lot of all exiled writers, yet the majority labored on under conditions which would appear totally inhibitive to creative work. The narrowing and stultifying effects of the exile are often discernible; they also became, of course, material of literary objectification. But the main work in exile reveals a remarkable evidence of the effective humanistic front which free German writers formed in the struggle against the tyranny over the minds and bodies of men. This is one of the functional features of the exile literature, and it might be found, if only in traces, even in the work of authors who, with Kesten, subscribe to the principle that true creative art is "beyond tendency and purpose, politics and morality." It is a fact beyond dispute that, while within the boundaries of the Reich, German Literature had to coordinate itself somehow if it wanted to deal with freedom and human problems of relevance beyond the framework of Nazi *Weltanschauung,* "hundreds and hundreds of German poets, authors and journalists, adequately or inadequately, have given loud and frank testimony as to the existence of another, *non-national-socialist* Germany, and thus maintained . . . the continuity of German autonomous culture."[41]

The present study does not assign to the German literature in exile qualities of integration which it does not have. The time has not come to say anything about it with a claim for finality; the forces and passions that animated it still reach out into the present day, and, according to partisanship and *Welt- und Kunstanschauung,* judgments will differ. Here the traditional ideal of scholarly objectivity as far as it is consistent with a firm commitment to a liberal-humanist faith will be adhered to, and it is the hope of the writer that the exposition of the problems connected with the writings in exile and the issues that gave them substance and direction will be at least of some value to literary-cultural history.[42]

Notes

1. This terminology is not undisputed. For definition of terms, statistics, literature and information about help rendered to the fugitives see: Kurt R. Grossmann and Hans Jacob, "The German Exile and the 'German Problem'" in *Journal of Central European Affairs,* IV, 2, pp. 165-185; Sir John Hope Simpson, *The Refugee Problem* (London, 1939); Stephen Duggan and Betty Drury, *The Rescue of Science and Learning* (New York, 1948); Paul Frings, *Das Internationale Flüchtlingsproblem 1919-1950* (Frankfurt/Main, 1951); D. P. Kent, *The Refugee Intellectual* (New York, 1953); W. Rex Crawford, ed., *The Cultural Migration* (Philadelphia, 1953); Norman Bentwich, *The Rescue and Achievement of Refugee Scholars* (The Hague, 1953); Helge Pross, *Die deutsche akademische Emigration nach den Vereinigten Staaten: 1933-1941* (Berlin, 1955).

2. Kent, *op. cit.,* p. 135. In the course of my studies, I counted more than 450 names of exiled writers who at some time during the Hitler regime published in German outside of Germany. This included, of course, authors of any kind of writing, literary or otherwise, from short book reviews to the well-known works of Thomas Mann. The actual number of writers is, of course, higher than the above figure.

3. German critics, until recently, have hardly concerned themselves with the literature created in exile. In Germany, some exiled authors have been published again with success. In the Soviet Zone of Germany, the publishing of exiled writers of leftist and communist persuasion has been promoted with special vigor. Here greater critical, if dogmatically fixed, attention has been paid to the literature of the exile

than in Western Germany. For a typical comment see: H. E. Holthusen, *Der unbehauste Mensch* (München, 1952) pp. 142 ff. Some outstanding histories of German literature of recent date either fail to mention or pay scant attention to the exiled writers and their works; for instance: *Annalen der Deutschen Literatur,* ed. by H. O. Burger, (Stuttgart, 1952); Wolfgang Pfeiffer-Belli, *Geschichte der deutschen Dichtung,* (Freiburg, 1954); Herbert A. Frenzel, *Daten deutscher Dichtung,* (Köln/Berlin, 1953). Works which, within the framework of their intellectual-spiritual pattern, give recognition to the exile and to some of its authors are: *Deutsche Literatur im XX. Jahrhundert,* ed. by Hermann Friedmann and Otto Mann, (Heidelberg, 1954); Wilhelm Grenzmann, *Deutsche Dichtung der Gegenwart* (Frankfurt/Main, 1953); Paul Fechter, *Geschichte der deutschen Literatur,* (Gütersloh, 1952). Important American books with analyses and bibliographies are: Harry Slochower, *No Voice Is Wholly Lost . . . ,* (New York, 1945) and Victor Lange, *Modern German Literature,* (Ithaca, N. Y., 1945). See also the articles on German writers in exile by Karl O. Paetel, W. Sternfeld, Harold von Hofe and others as listed in the bibliographies of the *PMLA,* etc. (See introductory note to the Bibliography).

4. F. C. Weiskopf, *Unter fremden Himmeln* (Berlin, 1947).

5. Walter A. Berendsohn, *Die Humanistische Front,* Vol. I, (Zürich, 1946). I had the privilege of reading the manuscript of the second volume in London and derived not only valuable information from it but found corroborative support for much of my own findings. Berendsohn's second volume now deposited in the Deutsche Bibliothek in Frankfurt/Main will be published presently.

6. *Verboten und Verbrannt,* ed. by Richard Drews and Alfred Kantorowicz, (Berlin and München, 1947).

7. Paul E. Lüth, *Literatur als Geschichte,* 2 vols. (Wiesbaden, 1947).

8. F. Martini, "Dichter der Emigration" in *Deutschland-Jahrbuch 1953* (Essen, 1953), pp. 601 ff.

9. On several occasions I was counselled by colleagues not to bother with this "insignificant, non-German" literature. After they had become acquainted with the scope and character of the literature in question, they regretted their earlier unfamiliarity with the field.

10. Quoted in *Das Wort,* I, 1, p. 4. Heinz Rabe accepted the refer ence *German Emigration 1933* as a sociological-political phenomenon only as a *formale Kategorie* (*Neues Tagebuch,* 1934, 17, p. 403). The same might be said of the term "Literature in Exile" when a first definition is attempted. For details of periodicals quoted, see bibliography.

11. In order not to have this study burdened with a tiring and—in view of the publications already cited—needless catalog of names and titles, I limited myself to material personally examined. From it I drew what appear to be reliably representative data. Some exceptions in the use of secondary sources are carefully noted.

12. *Das Neue Tagebuch,* 1934, 52, pp. 1244 ff. Quoted as *NT.*

13. *NT,* 1935, 1, pp. 1267 ff.

14. *NT,* 1935, 2, pp. 43 ff. In parenthesis Marcuse allows, of course, the existence of some kind of German "literature in exile"; by implication he permits the conclusion that it has at least one distinguishing mark: its emphasis on indignation.

15. *Ibid.,* p. 45.

16. *Almanach für das freie deutsche Buch* (Prague, 1935). About one-fourth of the authors mentioned in this publication were not German; among these were many Soviet writers. The almanac also announces literature in the field of social and natural sciences and is not confined to so-called belles-lettres.

17. The driving force in the activity of the German writers in Paris was Alfred Kantorowicz. See Berendsohn, *op. cit.,* p. 63 f.

18. For compendious bibliographies, see the summaries and titles in *NT, Das Wort, Internationale Literatur, Die Sammlung, Der Aufbau* (New York), and periodicals listed in the bibliography; *Fünf Jahre freies deutsches Buch* (Paris, 1937); *Das Buch* (Paris, 7 issues, 1938/1939). In addition to the bibliographies found in the postwar works already mentioned, attention may be called to the *Deutsche Nationalbibliothek,* Ergänzung I (Leipzig, 1949). Among its 5495 titles are a great number of "exile works." See also W. Sternfeld, "Die 'Emigrantenpresse'" in *Deutsche Rundschau,* 1950, pp. 250-259; and his articles in *The Wiener Library Bulletin* (London), Vols. III and IV.

19. Odd Eidem, *Diktere i Landflyktighet* (Oslo, 1937). My information about this work is not firsthand; my discussion is mainly based on Berendsohn, *op. cit.,* and a few other secondary references.

20. Cf. Werner Türk, "Dichter im Exil" in *Das Wort,* III, 5, pp. 122 ff.

21. *Ibid.,* p. 124.

22. Cf. Berendsohn, *op. cit.,* p. 69.

23. *Ibid.,* and Türk, *op. cit.,* pp. 123, 125.

24. Alfred Döblin, *Die deutsche Literatur: Im Ausland seit 1933* (Paris, 1938). I call attention to the critical review by F. Lion in *Mass und Wert,* 1939, 6, pp. 854-858, and the scathing attack on Döblin by Kurt Hiller in 1939, reprinted in *Köpfe und Tröpfe* (Hamburg/Stuttgart, 1950), pp. 127-135. In a study of a pronounced religious-irrational character pub-

lished after his return from exile, Döblin, then a Catholic convert, retained the earlier basic classification of German literature but recommended "a new tuning of its harps." See "Die deutsche Utopie von 1933 und die Literatur" in *Das Goldene Tor,* (Lahr im Schwarzwald), 1946, October/November, pp. 136-147, and December, pp. 258-269.

25. *Ibid.,* pp. 22 f. "In die tiefste Einsamkeit nimmt jeder Künstler, jeder Schriftsteller die Gesellschaft, in der er lebt, mit. Sie ist es, die mit ihm zusammen dichtet und formt, in der Sprache, in den Urteilen, Bildern und Begriffen, die er mitgenommen hat. Nicht stumm ist der Schriftsteller in der Einsamkeit. Ein tausendfaches Gespräch führt er nach allen Seiten und trägt in dieses Gespräch seine Eingebung hinein."

26. *Ibid.,* p. 29. In summarizing the ideas of Döblin, and those of others, I had to go beyond mere literal transcriptions in order to render an interpretatively correct picture.

27. Döblin does not state this explicitly, but his implication is clear. For an enumeration of the reasons pro and con regarding the term *Emigrantenliteratur,* see Berendsohn, *op. cit.,* pp. 69-75. Berendsohn himself and also Odd Eidem favor it.

28. "Fünf Jahre nach unsrer Abreise . . ." in *NT,* 1938, 5, pp. 114-117.

29. *Ibid.,* p. 115. Kesten himself uses the term against which he protests simply as a matter of necessary reference. After all is said and done, referral has to be made to this body of literature, and *de facto* Kesten, too, speaks of two literatures. Henry W. Nordmeyer used in his indispensable annual bibliography in Germanics the parenthetical reference: "(Reich and non-Reich)." *PMLA,* LIV, p. 1313 *et al.* Martin Gumpert chooses the term "Exile Literature" for the survey of German literature in the *New Int. Year Book,* Vol. 1939, p. 312. George N. Shuster speaks of "Emigré Literature," *ibid.* 1938, p. 287.

30. *Op. cit.,* pp. 854 ff. See note 24.

31. Berendsohn, *op. cit.,* pp. 75 *et al.*

32. Cf. Werner Milch, *Ströme. Formeln. Manifeste* (Marburg, 1949) pp. 81 ff.

33. O. M. Graf, "Die Unteilbarkeit der deutschen Literatur" in *Deutsche Beiträge,* 1950, 6, p. 447. Holthusen (*op. cit.,* pp. 142 ff.) describes the difficulties for the "two literatures" growing together again and concludes ". . . it will require a high degree of tact, patience and mutual concessions in order that the two German literatures, the emigrated and the non-emigrated, can again grow into one."

34. Karl O. Paetel, "Das deutsche Buch in der Verbannung" in *Deutsche Rundschau,* 1950, p. 755; and "Deutsche im Exil" in *Aussenpolitik* (Stuttgart), September, 1955, pp. 584 f. See also his monthly *Deutsche Gegenwart. Ein Informationsbrief.* Published from January, 1947, to December, 1948.

35. A phrase coined by Freiligrath, quoted by Oswald Mohr in his *Das Wort der Verfolgten* (Basel, 1945), p. 14. This work is a valuable anthology of German voices of the exile in historical order, from H. Heine to Th. Mann. See also a related collection, *Dies Buch gehört der Freiheit,* edited by Erwin Reiche (Weimar, 1950).

36. Arthur Rosenberg, "Zur Geschichte der politischen Emigration" in *Mass und Wert,* II, 3, pp. 371 ff. A typical view to the contrary is expressed by Ernst Jünger in his *Strahlungen* (Tübingen, 1949) p. 550, quoted approvingly by Holthusen (*op. cit.,* p. 143). Jünger states: *Der Schritt in die Emigration führt immer in ein schwächeres Element* (The step into emigration always leads into a less potent realm). Jünger's well-authenticated opposition to the dictatorship at home and his rank as a writer will not be disputed. But his dictum, made when he considered the possibility of staying behind in France as the Germans retreated from that country in 1944, was based on a fantastically different situation from that of the true exiles. Jünger no doubt realized that the Allies would not receive as an "emigrated writer" an officer who almost until the end had served under Hitler, no matter with what sincere mental reservations. His judgment about exile writing is colored by the rationalization of his situation. He shows no knowledge of the nature and the achievement of the literature in exile. By not giving the background of the statement, Holthusen's quotation is misleading. As a veteran officer of World War I of highest distinction and fame, Jünger held for a long time a unique position of immunity; by going back into the army, he went into "the aristocratic form of emigration." (This phrase was coined by Gottfried Benn; see his *Doppelleben* [Wiesbaden, 1950] p. 110. See also the reference to Edmund Wilson in note 9, ch. II.)

37. Hermann Kesten in *Klaus Mann zum Gedächtnis* (Amsterdam, 1950) p. 85.

38. Cf. Hermann Kesten "Der Preis der Freiheit" in *Die Sammlung,* (1933/34) pp. 238-244.

39. Quoted in *Neue Weltbühne* (1937), 32, pp. 988 ff.

40. O. M. Graf, *op. cit.,* pp. 438 ff.

41. Karl O. Paetel, "Das deutsche Buch in der Verbannung," *op. cit.,* p. 760.

42. Concerning my approach to literature, see Wm. K. Pfeiler, *War and the German Mind: The Testimony of Writers Who Fought at the Front* (New York, 1941), pp. 319 f.

Thomas A. Kamla (essay date 1975)

SOURCE: Kamla, Thomas A. "Konrad Merz: *Ein Mensch fällt aus Deutschland*—The 'Inner' and 'Outer' Exile of Youth." In *Confrontation with Exile: Studies in the German Novel*, pp. 35-44. Bern: Herbert Lang/Frankfurt: Peter Lang, 1975.

[*In the following excerpt, Kamla focuses on the ideas and career of Konrad Merz, an anti-fascist novelist who left Germany to write in exile.*]

Konrad Merz numbers among the younger writers who made their literary debut in exile. Written shortly after his flight to Holland in 1934, *Ein Mensch fällt aus Deutschland* (1936), an epistolary novel, describes the traumatic experiences of the uprooted emigrant who attempts to find some purpose to his new existence. The semi-integrated status in which Merz portrays his autobiographical hero at the end anticipates his own situation after 1945. Merz never returned to Germany to take up the law practice for which he had studied prior to his exile. A brief visit to Berlin after the war was such a depressing experience for him that it apparently made him feel more alienated than the condition of exile itself.[1] Since the end of the war he has been employed as a masseur in a hospital near Amsterdam. Merz's second and last novel to come out of his exile, *Generation ohne Väter* (1938), unfortunately was never published. No doubt it would have shed valuable light on the author's treatment of the youth issue in the work at hand.

Born in 1908, Merz belongs to a generation of youth caught up in the wave of political extremism in the 1920's. The problem of the youth vacillating between the poles of radicalism and liberal humanism is new to the category of novel presently under study. *Ein Mensch fällt aus Deutschland* gives such unusual expression to this problem that one is tempted to write it off as a simple lamentation of an existential predicament followed by an irrational, dirt-throwing denunciation of the regime responsible for putting the hero Winter into this dilemma. It is not surprising that Merz's name remained a virtual nonentity among the population of exiled literati. Certainly the more established humanistic writers would have envisioned little meaningful protest arising from a novel employing images of excrement and festering limbs as an expression of defiance towards Nazi Germany. The representative spokesmen of the established "other Germany" could only have looked with repugnance upon such "vile anarchy." Even Klaus Mann, a fellow younger writer always ready to promote new talent in Die Sammlung, would probably have drawn the line with Konrad Merz.

Despite this unfortunate nonrecognition, Merz is still very much a part of the exiled "other Germany" which sought to defend humanity against its barbaric abuse at home. But the astonishing way he approaches the dilemma of youth, seen in the dualistic position of Winter as both representative and defier of traditional humanism, undoubtedly accounts for this author's isolation among his contemporaries. Neither young nor old could have sympathized with a form of protest, emanating especially from the second half of the novel, that is divested of all reason—so it would seem. A critical glance at this highly problematic work is, therefore, long overdue.

As the novel opens we find Winter hiding out with his former classmate Heini, a left-wing anarchist wanted by the Nazis. Winter does not share his friend's radicalism; his alignment with this political fugitive is rather a sign of general protest felt by a betrayed youth. Essential to an assessment of Merz's intent is an understanding of Winter's historical insight into Hitler's rise to power. The protagonist does not seek to cancel out tradition through anarchistic revolt, as Heini and his clique of followers do, but recapitulates critically the developments leading up to and explaining the desperation expressed by his generation: "Weg mit dem Kaiser, her mit der Republik; her mit der Inflation, weg mit dem letzten Wohlstand. Dann die Scheinblüte, und dann blühten die Stempelämter. An jeder Haltestelle ein neuer Betrug. So war unser ganzes Leben: ein Fahrstuhl nach unten—und mit uns fiel auch unser Gott den Fahrstuhl hinunter. Dann kam Hitler: Erdgeschoss, aussteigen!"[2] We will see that Winter does not attempt to totally reject the past, but takes a position whereby he interacts dialectically with it. Merz regards him as a historical person, as one who criticizes the past but who also is a product of it. Winter emerges as a figure who must settle accounts with the old in order to bring about the new. Later in the novel he exclaims: "Dürfen wir auch deine Fehler lieben, Deutschland? Wir dürfen nicht: wir müssen" (77). Only by overcoming the mistakes of the past can a realistic future be envisioned, and the realization of a solution to the future will depend on the type of youth portrayed by Winter.

The dilemma confronting Winter in Germany is representative for those youth who did not seek to establish an identity in the late twenties and early thirties by taking extreme positions to the left or right: "Der Boden von Deutschland brennt. Schon fast ein Jahr lang wanken und fallen alle Balken in unserem Lande, und ich sollte so tun können, als ginge mich das wenig an? Oder ich sollte gar die Hacken zusammenschlagen, weil irgendein Stiernacken es befiehlt, mich bücken, ein krummer Hund werden, weil ich meine Dreigroschenhoffnung, mein ranziggewordenes Glück in Sicherheit bringen wollte?" (20-21). Dietrich, another school-mate of Winter's, typifies the dissatisfied youth who embarked on this reactionary path. Heini, the other comrade, has chosen the opposite road. The one will perpetuate the corrupt elements of society; the other, by the task assigned him to eliminate Hitler, will seek to eradicate these elements and, by committing this act, compromise the decency in man. The justification given this deed by Heini's anarchistic group recalls the revolutionary fervor of the expressionist generation (with which Merz felt an affinity): "Ein einziger Mensch müsse weg, damit Millionen leben können. Diese Tat sei nicht Mord, nicht Töten, sie sei Gebären, Lebenschaffen. Endlich sei es an uns, zu vollbringen, an der Jugend. Das Gesetz, darum ginge es, und das Gesetz seien wir" (15). Winter, an innocent bystander to this plot, interjects defiantly: "Eben um das Gesetzliche geht es. . . . Ihr kommt mir vor wie ein Verein für Selbstentleibung" (16). Still, Winter is linked by association to the conspiracy, and when the attempted assassination fails, he is forced into exile.

From a documentary standpoint, *Ein Mensch fällt aus Deutschland* sets the tone for the typical material problems of exile. An opponent of the Nazi regime must flee Germany to avoid imprisonment. Unable to make preparations for his exodus, he finds himself in exile without finances or passport. Since work permits are not issued to foreigners, especially to those who have crossed borders illegally, life in exile becomes a constant struggle for survival. Without identification papers the newly arrived refugee must avoid any confrontation with legal authorities; at the same time he is dependent upon the generosity of the guest country for his material existence. As so often happens, he must resort to peddling to earn a livelihood, an occupation which offers little assurance of continued survival.

In approximately the first half of the novel—before Winter sustains a leg injury and meets the Dutch physician Coy, the two incidents spurring him to defiant protest—the hero occupies an apolitical role not unlike that of certain other figures in the exile novel. The everyday problems of exile take precedence over a direct concern for the political oppression existing at home. The recurrent motif of "Durchhalten" in Merz's novel exemplifies a passive attitude emerging in other works, where numerous emigrants optimistically endure their misfortune in the knowledge that they will prevail if the Germany they once knew is to survive. In the initial stages of his exile Winter is portrayed in much the same way. A sense of responsibility towards the disgrace that has befallen Germany has not yet crystallized into open conflict. Winter psychologically withdraws from the present Germany by nostalgically seeking refuge in the past: "Deutschland. Ilse. Mutter. Aber nicht jenes Deutschland, ans Hakenkreuz geschlagen!" (62). (Ilse, the girl Winter left behind, eventually becomes an enthusiastic supporter of the brown-shirts.)

Merz's disjointed style initially reflects the personal conflicts related to the alienating experience of exile. Winter's flight from Germany is symbolic of a loss of identity. His experiences as an emigrant consist of repeated attempts to restore this identity, to establish roots in an antagonistic environment. His conversations, often internalized, serve the purpose of discovering whether he is who he is: "Ich sitze mir gegenüber" (36); "Ich sehe garnichts. Ich will ja nur . . . ja was will ich! Ich bin hierher gefallen . . . ich muss nun . . . ja was muss ich! Ich werde jetzt endlich . . . ja was werde ich!" (31). He finds himself in a perpetual state of movement, without direction or goal: "Da steht ein Baum. In der ganzen Strasse steht nur ein einziger Baum. Und nicht einmal dick. Er steht rechts, also muss ich nach links . . . nach links . . . nur nicht . . . bumm! In der ganzen Strasse steht nur ein einziger Baum, und gerade gegen den muss ich . . . ein richtiger Radfahrer würde ihn vielleicht garnicht treffen . . ." (39-40). Winter's inability to orient himself, to establish a self-identity, takes on the appearance of a timeless, universal uprootedness. Even repossession of his passport fails to alter his situation appreciably: "'Staatsangehörigkeit 'Preussen'. Ist das wahr? 'Gestalt: leider vorhanden'. 'Beruf: Ausländer'. 'Farbe der Augen: verboten'. 'Gesicht: unangenehm'. 'Besondere Kennzeichen: Hat mächtigen Hunger'. 'Wohnort: auf der Erde, postlagernd'" (76).

Merz's later departure from a treatment of an exile experience that is quasi-existentialistic to one that is violently polemic seems, at first glance, to lack structural continuity. We know from the pre-exile scenes in Germany that Winter is an active opponent of the Nazis, a fact born out by his association, however indirect, with an anarchist left-wing group. Why then should Merz delay the polemic aspect of the novel by spending so much time on his hero's personal encounters in Holland? Surely not for the purpose of leveling criticism against the red tape of a foreign bureaucracy. This aspect certainly presents itself, but there appears to be a more critical reason, one that ties in with Winter's experiences in Germany.

It would seem that Winter had been an exile figure from the very start, the result being that his actual exile status forms the physical extension of a spiritual uprootedness that had already existed at home. His search for identity already had its inception in Germany. Thus one form of exile, the inner, complements the other, the outer.

One might question the credibility of such a comparison by calling to mind the active political impression conveyed of Winter in Germany, an image hardly resembling that of an uprooted isolationist. Yet what Merz does is characterize Winter as a political opponent without a following. Winter's alignment with Heini signifies the spiritual bond of one youth to another, a bond which Heini vitiates, however, by his bloodthirsty anarchy: "Und . . . wenn ich kein Genosse bin von Heini, so ist er doch mein Freund, mein Bruder, ein Stück von mir: ich weiss in dieser Sekunde nicht einmal genau, wo er aufhört und wo ich beginne" (21). Winter's isolation is evidenced by his futile desire to champion a form of political opposition based on reason, on Gesetz, an undertaking naturally lacking aspirants in a period governed by irrationality and extremism. Winter's political stance, however noble it may be, was virtually outmoded at a time when the majority of German youth had swung to the left or right. In the second half of the novel the problem of Winter's dual exile experience assumes highly dramatic proportions, crystallizing in the conflict between the hero and both his radical peers in Germany as well as the humanistic "other Germany" whose idealistic tradition had indirectly brought on the disillusionment and resultant extremism of his generation in the 1920's.

That Winter includes himself as a member of a dissatisfied youth movement becomes clear in the one scene where he recalls the inspirational leadership of his fascist classmate Dietrich. Winter's relationship to Dietrich in school was marked by an ambivalence which in the present action of the novel helps to illuminate his conflict. On the one hand he identifies with Dietrich's rebellious pathos as an expression of freedom from the constraints of an unsympathetic system: "Er war der Apostel einer neuen Bewegung, die Deutschland Ehre und Kraft zurückbringen werde und Befreiung. Und danach suchten wir. Er steckte uns an, denn er war der Stärkste von uns" (143); yet he also recognizes the potential dangers erupting from a revolutionary fervor rooted in militancy and power: "Dann gingen wir mit ihm, Heini und ich. Und an diesem Tage wurden wir Feinde. Denn wo er Blut fühlte, fühlten wir Schminke, und wo er Taten sah, hörten wir Worte" (143). We know the path that Heini was soon to take. However extreme and irrational the political poles represented by Dietrich and Heini were, they still insured the group identity for which the youth of Germany had been searching. Ironically, Winter was forced into isolation because he foresaw the disastrous consequences. Idealism on the part of German youth was distorted into the partisan loyalties of communism and fascism. Winter stands, therefore, in opposition to the present as well as the past that had spawned it.

Merz characterizes this opposition by placing his figure in a double dilemma. On the one hand, Winter's insistence on reason and Gesetz implies a respect for the best of German tradition. This is revealed in his admiration for Goethe: "Man hasst ein ganzes Land und meint doch nur seine Krankheit. Und manchmal werde ich selbst irre daran, darum und darum soll es über mir sein, wenn ich mich abstaube, und wenn ich die Knöpfe an meine Hosen nähe, über mir sein, wenn ich meine Muskeln zurückschleppe in den Abend zu mir: das Bild von Goethe" (162). On the other hand, Winter literally profanes the machtgeschützte Innerlichkeit (Thomas Mann) of the recent German past for its failure to incorporate into reality the lofty ideals of its rich tradition. Merz leaves no doubt as to his polemic intent when, in a later episode, Winter assumes the duties of a "Kuhstallknecht" for a herd of cattle, one of which symbolizes the innocuousness of Germany's intellectual heritage: "Die Kuh Idealismus ist kurzsichtig, wir werden ihr eine Brille kaufen müssen, dieser abgemagerten Vergangenheit. Aber es lohnt sich nicht, sie gibt so unverschämt wenig Milch, sie wird wohl abgeschlachtet werden" (173). In this invective Merz is exposing a politically unconcerned society's ineptitude for dealing with the social realities of the day. Winter's admiration for Goethe and the travesty of idealism illustrated here are not to be construed, however, as contradictory. He is really opposing a regression to tradition, not its realistic application in society. It is an abstract idealism he makes a mockery of, one whose adherents had not put into practice the humane principles implied therein.

The other side of Winter's dilemma rests with his own generation. He is both one and at odds with the youth of his day. Whereas he identifies with his peers in their disillusionment over a politically inept Weimar Republic, many of whose constituents were descendants of the "rising" bourgeoisie under the monarchy, he cannot share the extremism underlying their desire to change things. Thus, when Dietrich is suspended from school for undisciplined behavior, Winter's reaction is one of both approval and rejection: "Wir wurden die besten Feinde" (144).

Merz goes so far as to idealize his main character by setting him up as a model of youth in Nazi Germany, but he also stains him with the guilt incurred by many members of his generation as they gathered in force to support the fascist movement. The last half of the novel shows Winter violently erupting from the twofold nature of his isolation. In the most loathsome of metaphors he proceeds to vent his wrath against a Germany for whose barbaric tyranny he expresses both guilt and rejection. Whether an "idea" workable for the future can be reconstructed from this extreme confrontation remains to be seen.

Werner Vordtriede has discussed various images and tones employed in the poetry of exile which can be partly exemplified in this novel, whose subjective, highly stylized language has a lyrical quality about it to begin with. Vordtriede refers to the emigrant lyricist who departs from a traditional art form by resorting to unesthetic metaphors. The artistic medium for conveying this iconoclastic imagery is the parody: "Dialektisch verbunden mit dieser schweren Traditionstreue ist die Exilparodie. Sie ist kein spassiges Randwerk, sie gehört zum Hauptwerk, ist Waffe gegen die Traditionsverderber zu Hause und zugleich ein Eigenkorrektiv."[3] Merz employs his language along similar lines whereby the polemic intent is to expose the inhumanity of Nazismus through the evocation of dehumanized imagery. Vordtriede goes on to mention "Hassdichtung" as one of the extreme forms of parody in exile: "Der Exilierte ist zunächst selber nichts als ein Opfer des Hasses, er will nicht hassen, nur als Gehasster wird er zum Hasser."[4] This hate frequently takes on the form of animal comparisons: "Das Hassgedicht hat aber die Fähigkeit, das Scheusslichste, den Kot, den Dreck, dichterisch möglich zu machen."[5] And so we see Merz executing such language as a vehicle of protest and satire against the animalism of a soulless regime:

> Jeder Fusstritt hat seinen Sinn, jede Blutsstrieme auf meinem Rücken hat ihren Wert. Saat unterm Schnee. Und sie wird aufgehen in jenem Sommer. Dafür bluten wir. Für jenen Sommer. Den wir vielleicht niemals erleben werden. Schon drei andere Säcke über dem Allerwertesten. Ob wir nun draussen bluten oder im Lande. Jeder Tropfen soll Saat sein. Wird Saat sein. Wir glauben es. Wir sind Dünger. Nur Dünger. Aber das sind wir!
>
> (127)

> Mein linkes Bein ist heiss. Es glüht wieder. Fieber. Dieser hündische Oberschenkel, der mich trägt. Und nicht tragen will. . . . Er will mich quälen, er will nach Berlin. Der Oberschenkel gehört mir.
>
> (128)

> Jetzt bin ich also Kuhstallknecht. Habe morgens und abends den werten Kühen den Strunk unter ihren Hinterausgängen wegzuschaufeln und abzufahren. Der

> wird dann draussen aufgeschichtet zu einem Denkmal. Die Kühe erkundigten sich erst, ob ich auch die Universitätsreife hätte, und nachdem ich ihnen das beweisen konnte, liessen sie mich, sichtbar befriedigt, an ihre Allerwertesten.
>
> (167)
>
> Immer wieder stampfte ich mit den beiden Dreckeimern an den Pfuhl und zog das Gestinke an den Tag. Es wurde nur langsam weniger, denn die Kühe legten immer noch mehr dazu, aus persönlicher Niederträchtigkeit; das floss durch die Rinne immer wieder in den Pfuhl. . . . Mein Körper war schwer wie selbst voll Kuhmist. . . . Ich möchte jedem, der mir in die Quere kommt, eins in die Schnauze hauen oder ihn abküssen. Bis zum letzten Vorrat.
>
> (171-72)
>
> Die Löcher an meinen Händen eiterten.
>
> (174)
>
> Als ich heute früh unserer werten Kuh Bügelfalte den Rücken säubern musste, schlug sie mir mit dem Schwanz ins Gesicht. Ich wollte ihr in den Hintern treten vor Wut, konnte es aber nicht, ich darf mich hier ja nicht mit Politik bemühen. Für Ausländer verboten.
>
> (184)

Two related events incite Winter to action. Hospitalized with an injured leg as a result of an automobile accident, he comes under the care of a Dutch physician named Coy, whose German husband is languishing in a Nazi concentration camp. Winter's festering leg refuses to heal and he associates this rotting limb with Germany's sickness: "Die Krankheit Deutschland tut mir mehr weh als mein Bein" (87). His sense of guilt prevents him from reciprocating Coy's affections and he escapes from the clinic. Finding work on a peasant's farm, he wallows in self-chastisement, associating his malady with dung as a symbol of Germany's corruption: "Hier riecht es doch nach Kuhdung, nach Pferdeäpfeln, nach Dreck, hier riecht es doch nach mir. Ich bin aus Deutschland geflohen, geflohen, ich Hund . . . ich Hund. Ich will bezahlen" (110). On the farm Winter attempts, through self-inflicted pain, to overcome his affiliation with a diseased country. Dehumanized images of decay, rot, filth, excrement are evoked as an indication of his desire to remove his burden of guilt. He wishes to atone for Nazi Germany's bestiality by self-degradation, by writhing in pain as a martyr for the transgressions of a barbaric regime.

Merz does not depict these indignities as an end in themselves. Winter is no masochist. However grotesque the metaphors may seem, they demonstrate a definite polemic function. Merz is exposing a barbaric ideology by employing images appropriate to the situation. His hero's conflict evolves from a desire to overcome, to supercede, the fascist path his generation had taken: "Das 'Dritte Reich' ist nicht *Deutschland*. Man sieht nur die Pickel und nicht das Gesicht dahinter" (162).

The author does not set off the real Germany from the false one, but views them dialectically. "Wir sind dort und hier," Winter states, "weil wir zu schwach waren, darum dort und darum hier" (149). That this antagonism does not stagnate, but symbolizes a dynamic struggle that begs for a historical solution is evidenced by frequent references to the future: "Was mir heute wehtut, das muss in Schweiss eingelegt werden für künftige Zeiten" (115); "wir werden zurückfinden nur, wenn wir überwunden haben" (149). The comparison between Winter's festering leg and a barbaric regime has a deeper level of meaning. By symbolically relegating Nazism to the level of decay and filth, Merz in effect strips his lampoon of all human qualities, thereby enabling Winter to overcome, and thus render nonexistent, any element of guilt—also a human quality.

This dialectical turnabout crystallizes in Winter's application of his festering limb—symbolic of his link with fascist Germany—to constructive action. A dynamic process associating past with future passes before our eyes in Winter's figurative working of the soil on the farm:

> Und dann kommt der gute Morgen.
>
> Der beginnt mit Unkrautausziehen. Unkrautausziehen, . . . das müsste jeder Mensch lernen, das müsste sehr zeitgemäss sein. . . . Das müsste man heute über die ganze alte Erde tun. Das wäre endlich ein Anfang. Oder ich muss Stangenbohnenpflanzen an die Stange binden. Damit sie aufrecht werden. Immer mit dem Köpfchen an die Stange. . . . Auch das müsste man über die ganze alte Erde tun. Gleich nach dem Unkrautausziehen. Du siehst, . . . ich arbeite nicht nur für meinen Bauch, die Arbeit geht in kommende Jahrzehnte.
>
> Und dann das Pflücken. Auch das will gelernt sein. Zum Beispiel die Erdbeeren . . . , die müssen mit festem Griff abgezogen werden. Aber das Pflücken, soweit sind wir auf der alten Erde noch längst nicht. Darum muss ich jetzt auch meistens nur Unkrautausziehen.
>
> (117-118)

The incisive critical tone of this passage reveals itself once again in Merz's use of dehumanized images as a means of exposing the inhumanity of Nazism. The complexity of politico-social ideas erupting from this symbolic process of nature is significant in that it underlines the basic structural character of the novel: by employing a negative form of protest (festering leg, "Unkraut") Merz unmasks the debasement of a barbaric regime, also a negative condition. He does not oppose the inhumanity of Nazi tyranny by depicting his hero as a model of decency. Fascist Germany had viewed humanity as a weakness to begin with; only the irrational and instinctual in man counted. Accordingly, Merz engages in an invective that the Nazis would understand. At the same time he imparts a dynamic aspect to Winter's criticism, one which develops beyond this purely negative stand by virtue of the positive qualities he possesses. In the metaphoric scene just described Merz does not predict a utopian society after the corrupt, objectionable elements have been "weeded" out. Rather his optimism is matched by a critical awareness of the constant reappearance of these elements. The kind of society on which a future Germany must build—typified in the figure of Winter—is one that must also realistically contend with and eradicate those reactionary elements that thrive anew ("Unkraut") even after they have been uprooted (the situation prevailing in Germany in the early thirties).

This interpretation is not as outlandish as it may first seem. In the scene which shows Winter reflecting on his school days with Dietrich in the twenties, reference is made to the type of apolitical bourgeois intellectual who ignores the blunders of the Republic and reminisces instead on the "good old days" of the Wilhelminian era: "In der Aula, vorne, über dem Pult, war ein Stehkragen, er erzählte etwas von Vernunft, und wir verstanden ihn nicht, er sprach gar von guten Zeiten und konnte wohl nur seine Gehaltstüte meinen, und dann pries er zaudernd und verlegen eine Republik, die nicht bestand" (143). These so-called pillars of society who had expelled the impudent Dietrich for crying "Deutschland erwache!" (144) were the same ones who eventually re-echoed this call by bowing to Hitler: "Jetzt sind wieder die dran, die mich damals aus der Schule geworfen haben, genau dieselben, sie haben sich nur mein Abzeichen angesteckt und andere Vorsitzende gewählt" (144). Looking to the future, after Nazi Germany ("Unkraut") has been "eradicated," Merz is quite perceptive in recognizing that the ills of society will not have been cured overnight. He envisions a future in which reactionary attitudes will continue to spread, but he also envisions a youth coming to maturity which, having suffered and learned from the past, will represent an enlightened, democratic segment of society that will retard the growth of reaction ("Unkrautrausziehen"), thus enabling the positive forces of society to grow ("Stangenbohnen," "Erdbeeren").

The most problematic area of the novel lies in Winter's sense of guilt over the wrongdoings of a movement he had denounced from the very start. Why should he bear the guilt of Nazi Germany's disgrace if he was not responsible for its emergence? The answer seems to lie in Merz's conception of youth in Nazi Germany. Winter acts as both heir of the old and harbinger of the new. As spokesman for the new he, by virtue of his own youth, must count himself amont the future leaders of Germany. Yet the new, the current moving force of history, has retrogressed to barbarism, a retarding state, and a part of Winter has fallen with it. The redeeming factor enabling Winter to transcend this backward state reveals itself in his humanity, that part of the "other Germany" that respects reason, justice, "Gesetz," which draws on and realistically applies the humane principles of Goethean tradition. The struggle against Nazi tyranny is still being waged ("Unkrautrausziehen"), but Merz does not allow his polemic to stagnate into mere opposition. Very likely he was of the opinion at the time that the fascist hegemony would appear as a brief phase of history, that the forces of corruption would soon induce their own dissolution. Thus the images of degeneration, decay, putrefaction. Merz looks beyond this phase of barbaric tyranny, anticipating a future that will be better because of its critical assessment of the past.

One might still be inclined, however, to question the credibility of a figure like Winter in his relationship to the future. Is he not, in the last analysis, still an isolated type without a following? Does not Merz characterize merely a dynamic struggle of ideas that lacks realistic backing? Where is there an indication of a presence of social forces during this period that would lend credence to the type that Merz draws? Such questions are not without foundation. If the other types representing the majority of youth—the Dietrichs and Heinis—ended in extremism, then there is not much left to recruit from. Merz makes it quite clear that Winter's political opposition was nonpartisan. It would seem then that he does create an isolated figure lacking representation in reality.

But youths are impressionable. It was not they who concocted the truculent theories of Germanic supremacy, racial purity, blood and soil, Volk and Führer. The credulous youths of the twenties were understandably intimidated by a political program that promised to restore social stability and national esteem. And a typical enthusiast of the new movement was Winter's "best enemy," Sturmführer Dietrich von Winterstein.

The relationship in this contradiction is not one-sided. The reverse side comes into play as well: that Winter is also Dietrich's "best enemy," suggesting that a reciprocal attraction of the two exists and that Merz is not condemning the rest of youth while singling out Winter as the exception. Rather he envisages in youth as a whole a redeeming quality quite absent in the totally corrupt fascist leadership. Winter indeed becomes Dietrich's "best enemy" when the latter joins him in exile!

Dietrich's presence in Holland is self-imposed. Other functionaries of the SA had relegated him to a lower position and, infuriated over this indignity, he comes to his political enemy and school friend for advice. His behavior is decidedly ambivalent at first. He is still the dedicated Nazi who clicks his heels, dons his SA cap, and flaunts his title, but who, behind this facade, is also looking for a rational meaning to the movement he has joined. It is Winter who tips the scale from the false to the real Germany for Dietrich. In a grotesque boxing match, where Winter literally beats Dietrich to his senses, Merz constructs a violent ritual symbolizing the struggle between the forces of reason and tyranny. Winter's victory has synthesized the "best-enemy" dualism of youth in the novel. His friend's transformation, his "cleansing," is not without psychological motivation, however. Prior to the confrontation Dietrich had exhibited an attitude towards humanity that directly refutes one of the main tenets of fascist ideology, namely, Jewish racial inferiority: "Du weisst, ich habe diese Seite niemals gedeckt. Ich habe denn doch zu grosse Achtung vor uns Deutschen, man hat mir niemals einreden können, dass sich 99 Deutsche von einem einzigen betrügen oder gar 'unglücklich' machen lassen. . . . Ich bin selbst aus zu reinem Geschlecht, als dass ich Judenhasser sein könnte. Diese habe ich jetzt kennengelernt. Davon gibt es im ganzen nur drei Sorten, sage ich dir: neidische

Schwächlinge, perverse Schweine, und die dritten sind selber ehemalige Juden" (163). After a short stay in Holland, Dietrich returns to Germany on a humane mission whose failure is really envisioned as a victory. While attempting to free Coy's husband from a concentration camp, he is caught and imprisoned. Winter's optimistic reaction to Dietrich's incarceration reflects the victorious expression of a generation's united opposition to tyranny: "Dietrich im Konzentrationslager . . . Das Schicksal ist doch grösser als unser grösster Wunsch! Was ich nicht konnte, das wird dort . . . er wird dort . . . er wird dort vielleicht erwachen!" (195). The implication of this optimistic outcry is that many youths who had initially regarded Hitler as a symbol of Germany's future would soon realize their mistake and join together in opposition. Despite his incapacitation through imprisonment, Dietrich nevertheless symbolizes the will of youth to resist. The satiric polemic still carried on by the exiled Winter in his role as a "Kuhstallknecht" reflects the spirit of the resistance to be undertaken in Germany.

At this early stage of exile such an optimism was not so ill-founded. Merz was not the only writer who believed that the anti-fascist opposition of the "other Germany" was the verbal counterpart of the real battle being wged at home. Many exiled writers had entertained the belief that Hitler's hegemony would crumble once the German people had come to their senses. If Merz had written his novel at a later period, one would be justified in viewing his confidence in a defiant youth as politically untenable. For, as time went on, it became evident that Hitler's most enthusiastic following came from these very ranks. Merz's premises seem to have been sound at the time he wrote the work. Unfortunately, the remaining years until 1945 did not bear them out.

Notes

1. Merz states in a personal letter dated August 13, 1972: "Die Friedhöfe vom Krieg. Ostberlin. Kein Haus, wo er gewohnt hatte, war noch Haus. Nur das letzte stand noch da. Es sprach nicht mehr mit ihm. Die Erinnerung ist eine Lügnerin, sogar unsre Fotos noch sind Lügner. Die Zeit vor Hitler ist der Zeit nach Hitler entnommen."

2. *Ein Mensch fällt aus Deutschland* (Amsterdam: Querido, 1936), p. 13. Subsequent references appear parenthetically in the text by page number.

3. "Vorläufige Gedanken zu einer Typologie der Exilliteratur," *Akzente*, 15 (1968), 570-71.

4. Ibid., 572.

5. Ibid., 574.

Egbert Krispyn (essay date 1978)

SOURCE: Krispyn, Egbert. "A Year of Decision." In *Anti-Nazi Writers in Exile*, pp. 45-58. Athens: University of Georgia Press, 1978.

[*In the following excerpt, Krispyn analyzes the political and social climate of Germany in 1935-36, commenting on why such writers as Thomas Mann and Arthur Koestler chose to continue writing in exile.*]

While the emigrants were arguing among themselves about the true nature of exile literature and its contribution to the antifascist cause, Hitler pressed forward relentlessly with his political battle plan for the stabilization and expansion of his power. His first objective was the Saar territory which since the end of World War I had been administered by the League of Nations. In January 1935, in accordance with the terms of the Versailles peace treaty of 1919, a plebiscite was held to decide the future of this French-German border region. The exiled and Saarlandian antifascists of all ideological hues naturally strongly opposed the reunification of the province with Germany and spared no effort to put their case before the people. To a large majority of the population of the area, the Nazi propaganda and the apparent political and economic achievements of the new regime in Germany proved to be irresistible. The overwhelming vote in favor of joining the Third Reich forced all those who had publicly expressed their opposition to National Socialism to join the ranks of the exiles.

The free, democratic, and legal decision of the Saarland to become a German province showed that Hitler had strong popular support. It made the ineffectiveness of the exiles in opening the eyes of the world to the real nature of the fascist regime painfully obvious. Kurt Tucholsky once again drew the only correct conclusion with his observation that the Germans really wanted National Socialism and that the exiles fooled themselves with their talk about a "better Germany" that they allegedly represented. Tucholsky's extreme but justifiable skepticism had from the beginning prevented him from joining the exile cause. Now his despair became so deep that he washed his hands of Germany completely. In a letter, he wrote: "I won't have anything to do anymore with this country whose language I speak as little as possible. May it perish—may Russia conquer it—I'm through with it." And a few days before his pessimism concerning the future drove him to suicide, he found a striking image for the illusoriness of the exiles' hopes and aspirations in the face of the world's shortsightedness and indifference: "My life is too valuable to me to place myself under an apple tree and ask it to produce pears. Not me."

Valuable as his life was to Tucholsky, he gave it up rather than witness the seemingly irreversible decline of the civilized Western world. A few months after Tucholsky's suicide, Hitler embarked on the next, decisive phase of his plans for world conquest. While in the annexation of the Saar region the Nazis had triumphed by legal means, they acted in open defiance of their international obligations when early in the following year they occupied the Rhineland. The Locarno Pact of 1925 had reaffirmed the stipulation of the 1919 Versailles peace treaty that Germany was not allowed to maintain military installations or troops in the area between the Rhine and the French border. This had been the price exacted by France in return for its approval of a moderation of Germany's World War I reparations payments. As was to be expected the continued demilitarization of this region rankled in the German people. It proved to be a fruitful propaganda topic for the Nazis in their attacks on alleged traitors and enemies of the state. Hitler's decision in March 1936 to send his armed forces into the territory was therefore enthusiastically applauded by the people. In a subsequent referendum both the Rhinelanders themselves and the rest of the Germans almost unanimously approved the action.

This illegal military occupation of the Rhineland was a direct challenge to the Allies. For a while it seemed as if the Führer's daring act would provoke France to military countermeasures. It was a very tense situation in which the fascist regime itself was at stake, but in the end the Western powers backed down and accepted the accomplished fact, letting Hitler get away with his flagrant, aggressive breach of the letter and the spirit of Locarno. The failure of the democracies to call the Führer's bluff in the remilitarization of the Rhineland was due to the adoption of an "appeasement" policy toward Germany. It reflected their more or less pious belief in the dictator's basic political sincerity and in the limited nature of his objectives.

All in all the Rhineland incident once more brought home to the exiles that they were acting in a political vacuum. Neither the statesmen of the Western powers nor the German people paid any attention to their warnings that the Führer would lead Germany and the rest of the world to disaster. This sobering experience of their isolation came at a time when the literary emigration was already in a state of anxious turmoil. There was widespread and deep concern not only for the continued existence of the exile publishing industry as such but also for its political integrity. At issue was a strange and never fully explained deal between the Nazis and the leading publishing house of Fischer.

Under the terms of the agreement the German authorities allowed the firm to split into two separate branches. The Jewish owner and his "non-Aryan" employees were permitted to leave the country and set up business as an exile publisher. For that purpose the Nazis even allowed them to take along a stock of some 780,000 volumes by those Fischer authors who were banned in Germany. Gottfried Bermann Fischer was further enabled to take nearly one half of the firm's business capital and his considerable private assets out of Germany as well. After an unsuccessful attempt to settle in Switzerland, the new exile publishing enterprise was with the Nazis' blessings founded in Austria. Meanwhile the non-Jewish section of the firm continued to do business inside Germany with works and writers that were acceptable to the authorities.

The whole arrangement was highly unusual and puzzling, particularly because it involved a most uncharacteristic generosity on the part of the fascists. It could not help but arouse uneasy feelings about the new venture among the exiles who had not forgotten that Fischer played a major role in the campaign to discredit Klaus Mann and his journal *Die Sammlung*. In view of the circumstances the ideological commitment of the new enterprise was highly suspect. This was an all the more serious concern, as the existence of the established exile presses was very much endangered by the Fischer venture. Operating on a shoestring, the original emigrant publishers would have very little chance of surviving the competition of the large, well staffed and lavishly endowed newcomer. It seems more than likely that the Nazis by agreeing to the Fischer deal also thought they were dealing a mortal blow to the genuine, politically incorruptible exile press. As it turned out "Bermann-Fischer" in due course became one of the most important and distinguished emigrant publishers. It worked in close collaboration with the Amsterdam based firms of Allert de Lange and Querido. After the German annexation of Austria the firm moved to Sweden, where it remained active throughout the Nazi period.

Indirectly Fischer's entry into the exile publishing field benefited the antifascist cause in a very different way as well, since it triggered a chain of events that led to Thomas Mann's long overdue public endorsement of and identification with the emigration. In Mann the exile establishment gained a sorely needed focal point and a widely respected and influential spokesman. His decision to throw in his lot with the refugees was all the more effective for coming so late. For a full appreciation of its impact and of Thomas Mann's extraordinary stature within the emigration it is necessary to trace his ideological development up to this point.

More than two decades earlier at the outbreak of World War I, he like many other prominent literary figures had been caught up in the wave of patriotic fervor that swept the country. He had given expression to his somewhat exalted feelings in several essays. Then his brother Heinrich Mann in a piece ostensibly dealing with the French writer Emile Zola launched a sharp attack on the intellectual supporters of misguided nationalism. Thomas quite rightly took it personally and countered with a voluminous work entitled *Observations of a Non-Political Person (Betrachtungen eines Unpolitischen)*, in which he took issue with the spirit of cosmopolitan intellectualism and aestheticism that in his opinion was contrary to the essence of German culture. Unfortunately very few people, not even brother Heinrich, had the perseverance to read the entire work. This general unfamiliarity with the details of his arguments caused widespread misunderstandings about Thomas Mann's political views, the most serious being the notion that the novelist utterly rejected democracy as a political system. In reality he criticized only the democratization of Germany along capitalist lines "in the Roman Western sense," and the "inner annexation of Germany by the empire of civilization" as opposed to the realm of culture.

Even those who on the basis of an incomplete reading and understanding of the *Observations* accused Thomas Mann of being a reactionary nationalist should have been aware that as early as 1923 he had renounced in no uncertain terms the opinions expressed in that work. At that time he delivered a speech "About the German Republic" ("Von deutscher Republik") in which he urged support for the Weimar state, which in many ways embodied the very ideas he had attacked in the *Observations*. From this point on he left no doubt whatsoever about his political stance. Five years before the Nazis came into power, their party press already abused him in print. The fascists even then regarded him as an adversary because of his alleged francophile outlook—the same thing he himself had held against his brother fourteen years earlier. In October 1930 Thomas Mann gave a lecture in Berlin in which he sounded an outspoken warning against National Socialism and came out in support of the Social Democrats. The Nazis, knowing what to expect, had infiltrated the audience and started fights and other disruptions in an effort to prevent Mann from speaking, but he refused to let himself be intimidated and calmly finished reading his paper.

Two years later again he gave a press interview in which he declared himself strongly opposed to Hitler and his party. Around the same time he expressed his antifascist attitude in a talk before Austrian laborers in the Vienna suburb of Ottakring. The Nazis also associated Thomas Mann with the bitingly satirical political cabaret "The Peppermill" ("Die Pfeffermühle") which opened in Munich on 1 January 1933. Even though the novelist was not directly involved in this enterprise, he certainly had strong links with its leading figures. His daughter Erika directed the cabaret and together with her brother Klaus wrote most of the texts which heaped ridicule on the National Socialists.

In February 1933 Thomas Mann had been invited to address the Socialist Cultural Society in Berlin. Since he was unable to attend personally he sent the text of his speech to be read for him. Although the meeting was banned by the Nazis his connection with this opposition organization was duly noted as further evidence of his hostility toward the new rulers. In a clear gesture of defiance Mann in December of the same year, while living in a colony of exile writers in the south of France, refused to join the official German literary organization, the "Reichsschrifttumskammer." Early in 1935 Thomas Mann had once more gone on record as an antifascist with his paper "Europe, Beware," which was distributed at an international conference in Nice.

But in the minds of many, not even all these demonstrations of Thomas Mann's political viewpoint were conclusive evidence of his critical attitude toward the new regime. Among both Nazis and exiles some uncertainty remained about the firmness of his commitment to the antifascist cause. His disavowal of *Die Sammlung* and the fact that he continued to be printed and published in Germany kept such doubts alive. Mann's studied and emphatic personal neutrality and aloofness toward the emigration did nothing to convince the exiles that his heart was in the right place. Their doubts were further strengthened by the fact that even at the beginning of 1936 the German authorities, despite Mann's repeated provocations, had not yet stripped him of his German citizenship.

Under these circumstances Thomas Mann was regarded as a somewhat dubious figure in emigrant circles at the time Fischer set up shop in Vienna. On that occasion Leopold Schwarzschild as editor of the journal *Neues Tage Buch* commented that the exiled writers included just about the entire German world of letters as far as it was worthy of note. With the same ambiguity that had marked some of his earlier utterances and actions, Thomas Mann burst into print to protest this view. In doing so he may have acted out of consideration for Fischer's remaining business interests in Germany and his own stake in them. In any case at this point the Swiss newspaper *Neue Zürcher Zeitung* became embroiled in the public controversy.

In the issue of 26 January 1936, there appeared an article by Eduard Korrodi, a Swiss journalist with pronounced Nazi sympathies. He entered into the argument between Schwarzschild and Thomas Mann with the intention of alienating the novelist from the emigration and claiming him for the fascists' side. To this end he reversed Schwarzschild's claim that practically all German authors of importance had left their native soil. Korrodi asserted that the exiles constituted a worthless segment of German literature. To bolster his opinion he said that they were all Jewish and that they wrote nothing but cheap novels. Korrodi went on to contrast Thomas Mann with these allegedly inferior writers. Mann was not really in exile; he just happened to have been living outside Germany since early 1933. He was a great artist and, moreover, he was not Jewish.

Thomas Mann proved to be above this kind of flattery. In an answering letter of February 1936 he stressed the great contributions the Jews had made to German literature over the centuries. In that connection he also took issue with the fascist notion that the Jews had to be eliminated to protect the German way of life. According to Mann, Nazi anti-Semitism was really directed against the essential Christian and ancient aspects of German civilization itself. He further corrected Korrodi's statement that the exiled authors were all Jewish by reciting the names of a number of them, including himself and his brother Heinrich, who were not. Mann also addressed himself to the Swiss journalist's attempt to downgrade exile literature because it consisted largely of novels. Mann made the point that this genre was not inferior but had established itself as the leading literary form in Europe generally. The novel was far more relevant to the politically turbulent times than any other kind of writing. Thomas Mann did not content himself with rebutting Korrodi's arguments; he condemned the Nazis in the strongest terms and, adding insult to injury, taunted that for the past three years they had been unable to decide whether to revoke his German citizenship. His letter concluded with an impassioned affirmation of his own allegiance to the emigration.

There continued to be exiles who had serious reservations about Thomas Mann. Some were envious of his great reputation or presumed prosperity. Others disagreed with his political or literary orientation. But by and large his outspoken reply to Korrodi made Mann the key figure of the emigration. His reputation as a champion of the exile cause was further solidified when the Hitler regime, convinced at last that he could not be wooed into their camp, deprived him of his German citizenship. The blacklist concerned was published in December 1936, but it did not leave Mann stateless. His prominence and his friendly private relations with President Beneš had enabled him to obtain Czechoslovak nationality for himself and his family.

Later in the same month the Nazis took further action against him. The University of Bonn announced that the honorary doctorate it had bestowed on the novelist many years before had been rescinded. Thomas Mann's reaction in this instance was more pithy than his letter to Korrodi, which out of consideration for the journalist's Swiss nationality had been couched in respectful terms. Mann's response to the dean of the university opened with a reference to the "depraved powers that are destroying Germany morally, culturally and economically" and concluded with the prayer that God might help the abused country and teach it to make peace with the world and itself. The document is a deeply personal statement of position and principles. Owing to the status of the author and the vibrant conviction of his words, it almost assumed the significance of a charter for exile literature as a whole.

Of particular interest was the passage dealing with the relation between the creative and the political concerns of the emigrants. Thomas Mann did not assign priority to one over the other but spoke out for a synthesis of the two on a linguistic level: "The mystery of language is great; the responsibility for language and its purity is symbolic and spiritual, it is by no means only of artistic but also of general moral significance, it is responsibility itself, human responsibility as such, also the responsibility for one's own people, keeping its image pure before the eyes of mankind, and in it the unity of humanity can be experienced, the totality of the human problem that does not allow anyone, least of all in these times to separate the spiritual-artistic from the political-social and to isolate oneself from the latter in an elevated 'cultural' realm."

As Thomas Mann was writing his letter to the dean of the University of Bonn, the struggle between the fascists and their opponents had moved beyond the literary sphere onto the battlefields of the Spanish civil war. Armed conflict had broken out earlier in the year as the final result of political tensions that had been building up in Spain for a long time. A left-leaning republican government had legally come to power, but the country's nobility and the Roman Catholic church banded together to overthrow it and establish a fascist regime instead. Socialists and Communists united in a popular front resisted this revolution from the right.

This internal issue took on implications of much greater magnitude. Hitler and Mussolini had entered into an alliance known as the fascist Axis and decided to use the civil strife in Spain as a dress rehearsal for their own planned war of conquest. In flagrant disregard of all international agreements, they supplied the forces of General Franco, the military leader of the right-wing insurrection, with troops and equipment. The new German air force, then being built up by Hermann Goering in defiance of the Versailles peace treaty, also took part in the civil war. Under the name "Condor Legion" it used the opportunity to train its pilots, test its airplanes under combat conditions, and experiment with new strategies of air warfare—particularly the bombarding of civilian population centers.

When the involvement by the Axis was first suspected but not yet proven, the German exile writer Arthur Koestler was assigned to investigate the matter as an undercover agent for the Communist Party. In the years before Hitler's rise to power he had worked as a journalist for the big Berlin newspaper concern of Ullstein. A Communist Party member since 1931, he took his political commitment seriously enough to pass on to the Marxists the diplomatic information that he came across in his professional capacity. In 1933 he was caught at this and lost his job in disgrace. He thereupon went to Russia, where he spent almost a year before moving on to Paris. He was active in the production of antifascist propaganda literature until the Communist Party ordered him to look into the question of German and Italian participation in the Spanish civil war.

Koestler's career as a spy in Spain came to an untimely end when he happened to run into a former newspaper colleague from Berlin who meanwhile had become a Nazi. He recognized Koestler, who posed as a right-wing journalist, and tipped off the fascists. Just one hour before a warrant for his arrest was issued, Koestler managed to flee to Gibraltar. Undeterred by this narrow escape he returned to Spain later in the year on other secret missions. Early in 1937 his luck ran out when the same informer succeeded in having him arrested by Franco's forces. The incident caused a furor, and all over the world much sentiment was aroused in his behalf. Eventually so much pressure was exerted on his captors that after some three months' imprisonment he was released on the condition that he would not return to Spain again.

Arthur Koestler was but one of many volunteers of different countries and from different parts of the political spectrum who had recognized the historic significance of the conflict in Spain. They wanted to contribute their share to the fight against the totalitarianism that threatened to engulf Europe. In contrast to Koestler's cloak-and-dagger activities most of those who came to the aid of the republicans did so as members of the International Brigades. These army units often bore the brunt of the military operations against the fascists. Not surprisingly the foreign volunteers included a goodly number of German exile writers. Dedicated to the cause of antifascism but frustrated by the ever more apparent political futility of their literary activity, they eagerly seized this opportunity to engage in a more direct confrontation with the enemy.

One of these literary exiles who took up arms against Franco was the novelist Gustav Regler, who ranked high on the Nazis' list of enemies. As a journalist in the twenties he had published a story that led to the public exposure and conviction of the perverted and criminal Julius Streicher, one of Hitler's oldest cronies and a prominent figure in the National Socialist movement. In 1933 Regler left the country and settled in Paris where he, like Koestler, took part in various antifascist publishing ventures. As a native of the Saar territory he also became involved in the propaganda battle that preceded the plebiscite of January 1935 and was much disheartened and disillusioned by the outcome.

In 1936 Regler, a somewhat unorthodox Communist, went to Moscow. He undertook this trip in connection with a projected biography of Loyola that was sponsored by the Party. Regler actually intended to criticize Stalin's ruthless dictatorship indirectly in his book by implying a comparison between the Russian strong man and the founder of the Jesuit order. During his stay in Moscow, Regler became aware that a political crisis was brewing involving the old-guard Communists in whose circles he mainly moved. In the middle of August the issue came out in the open with an official announcement that a number of prominent Leninists were to stand trial. They were charged with organizing and participating in the preparation of acts of terror against the leaders of the Party and the government.

This was the start of the infamous Moscow show trials that were to have ideological repercussions throughout the world. The Russian dictator was shown to resort to judicial murder of the real founders of the Soviet state in order to bolster his own absolute personal power. As a result Communists everywhere lost faith in the Stalinist version of their political gospel. Many Marxists broke with the Party but others clung to it in the desperate hope of somehow salvaging their ideals in spite of the grim and bloody realities in Russia.

Regler's reaction was typical in this respect. The trials confirmed all his worst fears about Communism, which up to this point he had hesitated to confess even to himself. He was dismayed and shocked by Stalin's callously cynical betrayal of the cause to which he had dedicated his life. Nevertheless he was not yet prepared to admit that the germ of totalitarianism was inherent in the ideological foundations of Marxism. He therefore sought to recapture on the battlefields of Spain the spirit of idealism that had originally led him to become a Communist. The Spanish civil war had broken out while Regler was in Moscow, and the progress of the conflict had been followed with passionate interest by him and everyone else as a decisive contest between the forces of good and evil. Now the military campaign seemed to offer a chance for him to cleanse himself of the corruption of Stalinist Russia. On the battlefield he might be able to atone also for his futile literary and propagandistic efforts on behalf of the Party, with which he continued to maintain a formal allegiance.

In the fall of 1936, after many bureaucratic delays and obstructions by the red functionaries, Gustav Regler went to Spain. He took with him a gift from the Communist International Writers Association for the republican forces. It consisted of a small truck, a press for printing pamphlets, a projector, and some propaganda films. When Regler had handed over this somewhat symbolic present he joined the forces that were defending Madrid against the troops of Generalissimo Franco. Gustav Regler was no newcomer to front-line action. While still in his teens he had served and been wounded in the First World War. Now he took an active part in the fighting around the Spanish capital. From that perspective he had nothing but contempt for the Communist Party officials who were attached to the republican army, for they seemed much more concerned with their own endless intrigues and power struggles than with the fate of the Spanish state.

A short time later Regler himself was appointed as a political commissar to the nationally and ideologically mixed twelfth International Brigade. (The numbering of these troop units started with eleven.) He carried out his functions in an undogmatic spirit. Rather than insist pedantically on absolute, rigid adherence to the dogmas of Communism, he used his influence to keep up the spirit of the soldiers. They certainly needed all the encouragement he could give them, since both in numbers and in quantity and quality of equipment they lagged far behind the enemy. Regler's unorthodox, humanistic faith in the power of the word manifested itself in the battle of Guadalajara in March 1937. Over the disdainful objections of militarists and Marxist stalwarts, he belabored the opposing Italian fascist troops with leaflets and rather highbrow propaganda speeches broadcast over large loudspeakers. This psychological warfare allegedly persuaded many of the fascist soldiers to defect to the republicans. In any case the engagement ended in the defeat of the revolutionaries. Three months later Regler was seriously wounded in the fighting around Huesca when a grenade hit his car, forcing the end of his active military career. When after four months he came out of the hospital he was sent to America to raise money for the loyalists.

Regler later used his personal experiences in the Spanish civil war to continue his struggle against the fascists by literary means. On his way to Mexico in 1939 he was for a while the guest of Ernest Hemingway, whom he had met and come to admire in Spain. In Key West he wrote his semiautobiographical novel *The Great Crusade* to which his host supplied a foreword. The book did not make any attempt to gloss over the tensions and frictions between the different political factions within the International Brigades. Regler also dwelt on the self-defeating dogmatic narrow-mindedness and paranoia of the official Communist Party representatives. Nevertheless *The Great Crusade* ended on a positive note. In the battle of Huesca that ended Regler's fighting days, the loyalists had scored a military victory over the forces of Franco. From a literary standpoint it was entirely justifiable to conclude the novel with this promising scene, yet in a larger context Regler distorted the truth about the Spanish civil war in closing his book on this upbeat note.

Guadalajara and Huesca were no more than retarding moments in a development that inevitably had to lead to the military defeat of the republicans. In March 1939 the fight was over and a fascist regime was established in Spain. Once again the world had ignored the handwriting on the wall. The legal government of Spain had in its hour of need been deserted by Russia no less than by the Western democracies who had failed to supply vitally important military and medical supplies and food. Some statesmen had paid lip service to the righteousness of the loyalist cause. In reality the republicans had been diplomatically and militarily abandoned by all those who refused to see the plight of Spain for what it was: the preamble to the most disastrous war ever waged. From this perspective Regler's ultimately rosy picture of the loyalist prospects in *The Great Crusade* was more than just a literary device to round out his story. It symbolized the desperate longing of the emigrant writers for some hopeful sign, some bright spot on the horizon. During six years in exile they had seen the international situation grow steadily worse. All resistance, whether with the pen or with the gun, appeared to be fruitless as the fascist scourge spread further and further. The exiles' hardship and sacrifice seemed wasted and the future more bleak than ever.

Günter Berghaus (essay date 1989)

SOURCE: Berghaus, Günter, "Producing Art in Exile: Perspectives on the German Refugees' Creative Activities in Great Britain." In *Theatre and Film in Exile: German Artists in Britain, 1933-1945,* edited by Günter Berghaus. Oxford: Oswald Wolff Books, Berg Publishers, 1989.

[*In the following essay, Berghaus traces the contributions of noted German artists living in exile in Great Britain after 1933.*]

Following Hitler's appointment as Chancellor on 30 January 1933 a number of laws were passed which enabled the Nazis to assume total control over the German population: a Law for the Reconstruction of the Civil Service (7 April), a Denationalization Decree (14 July), a Law for the Protection of German Blood and Honour, and a Reich Citizenship Law (13 September: the so-called Nuremberg Laws) and a Law for the Establishment of a Reich Cultural Chamber (22 September), to name just a few. A few weeks after Hitler's seizure of power the *Große Säuberung* began, the clearing out and elimination of left-wing and Jewish art and culture. On 10 May 1933 a burning of books was held, and in September 1933 Joseph Goebbels was charged with the formation of a *Reichskulturkammer,* a guild-like organization with compulsory membership for all artists working in the media of literature, theatre, music, film, radio, fine arts and journalism. In order to qualify for membership a proclamation of loyalty to the new régime was required; those who were not prepared to support the new cultural policy were barred from exercising their profession and having their work shown in public.

As a result of these measures many artists were arrested, deported or killed in prisons and concentration camps. Others went into so-called 'inner emigration'; but the majority of Germany's critical intelligentsia and creative artist community went into exile. Some of them were forced to leave Germany because they found themselves on the *Ausbürgerungslisten* (lists of expatriation) on account of their ethnic background or political record. For them, fleeing Germany was the only way to secure their physical survival. However, famous artists found themselves, generally, in a much more secure position than the so-called man on the street who was caught and put through the mangle of the Gestapo without anybody but his nearest friends and relatives knowing about his disappearance. The number of well-known artists who ended up in concentration camps or died in the torture chambers of the SS was very small indeed. A few prominent left-wing or Communist intellectuals fell into the hands of the Gestapo (e.g. Willi Bredel, Berta Lask, Egon Erwin Kisch, Ernst Busch, Wolfgang Langhoff, Hermann Duncker, Karl August Wittfogel), but none of them shared the ill fortunes of Carl von Ossietzky or Erich Mühsam.

Many artists were made extremely tempting offers by the new government in order to ensure their loyalty. Actors, for example, were given long-term contracts, paid holiday leave, free medical treatment and generous social security and superannuation schemes.[1] The Nazi rulers themselves must have been rather unsure about who could be classified as their supporter or enemy. The well-known case of Fritz Lang who was offered the chair of the *Reichsfilmkammer* and then decided to leave Germany, just a few hours after his audience with Goebbels,[2] may have been an extreme example, but it was indicative of the Nazis' attempt to prevent a cultural famine following their take-over. They were perfectly aware that the loss of one Thomas Mann could not be redeemed by the retention of ten Ernst Jüngers, Ernst Wiecherts or Hans Carossas.

The attitude of those artists who could be persuaded to stay in Germany after 1933 ranged from open support for the Nazis or restrained loyalty, to passive resistance or inner emigration. In the field of theatre one could mention the playwrights Gerhart Hauptmann and Max Halbe; the directors Gustav Gründgens, Heinz Hilpert, Erich Engel, Jürgen Fehling and Karl Heinz Martin; the designers Caspar Neher, Traugott Müller and Cesar Klein; the dancers Mary Wigman and Harald Kreutzberg; the actors Heinrich George, Werner Krauß, Paul Wegener, Eduart von Winterstein, Horst Caspar, Lothar Müthel, Friedrich Kayßler, Paul Hartmann; the actresses Käthe Gold, Marianne Hoppe, Käthe Dorsch and Paula Wessely. Although a number of prominent artists and a few of international repute stayed behind in 1933, their creative output over the next twelve years could not make up for the intellectual bloodletting caused by the exodus of no fewer than 2,000 writers (420 of them dramatists) and 4,000 theatre practitioners.[3] Some were overtaken by events at a time when they were travelling abroad and found 'that while one is away one's country is running away somewhere and one can't get hold of it anymore'.[4] Others were *Spätexilanten* (late emigrants) who initially tried to come to some kind of arrangement with the new régime but then decided to leave when the full extent of Nazi oppression and the cultural implications of their take-over dawned on them. Whether exiled by design or coincidence, few of the emigrants conceived of the possibility that their 'prolonged trip abroad' would actually last ten to twelve years. What initially looked like a short interlude in their lives soon grew into a veritable nightmare. Even the most starry-eyed artists, who had to experience the November pogroms of 1938 (*Kristallnacht*) and German expansion into Austria, Czechoslovakia and Poland to see clearly what was afoot, eventually became aware that the Nazi régime was proving to be a durable factor in German politics and was, in fact, developing into a major political force threatening European peace and security. The sooner they came to terms with the fact that their exile was more than just a passing phase the easier it was for them to build up a new existence abroad and to find a new purpose for their art.

Many artists, when they arrived in France, England, Sweden or wherever, expected to be received with the same friendliness they had experienced on their former trips to these countries. However, after 1933 things turned out to be very different. The friends, who had invited them to their country (and it was usually personal contacts that determined the artists' choice of exile country), may have given them a warm welcome, but the rest of the population was usually less enthusiastic about the possibility of a large refugee community in their midst.

Once-famous artists suddenly had to realize that they were virtually unknown figures in their guest country. The self-importance they had always attached to themselves, and the notion of international repute they thought they had achieved following an exhibition in Paris, a lecture tour in Scandinavia, or the granting of an honorary degree in Oxford, suddenly fell apart when an unimportant magazine declined to publish one of their poems because it was not considered 'good enough', or when they tried to secure the commission of a portrait or some book illustration, and their offer was rejected because nobody wanted to buy the work of an 'unknown artist'. This experience is reflected in Max Herrmann-Neiße's poem 'Ein deutscher Dichter bin ich einst gewesen' (Once I was a German poet), where he says:

> . . . hier wird niemand meine Verse lesen,
> ist nichts, was meiner Seele Sprache spricht;
> ein deutscher Dichter bin ich einst gewesen;
> jetzt ist mein Leben Spuk wie mein Gedicht.[5]
>
> (No-one will read my poems here,
> The language of my soul has no meaning.
> Once I was a German poet,
> Now my life is a spectre, just like my work.)

Most artists were not able to survive by their creative work alone. Many were forced to take any job offered to them in order to supplement their meagre income. They had to join the queue of other refugees on the labour exchange and compete with the native unemployed on the job market. As a result of this, the population's indifference towards these artists often turned into open hostility. The frosty atmosphere caused by xenophobia and anti-Semitism, the loss of self-esteem, and the sudden realization that they had been cut off from their old public and stood little chance of gaining access to a new market, led many artists into severe personal crises. Some were driven into isolation and despair and committed suicide (Kurt Tucholsky, Walter Hasenclever, Ernst Weiß, Carl Einstein, Stefan Zweig and Walter Benjamin, to name just a few), which seemed to be the only logical answer to Hasenclever's question: 'We are banished, we are homeless, we are cursed. What right do we have to live?'[6] Stefan Zweig confessed that after his move into exile 'I felt that I didn't quite belong to myself anymore. Something of my original and real self had been destroyed forever.'[7] As early as 1937, Ernst Stern wrote a book on this phenomenon entitled *Die Emigration als psychologisches Problem* (*Emigration as a Psychological Problem*). Klaus Mann, in his *Emigrantenroman Der Vulkan,* called this attitude 'Entwurzelungsneurose' (neurosis caused by uprooting a person), and Alexander Granach coined the term 'Emigrantenpsychose' (emigrant psychosis) for this.[8]

Artists who relied on language as a medium of expression (writers, actors, etc.) found it invariably frustrating to see themselves reduced to stuttering in a foreign language when their accomplished command of the German tongue had brought them justified acclaim in their homeland. One might assume that artists who used a visual language might have been in a better position and more able to transcend any national barriers and to continue their career in exile without too much of a hiatus. But this was far from being the case. The living and working conditions forced nearly all artists to relinquish their personal style and interest and to produce whatever might find a buyer on the market. For example, one painter who had come to England in the 1930s still remembers how his works were considered too expressionistic and how he was constantly asked to tone down his colours:

> As much as I have an accent in my language I have an accent in my painting. In German art of our century, expression and feeling comes into it a lot. Whereas mainstream art in Britain is more good taste and playing down feelings. The majority of English people find my paintings too emotive, too direct. English art is a refined understatement.[9]

The modes of expressions that had prevailed in the Weimar Republic (e.g. Expressionism, *Neue Sachlichkeit*) were known to only a few admirers abroad. When a courageous gallerist was prepared to organize an exhibition of one of these artists, the show was often greeted with consternation and revulsion by the local population and turned into what Ludwig Meidner called in his case 'a second class funeral'.[10]

Theatre artists did not fare any better, as the examples quoted on p. 33-41 reveal. The artistic traditions in the countries of exile were so different from those that had existed in Germany before 1933 that many artists felt that they could not elicit any desired response from their addressees, or that they were, as Leonard Frank put it, 'playing on a violin of stone, a piano without strings.'[11] As a result of this, artists had to turn to menial tasks in order to make a living. Stage designers had to do window decoration for department stores; painters worked in china factories and sculptors in toy shops; poets wrote advertisement slogans and composers little ditties for the radio. There were few who could agree with Schoenberg when he said: 'If immigration to America has changed me—I am not aware of it.'[12]

On the other hand, it would be misleading to assume that exile had only negative experiences to offer. The life of an émigré artist may have been hard but it also granted valuable lessons, which some of them later would not have missed for anything. Bertolt Brecht saw exile as a school for life and reminded his fellow emigrants that 'the Chinese poets and philosophers are wont to go into exile just as we are used to going to an academy'.[13] Egon Schwarz came to appreciate his exile experience as a blessing in disguise 'which led me away from the insularity, provincialism, the narrow-mindedness full of resentment and hostility of my middle-European existence'.[14] Alfred Kerr rhymed in a similar vein:

> Manchmal fühlt das Herz sich sehr erheitert
> (trotz der zugeschlagnen deutschen Tür):
> Weil die Flucht den Horizont erweitert,
> Ja, du dankst den Jägern fast dafür.[15]
>
> (Sometimes my heart cheers up
> (Despite the German door being closed):
> Because exile widens the horizon—
> I could nearly thank my persecutors for this.)

Hermann Kesten adjudged that 'we have found plenty of knowledge and experience of the ways of the world during our exile, which we can now use to enrich German literature with'.[16]

These quotations show that artists did not necessarily consider their exile a purely negative chapter in their lives. Therefore, Peter Laemmle's challenge: 'Shouldn't the exile scholars for once admit that exile, or the experience of exile, has changed the quality of literary texts, and has changed them in a negative sense?'[17] has to be treated with care. It is true that artists did not always create their best and most enduring works during their exile, but it was not always exterior circumstances which prevented them from achieving a level of quality which otherwise they would have been capable of. In many cases exiled artists continued a process already set in motion during the Weimar Republic, one which might roughly be described as 'deconstruction of High Culture'. New genres had sprung up in the 1920s (e.g. reportage, *Lehrstück*, photomontage, collage, etc.) because they were more flexible and versatile, and therefore more suitable to express contemporary artistic concerns. The small, 'operative' forms preferred by the exile artists must be seen in a similar light. Works of art should not be judged by 'absolute' aesthetic standards. Using criteria derived from other historical periods and applying them to creations which differ from those of previous centuries in aim and function will, by necessity, lead to distorted judgements. Any artistic product has to be assessed within the parameters or historical conditions which determine its creation, otherwise its specific qualities will easily be overlooked and misinterpreted. Since the circumstances under which the exiled artists were creating their works differed so fundamentally from those in pre-1933 Germany, these conditions have to be examined first before one can arrive at a critical, objective assessment of the artists' achievements in the various countries of exile. In our case this means that we have to study the political and cultural climate in Britain before we can come to a proper understanding of the theatrical activities generated by the German exiles.

Exile in Great Britain

Britain is a country with a high tradition of hospitality to foreigners and has, for centuries, offered refuge to those of every rank and station who sought asylum on her shores from persecution and economic plight in their own lands. During the nineteenth century, many Germans had to flee their country because of the anti-revolutionary backlash following the defeats of the 1830 and 1848 revolutions. Others decided to emigrate because of Germany's backwardness with regard to economic and scientific development. Because of her acclaimed liberalism Britain was a classic country of refuge for these men and women disenchanted with their homeland, and many Germans settled here, especially in London around Soho and Leicester Square, in St John's Wood and Camberwell.

Two of the most famous Germans to arrive in Britain were Karl Marx and Friedrich Engels. Other political thinkers and philosophers included Arnold Ruge, Gottfried Kinkel, Wilhelm Wolff, Eduard Bernstein and Wilhelm Liebknecht. Amongst the poets one can mention Ferdinand Freiligrath, Georg Weerth and Moritz Hartmann; amongst the publishers Nikolaus Trübner and Julius Reuter; amongst the scholars the orientalist Friedrich Karl Müller and Theodor Goldstücker, the Germanists Karl Buchheim, Eugen Oswald, Robert Priebsch, and many more. Some immigrants such as the engineer Wilhelm Siemens or the architect Gottfried Semper decided to return to Germany; others made England their permanent home and founded institutions which are still with us today (e.g. Johannes Ronge, who introduced the first kindergarten in England in 1851, or Karl Halle, who founded the distinguished Hallé Orchestra in Manchester).[18]

Between 1826 and 1905 there existed practically no restrictions on immigration to Britain and, by all accounts, the reception refugees found in this country was very friendly indeed. Lord Malmesbury, in a speech to Parliament on 5 April 1852, sums up the prevailing atmosphere of hospitality by saying:

> I can well conceive the pleasure and happiness of a refugee, hunted from his native land, on approaching the shores of England, and the joy with which he first catches sight of them; but they are not greater than the pleasure and happiness every Englishman feels in knowing that his country affords the refugee a home and safety.[19]

According to a census in England and Wales the number of foreigners resident in those two parts of the country rose from 50,289 in 1851 to 118,031 in 1881.[20] Most of these exiles had arrived in England on their own or with their nearest relatives. They found the political climate here more liberal and the economic structures more advanced than in their home country and therefore decided to stay and start a new life as British citizens. The situation changed drastically with the mass emigration of Russian Jews at the end of the nineteenth century. By 1901 the number of aliens resident in the country had risen to 247,758, nearly half of them being East European Jews who had arrived in Britain during the past two decades.[21] This large influx of an ethnically and culturally diverse group of immigrants and their settlement in a relatively small, confined area (the London East End) gave rise to anti-Semitism, which soon turned into general xenophobia during the Boer War (1899-1902). As a result of this, the Aliens Act of 1905 was passed and soon afterwards was reinforced by the Aliens Restrictions Bill of 1914, curtailing the right of asylum and giving the immigration officers the power to refuse entry to those immigrants they considered 'undesirable'. The outbreak of the Second World War caused an outbreak of Germanophobia and led to the internment of about 40,000 of the 50,000 Germans living in this country.

The restrictions of the Aliens Act of 1905 and 1914 were further reinforced by the Aliens Order of 1920 which stated that no alien was to be given leave of entry unless he was in the possession of a work permit or some visible means of support. These restrictions being still in force during the 1930s prevented Britain from becoming a country of mass exile after Hitler's seizure of power. The initial wave of emigration from Nazi Germany caused the British Cabinet to set up a committee under the chairmanship of the Home Secretary in order to consider the question of German refugees. It was judged to be in the public interest to

> try and secure for this country prominent Jews who were being expelled from Germany and who had achieved distinction whether in pure science, applied science, such as medicine or technical industry, music or art. This would not only obtain for this country the advantage of their knowledge and experience, but would also create a very favourable impression in the world, particularly if our hospitality were offered with some warmth.[22]

Since many of the applicants for exile status were neither prominent nor wealthy, they tried to enter the country as 'visitors'. Consequently, the Foreign Office instructed the Passport Control Department that 'such persons, especially those who appear to be of Jewish or partly Jewish origin, or have non-Aryan affiliations, should be discreetly questioned as to their family circumstances, and how their business or employment has been affected by recent events'.[23] Further instructions were to the effect that whilst any 'distinguished persons, i.e. those of *international* repute in the field of science, medicine, research or art' were to be granted a visa, those applicants who were not 'likely to be an asset to the United Kingdom' were to be refused entry. Amongst those regarded as '*prima facie* unsuitable' were

(1) Small shop-keepers, retail traders, artisans, and persons likely to seek employment.

(2) Agents and middlemen, whose livelihood depended on commission and, therefore, on trade activity.

(3) Minor musicians and commercial artists of all kinds.

(4) The rank and file of professional men—lawyers, doctors, dentists.[24]

As a result of these restrictions, only 5,500 of the 154,000 refugees who left Germany between 1933 and 1937 were granted asylum in Great Britain. Most of them were professionals, industrialists, scholars and academics who had personal contacts or family ties in Britain and who also managed to transfer a substantial part of their personal possessions from Germany to Britain.

This development took a drastic turn in 1938 following the invasion of Austria, the occupation of the Sudentenland and the anti-Jewish pogroms after the *Kristallnacht*. In 1938/39 more than 25,000 mainly Jewish refugees were admitted to Britain, and by the time war broke out the number of exiles from countries under Nazi rule had risen to 55,000. Nearly 90 per cent of them had left their home country because of the anti-Semitic coercive measures, and the rest were political exiles.

Because of the rather diverse ethnic, political and cultural background of these refugees it is difficult to speak of *a* German group of exiles in Great Britain. Besides the Reichsgermans there were the Austrians,[25] Czechs,[26] Hungarians, Poles, Rumanians, Yugoslavs, etc. Because of the apolitical nature of most of these refugees and because of the interdiction against forming political parties, most exiles organized themselves around *Kulturvereine* based on the emigrants' country of origin. Other popular meeting places were the clubs and coffee-houses, as well as the social events organized by the approximately 200 refugee charity bodies. Many English people looked at these refugee organizations with amusement and regarded the endless number of societies and associations that sprang up all over the country as a typical outgrowth of German club mania. Although this mentality cannot be completely denied, one should, however, not underestimate the cultural, political and social functions these innumerable clubs had.

A social analysis of the German emigrant population in Britain reveals that 27 per cent of the men and 17 per cent of the women had an academic profession, and 33 per cent were entrepreneurs and businessmen.[27] These refugees had been eager participants in the cultural life of their home countries, but a continuation of their former life-style was often out of the question when they arrived in Britain, partly for financial reasons, partly because they lived outside the centre of London where most of the cultural life was concentrated. But even when they had access to a theatre or music hall, a cinema or an art gallery, many of the immigrants did not avail themselves of these facilities. Their unfamiliarity with the English language and with English artistic traditions made it very difficult for them to appreciate cultural events aimed explicitly at British audiences.

This loss of a cultural identity came as a shock to many emigrants, since they had not expected that the process of adaptation to their new surroundings would be so difficult and long-lasting. The refugees' desire to keep in touch with their cultural traditions led to the foundation of several cultural associations which soon became a vital element in the life of the German émigré community. Out of the *Kulturbünde* grew a large number of projects and ventures such as journals, theatres, exhibitions, concerts, lectures, etc. which operated in two directions: they helped the refugees to overcome the feeling of loss inevitably connected with their emigration to another country, and they served to communicate the emigrants' concerns and interests to the native population. This latter element was, of course, of immense political importance. In most instances it was the left-wing artists and intellectuals who set up these enterprises. They had the self-confidence and political experience, and often the organizational skills, to build up a network of contacts with local parties and societies and to bridge the gap between the refugees and the British population.

A strong anti-Fascist attitude served as a common ground to unite the socially and politically diverse members of the refugee community. However, when it came to formulating a more precise programme for action, the differences of opinion and beliefs often proved to be an insurmountable obstacle for creating a popular front against Fascism. The economic, social and political causes for the rise of Fascism in Europe and National Socialism in Germany were interpreted and analysed by the émigrés in rather diverse terms. This often led to arguments and friction and caused serious ruptures within the organizations. Personal animosities, formations of cliques and coteries, ideological quarrels and political sectarianism enhanced the potential for discord and conflict. Not infrequently this led to the formation of splinter groups, which seriously weakened the effectiveness of the refugee organizations:

> For most of the Social Democrat refugees it was out of the question to get involved with the *Kulturbund* because of the active participation of Communists in the organization. Rejecting co-operation with the *League* (which, after all, was the largest and most effective organization of the German emigrants in Great Britain) even implied, for the SPD leadership, the boycott of purely cultural or literary events.[28]

In their initial stages, however, the refugee organizations knew few of these problems. The thousands of émigrés who had just arrived in Britain often led a lonely existence in tiny flats and dingy bed-sits; so if nearby there was a Refugee Centre they went there 'because there was a restaurant, so in that sense people met and I mean during the war, any restaurant where you got food and especially food to your liking, was a great attraction and I would say most people were attracted by that sort of thing, the dancing and the social events'.[29]

Whilst the first wave of immigrants had found it relatively easy to integrate into British society, the majority of the new arrivals in 1938/39 found the conditions of exile more difficult. They arrived in a country where few of them had any family ties, and where because of high unemployment it was extremely difficult to make social contact through work. According to Gabriele Tergit, 'around 1943 many refugees—at least in London—had never been in an English home, didn't know an English soul except the milkman, the postman and the greengrocer'.[30] Due to this lack of social contacts their command of the English language improved only slowly and they found it difficult to entertain normal relationships with the people who lived around them. As a result of this, most of the refugees hoped that their stay in Britain would be a short one and that soon they would be able to return to their native country:

> Each man might say to himself, or each woman for that matter, I've just come from Düsseldorf, I've just come from Mannheim, the war will finish, and I'll go back, because I'm a stranger here—I am truly a refugee. So it's better to keep together, and to retain each one's own culture, one's own interest, one's own language, one's own behaviour and so on because I don't know, tomorrow I might be able to go back. So you keep yourself to yourself.[31]

The only people many of them knew were other refugees who showed similar reactions to their new surroundings and went through similar experiences. Hence they frequented the same meeting places which offered social contacts and psychological support in a society which appeared alien and often hostile to them. When being asked why they spent so much of their spare time in the refugee clubs their typical answer was: 'When meeting other refugees one does not feel an outsider.'[32] This lack of integration into British society bred loneliness and depression, and without the Refugee Centres many of the emigrants would have ended their lives in utter despair. If there was no Centre near, a restaurant or a café could fulfil the function of acting as a social focal point for the local refugee population: 'The majority were refugees who were at a loose end with language difficulties here anyway and that was the only way they could spend a Sunday afternoon or a Saturday afternoon to get some strudel and a bit of music but it was as innocent as that.'[33]

Erich Fried, in a recent interview, remembered the refugee organizations 'as a basis of our existence, as employment agency, as cheap restaurants where you could have a decent meal, and as cultural organizations',[34] but he also underlined their political importance, especially for the younger generation of emigrants:

> The exile organizations had been called into existence by the political movements. There were Zionist ones (amalgamated with the English Zionists) who had a great run from the Jewish refugees. Then there were communist ones, who were the biggest. Not that the communist parties—the Austrian or German ones—had all that many members, but their propaganda was very efficient. The communists opened up restaurants, founded culture clubs, organized cultural programmes, lectures, cabarets, etc. in order to reach as many emigrants as possible, especially the young ones.... The youth organization of the communists—not the Kommunistischer Jugendverband, although that was the core—had immense influence. The mass organization Young Austria alone had about 2,000 members, which was quite a number. And with the German communists it was similar.[35]

The Refugee Clubs were, in the first instance, social meeting places, but since political discussions were a regular event, they often gained a reputation which put off some of the older, apolitical émigrés:

> I know my parents used to say, you know that's quite a left-wing club you go to and I said nonsense, nonsense because I was not a bit interested and I didn't want to know, all I was interested in was that I could meet some young people of my age and I was quite happy with that, I didn't want to get involved.[36]

Many of the younger refugees were less opposed to political activities, and they liked to come to the Centres because of the opportunity they offered for political debates and education:

> Questions such as what had all this been about, you know, Hitler coming to power and the war breaking out and where was all this leading and what was going to happen and in those days socialism certainly seemed a way out of all these difficulties and so our activities at the centre and the cultural activities were geared towards widening our knowledge about what that really meant and we had some marvellous programmes. We participated in a young group of actors and we participated in a choir and when the War broke out we went right up to the north of Scotland where we took songs from Czechoslovakia, songs from the Spanish War, from Germany and then we had 'Sprechchöre' but we didn't only do that, we wanted to let the Scots know how much we appreciated living here. We recited Burns at them with rather strange accents and they bore with us with a great deal of pleasure and even more tolerance.[37]

The biggest and most important exile organization in Britain was the Freier Deutscher Kulturbund (Free German League of Culture). Besides theatrical activities they organized exhibitions, concerts, readings, lectures, courses, published journals, books and pamphlets, and so on. Membership in the FDKB was open to British citizens, and in their public events directed at the native population the émigrés made the voice of 'the other Germany' heard in the country. They tried to explain to the British that 'Germans' and 'Nazis' were not the same, that Hitler and the NSDAP had seized power and were holding it largely through the use of terror and intimidation. They pointed out that there were Germans inside the Reich who were resisting the Nazi régime (as for example in the 1942 exhibition 'Allies Inside Germany', which had no less than 30,000 visitors[38]).

This 'two Germanies' doctrine found support amongst some members of the British government. In April 1941, the Foreign Office explained the reason behind their support for the German-language newspaper *Die Zeitung* by saying: 'It is part of [our general propaganda line] that we must admit the existence of two Germanies (a 'good' one and a Nazi one).'[39] But others held the opinion that while there were 'other Germans' there was no 'other Germany'. Many refugees found it more and more difficult to defend their position when it became evident that even at times of increasing war-weariness Hitler's hold over the German people remained strong and that there were few signs of a widespread and effective resistance movement. Especially amongst the exiled politicians of the Social Democratic Party (SPD) this led to a reconsideration of the political line to be taken with the British government. Instead of seeking a rôle of representing the German opposition against Nazism they regarded themselves as representatives of the 'better Germans' who were going to erect a new German state after the defeat of the Hitler régime.

The government's attitude towards the Hitlerites or the exiles depended largely on the political expediencies of the day and the opinions which gained influence in Parliament. In March 1933, immediately after Hitler's seizure of power, there were debates in Parliament as to what attitude the government ought to take towards the stream of Germans who were forced to leave their country. Some MPs maintained that Britain had always welcomed exiles from anti-democratic countries, whilst others supported a Conservative MP who proclaimed that 'hundreds of thousands of Jews are now leaving Germany and scurrying from there to this country . . . Are we prepared in this country to allow aliens to come in here from every country while we have 3,000,000 unemployed?'[40] In June 1933, the Marquis of Reading, a member of the House of Lords and himself a prominent British Jew, warned: 'We have well in mind, in our duty as British citizens, that we must take care that we do not add to the great unemployment existing in this country.'[41]

The refugees who tried to gain entry to Britain were at the mercy of the vagaries of the official line the government was taking towards Nazi Germany. During the period of appeasement the attitude towards the German refugees was 'carefully restrictive',[42] which meant that the exile question was handled in a manner avoiding any possible clashes with the diplomatic representations of the Hitler régime in Great Britain. The situation began to change after the Munich agreement, when Hitler's expansionist policies threatened the peace in Europe and eventually led to the Second World War. Germanophobia became rampant in Britain and sentiments against anything or anyone German were expressed even by educated people and by politicians who should have been able to distinguish between Nazis and the German victims of this régime. Sections of the British government spurred these anti-German feelings, and Robert Vansittart, Under-Secretary at the Foreign Office, proclaimed a doctrine according to which '80 per cent of the German race are the moral and political scum of the earth. You cannot reform them by signatures and concessions. They have got to be hamstrung and broken up . . . They are a race of bone-headed aggressors . . .'[43] The Foreign Secretary, Anthony Eden, stated in 1941: 'I have no confidence in our ability to make decent Europeans of the Germans and I believe that the Nazi system represents the mentality of the great majority of German people.'[44] Even William Gilles, International Secretary of the Labour Party, who had invited part of the SPD leadership to form a German shadow government in London, lost his trust in the German comrades and stated in 1943:

> The HQ regards these émigrés as individuals and does not accept that they are representatives of a party. The Germans' spirit is not really democratic. They are too easily led, much more prone to follow any warlord to the conquest of their neighbours' lands. An insignificant part of the SPD leadership became exiles . . . and there is not much basis for the opinion that they will have any influence after the war.[45]

In 1943 the British Institute of Public Opinion tested the British public's feelings towards Germany and reported that in reply to their question: 'What are your feelings towards the German people?' 45 per cent answered 'bitterness, hatred and anger', 20 per cent 'the Germans are getting what they deserve', and only 15 per cent stated any feelings of friendliness or pity.[46] These attitudes can be compared to an opinion poll carried out in the summer of 1939 when 70 per cent stated that refugees from Nazi Germany should be allowed to enter Great Britain (although 80 per cent of those in favour of giving these refugees leave of entry wanted to see restrictions attached to their entry permits in order to safeguard British workers and taxpayers[47]). Andrew Sharf, who analysed the British press's attitude towards the German refugees, sums up his findings by saying that public opinion displayed 'an anti-Semitic substratum lightly covered over by a mixture of vague humanitarianism and fear of German conquest'.[48]

The Jewish refugees who had sought asylum in Britain found themselves in the ironic situation that after having had to leave Germany because of their Jewish origin they were now treated as Germans and subjected to the same enmity as their Nazi oppressors. Erich Fried, when questioned about his experiences of xenophobia in those years, stated that on the whole the English had been friendly to foreigners, but exceptions to the rule occurred fairly regularly: 'Only occasionally one heard someone saying "Bloody German". Then one replied: "But I'm not really a German. I am a Jew." Then one could hear: "Worse still, bloody German Jew!"'[49] This inability to distinguish between Nazis and anti-Fascist exiles is mentioned again and again in the refugees' memoirs and personal recollections. The following statement of an exile employed in a Scottish household is typical of this experience:

> They had four sons in the British army and one of them was shot down by the Germans and I got the blame for that. I find Scottish people very nice people and I wouldn't change my life but all the time of the war they hated us, they could not understand the difference between a Jew and a German.[50]

Marion Berghahn interviewed a large number of Jewish exiles on the question of xenophobia and sums up her findings:

> In general, though, they were convinced of the fundamental decency of the English people, and were confident that the liberal traditions of England would retain the upper hand—although some expressed doubt, because 'after all, we believed that in Germany too'.[51]

The ambivalent feeling many refugees had towards the British population was further exacerbated when they looked for employment to match their professional training and expertise. Some were lucky enough to be issued with a work permit; but this still did not mean that they could find a position where they could use their professional training or which gave them an income comparable to what they had earned in Germany. Only a few of them were able to continue their secure middle class existence in Britain. More typical were the personal histories I was told by London émigrés, such as the case of a lady of good society who once commanded a large household with several servants in Berlin-Wilmersdorf and then became a maid in Putney; of a well-known lawyer from Vienna who had to work as a bank clerk; of a doctor from the *Charité* who became employed as a nurse at St Bartholomew's; or of a Germanist from Humboldt University who served as a farm hand in Cornwall. One can imagine how humiliating it felt for the mainly middle-class refugees to be pushed into the only work sector where a shortage of labour existed: domestic service. No fewer than 21,000 of the émigrés became employed as domestic servants[52] (usually the women, since many men refused to lower themselves to become members of the 'serving classes'). I quote from two interviews to give an impression of how reduced in their value these middle-class refugees felt:

> And I really must say, they wanted to exploit us all! At home, we'd all had maids of our own. And it wasn't so easy, suddenly to become maids ourselves. But they made no allowance for this, I must say.[53]

> [My wife found a] position in Glasgow. It was a large tailor's workshop producing women's uniforms. Her job was at the sewing-machine. There were large rooms with a lot of people and a lot of noise, dust and dirt. She really got to know proletarian working conditions there. She accepted this with her usual courage, but it

wasn't nice. . . . I often used to pick her up from work and would wait for her in front of the house in the city centre, in a narrow and rather unpleasant-looking street near the Clyde. After work the female workers would pour out. They were mostly very young girls who looked pretty dirty and unkempt. As a class they were below the shop employees, but gradually she even got used to these surroundings . . .[54]

The employment situation improved after 1940. The acute labour shortage caused by the outbreak of the war made it easier for the refugees to find work. Many of the exiles contributed to the war effort on the side of the anti-Fascist allies. No fewer than 9,000 men and 1,000 women volunteered for the British forces and 'conducted themselves', as Col. Arthur Evans, MP, told the House of Commons, 'in the best traditions of the British Army'.[55]

Similar praise and distinction were earned by a number of scientists who had come to Britain. In 1933 some 1,200 scholars had been dismissed from German universities, and by 1934 about 650 of them had decided to emigrate. Within two years, 287 of them had been placed permanently in some thirty countries, and 336 temporarily. The British share was fifty-seven permanent and 155 temporary appointments.[56] Most of them remained after 1945 and contributed to the advancement of science and learning in Britain. By 1955, no fewer than twenty-five had been awarded fellowships of the Royal Society, and three, Born, Chain and Krebs, had won the Nobel Prize. By 1977, fifty-three of them had become Fellows of the Royal Society and twenty-eight Fellows of the British Academy. Art History in British universities gained international status by the arrival of the Warburg Institute and of celebrated scholars such as Nikolaus Pevsner, Ernst Gombrich, Frederick Antal and Rudolf Wittkower.[57] The British publishing world profited from the arrival of George Weidenfeld, André Deutsch, Bruno Cassirer, Oswald Wolff, Walter Neurath (founder of Thames and Hudson), or Bela Horovitz and Ludwig Goldscheider (who transferred the Phaidon Press from Vienna to London). British sociology took a new course through the enormous influence exercised by Karl Mannheim. There was hardly any university or academic discipline which did not benefit from the exodus of the cream of German scholarship; in fact several pages could be filled if one were to compile a complete list of all German scholars who became distinguished professors, heads of department, directors of medical schools, or chairmen of scientific research institutions in Great Britain.[58]

Similarly beneficial to the country was the arrival of about 4,000 to 6,000 German industrialists, businessmen and entrepreneurs. Most of them were directed into regions of severe unemployment, and by 1939 about 300 firms had been established by refugee manufacturers, creating about 15,000 to 25,000 jobs. By 1947 this number had been increased to about 1,000 refugee manufacturing firms employing about 250,000 people.[59]

There are no exact figures available on how many of the émigrés went back to their country of origin after 1945. Most of the political exiles returned to their homeland in order to participate in the reconstruction of a democratic Germany, whilst the majority of the Jewish refugees made Britain their home. Their break with Germany remained final, partly because of their distrust and reserve towards the Germans; partly because their family ties had been broken up by the Nazis and there were no relatives left in Germany to go back to. When Karen Gershon questioned these émigrés about their attitude towards Germany,[60] even thirty years after the war many of them still felt bitter:

When I go back to Germany I smell blood.

(p. 154)

I wish them all to hell, do unto them what they did unto others.

(p. 135)

As late as 1951, when I paid my first visit to Germany since leaving in 1938, I murmured, when actually seeing the mounds of rubble that were once cities: 'Serves them right, serves them right, serves them right'.

(p. 139)

I have found that on a few visits to relatives my emotions have got the better of me. The old fears returned from the moment I set eyes on the man who inspects the passports.

(p. 139)

My attitude to Germany and the Germans is rather mixed. It varies between cynical admiration of their revival, to deepest revulsion about their past deeds.

(p. 136)

I do sometimes find myself resenting West German affluence and efficiency, and our recent purchase of a Volkswagen took some doing.

(p. 136)

All émigrés I spoke to over the last ten years see themselves as loyal Britons; yet culturally they have not broken with their past. They regularly frequent the German Film Seasons at the National Film Theatre, come to poetry readings at the Goethe Institut, or visit the performances of German theatre companies touring Great Britain. Many of them never set foot again on German soil. Some of Gershon's interviewees visited their old home town and found that 'the home is destroyed by bombs, a new generation lives in the town, their social and economic culture is alien . . . There is nothing there for me' (p. 140); or, 'I went back to my home town last year. It was completely destroyed and rebuilt and seemed to me like a strange place' (p. 141). Some of the Jewish émigrés occasionally return to Germany in order to visit a friend or relative, but their attitude towards the Germans as a people still remains ambivalent: 'I know quite a few individual German people whom I like very much, but as an anonymous nation I hate and fear them' (p. 140). Another former refugee explains why he takes a more philosophical view: 'How can I hate the Germans; my worst enemies, but also my best friends were German.'[61] They certainly feel more comfortable in Britain, although they cannot refrain from the occasional jibe about the British way of life. Marion Berghahn has studied the assimilation of German refugees into British society[62] and has found that their attitude towards their new home country is overwhelmingly positive. They have become integrated into British life, but socially they still carry the stigma of being 'Continental'. Their homes tend to exude a typical German notion of *Gemütlichkeit* and their eating habits are distinctly non-British.

Even the second generation of immigrants is still aware of their German-Jewish background. They were born in England, their friends are mainly English, but at the most they can say: 'I am British, though I shall never be English.'[63] In Marion Berghahn's study, even in the third generation, 99 per cent stated that they do not feel English. They see themselves above all as Jews, but different from the English Jews. One of Gershon's interviewees explains this by saying: 'We do not fit in completely because we are Jewish, yet not Jewish enough for English Jews.'[64] They do not feel German either, but then German-Jewish culture has always been different from the official German 'high-culture'. Berghahn describes their identity as 'German-Jewish ethnicity', where the German component becomes more diluted and the Jewish element merges more and more with the Anglo-Jewish culture. But at the present, forty years after the Holocaust, an important part of German culture of the past still survives in Britain because, as Marion Berghahn says, 'in England the Jews are permitted to be what, in the final analysis, they could not be in Germany: German Jews.'[65]

German Exile Theatre: The British Experience

In 1945, when many of the exiled theatre artists returned to their home country, they were greeted by a population which was crying out for theatrical entertainment. Between 1945 and 1948 no fewer than 419 theatre enterprises were called into existence,[66] but the fare the audiences were provided with consisted mainly of comedies, operettas and classical plays. Contemporary anti-Fascist drama accounted for only a small fraction of the repertoire. Hans Daibler has estimated that of the circa 500 plays written during the period of exile only 5 per cent were performed after 1945,[67] and most of these in the Soviet Occupied Zone.[68]

One of the few plays to be given repeated runs in several West German theatres was Friedrich Wolf's *Professor Mamlock*. Obviously audiences were interested in the play's political message—much to the distaste of the cultural establishment. On 13 December 1946 the *Kölnischer Rundschau* wrote: 'What are we to do with tendentious plays such as *Professor Mamlock*? We have been fed with this kind of stuff during the Third Reich . . . Now we want to see works which lift us out of the narrowness of our poor existence into higher spheres . . .'[69] While anti-Fascist drama was being pushed into the background the protagonists of National Socialist drama, such as Erwin Guido Kolbenheyer or Hanns Johst, experienced a renaissance in West Germany. The political climate of the Cold War and restoration period led to a situation where the exiles, just as the resistance movement, 'became for a second time victims of a political situation'.[70] A similar fate lay in store for the historians who had studied the cultural activities of the exiled artists and who wanted to inform the German public how the progressive and humanist traditions of German culture had been upheld and continued by the exiles outside the confines of the Third Reich. When Walter Berendsohn offered his manuscript of *Die humanistische Front* to the Munich publisher Kurt Desch the book was rejected because it was considered

> a sort of pamphlet of an émigré against the writers who remained in Germany. We have to and want to object to this book most emphatically because of its sad and disgraceful tendency . . . which not only obstructs our attempts of bridging the gap between us and the émigrés, but also contaminates the atmosphere between Germany and her neighbours with new poison.[71]

The theatre artists returning from exile with the intention of informing their fellow countrymen about their activities abroad received a fairly similar reception, i.e. total disinterest or distinct hostility. Apart from a few articles and brochures published immediately after the war,[72] no major study on exile theatre appeared until the early 1970s.

In 1973, the Academy of Arts in West Berlin organized an exhibition 'Theater in Exil' and a symposium on the same subject, and in the same year published the papers given at the conference. These events coincided with a research project organized by the Academy of Arts in Berlin (GDR) and the issuing of an *Arbeitsheft* containing a survey, entitled *Das antifaschistisch-demokratische und sozialistische deutsche Theater im Exil*. In West Germany the Hanser Verlag published Hans Christof Wächter's dissertation *Theater im Exil*. From then on, a major monograph on exile theatre has appeared nearly every year. . . . This sudden upsurge of interest in the exile period brought to a halt the irretrievable loss of valuable documents which had still been in the possession of the artists once involved with the exile theatre, or at least decelerated the rapid disappearance of material without which the history of exile theatre cannot be reconstructed. Since many of the theatre productions were badly documented in the first place, the personal scrapbooks of actors, directors or designers, containing texts, music sheets, photographs, or newspaper clippings are of considerable importance for the theatre historian. Unfortunately, many of these memorabilia do not have much of a sentimental value for the relatives of a deceased artist, which means that a large amount of unique documents has been destroyed and will no longer be available for future research.

It has been estimated that between 1933 and 1945 the exiled playwrights and theatre artists created about 724 dramatic works and 800 theatre productions, 108 radio dramas and 398 film scripts.[73] Only a few of the texts survive, and many productions were never reviewed in the exile or foreign press, which leaves us with very little evidence of how extensive the theatrical activity was and what artistic quality it did achieve. A systematic study of those documents that have been preserved in various archives and private collections makes us aware that an enormous variety of theatrical activities was instigated by the exiled artists. It is therefore misleading to speak of *the* exile theatre, when the diversity of theatrical ventures appears to be one of the most salient traits of the émigrés' theatre activities. The particular organizational or artistic shape of a theatrical enterprise depended on the artists involved, the composition of the exile community, the theatrical traditions of the host country, the financial and material conditions of the theatre, the political and legal framework under which they were operating and so on. Hence it is wise to avoid generalizations and sweeping judgements and to concentrate on specific descriptions and analyses of the theatrical work carried out in individual countries or theatres or by particular ensembles or artists.

The ten studies assembled in this volume offer an impressive picture of the range of activities carried out by the exiled theatre artists in Great Britain. Arising out of these essays a number of conclusions can be drawn. (These, of course, only reflect my own opinions and do not necessarily coincide with the views of the contributors to this volume.)

When comparing the German exile theatre in Great Britain with that in other English-speaking countries, especially the USA, it becomes apparent that the cultural climate in a receiving country was always more important for an artist's successful career than his or her command of the English language. While in the USA the refugee artists had relatively good chances of becoming integrated into the existing theatre structure, in Britain the co-operation with professional theatre institutions could be achieved only to a limited degree. Initially, the situation looked fairly promising. Many actors who were fleeing Nazi Germany seem to have regarded London as a favourite city in which to continue their theatrical career. On 21 December 1935, the exile journal *Das Neue. Tage-Buch* reported: 'The transplantation of the Berlin theatre of old makes constant progress. After Elisabeth Bergner, Lucie Mannheim, Grete Mosheim, Oskar Homolka, Fritz Kortner, Conrad Veidt, Paul Grätz and others, Ernst Deutsch is now also making his passage to the English stage.' It is interesting to note that between 1933 and 1938, when only a limited number of refugees had found asylum in Britain and only a small exile community existed in London, there were more productions of German plays in regular English theatre than in the following six years. Nick Furness, in his article 'The Reception of Ernst Toller and His Works in Britain' in the volume *Expressionism in Focus,* lists no fewer than nineteen productions of this dramatist, presented between 1933 and 1939, in British theatres. Toller, certainly, was the most widely performed German playwright in the country; but one should also mention some other notable productions of the pre-war era:

1933	Friedrich Schiller, *Kabale und Liebe* (perf. in German), Duke of York's Theatre, dir.: Leopold Jessner, des.: Caspar Neher
1933	Hermann Sudermann, *Heimat*, ditto
1934	Carl Zuckmayer, *The Golden Toy,* Coliseum, dir.: Ludwig Berger
1935	Kurt Weill, *My Kingdom for a Cow,* Savoy Theatre, dir.: Felix Weissberger, des.: Hein Heckroth
1936	Bruno Frank, *Young Madam Conti,* Savoy Theatre, dir.: Benn W. Levy, des.: Ernst Stern
c. 1936/37	Leo Lania, *Der Held* (mentioned in Wächter, p. 41)
1937	Walter Hasenclever (under the pseudonym Axel Kjellström), *Scandal in Assyria,* The London International Theatre Club at the Globe Theatre, London, dir.: John Gielgud, des.: Motley
1937	Walter Hasenclever, *What Should a Husband Do*? Theatre unknown; dir.: Robert Klein
1938	Bertolt Brecht, *Señora Carrar's Rifles,* Unity Theatre, dir.: John Fernald

It was a great loss to the English theatre that internationally renowned actors such as Fritz Kortner, Oskar Homolka or Ernst Deutsch could not be won permanently for the London stage. The same applies to directors such as Berthold Viertel, who directed only one major production in London, Max Catto's Gothic thriller *They Walk Alone* (1939: Shaftesbury Theatre).[74]

Only after 1938, when the mass immigration of German refugees to Britain set in, did an exile community with an active cultural life come into being. Whenever the exiled actors, directors, designers etc. did not find employment in the theatre, the film industry or at the BBC they offered their service to one of the exile theatre ventures that had sprung up after 1939: the Laterndl, the Kleine Bühne des FDKB, the Blue Danube, the Österreichische Bühne, the Lessing Theater, the Spieltruppe der Freien Deutschen Jugend, the Kulturbund-Spielgruppe, the Austrian Youth Players, the Oxford Refugee Theatre Company, the Kleinkunstbühne der Jacob Ehrlich Gesellschaft.

Due to the limited facilities these companies had at their disposal, short plays and revue shows were performed more frequently than full-length plays with large casts. The artists drew heavily on the traditions of cabaret and agit-prop, although some reviews indicate that even within the limitations of small budgets and restrictive technical apparatus attempts in the direction of psychological naturalism were undertaken. Experiments with new dramatic forms or innovatory theatrical languages are never mentioned. Even the three Brecht productions of the FDKB (the 'Informer' scene from *Fear and Misery of the Third Reich* in 1939 at the West Central Hall, the 'Rechtsfindung' scene from the same play in 1941 at the Toynbee Hall, and *Señora Carrar's Rifles* in the same double bill as *Rechtsfindung* in 1941) had been chosen solely for their political subject matter and were performed in a style that gave no indication of Brecht's importance as a radical innovator of the German stage.

The artistic quality of a production was largely determined by the technical facilities and the personnel available, and its formal characteristics were always subservient to the function of the production. The restrictions imposed by poor working conditions forced the exile theatres in their initial phase to use an Epic style similar to the one used by the working-class theatre collectives of the Weimar Republic. But later, when the facilities and finances allowed it, the style of many productions resembled those of a traditional Stadttheater of the Weimar period (see, for example, the last productions at the Kleine Bühne (Little Theatre) and the Laterndl).

The relationship between function and format of the exile theatre productions can be summarized under five headings:

(1) The performances were organized by refugee clubs and took place in the early evenings or at weekends, when there were no curfews and few work commitments. The theatres served as a meeting point for the refugees and fulfilled important social functions within the exile community.

(2) Many performances were given in the German language in order to help the refugees retain a cultural identity and serve as a reminder of the Weimar years when theatre had always played an important rôle in their lives. The retention of a cultural heritage reduced the feeling of loss which characterized other parts of the refugees' existence. Hence the emphasis on plays and scenes stemming from the traditional repertoire and the nostalgia which pervaded many performances.

(3) The rediscovery of the humanistic and democratic traditions in German theatre served to emphasize the existence of an 'other Germany' and to counterbalance the appropriation of part of the classical repertoire by the Nazis. Since these performances were directed at an exile as well as an English audience they were given in the English language.

(4) Plays and scenes written by authors living in exile often dealt with the everyday life of the refugees and offered help in coping with the exile situation and the innumerable problems attached to the émigrés' attempts at building up a new existence for themselves in a foreign country. These problems were dealt with in humorous little vignettes or sketches, but sometimes whole revues or serious plays were dedicated to this subject matter.

(5) Anti-Fascist plays and scenes performed in English served to enlighten the British public about what was happening in Nazi Germany. They tried to reveal the true nature of the Hitler régime and served as a counterbalance to the propaganda of the Nazis and their British allies. These performances aimed at having a strong emotional appeal, which was usually achieved by offering the spectator the opportunity to identify with the victims of Nazi oppression. The Brechtian method of appealing to the spectators' rational capacities and making use of the Alienation Effect was rarely employed.

It is difficult to assess what kind of response these productions received outside exile circles. Reviews in the national as well as exile press tended to be very positive because many of the reviewers were personal friends or acquaintances of the performers, and they tried to support these theatrical activities by writing encouraging reviews. Therefore, one cannot attach too much significance to their assessment of the artistic qualities of the productions. From most reviews it transpires that the critics were so impressed by the mere fact that the refugees were creating theatre under such adverse circumstances that they would not discourage these undertakings by petty carping or fault-finding, even if they thought that the productions left a lot to be desired.

The attempts of the National Socialist embassy and consulate to suppress the activities of the émigrés and to hinder the performances of anti-Fascist plays (successful, for example, in the case of Bruckner's *Die Rassen,* which Robert Klein, former director of the Deutsches Theater in Berlin, planned to produce in London in 1934[75]) can be interpreted as a sign that the exiles' influence on public opinion abroad was taken seriously by the government in Berlin. The exile theatres were considered to have a detrimental effect on the image the Nazi régime sought to propagate abroad, and they tried to counteract it by founding a Truppe für Auslandsgastspiele (Foreign Touring Company) under the auspices of the Reichsministerium für Volksaufklärung und Propaganda (Propaganda Ministry).[76]

But it is rather doubtful that the importance the Berlin government attached to the exiles' activities can serve as a truthful indicator of the actual effect the émigrés' propaganda work had on the population of their host country. In 1943, the Foreign Office requested MI5 to investigate the political activities of the German refugee organizations and was content to find, after they had received the secret service's report, 'First, that German exiles were very much on their good behaviour and less outspoken than their colleagues in the USA and second, that whatever their views, they had in fact been able to gain little influence on any action of British public life not excluding the Labour party with which their contacts are strongest'.[77] Although the majority of the population was aware of the presence of a considerable number of German immigrants in their country, only a few of them took an active interest in their political and cultural activities. Until the outbreak of the Second World War, the arts programme of the Nazi consulates exercised a considerable influence in Britain, and it was not only the Mosleyites who were impressed by the glamour of Nazi culture and admired Hitler's solution to the economic crisis of the early 1930s.

Amongst those members of the public who felt sympathy for the émigrés, only a few attended their theatre performances, and if they did, they did not necessarily find them to their taste. For obvious reasons, the performances in the exile theatres did not compare favourably to productions in the West End. But even when the German theatre artists managed to break into the commercial theatre world, only a few of them received a favourable reception. The gap between the German and British theatre traditions was immense: the works of Expressionist playwrights such as Ernst Toller were greeted with consternation, atonal music of the Viennese School was slated as 'sewing machine counterpoint', Jessner's famous *Treppen* were gazed at in disbelief, and many spectators found Kortner's acting style downright revolting.[78] The revolutions in European theatre from Craig and Appia onwards had left virtually no trace in Britain. Even the productions in 'experimental' theatres such as the Gate or Cambridge Festival Theatre were tame compared to what had been performed in Germany, Russia, France or Italy in the early part of the century. In Britain, the *pièce-bien-faite* variety of theatre reigned supreme, and the production methods can only be described as slapdash. Friedrich Richter, later to become one of the few commercial success stories of German émigrés working in the British commercial theatre, draws a vivid picture of this type of production:

> The Oxford Playhouse opens every week with a new play. How is it possible that the actors in Oxford can churn out a play in no less than six days (the seventh day is a Sunday when the theatre is dark and no rehearsals take place)? How is this in the long run possible? Well, first of all these plays are pure conversation pieces, and secondly these actors are incredible *routiniers* and play without director. True, the programme always mentions a director, and this person is also sitting in the stalls during rehearsals, but he very wisely keeps his mouth shut. He can't afford to hold up rehearsals by giving any hints or advice. There are six times four hours of rehearsals, half an hour of which is always taken up by a coffee break, when you go over into the foyer, have a cup of coffee, and become absorbed in a conversation with the charming English colleagues.[79]

The six days rehearsal period also applied to arts theatres such as the Gate or Festival Theatre,[80] which despite the Continental flavour of their repertoire do not hold any comparison to the Art Theatre in Munich or Moscow.

Kurt Schwitter's judgement on the English art scene: 'Nobody in London cares about good art. Only a few foreigners know what art is'[81] would have been fully endorsed by the German theatre folk. For anybody who had grown up with the richness and diversity of the Weimar art scene London must have looked like a cultural desert in the 1930s and 1940s. However, it would be unfair to fault the British for not lapping up the 'artistic manna' which the German exiles were dispensing to a 'culturally impoverished' country. There were enlightened, cultured, sympathetic visitors to the performances created by the German exiles, and they found many productions lacking in artistic quality and unsuccessful in evoking the gripping emotional experience the executing artists had aimed at. A plausible explanation for this is given by Brooks Atkinson in an analysis of the genre of anti-Fascist drama on the occasion of the New York première of Friedrich Wolf's *Professor Mamlock*. He finds that the persecution of the Jews and the atrocities committed by the Nazis are so appalling that a mere description on stage turns them into Grand Guignol or a horror show. In order to avoid this danger anti-Fascist theatre has to lay bare the causes of this evil and the mechanism that enabled it to grow to these proportions: 'The province of the playwright goes beyond surface events to the causes of action. What we need to know is how this relapse into ignorance and barbarism came about in one of the major nations of the world. . . . What the playwright should explain to us is not what, for we know that, but why.'[82]

The reason for the lack of response which many productions received cannot be explained solely by the audiences' lack of appreciation or by the poor technical facilities in the exile theatres. Amongst the artists there existed a misconception of how art could operate under the conditions of exile. In the theatre this not only applied to the format of a stage show, but also to the communication structure of a performance and the stage-audience relationship. Productions that would be a reasonable success in Germany cannot be expected to receive a similar reception in England, because the audience has a different cultural background and goes to the theatre with different expectations and references in mind. The mixture of agit-prop and nostalgia which characterized so many productions in the exile theatres was bound to be anathema to an English audience raised on French farces and West End comedies.

These critical notes do not mean to detract from the fact that despite many faults the productions organized by the exiled theatre artists, taken in their entirety, did have considerable political effect and did amount to a remarkable artistic achievement. But at the same time one has to be aware of their limitations. Exile theatre can be assessed objectively only by examining the productions within the framework of the social and cultural conditions of the country where they were presented. If the artistic quality of many performances in the exile theatres was not always of the highest standard, one can find good reasons for it. If the political effect was not always as powerful as expected, again—with hindsight—one can see why. To write a history of exile theatre, therefore, also means to write a history of the obstacles and restrictions under which the artists were operating. It is astonishing to see how much—despite the most detrimental circumstances—was actually achieved by the exiled theatre artists and how many traces this activity has left behind to the present day.

Notes

1. See Wolf-Eberhard August, *Die Stellung der Schauspieler im Dritten Reich*, Ph.D Thesis, Munich, 1973.

2. See his own account of the event in an autobiographical sketch, published by Lotte H. Eisner, *Fritz Lang*, London, 1976, pp. 14-15.

3. See Curt Trepte, 'Deutsches Theater im Exil der Welt', in Helmut Müssener and Gisela Sandqvist (eds), *Protokoll des II. Internationalen Symposiums zur Erforschung des deutschsprachigen Exils nach 1933 in Kopenhagen*, Stockholm, 1972, pp. 520-56, here p. 522.

4. Quoted in Peter de Mendelssohn, *S. Fischer und sein Verlag*, Frankfurt, 1970, p. 1253.

5. Max Herrmann-Neiße, 'Ein deutscher Dichter bin ich einst gewesen', in *Um uns die Fremde: Gedichte*, Zurich, 1936, p. 84.

6. Walter Hasenclever, *Gedichte, Dramen, Prosa*, ed. Kurt Pinthus, Reinbek, 1963, p. 407.

7. Stefan Zweig, *Die Welt von Gestern: Erinnerungen eines Europäers*, Stockholm, 1944, p. 466.

8. See Ursula Ahrens, 'Bericht über Alexander Granachs sowjetische Exiljahre 1935-37. Aus Briefen im Archiv der Westberliner Akademie der Künste erstellt', *Europäische Ideen*, no. 14-15, 1976, pp. 127-30, here p. 129.

9. See the interview in Marion Berghahn, *Continental Britons: German-Jewish Refugees from Nazi Germany*, Oxford, 1988, pp. 94-5.

10. Quoted in Michael Nungesser, 'Die bildenden Künstler im Exil', in *Kunst im Exil in Großbritannien 1933-1945*, Exh. cat., Berlin (West), 1986, pp. 27-34, here p. 31.

11. Leonard Frank, *Links wo das Herz ist*, Munich, 1952, p. 191.

12. See 'The Sounding Board: The Transplanted Composer', *Los Angeles Times*, 14 May 1950, part IV, p. 5.

13. Bertolt Brecht, 'Geburtstagsbrief an Karin Michaelis', in *Gesammelte Werke*, vol. 19, Frankfurt, 1967, pp. 477-8, here p. 478.

14. Egon Schwarz, 'Was ist und zu welchem Ende studieren wir Exilliteratur?', in Peter Uwe Hohendahl and Egon Schwarz (eds), *Exil und Innere Emigration II: Internationale Tagung in St. Louis*, Frankfurt, 1973, pp. 155-64, here p. 160.

15. Alfred Kerr, 'Exil', *Neue Weltbühne*, 4 Nov. 1937, pp. 1422-4, here p. 1423.

16. Hermann Kesten, 'Erinnerungen und Erfahrungen: Schicksale der Deutschen Literatur 1933-1953', *Deutsche Universitätszeitung*, vol. 8, 1953, no. 4, pp. 12-15; no. 5, pp. 14-17; here no. 5, p. 15.

17. Peter Laemmle, 'Vorschläge für eine Revision der Exilforschung', *Akzente*, vol. 20, 1973, pp. 509-19, here p. 518.

18. The history of the German exiles in Victorian England has recently been re-examined by Rosemary Ashton, *Little Germany: Exile and Asylum in Victorian England*, Oxford, 1986. Still informative on the subject is C.R. Hennings, *Deutsche in England*, Stuttgart, 1923. For a general characterization of German emigration to Britain in the nineteenth century see C.C. Aronsfeld, 'German Jews in Victorian England', in *Leo Baeck Institute Year Book*, vol. 7, 1962, pp. 312-29.

19. See *Hansard's Parliamentary Debates*, Third Series, vol. 120, London, 1852, col. 675.

20. See Bernard Porter, *The Refugee Question in Mid-Victorian Politics*, Cambridge, 1979, p. 4.

21. In 1850 the Anglo-Jewish community in Britain numbered about 35,000 persons. The 1871 census counts 32,823 Germans and 9,569 Russians and Poles in a foreign population of 105,000. The 1891 census counts 50,599 Germans, 21,448 Russian Poles and 23,626 Russians. In 1901 the Russian-Jewish population is believed to consist of 95,245 persons with 43,000 of them living in Stepney, where they form 18.19 per cent of the population. The census of 1911 lists 272,204 foreigners, 51,165 of them being German and 106,082 Russian and Polish Jews. All figures are taken from Lloyd P. Gartner, *The Jewish Immigrant in England, 1870-1914*, London, 1973, p. 49; Colin Holmes, *Anti-Semitism in British Society, 1876-1939*, London, 1979, p. 5; Colin Holmes, 'Immigrants, Refugees and Revolutionaries', *Immigrants and Minorities*, vol. 2, 1983, pp. 7-22, here p. 8.

22. Home Secretary's Memorandum to Cabinet Committee on Alien's Restrictions, 6 April 1933, Public Record Office, Kew, CAB 24/239; quoted in Bernard Wasserstein, 'The British Government and the German Immigration 1933-1945', in Gerhard Hirschfeld (ed.), *Exile in Great Britain: Refugees from Hitler's Germany*, Leamington Spa and New Jersey, 1984, pp. 63-81, here p. 68.

23. Foreign Office Circular to Passport Control Department Concerning Visas for Holders of German and Austrian Passports Entering the United Kingdom, 27 April 1938, Public Record Office, Kew, FO 372/3284/9, quoted in Wasserstein, 'The British Government and the German Immigration', p. 72.

24. Ibid.

25. Werner Röder, *Die deutschen sozialistischen Exilgruppen in Großbritannien: Ein Beitrag zur Geschichte des Widerstandes gegen den Nationalsozialismus*, Hanover, 1968, p. 23 gives their number as 12,000 in 1940.

26. A.J. Sherman, *Island Refuge: Britain and Refugees from the Third Reich 1933-1939*, London, 1973, p. 264 sets the number of Czech refugees in Britain at 6,000. Leopold Grünwald, *In der Fremde für die Heimat: Sudentendeutsches Exil in Ost und West*, Munich, 1982, p. 13 estimates that 3,000 of them were Sudentendeutsche.

27. See Röder, *Die deutschen Exilgruppen*, p. 25.

28. Ibid., p. 87.

29. Interviewee, quoted in Rainer Kölmel, 'Problems of Settlement: German-Jewish Refugees in Scotland', in Hirschfeld, *Exile in Great Britain*, pp. 251-83, here p. 272.

30. Gabriele Tergit, 'How They Resettled', in *Britain's New Citizens: The Story of the Refugees from Germany and Austria,* ed. The Association of Jewish Refugees in Great Britain, London, 1951, pp. 61-9, here p. 63. On unemployment and living conditions in Britain in the 1930s see Noreen Branson and Margot Heinemann, *Britain in the 1930's,* London, 1971. The refugee question is also dealt with in Malcolm Muggeridge, *The Thirties: 1930-1940 in Great Britain,* London, 1940.

31. Interviewee quoted in Kölmel, 'Problems of Settlement', p. 264.

32. Interviewee quoted in Karen Gershon (ed.) *We Came as Children: A Collective Autobiography,* London, 1966, p. 155.

33. Interviewee quoted in Kölmel, 'Problems of Settlement', p. 273.

34. 'Gespräch mit Erich Fried', in Michael Seyfert, *Im Niemandsland: Deutsche Exilliteratur in britischer Internierung. Ein unbekanntes kapitel der Kulturgeschichte des Zweiten Weltkrieges,* Berlin (West), 1984, pp. 151-6, here p. 155.

35. Ibid., p. 154.

36. Interviewee quoted in Kölmel, 'Problems of Settlement', pp. 274-5.

37. Ibid., p. 275.

38. See Cordula Frowein, 'Ausstellungsaktivitäten der Exilkünstler', in *Kunst im Exil in Großbritannien,* pp. 35-48, here p. 44.

39. Report in Public Record Office, Kew, FO 371/26554 c 1930, quoted in Anthony Glees, *Exile Politics During the Second World War: The German Social Democrats in Britain,* Oxford, 1982, p. 149.

40. E. Doran on 9 March 1933. See *Hansard Parliamentary Debates: House of Commons,* Fifth Series, vol. 275, London, 1933, col. 1352.

41. Quoted in Austin Stevens, *The Dispossessed: German Refugees in Britain,* London, 1975, p. 119.

42. Sherman, *Island Refuge,* p. 259.

43. Memorandum of 11 March 1940 in Public Record Office, Kew, FO 371/24418 c 5304, quoted in Glees, *Exile Politics,* p. 51.

44. Quoted in Glees, *Exile Politics,* p. 155.

45. Labour Party Archives, International Department, Middleton Papers, (M), Box 9, Letter to S.W. Smith and R.J. Davies of 21 September and 6 May 1943, quoted in Glees, *Exile Politics,* p. 103.

46. Public Record Office, Kew, FO 371/34461 c 12764, quoted in Glees, *Exile Politics,* p. 201.

47. See Andrew Sharf, *The British Press and Jews under Nazi Rule,* London, 1964, p. 199.

48. Ibid., p. 206.

49. Fried in Seyfert, *Im Niemandsland,* p. 153.

50. Interviewee quoted in Kölmel, 'Problems of Settlement', p. 261.

51. Marion Berghahn, 'German Jews in England: Aspects of the Assimilation and Integration Process', in Hirschfeld, *Exile in Great Britain,* pp. 285-306, here p. 295.

52. See Francis L. Carsten, 'German Refugees in Great Britain 1933-1945: A Survey', in Hirschfeld, *Exile in Great Britain,* pp. 11-28, here p. 13.

53. Interviewee quoted in Kölmel, 'Problems of Settlement', p. 259.

54. Ibid., pp. 263-4.

55. Quoted in Francis L. Carsten, 'German Refugees', p. 24. See also the statistics in Norman Bentwich, *I Understand the Risks: The Story of the Refugees from Nazi Oppression Who Fought in the British Forces in the World War,* London, 1950, pp. 176-7.

56. All figures are taken from Norman Bentwich, *The Rescue and Achievement of Refugee Scholars: The Story of Displaced Scholars and Scientists 1933-1952,* The Hague, 1953, pp. 1-2 and 13. See also Kurt R. Grossmann, *Emigration: Geschichte der Hitler Flüchtlinge 1933-1945,* Frankfurt, 1969, p. 217.

57. See Dieter Wuttke, 'Die Emigration der Kulturwissenschaftlichen Bibliothek Warburg und die Anfänge des Universitätsfaches Kunstgeschichte in Großbritannien', in *Kunst im Exil in Großbritannien,* pp. 209-15.

58. The most important names are mentioned in *Britain's New Citizens,* pp. 35-43 and Bentwich, *Rescue and Achievement,* pp. 80-92. See also Gerhard Hirschfeld, 'Die Emigration deutscher Wissenschaftler nach Großbritannien, 1933-1945', in Gottfried Niedhart (ed.), *Großbritannien als Gast- und Exilland für Deutsche im 19. und 20. Jahrhundert,* Bochum, 1985, pp. 117-40; and Bernard Wasserstein, 'Intellectual Emigrés in Britain, 1933-1939', in J.C. Jackman and C.M. Borden (eds), *The Muses Flee Hitler: Cultural Transfer and Adaptation 1930-1945,* Washington DC, 1983, pp. 249-56.

59. See Herbert Loebl, 'Refugee Industries in the Special Areas of Britain', in Hirschfeld, *Exile in Great Britain,* pp. 219-49, here pp. 221 and 246.

60. See Gershon, *We Came as Children.*

61. Quoted in Berghahn, 'German Jews in England', pp. 297-8.

62. See idem, *Continental Britons.*

63. Interviewee quoted in Gershon, *We Came as Children,* p. 168.

64. Ibid., p. 155. In the wake of the Jewish emancipation in the eighteenth century many German Jews had become integrated into German society and given up their Jewish culture. They despised their non-assimilated co-religionists, especially if they were *Ostjuden.* Many of these Eastern Jews had settled in Britain at the turn of the century and regarded the new influx of German Jews after 1933 with suspicion, resentment or aloofness. One refugee remembers: 'The Glasgow Jews took just as little interest in us. On the contrary, they to a certain extent resented the German-Jewish refugees. Most of the Glasgow Jews had come from Russia or Poland; their families had emigrated in the 1880s and 1890s, at the time of the pogroms there. Earlier, German Jews had looked down on them; now they avenged themselves by being very reserved towards us.' (Quoted in Kölmel, 'Problems of Settlement', p. 267. See also the interviews in Berghahn, *Continental Britons,* pp. 231-4.) These distinctions account for the fact that to this day there are culturally different Jewish communities living in Britain.

65. See Berghahn, 'German Jews in England', p. 304.

66. See Hans Daibler, *Deutsches Theater seit 1945,* Stuttgart, 1976, p. 90.

67. Ibid., p. 57.

68. See Werner Mittenzwei *et al., Theater in der Zeitenwende: Zur Geschichte des Dramas und des Schauspieltheaters in der Deutschen Demokratischen Republik 1945-1968,* vol. 1, Berlin (GDR), 1972, pp. 82-136.

69. Quoted in Gerhard Roloff, *Exil und Exilliteratur in der deutschen Presse 1945-1949,* Worms, 1976, p. 203.

70. Hans-Albert Walter in an interview with Heinz Ludwig Arnold, in *Akzente* vol. 20, 1973, p. 483. See also Erhard Bahr, 'Das zweite Exil: Zur Rezeption der Exilliteratur in den westlichen Besatzungszonen und in der Bundesrepublik Deutschland von 1945 bis 1959', in Donald G. Daviau and Ludwig Fischer (eds), *Das Exilerlebnis: Verhandlungen des Vierten Symposiums über deutsche und österreichische Exilliteratur,* Columbia, 1982, pp. 353-66: and Martin Mantzke, 'Emigration und Emigranten als Politikum in der Bundesrepublik der sechziger Jahre', *Exil,* vol. 1, 1983, pp. 24-30.

71. See the facsimile documents in Walter A. Berendsohn, *Die Humanistische Front: Einführung in die deutsche Emigranten-Literatur. Zweiter Teil: Vom Kriegsausbruch 1939 bis Ende 1946,* Worms, 1976, pp. 229-30.

72. See Curt Trepte, 'Freies Deutsches Theater in Schweden 1938-1945', *Theater der Zeit,* vol. 1, no. 2, 1946, pp. 22-4; Erich Freund, 'Deutsches Theater im Londoner Exil', *Theater der Zeit,* vol. 1, no. 4, Oct. 1946, pp. 20-4; Paul Walter Jacob (ed.), *Theater: Sieben Jahre Freie Deutsche Bühne in Buenos Aires,* Buenos Aires, 1946; Kurt Stern, 'Eine Bühne im Exil: Deutsches Theater in Mexiko', *Theater der Zeit,* vol. 2, no. 4, 1947, pp. 23-6; Erich Freund, 'Studio 1934: Die erste deutsche Bühne im Exil', *Theater der Zeit,* vol. 2, no. 7, 1947, pp. 30-2; Egon Larsen, 'Deutsches Theater in London: Ein unbeschriebenes Kapitel Kulturgeschichte', *Zick-Zack,* vol. 2, 1948, pp. 13-15; Paul Walter Jacob (ed.), *Theater 1940-1950: Zehn Jahre Deutsche Bühne in Buenos Aires,* Buenos Aires, 1950; Karl Otto Paetel, 'Deutsches Theater in Amerika', *Deutsche Rundschau,* vol. 81, 1955, pp. 271-5.

73. See Curt Trepte, 'Archiv Deutsches Theater- und Filmschaffen im Exil', *Mitteilungen der Deutschen Akademie der Künste zu Berlin,* vol. 5, 1967, no. 1, pp. 11-12, here p. 12 and Curt Trepte, 'Deutsches Theater im Exil der Welt', in Müssener/Sandqvist, *Protokoll des II. Internationalen Symposiums,* p. 522.

74. See Friedrich Pfäfflin (ed.), *Berthold Viertel (1885-1953): Eine Dokumentation,* Munich, n.d. [1969], p. 35; Berthold Viertel, *Schriften zum Theater,* ed. Gert Heidenreich, Munich, 1970, p. 531; Konstantin Kaiser, 'Theater im Exil: Das Beispiel Berthold Viertel', *Wiener Tagebuch,* no. 11, Nov. 1986, pp. 22-4; Eberhard Frey, 'Ethisches Theater: Berthold Viertels Theatertätigkeit im Exil', in Wolfgang Elfe *et al.* (eds), *Deutsches Exildrama und Exiltheater: Akten des Exilliteratur-Symposiums der University of South Carolina,* Berne, 1977, pp. 77-84, here p. 78.

75. See Joseph Wulf, *Theater und Film im Dritten Reich: Eine Dokumentation,* Gütersloh, 1964, p. 245.

76. See Georg Wilhelm Müller, *Das Reichsministerium für Volksaufklärung und Propaganda,* Berlin, 1940, p. 28.

77. Quoted in Glees, *Exile Politics,* p. 189.

78. In his autobiography, *Aller Tage Abend,* Munich, 1959, pp. 386 ff., 428 ff., 465 ff., Fritz Kortner paints an amusing picture of the London theater world and describes how the British tradition of underacting (he calls it 'Gefühls-Tiefstapelei' [p. 466] or 'Ausdrucksanämie' [p. 429]) forced him, who had always strived for expressiveness, to forgo his best qualities as an actor and to adapt to the 'charming virtuosity of a non-committal acting style' (charmante Virtuosität der Ausdrucksunverbindlichkeit, p. 428) which the British audiences favoured. See also the sources quoted by Alan Clarke in this volume, pp. 100-7.

79. Friedrich Richter, 'Auf Theatertour in England', in Renate Seydel (ed.), *. . . gelebt für alle Zeiten: Schauspieler über sich und andere,* Berlin (GDR), 1978, pp. 293-306, here pp. 296-7.

80. See Richard Cave, *Terence Gray and the Cambridge Festival Theatre,* Cambridge, 1980, p. 14.

81. Schwitter in a letter of 1 April 1947 to Louise Spengemann, in Kurt Schwitter, *Wir spielen, bis uns*

der Tod abholt: Briefe aus fünf Jahrzehnten, ed. Ernst Nündel, Berlin (West), 1974, p. 272.

82. Brooks Atkinson, 'Culture under the Nazis', *New York Times,* 25 April 1937, Section X, p. 1.

FURTHER READING

Criticism

Emery, Mary Lou. *Jean Rhys at "World's End": Novels of Colonial and Sexual Exile.* Austin: University of Texas Press, 1990, 219 p.

    Study of Rhys's works that emphasizes her treatment of the theme of exile.

Fuchs, Anne. *A Space of Anxiety: Dislocation and Abjection in Modern German-Jewish Literature.* Amsterdam: Rodopi, 1999, 200 p.

    Discusses the themes of separation and difference in the work of several Jewish authors, including Sigmund Freud and Albert Drach.

Iribarne, Louis. "Lost in the 'Earth-Garden': The Exile of Czesław Miłosz." *World Literature Today* 73, no. 4 (autumn 1999): 637-42.

    Comments on the themes and style of Miłosz's poetry written about and in exile from Poland.

Johnson-Roullier, Cyrina E. *Reading on the Edge: Exiles, Modernities, and Cultural Transformation in Proust, Joyce, and Baldwin.* Albany: State University of New York Press, 2000, 217 p.

    Examines selected writings of Marcel Proust, James Joyce, and James Baldwin in terms of their physical, intellectual, and emotional exile.

Mehlman, Jeffrey. *Émigré New York: French Intellectuals in Wartime Manhattan, 1940-1944.* Baltimore: The Johns Hopkins University Press, 2000, 209 p.

    Discusses the artistic and intellectual contributions of French intellectuals living in New York during World War II.

Peterson, Walter F. *The Berlin Liberal Press in Exile: A History of the "Pariser Tageblatt-Pariser Tageszeitung," 1933-1940.* Tübingen: Max Niemeyer Verlag, 1987, 287 p.

    Analysis of the Berlin liberal press, first at home in Germany, and then in exile in France just before the start of World War II.

Seidel, Michael. *Exile and the Narrative Imagination.* New Haven: Yale University Press, 1986, 234 p.

    Focuses on the theme of exile, both real and metaphorical, in the writings of six major novelists.

Stock, Noel. *Poet in Exile: Ezra Pound.* Manchester: University of Manchester Press, 1964, 273 p.

    Critical biography of Ezra Pound that discusses how his self-imposed exile, physical and emotional, from America influenced his life and works.

Literary Prizes

INTRODUCTION

Literary prizes have been awarded for centuries, but in the twentieth century they proliferated and became more global in nature and scope. They are awarded on various levels, from local and national to the international Nobel Prize in Literature; judges are usually prominent writers or professionals in the arts who are asked to choose from a field of prestigious nominees. Groups such as publishers, writers' associations, and foundations like the Pulitzer usually award prizes for works written during that year, whereas the Nobel Prize in Literature is intended to recognize lifetime achievement. Although a literary prize can be an economic boon to the publishers and writers involved, winning a major prize like the Pulitzer or the Nobel is especially significant because it enhances the reputation and career of the individual writer. In the last several decades, however, critics of literary prizes have raised questions about the fairness of selection criteria, the objectivity of the judging process, the judges' openness to and acceptance of diverse styles and minorities, and their susceptibility to literary fashions and cultural trends. Kjell Espmark has argued that the Nobel Prize in Literature has reflected a greater tolerance for new literary styles and movements in the last several decades, and Ralph Gunther has pointed out the multinational and multiethnic character of Nobel winners. On the other hand, William Pratt and Burton Feldman have explored possible reasons for what they consider some notable omissions among Nobel nominees over the years. Pulitzer Prizes have been similarly scrutinized by critics, especially in regard to their criteria and the influence of individual judges on controversial decisions. Thomas P. Adler has written about the treatment of such themes as politics and race relations in Pulitzer-winning plays.

REPRESENTATIVE WORKS

Samuel Beckett
Molloy (novel) 1951
En Attendant Godot [*Waiting for Godot*] (drama) 1952

Pearl Buck
The Good Earth (novel) 1931

Ivan Bunin
The Village (novel) 1910
The Well of Days (novel) 1933

Albert Camus
L'Etranger [*The Stranger*] (novel) 1942
La Peste [*The Plague*] (novel) 1947

T. S. Eliot
The Waste Land (poem) 1922

Ernest Hemingway
The Sun Also Rises (novel) 1926
A Farewell to Arms (novel) 1929

Hermann Hesse
Siddartha [*Siddartha*] (novel) 1922
Der Steppenwolf [*Steppenwolf*] (novel) 1927

Juan Ramón Jiménez
Platero y yo (poetry) 1914

Rudyard Kipling
Captains Courageous (novel) 1897
Kim (novel) 1901

Selma Lagerlöf
Jerusalem [*Jerusalem*] (novel) 1901-02

Sinclair Lewis
Arrowsmith (novel) 1925

Thomas Mann
Buddenbrooks [*Buddenbrooks*] (novel) 1901
Der Tod in Venedig [*Death in Venice*] (novella) 1912

Gabriel García Márquez
Cien años de soledad [*One Hundred Years of Solitude*] (novel) 1967

Arthur Miller
Death of a Salesman (drama) 1949

Gabriela Mistral
Sonetos de muerte (poetry) 1914

Eugene O'Neill
Anna Christie (drama) 1921
Long Day's Journey into Night (drama) 1956

Luigi Pirandello
Sei personaggi in cerca d'autore [*Six Characters in Search of an Author*] (drama) 1921

Jean-Paul Sartre
Huis-clos [*No Exit*] (drama) 1944

George Bernard Shaw
Mrs. Warren's Profession (drama) 1902
Man and Superman (drama) 1905

Henryk Sienkiewicz
Bez dogmatu [*Without Dogma*] (novel) 1891
Quo Vadis? [*Quo Vadis?*] (novel) 1896

John Steinbeck
Of Mice and Men (novel) 1937
The Grapes of Wrath (novel) 1939

Thornton Wilder
Our Town (drama) 1938
The Skin of Our Teeth (drama) 1942

Tennessee Williams
A Streetcar Named Desire (drama) 1947
Cat on a Hot Tin Roof (drama) 1955

William Butler Yeats
The Wild Swans at Coole (poetry) 1917
The Tower (poetry) 1928

OVERVIEWS AND GENERAL STUDIES

John W. Sahn (essay date 18 December 1987)

SOURCE: Sahn, John W. "What Are Book Awards For?" *Publishers Weekly* 232, no. 25 (December 18, 1987): 9.

[*In the following essay, Sahn comments on the characteristics and purpose of book awards in general, and on the National Book Awards in particular.*]

The recent surprise win of the National Book Award for Fiction by Larry Heinemann, author of *Paco's Story*, has made us think once more about the whole philosophy and purpose of book awards. The flurry of astonishment caused by Heinemann's win, in the face of such contenders as Toni Morrison and Philip Roth, was perhaps understandable, but hardly flattering to Heinemann, whose book was a remarkably eloquent evocation of the hideous legacy of the Vietnam War. And although the Fiction judges very wisely kept their own counsel about their deliberations, the impression was certainly left, willy-nilly, that the prize had been given this time not so much to the obvious "best book"—judged in terms of review accolades, that would certainly have been Morrison's—but rather to encourage a comparatively new writer who had written a striking book at a pivotal moment in his career.

There are, in fact, these days a number of remarkably generous grants and awards designed to do just that: in addition to the well-known MacArthur so-called "genius awards," there are the much newer Whiting Writers' Awards, which recently gave $25,000 each to 10 young writers for the third year in a row, and the even more lavish Mildred and Harold Strauss Livings, which give writers a quarter of a million dollars annually for five years. In contrast to these, the $10,000 for each of the two NBA [National Book Awards] winners, and $1000 each for all the nominees, is comparatively lean pickings.

The difference about the NBA, of course, is that it is an award made publicly, and chosen by a publicly known group of jurors. Sometimes, over the years, these jurors *have* made the obvious choices—and the list of NBA winners is a highly impressive one, including in this decade such writers as Styron, Updike and Doctorow; sometimes, like this year, they have seemed deliberately to flout expectations. So how do they see their role? None of the judges we spoke to on the subject would agree that they ever thought of anything but rewarding what they considered to be the best book of the year—though there was some reluctance to single out fellow writers, as exemplified by winner E. L. Doctorow's comment last year that literature "is not a horse race" and judge Gail Godwin's sad observation, also last year, that "we took three winners and created a winner and two losers."

The organizers of the NBA, which includes a blue-ribbon board of top publishing people and an able and energetic director, Barbara Prete, see their function essentially as drawing more national attention, and customers, to books.

They crave better and wider coverage—and in fact the decision in the past couple of years to make the winners known only on the night, in Academy Awards style, is a deliberate attempt to create more news value—and openly aspire to the commercial heft of Britain's Booker or France's Goncourt prizes.

Sometimes, however, the simultaneous desire for quality and hope for greater sales can be an uneasy mix. On more than one occasion Britain's booksellers have openly grumbled about the Booker winner, being clearly much happier when it has served to reinforce sales of an author who would have sold well anyway rather than to send customers after a book they might not, in the end, enjoy.

The clout of the NBA—or indeed of any major book award, including the Pulitzer and the Nobel—is not exactly hearty in America's bookstores, and perhaps never will be; the country is too big, unwieldy and heterogeneous for that. So perhaps the best service the NBA judges can render is to go ahead and make their choices without regard to whether the winning books are likely to win wide readership; neither to deliberately seek out dark horses nor shy away from bestsellers, but to pursue, as they swear they do, the best book, regardless.

As to how the occasion can be made more newsy, in a country where books are rather low on the scale of cultural priorities, it is noteworthy that the two most-discussed of the recent Booker occasions have both been ones on which feisty authors have stood up and spoken out frankly about the current publishing scene: Fay Weldon four years ago and P. D. James this year. While it may seem tough on publishers to ask them to pay $200 a seat to hear their dirty linen aired, there's no doubt that it makes news editors sit up. So in future, rather than such brilliant but airy exercises as William Gass engaged in last month, how about finding an eloquent, well-known author who has a broad vision of what publishing is and should be? (Philip Caputo, at a recent AAP [American Association of Publishers] symposium, was just such a speaker, and made the day.)

Perhaps no one will ever devise a way of giving book awards that can support the expectations everyone brings to them; in the meantime, the best the judges can do is look only for the best, without fear or favor, and let the publicity come as it may.

Marc Aronson (essay date May 2001)

SOURCE: Aronson, Marc. "Slippery Slopes and Proliferating Prizes." *The Horn Book Magazine* 77, no. 3 (May 2001): 271.

[*In the following essay, Aronson comments on the many prizes for children's literature now available, notes several problems with their criteria and administration, and suggests some ways to improve them.*]

I'm sure that nearly every reader of this magazine is in favor of supporting a more diverse children's literature that is in tune with the increasingly multi-ethnic environment in which we and our children live. I am equally convinced, though, that [American Library Association, hereafter ALA] ALA's sponsorship of three awards in which a book's eligibility is determined by the race or ethnicity of its creators is a mistake. For the Coretta Scott King, the Pura Belpré, and the (announced but as yet unnamed) Asian American awards, the creator's biography—ethnic credentials, if you will—predetermines the book's validity. I am convinced that this is wrong. It is the wrong way to bring more kinds of books to more kinds of readers; it is wrong in that it does not evaluate literature in its own terms but by extraneous standards; it is wrong because it is a very slippery slope down which we are already tumbling; and finally it is wrong because even as ALA sponsors more and more such awards, we have not openly discussed and debated their merits. Let's start now.

How can you question the Coretta Scott King Awards, I hear you protesting. Haven't they been a success? Well, yes and no. In one sense the [Coretta Scott King Awards, hereafter CSK] CSK has worked very well. When it was first envisioned by Mabel McKissack, Glyndon Greer, and John Carroll in 1969, no black artist or author had won major recognition from ALA (Arna Bontemps's *Story of the Negro*, a 1949 Newbery Honor Book, aside), and there were relatively few African Americans working in the field. Things were not a great deal better by 1982 when ALA recognized the award, although by that time two black authors, Virginia Hamilton and Mildred Taylor, had won the Newbery, and Leo and Diane Dillon (an interracial team) had secured two Caldecotts.

Fast-forward to 2000, eighteen years into ALA's involvement with the CSK, and another African-American author, Christopher Paul Curtis, had won the Newbery, while Walter Dean Myers had won the first-ever Michael L. Printz Award for YA [Young Adult] books. There is a steadily growing group of African-American artists that every important publisher, large and small, seeks to publish. In addition, there are small presses—and even the entire Jump at the Sun imprint at Hyperion—that are devoted to advancing the presence of African-American culture in children's books.

Though this rise in African-American creators and books cannot be linked solely to the CSK, I do not doubt that the recognition offered by the award, not to mention the passion and enthusiasm of the annual award ceremony, have had positive effects. And in the particular case of African Americans, you could argue that an exclusive award was necessary, especially in the early years. I recall hearing senior publishing people say such things as "blacks don't buy books" or "black books only sell to schools and libraries." In such an environment, it was probably necessary to force publishers, reviewers, and librarians to see how talented black artists and authors were, and to help launch careers that then took off on their own. When combined with Black History Month, the Coretta Scott King Awards created a sales channel that previously had not existed.

For those who have been ignored, denied their due place as creators, as readers, as a public, there is a pure existential value in being acknowledged. There is real power in saying, We are here, we do count, we have something to say. The more frequently and powerfully this point is made, the more new artists are likely to join the field.

But there is an undertow beneath this swell of success. By insisting on testing the racial identity of its winners, the CSK shifts its focus from literature to biography. Who you are, which box or boxes you check on the census form, comes first. Your community, your ethnicity, comes before your talent. And as long as the prize is essentially a community honoring and encouraging its own, it is not clear how the rest of the public is meant to react.

The danger, which to some degree has become the reality, is that this kind of rule balkanizes literature. There is less pressure on the general population to read, understand, appreciate, and develop a fine critical eye for African-American literature if a librarian can always think, "I don't have to read those books carefully. The Coretta Scott King Award takes care of that."

An even worse attitude that is all-too-often the outcome of a balkanized award system is, "I don't have any African-American kids in my library, so I don't need to buy books by or about African Americans." As myopic a judgment as that is, the rules for CSK invite it, because they set down a racial standard which others can put to their own uses. If you have to be black to win the award, do you have to be black to appreciate the winning book? The implication that only blacks can write well about blacks sets up the implication that only they can *read* well about them, too.

The danger in every award that sets limits on the kinds of people, or types of book, that can win it is that it diminishes the pressure on the larger awards, the Newbery and the Caldecott, to live up to their charge to seek the most distinguished children's books of the year.

Speaking as the first winner of the Robert F. Sibert Award for most distinguished informational book for children, I can attest to the mixed effects of receiving a special honor. On the one hand, I was very pleased not only to receive the committee's recognition but also to learn of all of the deserving books that were honored by the Sibert. And yet I could not help feeling sad that the only way we could be noticed was by a kind of admission of failure. It is only because members of the Newbery committees have historically been so averse to nonfiction that we needed the Sibert. Creating a new award is a concession that the other awards will never change.

Advocates of identity-based awards claim that if they select the best of their own literature, the surrounding world will appreciatively buy their selections so that all children grow up learning about all experiences. The problem is that if the award is *from* the community *to* the community, then it is up to the surrounding communities to decide if those experiences—which they are inherently excluded from completely understanding—are vitally important to them. If the award celebrates, instead, individuals who delve deeply into aspects of human experience, no literate, aware reader can afford not to read the books.

We should do everything in our power to encourage the growth of a more diverse literature, but not by predefining who will create it. We should do our best to encourage all readers to be receptive to every brand of literature. Which also means that we must be open to great art, no matter who creates it.

Oddly enough, the CSK committee rules admit this, in a back-handed way. A book is eligible even if only one of the creators is black. What sense does this make? Does the race of one offer a kind of guarantee or validation of the other? That assumes the "authentic" part of the pair has some kind of power over the other, when there is no reason to believe this is so. If this ruling is not about the truth-value of the book, it is strictly a matter of affirmative action: a set number of places are reserved at the table for African Americans, and therefore only they can sit in them.

But here's the trap you get into if you take your stand on affirmative action: you have conceded that you are using identity not as a guarantee of quality but rather to serve a different end: that of advancing the careers of people who may have had difficulty cracking the heedless publishing world. This means that a question of literary deservedness, however softly whispered, will always attach itself to the winners of these awards.

The insistence on ethnic credentials for certain awards has an echo effect on the others. Can any of you who are reading this honestly tell me that if you were sitting in a room with an almost entirely white group of fellow judges (as it would probably be) and a book on a black, or Latino, or Asian-American theme by a writer *not* of that group came up for consideration, you would be willing to select it as a winner? While award committees did this with some regularity in the past (Newberys for *The Slave Dancer* and *Sounder,* for example), the social pressure against doing so increases every time ALA endorses another identity-based award. These awards cause both white writers and writers of color to suffer the imposition of nonliterary criteria on their craft.

Speaking as an editor now, when a manuscript or portfolio comes to me that is related to an experience that I don't know well, I wonder whether the author has it right. And I also think it would be great if I could find a person from a group that is not well represented in publishing to do the art or text for a book that deals with an aspect of his or her culture. That is good sense and good publishing. But that uncertainty should not be codified as a rule someone else sets for me. The challenge is for me to learn enough to determine the value of the text or art myself, to judge it on its merits. And if I have difficulty making that judgment, then it is up to me to grow, to learn, to expand my knowledge.

Expanding the knowledge base of librarians and reviewers is where I think ALA should be turning its efforts. It should focus on diversifying its membership and training its members to appreciate the art and experience of all cultures. The focus should not be on the identity of the creator, which does not tell you anything about the work, but rather on learning how to judge all manner of works on their own terms.

The logic of this position becomes all the clearer when you think about the rules for the Belpré. What does it mean to be Latino? The Belpré rules specify that the winner's heritage must "emanate from any of the Spanish-speaking cultures of the Western Hemisphere." That is somewhere between silly and offensive. For one, it excludes citizens of and émigrés from the largest country in Latin America, Brazil. Brazilians, who are now a major immigrant group in Miami, speak Portuguese, not Spanish. If you include Portuguese-speaking cultures, then New England Cape Verdeans as well as the whole mixed South Asian, black, Amerindian, Chinese, English, Caribbean population—which often has some Portuguese mixed in—are Latinos.

An even more troubling problem this rule poses comes from the role Spanish has played in Latin American history. For indigenous peoples who speak Quechua, or Mayan, or Yanomami, Spanish has been the language of oppression. As these peoples immigrate to America, we are telling them they have to learn the language they resisted in order to celebrate their own culture. If ALA insists on having this rule for the Belpré, it is honor-bound to create a new award for indigenous peoples. Otherwise it is in the curious position of supposedly encouraging diversity by rewarding the suppression of native cultures.

The fact that Spanish could be imposed on reluctant peoples points out the most obvious fact about it: it is a language that anyone can learn. It is the very definition of the kind of knowledge an outsider can attain. That is good from my point of view, but it completely undermines the idea that who you are should have anything to do with what you are capable of understanding and creating.

In high school my Spanish teacher, who was Japanese-American, introduced me to Neruda, Darío, and, most of all, García Lorca. Reading those poets deepened me and made me understand more about the world. This is what I think awards from ALA should honor: great creators like these poets who, using traditions they deeply understand, add to the imagery, vocabulary, rhythmic pulse, and psychological insight that is our human heritage.

The Spanish requirement is one problem with the Belpré, but the idea of being Latino itself is another. Once you are in, you are in. So an arch-conservative Miami Cuban could win for writing about being a militant Chicano organizer; an elegant Argentinean émigré could be honored for a novel about being a poor Central American farmer (even though in Latin America that same Argentinean would be the butt of jokes for seeing himself as too European); a member of a family that had lived in the Southwest for hundreds of years could be selected for writing about a Puerto Rican shuttling between New York and Ponce. The umbrella definition of being Latino—which has no precise meaning—allows that person total freedom to deal with any Latino topic, while a person who does not use that term to define him or herself, no matter how knowledgeable about the specific subject he or she writes about, is forever banned from winning the prize. How can a requirement that is both ludicrously capacious and blindly restrictive make any sense?

The worst problem with the Belpré, though, is simply that it was the second ALA prize to include an identity clause in its rules. Two points define a line, which then contains an infinite number of points. Once the principle of identity is confirmed as valid, every group has a right to claim it, as Asian Americans soon did, with their new prize, and indigenous Americans should. Who will bet how soon mixed-race authors, those with disabilities, Muslims (and thus Jews, which, of course, then means Christians), will demand awards of their own? How can ALA say no to any of them? It has abandoned the idea that literature speaks to all and for all and has instead embraced the intellectually passé 1980s Cultural Wars concept that art is defined by a community by its own rules and for its own purposes. Now, any community has a right to demand its announcement at Midwinter, its award, its share of the honor pie.

Fortunately, we have two models that can show us how awards could be handled better. One is an award that honors books entirely based on identity—but not that of the author, only the themes in the books. I am speaking of the Lambda Literary Awards given by the Lambda Literary Foundation for excellence in books about the gay and lesbian experience. The "Lammies" carefully split honorees between gay and lesbian topics, and have many categories reflecting different types of books from young adult through academic. Their literature reflects an acute awareness of the differences among gay, lesbian, bisexual, and transgendered people. Yet nowhere do they specify anything about the sexual orientation, or even gender, of the author. The book wins, no matter who wrote it.

A second model is the award system of the Asian American Writers Workshop. It *does* pay attention to the ethnicity of the writer, and even has a category of award only for members of the workshop. I think that is perfectly right for them, as an advocacy group, to do. But they are not seeking an imprimatur from ALA. If a librarian reads over their awards list and decides that those are important books, fine. But that is the judgment of the individual librarian, not of a body that represents all librarians, and thus all readers and potential writers, across the country.

The more awards are defined by identity, the less relevant to the world-at-large they seem. I believe that ALA has been hasty in acceding to the demands of fervent advocacy groups without truly opening the issues to debate. So let's have it out. Let's discuss how best to foster the creation, reception, and dissemination of a truly diverse literature.

My suggestion is this: keep the CSK, Belpré, and Asian-American awards, but honor content alone, not identity. Use the very best judges and set the very highest standards for these awards—which may mean that all the winners turn out to be ethnically linked to their topics, but that will be a judgment based on merit, not an *a priori* assumption. Let those committees—who should have a deep knowledge of the cultures and literatures (as well as a knowledge of Culture and Literature) encompassed by the awards they are judging—struggle with judging a work strictly on its own merits, not its author bio.

I believe this will do even more to foster the best new talent from all groups; it will increase sales of the books, which will no longer be seen as only of interest to one community or another; and it will be intellectually honest. What more can you ask of an award?

THE NOBEL PRIZE IN LITERATURE

William Riggan (essay date summer 1981)

SOURCE: Riggan, William. "The Swedish Academy and the Nobel Prize in Literature: History and Procedure." *World Literature Today* 55, no. 3 (summer 1981): 399-405.

[*In the following essay, Riggan presents an overview of the background and method of the committee for awarding the Nobel Prize in Literature.*]

In presenting separate essays on the ten literary members among "The Eighteen" of the Swedish Academy, the Spring 1981 issue of *WLT* [*World Literature Today,* hereafter *WLT*] (55:2, pp. 197-256) was an attempt to introduce "The Swedish Writers Behind the Nobel Prize" as the ten prominent, engaging and highly individualistic authors that they are, in contrast to the occasional public image of them abroad as a monolithic group of aged men given to "musing the obscure"[1] in their annual Nobel selections. The criticism which these yearly choices call forth—whether of a literary, a journalistic or an ideological nature—often betrays a comparable misapprehension of the way in which the Academy approaches the task and reaches its decisions. Critics outraged at the failure to honor Tolstoy with the first Nobel Prize in 1901, for example, neglected to note that the great Russian novelist had not been formally nominated by any outside individual or group and thus could not even be considered by the Academy under the statutes it had formulated for selecting the prizewinner [Anders Österling, *Nobel: The Man and His Prizes,* hereafter *NMP*] (*NMP,* 91);[2] and charges of political opportunism in the 1980 choice of Polish poet and novelist Czesław Miłosz during a well-publicized labor crisis in Gdańsk evidently were prompted by a confusion of the *announcement* of the prize with the lengthy *deliberations* which had begun months if not years earlier and had, for all practical purposes, been concluded before the strikes became a daily page-one item. As a complement to the Spring issue's essays on ten of the Academicians, then, the following descriptive history may serve to clarify, at least in some measure, the Swedish Academy's work in choosing the recipients of the world's most well-known and remunerative literary award.

. . . . .

In an 1893 will Alfred Nobel included no specific bequest in regard to literature, making only general reference to rewards "for the most important and original discoveries or the most striking advances in the wide sphere of knowledge or on the path of human progress" and therefore evidently wishing to aid the exact sciences first and foremost (*NMP,* 85). The final will of November 1895, however, stipulated that one of five annual awards for "those who, during the preceding year, shall have conferred the greatest benefit on mankind" was to be given to "the person who shall have produced in the field of literature the most outstanding work of an ideal tendency"[3] and that this prize be distributed by "the Academy in Stockholm." Nobel's wish to promote the cause of letters, writes Academy member Anders Österling,

> . . . was inspired, first and last, by his own interest in literature, which had been developed in his earliest youth and was later stimulated by his continued language studies. He not only read but mastered five languages, including Russian; his poems in English, written in his late teens and still preserved, show an astonishing mastery of poetic diction and an unmistakably poetic instinct.
>
> Throughout his life, Alfred Nobel gave serious attention to literature and, as far as his absorbing and hectic existence permitted it, kept in touch with the literary developments of his time. In regard to his tastes, it is also known that he preferred works of an ideal tendency and consequently strongly disapproved of the contemporary naturalism represented, for example, by Zola. . . . As a reader of literature, he looked for the living core; the ideas expressed interested him more than the forms.
>
> Consequently, it was not by chance that he expressly stipulated that "an ideal tendency" was an essential qualification of literary works to be judged for the prize, even though the expression was vague and has caused endless arguments. What he really meant by this term was probably works of a humanitarian and constructive character, which, like scientific discoveries, could be regarded as of benefit to mankind.
>
> (*NMP,* 85-86)

The Svenska Akademien itself was founded in 1786, under the reign of King Gustavus III. Although based on the model of the Académie Française, the Swedish Academy is composed of only eighteen members instead of the former's forty—reputedly because Gustavus preferred the resonant sound of *En av De Aderton* (*One of The Eighteen*) to that of all other possible numbers, particularly the pinched nasal tones of *En av De Fyrtio* (*One of The Forty*). The Academy's principal duties were originally the promotion and preservation of Swedish language, literature, history and culture; since 1893 it has also published and periodically updated the *Svenska Akademien ordbok* (*Dictionary of the Swedish Academy*). The organization awards numerous grants and scholarships to individuals, to journals and to groups, with the total annual amount allocated for such awards, philological work, magazine publication and research roughly corresponding to that of three Nobel Prizes. Funds for these programs "are derived chiefly from an old newspaper monopoly and from donations which the Academy administers," writes current Permanent Secretary of the Academy Lars Gyllensten (*NPL,* 5).[4] The Swedish Academy also participates with the Music Academy and the Art Academy in the publication of *Artes,* a bimonthly journal devoted to literature and the arts. The journal is not an official organ of the three organizations, but the articles and features published there do represent their various areas of interest. Swedish Academy member Östen Sjöstrand is the Editor, and the Editorial

Board includes his fellow authors Lars Gyllensten and Artur Lundkvist as well as essayist and art critic Ulf Linde.

Members of the Academy, who are elected by the group itself for life and occupy specific "chairs" within the organization, are drawn "from Swedish cultural life and the humanities"; approximately half are themselves writers, the others being elected on the basis of their "literary leanings and expert knowledge of the Academy's various spheres of responsibility," Gyllensten continues. The organization "is not subordinate to any state or other authority. The governing body consists of a Director (chairman) and a Chancellor (vice chairman), who are elected for six months at a time, and of a Secretary, who usually remains until the age of 70—all of them members of the Academy. The Academy meets weekly and conducts its business in its own premises on the upper floor of the Stock Exchange (from the 18th century) in the old part of Stockholm" (*NPL*, 5).

Within a month of Nobel's death on 10 December 1896 the Swedish Academy was informed of the task entrusted to it by the magnate's will. There was evidently considerable hesitation and even reluctance among the members to assume this new responsibility, which some felt would so increase the Academy's workload as to force that body to neglect its traditional duties. That a majority of the Academicians did in fact ultimately vote in favor of acceptance was doubtless due to the persuasive force of the group's Permanent Secretary, Carl David af Wirsén, who argued:

> If the Swedish Academy refuses to assume this responsibility, the whole donation will be forfeited as far as literary awards are concerned, and by that very act the leading men of letters throughout Europe will be deprived of the opportunity to enjoy the financial rewards and the exceptional recognition for their long and brilliant literary careers which Nobel had in mind. A storm will blow up, a storm of indignation. The Academy's responsibility is great; if it definitely rejects the task, it will suffer sharp reproaches; in these reproaches may join future generations of our eighteen members who are to succeed us and who may find it strange that for reasons of personal convenience the members of today deliberately declined an influential role in the world of letters. The task is said to be foreign to the true purposes of the Academy. The work will, no doubt, be both new and arduous, but it can hardly be called foreign since it is of a literary character. A body that is to judge the literature of its own country cannot afford to be ignorant of the very best produced abroad; the projected prizes are to be given to the best living writers anywhere, and, consequently, as a rule, to the very men whose work ought to be familiar to the Academy members anyway.
>
> (*NMP*, 91).

To administer the huge fortune made available from the Nobel estate for the five prizes and to coordinate the work involved in the judging and presentation of the awards—though exercising no influence whatsoever on the prize deliberations and decisions themselves—the *Nobel Foundation* was established in early 1897. The Foundation is headed by an Executive Director and is managed by a Board of Directors whose members are elected by the several prize-awarding institutions,[5] to which they are responsible; the Executive Director is chosen by the Board, but the Chairman and Deputy Chairman of the Board are appointed directly by the Swedish government (*NPL*, 2). As of this writing (March 1981) the Chairman is Sune Bergström, a physician and professor at the Caroline Medico-Surgical Institute in Stockholm, and the Executive Director is Stig Ramel, a Doctor of Law; the other Board members are bank director Tore Browaldh (Deputy Chairman), professor Carl Gustaf Bernhard (Permanent Secretary of the Royal Academy of Sciences), bank director Lars-Erik Thunholm, and medical professor and novelist Lars Gyllensten (as noted above, Permanent Secretary of the Swedish Academy).[6] "In the course of the years," Gyllensten writes,

> . . . the Foundation has received a number of donations and grants from other quarters and has engaged in various scientific and cultural projects in line with the principal aims of the Nobel Prizes but in addition to the actual prize work. The international conferences known as the Nobel Symposia are one example. The Nobel Foundation acts as arranger and host at the ceremonies and festivities in connection with the presentation of the prizes, which takes place on 10 December, the anniversary of Alfred Nobel's death. The Foundation has nothing to do with the actual prize decisions, the choice of candidates, the practical work of assessment etc. All this is entirely in the hands of the prize-awarding bodies. . . . The ambition in administering the donation has been, and is, to maintain as far as possible the real value of the fortune and of the revenue (and thereby also of the prizes), and to place sufficient financial means at the disposal of the prize-awarding institutions for their increasingly widespread and expensive work of investigation. In 1901 . . . a prize was worth 150,800 kronor. In 1978 each prize amounted to 725,000 kronor [over $180,000].
>
> (*NPL*, 2-3)

Upon the establishment of the Nobel Foundation, the prize-awarding institutions began drawing up formal statutes and regulations detailing the procedures by which they would carry out the work of assessment and selection in their respective areas. The Swedish Academy's final proposals (submitted in the spring of 1900) placed particular stress on the need for strict and specific rules regarding the right to nominate candidates for the prize. Österling explains:

> In the case of the Swedish Academy the problem was all the more complicated as there were no other institutions of the same type anywhere in the world, except the French and Spanish academies. It would obviously have been unfair to limit the nominating rights to these two bodies, and it would have been equally inappropriate to grant such rights to any institution as a body, since the Academy's freedom of action might thereby be hampered by overwhelming external pressure. It was therefore proposed that the right to nominate can-

didates should be granted to the individual members of such institutions and not to the institutions themselves. The Academy felt, it was further stated, that by distributing the nomination rights so widely, it had tried to make sure that proposals could be made by duly qualified persons in all parts of the world and that no domestic or foreign literary organization of any importance should have cause to complain that the rights and privileges of its members had been slighted. The proposed text for the special statute was formulated as follows: "The right to nominate candidates for the Prize in Literature is granted to members of the Swedish Academy; and of the French and Spanish Academies which are similar to it in character and objectives; to members of the humanistic sections of other academies, as well as to members of the humanistic institutions and societies as enjoy the same rank as academies, and to university professors of aesthetics, literature, and history."

(*NMP*, 91-92)

The statute was altered in 1949 to broaden the range of groups regarded as competent to make nominations. The field now includes, according to Gyllensten, "members of the Swedish Academy and of other academies, institutions and societies similar to it in membership and aims; professors of languages or in the history of literature at universities and university colleges;[7] Nobel laureates in literature; and presidents of authors' organizations which are representative of the literary activities of their respective countries" (*NPL*, 7). Detailing the actual nomination procedure, Gyllensten continues:

> In order for anyone to be considered for a Nobel Prize, he or she must be proposed as a candidate for the prize by someone qualified to make such a proposal. . . . Nominations must be sent in writing to the Swedish Academy or its Nobel Committee before the end of January of the year in which the award is made. The reason for a nomination should be stated, but detailed analysis is not necessary. A person who has once been proposed for a Nobel Prize is not automatically regarded as a candidate in following years but can be proposed again. Also, the Nobel Committee or the Academy can, if it sees fit, reconsider a previously proposed name, if this is not among the nominations from outside. Applications to receive a prize are disregarded.
>
> In order to stimulate nomination, the Nobel Committee during the autumn sends out reminders or invitations to nearly 600 persons within the groups having the right to nominate candidates. The Committee endeavours to distribute such invitations all over the literary world and to vary the recipients each year. This procedure does not mean that others who are entitled to submit proposals do not have the right to do so—this right holds good even if no special invitation has been received.
>
> The Academy receives between three and four hundred nominations each year before 1 February. Many of the proposers nominate the same candidates, so that the number of suggested prizewinners is much smaller than the number of proposers—of recent years, the number of nominees has usually amounted to 100-150. Of these, only a few are new names which have not been proposed before—about a dozen. It does not occur that a candidate of any literary importance is proposed who is unknown to the Academy or the Nobel Committee. The names of the more important ones are sent in year after year. It is very unusual for anyone who has been proposed for the first time to receive the prize. As regards appraisal of the most qualified candidates, there is a clear consensus of opinion between many of the proposers from different parts of the world.

(*NPL*, 7-8)

In setting up a mechanism whereby it might handle the nominations most efficiently, the Swedish Academy established, prior to the very first prize, a *Nobel Committee,* which consists of five regular members plus one or more co-opted members appointed by the Academy. (The Committee presently includes Johannes Edfelt, Karl Ragnar Gierow, Lars Gyllensten, Artur Lundkvist and Anders Österling, with Östen Sjöstrand as a co-opted member.) Committee members are elected for three-year terms, receiving a yearly honorarium of approximately $1,200 (otherwise the Academicians receive no salary or stipend for their Academy work), and may be reelected without restriction; in fact, Österling has served on the panel continuously since 1921! The Nobel Committee, Gyllensten writes,

> . . . is responsible for the adjudication work necessary in dealing with the questions concerning the Nobel Prize in Literature. . . . This work goes on all the time, the whole year round. It is the Committee which gathers in the nominations from outside, supplementing the list if necessary, and which sees to it that the merits of the nominees are scrutinized sufficiently to give the [Academy] a solid basis for its opinion. . . . The Committee is aided in its work by a secretary (the head librarian of the Nobel Library) and a literary scholar engaged as professor at the Academy. [Presently these posts are held by Anders Ryberg and Knut Ahnlund respectively.] . . . The Nobel Committee's adjudication work is of course decisive for the Academy's choice, but this work is done in continual contact with the Academy as a whole and during discussions which can be carried on all the year round in connection with the Academy's regular meetings each week.

(*NPL*, 6, 4)

Assisting the Academy and the Nobel Committee in their work is the Academy's *Nobel Institute,* which consists of the *Nobel Library,* housed in the Academy's premises in the Royal Stock Exchange. The Library maintains a large collection of Swedish fiction, poetry, drama, essays and criticism for use in the Academy's regular activities, and also procures some 1,500-2,000 books annually in modern literature from throughout the world, in accordance with each year's list of Nobel Prize candidates. The total collection numbers approximately 150,000 volumes, making the Nobel Institute "the largest library in the Nordic countries as regards modern literature," adds Gyllensten. Moreover, "it is available to the public and is part of an interurban library service together with other public libraries. It is financed, however, entirely by private means from the Nobel Foundation and the Academy, without state or municipal grants. In addition to the head librarian and his assistants, the previously mentioned literary scholar works at the Academy's Nobel Institute" (*NPL*, 6-7).

All candidates proposed prior to 1 February by eligible individuals or organizations are placed on the year's list of nominations by the Nobel Committee, which may not exclude anyone so proposed. "This list," explains Gyllensten, "is put before the Academy as a whole during the first days of February. The Academy can then add new names, if necessary supplementing with those which for some reason, perhaps mere chance, have not been included. Nowadays the Academy, as well as the Nobel Committee, is more active in making such nominations than it was in the early days of the prize, when the members thought they should be very restrictive with their own proposals" (*NPL*, 8). All nominees on the supplemented list are appraised by the Academy, but "for one reason or another, many are unthinkable as Nobel laureates—perhaps because their production must be regarded as scholarship without the stipulated literary qualities, perhaps because their work, even if it does belong to literature, is far from having the necessary weight or quality, perhaps because they have obviously been proposed on grounds other than factual or literary ones (in some cases political, provincial, ideological and other motives appear as the decisive ones for the nomination in question)" (*NPL*, 9). The remaining names are then turned over to the Committee for thorough scrutiny. Gyllensten outlines the procedure at this stage of evaluation as follows:

> [The candidates'] works are procured in the original or in translation, if they are not already in the library. In cases where there is a paucity of translations and where candidates write in a language unfamiliar to the Academy's members or the experts, sample translations can be commissioned. With the aid of reference books, magazines, critical or scholarly reviews of literature etc. the Nobel Committee and its assistants familiarize themselves further with the nominees and their position in the literary world. Experts within or outside the Academy, at home and abroad, are commissioned to submit reports. Sometimes such assignments are given to individual writers, sometimes they are extended to include specific language areas or countries and certain literary schools or genres etc. Several investigations are made concerning most of the candidates of any importance and extensive information is collected about them. At the same time, the members of the Committee themselves read as much as they can of the candidates' works in the original or in translation and recommend books for the other members of the Academy to read.
>
> (*NPL*, 9)

Several factors pertaining to Alfred Nobel's will must be considered by the Committee and subsequently by the Academy as a whole in weighing each year's candidates: the nature of "literature," the "work" to be recognized, the "recentness" of that work, its benefit to "mankind" and the "ideal tendency" which it reflects. In 1900 the original Committee decided that "under the term 'literature' shall be comprised, not only belles lettres, but also other writings which, by virtue of their form and method of presentation, possess literary value" (*NMP*, 93); hence the subsequent selection of such laureates as Henri Bergson (1927), Bertrand Russell (1950) and Sir Winston Churchill (1953), although the Academy has adhered to a more purely belletristic line since Churchill's award. The will's stipulation that the prizewinners must have rendered their noteworthy service "during the preceding year," Österling writes, "is interpreted to mean that 'the awards shall be made for the most recent achievements in the fields of culture referred to in the will, and for older works only if their significance has not become apparent until recently.' The purpose of the new phrasing was, obviously, to clarify in a legally proper way the testamentary requirement which, in most instances, it would have been impossible to interpret in any other way" (*NMP*, 93). Gyllensten reasons:

> Literary works in particular often do not acquire their full importance until they are seen as a life's work or parts of a whole, as distinct from more ephemeral lucky shots in the literary market. This is also the background to the fact that many literary laureates receive their prize when they are well up in years and the greatness and creative context of their work is clearly apparent or when their significance to the age in which they live begins to be discerned. The insistence on topicality and on the benefit to mankind implies, however, the condition that what is to be rewarded shall still be a vigorous and fruitful literary creativeness on which the prize and its prestige can be expected to have a stimulating effect. This point of view has explicit support in what is known of Alfred Nobel's intentions with his donation.
>
> (*NPL*, 12-13)

The statutory regulation that the prizes be given for *a work* or *a writing* posed no dilemma for the prize-awarding institutions in the sciences and medicine, "but for the Swedish Academy it has been much more difficult to observe," Österling says. "Usually the literary awards have been given for an author's entire production, without specifying any particular work. At times it has been done, however, 'with special reference' to a particular book, as in the case of . . . Hamsun's *Growth of the Soil*, . . . Mann's *Buddenbrooks*, Galsworthy's *Forsyte Saga*, and Martin du Gard's *Les Thibault*" (*NMP*, 93). The condition that the prizes benefit "mankind" has been taken at least since World War II as an enjoiner to look beyond the somewhat limited geographic and cultural views of Nobel's day, to adopt a more "universalist" outlook, to take into account what is being offered by civilizations other than those of Scandinavia or Europe or North America, and to honor their outstanding achievements too (*NPL*, 13). Lastly, the will's directive that the prize in literature honor the person who has produced the most outstanding work "of an ideal tendency" has caused much perplexity over the years. Gyllensten explains:

> Just what Alfred Nobel intended is not clear. With the knowledge we have of his person and life, and of what he has expressed about his general outlook and aims,

the words "of an ideal tendency" have been taken to mean a striving for the good of mankind, for humaneness, common sense, progress and happiness. The fundamental idea has been interpreted as applying to literary achievements with constructive aims. All the same, there have sometimes been violent differences of opinion as to what was intended by "ideal tendency" in the strict sense. When considering the candidates nowadays, this expression is not taken too literally. It is realized that on the whole the serious literature that is worthy of a prize furthers knowledge of man and his condition and endeavors to enrich and improve his life.

(*NPL,* 15)

In December 1900 Esaias Tegnér, in his capacity as Director of the Academy, delivered an address which became something of a program declaration regarding the organization's approach to its new duty. He emphasized that the task was one which the Academy did not assume lightly, one which it in fact could not shirk, since the donor's millions had been given not to the Academy itself but to all mankind as represented by its foremost writers. His fervent hope was that a prize of such magnitude would in any event "have the effect of making a good piece of work known in much wider circles than would otherwise have been the case—and that it would be an excellent piece of work, if not in every instance the best available for a prize, he felt could be taken for granted" (*NMP,* 94). He foresaw the difficulties involved, but pointed up as well the Academy's uniquely favorable position for accepting such a task as that assigned by Alfred Nobel's will.

"The Swedish Academy," [Tegnér] proceeded, "certainly does not cherish the illusion that even once it may be able to award a prize in such a way as to escape criticism. Nay, it anticipates with certainty that such criticism will often be merited. But it consoles itself with the assurance that in the whole world there is no other institution which would not meet the same fate. . . . If there are drawbacks to being a small nation situated on the outskirts of the civilized world, there are also certain advantages. And when it is a question of a responsibility like this, a few of them become clearly evident. A person living on the border of a province is better able to decide which peaks inside it are the highest than an observer standing amidst the mountains themselves. In a different sense, this is also true of us. And in the fact that we are a small nation we have, in a way, a safeguard against partiality which the big nations lack: we shall less often be able to appear as contenders for the prize ourselves."

(*NMP,* 94-95)

Once its studies and preliminary discussions are completed—usually by early summer—the Nobel Committee submits to the full Academy a ranked listing of the candidates it deems most deserving of full consideration in the current year, together with information on the nominees' principal works, suitable secondary-source materials and available reports by Committee members and/or outside specialists. The Academy is in no way bound by the Committee's recommendations and may alter or add to the list as it wishes. Upon receiving the Committee's list, the Academy begins its deliberations, which occupy the major portion of the time at the group's weekly meetings until a decision is reached, usually by mid-October (*NPL,* 9-10). All nominations, investigations, deliberations and pollings are secret, and only the final choice is officially made public, at a time fixed by the awarding institution (*NPL,* 4). "In order for the voting within the Academy to be valid," Gyllensten notes, "it is required that at least twelve members shall take part and that a candidate shall receive more than half of the votes. The choice is made by secret ballot in writing. As a rule, all members of the Academy take part in the voting; if one or two cannot be present they send in their ballot papers. Usually the result is apparent after lengthy discussions and scrutiny, so that a large majority, or all, can agree on the prizewinner. No reservations concerning the majority's decision may be expressed, still less made public" (*NPL,* 10).[8] The awards, moreover, cannot be appealed against. In addition, the following regulations apply:

All prizes may be shared jointly by more than one person (a maximum of three). . . . The literary prize, however, is shared very seldom, as literary achievements rarely show the kind of affinity which often justifies a division of the scientific prizes. . . . A prize can be withheld and awarded the following year. Prizes may only be given to persons, except the peace prize which may also be given to an institution or a society. A deceased person cannot be put on the list of candidates for a prize, but if someone dies after having been chosen a prizewinner and before the prize has been presented, the prize can nevertheless be given. This is the exception, however. Any criteria other than actual merit may not be observed when the decisions are made—in other words, no regard shall be paid to race, sex, nationality etc.

(*NPL,* 4)

Once the final vote has been taken, the Academy notifies the new laureate (usually by telegram or phone), announces the decision publicly and issues a brief citation which is later printed on the Nobel diploma presented to the prizewinner by the Swedish King at the official award ceremonies on 10 December. Responsibility is then passed to the Nobel Foundation for issuing invitations to the recipient and his or her family and for arranging the round of festivities held in conjunction with the presentation ceremonies. The Academy does host a luncheon in honor of the laureate, however, and also sponsors the *Nobel Lecture* that most recipients consent to give, generally on 8 December or at another time shortly before or after the award presentations: "It is a rule for [the Nobel Lecture] to be given by the prizewinners in the other spheres, but not always in the case of the literature prize. If the lecture is not held, the prizewinner writes an essay or an article which the Nobel Foundation issues in its publication *Les Prix Nobel*" (*NPL,* 10).

. . . . .

Kipling, Yeats, Shaw, Thomas Mann, Pirandello, O'Neill, Eliot, Faulkner, Pasternak, Seferis, Beckett—like them or not, as you will, they are writers whose fame has endured and who are still read and admired the world over. Many of these were at the time by no means obvious choices for the Nobel Prize in Literature: Faulkner was lionized in France and Sweden and was prominent in the States in 1949 (though success at home had been long and slow in coming, and many of his books were in fact out of print) but enjoyed only a modest reputation in most other countries; and Seferis was only slightly more well known outside Greece in 1963 than was his compatriot Odysseus Elytis in 1979. The Prize focused the reading world's attention on their work, however, and that work has proved itself worthy of the scrutiny. The same is true to varying degrees in the cases of Lagerlöf, Tagore, Hamsun, Undset, Hesse, Lagerkvist, Asturias and Kawabata, and probably will prove so with 1978 laureate I. B. Singer. Meanwhile the fame of, say, Heyse, Sillanpää and Frédéric Mistral has shrunk from international to merely national or regional dimensions in literary history. "At the same time," concludes Österling,

> . . . it could be objected that a number of equally significant names are conspicuous by their absence; . . . and it is not to be denied that the history of the Nobel Prize in Literature is also a history of inexpiable sins of omission. But even so, it may perhaps be said that the mistakes have been comparatively few, that no truly unworthy candidate has been crowned, and that, if allowances are made for legitimate criticism, the results have reasonably matched the requirements and difficulties of an almost paradoxical assignment.
>
> Just as there are older prizewinners in whom a younger generation can take only a slight interest, so there are recent winners who, to the older people, would have seemed unthinkable. The coming of new generations, with inevitable changes in literary tastes, must obviously be reflected in the history of the Nobel Prize, and all the more clearly as time goes on. But under any circumstances it would be presumptuous to expect the Nobel Prizes to exercise any kind of guiding influence on the direction of literary progress. This has so far followed its own course, independently of the prizes, and will continue to do so in the future.
>
> (*NMP*, 133)

To point up the unique difficulties in choosing each year's recipient of the Nobel Prize in Literature is not to offer any apology for past choices but rather to state what should be readily apparent upon serious reflection. The criteria for assessment here "are necessarily more varied and often, too, more contradictory than in the case of medicine and other natural sciences," writes Gyllensten, himself both a teaching physician and a novelist; and those criteria are also more readily discernible—and therefore disputable—by the layman than are those for the exact sciences.

> A literary work has its roots in the traditions and the cultural setting of the age and country in which its author lives. The work reflects this background and acquires its full richness only through this interplay and only in those readers who are, or can put themselves, in sympathy with it. Literary works are more or less bound to the literary environment in which they are created, and the farther away from it one is, the harder it is to do them justice.
>
> The task of awarding the Nobel Prize in Literature involves the obligation of trying to find methods for keeping oneself *au fait* with what is happening in literature all over the world and for appraising it, either on one's own or with the aid of specialists. Finally, the prize awarders must try to familiarize themselves with the works of most value, directly or via translations, and to make a careful assessment of their quality with all the viewpoints conceivably necessary for a reasonable evaluation. It is obvious that no hard and fast criteria for such an appraisal can ever be laid down. One must accept a kind of pragmatical procedure and look to the fundamental idea in Alfred Nobel's will as a whole: it was a matter of encouraging science and literature and of disseminating them in an international perspective for the benefit of mankind, but not of handing out empty status rewards.
>
> (*NPL*, 11)

A given year's laureate may well turn out to be, in time, another Sully-Prudhomme, who received the very first award in 1901 yet today is all but forgotten even by his French countrymen. But he or she may also be another Pasternak, a Hamsun, a Seferis. Whatever posterity may reveal about a particular prizewinner, the Academicians take their year-round labors seriously, as I hope this outline of their history and procedures will indicate. The annual shots fired by much of the fourth estate at the Academy's choices thus are often as ill-considered as they are unoriginal, a perhaps natural ("the general public naturally does not like to be surprised by names it has never heard of before," *NMP*, 134) though regrettable reaction totally alien to the spirit of the Prize selections. Current fame is not a major criterion. Quality is. The Nobel Prize in Literature is not intended merely to echo and confirm popularity. It may also attempt to point out talent not yet recognized by most of the world's readers and critics. It may educate the many as it celebrates the one.

Notes

Ed. Note: We would like to thank the Swedish Academy's Permanent Secretary Lars Gyllensten for taking the time to read over this essay and check its accuracy prior to publication. His comments and corrections were most helpful in clarifying several points left unclear in the available published materials on the Prize procedures.

1. In its issue of 3 November 1975 *Time* wrote (p. 95): "In one of his great poems, Wallace Stevens speaks of 'musing the obscure.' That phrase seems to be the unspoken motto of the Swedish Academy. Last week it again passed over such notables as Vladimir Nabokov, Graham Greene and Saul Bellow to award the Nobel Prize in Literature to Eugenio Montale, 79, an Italian poet virtually unknown to the public outside his native land." The view is surprising, to say the least, in light of the same magazine's comments nine years earlier (3 June 1966), when "trans-

atlantic ignorance [was] relieved" by the appearance of Montale's *Selected Poems* in English: "a European writer of enduring importance, indisputably the most profound Italian poet of the 20th century. . . . Like Eliot, he has written very little . . . but that little he has written with iridescent precision." Evidently "times" change.

2. Anders Österling, "The Literary Prize," in *Nobel: The Man and His Prizes,* Norman, Ok., University of Oklahoma Press, 1951; second and third revised and enlarged editions were published in New York by Elsevier in 1962 and 1972 respectively. Parenthetically abbreviated as *NMP*.

3. The word used in Nobel's will is *idealisk* (ideal) and not *idealistisk* (idealistic), although the latter form is often used in translations of the will such as that which appears in *Nobel: The Man and His Prizes.* As Österling indicates, the term is best understood as expressing a preference for works possessing some positive, constructive purpose, although widely varying interpretations have been offered. Astronomer and mathematician M. G. Mittag-Leffler, for example, a good friend of Nobel, wrote that "he was an anarchist; by *idealisk* he meant anything that comprehends a polemic or critical attitude toward religion, royalty, marriage, or social organization in general" (see Richard Vowles, "Twelve Northern Authors," *BA* 41:1 [1967], p. 22). In any event, writes Lars Gyllensten, "*idealisk* is about as bewildering in Swedish as *ideal* is in English" (letter of 1 April 1981). For consistency, I have changed all references here to read *ideal* and not *idealistic.*

4. Lars Gyllensten, *The Nobel Prize in Literature,* Alan Blair, tr., Stockholm, Swedish Academy, 1978. Parenthetically abbreviated as *NPL*.

5. In addition to the Swedish Academy, the prize-awarding institutions are the Royal Academy of Sciences (physics and chemistry awards), the Nobel Assembly of the Caroline Medico-Surgical Institute (physiology and medicine) and the Norwegian Nobel Committee (peace). The prize in economics was added in 1969 and is actually sponsored by the Bank of Sweden "in memory of Alfred Nobel"; it is awarded by a special Prize Committee of economists from the Royal Academy of Sciences.

6. *Nobel Foundation Directory: 1979-1980,* Stockholm, Nobel Foundation, 1979.

7. The *Nobel Foundation Directory* (p. 11) qualifies this category as "professors of languages or in history of literature at universities and university colleges *selected by the Swedish Academy*" (my stress).

8. However, in the three editions of *NMP* Österling does give brief summaries of the Academy members' thinking and a hint of the course which the deliberations followed in many of the Nobel selections through 1970.

Kjell Espmark (essay date 1986)

SOURCE: Espmark, Kjell. "Intended for the Literature of the Whole World." In *The Nobel Prize in Literature: A Study of the Criteria behind the Choices,* pp. 131-44. Boston: G. K. Hall & Co., 1986.

[*In the following excerpt, Espmark explores the Nobel Prizes in Literature awarded after World War II, concluding that the committee's choices during that period reflect a new tolerance for different writing styles and literary movements.*]

The Nobel Prize in Literature seemed for a long time to be a European affair. Nobel's will indicated that the prize was to have an international aim, but in cautious wording: "It is my express wish that in awarding the prizes no consideration whatever shall be given to the nationality of the candidates, but that the most worthy shall receive the prize, whether he be a Scandinavian or not." The emphasis in the last clause on Scandinavian authors was reflected in the practice of the early Nobel Committee. In principle, however, the international scope of the prize is assured by its very conditions. A broader perspective is also implicit in Wirsén's speaking of the influential position "in world literature" available to the Swedish Academy. Yet the concept of universal literature was still to a high degree focused on European literature. Wirsén declared that if the task of administering the prize was not accepted by the academy, then "the leading men of letters throughout Europe" would be deprived of the opportunity to be recognized. Also representative of such a view was the wish expressed by the diplomat Bildt in a letter in 1904 that "to begin with we work round Europe."

A tentative move outside the European sphere was made in 1913 with the prize awarded to the Indian Rabindranath Tagore. In an important passage, to which we shall soon return, the 1922 report spoke of the danger of the Nobel Prize, "which is intended for the richly variegated literature of the whole world," being limited to "a less universal circle." Even the United States, however, had to wait until the 1930s before becoming part of the picture with the prizes to Sinclair Lewis (1930), Eugene O'Neill (1936), and Pearl Buck (1938). A further widening of the field did not occur until 1945, when Gabriela Mistral was hailed by Hjalmar Gullberg in his speech as "the spiritual queen of the entire Latin American world." The decision could have been made five years before, but the international situation prevented it. In this way both of the prizes given to writers outside Europe and North America up to that time were awarded in the margins, as it were, of the two world wars: one immediately before World War I, and the other immediately after World War II.

A further series of prizes to writers from the United States and Latin America scarcely altered this pattern. The rich culture of East Asia was first recognized in 1968 with the award to Yasunari Kawabata, for a "narrative mastery which with great sensibility expresses the essence of the

Japanese mind." The wording of the prize to Australia's Patrick White in 1973—"for an epic and psychological narrative art which has introduced a new continent into literature"—suggests how a new part of the world was incorporated into the history of the literary prize. But these occasional excursions outside European-American literature hardly fulfill the global responsibility that the academy more and more clearly faces. The vigorous literature of Africa has been neglected, like that of the Arabian countries, until very recently, and both Indian and Chinese voices have made increasingly determined claims for a more reasonable geographical distribution. At the same time, we can detect in recent years in both the Nobel Committee and the Swedish Academy a greater interest in taking this problem seriously. In an interview in the German magazine *Titel* in 1984, Lars Gyllensten said that attention to non-European writers is gradually increasing in the academy; attempts are being made "to achieve a global distribution."[1] The first fruits of this ambition were the prizes to Wole Soyinka in 1986 and to Naguib Mahfouz in 1988.

The new situation appears clearly in an exchange between the author Tsu-Yü Hwang and Gyllensten in *Göteborgs-Posten* (29 May and 24 June 1984). Tsu-Yü Hwang raised the question "whether an author writing in an 'uncommon' language has the same chance of a Nobel Prize as a Western author"; produced figures to illustrate the discrepancy between Scandinavian and English-language authors on the one side and Asian on the other ("of thousands of authors among the 800-1,000 million Chinese, not a single one has received the prize!"), and concluded that anyone who writes in an "uncommon" language and wants to be considered must "fulfill two equally important conditions: (1) He or she must have produced work showing to a high degree an idealistic tendency, and (2) He or she must find another author, preferably of the same exceptional caliber, who can translate his or her works into one of the main Western languages."

With regard to, among other things, the question of how much of the subtlety of the original text vanishes in translation, Tsu-Yü Hwang opted for the following model:

> After a certain period of time, say thirty or forty or fifty years, the academy realizes the suitability of giving the prize to an author who writes in one of those "uncommon" languages. Having thus decided, the members of the academy can take the time to consult experts from around the world in their search for suitable candidates. After reading representative works by those authors—mostly in translation—the academy should have the last word in selecting the winner.

Gyllensten admitted that in essentials, Tsu-Yü Hwang was right. A global comparison gave "the impression that a great injustice has been done." It was "clear that Europe has been favored," but many smaller regions of Europe did not appear in the list of winners, "in spite of the fact that they have been able to demonstrate a high level of literary culture." At the same time Gyllensten stressed that the Nobel Committee had from the beginning been aware of the problem and that he saw it as "stimulating, exciting even, to come to grips with." Concerning two of the proposed methods—"the use of experts and the deliberate aim to pay due attention to 'foreign' language areas"—he confirmed that these methods were "exactly how" the work was carried out. But the academy members could not delegate their task to experts but "must in the end make up their minds independently"; thus, when it came to non-European languages—and also to "minority" languages in Europe—they had to rely on translations. But the academy was not limited to what the commercial book market could offer. The academy could commission translators, "but of course not to an unlimited extent." Gyllensten thought the best way of breaking down linguistic and cultural barriers was to "promote the translation and publication of the literature one feels enthusiastic about."

But the academy could not content itself with waiting for a flow of good translations; it had to do what it could in the circumstances:

> In the case of writers we want to take up and treat fairly it is a matter of trying to acquire some understanding of the traditions and of the literary and cultural milieu out of which they write. A great deal of background reading is needed if one is to grasp something of what a writer from a culture other than one's own feels engaged in and wants to write about. And here, too, we must assume close cooperation between external specialists and those who will in the end reach a decision.
>
> Finally, we must be able to discriminate among the specialists, to choose them properly, and to arrive at a conclusion on the reliability, impartiality and so on of their reports. That is not always so easy. Many specialists are much too patriotic; others offer highly personal judgments; others give undue attention to their countrymen's position in a hierarchy conditioned by age; others apply political criteria, explicitly or implicitly etc. Cultural differences surfaced as well—attitudes towards age and other "diplomatic" considerations may well carry a different weight in Japan or China than they do in the West.

In this highly instructive article there was one idea particularly relevant to the present discussion, and that was the challenge of learning to understand the traditions and cultural milieu of an author from a distant cultural world—and then to judge the evaluation offered by his countrymen. The problem has been a constant, though not especially insistent, one in the earlier period. It can be glimpsed in the committee's cautious attitude toward Tagore in 1913. Among other aspects to be investigated were the connections between Tagore's poetry and that of the Vishnu cult; only then "may it be possible, for the guidance of independent evaluation, to distinguish between the original and the traditional elements in Tagore's religious mysticism and poetry." In fact, the academy was trying to judge the candidate's originality rather than attain a richer understanding of his work. Heidenstam made short business of it all with an argument that anticipated a later period's "pragmatic" line of thought; the problem of principle was not discussed further on that occasion. But it returned in 1922. In "the difficult choice" between Yeats and Benavente, the dilemma was formulated in words of great general relevance:

> In spite of a certain exclusive, aesthetically refined disposition, the Irishman, with his exceptionally highly developed English poetic culture, is more likely to master our emotions, to delight the lyrical sense that for us Swedes and for Germanic people in general plays such a large part in the enjoyment of art, than the Spaniard, representative as he is of a literature whose aims are quite otherwise. We must always reason with ourselves to maintain objectivity in our evaluation, but such objectivity is highly necessary. There is a real danger of the Nobel Prize, intended for the richly varied literature of the whole world, awarded by Nobel's countrymen, gradually being limited to a less universal circle, if our greater or lesser ease of access to the individuality of the different national spirits should affect our judgments. It is a matter of being on guard and assessing what is foreign to us not simply according to our own demands but according to its own conditions, and according to what we can gather of what it means where it has been created, and where tradition and culture facilitate comprehension of its content and form. With regard to both of the writers before us now there is reason to believe that each in his own place is a worthy representative of his people.

These words of Per Hallström's "on behalf of the committee" belong to a different epoch than Gyllensten's in 1984. For Hallström poetry reflected "the individuality of the national spirits"; Gyllensten spoke of "the traditions" and "the literary and cultural milieu" in which an author writes. But the problem is basically the same. It is still a question of trying to understand what the foreign work "means where it has been created, and where tradition and culture facilitate comprehension." One change since the 1920s, however, is that the academy's ambition to "gather" what it can has acquired wider geographical horizons; it is also more likely to resort to experts to acquire enough background understanding for it to make a reasonably empathetic assessment.

The desire apparent in 1922 to judge foreign work in accordance with its own conditions and frames of reference returned in Schück's report on the Portugese Correia de Oliveira in 1933. He found it scarcely proper "strictly to apply only our own Swedish taste to the works of one whose outlook and conception of life is remote from our own. . . . So far as it is possible for us we ought to try to understand and appreciate their way of viewing literature." The candidate in question was not "European," but appeared to base his work "on purely native traditions. . . . Several of his poems seem to *us* to be rather simple and trivial, but I suspect that the Portuguese see them with other eyes, while they in turn would not appreciate, for example, Fröding." Schück voted for Correia de Oliveira's *Job*—"even a non-Portuguese must recognize this poetic drama of ideas as a significant work of art"—and he suggested a complete translation of the work; only small parts were available in Swedish. This practical gesture, however, carried with it no solution to the problem of principle. Foreign literature, which in its own milieu was seen "with other eyes," continued to offer a difficult challenge. We note recurring expressions of the wish to "understand and appreciate" the literature of remote peoples. Bridging the distance in a real sense—that is, translating "remote" literature in a manner more thorough-going than the merely linguistic—is perhaps the most intimidating task facing those who in future will distribute the Nobel Prize in Literature.

The overall intention behind the remarks quoted above is to comply with Nobel's will in making the prize available worldwide. Early on, consideration was given to "the idea that the Nobel Prize, as far as possible, should circulate in turn between different countries." These words from 1904 refer to the possible objection to the Nobel Committee's candidate Mistral that the prize—which in 1901 went to Sully Prudhomme—"should not so soon afterwards go to France." The rightness of the argument was not denied, but reference was made to the fact that Mistral "nonetheless writes in an independent language, through the consolidation of which he has earned himself new honor." The committee had also to act with a certain haste, "in consideration of his advanced age." The principle recurred rather defensively when a majority of the committee proposed Swinburne in 1908. It had "not ignored the possible objection that last year's prize went to an Englishman and that reasons of expediency could well suggest that the prize should circulate among the different cultures." After duly recognizing the suitability of "such a circulation as a rule taking place," the committee claimed that "there is no real obstacle, when the circumstances are appropriate, to giving the prize to the same country in close, and even in immediate, succession." As it happened, the prize did not go to Swinburne and the principle was never tested on this point. Since then, two prize-winners from the same country have never been chosen in close succession. It is more significant that in 1922, "in the difficult choice" between Yeats and Benavente, the latter was given preference largely in consideration of the "omissions in the geographical distribution of the Nobel Prize." This line of reasoning recurs more recently. When in a letter in 1964 Gierow weighed Sartre and Auden against each other, one of his arguments against Sartre was "the series of French Nobel Prize winners—four Frenchmen already since the war"; it was therefore an argument in Auden's favor that "so far English literature has been remarkably little kept in mind." Another example is the prize to Böll in 1972; there was a certain pressure behind it because no literary prize had gone to Germany since 1929.[2]

Circulation of the prize, however, was for a long time restricted to Europe. The unrest noted in 1922 over the uneven distribution allowed the committee's horizon to cease immediately beyond England and Spain. The prize to Tagore in 1913 seemed like an expansive gesture, but in reality it illustrates this limitation. The proposal originated not in India but from a member of the Royal Society of

Literature in Britain, and the final decision was based on Tagore's English version of Gitanjali, without the aid of Oriental experts to assess the rest of his production. (One of the committee members, Esaias Tegnér, Jr., could in fact read Tagore in Bengali, but there is no indication that use was made of his expertise in the matter.) The impression of a narrow Eurocentric discussion persisted. It was not until 1929 that the committee expressed a wish "to greet with satisfaction the opportunity, through the medium of the Nobel Prize, to draw attention to the great and vigorous literature of the South American language area." Unfortunately, Venezuela's Rufino Blanco Fombona could not meet with the committee's approval as, "in the eyes of the non-Spanish world, a sufficiently important author to fill the place of a representative of his culture."

The prize to Gabriela Mistral did mark a breakthrough. It is known that in 1940 her candidacy was enthusiastically supported by Latin American spokesmen. When Valéry, who had been destined to receive the 1945 prize, died in the summer of that year, Gabriela Mistral, in Österling's words in a letter to Hallström on 2 August, had "a new chance. . . . I have nothing against it, bearing in mind the idea of a gesture to Latin America, which we have neglected." But it was not simply an effort to extend the award itself to that part of the world for the first time. The 1940 report, written by Hallström, also extends to Latin America the committee's willingness to "understand and appreciate" a foreign literature. This intention was already clear in Hallström's attempt to view the original "through the veils of translation. . . . Even for one who does not feel sufficiently at home in Spanish to have an ear sensitive to the harmony of the language, and who can but dimly guess his way into the associations that mean so much for lyrical beauty, even for such a reader it is possible to approach a fair appreciation by comparing original and translation line by line."

But his efforts went further than dealing with translation problems and were extended to gaining an understanding of "the emotional differences" between Spaniards and Swedes, and "not the least the [Spanish] poetic tradition and the means of expression it offers. . . . One must accustom oneself to finding genuineness in foreign dress." This ambitious reader was feeling his way into "the energetic and passionate language, compressed almost to breaking point, that streams from this poetess" and toward "the human being" behind the voice, its captivating personality that with its "unchecked, open-hearted, courageous, and spontaneous poetry has appeared as a revelation in her homeland." Here again we catch a glimpse of the wish—now extended beyond the European horizon—to understand what the literary work "means where it was created."

The result was a judgment that in one important respect resembled that of Schück on Correia de Oliveira—Hallström abstained from making objections conditioned by his own tradition in order to do justice to the genuine poetry he perceived in its foreign framework: "If she does not always attain to what we strangers are accustomed to seek in poetry, if the intellectual content does not seem to us to be particularly profound or new, this ought not to be decisive for our assessment, when we are able to get as far as appreciating the emotional sincerity and purity and without difficulty seeing that we are confronting a great personality."

It was harder to reach correspondingly fair evaluations of Asian literature. In the 1930s just finding serious candidates was a problem. One of the few was Sarvepalli Radhakrishnan. On the basis of the philosher Hans Larsson's highly positive report, the committee members in 1933 felt "lively interest" but expressed "the same doubts as usual about the suitability of awarding Nobel Prizes in the area of philosophy." Interest remained cool in the following years; occasional candidates from several Asian countries appeared in the late thirties but as a rule were promptly dismissed. The proposals, in some cases quite strange, illustrate a decisive weakness in the whole system. For areas outside the West not enough had been done to secure competent proposers. And the idea of the committee actively searching for such candidates, on its own initiative, was still a long way in the future. The process thus got no further than a state of willingness to promote, for example, new Chinese poetry, "for the appreciation of the Western world," if only a body of work could be found that was "aesthetically significant and captivating." In 1940 it was possible to consider, alongside Selma Lagerlöf, the "Chinese writer Pearl Buck recommends," Lin Yutang,[3] but the academy was not entirely convinced. A degree of help in finding one's way around this literature was available from the Asian specialist Sven Hedin. But the matter stopped there.

Nowadays, proposals come in from countries such as China, Japan, and India, as well as from various parts of the Arab world, and they are representative of their respective literatures in a manner quite different from such proposals in the 1930s. In the early 1960s the nominations from Japanese literature included Junichiro Tanizaki, first proposed by Pearl Buck in 1958; Junzaburo Nishiwaki, whose name was put forward by, among others, the Japanese Academy; Yasunari Kawabata, proposed by, among others, PEN of Japan; and Yukio Mishima, proposed by Americans.[4] In an interview with the London *Sunday Times* (23 November 1980), Artur Lundkvist revealed that there were by that time nominations from black Africa. To the question whether in the near future we might see a black prize winner, he replied, "That's possible." (A few years later he mentioned that his own candidate was Léopold Sédar Senghor, whom he also introduced and translated.)[5]

That the system for proposing candidates is not functioning as one could wish is apparent in an article in the 3 May 1985 issue of *Asiaweek*; it reported on the prevalent criticism that the Asian area has been neglected by the academy and listed the oft-named candidates Yasushi Inoue from Japan, Ba Jin from China, Pramoedya Ananta Toer of Indonesia, and R. K. Narayan of India.[6] The author of the article interviewed Gyllensten and learned that the nominations of Asian authors are not particularly numerous. Gyllensten ascribed this to special difficulties, such as a lack of consensus even among specialists, problems in developing criteria for the evaluation of authors with widely divergent cultural backgrounds and very different literary purposes, and (for nominations made from the West) a lack of translations. The journalist pointed out that in several countries those with the right to propose have neglected to make use of the right. Ba Jin, president of PEN in China, admitted that he was invited to make a proposal but did not reply. The other PEN groups in Asia have also let chances slip by. PEN of Thailand, for instance, is unfailingly contacted each year, but there has never been a response. Its president, Nilawan Pintong, is not sure if anyone from her country has ever been proposed: "Here in Thailand we have not done much in translation of literary work. We can have it submitted in our own language, but the fact is we have not found anything meritorious because we have not worked seriously to find it." This comment well illustrates the defeatism that so often prevents interesting candidates outside the West from even reaching the stage of being proposed.

The deficiencies in the system for proposing candidates have laid an extra responsibility upon the academy itself. Recently, the members of the Nobel Committee—and of the academy—have been making much greater use of their own right to submit proposals. The committee even asks for specialist reports on literatures that were simply not within sight in the earlier period. These reports locate particular works in their literary and cultural contexts and give some idea of the resonance and associative qualities of the language as it is handled in those works. These efforts to attain some kind of overview are reflected in the surveys included in the magazine *Artes* (published by the academies). That modern Arabic literature was no longer beyond the pale—as several critics had suggested—was clear from the fact that the first issue of *Artes* in 1984 was devoted to Arabic literature, with presentations and translations by, among others, Adonis (Ali Ahmed Said), Mohammed Dib, and Tahar Ben Jelloun.[7] Other issues have been devoted to Chinese and Indian literature.

How specialist knowledge is used to locate the worthiest representative of a literature that is both foreign and hard for Western readers to orientate themselves in is apparent in those parts of the Yasunari Kawabata background material that have been made public.[8] In this case, certain myths about the Nobel Prize meet reality. The myth was voiced by Irving Wallace when he said, "A Swedish official was flown to Tokyo to scout the field."[9] In reality, the process, from proposal to decision, took seven years. A preliminary investigation was entrusted in 1961 to a Swedish critic, who based his highly appreciative assessment of Kawabata on a number of works in German, French, and English translation. His evaluation was then supported by reports from three experts in the field: Professor Howard S. Hibbett of Harvard University, who regarded both Tanizaki and Kawabata as figures of world status; Professor Donald Keene of Columbia University, whose evaluation was equally high—in the choice between Kawabata and Mishima, he preferred Kawabata, the elder of the two; and the Japanese scholar Sci Ito, who concluded that after the death of Tanizaki, Kawabata was the only one really worthy of representing Japanese literature. On such a basis the academy was able—from the members' own reading of Kawabata in translation—to make a confident decision that for the first time went beyond the European linguistic horizon.[10]

Efforts have also been made, however, to ensure a significant level of linguistic and literary competence *within* the academy. English, German, and French have caused no problems. Competence in Spanish and Italian (and even in Provençal) has also been well represented. Academy members themselves have made significant translations, such as Gullberg's translations of Gabriela Mistral and Seferis, or Österling's of Quasimodo and Montale. And, of course, the academy continually obtains reports on European writers from outside sources. In the case of the Slavonic languages, this "extramural" aid has been necessary even if there has sometimes been a member with the relevant knowledge, such as Harald Hjärne. Language experts have been closely associated with the Nobel Institute from early on—first Alfred Jensen, then Anton Karlgren. Throughout the greater part of the Nobel Prize's existence the academy has also included eminent Orientalists—up to 1928, Esaias Tegnér, Jr., then from 1948 to 1974, H. S. Nyberg. When the Egyptian author Taha Hussein was proposed in 1967, the relevant specialist was at hand.[11] At an early stage recourse could also be made to a specialist in Chinese matters, Bernhard Karlgren.

None of those specialists, however, can be said to have shown a bold approach to the global task. More recently, the academy has often made use of a more active expertise with a view to the ever-widening scope of the Nobel commission. With the election of Artur Lundkvist in 1968, the academy acquired regular access to Sweden's foremost advocate for foreign literature, especially from the Spanish-speaking areas. An idea of his role in this widening of perspective can be suggested by two small items of information. On 26 May 1962, in *Stockholms-Tidningen*, he opened the first Swedish presentation of Patrick White's work with the words: "As far as I am aware, no Swedish critic or publisher has drawn attention to Patrick White. Yet he is something that nowadays is rather rare and special—a great epic storyteller who, in addition, is an admirable psychologist and stylist." Eleven years later it was Lundkvist who made the speech to the Nobel Prize winner Patrick White.

Competence in Spanish literature was further strengthened in 1970, when Knut Ahnlund, as the holder of a professorship attached to the Nobel Committee, began to serve as a specialist adviser. He has been a member of the academy since 1983, and of the Nobel Committee since 1984. With the election in 1985 of Göran Malmqvist, a translator and professor of sinology, the academy has secured the services of one of the West's foremost experts in modern Chinese literature, one who is also in close contact with specialists in Oriental literature in general.

The support of such expertise—from close at hand or from further afield—makes it possible for the academy to acquire an overview, to find its way, and to arrive at a preliminary conception of the worth of various candidates. But this cannot, of course, replace the personal study upon which the members of the committee and the academy must base their final decisions. For such study, when it comes to the more "remote" languages, reliance on translations is unavoidable. Over the years, the significance of translation has been a recurring theme in the reports. The doubts felt by the 1920s committee over Kostis Palamas is closely related to the difficulty of assessing the language of the original works. In 1931 it was expressly confirmed that the award to Bunin "shall relate to the works as they exist in their original language." It had been difficult for the academy members to understand the "stylistic mastery" attributed to Bunin by his countrymen; they relied on "cultivated Russian opinion, both among emigrants and at home."

This problem is a constant part of the work of the Nobel Prize. An important expedient can be seen in Schück's 1933 statement commissioning a translation of a work by Correia de Oliveira. The opportunities the academy had of "itself procuring translations" was touched upon, as we have seen, in Gyllensten's 1984 article. He added: "Paradoxically, this is easier with poets than with prose writers, since a poet can be reasonably represented by a quantitatively more limited body of text than that required by a prose writer." In several cases such exclusive translations—with eighteen readers—have played an important role in the recent work of the academy.

But even in such favorable conditions the problem of finding access to a foreign culture remains. Faced with this persistent dilemma, Artur Lundkvist adopted a position that stimulated reactions from around the world. In his article "Nobelpris åt vem?" ("The Nobel Prize to Whom?") in *Svenska Dagbladet* (12 October 1977) he described the task of the Nobel Prize as one of drawing "attention to achievements that have not been sufficiently regarded and to a high degree deserve recognition." He believed "that the smaller areas of literature, defined in terms of either language or nationality, suffer particularly" from the difficulties of acquiring an overall view of the "enormous range of contemporary literature." He continued:

> Those literatures that are great yet exist in languages to which we do not have ready access present another problem. The academy is often reproached for thus neglecting the literatures of Asia and Africa and other "remote" parts. But I doubt if there is so far very much to find there. It is a question of literatures that (with a certain exception, particularly in the case of Japan) as far as can be judged have not achieved that level of development (artistic, psychological, linguistic) that can make them truly significant outside their given context.

> The Nobel Prize is after all a Western institution and cannot reasonably be distributed on the basis of other than Western evaluations. In itself this may be regrettable, and I hope, of course, that these more distant literatures will soon enough catch up on the lead so far enjoyed by Western literature, so that they can fully participate in a global cultural exchange.

Lundkvist's views, repeated in an interview in the London *Sunday Times* on 23 November 1980, naturally met with sharp criticism in the Third World, not least from official Indian quarters. Quite objectively, there is good reason to question Lundkvist's idea of a qualitative *development* in literature, with a Western "lead" that Asia and Africa must "catch up" on. Even within the context of European literature that perspective is rather peculiar—in what sense do twentieth-century authors exist on a higher "level of development" than Sophocles, Dante, Shakespeare, or Tolstoy? And from the point of view of Asian literature, how is Western tradition superior to a tradition that includes on the one hand Tang poetry and *The Dream of the Red Pavilion,* and on the other, Firdausī, Rūmī, and Hāfiz?

Lundkvist was responding to the reproaches against the Swedish Academy for its alleged neglect of Asian and African literature. The same can be said of his views in the London *Sunday Times* interview: when asked how the Nobel Committee could judge the value of literature in countries such as China or India, whose cultures are altogether foreign, he replied that they were "primitive cultures" that he did not believe capable of "developing on a global scale." Such remarks, however, are not representative; they deviate sharply from the thoughtful self-questioning that can be traced from Hallström and Schück to Gyllensten.[12] The spirit of this tradition is perhaps best caught in Gyllensten's words, already quoted: "In the case of writers we want to take up and treat fairly, it is a matter of trying to acquire some understanding of the traditions and of the literary and cultural milieu out of which they write."

Further, Lundkvist's statement is incompatible with the modest practice that can be distinguished. The idea of a Western lead that only Japan has to a certain extent managed to close is hardly compatible with Österling's authoritative words on Kawabata. To him, Kawabata represents a cultural consciousness that *vindicates itself* against Western influence. Österling finds Kawabata capable—in his analysis of erotic episodes—of small, secretive nuances that "often put European narrative art in the shade." Those words in the speech to Kawabata well catch the spirit of the 1968 choice. They imply at the same time a criticism of the other candidate, Mishima, whose methods show a strong European inspiration.

The picture of the academy's Eurocentric policy has been significantly altered by the choices of Wole Soyinka in 1986 and Naguib Mahfouz in 1988. The awarding of two prizes so close in time to authors outside the European-American cultural sphere naturally raises the question of whether the academy radically changed course during the latter half of the 1980s. That a change is involved is abundantly clear, but it is less dramatic than may at first be thought. In 1984 Gyllensten expressed a desire—already felt by others in the academy—to achieve a global spread. But it takes time to realize such ambitions, and a few years had to pass before the first results were apparent. Obviously, even more time is required before a serious attempt to encompass—knowledgeably—the whole of the rich and variegated field of world literature will be possible.

The point ought to be made that, in the light of this more expansive policy, the procedure offered by Tsu-Yü Hwang—that we should first decide upon a neglected language area and then seek out the best candidate in it—is not being followed. Doing so would amount to a politicization of the prize. Instead, efforts are being made to extend the area under scrutiny so that in the course of the normal process of arriving at decisions it is possible to weigh sometimes a prominent Nigerian dramatist and poet, sometimes an Egyptian novelist, against candidates from parts of the linguistic atlas closer to our own—with all such evaluations continuing to be made on *literary* grounds. That more than one candidate from the same region may figure simultaneously in a choice does not detract from such a statement; the proposal of a candidate from one particular literature may, within the committee and the academy, evince a counterproposal in favor of another candidate from the same sphere.

Two of the more recent criteria that I have described do have a bearing on the final adjudication between different candidates. The matter can be illustrated by way of an indiscretion on the part of Artur Lundkvist shortly after the 1988 choice was made: in an interview in *Göteborgs-Tidningen* on 4 December, he revealed that he himself "had another Arabic author as a candidate—Adonis." The juxtaposition of the names of Mahfouz and Adonis is immediately significant to anyone at all versed in Arabic literature: the choice was between two pathfinders—more exactly, between the great pioneer of Arabic fiction and the more recent regenerator of Arabic poetry. The academy opted for the larger epic figure, while Lundkvist felt more strongly in favor of the younger, more exclusive poetic innovator. But alongside the "pioneer" criterion, applicable in both cases, the "pragmatic" aspect of the assessment had made itself felt, quite naturally. Mahfouz was admittedly no obscure genius—about ten of his works could be read in, among other languages, English and French—but his readership outside the Arabic area was greatly limited. A prize could be expected to function as a signal to a large number of potential readers, at the same time, of course, as it signified a just and overdue recognition of a rich contemporary literature. It should hardly need to be said that criteria of that kind can in the end only supplement a powerful experience of the artistic strength of the oeuvre in question.

This widening of the academy's horizons requires a constant effort to understand the cultural identity of the writing under consideration and to overcome as far as possible personal prejudices. Gyllensten's speech at the Nobel Festival in 1986 echoed his statement two years before about the importance of becoming acquainted with the environment of the writers the academy wants "to take up and treat fairly." In connection with Soyinka's description of his childhood in a small Nigerian village, he sketched a cultural background of just the kind it was necessary to try to comprehend: "We encounter a world in which tree sprites, ghosts, sorcerers, and primitive African traditions were living realities. We also come face to face with a more complicated world of myth, which has its roots far back in African culture handed down by word of mouth. This account of childhood gives a background to Soyinka's literary works—a self-experienced, close connection with a rich and complex African heritage."

Gyllensten observed that Soyinka's drama "is closely linked with the African material and with African forms of linguistic and mime creation." Of course, he also stressed that Soyinka is "familiar with Western literature, from the Greek tragedies to Beckett and Brecht"—an acknowledgment of the "wide cultural perspective" mentioned in the wording of the award. But the presentation lingered, significantly, on Soyinka's original milieu. Far from talking, like Lundkvist, of any Western "lead" that must be "caught up," Gyllensten focused on the genuine African provenance of Soyinka's drama, its roots in a "composite culture with a wealth of living and artistically inspiring traditions." His speech was a much more accurate testimony to the spirit behind the academy's recent attempts to address the prize to "the literature of the whole world."

Donald Keene has written that, through the award of the Nobel Prize to Kawabata, the Japanese novel tradition—the world's oldest—has been incorporated into "the world stream of writing."[13] It is in this wide assimilative process, rather than in any expectation that the Third World should catch up on a Western lead, that the Nobel Prize has its global future.

Notes

1. Ingmar Björkstén, interview with Lars Gyllensten, *Titel*, no. 4 (1984) ("man versuche jedoch eine globale Verbreitung zu erreichen" ["we must still try to reach a global distribution"]). Cf. Gyllensten in *The Nobel Prize in Literature* (Stockholm, 1978), 13.

2. See also Lundkvist's statement in an interview in *Aftonbladet* (10 December 1970): "There is a kind of rotation system whereby the same country should not recur too often."

   A question already apparent in connection with the strong Scandinavian representation during the neutrality policy of the 1910s is how often a Swedish or Scandinavian name may be allowed to emerge from the process. One answer is to be found in a speech by Tegnér in 1900: he thought that it would be "only as an exception" that a Scandinavian author would be worthy of the award, since "our northern nations are so small." He saw in this fact "a safeguard against partisanship," a safeguard that "the greater nations lack." Another answer was given by Heidenstam when in 1913 he recalled that the Nobel Prize was nonetheless a Scandinavian award (letter to Per Hallström, 8 April 1913).

A more recent attitude is reflected in Gyllensten's objection to the idea, raised in a newspaper debate, that Swedes should be more or less excluded:

> Oddly enough, such claims are made only concerning the literature prize. To exclude Swedes or Scandinavians, however, would be in violation of the statutes. In regard to the prizes hitherto awarded to Swedes, it can be said that in all cases the prize winners were nominated by proposers outside Sweden, most of them over a period of many years and from several quarters. Naturally, they themselves did not take part in the work of assessment when their candidacies were being dealt with
>
> *(The Nobel Prize in Literature,* 14).

A certain disagreement with such a line of thought can be detected in Lundkvist's remark in an interview that the Nobel Prize should not be given to a Swede (*Aftonbladet,* 10 December 1970; see also *Dagens Nyheter,* 30 December 1984).

3. Selma Lagerlöf to Per Hallström, 12 February 1940 (LUB). The name of Pearl Buck's candidate, first proposed in 1938, was revealed by Strömberg in the Kawabata volume of *Nobel Prize Library.* The letter also names several of the 1940 candidates in addition to "that Chinese writer"; Lagerlöf pities the secretary "for once more having to consider Jensen, Falkberget, and Palamas."

4. See Strömberg's introduction to the Kawabata volume of *Nobel Prize Library.*

5. Artur Lundkvist interview in the Czech press, cited in *Dagens Nyheter,* 30 December 1984. His other favorites for the prize were André Brink and Claude Simon.

6. Other names put forward by *Asiaweek* were Nick Joaquin and F. Sionil José from the Philippines, Kenzaburo Oë from Japan, Ding Ling from China, Kim Tong Ni from South Korea, and the deceased Faiz Ahmed Faiz from Pakistan. The unsigned article was by Isabella Wai.

7. *Artes,* no. 4 (1984) includes translations by Sabur, Bayyāti, Sayyāb, and Bachir Hadj Ali.

8. See also Strömberg's introduction to the Kawabata volume of *Nobel Prize Library.* In fact, the specialist support was greater than Strömberg suggests, a fact that unfortunately cannot at present be illustrated.

9. David Wallechinsky and Irving Wallace, *The People's Almanac* (New York, 1975), 1104.

10. Tagore was assessed, as we have seen, on the basis of his own translation of his work into English, which, it was stressed, gave the translation the character of an original work. Hebrew—Agnon's language—also belongs to a European perspective.

11. Strömberg's introduction to the Asturias volume of *Nobel Prize Library.*

12. In connection with such sensational statements by Lundkvist, it should be mentioned that the material gives no support to the widespread notion that he had a decisive influence on a line of choices and rejections in the last two decades.

13. *New York Times Book Review,* 8 December 1968.

William Pratt (essay date spring 1988)

SOURCE: Pratt, William. "Missing the Masters: Nobel Literary Prizes in English, 1967-1987." *World Literature Today* 62, no. 2 (spring 1988): 225-28.

[*In the following essay, Pratt speculates on the reasons why some of the most famous writers in British and American literature have not been awarded the Nobel Prize in Literature.*]

What do Mark Twain, Henry James, Thomas Hardy, Joseph Conrad, Robert Frost, D. H. Lawrence, James Joyce, F. Scott Fitzgerald, Wallace Stevens, Ezra Pound, W. H. Auden, Robert Penn Warren, Willa Cather, Virginia Woolf, Marianne Moore, Katherine Anne Porter, William Carlos Williams, and Robert Lowell all have in common? They happen to be British and American writers of this century who have *not* won the Nobel Prize in Literature. And what do Rudyard Kipling, John Galsworthy, Sinclair Lewis, Pearl Buck, and William Golding all have in common? They are British and American writers who *have* received the Nobel Prize. Comparing the unlaureled with the laureled, one might reasonably conclude—as Robert Spiller did in his 1967 *Books Abroad* survey of the Nobel literary prizes in English—that "the Nobel Prize in Literature is not really a literary award in the modern sense and was never intended to be."

There have always been critics ready to dismiss the Nobel Prize as either inconsequential or merely political, but to do so is to ignore the names left out of the list above; for whatever sins of omission and commission may be charged to the Swedish Academy, it has chosen enough distinguished Nobel laureates in English alone to crown anyone's canon of major twentieth-century writers: William Butler Yeats, George Bernard Shaw, Eugene O'Neill, T. S. Eliot, William Faulkner, and Ernest Hemingway. If anyone needs proof that the Nobel Prizes are truly literary, there it is, and if we note that two of these six writers are poets, two are dramatists, and two are novelists, we find a pair of major artists at the top of each of the twentieth century's three major literary genres. Some may object that the merit is not equally distributed among genres, and that between Yeats and Shaw, for instance, or O'Neill and Faulkner, distinctions could be made on purely literary grounds—modern drama, in short, does not measure up to modern poetry or modern fiction in artistic excellence. Still, the balance is certainly there, and so is the evidence that the Swedish Academy has done its job well. It has recognized at least a half-dozen writers in English in this century, in the major literary categories of poetry, drama, and fiction, writers who, according to the terms of Alfred Nobel's will, "shall have produced in the field of literature the most outstanding work of an ideal tendency." To these six acknowledged masters, some might want to add more recent prize-winners such as John Steinbeck, Samuel Beckett, or Saul Bellow, but these are more open to question than the first six; the same is true of the remaining two Nobel laureates in English, Bertrand Russell and Winston Churchill, who are certainly esteemed in their respective roles of thinker and leader but are not in the strict sense literary artists. All in all, taking in the complete list of seventeen writers of English who have won Nobel Prizes during the nine decades the awards have been offered, and conceding that fame and popularity are likely to weigh more heavily than true literary excellence in any contest—still, without claiming that Nobel Prizes are divided evenly between writers of genius and popular favorites, a record of six out of seventeen is not bad. One bull's-eye for every three tries is not quite the 50-percent success with which Spiller was willing to credit the Academy, but it is a record honorable enough to argue against his conclusion that Nobel Prizes are not "really literary."

In fact, T. S. Eliot came much nearer the mark when, accepting his Nobel Prize in 1948, he said that to speak of it as "the highest international honor that can be bestowed upon a man of letters, would be only to say what everyone knows already."[1] No Nobel laureate has ever been in a better position than Eliot to appreciate the work of the Swedish Academy, since he was not only a poet of the first rank in both Britain and America, but a critic who was a principal shaper of the literary taste of his age. He made his acceptance speech an occasion for giving "my own interpretation of the significance of the Nobel Prize in Literature," which was that it represents "the election of an individual, chosen from time to time from one nation or another, and selected by something like an act of grace, to fill a peculiar role and become a peculiar symbol"—a symbol, quite simply, of the value of literature to the human race. No higher significance need be sought: if the prize honors some writers more than they deserve, whereas others bring honor to the prize, the net result is that literature, being by its nature "of an ideal tendency," just as Alfred Nobel stated in his will, has been annually held up before the world as a benefit to mankind, comparable to the benefits of medicine, physics, chemistry, and peace (economics is a latecomer not included in Nobel's original bequest). Since literature is the only art so honored, it enjoys a unique status among the Nobel Prizes and draws more than its share of skepticism and controversy. If Nobel Prizes were given in architecture, painting, sculpture, music, or dance—who knows?—they might be equally controversial, but the debate about the literary prizes might be a little less intense.

In any case, it is to the credit of those entrusted with choosing the winners of the Nobel Prize in Literature that it has such high standing with writers as well as readers the world over; for the prize must be awarded to someone every year, and the good writers in any age will always outnumber the great. A few great writers are enough to establish the standard, and clearly, some of the greatest in our century have been Nobel Prize winners. I suppose it could be argued that until 1923, when Yeats won the laurels, the Nobel had not reached its highest level of excellence, at least in the English-speaking world, but since then, no serious writer of English could doubt that the standard is potentially of the very first class. Moreover, the importance of the Nobel Prize to a writer's career is fully illustrated by the case of Faulkner, whose international fame largely dates from the time when he received his Nobel in 1950, proving that the Academy may occasionally be inspired to honor a great writer as yet unappreciated in his own language and justifying William Riggan's conclusion in "The Swedish Academy and the Nobel Prize in Literature: History and Procedure" [*World Literature Today,* hereafter *WLT*] (*WLT,* Summer 1981): "The Nobel Prize in Literature is not intended merely to echo and confirm popularity. It may also attempt to point out talent not yet recognized by most of the world's readers and critics. It may educate the many as it celebrates the one."[2]

In the twentieth century it might even be said that being summoned to Stockholm is the equivalent of being invited to Florence in the time of the Medici or to London in the time of Elizabeth I: almost every talented and ambitious writer dreams of being recognized by the Nobel Committee, which has become the royal patron of a democratic age. That the Academy has sometimes withheld its patronage until a writer's career was virtually over, that it has overlooked many deserving authors, and that it has honored many less-deserving ones all seem to me inevitable in any competition which must confer a yearly award; and if I find, when I turn to the Nobel Prizes in English for the past twenty years, that none reaches the very highest standard, I am inclined to think the cause is less a lowering of the standard than a broadening of the range of national and ethnic identities which, for a world-embracing language like English, naturally enter into consideration for an award with the international prestige of the Nobel.

I say this, knowing that the four English-language writers who have won Nobel Prizes in Literature since 1967 would not have been my choices. No, if I had been a member of the Swedish Academy in these last two decades, instead of giving prizes to Samuel Beckett, Patrick White, Saul Bellow, and William Golding, I would have voted to confer the prize on Ezra Pound, W. H. Auden, Robert Penn Warren, and Robert Lowell. If I had met fierce opposition from my fellow Academicians to these undisputed masters, I would have been ready to propose four acceptable alternates: Katherine Anne Porter, John Crowe Ransom,

Marianne Moore, and Allen Tate. These choices are not mere fantasy, because all the writers were alive two decades ago (and one, Warren, still is); and if I had occupied a seat on the Nobel Committee of the Swedish Academy (more to be desired by any true lover of literature than a seat on the New York Stock Exchange), I would have argued that any of these eight writers deserved the prize more than any of the four who actually received it. I would have based my advocacy on literary merit alone, of course, but then I would have had to contend with my fellow Academicians' notions of what constitutes literary merit and with other considerations as well, which undoubtedly influenced their choices: for instance, that Beckett, whose Nobel citation hailed him for "introducing new forms to the novel and drama," was born in Ireland but has lived in Paris and written in French as well as English; that White "for the first time has given the continent of Australia an authentic voice"; that Bellow, credited with the "subtle analysis of contemporary culture," was born in Canada of Jewish parents and has lived and written in the United States; and that Golding, who "illustrates the human condition in the world today," was born in London. The geographic and ethnic scope of the Nobel Committee's choices is, I admit, wider than mine would have been; and they had, besides the privilege of choosing the winners, the responsibility of justifying their choices, first to their fellow Academicians and then to a world audience, whereas I can confer my awards freely, without dispensing huge sums of money or facing the risk of having them seriously challenged. Still, my point of view is simply that the Nobel laureates of the last twenty years in English have added no special luster to the prize, despite the fact that in this same period there were living masters who might well have done so, had they been chosen instead.

. . . . .

Reflecting on the actual choices rather than on my own wishes, I see that they do bear out Herbert Howarth's observation in the 1967 *Books Abroad* symposium that prose has prevailed over poetry in the Nobel Prizes, "as if the judges have either thought prose more beneficial to the world than poetry, or have found it easier to reach conclusions about prose and particularly about the novel." All four of the laureates in English in the last two decades are indeed novelists—though Beckett is better known as a dramatist and is therefore the most original choice among them. Beckett is an original choice in another respect too. It has been contended by some critics that Alfred Nobel's will, with its "idealist" emphasis, has prevented some worthy writers in the past from being nominated: Theodore Dreiser, say, or Robinson Jeffers; and it is at least on record that Ezra Pound, a writer high on the list of nonwinners, when asked jokingly in the twenties by another nonwinner, Wyndham Lewis, whether Pound might not secure a Nobel for him, replied sarcastically, "NO, the Nobel Prize is for idealists."[3] Still, if the suspicion of some kind of liberal humanitarian bias in the literary awards were ever justified, it has been permanently laid to rest by the award to Beckett, since no more nihilistic writer is ever likely to gain a world audience than he. Golding too, at least in his best-known novel, *The Lord of the Flies,* has written comparably pessimistic—it might even be termed atavistic—fiction, demonstrating, according to his Nobel citation in 1983, that "evil springs from the depth of man himself." So perhaps one conclusion that can reasonably be drawn from the winners of the last twenty years is that idealism, at any rate of the patently uplifting variety (Pearl Buck may be the example most critics would cite, since she is otherwise hard to account for), is no longer a requirement for the Nobel Prize in Literature.

Another discernible trend of the last twenty years has an indirect bearing on my topic of English-language authors and the Nobel: four of the laureates since 1967 have been writers in exile, two Polish and two Russian, all of them now living in the United States and either writing in English or being translated immediately for English-speaking audiences. I refer to Aleksandr Solzhenitsyn (1970), Isaac Bashevis Singer (1978), Czesław Miłosz (1980), and most recent of all, Joseph Brodsky in 1987.[4] These writers may well be claimed as half-American—thus doubling the list of Nobel laureates in English—and since two of them, Miłosz and Brodsky, are poets, they help enrich the literary variety of the list as a whole. Miłosz's prose, especially his *Visions from San Francisco Bay,* and Brodsky's prose, especially the essays in his recent collection *Less Than One,* are written from the point of view of their adopted land as much as of their native countries, and they are eagerly read, as are Solzhenitsyn's accounts of the Soviet gulag and Singer's stories of the Warsaw ghetto, as contributions to American literature as much as to Polish or Russian literature. Brodsky was quoted as saying, in response to the news of his Nobel Prize: "I'm the happiest combination you can think of. I'm a Russian poet, an English essayist, and a citizen of the United States."[5] The Irish poet Seamus Heaney (who is also American half the year when he teaches at Harvard) congratulated Brodsky on his bilingualism, remarking wryly of the Russian poet that "in order further to impose upon English the strangeness and density of his imagining, he is now the official translator of his own lines."[6] Certainly the presence of so many foreign Nobel laureates in an English-speaking country is bound to enrich the native literary tradition, probably in unpredictable ways—as Beckett in Paris has given the French drama of the absurd an Irish flavor. Already, Solzhenitsyn, Singer, Miłosz, and Brodsky are as familiar to educated readers in America as any contemporary American writer would be—more familiar, probably than they can be to audiences in their native Poland and Russia, where the official disapproval of writers in exile, even if they are Nobel Prize winners, is bound to limit their outreach.

Part of the distinction of English-language literature's Nobel Prizes in the last two decades, I am thus convinced, comes from writers who enjoy bilingual audiences, not simply from writers whose native language is English. It may be they are harbingers of a more international tradition in literature generally, which the Nobel is uniquely situated to honor. If cosmopolitanism seems the order of the future, however, there is much nationalism and regionalism inherent in literary expression that will probably never die out. Indeed, if someone should ask me (happy chance!) to choose where the next Nobel Prizes might come from in the English-speaking world, I would think first of two fairly small regions which have produced some of the finest literature in this century: Ireland and the American South. True, Yeats and Shaw and Beckett are Irish writers who have already won Nobels, but there are at least two more Irish writers today whose work has a growing international reputation: Seamus Heaney in poetry[7] and Brian Friel in drama. True too, Faulkner was a Southern writer and a Nobel laureate, but of living writers in English, surely none is more deserving of the honor at present than Robert Penn Warren, who has received every other conceivable prize for his poetry, his novels, and his essays and who in his eighties is as prolific as ever, a man of letters in the grand style.[8] I would also suggest that, with his new novel *A Summons to Memphis,* Peter Taylor has crowned a career in fiction that arguably deserves something higher than the Pulitzer and Hemingway prizes he has won, leaving only one possibility, the Nobel. As Eliot put it in 1948, Nobel Prizes are a recognition that "an author's reputation has passed the boundaries of his own country and his own language" and is worthy of a world audience; and though there are never many such authors to choose from, there have been a surprisingly large number of them in the twentieth century—most of whom, unfortunately, have not received the Nobel Prize. As Hemingway, one of the lucky ones, acknowledged in his Nobel acceptance speech in 1954, "No writer who knows the great writers who did not receive the prize can accept it other than with humility."[9]

Though it is certainly presumptuous to say what writer in English most deserves future recognition by the Swedish Academy, I would count it a guarantee of literary quality if the next Nobel Prize went to Heaney or Friel, Warren or Taylor. If I were asked, however, not to choose but to bet on the next Nobel Prize recipient in English, I would not put my money on either an Irishman or a male Southerner, but on a woman—say, Margaret Atwood in Canada or Nadine Gordimer in South Africa, or a black writer such as Toni Morrison in the United States, or even, with a little bit of luck, on that thoroughbred of living women writers, Eudora Welty.[10] To predict that a woman will win the next prize is to admit that the Nobel is often political and social as well as literary, and any honest survey would have to concede that fact; still, I would maintain that its emphasis has often been on the literary rather than the political or social side, and I would at least hold out the hope that, when the next Nobel Prize in Literature is announced for an English-speaking writer, he or she will be the kind of literary artist who, like some of the writers of the past, is not only honored by but brings honor to the prize.

Notes

1. *Nobel Lectures: Literature, 1901-1967,* Horst Frenz, ed., London, Elsevier, 1969, p. 435.

2. Riggan's article is in *WLT* 55:3 (Summer 1981), pp. 399-405; the quoted passage is from p. 405.

3. *Pound/Lewis: The Correspondence of Ezra Pound and Wyndham Lewis,* Timothy Materer, ed., New York, New Directions, 1985, p. 161.

4. On these four authors, see the following: on Solzhenitsyn, *BA* 45:1 (Winter 1971), pp. 7-18, and *WLT* 53:4 (Autumn 1979), pp. 573-84; on Singer, *WLT* 53:2 (Spring 1979), pp. 197-201; on Miłosz, *WLT* 51:4 (Autumn 1977), pp. 570-71, and 52:3 (Summer 1978), pp. 357-425; on Brodsky, *WLT* 57:2 (Spring 1983), pp. 214-18.

5. Quoted by Francis X. Clines in "A Writer Reflects on the Fortunes of Literature and the Russian Language," *New York Times,* 23 October 1987, p. 8.

6. Seamus Heaney, "Brodsky's Nobel: What the Applause Was About," *New York Times Book Review,* 8 November 1987, p. 63.

7. On Heaney, see *WLT* 57:3 (Summer 1983), pp. 365-69.

8. On Warren, see *WLT* 55:4 (Autumn 1981), pp. 626-27.

9. *Nobel Lectures,* p. 501.

10. On Atwood, see *WLT* 60:1 (Winter 1986), pp. 47-49; on Gordimer, *WLT* 52:4 (Autumn 1978), pp. 533-38, 59:3 (Summer 1985), pp. 343-46, and 62:1 (Winter 1988), pp. 76-77; on Welty, *WLT* 51:4 (Autumn 1977), pp. 579-80.

Ralph Gunther (essay date 1993)

SOURCE: Gunther, Ralph. "If a Traveler Comes to Florence—" In *Giants in Their Field: An Introduction to the Nobel Prizes in Literature,* pp. 1-25. Potomac, Md.: Scripta Humanistica, 1993.

[*In the following excerpt, Gunther presents a biographical survey of some of the Nobel Prize in Literature winners, focusing on their diversity.*]

If a traveler comes to Florence, to the graceful city in the hills of Tuscany where the poet Giosuè Carducci first went to school, he may simply stroll along a riverside street and wind up in a café, unaware of the artistic treasures around him. Or he may visit a priceless collection of paintings by Titian, Raphael, Tintoretto and Veronese, or go to the Galleria dell'Accademia and gaze at the magnificent 'DAVID' by Michelangelo—and suddenly fall under the spell of the birthplace of the Renaissance! Of course, a traveler may never reach Florence. In fact, hundreds of millions of people will never set foot in that city. They will never stand in the Piazza del Duomo, one early morning, to watch the rise of a new day over the Cathedral of Santa Maria del Fiore. They will never walk across the Ponte

Vecchio, the covered bridge over the Arno River, in search of the famous Florentine museum, the Pitti Palace. They will never step into the Church of San Lorenzo to admire its sensuous carvings. Many millions of people will never even travel to Italy—or to France, or to Spain, or to Poland, or to any other country in the Old World with a rich history and with deeply embedded traditions. Thus they will miss the feeling, so perceptible in Florence, that up to the time of the Renaissance human beings were only part of a crowd, not the developers of a sense of their own individuality.

But they need not be the poorer for it.

They may, one day, come across an exceptional book about Italy. If fortunate, they will chance upon a novel by Grazia Deledda, or upon the lyrical poems by Salvatore Quasimodo, imbued with a deep Mediterranean sensitivity. In time, they may even come under the spell of books which will whisk them to other countries, perhaps the great stories by Mikhail Sholokhov about Russia, or by Pearl Buck about China; or the colorful tales by Rudyard Kipling about India. And when they stumble over a little boy and his donkey wandering through the countryside of Andalusia, in southern Spain, a walking tour narrated with infinite charm by the poet Juan Ramón Jiménez, they will realize that one of the most creative ways of bringing the past into the present, of capturing the mood of an era, is reading. A skill in existence for over two thousand years, it allows the mind to explore the works of those who express themselves with beauty of thought and language. It also allows the mind to discover that people whose sightseeing is inward can in themselves find all they need for transport, and that such is a marvelous mode of journeying. Not just to learn that Florence was founded scant decades after the mass migration of Germanic tribes all over Europe in search of a new homeland, a trek that brought them up against Rome and the Consul Gaius Marius; or that twenty centuries later, a young author, Hermann Hesse, following his first visit to the city on the Arno, would suddenly become aware of his dislike for modern civilization. But to realize that there are other treasures in the world, treasures equal to those in the galleries of Florence and far more within reach of everyone: the works of the great masters of the pen!

Some of these works, written by men and women who achieved immense stature in the field of letters, may contain the true account of a person's life. In 1906, Winston Churchill brought out a two-volume biography of his father, Lord Randolph Churchill, which became a landmark in British biographical literature. The biographies of Michelangelo and Gandhi, among others, sprung from the pen of Romain Rolland, throw a special light on the author's mind as a pacifist. Yasunari Kawabata kept a diary describing his grandfather's final days, and the effect of this on his own mind—a stunning first literary achievement for a sixteen-year-old. Ivan Bunin published a novelized autobiography, *The Well of Days,* a moving evocation of his youth in the land of the Czars, which became the key to his Nobel Prize in 1933. Pearl Buck, famous for her novel *The Good Earth,* wrote the biographies of her parents, the missionary pair in China, which became paramount in the Swedish Academy's decision to award her the Nobel Prize in 1938. André Gide's confessional literature, descriptions of the conflict between desire and restraint, led to illuminating meditations on life, and to the Nobel Prize in 1947. Eyvind Johnson wrote a four-volume masterpiece, *The Novel About Olof,* considered one of the finest examples of the Swedish semi-autobiographical genre; it brought him the Nobel Prize in 1974.

Other works may contain the account of particular streams of thought, or the account of real happenings in the life of a people. Romain Rolland wrote a powerful essay of pacifist protest, *Above the Battle Field,* which led to his Nobel Prize in the middle of the First World War; Rudolf Eucken, already a Nobel laureate, famous for his stand on the meaning and value of life, dedicated his latest philosophical work, *The Representatives of German Idealism,* to his two sons who were fighting in that war. Winston Churchill wrote a superb history of the Second World War, which gained him the Nobel Prize in 1953. By that time, Jean-Paul Sartre had published his most important work, *Being and Nothingness,* an impressive essay on Existentialism, the philosophical movement which stresses individual existence and holds that man is totally free and responsible for his acts—Albert Schweitzer, who had exercised that freedom and assumed responsibility for the needy in the jungles of Africa, accepted a Nobel Prize; his nephew, Jean-Paul Sartre, would decline one.

But most works in literature are fictional narratives. Combined with poetry and drama, they are the backbone of all writings of an imaginary character which possess permanent value. Selma Lagerlöf's classic, *The Wonderful Adventures of Nils,* the story of a little boy who flies on gooseback over Sweden at a time when aviation was still experimental, captivated people all over the world, and led to her Nobel Prize in 1909. *The Forsyte Saga,* a trilogy by John Galsworthy, became so popular that it was continued in two further trilogies; it won him the Nobel Prize in 1932. *The Thibaults,* another sensational, multi-volume family chronicle by Roger Martin du Gard, was crowned with the Nobel Prize five years later—even before completion! Naguib Mahfouz finished his most celebrated work, the *Cairo Trilogy,* in the early 1950s; considered a sort of Egyptian *Forsyte Saga,* the first volume of this trilogy, *Palace Walk,* appeared in America, in English translation, only in the winter of 1990, when the two daughters of the author had already traveled to Stockholm to accept the Nobel Prize in their father's name. Gabriel García Márquez had been thinking about *One Hundred Years of Solitude* for more than twenty years when, suddenly, the elusive plot took shape in his mind, the pieces of the story fell into place; he was driving through the mountains of México at the time, to Acapulco, and very likely had not the vaguest idea that he, too, would be invited to Stockholm as a result of it. Today the titles of novels like *The Magic Mountain, The Silent Don, The Grapes of Wrath,*

For Whom the Bell Tolls, Doctor Zhivago and *Lord of the Flies* may be as familiar to readers as the names of theatre plays like *The Blue Bird, Six Characters in Search of an Author, Desire Under the Elms, Murder in the Cathedral, Waiting for Godot* and *Kongi's Harvest,* the latter wildly applauded at the first 'Festival of Negro Arts' held in Dakar, Sénégal—all created by authors who, together with a number of poets, received the Nobel Prize in Literature and attained international renown.

The history of the prizes reads like a compendium of fairy tales. The first German winner of the Nobel Prize in Literature was born under Danish sovereignty and owed allegiance to King Frederick VI of Denmark. When the next Danish monarch, King Christian VIII, gave him a purse to travel to Italy and study Latin inscriptions, he unwittingly contributed to the creation of a masterpiece, the monumental *History of Rome.* The first British winner of the Nobel Prize in Literature was born in India, far from the island from where Queen Victoria ruled her empire. He produced a body of work, on the Asian subcontinent and in North America—poems, stories, and two magnificent 'Jungle Books'—which spread his fame through the English-speaking world even before he reached the age of thirty. The first Greek winner of the Nobel Prize in Literature was born in Asia Minor, not far from the place where Cassandra, a king's daughter, had trembled at the sight of a wooden horse. He had to flee the threat of Turkish domination when only fourteen, but he carried with him the spirit of Homer, and later wrote a series of related poems, based on episodes and peoples from the Odyssey, which was hailed as a work of art along the coasts of the Mediterranean and beyond. The first Israeli winner of the Nobel Prize in Literature was born in Galicia, a multi-ethnic province in eastern Europe, then part of the dual Austro-Hungarian monarchy. He emigrated to Palestine, a land under Turkish domination, while still in his teens. When he reached Jaffa, he wrote a major tale which he signed for the first time with the pen name that would make him famous as one of the outstanding figures in modern Hebrew fiction. Thus Theodor Mommsen, Rudyard Kipling, George Seferis, and S. Y. Agnon came into prominence in the field of letters. Eventually, the birthplace of George Seferis fell to the Turks and was renamed Izmir, the name it had lost many decades earlier. But Palestine was wrested from the Turks by the British, who pledged to support a Jewish national homeland there; it became the State of Israel.

What is the Nobel Prize?

It is the prize of all prizes! Conceived to honor the great minds of the world, it comes from a peninsula washed by chilly seas—a peninsula which Eyvind Johnson, not yet ready for *The Novel About Olof,* would leave as a stowaway on a ship, and which Bertrand Russell, well-known for *The Principles of Mathematics,* would have to swim to if he wanted to live. Awarded on the eve of winters, the prize consists of a gold medal, a diploma bearing a citation, and a sum of money. Its first appearance goes back to the year 1901, the year in which Rudyard Kipling published *Kim.* And like *Kim,* the magnificent story of a boy who grows up in India, the prize has no equal.

To determine the origin of that prize, one has to turn to northern Europe in the nineteenth century. One man, Alfred Bernhard Nobel, was responsible for its inception. Born in Stockholm, on October 21, 1833—when Theodor Mommsen was already close to sixteen—he spent the first years of his life in Sweden. When he was four, his father moved to Finland, then to Russia. Five years later, the boy and the rest of the family joined him in St. Petersburg; there he would be tutored privately, become proficient in languages, and acquire a suitable education. When he was seventeen, he began to travel and to sojourn in other countries. From his father he inherited a talent for invention, on his own he developed an affinity for literature. In time, his attention turned to chemistry: he invented dynamite and blasting gelatine! Then he produced explosives and detonators and, before long, became a successful industrialist and immensely wealthy. There were several accidental explosions, one of which caused the death of his brother Emil, aged twenty-one. Inevitably, the military use of his inventions came about. He had always thought that his explosives, by their very destructiveness, would help prevent wars, and he began to view mankind with pessimism. He came to admire Herbert Spencer, the British writer on education who adopted the Darwinian theory and built a philosophy based on evolution as the ultimate principle in the universe. He never married. When he died on the Italian Riviera, in 1896, he had made the provision for an extraordinary prize, a prize to be given annually to those who during the preceding year had conferred 'the greatest benefit on mankind'. Later called the Nobel Prize, he asked that it be divided into five equal parts: one for the most outstanding work of an idealistic tendency in the field of literature, one for the most important discovery in physiology or medicine, one for the most important discovery or invention in the field of physics, one for the most important chemical discovery or improvement, and one for the best work of fraternity among nations, including the abolition or reduction of armies and the holding and promoting of peace congresses. In a will written in his own hand, he requested that his capital be invested in safe securities, and that it constitute a fund, the interest of which should be distributed annually in the form of prizes in these fields. It would take several years to work out the stipulations of that will. He expressly wished that the nationality of the candidates be disregarded, so that the most worthy, whether Scandinavian or not, would be able to receive the prize.

The first winner of the Nobel Prize in Literature was the French poet René-François-Armand Prudhomme, better known as Sully-Prudhomme. A dictionary of world authors, published in France in 1984, closes a brief entry on him with the astonishing remark: "Who remembers that he was, in 1901, the first Nobel Prize in Literature?" Covering a period of more than nine decades, that prize has since been awarded more than 80 times, spanning nationalities from more than 30 countries and original works written in more than 20 languages. The most coveted of prizes, summarized by a former President of the Royal Swedish Academy of Sciences as 'the highest recognition of intellect that can be bestowed on a man or woman', its recipients—novelists, poets, playwrights, philosophers and historians—are often spoken of as members of the most exclusive 'Club' in the world. A lot of people may not remember Sully-Prudhomme today. Perhaps none but a handful of scholars and the odd dilettante know that he turned to prose-writing only at the end of his life; but to many he is still the shy poet who wrote "Le vase brisé," a beautiful poem about a broken vase, and the young man who made a remarkable translation of Lucretius into French verse. The announcements of the winners of the Nobel Prize are made in Stockholm, in the fall, and are the culmination of intense expectations worldwide. The prize in literature, as well as the prizes in physiology or medicine, in physics, in chemistry and, more recently, in the economic sciences, is presented by the King of Sweden in the Concert Hall in Stockholm. The peace prize, the only Nobel Prize given in Oslo, is presented by the Chairman of the Norwegian Nobel Committee in the Assembly Hall of the University of Oslo, in the presence of the King of Norway and the royal family. These ceremonies, which take place every year on December 10, are glittering social events in both cities.

The early years of the Nobel laureates contain their own measure of importance. Some were born into great wealth, others saw the light of day in great poverty. Some earned degrees as a matter of course, others followed the paths of education by the sweat of their brows. W. B. Yeats received his first formal instruction when many of his peers were already school-wise; his father first gave him lessons at home. Some disliked their schools with a passion: Maurice Maeterlinck spoke of his stay at the Collège de Sainte-Barbe as 'seven years of tyranny', and Gerhart Hauptmann described his years at the Realschule in Breslau as 'a time of everlasting toothache'; at Cheltenham College in England, Patrick White spent 'four detestable years of his life'; in the Balkans, Ivo Andrić called his high school 'a wasteland'—Some had schooling that was scant beyond belief, but they managed to draw on personal reserves of willpower and determination and, in time, to become self-educated and vastly knowledgeable. A sizable number would publish their works under names different from those received at birth. José Echegaray, the first author from the Iberian Peninsula to become a Nobel laureate, began his writing career with books about geometry and thermodynamics, hardly the subjects from which literature is made; an engineer by profession, he later wrote his first neo-Romantic plays under the pseudonym JORGE HAYASECA, and became one of the most popular playwrights in the history of the Spanish Theatre. Karl Gjellerup, one of two authors from the Danish island of Sjaelland to win a Nobel Prize, published his first novel under the pseudonym EPIGONOS—and studied watercolor in Rome, stepping into the footprints of a poet from Sweden, Verner von Heidenstam, who had studied watercolor there before him. Hermann Hesse's *Demian,* which became a household word with every generation following 'the war to end all wars', saw its maiden print under the pseudonym EMIL SINCLAIR; although the *Boston Transcript* called it 'a nightmare of abnormality, the crazed dream of a paranoiac', its place in the line of great German novels could never be shaken. A few authors adopted the names of the land they lived on as children: HAMSUN, KARLFELDT, SILLANPÄÄ, LAXNESS are actually place names, the names of farms and homesteads; they originated the pen names Knut Hamsun, Erik Karlfeldt, Frans Sillanpää and Halldór Laxness, symbols of excellence in world literature. One name change was an accident: the misspelling of Stanislas Rejment's name on a Russian document, when he was sixteen, led to Wladyslaw Reymont, the name that would make him famous as the author of *The Peasants,* one of the finest tetralogies to come out of Poland. When a spokesman for the Swedish Academy announced Ricardo Eliecer Neftalí Reyes Basoalto as the winner of the 1971 Nobel Prize in Literature, the audience sat mystified, thinking that an obscure person had been chosen for the prestigious prize. Then the speaker, having made a pause, added with a smile: "—better known as Pablo Neruda", and everybody burst into applause upon hearing the familiar name. A pseudonym, the name had first been used in a poetry contest in the south of Chile, when the aspiring poet was fifteen. Fifty-two years later, by then renowned, the poet's residence was the Chilean Embassy in Paris, and his poems were read on every continent. Another Latin American, Miguel Angel Asturias, whose residence was the Guatemalan Embassy in Paris, had won the Nobel Prize four years earlier; the Swedish Academy had announced his laureateship on his birthday. The two ambassadors were friends, and had written a book together; they had also known conflict with political leaders, and had tasted exile.

The status of belonging to a country held significance for a number of Nobel laureates: loss of citizenship, the acquisition of a new one, the regaining of an old one were their lot. The first Russian exile, Ivan Bunin, who spent the final decades of his life in France, is sometimes referred to as French, though no proof of his having asked for that nationality is apparent. Saint-John Perse, born on an island in the Caribbean, and Claude Simon, born on an island in the Indian Ocean, were French citizens; so was Albert Camus, born on the African rim of the Mediterranean. Patrick White, a fourth-generation Australian, was born in London. Henri Bergson, who was born in Paris, was a British citizen; he applied for French citizenship only when he completed his 'baccalauréat' at the Lycée Condorcet, the school where some time later Jean-Paul Sartre would teach. Thomas Mann, who in the 1930s became a Czech citizen and in the 1940s an American citizen, is universally known as a German writer; he spent his last years in Zürich, the city where Theodor Mommsen had started the *History of Rome.* Elias Canetti and T. S. Eliot became British citizens: the former, born on the eastern Balkan Peninsula by the Black Sea, is widely considered a Bulgarian; the latter, born in America, is only spoken of as a Briton. In the 1970s, within a time span of twenty-one months, two authors were thrown out of Russia, Joseph Brodsky and Aleksandr Solzhenitsyn, one on his way to a Nobel laureateship, the other already there. Stateless, they came to America, to the country whose next four winners of the Nobel Prize in Literature were in for a rare common denominator: they would be foreign-born, and their mother tongues would not be English!

Progress, with its relentless element of change, has left deep traces in the twentieth century. Its effect on human creativity, and on the development of nations, may never be fully measured by present-day generations. Provençal, the language in which the first cultivated vernacular lyric poetry of Europe had been written, reached the edge of extinction. The use of the telephone did away with much of spontaneous letter writing. The advent of television brought a new, passive quality to the life styles of many people, and reshaped the reading habits of the young. Jet travel made the crossing of continents as easy as taking a bus to a destination a few miles down the road—albeit not with the same spirit of adventure which little Nils Holgersson had experienced from the back of a goose. When Gabriela Mistral, a girl not yet in her teens, stood for the first time in front of the Pacific Ocean, in total awe, the Chilean skies were not yet rent by airplane engines. Did she sense that she would never follow the sun across that ocean? Was her young mind already playing with the sound of words, with rhythmic sequences? She could hardly have known that her future was tied to children, and that this would one day anger the followers of Generalissimo Franco in war-torn Spain; or that a young artist from Romania would one day proudly illustrate a book of hers. What did Harry Martinson think, a boy just in his teens, when he stood by the Kattegat and caught his first view of the schooner 'Willy', the ship that would take him away as a cabin boy? Did the forerunners of poetry course through his mind, or the years of intercontinental vagabondage which beckoned on the horizon? Was he already the holder of beliefs that would make him run to the defense of a small country which had suddenly come under attack from a powerful neighbor? He could hardly have known that he would one day be invited, like the South American girl who had gazed at her own ocean, to stand before the King of Sweden and receive a Nobel Gold Medal. What did the German Consul in Geneva think when he learned that Romain Rolland refused the Goethe Medal, a great honor from the city of Frankfurt? In a letter addressed to him, in the spring of 1933, the French pacifist and Nobel laureate wrote that he could not accept an honor from a government which allowed the crushing of rights and the proscription of the Jews. Shortly thereafter, Hitler issued a decree forbidding German citizens in future to accept a Nobel Prize. It is not difficult to imagine what Aleksandr Solzhenitsyn thought, in the spring of 1978, when the American press reacted to his Harvard Commencement address by defending the 'decadent' qualities of the West as the price for freedom; the social erosion that had begun in the cities in freedom-loving America had not merited a newspaper outcry yet. But it will forever be a matter of speculation what Ernest Hemingway, a correspondent in several wars, would have thought of women in the 1980s fighting for admission in an all-male military academy at West Point.

When Alfred Bernhard Nobel affixed his signature to his will in Paris, in 1895—three quarters of a century before Pablo Neruda arrived in that city as the Ambassador of Chile—dynamite had been used to blast open the oil fields of Baku. Dynamite had also been used to blast a tunnel through the Alps, to blast a canal across a stretch of Greece, and to blast people into oblivion in the Franco-Prussian War of 1870-1871, the war from which a young Pole, the brother of Henryk Sienkiewicz, never returned. The Swedish inventor, to whom war was 'the horror of horrors', was to think in vain about the invention of a device with such powers of destruction that wars could be stopped forever. Five years after it was written, and following innumerable discussions, painstaking research, and thorough planning, the feasibility of implementing that will was accepted by the prize-awarding bodies. Early in the summer of 1900, King Oscar II of Sweden announced the creation of the Nobel Foundation, a nongovernment organization, which would be responsible for administering the considerable funds of the Swedish inventor's fortune, and of safeguarding the financial basis of the prizes. The task of selecting the winners would involve the most careful scrutiny by the members of two ACADEMIES and of one NOBEL ASSEMBLY in Sweden, and by the members of one NOBEL COMMITTEE in Norway. The first prizes were awarded the following year, in 1901, on December 10, the fifth anniversary of Alfred Bernhard Nobel's death. In time, as if in response to a guest from another era, two atom bombs exploded in a populated archipelago in the Pacific, and people suddenly began to wonder about the unbroken succession of civilization.

The twentieth century is often called the 'Century of Violence'. As the last of its ten decades begins its journey through time, it is unlikely that many Nobel laureates—or for that matter the millions of people who use a pen every day and do not receive a prize for their labors—will find fault with that denomination. Two of the Nobel Prize winners in Literature ended their lives by their own hand, one in the Far East, the other in the American Far West; a third was killed in an automobile accident in France. In 1918, while the First World War was still raging, Anatole France predicted that it carried the seeds of three or four equally horrible wars. Sir Rabindranath Tagore surrendered his knighthood the following year, in protest against the shooting of four hundred unarmed demonstrators at Amritsar, in northern India. Arson destroyed the home of S. Y. Agnon in Europe; years later, rioters would ravage his home in the Middle East. In China, Pearl Buck narrowly escaped death when Communist forces took Nanking and began to hunt down foreigners. Ernest Hemingway was severely wounded in one world war, Heinrich Böll in another; in between, Camilo José Cela was wounded in the Spanish Civil War, the war which saw the Madrid home of Vicente Aleixandre bombed out before the city surrendered. In Paris, in a peaceful street, a bored panhandler pushed a knife into Samuel Beckett's chest, only just missing the heart; in the same city, the apartment of Jean-Paul Sartre would be blown up by right-wing terrorists. During the Second World War, when men of letters became involved in the Résistance, Czeslaw Milosz, who lived in Warsaw, wrote under the name JAN SYRUC, Albert Camus, who lived in Paris, under the names ALBERT MATHE and BAUCHART; in spite of precautions, the latter barely escaped being caught by the Gestapo at least once. Nazi hoodlums roughed up Pablo Neruda in Cuernavaca, México. In Florence, the Fascists kept Eugenio Montale under surveillance; in Bergamo, the birthplace of Donizetti, Salvatore Quasimodo landed in prison. Further north, the relatives of Nelly Sachs were quietly murdered; while she was being saved from certain death by a Nobel laureate whom she would never meet, Sigrid Undset had to hide from machine-gunning planes in the snow fields of Norway: both women reached Sweden—and sanctuary—after many hardships, in the ninth month of the war, neither aware of the plight of the other. George Seferis, one of the first intellectuals to openly criticize the dictatorship of the 'Colonels' in Greece, became the victim of official harassment and vilification in the last years of his life. In her country on the southern tip of Africa, Nadine Gordimer was labeled a very disloyal citizen for her writings on the theme of 'apartheid'. At the time of the Olympics in México, the willful shooting of Mexican student demonstrators, sanctioned by the government, caused Octavio Paz to register strong protests and to resign from his post as Ambassador of México to India. In his homeland on the south coast of West Africa, Wole Soyinka received death threats for defending the right of an author to have his work published. Violence and irreverence for life were no less evident in the previous century: Henrik Pontoppidan, wide-eyed, had watched foreign armies march into his native Jutland when only six; Winston Churchill, freshly out of Sandhurst, with battle cries from India and Africa still to ring in his ears, had first been shot at on a sparkling island in the Caribbean.

Yet, the stand taken by the Nobel Prize winners in Literature in the face of violations of rights, in the twentieth century and earlier, can only be called an endorsement of peace. As the clouds of war sailed over Europe, Carl Spitteler, whose element was the mythical epic, wrote a politically influential tract on neutrality. Henryk Sienkiewicz, in Switzerland for the purpose of organizing help for the Polish towns and villages that were being destroyed in the First World War, made a famous appeal to the civilized world on behalf of his country. Thomas Mann gave a courageous speech in Berlin, asking the German people to resist the power build-up of the Nazis; before long, he was an exile. André Gide brought about legal reforms which led to the curbing of industrial concessions in the colonies; in a public debate in 1935, he emphasized the essential relationship of his literary campaigns with oppressed peoples or races, or with human instincts. In the same year, François Mauriac condemned Mussolini's assault on Ethiopia. Pär Lagerkvist wrote a play decrying Fascism. Romain Rolland worked unceasingly for the improvement of relations between nations: his home in Switzerland was visited by world leaders. Jaroslav Seifert wrote poems about Prague which became an inspiration to every Czech patriot during the German occupation of central Europe. Nelly Sachs, a refugee in Sweden, wrote the awe-inspiring poetry which called attention to the soul of her people, a people almost annihilated in the Second World War. In America, in the 1960s, Saul Bellow served on an ad hoc committee aimed at ending the war in Vietnam. Prose works by Heinrich Böll became devastating attacks on the futility of war. Pablo Neruda traveled to Peking in the name of the World Peace Council to hand the INTERNATIONAL PEACE PRIZE to Mme Sun Yat-sen, the wife of the first President of China. Pearl Buck, who had grown up in China, established a foundation to assist fatherless, and often stateless, half-American children throughout Asia. Gabriela Mistral made the first global appeal for funds for the poor children of the world, and helped in the creation of the United Nations Children's Fund, or UNICEF. Gabriel García Márquez served on a tribunal which investigated the abuse of human rights in Latin America; he founded a human rights organization called 'HABEAS', in México. Naguib Mahfouz openly approved the 1979 Treaty between Egypt and Israel, unmindful that several Arab countries would henceforth prohibit the sales of his books. Aleksandr Solzhenitsyn assigned proceeds from the sales of *The Gulag Archipelago* to help families of imprisoned dissidents in the Soviet Union. Bertrand Russell, just months away from his ninetieth birthday, was handed a jail sentence and served time in prison for participating in a 'BAN-THE-BOMB' demonstration in London—the same year in which Jean-Paul Sartre's apartment was blown up in Paris!

When Egypt and Israel agreed to end the state of war which had existed between them for nearly thirty years, the leaders of both countries became the recipients of the Nobel Peace Prize. At present, the Nobel Prize is given in six fields. For each field there is a Nobel Committee, totalling five Swedish committees and one Norwegian committee. The Swedish Academy appoints the committee for literature. The Karolinska Institute of Stockholm appoints the committee for physiology or medicine. The Royal Swedish Academy of Sciences appoints three committees, one each for physics, chemistry and economics; the latter was added in 1968, when the Bank of Sweden instituted a prize in the economic sciences, a prize first awarded in 1969. The Norwegian Parliament, or 'Storting', appoints the committee for peace. The regulations governing that committee date from 1905, the year in which the political union between Sweden and Norway came to an amicable end. Each Nobel Committee is made up of five members, and is free to avail itself of advice from experts and specialists anywhere in the world.

A number of creations of the Nobel laureates were set to music, others were immortalized on the screen. Films based on such creations have won many prizes at national and international film festivals. The talking picture in which Greta Garbo's voice was first heard was *Anna Christie*, the screen version of the play for which Eugene

O'Neill had received a Pulitzer Prize. Several poems by Odysseus Elytis found expression in the catching melodies of Míkis Theodhorákis of Greece. Works by Frédéric Mistral, Maurice Maeterlinck and Gerhart Hauptmann, to mention but a few, led to the operas *Mireille, Pelléas and Mélisande* and *The Sunken Bell,* cherished by opera lovers around the world. Musicians sometimes intervened directly in the lives of distinguished authors: when Aleksandr Solzhenitsyn was hounded by his Russian detractors, cellist Mstislav Rostropovich gave him shelter in his 'dacha' near Moscow. Bernard Shaw and T. S. Eliot sparked musicals which were acclaimed by millions! In February 1941, Maurice Maeterlinck, a refugee from the war in Europe, became the guest of the city of Philadelphia, and for the first time attended a performance of *Pelléas and Mélisande,* the opera he had persistently refused to see for almost forty years. The first Italian sound film, *Song of Love,* was based on a story by Luigi Pirandello. However, adaptations of the literary productions of the Nobel Prize winners were not limited to films or music. A novel by Selma Lagerlöf was adapted for the stage by Gerhart Hauptmann, and received a memorable première in Berlin under the direction of Max Reinhardt. William Faulkner's novel *Requiem for a Nun* was rewritten for the stage by Albert Camus, and premièred in Paris in September 1956; in the same month, an editorial board in Moscow, unwilling to recognize a masterpiece, rejected Boris Pasternak's manuscript of *Doctor Zhivago,* the work which would then be smuggled to Italy. Hermann Hesse's novel *Narcissus and Goldmund,* an adventure for the senses and the spirit, was made suitable for dance and became the narrative ballet *Equinox*; commissioned for the Pennsylvania Ballet, its world première took place in Philadelphia—just steps away from where Maurice Maeterlinck had watched a play of his unfold as an opera.

Some of the creations of the Nobel Prize winners in Literature produced effects of a different kind: they failed to find favor with people who, occasionally, were in position to decide their fate. Thus several of their writings were placed on the Vatican 'INDEX' of Forbidden Literature; the act of reading a book listed there, or part of it, excluded a Roman Catholic from his Church with absolute finality. In 1909, a Joint Select Committee on Stage Censorship declared all the plays by Bernard Shaw to be 'conscientiously immoral'. In 1940, a Supreme Court judge annulled Bertrand Russell's teaching contract with the City College of New York, on the grounds that he was 'an advocate of immorality'; one of his books, *Marriage and Morals,* published earlier, favored 'temporary marriages' for college students—a concept too advanced, at the time, for parents of students in America, and elsewhere, who did not yet consider coed dormitories essential to higher education. Officials at Harvard were quick to announce that the Supreme Court decision would have no effect at Harvard, where the British philosopher was scheduled to give the 'William James Lectures' in the fall. In 1980, a school board in the State of Iowa banned *The Grapes of Wrath* from use in sophomore English classes, the remarkable work by John Steinbeck which a reviewer for the *London Times* had termed 'one of the most arresting novels of its time'. A landmark in American culture, the work had won a Pulitzer Prize, had received two Oscars for its 1940 film version, and had led to the Nobel Prize in Literature in 1962. That it would become a famous stage production, in England and in America—and win a Tony Award in 1990—could in all likelihood not have been foreseen by any school board. In the Germany of Adolf Hitler, huge bonfires settled the matter of disapproved books: the works of Upton Sinclair, Halldór Laxness, Lion Feuchtwanger, Sigrid Undset, Jack London, Thomas Mann, Jakob Wassermann, Ernest Hemingway, Sigmund Freud, and countless other writers, perished in flames. In 1986, during the spring of the southern hemisphere, more than 14,000 copies of the novel *Clandestine in Chile: The Adventures of Miguel Littín* were burned by the military authorities in the harbor of Valparaíso; at about the same time, its author, Gabriel García Márquez, was attending the political talks being held in Cuba in support of the Contadora Peace Process for Central America. Countries in which the works of the Nobel laureates, or of the Nobel laureates-to-be, were officially banned or censored, at one time or another, include Ireland, South Africa, Spain, Germany, the United States, Italy, Great Britain, Egypt, France, Chile, Russia, Guatemala and Nigeria. Joseph Brodsky, who had been jailed for his poetry while in his twenties, and whom the Swedish Academy announced as the winner of the Nobel Prize in Literature for 1987, may have expressed the thoughts of all book lovers when, in December of that year, he said: "There would be less grief in the world if leaders were chosen on basis of what they read rather than their political programs; as a form of moral insurance, literature is more dependable than system of beliefs or philosophical doctrine." Did he have an intuition of what the future held for the imprisoned playwright Václav Havel of Czechoslovakia? Or of the commitment which the novelist Mario Vargas Llosa was ready to make for Perú?

The nominations of candidates for the Nobel Prize are made by invitation only. The invitations are sent out in the last months of the year preceding the award. Every year a number of prominent people are invited to send in their nominations; those contacted, in countries throughout the world, include intellectuals, scholars, professors, members of academies, previous Nobel laureates, and individuals, or groups of people, foremost involved in peace activities. The invitations to submit proposals are strictly confidential, as are the names of the candidates proposed. The deadline for the proposals is FEBRUARY 1 of the year in which the prizes are to be given. On that day, the real toil of the Nobel Committees begins: the careful examination of each candidate's work, the collecting of information, the sifting of data, the writing of reports. By the time these tasks have been completed, usually in the summer or the early fall, several thousand people—among nominators, committee members, specialists, and consultants—will have participated in, or contributed to, the confidential evaluating process of the nominees. Then the reports and recommendations are sent to the prize-awarding bodies which have the right to make final decisions: the SWEDISH

ACADEMY (with 18 members), the ROYAL SWEDISH ACADEMY OF SCIENCES (with some 75 members), the NOBEL ASSEMBLY of the Karolinska Institute (with 50 members), and the NORWEGIAN NOBEL COMMITTEE (with 5 members), actually the committee elected by the 'Storting', the only Nobel Committee with the right to decide a prize by itself. . . .

[The] profiles of the Nobel laureates contain descriptions favoring the early years of their lives. Like brush strokes on a canvas, applied sparingly, they seek to capture the likeness of people whose presence in the world of letters goes far beyond the ordinary. Only two of the Nobel Prize winners in Literature were historians, fewer than half a dozen were philosophers. The majority were men and women whose literary productions place them firmly in the ranks of novelists, poets, and dramatists. The narratives of many of their works run the gamut from exciting to spellbinding. Jacinto Benavente's peasant tragedy, *The Passion Flower*, on its first visit across the North Atlantic, totalled more than 850 performances in America alone! Some 80% of the works of the Nobel laureates were written in languages other than English. Translations into English, or into languages other than the original, follow no pattern that is discernible. The English version of *L'Arrabbiata*, the work which established Paul Heyse as the creator of the modern psychological novella, appeared more than ten years after it was first published in Germany; on the other hand, *The Intelligent Woman's Guide to Socialism and Capitalism*, a piece of Bernard Shaw's expository prose, was translated into Yiddish by Hinde Esther Singer, the sister of Isaac Bashevis Singer, less than one year after its original publication in England. It is perhaps symbolic that in the feud between Islam and Christianity the *Cairo Trilogy* by Naguib Mahfouz, written in Arabic, was first translated into Hebrew, the language of Israel, and that both languages arise from a common source. Each biography is accompanied by a list of the author's more popular creations, and includes date of first publication and genre. Accuracy has been pursued to a fine point. Complete accuracy remains a matter of debate: errors of dating are repeated from one reference book to another, and mistakes will slip into even the most reputable of encyclopaedias. Rudyard Kipling's age on being awarded the Nobel Prize is frequently given as 42, when in reality it was 41. Joseph Brodsky is widely cited as the second youngest Nobel Prize in Literature, but his actual standing is sixth in line to that claim. And it seems to be accepted that the Nobel Prize to Romain Rolland was awarded in 1915, to Carl Spitteler in 1919, to Bernard Shaw in 1925, to Grazia Deledda in 1926, to Henri Bergson in 1927, and to William Faulkner in 1949—when neither author received the prize in those years!

The lives of the Nobel laureates are filled with a vibrancy that has shaped their course for more than one hundred seventy years. Theodor Mommsen, who was born in 1817, had a long and happy marriage to Marie Reimer and produced sixteen children; he won the Nobel Prize in 1902. Bjornstjerne Bjornson, who was born in 1832, had a celebrated career as an orator and was often referred to as 'the uncrowned king of Norway'; he won the Nobel Prize in 1903. However, the Nobel Prize in Literature was not awarded every year. On occasion, when there were not enough votes for a winner, the prize was put on reserve. In 1914, the dramatic change in the world situation made the Swedish Academy decide, for the first time, to omit the distribution of the prize entirely, a decision it would make six more times in the next twenty-nine years. During some of the war years, when the Nobel Prize was in fact given, no official ceremonies were held, either in Stockholm or in Oslo. Only one author made it to Sweden in those years, Frans Sillanpää of Finland. As the Second World War had already broken out, he avoided the danger of a sea trip across the Baltic. Instead, he took the long and hazardous route overland, around the Gulf of Bothnia; a journey which at intervals required his trekking through ice and snow, first along the Finnish coast, then along the coast of Sweden. When he finally reached Stockholm, the Swedish Academy honored him with a private dinner, at which time he was handed his prize. Less than five years later, William Golding sailed his rocket-launching craft to the coast of France for the D-Day invasion of Europe.

Alphabetic writing came into use for literary purposes in the middle of the seventh century B.C. Literary creations have influenced religious and secular affairs ever since. Today the written word is mankind's greatest legacy, and the Nobel Prize winners in Literature occupy an eminent place therein. In a world in which statements of faith in human values are being put to the test with bewildering frequency, Johannes Jensen's novel *The Long Journey* acquires new meaning: it is a magnificent, six-volume tale of the Darwinian theory, in which poetry, symbolism, and myth combine to produce a work of epic dimensions. T. S. Eliot thought that no art could be more stubbornly national than poetry, but myth, the indispensable element of timelessness, is equally part of the heritage of nations. The books written by the Nobel Prize winners in Literature are not always displayed prominently in bookstores or libraries, or even in schools, but many of them hold the key to a world of incredible adventure, a world which Isaac Bashevis Singer—who wrote in Yiddish, a language not supported by any government—was sure was only once removed from the true world.

A breathtaking world, action-packed, abundant in symbols, leading triumphantly to the power of one's own imagination.

A wondrous world, filled with distinct voices, created by weavers of tales whose molds were broken when they made them.

A stirring world, in which the works of the great masters of the pen, of late also Derek Walcott's, are guiding signals to modern consciousness—perhaps for as long as the green hills of Tuscany stand guard over the birthplace of the Renaissance.

Untouched by time, in Jerusalem, a sign in the street where an immigrant from Galicia once lived reads:

'QUIET, AGNON IS WRITING!'

Burton Feldman (essay date 2000)

SOURCE: Feldman, Burton. "The Nobel Prize in Literature." In *The Nobel Prize: A History of Genius, Controversy, and Prestige,* pp. 55-113. New York: Arcade Publishing, 2000.

[*In the following excerpt, Feldman presents a detailed overview of the winners, criteria, and limitations of the Nobel Prize in Literature.*]

For a portrait of what the Nobel Prize in Literature is not, one can't do better than Irving Wallace's novel *The Prize*. Published in 1962, it quickly became a best-seller and a hit movie, and no wonder, considering its sensational plot. The young, "lanky" author is dead drunk when he learns he has won the Nobel Prize. Embittered since his wife died, and a romantic rebel against social convention, he very reluctantly agrees to accept the award: he can use the money. But winning the Nobel Prize is the least of his triumphs in the book. In Stockholm he falls in love, plunges into a wildly complicated spy chase in which he singlehandedly unravels a plot to abduct a science laureate to the Soviet Union, and solves everything just as the stately Nobel ceremony itself gets under way. Even aside from such a farrago, the writer-hero is much too young to have won a literature Nobel—by the time they are chosen, most literary laureates are too old to chase anyone. But then, *The Prize* paints the Nobel ceremony and literature laureates as the exciting things that thrillers and Hollywood wish they were.

Some offended mutterings arose about Wallace's preposterous sensationalizing of the exalted Nobel ceremony. Certainly, no very wild things seem to happen there. The acme of exciting behavior was probably reached by the Norwegian novelist Knut Hamsun, who won the 1920 prize. Hamsun started drinking riotously the night of the ceremony, pulled the whiskers of an "elderly Nobel committee man," and then snapped his finger against the corset of his fellow Norwegian laureate Sigrid Undset (literature, 1928) and cried, "It sounds like a bell buoy!"[1]

If the Nobel in literature is not exactly a thriller like Wallace's novel, it might however be compared to a ghost story. At least, as the king bestows the medals, a great ghost compounded of all the great writers ignored by the Nobel haunts the festivities. No prizes went to Tolstoy or Ibsen or Joyce or Virginia Woolf or Rilke, to Wallace Stevens or Vladimir Nabokov or Paul Celan. To exclude such figures is like a Nobel Prize in Physics that passed over Einstein, Bohr, Heisenberg, and Feynman, just to start.

Indeed, the world's most prestigious literary award has become widely seen as a political one—a peace prize in literary disguise. For the Nobel judges, it is charged, art and social reform are inseparable. Writers indifferent to moral uplift like Nabokov imperil their chances. An exception or two, such as Samuel Beckett in 1969, proves the rule.

Writers of political taste disapproved by Nobel judges certainly risk being blackballed, as seems to have happened to Bertolt Brecht, André Malraux, Ezra Pound, and Jorge Luis Borges.

THE NOBEL LITERARY MUSEUM

Reading through the Nobel list across the century is a curious experience: one is apt to think more about those absent than present. From 1901 to 1945, the list is depressing. Of the forty laureates in that period (awards were omitted in some years), only Kipling, Hamsun, Yeats, Shaw, Mann, and Pirandello have held stature. Hauptmann and Maeterlinck were once esteemed. The others are largely unread or unreadable, such as Sully Prudhomme, José Echegaray and Frédéric Mistral, Henryk Sienkiewicz, Selma Lagerlöf, Paul Heyse, Romain Rolland, Verner von Heidenstam, Gjellerup and Pontoppidan, Carl Spitteler, the philosopher Rudolf Eucken (so forgotten that even philosophers are usually surprised he was a philosopher), Anatole France, Jacinto Benavente, Władyslaw Reymont, Grazia Deledda, Erik Karlfeldt, John Galsworthy, Ivan Bunin, Pearl Buck, Frans Sillanpää, J. V. Jensen.

In that same period, the Nobel judges ignored or rejected all of the following (a deep breath is advised before reading): Leo Tolstoy, Emile Zola, Mark Twain, Henry James, Henrik Ibsen, August Strindberg, Henry Adams, Thomas Hardy, Machado de Assis, Pérez Galdós, Joseph Conrad—and this is only the generation bridging 1900.

It takes a heroic blindness to miss everyone in so illustrious a list. But the Nobel committee managed to do as poorly in the next generation as well, missing or rejecting writers as towering as the century provides: Marcel Proust, Rilke, Joyce, Virginia Woolf, Gertrude Stein, Theodore Dreiser, D. H. Lawrence, Karel Čapek, Jaroslav Hašek, Willa Cather, Hugo von Hofmannsthal, Chaim Bialik, Miguel de Unamuno, George Santayana, José Ortega y Gasset, Alfred Döblin, Stefan George, Robert Musil, Karl Kraus, Arno Schmidt, H. G. Wells, Andrei Bely, Aleksandr Blok, Georges Bernanos, Fernando Pessoa, César Vallejo.[2]

After 1945 the Nobel committee began a sort of reparations campaign to honor neglected modernist pioneers. At long last, T. S. Eliot, Hemingway, François Mauriac, Juan Ramón Jiménez, and Boris Pasternak became laureates. Since about 1970 the prizes began to catch up with writers whose careers were still flourishing: Samuel Beckett, Pablo Neruda, Saul Bellow, Toni Morrison, Naguib Mahfouz, Derek Walcott, Seamus Heaney.

But again, great ghosts haunt the list. Since 1945 the Nobel Prize has denied (to list only the departed) Colette, Robert Frost, Wallace Stevens, W. H. Auden, William Carlos Williams, Anna Akhmatova, Hermann Broch, Bertolt Brecht, Giuseppe Ungaretti, Louis-Ferdinand Céline, Evelyn Waugh, Gunnar Ekelöf, Luis Cernuda, Hugh MacDiarmid, Ignazio Silone, Marguerite Yourcenar, Raymond Queneau, André Malraux, René Char, Yannis Ritsos, Jorge

Luis Borges, Paul Celan, Witold Gombrowicz, Philip Larkin, Jean Genet, Italo Calvino, Alberto Moravia, Thomas Bernhard, Eugène Ionesco, Primo Levi, Danilo Kiš.

"Old Age Pension Prizes"

When pioneers like T. S. Eliot or André Gide or Hemingway began to receive prizes, most were so famous that their prize seemed only an anticlimax. These and others were usually long past their productive years. Eliot wryly described the prize as a nail in an author's coffin. The critic Herbert Howarth put it as gravely: the Nobel prize is like "a deathmask on fulfilled grandeur."

But long-delayed prizes continue: the Spanish novelist Camilo José Cela was at last honored in 1989 at age 73, almost fifty years after the innovative work that won him the prize. Of laureates since 1984, the Czech poet Jaroslav Seifert was 83 years old when honored, the French writer Claude Simon 72, the Egyptian novelist Naguib Mahfouz 77, the Mexican poet Octavio Paz 76, the Polish poet Wisława Szymborska 73, the Portuguese novelist José Saramago 75. When the Northern Irish poet Seamus Heaney was honored at 56, he could seem positively boyish by comparison. The youngest laureate ever was Kipling back in 1907—at age forty-two.

Such long delays allow the Nobel judges to have their cake and eat it too, avoiding controversy yet claiming to honor boldness. Eliot in the 1920s and 1930s was a rebellious sort the Nobel then spurned. But by 1948 he had become venerable and mainstream, and his prize could seem an appeal to tradition against some of the new rebels—say, the French dramatist Jean Genet, whose plays mockingly pulled down all respectable social and sexual values, and who was never Nobelized.

Long delays have made laureates of some who happened to outlive their unhonored contemporaries, and thereby became stand-ins for them. Anders Österling, the permanent secretary of the Swedish Academy from 1941 to 1970, is supposed to have admitted that the Nobel Prize given to the Russian novelist Bunin in 1933 was "to pay off our consciences on Chekhov and Tolstoy."[3] The Nobel citation for Juan Ramón Jiménez (1956) says:

> This year's laureate is the last survivor of the famous Generation of 1898. . . . When the Swedish Academy renders homage to Juan Ramón Jiménez, it renders homage to an entire epoch in the glorious Spanish literature.

This generous homage to a past generation was in fact caused by earlier Nobel neglect of a group of writers who in 1898 set out to revive Spanish writing, Antonio and Manuel Machado, Ramón del Valle-Inclán, Miguel de Unamuno, the Nicaraguan Rubén Darío (then living in Spain), and Jiménez among them. Jiménez is an excellent poet. But making him a stand-in for a neglected generation renders his own honor ambiguous. Did he deserve the honor on his own, or because the others died ignored and he happened to live so long? He was seventy-five when honored.

The citation for the Greek George Seferis (Nobel 1963) says: "Now that Palamas and Sikelianos are dead, Seferis is today the representative Hellenic poet." Palamas lived until 1943, Sikelianos to 1951, and Kazantzakis to 1957, yet none was honored. To the living belong the spoils, when the Nobel feels it is time to reward a Greek poet?

Paul Valéry's Nobel Prize was delayed so often that his death "regretfully" intervened in 1945. The next French poet honored was Saint-John Perse (1960). But would Perse have won if Valéry hadn't died "too soon"? The citation to Perse tactfully did not mention Valéry explicitly but surely invoked that poet by its praise of Perse's "rhetorical tradition inherited from the classics." And here is the German-Swiss novelist-poet Hermann Hesse (1946), another stand-in. The citation: "Since the death of Rilke and [Stefan] George, he has been the foremost German poet of our time." In short, if either Rilke or George were then alive, Hesse would not have become the laureate. The Spanish poet Vicente Aleixandre (Nobel 1977) was similarly the proxy for the dead Lorca, Jorge Guillén, Rafael Alberti, and Luis Cernuda.

Faulkner's citation suggests that his prize was partly meant to ease the Nobel conscience for neglecting Joyce. "Side by side with Joyce—and perhaps even more so—Faulkner is the great experimentalist among twentieth-century novelists." (The *great* experimentalist? One wonders if the Nobel judges had taken a look at *Finnegans Wake*.) Beckett's prize in 1969 may also have been a gesture toward Joyce, who was Beckett's mentor.

Part of the reason for honoring Joseph Brodsky, the Russian émigré to the U.S., was as a stand-in for an entire generation ignored by Nobel judges—the great line of Russian poets from Aleksandr Blok to Osip Mandelstam, Marina Tsvetaeva, and especially Anna Akhmatova. Brodsky was Akhmatova's favorite young poet. Else why a prize so young, at age forty-seven, and soon?

As the list of laureates makes clear, the Nobel Prize in Literature is still far from being the global award it claims to be. Its prizes have repeatedly gone to writing in a few major European languages, primarily English, French, German, Spanish—not to mention fourteen prizes in the Scandinavian languages, one-seventh of all awarded. Literature in India has been honored only once—Tagore in 1913, which was really another prize in English, since it was awarded on the basis of a translation. No Chinese writer has ever won the prize, though two Japanese writers have become laureates, by the luck of superb translations. Arabic, which spans the world and has a rich literary tradition, won its first and only prize in 1988 (the Egyptian novelist Mahfouz). Nothing in the Bantu languages, or Turkish, or the Malayan group.

Is it possible that no Chinese writer has ever measured up to Nobel standards? And none in India since 1911? That only one writer in Arabic can be found? One can easily imagine that so great a Hebrew poet as Chaim Bialik (died 1934) was invisible to Stockholm. The fact is that the Swedish Academy lacks the linguistic competence needed for a truly international jury, which is not surprising. Perhaps only three or four of the greatest universities in the world have such resources. Unprepared to read fluently and directly in major and populous languages such as Chinese, Arabic, or Hindi, not to mention minor ones, the Nobel committee is overly dependent on translations, whose occurrence and quality are notoriously capricious. One would assume that Nobel judges would all be fluent readers of French. But it has been claimed that the French novelist Claude Simon's Nobel award (1985) gained immeasurably from a Swedish translation of all his work just before his prize.[4] And that the French poet Saint-John Perse won his prize only because of the Swedish diplomat Dag Hammarskjöld's enormous influence and tireless promoting.

The Nobel Prizes in science and peace are true international awards; the literature prize is not. Unless it soon moves beyond its familiar linguistic horizons, it may end up a glorified Pulitzer Prize. It treads a fine line here. If it dutifully starts distributing the prize around the globe, it can become less a literary than an international goodwill prize.

The Nobel seems at least to be trying to close the gender gap. In almost a century, only nine women have been literary laureates: six in the first ninety years, but three since 1991 (Gordimer, Morrison, Szymborska).

The Nobel Replies to Its Critics

The Nobel literary jury has ringed itself with four main lines of defense.[5] A favorite official plea is that if Conrad and Joyce were bypassed, this was unfortunately because they were "never nominated." The official history of the Nobel literary awards trots out this bureaucratic disclaimer quite often, as if the rules regrettably tied their hands. But of course the Nobel committee itself selected those very nominators who, while ignoring a Joseph Conrad, did nominate Pierre Loti, Emile Faguet, Paul Bourget, Gaspar Núñez de Arce, Ramón Menéndez Pidal, Upton Sinclair, or Margaret Mitchell. Even if its nominators were so undiscerning, members of the Swedish Academy and its committee can enter nominations. If they chose not to do that, the fault is their own.[6]

Another favored argument, also wearisomely bureaucratic, takes the form "died too soon before could be properly evaluated." Frequently cited instances are C. P. Cavafy, Rainer Maria Rilke, Virginia Woolf, James Joyce, D. H. Lawrence, and Franz Kafka. Certainly, discovering the Alexandrian poet Cavafy (d. 1933) or Kafka or Anton Chekhov would have been a miraculous long shot: Cavafy and Kafka published very little before their early deaths; Chekhov died in 1904.

Neglect of others is not so easily explained away. True, Rilke died in 1926, only three years after writing his masterpieces, the *Duino Elegies* and *Sonnets to Orpheus*. But those poems, great as they were, were only the capstone of a brilliant career. Since 1899 his published work had given him outstanding claim as one of the greatest poets in the German language. Yeats, who came to greatness around 1910, won in 1923—why not Rilke about the same time? Many critics have suggested that Yeats's award was politically motivated: Ireland had just become independent. But Rilke, born in Prague, wandered restlessly and had no nation, thus no Nobel "identity" or support from a national academy or critics.

D. H. Lawrence died in 1930, but had an international reputation by the mid-1920s. Joyce and Woolf died in 1941, both recognized as masters.[7] Proust is more problematic. He published the first volume of his great work, *À la recherche du temps perdu*, in 1913, and the second and third parts in 1919 and 1921. In 1920 he won the prestigious Prix Goncourt. Why was the Nobel committee in doubt that Proust was a deserving choice, when many international observers very early on thought him the greatest living novelist? True, he died only three years after finishing his great cycle. But this masterpiece had been available for nine years before he died, and the Nobel judges needed only nine years to honor Sienkiewicz for his *Quo Vadis*—"displacing Tolstoy," claimed a Nobel evaluator—and only three to make Pearl Buck a laureate.

An unspoken implication here is that the Nobel Prize in Literature cannot rush into things like lesser prizes, as the Prix Goncourt did in crowning Proust. The supreme international dignity and status of the Nobel, its great renown and prestige, require doing nothing precipitate. Alas, this lofty principle, useful against a Woolf or Joyce, has also been passed over at will, as with Buck, Sinclair Lewis, Joseph Brodsky, or Gabriel García Márquez.

A third defense often raised is related to the limitations of committees. Nobel defenders, with suitable murmurings of regret after the fact, acknowledge that certain kinds of writers (Tolstoy, Ibsen) were simply not acceptable to certain committees, especially during the first half of the century. This bias went under the rubric of "idealism"; we shall return to it shortly because it remains a major factor.

The final line of defense is to admit that mistakes have been made, but insist that the record on the whole is quite good. Thus, in the official history of the prizes, Anders Österling of the Swedish Academy begins roundly conceding the mistakes: "It is not to be denied that the history of the Nobel Prizes in Literature is also a history of inexpiable sins of omission." This is strong language. Yet loyal committeeman Österling immediately paints the brighter side:

> But even so, it may perhaps be said that the mistakes have been comparatively few, that no truly unworthy candidate has been crowned, and that if allowances are made for legitimate criticism, the results have reasonably matched the requirements and difficulties of an almost paradoxical assignment.[8]

This last statement of course expiates the "inexpiable" omission of Tolstoy, Rilke, and all the rest. After all, if the mistakes have been few, if no truly unworthy candidate has been crowned, and "if allowances are made for legitimate criticism" (whatever that may mean), who has any reason to complain?

For the moment, let us consider the optimistic side. Surely, if Czesław Miłosz, Saul Bellow, Toni Morrison, and Günter Grass have become laureates, the Nobel must be making progress. Better late than never. However hesitantly, the award has also begun to move beyond Europe with an occasional award to the Mideast, Japan, Africa. This sort of piecemeal improvement encourages some to believe that one or another remedy will cure the Nobel of its lapses. Let the judges embrace new stirrings. Let them become fluent in Chinese or Estonian. Let them not play so many safe bets among the unobjectionably good but do as the Swedish statesman Dag Hammarskjöld was said to urge, when protesting awards to the superfamous such as Hemingway or Churchill: "Oh—if once we could show a touch of daring!"[9]

Yet this sort of progress is at best only patchwork. Two main obstacles are the heavy moralistic-political emphasis and the committee system.

The Nobel Committee as Boyg

In Ibsen's *Peer Gynt* there is an all-devouring, formless monster called the Boyg. The Danish critic Georg Brandes (1842-1927) interpreted this as "the Spirit of Compromise."[10] The world of course leans on committees to arrive at a working consensus—which means being willing to cooperate and compromise. Safe choices are apt to be preferred to the trouble-making sort. The Nobel Prize is the work of committees. But a committee is a poor way to evaluate literature.

Nobel's will did not set up a committee to sift and nominate laureates. That was done by the Nobel Statutes of 1900. Practicality was and remains the reason. World literature—and the Nobel claims to deal with nothing less—is fragmented into hundreds of languages and diverse nations. There is so much of it, and so indigenous, that only a committee with a huge network of specialists can possibly cope with it, even in the most limited way. Literary "experts"—scholars, linguists, critics, historians, librarians—are required. As noted, luckily for the new Nobel literary committee of 1901, literature was then becoming institutionalized and professionalized as never before in history. This is why professors dominate the Nobel's nominators and judges; they already know how to work inside a bureaucracy.

Practicality is also the answer when the Nobel jury is reproached—continually—for having ignored this or that eminent writer. It responds, fairly, that there are too many worthy writers for any annual prize to honor. The official solution to this dilemma has been set forth recently by the chair of the literature committee, Kjell Espmark: What the Swedish Academy "cannot afford is giving [the] Nobel's laurels to a minor talent." One might counter that what the Nobel really cannot afford is giving its laurels to any but writers of the caliber of Tolstoy, Joyce, or Woolf. This is said not to be feasible. The Nobel jury receives two hundred nominations a year from respected nominators; these must be closely evaluated by committee members and their far-flung network of advisers; thick reports must be assembled to guide the academy's decisions. Doubtless some writers are "great" and some only "good." But any committee or academy member who claims to know who the geniuses are will only set off a long wrangle. Better to wait twenty or thirty years to learn who is worthy. As for "greatness," leave that to posterity.

The difficulty of getting agreement about how to rank contemporary writing is at least one reason why every account of the Nobel jury reports their often bitter electioneering. Some writers—the great poet Pablo Neruda, for example—openly campaign for a prize, thus creating factions on the jury. Even without this, the Swedish Academy and its committee seem to indulge in constant infighting. Some publish public denunciations of fellow members.[11] Others confide to journalists their contempt for their colleagues: one described the present permanent secretary, Sture Allen, as "an intellectual accountant" and as someone "who doesn't even read."[12] But of course the committee system itself, with its outlying bureaucracy of academic consultants and nominators long experienced in partisan maneuvers, is apt for intrigue.

Meanwhile, everyone realizes that a compromise must somehow be cobbled together in a few months so that the next prize can be announced by October. The committee and academy count up individual preferences and prejudices, and the majority wins. The decision is always presented to the public as a unanimous choice.

Using such a commmittee process is outlandish only for the literature award. Committees work quite well for the sciences. Robert Oppenheimer once wrote that "there is something inherently comforting about a panel of experts" because slanted and merely personal ideas can be corrected.[13] For science, yes: the best experts there must approve the work or else it is stillborn. But superior literary prizes are harder to choose than science prizes. Science speaks a common language around the globe, and is a cumulative, collective enterprise; theories can often be tested quickly by rigorous experiments. Literary works stand on their own. Comparisons are anyone's right and gamble.

The Swedish Academy is a self-perpetuating enclave: it elects its own successors and, like other bureaucracies, tends to preserve its character, including its fractious nature. Discussions and negotiations are secret and sealed, to ensure freedom of decision, but of course such secrecy also insulates it from outside criticism. As noted, a member cannot resign but can stop attending meetings and can refuse to vote. In 1989 two of the academy's members withdrew, protesting the body's refusal to denounce Iran's death sentence on Salman Rushdie. At present, three or perhaps four members of the academy are boycotting votes. This can produce very narrow margins, since twelve votes of the eighteen-member academy are needed to award a prize.

Certainly, the Nobel committees have changed character over the years. Espmark, who has documented this in detail, is sharp with critics of the Nobel system who make sweeping charges about the defects of the awards while not being "historical" about how each particular committee "had its special character and its own criteria."[14] The German naturalistic playwright Gerhart Hauptmann was thus anathema to the first committee but acceptable to the new one in 1912. That new committee sought the "great style," with Goethe's example of high classicism and universal appeal in mind. After 1945 there came another shift, honoring neglected modernist "pioneers." From about the 1970s a "pragmatic" attitude has prevailed.

Espmark's behind-the-scenes explanation is, however, beside the point. As the American critic Herbert Howarth has put it,

> As soon as one asks about a prize-man not "Was he the best man?" but "Why did the judges select him?" one is likely to perceive he was chosen for reasonable reasons; and one reports these; and in so doing willy-nilly defends the good instead of demanding the best.[15]

That is a succinct indictment of the committee system. Why certain judges did not choose Rilke or Joyce has the same sort of interest, finally, as an insider's details on how a political campaign was run. It can be absorbing, but what really matters is only that, for example, a Lincoln was elected or not. The rest is details for the archivist to pick over.

Yet the literature committee has undoubtedly improved, and the literature prize has become much more consistently a "literary" prize. The old bogey of "idealism" has been tamed if not altogether exorcized. But this change happened also because recent committees are in a luckier historical position than earlier ones. The recent sustained improvement of the prizes begins just after the once baffling "experimentalism" of early modernism—*Ulysses, The Waves, The Castle, Duino Elegies*—finally filtered into broad literary usage and also became familiar to a wide readership. The early moderns—"difficult" or "immoral" or "inaccessible"—were the ones who frightened the literary judges for more than half of the twentieth century. Nobel laureates in the last three decades obviously owe a diffuse and incalculable artistic debt to those forerunners—and also the Nobel's new welcome mat. The Nobel judges have become more open; so has everyone else. Late-twentieth-century writing does not bristle with the old shock and strangeness because it does not need to. That necessary battle was fought and won earlier. The Nobel committee presents its 1969 award to Samuel Beckett as a breakthrough. But the breakthrough for Beckett's own innovations was prepared decades before. Thus his *Waiting for Godot* and other plays, and even his novels, have enjoyed popular success as no early avant-gardist's did.

Are there any alternatives to the present committee system? Espmark complains that the nomination of *Gone with the Wind* showed up "a weak aspect of whole selection system," by which he means "the significant degree of incompetence" among nominators.[16] It is misleading to narrow that problem to *Gone with the Wind*. Nominators are usually as incompetent when it comes to *Mrs. Dalloway* or *Mother Courage*. Faced with the strangeness and newness that great writing often involves, the Nobel's eminent professors and critics are quite as fallible as the rest of us. Each year the Nobel jury faces a challenge that very few minds in history have been able to solve, and then only erratically: to know which literary works truly surpass others now, and will continue to stay alive for generations to come. In short, to predict how posterity will think, fifty or a hundred years from now. Each year's Nobel literary award is just such a gamble on the future. The Nobel's task is not to decide that the old Eliot was a great poet—everyone knew he was—but to have decided the younger Eliot was. Otherwise the Nobels degenerate into "old age pensions" or honorary degrees.

But literary reputations are among the riskiest businesses known. Kipling's stature sank for years, but now keeps rising fitfully. Sinclair Lewis—peculiarly hailed by the Nobel citation as an American "humorist"—and his once-shocking *Babbitt* and other novels have largely vanished from the minds even of Americans. Eliot and Hemingway do not rate as the colossi they once seemed; the stock has already fallen on Solzhenitsyn, even as he continues to publish.

The predictive gift is the rarest sort of critical intelligence. It has little to do with being a great scholar or critic or writer. Extraordinarily few have shown genius in the stock market of fame. In the English-speaking world, Ezra Pound is perhaps the best known. He had an uncanny eye for what was new, superb, and lasting. He proved it with his prescient judgments on the as yet unknown Robert Frost and James Joyce, the still obscure T. S. Eliot, the not yet famous Ernest Hemingway, and with his quick appreciation of Yeats's new style of poetry from 1910. No matter that Pound was wildly unbalanced about fascism and uneven in his own poetry. He would have made the perfect scout for the Nobel literary committee. Eliot and Hemingway could have been honored in midcareer, and Joyce, Frost, and Gertrude Stein made laureates as they deserved, to the future glory of the Nobel Prizes. Prophetic readers like Pound can recognize genius when they see it, light-years ahead of the rest.

Except that no Nobel committee could tolerate any such arch-spirit of the anti-Boyg.[17]

The Iron Corset of Idealism

Here is the other main stumbling block. Alfred Nobel's will contained only the following terse criterion for the literary award: it "should go to the person who shall have produced in the field of Literature the most distinguished work of an idealistic tendency." This sentence has bedeviled the prize. Should the award go to a specific work, or to an author's lifetime achievement? Honoring only works done "in the preceding year," as the will earlier and broadly stated, would have hamstrung the literary awards intolerably. The Nobel jury has mainly honored a writer's lifetime work, but occasionally a specific work has been singled out for the award (Thomas Mann's *Buddenbrooks,* John Galsworthy's *Forsyte Saga*).

The prickliest part was the phrase "of an idealistic tendency." Surely Nobel meant high-minded moral goodness? A minority view, however, startlingly maintained the opposite. The prominent Swedish mathematician Mittag-Leffler, who had known Alfred Nobel, claimed that the inventor intended "idealism" to mean a sceptical, even satirical attitude to religion, royalty, marriage, and the social order in general. Or so he was reported as saying by the aforementioned Danish critic Georg Brandes, one of the great early champions of Nietzsche, and himself a nominee for a Nobel.[18]

Many of Nobel's own writings are indeed sceptical and caustic—his play *Nemesis,* written only a year before he died, or the satirical *In Lightest Africa* and *The Bacillus Patent.* And he could be strangely ironic, as in his plan to set up that lavish mansion where prospective suicides could die amid luxury, rather than drown in the cold, filthy Seine. To Österling, Nobel's literary tone recalled Strindberg's mordant attacks.[19] That was strong backing for "idealism" as an ironically subversive force.

But can a grand international prize be devoted to subversive irony of this sort? And backed, no less, by a solemn academic institution and the Swedish government itself? It is unthinkable. The opposite and respectable view prevailed. Österling inadvertently describes how this was managed. While conceding that Nobel himself frequently spoke as if "an enemy of all religious faith, [even] an out-and-out atheist," Österling nonetheless pronounces this "so-called atheism . . . in reality . . . very close to Platonism and Christianity."[20] As shall be seen, this conversion of nay-saying into an optimistic and reassuring "idealism" threads decisively through all Nobel literature prizes to the present.

The first champion of such a view, the iron force in the first Nobel jury from 1901 to 1912, was Carl afWirsen (the prefix *af* denotes nobility in Sweden). Born in 1842, he was permanent secretary, or director, of the Swedish Academy from 1901 until his death in 1912. This moribund academy included no critic of real power and one minor poet, Carl Snoilsky (1841-1903), who wrote in the Swedish neoromantic manner of the 1860s. Ibsen and Strindberg, who could have revitalized things, had long before been blackballed. The rest of the first Nobel committee chosen by the academy in 1901 included Elias Tegner, orientalist (1841-1903); Carl Nyblom, Uppsala literature professor (1832-1907); and Carl Odhner, historian (1836-1904).

As their birth dates suggest, these judges were elderly Victorians who showed it. So were the rest of the eighteen members of the Swedish Academy. Assigning them the Nobel Prize in Literature was quixotic. As twentieth-century literature entered its first great period of innovative achievement, it was disinherited by the Nobel jury set up to honor it. As one late-nineteenth-century observer put it, the guardians of Swedish culture were like "elderly men . . . who after a particularly refined dinner with a plenitude of wines, are discussing religion and the affairs of state over their glasses of arrak punch."[21] Strindberg, in his *New Realm* of 1884, pilloried the hypocrisies and pettinesses of Swedish culture that Wirsen embodied. Nor did Strindberg spare the Swedish Academy's eighteen "immortals" who thought of themselves as carrying on the traditions of the Académie Française, their "foster-parent" institution. Strindberg lived to 1912 but of course never won the Nobel Prize.

Wirsen was wonderfully unequipped to lead the Nobel assignment. Even back in 1889, he despised what he saw as a perverse new literature flooding the world. As chair of the Nobel jury, Wirsen used "idealism"—reactionary, respectful of State and Church and Society—as a stick to beat off Emile Zola as "lurid" and "spiritless and often grossly cynical." Ibsen, the greatest dramatist of the nineteenth century, was evaluated as "totally atheistic and, in ethical-sexual questions, highly adventurous in outlook." Hardy was unacceptable because his God "lacks any sense of justice or mercy."[22]

It was especially Tolstoy, widely and rightly admired as the greatest living writer, who put the committee in a terrible fix. Blessedly for the committee, a technicality saved them in 1901. Tolstoy had not been "duly nominated" that year. The very first Nobel Prize in Literature, in 1901, went to Sully Prudhomme, suggesting that he was the world's foremost living poet. He was in fact as forgettable a poet as can be found in the Nobel's long list of mediocrities. His poetry was of the mid-nineteenth-century French Parnassian sort, sculpted in line, refined in taste, quite vacant—or, as the Nobel citation chose to put it, "noble, melancholy, and thoughtful." When he became the laureate at age sixty-two, his productive years were long past. He was, however, a member of the Académie Française, strongly supported by that parent organization of the Swedish Academy, and thus a reassuringly respectable choice: no wild writers need apply.

Tolstoy's exclusion caused forty-two Swedish writers, artists, and critics to protest. The Nobel committee evaluated Tolstoy's work as containing "ghastly naturalistic descriptions" and "negative asceticism" and abhorrent religious, fatalist, and anarchist sympathies. But in 1902, again blessedly for the Nobel committee, Tolstoy declared himself happy not to receive such a valuable prize, since "money brings nothing but evil."[23] Saved from the terrible fate of honoring Tolstoy, the Nobel committee instead made a laureate of the German Theodor Mommsen, whose monumental history of ancient Rome dated all the way back to

1845-56, with a last volume in 1885. Mommsen was then eighty-five years old, and his work was hardly "recent" or of surpassing literary merit.[24] No matter: however aged and dormant, Mommsen rescued the Nobel committee from having to honor the "morbid" Emile Zola or his ilk.

In 1903 another crisis arose. The Norwegian Ibsen, greatest dramatist of the past century, was now a candidate. But, subverter of authority and champion of individual freedom, he was all too unacceptable to the Nobel jury. They found a proxy in another Norwegian dramatist, Bjørnstjerne Bjørnson.

In recent years Nobel officials have impatiently insisted that "idealism" is a dead and discarded issue. Now only the "best" writing is what matters.[25] Espmark declares that idealism of the "patently uplifting variety" is no longer a Nobel requirement, that only literary "integrity" matters, whether corrosive or uplifting. He cites prizes to Samuel Beckett and Camilo José Cela as honoring those who "uncompromisingly" depict the "human predicament." The American critic Alexander Coleman once wrote that "it would be easy to say that that Academy does anything it wishes, wrapping itself in the flag of idealism only at the hour of the ceremony." But, he went on, it has in fact always endorsed such idealism. (He also suggested that, as there used to be Kremlinologists, so there should be Nobelogists, who could divine the hidden tendencies of this secretive organization.)[26]

Certainly, the issue is not dead. When the Polish poet Wisława Szymborska won in 1996, the *TLS* reviewer still felt obliged to insist she had won for merit, not "for being a moral comforter to humanity, nor for being a literary activist indicating what the correct lines or parties are."[27]

The Nobel literary judges are doubtless sick of the issue. In 1997, indeed, it seems that their collective gorge rose and they provocatively chose Dario Fo, who is an actor, stand-up comedian, performance artist—almost anything but a writer in the sense of Yeats or Mann. After that, who could dare call the Swedish Academy old-fashioned?

But not much has really changed. In 1901 the Nobel citation lauded its very first laureate, the French poet Sully Prudhomme, for tirelessly seeking

> evidence of man's supernatural destiny in the moral realm, in the voice of conscience, and in the lofty and undeniable prescriptions of duty. From this point of view, Sully Prudhomme represents better than most writers what the testator called an "idealistic" spirit in literature.

Ninety years after Sully Prudhomme, the 1991 Nobel award went to the South African novelist Nadine Gordimer, praised in the Nobel citation for "her involvement on behalf of literature and free speech in a police state where censorship and persecution of books and people exist." This is still the Nobel idealism of 1901, only now politicized and liberal rather than spiritualized and conservative.

In 1986 Wole Soyinka of Nigeria ended his Nobel lecture with these words: "The prize is the consequent enthronement of its complement: universal suffrage—and peace."

But as in Sully Prudhomme's case, high ethics or worthy politics do not make anyone's writing better or worse. Gordimer is a good novelist, yet one cannot forget—nor does the Nobel citation let us—that she was also a leading white South African activist against apartheid. While any comparison here will seem invidious, unavoidably, it may be said that Doris Lessing, also a white African but long removed to Europe and not such an activist, has thus far been passed over for a prize—although Gordimer has arguably never written a novel to match Lessing's brilliant, disturbing *The Golden Notebook*.

Kjell Espmark complains that such remarks are typical of the "armchair politicizing" surrounding Nobel literature prizes. But the cause lies not in the armchair critic but in the Nobel citations themselves. A sceptical reader is urged to read through the last century's citations for proof. In 1967, for example, the Guatemalan novelist Miguel Angel Asturias was praised for protesting against imperialism, tyranny, slavery, and injustice, and his citation concluded: "This was indeed what Alfred Nobel hoped to promote by his Prizes." His fellow Caribbean, V. S. Naipaul, though a more powerful writer, continues to be ignored, likely because of his scathing portraits of the Third World.

Now as then, too, the Nobel citations tend to nudge writers into an "affirming" mode. One recalls how Nobel's own "out-and-out atheism" somehow emerged "Christian." Did T. S. Eliot wince when his citation rephrased his idea of tradition to harmonize with Nobel sentiments? "The existing monuments of literature form an idealistic order . . ." was not quite what Eliot meant.

Some laureates have resisted Nobel uplift. The fastidious French poet-diplomat Saint-John Perse (Nobel 1960), after being lauded for exalting "man's creative powers," uncompromisingly concluded his acceptance speech by saying, "It is enough for the poet to be the bad conscience of his age." The most eloquent rejection of the Nobel's hectoring came from the Northern Irish poet Seamus Heaney. In 1995 he was honored for his remarkable poetry but also and inevitably "for concerning himself with analysis of the violence in Northern Ireland." Heaney's own views, however, indicted the Nobel's motives here. Poetry, he wrote, offers an alternative to reality

> which has a liberating and verifying effect upon the individual spirit, and yet I can see how such a function would be deemed insufficient by a political activist. . . . Engaged parties are not going to be grateful for a mere image—no matter how inventive or original—of the field of force of which they are a part. They will always want the redress of poetry to be an exercise of leverage on behalf of their own point of view; they will require the entire weight of the thing to come down on their side of the scales.[28]

Reading through the citations, indeed, one sometimes wonders if the Nobel judges recognized who or what they were honoring. In 1923 an earlier Irish poet, William Butler Yeats, became the laureate. Only two years before, he had published "The Second Coming," with its unforgettable vision of the nightmare settling on modern civilization. This apocalyptic vision is the voice of the devil's advocate condemning the Nobel's usual optimistic and middle-of-the-road view. Was the Nobel committee listening? One doubts it, since their citation for Yeats praised him as if he were still the dreamy Celtic Twilight poet of 1900. The citation incredibly described Yeats's 1910 volume *The Green Helmet*—where he began his "passionate syntax" to handle prosaic themes and responsibilities—as "a merrily heroic myth of a peculiarly primitive wildness."[29]

Such idealistic uplift and call for social betterment explain much about the Nobel choices that is otherwise mystifying. The prize to Pearl Buck in 1938 suggests she swept the Nobel judges off their feet.[30] Her famous trilogy on China, including *The Good Earth,* came out between 1931 and 1935. Three short years later, she was a Nobel Prize winner. The Nobel literary judges have rarely moved so fast. To honor her, the Nobel committee had to ignore Dreiser (whose *An American Tragedy* came out in 1925), Fitzgerald (*The Great Gatsby,* 1926, and *Tender Is the Night,* 1934), Hemingway (*The Sun Also Rises,* 1926, and *A Farewell to Arms,* 1929), and John Dos Passos, whose great trilogy *U.S.A.* (completed 1936) made the young Jean-Paul Sartre call him the greatest writer in the world. However exaggerated that was, Dos Passos deserved a Nobel Prize for his work through the 1920s and 1930s. On literary merit, the choice of Buck was dubious. But her Nobel citation sings a paean to her sympathy with the plight and dignity of Chinese peasants. Buck built "idealistic" international bridges between East and West in *The Good Earth* and sequels which became famed best-sellers through the world. Buck's heart was in the right place, though her prose remained as flat as ever, with the moral complexities flattened as well. Still, worrying about her literary merit may be irrelevant. In the official Nobel history, Österling astonishingly says that the "decisive factor in the Academy's judgment" was her "incomparable" biographies of her parents, both missionaries in China.[31]

Is it only coincidence that the last two prizes to Americans writing in English have gone to Saul Bellow and Toni Morrison? Bellow is "Jewish-American," and Morrison "African-American," and both can therefore stand as "minority" writers. One can scarcely believe that the Nobel judges chose such extraordinary writers even partly on so narrow a basis. And yet, the American laureate preceding them was John Steinbeck (1962), famous for his *Grapes of Wrath* set in the 1930s Depression. His selection as a Nobelist puzzled many American readers, since he was preferred over Robert Frost, W. H. Auden, Wallace Stevens, Marianne Moore, William Carlos Williams, John Dos Passos, and others. It puzzled Steinbeck as well. The suspicion that this was yet another politicized prize gained credence with a report from a Swedish source that the Nobel judges saw Steinbeck's award in 1962 "at least in part, as a social gesture in support of the tormented South. As if Americans would easily make the connection between the 'okie' of the Thirties and the Negro of the Sixties!"[32]

Modernism at Arm's Length

Herbert Howarth has astutely summed up the situation of the Nobel Prize in Literature:

> The Nobel's penitent longing for a better world will be answered whenever the Academy gives the Prize not to the best-wishing maker but to the best maker—even if the best maker appears to wish ill.[33]

But the Nobel has tended to shun writing of a modernist sort as too "difficult" or "morbid" or "inaccessible," or simply ignore it. The first Nobel Prize in 1901 came as the Dreyfus Affair split France for decades to come. That was a tiny but apt prelude to twentieth-century world wars, totalitarianism, and other nightmares. To many, human history has sometimes seemed to be radically disconnecting from its past and anchor. "Man is falling toward an X," Nietzsche said.

The Nobel's shying from literature too intimate with the dangers and extremism of our age shows in the number of awards to less disturbing writers. Up to 1945, the Nobel judges awarded nineteen prizes to fiction writers. Eleven of those went to the "saga" genre, mostly many-volume renderings of rural or folk and traditional ways of life, vanishing or vanished—which spoke not only *of* an earlier era, but *like* one. Of course, some saga laureates far transcend this genre, such as Halldór Laxness of Iceland (1955). Still, the Nobel committees favored the way the saga practitioners usually held at a safe distance the anarchic modern world so intimately linked to the city, the new unrooted intelligentsia, the energies of revolution and change. They were also accessible to a popular audience. There has always been a populist streak in the Nobel literary jury.[34]

Saga prizes began as early as 1905 with the prize to Sienkiewicz, author of *Quo Vadis*. In 1908 Lagerlöf became a laureate for her *Gösta Berling's Saga*. In 1915 the indefatigable Romain Rolland won the Nobel for his *Jean-Christophe* (1903-12), which runs to ten volumes. Modernist literature was already on the scene in force—Pound and Wyndham Lewis's *Blast* of 1914, or the Italian Futurists of 1909 who sang of "glorifying war . . . the only hygiene of the world." Rolland instead preached being a "good European" via art—his French hero Jean-Christophe was captivated by German music. In 1917 two Danish novelists shared the prize: Henrik Pontoppidan and Karl Gjellerup. The Nobel's wish to award "neutral" prizes during the war made this possible. Any other reason for choosing Gjellerup remains a mystery. Pontoppidan however was in the saga line, with his eight-volume *Lykke-Per* (Lucky Peter, 1898-1904) and his five-volume *De Dödes Rige* (The Realm of the Dead, 1912-16).

The only other novelists honored up to this point had been Kipling (1907), Hamsun (1920), and Anatole France

(1921). In 1924, however, the prizes reverted to saga writers with the Polish Reymont (Conrad, unhonored, died that year), and the 1928 winner was the Norwegian Sigrid Undset, whose *Kristin Lavransdattar* is set in fourteenth-century Norway. One may add the Italian Grazia Deledda (1926), who explored the life of Sardinian peasants. Perhaps also Thomas Mann in 1929. His 1900 novel *Buddenbrooks*, his closest approach to the saga genre up to the time of his award, was singled out in the Nobel citation, which passed over his 1926 masterpiece *The Magic Mountain*, a portrayal of modern diseased civilization, in a single phrase. In the 1930s three of the four fiction prizes again went to saga writers. John Galsworthy won in 1932 for his *Forsyte Saga*. If his subject was the gentry rather than the folk, the results could be as deadening. Someone has noted that Galsworthy's popularity abroad came from his portraying the English precisely as foreigners liked to imagine them. In 1937 the prizewinner was the Frenchman Roger Martin du Gard, whose best-known novel, still worth reading if one can persevere, is *Les Thibault* (1922-40), another many-volume, closely realistic chronicle, this time about the tensions and crises of a pre-1914 bourgeois family. He is an impressive writer, perhaps lacking only that final carrying surge of poetic verve or imaginative daring that lifts such writing above its steady level. In 1938 came Pearl Buck with her trilogy saga about China. In 1944 the prize went to J. V. Jensen of Denmark, whose six-volume saga moves with evolution from the great apes to early human history. After John Steinbeck came the Australian Patrick White (1973) for his masterpieces *The Tree of Man* and *Voss*, though White surmounts any genre, as does Faulkner—who indeed did write a full-fledged saga, which perhaps influenced the Nobel judges to honor him in 1949.

Other laureate practitioners of the saga genre are Ivo Andrić (1961) and Mikhail Sholokhov (1965). Their work falls in the period when the Nobel Prizes collided with the Cold War, and needs looking at now.

Political Pressures from Within and Without

The Swedish Academy bristles at any suggestion that its awards have been influenced by politics. But as Henry Thoreau (pre-Nobel) once wrote: "Some circumstantial evidence is very strong—as when you find a trout in the milk." And some large trout swim in the milky Nobel record. In 1912 the Catalan writer Angel Guimera was denied a prize lest honoring him offend the Spanish government. Spain had conquered Catalonia centuries before, but memories are long there. The Nobel committee justified this rejection as "promoting peace."[35]

From the 1920s, some writers went right (D. H. Lawrence, Yeats, Pound, Hamsun), some left (Brecht, Aragon, Sartre, Auden). Some were card-carrying members for longer or shorter periods (Neruda in the Communist Party, Pirandello in the Fascist); some became totalitarian propagandists (Pound, or the Soviet poet Mayakovsky). T. S. Eliot was on the right, Hemingway on the left.

Intentionally or not, the Nobel by long delays diluted such contentious disputes into its own softer idealism. By honoring Eliot and Hemingway only after 1948—after the Spanish Civil War and the defeat of fascism—the Nobel could present them as elder statesmen in a "republic of letters," with their earlier energizing differences covered over by ceremonial plaudits.

At the height of the Cold War, from about 1950 to 1970, the Nobel jury found itself dogged by politics as never before. The media, East and West, were eager to turn Nobel awards into simulacra of Big Power hostility or detente. The Swedish Academy could have tried to finesse this by choosing laureates as far as possible from Cold War partisanship. Instead they bravely plunged in, and did well in resisting outside censorship. But they indulged in some political censoring of their own.

First, the outside pressures. The most sensational disputes about Nobel neutrality involved the Soviet Union. Take the following chronology of prizes during the Cold War:

1955 Halldór Laxness

1956 Bertolt Brecht dies (never a laureate)

1957 Camus

1958 Pasternak

1961 Andrić

1964 Sartre

1965 Sholokhov

1967 Anna Akhmatova dies (never a laureate)

1970 Solzhenitsyn

1971 Neruda

1972 Böll

Laxness, the Icelandic novelist, won the first Nobel involving the Cold War. He had long championed the Stalinist regime; the Soviets were gratified. Almost immediately after, however, came three prizes in a row applauded by the anti-Soviet bloc. Camus eloquently opposed Soviet repressive policies and totalitarian premises, and was accused by Communists of winning the prize because he was a lackey of capitalism. Pasternak won the first literature prize ever awarded to a Soviet citizen, mainly for his novel *Doctor Zhivago*, but he had published this novel in the West without permission, and the regime denounced its new laureate as a Judas, "a foreign stain on our socialist country," and a traitor. The Soviet authorities refused to let Pasternak go to Stockholm to receive his prize. Nor did the 1961 award to the Yugoslavian novelist Ivo Andrić please Moscow: Yugoslavia was then led by Marshal Tito, who had broken free of the Soviet empire and remained defiant of the Kremlin.

Only a few years later, as if in reverse, three Nobel Prizes in four years went to Soviets or their apologists. This about-face suggested to many that the Nobel committee was making amends to Moscow, especially for the Pasternak offense. When Sartre was awarded the prize in 1964 he was the most powerful intellectual in France—probably in the world—defending Soviet policies or the allegedly higher virtues of totalitarianism. Sartre however declined the prize, the first to do so voluntarily since Tolstoy in 1902. The Swedish Academy, grown wiser since the Tolstoy fiasco, refused to withdraw his award. Some suggested that Sartre was in a pique because his rival Camus had won first. Sartre's own explanation was that he never accepted public honors; only an unaffiliated writer could speak freely about politics. Accepting the Nobel Prize, he claimed, turned one into a spokesman for that institution. Speaking of himself in the third person, he said that "Jean-Paul Sartre, Nobel Prize winner" would thenceforth be appended to every statement he made; "he is in a way inevitably coopted by simply being crowned. It's a way of saying, Finally he's on our side."[36] For the same reason, Sartre claimed he would never accept a Lenin Prize, although he declared his sympathies lay entirely with the Soviet Union versus the West, and the Nobel Prize, "objectively speaking," lined up against the Soviet Union. It was after all "an honor restricted to Western writers and Eastern rebels."[37] By such a rebel he meant Pasternak, and regretted that Sholokhov was not honored before Pasternak.

Indeed, right after Sartre, Sholokhov became the laureate. His famous *The Quiet Don* (1927-32) is a saga of the sort long beloved by Nobel committees. Sholokhov was also the "good" Soviet writer.[38] He had denounced the award to Pasternak (in later years he recanted this), and the Soviet leaders permitted him to accept his Nobel in person. Then in 1967 the Guatemalan Asturias won; highly sympathetic to the Soviet Union, he had spent much of his life fighting Latin-American dictators and U.S. greed: his "banana trilogy" attacks the rapacity of the United Fruit Company, at its peak in the 1920s.

In 1970, however, the Nobel made a laureate of Solzhenitsyn, the great scourge of the Soviet regime. He had been imprisoned in labor camps and "internal exile" from 1945 to 1956 on trumped-up charges; these experiences launched his epochal history of the Gulag, the huge invisible Soviet prison system. During the "thaw" initiated by Khrushchev in 1965, Solzhenitsyn published *The First Circle* (1968) and *The Cancer Ward* (1968-69), both cited by the Nobel judges. He had also become a leader of public protest against the regime. The Soviet authorities derided his prize as "political enmity" or worse. Espmark reports that the Nobel jury refused a request by the Swedish Foreign Office to drop the prize to Solzhenitsyn.[39] Solzhenitsyn declined to leave the USSR to accept his prize, lest the Soviet leaders refuse to let him return.

Then, one year after Solzhenitsyn, another possible flip-flop: the Chilean poet Pablo Neruda took the prize. He had served long years as a loyal Stalinist, in and out of Russia. Was this prize an effort to soothe Soviet resentment about Solzhenitsyn?

The Cold War staggered on, but from 1971 the prizes no longer ricocheted back and forth. After Solzhenitsyn it was seventeen years before another Russian writer won the prize—and he was then living in exile: Joseph Brodsky (1987). Later prizes went to several who had lived under Soviet oppression: Miłosz of Poland (1980), Jaroslav Seifert of Czechoslovakia (1984), and the Polish poet Wisława Szymborska (1996). The poet and critic Octavio Paz and the novelist Carlos Fuentes had long been the leading Mexican candidates for the Nobel award. For years, they had also been political opponents—Fuentes on the Marxist side, Paz against. Paz won the 1995 Nobel Prize. In 1989 the Soviet Union itself collapsed, and Cold War prizes with it.

THE NOBEL, THE STALIN, AND THE "HITLER" PRIZE

Among the laureates just named, several of the Stalinist defenders had accepted Stalin Prizes. Why was a Stalin Prize acceptable to Nobel judges when a "Hitler Prize" would not be? (No Hitler Prize actually existed; it is meant to indicate those who might have accepted such an honor had it been available.)

That question cannot be lightly dismissed. The Stalin and Lenin Prizes, after all, honored a tyranny which lasted much longer than Hitler's and outmatched him in numbers of innocent victims. The Nobel committee's response to this was peculiar, to say the least. When Laxness was honored in 1955, he had accepted the Stalin Prize only two years before, although much was known by then about Stalinist terror and murder. Yet to go by his Nobel citation, the jury's main concern was only whether Communism had diminished his art. In his 1963 autobiography, *Skalditimi,* Laxness caused an uproar among his former ideological allies by denouncing Soviet Communism.

Neruda received a Lenin Peace Prize in 1950, and a Stalin Peace Prize in 1953. In 1954 this very great poet actually fawned on Stalin as "the high noon, the fulfillment of men and peoples."[40] Neruda hungrily sought the Nobel Prize, but was balked by the Swedish poet Gunnar Ekelöf, a member of the Nobel committee. Ekelöf suspected that Neruda had been involved in Trotsky's murder in Mexico in 1940; Neruda had been a Chilean diplomat in Mexico at the time.[41] Ekelöf died in 1968, and three years later Neruda was the laureate. In his *Memoirs* of 1963, Neruda recanted his Stalinism, though not his Communism. But the poems honored by the Nobel Prize had been written in his Stalinist years. Once more, the Nobel judges worried only whether Neruda's art had been compromised. So too with Asturias, who had accepted a Lenin Peace Prize in 1966, the year before he won the Nobel award.

The Nobel committee was not so lenient to writers on the right. As Dag Hammarskjöld in 1959 explained to Pär Lagerkvist (the 1951 Nobelist) about his objections to a prize for Ezra Pound:

> I have no objection to a Nobel Prize being given to an author who is mentally unbalanced. . . . But Pound [fell] victim to anti-Semitism. . . . such a "subhuman"

reaction ought to exclude the possibility of a prize intended to lay weight on the "idealistic tendency." . . . I do not know exactly what the words "idealistic tendency" mean, but at least I do know what is diametrically opposed to what they can reasonably be assumed to signify.[42]

Racism is a horror. But if, as Hammarskjöld says, some acts are so foul that they should preclude any Nobel award at all, one can only ask again: why is killing people for belonging to the "wrong" race worse than killing them in gulags for belonging to the "wrong" class? The victims are both as dead, the motives are both as subhuman.

In 1979 Karl Vennberg, a Swedish critic, challenged the Nobel's claim that it judged literature apart from politics. If so, he asked, why didn't the academy award Ezra Pound a prize? "The private politics of an author amount after all to an aberration that dies with his historical epoch."[43] Even vehement Marxists no longer condemn the "reactionary" Balzac. A member of the Swedish Academy, Artur Lundkvist, disagreed with Vennberg: "the limited merits" of Pound's work could not make up for his "shameful outpourings of psychopathic hatred and evil."[44] Did Lundkvist mean that a less limited writer than Pound, but also a fascist, could be awarded the prize? He did not clarify this delicate point.

But there was such a writer. Lundkvist lumped the French novelist Céline with Pound as too limited in achievement, and too shamefully full of hatred, to be prizeworthy. Céline was the pen name of Louis-Ferdinand Destouches (1894-1961), a physician who worked selflessly for the desperately poor. From 1938 he also published tracts filled with ravening hatred of Jews—Pound's is feeble by comparison. But Céline was a writer whose "aberrations" did not diminish his work any more than Stalinism did Neruda's. One of the powerfully disturbing writers of our age, he deserved the Nobel Prize for his *Journey to the End of the Night* (1932) and *Death on the Installment Plan* (1936). Reading those novels, even now, one can feel the world's pious verities trembling beneath one's feet, and see how a rising hatred might well bring down the temples—as almost happened. In the fateful 1930s, the decade of Céline's horrific visions, the Nobel laureates included the tepid Galsworthy, Bunin, Pearl Buck, Frans Sillanpää, and J. V. Jensen.[45]

The Nobel judges have waged a Cold War of their own against other writers whose politics displeased them. Jorge Luis Borges, the Argentine poet, fictionist, and essayist, utterly deserved a prize but never won. A Nobel judge, Artur Lundkvist again, said he would blackball Borges because he accepted an honor from the dictator Pinochet. Lundkvist said he much admired and even had translated Borges, but "his political blunders, this time in a fascist direction . . . make him in my opinion unsuitable on ethical and human grounds for a Nobel Prize."[46] Borges was as far from being fascist as was Churchill. But neither the greatness nor the uniqueness of Borges's art could override this political veto. André Malraux felt he was also vetoed as too conservative (a Gaullist!) by the Stockholm judges.

The most telling case is not of a conservative but of a Communist: Bertolt Brecht, the famed author of *Mother Courage, The Threepenny Opera, Galileo,* and many other great plays from 1922 to his death in 1956. Brecht was clearly blackballed for political reasons. There was no other possible reason to delay or reject him. From the 1930s, Brecht was as great a dramatist as Europe produced, and one of Germany's best poets as well. Few writers deserved the prize more than he did. But he died unhonored—first nominated only in the year of his death, according to Espmark. Why nominated so very late? In his case, the judges did not "need more time for evaluation," as they often say. Espmark merely notes that Brecht's "tendentious" Communism kept him from being honored earlier. As an ideologue, he was of course tendentious: so are all ideologues. But that cannot be said about his dramas, which generously enlarge the meaning and mystery of life.

As for "benefit to mankind," as Nobel set forth in his will, why wasn't Arthur Koestler made a laureate, at least for *Darkness at Noon* (1940)? That novel helped shift European history from darkness at a crucial moment, circa 1948. Of how many poems or novels in any century can that be said? And the Nobel Prize, as seen, has singled out certain works as deserving the prize.

Sadly, one cannot say that the Nobel committee or the Swedish Academy has always been willing to fight very hard to back up its liberal or idealistic aims. In 1989 two members of the academy—Kerstin Ekman and Lars Gyllensten, publicly resigned, charging that the academy would not openly support the Anglo-Indian Salman Rushdie against the Iranian call for his assassination. Rushdie is not a laureate; if he were, that title might help protect him. But not necessarily. The Nigerian dramatist Wole Soyinka (Nobel 1986) was imprisoned in his homeland by the military junta from 1967 to 1969 and forcibly exiled in 1983. Despite his prize—or, more likely, because of the international attention it attracts—he has again been in exile since 1994; in early 1997 the regime charged him with treason, which carried the death penalty.

Soyinka's award points up how reluctantly the Nobel Prize guardians have moved outside the orbit of Europe and European languages. This is true not only of Asian nations and languages but of those on the margin of Europe itself, such as Greece, which won its first prize only in 1963, to the poet George Seferis. Israel and Egypt are Mediterranean countries, only a skip away from Greece—but the Hebrew and Arabic languages can seem light-years away. Still, Israeli literature won its first award as early as 1966, to the novelist Shmuel Y. Agnon, who wrote in Hebrew. Part of the reason was that he shared the prize with the Jewish poet Nelly Sachs, who wrote in German. Sachs, born and raised in Germany, fled to Sweden in 1940. After the Holocaust was revealed, her poems caught fire for a memorable decade or so. She can be haunting to the bone but also repetitive; Stephen Spender said that all her poems seem the same poem. Agnon is the greater writer. Why did they share the prize? According to the Nobel citation, because they shared a "kinship":

> to honor two writers who, although they write in different languages, are united in a spiritual kinship and complement each other in a superb effort to present the cultural heritage of the Jewish people through the written word.

By having them share a prize, the American critic Theodore Ziolkowski commented,

> the Swedish Academy has succeeded in making itself ridiculous and in reducing the Nobel Prize to a farce, so blatantly tactical, so palpably non-literary are the reasons for its choice.[47]

"It would have been more honest," he concludes, if Sachs had been given the 1966 peace prize, and Agnon the literary award alone. He adds that though Sachs wrote in German, her award was as much another prize for Swedish literature, since she had had no connection with Germany or its writing for thirty years. But others have claimed that, far from having no connection with Germany, her poems had a too intimate connection which the Germans sought to evade: the death camps. Her major book of poems is titled *The Chimneys*. It has been plausibly argued that Sachs's prize was prompted by West Germany's wish in the 1960s for reconciliation with the Jews. Several high German prizes went to her just before the Nobel. But the distinguished German-Jewish poet Hilde Domin claimed that by thus locking Sachs into being "a poet of the Holocaust," the Germans could ignore her role in German writing and the German past. This freed the Germans "from the obligation to live with such poems." Certainly the strain wracked Nelly Sachs. She spent three years in a mental asylum, suffering from persecution mania. Her Nobel Prize came in the middle of this siege. She died in 1970.[48]

If non-European languages like Hebrew or Arabic can handicap a writer, being without a nation has excluded some from any consideration. Exile is not the issue here, but that small nations can be swallowed up by their neighbors and disappear. Up to the collapse of the Soviet empire, for example, no Latvian or Lithuanian as such could ever win an award; they did not even exist: they were all "Soviet" writers.

The far-ranging effects of a Nobel award in this context have been sharply noted by Czesław Miłosz, the Polish poet and 1980 Nobelist. Until recently, he said in 1983, the literary map of Europe had several blank spots. England, France, Germany, and Italy were distinct. So too Spain, Portugal, Holland, Belgium, and Scandinavia. Moscow and Russia bulked large to the east. But for Eastern Europeans like Ukrainians and others, the "white spaces" could easily have borne the old inscription found on medieval maps: *Ubi leones* (*Here be lions*). That blank space included cities like Prague ("mentioned sometimes because of Kafka"), Warsaw, Budapest, and Belgrade. The effect of this kind of literary map is by no means negligible, said Miłosz:

> The images preserved by a cultural elite undoubtedly also have political significance as they influence the decisions of the groups that govern, and it is no wonder that the statesmen who signed the Yalta agreement so easily wrote off a hundred million Europeans from those blank areas.[49]

Miłosz refers, of course, to how Churchill and Roosevelt ceded Eastern Europe to Stalin in 1945. Would a less provincial and parochial Nobel attitude to Eastern European writing have made a difference at the time of Yalta? Miłosz suggests yes, and his point cannot easily be set aside. Because of prizes to writers like García Márquez, Octavio Paz, Miguel Angel Asturias, and Pablo Neruda, Latin America is no longer one of the blank places in world consciousness. The effect of a Nobel award can be incalculably important.

A Handful of Poets, and Fewer Playwrights

Since 1901 the Nobel literary awards display a curious statistic. Although laureates have often crossed genres, generally fiction writers have won almost three times as often as poets, and eight times more often than dramatists. Up to 1999, of ninety-six laureates—there were no awards in some years—poets have won twenty-six whole prizes and shared six more times. Dramatists have won seven whole and three or four shared prizes; the rest are almost all fiction writers. The above number does not include writers who also wrote poems but were more famous in other genres, such as Kipling or Beckett. Why this disbalance? One can hardly conclude that our century has been so lacking in worthy poets and dramatists.

Poetry competes with fiction under two obvious handicaps. Great modern poetry often has seemed "obscure" to general readers and the Nobel committee alike. As late as 1960, the citation for the French symbolist poet Saint-John Perse apologized for his "difficulty," by which time such modernism was an undergraduate school subject. And of course, fiction "travels" much better in translation than poetry. It would be interesting to know what languages the Nobel committee of 2000 read fluently in the original.

Since the Nobel judges depend so heavily on translations of verse, poets from minor European languages are at a disadvantage—if the Polish Szymborska had not been available in German and Swedish translations, would she ever have won?—and those from non-European languages all the more so. Nobel officials often point to the Indian laureate Tagore (1913) as an example of an early non-Western poet on their list. Unfortunately, although Tagore did write originally in Bengali, he won the Nobel Prize because of his English translation of the collection *Gitan-*

jali (*Song Offerings*). This once roused great enthusiasm in the West as an expression of Indian wisdom, and still has many admirers. It reads like a late-Victorian effusion edged with vague melancholy: "This frail vessel thou emptiest again and again, and fillest it ever with fresh life." A Nobel committee member, Verner von Heidenstam, a later laureate, claimed that just as knowing only a selection of Goethe's poems would convince us of his greatness, so too with Tagore. Reading some of Goethe in the original German, if you know German, and deciding he is a great poet is one thing. To read Tagore only in an English translation and conclude he must be a great Bengali poet is fatuous. And of course the Nobel judges could not read Bengali.[50]

If the Nobel has heavily favored fiction over poetry, it has almost disinherited drama. Its eight awards (shared or whole) are: Bjørnson (1903), Maeterlinck (1911), Hauptmann (1912), Shaw (1925), Pirandello (1934), O'Neill (1936), then a fifty-year wait until Wole Soyinka (1983) and, after another decade, Dario Fo (1997).

But one can argue that the twentieth century was a great age of drama: Ibsen, Strindberg, Chekhov, Claudel, John Millington Synge, Sean O'Casey, Brecht, Brian Friel, John Osborne, Harold Pinter, Athol Fugard, Ugo Betti, Giraudoux, Jean Anouilh, Fernando Arrabal, Eugène Ionesco, Tennessee Williams, Edward Albee, Friedrich Dürrenmatt, Max Frisch, Peter Weiss, Vaclav Havel, Michel de Ghelderode, Peter Barnes, Tom Stoppard.

Some reasons for ignoring Chekhov, Strindberg, and Brecht have been mentioned. As for the mighty Ibsen, the Nobel committee derailed his nomination in 1903 by selecting Bjørnstjerne Bjørnson, inferior but more gratifyingly "idealistic." The committee resorted to some astonishing arguments to justify barring Ibsen. One was that "the genius of Ibsen had unquestionably burnt out."[51] Between 1892 and 1899, Ibsen had merely written *The Master Builder, John Gabriel Borkman,* and *When We Dead Awaken!* A historian of Swedish literature has remarked that Bjørnson would still be one of Norway's national heroes if he had never published a line—as a supreme orator, political influence, and publicist. Wirsen's citation did not fail to mention that Bjørnson had written the Norwegian national anthem. Ibsen himself said that Bjørnson's life was his best work. Of course, Bjørnson's choice effectively put Ibsen out of the running, since Scandinavians could not be honored too frequently. Ibsen died in 1906. Once that happened, however, the worry about too quickly honoring another Scandinavian quickly faded. Only three years later, in 1909, the Swedish novelist Selma Lagerlöf was made a laureate.

Paul Claudel, perhaps the greatest French dramatist of this century, did his major work before 1920. The Nobel committee thus had ample time to come to know his work before he died in 1955. In 1926 he was a candidate for the prize. The evaluation praised the richness of his work and style but, with the usual Nobel nervousness about any "difficult" writing, worried about joining "this strangely esoteric poetry with the publicity of the Nobel Prize." Espmark sums up the objections: "unnaturalness" and "unreality" versus "immediate" accessibility. Claudel was passed over. In 1937 Claudel was again rejected as too "difficult." Österling, the permanent secretary of the Swedish Academy in the year before Claudel's death, called him "France's leading poet"[52] but complained that, in the dramas, the religious symbolism stifled the aesthetic side. W. H. Auden wrote that Time worships language and

> Will pardon Paul Claudel,
> Pardons him for writing well.

The Nobel jury apparently could not accept posterity's strange excuse, Claudel was vetoed.

In 1997 the prize went to the Italian Dario Fo, whom many consider not a dramatist but a writer of scripts for his own performances. He is a vivid and popular actor of farce and satire, aimed mostly at political but also at other targets—the Vatican, anti-abortion, graft, genetic engineering. In each performance he improvises at will, so that his scripts are never quite available in permanent form, but remain prompt-books. He is the first postmodern "playwright"—or performance artist—in the Nobel list. One remembers that Charlie Chaplin was once nominated for the literature prize, since he too wrote his own scripts, but was rejected as not truly a dramatist. Yet Chaplin's films now exist in more permanent form than Fo's scripts.[53]

PHILOSOPHY AND HISTORY

History entered the Nobel literary canon with the 1902 award to the German historian Mommsen. Only one other award to a historian—Churchill in 1953—has ever been given. Philosophy arrived when Eucken of Germany won the 1908 prize. After a two-decade pause, the French philosopher Henri Bergson was honored in 1927. A quarter century later, in 1950, came the British philosopher Bertrand Russell. Jean-Paul Sartre was honored both as writer and philosopher in 1964.

Trying to discover a pattern or principle in these prizes is hopeless. Committee quirks seem the only explanation. Eucken was a last-ditch compromise candidate when the judges deadlocked over Swinburne and Lagerlöf.[54] Bergson was a candidate from 1915, but his militant French patriotism kept him from being honored during the war. A magnificent stylist, he was the most popular philosopher in France; savants and society hostesses and Proust attended his lectures. Whatever else, the Nobel conservatives saw him as a staunch opponent of the materialists. Not least, Bergson brought to Stockholm the prestige of the French intellectual world and the Académie Française.

But the American philosophers William James (d. 1910) and George Santayana (d. 1952) were as fine stylists as Bergson, and his intellectual peers. Santayana should have been a candidate from 1920 on, but there is no sign he was ever nominated. The American Henry Adams (d.

1918), who wrote *Mont-Saint-Michel and Chartres* as well as *The Education of Henry Adams,* and some first-rate American history, was ignored. The Spanish philosopher and cultural critic José Ortega y Gasset (d. 1955) deserved a prize, but he too may never have been nominated. Though Benedetto Croce was a candidate and strongly recommended, the Italian was rejected in 1933 perhaps because the judges were then disinclined to move away from strictly literary fields. The Spaniard Unamuno was rejected in 1935 as too "abstract," which may surprise anyone who has read his *Tragic View of Life* (1913) or his *Meditations on Don Quixote* (1914). J. G. Frazer, author of *The Golden Bough* in 1915, was rejected because his work was "too old." Freud, a master of German style, was set aside as having "a sick and distorted imagination"[55] and as really belonging in the field of medicine, where he was also denied a prize.

Bertrand Russell began as a philosopher of mathematical logic as forbiddingly technical as possible. But he then shifted to intellectual popularizations of any subject under the sun—science, history, psychology, pedagogy, political thought. Like George Bernard Shaw, Russell turned into a long-lived and revered perpetual enfant terrible; his Nobel chances were certainly helped by his receiving the prestigious British Order of Merit the year before. He was surely a lucid philosophic expositor, but even the Nobel judges could hardly believe that amounted to great literature.

Mommsen was eighty-five when named a laureate, a living monument of historical scholarship. Churchill himself was a living monument of history. His six-volume *The Second World War,* published from 1948 to 1954, provided a "literary" reason for making him a laureate, but the Nobel jury suggests it was thinking as much or more of his oratory during World War II.[56]

Nobel Identities: Language and Nation

Nobel laureates have always been identified by nation. But with the literary prizes, language provides a more accurate reckoning. Nations divide, redivide, and sometimes vanish. A laureate's nation is not always easy to determine. Languages are stabler. Czesław Miłosz, the poet and Nobel laureate who writes in Polish, was born and raised in Lithuania, which together with part of Poland was then under Russian rule. Miłosz has lived many decades in America, but the Poles rightly count him as one of their own, as Russians do the émigré poet Joseph Brodsky, an American resident to his death. Languages ignore all such political happenstance. Isaac Bashevis Singer is part of Yiddish writing, for which there has never been, and now will never be, a nation.

The Nobel Prize in Literature has of course mostly honored the major European nations. But being a Great Power does not guarantee success. Germany did moderately well until 1929, when Thomas Mann took the prize, but has had only two prizes since then, spaced almost thirty years apart: to Heinrich Böll in 1972, and to Günter Grass in 1999. But though a nation may not do well, its language can. Although Germany has earned only seven prizes, the German language also lives in Austria, Switzerland, and here and there in Central Europe; Kafka and Rilke, both from Prague, wrote in German. The German language has a total of eleven laureates, including two from Switzerland plus the German-writing Canetti and also counting Nelly Sachs. Spain has won only five awards, but Spanish-language Nobels have mounted up impressively: Spain after all colonized a continent. Of the thirteen nations in South America, nine speak Spanish, as do all countries in Central America; Brazil, with no winners, uses Portuguese. There are now five Latin-American laureates, all but one in the last third of the century.

English has spread even further. Prizes here now dominate the Nobel list—twenty-one awards, including writers from Great Britain, the U.S., Ireland, Australia, South Africa, Nigeria, and the West Indies.

France, with a very high total of eleven up to 1965, has had only one prize in the last thirty years. Italy has won six, Poland four, and a handful of others one or two.

Scandinavian nations have had the extraordinarily high total of fourteen laureates. But the Swedish Academy's generosity to its own and neighboring writers has ceased, at least for the moment: the last Scandinavian laureates were in 1974. One of the Scandinavian prizes was to the Finnish novelist Sillanpää; Finland is a Scandinavian nation but Finnish isn't a kindred language, which shows how complicated counting Nobels by nations can get.

Nobels in English

Laureates from Great Britain and Ireland

1907 Rudyard Kipling, fiction

1923 William Butler Yeats, poetry (Irish Free State)

1925 George Bernard Shaw, drama

1932 John Galsworthy, fiction

1948 T. S. Eliot, poetry

1950 Bertrand Russell, philosophy

1953 Winston Churchill, history

1969 Samuel Beckett, fiction and drama (Irish-French)

1983 William Golding, fiction

1995 Seamus Heaney, poetry

As a representation of Great Britain's best writing in the twentieth century, this list is of course absurd, and the Nobel judges realize it.[57] Without the Irish component of Yeats, Shaw, Heaney, and Beckett and the Anglo-American Eliot, the English fiction list shrinks to Kipling, Galsworthy, and Golding: not brilliant. The Nobel jury, at least, has not been able to find any native English, or Scottish or Welsh, writers of true distinction.

Instead of the undistinguished Galsworthy, a more competent Nobel jury would have chosen Virginia Woolf, James Joyce, Joseph Conrad, D. H. Lawrence, Sean O'Casey, or E. M. Forster. As noted, Golding's merits were so disputable that a Swedish Academy member, in a rare breach of Nobel secrecy, publicly dismissed him as a nonentity. Among his contemporaries, the Nobel jury could have honored Evelyn Waugh, Anthony Powell, Philip Larkin, Graham Greene, Anthony Burgess, Hugh MacDiarmid, or Doris Lessing.

Early unsuccessful British candidates included the philosopher Herbert Spencer, too "agnostic"; George Meredith, too "often artificial and febrile"; and Thomas Hardy, vetoed for his unGodly novels—his present high status as a poet came after his death in 1928. There was also the Victorian poet Algernon Swinburne, whose best work by 1901 lay more than thirty years back. He lost out in an inimitable Nobel comedy. Swinburne's perverse, sometimes sadistic touches ("O lips full of lust and laughter, / Curled snakes that are fed from my breast, / Bite hard . . .") and his pagan anti-Christianity had often shocked his Victorian readers, and he also once sang songs of revolution. The reactionary Wirsen nonetheless enthusiastically backed him for an award. He blamed Swinburne's excesses on the wicked Baudelaire's influence; he was also pleased that the old Swinburne, come to his senses, now censured libidinous poets like Whitman and stoutly championed monarchy. But Swinburne lost out in 1908 and died soon after.

Some of those passed over by the Nobel judges could comprise a Great Books collection:

Joseph Conrad: Conrad desperately hoped to win the award, always anxious about his reputation and always in financial straits until the last few years of his life. He had high claims as the world's finest sea writer, but also for such novels as *Lord Jim* (1900), *Heart of Darkness* (1902), and the extraordinary sequence of political novels *Nostromo* (1904), *The Secret Agent* (1907), and *Under Western Eyes* (1911). Conrad, never very practical, pinned his hopes for a Nobel Prize on his novel *The Rescue* (1919-20), not one of his best. But the 1919 prize went to the Swiss poet Carl Spitteler. Conrad hoped that after the 1923 prize to Yeats, a novelist would be chosen next—perhaps Conrad himself. In 1924 it was indeed a novelist, and a Polish one—Władysław Reymont. Conrad died that same year. Espmark claims that Conrad had never been nominated for the Nobel award from Britain or the U.S.,[58] though he later adds that "not a single legitimate proposal" was made. This is cryptic: had Conrad been nominated or not? Conrad's reputation was high not only in Britain and the U.S. but in France. A simpler reason doubtless kept Conrad from a prize. If the Nobel jury could not see the Yeats of 1923 except in terms of his Celtic Twilight self of 1900, what could they make of a Pole writing exotic English about terrorists and nihilists, as in *Under Western Eyes* and *The Secret Agent,* or strange and sinister colonialists as in *Heart of Darkness*? T. S. Eliot quoted from Conrad, unidentified as from a classic, in his *The Waste Land* and "The Hollow Men" of the early 1920s; but the Nobel judges at that time also found Eliot indigestible.

D. H. Lawrence: Lawrence's "international breakthrough" occurred in the 1920s, Espmark concedes, but Lawrence died in 1930, "too soon to be evaluated." Lawrence had by then written *Sons and Lovers* (1913), *The Rainbow* (1915) and *Women in Love* (1921), *The Plumed Serpent* (1926), and *Lady Chatterley's Lover* (1928), as well as much powerful short fiction. But it is useless to repeat that the Nobel jury needed only three years to honor Pearl Buck, less than ten for others like Sinclair Lewis or Sienkiewicz. Espmark broaches the real reason Lawrence was never honored: it was unlikely that the Swedish Academy of those days "would have been capable of realizing the importance of this controversial figure." In short, Lawrence would never have won a prize no matter how long that hostile jury "evaluated" his works.

Virginia Woolf: If they ever read her, the Nobel judges might have wondered if Woolf's lyrically allusive *Mrs. Dalloway* (1925) and *To the Lighthouse* (1927), not to mention the dazzling poetic formalisms of *The Waves* (1931) and *The Years* (1937), were in fact novels at all. In Nobel view, she was all those things they disliked and feared—"difficult," "eccentric," "exclusive," their code words for a writer without popular appeal.

James Joyce: As usual, we are told that Joyce was never nominated. In 1923 Desmond Fitzgerald, a minister of the new Irish Free State, wrote Joyce that Ireland should propose him for a Nobel prize. Joyce commented that such a move not only would not get him the prize but would probably get Fitzgerald sacked.[59]

Defending the Nobel jury, Espmark claims that Joyce's "stature was not properly recognized even in the English-speaking world." This is limp. *Ulysses* was published in 1922, and within ten years, discerning and influential critics—T. S. Eliot, Pound, Edmund Wilson, Ernst Robert Curtius, and others of that rank—"properly" recognized him as one of the world's greatest living novelists. Espmark concedes this by saying that Joyce would doubtless have been honored as a "pioneer" like Eliot in 1948 if he had only lived until the post-war years. But Joyce died in 1941. In 1947 or so, he would have been worthy of a prize, but not six years before? The Nobel litany of "died too soon" thus really seems to mean "didn't live long enough for us."

Laureates from the United States

1930 Sinclair Lewis, fiction

1936 Eugene O'Neill, drama

1938 Pearl Buck, fiction

1949 William Faulkner, fiction

1954 Ernest Hemingway, fiction

1962 John Steinbeck, fiction

1976 Saul Bellow, fiction

1978 Isaac Bashevis Singer, fiction in Yiddish (resident in the U.S. when awarded prize)

1980 Czesław Miłosz, poetry in Polish (resident in the U.S. when awarded prize)

1987 Joseph Brodsky, poetry in Russian (resident in the U.S. when awarded prize)

1993 Toni Morrison, fiction

As a record of great American writing, this is as peculiar as that of Britain. First, the Nobel Prize ignored giants such as Twain (d. 1910, apparently never considered) and Henry James. In 1911 Edith Wharton, Edmund Gosse, and William Dean Howells began a campaign to get James the Nobel award. He deserved it, was ill, and badly needed the money. They did all the right things: they gathered eminent supporters; they had impressive letters sent to the Nobel committees spelling out James's towering position as an Anglo-American novelist. It had no effect. The Nobel jury read the letters but, as James's biographer Leon Edel puts it,

> the Northern judges of the world's literature had not read James. They had not read about him in the newspapers; he was intensely private. Moreover, they tended to be influenced by the degree to which foreign writers were popular in other countries than their own and the extent to which they were translated. James had been very little translated. He considered himself—and most translators agree—untranslatable.[60]

The evaluators of James, as Espmark reports them, admit he had fine style, but with wondrous blindness claimed his novels were too often only "conversation and situation novels," and he "lacks concentration." *The Wings of the Dove* had "an improbable and odious subject."[61]

After no prizes at all to Americans until 1930, three came in quick succession to Lewis, O'Neill, and Buck. Was the Nobel committee trying to make up for past neglect? Perhaps they were truly smitten by what seemed fresh new voices. But Sinclair Lewis has faded dramatically. It is difficult now to recapture the excitement of Lewis's early novels, each a devastating satirical blow at American complacency: *Main Street* (1920), *Babbitt* (1922), *Arrowsmith* (1925), *Elmer Gantry* (1927). He was the deadly deflater of twenties boosterism and American brashness. His satire had a photographic perfection in which every fatuous flaw in the target loomed up at one. But when the provincialism and hectic phoniness of the 1920s gave way to the deeper problems of the Depression, he seemed at sea. He lived to 1951 and turned out novels regularly, often best-sellers, too often bloated and formulaic.

Why was Lewis chosen as the first American Nobelist? The Nobel committee claimed he was beginning a new national literature. Having earlier passed over Twain and James, they now managed to ignore other new makers of American writing far more important than Lewis. In fiction alone, there was F. Scott Fitzgerald, Ernest Hemingway, Willa Cather, and Theodore Dreiser. In his Nobel acceptance speech, Lewis honorably and generously suggested that Dreiser was more deserving of the Nobel award: "more than any other man" he was the real pioneer, "marching alone, usually unappreciated, often hated," but "he cleared the trail from Victorian . . . timidity and gentility." A better description of exactly the sort of writer the Nobel juries of that time would never honor could hardly be given.

Faulkner's award was one of the Nobel's finest moments: they actually picked a writer who had been dismissed in the United States and Britain as perverse, grotesque, impenetrable, or a mere regionalist, and most of his books were out of print. The *New York Times* derided his prize: "Incest and rape may be common in Faulkner's Jefferson, Mississippi, but they are not elsewhere in the United States." As for Hemingway, he was one of the world's supercelebrities when he won the prize, but though he was only fifty-five, his career was essentially over. The Swedish Academy praised *The Old Man and the Sea* (1952) as a masterpiece and a sign of Hemingway's regenerated powers; it was neither. Then came John Steinbeck, described by the Nobel citation as embracing all America in his sympathy for its mountains and coasts, its oppressed and misfits and ordinary folk—the citation in its turn embracing all of Steinbeck by devoting a paragraph of praise even to *Travels with Charley* (1962), Steinbeck's book about touring the country with his dog in a truck named Rosinante. Far more gifted than Pearl Buck, Steinbeck is however also her closest relative on the Nobel's American list.

The prizes to Saul Bellow and Toni Morrison have rightly received wide approval. Bellow, with Beckett, is the greatest comic novelist on the Nobel list; Faulkner is a contender. Another supreme comic master unjustly denied a Nobel Prize was Vladimir Nabokov (1899-1977). Perhaps the Nobel committee, blinking like a mole at too much sunlight, judged *Lolita* (1955) obscene, *Pale Fire* (1962) too eccentric, and the enchanting *Pnin* (1957) too slight.

A real test of the Nobel's maturity, openness, literary wisdom, and determination to honor genius would have been a prize to Gertrude Stein. Her novel *Three Lives* (1903) has lost none of its audacity and freshness (in both senses); nor has *Tender Buttons* (1915) or *The Making of Americans* (1925) or *Operas and Plays* (1937). But for such a "difficult" and "eccentric" writer, her chances were zero. She died in 1946.

To date, American laureates have all been fiction writers, with O'Neill the only dramatist. No American poet has ever been honored. Worthy candidates have hardly been lacking. By the 1920s, an American renaissance in poetry was spilling over: Robert Frost, Wallace Stevens, Marianne Moore, Hart Crane, William Carlos Williams, Ezra Pound, to name only the most prominent. If a Nobel Prize is ever given to an American poet, the future poet-Nobelist is going to have to contend with these potent ghosts, and the comparisons will likely not be polite.

Why no American poets? The Swedish judges patently lacked a sense of what was new and good in American poetry. And the Nobel's disdain for "difficult" writing put most of the above poets out of court automatically—except Robert Frost. Up to the late 1950s, Frost was still widely seen in the United States as the homespun philosopher of rural New England folkways; the sense of his darkly ironic, even nihilistic side spread slowly. He was America's most popular poet of the time. He wrote always in disciplined meter and style, and could never be accused of formal eccentricity. Indeed, if any poet seemed ideal for the Nobel Prize in the Swedish Academy's own terms, it was Frost. Why then did he never win? Our cicerone to the Nobel committee, Espmark, notes without further explanation that the Swedish statesman Dag Hammarskjöld thought Frost lost out to Hemingway for "political" reasons.[62]

Frost lived until 1963, Stevens to 1955, Williams to 1963, Moore to 1972.

The one "American" poet who came close was W. H. Auden, who died in 1973. Here arises another nationality tangle: Auden had lived in the United States for thirty years, and became a citizen; if Eliot was counted English, didn't Auden count as American? In 1965 the two leading candidates apparently were Auden and Sartre. Sartre was deemed the philosophy pioneer, Auden the literary innovator. Sartre won; Auden's best work was thought "too far back in time." In 1967 Auden came up again with Miguel Angel Asturias of Guatemala and Graham Greene as his rivals. But now Auden was set aside by a Nobel swing of mood against honoring too well-known writers: why bother to celebrate the celebrated? The same argument obviously worked against Greene; Asturias won.

ENGLISH-LANGUAGE LAUREATES FROM ELSEWHERE

1973 Patrick White, fiction (Australia)

1986 Wole Soyinka, drama (Nigeria)

1991 Nadine Gordimer, fiction (South Africa)

1992 Derek Walcott, poetry (West Indies)

Patrick White (1912-1990) dominated Australian writing in his lifetime and still does. His is no provincial reputation; White is properly seen as one of the great writers of the twentieth century in any language. Soyinka and Gordimer are two from a vast continent of important writers, as yet scarcely noticed by the Nobel committee. Soyinka is a major dramatist, Gordimer a distinguished novelist. But prizes to African writing in English could as rightly have gone to the Nigerian novelists Chinua Achebe (b. 1930) and Amos Tutuola (b. 1922), the Ghanaian poet Kofi Awoonor (b. 1935), the Kenyan novelist Ngugi wa Thiong'o (b. 1938), J. M. Coetzee (b. 1940) of South Africa. Or the major poets Léopold Sédar Senghor or Aimé Césaire, who wrote in French. There may also be worthy prize candidates who write in native African languages or in Portuguese. Walcott's poetry focuses on his West Indian roots, but he draws eclectically from European and American modernism, Greek myth, and much else. V. S. Naipaul is from Trinidad but, as earlier noted, has been passed over by Stockholm.

NOBELS IN FRENCH

LAUREATES FROM FRANCE

1901 Sully Prudhomme, poetry

1904 Frédéric Mistral, poetry (shared with Echegaray of Spain)

1915 Romain Rolland, fiction

1921 Anatole France, fiction

1927 Henri Bergson, philosophy

1937 Roger Martin du Gard, fiction

1947 André Gide, fiction

1952 François Mauriac, fiction

1957 Albert Camus, fiction

1960 Saint-John Perse, poetry

1964 Jean-Paul Sartre, philosophy and fiction

1985 Claude Simon, fiction

Anatole France used to be thought a sceptical Epicurean, Martin du Gard an epic novelist of the bourgeois, Gide an intellectual in the guise of novelist, Mauriac a novelist of Catholic guilt on the rack. Their reputations have faded, Mauriac's perhaps the least.

Albert Camus was the first laureate (1957) from the World War II generation. He wrote existential philosophy in *The Rebel* (1951), and novels of the "absurd" with classic control: *The Stranger* (1942), *The Plague* (1947), *The Fall* (1956). Camus agonized over his award. He thought André Malraux more deserving; and he worried that all his writing from then on—he was only forty-four when he became a laureate—would have to live up to his Nobel reputation. His prestige as a Nobelist and his Algerian birth made him a large political target during the Algerian crisis exploding at that time. But three years later, in 1960, Camus was dead in a car accident.

His onetime existentialist ally and then political opponent was Jean-Paul Sartre, the combative lion of that generation of French intellectuals. But after Sartre's refusal of the 1964 prize, no French writer won for twenty years. Many French saw this as the Swedes' revenge. Others pointed out that Beckett's prize in 1969 was half for writing in French. In 1985 the novelist Claude Simon finally brought France a "full" laureate. A candidate since the 1960s, heavily influenced by Faulkner, Simon's stylistic explorations or obsessions make him one of the few strenuously avant-garde prose writers on the Nobel list.

Among the excluded:

André Malraux: The omission of Malraux (1901-1976) is one of the Nobel's great lapses. He began as a novelist and in midcareer moved into art history, with his famous *Voices of Silence* (1951) and *The Imaginary Museum* (1953), and other works including innovative biography and autobiography. In 1969, after Camus and Sartre had become laureates, many expected Malraux finally to win. He had long been a prominent candidate. But Beckett was chosen instead as the French representative. Malraux believed that the Swedish Academy refused to honor him because they considered Gaullism to be semifascist; Malraux served as a minister under de Gaulle. The Nobel's explanation, according to Espmark, was that Churchill's Nobel Prize, given when he was prime minister, raised charges of political favoritism. Since then, the Swedish Academy chose to honor no writer holding political office. This is supposedly why Léopold Sédar Senghor, president of the Republic of Senegal from 1960, was not honored. But Senghor stepped down in 1980. And why, when de Gaulle was out of office and Malraux not a minister, wasn't he honored then? One is forced to conclude Malraux was right: the Nobel jury's politics vetoed not his work but his Gaullism.

Colette: Sidonie Gabrielle Colette (1873-1954) was so brilliantly the writer of sensuous life, landscape, longing and love, that she was also often confined to a narrow and quintessentially feminine carnality. For the same reason, she has been charged with being trapped in the fin-de-siècle, in the demimonde, in childhood memory and adolescence wakening to sexuality and life. Yet she was a writer of overwhelming natural power, perfect instinct, and inexhaustible vitality. Colette still seems to await adequate appreciation. But after novels like *Chéri* (1920) and memoirs like *Sido* (1929), and her prolific output before and after, she should have been honored in the later 1930s, when she easily outclassed the Italian Grazia Deledda or the Danish J. V. Jensen, to mention no others.

Paul Valéry: Scheduled to be the laureate for 1945, Valéry died in July of that year. The Nobel jury had awarded a posthumous prize in 1931 to the Swedish poet and member of the Swedish Academy Erik Karlfeldt, but decided against this with Valéry, probably since there were many protests that Valéry should have been honored a decade or so before. Valéry's selection was meant as a sign that the Nobel had somewhat abandoned its resistance to "difficult" modernist poetry. A new committee had been appointed, the same that soon honored Faulkner; the next poet selected, Eliot in 1948, was in Valéry's symbolist tradition, as was Perse in 1960, and both were also used to pay homage to Valéry.[63]

Of the three poets among French laureates, only Perse has great distinction, the two others being Sully Prudhomme and Frédéric Mistral. But there has been a crowd of superb poets in French: Louis Aragon, Blaise Cendrars, René Char, Henri Michaux, Pierre Reverdy, Francis Ponge, Yves Bonnefoy, Mohammed Dib, Aimé Césaire.

And why did Marguerite Yourcenar never receive a Nobel?

Nobels in German

Though the few Nobel awards here suggest otherwise, twentieth-century writing in German has been one of modern literature's richest areas, as well as one of the richest mixes of participating nationalities. Poets included Rilke from Prague, Hofmannsthal from Vienna, Paul Celan from Romania, Stefan George and Arno Holz and Peter Huchel from Germany, Carl Spitteler from Switzerland. In fiction and drama, Thomas Mann, Günter Grass, Heinrich Böll, and Bertolt Brecht from Germany; Kafka from Prague; Hermann Broch, Robert Musil, Thomas Bernhard, and the satirist Karl Kraus from Austria; Hermann Hesse and the dramatists Max Frisch and Friedrich Dürrenmatt from Switzerland. With all this talent, the Nobel has netted seven Germans, two Swiss, and two émigré writers. Of these probably only Thomas Mann is of undoubted first rank. How, even in the erratic history of Nobel committees, could so many have been missed by so few?

Laureates from Germany

    1902 Theodor Mommsen, history

    1908 Rudolf Eucken, philosophy

    1910 Paul Heyse, poetry

    1912 Gerhart Hauptmann, drama

    1929 Thomas Mann, fiction

    1972 Heinrich Böll, fiction

    1999 Günter Grass, fiction

Laureates from Switzerland

    1919 Carl Spitteler, poetry

    1946 Hermann Hesse, fiction

Other German-Language Laureates

    1966 Nelly Sachs, poetry (Sweden)

    1981 Elias Canetti, fiction (Bulgaria-Austria-Britain)

Germany's Nobel list is perhaps the strangest of any major European country: four to 1912, then only three in almost ninety years following. Hauptmann, Spitteler, and Heyse were a generation older than Thomas Mann. But Mann's generation is the one strikingly missing from the Nobel awards. Mann (born 1875) was almost an exact contemporary of Rilke (b. 1875), Kafka (b. 1883), Hofmannsthal (b. 1874), Musil (b. 1880), Karl Kraus (b. 1874), Broch (b. 1886), Alfred Döblin (b. 1878). The Nobel judges missed them all. Kafka published too little. The others had the bad luck, with the Nobel in mind, to come to maturity from around 1900 to about 1940—true even of Brecht, born 1898, because of his precocity—when the Nobel strongly disdained modernism.

They also came from unlucky lands: Germany and Austria with their wars and Nazi interregnum, or Central Europe with its contentious small nations and minorities—Czechs, Slovaks, Serbs, Bosnians, Croatians, Poles, Romanians, Bulgarians, Hungarians—often swallowed up by powerful neighbors or thrust into precarious, short-lived independence. Small, fractured, inwardly clashing nations scarcely provide the sort of prestigious nominations and organizational support possible in France or the U.S. In this Mitteleuropa, even becoming visible through translation was difficult, since it was often a point of honor not to know a major language like German or Russian.

Remarkably, there is as yet no Austrian laureate, unless one counts the émigré Canetti.[64] Yet Vienna, in concentration of genius, easily rivaled Paris before Hitler arrived in 1938. Perhaps these Central Europeans were too precocious about the tremors and disorientations of modernity—the Central Europeans knew disorder and fragmentation, as it were, in their bones and history, "along the blood," in a way not available to the French or British, or Swedes. The Nobel committee took fifty years or more to begin to catch up with them. And by then, the 1870s generation were dead or "too old" or still undiscovered. Robert Musil's great novel *The Man without Qualities* (written 1930-43), like those of the Austrian Joseph Roth (1894-1939), is only now coming into its own.

Of this lost generation, special mention must be made of Hermann Broch and Hugo von Hofmannsthal. Broch's epical, many-layered, prose-poetical *The Death of Virgil* (1945) puts him on the level of Proust, Mann, and Joyce. Thomas Mann and Einstein were among those nominating him for a Nobel Prize. The Nobel evaluator felt that *The Death of Virgil* lacked a wide following (true, but irrelevant) and that it mixed narrative, poetry, philosophy, and history to excess (how define "excess"?). Broch died in 1951. By the 1980s the Nobel jury was finally ready to cope with such writing and they chose the lesser Canetti. Hofmannsthal is best known as the librettist for Richard Strauss's operas, but as a poet and dramatist, and analyst of the disintegration of language, he has few superiors.

The novelist Günter Grass, Rabelaisian in energy and enormities, is also outspoken and truculent politically. In 1972, when the Nobel judges finally selected their first postwar German laureate, they passed over Grass—who by then had published *The Tin Drum, Cat and Mouse,* and *Dog Years*—and instead chose the excellent but also more respectable Heinrich Böll, who spoke for decent, middle-of-the-road Germans. Grass finally won in 1999, aged seventy-three.

Of recent writers, the poet Paul Celan is among the Nobel's most serious lapses. Celan was a Romanian Jew born in 1920, who survived the Holocaust, worked in Paris, and wrote poetry in German. Any discussion of modern writing must soon move him into the forefront. His subject was the Holocaust and in his style—the chopped syntax, the words burdened with silences and derailments—that horrifying experience leaks through like blood at every point. But he committed suicide in 1970, aged fifty, while the Nobel evaluators were still cautiously deciding if he measured up to Nobel standards. Was he perhaps not old enough for a prize? One wonders if the Russian poet Brodsky, honored so young and quickly, was another of the Nobel's stand-ins here.

Nobels in Scandinavia

Scandinavian Laureates

1903 Bjørnstjerne Bjørnson (Norway)

1909 Selma Lagerlöf (Sweden)

1916 Carl Verner von Heidenstam (Sweden)

1917 Karl Gjellerup (Denmark); Henrik Pontoppidan (Denmark)

1920 Knut Hamsun (Norway)

1928 Sigrid Undset (Norway)

1931 Erik Karlfeldt (Sweden)

1939 Frans Sillanpää (Finland)

1944 Johannes V. Jensen (Denmark)

1951 Pär Lagerkvist (Sweden)

1955 Halldór Laxness (Iceland)

1974 Eyvind Johnson (Sweden); Harry Martinson (Sweden)

One may perhaps add Nelly Sachs, though she wrote in German and is considered above.

This is fourteen or perhaps fifteen Nobel Prizes to Scandinavian writers—against twelve for France and seven for Germany. One might thus assume we are dealing with a very major body of world writing. But only Hamsun's reputation, and recently Martinson's, has grown. Sillanpää is often said to have won because the Nobel wanted to reward Finland for its brave resistance to the Soviet Union in the 1939 war; Espmark refutes that, pointing out that the USSR attacked Finland on 14 December 1939, months after Sillanpää had been named. But wasn't the Soviet threat discernible months before? Harry Martinson's epic poem *Aniara* is a haunting masterpiece of humans leaving the earth as the space age begins; perhaps Martinson lacks the international fame he deserves because the list's general Scandinavian mediocrity makes him suspect.

It could have been a much more impressive list. To start, there were Ibsen, Strindberg, Georg Brandes, and Isak Dinesen. Was the superb Swedish poet Gunnar Ekelöf (1907-1968) omitted only because by then the list was already swollen with not-so-great Northern writers? And has the arresting Swedish poet Tomas Tranströmer been denied because adding another Swede might be too embarrassing now?

Nobels in Italy

Italian Laureates

1906 Giosuè Carducci, poetry

1926 Grazia Deledda, fiction

1934 Luigi Pirandello, drama

1959 Salvatore Quasimodo, poetry

1975 Eugenio Montale, poetry

1997 Dario Fo

As poet and critic, Carducci was a dominating figure in Italian literature in the last third of the nineteenth century. His is the aura of an emancipator. From midcentury, he challenged a decayed romanticism with an invigorating classicism, and at a time when Italy preferred even poor translations of mediocre French poetry or fiction to its own living best, he helped restore Italian writing to dignity in its homeland. This was the period of his great *Odi barbare* (1877-89), of many sonnets, and of poems celebrating Shelley, Rome, and Dante's church.

Grazia Deledda was self-educated and wrote against all the odds for a woman at that time in that place. Her Sardinian landscapes and peasants, the social world that seemed as fixed and archaic as the earth, are real yet not compelling. The Nobel committee of the 1920s, Espmark notes, considered her an example of the Goethean "great and noble simplicity" they had chosen as their model. One suspects this was another way for the Nobel to finesse the challenge of modern writing, the greatest of which did not meet, nor wish to, Goethean neoclassical standards.

Pirandello is still perhaps the most famous Italian writer of this century. He anticipated the modernist theater, experimental, existential, and absurd. Unfortunately, "Pirandello" too often narrows down to one or two of his plays, *Six Characters in Search of an Author* and *Right You Are, If You Think You Are.* He wrote more than forty plays, seven novels, a hundred-odd short stories, and a great weight of criticism and essays.

Salvatore Quasimodo's Nobel Prize before Montale's seems to have depended crucially on a brilliant English translation by the American poet and translator Allen Mandelbaum, which came out at the opportune moment. That Quasimodo wrote some lovely verses, says Ragusa,

> and that at a certain point he rejected the poetics of Hermeticism to turn to a more readily graspable diction seem insufficient reasons for the decision of the Nobel committee at the expense of alternate possibilities.[65]

Montale has great humanity. But the unanointed Giuseppe Ungaretti (1888-1970) was a greater poet, of such compact power that he can make all other poets garrulous.

Nobels in Russia/USSR

Russian Laureates

1933 Ivan Bunin, fiction

1958 Boris Pasternak, poetry and fiction

1965 Mikhail Sholokhov, fiction

1970 Aleksandr Solzhenitsyn, fiction

1987 Joseph Brodsky, poetry

Twentieth-century Russian literature has been extraordinarily rich, but almost three entire generations were murdered or had their careers chopped short by the Soviet regime, or emigrated—the young Nabokov, for example. In 1925 the Communist Party declared total censorship privilege over all art. In 1932 the Soviet Writers Union took over direct control of publishing and support. A short list with dates suggests how some of the greatest writers had no chance at a Nobel award:

> Andrei Bely, fiction, 1880-1934 (remained in USSR; no important work after 1920s)
>
> Aleksandr Blok, fiction, 1880-1921 (died from overwork)
>
> Vladimir Mayakovsky, poetry, 1893-1930 (suicide)
>
> Osip Mandelstam, poetry, 1891-1938 (died in prison camp)
>
> Eugene Zamyatin, fiction, 1884-1937 (exiled in early 1930s)
>
> Marina Tsvetaeva, poetry, 1892-1941 (suicide)
>
> Isaac Babel, fiction, 1894-1941? (murdered in purges)
>
> Mikhail Bulgakov, fiction, 1891-1940 (major work banned during lifetime)
>
> Anna Akhmatova, poetry, 1889-1966 (mostly unpublished from 1920s; publicly denounced 1946)

Of those who matured during and after the revolution, Boris Pasternak was the first of a meager handful to become a laureate. Pasternak's *Doctor Zhivago* is, however, often said to be rivaled or surpassed by Bulgakov's novel *The Master and Margarita,* allowed into print only sixteen years after the author died. Anna Akhmatova survived by the skin of her teeth, and from the 1950s gained international notice, but the Nobel jury let her die unhonored. It is one of the Stockholm mysteries. Isaiah Berlin, the famous Oxford don and Russia expert, visited her during the war and shortly after, and knew her great worth. Was he ever a Nobel nominator, and if not, why on earth not? There appears only one reason he might not have nominated her—that she might thereby suffer more official harassment. But if the Nobel jury were concerned about that, why then did they expose Pasternak to even worse possible harassment, since his "crime" of publishing a historical novel in the West about the Soviet world was more flagrant? Akhmatova is as great a loss to the list as anyone namable.

Ivan Bunin (Nobel 1933) survived by leaving the Soviet Union in 1920 and never returning. He kept writing in Russian, and happily was widely translated, by D. H. Lawrence among others. It is difficult to see Bunin as anything but a minor writer, but the Nobel citation, laying stress on his link with Russia before the Communists, and even bringing in Tolstoy, suggested Bunin was preserving the great pre-Bolshevik tradition. Even by the time of Bunin's award, however, Nabokov was often considered the best Russian émigré writer. It is known that Aleksandr Solzhenitsyn, for all his apparent distance from Nabokovian playfulness and dandyism, nominated him for the Nobel Prize. Nabokov never won—he seems to hold the record as the writer who should have won a Nobel in either or both of two different languages.

Nobels in Poland

Polish Laureates

1905 Henryk Sienkiewicz, fiction

1924 Władysław Reymont, fiction

1980 Czesław Miłosz, poetry

1996 Wisława Szymborska, poetry

Sienkiewicz's *Quo Vadis* appeared in 1896 and over the next few decades sold millions of copies. The Nobel judges have often been greatly impressed by the international popularity of a writer—it can seem a testimony of worth—and here was one indeed.

By the time Reymont's historical novels were honored, Polish writing was starting to remake itself into writing as vital as any in the world. In the 1920s new movements sprang up. Before and after the Second War there were such fiction writers, to mention only those best known in the West, as Tadeus Borowski, Witold Gombrowicz, Bruno Schulz, Jerzy Peterkiewicz, the science-fantasist Stanisław Lem—and such Yiddish writers as I. J. Singer, brother of the Nobelist I. B. Singer. Poets included Miłosz, Alexander Wat, and the slightly younger Zbigniew Herbert, Tadeus Resewicz, and Adam Mickiewicz. In the 1980s, the later Russian Nobelist Joseph Brodsky was not alone in saying that everyone should learn Polish because the century's most interesting poetry was being written in that language.

Miłosz came to maturity in the 1930s, in a Poland wracked between the Soviets and Nazis, and inwardly by its own many tensions; he witnessed firsthand the destruction of the Warsaw ghetto; in 1951, he went into exile. His poetry brims with extraordinary richness, an unsettling blend of generosity and bitterness, open to all experience. The next Polish laureate, in 1996, was another poet, Wisława Szymborska (b. 1923). Younger than Miłosz, she is little known in the West. She has been called one of the least prolific major poets of our time. No one else quite so casual and commanding comes to mind.

And should Isaac Bashevis Singer be added to the Polish list? The puzzling notion of nationality arises again. He lived in Poland, mainly Warsaw, until he was thirty-one, writing in Yiddish, publishing there his famous story "Satan in Goray." In 1935 he emigrated to the U.S., but he kept writing in Yiddish and setting his fiction most often in Poland. After James Joyce left Ireland, he kept writing about Dublin, and remained an Irish writer. So should Singer be listed among "Polish" writers?

Nobels in Spanish

Spanish-Language Laureates

1904 José Echegaray, drama, Spain

1922 Jacinto Benavente, drama, Spain

1945 Gabriela Mistral, poetry, Chile

1956 Juan Ramón Jiménez, poetry, Spain

1967 Miguel Angel Asturias, fiction, Guatemala

1971 Pablo Neruda, poetry, Chile

1977 Vicente Aleixandre, poetry, Spain

1982 Gabriel García Márquez, fiction, Colombia

1989 Camilo José Cela, fiction, Spain

1990 Octavio Paz, poetry, Mexico

The awards to Echegaray and Benavente, both deemed lightweight writers, roused scepticism and protests in Spain. No prizes thereafter for Spain for thirty years, until the award to Jiménez. He was famous in Spain for his *Platero y yo* (1917) and later symbolist poetry, but, as noted, his prize was partly to honor a generation passed over by the Nobel jury. So too with Aleixandre.

The opening of Latin America to the Nobel Prize was bound to cause disputes about awards. The continent seemed overflowing with talent. Was Gabriela Mistral really a more deserving poet than César Vallejo of Peru, or did she simply outlive him—he died in 1938, aged forty-six—and so be there when the Nobel jury decided it was time to honor the first South American?[66] Mistral's award also blocked one to the eminent Chilean poet Vicente Huidobro, whom many believe superior to Mistral. The prizes to Neruda, García Márquez (*One Hundred Years of Solitude*), and Octavio Paz seem universally approved.

Against Latin America's two fiction laureates, Spain has one: Camilo José Cela, who reinvigorated Spanish fiction after the Civil War, especially by his *The Hive* (1951), whose hero is Madrid itself, traversed by 116 characters. It remains a puzzle why the Nobel judges delayed Cela for more than forty years, or after such a delay, honored him.

Two Argentines were never honored, to the Nobel's impoverishment: Julio Cortázar (died 1984) and the incomparable Jorge Luis Borges (died 1986).

And not until 1998 was the first Portuguese laureate named: the novelist José Saramago, at age seventy-five.

Japanese Nobels

Laureates from Japan

1968 Yasunari Kawabata, fiction

1994 Kenzaburo Oe, fiction

Of all Asian nations, Japan alone has won two Nobels. The remarkable interest from the 1950s of English and French translators in Japanese literature helps account for this, as well as Japan's own determined effort to westernize itself. Its first great modern novelist, Natsume Soseki (1867-1916), studied in England from 1900 to 1902, and the influence of European writing showed in his work only a few years later. A great and subtle novelist, of undoubted Nobel caliber, he remained untranslated before his death.

In the decades after the Second World War, when enough translations were at hand, two writers attracting world attention were Jun'ichiro Tanizaki (1886-1965) and Yukio Mishima (1925-1970). Tanizaki's subjects were unpredictable and startling: *The Makioka Sisters* (1948) seemed to some Western readers as clinically obsessed with disease as Mann's *The Magic Mountain*. His novel of a man masochistically submitting to lovely women for a glimpse of higher beauty (*Diary of an Old Mad Man*) is at once bizarre and brilliantly perceptive. But he won no Nobel. Perhaps, as a critic of Japanese literature pointedly noted, "his resolutely aesthetic focus, meager in what might be called redeeming social values," greatly reduced his Nobel chances.[67] The flamboyant Mishima committed ritual suicide in 1970 when he was forty-five.

The first laureate was Kawabata. His prize raised two questions that emerge about every non-Western Nobel Prize. Are the Nobel jury drawn to works showing Western influence, since these can be compared more readily to what they know? Or the opposite: do they seek what seems to them unwesternized, exotic, "other," redolent of strangeness? Many Japanese deemed Kawabata's novels quite inwardly Japanese. To go by their citation, the Nobel judges must have thought so too. He was lauded "for his narrative mastery which with great sensibility expresses the essence of the Japanese mind," and he thus contributes to "spiritual bridge-building between East and West." Kawabata is assuredly a great writer, so far as one can tell from an English translation that must render experiences of a fragmented modern kind narrated in prose that often seems like haiku.

The second award went—almost thirty full years after Kawabata's—to Kenzaburo Oe. His story is unusual and moving. He began writing fiction after a son was born brain-damaged. The experiences of Hiroshima survivors affected Oe's decision here as well: writing was "a way of exorcism." The son, though remaining mentally handicapped, emerged as a remarkable composer; the father won the Nobel Prize. Oe says he was greatly influenced by fellow members of a writers' group he belonged to, including Kobo Abe, best known for *The Woman in the Dune*, and Masuji Ibuse, who wrote *Black Rain*. Both died before Oe became a laureate; in a sense, he is another stand-in. Since winning the prize—and with his son's success as a composer—Oe has decided to stop writing novels, and perhaps try a different literary form.

The Nobel "Out There"

Artur Lundkvist, a member of the Nobel jury, once bluntly commented that while the Swedish Academy is reproached for neglecting writing in Asian, African, and other regions,

> I doubt if there is very much to find there. It is a question of literatures that [he cites Japan as an exception], as far as can be judged, have not achieved the level of development (artistic, psychological, linguistic) that can make them truly significant outside their given context.

This was taken by many as arrogantly Eurocentric. But Lundkvist was raising a real if politically unpalatable possibility: "The Nobel Prize is after all a Western institution and cannot reasonably be distributed on the basis of other than Western evaluations."[68]

The literature Nobel is rooted in the centrality of the book and writing. What happens when such a self-contained artifact doesn't matter? Or when literature exists in ritual or political contexts that baffle analysis in Western terms? Or if, even among people of the Book, taking up Western literary forms is to be resisted, as among Islamic fundamentalists, in the name of national or religious integrity? The conviction can arise, as Lundkvist attests, that there is little of worth to find "out there"—at least for the Nobel Prize as now known.

There are other mountainous problems. In countries as vast as China and India, the number of writers about whom even the best-informed Western expert knows essentially nothing is staggering. It would take a generation of monumental labor and endless computerizing simply to read, tabulate, and sort them out, to get the lay of the literary landscape and the start of a feel for its special topography—and we are not yet speaking of translating or critical evaluation with sufficient cultural and linguistic intimacy and sympathy. The languages of Indian literature include Hindi, Kashmiri, Punjabi, Gujarati, Marathi, Bengali, Maithili, Tamil, Assamese, among others; prosodies can vary dizzyingly, as do the assumptions underlying imagery and themes, variously springing from Hindu, Buddhist, and Islamic roots. The important African novelist Ngugi wa Thiong'o, after establishing a reputation with novels in English, began writing in Kikuyu, his native tongue.[69]

What to do? The Novel committee, as befits a committee, has sought the help of other committees and organizations such as PEN groups, and meanwhile beefed up its own resources—in earlier times with an Arabic scholar and someone who could read Tagore in Bengali (but chose not to!) and more recently with an expert on modern Chinese literature along with a member who can read Russian. Other specialists have been consulted.[70]

But this is like pitting a few sandbags against a flooding Mississippi. The sheer diversity of languages in the world is overwhelming. One needs a small army of linguists just for India, another for Africa. And linguists are beside the point here anyway, since one needs literary critics gifted enough to spot the very best, and there have never been enough of those anywhere.

There is also the Nobel's constant fear of being labeled politically biased. Should the committee select some neglected language area and then systematically search for the "best" writer? No: "Doing so would amount to a politicization of the prize."[71] But the alternative is to wait until, somehow, a writer from a "remote" area becomes prominent enough to be nominated as a candidate.

Yet it needs no emphasizing that writers' contemporary reputations often owe as much to chance and manipulation as to merit. In the West, with its free competitive cultural and economic markets, much depends on skill at promotion and self-advertisement. Advertising money spent by publishers can grease the slide. But how does it work in

Somalia, or Sri Lanka, or Syria, or Surinam? The media and universities there are often government-controlled; scholars and critics usually command little international clout; professional literary societies may not exist and individual scholars may be poorly informed; translations, if any, may be rare or amateurish.

It cannot be doubted that the Swedish Academy acutely understands the difficulties involved in all this as well as anyone. But to have a resident specialist in Chinese and the like will not help much. Even in France or the U.S., where the scrutiny and assessment of contemporary writing is incessantly done by hundreds of experts, there is not the slightest guarantee that such effort locates the best writers. What then are the chances in an India with its multitudinous languages and subcultures? Or in a small African nation?

Can anything help? At the end of almost a century of awarding prizes, the Nobel is still quite unadventurous in its move out into global literature. But perhaps it is not unadventurousness, after all. Perhaps a certain realism is setting in, now that the easier awards (i.e., major Western) have been made. Perhaps the committee will reorganize itself radically to cope with the strange swarming mass of literary and linguistic usages "out there." Perhaps it will redefine what it means by "literature." Or perhaps it will stand pat, and wait for arbitrary market and other chance forces to flush up an author from a distant land who then, willy-nilly, becomes a "major candidate." This hardly seems satisfactory, but radical surgery on the Nobel doesn't seem likely either. Perhaps its slogan should be the very last remark of Beckett's narrator in *The Unnamable*: "You must go on, I can't go on, I'll go on."

Finale

The Nobel Prize in Literature is bedeviled by its history. A physicist who nominated Einstein added the warning: imagine how the Nobel scientific list will look fifty years from now with Einstein missing. The Nobel Literature Prize demonstrates the truth of that remark. But the prize has indeed changed greatly and for the better. At least in the last three decades, the awards have kept a high level. If this can only continue for another thirty years or so, the weak laureates of the first half century will gradually be forgotten. It is a high-risk task, given the uncertain nature of literary reputations, to say nothing of the uncertain future of literature itself.

Long before the Nobel existed, Herman Melville worried this same problem. Melville of course lost his own readership with *Moby Dick*, and in our century would never have won a Nobel Prize (too obscure, misanthropic). Here he is prophetically taking up our concern. He is thinking not of glorified prizes but of the literary establishment that sets the taste for the public and the age. He is writing about Hawthorne, trying to persuade the reader to see how great Hawthorne is right now, and not to leave him hanging until "posterity" (or any Nobel authority) hands down a verdict:

Give not over to future generations the glad duty of acknowledging him for what he is. Take that joy to yourself, in your own generation; and so shall he feel those grateful impulses on him, that may possibly prompt him to the full flower of some still greater achievement in your eyes. And by confessing him, you thereby confess others; you brace the whole brotherhood. For genius, all over the world, stands hand in hand, and one shock of recognition runs the whole circle round.

Notes

1. Wallace, *Writing of a Novel*, 161. The novel referred to in the title is *The Prize*.

2. In these same decades (1910-40) the Pulitzer Prizes in the U.S. chose the same sort of middlebrow writers: Booth Tarkington, Edna Ferber, Louis Bromfield, Julia Peterkin, Oliver LaFarge, Pearl Buck, Margaret Mitchell, J. P. Marquand, and Marjorie Kinnan Rawlings (of *The Yearling* fame). Like the Nobels, the Pulitzers occasionally landed a good one: Cather, Sinclair Lewis (who refused the prize), Thornton Wilder. But in this same period they blackballed Fitzgerald, Hemingway, Dos Passos, and Faulkner.

3. Frenz, "What Prize Glory?" 44.

4. Brown, "Twenty Years and Two Laureates," 208.

5. Kjell Espmark, *The Nobel Prize in Literature* (1986) is the indispensable study of the voting and nominating records of the Nobel literary committees from 1901 to 1986. This chapter is crucially indebted to his work. His book resulted from unrestricted access to the otherwise sealed Nobel archives. He has been chair of the Nobel literary committee since 1988. In every sense an insider, he views the Nobel awards in terms of the various committees' historical biases, needs, and constraints. He writes neither to defend nor to attack the Nobel choices and fairly gives evidence on both sides, but places them in the historical context of the Nobel committees. This is a healthy corrective to any naive notion of how the prize originates. But besides seeing how the prizes reflect the personalities of the committees, they must finally be judged on their own terms, and that is a different story. On that side, the Nobel Prizes do present themselves to the public in terms of "timeless" excellence. The history of the American presidency cannot be understood in terms of election campaigns. See Herbert Howarth's trenchant comment in the text for the limitations of an approach like Espmark's, and also the Finale section.

6. Ödelberg, *Nobel*, 91.

7. Espmark, *Nobel Prize in Literature*, 153.

8. Ödelberg, *Nobel*, 136.

9. Espmark, *Nobel Prize in Literature*, 79.

10. For "the Boyg," see Levin, *Memories of the Moderns*, 115-16.

11. Specter, "The Nobel Syndrome," 48. The next quote in the text about Sture Allen is also from Specter, 48.

12. Perhaps this animosity is why Sture Allen remains permanent secretary, while Kjell Espmark has chaired the committee since 1988. Up to 1986, the permanent secretary also chaired the committee.

13. Oppenheimer, *The Open Mind,* 119.

14. Espmark, *Nobel Prize in Literature,* 146.

15. Howarth, "Petition to the Swedish Academy," 6.

16. Espmark, *Nobel Prize in Literature,* 64.

17. One of the most successful awards of prizes without a committee occurred in 1914, when the philosopher Ludwig Wittgenstein, whose family was wealthy, decided to give 100,000 Austrian crowns (then worth about approximately £4,000 or $20,000, almost the size of a Nobel Prize) to needy Austrian artists. Wittgenstein asked an Austrian editor, Ludwig von Ficker, to decide. Ficker split the money among three artists: Rilke, Georg Trakl, and Carl Dallago.

18. Espmark, *Nobel Prize in Literature,* 4-5.

19. Ödelberg, *Nobel,* 77.

20. Ibid., 9.

21. Ruth, "Second New Nation," 53.

22. These quotes, respectively, are from Espmark, *Nobel Prize in Literature,* 10-11, 17, 18, 25.

23. Ibid., 16-17.

24. The classical scholar G. W. Bowersock, in a review of a translation of Mommsen's *History of Rome,* claims the work still had relevance when honored in 1902, and that perhaps the Nobel jury believed it could push the eighty-five-year-old author into finishing his missing volume 4. They were wrong. See Bowersock, "Rendering unto Caesar."

25. See Espmark, *Nobel Prize in Literature,* 164-65.

26. Coleman, "Why Asturias?" 1-3.

27. Sommer, "The Air You Breathe."

28. Heaney, *Redress of Poetry,* 2.

29. *Nobel Lectures in Literature 1901-67,* 196.

30. Wallace, *Writing of a Novel,* 17. Wallace claims he was told that Buck scarcely bowled over the academy. Ten of the eighteen members voted against her, but Sven Hedin and Selma Lagerlöf changed their minds. Hedin was Wallace's informant.

31. Ödelberg, *Nobel,* 115.

32. Vowles, "Twelve Northern Authors."

33. Howarth, "Petition to the Swedish Academy," 5.

34. The influential Swedish critic Sven Delblanc, writing in 1982, claimed that saga fiction appealed so much to the Nobel judges and Swedish readers because Swedish writers were more comfortable dealing with their country's past than its present. But this past is painted darkly, so that readers—while escaping the present—can also say that things aren't so bad now. Quoted in Gustafsson, "Silences of the North," 97.

35. Espmark, *Nobel Prize in Literature,* 38.

36. Contat and Rybalka, *Writings of Jean-Paul Sartre,* 455. For Sartre's pro-Communism and Nobel "objectivity," see Espmark, *Nobel Prize in Literature,* 109-12.

37. Contat and Rybalka, *Writings of Jean-Paul Sartre,* 453.

38. Sholokhov wrote *The Quiet Don* (more than a thousand pages) between the ages of twenty-two and twenty-five. The first volume appeared in 1928, and there were immediate charges that Sholokhov had plagiarized a Cossack writer; evidence for and against has been advanced, but the case remains unsettled. His writing during the rest of his life never came near matching the *Don* work. See Scammell, "The Don Flows Again."

39. Espmark, "Nobel Prize in Literature" on Nobel website, 8.

40. Bizzarro, *Pablo Neruda,* 135

41. Specter, "The Nobel Syndrome," 52.

42. Espmark, *Nobel Prize in Literature,* 108. Also Espmark, "Nobel Prize in Literature," Nobel website, 4, states that Hammarskjöld negotiated "on the Academy's commission" for Pound's release from St. Elizabeth's Hospital, where he was confined after World War II. Espmark cites this as an instance of the academy's "generosity." But if the Swedish Academy thought Pound not mentally ill—and thus fit to be released from the mental asylum—shouldn't they have concluded he had committed treason against his country and belonged in jail?

43. Espmark, *Nobel Prize in Literature,* 109.

44. Ibid.

45. On Céline, see Steiner, "Cry Havoc," 35-46.

46. Espmark, *Nobel Prize in Literature,* 115.

47. Ziolkowski, "German Literature and the Prize," 1.

48. See Bahti and Fries, *Jewish Writers,* for a general discussion; for Sachs's mental suffering, 35; for Domin, 3 and 49 (Sachs's "poetry belongs to the best produced in the German language during this century"); for the German isolation of Sachs as a Holocaust poet, 8, 49-50, and passim.

49. Miłosz, *Witness of Poetry,* 7. For a survey of the nations and writers involved, see Czerwinski, "For Whom the Nobel Tolls."

50. Dutta and Robinson, *Tagore,* report that in the 1920s and 1930s he was one of the most popular lecturers in the world.

51. Ödelberg, *Nobel,* 94.

52. Dates and comments on Claudel are given in Espmark, *Nobel Prize in Literature,* 54, 59, and 161.

53. The film critic Stanley Kauffmann suggested Nobel awards for screenplays, with Ingmar Bergman or Akira Kurosawa as eligibles.

54. Ödelberg, *Nobel,* 97.

55. Espmark, *Nobel Prize in Literature,* 67.

56. Ödelberg, *Nobel,* 123.

57. Österling in Ödelberg, *Nobel,* 1st ed., 132: the prizes "obviously cannot serve as a representative picture of the literary standards in each country."

58. Espmark, *Nobel Prize in Literature,* 42, 152; for "not a single legitimate proposal," 190.

59. Ellmann, *James Joyce,* 546. For Joyce's non-nominations, see Espmark, *Nobel Prize in Literature,* 152.

60. Edel, *Henry James: The Master;* 476.

61. Espmark, *Nobel Prize in Literature,* 26.

62. Ibid., 106.

63. Ibid., 74, on Valéry as "difficult"; 59 and 80 on earlier Nobel evaluations of Valéry.

64. In a letter to the *New York Times* (18 October 1981), the German literature scholar Roman Karst protested that the *Times* had described Canetti as "the first Bulgarian" to win the Nobel in Literature. Karst pointed out that Canetti left Bulgaria at age six, lived in Austria from 1921 to 1938 and wrote his major works there, and, alluding to his debt to that city's writers Nestroy and Karl Kraus, said, "I am a Viennese writer."

65. Ragusa, "Carducci, Deledda, Pirandello, Quasimodo."

66. More intriguing gossip from Irving Wallace: a Nobel committee member told him that Mistral was chosen over Croce, Hesse, Sandburg, Jules Romains, and others because a Nobel judge and poet, Hjalmar Gullberg, fell in love with her verse and translated it all into Swedish—and single-handedly swayed the entire vote. See *Writing of a Novel,* 19.

67. Yoshio Iwamoto, "The Nobel Prize in Literature, 1967-87: A Japanese View," 218.

68. Espmark, *Nobel Prize in Literature,* 141.

69. Preminger, *Princeton Encyclopedia of Poetry,* 389-90. For Ngugi, see Sturrock, *Oxford Guide to Contemporary Writing,* 13.

70. See Espmark for the Bengali scholar. Espmark thus claims that the academy's "linguistic competence has, as a rule, been high," in "Nobel Prize in Literature," Nobel website, 7.

71. Espmark, *Nobel Prize in Literature,* 142.

THE PULITZER PRIZE

W. J. Stuckey (essay date 1981)

SOURCE: Stuckey, W. J. "Joseph Pulitzer and His Prizes." In *The Pulitzer Prize Novels: A Critical Backward Look,* pp. 3-25. Norman: University of Oklahoma Press, 1981.

[*In the following excerpt, Stuckey provides biographical and historical context for Joseph Pulitzer, the founder of the Pulitzer Prizes, and for the award itself.*]

The life story of Joseph Pulitzer, founder of the Pulitzer prizes in journalism, letters, and music, fits beautifully into a familiar pattern of American success. Pulitzer arrived in this country in 1864 at the age of seventeen, without money and with almost no competence in the English language. By a combination of hard work, shrewdness, thrift, perseverance, some luck and some opportunism, he made his way relentlessly to financial eminence. When he died in 1911, Pulitzer left a fortune of almost nineteen million dollars, including two large and prosperous newspapers, the St. Louis *Post-Dispatch* and the New York *World*.[1]

Like some other self-made millionaires of the late nineteenth century, Joseph Pulitzer also left behind an ambiguous reputation as both an exploiter and a benefactor of the public. Pulitzer's newspapers helped expose public and private abuse of power and led campaigns for political and social reform, but they were also blamed, even by sympathetic critics, with helping debase the standards of American journalism through stunts, sensationalism, and in other ways that catered to the taste of the masses.[2] Pulitzer himself seemed to have felt that in the conduct of his newspapers he had been a model of integrity. For despite what might seem to more objective observers as a deliberate courting of the lowest taste, Pulitzer evidently felt that in turning out a "cheap," "bright," "interesting" newspaper, he was giving the people what they required. The profits he made from the pennies of the poor were not just so much money in the bank; they were a return on service rendered the public. In his newspaper columns and feature articles, he brought news down to the people's level; on his editorial page he took issue with the "purse potentates" and battled for the people with "earnest sincerity."[3]

Whatever Pulitzer's deepest motives may have been and whatever his severest critics may have thought these were, his devotion to the interests of the common people and his own self-interest were, in his mind, inseparable. Though rich and successful himself, he despised the privileged classes and still emotionally identified himself with the poor and the disenfranchised, a class to which his early poverty and immigrant status had consigned him. Pulitzer was also a moral pragmatist. That is, he knew from practical experience that to expand and prosper in mid-nineteenth-century America, a newspaper had to be not only cheap and popular but also "morally" sound. Without morals, he once wrote, no newspaperman can hope to succeed.[4] If this seems crass and hypocritical, it is also commonsensical, in the tradition of Ben Franklin.

While he was still a fairly young man, Pulitzer's health failed and he had to surrender direct management of his newspapers to subordinates. Although he continued to keep in touch, receiving reports and issuing commands by telegram or cable, he now had time for other things, including the disposition of his fortune and the establishment of several endowments, including one for his favorite project, a journalism college. The establishment of such a school, Pulitzer felt, would raise the standards of American newspapers and put journalists on somewhat the same footing as doctors and lawyers. He did not mean to make scholars or intellectuals of apprentice journalists, of course, but only to give them enough history, law, literature, and morality to help them carry on their careers successfully.[5] In 1890, Pulitzer approached Harvard University with an offer of one million dollars if the university would undertake sponsorship of his school. The offer was turned down by President Eliot. Two years later, Pulitzer made a similar proposal to Columbia University, and it was also rejected by President Low and the university's trustees.[6]

Off and on for another ten years Pulitzer brooded over his project, revising, polishing, and attempting to make it more acceptable to the academic world. Then in 1903 he submitted a revised plan to Columbia University's new president, Nicholas Murray Butler. President Butler, as it turned out, was more sympathetic to the idea of a college of journalism. This time the Columbia trustees accepted the one million dollars and undertook to establish Joseph Pulitzer's school.[7] Then, while public announcements were being prepared, Pulitzer began negotiations with Columbia for the establishment of another favorite project, a series of annual prizes and scholarships in journalism and letters. To persuade the trustees to undertake this additional responsibility, Pulitzer offered to add another million dollars to the endowment of the new journalism school—provided that half the income from this additional million would be given away each year as cash prizes in journalism and letters. This second million with its attendant responsibilities was also accepted by Columbia, and establishment of the Pulitzer prizes was thereby assured.[8]

In his negotiations with Columbia, Pulitzer displayed some of the same stubbornness that had characterized many of his dealings with subordinates on the *World*. He was willing to put his journalism college and yearly prizes into Columbia's care, but he wished to make certain that they would be managed according to his specifications. Although he was too ill himself to take a hand in setting up the journalism school, he made certain that its initial character was shaped by journalistic rather than academic minds: he arranged with Columbia for the creation of an Advisory Board, to be appointed by himself, to help launch his college and to take charge of the prizes in letters and journalism.

Although Pulitzer gave this board the authority to determine the standards of excellence to be looked for in the prize-winning works, he could not forbear stipulating the standards by which he meant the board to be guided. The intent of these terms as Pulitzer set them down was quite explicit, though the meaning was exceedingly vague. For the four prizes in letters (that is, for the novel, an original American play, a work of American history, and an American biography), the judges were instructed to look mainly for patriotism, good manners, and good morals. Only the prize in American history was to be given "for the best book of the year" in that category. The novel prize, according to official announcements, was to be awarded "annually, for the American novel published during the year which shall best present the wholesome atmosphere of American life and the highest standard of American manners and manhood. $1000."[9] This wording, given out to newspapers and repeated year after year to jurors in letters of instruction and enshrined in the yearly announcement of the novel prize-winner, was not exactly as Joseph Pulitzer had specified it. In his detailed instructions to Columbia, Pulitzer had stipulated that the prize-winning novel should reflect "the *whole* atmosphere of American life"; someone in the Columbia administration—Nicholas Murray Butler, presumably—changed *whole* to *wholesome*.[10] From the standpoint of consistency the change made sense, of course, but in coming out explicitly for wholesomeness the Columbia authorities would make it more difficult for their best jurors to exercise their own judgment, and would encourage the rest to play it safe and pick books that would not offend "respectable" taste.

From a certain point of view it could be said that the Pulitzer authorities were simply creatures of their own time, merely translating into too simple language the taste and prejudice of the late Victorian age. One recalls, for instance, from Henry James's famous essay, "The Art of Fiction," that Walter Besant listed as one of the chief requirements for the novel a "conscious moral purpose."[11] The phrase "conscious moral purpose," of course, admits the possibility of a writer's including in his novel both "bad" and "good" characters, whereas the phrase "presenting the wholesome atmosphere of American life" and "the highest standards of American manners and manhood" suggest that only books fit for a Sunday school library qualified for a Pulitzer prize in fiction. Certainly Hawthorne's *The Scarlet Letter,* Melville's *Moby Dick,* Twain's *Huckleberry Finn,* or Crane's *The Red Badge of Courage* could not have qualified. Nor could James's *The Ambassadors,* nor, technically even Howells' *The Rise of Silas*

Lapham, which comes closer to fulfilling the spirit of these conditions than any other important American novel published during Pulitzer's lifetime.

Naïve as such literary standards were, they would not have caused as much difficulty in the 1880's or even in the early 1900's as they did after 1917, the year the first prizes were awarded: for by then American fiction had begun to mirror and often encourage the social revolution that was sweeping away the code of polite behavior that governed the public lives of middle-class Americans—a generally accepted standard that might have given the Pulitzer terms some relevance. In fact, the success of much of the new fiction—John Dos Passos' *Three Soldiers,* Sinclair Lewis' *Main Street,* F. Scott Fitzgerald's *This Side of Paradise,* and Ernest Hemingway's *The Sun Also Rises*—was to depend in part on the reader's awareness that the standards of conventional morality were being questioned. By 1925 the criteria set down by Pulitzer (and amended, presumably, by Nicholas Murray Butler) were irrelevant even to second- and third-rate American novels.

It is to Joseph Pulitzer's credit that, although he left his administrators a set of naïve literary standards, he also left them the means to set themselves free. Pulitzer's will provided that any of the conditions he had drawn up for the granting of these prizes could be changed by the Advisory Board when rendered necessary by the passing of time or if such changes or alterations seemed "conducive to the public good."[12] Almost from the beginning there were problems with the official terms. Younger jurors in particular felt constrained by the emphasis on "wholesomeness." The Advisory Board, however, doubtless at the insistence of Nicholas Murray Butler, held onto these terms for eleven years and then changed them only after the award to *The Bridge of San Luis Rey* in 1928 had clearly violated the requirement that the prize novel deal with American life. After that decision, *wholesome* was dropped back to the *whole* of Pulitzer's original wording and the "manners and manhood" clause was eliminated. The new terms for the novel prize, to be applied in the 1929 contest, then, read: "For the American novel published during the year, preferably one which shall best present the whole atmosphere of American life." The Advisory Board had dispensed with the moralism and uplift, but by reintroducing that ambiguous word *whole* and adding an ambiguity of its own, had further muddied the waters. What was meant by *the* American novel? And by *whole,* did the authorities mean that to qualify for a Pulitzer prize a novel had to get *all* of American life into one novel? Or did *whole* simply mean that the prize-winning novel might include the sordid as well as the wholesome aspects of American life—whatever these might be?[13]

The following year, evidently in an attempt to clear up the confusion, the authorities announced that they had formulated another new set of requirements for the novel: The Pulitzer prize in 1930 would be given for "the best American novel published during the year, preferably one which shall best present the wholesome atmosphere of American life."[14] These new conditions, which read like a statement of compromise between literary critics and public moralists, were certainly more precise than the last version. However, by retaining the equivocal adverb "preferably," the authorities seemed to acknowledge the "best" American novel might not be wholesome, which could hardly have pleased the moralists. And so the next year, 1931, the Pulitzer authorities announced a third set of conditions, which came out unequivocally for excellence as the only official criterion for the fiction prize. The Pulitzer novel prize would now be given "for the best novel" published during the year by an American author.[15]

But more changes were to come. So much controversy was stirred up in 1934 when the Pulitzer officials rejected their drama jury's vote for Maxwell Anderson's play, *Mary of Scotland*—jurors were resigning and denouncing the Pulitzer officials in print and on the radio—that the authorities again altered the terms of the novel as well as the drama awards, giving preference once more to American material. Henceforth, the novel prize would be given "for the best novel published during the year by an American author, preferably dealing with American life."[16]

The critics were not silenced, however. One disaffected drama juror, Clayton Hamilton, continued to attack the drama selections and, in 1935, disgruntled New York drama critics founded a rival drama prize, the New York Drama Critics Circle Award.[17] In an obvious attempt to put a stop to such criticism, or to cut the ground from under their critics' feet, Pulitzer authorities in 1936 made a fifth change in the official prize conditions. Instead of claiming to select the "best" novel [play, and so forth] of the year, they would now simply give their prize to "a distinguished novel of the year."[18] The new terms, of course, amounted to little more than word-juggling. The fact that the Pulitzer officials continued to single out one work from the hundreds produced each year implied (whether they wished to admit it or not), that, for reasons unspecified, the chosen work was thought to be the best one published in that year.

Since 1936 one more alteration has been made in the official terms under which the novel award is made. In 1947 the word "novel" was dropped and the phrase "fiction in book form" was substituted.[19] These are the terms under which the awards have since been made. Considering the many fine collections of short stories that have appeared in this country before 1947—by Ring Lardner, F. Scott Fitzgerald, Ernest Hemingway, Caroline Gordon, Katherine Anne Porter, and many others—this change was long overdue. Regrettably enough, the Pulitzer authorities appear to have been motivated less by a desire to broaden the scope of the award than to accommodate James A. Michener's *Tales of the South Pacific,*[20] a poorly written collection of journalistic sketches that could not qualify under the old conditions.

During the early 1920's, when the Pulitzer prize was not well known, officials of Columbia University disseminated information about the prize selection procedure. It was explained that the Pulitzer prizes were awarded as the result of a "national competition" in which writers from all parts of the United States competed. In order to enter a book in the contest, it was said, novelists or their agents (that is, their publishers) had only to submit a letter of nomination and a copy of the book to the Pulitzer authorities. The novels so nominated were then read by a three-man jury of "experts" who met together, nominated the prize-winning work, and passed on their recommendation to the Advisory Board of the School of Journalism. The board, at its annual meeting in May, then voted to accept or reject the recommendations of its juries and passed on its decisions to the trustees of Columbia University for approval and official certification.[21]

Columbia officials said nothing publicly about how the jury reached its verdict, but some jurors did talk about what went on behind the scenes. As a consequence, the jury procedure became public knowledge. After the jury was appointed, each member was provided with a list of the novels that had been formally "nominated" and the process of narrowing the field began. First, the committee eliminated all works thought ineligible, then it read and rejected all but three novels which the jury agreed were the best of the lot. When that list was complete, a final vote was taken. Each juror ranked the candidates in the order of his preference and sent his ballot to the chairman of the jury, who then totaled the results (giving three points for a first place vote, two for a second, and so forth) and forwarded to Columbia the name of the candidate that had received the largest number of points. At its annual meeting in May the Advisory Board then voted on the recommendations of its juries. This nominating procedure was in effect (officially, at least) from 1918 until 1934 when, because of the public dispute with drama jurors, a new system was officially instituted. Beginning in 1934 all literature juries were instructed not to recommend one candidate for the prize, but instead to submit the names of several possible contenders along with the jury's reasons for recommending each one. The final decision was then made by the newspaper publishers and editors who served on the Advisory Board.[22]

The role of the Advisory Board in the yearly decisions before the 1950's has never been made entirely clear. Though legally free to do as it chose, the board for many years left the choice of prize-winning books pretty much to the juries, intervening only when asked to do so by President Butler and then merely to follow his instructions.[23] Even after the alteration in 1934 of the nominating procedures, the juries apparently continued to make the final selection by pushing one candidate harder than others, the Advisory Board acting only when a jury could not agree on a top contender. Whether in those instances the board actually read all of the books nominated by the jury, or whether it based its decision on the jury's comments (and Butler's suggestions) is an open question. It did happen occasionally that a board member pushed his own preference which, whether nominated by the jury or not, might end up with the prize, as *Tales of the South Pacific* did in 1948.[24]

But whatever role the Advisory Board played from year to year, it was always under the watchful eye of Nicholas Murray Butler, who was the real power behind the scenes. Nothing could be done that Butler did not approve. He had a long-standing, jealous regard for the Pulitzer prizes, particularly for the novel prize, and saw it as a means of attracting national attention to the university. Butler's influence extended from the beginning in 1917 until his retirement in 1942. Though he apparently never worked to get any one candidate the prize (he may, however, have pushed for Ellen Glasgow's *In This Our Life* in 1942), he saw to it that only the kind of books he approved were finally selected.[25] He did this primarily by making certain that only his sort of people were appointed as jurors. In the early years when juries were filled from the rosters of the American Academy of Arts and Letters (of which Butler was president), and from its affiliate organization, the National Institute of Arts and Letters, Butler either made the selection of jurors personally or allowed a trusted underling to do so.[26] He also reviewed the jury lists each year in light of recent performances and made decisions about whether a change in personnel was in order—for he was sometimes disappointed in the decisions of his jurors. But if a jury let him down by picking a candidate he did not like, he took his case to the Advisory Board and got what he wanted. Butler's power was such that when the Advisory Board voted, over his strenuous objections, to give *For Whom the Bell Tolls* the 1941 Pulitzer prize, he threatened to refuse to submit the board's decision to the trustees and the board backed down. No prize was given in 1941.[27]

After Butler's retirement in 1942, the center of power began to shift. Subsequent presidents of Columbia stayed out of the Pulitzer prize decisions and the Advisory Board began to assert itself. With the retirement of many older members in the 1950's the board was reconstituted and began to take a more active role in the selection of the prize-winners. Whereas formerly it had more or less followed the advice of juries, it gradually developed "consultative committees" which acted as super juries, regularly reading all of the recommendations by the juries and making its own recommendations to the full board.[28] If the "jury of experts" disagreed among themselves, the board's own subcommittees made a final decision; or if the board's subcommittee members disliked all of the juries' candidates, it substituted its own candidate or recommended withholding the prize.

From the beginning Columbia made it official policy to keep the names of jurors secret, not only in the months preceding announcement of the winners (when such secrecy would be justified), but for years afterwards as well. In the 1920's, when the prize decisions were beginning to stir controversy, President Butler did offer the assurance that the men who served on the Pulitzer juries were "invariably men of the highest competence and reputation."[29] Later, in 1951, in a letter to the editors of the *Saturday Review* who had been agitating for the disclosure of jurors' names, Carl W. Ackerman, then Dean of Columbia's Journalism School, asserted that the jurors' names could not be made public but assured his readers that the Pulitzer jurors were all faculty members of prominent universities. This claim was true for 1952, but had not been true during the preceding nine years.[30]

Other than Butler's vague assurance and Ackerman's misleading letter, the Pulitzer authorities kept quiet about their jurors and since the mid-1920's even kept jurors from talking in public. In the earliest years, however, before the lid was entirely fastened down, there were numerous "leaks." Jurors, angered at being overruled, spoke out publicly, revealing their own identity and sometimes that of others. Enough names came out in those years so that a reader interested in penetrating the facade of Pulitzer secrecy could put together a fairly accurate roster of the men who served on the seven earliest juries and who thus helped give the Pulitzer novel prize its distinctive character.[31] In 1974, when the names of all Pulitzer jurors were finally published, readers had confirmed what earlier evidence had clearly suggested: Pulitzer judges—whatever their talents—were not always as Nicholas Murray Butler had portrayed them, "invariably men of the highest competence and reputation."

Among the jurors who helped establish the Pulitzer fiction prize were Robert Morss Lovett and Stuart Pratt Sherman, academicians with some experience in journalism and book reviewing. Lovett was briefly an editor of the *New Republic* (1921), a longtime professor of English at the University of Chicago (1904-36), and author of books on Edith Wharton and on the contemporary novel, though he was best known as coeditor of a history of English literature. Stuart Pratt Sherman, probably the best known of the academic jurors, left a professorship at the University of Illinois to become editor of the book section of the New York *Herald Tribune* in 1924 where he established a reputation as a highbrow interpreter of contemporary literature and an authority on culture. Lovett and Sherman were both committed to the view that the best American fiction should propagandize for social improvement. Lovett's concern, however, was with broad social change, Sherman's with cultural uplift. In 1929, for instance, Lovett voted to give the novel prize to *Boston,* Upton Sinclair's novel about the Sacco-Vanzetti case because he approved its social message; and in 1920, when the jury (of which Lovett was a member) voted to give the prize to *Main Street* and were overruled in favor of Edith Wharton's *The Age of Innocence,* Lovett publicly protested. Mrs. Wharton's novel was an exercise in nostalgia, he said, whereas *Main Street* was a living commentary on the American scene, leading "its readers to purge the small-town atmosphere of certain unwholesome tendencies. . . ."[32] Lovett's defense of *Main Street* echoed some of the official phraseology of the Pulitzer award and was no doubt designed in part to embarrass Columbia officials who had overruled the jury. But there is little doubt that *Main Street* appealed to Lovett's critical sense as thoroughly as had the novels of Booth Tarkington, Upton Sinclair, and Margaret Ayer Barnes—all of whom Lovett admired and helped to give Pulitzer prizes.[33]

Stuart Pratt Sherman also served on the jury that had picked *Main Street* for the 1920 award, and though he did not publicly protest being overruled, he subsequently published an essay on Lewis in which he took somewhat the same line of defense Lovett had, except that his interest was less in altering the atmosphere of small-town life than in jolting the average reader into an awareness of his low cultural condition and starting him on the road to self-improvement.[34] Sherman's particular point of view is more fully spelled out in an essay in which he explained his theory of cultural salvation. Young men and women would be saved from unhappiness and discontent by service, he said, not service of the old-fashioned sort, such as missionary work in Africa or even in the Y.M.C.A., but the service of work—"all work that is done as it should be done whether of the hands or of the brain." Such work, Sherman said, "whatever it is," has "something of the peace and satisfaction of religious devotion."[35]

Sherman's theories about service and work are pertinent here because they so closely resemble sentiments expressed in several Pulitzer prize novels, particularly *His Family, The Magnificent Ambersons, So Big,* and, especially, *Alice Adams,* which he helped give a Pulitzer prize in 1922. Sherman's theories could also be used to gloss more recent winners such as *Arrowsmith, The Store,* and even *Grapes of Wrath*—prizewinners that Sherman had no hand in selecting. Of all the jurors, Stuart Pratt Sherman best epitomizes Pulitzer standards of literary excellence, not only because of his "uplift" theory of fiction and his veneration of the work ethic but also because artistic excellence seemed to have so little place in his critical judgment.

Other jurors who served in the early years and who left their stamp on the Pulitzer novel prize were men distinguished in ways other than by fiction writing or literary criticism. Robert Grant had published novels, but was best known as a judge in the Massachusetts state courts.[36] Edwin Lefèvre, an engineer-journalist, wrote cashbox romances in the tradition of Horatio Alger.[37] Samuel McCord Crothers was a Unitarian minister whose chief literary distinction appears to have been a volume titled *The Gentle Reader,* in which he announced that the English novel had reached its highest development with Fielding and Richardson. In that same book Crothers also remarked that "the greatest thing [about the novel] is still action, and we eagerly turn the pages to see what is going to happen next—unless we are reading some of our modern realistic studies of character. . . . But when we turn to the poets, we are in the land of the lotus-eaters. . . . The atmosphere is that of a perfect day."[38] Crothers, Lefèvre, and Grant served only briefly—Lefèvre one year, Crothers, three, Grant four.

Like Lovett and Sherman, most of the early jurors were academics, many with some professional interest in contemporary fiction. However, the academic juror with the longest tenure (seventeen years) was Jefferson Butler Fletcher, who taught comparative literature at Columbia University, specializing in the Italian Renaissance.[39] Fletcher's chief publications are *Religion of Beauty in Women* and *Platonic Love* and a translation of the *Divine Comedy* for the Home Library. An academic juror with more apparent qualifications as a judge of contemporary fiction was Richard Burton, sometime head of the English Department at the University of Minnesota and lecturer on contemporary fiction at Columbia and the University of Chicago. Burton served for four years as a fiction juror and then resigned when the Advisory Board overruled the jury he had chaired.[40] Among Burton's literary pronouncements was the assertion that fiction writers of the nineteenth century were too much preoccupied with technique at the the expense of thought and character.[41] He also said that the chief function of American fiction was to teach

> the different parts of the land to know each other and so to realize the variety and vastitude of our national life.... The novel, in this thought, is a mighty civilizer, drawing men together as do the wonderful material uses of electricity, and for for the higher purposes of a comprehensive sympathy and love.[42]

Bliss Perry, professor of American literature at Harvard, also served for four years, and like his colleagues Sherman and Lovett regarded fiction as a vehicle for social propaganda. In his book *The American Mind,* Perry argued that the period of rugged individualism was over in the United States and that a new era of socialism was dawning. Individualism would not be dispensed with, Perry said, but there would now be a new and proper blending of individualism with fellowship, a mystical union in which

> we shall not forget the distinction between "each" and "all," but "all" will increasingly be placed at the service of "each." With fellowship based upon individualism, and with individualism ever leading to fellowship, America will perform its vital tasks and its literature will be the unconscious and beautiful utterance of its inner life.[43]

What that inner life might consist of is suggested by Bliss Perry's remark in another context that, to be genuinely American, a novel or poem had to reflect what Perry said were the typical qualities of the American people: democratic, optimistic, idealistic, and "fundamentally wholesome." On the basis of these alleged national characteristics, Perry disparaged the achievement of Emily Dickinson, Poe, and Hawthorne, and praised Longfellow, Whittier, James Whitcomb Riley, Winston Churchill, and Sam Walter Foss, who wanted "to live in a house by the side of the road and be a friend to man."[44] For Perry, the novelist par excellence of democratic America was Fenimore Cooper, "who cared nothing and knew nothing about conscious literary art; his style is diffuse, his syntax the despair of school teachers, and many of his characters are bores."[45] Perry's description of what he took to be Cooper's virtues might be applied to a good many Pulitzer novels, though one would not wish to call them virtues.

Another Pulitzer juror much more widely known than Perry was Professor William Lyon Phelps, fondly known to many Yale undergraduates as Billy Phelps, an indefatigable writer, lecturer, and public moralist, who once brought the boxer Gene Tunny to his class to lecture on Shakespeare.[46] In one of his essays Phelps expressed the opinion that *Bob, Son of Battle* was the best English novel published between *Tess of the d'Urbervilles* (1891) and *Joseph Vance* (1906).[47] He served on the drama and poetry juries as well as on the novel jury and doubtless represented exactly that blend of moralism and literary boosterism that most satisfied Nicholas Murray Butler. Phelps helped select the first four Pulitzer prize novels before moving on to another jury.

Bliss Perry served on two fiction juries, Sherman on three; Lovett and Fletcher, however, continued to serve up to the beginning of World War II. Fletcher was chairman of the novel jury from 1930 through 1937, years when Fitzgerald, Hemingway, and Faulkner were eligible with some of their finest work. Fletcher continued to serve as a member of the novel jury through 1942, a year when the committee was composed entirely of Columbia faculty members.[48] In the following year, 1943, after Butler's retirement and the ascension to power of Carl W. Ackerman, dean of the Journalism School, the makeup of the novel jury changed significantly. Whereas early juries had been filled largely with academics (some with Columbia connections), juries from 1943 on were composed largely of journalists.[49] Except for a three-year period (1952-54) when academics were again in the majority, journalists have usually dominated the fiction juries. Even more significant than this shift from academic to journalistic influence, however, is the astonishing absence from Pulitzer juries of professional novelists. In the fifty-seven years from 1917 to 1974 (out of a total of 155 jurors) only five professional novelists served on the Pulitzer novel juries,[50] a lack which may in part explain the choice of so many amateurish books and the absence from the Pulitzer prize list of most of our best novels and short-story collections.

The history of the Pulitzer prize novels, however, is not merely a history of omissions nor of books plucked hastily from best-seller lists. Juries deliberated and recommended, the Advisory Board confirmed or overruled or made its own decisions, and during his long tenure Nicholas Murray Butler monitored the results and sometimes had them altered. The outcome of this elaborate procedure—complicated by changes in jury membership, the vicissitudes of publishing, fluctuating reputations, and shifts in public taste—constitutes, nonetheless, a fairly substantial body of fiction that, except for notable exceptions, is surprisingly consistent in quality and in point of view....

Notes

1. Don C. Seitz, *Joseph Pulitzer: His Life and Letters* (New York, 1924).

2. Frank Luther Mott, *American Journalism* (New York, 1941), 430-45.

3. *Ibid.*, 434.

4. Seitz, *Joseph Pulitzer*, 447.

5. Joseph Pulitzer, "The College of Journalism," *N. Amer. Rev.*, Vol. XLXXVIII (May, 1904), 641-80.

6. Seitz, *Joseph Pulitzer*, 436.

7. *Ibid.*, 445.

8. *Ibid.*, 445-48.

9. For the terms of the other prizes in letters see Appendix A. The poetry prize, added in 1921, also specified only excellence as the criterion for a Pulitzer prize. See John Hohenberg, *The Pulitzer Prizes* (New York, 1974), 18-20, 68-69; Wyman Barrett, *Joseph Pulitzer and His World*, 263; and Seitz, *Joseph Pulitzer*, 463-64.

10. Hohenberg, pp. 55-57.

11. Henry James, "The Art of Fiction," *The House of Fiction*, ed. by Leon Edel (London, 1959), 42.

12. Barrett, *Joseph Pulitzer and His World*, 264.

13. Robert Morss Lovett, "Pulitzer Prize," *New Republic*, Vol. LX (Sept. 11, 1929), 100-101; *New York Times*, May 13, 1930, p. 1; Hohenberg, *The Pulitzer Prizes*, 56-57, 88-89.

14. *New York Times*, May 14, 1929, p. 14.

15. *Ibid.*, Nov., 18, 1931, p. 25.

16. *Ibid.*, May 12, 1934, p. 27.

17. Clayton Hamilton, "Poor Pulitzer Prize," *Amer. Mercury*, Vol. XXV (May, 1935), 25-32; *New York Times*, May 7, 1935, p. 21, and May 5, 1936, p. 18.

18. *New York Times*, May 7, 1936, p. 21.

19. *Ibid.*, May 11, 1947, p. 45.

20. See Chap. VII below.

21. *New York Times*, Nov. 27, 1921, p. 3.

22. Hamilton, "Poor Pulitzer Prize," *Amer. Mercury*, Vol. XXV (May, 1935), 25-32; Robert Morss Lovett, "Pulitzer Prize," *New Republic*, Vol. XXVII (June 22, 1921), 114; and *New York Times*, May 12, 1934, p. 17.

23. Hohenberg's semi-official history, *The Pulitzer Prizes*, makes numerous references to the role of the Advisory Board, but the full story of what went on behind the scenes has yet to be told.

24. See pp. 138-39 below. In addition to *Tales of the South Pacific* (1948), the Advisory Board also selected *For Whom the Bell Tolls, In This Our Life* (1943), *The Town* (1951), *The Travels of Jaimie McPheeters* (1949), *A Death in the Family* (1958), and *Advise and Consent* (1960). Hohenberg, pp. 146-47, 200-203, 256-60.

25. See Hohenberg, pp. 146-47. Butler may also have been responsible for the 1921 prize being taken from *Main Street* and given to *The Age of Innocence*. See pp. 39-42 below.

26. F. D. Fackenthal was Butler's chief liaison with the juries. See Hohenberg, p. 26.

27. See pp. 122-23 below.

28. Hohenberg, pp. 229-31, 235, 255.

29. *New York Times*, March 30, 1925, p. 5.

30. *Saturday Review*, Vol. XXXIV (July 14, 1951), 26. See Appendix C for a list of the jurors for those years.

31. See W. J. Stuckey, *Pulitzer Prize Novels: A Critical Backward Look*, 1st ed. (Norman, 1965), 16-25. Newspapers at the time reported that Sinclair Lewis was a fiction juror in 1936, a report that has since proved false. See Hohenberg, p. 93.

32. "Pulitzer Prize," *New Republic*, Vol. XXVII (June 22, 1921), 114, and pp. 40-42 below.

33. Lovett lavishly praised *The Magnificent Ambersons* in a review in *Dial* (*Book Review Digest*, 1918, p. 431). In *Preface to Fiction* (p. 83), he mentioned *Years of Grace*, which he had helped select for a Pulitzer prize, as an American example of the genealogical novel. He had also said that since the novel is "essentially popular," it "should demand of the layman no deeply specialized knowledge." (p. 10).

34. *The Significance of Sinclair Lewis* (New York, 1922).

35. *The Genius of America: Studies in Behalf of the Younger Generation* (New York, 1923), 171-95.

36. Among Grant's books are *Jack Hall* (Boston, 1888); *Jack in the Bush* (New York, 1893); *The Reflections of a Married Man* (New York, 1892); *The Opinions of a Philosopher* (New York, 1893); *Unleavened Bread* (New York, 1900), a novel about Selma, a social climber from the Middle West, which Hamlin Garland characterized as a "good book with sociological significance . . . true and broadminded," in *My Friendly Contemporaries* (New York, 1932), 363; *The High Priestess* (New York, 1915); *Occasional Verses, 1873-1923* (Boston, 1926).

37. According to *Who Was Who in America, 1943-1950* (II, 317), Lefèvre studied engineering at Lehigh University, was "in Journalism." His publications include *Wall Street Stories* (New York, 1901); *H. R.* (New York and London, 1915); *The Plunderers* (New

York, 1916); *To the Last Penny* (New York and London, 1917); *Reminiscences of a Stock Operator* (New York, 1923).

38. Pages 46-47.

39. Fletcher served from 1922 through 1925 and from 1927 through 1942.

40. For a fuller account of the incident see p. 80 below. According to Hohenberg, *The Pulitzer Prizes,* p. 89, Burton asked to be relieved because his lectures on contemporary fiction subjected his public statements to misrepresentation. Burton (who also served on the jury that gave the 1927 prize to Louis Bromfield for *Early Autumn*) was at one time managing editor of *The Churchman,* literary editor of the *Hartford Courant,* head of the English department of the University of Minnesota (1898-1902, 1906-25), and lecturer on literature at Columbia (1921-33). He also served on Pulitzer juries in drama, poetry, and biography from 1920 to 1940. Among his published works are *Literary Leaders of America* (New York, 1903), lectures for the Chautauqua Society, and *Forces in Fiction and Other Essays* (Indianapolis, 1902).

41. *Literary Leaders of America,* 202.

42. *Ibid.,* 314.

43. Pages 248-49.

44. *The American Mind,* p. 245.

45. *A Study of Prose Fiction* (New York, 1902), 235-60. Other publications by Perry include *Walt Whitman: His Life and Work* (Boston and New York, 1906); *The American Spirit in Literature* (New Haven, 1918); *A Study of Poetry* (Boston and New York, 1920); *Emerson Today* (Princeton, 1931); *And Gladly Teach* (Boston and New York, 1935).

46. *Autobiography with Letters* (New York, 1939), 793-94.

47. *Essays on Modern Novelists* (New York, 1910), 171. Phelps, who was Lampson Professor of English at Yale for thirty-two years, had a national reputation as a genial, morally upright intellectual with the common touch. Among his more than two dozen published books are *The Advance of the English Novel* (New York, 1916); *The Advance of English Poetry in the Twentieth Century* (New York, 1918); *Essays on Modern Dramatists* (New York, 1921); *Human Nature in the Bible* (New York, 1922), *Happiness* (New York, 1927); *What I like in Poetry* (New York, 1934).

48. The other two Columbia faculty members were Joseph Wood Krutch and Gilbert Highet.

49. See Appendix C.

50. These include Hamlin Garland, Dorothy Canfield Fisher, Elizabeth Janeway, Jean Stafford, and Elizabeth Hardwick. Sinclair Lewis was erroneously reported as a member of the 1936 jury that chose *Honey in the Horn* by H. L. Davis. *New York Times,* May 5, 1936, p. 18, and Hohenberg, p. 93.

Thomas P. Adler (essay date 1987)

SOURCE: Adler, Thomas P. "The Fifth Horseman of the Apocalypse—Race." In *Mirror on the Stage: The Pulitzer Plays as an Approach to American Drama,* pp. 68-84. West Lafayette, Ind.: Purdue University Press, 1987.

[*In the following excerpt, Adler discusses some Pulitzer Prize-winning plays that dealt with the subject of race relations, noting how the plays reflect their historical context.*]

It would be over fifty years after the establishment of the Pulitzers and well over forty years after the first Broadway production of a work by a black writer (Garland Anderson's *Appearances* in 1925) before a black playwright would receive the drama award. Racial issues, however, not only surface in but dominate a number of American plays from the mid-nineteenth century on, including such well-known ones as George Aiken's adaptation of *Uncle Tom's Cabin* (1852), Dion Boucicault's *The Octoroon* (1859), Edward Sheldon's *The Nigger* (1909), O'Neill's *All God's Chillun Got Wings* (1926), Langston Hughes's *Mulatto* (1935), and Louis Peterson's *Take a Giant Step* (1953). In her study *Negro Playwrights in the American Theatre 1925-1959,* Doris Abramson argues that the earliest plays by black authors—*The Escape; or a Leap for Freedom* (1858) by William Wells Brown and *Caleb, the Degenerate* (1903) by Joseph S. Cotter—inaugurate the "two strains," respectively, of "protest against . . . the status quo" and of "acceptance of the status quo" in works "directed more against the attitude of [the blacks] than against white society" that will continue well into the twentieth century.[1] Abramson's book also makes clear the artistic concessions and compromises that playwrights made in treating the volatile issue of race so that their works would be palatable to commercial theatergoers.

Central to a consideration of any protest drama is, of course, the question of audience. If the protest is directed against the political and social values of the bourgeois establishment who make up, in large part, the audience of the commercial Broadway theatre, then it will likely be guarded and muted, only mildly reproving. The first two plays discussed in this chapter—one having to do with the cultural and racial differences between Americans and Polynesians, the other with anti-Jewish (and in some senses anti-intellectual) sentiment—are cases in point: despite their considerable protest against these forms of racism and prejudice, it is difficult to dispel the notion that either *South Pacific* or *Talley's Folly* is anything more than *just* theatre and theatre as an escapist withdrawal into a kind of fantasyland at that. Both works employ stage space and even the theatre metaphor in a very similar fashion: the characters retreat from society—in the first instance to an island, in the second to a boathouse—in the same way that the audience come into the theatre. In each, the theatre is where the audience go to dream, where the unlikely comes to pass; the romance will be remembered, while the reality will be filed away. What occurs on that island, or in that boathouse—that is, in the theatre—seems remote from the world outside, and so the connection between art and life is not forced home in any astringent manner. It is there for the taking or the leaving.

When it came time for the 1950 awards, the drama jury recommended Gian Carlo Menotti's "opera" *The Consul*—which received the music prize instead. The advisory board, ignoring the jury's selection, chose Richard Rodgers and Oscar Hammerstein's *South Pacific*, based on James Michener's *Tales of the South Pacific*, winner of the 1948 Pulitzer for fiction. (It especially pleased Rodgers that he as composer shared as an equal contributor in the award, since George Gershwin's name had not appeared on the citation for *Of Thee I Sing* eighteen years before.) Somewhat less Pollyanna-ish than the majority of musicals that preceded it, *South Pacific* boasts a more than usually full plot. Drawing mainly on three Michener stories, "Our Heroine," "Fo' Dolla," and "The Remittance Man (The Cave)," with a lesser debt to two others, "Dry Rot" and "A Boar's Tooth," *South Pacific* charted new territory for the musical: because neither the main plot concerning the French planter Emile DeBecque and the Navy nurse Nellie Forbush nor the subplot (really a double plot because it parallels and comments upon the other so neatly) between the American Lieutenant Cable and the Polynesian girl Liat is comic, a third plot strand involving Luther Billis and Bloody Mary was added, as Rodgers notes, for "comic leavening."[2] Furthermore, the show lacks extended dance routines, the only one of Rodgers and Hammerstein's classic musicals of the late 1940s and early 1950s not to include a ballet sequence.

South Pacific explores two major concerns: the tension between isolation and commitment in personal affairs and politics and the racial prejudice between cultures thrown together by war—the latter the subject two decades later of Rabe's much angrier *Sticks and Bones*. The first concern revolves around the pull between public and private duty, a popular motif before the war—and in Sherwood's plays—but one that by the late 1940s had lost some of its social edge. Tied in with this is an emphasis on love as a means of overcoming the separateness and estrangement endemic to the human condition. As the lyric to the haunting "Bali Hai" says, "Mos' people live on a lonely island, / Lost in de middle of a foggy sea," longing for someplace where their special "hopes" and "dreams" might live.[3] But that searched-for place might, significantly, be only another "island," romantic and dreamlike, since love between different races evidently cannot exist within the framework of the advanced social structure called civilization.

This concern about racial hatred and whether it is born into a person or generated through training and environmental attitudes seems to receive, Rodger's disclaimer against intending any "propagandistic message" notwithstanding, the major emphasis. Almost twenty years before *South Pacific*, Jerome Kern, Hammerstein, and Edna Ferber treated the subject of miscegenation in *Show Boat*, which might justifiably be called the first modern musical play; in *South Pacific*, however, the races are not black and white but Caucasian and Oriental. The racial issue, which appears in both major plot lines, is encapsulated in Cable's act 2 song, "You've Got to Be Taught," which, contrary to Nellie's belief that her racial attitudes are emotional predispositions born in her, proposes that these are acquired hates and fears inculcated into the children: "It's not born in you. It happens *after* you're born" (p. 346). This song constitutes the thematic center of the play.

Emile, the fugitive running away from a past in which he killed a man who tried to corrupt and take over a town, and Nellie, the "corny, cock-eyed optimist" (as she dubs herself in a lyric indicative of Hammerstein's consistently hopeful philosophy) who is running towards something, contrast with one another. If Emile once chose active involvement while the rest of the world just sat by and watched (is the man he killed to be seen as a symbol for Hitler or Benito Mussolini?), he now opts for savoring the sweetness of life with Nellie rather than risk losing her in a show of patriotic heroics. The hero and heroine's falling in love at first sight on an "enchanted evening" is as predictable and conventional as in most musicals (a truly unsentimental view of love and marriage will not come in a musical until almost a quarter century later with Sondheim and George Furth's *Company*). The dramatic "Twin Soliloquies," with some of their lyrics taken directly from Michener's words, help make the too-sudden love more plausible and effect suspension of disbelief by openly admitting the artificiality and even ritualizing it through rhyme. Later, the Thanksgiving Follies segment employs the show-within-the-show, casting the audience in the role of American troops watching a musicale, thus furthering the breakdown of the barrier between auditorium and stage begun when Bloody Mary addresses the audience as customers for her exotic wares.

When Nellie runs off after learning that Emile had two children by his Polynesian wife, which momentarily destroys any chance that she could still consider marrying him, Emile decides to accompany Cable on a dangerous reconnaissance mission; he involves himself not from any sense of patriotism, but only from a feeling of having nothing left to live for. Cable dies, but his "springtime" love for Liat has already been cut short by the realization that he could never cross the racial prohibition against intermarriage except on an island where spells are cast and dreams come true—in the theatre. Even with his death, the war as pictured here is hardly realistic, seen instead through the nearsighted lenses of postwar euphoria with Billis as guide: exotic locales and customs, get-rich-quick schemes with the natives (as in *Teahouse*), and clowning around and sexual high jinks with the nurses. The unhappy ending of the subplot renders Emile's return and reunion with a chastened and wiser Nellie indispensable for the musical comedy audience. Yet if *South Pacific* makes no very substantial statement about war, or even about love, it does make a provocative one about racial attitudes and prejudices: to see them as *learned* responses implies that someday they might be unlearned and eradicated.

Given the strain of anti-Semitism that continues to exist just under the surface of American society, as evidenced in its most pronounced form by the renewed stirrings of the neo-Nazis in the late 1970s, it is perhaps not surprising to find Lanford Wilson exploring the issue in his 1980 prize play. Set on July 4, 1944, *Talley's Folly* is a slight, sentimental effort, somewhat redeemed by its endearing and engaging central couple: Matt Friedman, a liberal in his early forties, and Sally Talley, a nurse headed for self-imposed spinsterhood, who are misfits in the real world but, finally, fit together almost too neatly by the prestidigitation of some mischievous angel or crazy Providence. As misfits fearing the hurt of rejection, the egg serves as their overriding symbol: "Crack our shells, never be any use again . . . individuals. We had to keep separate, private."[4] Wilson disguises the slightness of his play in two ways: by the paranoid Matt's Jewish comedy routines (including Bogart imitations and farcical pratfalls) that Matt uses as ploys to cover his own vulnerability and keep cynicism at bay and by the Wilder-like frame of Matt as narrator/stage manager/central character addressing the audience. The latter device, rather than apologize for, actually calls attention to the saccharine, fairytale nature of the play. Here the nonrepresentational form is not integral to the content; rather, it is a clever ploy. What audience, warned beforehand not to expect more than its author is prepared to deliver, could fail to like a play that wears its heart so openly and unashamedly upon its sleeve?

Folly is, essentially, a play of character revealed largely through exposition and some lengthy monologues. Matt, because of the history of his wandering family, considers himself non-nationalistic and feels little allegiance to any political cause or "ism," distrusting them all because "in no time at all you start defending isms like they were something tangible" (p. 46). When he tells Sally the tale of his past—of a Prussian father and Ukranian mother "indefinitely detained" by the Germans in World War I, of a Latvian sister tortured by the French so that their father would divulge information he did not have, and of himself, born in Lithuania and arriving as a refugee with his uncle and family from Norway via Caracas—he distances the story by narrating it in the third person, almost as if it were a parable or folk tale. Only unconsciously does he slip into the confessional, first person "I." Although he escaped the draft because of his age, he is not unaffected by the war (which governments deliberately prolong, he thinks, for economic stability). Since the way of the world for Matt has always been that "life was war, war was life" and since he feels uncertain whether there will even be a time after this war, he refuses to "bring into this world another child to be killed for political purposes" (p. 40), and so he hesitates to marry Sally. In one of the running gags expressing his belief that "the car" (America) "is out of gas" (hope) (p. 50), he foreshadows the emotional and physical aftershock of Vietnam that will be felt by the characters in Wilson's sequel, *Fifth of July*, which occurs thirty years later.

For herself, Sally yearns on this Independence Day to break free from a restrictive family that is antiliberal, anti-Semitic, and anti-German—and so anti-Matt. Yet political, religious, and racial intolerance are not the only things preventing her marriage. She was engaged once before to her high school sweetheart and fellow "golden" child, and their marriage portended a merger of the two families. But her father committed suicide in the Depression, and—in the secret the audience waits to have revealed—an illness left Sally sterile. Once her misconception that Matt was only *saying* he would never father a child so as to spare her the burden of not being able to give him one is cleared up, then these two, made for each other, can come together. Such a resolution has been inevitable all along, and if Wilson equates himself with the Providence who through sleight-of-hand finally brings them together, he delays that union until the last possible moment.

The "folly" of the play's title and the setting of the action is a boathouse that Sally's Uncle Everett, a free spirit like Matt, constructed in place of the gazebo that he had hoped to build. For Sally, it is a place of escape, of "magic." Matt and Sally leave this place to return to a family and a community unprepared to accept them, to one which will ostracize them, just as Matt, the stage manager again at the end, sends the audience out from the theatre exactly ninety-seven minutes later and back into their imperfect world where the only certain value seems to be love on a very selective and limited basis. A dissonance exists between what Matt calls the "waltz" or "valentine" of this "once upon a time" bauble the audience has been watching and the prejudice that pervades the world. Maybe only art, the play, can make that reality bearable or lead the way to a change.

Certain dramas written by black authors in the 1950s and 1960s might well have been honored with the Pulitzer, for example, Lorraine Hansberry's *A Raisin in the Sun* or LeRoi Jones's *Dutchman*, which both explore, in Jones's words, "the difficulty of becoming a man in America."[5] If Hansberry upsets many among a black audience by not questioning critically enough whether the dream that her protagonist pursues has been irreparably tainted by white values, she does examine the ethic that equates "being somebody" with material success while urging a new generation of black men to achieve dignity by coming into their own as husbands and fathers. As Clinton Oliver suggests, however, *Raisin*, though written by a black, is intended as "bourgeois or middle class drama" and so "is essentially integrationist." Yet he is quick to deem that "an oversimplification. The segregation of the Negro from the mainstream of American life has made his art necessarily a reflection of this fact, and is therefore in its profoundest aspects, separatist"[6]—as *Dutchman* more obviously approximates. If Jones annoys many in an establishment audience by his insistence that white society has emasculated the black man, at the same time he still emphasizes how an assimilationist stance by blacks subverts selfhood; the blacks' justifiable hatred and impulse towards violence might even be seen as channeled into and sublimated in artistic creation. Before 1970, however, the two plays focusing on black/white issues that won the drama Pulitzer were both written by whites.

Paul Green's *In Abraham's Bosom,* the first off-Broadway and the third regional drama to win the Pulitzer (for 1927), is, more importantly, the first specifically Southern play and the first about the black experience to be honored. Green (who later collaborated with Richard Wright on the dramatization of *Native Son*), adapted *Abraham's Bosom,* which covers a period of eighteen years beginning in the 1880s, from three of his one-act plays, accounting for the looseness of its structure and abundance of material and detail. The looseness is justified partly by the chronicle nature of the play and mitigated further by patterning the work as one man's odyssey towards selfhood. Moreover, an impressive, heightened rhetoric, appropriate because historical and biblical myths overlay the action, helps direct attention away from the structural flaws. Even though the Abraham whom Green alludes to in his title (taken from a well-known Negro spiritual) is the Old Testament patriarch, the mainly white audience might well connect the self-taught Abe McCrannie's efforts to educate and thus emancipate his people with those of Lincoln. McCrannie gives his son the name Douglas, evidently in honor of Frederick Douglass, the freed slave turned abolitionist and orator whom McCrannie himself emulates and may even be partly modelled after. That Douglas fails so miserably in living up to his namesake and in being the obedient son that Isaac was to Abraham, or like Moses in delivering his people out of the wilderness, are only a few of the play's multiple tragic ironies. Along with the patterning of fathers and sons, the archetypal antagonism between Cain and Abel underpins the work. As the mulatto McCrannie kills his white half-brother, Lonnie, the moral categories of good and evil become confused with the racial coloration. Finally, as frequently happens in American literature, the white/good and black/evil stereotypes are inverted and their validity questioned.

An action Abe performed two years before the play opens began his troubles; he buried a black man lynched for attacking a white woman and was saved from the angry mob only by the intercession of his father, the Colonel, who, though inwardly proud of Abe's strength and intelligence, must respond to his son in public in the way society demands that its leaders act towards blacks. So when Abe retaliates against the jealous Lonnie for striking him, the Colonel whips Abe, calls him a slave, and banishes him. The action picks up in Abe's two-room cabin in the springtime three years later; adorning the walls is a calendar picturing a slave leaving his chains with the caption, "'We Are Rising,'"[7] which foreshadows the aspiring Abe's own ascendency. His wife, Goldie, has just given birth to their third child—and first to survive—a son; and the Colonel, praising Abe's perseverance in contrast to Lonnie's laziness, gives Abe the house and land, as well as permission to teach at the black school. But in this play where the mood is a seasonal, shifting sistole and diastole of joy and grief, the winter—with the ragged field showing through the window—finds Abe beleaguered by the angry parents for having beaten one of the recalcitrant youths. Fifteen years later, on a dying winter day in Durham, Abe is devoid of funds and of any hope for his son; breaking the bond of kinship with Douglas, he even demands that the boy change his name. Instead of the Douglas/Abe relationship mirroring that of Abe and the Colonel, it more closely repeats the Lonnie/Colonel pattern. Deciding that their time in the urban hell has been a dark night of the soul, they return to the country and, close to the soil, make a new beginning. When Lonnie steals his crop and threatens him, Abe kills Lonnie in self-defense. Seeing himself as another Cain, deserted by God, Abe comes close to despair; stones are pelted through his window, and he is finally shot down like a dog.

In killing Lonnie, Abe kills not only his half-brother but tries to exorcise the white side of himself that has always existed so precariously with the black. Abe is a divided self, a constant struggle ensuing between his intellectual aspirations and his instinctive emotional drives; as one of the minor black characters analyzes it, his "nigger" heart lives in opposition to his "white" head. Acts 5 and 6, during which Abe kills Lonnie, seem indebted in their psychological use of stage setting to two of O'Neill's plays which feature blacks, *All God's Chillun* and *The Emperor Jones*. At one point, great leaping shadows that expressionistically objectify Abe's inner turmoil fill the cabin; later, when Abe is pursued in the moonlight, the trappings of civilization, such as learning and speech, fall away from him just as Jones sheds them in the forest. After killing Lonnie, Abe senses his spirit in the wind and sees the tree branches as menacing hands; he hallucinates, envisioning a lynching, ghosts and haunts, and finally a young Negress and a dandified white man coupling like "hawgs." It is Abe's vision of the primal scene, and the child they conceive is himself. This contributes to the impression of Abe as a victim of his birth, who seems in the evil he does mainly to *react* to outside stimuli rather than to act, making him less tragic a figure than Green evidently intended he would be.

No matter how sympathetic an audience might be to Abe today, the play is not only a pessimistic and unlightened examination of the racial question, but even a reactionary one. Certain of its ideas do retain their viability: violence is not the solution; the urban ghettos are as enslaving as the cotton fields. On at least one point—the necessity for breaking down the idea of God as exclusively white—the play was even prophetic. Abe moves, in fact, from a belief that black oppression means a white God rules the universe to a recognition that God encompasses both black and white. But the work's central emphasis, voiced by Abe himself, clearly places the burden on the black man for his own lot: it is not white society that must change, but the black man who will rise only when he has first freed his mind through education. In Green's amelioristic approach, blacks are not yet ready to be the equals of whites—a viewpoint that may have made the play palatable to audiences of the 1920s but which renders moot any question of reviving the work today. Green, along with Abe and the minor black choral figures who reject Abe's way and opt instead for maintaining the status quo with the whites as superior, carefully prevents the whites in the audience from feeling guilty, even makes them feel complacent, which severely vitiates any grandeur the play possesses in characterization and language. Two Pulitzer plays on the racial issue from the late 1960s do, however, distribute the blame more equitably.

For over two decades now, the center of original theatrical activity in America has been shifting from on Broadway to off, even to the regional theatres, and a number of the more recent Pulitzer plays, like Howard Sackler's *The Great White Hope*, which won the award in 1969 but first opened at Washington's Arena Stage in 1960, reflect this trend. *White Hope* covers roughly the same time period in American history as *In Abraham's Bosom* and falls even more clearly into the chronicle-cum-tragedy form than does Green's work. But it owes just as much, as Gerald Weales notes,[8] to the Brechtian epic theatre for its episodic structure, its style that blends song with dialogue, and its social commitment, though it does not depend on estrangement devises to stimulate an intellectual reaction at the expense of emotional involvement. Although several earlier American plays demonstrate some dependence on Brechtian techniques, Sackler's is so far the only winner wholly in the neo-Brechtian mode.

As a chronicle-cum-tragedy, Sackler's work details the desperate attempts of the white establishment, reaching even to the White House, to find a "great white hope" capable of defeating the black heavyweight boxing champion, Jack Jefferson, a thinly disguised portrait of Jack Johnson. As if his race were not embarrassment enough to white strangleholds of power and authority, the married Jefferson further fuels the hatred by openly living with his white mistress, Ellie, eventually violating the law by taking her across the state line. Yet the conflict becomes one not simply of law versus love, but of the necessity to sacrifice personal integrity to the public role that America thrusts upon her culture heroes; for the white Kid who finally defeats Jack is as much a martyr to racial bigotry as is Jack: "his smashed and reddened face . . . barely visible" as he is borne out through the jubilant crowd, he is dehumanized by being turned into an object, a parody of "the lifelike wooden saints in Catholic processions."[9]

His determination to define his life on his own terms makes Jack, hounded out of country after country, reduced to playing Uncle Tom to Ellie's Little Eva on the cafe circuit in Budapest and even to selling his gloves to survive, less the victim (as Abe is) and more the tragic sufferer, Promethean in his defiance of established codes. What topples him is not only his freely chosen burden of Ellie but also the unsought burden of being manipulated by his own race—most of whom long either to be assimilated into white society or kept in their lowly place. Despite his wanting to fight only for himself and not to deliver the black race, others force a Messianic role upon him until the gold belt becomes his albatross: "Ah'm stuck widdit, see, a hunk of junky hardware, but it don't let go" (p. 137). If the majority of blacks quickly lionize him, some who are making inroads into the white power structure hasten to vilify him for fear that their own standing will be jeopardized, while others want nothing more than to remain subservient, like his mother who "tried to learn him like you gotta learn a culled boy" (p. 75). So Sackler's play is a two-edged sword, cutting at both blacks and whites, as Jones does in *Dutchman*.

Sackler never adequately dramatizes the relationship between Ellie and Jack, and yet on its outcome hinge the final choices that determine Jack's heroism. The same skepticism about the option of interracial marriage as a step towards integration pervades *White Hope* as underlies Green's drama. Ellie claims him to be kind and sensitive, yet the audience never sees this—unless the embarrassing sexual banter in the cabin is to be accepted as proof; when Jack's resentment boils over, he takes it out on her, forcing her to leave, which leads to her suicide. After her body is brought in, Jefferson decides on retaliation against what "they" have done; he refuses to throw the fight and will do his best to triumph. In the process, he endures a terrible battering, finally securing his freedom from control and his sense of dignity.

In place of depth, Sackler provides expansiveness through the panoply and pageantry of the chronicle form to which are added blackouts—with sound effects used as transitions or bridges as they would be in radio or film—and spirituals, blues, and pop tunes to punctuate the short scenes. Frequently, characters interrupt their longer speeches with single lines of direct address, further breaking the illusion of reality and establishing this as a convention, so that the five long speeches—three directed to the whites in the audience and two to the blacks—are prepared for. In the first of the three addressed to whites, Cap'n Dan, a former champion turned referee, declares that having a black wear the heavyweight crown is "like the world's got a shadow across it" (p. 42). In the second, Ellie's mother reiterates the numerous stereotypical connotations of the word *black*—"the dark to be afraid of, pitch black, black as dirt, the black hole and the black pit, what's burned or stained or cursed or hideous, poison and spite and the waste from your body and the horrors crawling up into your mind" (p. 135)—demonstrating how language can be used to foster and support prejudice, corrupting its original function. Just as Green takes pains not to annoy his white audience, Sackler allows the liberals to feel self-satisfied and morally superior, while at the same time playing to the white silent majority, as when he allows

Dixon to echo their fears: "Give it some thought next time you're alone on the streets at night" (p. 111). The Brechtian form, however, demands less ambiguity and a clearer demarcation between heroes and villains and a more consistent social philosophy than the fence-straddling for the commercial theatre apparent here.

Two speeches addressed to the probably few blacks in the audience create additional difficulties. The first, by a character named Scipio who is totally extraneous to the play's action, speaks out for black pride—taunting the blacks by asking, "How white you wanna be?" (p. 71)—and holds up Jefferson as an example of selling out to the white value structure in a new brand of slavery. He urges them to take pride in their black civilization and culture: "Time again to make us a big new wise proud dark man's world—again!" (p. 72). The second black monologuist and final commentator is Jack's estranged wife, Clara, motivated by personal jealousy and vengeance against Jack for having turned his back on black women and succumbed to the white woman's mystique of black male sexuality. Costuming her in a garment stained by blood and excrement makes her appearance unnecessarily sensational. But then Sackler depends on broad strokes and effects throughout rather than on subtlety to propel his play, which is as much shadowboxing as the real thing.

Even before Green wrote *In Abraham's Bosom,* authors were beginning to formulate an aesthetic for a black drama that would address itself largely to a black audience. In his 1925 essay called "Play-writing," Mark Seyboldt, while granting that black playwrights must continue to be aware of "two different audiences," one "used to theatre going" and the other not, urged them to be "'mainly interested in the second audience; we want colored folk to add the new diversion of drama to their lives. . . . It will stimulate and broaden cramped lives.'"[10] By the following year, 1926, in a manifesto written for the Krigwa Players' Little Negro Theatre in Harlem, W. E. B. DuBois was arguing that "'The plays of a real Negro theatre must be: 1. *About us.* . . . 2. *By us.* . . . 3. *For us.* That is the Negro theatre must cater primarily to Negro audiences. . . . 4. *Near us.*'"[11] By the late 1960s, the notion not just of two audiences but of two Americas had become a sad fact of American society, and the Black Arts Movement had linked itself inextricably with, and become an instrument and expression of, Black Power—an understandable alliance for the drama since, as Larry Neal asserts, "theatre is potentially the most social of all the arts."[12] Adopting Frantz Fanon's belief in the inability of "acquir[ing] the oppressor's power by acquiring his symbols," Neal proposes that "a 'black aesthetic'" must replace "the Western aesthetic [that] has run its course" as a viable "cultural sensibility": "The motive behind the Black aesthetic is the destruction of . . . white ways of looking at the world. The new aesthetic is mostly predicated on an Ethics which asks the question: whose vision of the world is finally more meaningful, ours or the white oppressors?" (pp. 29-30). Though neither seems addressed to an exclusively black audience, the two plays by blacks that have won the Pulitzer, perhaps especially the first, participate in the agenda that Neal envisions for black drama.

Charles Gordone, the first of only two blacks thus far to win the Pulitzer for drama, frames the action of his "Black Black comedy" and 1970 award play, *No Place to Be Somebody,* by employing a nonrealistic technique. The frame hints that the entire play may be occurring in the mind of the apocalyptically named apprentice playwright, Gabe Gabriel—may, in fact, be the play he is writing. The nonillusionistic devices, including long narrative passages and poems, function more satisfactorily than the similar ones in *White Hope* because Gordone establishes the illusion-breaking conventions earlier and employs them consistently. *No Place* departs from the traditions of the barroom drama in America (evident in such plays as Saroyan's *The Time of Your Life,* O'Neill's *The Iceman Cometh,* and Jack Gelber's *The Connection*) in that although some of the bar's habituees gravitate to it as a protective womb or source of intoxicating illusions or forgetfulness, it is not, finally, a haven of safety and security. It becomes, instead, a testing ground for people's perception of race and the black movement.

The rather cluttered melodramatic action, reminiscent of a grade-B gangster movie, can be dealt with quickly; it is important mainly for the effect that it—real or imagined or both—has upon the light-skinned Gabe and, by extension, the black race in general, in the change from nonviolence to violence. Since the events are melodramatic, Gabe can participate in actions which, lacking subtlety, ambivalence, and ambiguity, force reactions that reveal his progression. Gabe writes his play in a bar owned by Johnny Williams, a black pimp intent on leading a Black Mafia, who equates respect for the law with the white way. In his stable are two black (Evie and Cora) prostitutes and one white (Dee). Frequenters of the establishment include Shanty, a hypster white drummer who dreams of winning Cora through his music, which supposedly proves he has as much soul as any black; and Melvin, a black dancer. Arriving at the bar after a long absence in prison is Sweets Crane, a reformed black racketeer and Johnny's surrogate father. Sweets, challenging Uncle Tomism, regrets that Johnny has aped his "bad points" and expresses disdain "for giving Johnny the worst sickness of all: the Charley fever."[13] Coming into the bar for the first time are two whites, Mary Lou (daughter of Judge Bolton) and Ellen, both civil rights picketers. The judge, it happens, has risen to office by acquitting two Italian mobsters on charges of bribery and murder, and Mary Lou willingly turns over a file incriminating him to Johnny. Dee, jealous of Johnny's attention towards Mary Lou, degrades herself by putting on black face and ultimately commits suicide. Sweets, after willing everything to Johnny provided he reform, knifes Mafucci and is himself killed in an altercation over the files. Johnny taunts Gabe, who has "no stomach" for this personal war against whites and refuses to hand over the information, with being a "lousy, yellow, screamin' faggot coward" (p. 113) and threatens to kill him. In a pattern that closely repeats the action of Albee's *The Zoo Story,* Johnny drives

Gabe to kill him so that Gabe can no longer be the uninvolved, nonviolent observer, the passive commentator who speaks through words rather than actions.

Gabe addresses the audience directly in three of his poems. The first is a satiric work about a Whitmanesque speaker at a civil rights protest rally who tries to embrace all blacks, pleading for solidarity rather than violence, but receives no response. The second narrates a fable about blacks who move into the white world, go unaccepted, and finally return to the black world, only to find rejection there as well. This poem, which begins with Gabe intoning the old Protestant hymn, "Whiter Than Snow," underscores (like Mrs. Bachman's monologue in *White Hope*) and simultaneously undercuts the stereotypical association of whiteness with moral rightness and purity. Gabe's final verse insists, "There's mo' to bein' black than meets the / Eye" (p. 79), yet it ultimately defines blacks by the same stereotypes that they themselves help the whites to perpetuate. Gabe symbolizes his own prescience as black poet and suggests the violent course of action he will follow through the mock communion in which he eats a gun and drinks a Molotov cocktail.

Just as Sackler introduced Scipio, the black militant, Gordone brings on an equally unprepared-for character named Machine Dog, dressed in a military uniform and given to Nazi-like salutes. Whether he exists only in Johnny's imagination, or only as a tempter in Gabe's mind, is not clear; what is clear is that Machine Dog serves as a kind of *deus ex machina* (perhaps that wryly accounts for his name), delivering an edict canonizing Johnny as a heroic martyr for his people. His revivalist monologue delivered immediately after Gabe kills Johnny is rhetorically confusing and probably an obfuscation for an audience in the theatre, though it appears to be a series of charges against the blacks for failing to aid the revolutionaries.

In the epilogue, Gabe appears one last time, now dressed in a new role as a woman in mourning, to utter a jeremiad in biblical phraseology that recalls the prologue. Contrary to Walter Kerr's belief that the "Epilogue" is "false to the play's tone . . . too thin and obvious in its humor for the weightiness of the text as a whole and should . . . be dropped,"[14] it marks the essential end-product of Gabe's development. Appropriately dressed in the widow's weeds that had become so familiar an American sight by the end of the 1960s, Gabe—and through him, Gordone—mourns the years of dehumanization and degradation that the people have allowed themselves to suffer, mourning, too, the end of nonviolence as a solution for himself and for his race. The play's title suggests that finding and living by one's own proper identity is a near impossibility for the blacks in this society, that there is, literally, "no place" for them "to be somebody" except by aping Charley's ways, which ironically only renders each of them even more of a "nobody." The epilogue rounds out the play thematically by suggesting the frightening impasse at which the struggle for racial equality has arrived.

With *A Soldier's Play,* Charles Fuller became in 1982 the second black to win the drama Pulitzer. His play, which mixes yet finally transcends two perennially popular forms, the whodunit and the courtroom melodrama, is acted out on a nonrealistic set in the shape of a "horseshoe-like half circle" resembling a courtroom. It opens with a tantalizingly incomplete reenactment of the 1944 murder of a black tech sergeant, Vernon C. Waters, near an army base in a small Southern town; by the time it ends with a complete reenactment of Waters's death, suspicion has shifted from the Klan, to two white officers, and finally to the two guilty black soldiers. In its overall physical conception of the setting and its fluid, cinematic shifting between present and past, Fuller's work recalls Peter Shaffer's *Equus,* also an investigation of sorts, albeit a psychiatric one. During the criminal investigation, testimony about the past is not simply recited but is acted out (again as in *Equus*), the audience sometimes viewing the past within the past. Because of the courtroom setting, the audience becomes implicated in the action as spectators at the inquiry and even as a tribunal or jury assessing guilt and innocence. When the killers are revealed, however, the complex question of guilt still resonates.

Capt. Richard Davenport, dispatched from Washington to conduct the investigation, functions as the play's most obvious narrator, establishing the time frame as he probes the witnesses. But as these witnesses testify, they, too, become narrators, helping to distance the theatre audience, as Brecht does, and permitting it to analyze the events with a degree of objectivity. The white company commander, Capt. Charles Taylor, has been so acculturated with the stereotypical white-as-master/black-as-servant division that he finds it difficult to accept Davenport's authority, especially before he learns that he has been betrayed by the white superiors who have tied his hands out of fear the scandal will spread. Yet Davenport, who has always tried to be a source of pride for his fellow blacks, ultimately wins Taylor's support and respect because he is "not your yesserin' colored boy."[15] That Taylor attains this new attitude because of Davenport's conduct and despite his skin color is one of the positive notes in an otherwise pessimistic play, and it is signalled by Davenport's finally shedding the tinted glasses he has hidden behind. But Davenport's awareness, expressed in his preachy summation, that "the madness of race in America" (p. 84) has made blacks as well as whites small of heart counterbalances Taylor's growth.

Waters, under the tutelage of his "Daddy," came to regard the army as the only avenue open to blacks for entrance into the white power structure. He became, though, as racist as any white, psychotically obsessed in his preaching against "lazy, shiftless Negroes." Peterson, one of the black soldiers, hints at the analogy between Waters and Hitler; Waters, indeed, developed his own version of the Nazi plan for a master race by campaigning to eradicate certain kinds of blacks he despised. One of these, the gentle musician C. J. Memphis, embodied for Waters all the worst features of the "cotton-picker, singin' the Blues, bowin' and scrapin'—smilin' in everybody's face" black (p. 55). So the megalomaniac Waters, like Lula who represents white society in Jones's *Dutchman,* goaded C. J. into reacting against him, only to break him—a pattern of action that (again like Lula) he had successfully followed elsewhere. C. J. commits suicide in prison, prompting Peterson's eventual vengeance against Waters. Waters, attempting to gain an entree into white authority structures by hating his own race, redefined himself in terms that masked his true identity. Because he tries to deny his brotherhood with other members of his race, Waters reverts when drunk to an animalistic black every bit as stereotypical and onerous as the shuffling Uncle Toms he has goaded to death. His futility at the point of his own death resides in his recognition that those in power who successfully connive to have him do their dirty work for them "still hate [him]" (pp. 4, 82). By repressing his racial identity, he has enslaved himself.

As important to the total impact of the play as Waters's and Davenport's attempts—the first despicable, the second admirable—at discovering a social role that can mesh with a private role without any concomitant loss of integrity, are the modes of response of the minor characters. In his handling of them, Fuller is at his most subtle and complex. At opposite sides of the stage hang two pictures: one of FDR in Taylor's office; a second of "Joe Lewis in an Army uniform" above the words "We'll Win Because We're on God's Side" (p. 3) in the soldiers' barracks. The portrait of FDR serves as a reminder that the avenue of political action was largely closed to blacks, despite the generally liberal stance of the Roosevelt years, and would remain closed to them for two more decades. The poster of Louis suggests that the way to success most available to blacks was—and this remained true for a long time afterwards—sports; in fact, the black soldiers segregated in this barracks are being exploited for their success in the Negro Baseball League. They yearn to fight in the war against Hitler and the Japanese, but they fail to see any connection between Hitler's oppression of the Jewish people and white oppression of blacks, and between themselves as victims of American racism and the Japanese in America as victims during World War II. They want only to be called up into the game of war (certainly one of the connotations of the title *Soldier's Play*) and are elated when they finally receive equal treatment and are shipped out—though they do not understand the hypocrisy of America's missionary zeal abroad when coupled with its moral astigmatism over racism at home. Ironically, the entire squadron, black soldiers and white officers, die almost as soon as they see action. Fuller's drama is thus more radical and subversive than at first appears, taking a stand against all power structures that abuse people by too narrowly defining their roles or by inculcating distorted values. Certainly in Fuller's America both sides, black and white, are guilty, and both sides lose. Fuller arraigns both society as a whole and his specific audience who, unless they actively protest the status quo, are tacitly furthering it.

Not until Gordone's *No Place to Be Somebody,* which premiered at Joseph Papp's Public Theatre, and Fuller's *Soldier's Play,* first produced by the Negro Ensemble Company, are there Pulitzer plays about the black experience that do not bow to commercialism, partly—maybe even primarily—because they were addressed to a black audience as well as to a white. *In Abraham's Bosom* and *The Great White Hope,* written by whites with an almost exclusively white audience in mind, both sacrifice some of their dramatic consistency and integrity to make their material palatable to paying customers; they both insist on straddling the fence, critical of the manner in which blacks have been oppressed and yet careful not to make whites feel too guilty or uncomfortable. *No Place,* the most theatrically complex of all these works, and *Soldier's Play* both rely on conventional, easily recognizable forms—the gangster movie in the first, the courtroom melodrama in the second—used in unconventional ways to dramatize the dilemma blacks face in a white society: how to discover a black identity that is not defined by a white power structure and value system and so is no better than what it attempts to change or replace. Yet blacks in these plays who try to goad their fellow blacks out of complacency risk becoming as oppressive as their own oppressors. As one of the characters in August Wilson's recent *Ma Rainey's Black Bottom,* about racism and rage in Chicago in the 1920s, sums up the problem, "As long as the colored man look [sic] to white folks to put the crown on what he say . . . as long as he looks to white folks for approval . . . then he ain't never gonna find out who he is and what he's about."[16] One of the most pernicious cultural inheritances—and one, ironically, fostered and sustained by literary symbolism—which these playwrights as far back as Green have attempted to expose, is the antithetical way of perceiving experience that sees white as synonymous with right and good and black as synonymous with wrong and evil. This mind-set is now so ingrained in the consciousness (and racial unconscious) that to alter it will demand, Sackler and Gordone and Fuller know, a change not only in their audience's way of thinking but also in their very habit of being.

Five of the six Pulitzer dramas that examine the racial issue break, to a greater or lesser extent, the confines of strict realism. *Soldier's Play, No Place to Be Somebody,* and *Great White Hope,* by employing Brechtian distancing devices, all preach directly to an audience aware that they are watching a play. The stage in the last two even becomes at times a lectern or platform, except that the messages sent are occasionally confusing and/or obscure, probably because of uncertainty about the nature of the audience in a volatile and unstable time. *South Pacific*—which at one point casts the theatergoers in the role of American troops enjoying a musicale-within-the-musical—and *Talley's Folly* force their audiences to think about the experience of going to the theatre, intimating that only in a place of romance and illusion removed from the real world (the island Bali Hai, Uncle Everett's boathouse) can racial differences be ignored and overcome in love relationships. Yet both are only gently corrective of civilization's failure, with the playwrights' intention to entertain remaining preeminent. It might even be that the theatre metaphor itself in each of these works, because it emphasizes the illusionary nature of what happens up on the stage, acutally helps shield the audience from the racial issues; both of them, to extend Matt's categorization of *Folly,* might well be called "valentines" sent to their audiences. *Folly,* however, more so than *South Pacific,* adopts the paradigm of sending its audience back out into society to face and maybe to solve the problem, a strategy that *White Hope* and *No Place* and, to a lesser degree, *Soldier's Play* follow as well. Most prominently in *Soldier's Play,* the stage of the action moves out into the audience as they watch the play; they become aware of themselves as a jury weighing the evidence and passing moral judgment on the American political and military system as the radical protestors have always done.

Notes

1. Doris E. Abramson, *Negro Playwrights in the American Theatre 1925-1969* (New York: Columbia University Press, 1969), p. 8.

2. Richard Rodgers, *Musical Stages: An Autobiography* (New York: Random House, 1975), p. 222. In his autobiography, *Josh: My Up and Down, In and Out Life,* the musical's director, Joshua Logan, lays claim to having supplied much of the libretto: "After three fourths of the first act, I realized Oscar was throwing me lines for Emile Debecque, Bloody Mary, and sometimes for Captain Brackett, and I was doing all the rest" (New York: Delacourte Press, 1976, p. 222). Although he feared "'no one will ever know I wrote a word of it,'" at Rodgers and Hammerstein's own insistence, his name was added to the award citation (Hohenberg, *Prizes,* [see chap. 3, n. 4], p. 201).

3. Richard Rodgers and Oscar Hammerstein II, *South Pacific,* in *Six Plays* (New York: Modern Library, 1959), p. 294. Further references appear in the text.

4. Lanford Wilson, *Talley's Folly* (New York: Hill and Wang, 1979), p. 35. Further references appear in the text.

5. Quoted in Abramson, p. 276.

6. Clinton F. Oliver, "The Negro and the American Theater," intro. to *Contemporary Black Drama from "A Raisin in the Sun" to "No Place To Be Somebody",* eds. Clinton F. Oliver and Stephanie Sills (New York: Charles Scribner's Sons, 1971), p. 24.

7. Paul Green, *In Abraham's Bosom,* in *Pulitzer Plays,* p. 396. Further references appear in the text.

8. Gerald Weales, *The Jumping-Off Place: American Drama in the 1960s* (New York: Macmillan, 1969), p. 292.

9. Howard Sackler, *The Great White Hope* (New York: Dial Press, 1968), p. 186. Further references appear in the text.

10. Quoted in Oliver, p. 19.

11. Quoted in Oliver, p. 20.

12. Larry Neal, "The Black Arts Movement," *The Drama Review,* 12, 4 (Summer 1968), 33.

13. Charles Gordone, *No Place to Be Somebody* (Indianapolis: Bobbs-Merrill, 1969), p. 39. Further references appear in the text.

14. Walter Kerr, "Not Since Edward Albee . . . ," *The New York Times,* 18 May 1969, D22.

15. Charles Fuller, *A Soldier's Play* (Garden City: Nelson Doubleday, 1982), p. 3. Further references appear in the text.

16. August Wilson, *Ma Rainey's Black Bottom* (New York: New American Library, 1985), p. 25.

Thomas P. Adler (essay date 1987)

SOURCE: Adler, Thomas P. "The Political Animal." In *Mirror on the Stage: The Pulitzer Plays as an Approach to American Drama,* pp. 85-95. West Lafayette, Ind.: Purdue University Press, 1987.

[*In the following excerpt, Adler analyzes the treatment of American politics in a group of Pulitzer Prize-winning plays, concluding that their authors' lack of inventiveness in dramatic technique reflects their acceptance of the political status quo.*]

In his history plays, Shakespeare attempts to define the qualities of the good king, proposing a relationship between the health of the body politic and the moral nature of its rulers. This link was not original with the Renaissance; anthropological studies reveal that ancient societies knew "the king must die" so that the wasteland could be made fertile. Shakespeare's perspective is further characterized, however, by the suspicion he casts upon the ability of the ruler to maintain his personal integrity when it inevitably comes into conflict with his position of power. This question of the relationship between a ruler's personal moral integrity and the exercise of political authority pervades the Pulitzer prizewinning dramas about presidents and mayors and members of Congress, though these dramatists' points of view about the political system's effect upon its elected rulers are generally less skeptical and more sanguine than Shakespeare's. Although audiences much loved the two plays among this group that feature a revered historical figure as their subject—Lincoln and LaGuardia—taken as a whole these political plays are the least substantive of all the Pulitzer dramas, lacking much theorizing about history and the political man, such as readers and viewers continue to receive from Shakespeare's chronicle plays.

What may, in part, account for the relatively unchallenging nature of these works—from both a dramaturgical and an ideological perspective—is the playwrights' hesitancy to criticize the audience/electorate too openly for the lack of wisdom exhibited by the rulers it elects, perhaps out of fear that such criticism would be seen as directed against the democratic system itself. Yet at least the first three plays to be discussed here implicitly espouse a notion of the electorate not unlike that found in the writings of Alexis de Tocqueville and John Stuart Mill, both of whom, while prizing individual conscience and character, sensed that majority rule may mean that mediocrity rules. Tocqueville, who seems to have taken over from religious thought into political philosophy the belief in an "inner light" that guides the individual, knows that the majority opinion may be intolerant of the minority viewpoint in its midst, enforcing conformity rather than independence in thought and action. As he writes in *Democracy in America,* "What is a majority, in its collective capacity, if not an individual with opinions, and usually with interests, contrary to those of another individual, called the minority?"[1] Mill goes further in his suspicion that collective rule by the majority tends to level everything down to a kind of uniformity, an average that prevents the exceptional from flowering except when a society is willing to counter this by permitting and nurturing an indispensable aristocracy of thought and character: "No government by a democracy or a numerous aristocracy, either in its political acts or in the opinions, qualities, and tone of mind which it fosters, ever did or could rise above mediocrity, except in so far as the Many have let themselves be guided (which in their best times they have always done) by the counsels and influence of a more highly gifted and instructed One or Few."[2] For most of the playwrights here, this expressed need for exceptional persons to lead society inevitably conflicts with their preception of the audience's predisposition against even righteous individuals who appear to reject the wisdom and will of the collective majority. This timidity in making the audience examine its potential flaws as a citizenry finally constricts the forcefulness of many of these political dramas.

Of Thee I Sing, one of the earliest important American musicals and the first of only a half-dozen to win the Pulitzer, must have seemed at least a quirky and at best a daring and rebellious choice for the prize in 1932, since it received the honor over a number of serious dramas, including O'Neill's *Mourning Becomes Electra.* (At that time, no provision was made for composers to share in the drama award, so the citation named librettists George Kaufman and Morrie Ryskind along with Ira Gershwin who contributed the perky and biting lyrics, but not his brother George Gershwin who wrote the music.) Kaufman and Ryskind's farcical book moves in broad strokes, much like a political comic strip. The nature of *Of Thee I Sing* as an irreverent lampoon can best be seen in the still amusing treatment of the much-maligned and joked-about vice-president, Alexander Throttlebottom; his very name, naturally, occasions malapropisms galore—including "Gottabottle," "Bottlethrottle," and "Teitelbaum." A "hermit" before the kingmaker Fulton picked his name out of a hat to serve as John P. Wintergreen's running mate, Throttlebottom poses a distinct liability to the ticket, sure to precipitate a loss if anyone as much as sets eyes on him. After the ticket wins, he intends to resign so that his mother will not be embarrassed, he loses his pass to the inauguration, he can only gain entrance to the White House by joining a tour, and he cannot obtain a library card because he lacks the necessary references. He is so totally inept that when he does preside over the Senate (confusing the senators with the ball team), he institutes a musical roll call, pays tribute to Paul Revere's long-dead horse Jenny, and fills up his time knitting baby clothes. Yet his historic function—to assume the duties the president cannot in times of incapacitation—and his dramatic role dovetail when he unexpectedly realizes, before anyone else, the solution to the president's romantic difficulties: Throttlebottom can be the essential fourth party who "squares the triangle" by marrying the president's cast-off girl, thus allowing a resolution to the love plot.

Wintergreen, lacking a platform on which to run, takes the unsolicited advice of a hotel chambermaid and runs on "love," complete with a beauty contest to find a Miss White House to become the First Lady. The national committee picks Diana Devereux, a dumb blond sexpot, whom they later try to legitimatize through claiming that she is the "illegitimate daughter / Of an illegitimate son / Of an illegitimate nephew / Of Napoleon."[3] But Wintergreen's heart goes to Mary Turner, famous for her corn muffins made without corn. Diana claims such breach of promise is a "communistic plot," but the Supreme Court justices, after going into a football huddle, decide in Mary's favor because she is pregnant and so "posterity is just around the corner" (p. 737)—the closest reference to the raging Depression in this piece of escapist fluff.

While this outcome satisfies the demands of the musical comedy audience for a happy union between hero and heroine, it fails to conclude logically the sequence of political satire; it can, moreover, only uphold the inner logic demanded of farce if it is taken as a satiric jab at the audience's own desire for a romantic ending. Wintergreen is, though, a far cry from the typical hero; that Kaufman and Ryskind paint him so darkly at the beginning makes the later shift to greater sympathy implausible. Wintergreen nominated himself as presidential candidate, but not until the sixty-third ballot, and will play dirty in order to force himself down the populace's throats; and only his "delicate condition" as an expectant father prevents his impeachment once elected. Even in these premedia-mad days, image supercedes issues, although they, too, lack substance: a dearth of Chanel No. 5, bringing back black cotton stockings, and changing the name of the Virgin Islands since the connotations prove bad for trade. *Of Thee I Sing* seems, finally, despite its fun, to have a critical attitude towards the majority hidden beneath its good-natured face: if the electorate is so blind and allows itself to be manipulated by a do-nothing administration, then maybe it gets the rulers—and "heroes"—it deserves.

Perhaps *Of Thee I Sing* does well not to have a hero, since the next year in *Both Your Houses,* Maxwell Anderson cannot resist making his hero too good to be convincing, although the playwright intends that his ideas take precedence over character credibility. Anderson, author of such works as *Winterset* and *Elizabeth the Queen,* stands as virtually the sole poetic dramatist in the American theatre, yet he won the 1934 Pulitzer for a prose play; ironically, he considers *Houses* "by all odds his worst" offering.[4] Essentially a polemical tract parading as political satire, it follows the career of a United States congressman. The transparency of the play's moral conflicts is thrust at the audience through the too-schematic name symbolism. The naive hero-writ-large is named Alan McClean; he is surrounded by a tainted politician named Simon Gray and a wise old politico totally without guile named Solomon (what else?) Fitzmaurice. Although the play boasts a refreshing turn in that the guy does not get the girl—in this instance the daughter of his foe—Alan's idealism is never challenged; because he never finds himself truly on the defensive, there is little internal conflict or possibility for growth. What exists in abundance is authorial commentary, including an unexpected dose of cynicism about the democratic system that faces its greatest challenge because of a disinterested and apathetic electorate—a criticism Anderson can afford to make more explicitly, albeit more heavy-handedly, than Kaufman and Ryskind could within the scope of an entertainment.

Alan arrives in Washington a political neophyte, wide-eyed and uncompromising. Son of a newspaperman, wearer of mail-order clothes, and devotee of Thomas Jefferson, he lost his college job because of his social commitment and now, like an earlier-day Ralph Nader, even has his own election investigated for possible abuse. Assigned to the appropriations committee, he discovers that all the other members are out to get something for themselves and their constitutents by tacking amendments onto a bill for a dam. Alan's instinct to hate the system but maintain faith in the citizenry seems confirmed by the facts at this point. Solomon, as Anderson's *raisonneur,* does not, however, hold such a complimentary view of the voters; a former radical who is frank about his own motives and about the evils that daily creep into the American system—for example, using taxpayers' money for patrolling the Canadian border to prevent an invasion of Japanese beetles from the Southwest—he counsels Alan that reform is not possible. Better to concentrate on the individual virtue of being fully humane, which in this instance pragmatically means not revealing the former corruption of Senator Gray that would now wreck his life. When one considers the magnitude of the evil (Warren G. Harding was nothing, supposedly, compared to this), the Messianic fervor of youth must naturally buckle under. Alan decides to undermine the system by arranging to have so many extra appropriations tacked onto the bill that it will surely invite a presidential veto. Since the vote is strong enough, however, to override the veto, his scheme backfires. Consequently, Alan has accomplished more harm than good; inadvertently he has taught his unethical colleagues a tactic that will mean even bigger expenditures in the future.

Rationalizing that even honest people are corrupt and that honesty is perhaps impossible under the American system, Gray plays the devil's advocate who receives a partial nod from Anderson. For Anderson hints that something negative infests the very core of the process, some choice made long ago that is partially responsible: the pragmatic robber barons, embodiments of the height of capitalistic enterprise, showed that graft could guarantee prosperity. Yet the voters themselves have a great faith in the promise of the democratic system, and Anderson follows Tocqueville and Mill in suggesting that they must be awakened out of their mediocrity: Solomon claims "no word" or "figure of speech [can] express the complete and illimitable ignorance and incompetence of the voting population."[5] Anderson's "Don Quixote" finally realizes that, far from perfect, this is perhaps not even the best method of government and that revolution is long overdue. But neither the ignorant and incompetent voters nor the Congress appear likely to take action to change things. Maybe Anderson is actually warning against allowing an attitude to develop that will make the country susceptible to precisely what was beginning to occur in Germany, where a sleeping, apathetic people were awaking to find that the monster in their nightmares was real and that they themselves had helped to create it.

If *Both Your Houses* focuses on politicians already in positions of power, *State of the Union*—loosely based on Wendell Willkie's campaign and the prizewinner for 1946—details that rise to power. The emphases in the two works are, nevertheless, virtually identical, though *Union,* more comedic, hits less bullishly. As the coauthors Howard Lindsay and Russel Crouse comment, they desired "'to stir the conscience of the individual citizen . . . to say certain things but to do so amusingly.'"[6] *Union,* like *Houses,* is basically an actionless play, though with a slightly less idealized hero who ends, however, in essentially the same stance as Alan. The playwrights siphon off their indignation through Mary, the candidate's wife, just as Anderson does through his character Solomon. Both plays, too, involve questions of ambition versus integrity, of public morality versus personal relationships. The word *union* in Lindsay and Crouse's title combines a political with a private connotation; the third point in the triangle involving Mary and Grant Matthews is sometimes the political game yet is just as often the other woman, the big-city newspaper publisher Kay Thorndike. In fact, the romantic relationship becomes almost more central than the political conflict in this comedy of manners that only rarely reaches the high level of epigrammatic wit characteristic of the form; about the best the authors seem able to muster are quips such as, "Politics makes strange bedfellows" or "Our personal relations are strictly political."[7]

State of the Union examines the role of the woman behind the political figure. Kay builds up Grant's self-confidence, while Mary—who bemoans the fate of the politician's wife long before it became fashionable to do so—sees her primary function as keeping Grant's ego in check, her worst days being those when he falls prey to the "big man" complex. For Grant is another "Sir Galahad," totally untutored in the seamier side of political reality, determined to campaign and win while remaining morally unscathed. Such a "streak of decency" can be a burden since, for the man of conscience, every decision becomes a moral choice. Politics, which initially seems to keep Grant and Mary apart, ironically brings them closer together as she senses the return of the idealistic boy she wistfully recalls from their honeymoon days. If the campaign turns back the clock on a marriage gone stale, it also forces them to confront large ethical issues. Grant is an unassuming and yet charismatic figure, not as pure as Alan (he vaguely admits to having paid hush money in the past), but one who continues to have faith in the American people and insists on appealing to their best rather than their worst instincts—refusing, for example, to trade on the emerging Cold War hatred against the Russians. What does surprise him is the cynicism of the political giants who take advantage of the "lazy . . . ignorant . . . prejudiced" people. These lawmakers tend to view politics as a game, and it is in such "political" plays as *Of Thee I Sing* and *State of the Union* that the game metaphor so prevalent in political rhetoric of the 1960s and 1970s first enters American drama. As James Conover, the kingmaker, remarks in one of the more obvious expressions of this metaphor: "In this country, we play politics and to play politics you have to play ball" (p. 222). Grant, finally, refuses to cooperate, deciding that he cannot be a candidate on anyone's terms but his own; instead he will be a gadfly from the sidelines—a resolution identical to the one reached by the former political candidate in Robert Anderson's *Come Marching Home* from the same season. In assuming this role of watchdog, Grant does only what every good citizen must: there can be no such thing as an apolitical stance within a truly democratic society.

Fiorello! (the 1960 Pulitzer winner) raises the identical question asked by the other prize plays discussed so far in this chapter: namely, is it possible for the public servant to retain his high ideals and moral values and still succeed politically? The play answers the question uncharacteristically, however, by providing a resoundingly affirmative response in the person of the title character. Since this musical appeared at the tag end of an age of relative stability and optimism—after the second World War and the Korean conflict and in a nation led by a popular and revered hero—it is not surprising that it dwells on a man who was one of America's best-loved politicos rather than on the issues. Selected by the advisory board and not the choice of the drama jury (which gave its nod to Hellman's *Toys in the Attic*), *Fiorello!* can in no way be considered a landmark American musical; rather, it is an old-fashioned, if thoroughly professional show with a score by composer Jerry Bock and lyricist Sheldon Harnick—later of *Fiddler on the Roof* fame—and a book by George Abbott and Jerome Weidman.

The man affectionately known as "the Little Flower" first appears, in a frame that inexplicably occurs only at the beginning, reading the comics over the radio to his adoring constituents. If he possesses an ingratiating political style, complete with theatrical props and costume, he evidences as well a real empathy and concern for the common people. His enemy and theirs is the Establishment: the exploiters who murdered his father during the Spanish-American War, the owners of the sweatshops who take advantage of women workers, and the ward bosses of Tammany Hall. But amidst the corruption of the political machine and even of the courts, as exposed in the memorably satiric number, "A Little Tin Box," Fiorello remains totally incorruptible, always "on the side of the angels."[8] Along with this incorruptibility runs a strain, however slight, of self-righteousness; his aide Ben warns him against being totally uncompromising and falling prey to the great-man syndrome or, worse still, to self-aggrandizement. For Fiorello, without any power base except the people, must merchandise himself through the media, as later politicians will become masters at doing. If Fiorello as showman capitalizes on the theatrical aspect endemic to politics, that remains preferable to reducing politics to a game (as described in the lyric "Politics and Poker") in which "usually you can stack the deck!" (p. 26). Fiorello, nevertheless, stands by his principles: he is independent, anti-isolationist—he even enlists in the Army—slightly Marxist in his economic theory of money as the root of all evil, and tentatively revolutionary in his insistence on placing the individual citizen over and above the law.

Like virtually every musical, *Fiorello!* involves a love triangle and includes a comic subplot. The latter, between Dora and Floyd, a policeman turned sewage treatment entrepreneur, underlines the corruption of Tammany Hall, which Floyd finds synonymous with "tyranny" because it runs on patronage and protection. In the main love plot, Fiorello first marries Thea, a political activist, realist, and something of a New Woman; after her death, he marries his secretary Marie, a confirmed romanticist. Thea first attracts Fiorello because she is the underdog, spokeswoman for the put-upon garment workers; he associates her courage in standing up against those who say women should stay in their place and in sacrificing herself for a cause with that of "Joan of Arc," just as she regards his commitment to causes as the actions of a "Sir Galahad." If Thea is the public person, Marie is the private one for whom the laws of love and family reign supreme and for whom marriage is the only role; she would "outlaw bachelorhood," "rid the country / Of contempt of courtship" (p. 50), and "marry the very next man who asks [her]" (p. 33) before it becomes too late. This elegiac tone pervades Thea's song, "Til Tomorrow," which ritualizes the passing of time in a foreboding way. When Thea dies, Fiorello has just been defeated in his bid for mayor, so his political and personal misfortunes mesh. He must pick himself up and begin anew, through hard work and determination. Marie forces him to take hold, in her traditional role as the woman behind the man, and he emerges victorious.

Not all American musicals express an elemental faith in America and American savvy and self-reliance, but *Fiorello!* assuredly does, for it looks back nostalgically at a period of war and Depression and suggests that these can be overcome. It remains a too sanguine and sentimental look, though, with the tension between public and private morality never translating into a real conflict for the central figure.

The pattern of two very different women and their impact upon a public figure from *Fiorello!* and *State of the Union* appears even earlier in Robert E. Sherwood's *Abe Lincoln in Illinois,* which won the 1939 Pulitzer. Sherwood reportedly admired John Drinkwater's *Abraham Lincoln,* which (complete with verse prologues) premiered in New York in 1919 and began where Sherwood's would leave off, with President-elect Lincoln preparing to leave Springfield for Washington. Had Drinkwater been American rather than British, his work would probably have won the prize over O'Neill's *Beyond the Horizon*; the advisory board, in fact, issued a statement "record[ing] their high appreciation" of Drinkwater's play and "regret[ting] that by reason of its foreign authorship, [it] was not eligible for consideration."[9] Sherwood's main source, however, was Carl Sandburg's *Abraham Lincoln: The Prairie Years* (1926)—itself disqualified from consideration for the history award because of a prohibition then in effect against honoring books about Washington and Lincoln—with a lesser debt to works by William H. Herndon, Nathaniel Wright Stephenson, and Albert J. Beveridge, as well as to Lincoln's own writings.

The action of Sherwood's episodic but economically handled chronicle play is less important than the characterization of Abe, which reveals a psychological complexity missing from the portraits in the other "political" plays, making the work most compelling in those scenes that attend to Abe's inner life. Sherwood's Abe is a Hamlet-like creature: rootless, and so thrown back on the elemental influences in his life; a loner with a low opinion of himself; melancholic and misanthropic, yet, like Swift, someone who "likes people one-by-one, but not in crowds, mobs, or armies."[10] His virtues arise from and are inextricably bound up with his frailties and flaws. John Keat's poem, "On Death," which Abe reads aloud at the end of scene 1, serves as a leitmotif for the work; not only does it establish a somber tone that presages the deaths of Ann Rutledge and (outside the play) of Abe himself, but it also relates as well to Abe's instinctive desire to retreat from the burdens of public life and succumb to a death wish. His political leanings, in fact, are not towards withdrawing but from never entering the arena in the first place. Abe seems at times more than half in love, even obsessed, with easeful death; oftentimes he gloomily repeats the phrase, "If I live. . . ." Yet since Keats firmly places his emphasis on awakening from "a life of woe" that "is but a dream" to immortality, man's "future doom" will actually be a respite from pain and a dying in order to rise. Part of Abe's immortality, that he could only vaguely have guessed at, comes from the process whereby his life enters the realm of myth. To win Ann, who frees his emotional or romantic side, would have made a reality of all that Abe read about in books of poetry; she helps him have faith in the beauty and purity of people and solidifies his belief in God. She would have distracted him, however, from the call to duty and so not have been a positive influence on his political career. The sketchily characterized Mary Todd, a disillusioned and mentally unstable woman, exerts just the opposite influence; she succeeds in being the shaping force behind Abe's life, not so much directing his ambition as instilling it. But a gulf exists between them, her emotional reticence matching his own. Winning the highest office in the land does not guarantee contentment; in fact, duty and personal happiness seem incompatible. That it is Mary, and not Ann, who is temperamentally more suited to becoming a president's wife only underscores this.

In writing about Abe, Sherwood pens his own intellectual and spiritual autobiography, and a biography of the nation as well. As he remarks, "Lincoln's life . . . was a work of art, forming a veritable allegory of the growth of the democratic spirit."[11] Abe as the common man is also Everyman, the protagonist of a morality play; there is, he admits, a civil war "going on inside [him] all the time. Both sides are right and both are wrong and equal in strength" (p. 326), since the struggle is between two imperatives, a hatred of force (war) and an equally intense hatred of slavery (life under dictatorship). Abe's private battle reflects the public one in 1938, mirroring for the audience not so much the Civil War as the trial facing the American people on the eve of World War II. Sherwood employs the history play for a traditional purpose: to present the past as lesson for the present. As much as Americans in 1938 hate war, they must hate even more the threat to humanity's freedom posed by the Nazi tyranny. Man, like Abe, "cannot go on to the end of [his] days avoiding the clutch of his own conscience" (p. 325); he must decide that a "wrong" law "must be changed, if not by moral protest, then by Force!"—and that "some ideals are *worth* dying for" (p. 333). Lincoln, "who is against slavery, but even more opposed to going to war," must declare war; by doing so, however, he becomes a timeless model for the audience, in the same way that he inspired Sherwood to understand that "a natural, intellectual, and moral world must be cultivated" (p. 353). Sherwood underscores Abe's role as an example for all seasons when the crowd at play's end bids Lincoln farewell by singing the chorus from "The Battle Hymn of the Republic," interpolating a line from the earlier "John Brown's Body," which, significantly, has its source in a Negro spiritual: "His soul goes marching on" (p. 353). This apotheosizes Abe, confirming his place on the level of ahistorical myth.

This group of Pulitzer plays seems not to look too hard or too critically at the conduct of America's leaders. Given the almost inevitable conflict between maintaining private integrity while wielding public power, these playwrights could potentially have drawn protagonists open to tragedy, but only Sherwood's Abe, forced to choose between two morally good objectives—union and an end to slavery—approaches that possibility. If Abe is a secular saint, he is a troubled one; public service not only exacts the price of personal happiness, but to follow one's conscience in the political arena means waging a war within oneself. Perhaps partly because of the play's facticity and because of what an audience cannot help but bring to it, Abe's battle seems compelling in a way that the heroes' conflicts in *Both Your Houses* and *State of the Union* do not. With their idealists under fire for their integrity, those two plays bear a relationship to works such as the populist filmmaker Frank Capra's *Mr. Smith Goes to Washington*. They offer their audiences the comfortable facade that they are doing some hard, sophisticated thinking about complex issues and that the "other man" is the guilty one while they are "on the side of the angels." These are not, however, serious social problem plays. They cater to the vague discontent everyone experiences with any imperfect—because human—political system. Although they may mildly criticize the system, especially the corrupt, or at least morally compromised, power brokers, they might also, albeit unintentionally, help to buoy up the status quo, creating an even more deeply rooted and insidious complacency among an audience generally disinclined to admit that what Tocqueville and Mill feared about the majority within a democracy might be true. Furthermore, the naiveté of the hero in *Both Your Houses* is hardly less unappealing than his near perfection, and the self-righteous attitude Anderson assumes towards his audience results in a rather dour play. *State of the Union*, of course, appeared in the aftermath of one of America's greatest victories, during a period of national euphoria when any questioning of the system's goodness was not yet in fashion; but such uncritical acceptance fed directly into the tyrannical rejection of the least ideological difference during the Joseph McCarthy years.

Of Thee I Sing, with its government that trivializes the issues and depends solely on image—and is permitted to do so by the gullibility of an unenlightened electorate—might have been the *Doonesbury* of the Depression; instead, it offers little except the escapist medicine of laughing the country's troubles away. *Fiorello!*, too, though bright and snappy, is little more than an exercise in nostalgia for a simpler time, as if its writers intuitively sensed that political and social turmoil were just around the corner and that theatergoers would not want to confront those in their entertainment. In *Fiorello!*, *State of the Union*, and *Both Your Houses*, moral principles comfortably survive, if they do not completely triumph. Sherwood alone dares to leave his audience with the darker possibility that the leaders of the nation and her citizens might indeed have diminished since the days of the Declaration. As Abe states the challenge: "We gained democracy, and now there is the question of whether it is fit to survive. Perhaps we have come to the dreadful day of awakening, and the dream is ended" (p. 352). That these "political" Pulitzer plays generally lack the technical variety and virtuosity of so much of the best American drama may help account for their thinness. Their authors' unwillingness to question the spectators' traditional aesthetic assumptions about how drama works, to break down the invisible barrier between stage and auditorium, characters and audience, mirrors their hesitation to challenge—as Tocqueville and Mill were not afraid of doing—the spectators' long-held but probably unexamined political views. Unadventuresome techniques and timidity in ideas are, for these Pulitzers at least, two sides of the same coin.

Notes

1. Alexis de Tocqueville, *Democracy in America*, trans. George Lawrence (New York: Harper & Row, 1966), p. 231.
2. John Stuart Mill, *On Liberty*, ed. David Spitz (New York: W. W. Norton, 1975), pp. 62-63.
3. George S. Kaufman, Morrie Ryskind, and Ira Gershwin, *Of Thee I Sing*, in *Pulitzer Plays*, p. 729. Further references appear in the text.
4. Quoted in Toohey, *History*, (see chap. 2, n. 6), p. 109.
5. Maxwell Anderson, *Both Your Houses*, in *Pulitzer Plays*, p. 773.
6. Quoted in Cornelia Otis Skinner, *Life with Lindsay and Crouse* (Boston: Houghton Mifflin, 1976), p. 200.
7. Howard Lindsay and Russel Crouse, *State of the Union*, in *50 Best Plays*, Vol. III, pp. 185, 200. Further references appear in the text.
8. Jerome Weidman, George Abbott, and Sheldon Harnick, *Fiorello!* (New York: Random House, 1960), p. 9. Further references appear in the text.
9. Hohenberg, *Pulitzer*, (see chap. 3, n. 4), p. 48.
10. Robert E. Sherwood, *Abe Lincoln in Illinois*, in *50 Best Plays*, Vol. II, p. 309. Further references appear in the text.
11. Quoted in John Mason Brown, *The Worlds of Robert E. Sherwood: Mirror to His Times 1896-1939* (New York: Harper and Row, 1965), p. 370.

FURTHER READING

Biography

Frenz, Horst, ed. *Nobel Lectures, Including Presentation Speeches and Laureates' Biographies: Literature, 1901-1967*. Amsterdam: Elsevier Publishing Company, 1969. 640 p.

Collection of biographies, Nobel citations, and acceptance speeches of laureates from 1901 to 1967.

Criticism

Beasley, Maurine Hoffman and Richard R. Harlow, eds. *Voices of Change: Southern Pulitzer Winners*. McLean, Va.: University Press of America, 1979, 145 p.

Collection of interviews with Southern Pulitzer Prize-winning playwrights.

De Nooy, W. "Gentlemen of the Jury . . . : The Features of Experts Awarding Literary Prizes." *Poetics* 17, no. 6 (December 1988): 531-45.

    Detailed study of the criteria used to select jury members for Dutch literary prizes.

Marrouchi, Mustapha. "Fear of the *Other*, Loathing the Similar." *College Literature* 26, no. 3 (fall 1999): 17-58.

    Discusses the role and treatment of third world, minority, and postcolonial literature in the awarding of literary prizes.

Oehlschlaeger, Fritz H. "Hamlin Garland and the Pulitzer Prize Controversy of 1921." *American Literature* 51, no. 3 (November 1979): 409-14.

    Explores Garland's role in the controversy surrounding the awarding of the 1921 Pulitzer Prize for the novel to Edith Wharton's *The Age of Innocence* rather than to Sinclair Lewis's *Main Street*.

Stuckey, W. J. *The Pulitzer Prize Novels: A Critical Backward Look*. Norman: University of Oklahoma Press, 1981, 277 p.

    A history of the Pulitzer Prize for novels from its inception to 1977.

Toohey, John L. *The Pulitzer Prize Plays*. New York: The Citadel Press, 1967, 344 p.

    Provides synopses, production credits, and history of reviews for Pulitzer Prize-winning plays from 1916 to 1967.

Wilhelm, Peter. *The Nobel Prize*. London: Springwood Books, 1983, 111 p.

    Overview of the ideas of Alfred Nobel, the Nobel Foundation, selection criteria for prizes, and various statistics about the prizes and winners.

Modern French Literature

INTRODUCTION

The history of French literature is closely linked to the state of French politics, ideology, and culture, often reflecting and shaping these realities in France. Equally important is the place given to the French language; language has often been perceived in both French literature and critical study as being instrumental in creating the order and hierarchy of society. The political and social dimensions of the French literary canon, therefore, are central to the study of modern French literature.

French writers have consistently used their work to expostulate political and philosophical ideology, and thus, the relationship between literature and social and political attitudes has been acutely important in French society. Many scholars of French literature have remarked on the importance the French place on literary figures in their society, including electing a number of them to political power. And often, French opposition literature has had enormous influence with the citizenry of France as well as intellectuals throughout Europe. Although politically motivated literature has seen a decline in France in the latter half of the twentieth century, primarily due to the increasing popularity of other media, the French literary scene continues to experiment with new forms and techniques, now focusing more consciously on the development of form rather than content.

At the beginning of the twentieth century, however, the French literary scene was dominated by the popularity of naturalist writers and their mode of realistic, mostly linear narratives, reflecting the social and political realities of their time. A significant change to this legacy began in the works of such authors as Marcel Proust, and his novel *À la recherché du temps perdu* (1954; *Remembrance of Things Past*), published posthumously, is considered one of the seminal works marking the departure from naturalist thinking. With its examination of the nature of literature in the narrative, as well as its themes of the search for permanence and coherence in human identity, Proust's writing, note critics, is a blend of realism, philosophy, and psychology, and ultimately represents the struggle between reality and experience versus the primacy of art. The advent of World War I, the most violent and widespread conflict in human history at the time, had engendered in many French intellectuals the feeling that the entire European cultural tradition had been dishonored. Many writers saw the slaughter of thousands as deeply disheartening, final proof of the negative impact of the culture of rationalism on which the common language and culture of the time was based. This disillusionment was in part what led to the creation of the Dadaist movement. Although it originated in Zurich, Switzerland, in 1916, the main activity of this movement took place in France, involving such authors as Tristan Tzara, André Breton, Louis Aragon, and Benjamin Péret. The movement eventually evolved into the Surrealist philosophy, focusing on an agenda of literary and political revolution.

By the 1930s, however, there was a growing tension between writers and political figures, symbolized most clearly by the relationship between the Surrealists and the French communists, leading to an acute polarization along political lines among French intellectuals. André Malraux, disheartened by the decline of western culture in the face of western bourgeoisie individualism in the colonies, wrote *La Condition humaine* (1933; *Man's Fate*), a novel that reflects his perception of the struggle between these opposing forces. The beginning of World War II forced a new strain of French literature to emerge, where the writing mainly became a branch of political and military activity of collaboration or resistance. At the end of the second World War, the French literary scene was dominated by Existential activity and the work of such authors as Jean-Paul Sartre, who aimed to establish existentialist values as a replacement for the bankrupt values of prewar France. Sartre explored issues of commitment in such works as *L'Être et le néant* (1943; *Being and Nothingness*) and *L'Âge de raison* (1945; *The Age of Reason*). Another major literary figure of the time was Albert Camus, whose *L'Etranger* (1942; *The Stranger*) epitomized his philosophy of revolt. Camus rejected the possibility of an afterlife, believing only in the certainty of death.

While the idea of the French Resistance remained an integral part of French popular literature well into the 1960s, several writers began to question the myth of French national unity and sacrifice as exemplified by the Resistance, and works of such authors as Roger Nimier offered an alternative, disillusioned view of the bond forged during the war. However, it is Samuel Beckett who is often regarded as the most serious challenger to the humanist ideals of the postwar years. In works such as *En attendant Godot* (1952; *Waiting for Godot*) Beckett put forth the challenge to the existing novel tradition, facilitating the move away from Existentialist literature. Now concern focused on language and narrative technique and not political and ethical ideology, and a new phase of experimentation emerged. Based on the narrative techniques of American authors such as William Faulkner and John Steinbeck, the *nouveau roman* (new novel) created a new relationship between author and reader.

Equally relevant in the development of modern French literature is the growth of French theater, which in many ways paralleled the development of French fiction. During the early half of the twentieth century and even up to the Second World War, French theater was mainly based in Paris. A major change occurred at the end of the war, when performances moved away from Paris and into the rest of the country. Evolving from an austere and elite literary style to a more diverse mixture that allowed for a wider selection in performance and production, French theater in the 1930s, led by such directors as Jacques Copeau, saw a revival of the classics as well as staging of quality contemporary plays. Copeau, along with Louis Jouvet, Charles Dullin, and others formed what became known as the Cartel, the objective being to promote respect for the text, simplicity in staging, and poetic impact in contrast to spectacular effect. After the 1940s, theater activity focused in Paris again, with new writers emerging, showcasing complex dramas of multiple viewpoints. The period between the 1930s and the 1940s, led by the Cartel, is often referred to as one of the best in French theater, with both new and established authors writing. Major authors of the time included such established playwrights as Camus, Sartre, Henry del Montherlant and Marcel Aymé, as well as newcomers to the literary scene such as Eugène Ionesco, Vauthier, Beckett, and others. In the 1970s, French theater had evolved again, with playwrights now used more as literary consultants rather than creators of the script that actors then produced. Instead, as David Bradby notes in his book on modern French theater, the writer became almost secondary to the production and actors.

A major trend in the critical study of modern French literature has been the marginalization of women authors. Much of this rejection is traced to the dominance of fascist and other right-wing political influences in France in the early twentieth century. In their book discussing fascism and French politics, Richard Golsan and Melanie Hawthorne discuss the role of women in fascist ideology and psychology as well as in the history of fascist movements, parties, and regimes. They suggest that male sexuality and misogyny form crucial building blocks of the fascist male psyche that dominated France through the early twentieth century, shutting out the feminine perspective in both political and intellectual arenas. The postwar years, however, have seen a revival of female writing as well as interest in critical study of female authors who continued to write during the war years, including Simone de Beauvoir, Nathalie Sarraute, and others.

REPRESENTATIVE WORKS

Simone de Beauvoir
L'Invitée [*She Came to Stay*] (novel) 1943
Le Sang des autres [*The Blood of Others*] (novel) 1945
Le Deuxième Sexe [*The Second Sex*] (prose) 1949
Mémoires d'une jeune fille rangée [*Memoirs of a Dutiful Daughter*] (prose) 1958
La Femme rompue [*The Woman Destroyed*] (novel) 1968

Samuel Beckett
Malone meurt [*Malone Dies*] (play) 1951
Molloy (play) 1951
En attendant Godot [*Waiting for Godot*] (play) 1952
L'Innommable [*The Unnamable*] (play) 1953
Mercier et Camier [*Mercier and Camier*] (play) 1970

Yves Bonnefoy
Du mouvement et de l'immobilité de Douve [*On the Motion and Immobility of Douve*] (poetry) 1953
L'Improbable (poetry) 1959
Pierre écrite [*Words in Stone*] (poetry) 1965
Un rêve fait à Mantoue (poetry) 1967

Albert Camus
L'Etranger [*The Stranger*] (novel) 1942
Le Mythe de Sisyphe [*The Myth of Sisyphus*] (novel) 1942
La Peste [*The Plague*] (novel) 1947

Michel Deutsch
Dimanche (play) 1974
Partage (play) 1981

Marguerite Duras
Un Barrage contre le Pacifique [*The Sea Wall*] (novel) 1950
Moderato cantabile (novel) 1958
Le Ravissement de Lol V. Stein [*The Ravishing of Lol V. Stein*] (novel) 1964
L'Amour (novel) 1971
L'Amant [*The Lover*] (novel) 1984

Violette Leduc
La Bâtarde (autobiography) 1964

André Malraux
La Condition humaine [*Man's Fate*] (novel) 1933

Georges Michel
La Promenade du Dimanche [*The Sunday Walk*] (play) 1967
Arbalètes et vieilles rapiers (play) 1969

Roger Nimier
Les Éspées (novel) 1948
Le Hussard Bleu (novel) 1950

Paul Nizan
Antoine Bloyé (novel) 1933
Le Cheval de Troie [*The Trojan Horse*] (novel) 1935
La Conspiration [*The Conspiracy*] (novel) 1938

Georges Perec

Zazie dans le metro (play) 1959

La Disparition [*A Void*] (play) 1969

La Vie ode d'emploi [*Life, A User's Manual*] (play) 1978

Marcel Proust

Du côté de chez Swann [*Swann's Way*] (novel) 1913

Sodome et Gomorrhe (novel) 1922

Le Temps retrouvé [*The Past Recaptured*] (novel) 1927

À la recherché du temps perdu [*Remembrance of Things Past*] (novel) 1954

Nathalie Sarraute

Portrait d'un inconnu [*Portrait of a Man Unknown*] (novel) 1948

Martereau (novel) 1953

Le Planétarium [*The Planetarium*] (novel) 1959

Entre la vie et la mort [*Between Life and Death*] (novel) 1968

Jean-Paul Sartre

La Nausée [*Nausea*] (novel) 1938

L'Être et le néant [*Being and Nothingness*] (novel) 1943

Les Mouches [*The Flies*] (novel) 1943

L'Âge de raison [*The Age of Reason*] (novel) 1945

Le Sursis [*The Reprieve*] (novel) 1945

Michel Tournier

Vendredi ou les limbes du Pacifique [*Friday, or The Other Island*] (novel) 1967

Gaspard, Melchior et Balthazar [*The Four Wise Men*] (novel) 1980

Gilles et Jeanne (novel) 1983

Michel Vinaver

Les Coréens (play) 1956

Iphigénie Hotel (play) 1977

OVERVIEWS AND GENERAL STUDIES

Jennifer Birkett and James Kearns (essay date 1997)

SOURCE: Birkett, Jennifer, and James Kearns. "Changing Forms and Subjects." In *A Guide to French Literature: From Early Modern to Postmodern*, pp. 200-75. New York: St. Martin's, 1997.

[*In the following essay, Birkett and Kearns provide a detailed history of modern French literature, including an overview of novels, plays, and poetry.*]

I THE NOVEL

1914-39: NEW IDEAS AND FORMS

The most profound challenge to the Naturalist legacy in the novel came from Marcel Proust (1871-1922) in *À la recherche du temps perdu* (published 1913-27). All of Proust's early work was in one form or another a preparation for this novel, which he began writing in July 1909.[1] Reading Ruskin had confirmed his sense of the over-riding importance of art; translating him had reinforced the apprenticeship of writing also evident in his pastiches of the style of major French writers.[2] In the fragments of *Jean Santeuil*, he described the pleasure derived from identifying elements common to sensations in the past and present. In *Contre Sainte-Beuve*, what began as an attack on the biographical approach to literary history developed into a series of autobiographical texts in which essential characters and themes of *À la recherche* were developed towards their final form. Just as the critical work extended into episodes of fiction, the novel incorporated across its length an analysis of the nature of literature, ending with the narrator's discovery of the means to write the novel which Proust was drawing to a close.

The search for lost time is the search for the permanence and coherence of human identity.[3] Predicated on the essential truth announced at the outset that 'nous ne sommes pas un tout matériellement constitué, identique pour tout le monde' ['we are not a materially-constituted whole, identical for everyone'], but that 'notre personnalité sociale est une création de la pensée des autres' ['our social personality is the creation of the thoughts of others'], it is a lifelong journey through the damage which the passage of time inflicts on knowledge of the self and others. Fashionable upper-class Parisian society of the Third Republic is the arena for the meaningless and inauthentic action whose false values and empty rituals replace knowledge in a world subjected to time. Extending Flaubert's ironic deconstruction in *L'Éducation sentimentale* of Balzac's energised city, Proust shows characters and events as reference points for rituals of social acceptance or exclusion which are vicious and intensely comic at the same time. The Dreyfus Affair is an 'erreur mondaine' ['social gaffe'] through which Madame Verdurin loses ground in the social race; the First World War demonstrates the stupidity of the baron de Charlus's conversation. History is refracted through, and reduced to, the shifting and ephemeral anecdotes of society gossip.

If time condemns social aspirations and relationships to a meaningless formalism, it is no less destructive of love. Since time renders knowledge of the self and others impossible, love in *À la recherche* is a doubly sterile delusion of power, a projection of imagination and desire onto others which always carries the seeds of its own destruction. Each major relationship (Swann with Odette, the narrator with Albertine, Charlus with Morel and so on) repeats the same infernal sado-masochistic sequence of pain inflicted and endured, of a desire for mastery which fuels jealousy and provokes lies and silence.

Only at the end of the novel does the narrator realise that the experience of society and love, worthless in itself, finds its necessity in art. Real without being imprisoned in time, ideal without being devoid of reality, the sensations experienced in the Guermantes courtyard convene past and present in what the narrator describes as time in the pure state, abolishing contingency and the fear of death. The lessons of the madeleine and Martinville steeples episodes in *Combray* can at last take their true place in this self-discovery and in the literary project which flows from it, in the synthesis of sensation and memory in which the necessary relationship between past and present may be demonstrated. Metaphor and simile, which annul restrictions of time and space and fuse abstract thought and physical sensation in a single association, provide an essential linguistic counterpart to this victory over the negative effects of time.

Proust's novel is a compendium of fictional models, its whole extending far beyond the sum of their parts: realist (its sociohistorical analysis); psychological (its involvement of the reader in the narrator's introspective response to experience); developmental (the narrator's sentimental education from childhood to middle-age); confessional (first-person revelation of a life); Wagnerian (its length, and the strategic role of themes and symbols linked by the leitmotif technique). It offers an extended history of its own creation as the narrator eventually abandons the example of the false artists and aesthetes (Swann, Charlus) for the lessons of the true (Vinteuil, Elstir, Bergotte) and, in the novel's circular structure, decides at the end of *Le Temps retrouvé* to write the history of a narrator becoming a writer. Each volume reproduces the same sequence of the aspiration to an ideal world of essential terms followed by the confrontation of this ideal with the reality of experience. The repeated failure of this confrontation brings the narrator to the very brink of defeat—from which victory is snatched in the closing moments of the quest. At the centre of this vast cycle, the Proustian narrator moves between the multiple levels of past and present experience, reflecting on the nature of narrative in ways which have offered subsequent writers enormous potential to extend the means of fiction.

The work of André Gide (1869-1951) is dominated by the conflict between the desire for authenticity and the moral, intellectual and social systems which oppose it.[4] Following the death of his father in 1880, Gide was raised by his mother and his Scottish governess in an intense Protestant austerity. In the mid-1890s he undertook two journeys to North Africa, during which he experienced what he felt to be a spiritual rebirth through the discovery of his homosexuality, the life of the senses and openness to experience. These discoveries intensified the conflict between self-denial and desire for experience with which he had struggled throughout adolescence. In the course of his life this conflict between the temptation and the fear of desire, between submission and resistance to authority, took many forms and Gide used the act of writing to analyse its contradictions critically and thereby deliver himself from them. Each of his books, he said, carried within itself its own contradiction.

In Gide's *récits,* a first-person narrator confronts with varying degrees of lucidity and self-deception the consequences of an ethical choice taken to destructive limits. In *L'Immoraliste* (1902) Michel sacrifices his wife to his theory of immoralism. Formulated five years earlier in *Les Nourritures terrestres,* this philosophy of *disponibilité* and of freedom from external moral constraints had as its object the search for God, deemed the source of all experience. In *L'Immoraliste,* it has become a self-serving cult of force and independence which leaves the narrator with anguish and doubt. *La Porte étroite* (1909) re-enacts the destructive outcome of *Les Cahiers d'André Walter* (1891), Gide's first published work. Alissa's mystical ideal of virtue and self-sacrifice in the name of a silent God lead to desperate solitude and ultimate tragedy. In *La Symphonie pastorale* (1919), the pastor's deception of self and others leads Gertrude to the fatal despair of the knowledge of sin without the knowledge of forgiveness; her death highlights the dangers of the pastor's self-interested interpretation of the Scriptures, choosing between a religion of law and one of love. In these *récits,* the use of the first-person narrator paradoxically achieves what Gide called the height of objectivity, because without authorial intervention, the narrator, recounting experience in her or his diary and letters, unwittingly betrays the self-deception and sophistry which kill. For this reason Gide referred to his *récits* as 'ironic' books. The difficulty of self-knowledge implies a permanently critical, ironic mode of writing.

This ironic mode found its fullest development in Gide's *soties,* a term taken from the medieval popular comic play in which actors masqueraded as fools. *Paludes* (1895), his satire on Symbolist attitudes to the relationship between art and life, and *Le Prométhée mal enchaîné* (1899), his modernised version of the Greek myth in which Prometheus discovers immoralism, illustrate its possibilities but its most powerful demonstration comes in *Les Caves du Vatican* (1913), an hilarious spoof adventure story of an alleged abduction of the Pope and his replacement by an imposter. Composed at the height of the Catholic revival, this ferocious satire of uncritical allegiance to systems of belief centres on the Vatican cellars, underground passages which link the residences of the true and fake Popes and so serve as a metaphor for the unfathomable distinctions between appearance and reality and for the threat of the counterfeit in every area of experience, from Protos's disguised crooks to Lafcadio's false *acte gratuit*. As in his *récits,* Gide in *Les Caves* makes the problematics of writing central to the burlesque escapades. Autonomous pantomime characters, shifting narrative points of view, a decentralised and open-ended plot structure, a profusion of coincidences and word-play represented Gide's most sustained subversion to date of the nineteenth century's practice of the realist and psychological novel.

In this respect it was an essential preparation for *Les Faux-Monnayeurs* (1926). This was the only one of his texts which Gide described as a novel, for he tried to fulfil there the encyclopaedic ambition of Balzac and Zola to depict modern society (which Gide saw as threatened by inauthenticity at every level) while showing at the same time the conflict between the reality of this society and our representation of it. In *Les Faux-Monnayeurs,* the moral focus of the *récit* and the narrative innovations of the *sotie* are combined and multiplied. The threat of the counterfeit provides unity across the range of characters and themes (Bernard and the family, the Oliver/Édouard couple and homosexuality, Passavant and writing) while the narrative system unpacks realist conventions of linear time, fixed characters, absolute knowledge and closed structure. The multiple narrative points of view created by these procedures are themselves displaced by the *mise en abyme* technique which shows Édouard writing *Les Faux-Monnayeurs* and keeping a diary, the *Journal des Faux-Monnayeurs,* and an 'author' intervening in the text to judge his characters, as does Gide himself.

Gide was also the most prominent founder member in 1909 of the *Nouvelle Revue Française,* which became, particularly from 1919, when Jacques Rivière (1886-1925) took over as director, one of modern France's most famous literary reviews. Despite the review's commitment to independence from political programmes, Gide was passionately involved with some of the central moral and political issues of his time and ours—homosexuality (*Corydon,* 1924), the failures of colonisation (*Voyage au Congo* and *Retour du Chad,* 1927-8) and those of Stalinism (*Retour de l'URSS,* 1936). His experimentation with new narrative practices, though complex and somewhat contrived, his use of narrative to work through the contradictions and potential dangers of intellectual systems, his continued reflection on the nature of autobiographical writing in the diary he kept throughout his life, all stemmed from his sense of the importance of self-knowledge at a time when the systems of thought which had underpinned the literature of the nineteenth century were losing credibility. For these reasons, his work makes an essential contribution to the development of twentieth-century sensibility.

The Great War and its Aftermath

The work of Proust and Gide provided from the 1920s two of the most important models of the implications for narrative practice of the re-examination of that positivist ambition which for much of the nineteenth century had given literature coherence and direction. By then, however, these issues had been engulfed by the catastrophic devastation of the Great War (1914-18).

The sense that the entire European cultural tradition had been dishonoured by the war was widely felt; Paul Valéry expressed it powerfully in his famous essay of 1919, *La Crise de l'esprit.*[5] Despite the unprecedented scale of the slaughter, certain writers found it possible to view the war positively, transforming it into a nostalgic ideal of heroic comradeship and purification through sacrifice. But at the other end of the cultural spectrum, one faction of the avant-garde saw it as the justification of its contempt for the culture responsible for the industrialised carnage in the trenches, and an opportunity to unite the European avant-garde in the great task of destroying through derision the rationalist tradition on which bourgeois language and culture was based. This faction formed the Dada movement in Zurich in February 1916. Its main activity however took place from 1920 in Paris where its leading figure, Tristan Tzara (1896-1963), linked up with the French pre- and post-war avant-gardes and, in particular, with the *Littérature* group, created in 1919 by André Breton (1896-1966), Louis Aragon (1897-1982) and Philippe Soupault (1897-1990) and quickly reinforced by Paul Éluard (1895-1952) and Benjamin Péret (1899-1959). Together they channelled Dada's provocative and nihilistic agitation in the direction of the Surrealist programme of literary and political revolution.

The wave of euphoric nationalist and revanchist sentiment which greeted the declaration of hostilities in August 1914 was soon confronted by the atrocious facts of the trench warfare into which the conflict settled from its first winter. Public ignorance of the realities of modern warfare, and the divorce between these realities and the official propaganda emanating from incompetent and deceitful military and political authorities, created, for writers seeking to describe authentically the experience of the trenches, the problem of finding words for what was unprecedented, and literally unspeakable. Though there were some reference points in the French novel tradition to help them—the description of the battle of Waterloo in Stendhal's *La Chartreuse de Parme,* that of the battle of Sedan in Zola's *La Débâcle,* for example—the sheer scale and horror of the carnage called for new types of description of death, mutilation and survival and a wider range of linguistic registers, incorporating dialect, slang and obscenity. Limited points of view and episodic, disjointed sequences of events displaced the purposeful actions of linear narratives, which were inappropriate for the sudden catastrophes visited upon soldiers unable to comprehend the forces that a modern technological civilisation had unleashed upon them.

The two most famous novels of the Great War, *Le Feu* (1916) by Henri Barbusse (1873-1935) and *Les Croix de bois* (1919) by Roland Dorgelès (1886-1973), offered different responses to the chaos. Despite the censorship to which its initial serialisation in a left-wing review was subjected, *Le Feu* outraged conservatives, but its strong fusion of documentary realism and pacifist, internationalist vision of a society of equality and brotherhood made it a huge critical and commercial success.[6] *Les Croix de bois* recounted the fear, suffering and will to survive which marked day-to-day life in the trenches, where horror was displaced by moments of intense release and humour. Unlike *Le Feu, Les Croix de bois* contained little political analysis or vision and this distinction between the two novels also characterised the post-war directions taken by the authors. Both before and after joining the Parti Communiste Français (PCF) in 1923, Barbusse played a leading role in efforts to create a collective revolutionary consciousness among intellectuals, notably through the reviews *Clarté* and *Monde,* of which he was the founding editor (in 1919 and 1928 respectively), and through his contribution to the debate on proletarian and popular literature.[7] In *Le Réveil des morts* (1923), Dorgelès vented his sense of outrage that the society which had survived the war was failing in its moral obligations to the war dead. Having done so, he turned to writing travel literature and escapist, nostalgic chronicles of an idealised and carefree bohemian life in pre-war Montmartre.

The Inter-War Years

In the novel the end of the war triggered a wide range of responses. Not surprisingly, anti-war sentiment was prominent among them, while the implications of the war for religious faith, spiritual values or cultural and intellectual issues of the sort raised by Valéry in 'Crise de l'Esprit' also became important themes. At the same time, other novelists responded to a powerful public need to draw a veil over 1914-18, and this led to a sharp increase in the production and consumption of thrillers and of travel and adventure novels. Exotic geographical, historical and social locations had in any case long since been the staple diet of popular and escapist fiction. In the post-war euphoria of the *années folles,* the adventure novels of Pierre Benoît (1886-1962) achieved huge sales.[8]

On another level, novelists whose work came into the imprecise and wide-ranging category of the poetic novel again took up pre-war criticisms of what were considered to be the artificial and superficial observation and organisation of external reality in Naturalist fiction. The 1920s novels of Jean Giraudoux (1882-1944) contained sequences of loosely-related episodes which showed the poetic sensibility's subjective transformation of everyday life. This formula, in which the mechanisms of prose poetry and fiction collaborated within the narrative structure, was a focus for much discussion of narrative theory during this period.

The most important group of novels referred to at that time under the term 'poetic novel' was that of the regional *roman rustique,* which tapped into a demand for something more profound than the conventional pastoral of rural local colour. The desire to escape modern urban industrial society through a return to the values of a mythical *France profonde* reflected the wish to re-establish contact with more stable rhythms associated with the ancestral relationship between people and land, far removed from the brutal contingencies of modern history. André Chamson (1900-83), with his historical novels of the Cévennes (published 1925-8), and Maurice Genevoix (1890-1980), with *Raboliot* (1925), were important figures in this development, but it was in the work of the Swiss francophone novelist Charles-Ferdinand Ramuz (1878-1947) and that of Jean Giono (1895-1970) that the regional novel briefly appeared central to the intellectual and formal developments taking place in the novel of the period.

In Ramuz a lyrical and mystical vision of the mysterious forces in nature which both threaten and enhance those in contact with them was expressed in distinctive verbal rhythms and syntactic disjunctions. In a cycle of novels known as the Pan trilogy (published 1929-30), Giono created a myth of rural life in which the ancestral gestures and rhythms of day-to-day experience confront the mysterious forces of nature. In *Le Grand Troupeau* (1931) he returned to his loathing of war. As is indicated by the metaphor of the flock contained in the title, the novel contrasts apocalyptic scenes of soldiers led like lambs to the slaughter with descriptions of the cyclical continuities and force of life within peasant society. The interwoven themes and images of war and land bring to the surface the relationship between anxiety about the nature of modern experience and the values for which the regional novel of the 1920s was the vehicle. Nevertheless, the novel retains a guarded optimism that the force of life exemplified in peasant society will overcome even as violent an assault on its values as that of the Great War.[9]

It was no coincidence that in 1931 Giono returned to the theme of war or that he depicted it then as an essentially totalitarian phenomenon. After an initial rush of war novels of the 'lived experience' type, the Great War began to serve as a metaphor for the post-war world it had engendered. An early case in point is that of *Le Diable au corps* (1923), in which Raymond Radiguet (1903-23) showed, through an affair between an adolescent and a young woman whose husband was fighting at the front, the premature cynicism of an adolescent growing up in the exceptional situation created by the war. The youth's calm amoralism and the negative portrayal of the female characters created a huge *succès de scandale* at a time in the early 1920s when 'official' accounts of the war were stressing heroism, self-sacrifice and just revenge.[10]

As the 1920s progressed, the growing impact of the ideological systems of Communism and National Socialism drew intellectuals in every sphere towards contemporary historical and political issues. The publication of *La Trahison des clercs* (1927), in which Julien Benda (1867-1956) denounced what he considered this betrayal of the intellectual's responsibility for detached speculative thought, and the reaction his work provoked, crystallised this trend. Any hopes Benda might have had of convincing his fellow-intellectuals of the need to withdraw to some ivory tower of pure ideas were ended by the economic and political crisis triggered by the Wall Street Crash in 1929. The Great Depression and its political consequences created for many writers the sense of living after one war and on the verge of another, and refocused their interest on the nature of modern history and its origins in the Great War.

The Great War is the first of the four locations in which Louis-Ferdinand Céline (1894-1961) situated his *Voyage au bout de la nuit* (1932), in which modern life is depicted as a sinister farce played out initially in the military context of war and later in the economic and social context of peace. In this radically pessimistic variation on *Robinson*

Crusoe, dehumanising victimisation exercised by a ruling elite is the general law in all four locations (trenches and military hospital, African colonies, American factories, Parisian suburbs) down whose long, dark night the protagonists, Barmadu and Robinson, wander. In his second novel, *Mort à crédit* (1936), the death is that of the *petite bourgeoisie* to which the narrator's family belongs, while the credit is that of the new technological economy which is the source of its ruin. The novel recounts the narrator's hopeless childhood and adolescence, spent in growing conflicts with his family. This second novel took further than the first Céline's efforts to inject into the literary tradition the energy and authenticity of popular spoken French and slang and his experimentation with expressive, stylised punctuation. The scandalous nature of the themes and language in both novels, and the predominantly sociopolitical readings they encouraged, notably in view of Céline's notorious pro-fascist sympathies immediately before and during the Second World War, were originally the basis of his reputation. Later, *nouveau roman* experimentation in the 1950s and 1960s helped to promote awareness of his subtle and complex reworking of the Proustian legacy in the French novel.[11]

The ironic reversal of the values of the Great War from heroism to farce is also present in the work of Pierre Drieu la Rochelle (1893-1945). Leading the charge at the battle of Charleroi in October 1914, Drieu had apparently experienced a mystical, purifying vision of the union of intellect and action, after which life in post-war Paris appeared as one of cultural and political decline. In the title story of his collection *La Comédie de Charleroi* (1934), heroism has become a 'comédie', farcically ill-adapted to the forms of modern warfare, which reduced heroes to cannon-fodder, and irrelevant to the post-war world order, in which the USA and the Soviet Union were replacing the old European empires. In the story, a middle-aged narrator speaking at an unspecified time in the 1930s tells of his return to the battlefield in 1919, in the course of which he had recounted the 1914 battle to the mother of his fallen comrade. Through the interplay between these three narrative moments, Drieu shows how the war prefigures the unviable, divided society created in Europe by the advanced industrialised civilisation of the post-war years. As the collection was appearing, Drieu was finding his own solution to the problems it raised: the fascist riots of February 1934 precipitated his conversion to the fascist cause. The intellectual itinerary of the fascist is the subject of his novel *Gilles* (1939).[12]

Les Thibault (1922-40) by Martin du Gard illustrates a different aspect of the impact on fiction of the retrospective assessment of the Great War. Planned in 1920 as a modern version of the classical chronicle of the lives of two antithetical brothers, the cycle traces the development of Jacques and Antoine Thibault in relation to the pre-war values of their authoritarian father. The final volume, *L'Été 1914* (1936), marks the eruption of modern history, in the form of the declaration of war, into the private destinies of the brothers. Within a conventional naturalist technique,

Martin du Gard presented an analysis of human relationships deepened by his study of Freudian descriptions of sexuality, and by what Camus called a 'shared misery', in which the subject is both limited and empowered by its recognition of the force of collective realities.[13] As such, he appears in histories of French literature as a transitional figure between the nineteenth-century Naturalist and the mid-twentieth-century existentialist novels.

The nature of collective experience is central to the other major novel cycle of the inter-war period, the 27-volume *Les Hommes de bonne volonté* (published 1932-46), in which Jules Romains tried to integrate the theories of unanimist collective realities developed in his pre-war poetry (see above, p. 181) with an account of history in the making, based on the realist model.[14] The two volumes (15 and 16) which deal with the battle of Verdun are thematically and structurally central. They illustrate unanimist principles in the sense that the sum of the limited and distorted individual narrative points of view before and during the battle is less than the whole, transcendent overview of their collective relationships. The cycle of novels strikes an uneasy balance between fatalistic submission to contingent, uncontrollable forces and faith in the possibility of individual action which might channel these forces in directions beneficial to the collectivity.

By the mid-1930s one of the clearest signs of the heightened awareness of the novel's engagement with modern history was that of the complex, difficult relationship between the Surrealists and the French Communist Party.[15] By that time Aragon was the sole survivor in the Party of those members of the group who had joined in 1927, and his support for the theory of socialist realism alienated them still further. Aragon used the term to describe *Antoine Bloyé* (1933), the first novel by his fellow Communist Paul Nizan (1905-40). Whereas Aragon considered socialist realism to be the means to bring together the political and cultural levels of revolutionary struggle, Breton thought it a sterile dogma indicative of the Party's subservience to Stalinist cultural orthodoxy. In *Pour un réalisme socialiste* (1935), Aragon claimed that the Surrealists had sought to submit Marxism to Freudian theory without regard to socio-economic conditions. But like Breton (in *Nadja,* 1928), he was the author of a classic Surrealist prose text.[16] In *Le Paysan de Paris* (1926), a narrator creates from chance encounters and observations triggered during visits to the Passage de l'Opéra, scheduled for demolition, and the Buttes-Chaumont gardens, a collage of dialogues, memories, inventories and newspaper cuttings which reinvent the city as an adventure of the imagination. With his conversion to socialist realism, Aragon did not, however, simply abandon the effort to create a new type of novel which *Le Paysan de Paris* had represented.

During the 1930s Aragon published *Les Cloches de Bâle* (1934) and *Les Beaux Quartiers* (1936), the first two of a cycle of novels which would be called *Le Monde réel*. *Les Cloches de Bâle* shows the condition of three women in French society between 1897 and 1912 (the latter being the date of the Basle Congress of European Socialists, which gave the novel its title). Diane de Nettencourt is a high-class prostitute whose life illustrates the corruption, duplicity and waste inherent in the bourgeois capitalist system. Clara is the emerging proletariat and Catherine represents that sector of the bourgeoisie that tried and failed to rebel against its class through social and political education. In contrast, the epilogue introduces the German militant Clara Zetkin as a model of the new emancipated political woman. In *Les Beaux Quartiers,* the classical fictional device of two brothers following opposing paths, one towards wealth and power, the other towards left-wing political commitment, is used to represent pre-war Paris, its *Belle Epoque* decadence and its political agitation. The novels have a political objective absent from *Le Paysan de Paris* but draw on a variety of narrative forms and tones already present in Aragon's work of the 1920s.[17]

The other essential figure of French socialist realism, the militant novelist and journalist Paul Nizan, had already established his Communist credentials with his attacks on colonialism in *Aden Arabie* (1931) and on the idealist philosophical tradition of the French university system in *Les Chiens de garde* (1932) when he published *Antoine Bloyé* (1933).[18] This novel recounts the life of a railwayman who betrays his working-class origins in favour of integration with the petty bourgoisie and pays, through alienation and solitude, the price of his lack of political lucidity. His life is analysed by his son, compassionate towards his politically uneducated and manipulated father but aware, as a committed Communist, of the ideological mechanisms which have led him to betray his class. This problem of the complexities and self-deceptions of political commitment, and the consequent need for lucid self-criticism, is taken further in *La Conspiration* (1938), Nizan's most accomplished novel.[19] He broke with the French Communist Party in September 1939 following the signing of the German—Soviet non-aggression pact and was, as a result, denigrated as a traitor by the Party (and, in particular, by Aragon).

The commitment to socialist realism created difficulties for Communist novelists working within a culture which had not yet carried out its own revolution and whose reading public was therefore from the Marxist point of view an accomplice to the forms of sophistry and mystification by which the ruling class maintained its position. The need to show the development of the proletarian class consciousness from which revolution would spring, to analyse the economic and historical factors which produced the situation in which characters found themselves, and to show how the forces of reaction worked from mysterious centres of power to frustrate the emergence of a revolutionary situation—all these created difficult issues of narrative technique in a culture in which pre- (or counter-) revolutionary narrative traditions were so strongly established.

It is hardly surprising, given the pressure of circumstances, that Aragon and Nizan made use of mechanisms readily available in the French nineteenth-century realist tradition, even though it represented the triumph of the bourgeois ideology to which they were opposed. These mechanisms included the use of the Balzacian omniscient narrator, able to relate individual action to the wider socio-historical context; the description of places and objects onto which a Marxist perspective of economic determinism might be grafted; the creation of characters as types representative of class commitments; and the representation of the city and its streets and buildings as signs of the social organisation enacted there. As a result, Aragon and Nizan were attacked for relaying a revolutionary message through conservative narrative techniques, and the seriousness with which they struggled with the issues of narrative technique and the interest of the solutions they brought were overlooked.[20] Only from the mid-1950s did different historical circumstances make it possible to consider these issues from new perspectives. These included Aragon's own fiction from 1956, and Nizan's rehabilitation, begun in 1960 with the famous preface by Jean-Paul Sartre (1905-80) to a new edition of *Aden Arabie* and extended by the rediscovery of *Chiens de garde* in the student upheavals of May 1968.

In addition to their political novels, Nizan and Aragon were essential figures in the controversies which in the course of the 1930s increasingly polarised French intellectuals. If, at the beginning of the decade, the 'spirit of 1930' was for many of the younger generation of intellectuals still a largely-unfocused rejection of contemporary political and social structures, by the mid-1930s polarisation had taken place on political lines. The choice appeared clear between the communist/socialist rapprochement, which led in 1936 to the election of the Popular Front government under Léon Blum, and the conservative Right, which aligned itself with the fascist opposition to this development. The outbreak of the Spanish Civil War in 1936 was a defining moment in this process of polarisation in the period leading up to the Second World War.[21]

The work and political activity of André Malraux (1901-70) was directly involved with these events and the issues they raised.[22] Like Gide in the Congo, Malraux had discovered in the Far East the decline of European culture, and in the alien gaze of the colonised he saw reflected the crisis of Western bourgeois individualism (*La Tentation de l'Occident,* 1926). With the death of God there was no universal human nature created in His image and likeness. There was only the human condition, the tragic state of being in an unstable world. With no prospect of an afterlife, the choice was either to reconcile oneself to living in a meaningless world of atomised subjectivities or to struggle to create new meanings through revolt against the tragic vision of human destiny.

For those who chose struggle, the historical situation in which they did so made available a further choice between individual and collective action. In Malraux's novels the characters who act seek either to project into the world the values of self-realisation or to submit these values to a collective discipline which will transform political and social reality for the group with which they identify. The tensions between the two forms of action, between what Malraux presents as the anarchist urge to be and the communist urge to do, underpin the structure as well as the ideological and ontological debates which the novels enact. In *La Condition humaine* (1933), the representatives of both types of action within the revolutionary community engaged in the Communist uprising in Shanghai in April 1927 are doomed in advance, victims of the political expediency of the Communist International in Moscow, which sacrifices them to its own wider strategy of class alliances with bourgeois parties. In this situation the dichotomy between being and doing is transcended only negatively, in the faith in the value of martyrdom, and the belief in the right to choose how one dies, which unite the two groups.

The vision of hope, tragic in *La Condition humaine,* is epic in *L'Espoir* (1937), in keeping with the fact that in 1937 the outcome of the Spanish Civil War was still uncertain. Between the anarchists whose commitment to a personal ethic of immediate and absolute freedom leads only to the lyrical illusions of the initial phase of the conflict (Part I), and the Communists whose collective discipline and organisation, however important strategically, threaten the ideals for which the war is being waged, certain characters (Manuel, Magnin, Garcia, Scali) represent in different forms the ambition to produce effective military and political action which embodies an idealism of liberty and fraternity.

For Catholic novelists the essential issue during this period was not the death of God but the mystery of His existence. In the work of François Mauriac (1885-1970), the certainties and doubts of modern Catholic faith and, in particular, the difficult relationship between free will and divine knowledge, underpin the theory and practice of fiction.[23]

With *Le Baiser au lépreux* (1922), a tragic allegory of marital incompatibility whose conflict between creative and destructive dynamics can be resolved only in self-sacrifice, the essential themes, types and settings of Mauriac's fiction are in place. In *Thérèse Desqueyroux* (1927), Mauriac explored technical and ontological issues involved in the relationship between author and character. On the one hand, Thérèse extends the movement towards the greater psychological indeterminism of characters which Mauriac (like Gide before him, notably in *Les Caves du Vatican*) had seen as the legacy of Dostoievsky and the Russian novel, and which might express what Mauriac thought of as the illogicality of life. On the other, she inherits the Jansenist predestination which imprisoned Phèdre in a logic of destructive action. In the stifling, claustrophobic physical and moral landscape of the materialistic provincial society in which much of Mauriac's fiction is set, her solitary confinement, real and symbolic, concentrates the tensions of her struggle to find, within the narrow range of freedoms created for her by Mauriac's subtle, flexible use of narrative point of view, her essential but indefinable self in the face of the destiny which drives her to destroy herself and others.

In a sequel, *La Fin de la nuit* (1935), Mauriac attempted to write the happy ending of her redemption but stopped short because, as he put it in his preface, he was unable to *see* the priest who would receive Thérèse's confession. The Communist Nizan saw this as the resistance and protest of the novelist against the theologian, proof that the aesthetic demands of Mauriac's system of characterisation blocked the religious apologetics and that this impasse devalued his fiction and theology. The existentialist Sartre saw it as an example of Mauriac's bad faith, denying freedom to his characters to create themselves, through his authorial omniscience, and disguising this denial by means of the ambiguities of his narrative point of view.

Georges Bernanos (1888-1948), unlike Mauriac, sided with the traditionalists against the modernists in the controversies which divided the Catholic Church in the 1920s, and, more than Mauriac, he drew for his fiction on themes central to the Catholic revival at the turn of the century. He stressed the metaphysical reality and power of evil, the need for a militant faith with which to sustain the relentless struggle against it and the importance of willed submission of the self to God's hidden purposes. In *Journal d'un curé de campagne* (1936) the curé of Ambricourt keeps a diary which recounts his own version of Christ's agony on the Way of the Cross. Like Christ, he experiences the anguish of physical and moral suffering through a series of struggles against multiple forms of darkness (his own illness, the incomprehension of the villagers, loneliness, the temptation of suicide). In this novel, thematic elements and stylistic features present from the beginning in Bernanos's fiction (the importance of childhood, the relationship between natural and supernatural, and between physical and spiritual) achieved a new depth through the use of the first-person diary form, both because of the confrontation it permitted between the priest's experience and the trials of his faith, and through its erasures and omissions, which suggest the priest's anguish at the invisibility of God.[24]

Despite their holding different viewpoints, both Mauriac and Bernanos found in the reality of faith a firm framework within which to explore the limitations of nineteenth-century models of the psychology of individualism. In exploring the complexity and difficulty of faith, they confirmed their own commitment to this individualism. One result of this was that both distanced themselves (albeit in different ways and to different degrees) from what they saw as the failure of the Catholic Church to dissociate itself from fascism. This relationship between Christian commitment and the craft of fiction was one manifestation of the growing recognition by intellectuals during the 1930s of the need to break down the barriers between action, writing and professional or confessional philosophy.

Benda and Nizan had taken prominent parts in this debate but in the final years of the inter-war period it was Sartre, versed in the German philosophical tradition from Kant to Heidegger and a committed atheist, who produced in *La Nausée* (1938) the most wide-ranging attack on the philosophical system which underpinned the French novel.[25] In a world which the lack of religious faith leaves bereft of inherent structure and necessity, the relationships in which we invest meanings—those between words and objects, objects and people, body and mind, past and present—prove to be no more than reassuring conventions designed to keep at bay the arbitrary nature of existence. The narrator, Roquentin, experiences a series of panic attacks at his discovery of existence without meaning or necessity, until he finally understands, listening to the jazz song 'Some of these Days', that art exists in a radically different form from that of other objects. Whereas objects simply *exist*, brutish and shapeless, art *is*; human creativity can set up a model of a coherent, necessary world, simply by practising variations of form, on a theme of its own choice. Existence precedes essence, but art brings both together. The philosophy of existentialism, of which Sartre was, from the publication of *La Nausée*, the best known representative, required the individual to recognise and accept the terrible but empowering freedom of contingency. The outbreak of the Second World War in September 1939 would give a dramatic new relevance to existentialism's ambition to fuse writing, thought and action in the world.

After 1939: Commitments and Interrogations

In May 1940, the German army swept through Northern Europe, reaching Paris on 14 June. The invasion brought an end to the eight months of phoney war which had followed the declaration of hostilities on 3 September 1939. It triggered a mass French exodus southwards during the summer of 1940 and, in association with these dramatic events, a substantial literature of primarily documentary interest.[26] Following the armistice, the literature of collaboration returned to simple explanations already familiar from the débâcle of 70 years earlier. Crushing military defeat was no more than France deserved for the decadence of the pre-war years. The experience was an opportunity for self-appraisal and renewal or for a return to the supposedly essential virtues of traditional, rural France.

Among the most famous literary figures associated at the time with the Vichy regime, collaboration took different forms and involved various levels of commitment. *La Solstice de juin* (1941) by Henry de Montherlant (1896-1972) contained themes which supported collaborationist ideology, but in his own life Montherlant placed the lucidity and independence of the creative writer above collaboration. Drieu la Rochelle became the editor of Gallimard's prestigious pre-war literary journal the *Nouvelle Revue Française*, which published during the period 1940-3 a mixture of pro-Vichy polemic and ostensibly apolitical literary criticism. Céline produced a series of ferocious anti-Semitic pamphlets. The journalist Lucien Rebatet (1903-72) was Céline's equal in anti-Semitism and wrote a violently anti-Republican account of the final years of the Third Republic, *Les Décombres* (1942). But it was Robert Brasillach (1909-45), as editor of the fascist *Je suis partout*, who most consistently promoted the fascist cause and who, along with Drieu, paid the heaviest price when the liberation of Paris in August 1944 ushered in the *épuration*, the purges of collaborators, real or invented. Montherlant was investigated but simply forbidden to publish for a year. Céline fled into exile in Denmark. Rebatet, condemned to death in 1946, was reprieved and, in the course of the six years he spent in prison, wrote *Les Deux Étendards,* a novel on his sentimental education into cynicism and disillusionment. Drieu committed suicide and Brasillach was executed by firing squad after a trial which became a focus for the post-war debate on the responsibilities of the writer.

The literature of resistance grew slowly at first in a country divided (until November 1942) between the Northern, occupied zone and the Southern, 'free' zone administered from Vichy.[27] For the reasons we shall see, poetry was the exception. In fiction, the emergence of Resistance sentiment achieved a significant break-through with the creation in 1941 of the clandestine *Éditions de Minuit*, whose editor, Vercors (pseudonym of Jean Bruller, 1902-91), wrote and published the collection's first novel, *Le Silence de la mer* (1942).[28] In the novel, silence is the most powerful form of passive resistance to the occupier and the most eloquent expression of the victory of French humanist values over a hateful ideology. Silence thwarts the efforts of the francophile German officer von Ebrennac to blur the distinctions between friend and enemy and forces him to face the evidence of his self-deception.[29]

In the area of active resistance, *Pilote de guerre* (1942) by Antoine de Saint-Exupéry (1900-44) showed the efficacy in the context of war of the intellectual and spiritual humanism developed in the adventure of aviation, with its heightened awareness of the interdependence of the individual and collective and of the contrasting beauties of earth and sky. These themes were already in evidence in his pre-war novels (notably *Courrier Sud,* 1928, and *Vol de nuit,* 1931).[30] In *Drôle de jeu* (1945), Roger Vailland (1907-65) created one of the major novels of the Occupation years, with its analysis of the nature of Resistance and language in occupied Paris.[31]

Under the Occupation, literature was primarily one branch of the political and military activity of collaboration or resistance. With the liberation of Paris and the end of the war it returned to its more specialised forms of intervention in the cultural domain. The immediate post-war period was dominated by the existentialist sensibility (see above, pp. 190-2), in which concepts such as commitment, responsibility and situation, erasing the boundaries between philosophy, literature and action, had acquired enormous prestige through the Resistance effort. The publication of *L'Être et le néant* (1943) and *L'Âge de raison* and *Le Sursis* (both 1945), the first two volumes of his intended trilogy of novels *Les Chemins de la liberté,* and the first performances of his plays *Les Mouches* (1943) and *Huis Clos* (1945), made Sartre a paradigm of this sensibility. No sooner was Paris liberated than he began working to establish in the cultural domain the existentialist values which he hoped would prevent a return to the bankrupt values of the pre-war Third Republic he had attacked in *La Nausée*.³² He set about founding a literary review, *Les Temps Modernes,* whose first issue appeared in October 1945 and in which he outlined the theory of *littérature engagée,* which he then revised and expanded in *Qu'est-ce que la littérature?* (1947).

Within the theory of *littérature engagée* the relationship between commitment and literature, between political and aesthetic freedom, remained a difficult issue, but as the post-war period settled into Cold War confrontation between the United States and Soviet Union, the search for a third way between the two blocs led Sartre to engage his theories of situation, choice and action on behalf of the Rassemblement Démocratique Révolutionnaire (RDR) launched in 1948. His departure from the group in October 1949 was a clear sign of the dissensions undermining the unity of purpose which the Resistance effort had encouraged. Another was his disagreement with Camus following the publication of the latter's *L'Homme révolté* (1951).

As the author of *L'Étranger, Le Mythe de Sisyphe* (both 1942) and *La Peste* (1947), and as a journalist who had worked in the Resistance movement, Albert Camus was a major figure in the post-war literary debate. Since he too rejected the prospect of an afterlife and believed that the only certainty was death, the essential issue was how one lived with this knowledge. Awaiting death in his cell, Meursault (*L'Étranger*) discovers through his confrontation with the priest the meaning of the absurd and with it the knowledge of the significance of the present when it is emptied of that form of resignation which is hope for the future.³³ In *La Peste,* this lesson acquired on the individual level takes collective form through the allegorisation of the experience of the Occupation. Faced with the moral and metaphysical absurdity of arbitrary, unjustified suffering, the only choice is between solitude and solidarity, and the only solution is revolt. The journalist Rambert initially refuses solidarity, only to discover through his experience of a child's death the obligation of collective resistance. Putting into practice Camus's own reformulation (in *L'Homme révolté*) of the Cartesian *cogito ergo sum,* 'I revolt, therefore I am', he joins Rieux and Tarrou in their ethics of service. Human happiness, the goal of ethics in a world without God, is a ceaseless struggle against the forces of the plague and cannot be achieved alone.

Transposed into the political philosophy of *L'Homme révolté,* the two fundamental values of revolt—happiness and freedom—placed Camus at odds with Marxism's commitment to scientific models of historical materialism, which for Camus led inevitably to political and intellectual terrorism. The result was a public dispute with Sartre, more closely identified with the Communist cause, and the relative decline of Camus's reputation in literary, intellectual and academic circles in which Communist sympathies were still powerful. When this dominant position of Marxist thought began itself to be called into question, notably from the late 1970s, Camus's critical fortune enjoyed a strong revival. The critical and commercial acclaim which greeted the publication in 1994 of *Le Premier Homme,* the strongly autobiographical novel on which Camus was working in the year prior to his death, powerfully reaffirmed this revival.

Sartre's withdrawal from the RDR and his break with Camus confirmed that the sense of common purpose which had brought writers together during the Occupation was being eroded by their post-war dissensions in the political sphere. At the same time, the legend of the French Resistance was serving as an important source of legitimacy for the coalition of left-of-centre parties in government during the Fourth Republic (1946-58) and for de Gaulle, who was returned to power in May 1958 to resolve the Algerian conflict. Significantly, certain major texts intended to project the forms of the *prise de conscience* that occupation and resistance had produced were not completed. Sartre had intended *Les Chemins de la liberté* to provide a more collective destination for the escape from contingency than Roquentin's Proustian idealisation of art in *La Nausée,* but though the third volume, *La Mort dans l'âme,* appeared in 1949, the fourth and final volume, *La Dernière Chance,* remained unfinished. In the face of the difficulties encountered in determining a practice of the novel which would reconcile existentialist freedom and Marxist theory, Sartre's faith in *littérature engagée* declined in favour of more direct political commitments and a critique of literature which led him towards autobiographical writing (*Les Mots,* 1953). Similarly, Malraux failed to complete *Le Combat avec l'ange* and Aragon rewrote *Les Communistes,* publishing the definitive version only in 1967.

Committed writing remained a powerful idea among the left-wing intellectuals from whom the Resistance movement had drawn its main support. But with the emergence of the Cold War, writers on the political Left were increasingly faced with the choice between responsibility for a general commitment to humanist values on the one hand and allegiance to a particular party line on the other. Communist writers were expected to adhere to an increasingly intransigent Stalinist orthodoxy of socialist realism which left unresolved the difficult problem of the relationship between from and content in literature. Though several major novelists practised forms of socialist realism in the early post-war period (notably Roger Vailland and Pierre Courtade³⁴), the Soviet invasion of Hungary in 1956 and the beginnings of de-Stalinisation in the Soviet Union further weakened its credibility.

The legend of the French Resistance was relayed through a wide range of popular cultural forms until the late 1960s—until, that is, the first post-war generation reached maturity and de Gaulle, baffled by the events of May 1968 and defeated in the referendum of April 1969, withdrew from political life. In the novel, however, this myth of the Resistance as national unity, heroism and self-sacrifice was challenged from an early stage after the end of hostilities.

The novels of Roger Nimier (1925-61), *Les Épées* (1948) and *Le Hussard bleu* (1950), proposed a distinctly unheroic reality of collaboration and offered a sardonic, disillusioned commentary on the humanist commitment of much writing of the immediate post-war period. Marcel Aymé (1902-67) in *Uranus* (1949), set at the time of the Liberation, presents the Resistance ideal as an official discourse to which lip-service must be paid in order to stay healthy at a time when the country is embroiled in vicious settlings of political scores and when the Resistance groups are now rivals for power. In *Au bon beurre* (1952), Jean Dutourd (b. 1920) ridicules the opportunistic switching of allegiances as supporters of Vichy and Pétain seek to establish Resistance credentials with which to turn the *épuration* to their own advantage. In these texts the universal humanist ideal central to the Resistance message confronts the sordid realities of the *années noires*.[35]

The most radical challenge in fiction to the dominant humanist ideal of the post-war years, however, came in the work of Samuel Beckett (1906-90).[36] Growing up as a Protestant in Dublin was an early experience of life at the edges of a world in change. This was reinforced from 1928 by his move to Paris where he made contact with the brilliant, cosmopolitan avant-garde gravitating around James Joyce and fostering wide-ranging literary experimentation. In Beckett this was filtered through his readings of literary and philosophical tradition (most notably Dante, Proust, Joyce, Descartes, Pascal, Sartre, Wittgenstein). He began writing short stories, poems, essays, translations, and produced his first novel, *Murphy* (1938), which went largely unnoticed in the immediate pre-war context. His wartime experience in the Resistance confronted him with the bankruptcy of the ideals which European culture claimed to uphold and in 1943, whilst in hiding, he wrote his last novel in English, *Watt*, a comic investigation of the 'meaning of unmeaning' which would dominate his subsequent work.

In the immediate post-war years Beckett's writing flowered in an extraordinarily productive period which included *Mercier et Camier* (1946, published 1970), his trilogy of novels, *Molloy, Malone meurt* and *L'Innommable* (1948-9, published 1951-3), and, for the theatre, *En attendant Godot* (1948, performed 1952). In *Molloy,* two monologues recount two symmetrical searches, Molloy's for his mother, Moran's for Molloy. Both peter out in atrophy and the impossibility of discovering the source of meaning and being. The text makes the same forward journey towards an ending which may or may not be merely another false departure. Imprisoned in the chain of being whose law is unexplained suffering and in the arbitrary, self-contained system of language whose relationship to the world is a mystery, the desire for silence and urge to speak are all that remain. In *Malone meurt,* Malone invents absurd doubles so as to sustain a flow of words with which to keep the game in motion on the unlikely chance that some break through the barrier of language into meaning will occur. In *L'Innommable,* the first-person narrator dismisses all previous selves and their pointless searches, and struggles on through new and increasingly grotesque incarnations in which words, emptied of their traditional claim to narrate and invent, are voices in the mind, saturating the silence yet without belonging to the self. Beckett's trilogy conveyed in unique depth the philosophical and literary interrogations of modern experience and, in doing so, facilitated the wide-ranging challenge to the novel tradition emerging in the 1950s as existentialism's relationship with literature began to lose credibility.

New Novel Commitments

Existentialism's influence waned as dissension increased among writers associated with it, as did the public desire to draw a veil over the bitter divisions of the Occupation and *épuration*. Emphasis in the novel moved away from political and ethical commitments towards concerns about language and narrative technique. These had been central issues in the work of Proust and Gide and were a significant legacy of French translations of the Russian novel, but the political crisis from 1930 had made them appear less urgent than engagement with the ideological divisions with which Europe was confronted. In practice, however, novelists with a political, religious or philosophical position to convey were led more, not less, to address questions of narrative technique. Céline had explored the use of fractured narratives and innovative language and syntax. The novels of the socialist Aragon and of the fascist Drieu la Rochelle had illustrated ways in which an apparently unproblematic representation of perceived truths about the world may be undermined by the language of fiction with which they are represented.

The 1930s had also seen the discovery by French writers of a whole series of major American novels in translation, beginning in 1931 with Faulkner's *Sanctuary* and continuing with the works of Hemingway, Dos Passos, Steinbeck and Caldwell. The techniques associated with these novels—simultaneity of action, narrative fragmentation and impersonality, and the assimilation of forms of popular culture such as the cinema and the detective novel—whether seen as symptoms of the alienation of modern civilisation or of the freedom enjoyed in a culture unfettered by literary traditions, were gradually assimilated into French narrative practice. Malraux's *L'Espoir,* with its rapid shifts of narrative focus, is a well-known case in point. Sartre considered Dos Passos's *U.S.A.* a model for the integration of history and fiction and adopted in *Les Chemins de la liberté* certain of its technical features, such as the simultaneous presentation of events. In *L'Étranger,* Camus used narrative procedures derived in part from Hemingway to show that the model of psychological interiority used by the prosecuting counsel to secure the death penalty for Mersault entirely failed to explain Mersault's action.

Wider intellectual developments in science and philosophy had also undermined the positivist relationship between consciousness and the world from which nineteenth-century realism had derived its mimetic ambition. The phenomenology of Merleau-Ponty, with its emphasis on the subjectivity of perception and representation, was providing an alternative philosophical context for fiction to that of the German philosophy on which existentialism had drawn. By the early 1950s a substantial body of narrative theory and practice operating within a changing intellectual framework was available to novelists hostile to the concept of existentialist *littérature engagée* and ready to embark on a new phase of experimentation.

By the end of the decade, this experimentation had achieved a collective status in what was by then known as the *nouveau roman*.[37] The term was adopted as a means of grouping together novelists whose writing during the 1950s appeared to share a determination to work out in the practice of fiction the implications of the cultural and intellectual changes which had taken place in the period 1930-50. As is frequently the case with literary labels, the term referred more to a series of shared objections to traditional forms of the novel than to any common programme of writing. The new novelists rejected the plots, characters, linear chronologies and omniscient narrators of the nineteenth-century tradition, which had expressed that century's belief in a knowable, representable world of which man was the centre and purpose. From this perspective the existentialist committed novel was no more than the latest form of this outmoded anthropomorphism and was dismissed in favour of a commitment to explore, from within, the theoretical and practical issues involved in the production of fiction from the raw materials of impressions, perceptions and feelings. Characters, far from denoting real people in a real world, were the supports on which to hang the exploration of mental states and the production of language. The *nouveau roman* sought to forge a new relationship between writer and reader on the basis of their complicity in the adventure of writing, an adventure in which the creation of narrative becomes in a self-referential way the subject of narrative.

Not surprisingly, this radical departure from a literary tradition in which the novel was expected to enact serious ethical or political dilemmas judged to be central to the human condition was initially attacked as antihumanist or dismissed as a self-indulgent game. The new novelists (notably Robbe-Grillet in *Pour un nouveau roman*, 1963) responded that to oblige the human mind to recognise that the world has no inherent meaning or stability on which to base identity, knowledge or absolute moral values, to free it from complacent acceptance of the comfortable falsehoods it prefers to these difficult truths, was a profoundly political act and more authentically humanist (in the widest sense of dealing with the reality of human experience) than the committed literature to which it was opposed.

In the early novels of Alain Robbe-Grillet (b. 1922), a narrator's eye charts the material world in meticulous detail, either investing it with obsessions or desires or travelling across its impenetrable surface.[38] The traditional role of description—that of establishing relationships between an observer and a meaningful universe—is dispensed with in texts which at the same time rework some of the novel's most stereotypical genres and myths (the detective story and the Oedipus myth in *Les Gommes* of 1953, the novel of adultery and the colonial novel in *La Jalousie* of 1957). In *Dans le labyrinthe* (1959) a complex network of narrative paths and passages link three labyrinths, those of an anonymous town, a delirious character's mind, and an author's creation of a text. At specific junctions in the text the reader is moved from one labyrinth to another and continually obliged to re-establish bearings as the signposts operative at one narrative level (the soldier's fear and alienation in his efforts to deliver his parcel) suddenly stop working in another (the text's foregrounding of its own manoeuvres). From *La Maison de rendezvous* (1965) Robbe-Grillet's novels combine and interrogate the fictions triggered by the most powerful collective myths (sadomasochistic eroticism, political revolution, secret agencies), cultural objects (paintings, poems, musical arrangements), mathematical figures (triangles, circles). Within each text the construction of meaning is provisional, frustrating the reader's search for reassuring fictions with which to counter the anxieties and unintelligibilities of modern experience.

The work of Michel Butor (b. 1926) represents in even wider terms this continual exploration of the nature of writing. Beginning with novels, each of which explored new forms of fiction's internal architectures, and with literary criticism distinguished by its cosmopolitan range, Butor's writing extended into other forms of aesthetic and cultural production (including music, painting, utopian philosophy, ethnography, dreams), each relationship a new exploration of language's capacity to produce and organise text. In his first four novels, he focused on the nature of fictional time and space.[39] In *Passage de Milan* (1954), which reconstitutes twelve hours in the lives of the inhabitants of a Parisian block of flats, the simultaneity of chronology and architecture structures the narrative. In *Emploi du temps* (1956), the narrator keeps a diary in an attempt to understand the physical and psychological geography of a city which threatens to envelop him in its labyrinthine streets and multiple layers of time between present and legendary past. *La Modification* (1957) explores the mechanisms of second-person narration and the relationship between internal and chronological time. In *Degrés* (1960), the attempt to recount the hour of a school lesson forces the narrator to face up to the extent to which experience evades language and to the consequential need to invent the real.

On her own admission, the entire work of Nathalie Sarraute (b. 1900) was present in embryonic form in her first novel, *Tropismes*, published in 1939 but largely unknown until its second edition (1957).[40] Tropism is the response of an organism, especially a plant, to an external stimulus and Sarraute used the term as a metaphor for the intense, pre-verbal psychological activity situated on the edge of consciousness and of which the family unit is the most common and most powerful trigger. In Sarraute, the family is the theatre for the ceaseless movement of advance and retreat produced when two centres of tropistic life enter into contact with each other. In each novel Sarraute takes up the challenge to create a verbal form for these indefinable movements, an internal 'sub-conversation' which negotiates with that public, social discourse whose polite, formulaic platitudes are designed to neutralise its complex, elusive and potentially explosive energies. These negotiations do not produce characters or plots of the type the traditional psychological novel displayed, nor the laws of an essential self grounded in involuntary memory on behalf of which Proust had challenged the earlier practice of the psychological novel. Instead they reveal a new type of psychological material, with the invention of a language for the basic, instinctive urges of attack and defence, embrace and rejection, which constitute the power struggles in which human beings are ceaselessly engaged.

The publication of *Moderato cantabile* (1958) drew Marguerite Duras (1914-96) into brief and provisional association with the *nouveau roman* group, for the novel marked a break with the more traditional forms of characterisation through which her earlier work had represented woman's struggle against the confinements of patriarchal society.[41] The experiment was the vehicle for a more radical refusal of such authoritarianism. The piercing cry which interrupts the music lesson in *Moderato cantabile* triggers a series of encounters between Anne Desbaresdes and Chauvin which, through the imaginary reconstruction of the murder in the café, lead Anne gradually to destroy her conformist, externally imposed social self in order to attain an absolute form of freedom and self-knowledge. *Le Ravissement de Lol V. Stein* (1964) takes the formal experimentation and, with it, the understanding of woman's emancipation a stage further. Abandoned by her fiancé for another woman, the heroine is so entranced by the power of the love she feels between them that she experiences abandonment as a form of liberation. Released from the prison of her socially-defined role as member of a couple into a new and creative loss of identity, she is free to share as observer in the mystical, total power of lovers' passion.[42] The loss of identity, the breakdown into fragmented states of mind which this self-effacement produces, is expressed through the silences or gaps which frustrate meaning and narration but in which the narrative voice seeks to translate the unknown of female experience.

The novels of Claude Simon (b. 1913) show the continual search for narrative procedures able to describe the inscription in the present of the multiple forms of memory (personal experience, family archive, collective history) and the ways in which the language which effects this fusion of present and past time in turn generates and structures the production of narration.[43] Thematic elements common to the sequence of novels embrace the major themes of modern writing (the nature of time, the presence and displacement of desire, the awareness of death), but with each novel, Simon deepens his analysis of their role in the operations of the mind and in the processes of writing itself. A brief comparison between, for example, Malraux's *L'Espoir* and Simon's *Le Palace*, in which an experience of the Spanish Civil War forms the common narrative base, demonstrates the extent to which Simon's fiction abandons the existentialist values sustaining that of Malraux in favour of a fatalistic initiation into the lack of human control over cycles of history repeating themselves regardless.

Simon's central work, *Histoire* (1967), draws together the strands of the exploration of the past contained in the earlier novels. Through the description of a collection of postcards sent by the narrator's father to his mother and the evocation of a twenty-four hour period in the narrator's life, the text constructs a complex collage of language in which the tension is sustained between representation of human feeling in search of an ever-elusive autobiography and the capacity of language to produce text through its own material, non-representational associations.[44] Hence Simon's departure from the traditional conventions (chapters, paragraphs, punctuation), which served to organise works of fiction but are quite inadequate to address these operations of the mind and language.

The sustained analysis of universal themes of fiction gives Simon's work an epic range and power lacking in other members of the new novelists group. His increasingly radical reflection on the act of writing has taken his work beyond fiction in the accepted sense, beyond representation of the events of personal or collective memory to the play of language itself, as it defers satisfaction of the aspiration to stable definition and meaning. Instead, the text is structured on the basis of internal formal design, in a manner related to the modern painting with which Simon is so familiar.

The unpredictable exploits and failings of memory are also an important element of the work of Robert Pinget (b. 1919) for they combine to generate narrative sequences which unfold, miscarry, return, lead in other directions or nowhere, scraps of conversation in which the act of speech is as central as the content.[45] In *L'Inquisitoire* (1962), a half-deaf servant is interrogated about his masters, and the wanderings through the labyrinth of his memory, prompted by the questioning, lead to no resolution of the enigma but to a reconstruction of the process of story-telling. Pinget's increasingly refined exploration of the nature of narrative voices bears the mark of his friendship and collaboration with Beckett. Claude Ollier (b. 1922) used some of the most familiar narrative forms (the colonial novel in *Mise en scène,* 1958; science fiction in *La Vie sur Epsilon,* 1972) to undermine the description in traditional fiction of the narrator's relationship to the world and to the act of writing.[46] Claude Mauriac (1914-96, son of François Mauriac), whose critical texts *L'Alittérature contemporaine* (1958) and *De la littérature à l'alittérature* (1969) made him one of the most informed commentators on contemporary writing, built on his study of Proust (*Proust par lui-même,* 1953) to show the nature of subjective time through the structure of fiction itself, notably in *Le Dîner en ville* (1959) and *La Marquise sortit à cinq heures* (1961). The eleven volumes of his memoirs, *Le Temps immobile* (1974-91) constitute a vast reflection on the nature of sensation and memory.

. . . . .

Public perception of the 'new novelists' as a coherent group continued through the 1960s and 1970s but their work increasingly diverged. Simon (*Les Géorgiques*, 1981) and Sarraute (*Disent les imbéciles*, 1978) continued to produce work of major importance by extending the intellectual and formal parameters established in their work of the 1950s. With *Mobile* (1962) and *6 810 000 litres d'eau par seconde* (1965), Butor abandoned the novel in favour of freer forms of textual production. Robbe-Grillet and Duras turned increasingly to film-making and the possibilities it offered for the creative interplay of their written and filmic texts.[47] But quite apart from the intrinsic value and interest of their work, the impact of the original group of new novelists in an increasingly mediatised French literary and educational environment has been significant. Their active and productive relationships with the institutions of literary criticism and the teaching of literature in higher education both in France and abroad has ensured a wide circulation of their commitment to a more creative role for the reader in the practice of fiction and encouraged the fundamental reappraisal of the work of earlier novelists which has taken place since the 1950s, notably under the impulse of the *nouvelle critique* with which the *nouveau roman* was initially associated.

As the 'new novelists' pursued their different practices of fiction, other experimental writing parallel to theirs created an analogous group identity. In November 1960, a group of writers and mathematicians committed to research into literary forms with the potential to generate new types of writing formed Oulipo (the *Ou*vroir de *litt*érature *po*tentielle).[48] Its most important member was Raymond Queneau (1903-76), its (subsequently) most important recruit Georges Perec (1936-82). In 1959, when he achieved the huge success of *Zazie dans le métro*, a modern Parisian version of *Alice in Wonderland*, Queneau had been a major literary figure for nearly thirty years. In 1933 he had published his first novel, *Le Chiendent*, which he began as an attempt to translate Descartes's *Discours de la méthode* into spoken French. This attempt to end the linguistic divorce between academic philosophy and the language of the streets was another example of the ambition to transform philosophy from a theory of knowledge into a committed analysis of existence and was contemporaneous with Céline's radical extension of narrative language. In addition, its playful yet serious combination of mathematical constraints against which to construct fiction—the text consists of 91 (7 × 13) sections—made it a precursor of Oulipo experimentation, which in 1960, as *Le Chiendent* had already done in 1933, sought to reject the twin legacies of Jarry's 'science of imaginary solutions' (which he called pataphysics) and Surrealism's automatic writing.

The Oulipo writers did not of course discover the idea that formal constraints stimulate rather than obstruct creative writing but they took it to far greater lengths than before. Their arbitrary phonetic, syntactic and alphabetical restrictions made enormous demands on the writer's ingenuity and had two main effects: first, to reaffirm the capacity of language to create texts from within its own operations and thereby shape our perceptions of reality; secondly, to free the writer from the obligation to create politically or philosophically committed literature, which for the Oulipo group was a far more alienating constraint. Perec's *La Disparition* (1969) is a novel written without a single 'e', the most common letter in French, while the same vowel is the only one used in *Les Revenentes* (1972). His *La Vie mode d'emploi* (1978) is an astonishing construction based on a mathematical puzzle known as the Magic Square, thought to have been first used by Dürer, the German Renaissance painter and engraver, of which Perec used a specially-adapted form.[49] Though such fiendish ingenuity is not in itself inherently literary, Perec combined it with an exceptional knowledge of a wide range of writing, and a powerful desire to explore the anguish of the human condition.

Perec's first novel, *Les Choses* (1965), was subtitled 'une histoire des années soixante' ['a story/history of the 60s'], a study of the consumer ideology which for a young Parisian bourgeois couple, Jérôme and Sylvie, replaces political commitment as the form of their relationship to society. They fail to get involved in the central political issue of their youth, the Algerian War, and instead define themselves in relation to the objects of bourgeois desire as they appear in the advertisements in *L'Express* magazine. *Les Choses* is closely related to Barthes's study of social signs in *Mythologies* for it shows the way in which the most everyday objects are invested with meaning and participate in an economy of signs. Perec does not condemn consumer society (though with the advantage of the hindsight provided by the events of May 1968 it was widely believed that he had done so) but encourages the reader to recognise the form of its manipulations, something Jérôme and Sylvie fail to do. *Les Choses* was followed by two entirely different works, the hilarious *Quel petit vélo à guidon chromé au fond de la cour?* (1966) and the dark *Un homme qui dort* (1967), by the period of involvement with Oulipo and its formal and linguistic acrobatics, and by the post-Oulipo writing of his final years.

The unity within the diversity of these and other Perec texts is located at a deeper level, in the autobiographical condition of the writing, but it must already be obvious that with Perec this relationship is exceptionally complex. In *W ou le souvenir d'enfance* (1975) he stated that his writing was born out of the horror of the war in which his father was killed in 1940 and the concentration camp into which his mother disappeared in 1943. Dedicated to the 'E' which disappeared from *La Disparition* and to the homophonous 'eux' of his lost parents, it explores the relationship between autobiography and literary reconstruction, which has itself become a significant development in the contemporary novel. The oblique fragments of a remembered and imagined relationship with his parents are forms of his inner need to address the personal grief of their loss and the universal grief of the holocaust through writing, the decisive sign of presence in the world. This association of personal anguish and passion for the creative power of language gives Perec's work a depth and range which make him one of the essential literary figures of the century.

. . . . .

By the late 1960s, just as the *nouveau roman* had established itself as the French novel's official avant-garde, taught on university syllabuses as the culmination of the experimental, self-referential tradition of fiction going back to Proust and Gide and representing what now appeared to be the central twentieth-century trend, it was caught in a crossfire of new developments: on the one hand, a return to story-telling and myth-making; on the other, more radical forms of experimentation. The commercial and critical acclaim which greeted the rewriting and re-siting of the Robinson Crusoe story by Michel Tournier (b. 1924) in *Vendredi ou les limbes du Pacifique* (1967), resulted from Tournier's use of a very familiar narrative to produce a powerful contemporary criticism of Western society's consumer culture and express a renewed aspiration to alternative forms of spirituality.[50] The reworking of the literary and philosophical traditions of Defoe's novel through contemporary theories of the material imagination and structuralist analysis of myth met a demand for the novel of ideas which for those unsympathetic to *nouveau roman* experimentation had been unanswered since the passing of the existentialist novel.

In his subsequent writing, Tournier continued to develop his interest in the German metaphysical tradition, which he had studied in Tübingen after the Second World War, exploring the themes of the ogre (*Le Roi des aulnes*, 1970), twinship (*Les Météores*, 1975), the Magi (*Gaspar, Melchior et Balthazar*, 1980), Gilles de Rais and Joan of Arc (*Gilles et Jeanne*, 1983) and exile (*La Goutte d'or*, 1986). Tournier described these narratives of quest and initiation by ordeal as a 'mystic Naturalism'. On the one hand, he makes full use of nineteenth-century narrative procedures (description, character, plot). On the other, this Naturalism serves texts which, though historically located (*Le Roi des aulnes*, for example, set in 1938-44, reworks allegorically some of the most sinister episodes of the Second World War), present themselves as re-narrations of a timeless story, in which the novelist explores alternative forms of sexuality and social organisation.

Other forms of rejection of the technocratic direction of Western culture can be found in the work of Jean-Marie Le Clézio (b. 1940), notably in *L'Extase matérielle* (1967), *La Guerre* (1970) and *Désert* (1980).[51] His characters share an intense commitment to the value of life and to reconciliation with the self and the natural world, continually threatened by the destructive elements of modern, technocratic civilisation. In *La Guerre*, the aggression of modern cities induces panic and a desperate nostalgia for an ideal, lost world in which to experience a purifying calm. It is the world from which Lalla, the heroine of *Désert*, is exiled to Marseilles, whose wretched squalor fails to extinguish the light and purity of her desert origins, to which she eventually returns. To the spiritual light of such communion with the elements of the natural environment corresponds the author's intense observation of the world and a prose style of diversity and virtuosity with which to inscribe its depth of meaning for a public increasingly insecure about the implications of technological advance.

Tournier's use of intertexuality and Le Clézio's poetic description of detail may be said to participate, albeit tangentially, in experimental forms of writing with which in the 1950s and 1960s the *nouveau roman* was identified. In contrast, Patrick Grainville (b. 1947), associated with Tournier and Le Clézio in the use his fiction makes of myth, is well known for his contempt for the *nouveau roman*, which he dismissed as introverted and self-seeking.[52] His best known novel, *Les Flamboyants* (1974), links up with neo-Romantic primitivism and its myth of Africa, seen as the repository of ancient and more authentic force and physicality lost to the degenerate rationalism of Western, Christian culture. In Grainville's work, this otherwise well-worn literary theme is renewed by the sheer drive of his language. In its excess and vitality it evokes the transformative energies of the erotic imagination which are released when the individual makes contact, beyond the constraints of modern experience, with the submerged but still vital forces of earlier cultures.

. . . . .

Another and more explicit opposition, from within, to the official modernism of the *nouveau roman* was forming in the late 1960s around the review *Tel quel*, founded in 1960 as an extension of the anti-existentialist context to which the *nouveau roman* had contributed. By the end of the decade, the *roman tel quel* had taken *nouveau roman* experimentation a stage further and replaced the production of *fiction* with the production of *text*. For over twenty years, *Tel quel* was the essential focus for the discussion of experimental writing and its relationship to radical contemporary literary, psychoanalytic and political theory.

It was in his fourth novel, *Drame* (1964), that Philippe Sollers extended the *nouveau roman*'s deconstruction of traditional fictional forms.[53] The text alternates first-person and third-person segments of poetic prose in which a divided subject observes and narrates the production of narrative, and its relationship to the mysterious experience of identity, language and engagement with the world. The conventional linearity of narrative is abandoned for the spatial configurations of the chessboard, whose sixty-four squares are represented in the sixty-four segments of text. Compensating for this loss of sequence, on which narrative representation was traditionally based, is the freedom to explore the power of language to generate text. The political and cultural crisis of May 1968 encouraged the *Tel quel* group to situate the act of writing in relation to the revolutionary project (*Théorie d'ensemble* 1968), and to explore the link between literary and political avant-gardes in a variety of ways throughout the early 1970s. Sollers's *Nombres* (1968) staged in its text an opposition between what *Tel quel* saw as the productive, dynamic language of the Chinese ideogram and its domesticated Western counterpart, at a time when Mao's Cultural Revolution and the American crisis in Vietnam had given this opposition a powerful political reality. *Lois* (1972) and *H* (1973) continued this experimentation with the material nature of language. By the second half of the 1970s, however, *Tel quel* had broken with Marxism and was turning again to America, since 1945 the most important initiator of avant-garde practices in the arts.

From his intense involvement for over a decade with theoretical and practical issues relating to the nature of the avant-garde, Sollers finally concluded that the avant-garde in advanced Western societies had failed to effect social transformation and that its organic relationship to the dominant culture would prevent it from ever doing so. His conclusion marked the end of a tradition, which can be traced back to the first-generation Romantics, of the writer seeking to achieve transformation of the world through the revolutionary literary act. In 1983, the year in which *Tel quel* was dissolved, Sollers published *Femmes,* an American journalist's narration of erotic experience, the rise of feminism and the cosmopolitan extensions of mediatised cultural happenings. Within weeks, the *enfant terrible* of post-war French writing was up there on the bestseller lists.

MAY 1968: STRUCTURES IN THE STREETS

In many respects *Tel quel* was the post-war equivalent of Surrealism's pre-war attempt to bring together literary and political change. This explicit effort at convergence was only one of the forms in which the events of May 1968 impacted on French writing. Though these events failed to achieve direct political transformation of French society (the legislative elections of June 1968 returned the largest-ever Gaullist majority), they played the crucial role of bringing to the surface underlying tensions in many areas of French private and public life, with far-reaching consequences for literature.

One such consequence, the raising of feminist consciousness, is discussed in detail below (see pp. 276-93). Another was the revision of the official history of the war period which accompanied the end of the Gaullist phase of the Fifth Republic. Huge amounts of historical material began to appear which shed light on the hitherto hidden realities of the *années noires.*[54] For novelists who belonged to the generation born during or immediately after the war, this historical revisionism was intimately related to a search for the self: these hidden realities were those of their own parents' experience of war and Occupation, which official history had silenced.

This search made the work of Patrick Modiano (b. 1945) one of the most significant examples of 1970s writing.[55] Driven by his own cosmopolitan Franco-Jewish background to go in search of origins and to explore the collective memory, real or imaginary, of the Occupation, and by his profession to locate himself in relation to his predecessors in the novel, Modiano wrote a trilogy of novels (*La Place de l'Étoile,* 1968; *La Ronde de nuit,* 1969; *Les Boulevards de ceinture,* 1972) which show characters moving through a shadowy world of false names, false papers and blurred identities, biographical and moral. Marginal, stateless people slip in and out of roles of collaboration, black marketeering and Resistance as much by accident as by design (a theme also prominent in the film scenario Modiano wrote with Louis Malle for *Lacombe Lucien,* 1974). *Villa triste* (1975) inaugurated a new phase of his writing in which echoes of the Occupation period remain but in which the emphasis shifts to a more general quest in search of lost time. It is of course the Proustian theme but without the Proustian revelation of the transcendent significance of art. Building on the fragility of memory's lost traces and false trails, Modiano creates novels in which the conventions of detective fiction, autobiography and the psychological portrait are set against each other in ways which reflect the hesitations of the modern subject in the face of the unfathomable reality of experience.

The events of May 1968 themselves became the subject or context of fiction. Through them, the question of the literary mediation of specific political and social events was now raised in terms of the wide-ranging developments in French fiction since the 1950s.[56] Pascal Lainé (b. 1942) was a teacher in a *lycée technique* during the events and in his second novel, *L'Irrévolution,* he shows a teacher's efforts to communicate to working-class children in a small provincial town the revolutionary spirit and project of May 68. Their refusal to be enlisted in the political programme of this representative of a class-based culture foreign to their own obliges the teacher to recognise the inauthenticity of his political discourse, his collaboration with a system he claims to despise and, by extension, the failure of a revolution which the participants had no interest in realising. He discovers his own existentialist bad faith in a post-existentialist age in which humanist solutions of the type proposed by Sartre or Camus seem no longer credible. The working-class children are victims of the historical division in French society between those who participate in the dominant culture and those who are controlled or marginalised by it, a division increased by post-war consumerism. The novel placed in the context of May 1968 questions already raised in *B. comme Barrabas* (1967) about the difficulty of self-knowledge and the ambiguities of narration. In *La Dentellière* (1974), Lainé extended his analysis of the failed experiment in class communication by showing the doomed relationship between Pomme, a passive, silent drudge in a hairdressing salon, and Aiméry, a privileged student of the École des Chartes, who undertakes to mould her in terms of the cultural stereotypes of femininity within which male image-makers imprison women. His inability to gain purchase on Pomme's unfathomable, inarticulate self is mirrored in the very visible and highly self-conscious shifts of narrative tone and viewpoint which confront the reader with the artificial nature of the construction of identity through language. In subsequent texts Lainé continued this exploration of narrative practices by re-working literary models (Queneau, Proust, the eighteenth-century libertine novel).

Novelists of wide-ranging ideological and narrative commitments responded to the events in one form or another in their fiction. The neo-Romantic libertarian agenda of May 1968 was expressed in Duras's *Détruire, dit-elle* (1969), in which a conventional bourgeois married woman discovers revolt and freedom from the conventions and fears of her class. In Sarraute's *Vous les entendez?* (1972) the events provided a wider theatre for the generation gap, which is encapsulated in the contrasting reactions of seriousness and laughter between a father and his children to an *objet d'art* the father is proud to own. At the other extreme of narrative practice, the traditional novelist J.-L. Curtis (1917-95), in *L'Horizon dérobé* (1979), showed young people disillusioned with the society of their parents, participating in the events as a final youthful fling before taking their allotted place in this society. The humanist convictions of Robert Merle (b. 1908) are seen in *Derrière la vitre* (1970), in which, in the Arts Faculty of Nanterre, where the events of May 1968 began, a new generation of would-be revolutionaries dream of an alternative fraternal society.

. . . . .

The French novel since 1980 can be seen as pursuing the engagement with post-war social and cultural change which the events of May 1968 had so dramatically brought to the surface. The problematical relationship between writing, knowledge and history appears to underpin its most significant trends.[57] New narrative domains have developed from widely differing points of origin. The particular importance of women's writing, and of francophone literature, will be considered in more detail below. Both are renewing French narrative's themes and forms. The growth of gay writing, itself stimulated by the changes in attitudes to sexuality which followed 1968, was reinforced by the AIDS crisis—most notably in *À l'ami qui ne m'a pas sauvé la vie* (1990) by Hervé Guibert (1955-91).[58]

Alongside these very visible general signs of the changing narrative field, there were in the course of the 1980s some revealing individual developments. We have already seen Sollers drawing a line in 1983 through the avant-garde and, by implication, through the writer's relationship to the world with which the avant-garde project had been associated. In 1984, Duras's *L'Amant* became the publishing event of the year, achieving sales usually associated with the bestseller thriller or adventure market. It did so because it brought together an author who was one of the historical figures of French post-war writing, a series of contemporary literary, political and cultural issues (the search for female self-knowledge and self-representation, woman's relationship to eroticism and to political change, the colonial experience, the nature of autobiography), and a literary form which told an apparently simple story without abandoning, the subtleties of characterisation and of motivation associated with Duras's work. The media's ability to package literature delivered a huge commercial success reinforced on the critical level by the award of the Goncourt prize for the outstanding French novel of the year. Not surprisingly, the screen adaptation followed. In 1985, Claude Simon was awarded the Nobel Prize for literature and thereby received consecration for his continued exploration of the problem of narrative and of the individual's difficult relationship to history, so powerfully renewed in *Les Géorgiques*. These and other examples suggest that the distinction between 'serious' and 'mass' fictional forms has to some extent been eroded and that the forms and implications of the experimentation introduced in the post-war period have become assimilated by the reading practices of a wider public.

The 1980s saw the emergence of a number of novelists who, when taken together with Modiano, might be said to have best expressed both the dominant modern sense of the subject deprived of presence and universality of meaning and the conscious decision to open literature to the contemporary culture of popular and mass art forms. Jean Echenoz (b. 1956) weaves together narrative models drawn from the forms of popular fiction (detective and spy novels, science fiction and comic strips) in exuberant, at times hilarious, narratives (notably *Cherokee*, 1983; *Lac*, 1989; *Nous trois*, 1992), but the proliferating adventures and comic-book characters reproduce the incoherence of a world in which the subject seems to have lost control over events. Daniel Pennac (b. 1944) is best known for his four-part cycle of novels (*Au bonheur des ogres*, 1985; *La Fée carabine*, 1987; *La Petite Marchande de prose*, 1989; *Monsieur Malaussène*, 1995) in which we find the same narrative energy, naive characterisation and use of popular forms as in Echenoz but with a slightly more optimistic sense that despite the mendacity and inauthenticity of the world, despite the multiplicity of false trails in modern experience, the possibility of creating meaning and ethical purposes survives. This sense permeates Pennac's superb essay on the pleasures of reading, *Comme un roman*, which was a huge commercial and critical success on its publication in 1992. Sébastien Japrisot (b. 1935) is a good example of the genre writer (exponent of the detective novel such as *Piège pour Cendrillon*, 1965, which plays with the conventions of the genre) who has emerged as a major novelist, particularly with *Un long dimanche de fiançailles* (1991), a quest narrative on the themes of war and memory.

In a postmodern age deprived of universality, the novel may be adopting less heroic stances and more self-reflective irony. And it seems possible that this general trend has been to some extent reinforced by the socio-political context of recent years, in which the socialist project which triumphed in the presidential and legislative election victories in 1981 has been forced from 1983 to face the economic realities of internationalised money markets and in 1986-8 to accept 'cohabitation' with the conservative political parties. In politics and literature, confrontation with the realities of the modern world was in the 1980s a difficult narrative. Be that as it may, the reinvigoration of narrative through its extension into mass forms—the detective novel in particular—offers a potentially powerful source of renewal.

. . . . .

The path through some of the major trends in French postwar fiction leads us to the threshold of a new century, in which the creation of fictions is likely to be subjected to conditions quite different from anything experienced so far. The French novel, particularly since the Revolution, has to some extent always been technology-driven, so it is certain that the mediatisation of Western culture and the revolution in information technology on which it is now embarked will transform the means and modes of fiction. Some of the implications are already evident; for example, the demise of the concept and practice of the avant-garde as it evolved in the early stage of the nineteenth century out of the cultural developments associated with the Revolution. The literary and cultural space which this classical avant-garde occupied has, like every other public space, been occupied by the media, whose capacity to transform all cultural products into spectacle was seen in the extraordinary impact of the televised book programme *Apostrophes*, France's most popular television programme between 1975 and 1990.[59] Just where the information superhighway will take the novel, where the Internet's transformations of narrative's themes, forms and modes of production will leave the tradition established by the writers discussed above, in what forms it will generate reassessment of the history of the French novel traced here, is of course a matter of conjecture. The narration of the relationship of world and subject will continue but in forms which remain to be seen.

II POETRY AND ITS PURPOSES

POETRY OF THE NEW, 1914-39

In the closing years of the century, reaction to the Symbolist movement in poetry most frequently involved a return to the modern, urban world. Its increasingly complex, fragmented reality was a source of both excitement and anxiety.[60] The very elements which offered the hope of renewal also frustrated the self's aspiration to stability and unity. In the poetry of Guillaume Apollinaire (1880-1918), a rootless cosmopolitan background reinforced a sense of fragmented identity. On the one hand, this created an elusive search for the self expressed in tender melancholy or nostalgic melody. On the other, it encouraged an aggressive commitment to the new, particularly from 1904, when Apollinaire's contacts with avant-garde painters and poets gave him a pivotal role in the efforts to create verbal and visual forms appropriate to the new century, and to the new world that scientific and technological change was creating.[61]

The dominant feature of *Alcools,* a selection of his poetry written between 1898 and 1913, is a multi-directional lyricism which weaves together the self's search for meaning in mythical, mysterious landscapes of Symbolist inspiration and in the associations and discontinuities of modern urban experience. The dominant theme is that of the journey, which may be in time or space, through personal or collective memory, and may be liberating adventure or aimless wandering. Such thematic links between the poems emphasise the range of voices used. Lost love is evoked with haunting simplicity in 'Le Pont Mirabeau', in which the poignant refrain softens the transitions between pain and resignation. 'La Chanson du Mal-Aimé' retains the range and intimacy of the private feelings of desire, anger and pain in a vast historical and mythological epic in which the disconnections between episodes are balanced by the formal continuities of rhyme scheme, strophic structures and repetitions. In 'Zone', the industrial landscape at the edge of the city, where the poet wanders between sensations and memories, and the combination of free verse and rhyme or assonance, denote the tensions between familiarity and insecurity which characterise the modern city. The proliferation of ready-made sights and sounds simultaneously invites and frustrates personal revelation. As in the Cubist painting of Pablo Picasso (1881-1973) and Georges Braque (1882-1963), who sought to represent the complete structure of the object and its relationship of volume and space by juxtaposing different views of it in interlocking planes, in 'Zone' the use of the historic present tense, which displays past and present in a single moment, and of abrupt shifts between first-person and second-person pronouns produces an interplay of fragmented, discontinuous selves in a modern collage of human feelings.

The poems of *Calligrammes* (1918) form a diary of the poet's immediate pre-war days, the mobilisation and his experience of the war. The title of the volume refers to the picture poems, in which the typographical phrase mimes the visual form of the object represented. Mallarmé's *Coup de dés,* republished in 1914, had made such experimentation topical but Apollinaire's picture poems had other terms of reference in Cubist painting, on which he had already published *Les Peintres cubistes* (1913), and in the work of Sonia and Robert Delaunay (1884-1979 and 1885-1941 respectively), which he had baptised Orphism in 1913.[62] Words take on a pictorial function through graphic arrangements and multiple typographies and the poet draws heavily on the sound patterning of alliteration, assonance, onomatopoeia and repetition to extend the forms by which meaning is produced in ways analogous to Cubist collage. In 'Lundi rue Christine', the juxtaposed fragments of conversation create montage effects reinforced by links of sound and theme. In the visually more conventional poems, Apollinaire exploits the expressive potential of the relationships between free and traditional verse and draws on all the resources of vocabulary, sound and rhythm to represent the real experience of war in its modern and mythical dimensions. In the final sequence, the more experimental forms become less frequent, the tone more measured. The final poem, 'La Jolie Rousse', takes stock of the journey accomplished and pleads for tolerance for the avant-garde poet searching for a new language.

Apollinaire's support for Orphism was only one of the productive exchanges between literature and painting in which the Delaunays were involved and which were central to definitions of modernism in the immediate pre-war period. The catalogue of the 1913 Berlin exhibition in which Robert Delaunay showed ten of his *Windows* series contained the first published version of Apollinaire's poem 'Les Fenêtres', republished five years later in *Calligrammes*. Delaunay then produced a simultaneist poem-painting on Rimbaud's *Alchimie du verbe* (1914). In 1913, Sonia Delaunay illustrated the six-foot-long folding sheet of twelve panels which contained *La Prose du Transsibérien* by Blaise Cendrars (1887-1961).[63] Labelled the 'first simultaneous book', it recounts in free verse the multiple forms of the modern world and their relationship to the journey of memory. With Cendrars, as with Apollinaire, the formal invention is not gratuitous. Its abrupt shifts of tone, rhythm and voice produced by the accelerating rhythms of real and imagined journeys register the poet's efforts to synchronise external stimuli and inner world and the excitement and anguish created by a confrontation from which only provisional stability can be achieved.

Among the group of writers and painters who, along with Apollinaire and Cendrars, worked side by side in Montmartre in the immediate pre-war years, Pierre Reverdy (1889-1960) and Max Jacob (1876-1944) made, in quite different terms, major contributions to the poetic theory and practice of modernity. For Reverdy, poetry was to be found 'dans ce qui n'est pas' ['in that which is not'],[64] in a solitary, often anguished exploration of everyday experience. Confined within the walls of a room or the limits of a garden, the poet looks for meaning and purpose in the diffuse and shifting presence of reality. In poems such as those in *Ardoises sur le toit* (1918), fragments of language combine the suggestive power of images with that of unusual and seemingly random typographical arrangements to create a quiet but profound tension between aspiration and disappointment. Jacob's prose poems of *Le Cornet à dés* (1916), on the other hand, are verbal pyrotechnics. Contemporary political and artistic topics, the poet's memories, reading, verbal games, pastiches of literary genres and tones, all crackle in the associative logic of language. Both poets were associated with contemporary developments in painting. Jacob described his work as Cubist realism.[65] Reverdy's essay 'Sur le cubisme', published in the newly founded avant-garde review *Nord-Sud* (1917), provided a theoretical framework for analogies between Cubist painting and literature.[66]

Essential features of what came to be seen as the modern spirit of French poetry were therefore in place before the outbreak of the First World War. The war's impact on poetry was as profound as it was on the novel but less direct. There was no French equivalent of the great flowering of English war poetry. Among the three poets who had sought in the pre-war period to open the poetic to the new and the everyday, Apollinaire was alone in doing so in the context of the war itself.

In some ways, the most important poetry written during the war was that of a poet who wrote by disengaging himself from contemporary events. In 1919 Paul Valéry described the First World War as the failure of European culture, yet he wrote his major poetical work, 'La Jeune Parque', at the very time the world seemed to be going up in flames.[67] He had embarked on the poem in 1912, when, encouraged to revise his early work for publication, he had returned to writing poetry after a twenty-year absence. In the early 1890s he had published poems in Symbolist reviews, and frequented Mallarmé, whom he worshipped, but he gave up literature after the spiritual crisis he experienced during the night of 4-5 October 1892. Its upshot was his decision to focus on the power of the mind to observe thought and feeling in action rather than to make these thoughts and feelings the object of literature. It gave him an intellectual method through which to recover from what he considered to be the destructive effects of thoughts, feelings and images on his sense of self. The critical writing which resulted has made him one of the foremost French intellectuals of the century, while the poetry written after his long silence is one of the most profound reflections on the nature of poetic language itself.

The subject of 'La Jeune Parque' (1917), a dramatic monologue of over 500 lines, is the self-questioning consciousness as it feels its way through a night-long struggle with conflicting experience and aspiration (sensuality and abstraction, desire and memory) towards the dawn light of harmonious self-knowledge. The complex thematic modulations, as Valéry called them, are themselves reinforced by the formal constraints derived from his commitment to classical prosody. Hostile to many early twentieth-century manifestations of the modern (Freudism, Marxism, feminism, Cubism, Surrealism), he rejected such recent developments in French prosody as free verse in favour of the classical alexandrine, whose rigour and expressive potential of sound patterning combine in the poem as both creative process and drama of the intellect. The poems of *Charmes* (1922) maintain the intellectual ambition in a wide range of forms and registers of exceptional technical virtuosity. The most famous poem of the collection, 'Le Cimetière marin', originated according to the poet in purely formal considerations (the expressive potential of the ten-syllable line, its use in six-line stanzas themselves organised in terms of thematic contrasts), around which he modulated the movements of the mind in its dialogue between light and darkness and its ultimate celebration of life.

Such commitments and procedures could hardly have been more removed from those of the Surrealist movement which dominated French poetry of the inter-war years. The revulsion felt by certain writers at the slaughter of the First World War strengthened the ambition to channel avant-garde literary activity towards a wider transformation of culture and society. They aimed to do this by unleashing desire and its forms of expression against the rationalist ideologies which in their view constrained or censured freedom. This would enable a new fusion of the real and the imaginary, a surreality, to be created to transcend the system of oppositions and hierarchies which this discredited Western ideology sustained. The Surrealist movement was the result of a series of connections: the meeting in 1917 of Aragon, Breton and Soupault, their shared discovery of Freud's work on the unconscious operations of the mind, their reading of nineteenth-century poets who had in their different ways practised forms of poetic language outside the didactic, Parnassian aesthetic (notably Baudelaire, Nerval, Lautréamont, Rimbaud, Mallarmé, Jarry), their contacts with avant-garde activity in Paris, and their meeting with Tzara, whose effect was to radicalise their opposition to the dominant culture. Thanks primarily to Breton, its chief theoretician and publicist, and despite (or because of) doctrinal disagreements and conflicts of personalities, Surrealism created a collective impetus which made it a major source of literary and cultural developments between the wars. From Paris, it spread quickly abroad, becoming the first truly international avant-garde movement.[68]

Language and linguistic experimentation were a central focus of Surrealist activity. To the alternative nineteenth-century tradition of poetic language noted above, the Surrealists added Reverdy's description of the poetic image and their understanding of Freud's work on dreams. In 1918, in *Nord-Sud,* Reverdy had defined the image as a pure creation of the mind, the juxtaposition of two more or less distant realities. The more distant the relationship, the greater the image's power. This definition substantiated Lautréamont's description of the poetic beauty of the chance encounter, on a dissecting table, of a sewing machine and an umbrella.[69] Freud's work on word association and dreams had suggested that a huge, untapped source of pre-rational mental activity was readily available. In the *écriture automatique* ['automatic writing'] of *Les Champs magnétiques* (1920), Breton and Soupault showed that when the rational mind's control over the instinctive urge to verbalise was removed, powerful repressed energies were released into language in the form of free verbal play. Such free association with the sounds and meanings of words would reveal the Surrealist dimension of the imaginary hidden within the real, the extraordinary hidden within the everyday of modern experience. As the Lautréamont example had shown, such verbalisation was intensely visual, hence Surrealism's impact on painting.

Not surprisingly, given the ambition, present in the Surrealist project from the outset, to extend this liberation into every aspect of cultural and social life, the Russian Revolution of 1917 became a crucial reference point for the revolution in literature. In 1927 the group's leading figures (notably Aragon, Breton, Éluard) joined the PCF (Parti Communiste Français), but the need to reconcile Marx and Freud—political transformation and the Surrealist commitment to liberation from intellectual and cultural constraints—remained a source of powerful tensions. The Marxist subordination of the latter to the former obliged Surrealists sooner or later to choose between the two. Breton's second manifesto (1929) showed the extent of dissensions within the group on this issue and though he restated his faith in the necessary relationship between Surrealism and revolution, relationships between him and the Communists were increasingly strained. In 1932 Aragon chose the Party, rather than the Surrealist, line; three years later Breton's *Position politique du surréalisme* consummated the divorce between the group and the Party. The emergence of the fascist threat in the 1930s nevertheless ensured that Communists and Surrealists remained allies in practice if not in theory.

Many of the major poets of the period were marked in one way or another by the Surrealist movement, usually adapting it to their own commitments and forms of expression. Paul Éluard (1895-1952), one of its founders, embraced wholeheartedly its liberation of the imagination but submitted its discoveries to the constraints of theme and the disciplines of rhythm.[70] His work contains some of Surrealism's most powerful images but their power derives less from their exploration of the unconscious *per se* than from the relationships they establish in the poem with other forms of human experience and the network of thematic and formal associations in which they participate. His poetic voice is a highly personal one but even in his free verse the familiar rhythms and patterns of the French poetic tradition can usually be discerned behind it. He brought to poetry his sense of the wonder of everyday experience and his conviction that the language of poetry could be liberated by and for everyone. The element common to these features of his work was his conviction that love was the source of the imagination's most creative, transformative energies and of the individual's most profound moral and political choices; love, for Éluard, was a truly revolutionary force. In *Capitale de la douleur* (1926) and *L'Amour, la poésie* (1929), love may bring the anguish of solitude and loss of self, but it is the ecstatic celebration of love shared which provides in both collections the most memorable verse. In 'La Courbe de tes yeux fait le tour de mon cœur', the sensations of light, water, wind and air generated by the eyes of the loved woman trigger in the poet both an intense erotic intimacy and an unlimited expanse of feeling.

Despite increasing internal dissensions within the Surrealist group, Éluard took part in collective efforts such as the poems of *Ralentir travaux* (1930), written with Breton and René Char (1907-88), and the automatic writing of *L'Immaculée Conception* (also 1930), on which he again collaborated with Breton. Like Breton, he was expelled from the Communist Party in 1933 but from 1936 the Spanish Civil War and his friendship with Picasso led him towards poetry of a collective humanism (*Cours naturel,* 1938; *Donner à voir,* 1939). This transition to a more explicitly political poetry led to Éluard's break with Breton in 1938 but would form the basis of his inspiring Second World War and Resistance poetry.

Among the earliest members of the group, Bejamin Péret (1899-1959) and Robert Desnos (1900-45) illustrate the diversity of poetic practices and intellectual commitments the Surrealist movement embraced during the inter-war years. Péret remained the most intransigent in terms of its original aesthetic and political ideals, and the most loyal to Breton's conduct of the movement. His unswerving contempt for all the forces which oppress, and a complete faith in the power of the imagination to liberate, fuelled the explosive mixture of vicious satire, burlesque verve and absurd linguistic and logical games which characterise his poetry (*Je ne mange pas de ce pain-là,* 1936). Like other Surrealists, Péret's anarchist faith led him to oppose Communist political orthodoxy, in his case by actively supporting Trotsky against Stalin, but his political commitment extended to fighting in Spain against Franco from 1936. Desnos, in *Rrose Sélavy* (1922-3), a collection of word-games which he claimed to have written in a transatlantic séance with the artist Marcel Duchamp, took Surrealist experimentation with hypnosis and automatic writing further than most, using with humorous, subversive and highly poetic results every manner of word- and sound-play to generate images and ideas outside the control of logic. In *À la Mystérieuse* (1926), he channelled this exceptional verbal virtuosity towards the poignant search for an inaccessible love. Surrealism's public commitment in 1927 to the PCF alienated Desnos, who was too much of an individualist to subscribe to any political programme, and his poems of *Corps et biens* (1930) represent his summary of his Surrealist years. Despite such divergent trajectories, both Péret and Desnos in their different ways later played significant roles in the French Resistance.

As important early members like Desnos and Queneau broke with the group in the late 1920s, there were new arrivals, notably René Char. He participated in the group's activities (working with Breton and Éluard on *Ralentir travaux*) and this participation, though brief, made a lasting impact on him. It was brief because he was soon uncomfortable with group formulae for poetry; it was lasting because Surrealism's central belief in the power of poetry to transform human existence was one he never abandoned. Though the poems of *Le Marteau sans maître* (1934) were written during this phase and appeared under the aegis of the Éditions surréalistes, they show that Char was already moving on. In Surrealist terms they present themes (such as poetry as mystery and spiritual combat) and forms (such as the prose poem) which were not inherently Surrealist and whose power would be reinforced by Char's experience of the Second World War.[71]

For poets indifferent to Surrealist performances of automatic writing or opposed to their assault on the fixed forms of the poetic tradition, poetry continued to represent an intellectual and spiritual journey, closer to Hugo than to Breton, in a language organised into recognised patterns of sound and image. *Anabase* (1924) by Saint-John Perse (pseudonym of Alexis Saint-Léger Léger, 1887-1975) is, in its author's words, an 'expédition vers l'intérieur', a journey into the interior through vast, undefined spaces of nature and memory. It is a rare example of a modern epic poem, weaving together the history of a people and of a poet, an Eastern and mental landscape.[72]

Jules Supervielle (1884-1960) possessed a Surrealist sense of the imagination's magical transformation of the real, but in collections such as *Gravitations* (1925) and *La Fable du monde* (1938), the vastness of his exploration of time and space has greater affinity with Romantic poetry than with Surrealism. It differs from Hugo in the humour and lightness with which this exploration is recounted, even if certain poems do express the poet's alarm for a world which appears to have broken from its moorings.[73] More often, however, this cosmic vastness finds a human scale in the organic relationships between the animal, vegetable and mineral universe. Supervielle's imagination performs a vast humanist embrace of the world, taking in the most distant stars and the most familiar objects. Despite the intense desire for understanding, there is a deep innocence and gentleness in his work; despite the difficulties of understanding, there is no rage or despair. In formal terms, Supervielle appears to move effortlessly between regular or fixed forms, free verse and the *verset* (a short sequence subdivided like the Biblical text), in which the choice of form and patterning is determined by the nature of the poetic substance to be expressed. It is a very deliberate, crafted relationship between thought and rhythm quite opposed to Surrealist experimentation with automatic writing but which has won for Supervielle an audience which seems certain to grow.

Henri Michaux (1899-1984) began writing in the ambiance of Surrealism in the sense that it was his discovery of Lautréamont's work in 1922, followed by that three years later of contemporary painting (Klee, Ernst, Chirico), that precipitated his faith in the transformative energies of verbal and visual signs. Compulsive in his commitment to voyages of discovery within and outwith the self, to experimentation of all kinds (in the borders between prose and poetry, the narratives of European myths, the visual arts, linguistic research, drugs), he invented landscapes which were war-zones for the raging contradictions of his fragile, fragmented self. This experimentation seeks to liberate the unknown within the self and results in a poetry of relentless, turbulent, occasionally fluid rhythms. Michaux is in this respect a distant relation of the Rimbaud of the 'Bateau ivre' and the prose poetry. His utopian hallucinations are more private than those of Rimbaud, and they lack the latter's political project. But they have a lucidity in which humour plays an important part and whose effect is moving as well as alarming.[74]

Like Michaux, Francis Ponge (1899-1988) was largely unclassifiable in terms of inter-war poetic practice, though for quite different reasons. He began writing, he tells us, as a result of the difficulties he encountered when, having tried and failed to express himself, he tried, and failed again, to describe objects. He decided to publish his accounts of these failures to describe. The result was *Le Parti pris des choses* (1942), in which Ponge confronts the difficulty of description and, in the process, transforms the reader's perceptions of the object described and of the nature of the language involved. The liberating potential of this repeated renewal of language and perception would echo down the twentieth century. Published in 1942, the collection was one example of the effort made by a Resistance poet to reclaim the language from the German occupier. In the post-war period, it (and subsequent Ponge texts) was identified in what became a trend of poetry devoted to the description of the visible world, in opposition to the Surrealist legacy of the imagination. Later still, it was adopted by the *Tel quel* group as a model of language's power to generate text.[75]

THE SECOND WORLD WAR

The period of Occupation and Resistance witnessed a remarkable revival in the public fortunes of poetry in France. Hardly had the armistice been signed than poets hostile to it began to circulate poems clandestinely.[76] Given the circumstances, poetry had obvious advantages over other forms of literary production. It used less paper and print. It could be memorised and transmitted orally. Its concision, density of language and use of symbolism and allusion gave it more powerful forms of expression than prose and made life difficult for censors. Moreover, there is a sense in which poetry is by its very nature oppositional, that 'good poetry is by definition protest and resistance, and cannot thrive on resignation or acceptance of the status quo'.[77] On the other hand, its effectiveness as an instrument of resistance depended on the reader recognising her or his place in a community of language and culture which the poetic tradition embodied. For this reason poets who were committed to the Resistance tended to abandon the introspective and esoteric forms of expression which since the late nineteenth century had distanced much contemporary poetry from its potential audience. Instead, they returned to more familiar rhythms, forms and language likely to prove more accessible to the wider public they now wished to reach. Some poets (Péret, for example) believed that political poetry was a contradiction in terms and refused to write during these years; others (Reverdy, Char) continued to write but refused to publish until after the war. But many poets wrote, circulated and published work which, taken together, redefined the relation between poetry and the circumstances in which it is written.[78]

The extreme situation of 1940-4 provoked in many poets a deep sense of outrage and revolt, and the challenge to create forms of poetic language capable of communicating these feelings to others. The extent of their moral and political commitment and the engagement with language that resulted from them led in many cases to poetic creativity of exceptional range and quality. The outstanding example was Aragon, who, after a decade in which his greatest creative effort had been invested in the novel, launched with *Le Crève-cœur* (1941) a collection of volumes of poetry and critical writing on poetry which made him during this period an essential voice of Resistance poetry.[79] Other poets who, like Aragon, had been associated with the Surrealist movement from its beginnings, were also actively committed to the Resistance cause. In the case of Éluard, the experience of Occupation and Resistance strengthened the humanist themes present in his poetry of the 1930s (such as faith in a universal fraternity, or the power of the mediation of love), while in 'Liberté' he created the single most famous Resistance poem. Desnos's clandestine poetry celebrated liberty and castigated oppression in a poetic language which drew heavily on the rhythms and tones of popular speech and for which he ended up in a concentration camp, where he died.

As leader of the Basses-Alpes section of the Forces françaises combattantes, Char played a significant part in the Resistance effort and the work published in 1948 under the title *Fureur et mystère* tells of his fury at the obstacles which historical reality was placing against the poet's ambition to transform the real, and of the mystery which poetic language projects into the present. Prose poems, notes on clandestine activity, poems of Provence and Alsace landscapes are followed by what Char calls the 'poème pulvérisé' ['pulverised poem'], fragments of emotion and sensation from which language seeks to establish a basis for a universal community of feeling. The distinct tensions Char's poetry creates made him one of the essential figures in post-war French poetry. From a non-Surrealist perspective, the Catholic poet Pierre Emmanuel (b. 1916-84) sought to establish the relationship between the historical reality of the war and human destiny in its ambition for the divine. In these and many other cases, the experience of Occupation and Resistance led poets to reformulate their understanding of the relationships between poetic, political and spiritual aspirations.[80]

In 1941, Aragon's anger at the phoney war of the winter of 1939-40 and at the débâcle of June 1940 was expressed in the poems written in the twelve-month period from October 1939 and published in *Le Crève-cœur*. Their impact was enormous for they not only found words for the feeling of calamity which had engulfed the French in June 1940 but also demonstrated Aragon's conviction that poetry could help to regenerate the values of national unity and common culture necessary to overcome the sense of hopelessness and isolation which had resulted from the débâcle. In addition, this national poetry derived much of its emotional force from the poet's love for his wife, Elsa Triolet. Their enforced separation was a source of despair and anger, a form of death comparable to the collapse of unity in national life. So, in 'Les Lilas et les roses', their separation and the news that Paris has fallen to the Germans are '. . . les deux amours que nous avons perdus' ['. . . the two loves we have lost']. But their love was also an affirmation of the solidarity at the heart of private and public life which fascism could not defeat. This reciprocal relationship between his love for Elsa and for his country remained a major theme in the two collections which followed, *Les Yeux d'Elsa* (1942) and *La Diane française* (1944).

One of the ways in which Aragon sought to represent love as a profoundly political response to fascism was to adopt the forms of medieval courtly love poetry. In this tradition of twelfth-century 'amour courtois', the knight placed his courage at the service of love and was loved in return, since his virtues were both a homage to his lady and a service to the Court community of which he was part. This 800-year-old poetic tradition seemed contemporary to Aragon in the early 1940s for it promoted the social values of the feminine over fascism's cult of masculine force. It was one example of the attempts made by poets to recreate the sense of national unity vital to the Resistance effort by drawing on France's geography, history and culture. In their poetry, French placenames appear repeatedly—Paris, inevitably, but also towns, villages, provinces and rivers. The most famous example is 'Oradour', by Jean Tardieu (b. 1903), written when news reached him in Paris of the atrocity perpetrated against the inhabitants of the village of Oradour-sur-Glane on 10 June 1944. Tardieu's poem made the name of the village synonymous with horror itself through the relentless rhythm of its repetition across the text.[81] Similarly, historical reference and analogy was used to sustain the idea of the nation in the face of Nazi myths of superiority founded on race. Multiple references to the Middle Ages, whether historical or literary, remind the reader of the emergence at that time of a French national culture. Joan of Arc is invoked as an earlier representative of the struggle for sovereignty; the Revolution and its Marseillaise, the Paris Commune and its Internationale contribute their exploits, martyrs and anthems to the values of international brotherhood and resistance to oppression. A wide range of literary references drawn from high and popular forms underline this sense of a community of culture at a time when the culture appeared to have collapsed in the face of Nazi aggression.[82]

For poets the most powerful instrument of resistance was, however, the language itself, and the most urgent need seemed to be to reclaim it from collaborators who were placing it at the service of an alien, destructive ideology. For many poets, this involved returning to the traditional rhythms of French poetry, to forms of versification anchored in the collective memory, in order to adapt them to the contemporary experience of defeat and resistance. This effort to create modern rhythmic patterns from within established ones took place at every level of the system of versification, from the use made of the most familiar fixed forms and line lengths to the organisation of stanzas and the creation of rhyme.

Once again, Aragon's poetry contains many examples. In *Le Crève-cœur,* for example, he uses a wide variety of stanza structures, ranging from the most familiar, the quatrain ('Le Temps des mots croisés' is made up of thirteen quatrains in cross rhyme, *abab*), to the less familiar, such as the stanza of six lines (*sizain*) in 'Zone libre', nine (*neuvain*) in 'Pergame en France', or ten (*dizain*) in 'Le Poète international'. The same poem may combine several different stanza structures (cf. 'Vingt ans après', 'Les Amants séparés') to exploit the sharp changes of rhythm and tone which such combinations may reinforce. 'Tapisserie de la grande peur' is an unusual case of a single-stanza poem of 32 lines, in which three four-line sequences of embraced rhyme (*abba*) are interrupted by a sudden switch to four lines in cross rhyme (lines 13-16), followed by a return to the embraced rhyme pattern for the rest of the poem. The effect of the sudden switch is to give an exceptional emphasis to the word in the rhyme position of line 15, where the break from the embraced rhyme scheme adopted up to that point is recognised. This emphasis which the word ('rapaces') derives from the rhyme scheme is added to that from the phonetic patterning in which it is also involved (with 'Espace', 'passe' and the other elements in /a/ and /s/). This is only one small example among many in the same poem in which Aragon uses the different levels of the French verse system to evoke the sense of panic which accompanied the *exode* from Northern France in June 1940.

The two most common line lengths in the French system are the alexandrine and the octosyllable. In his essay 'Crise de vers', Mallarmé had called the alexandrine 'la cadence nationale' ['the national cadence'], and the war poets used it for the history of shared feelings and rhythms it brought with it. Equally, the flexibilities which nineteenth-century poets from Hugo onwards had brought to its traditional 6/6 structure gave precedents for expressing profound feelings by showing a line's rhythm pushing against the alexandrine's well-established rhythmic constraints.[83] The octosyllable, on the other hand, had been a feature of more popular poetic forms and the war poets used it to connect their poetry to the familiar rhythms of folk song, with its emphasis on the spoken word, which lodged in the reader's memory. The *vers impair,* whose virtues Verlaine had extolled in his poem 'Art poétique', could be used in combination with the standard twelve- or eight-syllable line to create effects of emphasis or surprise through the switch between even and odd line lengths (as in Éluard's 'Faire vivre', in which the change to seven syllables in the final three lines of the poem underlines the sharp change of theme and tone on which the poem closes).

Fixed-form poems such as the sonnet, which had undergone a spectacular revival in the nineteenth century, also had deep roots in the collective memory. The dilemma facing Resistance poets in negotiating the relationship between expression and constraint was central to the ways in which the French sonnet worked, and its concision and familiar rhyme schemes made it easier to memorise. Jean Cassou (1897-1986) wrote his *Trente-trois sonnets composés au secret* (published in 1944) while in solitary confinement and their profound humanist values emerge more powerfully from the poet's respect for the constraints of the regular sonnet form. Desnos, on the other hand, in his sonnet 'Le Legs', which was published in the 1943 anthology *L'Honneur des poètes,* and opened with a reference to Victor Hugo, France's most famous nineteenth-century political exile, used an irregular rhyme scheme in the quatrains (*abba* in the first, changing to *baab* in the second) to reinforce his contempt for the Nazi leaders and French collaborators named there. Aragon adopted the earlier fixed forms of the *complainte* and *romance* for the same purpose of drawing upon familiar forms and reminding readers of the human and national values invested in these forms.

For Resistance poets, the problems of poetic language varied according to whether the poem was written as a private expression of feeling, without the intention to publish, or whether the aim was publication and, if so, whether this publication was intended to take legal or illegal form. Many poets wrote work of all three types but of the three, the attempt to publish a Resistance poem legally created particular problems, since the poet was obliged to choose themes and terms which censors would fail to recognise as an expression of resistance but which the poem's intended audience would identify as such. In this way, every contraband poem published represented a small victory over the forces of oppression. In this, as in many other aspects of Resistance poetry, Aragon played a major role, both by placing contraband verse in a French literary tradition (that of medieval troubadour poetry in which the lover declares his feelings to the lady under the nose of the husband, who fails to recognise the message), and by the examples he provided in his own poetry. To quote just one case in point, 'Santa Espina', in *Le Crève-cœur*, contains on one level a religious theme to which the authorities could hardly object and, on another, references to the Spanish Civil War and Catalonian anthems which would be unmistakable for those who had taken part in activities in support of Republican Spain's struggle against Franco.

SOME POST-WAR DIRECTIONS

The euphoria which greeted the liberation of France was of short duration. As was the case in the French novel, the ideals which had fuelled Resistance poetry were no match for the realities of the *épuration*, for the political expediencies surrounding the creation of the Fourth Republic, or for the ideological divisions which culminated in the Cold War. Symptomatic in this respect are the bitterness evident in Aragon's poems in his *Nouveau Crève-cœur* (1948) and the decline in his own position from the quasi-official status of *poète national* he had enjoyed at the Liberation. Though the publication of war poetry continued into the early post-war years, and though it was in some cases work of major significance (Char's *Fureur et mystère*, for example), it appeared at a time when the energies which the themes and forms of French war poetry had derived from the collective nature of resistance to oppression were receding. Poets withdrew once more into their more private spaces, where poetry could resume its broader historical development along the paths opened up in the latter part of the nineteenth century and which the events of 1939-45 had interrupted. In this respect, two collections of poetry published in the immediate post-war period signalled this renewed distance between the private and public spaces of poetry. The first, published in 1945, was the Pléiade edition of the complete works of Mallarmé, whose status in the post-war theory and practice of French poetry would not cease to grow. The second, the following year, was *Paroles* by Jacques Prévert (1900-77), whose poems of the everyday, liberating in their spontaneity, anarchic in their humour, full of the sights, sounds and rhythms of the street, have become classics of popular culture.

The major pre-war figures and the poets who had emerged during the war wrote on into the later stages of the century. Saint-John Perse, in *Vents* (1946) and *Amers* (1958), pursued his dialogue with the elements, and their relationship to human mortality and desire. In *Épreuves, Exorcismes* (1945), Michaux continued, as the title suggests, to develop his practice of poetry as exorcism of the obsessions and terrors of his private self; but from the post-war years, it is his interest and experimentation in different visual art forms which, more than his poetry, represent the new departures in his work. In *Babel* (1951), Pierre Emmanuel renewed his ambition to practise what he called the spiritual exercise of poetry, in this case a mystic contemplation of the rise and fall of humanity's Promethean ambitions.

Among the poets who began publishing in the post-war years, Yves Bonnefoy (b. 1923) has been the major revelation. In *Du mouvement et de l'immobilité de Douve* (1953) he explores the indispensable presence of death at all the transactions of experience. It is the common fate whose recognition is the essential prerequisite of knowledge. The poet's task is to find words with which to describe the presence of things permanently threatened by disappearance. In the poem, Douve is an enigmatic female figure who progresses through stages of death towards what the final section of the work calls the 'true place' of meaning in the material world, towards that sense of plenitude which the consciousness of mortality heightens. At certain moments experience of the natural world can be so intense as to fill the consciousness with an intimation of immortality, and poetry seeks to stabilise, however briefly, these hints of transcendence. This search for what Bonnefoy calls 'presence' and for the relationship between it and the language of poetry has been the focus of all his creative and critical writing.[84]

Philippe Jaccottet (b. 1925) published in the 1950s two volumes of poetry (*L'Effraie*, 1953, and *L'Ignorant*, 1958) in which the world is perceived in the fragile beauty of its surfaces, elusive and enigmatic. His work shares with that of Bonnefoy this intense focus on the real, which aims to discipline the unfettered imagination of the Surrealist legacy and to oblige poetic language to respect the smallest elements of the real, which are poetry's subject. As in Bonnefoy, such attention to the here and now seems to invite the belief in some form of permanence, however far removed, however circumscribed by the interrogative forms his language takes. It appears as a pale shadow of the Romantic faith in the correspondences between the external world and the ideal. In the late twentieth century, Jaccottet seems to imply, such permanence could at best be provisional. Modern poets can no longer claim to reveal the meaning of the world as confidently as predecessors did but, despite the limitations of subjectivity, they can still manifest in language the means to involve others in human and social vision and ambition. Jaccottet took this further in *Airs* (1967), brief, limpid poems modelled on the Japanese *haiku*, in which fleeting sensations of nature open out onto the poet's interrogations of the meanings such beauty might contain.[85]

The seriousness with which this search is conducted remains even when the means appear to be playful. The Oulipo experimentation practised in the novel (see above, pp. 229-31) took place in poetry too, notably in the work of Jacques Roubaud (b. 1932). His *Trente et un au cube* (1973) is, as its title suggests, a collection of 31 poems, each with 31 lines, each with 31 syllables, themselves distributed on the basis of a Japanese poetic form, the *tanka* (5 + 7 + 5 + 7 + 7). In addition, the poems openly recycle texts of different types, French and translations into French, in what amounts to an anthology of post-war experimental practices. But the seriousness of the game as a reflection of the power of language to rewrite itself, of the role of formal constraints in the process of writing, can be seen in the context of Roubaud's other efforts in the theory and practice of poetry, in particular his important study of French versification (*La Viellesse d'Alexandre*, 1978) and his contribution to the publications of the *Change/atelier* group, which included the definitive version, edited by Mitsou Ronat, of Mallarmé's *Un coup de dés* (1980).

It would not be difficult to find other examples of the faith which post-war poets continue to retain in poetry's power to trace a spiritual or philosophical journey from which to bring back alternative representations of being in the world. The work of Eugène Guillevic (b. 1907), Jacques Dupin (b. 1927), Michel Deguy (b. 1930) and Jean Daive (b. 1941), who, from different points on the generational and intellectual map, pursue the search for what Guillevic described (in *Vivre en poésie*, 1980) as the sacred in everyday life, provides further cases in point. This faith sustains the great vitality of contemporary French poetry. With hindsight, the intellectual upheavals which have taken place in the French cultural field since the late 1950s have tended to reinforce and generalise the terms of the discussion of the means and ends of poetry which Mallarmé formulated one hundred years ago. The 'initiative' which he 'ceded to words' has become the new orthodoxy. Yet this initiative has resulted not in a Surrealist vision of total freedom or automatic writing but in the continuing interrogation by poets of the relationship of modern experience to the language of poetry, of the nature of this language, and of its relationship to the French poetic tradition, its fixed forms, its systems and practices of versification. The one essential post-war cultural and political development which as yet lies outside these terms is that of women's writing (see below, pp. 276-93). As far as poetry is concerned, it is clear that a substantial number of French women are currently writing and publishing poetry and it may well be that the events of May 1968 were a defining moment in this development. Yet contemporary French poetry appears not yet to have engaged with the issues within feminist debate (for example, the distinction between 'écriture féminine' and 'écriture féministe').[86] Whether (and, if so, in which ways) this new voice of French poetry will enter and redirect the mainstream of French poetry is another question for the future.

III Theatre: Language in Performance

The Current of Change

Twentieth-century French theatre, said Jean-Louis Barrault (1910-94) in his *Réflexions sur le théâtre* (1949), is a protean form, reflecting a society that lives between two currents. One current pulls it to the past, described by Barrault as the great bourgeois epoch whose close we sometimes seem to be living, and is responsible for the prolonged life of conventional theatre and the 'boulevard' play. The other directed towards a still-underfined future, rushes forward to create channels of its own, towards dramatic forms still in the making.

This second current, starting up in the 1890s and given strength and direction in the early twentieth century by the attack on commercialism launched by the director Jacques Copeau (1879-1949), has transformed concepts of theatrical place and space, the roles of actor, director and playwright, acting styles and directing techniques, the relation between written text and performance and the relation between public and play. One of the few collective experiences still remaining to a fragmented society, theatre has become a rallying-place for avant-garde challenges to conventional ways of seeing. Increasingly materialist in its concept of itself—preoccupied with presenting the human body in its multiple and active relationships with the living world—seeking to liberate the imagination and the senses, theatre dispenses an excitement totally different from that of the cinema, whose challenge from the early years of the century forced it into radical self-examinations.

Antonin Artaud (1896-1948) argued the superiority of the theatrical over the cinematic image, which, he said, however poetic, is only film, and fixes imagination in a single visual form. Theatre allows imagination to pursue its own images and, most important, its medium is living matter, with all its challenges and resistances (*Le Théâtre et son double*, 1938). Paul Claudel, writing in 1929, had already seen further. Film for him was another creative resource, alongside music, poetry and action, to release the audience's imagination from the limits of the real. Film could open up the fixed décor of the stage to project the shifting variations and possibilities of dream ('Note sur *Christophe Colomb*', 30 December 1929).[87]

From the start of the modern period, theatre was on the move.[88] Narrowly bounded from the mid-nineteenth century by boulevard theatre and the Comédie Française, its spaces expanded to include the privately run little theatres of the 1880s (which reappeared in the 1950s and 1960s), State-subsidised drama centres, the open-air festival venues pioneered by Jean Vilar (1912-71, founder in 1947 of the Festival d'Avignon), working factories, with their hastily improvised stages (again pioneered by Vilar, in the 1950s) and in 1968, the streets. From the 1910s, a steady process of decentralisation marked a search for wider audiences in the popular classes. Jacques Copeau (1879-1949) moved his Théâtre du Vieux-Colombier from the boulevards to the Latin Quarter in 1913. His book on *Le Théâtre populaire* (1941) argued for the need to break with Paris altogether. In 1945, Jeanne Laurent, in the socialist Ministère des Beaux-Arts, moved drama to the provinces by establishing the Centres Dramatiques Nationaux. In the 1960s, under de Gaulle, André Malraux followed with the Maisons de Culture. Pompidou swiftly turned off the tap after the events of May 1968. It was switched on again in the early 1980s with Mitterrand as President by Jack Lang, Arts Minister in a socialist government with a programme of political reform based on regionalisation.

Acting styles evolved to reflect the shift away from the notion of individual 'star' performance and towards ensemble production. The single-author script was no longer the sole mover of the drama. Body language, mime and mask, or the equally potent language of objects, were held to communicate more complex meanings, more effectively, than the word alone. Eastern theatrical traditions could offer whole languages of gesture and movement which attached different meanings to the different kinds of movement of different parts of the body, reaching the same complexity and subtlety as the West had brought to the elaboration of its verbal codes.[89] Performance became a collaboration between actors, playwright and director in which the latter increasingly took the major part, inventing and disseminating new acting techniques.

Jean-Louis Barrault's *Réflexions sur le théâtre* gives a glimpse of the networks of influence and mutual reinforcement which grew out of Jacques Copeau's school. Barrault studied with the actor-director Charles Dullin (1885-1949), whose teaching emphasised the body and its expressive powers and the importance of the mask. Dullin introduced him to the ideas of Copeau, the Russian director Constantin Stanislawski and the scenic designer Edward Gordon Craig. From Craig, he acquired the notion of theatre as a collective craft where the actor shares the work of carpenter and electrician, helps with costume design and learns how the music works. He learned about mime from the actor Étienne Decroux, formerly of Dullin's troupe, and developed his own techniques of breath-control and gesture. Barrault's first production, *Autour d'une mère* (1935), based on William Faulkner's modernist novel *As I Lay Dying*, was an exploration of the expressive powers of the body, which filled the stage with controlled movement, stylised gesture and non-verbal vocal sound.

The exceptional actor or actress continued to be a focal point in the production, with such stars as Louis Jouvet, Barrault himself, Madeleine Renaud, Gérard Philipe, Edwige Feuillère. But the later 1960s and early 1970s saw productions collectively devised by the acting group, whether working with a text or improvising their own themes. New relationships were established with the audience, or rather, the various audiences to which different productions were addressed.

Alongside these changes ran a continuing discussion of the relationship between the written playtext and performance. This has caught up many of the twentieth century's other debates on the origins of authority, the relations between writing and speech and between tradition and innovation, and (that false dichotomy inherited from the eighteenth century) whether understanding comes through reason or the senses.[90] More often than not, the best twentieth-century dramatic performances have been generated in negotiation with a script. A poet who can write for the page cannot necessarily transfer his talents to the stage, as Symbolist theatre discovered in the 1890s with plays by Verlaine, Mallarmé, Laforgue. But dramatic poetry, written for the human body to unleash the energies of language as part of a total discourse incorporating gesture and sound, breath-rhythms and body movements, and underlining the connections of speech and action, is quite another matter.

Stepping Stones

In the period 1870-1920, the commercial theatre waxed fat on the continuing popularity on the boulevards of the farces of Georges Courteline (1858-1929) and Georges Feydeau (1862-1921), limiting its investment in new work to plays such as Edmond Rostand's tragi-comedy in verse, *Cyrano de Bergerac* (1897). Innovation came first from neighbour countries in Northern Europe through such diverse influences as Wagner, Ibsen, Strindberg and Maeterlinck, channelled through the little theatres of the Symbolist and Idealist movements. Home-grown Idealist drama consisted mostly of minor productions by minor playwrights, often with occultist sympathies (Villiers de l'Isle-Adam, Jules Bois, Joséphin Péladan), which foregrounded the text at the expense of performance.

Two dramatists from this period set the perspectives for twentieth-century theatre. In works such as *Partage de midi* (written 1905, staged 1948), *L'Annonce faite à Marie* (staged by Lugné-Poë, 1912), *Le Soulier de satin* (written 1919-24, published 1929, and staged 1943), the Symbolist Paul Claudel (1868-1955) dedicated his talents to the revival of the religious and political ideologies of the Right. For Claudel, spiritual and material worlds were joined in close communion, and his drama, built on Catholic doctrine and symbol (the Fall, the Cross, redemptive sacrifice, reparatory suffering, the Communion of Saints, the Providential direction of History), aimed to remake the connections between them in the contemporary imagination. The Wagnerian influence is strong in his work. In a programme note dated 30 December 1929, for the Berlin production of his play *Le Livre de Christophe Colomb*, he pointed to Wagner's interest in the subtle connections of rhythm and sonority that link the spoken word with music and enable the artist to transport his audience out of their present into a narcotic other-world of his own creation. In the 1930s, Claudel added to this discourse the techniques of the sacred lyrical drama of the Japanese Nô theatre, with its emphasis on ritual gesture, liturgical costume, and the use of the Chorus to provide a doubling commentary on the action ('Le Festin de la Sagesse', *La Revue de Paris*, 1 July 1938).

Claudel's theatre came into its own in the 1940s. Its search for a dramatic language which could make plain the tragic tensions between despair at a stifling present and longing for a liberating future is exactly that of the left-wing political drama of Sartre and Camus, who admired Claudel's work in this respect despite their antipathy to his religion and his politics. Jean-Louis Barrault, by then at the Comédie Française, was the first to realise the potential of his work and to stage Claudel's two evocations of star-crossed love, the epic and spectacular *Le Soulier de satin* (performed 1943) and the more intimate psychological drama, *Partage de midi* (performed 1948). Barrault's actors were excited by the technical challenges of a language which married mime and diction, the 'breathed' character of Claudel's prose-poetry, the loaded meanings to his words, and the drumming rhythms of his lines. The audience was, to Barrault's delight, overwhelmingly receptive to innovations which marked an energising reorientation of the theatrical enterprise.[91]

Equally influential, but set at the opposite political pole, was the work of Alfred Jarry (1873-1907), whose monstrous farce *Ubu roi* (1896), in a single two-night run, unleashed anarchy.[92] This parody of Shakespeare's *Macbeth*, set in a parody of Poland, was a provocative onslaught on the Third Republic, indicted for its small-mindedness, obsession with money and power, blinkered positivism, worship of technology and disregard for humane values. Two years before the Dreyfus Affair, the play stirred the same mud and released the same poisons. In his theoretical statements on drama, written mostly in 1896-7 ('De l'inutilité du théâtre au théâtre', 'Réponse à une questionnaire sur l'art dramatique', 'Questions de théâtre'), Jarry presented theatre as a visual, performative act, in which decor, mime and masks were as important as words. The puppets and robots who gesture and fawn mindlessly around the grotesque tyrant Ubu are the human wreckage on which the ballooning, predatory ego feeds. At the same time, for the fantastic horror of the play to achieve its full dimension, Jarry needed to depict the wreck of language, the gap between the words of modern culture and the meaning they create. Ubu's pompous rhetorics, parodies of medieval epic, Shakespeare, and Racinian tragedy, contrast sharply with his venal, cowardly and cruel acts. Jarry dramatised the processes by which culture is taken captive by an opportunistic bourgeoisie.

There are formal analogies between Jarry's work and that of his closest contemporary, Guillaume Apollinaire, whose verse play *Les Mamelles de Tirésias,* staged in 1917 under the tag 'drame surréaliste', bolstered its comedy with music, acrobatics and Chorus. But his direct heirs for both form and political intention were the Dadaists and Surrealists, who emerged in the 1920s and then again in the 1960s: Roger Vitrac, for example, whose *Victor, ou les Enfants au pouvoir* (1928) was revived in the 1962-3 season and who with Artaud was co-founder of the Théâtre Alfred Jarry in 1926.

In 1920-40, a stylish commercial theatre, fed by the prolific pens of Jean Cocteau (1889-1963), Jean Giraudoux (1882-1944) and Jean Anouilh (1910-87), produced much entertaining formal innovation but little substance. Isolated against this lightweight backdrop, Antonin Artaud identified a demand from the younger generation, against the establishment grain, for a culture which could reconnect human sensibility to historical event. Modern youth, he said, was opposed to bourgeois capitalism and like Karl Marx was sensitive to 'le déséquilibre des temps où monte la personnalité monstrueuse des Pères basée sur la terre et sur l'argent' ['the unbalance in times when the monstrous personality of the Fathers, founded on money and land, is on the ascendant'].[93] In response to that demand, he proposed his own concept of a Theatre of Cruelty. This theatre was not necessarily cruel in the sense that it staged violence and crimes, though it often could. (Artaud's own play *Les Cenci,* 1935, rewrote the exploration by that other revolutionary, the English poet Shelley, of murder and incest within the patriarchal family.) Rather, its cruelty lay in tearing an audience away from the conventions that pad the edges of everyday existence and confronting it with the terrible thrill of being alive, part of the blind, zestful drive of creation ('Lettres sur la cruauté', 1932). Such a theatre required a new dramatic language, seen in action in the body-centred ritual forms of the Balinese Theatre in Paris in 1931. This became the basis of Artaud's radical rethinking of theatrical form and function in *Le Théâtre et son double* (1938), whose impact was only felt on its reissue in 1944 and which fed powerfully into the New Theatre of the late 1950s.

Theatre, Artaud argued, like plague, should shake its audiences with paroxysms of feeling, push them (in imagination) to extreme gestures and disclose repressed depths of eroticism, cruelty and violence. It was essentially a symbolic form, producing a double of reality, probing the myths and fables of the cultural inheritance to evoke their dark underside ('Le Théâtre et la peste'). Words in such a theatre played a supporting role to the spectacular. The stage was a space to be filled with the concrete language of drama, which addresses itself to the unconscious, through the senses ('La Mise-en-scène et la métaphysique'). Creating the 'blaze' of energies and images which constituted ideal drama required a synthesis of music, dance, mime, vocal intonation, architecture, lighting and decor.

In the 1940s and 1950s, the drama of Jean-Paul Sartre and Albert Camus plunged theatre directly into history and politics.[94] Sartre's writing for the theatre doubles his political trajectory from optimistic faith in the revolutionary potential of France and Europe to deep disillusionment. *Bariona* (1940), written and staged in Sartre's prisoner-of-war camp, celebrated the collective rise of the local people to save the Holy Family from the Roman legions. *Les Séquestrés d'Altona,* produced in 1959 to indict French policy in Algeria, showed the impotence of individuals locked into family, nation, and a Europe bankrupted by past collusions with tyranny. All his plays deal with the problematic relation of character to historical situation, and with the individual subject's ability to turn intellectual desire for change into effective action. Their aims are theorised in *Qu'est-ce que la littérature?* (1947) and in the articles and interviews collected in *Un théâtre de situations* (1973). A Sartrean play is written to demystify conventional notions of human nature and motivation and to show how individuals are constructed by the situation—the complex of private, political, ideological and material relations—in which they are placed ('Forger des mythes', June 1946).

Serious bourgeois theatre continued to formulate its studies of contemporary issues as accounts of the psychological crises of the classically constituted hero (for example, the plays of Henry de Montherlant, *La Reine morte*, 1942; *Le Maître de Santiago*, staged 1948; *Port-Royal*, 1954). Sartre's analyses started from a situation in crisis, posing conflicts of moral and political values ('Pour un théâtre de situations', November 1947). Within that situation, individuals, caught in new lights and perspectives, confronted or dodged their contradictions and made or failed to make the choices that change worlds. Such a concept of character was meat and drink, as Barrault noted, to the modern director, concerned with the representation of the crosscurrents of body language and speech. Sartre described the challenge of writing for popular theatre as one of re-establishing the connections between word and action ('Théâtre populaire et théâtre bourgeois', September-October 1955) and gave careful attention to the technical problems involved in giving contemporary colloquial dialogue a capacity for precise significance that could match the language of classical drama ('Forger des mythes'). Every word uttered in the theatre should itself be an act: 'une manière d'agir . . . serment ou engagement ou refus ou jugement moral ou défense des droits ou contestation des droits des autres' ['a mode of action . . . an oath, a commitment, a refusal, a moral judgement, a defense of rights or a challenge to the rights of others'] ('Le Style dramatique'). Conversely, the written word needed the actor's gesture to complete its movement towards meaning.

In *Qu'est-ce que la littérature?*, Sartre argued that all writers must recognise the class standpoint from and to which they speak, and commit themselves to the cause of the oppressed. A play must find the appropriate myths to make visible the formative conflicts and preoccupations of its audience, generating an understanding that can be turned into political action. The myths could be, as in *Les Mouches* (staged 1943), a new version carved out within the shell of Ancient plots. More often, his plots were modern, encapsulating in vivid (melo-) drama those moments of confrontation and choice that were part of everyday life in post-war Europe. *Huis clos* (1944) brought together in a Hell of eternal futility three characters who limited their horizons to private life, and selfishly built their own happiness at the cost of the lives around them. *Morts sans sépulture* (1946) presented an arrested Resistance group, facing torture and death, struggling to fix their choices for the greater public good. *La Putain respectueuse* (1948) raised the issues of racist and sexist oppression. *Les Mains sales* (staged 1948) dramatised the failure of a young middle-class intellectual to break with his idealist conditioning and make choices which would further collective freedom.

Albert Camus's dramatic career began with the theatre collective he helped found in Algeria in 1937. For his models, he looked not to Brecht but to Shakespeare, the Spanish Golden Age and French Classicism and, among contemporaries, the novelist Faulkner, whose *Requiem for a Nun* he adapted for the stage. In all these periods, he saw a moment of major historical change, poised between present despair and future unknown and presenting a cluster of inevitably tragic choices. In their representative authors he prized the ability to represent those tragic tensions with heroic simplicity. His first text, written with the collective in 1936, *Révolte dans les Asturies* (published 1962), an account of the repression of the miners' rebellion in the Spanish Civil War, was banned from production. Its experimental features included a stage that surrounded the audience, locking them into the action, a stylised emphasis on the group (miners and ministers in opposition) rather than the individual actor, mimed battle scenes, and some skilful interplay of sound and presence. Radio news voice-overs, tracking the revolt and its defeat, indicated the dominance of distant Barcelona, and a closing scene of disembodied, imprisoned voices in the dark gave a powerfully lyrical presentation of crushed hope. Later work, more severe philosophical investigations of political problems, was less exciting dramatically. *Caligula* (written 1936-9, performed 1945) was an exploration of the meaning of freedom in an Absurd world, and of the tensions that exist between the individual's power to exercise his freedom and the freedom of others. *Les Justes*, which opened in 1949, explored the question of whether murder can be politically justified, comparing the different responses of a group of terrorists in 1905 in theory and in practice.

The 1950s and 1960s saw an acceleration in the dual emphasis on performance and politics, encouraged by a fresh wave of influences from abroad. The Piccolo Teatro de Milan, which in 1949 put down the first marker for a Marxist and materialist political theatre, returned regularly to Paris through to the 1960s. Brecht's Berliner Ensemble arrived in 1954, with its techniques for engaging the audience's enthusiasm while also positioning it to consider a case from a distanced, objective perspective (the 'alienation effect'). The Théâtre des Nations welcomed performances by the Peking Opera in 1955 and by Japanese Nô companies in the 1950s and 1960s. In 1959, Joan Littlewood presented the work of Brendan Behan and her own *Oh What a Lovely War*. The 1960s saw translations from the English New Theatre of Harold Pinter, Edward Bond, John Osborne, Tom Stoppard and Arnold Wesker. Piscator was directing in Paris in the 1950s, and his *Political Theatre* appeared in French translation in 1962. The American Theatre anarchist collective, with Judith Malina and Julian Beck, touring Europe in 1964-8, appeared at the Théâtre des Nations. In 1966, Jerzy Grotowski of the Warsaw Theatre Laboratory came with his 'poor theatre', in which the sole means of representation was the actor's body.

In France, the first impulse was to seek to re-address tradition and turn it to serve the needs of the present. Jean

Vilar, director of the Théâtre National Populaire (1951-63), and Roger Planchon, founder of the Théâtre de la Cité in Villeurbane, an industrial suburb of Lyons, offered productions of Racine, Molière and Shakespeare which reconstructed the original historical reality explored by these dramatists and added a second dimension that explored conflicts in contemporary France. But in France as in England, it was new plays that gave directors such as Vilar, Roger Blin, Barrault and Jean-Marie Serreau their greatest stimulus and made the mid-century French theatre a place where major critiques of power relations and practices were being undertaken at the level of structures and language. The great dramatists of the Absurd—Genet, Beckett, Ionesco—embraced the flow of that second, innovatory current of theatre identified by Barrault and declared its philosophical and political implications. In the theatre of performance, concepts of authority and meaning are completely transformed. 'Meaning' is not a noun, a message, a truth to be handed over on a plate. 'Meaning' in this theatre is a verb, a process of construction, an act of making made afresh from moment to moment. Meaning can be seen and understood on stage, modelled within given, pre-constructed forms, but not definitively lodged in any. It is a working congeries of many discourses, mutually transformative, and all showing their constructed nature, their status as human productions. To a culture still committed to rationalist and religious absolutes and to notions of essential structures and unchanging truths, Absurd drama presented the liberating alternative of an Absurd universe. In the beginning was not the Word; beginning is speaking and seeing.

The first signs of change appeared at the end of the 1940s in the first representations of the alternative world of Jean Genet (1910-86), *Les Bonnes* (staged 1947) and *Haute Surveillance* (1949). In his lyrical evocation of the murderous venom of the maidservant-sisters, and the snarling criminals in the death cell, Genet presented original and shockingly celebratory emblems of the eroticism and violence whose repression constitutes the limits of the bourgeois order. The Surrealist philosopher and prose-writer Georges Bataille, in a review of *Haute Surveillance* on its publication in 1949, wrote of the power of Genet's theatre to rediscover in the forbidden places of the modern world the sacred thrill and heroic grandeur of classical tragedy, which had slipped, he said, out of the reach of a mediocre bourgeoisie.[95]

Genet's lyrical drama is a production of the lived relations of power between individuals and between individuals and society. These relations, political and economic in their origins, are seen, in the tradition of Artaud, as experienced most profoundly in the erotically-charged myths and symbols by which a culture lives. A culture focuses and displays or conceals its repressions, fears, desires and latent powers in certain images, which then become forms through which the culture can be manipulated. These forms, perceived as 'natural', are in fact constructions, ideological illusions which individuals live without questioning. All power, Genet told an interviewer, shelters behind some kind of theatricality, and only the theatre, the place of avowed illusion, has the means to lift the veils.[96] The erotic dressing-up games in the brothel (*Le Balcon*, published in 1956 and first produced in 1957), the play-rehearsals undertaken by blacks for the entertainment of whites (*Les Nègres*, first performed 1959), and the criss-crossing of screens over the stage of the Algerian War (*Les Paravents*, published 1961, first staged by Roger Blin in 1966) are so many emblems of the illusionary processes by which participants in a society collude to create the society's self-image.

'Comment jouer "Les Bonnes"', Genet's preface to the published text of *Les Bonnes* (1947), explained that the function of theatre was to externalise in scenic images and rhythms the buried processes of individual and social dream. To this purpose, scenic techniques and acting style must blend realism and artifice, introducing an edge of surrealism that frees convention-blunted perceptions for new kinds of understanding. Sartre spoke of the 'whirligigs' of a drama that disorientates spectators, tossing them to and fro from the true to the false and the false to the true (*Saint-Genêt: comédien et martyr*, 1952, Appendix 3). Genet had wanted the women in *Les Bonnes* to be played by adolescent boys, as part of a process of stylisation which could turn the women from individuals into symbols of femininity and so release the spectators from preconceptions and let them think creatively about the feminine function. The feminine is a central concept in Genet's work, representing that repressed, marginalised and dependent element in the psychological and social unit which colludes with and reproduces its own subjection but is also a potential source of hostile energies, permanently on the edge of revolt.

One of the great conjuring-tricks of ideology is its presentation of everyday life as a harmonious order. The jarring contrasts and discrepancies set up by Genet's drama scar and crack this smooth surface. In *Les Nègres*, the disruption comes in the foregrounding of the acting, the make-up, the masks, and also in the mixing of linguistic registers, juxtaposing the colloquial and the lyrical, in which the blacks make their challenge. Invisible gaps and divides in society are made visible. In *Le Balcon*, the brothel's clients and visitors (the Judge, the General, the Bishop) act out their fantasies in what look like discrete private rooms but are all essentially the same space. When the social battle-lines are drawn, the establishment figures line up together on the balcony and the real divide is disclosed, between those on high and the anonymous crowds struggling off-stage, out of the reckoning.

The collaboration between Samuel Beckett (1906-89) and Roger Blin on *En attendant Godot* (1953), staged at the Théâtre de Babylone, marked the opening of another potent investigation into the capacity of drama to reformulate the relationship of meaning and form, glossed by discreet reference to the deep structures of self-deception, exploitation, collusion and illusion which have shaped Western civilisation.[97] Like the full-length stage plays that followed, in French and English (*Fin de partie*, 1957; *Krapp's Last Tape*, 1958; *Happy Days*, 1961), and then the ever-shorter pieces written for stage, radio and television (*Cascando*, written 1962; *Eh Joe*, produced in 1966; *Not I*, premiered in 1972; and *Catastrophe*, in 1982), *Godot* was an experiment that put the spotlight on discourse. Or more accurately, it explored the relationship between discourse and the referent: that is, the universal silence which human perception, movement and speech punctuate into significance.

Beckett's genius was to marshal the left-over materials of the theatrical tradition—a minimum of décor, a diminishing number of characters, and a ragbag of rhetorics—into a set of relationships and exchanges which, realised in the rhythms of performance, model the absurd void of significance that constitutes the lived present of European culture. Habit, and the patterns of familiar routine, Beckett's dramas demonstrate, give the illusion of order, direction and sense to contemporary life. Speakers mouth rhetorics moulded around concepts—God, Reason, Nature—without substance. Life's lack of any absolute structure is modelled by the movement of the dramatic performance.

Beckett's plays play at stretching and shrinking time and space. Passing the time is the object of his characters, as it is the sole object of life demystified of religious absolutes and orientations. Time goes fast or slow depending how it is lived. The movement of the world is fixed by the situation of its speakers. Clov, the servant in *Fin de partie* (produced 1957), turns on Hamm, his master, refusing to differentiate 'yesterday' from any other day, when all days are equally grey and empty. In *En attendant Godot*, the destitute friends Vladimir and Estragon congratulate one another on a well-timed exchange of dialogue that has filled at least a minute with distraction. In the same play, Pozzo, the capitalist exploiter fallen on hard times, defines life as a fleeting awareness, empty of human feeling (a woman gives birth straddling the grave, light flickers, then darkness falls again). Objects, sparsely placed in this devastated world, are points in which meaning can be located. Radishes, turnips, boots keep people going in a literal sense (*En attendant Godot*), as well as in the sense of providing a subject to talk about. Winnie's handbag and toothbrush (*Happy Days*) perform the same function, as does, more ominously, her revolver. In the hands of the masters, both objects and language are politicised and turned into instruments of control. Pozzo rules through his whip, watch and food hamper; Hamm, with his whistle and his key to the food cupboard.

Beckett manages his world of frightening absurdity with black humour, humanly lurching between the grotesque and the sublime. Life, says Estragon, is a circus. As Beckett stages it, it is knock-about farce, shot through with cruelty, pain and terror. Terror comes with the realisation that being is self-authoring and self-perceiving (a recognition process brilliantly mimed in the silent comedy *Film*, 1963), and with the acknowledgment of the shortness of the time which the human voice has to find itself (*Breath*, 1969). At the end of the day, confronting the terror head-on is the heroism of the ordinary human. The light goes out on Krapp, playing over to himself the tapes of his past life, as he teeters on the brink of seeing what he is and has been, embracing it, and letting it go.

From a conservative and idealist position, Eugène Ionesco (1912-94), Romanian-born, settled in Paris from 1938, offered a critique of contemporary rhetoric superficially similar to Beckett's but different in its intentions and in the corrosive despair by which it is animated.[98] Ionesco denounced the stereotyped, robotic nature of modern society and its inhabitants, reduced to absurdity by their identification with their social functions, not human beings but effects of ideology ('Le Rôle du dramaturge', *Notes et contre-notes*, 1962). His black comedies, brilliantly visual, staged the monstrous absence of meaning from the forms that claim to communicate it. *La Cantatrice chauve* (first produced 1950) displayed the absurdity of language, the arbitrary nature of grammar and syntax, the lack of correlation between sound and sense, and the conventional nature of the narrative forms by which all these elements are constructed into a semblance of meaning. Ionesco emphasised the deceitfulness of the 'story', with its assumptions of a beginning, a middle and an end, which cocoons listeners in the prejudice that coherence and meaning exist. In his own plays, storyline was replaced by layered sequences of intensifying panic, where the real toppled over the edge into the disproportions and distortions of nightmare ('Entretien avec Edith Mora', *Notes et contre-notes*). The old couple in *Les Chaises* (1952) are gradually pushed off-stage by a proliferation of empty chairs. In *Amédée ou comment s'en débarrasser* (1954), a corpse swells to fill the stage. Panic breeds violence, not least in those who hold power. The teacher in *La Leçon* (1951), who kills his pupil with the language of authority, belongs to the same totalitarian impulse that in *Rhinocéros* (1960) takes over the whole world, leaving one solitary romantic standing symbolically in a crumbling house.

None of this ground-breaking new work was political in the simple, dogmatic sense. The work that declared itself political did not have the same intellectual and dramatic force: that of Arthur Adamov (1908-70), for example (*Paolo Paoli*, 1957), or the plays of Armand Gatti (b. 1924), which are interesting for their attempts to make the audience a working part of the production (*Chant public devant deux chaises électriques*, 1966, on the execution of Sacco and Vanzetti; *V comme Vietnam*, 1967; *Les Treize Soleils de la rue Saint-Blaise*, 1968, written in collaboration with the audience during the May events; and *La Colonne Durruti*, 1974). The 'théâtre panique' or 'théâtre de cérémonie' of Fernando Arrabal (b. 1932) is effective as spectacle but less so as political analysis, from *Le Cimetière des voitures* (1958) to the scatalogical black humour of *L'Architecte et l'Empereur d'Assyrie ou Joseph K tenté par la mégalomanie* (staged 1967).

After the Events

May 1968 took theatre onto the streets.[99] A meeting organised by Roger Planchon in his Villeurbane theatre led to the 'Declaration of Villeurbane' that cultural action should be an exercise in politicisation and must invent ways to help a public accustomed to impotence to practise creativity and freedom of choice. Theatre unions took part in the general strike, demanding changes in theatre administration. The predictable government withdrawal of subsidies for popular and political theatre provoked further demonstrations.

The independent troupes who came to prominence from late 1969 in the regions and Paris made significant advances in improvisation, collective creation and audience participation. Jacques Kraemer's Théâtre Populaire de Lorraine, founded in 1963, dramatised the crises associated with the iron and steel industry (*Splendeur et misère de Minette la bonne Lorraine,* 1969; *Les Immigrés,* 1972). André Benedetto's Nouvelle Compagnie d'Avignon, founded in 1966, gave a dramatic voice to such issues as Occitanian independence, the Vietnam War, revolution and class struggle. In Paris, the Théâtre de l'Aquarium, a student company turned professional in May 1970, satirised urban exploitation and the abuses of the press. Jérôme Savary's troupe, Le Grand Magic Circus et ses animaux tristes, embarked on a series of riotous productions, subversive in their sheer exuberance.

Of all such companies, the most influential and successful was Ariane Mnouchkine's Théâtre du Soleil, founded in 1964, which first established its distinctive identity in *Les Clowns* (1969), a production built up through a process of individual and collective improvisation, with its thematic centre the relationship between actors and their society.[100] Mnouchkine's multi-stage spectacular presentations swept the audience into the actors' critique of the contemporary State. The latter was attacked at its Revolutionary foundations in *1789, La Révolution doit s'arrêter à la perfection du bonheur* (1970), which offered from fairground trestle stages a panoramic, carnival analysis of the origins of the Revolution and its take-over by the bourgeoisie in 1791. *1793, La Cité révolutionnaire est de ce monde* (1972) recreated the private lives of commoners in a revolutionary community and contrasted their disappointed aspirations with the triumphalist claims of bourgeois history. *L'Âge d'or* (1975), plotted on the struggles of an immigrant worker, satirised the materialism of modern France.

The emphasis on collective creation from the 1970s onwards resulted in the temporary marginalisation of the writer. At the beginning of the eighties, David Bradby has noted, the important names in French theatre were still those of directors: Barrault, Planchon, Mnouchkine, Chéreau, Vincent, Vitez.

Recently, women directors and writers have become more numerous.[101] Their work is marked by a common motif of resistance to the confinement of meanings in rigid forms and categories and to the definition of an authoritative subject centre. Marguerite Duras's *India Song* (1972), which received its first performance in England in the summer of 1993, constructs a complex web of dialogues between voice-overs, voices off-stage, sound and music, combined with the spectacle of silent actors on-stage to model the slips and shifts of gendered desire (male and female, homosexual and heterosexual). Duras has also directed her own play, *Savannah Bay* (1983). Simone Benmussa, playwright, director and editor of the *Cahiers Renaud-Barrault,* is especially interested in turning non-theatrical texts into theatre. Her own *La Vie singulière d'Albert Nobbs,* adapted from George Moore's study of transvestism, appeared in 1977, and *Enfance,* adapted from Nathalie Sarraute's memoir-dialogue, in 1984. But Benmussa is best known for her adaptation and direction of Hélène Cixous's *Portrait de Dora* (1976), on which she comments in *Benmussa Directs* (1979). For this performance, different stage levels, voice-over, film projections and lighting effects were used to catch the swirl of significations around the split subject that is Dora: the shifting subject positions, complex interrelations of male and female desire, the overlapping time-planes of Dora's dream-recollections and Freud's crude interrogations. The movement of representation aims to displace Freud from the spotlight, prising away from him control of his case-study narrative and releasing Dora from the object-status in which it scientifically imprisoned her.

The most adventurous of the women directors remains Ariane Mnouchkine, though her adaptations of Shakespeare in the early 1980s and her attempts at contemporary epic have been criticised for allowing history to fall back into myth and for sacrificing analysis for an oversimplifying single vision. Her productions of Hélène Cixous's dramatisations of the Cambodian catastrophe (*L'Histoire terrible mais inachevée de Norodom Sihanouk, roi du Cambodge,* 1985) and the making of Gandhi's India (*L'Indiade,* 1987) were not helped by texts which themselves seem to have exchanged feminist ambition for myth-making and gesture.[102]

Published plays were still few in the early eighties, but the situation was eased by subsidies from Jack Lang's Ministry, to help young writers. Two dramatists have dominated in recent years, both advocates of the written text. In his preface to the collection of dramatic commentaries developed in his seminars held in the 1980s at the universities of Paris III and Paris VIII (*Écritures dramatiques: Essais d'analyse de textes de théâtre,* 1993), Michel Vinaver emphasised the double nature of the dramatic text, which is produced both for representation and for private reading, and where spoken word and action are intimately connected. His closing pages, however, gave primacy to the text: 'l'œuvre est tout entière dans son écriture même, et l'écriture n'est pas quelque chose qui change en cours de route' ['the work is entirely in the writing, and the writing is not something that changes as you go along']. Bernard-Marie Koltès (1945-89) included in the Notes to the text of *Roberto Zucco* (1990) an impressioned plea for more new plays to be staged and fewer rewrites of the classical repertory, and a statement that the room for collaboration between writer and director (in his case, Chéreau) is limited to the narrow space between the points when the writing is finished and rehearsals begin.[103]

From his first play, *Aujourd'hui, ou les Coréens* (staged 1956), to his most recent, *L'Émission de télévision* (1990), Michel Vinaver (b. 1927) has produced multi-layered political drama, which recognises the construction of so-called private experience by the webs of political and economic discourse. The marketing ethos and its transformations of the world of work and the individual subject inspired both the comic epic *Par-dessus bord* (1969) and the shorter *Les Travaux et les jours* (1980). The legal system is the focus of *Portrait d'une femme* (1988), where the heroine confronts judge, lawyers and witnesses in Court, object of an interrogation that emphasises the theatrical and constructed nature of her experience. Actors change costume and scenery in full view of the audience. Juxtaposed sets make it possible to offset against each other dialogues between different sets of characters and to use flashbacks to build up a picture of the complex machinery of the patriarchal State that has made of Sophie the prisoner in the dock. *L'Émission de télévision* (1990) evokes the anxieties generated around individuals who must redefine themselves as they cross the gulf between the world of work and the no man's land of unemployment, and who suddenly find themselves called to account not only by the stereotyping machinery of law but by the even more powerful machine of the media. No music, no scenery and a minimum of props leave language in full possession of the stage. Stage-directions specify the movement of lighting over different parts of the stage to indicate fragments of a reality made of various times and places: 'Un peu comme si le spectateur, muni d'une télécommande, zappait face à l'espace du jeu' ['As though the spectator is zapping the playing space with a channel-changer'.]

Vinaver articulates and mobilises the anxieties of audiences caught in the sticky, quivering webs of contemporary life, which become substantial matter for analysis through the language of his drama. As the examining magistrate and would-be orchestrator of the action in *L'Émission de télévision* comments: 'En cinq jours, j'ai vu des situations basculer / Je travaille une matière vive' ['I've seen situations turn upside down in five days; I work on living material']. Koltès, in contrast, again in the Notes to *Roberto Zucco*, rejoices in the capacity of theatre to refuse the weight of the so-called real. For him, like Genet, theatre is the only place that does not claim to be real life. Rather, 'C'est comme le lieu ou l'on se poserait le problème: ceci n'est pas la vraie vie, comment faire pour s'échapper d'ici?' ['It's the place where you can pose the problem: this isn't real life, how do we get out of here?'].

Koltès's plays give glimpses of the possibility of other realities, admittedly inaccessible, but whose evocation briefly lifts the darkness of the prisonhouse. *Combat de nègre et de chiens* (1983), set in colonised Africa, evokes the tantalising world of the enslaved black that itself defies definition but defines and denounces the limited horizons of its brutal and impotent white masters. (There is always, notes Koltés, a black lurking at the edge of his dramas—an intimation, we should understand, of an Otherness which is never the reassuring reflection that the gazer in the mirror thinks he can see.) In these and subsequent playful exercises in moral and political paradox (*Quai ouest*, 1986; *Dans la solitude des champs de coton*, 1987), Koltès's representative character is not the magistrate but the criminal, the mad murderer-hero Roberto Zucco, climbing onto the prison roof, slipping past the guards, demonstrating and creating a new logic of existence, seductive and liberating. Against playwrights who explore the 'Why?' of a narrative, its rationale, Koltès argues for the importance of simply showing the 'How?', taking an empty space, setting in it an unexpected collocation of characters, and seeing what develops.

The result is a concept of theatre which is in every sense play with the logic of language. The dialogue is a comic match for Molière's, simultaneously pastiche and parody, catching with a discreetly unifying hint of lyrical movement the precise inflections and distinctive styles of individuals who are chiefly performers of social functions (sons and mothers, big brothers and little sisters, prisoners and guards, slaves and masters). But alongside the fun is a distinct sense of awe at the ability of language to model the constraints of time and space, and this, increasingly, was what Koltès tried to stage. Out of his own dramatic experience he reinvented the classical theatre of speech and presence:

> [J]'ai découvert la règle des trois unités, qui n'a rien d'arbitraire, même si on a le droit aujourd'hui de l'appliquer autrement. En tous les cas, c'est bien la prise en compte du temps et de l'espace qui est la grande qualité du théâtre. Le cinéma et le roman voyagent, le théâtre pèse de tout notre poids sur le sol.
>
> [I have discovered the rule of the three unities, which is by no means arbitrary, though we are entitled nowadays to apply it in different ways. In any event, the distinctive feature of theatre is the account it takes of time and space. Cinema and novel can go travelling; theatre stands us full square on the ground.]
>
> (Notes to *Roberto Zucco*)

Notes

1. This was only fully realised in the 1950s with the publication of his unfinished novel *Jean Santeuil* and his critical work *Contre Sainte-Beuve*. For full details see the 4-volume Pléiade edition of *À la recherche du temps perdu*, ed. Jean-Yves Tadié (Paris: Gallimard, 1987-9).

2. He translated *The Bible of Amiens* (1904) and *Sesame and Lilies* (1906). His collected *Pastiches et mélanges* were published in 1919.

3. See Jean-Yves Tadié, *Proust et le roman* (Paris: Presses Universitaires de France, 1971); Jean-Pierre Richard, *Proust et le monde sensible* (Paris: Éditions du Seuil, 1974); Maya Slater, *Humour in the Works of Proust* (Oxford: Oxford University Press, 1979); J. M. Cocking, *Proust* (Cambridge: Cambridge Univer-

sity Press, 1982); Leighton Hodson (ed.), *Marcel Proust. The Critical Heritage* (London and New York: Routledge, 1989); Julia Kristeva, *Le Temps sensible. Proust et l'expérience littéraire* (Paris: Gallimard, 1994); Michael Sprinkler, *History and Ideology in Proust: 'A la recherche du temps perdu' and the Third French Republic* (Cambridge: Cambridge University Press, 1994).

4. See William W. Holdheim, *Theory and Practice of the Novel. A Study on André Gide* (Geneva: Droz, 1968); David H. Walker, *André Gide* (London: Macmillan, 1990).

5. See Paul Valéry, *Œuvres,* ed. Jean Hytier, 2 vols (Paris: Gallimard, Bibliothèque de la Pléiade, 1960), vol. I, pp. 988-1014.

6. See Maurice Rieuneau, *Guerre et révolution dans le roman français 1919-1939* (Paris: Klincksieck, 1974); Frank Field, *Three French Writers and the Great War* (Cambridge: Cambridge University Press, 1975); Holger Klein (ed.), *The First World War in Fiction* (London: Macmillan, 1976); John Cruickshank, *Variations on Catastrophe: Some French Responses to the Great War* (Oxford: Clarendon Press, 1982); Jean Relinger, *Henri Barbusse: écrivain combattant* (Paris: Presses Universitaires de France, 1994).

7. See John Flower, *Literature and the Left in France* (London: Methuen, 1985).

8. See E. Tonnet-Lacroix, *Après-guerre et sensibilités littéraires (1919-1924)* (Paris: Publications de la Sorbonne, 1991).

9. On Giraudoux and the poetic novel see 'L'Âge du roman poétique (1920-1930)', in Michel Raimond, *La Crise du roman* (Paris: José Corti, 1967), pp. 224-43. On Ramuz see David G. Bevan, *The Art and Poetry of Charles-Ferdinand Ramuz* (New York: Oleander Press, 1977). On Giono see Pierre Citron, *Giono, 1895-1970* (Paris: Éditions du Seuil, 1990).

10. See Calogero Giardina, *L'Imaginaire dans les romans de Raymond Radiguet* (Paris: Didier, 1991).

11. See Nicholas Hewitt, *The Golden Age of Louis-Ferdinand Céline* (Leamington Spa, Hamburg, New York: Berg, 1987); Ian Noble, *Language and Narration in Céline's Writings* (London: Macmillan, 1987).

12. See Robert Soucy, *Fascist Intellectual: Drieu la Rochelle* (Berkeley and Los Angeles: University of California Press, 1979); Marie Balvet, *Itinéraire d'un intellectuel vers le fascisme: Drieu la Rochelle* (Paris: Presses Universitaires de France, 1984); Rima Drell Reck, *Drieu la Rochelle and the Picture Gallery Novel: French Modernism in the Inter-War Years* (Baton Rouge: Louisiana State University Press, 1990).

13. See Camus's preface to the two-volume Pléiade edition of Martin du Gard's complete works (Paris: Gallimard, 1955), vol. I, pp. ix-xxxi.

14. See Olivier Rony, *Jules Romains ou l'appel au monde* (Paris: Laffont, 1992).

15. See Alan Rose, *Surrealism and Communism. The Early Years* (New York: Peter Lang, 1991).

16. See Roger Cardinal, *Breton: 'Nadja'* (London: Grant and Cutler, 1986).

17. See Jacqueline Lévi-Valensi, *Aragon romancier* (Paris: SEDES, 1989).

18. See W. D. Redfern, *Paul Nizan: Committed Literature in a Conspiratorial World* (Princeton: Princeton University Press, 1972); Bernard Alluin and Jacques Deguy (eds), *Paul Nizan écrivain* (Lille: Presses Universitaires de Lille, 1988); Michael Scriven, *Paul Nizan: Communist Novelist* (London: Macmillan, 1988).

19. See P. M. Cryle, *The Thematics of Commitment* (Princeton: Princeton University Press, 1985), ch. VI, pp. 218-41.

20. See Susan R. Suleiman, *Authoritarian Fictions. The Ideological Novel as a Literary Genre* (New York: Columbia University Press, 1983).

21. See J. E. Flower, *Writers and Politics in Modern France* (London: Hodder and Stoughton, 1977); Mary Jean Green, *Fiction in the Historical Present: French Writers and the Thirties* (Hanover and London: University Press of New England, 1986); Alice Yager Kaplan, *Reproductions of Banality: Fascism, Literature and French Intellectual Life* (Minneapolis: University of Minnesota Press, 1986); Geraldi Leroy and Anne Roche, *Les Écrivains et le Front Populaire* (Paris: Presses de la Fondation Nationale des Sciences Politiques, 1986); Nicholas Hewitt, *'Les Maladies du Siècle': The Image of Malaise in French Fiction and Thought in the Inter-War Years* (Hull: Hull University Press, 1988).

22. See Cecil Jenkins, *André Malraux* (Boston: Twayne, 1972); Thomas Jefferson Kline, *André Malraux and the Metamorphosis of Death* (New York and London: Columbia University Press, 1973); Robert S. Thornberry, *André Malraux et l'Espagne* (Geneva: Droz, 1977); Barrie Cadwallader, *Crisis of the European Mind: A Study of André Malraux and Drieu la Rochelle* (Cardiff: University of Wales Press, 1981); David G. Bevan (ed.), *Via Malraux: Essays by Walter Langlois* (Wolfville: The Malraux Society, 1986); Geoffrey T. Harris, *André Malraux: A Re-evaluation* (London: Macmillan, 1995).

23. See Malcolm Scott, *Mauriac: The Politics of a Novelist* (Edinburgh: Scottish Academic Press, 1980) and *The Struggle for the Soul of the French Novel: French Catholic and Realist Novelists 1850-1970* (London: Macmillan, 1989); John E. Flower and Bernard C. Swift (eds), *François Mauriac: Visions and Reappraisals* (Oxford, New York, Munich: Berg, 1989); *François Mauriac et les romanciers de l'inquiétude de 1914 à 1945* (Paris: Grasset, 1991).

24. See Gerda Blumenthal, *The Poetic Imagination of Georges Bernanos* (Baltimore: Johns Hopkins University Press, 1965); J. E. Flower, *Bernanos: 'Journal d'un curé de campagne'* (London: Edward Arnold, 1970); Colin W. Nettlebeck, *Les Personnages de Bernanos romancier* (Paris: Minard, 1970).

25. See Paul Reed, *Sartre: 'La Nausée'* (London: Grant and Cutler, 1987); Jean Deguy, *'La Nausée' de Jean-Paul Sartre* (Paris: Gallimard (Foliothèque 28), 1992).

26. See Anthony Cheal Pugh (ed.), *France 1940: Literary and Historical Reaction to Defeat* (Durham: University of Durham, 1991).

27. See Frederick J. Harris, *Encounters with Darkness: French and German Writers on World War II* (Oxford: Oxford University Press, 1983); Margaret Atack, *Literature and the French Resistance: Cultural Politics and Narrative Forms, 1940-1950* (Manchester: Manchester University Press, 1989). On the liberation see *French Cultural Studies*, V, 15 (October 1994), pp. 219-300 (special issue on 'Culture and the Liberation'); H. R. Kedward and Nancy Wood (eds), *The Liberation of France: Image and Event* (New York and Oxford: Berg, 1995).

28. See Jacques Debû-Bridel, *Les Éditions de Minuit. Historique et Bibliographie* (Paris: Éditions de Minuit, 1954).

29. See William Kidd, *Vercors: 'Le Silence de la mer' et autres récits* (Glasgow: University of Glasgow, 1991); James W. Brown and Lawrence D. Stokes (eds), *'The Silence of the Sea'/'Le Silence de la mer': A Novel of French Resistance during the Second World War by 'Vercors'* (New York and Oxford: Berg, 1992).

30. See S. Beynon John, *Saint-Exupéry: 'Vol de nuit' and 'Terre des hommes'* (London: Grant and Cutler, 1990).

31. See J. E. Flower, *Roger Vailland: The Man and His Masks* (London: Hodder and Stoughton, 1975).

32. See Christina Howells, *Sartre's Theory of Literature* (London: Modern Humanities Research Association, 1979); Mark Poster, *Existential Marxism in Post-War France* (Princeton: Princeton University Press, 1975); Rhiannon Goldthorpe, *Sartre: Literature and Theory* (Cambridge: Cambridge University Press, 1984); Charles G. Hill, *Jean-Paul Sartre: Freedom and Commitment* (New York: Peter Lang, 1992); Christina Howells (ed.), *The Cambridge Companion to Sartre* (Cambridge: Cambridge University Press, 1992); Andrew Dobson, *Jean-Paul Sartre and the Politics of Reason: A Theory of History* (Cambridge: Cambridge University Press, 1993).

33. See John Cruickshank, *Albert Camus and the Literature of Revolt* (Oxford: Oxford University Press, 1959); Bruce Pratt, *L'Évangile selon Albert Camus* (Paris: José Corti, 1980); Susan Tarrow, *Exile from the Kingdom: A Political Re-reading of Albert Camus* (University of Alabama Press, 1985); Philip Thody, *Albert Camus* (London: Macmillan, 1989); J. C. Isaac, *Arendt, Camus and Modern Rebellion* (New Haven and London: Yale University Press, 1992); J. McBridge, *Albert Camus: Philosopher and Littérateur* (New York: St Martin's Press, 1992); Jean Guérin, *Albert Camus: portrait de l'artiste en citoyen* (Paris: F. Bourin, 1993); Ray Davison (ed.), *L'Étranger* (London: Methuen, 1988); Adèle King (ed.), *Camus's 'L'Étranger': Fifty Years On* (London: Macmillan, 1992); E. J. Hughes, *Camus; 'Le Premier homme', 'La Peste'* (Glasgow: University of Glasgow French and German Publications, 1995).

34. See J. E. Flower, *Pierre Courtade: The Making of a Party Scribe* (New York and Oxford: Berg, 1995).

35. See Nicholas Hewitt, *Literature and the Right in Post-War France: The Story of the 'Hussards'* (New York and Oxford: Berg, 1996); Christopher Lloyd, *Aymé: 'Uranus'/'La Tête des autres'* (Glasgow: University of Glasgow French and German Publications, 1992).

36. See Deirdre Bair, *Samuel Beckett: A Biography* (London: Vintage, 1990); Leslie Hill, *Beckett's Fiction: In Different Words* (Cambridge: Cambridge University Press, 1990); David Watson, *Paradox and Desire in Samuel Beckett's Fiction* (London: Macmillan, 1991).

37. On the *nouveau roman,* see the important collections of essays by Alain Robbe-Grillet, *Pour un nouveau roman* (Paris: Gallimard (Coll. Idées), 1963); Nathalie Sarraute, *L'Ère du soupçon* (Paris: Gallimard (Coll. Idées), 1964); Michel Butor, *Répertoire,* 5 vols (Paris: Éditions de Minuit, 1960-75). See also Jean Ricardou, *Problèmes du nouveau roman* (Paris: Éditions du Seuil, 1967) and *Le Nouveau Roman* (Paris: Éditions du Seuil, 1973); *Nouveau Roman: hier, aujourd'hui,* 2 vols (Paris: UGE (Colloque de Cérisy), 1972); Stephen Heath, *The Nouveau Roman* (London: Elek, 1972); Ann Jefferson, *The Nouveau Roman and the Poetics of Fiction* (Cambridge: Cambridge University Press, 1980); Celia Britton, *The Nouveau Roman: Fiction, Theory, Politics* (London: Macmillan, 1992).

38. See John Fletcher, *Alain Robbe-Grillet* (London: Methuen, 1983); Raylene L. Ramsay, *Robbe-Grillet and Modernity: Science, Sexuality, and Subversion* (Gainsville, Tallahassee, Tampa: University Press of Florida, 1992).

39. See Elf Jongeneel, *Michel Butor et le pacte romanesque* (Paris: José Corti, 1988); Jean Duffy, *Butor: 'La Modification'* (London: Grant and Cutler, 1990).

40. See Valerie Minogue, *Nathalie Sarraute and the War of the Words* (Edinburgh: Edinburgh University Press,

1981); Sheila M. Bell, *Nathalie Sarraute and the Feminist Reader* (London and Toronto: Associated University Press, 1993).

41. See Marcelle Marini, *Territoires du féminin: avec Marguerite Duras* (Paris: Éditions de Minuit, 1977); Micheline Tison-Braun, *Marguerite Duras* (Amsterdam: Rodopi, 1985); Sharon Willis, *Marguerite Duras: Writing on the Body* (Illinois: University of Illinois Press, 1987); Leslie Hill, *Apocalyptic Desires* (London: Routledge 1993); David Coward, 'Marguerite Duras', in Michael Tilby (ed.), *Beyond the Nouveau Roman* (London and New York: Berg, 1990), pp. 39-63. On *Moderato cantabile* see David Coward, *Duras: 'Moderato cantabile'* (London: Grant and Cutler, 1981).

42. See Renate Günther, *Duras: 'Le Ravissement de Lol V. Stein' and 'L'Amant'* (London: Grant and Cutler, 1993).

43. See *Claude Simon: analyse, théorie* (Paris: UGE (Colloque de Cérisy), 1975); Celia Britton (ed.), *Claude Simon* (London and New York: Longman, 1993); Mary Orr, *Claude Simon: The Intertextual Dimension* (Glasgow: University of Glasgow French and German Publications, 1993); Alastair Duncan, *Claude Simon: Adventures in Words* (Manchester: Manchester University Press, 1994).

44. See Anthony Cheal Pugh, *Simon: 'Histoire'* (London: Grant and Cutler, 1982).

45. See Robert M. Henkels, *Robert Pinget: The Novel as Quest* (Alabama: University of Alabama Press, 1979).

46. On Ollier see the *Review of Contemporary Fiction*, 8 (Summer 1988).

47. See Susan Hayward and Ginette Vincendeau (eds), *French Film: Texts and Contexts* (London: Routledge, 1990); Jill Forbes, *The Cinema in France: After the New Wave* (London: British Film Institute/Macmillan, 1992).

48. See Jacques Bens (ed.), *Oulipo, 1960-1980* (Paris: Christian Bourgeois, 1981); Warren F. Motte (ed.), *Oulipo: A Primer of Potential Literature* (Lincoln: University of Nebraska Press, 1986). See also Claude Simonnet, *Queneau déchiffré* (Paris: Julliard, 1962); C. Sanders, *Raymond Queneau* (Amsterdam and Atlanta: Rodopi, 1994). On *Zazie dans le métro* see Walter Redfern, *Queneau: 'Zazie dans le métro'* (London: Grant and Cutler, 1980); Michel Bigot, *'Zazie dans le métro' de Raymond Queneau* (Paris: Gallimard (Foliothèque, 34), 1994).

49. See D. Bellos, 'Literary Quotations in Perec's *La Vie mode d'emploi*', *French Studies*, LXI, 2 (April 1987), pp. 180-94 (p. 186). See also Warren F. Motte, *The Poetics of Experiment: A Study of the Work of Georges Perec* (Lexington, Kentucky: French Forum, 1984); Claude Burgelin, *Georges Perec* (Paris: Éditions du Seuil, 1988); David Bellos, *Georges Perec: A Life in Words* (London: Harvill Press, 1995).

50. See Serge Koster, *Tournier* (Paris: Veyrier, 1985); Arlette Bouloumié, *Michel Tournier: le roman mythologique* (Paris: José Corti, 1988); Colin Davis, *Michel Tournier: Philosophy and Fiction* (Oxford: Clarendon Press, 1988); David Gascoigne, *Michel Tournier* (New York and Oxford: Berg, 1996).

51. See Germaine Brée, *Le Monde fabuleux de J. M. G. Le Clézio* (Amsterdam: Rodopi, 1990); Jean Ominus, *Pour lire Le Clézio* (Paris: Presses Universitaires de France, 1994).

52. See David Gascoigne, 'Patrick Grainville', in Tilby (ed.), *Beyond the Nouveau Roman,* pp. 229-55.

53. See Roland Barthes, *Sollers écrivain* (Paris: Éditions du Seuil, 1979); Leslie Hill, 'Philippe Sollers and *Tel Quel*', in Tilby (ed.), *Beyond the Nouveau Roman,* pp. 100-22; Edmund J. Smyth (ed.), *Postmodernism and Contemporary Fiction* (London: Batsford, 1991); Malcolm Pollard, *The Novels of Philippe Sollers: Narrative and the Visual* (Amsterdam and Atlanta: Rodopi, 1994).

54. See Colin W. Nettlebeck, 'Getting the Story Right: Narratives of World War II in Post-1968 France', *Journal of European Studies* 15 (1985), pp. 77-116; Alan Morris, *Collaboration and Resistance Reviewed: Writers and the 'Mode Rétro' in Post-Gaullist France* (New York and Oxford: Berg, 1992).

55. See Colin W. Nettlebeck and Penelope Ann Hueston, *Patrick Modiano: pièce d'identité* (Paris: Minard, 1986); Alan Morris, *Patrick Modiano* (New York and Oxford: Berg, 1996).

56. See Patrick Combes, *La littérature et le mouvement de Mai* (Paris: Éditions de Minuit, 1984); Keith Reader, *The May 1968 Events in France: Reproductions and Interpretations* (London: Macmillan, 1993).

57. See Jean-Claude Lebrun and Claude Prévost, *Nouveaux Territoires romanesques* (Paris: Messidor Éditions Sociales, 1990); Colin W. Nettlebeck, 'The "Post-Literary" Novel: Echenoz, Pennac and Company', *French Cultural Studies,* V, 14 (June 1994), pp. 113-38.

58. See Christopher Robinson, *Scandal in the Ink: Male and Female Homosexuality in Twentieth-Century French Literature* (London: Cassell, 1995).

59. See Stephen Health, 'Night Books', in David Hollier (ed.), *A New History of French Literature* (Cambridge, Mass. and London: Harvard University Press, 1989), pp. 1054-60; and Nettlebeck, 'The "Post-Literary" Novel', pp. 117-18.

60. See Peter Broome and Graham Chesters, *An Anthology of Modern French Poetry, 1850-1950* (Cambridge: Cambridge University Press, 1976) and *The Appreciation of Modern French Poetry, 1850-1950* (Cambridge: Cambridge University Press, 1976).

61. See Anne Hyde Greet, *Apollinaire et le livre du peintre* (Paris: Minard, 1977); Margareth Wijk, *Guillaume Apollinaire et l'Esprit Nouveau* (Lund: W.K. Geerup, 1982): Antoine Fongaro, *Apollinaire poète: exégèses et discussions 1957-1987* (Toulouse: Presses Universitaires du Mirail-Toulouse, 1988).

62. See Claude Debon, *Guillaume Apollinaire après 'Alcools'. I: 'Calligrammes', le poète et la guerre* (Paris: Minard, 1981); Willard Bohn, *Apollinaire, Visual Poetry, and Art Criticism* (Lewisberg: Bucknell University Press: London and Toronto: Associated University Presses, 1993).

63. See Monique Chefdor, *Blaise Cendrars* (Boston: Twayne, 1980).

64. Pierre Reverdy, *En vrac* (Monaco: Éditions du Rocher, 1956), p. 139. See Clive Scott, *Reading the Rhythm: The Poetics of French Verse, 1910-1930* (Oxford: Clarendon Press, 1993).

65. See René Plantier, *L'Univers poétique de Max Jacob* (Paris: Klincksieck 1963); Gerald Kamber, *Max Jacob and the Poetics of Cubism* (Baltimore and London: The Johns Hopkins Press, 1971).

66. See Mary Ann Caws, *La Main de Pierre Reverdy* (Geneva: Droz, 1979); Michel Collot, *Horizon de Reverdy* (Paris: Publications de l'École Normale Supérieure, 1981); Andrew Rothwell, *Textual Spaces: The Poetry of Pierre Reverdy* (Amsterdam: Rodopi, 1989); 'Pierre Reverdy 1889-1989', *Nottingham French Studies*, 28, 2 (Autumn 1989).

67. See Christine M. Crow, *Paul Valéry: Consciousness and Nature* (Cambridge: Cambridge University Press, 1972), and *Paul Valéry and the Poetry of Voice* (Cambridge: Cambridge University Press, 1982); Brian Stimpson, *Paul Valéry and Music* (Cambridge: Cambridge University Press, 1984).

68. See Sarane Alexandrian, *Le Surréalisme et le rêve* (Paris: Gallimard, 1974); J. H. Matthews, *The Imagery of Surrealism* (Syracuse: Syracuse University Press, 1977); Marcel Jean, *Autobiographie du surréalisme* (Paris: Éditions du Seuil, 1978); Robert Stuart Short, *Dada and Surrealism* (London: Octopus Books, 1980); Keith Aspley, *André Breton the Poet* (Glasgow: University of Glasgow French and German Publications, 1989); Mark Polizotti, *Revolution of the Mind: The Life of André Breton* (London: Bloomsbury, 1995).

69. Lautréamont, *Les Chants de Maldoror*, in *Lautréamont: Germain Nouveau, Œuvres complètes*, ed. Pierre-Olivier Walzer (Paris: Gallimard, Bibliothèque de la Pléiade, 1970), p. 225.

70. See Jean Yves Debreuille, *Éluard ou le pouvoir du mot* (Paris: Nizet, 1977); Jean-Charles Gateau, *Paul Éluard et la peinture surréaliste* (Geneva: Droz, 1982); and *Paul Éluard, le frère voyant* (Laffont, 1988); Clive Scott (ed.), *Anthologie Éluard* (London: Methuen Educational, 1983).

71. On Péret, see Jean-Michel Goutier, *Bejamin Péret* (Paris: Veyrier, 1982). On Char, see Jean-Claude Mathieu, *La Poésie de René Char, ou Le Sel de la Splendeur*, vol. I: *Traversée du surréalisme*; vol. II: *Poésie et résistance* (Paris: José Corti, 1984-5); Michael Bishop, *René Char, les dernières années* (Amsterdam: Rodopi, 1990); Eric Marty, *René Char* (Paris: Éditions du Seuil, 1990).

72. See Roger Little, *Saint-John Perse* (London: Athlone Press, 1973); Marie-Laure Ryan, *Rituel et poésie: une lecture de Saint-John Perse* (Berne: Peter Lang, 1977); Mireille Sacotte, *Saint-John Perse* (Paris: Pierre Belfond, 1991).

73. See J. A. Hiddleston, *L'Univers de Jules Supervielle* (Paris: José Corti, 1965); Robert Vivier, *Lire Supervielle* (Paris: José Corti, 1971); Paul Villaneix, *Le Hors-venu, ou le personnage poétique de Supervielle* (Paris: Klincksieck, 1972); Yves-Alain Favre, *Supervielle: la Rêverie et le chant dans 'Gravitations'* (Paris: Nizet, 1981).

74. See Malcolm Bowie, *Henri Michaux: A Study of his Literary Works* (Oxford: Clarendon Press, 1973); Jean-Pierre Martin, *Henri Michaux: Écritures de soi. Expatriations* (Paris: José Corti, 1994).

75. See Ian Higgins (ed.), *Le Parti pris des choses* (London: Athlone Press, 1979) and *Francis Ponge* (London: Athlone Press, 1979); Jean Pierrot, *Francis Ponge* (Paris: José Corti, 1993).

76. See Pierre Seghers (ed.), *La Résistance et ses poètes*, 2 vols (Paris: Marabout, 1978); Jean Gaucheron, *La Poésie, la Résistance* (Paris: Les Éditeurs français réunis, 1979); Ian Higgins (ed.), *Anthology of Second World War French Poetry* (London: Methuen, 1982).

77. Higgins, *Anthology of Second World War French Poetry*, p. 27.

78. Ibid., pp. 19-24.

79. See Maxwell Adereth, *Aragon: The Resistance Poems* (London: Grant and Cutler, 1985).

80. On Emmanuel, see Alain Bosquet, *Pierre Emmanuel* (Paris: Seghers, 1959). On the importance of Pierre Jean Jouve for Emmanuel, see Margaret M. Callander, *The Poetry of Pierre Jean Jouve* (Manchester: Manchester University Press, 1965).

81. See Ian Higgins, 'Jean Tardieu's Oradour', *French Studies*, XLVIII, 4 (October 1994), pp. 425-38.

82. See the Higgins anthology of Second World War French poetry for examples of all of the types of reference discussed here.

83. See Claude Marie Beaujeu, *L'Alexandrin dans le 'Crève-cœur' d'Aragon* (Paris: Presses de l'Université de Paris-Sorbonne, 1993); Adareth, *Aragon: The Resistance Poems*, pp. 53-70; and Higgins, *Anthology of Second World War French Poetry*, pp. 31-44.

84. On post-war French poetry, see C. A. Hackett, *New French Poetry. An Anthology* (Oxford: Basil Blackwell, 1973); Michael Bishop, *The Contemporary Poetry of France: Eight Studies* (Amsterdam: Rodopi, 1985); Michel Baude and Jeannine Baude (eds), *Poésie et spiritualité en France depuis 1950* (Paris: Klincksieck, 1988); Marie-Claire Bancquart, *Poésie 1945-1960, les mots, la voix* (Paris: Presses de l'Université de Paris-Sorbonne, 1989); Richard Stamelman, *Lost Beyond Telling: Representations of Death and Absence in Modern French Poetry* (Ithaca and London: Cornell University Press, 1990); Martin Sorrell (ed. and trans.), *Modern French Poetry: A Bilingual Anthology* (London: Forest Books, 1992). On Bonnefoy, see John T. Naughton, *The Poetics of Yves Bonnefoy* (Chicago and London: University of Chicago Press, 1984); Daniel Leuwers, *Yves Bonnefoy* (Amsterdam: Rodopi, 1988).

85. See Marie-Claire Dumas (ed.), *La Poésie de Philippe Jaccottet* (Paris: Honoré Champion, 1986).

86. On Deguy, see Michael Bishop, *Michel Deguy* (Amsterdam: Rodopi, 1988); Jean Moussaron and Jacques Derrida, *La Poésie comme avenir. Essai sur l'œuvre de M. Deguy* (Grenoble: Syllabe, 1992). On Dupin, see Maryann De Julio, *Rhetorical Landscapes: The Poetry and Art Criticism of Jacques Dupin* (Lexington, Kentucky: French Forum, 1992); E. Loze, *Approaches de Jacques Dupin* (Amsterdam: Rodopi, 1993). On Guillevic, see Gavin Bowd, *Guillevic, sauvage de la modernité* (Glasgow: Glasgow University French and German Publications, 1993); Michael Brophy, *Eugène Guillevic* (Amsterdam: Rodopi, 1993). On recent women's poetry, see Martin Sorrell (ed. and trans.), *Elles. A Bilingual Anthology of Modern French Poetry by Women* (Exeter: Exeter University Press, 1995).

87. For a history of the development of film in France, see Susan Hayward, *French National Cinema* (London and New York: Routledge, 1993).

88. Two invaluable sources for this section have been David Bradby, *Modern French Drama 1940-1990* (Cambridge: Cambridge University Press, rev. edn 1991), with its thorough accounts of the material practices of contemporary French theatre and the work of key directors and details of the staging of individual plays; and David Bradby and David Williams, *Directors' Theatre* (London: Macmillan, 1988). See also Geneviève Serreau, *Histoire du 'nouveau théâtre'* (Paris: Éditions Gallimard, 1966); John Fletcher (ed.), *Forces in Modern French Drama* (London: University of London Press, 1972); Bettina L. Knapp, *French Theatre, 1918-39* (London: Macmillan, 1985); Jean Duvigneaud and Jean Lagoutte, *Le Théâtre contemporain: culture et contre-culture* (Paris: Librairie Larousse, 1974); Henri Béhar, *Le Théâtre dada et surréaliste* (Paris: Éditions Gallimard, 1979).

89. Keir Elam, *The Semiotics of Theatre and Drama* (London and New York: Methuen, 1980).

90. A difficult but rewarding consideration of issues appears in Jacques Derrida's essay on Antonin Artaud, 'La Parole Soufflée', *Tel quel,* no. 20 (Winter 1965), coll. in Jacques Derrida, *Writing and Differance,* trans. Alan Bass (London: Routledge and Kegan Paul, 1978).

91. See Jean-Louis Barrault, *Réflexions sur le théâtre* (Paris: Jacques Vautrain, 1949), *passim,* for Barrault's collaboration with Claudel. See, on Claudel, Jacques Madaule, *Le Drame de Paul Claudel* (Paris: Desclée de Brouwer, 1947); Michel Lioure, *L'Esthétique dramatique de Paul Claudel* (Paris: Armand Colin, 1971). For background see Richard Griffiths, *The Reactionary Revolution: The Catholic Revival in French Literature* (London: Constable, 1966).

92. See Roger Shattuck, *The Banquet Years: Origins of the Avant-Garde in France, 1985 to World War I* (New York: Vintage Books, 1968); Michel Arrivé, *Les Langages de Jarry* (Paris: Klincksieck, 1972); Henri Béhar, *Jarry dramaturge* (Paris: Nizet, 1980).

93. 'Trois conférences prononcées à l'université de Mexico. I: Surréalisme et révolution' (26 February 1936), coll. in Antonin Artaud, *Messages révolutionnaires* (Paris: Éditions Gallimard, 1971). Other pieces by Artaud referred to are collected in *Le Théâtre et son double* (1938).

94. See Sartre's theoretical writings, coll. in Jean-Paul Sartre, *Un théâtre de situations,* ed. Michel Contat and Michel Rybalka (Paris: Gallimard, 1973); also Robert Lorris, *Sartre dramaturge* (Paris: Nizet, 1975). See Camus's theoretical writings, coll. in Albert Camus, *Théâtre, récits, nouvelles,* ed. Roger Quilliot (Paris: Gallimard, 1962); also Ilona Coombs, *Camus, homme de théâtre* (Paris: Nizet, 1968); Edward Freeman, *The Theatre of Albert Camus: A Critical Study* (London: Methuen, 1971).

95. Georges Bataille, 'Notes: La question coloniale. D'un caractère sacré des criminels (Genet)', *Critique* no. 35 (April 1949), pp. 365-71 and 371-3; rpt. in *Œuvres complètes XI: Articles I (1944-49)* (Paris: Éditions Gallimard, 1988), p. 469. See, on Genet, Richard N. Coe, *The Vision of Jean Genet* (London: Peter Owen, 1968); Richard C. Webb (ed.), *File on Genet* (London: Methuen Drama, 1992); Edmond White, *Genet* (London: Chatto and Windus, 1993).

96. 'Jean Genet talks to Hubert Fichte', tr. Patrick McCarthy, *The New Review,* IV, 37 (April 1977), pp. 9-21; first published in German, *Die Zeit* (20 February 1976), p. 17.

97. See Dominique Nores (ed.), *Les Critiques de notre temps et Beckett* (Paris: Garnier Frères, 1971); James Knowlson and John Pilling, *Frescoes of the Skull, the Later Prose and Drama of Samuel Beckett* (London: John Calder, 1979); Ruby Cohn, *Just Play: Beckett's Theater* (Princeton: Princeton University Press, 1980); James Acheson and Kateryna Arthur (eds), *Beckett's Later Fiction and Drama* (New York:

St Martin's Press, 1987); Jonathan Kalb, *Beckett in Performance* (Cambridge: Cambridge University Press, 1989); Christopher Ricks, *Beckett's Dying Words* (Oxford: Clarendon Press, 1993); James Knowlson, *Damned to Fame: The Life of Samuel Beckett* (London: Bloomsbury, and New York: Simon and Shuster, 1996).

98. See, on Ionesco, Richard N. Coe, *Ionesco: a Study of his Plays* (London: Methuen, rev. edn 1971); Emmanuel C. Jacquart, *Le Théâtre de dérision: Beckett, Ionesco, Adamov* (Paris: Gallimard, 1974).

99. See Philippe Madral, *Le Théâtre hors les murs* (Paris: Éditions du Seuil, 1969); Judith Graves Miller, *Theater and Revolution in France since 1968* (Lexington: French Forum, 1977).

100. See Bradby and Williams, *Directors' Theatre*; and Ruby Cohn, 'Ariane Mnouchkine: Playwright of a Collective', in Enoch Brater (ed.), *Feminine Focus: The New Women Playwrights* (New York and Oxford: Oxford University Press, 1989), pp. 53-63.

101. See essays in Brater (ed.), *Feminine Focus,* especially Sue-Ellen Case, 'From Split Subject to Split Britches'; Elin Diamond, 'Benmussa's Adaptations: Unauthorized Texts from Elsewhere'; Jeannette Laillou Savona, 'In Search of a Feminist Theater: *Portrait of Dora*'; and Sharon A. Willis, 'Staging Sexual Difference: Reading, Recitation and Repetition in Duras's *Malady of Death*'. Also see Celita Lamar, *Our Voices, Ourselves: Women Writing for the French Theatre* (New York: Peter Lang, 1991).

102. On Cixous, see also Morag Schiach, 'Staging History', Chapter 4 in *Hélène Cixous: A Politics of Writing* (London and New York: Routledge, 1991); Jennifer Birkett, 'The Limits of Language: The Theatre of Hélène Cixous', in John Dunkley and Bill Kirton (eds), *Voices in the Air: French Dramatists and the Resource of Language* (Glasgow: University of Glasgow French and German Publications, 1992).

103. A good introduction to Vinaver and Koltès is the anthology in English, David Bradby and Claude Schumacher (eds), *New French Plays* (London: Methuen Drama, 1989). On Vinaver, see Anne Ubersfeld, *Vinaver dramaturge* (Paris: Librairie théâtrale, 1989).

FRENCH THEATER

David Bradby (essay date 1984)

SOURCE: Bradby, David. "Introduction: The Inter-War Years." In *Modern French Drama: 1940-1980,* pp. 1-15. Cambridge, England: Cambridge University Press, 1984.

[*In the following introduction to* Modern French Drama: 1940-1980, *Bradby presents a brief overview of the state of French theater following World War I.*]

When the second war broke out in Europe, the French theatre had come to the end of an era. The inter-war period had witnessed the triumph of literary drama and poetic production style; Jouvet, Dullin and other outstanding directors had achieved world-wide fame with glittering productions of plays by a new school of playwrights led by Giraudoux, Cocteau, Salacrou. By the end of the thirties, this literary and poetic theatre was firmly established in the public eye as the distinctive French contribution to modern drama. It received the official seal of approval when Jacques Copeau, the man who was considered to be its chief architect, was appointed director of the Comédie Française in 1940.

Four decades earlier, at the time of *la belle époque,* Copeau had set himself the task of purifying the decadent elements of the French stage. His career in the theatre started, not as a director, but as an author and critic. In the early years of the century he published a series of theatre reviews in which he developed a searing criticism of the state of Parisian theatre. The terms of his attack were more moral than artistic: he claimed that the modern theatre was guilty of cunningly corrupting the public's tastes in order that they might more easily be satisfied. He accused the actors of vanity, the theatre managers of rapacity, and claimed that 'fine craftsmanship' and 'aesthetic dignity' were dead (see Borgal, 1960: 29-42). He was offended by superficial bedroom farces, and by lavish productions in which sensational stage effects were sought as ends in themselves.

In place of this corruption, he wanted to see a theatre that was simple but inventive, one in which the play and its performance became an integrated whole, and in which the audience's attention would be directed towards the playwright's ideas rather than towards the effects displayed by actor or designer. He could see no evidence of good playwriting among his contemporaries, and claimed that the only way to make a new beginning was to return to Molière and Shakespeare. He valued these playwrights, not only for the quality of their ideas, but also for their ability to write plays that found natural expression in performance, plays that did not call for extraneous spectacular effects: 'with them there is no intermediary between poetic creation and its true theatrical realisation. Dramatic invention and stage production are merely the two phases of a single action' (Borgal, 1963: 18).

In 1913 Copeau founded the Théâtre du Vieux-Colombier in the student quarter of Paris, far from the fashionable boulevard theatres, where he hoped to produce a repertoire of plays combining revivals of the classics and good plays of the previous decades as well as occasional new plays of quality. For a theatre that is now considered to have been so influential, the Vieux-Colombier company had a remarkably short and troubled existence. It played for only one season before war broke out, then spent two seasons (1917-19) in America before returning to Paris, where it performed for only four and a half seasons before its final dissolution. Moreover it did little to reveal vigorous new playwrights: the only new play of lasting merit 'discovered' by Copeau was *Le Paquebot Tenacity* by Charles Vildrac (1920). But for Copeau the founding of his theatre school was more important than the success or failure of these professional seasons, since he believed that the profound transformation of the French stage would take a generation. This theatre school flourished alongside the theatre in the early twenties and it followed Copeau to his home in Burgundy when he withdrew from the Vieux-Colombier in 1924.

The training given at the school was based on a quasi-religious search for truth through a mystical trinity of qualities: *le Beau, le Bien* and *le Vrai*. Emphasis was laid on cultivating the complete man, not just the technical faculties, and on training actors to work for the group rather than for themselves. Discipline was harsh, control of the body a major priority. The early stages of training relied solely on physical exercise and cultivation of expressive faculties of the body, with an absolute ban on using words. After he had left Paris, he continued to work along similar lines with a shifting group of followers known for a while as Les Copiaus, later branching out on their own as La Compagnie des Quinze.

One of Copeau's central preoccupations was with the need for the skills of playwright, actor and director to be so closely integrated that they became indistinguishable. Another was the need to develop a new performance vocabulary of modern types similar to the old masks of the Commedia dell'arte. In both these respects, though he himself failed, he anticipated later developments. The Compagnie des Quinze helped to realise the first by taking on André Obey as resident dramatist and working closely with him on a number of plays, the most successful of which was *Noé* (1931). The practice of employing a resident dramatist has become much more common since the war, especially in some of the decentralised companies. The second aim was to be fulfilled, quite literally, by the Théâtre du Soleil in 1975 with their play *L'Age d'or* (see chapter 9). In order to achieve these aims, Copeau believed that the Italianate theatre with boxes, footlights, and trompe-l'oeil scenery must be abandoned in favour of something more like the Elizabethan stage. His architectural restructuring of the stage of the Vieux-Colombier became a model for later directors, actors and designers with similar aims.

During the 1930s Copeau occupied a more marginal position in the French theatre, acknowledged as the originator of a great movement of renewal, but doing relatively little in the way of production work. There were some notable exceptions however, especially two open-air festival productions in Florence of large-scale plays on religious themes. In their attempt to do more than just entertain, and in their use of multiple acting areas, these productions also anticipated the work of the Théâtre du Soleil. Copeau's name was often mentioned during this period, as a likely director of the Comédie Française. When his appointment finally came, it was in 1940 as the replacement for Edouard Bourdet, knocked down by a car in the black-out. Bourdet had been appointed under the Front Populaire to reform the old institution. He had initiated a system of inviting in guest directors (of whom Copeau was one) and survived the fall of the Government that appointed him. But 1940 was the worst possible time for someone with Copeau's reforming zeal to take over that post. He was not prepared to treat the Vichy authorities with tact and only kept the post for a few months.

At the end of the thirties, Copeau's authority was considerable and his reputation high. He was respected by the public for having tried to make long-term changes in the standard of French theatre. He was respected by actors and directors, many of whom he had taught, for having set his standards high and having restored some dignity to the profession. But this did not prevent him from becoming caught, early in 1940, in an uncomfortably contradictory position. As director of the Comédie Française, he was expected to foster the tradition of preserving high culture for the Parisian upper bourgeoisie. But as early as 1924, his rationale for a school had included the necessity of decentralisation, so that the theatre could escape from the destructive influence of Paris. After his short term at the Comédie Française, it was this second aspect of Copeau's work that reaffirmed itself in his publication of *Le Théâtre populaire* (see chapter 2).

Copeau had many disciples, among whom he considered the most important to be Louis Jouvet and Charles Dullin. Both had broken away from the Vieux Colombier at a relatively early date, Jouvet in 1922 and Dullin in 1918. Dullin, in fact, performed for only one season with Copeau, though he afterwards claimed that he had learned more from Copeau in that year than in the whole of his previous career (Borgal, 1963: 106), and like Copeau he set up a school which functioned alongside the theatre. But it was the establishment of the Cartel in 1927 that has rightly been seen as one of the chief factors in prolonging and confirming Copeau's ideas. The Cartel was a loose association between four theatres, run by Jouvet, Dullin, the Pitoëffs and Baty. All four agreed to a common policy which was summed up in a manifesto which appeared in *Entr'Acte,* a review published by Jouvet's theatre. The values expressed in the manifesto are similar to those of Copeau's 1913 manifesto ('Un essai de rénovation théâtrale'): respect for the text, simplicity and truthfulness in staging, the search for poetic impact rather than spectacular effect. Their attitude towards the public was also similar. They asked for intelligent participation, offered lectures and other supplementary events, and insisted on starting punctually. At a time when theatres were not expected to start for at least half an hour after the advertised time, this was quite a bold step and involved Dullin in a prolonged battle with the press when a critic arrived to find the doors closed and the play begun. The four Cartel directors also pledged themselves to publish each others' programmes and so to try to extend the audience that each was building up.

In the late 1930s, Jouvet had built up almost as much prestige as Copeau. He had been a teacher at the Conservatoire since 1934, and had been offered the directorship of the Comédie Française in 1936 (he refused, suggesting that Bourdet be asked to direct, taking on Copeau, Dullin, Baty and himself as guest directors, a solution that was accepted). He was known as the director who had revealed Giraudoux to the theatre-going public and who continued a fruitful collaboration with him, but who also triumphed with classical productions, such as his 1938 *L'Ecole des femmes* and with modern comedies such as Jules Romains' *Knock ou le triomphe de la médecine*. Jouvet had more of the showman and less of the professor in him than Copeau, but he retained from his period with Copeau an emphasis on the coming together of text and performance in a united artistic whole: 'I only discover the meaning of a play through the work of staging: sets, movements, rhythms and diction are all essential elements for me in the discovery, experience and understanding of a play' (Borgal, 1963: 80).

In his partnership with Giraudoux, Jouvet had achieved what Copeau had only dreamed of: a working relationship with a writer such that writing and staging became two parts of the same creative process. Some of the plays produced by this tandem still seem masterpieces of theatrical invention—*Intermezzo*, for example—while others now seem excessively wordy. Jouvet and Giraudoux's biggest success of the 1930s, *La Guerre de Troie n'aura pas lieu* is one of those that now seem wordy. The scenic inventiveness of Jouvet helped to put across plays of the latter kind, where the dramatic action is weak. Jouvet did not regard the lack of action as a serious weakness provided that the literary qualities of the text were sufficient. He always insisted that good drama was, in the first place, good writing. But his idea of good writing included notions of rhythm, poetry, pace etc. He claimed that the theatre's job was not to make its audience understand something but to make them feel it deeply. In *L'Impromptu de Paris* Giraudoux wrote a part for Jouvet in which he explains: 'Luckily the best theatre audience does not respond with its intellect but with its feelings . . . People who insist on understanding a play in the theatre are people with no understanding of theatre' (1959b: 187). For the next generation of writers and directors the example of the collaboration between Giraudoux and Jouvet became an important encouragement.

Another aspect of Jouvet's work was also to be taken as an example by directors in the post-war period: his film career. At a time when there was almost no public subsidy at all for theatres like those of the Cartel, one way to subsidise theatre production was to take on a film role during the summer months when the theatres in Paris are closed. Jouvet, who excelled in comic roles on the stage, had an extraordinarily powerful screen presence. Where his acting style on stage was large, even grotesque, his film style was restrained, muted, with a constant hint of mystery beneath the surface. His face became extremely well known in the late thirties through taking roles in a number of films such as Renoir's *Les Bas-Fonds* (1936) or Carné's *Hôtel du Nord* (1938). His example was followed by several post-war directors for the same reasons, notably Barrault and Dasté.

Dullin, like Jouvet, had a conception of theatre that was not content to mirror reality, but that viewed it as a world apart governed by its own laws, a poetic world in which the life of the imagination took precedence. He claimed to find his models in the Commedia dell'arte and the Japanese theatre, from which he also borrowed some of the techniques fused in his school. An impression of work at the school given by Artaud: 'We act with our deepest hearts, we act with our hands, our feet, all our muscles, and all our limbs. We feel the object, we smell it, we handle it, see it, hear it . . . and all to find there is nothing there, no accessories. The Japanese are our immediate masters, our inspiration, and so is Edgar Poe. It is wonderful!' (cit. Knowles, 1972: 19).

As well as Artaud, Dullin attracted Jean-Louis Barrault, André Barsacq, Roger Blin, Jean Vilar, Maurice Sarrazin, Claude Martin, Alain Cuny, Jean Marchat, Madeleine Robinson, Jean Marais, Marguerite Jamois and many others to his school. He made it possible for Barrault to try out his early experiments in total theatre: *Autour d'une mère* (1935) and *La Faim* (1939). Through this school, and the example of his productions, Dullin influenced a very large number of the young generation of actors, directors and writers. His conception of the theatre was demanding and all-embracing. He saw it as a force for cultural and social regeneration. Not finding many modern plays that matched these ambitions, he produced many versions of plays from the classical repertoire, particularly the Greeks and the Elizabethans, with maximum use of colour, mime, music, and a rich deployment of stage resources. His most famous productions of the period were probably *Volpone* (first produced in 1928) and *Richard III* (1933).

Being interested in a global all-inclusive theatre, he naturally laid some stress on the ancient Greeks, producing two of Aristophanes' plays. Sartre gave some lectures to his school in the early years of the Occupation and *Les Mouches* was a natural choice for production by Dullin. Sartre records that he learnt his craft as a dramatist through watching Dullin rehearse. He would say to the actors: 'ne jouez pas les mots—jouez les situations' (do not act the words—act the situations. Sartre, 1969). Sartre made this his guiding principle as a playwright, as he showed by his constant references to 'un théâtre de situations' (see chapter 3).

Among the modern authors regularly produced by Dullin before the war were Pirandello and Salacrou. Salacrou also showed how much he learnt from Dullin about theatre as a total art form in the prefaces and notes to his plays. These present striking similarities with pronouncements by Sartre at the same time, demonstrating the influence of Dullin on both writers. But something shared even more strongly by all three was the conviction that the theatre could not survive without broadening the social basis of its audience. This was one of Dullin's favourite themes and in 1937 he was commissioned by the Front Populaire government to write a report on the decentralisation of the theatre. The report produced no action at the time, but was influential after the war (see below pp. 14-15).

Georges Pitoëff and his wife, Ludmila, shared with Dullin and Jouvet a belief that theatre is not best suited to the naturalist mode of representing reality. Before coming to Paris, the Pitoëffs had worked for several years in Russia (where the father of Georges had been manager of the Tiflis state theatre), had undergone and rejected the influence of Stanislavsky, and had worked as producers in Geneva for seven years. In the theatre which they directed from 1922-39 they therefore brought to the French audiences many plays by foreign authors, especially Chekhov, Pirandello, Shaw, Schnitzler and Molnar. But their stage style was characterised by simplicity and imaginative qualities closer to the work of Copeau or Jouvet than to the Expressionists in Germany or their contemporaries in post-revolutionary Russia. They held that the production of any given play had to give scenic form to the invisible forces contained in that play. A famous example of this was their setting for Shaw's *Saint Joan* (1925) which stressed the idea of saintliness by using a permanent scenic structure reminiscent of an altarpiece: a central gothic arch with two half arches on either side, and stage groupings that concentrated the audience's attention on the upward thrust, suggesting a constant movement heavenward. The Pitoëff couple also put on a large number of plays by contemporary French authors, including Lenormand, Cocteau, Anouilh and Claudel, but failed to find an author with whom to work on a regular basis as Jouvet did in Giraudoux.

The fourth member of the Cartel was Gaston Baty, whose productions were responsible for bringing the stage techniques of Expressionism to the Parisian theatre. His general tendency was away from the simplicity and dependence on the actor that characterised the other three members of the group and towards complex staging using multiple levels and picturesque settings. Like Craig, he had a life-long interest in puppet theatre and shared with him an ambitious view of the role of the producer. Unlike the other three Cartel members, he was not an actor and this perhaps explains why he paid as much if not more attention to the pictorial elements of staging as he did to the actor. He was particularly remembered for his attack on the excessive verbosity of French theatre, an attack that had something in common with Artaud's later fulminations. His choice of emphasis was expressed as follows: 'Painting, sculpture, the dance, prose, verse, song, music, these are the seven chords stretched side by side on the lyre of drama' (cit. Knowles, 1972: 36).

The work of Copeau and the Cartel has been exhaustively studied by French theatre historians and large claims have been made for it. Undoubtedly, it succeeded in establishing high standards of acting, production and design, during the inter-war period. It also succeeded in broadening the outlook of the French theatre, showing that foreign plays (e.g. Pirandello or Chekhov) and foreign classics (e.g. the Elizabethans) could have a popular appeal and could be made to speak in a direct way to contemporary French audiences. These were lessons not lost on French theatre after the war.

The Cartel directors did not wait for theatre historians; they made large claims for themselves. Dullin wrote that in the renewal of French theatre the directors had come to the rescue of the authors, teaching them the forgotten skill of writing for the theatre: 'authors seem to have lost contact with the theatre . . . It is they who are responsible for the excessive, sometimes damaging importance of theatre directors. It is from this misfortune that we have the new barbarism "retheatricalisation of the theatre". To speak plainly, the directors are forced to teach the authors what they no longer know, that is to say the rules of the theatre game' (cit. Gouhier, 1943: 228-9).

This claim can probably be justified. On his own admission, Sartre learnt how to write for the theatre by watching Dullin. He had written only fiction and essays before the war; afterwards he was to become one of France's most successful dramatists. In a more general way, the tendency of authors to write plays that seem to require performance is a great deal more marked in the post-war period than it was in the inter-war period. The point can be rather sharply exemplified by contrasting Giraudoux with Genet, both authors brought to the stage by Jouvet. While Giraudoux's work always remained essentially that of a man of letters, Genet's is unmistakably that of someone who has a very sophisticated grasp of the nature of a performance art. It seems likely that by the end of the thirties the reforms and innovations brought about in the art of the theatre by Copeau and the Cartel had become sufficiently embedded in the consciousness of playgoers, playwrights and professional theatre workers to bring about that *rethéâtralisation du théâtre* claimed by Dullin.

What neither Copeau nor the Cartel could bring about was the larger cultural revolution that they had aimed at. The subsidies they received were almost non-existent, their theatres were small and depended on a regular audience of well-educated middle class Parisians. In these circumstances, it was not possible for them to become centres of social and cultural regeneration. But it is to their great credit that they understood this clearly and pointed towards the solution, especially Dullin in his report and Copeau in *Le Théâtre populaire*. The programmes of the successful decentralised theatres of the fifties were modelled very closely on the kinds of repertoire that had characterised the work of the Cartel between the wars, a fact that the directors of these theatres have been the first to recognise. Jouvet, Dullin and Baty all gave their active support to the establishment of these centres. . . .

Less influential at the time than the tradition of Copeau and the Cartel, but equally efficient at capturing the headlines was a tradition of avant-garde theatre which looked back to Apollinaire and to Jarry. The performances of *Ubu Roi* at the Théâtre de L'Oeuvre in 1896, which had provoked Yeats' famous dictum, 'After us, the savage god', were venerated by the inter-war avant-garde as the first manifestation of a truly modern consciousness. *Ubu Roi* still retains its aggressive and subversive power. In the course of its brief parodistic action, everything is distorted, vilified, denounced. Its spirit is well summed up in Jarry's own comment: 'We must get rid of certain notoriously horrible and incomprehensible objects, which uselessly clutter up the stage, particularly the sets and the actors' (1962: 140).

Jarry died young in 1907 but his writings were admired by Apollinaire, who also wrote a Surrealist play *Les Mamelles de Tirésias,* and by the Surrealist group, who republished some of Jarry's more obscure works. Breton, the leader of the Surrealists, who maintained a dictatorial control over the movement, always admired *Ubu Roi.*

This admiration was shared by Antonin Artaud, whose first theatre project was named 'Le Théâtre Alfred Jarry'. Artaud's life and work belong almost entirely to the period before the war, and yet, by 1939, he was still a relatively unknown figure. His influence did not extend beyond a narrow circle of Parisian friends until after the war, but since then it has assumed ever greater proportions, until he is now seen as the most influential French man of the theatre this century. His work has been interpreted by innumerable critics and there is no study of the modern theatre that does not devote a section to him. It will therefore not be necessary to summarise his work here. What we shall discuss, in later chapters of this book, is how his ideas have been interpreted and used, sometimes misinterpreted and misused, by theatre practitioners since the war.

In the theatre since the war he has chiefly been known through his collection of essays *Le Théâtre et son double.* This book, almost unnoticed at its first publication in 1938, only became generally known after its re-issue in 1944. It is not a simple theatre handbook, but a visionary work, in which Artaud proclaims an entirely new conception of theatre. He shares Jarry's desire to sweep away all the trappings of the French stage as he found it in the twenties and thirties. But he goes beyond Jarry for he also has a positive vision of what should exist in its place. It is an idea of theatre that is fundamentally religious, although it does not proceed from any established religion. It assumes that the function of theatre is to group people together in order to touch and release the hidden springs of life and the dark wells of emotion that the routine of so-called civilised life normally obscures.

In order to achieve this, Artaud insists on the necessity of doing away with the rationalistic theatre of the word as enshrined in the classic French tradition. Instead (like Mallarmé in his *Crayonné au théâtre,* 1887) he stresses the ways in which theatre can release irrational forces and communicate by means other than words. In a much more violent, apocalyptic tone, he echoes Baty's call for the expressive use of sounds, lights, colours, movements and appeals to complex sign systems that would enable the actor to become a moving hieroglyph. Suffering and cruelty are never far from his preoccupations and a number of critics have suggested that although he failed in productions like *Les Cenci* (1935) to bring his 'theatre of Cruelty' to fulfilment, he achieved it in his own life. This idea was suggested by Gide, by Barrault and by many others, and given detailed expression by Alain Virmaux in his definitive study *Antonin Artaud et le théâtre.* It is summarised by Esslin, following Virmaux: 'The plays Artaud wrote and produced were far from perfect, but his own life was the perfect tragedy perfectly enacted. That is why its impact continues beyond the grave' (1976: 115).

Artaud was expelled from the Surrealist movement by André Breton in 1928. After his departure, the official Surrealist group made little contribution to innovation in the theatre, partly because of Breton's mania for poor melodrama. It is a curious fact that Jarry and Ionesco, the two major dramatists whose work would seem to qualify as Surrealist, were both active outside the inter-war years, when the impact of Surrealism on poetry and painting was so decisive. Throughout the inter-war years, the main centre of Surrealist experimental theatre was the Laboratoire de Recherches Art et Action run by Madame Akakia-Viala, Louise Lara and Edouard Autant. Their aim was:

> Renewal of theatre, both form and content . . . creation of synchronism between the different forms of dramatic expression; evocation of the abstract by concrete means; use of old themes and myths, not disinterred and restored but brutally renewed . . . recourse to the fantastic and the grotesque to convey thoughts of gravity and concepts of the deepest pathos.
>
> (cit. Vais, 1978: 35)

This programme suggests clear affinities with Ionesco's stated aims in the theatre and so it is not surprising to learn that his first acting role (in 1948) was in a production by Akakia-Viala and that his first play was produced by Nicolas Bataille, who had also worked with members of Art et Action. This group had a long life, beginning before the First World War, and only coming to an end in 1952, when the New Theatre was almost established.

Among the various experiments in Surrealist playwriting that took place between the wars, the work of Vitrac stands out. His *Les Mystères de l'amour* produced at Artaud's Théâtre Alfred Jarry in 1927 had been an attempt to construct a play using the principles of automatic writing. His *Victor ou les enfants au pouvoir* (1928, also Théâtre Alfred Jarry) was a parody of the bourgeois *drame* in which the sordid greed and licentiousness of the French middle class mentality was exposed by the naive view of a precocious boy genius, only nine years old but already six feet tall. This play also looks forward to Ionesco's early work and has been successfully revived a number of times since the second war. Vitrac continued to write until his death in 1952, using a farcical, music-hall style to satirise the bourgeoisie, though his plays did not at first reach beyond avant-garde audiences.

Cocteau was known as a playwright on the fringes of Surrealism but his light-hearted early works such as *Les Mariés de la Tour Eiffel* (1921) had given way to ponderous reworkings of Greek myths and so, despite his tendency to shock, and the whiff of scandal that always surrounded his activities, he was not seen as a threat to the traditions of French literary theatre. In fact it was quite the reverse: he and Giraudoux were seen as the chief standard-bearers of the new literary revival, in which poetic plays on classical subjects were once more holding the stage as they had done in the *grand siècle*. It was Cocteau's film *Le Sang d'un poète* (first released 1932) that qualified for the epithet Surrealist rather than any of his recent plays.

Cocteau's interest in adapting Greek myth was shared by other writers, notably Giraudoux, Gide and Anouilh who, along with other authors, whose reputations have not survived, were thought of as a new school of literary dramatists. It is perhaps natural that in a culture so dominated by the awareness of its neo-classical writers, especially Racine and Corneille, any literary revival should also turn back to the classical myths. They offer a chance to deal with the great subjects and an escape from the apparent mediocrity of contemporary life. For theatres appealing to the educated class they also offered something familiar, an assurance that the quality of 'culturedness' was being preserved despite occasional anachronisms, vulgarities, or hints at contemporary events, like the long scarf of Cocteau's Jocasta, so reminiscent of the one that strangled Isadora Duncan when it became entangled in the wheel of a sports car.

But by the end of the 1930s, the strains imposed on the classical material by successive adaptations were becoming too great. The only successful attempts after 1939 were Sartre's *Les Mouches* and Anouilh's *Antigone*, both of which in different ways challenge the assumption that classical material makes for literary quality (see chapter 3). However, it did not become immediately apparent to many people involved with French theatre that the classical adaptation had seen its best days. The matter was complicated by the association of classical material and the verse play. Various attempts at verse drama, particularly those of Claudel during the war and T. S. Eliot after the war (Eliot's work had a considerable vogue in France just after the war) led many people to believe that the literary/verse/classical play was in the vanguard of French theatre. This helps to explain why, when the New Theatre of Genet, Adamov, Ionesco and Beckett first appeared, it took so many people, especially the critics, unawares.

At the outbreak of war, Anouilh was just becoming known as one of the most important young French dramatists. In some respects his early plays seem very clearly a part of the inter-war literary theatre movement. His dialogue displays a debt to Giraudoux in its use of wit and whimsy, and his frequent use of a play within the play shows that he had also learnt from Pirandello. But there are other aspects of these plays that look forward to the theatre of the forties and explain why Sartre was able to claim him as an Existentialist playwright (1973: 55-67). They are partly a matter of theme and partly of style. In theme, Anouilh's early plays develop with some bitterness a protest against class distinctions and a belief that someone who has had to suffer the privations of poverty in childhood can never entirely break free from the experience. In *Le Voyageur sans bagage* (1936), Anouilh also develops the idea that we have no fixed centre to our identity, but are the victims of the images that others have of us. This theme is developed in a manner reminiscent of Pirandello but which also looks forward to Sartre.

In style, Anouilh's early plays make a clear departure from the psychological case-study drama that was common between the wars. His characters are not subtle or rounded individual case histories: they are much more like types or masks. In fact, as has frequently been pointed out, they exist by virtue of their relationship to the other characters, the young innocent girl contrasting with the corrupt old baroness and so on. Their qualities appear in their actions and encounters rather than in soliloquies or investigations and for this reason they appealed to Sartre. Above all, Anouilh's work of this period was significant in establishing a style that was dramatic, playful, poetic, able to deal with contemporary subjects without being simply mimetic or naturalistic.

For the first collected publication of his plays in 1942 he divided them into *pièces roses* and *pièces noires*, and it was his first *pièce rose*, *Le Bal des voleurs*, that made a hit with the public. It was produced by André Barsacq with the Compagnie des Quatre Saisons in 1938 and revived by him in 1940 as his first production at the Atelier theatre, where he had succeeded Charles Dullin. The play's themes, of the division between rich and poor and the innocence of idealistic love, are similar to those of Anouilh's *pièces noires*, but they are dramatised in a comic, playful manner that never allows the social reality to intrude too much or to spoil the colour and sentimentality of the treatment. This was the beginning of a fruitful collaboration between Barsacq and Anouilh that was to continue for three decades.

Towards the end of the thirties in France there was much discussion of a mass theatre for the masses. This contrasted sharply with the practice of Copeau and the Cartel and had great appeal, especially in left-wing circles, as something radically new. In fact it was not very new: experiments in mass theatre having been conducted in both Russia and Germany throughout the twenties. In France, too, there had been a brief period when Firmin Gémier had attempted popular play production on a massive scale. In 1911 and 1912 he had already attempted an ambitious touring venture with a travelling theatre, the Théâtre National Ambulant. For the 1919-20 season he hired the Winter Circus, where he mounted two massive spectacular shows. The first was *Oedipus*, by Saint-Georges de Bouhélier, with a cast of over 200 including Olympic athletes. This was followed by a provençal nativity play *La Grande Pastorale*, directed by Baty. Gémier's stated aim was 'To create an atmosphere in which each member of the public is in communion with his neighbour and with the author in a sort of social religion' (1925: 72-3). As Gémier saw, this aim was better served by the public festivity than by the French theatre of the time. In 1920, as a result of a long campaign, Gémier succeeded in getting a Théâtre National Populaire established with himself as director, and organised a grand open-air festivity on the esplanade of Les Invalides to celebrate its inauguration. Unfortunately, Gémier had to put up with using the Trocadéro theatre, situated in the heart of the fashionable sixteenth arrondissement, so that it could never become a theatre for the masses. Even under Jean Vilar in the fifties, elaborate bussing arrangements had to be made if an audience was to be drawn from the working class areas. Furthermore, Gémier was allocated no money for a resident company, so his theatre had to function as what is now called a garage, receiving productions brought in from other theatres.

Gémier's achievement was to establish the first official Théâtre National Populaire and so lay the foundations for the successful work there of Vilar in the fifties. His failure was to confuse the theatre of massive means with theatre for the masses. The same confusion could be seen at work in the cultural policies of the Front Populaire government that came to power in 1936. For the International Exhibition of 1937 various shows were commissioned, including a composite show entitled *Long live liberty* and J. R. Bloch's play *Naissance d'une cité,* which was performed at the vast Vélodrome d'Hiver and described by Bloch as total theatre. These were inspired, to some extent, by the mass performances that had been a feature of socialist trade union gatherings in Germany in the twenties. By 1937, all such performances in Germany had been superceded by the Nazi mass rallies, and the French festivities were doubtless conceived in part as an alternative or rival form of mass celebration. The precision and power of the Nazi rallies certainly made a considerable impact on people all over Europe, who saw pictures of them on newsreel films, heard them broadcast on radio or experienced Leni Riefenstal's recreations. So hypnotic did they appear that for a long time after the war the very notion of a mass gathering seemed politically suspect.

There were many who took this view at the time of the Front Populaire but the government's commitment to mass shows was the outcome of a political struggle that had been going on among groups of the left for the whole of the thirties. There were many who favoured the promotion of agitprop work performed by small teams going out to find a popular audience in factories, streets or clubs. They argued that only in this way could hard political content be communicated and genuine two-way discussions be initiated. Others wanted to promote large-scale mass performances into which people of all classes would feel drawn, and through which the concepts of brotherhood or nationhood could be celebrated and confirmed. At first these two strategic approaches split fairly neatly into communist and socialist, the former favouring agit-prop and the latter favouring mass shows. But in the middle thirties the Soviet government put pressure on western communist parties to collaborate with the socialists and establish popular fronts, with the result that the agitprop movement was sacrificed.

This had the effect of cutting short the very promising theatre work of Jacques Prévert and the October Group. The plays performed by this group, most of which were scripted by Prévert, were characterised by a combination of playful wit and biting political satire. A good example is *La Bataille de Fontennoy* (1933) which anticipated Joan Littlewood's *Oh! What a lovely war* by presenting the First World War as a game in which lives are sacrificed in the name of hypocritical idealism while the spectator-population bays for blood. This sort of work was performed at trade union meetings, workers' halls, or in the open air. It was supported by a Fédération des Théâtres Ouvriers de France, which selected the October group to represent them at the Moscow Theatre Olympiad of 1933, where they won the first prize. But in 1936, when the Front Populaire came to power, the Fédération put all its energies into following the new fashion for massive displays of unity. Small groups like October were starved of funds and had to cease operation. It is difficult to assess the real importance, at the end of the thirties, of the political theatre movement, whether of the small agitprop or the mass festival variety. Much of the documentation was destroyed during the Nazi Occupation. What is certain is the failure, at a political level, of socialist and communist parties to prevent the rise of fascism in Europe discrediting these kinds of theatre, which had been associated with the left. It was not until 1968 that a new generation of theatre practitioners in France rediscovered the value of political theatre outside normal theatre buildings.

If the spirit of the Front Populaire survived anywhere, it was not in the theatre but in films. Already in 1936 *La Vie est à nous* had been made to celebrate the victory of the Front. This frankly propagandistic film was directed for the Communist Party, by Jean Renoir, André Zwoboda and Jean-Paul Le Chanois, and included almost all the October Group actors. The year before, Prévert had been Renoir's script writer on a film combining social polemic with brilliant dialogue, film technique and human observation: *Le Crime de Monsieur Lange.*

Renoir followed this by making a series of films with social preoccupations, among which are his acknowledged masterpieces. They include *Les Bas-Fonds* (1936) *La Grande Illusion* (1937) *La Marseillaise* (1937) *La Bête humaine* (1938) and *La Règle du jeu* (1939). Although Renoir did not collaborate again with Prévert, many of the October Group actors played small parts in these films which were animated by a broadly similar concern for the oppressed or exploited and a profound anti-militarism, although these themes were not expressed with any of the political force that had characterised October's work. Prévert established a working relationship with Marcel Carné and between them they were responsible for a number of very successful films that managed to keep alive something of the spirit of the Front Populaire during the years of Occupation. They include *Drôle de drame* (1937) *Quai des brumes* (1938) *Le Jour se lève* (1939) and *Les Enfants du paradis* (1943-44).

Alongside the left-wing demand for mass theatre or political theatre in the thirties, there had developed a trend which could loosely be described as Catholic theatre. Its most spectacular achievement was to stage Arnoul Gréban's sixteenth century *Mystère de la passion* on the square in front of Notre-Dame, an event that was to find an echo after the war in the great festival of religious drama held at Chartres immediately after the armistice, led by the Compagnons de la Saint-Jean (see chapter 2). But this trend had a more lasting influence on post-war theatre through the work of Léon Chancerel.

Chancerel had been one of Copeau's select group Les Copiaus, but did not join the Compagnie des Quinze in 1931. Instead, he began to set up a nation-wide network of theatre groups within the Boy Scout movement performing plays which frequently had a religious theme. He also formed a professional touring group Les Comédiens Routiers and a children's theatre Le Théâtre de l'Oncle Sébastien. In their repertoire the Comédiens Routiers did not concentrate solely on Catholic plays. They had a particular success with Molière's *Les Fourberies de Scapin,* developing the work that Copeau had begun with improvised farce, masks, acrobatics and the search for a modern Commedia dell'arte. Among those who worked in Chancerel's group were Maurice Jacquemont, Olivier Hussenot, Jean-Pierre Grenier, Yves Joly and Hubert Gignoux, all of whom were to become directors of Centres Dramatiques after the war.

The aims and methods of Chancerel's group were very similar to those of left-wing theatre groups, both emphasising unity, community and the importance of a combined front against fascism. Ideological motivation was considered an important factor in French theatre in the late thirties and Copeau was not the first to say that the theatre of the future would be either Christian or Marxist (see below p. 31).

The first socialist government that France had ever had, the Front Populaire, was also the first government to accept that the state had a responsibility to subsidise theatre that went beyond the Comédie Française. The Minister of Culture Jean Zay was keen to develop a policy of decentralisation of the theatre and commissioned Dullin to prepare a report. In this report Dullin identified *la centralisation* as the chief source of the lamentable state of French theatre outside Paris. Even in Paris itself he claimed that the people had been systematically removed from the proximity of theatres, so that the theatre-going public had become restricted to a small class. The solution proposed by Dullin was the division of France into *préfectorats artistiques*. These should be 'broad enough not to degenerate into parochialism or artistic bureaucracy' (1969: 161-2). From the 'capital' of each *préfectorat,* theatre groups (as well as groups of musicians, artists, etc.) would reach out into the surrounding country by a system of arranged tours and visits.

For this to work however, he made it clear that the financial basis of theatre would have to be changed and the theatres taken out of the hands of speculators. He was convinced that the state could and should take a hand in this. He applauded the plan, already under discussion, to construct three large new theatres in the workers' suburbs of Paris, suggesting that this principle should be extended to the provinces as well. He then developed some detailed ideas on how the new theatres should be built. The major features of his recommendations were the need for a flexible stage space and for the theatre to be provided with a library and good facilities for the actors. He then went on to discuss repertoire, stressing the need for a dazzling appeal to the imagination in the early productions of the new theatres: an ideal choice would be *Le Cid,* for 'the people will instinctively follow sublime tragic action if this action is presented on the necessary scale' (1969: 172). Each theatre should have its own company, with its own touring circuit, 'that means a central establishment with an administrative staff and workshop' (ibid. 174).

This report was shelved soon after it had been written because the Front Populaire government fell from power and the political will to implement it vanished. But when, after the war, there was once again a French government with the will to act, this report was rediscovered and acted upon. Dullin's model had been well thought out; the organisation of the first Centres Dramatiques was remarkably similar in its details to what he had suggested. After 1968, there was some criticism of a cultural policy that traded on the fact that 'the people will instinctively follow sublime tragic action', but the success of Vilar with *Le Cid* and of the Centres Dramatiques with similar heroic productions of the classics showed that Dullin understood his audience. He never patronised ('above all never say: they won't understand any of that', ibid. 172) and the directors who succeeded in the post-war decentralisation movement were all characterised by a similar respect for their new theatre-going public. Dullin's comments on the best production style for such work provide a useful summary, both of what he and the Cartel had achieved and of the style that was to predominate in the Centres Dramatiques:

> For new plays, a production style that is ingenious, using simple means, but profound and subtle, employing truthful performance to evoke the play; the time will come when the attraction of novelty has worn off and these new peoples' theatres (*théâtres populaires*) will once again be in competition with cinema, lavish operetta, etc. The best productions are generally the least expensive because there is more room for the spirit of the piece than for cardboard frippery.
>
> (1969: 173)

The theatre at the end of the thirties was very different from what it had been when Copeau began to write his drama criticism: it had become acceptable to think of theatre as educational, even uplifting, instead of dismissing it as a corrupting influence. Three influential forces had contributed to this change: the independent directors of the Cartel, the school of literary playwrights, and the political and religious bodies that had begun to see the theatre's usefulness to them. As a result of this change in attitudes, the foundations of much of the post-war development were already in place. The organisational and artistic strategies for decentralisation had been thought out, if not yet fully accepted, the need for plays of sufficient quality to make demands on their audience had been demonstrated, and the necessity for state involvement on a large scale had been understood.

The consequences of all this were, however, far from clear to most people working in the French theatre. Very few foresaw the major split that was to occur after the war between private- and public-funded theatres or between Paris and the provinces. There was almost no hint, either, of the major intellectual currents that were to dominate the post-war theatre: Existentialist, Marxist, Surrealist. In this respect the playwrights of the ensuing four decades were to make a series of startling new beginnings. Theatre people in France at the end of the thirties were surprisingly insular: very few had travelled widely in Europe or paid much attention to developments in other countries. Pirandello's work had made its influence felt, but that of Brecht and the German Expressionists was hardly known at all. Directors of major international stature such as Meyerhold and Piscator also remained unknown outside a very restricted circle. Many of the new beginnings of the post-war period were to be fuelled by the discovery of such major precursors. The impact of foreign influences was to be all the greater for being retarded by the isolation imposed by four years of German Occupation.

David Bradby (essay date 1984)

SOURCE: Bradby, David. "Playwrights of the Seventies." In *Modern French Drama: 1940-1980*, pp. 224-49. Cambridge, England: Cambridge University Press, 1984.

[*In the following essay, Bradby discusses major French dramatists and directors of the 1970s, focusing on both playwriting and staging issues.*]

In the course of the seventies, major changes have taken place in French playwriting which are still difficult to assess. In the excitement of the *création collective* experiments, during the early years of the decade, the traditional role of the playwright almost seemed to have disappeared: instead of starting with a text, theatre companies started from an idea, theme or situation; where playwrights were still employed, it was as literary advisers or adaptors, serving the interests of actors and directors. Among the factors contributing to this situation were: the emphasis on group responsibility; developments in literary theory; the questioning of established artistic methods; and the all-pervading '*gauchisme*'. *Gauchisme* was the pejorative name given to that brand of extreme intellectual left-wing attitude that proclaims the revolution now. Among actors, it led to the insistence that, as the 'proletariat' of the theatre, they had to be free to speak with their own voice. To speak a text written by someone else, especially if that someone was a professional writer (i.e. 'bourgeois individualist'), was to accept an oppressive and authoritarian practice: all theatre texts had to be the result of a collective voice. It was the squabbles arising from just such a superficial approach that had made Gatti's *Treize Soleils de la rue Saint Blaise* so unsatisfactory (p. 161).

In places where such crude over-simplifications were avoided, the writer did not necessarily fare any better, because of the predominance of 'directors' theatre'. The brilliant success of Planchon's methods had produced many imitators. The tendency towards a theatre of images had been further reinforced by the impact of Grotowski, the Living Theatre, Bread and Puppet, Bob Wilson and other similar foreign companies, whose work drew its power from images as much as from texts. Foreign influences of this kind continued to play an important role throughout the seventies, especially after the discovery of Tadeusz Kantor. It was these models that fired the imaginations of many of the new young directors and companies.

The power of the director was further reinforced by a change in the government's method of paying subsidies. Annual subsidies for a given theatre had always been paid to a named director rather than to an author or company, but extra money was available for the staging of new plays under the 'Aide à la Première Pièce' (originally established by Jeanne Laurent in 1947). After 1967 this was replaced by a 'Commission d'Aide à la Création Dramatique' (see Allen, 1981: 247). Under the new system, the director no longer had to find an unperformed playwright, but could claim the subsidy for a *création collective* or an adaptation of the kind discussed in the previous chapter.

The new playwrights of the forties and fifties had seen their work performed in the privately-owned Parisian 'art' theatres. During the sixties, the state-owned theatres had, to a large extent, taken over as the main presenters of new plays. But as the recession of the seventies began to make itself felt, the surviving Parisian theatres were no longer able to take risks and, as we shall see, the state theatres also ran into financial difficulties. The result was a sudden reduction in the number of outlets for new writing.

In this situation it became fashionable to declare that the era of the playwright was past. After all, had not writers of real quality, such as Gatti, chosen to abandon playwriting in search of new, collaborative forms of expression? This climate of ideas found its counterpart in structuralist and post-structuralist literary theory, which was proclaiming the 'death of the author'. By this was meant that works of literature should no longer be viewed as if they were letters, written by one person to convey information to another. Rather, they should be seen as slabs of discourse, whose meanings are constructed as much by the different readers as by the author who first set them down. Moreover, the old-fashioned notion of meaning was itself called into question and the suggestion made that there is in fact no such thing as a stable meaning that can be located in a literary text (see for example Eagleton, 1983: 127-45). The impact of these theoretical developments contributed to the fashion for the production of adaptations rather than of play texts (see pp. 221-3). As the intentions and the authority of the author lost much of their traditional importance, so it became more frequent for directors to put together 'colleges' of texts drawn from many different literary periods and genres. The tradition of literary introspection was particularly favoured: texts that call into question the whole basis upon which we sum up and judge a human character. These preoccupations were to come to the fore in the work of certain playwrights, too, especially those playwrights known as *le théâtre du quotidien*. But, as we shall see, their writing was also fuelled by social considerations.

The crisis that faced playwrights in the early seventies also had straightforward economic causes: put simply, many of the larger decentralised theatres had become too expensive to run. By the middle seventies the large building programme begun by Malraux, and which had carried on under its own momentum, had resulted in the existence of fifteen Maisons de la Culture, four national theatres, eighteen Centres Dramatiques and a further two dozen or more theatre companies of some size, all competing for subsidies. During the seventies around 0.5% of the national budget was devoted to the arts (as against 0.3% in Britain), but as the increase in labour costs and the general rise in inflation made the theatre more expensive, it became apparent that most of the government subsidies were being spent on administrative and running costs. Simply to keep a large theatre or Maison open was absorbing so much of the money that the creative work, for which the whole structure was supposed to exist, was being starved of funds. Often the only solution seemed to be to abandon creative work altogether and simply open the theatre to touring productions. This practice became known as 'garaging'.

The situation was aggravated by the suspicious attitude of successive Ministers of Culture towards the theatre. The ruling class had been profoundly shocked by the events of 1968. They were determined to do what they could to prevent state subsidy going to those whose professed aim was revolutionary socialism. On his appointment as Minister of Culture in 1973, Maurice Druon declared that he would not tolerate people who came to him with a begging bowl in one hand and a Molotov cocktail in the other. This inflammatory remark produced outraged response from theatre workers all over France, culminating in a massive demonstration by the Action pour le Jeune Théâtre. They claimed, with some justification, that it suited the Ministry very well to have a state-subsidised theatre so top-heavy with administrative costs that it could mount few new productions. Matters appeared to have reached an impasse during the last years of Giscard d'Estaing's presidency. Even the Association Technique pour l'Action Culturelle, which had performed a vital role in publishing regular news of activities throughout the decentralised theatres, was forced out of business. It became common to declare that 'decentralisation was dead'.

Like most slogans, of course, this gave only a very one-sided view of the true picture. Despite a hostile financial climate, the period of the seventies was marked by a constant increase in the number of new young theatre groups springing up in the provinces. Moreover, many of the major theatres continued to perform original work, notably the T.N.P.-Villeurbanne, the Comédie de Caen and the Théâtre National de Strasbourg. The work of the Strasbourg theatre was particularly influential and provides a good example of the profound change that was taking place in the practice of French playwrights.

In 1975 Jean-Pierre Vincent was appointed director of the Strasbourg theatre. He had made his name with productions of Brecht, Büchner, Vyshnevsky, as well as modern French plays by Rezvani and Grumberg, and a very successful revival of *La Cagnotte* by Labiche. He was an admirer of Peter Stein and had worked in Germany. From his appointment in 1975 until his move to direct the Comédie Française in 1983, Vincent established a pattern of working practice modelled on that of the German civic theatres. He drew the Strasbourg acting school into close collaboration with the professional theatre company and appointed two 'dramaturges'—Bernard Chartreux and Michel Deutsch. Their function was not just to act as literary advisers, but to write new material for performance by both the company and the students, mostly adaptations of non-dramatic work, such as Zola's *Germinal,* which formed the basis of the first production by Vincent at Strasbourg. The position of Chartreux and Deutsch typifies that of many playwrights in France today: they work from within a professional theatre company. This means that although they may write their own plays, they will also spend much of their time working on projects commissioned by the director, who thus reinforces his predominant role in the production of new theatre work.

In order to protect the interests of the independent author, an organisation called Théâtre Ouvert was established in 1970 by broadcaster and publisher Lucien Attoun. At first this consisted only of play-reading sessions at the Avignon festival, broadcasts on France-Culture and a special series of publications for Stock. But its activities have increased to include work at other times of the year and in other places. It now owns its own premises, at the Jardin d'Hiver in Paris, where it arranges for small-budget productions of new plays, usually directed by the author himself. The list of authors helped by Théâtre Ouvert during the seventies runs to nearly 200. It includes Gatti, Grumberg, Deutsch, Wenzel, Kalisky and Vinaver. It has shown that despite a changed intellectual climate and a reduction in the number of outlets for new work in the French theatre, plays of quality are still being written (see Jeffery 1984a).

The main casualty of the changes and cutbacks in the seventies was the particularly Parisian tradition of the lyrico-whimsical play, examples of which had featured in every Paris theatre season since the war. Its authors had resisted the polarisation into Brechtian or absurdist camps, combining sardonic social comment with humorous situations, often more or less 'absurd'. This tradition included writers such as Schéhadé, Dubillard, Billetdoux, Félicien Marceau, as well as Audiberti and Vauthier, who had made the link between the avant-garde and the boulevard in Paris during the fifties before their rediscovery by Maréchal in the sixties. New authors of secondary importance, writing in a similar style, emerged in the course of the sixties, notably Romain Weingarten and René de Obaldia.

Weingarten's *L'Eté* was a big success in the Paris season of 1966/7. It depicts two talking cats and two children, through whose eyes the relationship of two lovers (never seen on stage) is observed. It sparkles with *bons mots* and insights into adolescent psychology. It also offers two very amusing acting parts for the cats (played by Nicholas Bataille and Weingarten himself). But it marked no significant new departure. Much the same can be said of Obaldia's plays, the first of which, *Génousie,* had been part of Vilar's 1960 season of new plays at the Récamier. His *Le Satyre de la Villette* was produced in 1963 by André Barsacq, who had produced so many of Anouilh's early plays. In 1965 *Du vent dans les branches de sassafras* provided the great comic actor Michel Simon with one of his last triumphs; the play is a spoof western, in which Simon took the part of an accident-prone cowboy. Obaldia's plays always present slightly unexpected characters in strange situations, but their verbal antics are neither so 'absurd' as those of Ionesco, nor so precocious as those of Arrabal, nor so cynical as those of Vian.

Jean-Claude Grumberg

This variety of whimsical writing, which had flourished in the fifties and sixties has almost entirely died out since the beginning of the seventies. The playwrights who now make the link between the boulevard and the avant-garde are those who have managed to combine the lessons of the New Theatre with the discoveries of the *théâtre populaire* movement and of Epic theatre. The outstanding example is Jean-Claude Grumberg. Grumberg was born in 1939 in Paris of immigrant Jewish parents. Soon afterwards, his father was deported during the purges of the Occupation. He never returned and so his mother went out to work as a seamstress in the clothing trade to support her children. Becoming first an apprentice tailor, then an actor, Jean-Claude only began to write for the stage in the middle sixties. His first plays, heavily influenced by the New Theatre, dealt with the themes of racism and intolerance through violent images of incomprehensible conflicts taking place in everyday circumstances. They aim to create a sense of the grotesque by introducing into conventional situations a language so violent and cruel that the spectator experiences the shock of seeing, in the open, the normally hidden or unconscious desires and drives of the characters.

This was also the style of writing employed in the play that gave Grumberg his first commercial success, *Amorphe d'Ottenburg,* published by Stock in 1970, and produced the following year by J.-P. Roussillon at the Odéon theatre on a set resembling an enormous spider's web. The play is a parable of Nazism, with the dumb Amorphe as Hitler, his parents as the establishment powers who encouraged him, Uncle Merle as the Pope and an evil hunchback who represents the finance and business houses which benefited from the Nazi régime and came out of it even stronger than before. Most of the time, the play works as a parody of gothic melodrama, and its force is to demystify the process through which high-sounding ideological motives are made to cover base instincts. Amorphe has an irresistible compulsion to stab in the back anyone who is old and helpless. This liquidation of the infirm is an enormous boon to the Ottenburg economy and so his crimes are covered up by his father, the Lord of Ottenburg. When Amorphe kills the 'troubadour' (in fact a neighbouring prince in disguise) it seems as though he has gone too far, but his father succeeds in winning back sympathy for him by a forceful speech about the parasitism of all artists and musicians.

There is a strong influence of Jarry in the cruelty, systematic distortion of truth, and general base egotism of most of the characters in the play. This influence is also visible in the language, especially in the use of archaic French for scurrilous purposes and in the names of the Lord of Ottenburg's opponents, Stanislas, Matolas and Pamolas, recalling the good King Wenceslas of *Ubu Roi* and his noble son Bougrelas. There is a grotesque quality to the language throughout, well exemplified by the play's running gag which is in the murderous but mute Amorphe's struggles to articulate his own name. He finally succeeds as he mounts the throne over the dead bodies of father and uncle and his stammering of his name is taken up by those around him as a battle cry: 'A mort . . .' (Death to . . . ; 167). Those opposed to Amorphe appear just as corrupt as he is, interested only in how they can keep their own peasantry down with less blatant methods than those used by Amorphe. After a prolonged war, they conquer Ottenburg and kill Amorphe, but the hunchback saves his skin by presenting the victors with his perfectly kept account books. The audience's horror is shifted from its focus on Amorphe himself to the evil financial genius and suddenly, at the final curtain, we see a whole line of hunchbacks, each holding account books.

As a black farce the play is successful; as a political allegory it is less so. This is because the generalised nature of the vaguely medieval setting prevents the author from treating the problems of the relationship between power and finance in any but the most schematic way. Rather than discovering anything new about Nazism, the spectator's pleasure is limited to the amusement of exerting his wits in the recognition of the models to which each character refers. The parallel with the history of the Third Reich only becomes clear as the play progresses, so that recognition dawns slowly. Grumberg attempted to give the play a more general significance by making each character speak and act in the name of 'Gott' but, once again, since the terms of the analysis are so vague, nothing significant is revealed about the causes or effects of religious persecution. The play is both entertaining and brilliantly theatrical but there is a certain incongruity between this and its subject-matter.

Grumberg's subsequent plays show him turning more towards real events and situations and drawing more on his own personal experience. They also show an increased, self-consciously critical attitude towards the problems of form. This is most clearly evident in *Dreyfus,* in which the problem of how to write and present a play about anti-semitism is the central concern of a group of Polish Jews who are themselves the victims of anti-semitism. *Dreyfus* was first produced by Jacques Rosner at the Théâtre du Lambrequin, Tourcoing, the new name given to the Centre Dramatique du Nord when Rosner became its director in 1971.

Its content is more specifically political and its setting is precisely identified in a Yiddish-speaking suburb of a Polish town, where an amateur theatre group is working on a play (by one of their members) about Dreyfus (see fig. 19). The time is around 1930 and the play dramatises the murderous incongruity of people struggling to understand the anti-semitism of a previous generation while failing to see the growth of the new, more brutal anti-semitism in their own time.

The play turns on two questions: how is it possible to understand anti-semitism? and how is it possible to represent it in such a way that the audience will learn something that they can use? The first question is not really answered. The central character, Maurice, the one who has written a play about Dreyfus, concludes that it can only be understood in the context of a large Marxist theory of history, but this intuition only emerges at the very end of the play in a letter sent by Maurice to his friends. Most of the characters in the play remain completely baffled by the hostility they face, clinging all the more strongly to their Jewish identity. They cannot understand Maurice's fascination with the fact that Dreyfus did not even consider himself as a Jew, but was first and foremost an officer, thinking of himself simply as a French soldier. This was why the accusation of treason hit him so hard: it created a difference of species that had not existed before.

It is in the discussions about Dreyfus' view of himself that the answer to the second question is developed: Maurice insists that their play must show that there is essentially no difference between Jew and Gentile, that indeed the supposed differences do not emerge until someone needs to find a victim to protect himself from blame. Maurice has to struggle for his understanding of these issues against the traditionalism and inflexibility of his colleagues. Arnold, for example, sees the whole subject in melodramatic terms and would like to perform the whole play as a piece of traditional Yiddish theatre with song and dance routines. Motel, the tailor, believes that the only important ingredient of the play will be the costumes. Michel, the actor playing Dreyfus, finds it quite impossible to understand his role until one night a rehearsal is broken up by a couple of violent anti-semitic drunks. Michel terrifies them by charging, in his officer's uniform and with drawn sword. By not adopting his usual apologetic, self-effacing posture, he has stepped outside himself, realized that he need not be imprisoned by ideas of racial groups. Maurice's play is never finally performed. He leaves for Warsaw, where he joins the communist party, explaining his discovery of the concept of direct action to his former friends by letter.

Grumberg's play is well constructed. It draws richly on the Yiddish tradition for some very funny and some very moving dialogue. It employs the device of the play within the play most effectively, unashamedly exploiting the stock devices such as the scene in which the young lovers enact a declaration of love that turns into the real thing. The general atmosphere of the small, protective Jewish community is depicted with warmth and affection. Above all, Grumberg conveys a kind of amazement that such a group of people can persist in an almost blind idealism in the face of a brutally hostile world. But as in the case of *Amorphe d'Ottenburg,* the play is too self-contained to really illuminate the historical themes upon which it touches—they become submerged beneath the brilliantly observed surface detail of the Jewish community, and the large questions raised by the play remain unanswered.

What links *Dreyfus* with *En r'venant d'l'Expo* (1975) is an element of self-consciousness about the formal devices employed. In *Dreyfus* we saw a theatre group struggling to put on a play. Here we are asked to consider the function of the *cafés concerts* in the period leading up to the First World War. Once again, the play is extremely well constructed, the opening scenes, at the Universal Exhibition of 1900, being a particularly successful piece of dramatic exposition. The idea of showing how *la belle époque* led up to the First World War had already been used by Adamov in *Paolo Paoli*. While Adamov exploited the hypocrisies of the bourgeois *commerçants,* Grumberg attempts to juxtapose the sincere idealism of the syndicalist movement with the frivolity of the *cafés concerts.*

This enables him to use the popular songs of the period to some effect, although the play rather disappointingly shows only the superficial or escapist aspects of popular songs, failing to show how they could also be subversive. Rather like Maurice in *Dreyfus,* the syndicalists of this play are great idealists, believing up until the last moment that war is impossible since the workers' International will simply call a universal strike to prevent it. As a piece of documentary drama about the period, it is fascinating; as a piece of political theatre it seldom goes beyond stating the obvious.

The attractions of the play are in its surface texture rather than in its overall coherence. The setting of the play's opening scenes in the Universal Exhibition is particularly successful, since an exhibition provides the ideal public meeting point where the social and political clichés of the period are rehearsed, but where more intimate family and sentimental relationships can also be developed. Everything that occurs amongst the imposing exhibits is superficial and meretricious, from the curé's homily on the value of colonial wars because of the glorious deaths they provide, to the invocation of Joan of Arc by the Anglophobe. The various bugbears of the period are introduced: the Jews, the revolutionaries, indiscipline of any kind; and the exposition of plot is achieved with great vitality, economy and humour of dialogue and character.

The remainder of the play alternates between the *café concert* and the workers' hall. The *café concert* revels in jingoistic songs designed to stir up militaristic fervour, while in the workers' hall the union meets to discuss the politics of peace. The link between the two worlds is Louis, son of a waiter who begins to make a hit as a singer at the café, but realises the destructive effects of his songs and so searches for an alternative. The difficulty is that the second half of the play tends to degenerate into a series of debates with little dramatic force—a tendency already evident in *Dreyfus*. There is a debate about whether popular songs should do more than 'faire oublier'; there is a debate about pacifist politics. But in the end what is shown to matter is not these reasoned discussions, but the sheer emotional force of a militaristic song or the call to arms in 1914. In the end the pacifist workers have to admit their impotence in the face of the emotive power of nationalism, however false and short-sighted it may be.

The overall effect of the play is thus rather fatalistic. In the syndicalist scenes the writing expresses Grumberg's evident sympathy for their cause but the main emphasis of the action is on the disunity within the movement. Similarly, the author shows evident dislike of the chauvinistic traditions of the *cafés-concerts*, but stresses their attractions by including a number of examples of such songs. The message, that superficial passions and resentments are more powerful than reason, was emphasised most effectively by Jean-Claude Penchenat in his production of the play for the Théâtre du Campagnol (1979). The play was staged in a large arena which allowed the audience to feel they were part of the crowds at the exhibition or the clients at the *café-concert*. A last scene was added, in which the on-stage band played heroic military music while all the characters joined in a military parade. As they marched around the arena, their expressions and gestures became gradually more violent and hysterical until we were faced with a powerful, literal image of the lunacy and bestiality of war.

Grumberg's most recent play *L'Atelier* opened at the Odéon in 1979. It transferred to a boulevard theatre where it enjoyed a long run. It is a largely autobiographical story of Jewish survivors of the Nazi Occupation, and the pain of surviving when so many have died. It depicts the life of a small clothing workshop between 1945 and 1952. The action is entirely confined to the workshop so that everything the audience learns is filtered through the work process. This is treated entirely naturalistically. In the Odéon production (Grumberg both acting and helping to direct), the actresses playing the six seamstresses did not pretend to sew: they really did it and the audience saw whole suits take shape before their eyes as the evening progressed. To live through such a period was, the play suggests, a matter of survival. It was essential for the women to produce suits sufficiently fast and cheaply to stay ahead of the competition so that there would be a through-flow of cash enabling all who worked there to eat. The moments of crisis or movement on stage occurred when a consignment had been returned or deliveries were not going smoothly. At such points Léon, the owner, shouted and screamed at the women, who accepted it because they knew it was their survival as well as his that was at stake. This work was the most vital and most physically demanding thing in their lives and so had to be presented as such.

But the play does not develop a denunciation of the alienating effect on the women of having to sell their labour. Its mood remains broadly nostalgic, emphasising the simple contradiction that although the workshop was experienced as a treadmill, it also gave respite from the anguished loneliness of those who had survived the holocaust. Simone, the character based on Grumberg's mother, has to spend every waking hour that she is not in the workshop searching for news of her deported husband and caring for her children. The occasional moments of emotional depth occur when she is working late, alone in the workshop, and hears from Léon, or from the presser, about other men's experiences of deportation. The ending of the play comes with the collapse of Simone, exhausted from the years of privation and hard labour. The news that she has been taken to hospital is brought to the workshop by her son, aged about eleven. Grumberg, at this point, gives way completely to the sentimental tone as the women all kiss him and he announces that soon he will be old enough to do a man's work so that his mother need no longer go out to support him and his brother.

After flirting with the methods of the Absurd and the Epic, Grumberg here returns to the most traditional form of naturalism: he relies on reproducing, by means of set, costumes and actors' behaviour, an imitation of a real workshop so perfect that his audience will believe in its reality. So long as they are convinced by the imitation, they will experience the play's events through the eyes of the fictional characters, identifying with their sufferings and delights. Because the method has been well established for more than a century, an audience expects a story of high emotional voltage before it will allow itself to be convinced. The holocaust supplies the necessary power: suffering of such magnitude compels the submergence of one's own identity in awe-struck sympathy with the sufferings of the characters on stage. The final descent into sentimentality confirms our sense that although unquestionably a master of his craft, Grumberg has, for the time being, abandoned experiment with dramatic form for the well-tried formulae of the past.

GEORGES MICHEL

Another playwright whose early work brought the methods of the Absurd to bear on the real world was Georges

Michel. Michel is a watchmaker who lives in Paris and who shares Grumberg's Jewish proletarian origins. He was adopted in the early sixties by Sartre, who published his first play, *Les Jouets,* in *Les Temps Modernes* in 1963 and also provided a preface for his play *La Promenade du dimanche* in 1967. Michel's plays employ the dramaturgical methods of literalisation that were so successfully used by the New Theatre playwrights, presenting grotesque concrete images of the fears and fantasies of social conformism. *La Promenade du dimanche* depicts a typical French bourgeois family on its Sunday afternoon stroll. The dialogue is composed almost entirely of clichés; the common clichés of family life which are used to train children to accept authority and which were employed to similar effect in Ionesco's *Jacques ou la soumission.* But in Ionesco's plays both language and the world may be transformed: the deep subjective needs of Jacques and Roberte can be expressed through the ecstatic evocation of the flaming horse (Ionesco, 1954: 122).

No such transformation occurs in Michel's plays. The only unexpected occurrences are incursions of sudden violence, as first the grandfather, then the grandmother, and finally the little boy are shot or knifed. But these acts of violence produce no change in the survivors, for whom the cliché has become an impenetrable defence. When the grandfather is killed the mother simply comments:

> It's an unlucky day . . . it started badly . . . I could feel it. First of all the fuses went this morning, it was an omen . . . then the waste pipe was blocked in the bathroom. I've always said: it goes in threes . . . well, at least we shan't have any more today.

(1968a: 12)

She is wrong, as her own death is shortly to show. Every so often on their walk the family passes a scene of torture or brutality, but a cliché response is always to hand: 'he's only doing his job' or 'it's not our business to interfere'. The consequences of blind acceptance of authority enshrined in such statements take literal shape before their eyes without ever altering their behaviour: as their son lies dead, the mother shouts,

> Your father's right; come on, that's enough now, get up, get up, you hear me? All right, you'll have no pudding . . . no pudding, you hear?

(ibid.: 75)

The characters in most of Michel's plays behave, in similar fashion, like programmed automata. The only exceptions are children, who are presented as creatures with a certain naïve independence, still able to question the solidified clichés that have become the adults' stock responses to whatever experiences they encounter. *Arbalètes et vieilles rapières* (1969) contains one such child, who begins by questioning the need for war, but ends up indoctrinated with chauvinistic and militaristic propaganda, to the point where he is transformed into a bundle of senseless aggressive drives, ready to kill anything that crosses his path.

The violence in this play is not physical but verbal. The coagulated clichés of aggression and chauvinism are what drive the people to war, and the two opposing armies find that they, too, coagulate in the final scene, where, after hurling insults at one another, they freeze 'in an arrogant warrior's pose such as may be seen in our war memorials' (98), while the sound of bombs exploding fills the theatre. The merit of Michel's plays is that they do not remain at the level of cliché, but attempt to show how the reliance on pre-digested ideas and expressions places one entirely at the mercy of the dominant ideology and, ultimately, blinds one to the reality of violence. In *Arbalètes et vieilles rapières* the boy's family is incapable of seeing that the indoctrination they put him through is literally one of *alienation*: he ends up *aliéné*, i.e. mad. In *L'Agression,* produced by Wilson at the T.N.P. in 1967, a group of passers-by is equally incapable of understanding the revolt of a group of adolescents as they try to fight back against the subtly aggressive forces of the consumer society.

Un Petit Nid d'amour (1970) shows how the fears generated in people by the consumer society may be played on in order to create a hysteria of acquisition which also culminates in violence. It is a very simple story of a young couple falling in love and setting up house together. Michel cleverly exploits all the clichés of the *Love Story* variety to show how their ideological basis relies on the determination to feather one's own nest at the expense of others. The salesman, who is always near at hand, is able to persuade them to keep changing their house for one with thicker walls, first just to keep out the noise, later to defend themselves against enemies, real or imagined. In the end they acquire a nuclear bunker; the last scene of the play shows them shooting down someone who was asking for help and retiring into their bunker with the words:

HIM

> Did you see how he insisted on coming in?

HER

> Our little love-nest is not a dormitory, after all! *They kiss.*

(79-80)

In the aftermath of 1968 Michel wrote *La Ruée vers l'ordre* (a pun on the French translation of *the goldrush: la ruée vers l'or*). In this, for the first time, he attempted to treat public figures in the same manner as the couples and families of his early plays. It shows the President of France calming his panic-stricken cabinet, making a televised appeal to the nation, and winning an election campaign, after which the population is force-fed on the benefits of the consumer society. The play is a series of rather predictable left-wing images, although one or two of the scenes have considerable power, especially the preparation for the President's broadcast, in which we see just how the correct, reassuring image is constructed by the media men. There are also some good passages on the abuse of language in modern consumer societies, saturated by advertising, that compare with *L'Aboyeuse et l'automate* by Cousin and *Off limits* by Adamov. But the paradox of Michel's writing is that it has the greatest force when it is least applicable to a specific historical case. It is a style that aims to reveal the violence concealed behind familiar structures and, as such, must work with typical cases. As soon as it is applied to a precise set of circumstances, such as France in 1968, the results are bound to seem oversimplified. Its appeal lies not in historical investigation but in the intensely literal enactment of situations we all recognise to be real. Similar methods were to be employed by the writers of the *théâtre du quotidien* that flourished in the seventies.

Le théâtre du quotidien—Kalisky, Deutsch, Wenzel

This was the name given by critics to a school of playwrights influenced by the new authors and film makers of Germany and Austria. In the course of the seventies many translations from German were performed in France, especially at the Comédie de Caen, where Michel Dubois and Claude Yersin produced Handke (1972), Kroetz (1973) and Fassbinder (1975). In the work of these authors, audiences were confronted with fragmentary scenes showing ordinary, often inarticulate people in very ordinary situations, which were nevertheless presented in a style of heightened realism. Behind the ordinariness of the situations, the hidden violence of contemporary social structures emerged with great force.

The French writers we shall now examine employ similar dramatic methods: not linear plots, but a discontinuous structure of fragmented reality; not well-rounded characters in control of their language, but a demonstration of how language can control and articulate character. Together with Georges Michel, Kalisky, Deutsch and Wenzel all illustrate Vinaver's contention that modern man is 'both crushed by a system but at the same time in perfect communion with it' (see below pp. 246-7). Kalisky's cycling champion in *Skandalon* (1970) is a man who allows his life to be constructed entirely by the *interests* of others: the financial interests of his backers and trainers; the sexual interests of his friends and wives; the interest the journalists take in building up an idol and then destroying him again. He consents in the whole process, becoming pure object; as a subject he has no existence. When his second wife sees his status as champion on the decline, and tries to persuade him to give up racing, she is talking to an absence. He only exists as the champion; there is no longer any private individual 'behind' this public figure who could take an alternative path. He can only use the arguments of his backers that justify the brief glory of the racing cyclist: he articulates his own oppression.

The plays of Michel Deutsch exhibit characters who are similarly constructed from alien forms of discourse. Deutsch's work exemplifies the logical end-point of existentialist attitudes towards character which had been explored by Sartre in the fifties and Gatti in the sixties. In Deutsch's plays the idea of the character as a fixed entity has entirely vanished. Like Sartre, he sees human beings not as creations but as shapeless emergent existences. Sartre, however, used the dramatic situation to show the process through which these existences acquire an essence: he showed characters who, in choosing a course of action or a value, choose themselves. In this philosophy, a character can only be summed up after death, since every new moment of life presents new choices, and this is why Sartre needed the fiction of hell for *Huis clos*.

Deutsch reduces the scope of his enquiry, pinpointing not a whole life but particular moments. His characters are a collage of the many different types of behaviour of the different people they have encountered in their lives. They have copied a phrase here, an action there, and frequently these different elements contradict one another quite blatantly. As well as being shaped by other people, Deutsch's characters are constructed and deconstructed by the various public institutions that dominate their lives. Because his characters owe their reality to these other people and institutions outside themselves, the dividing lines that separate one character from another can never be established with absolute clarity. A recent play by Deutsch, *Partage* (1981), showed two of the Manson girls, after their murder of Sharon Tate, trying to make sense of their actions. In his programme note, Deutsch wrote 'They tear one another apart, devour one another, tremble, become motionless, close their eyes . . . One becomes the other who becomes the one who is the other. The boundaries are uncertain, hazy. There is no exact dividing line between them.' The play is a rite of attempted possession and expiation in which each girl tries to articulate her own character in an acceptable manner, projecting onto her companion those things she cannot face up to. Much more simply, one of Deutsch's earliest plays, *Dimanche,* published in 1974 and produced at Strasbourg in 1976, shows a girl whose personal reality is lost in her desire to become a perfect majorette. The alien, mechanical image of a long-legged American high-kicker imposes itself upon her to the point where she can live only for her training, submerges her subjective reality in the pursuit of this image, and dies of exhaustion.

A similar change in the subjective realities of two women is shown in *Convoi* (1980), set in the south-west of France during the German Occupation. Anne, a sixty-year-old peasant woman, takes in an eighteen-year-old Jewish refugee. She christens her Marie, treats her like a daughter, behaving as if the girl were a young cousin or niece who had lost her memory. For a while 'Marie' almost becomes Anne's daughter. But she cannot rid herself of the memory of the concentration camps or the columns of refugees being strafed by planes. Neither is she allowed to live in isolated exile, independent of Anne's family and neighbours. When the Germans invade the 'free zone' she is denounced, and the militia come to arrest both women. Jean-Pierre Vincent, who directed the play at Strasbourg in 1980, commented that the theme of the play was 'exile, physical exile or interior exile, a certain reaction to misfortune' (Deutsch, 1980: 109). He also suggested that all of Deutsch's characters could be summed up by a phrase from *Ruines*: 'you are pierced with slices of text' (*vous êtes traversés par des pans de texte*) (ibid.). They are martyred by their language, invaded and defined by it without wanting to be.

The outbursts of Marie in which she evokes her suffering have great lyrical force, but, outside of these passages, Marie seems inarticulate. Many of Deutsch's characters display this linguistic schizophrenia. The character named Jules in *La Bonne Vie* (produced by Vincent at Strasbourg in 1976) is a factory worker whose conversation consists of the most banal clichés interspersed with extraordinary, dream-like statements, e.g. 'In the Bois de Boulogne, coming back from work the other night, I caught sight of a pterosaurus. It was gliding on the rising air currents in search of carrion' (1975: 51). Jules' mind is filled with undigested chunks of unrelated text, or language. In order to improve himself he has been reading about evolutionary theory. He is also a devoted follower of 'Boggy'—Humphrey Bogart. At the end of the play the Bogart language overwhelms him entirely and articulates his destruction, as he talks through what might be one of Bogart's last scenes in the role of the tough guy driven into a corner finally having no alternative but to shoot both himself and his girl. The characters have little or no control over these slices of language which appear and then disappear, like icebergs, occasionally colliding with one another.

Most of Deutsch's characters are drawn from the bottom rungs of the social scale, peasants or urban workers. He has explained that at first he believed that their speech must be recorded and copied. 'That did not last long. I realized that the only thing that one could record was *silence* and the rhythm of that silence; the speech of these people escaped me' (Sarrazac, 1976: 97). But, unlike Kroetz, he did not reproduce the silence of the inarticulate in his plays. This would have been to fall into the 'ever-present threat' of 'reactionary naturalism' (ibid.). Instead, he introduced other discourses struggling for supremacy: the slogans of advertising, the small-talk of the secretarial office, the glamourised dialogue of Hollywood westerns. The emotional force of his plays arises from his use of dramatic irony: the audience observes characters struggling for independent life who are so deeply alienated that they seize on just that language or behaviour that is the very instrument of their destruction.

Violence is a constant factor in Deutsch's work, and while he is alert to the danger of naturalism, he does not always avoid the opposite danger of melodrama. Sometimes he even seems to welcome it, as in *L'Entraînement du champion avant la course*, a bloody tale of a man who murders his mistress (a butcher), and is poisoned by his wife. But the violence is only an extreme aspect of both the language and the behaviour imposed on his characters by external forces. In order to achieve a contemporary realism, Deutsch feels that it is essential to see that 'power relationships do not simply express themselves through state apparatus but they pierce us through completely, *pierce through our bodies*' (Sarrazac, 1976: 95). Some of his plays present scenes of almost unbearable violence, like the penultimate scene of *La Bonne Vie*, when Marie finds herself miscarrying in the toilets of a café. But the violence is not presented aggressively. It is violence suffered, helplessly.

What prevents these plays most of the time from seeming melodramatic, inflated or superficial is the fragmentation of the action. In traditional melodrama the causes and effects are too easily explained: the stereotype wicked landlord oppresses the poor widow because he is a greedy monster with no pity. But in Deutsch's plays the stories are so disjointed that the audience is never allowed to supply simple explanations of this kind. Instead, they are confronted with the irreducible reality of suffering and alienation and encouraged to look for explanations that lie outside the fictive world of the play. This is achieved partly by questioning the familiar expressions of everyday experience. Sarrazac (1981: 72) points out the centrality of the table in many of Deutsch's plays as an expression of the woman's everyday experience of reality. On it she has to provide, share out, labour, sometimes even offer herself to be shared out as in the case of *L'Entraînement,* in which the table is a butcher's chopping block. Deutsch explodes the whole concept of the bourgeois interior as a location for meaningful action. The interiors in his plays are evacuators of meaning: they contain nothing but destructive forces and the harder a character tries to deny this, like the butcher in *L'Entraînement,* the more destructive is the final result.

Deutsch has said that his aim is to present moments of revolt since even in the most oppressive situations 'there are always actions with a liberating content' (Sarrazac, 1976: 97). He gives, as an example, the moment in *L'Entraînement* when Maurice's wife and his mistress meet and discover that by coming together they can find a comfort and strength that is not possible while they remain separated in the roles of wife or mistress. But this is a very brief, utopian moment in the depiction of an otherwise violent and sordid reality. Where Deutsch is most successful in provoking a *prise de conscience* is in his whole treatment of women. For although their character outlines may be blurred by shifting contradictions, their physical reality is presented with great feeling and truth. Released from the traditional imagery of saintly, maternal love, or devilish, sexy seduction, their immediate problems are all to do with the realities of physical existence.

Jean-Paul Wenzel was responsible for founding a company entitled 'Le Théâtre du Quotidien', which performed *L'Entraînement* in 1975 under his direction. He has also written a number of plays, the best known being *Loin d'Hagondange*. This shows an ordinary working class couple at the end of their lives. After an unremarkable working life in Hagondange, they have retired to a little love-nest in the country, where they quietly die of boredom. Like the couple in Georges Michel's *Un Petit Nid d'amour*, they have accepted the model of married bliss that fits the needs of consumer society: they have cut themselves off from community life and concentrated instead on acquisitions. All their energies have been directed towards the purchase of the ideal retirement house. Now that they are there, they have no mental or spiritual resources with which to fill it or give it meaning. Without the familiar clichés of the husband's workaday routine to fall back on, the couple have nothing to say to one another. The husband continues to go to work in his garden shed each day, as he had previously gone off to the steel-works, the wife continues to clean up a house that never gets dirty. Their words express the alienation that has been forced upon them in the course of a working life: nothing of passion or personal value is left. Their language simply reproduces the slogans and clichés with which they have been force-fed.

Loin d'Hagondange was a sudden success for Wenzel, particularly after its production by Patrice Chéreau (T.N.P. 1977), who set the couple's retirement house in a Surrealist desert landscape. Chéreau's production exploited to the full the quality that much of the *théâtre du quotidien* shares with Pinter: its use of silence. The emptiness of these two old people's lives, their unspoken desires and repressed longings were conveyed as much by the intervals between their words as by the words themselves. Wenzel's subsequent plays have tended to develop the theme of latent violence, rejecting the passivity of the old couple in *Loin d'Hagondange*: 'I felt that the sentimentality of *Loin d'Hagondange* reassured and comforted too many people, that it veiled the violence of daily life that is contained in the play' (1982: 12). In his next play, *Marianne attend le mariage* (1975), he showed this violence erupting openly in a working class family, where one of the daughters is made to feel so guilty about a minor shop-lifting incident that she commits suicide and provokes the disintegration of the family group.

The authors of *le théâtre du quotidien* are always in danger of belittling their working class characters, of emphasising their alienation and victimisation to the point of patronising or even scorning them. This is why Deutsch insists that he wishes to avoid 'reactionary naturalism', i.e. the mere stating of lamentable facts. In his best plays he escapes from this danger by an approach that is more questioning than stating: he probes at the very concept of character, calling into question the received ideas of fixed personality and conscious value choices. His most successful plays are those like *Convoi*, in which the interplay of public violence and private suffering is evoked by means of a precise historical situation. The result is not 'reactionary naturalism' but a surprising revelation of a situation that had at first seemed familiar. By contrast, the stereotyped characters of Georges Michel's plays seem excessively arid by the end of a performance, lacking the detail and complexity of lived experience.

The work of the authors I have been discussing is an attempt to come to terms with the fragmented reality of a daily life which can no longer be made sense of, where both the personal motivations of individuals and the behaviour of public bodies seem beyond control. Their authors see them as political plays, provoking a *prise de conscience* in their audiences, but eschewing the neat demonstration formulae of plays which try to show how to have a revolution. Where they succeed, it is by their use of contradiction and discontinuity. In this way they demonstrate rather than discuss the broken lives that they choose to dramatise. Because of this, they all rely heavily on the immediacy of performance. Where the drama is chiefly one of language, the different forms of discourse must be enacted, permitting the language to establish its own rhythms and to impose its own life (or death) on the characters. Frequently these dramatists leave considerable scope to the director and actors to fill the spaces in the text with appropriate actions that will challenge its claims to dominance. Attempts to define a new relationship between text and action in this fragmented world have led to impressive experiments in staging such as Chéreau's production of *Loin d'Hagondange* (see Burgess: 1977) or a montage of fragmented scenes from many different plays including extracts from Molière, Beckett, Büchner, Brecht, Handke, Kroetz, Deutsch and Wenzel at the Comédie de Caen entitled *Le Désamour* (1980). For this production a multiple set was constructed that used all the spaces in the theatre, representing a street and a three-storey block of flats with the front wall removed. The audience itself was fragmented, not sitting in a single block, but separated into male and female and placed on different sides of the structure so as to observe the different scenes from different points of view. To many critics, this production appeared to represent the culmination of a decade of experimentation in new writing and staging methods, because it had found a concrete form of expression for the drama of multiple viewpoint towards which writers of the *théâtre du quotidien* school had been reaching (see *Loisir* (Caen) 35, 1980).

In the work of authors such as Kalisky, Wenzel and Deutsch, we can see a fusion of the discoveries of both New and Epic theatre. From Epic theatre they have acquired a skill in presenting lived experience in such a way as to reveal its socially determining factors. From the New Theatre, they have borrowed what Kalisky calls 'an interpenetration of space, of locality, of time, of consciousness, giving rise to new realities, ephemeral, unfixed' (1978: 223). Kalisky's later plays demonstrate this 'interpenetration' at work. In *Dave au bord de la mer* (1978), we see the experiences of Saul, David and Jonathan from the Old Testament superimposed on the relationships of a group of modern Israelis facing the threat of terrorist attack. Or, rather, the surface of the twentieth century characters' reality is constantly disturbed by the eruption of the mythical archetypes. The result is a fascinating attempt to show how the violent lives of modern men and women are experienced through the reliving of subconscious mythical models. Kalisky presents a multiple view of his characters' reality, refusing to provide his audience with a single, authoritative interpretation.

Michel Vinaver

The outstanding playwright of the seventies, also employing a drama of multiple viewpoint, is Michel Vinaver. In fact Vinaver's early plays were written in the course of the fifties, but the experienced a long fallow period during the sixties, becoming identified with the *théâtre du quotidien* in the middle seventies. Vinaver's first play, *Aujourd'hui ou les Coréens,* had enjoyed some success two decades previously: it had been produced by Planchon at the Théâtre de la Comédie in 1956, by Jean-Marie Serreau at the Alliance Française in 1957, by Charles Joris with the company that was to become the Théâtre Populaire Romand in 1959 and by Gabriel Monnet at the Comédie de Saint Etienne in 1960. But Vinaver wrote only one other full-length play, *Iphigénie Hotel,* before *Par-dessus bord,* written at the end of the sixties.

The action of *Aujourd'hui ou les Coréens* alternates between half a dozen French soldiers in the Korean war who have lost contact with their company and a group of Korean villagers. One of the soldiers stumbles on the village, where he is accepted and becomes integrated into the village life. In the course of this process the fixed ideologies and labels that have hitherto structured his experience of life fall away and simply lose their use. In a perceptive review, Barthes noted that '*Aujourd'hui,* as its title indicates, offers the present as a material that is *immediately* structurable and contradicts the traditional dogma of Revolution as an essentially eschatological time span' (1978: 59). Vinaver's original insistence on the immediate experience of the here and now as his basic dramatic material was to be the basis of his mature plays in the seventies. Both *Les Coréens* and *Iphigénie Hotel* are youthful plays in which he can be seen trying out a new form that would allow him to escape from the false alternative: either political theatre or absurdist theatre. The result is two plays concerning violent events but recounted, as it were, from a distance. In *Les Coréens* the villagers are awaiting the arrival of the liberation army, but the French forces fall back more quickly than expected, the army presses ahead and does not, after all, come to the village. In *Iphigénie Hotel,* the fall of the Fourth Republic is experienced by a group of tourists cut off in a hotel in Mycene, listening to unreliable radio reports. Instead of presenting historical events at first hand, these plays present history as experienced by the mass of people, having only partial information, feeling cut off from the centre of interest, yet discovering themselves in the seemingly unimportant details of everyday life.

In between *Iphigénie Hotel* and *Par-dessus bord* there was a period when his energies were fully absorbed by the multi-national corporation for which he worked. Moreover, he was unable to see how to bridge the gap between the cut-throat realities of a big international business concern and the fictions of theatre. He finally overcame this difficulty by writing *Par-dessus bord,* a work of enormous dimensions that would take at least eight hours to stage in its entirety, but in which melodrama is rigorously excluded by a style that is faithful to Vinaver's special feel for the everyday. Later, he explained that the centre of his creative life had always been located in the experience of 'astonishment at being permitted the simplest of things, such as opening a door, running, stopping, etc . . . all my (literary) activity has been an attempt to penetrate this territory of the everyday, which was never *given* to me but which had to be discovered, forced open. In other words, for the writer that I am, nothing exists before writing; to write is to try to give consistency to the world and to myself within it' (Vinaver, 1979: 73).

With this style of writing, the challenge was of course to avoid boredom, since 'the everyday is what is both repetitive and flat. An alchemy must operate so that the most uninteresting magma is transmuted into an object of enjoyment and understanding' (Vinaver, 1982: 132). The success of productions, both of *Les Coréens* in the late fifties and of his more recent plays, shows that in performance his texts do achieve this alchemical operation, and the fascination of Vinaver's theatre is to discover how this is done. The most striking feature of his plays is that they are not committed in the usual sense of the word, they do not take sides or present the pros and cons of an idea or situation. At first sight they are in fact more like stream of consciousness novels than plays. The text of *Iphigénie Hotel* seemed so undramatic that no director would take it on until Vitez produced it in 1977. As a director, Vitez likes to work by contradictions. Rather than construct a unified character, he encourages his actors to look for discontinuities, to show abrupt, even inexplicable changes of mood. He also encourages them to play against the text so that a tension emerges from, say, a suave piece of writing and a jerky delivery, or vice versa. He was attracted by the rather undramatic nature of Vinaver's work and appreciated his attempt to write 'not so much *for* the theatre . . . but rather against the theatre' (Vinaver, 1982: 294-5). Vinaver, in turn, appreciated Vitez's 'rare virtue of considering a text for what it is, as a *non-soluble element*' (ibid. 286). He considers that the best texts do not necessarily transfer easily to the stage but that 'what is productive are the tensions caused by the meeting of text and performance' (ibid. 151). The dialogue in his plays since *Par-dessus bord* is entirely devoid of punctuation except for the use of question marks. Sometimes the name of the speaker is not even specified. There is very little in the way of stage directions. The result is a verbal texture of great complexity and ambiguity. On the page it appears to be an unstructured copy of conversations that might be overheard in a great many everyday situations. But in performance the effect is more like that of exposing a cross-section of a human brain. On the bared surface are revealed mental or spiritual movements that range from the most superficial to the most profound, from those easily accounted for to those that are seemingly incomprehensible. Each page of text offers the possibility of many different interpretations because different kinds of statement jostle with one another quite unseparated by the verbal fabric, and leaving a permanent uncertainty about what the characters may be *doing* as they speak a given line.

One way of understanding Vinaver's writing is to compare it to painting. He is fond of such comparisons and has even written that he wishes he had been born with a talent for painting or composing rather than writing, carrying the ability to work simply with form, tone and rhythm (1979: 74). He claims that his work deals not so much with people, ideas, conditions, as with the relations between these things, just as Braque claimed that the important thing in his pictures was less the objects depicted than the space between them. This comparison is both accurate and helpful, for the discontinuities and contradictions of Vinaver's style are the marks of the first thoroughly successful drama of multiple viewpoint. Just like Picasso, Braque, Joyce, Eliot and the whole Modernist school of painters, poets and novelists, Vinaver's fragmented viewpoint is both statement and formal device. It states the impossibility of ever reaching the unified, coherent world view and asserts that only *meanings* not *meaning* can be found. It is not surprising that this drama of multiple viewpoint should have arrived in the theatre so slowly and so tentatively. The experience of theatre is immediate and cannot easily be interrupted or held at a distance like paintings, poems or novels. Vinaver wanted to find a way of combining the immediate experience with self-conscious reflection on the problems of fragmented vision. He could see that in some way the usual linear form of dramatic story-telling had to be changed, something new put in its place. That something, he describes as the very material of human intercourse, the texture of language itself (see 1982: 310).

In this way Vinaver is able to write plays that reflect both on society and on the means available to the theatre for depicting that society: his plays are both socially satirical and theatrically satirical. *Par-dessus bord,* written at the end of the sixties, employs elements of all the theatre styles fashionable at that time: total theatre, archaic myth, nudity, happenings, music theatre, dance theatre, etc. etc. It has a Rabelaisian quality; the subject is a toilet-paper manufacturing business and its attempts to change with the times: both from hard and crinkly to 'soft strength' and from the methods of an old-fashioned family firm to aggressive American marketing techniques. The story is commented on from within at different levels. The most obvious comments come from Passemar, who is both on the management staff of the firm and an autobiographical figure for Vinaver. His comments and interruptions have the same self-conscious ironic quality as those of Gide in *Les Faux-Monnayeurs.* Passemar gives us a running commentary on both theatrical and management techniques. Another commentator figure who intrudes is an old-school professor lecturing on Norse myths. Linked to his lectures is a group of dancers who want to use the myths for a mime and movement performance. The incomprehensible battles of the Norse gods provide an ironic counterpoint to the equally incomprehensible manoeuvres of the business world. There is also a group of jazz musicians who arrange 'happenings' in order to increase their popularity with a certain middle class public. This provides scope for the author to introduce discussion of the ultimate temptation in the happening: to create an event through other people's blood and suffering. The happenings of a tired avant-garde are contrasted with similar *Aktionen* inflicted by the Nazis on Jewish groups in Poland.

As well as this kind of comment, the social and economic function of a business like the toilet-paper firm is presented from a number of different viewpoints: that of the travelling salesman; of the secretaries; the various heads of department; the different members of the owning family; a banker; a Dominican father and the marketing consultants who come in to advise on plans for expansion; as well as the American president of the competing firm, who finally concedes defeat but buys them up as a profitable subsidiary. The play presents a kind of war of different languages: office jargon; franglais marketing jargon; old-fashioned academic language; new media slang; jazzmen's roughtalk; salesmen's smoothtalk; high-finance talk, etc. It is through the juxtaposition of these different languages that Vinaver scores his best ironic effects. For example, the story of the killing of Baldr, the visionary hero whose good judgements could never be put into practice, is enacted by the dancers immediately before the crushing analysis of the firm's management methods by Donohue and Frankfurter, the American marketing consultants. The two different ways of talking about the painful relinquishing of the old values reverberate against one another.

Many of the play's high points are achieved through Vinaver's sensitivity to the humorous possibilities inherent in displaying the place of linguistic manipulation in people's relations with one another and with their social conditions. Two scenes, one near the beginning and one near the end, depict the firm's annual office party. They are written like choral passages in Greek tragedy with no attribution of lines to speakers. The effect they create is of a group voice expressing a guarded loyalty towards the firm, a sense of outrage at the behaviour of fellow employees who have overstepped the unwritten rules of management, a grudging admiration for business success and a generalised feeling of being taken for a ride. These responses to the firm are interwoven with concerns of a more personal nature, so that the overall effect of the passage is to suggest how corporate life invades private life and vice versa. The choric device is used again for an outrageously comic 'brainstorm' session, in which the firm's executives get together to practise free association so as to produce a new name for their product. The final choice, 'Mousse et Bruyère' is only one of a list of some 200 similarly fatuous ideas, including such suggestions as 'Gair Sourire', 'Doux Baiser', 'Chaud Baiser' or 'Toison d'Or', 'Mon Plaisir', 'Sable d'Or', 'Vigne Vierge'. More insidious, as John Burgess has pointed out, are the passages in which the marketing consultants are able to manipulate the glib commercial jargon and newspeak of international commerce to mask the sterility of the economic competition and the inhumanity of the procedures it dictates (1974b).

Out of this rich kaleidoscope, Vinaver thought, the material for several different productions could be extracted. In 1956 and 1957 he had felt that neither of the two productions by Planchon and Serreau conveyed the full *Coréens,* but that taken together they did. He allowed Planchon to rewrite his own version of *Par-dessus bord* in the hopes that other productions would follow. In fact Vinaver was disappointed. The situation had changed, Planchon was no longer an interesting young outsider but the acknowledged leader, and no other producer was ready to invite invidious comparisons. What had impressed Planchon about the play was its documentary accuracy (the development of the toilet-paper industry in the seventies was, in fact, almost exactly as predicted in the play). He admired Vinaver's unique insight into the business world, and his vivid sense of contemporary dialogue. But he could see no solution to staging it as written, since it calls for many of the different actions to overlap or take place simultaneously. He therefore looked for a solution that would achieve the effect of fragmenting the story and ironically undermining it, but by scenic rather than verbal means. He used a technique that he had perfected over a long period, introducing features of the American musical comedy form to undermine the American economic conquest of French business. He considered that seeing American advertising consultants moving like Gene Kelly while discussing submerged drives and sales psychology had just the right derisive effect. Many of the subsidiary actions were cut and the whole play treated in a highly theatrical manner (see fig. 20).

Planchon claimed that it was permissible to treat Vinaver's text in this way *because* it was so brilliantly exact about what life is like in business. He contrasted it with *Paolo Paoli* which, he said, had required a realistic production because Adamov did not really know business life from the inside, but 'the truth of Vinaver's play is so strong, at the textual level, that everything can be transposed' (1975b: 36). At the time, Vinaver accepted Planchon's manipulation of his text, but, in later comments, he regretted the fact that in Planchon's production the linear story-line had once again become predominant and he felt that a production reproducing more faithfully the texture of the original might have been possible. He was no doubt encouraged by the faithful production in 1980 by Jacques Lassalle of *A la renverse,* a second play about the fortunes of a French firm, this time a manufacturer of sun-tan cream. The play presented many of the same features as *Par-dessus bord,* including the use of choral passages, though it was a more manageable length for stage performance. In between these two major works, Vinaver had written four shorter plays: *La Demande d'emploi* (produced in Paris and Lausanne in 1973 and in Caen in 1975); *Dissident, il va sans dire* and *Nina, c'est autre chose* (T.E.P. 1978); and *Les Travaux et les jours* (Annecy 1980).

Les Travaux et les jours is a masterpiece. Its title is borrowed from Hesiod (with overtones of Proust's *Les Plaisirs et les jours*) and demonstrates Vinaver's tendency, like T. S. Eliot whom he admires, to fill his work with obscure references to the ancient world. By studying this play we can discover the quintessential Vinaver more easily than from *Par-dessus bord* because this play is so much more pared down. It has a cast of only five and is set in the after-sales office of a firm making coffee grinders. There are three secretaries who take phone calls from the customers and explain how and where to send the machines for repair. In addition, there is the office manager and one blue-collar worker with a workbench at which he repairs urgent or special cases.

The three women talk amongst themselves when they are not on the phone—and sometimes even in the middle of a call—revealing not only the development of the firm but the progress of their private lives as well. Theirs is a world in which people are supposed to give meaning to their lives through their work. It is also the world of immense technical improvements in communications equipment. Through this work that is supposed to satisfy, and this equipment that is supposed to improve communications, the five characters live out their frustrated and fragmented lives. The only language that any of them can speak with perfect fluency is the language of the firm's promotional publications. But the more thoroughly they have mastered it, the more of themselves they have invested in it, the more it lets them down in the end.

To a greater or lesser extent each character finds a way of preserving his or her personal integrity. It is easiest for the men because in the unwritten law of the office world they always dominate: Guillermo by virtue of his proletarian past, Jaudouard by virtue of his power as boss. Each of the three women finds herself in competition for the favours of one or both of these men. In addition they cannot help noticing that many of the people who ring up do so less because of their broken coffee grinders than because they need to talk to someone. Beside these demands on them, they struggle to establish some space for their own emotional needs but end up simply articulating their own oppression: the comforting phrases that they offer to one another when troubles come are the echo of those they offer to the customers. Vinaver's analysis of modern man is that he is 'both crushed by a system but at the same time in perfect communion with it' (1982: 286). This paradox had been exploited by Adamov, particularly in *Le Ping-Pong,* but without quite the same vividness of lived everyday reality: *Le Ping-Pong* was still to some extent a dream play. Vinaver's play follows rigorously the pattern of real life: the company is bought up, economies are discussed, the work force goes on strike. The girls cope heroically with increasing calls, explaining to anxious customers that repairs will continue—as soon as the situation is normal. But as soon as this is so, it transpires that the after-sales service will be a victim of the economies. There will be no one to talk to callers; instead a computer will be installed to send the customer one of a range of 64 standard replies drawn up in advance. In the end only the youngest of the three is kept on because she has made eyes at the appropriate director in the lift.

The story element has been reduced to a minimum and is fairly ordinary. The play's brilliance is in Vinaver's dialogues which are ambiguous and fragmentary, mixing up different streams of consciousness and sequences of ideas.

Questions and answers do not correspond, they are interrupted by other lines of discussion, but through these shifting perspectives five different worlds are built up, each with a point of intersection in the office, but reaching beyond it, too, into the subconscious and emotional worlds of the characters. The method avoids all the usual traps of melodrama, sentimentality or didacticism by this subtle interweaving of themes and languages.

It is instructive to compare this play with Grumberg's *L'Atelier* (see above p. 232). Both plays present a group of women in their place of work dominated by structures of male authority. In *L'Atelier*, Grumberg skilfully arranges every event in a sequence that appears to be self-explanatory and gives the impression of reality. Vinaver, on the other hand, asks his audience to abandon this privileged perspective and to experience something of the confusions and ambiguities of the characters themselves. He makes it difficult for his audience to lose themselves in sympathy with the characters, because they are constantly having to re-assess the truth of those characters' situations. In Grumberg's play we are not invited to doubt or to question the veracity of the narrative. In Vinaver's we receive as many different versions of the events as there are characters on stage. All have a different understanding of what is happening to them and the play does not gradually reveal the falsehood of one view set against the truth of another: it obliges us to construct the reality of the situation as we go along from the patchwork of views, emotions and actions that appear before us. The play asks its audience, not to admire a particular behaviour pattern, but to work out what freedom of action is available to a given character in a given situation. Each slightly different image of the modern world that is presented carries an ethical and political value. The spectator must constantly accept or reject these values. In Vinaver's play the humour arises from the discrepancies and disjunctions between things that appear to the characters on stage to fit together but can be seen not to do so by the audience. They leave the theatre having had their emotions touched by an understanding of how we all love the system that destroys us—how easily we project human values onto an inhumane enterprise that serves only efficiency and profitability. In both plays the problems of a whole society are evoked through a microcosm. But Grumberg's microcosm is self-contained, specific to a particular class group. Vinaver's is at once more limited and more open. We do not receive the same sense of a homogeneous group. But we do see how everything hangs together—how a decision taken in an American boardroom may influence the emotional development of a French secretarial worker.

When Vinaver talks about his own writing, he emphasises the importance, in dramatic dialogue, of being able to set in relation one to another elements having, at the outset, nothing in common, so that 'a line by a character who is not in any way part of the dramatic situation of the character who spoke the line before will nevertheless influence the situation in question' (Vinaver, 1982: 288). What is offered to the spectator is a collage of fragments which generate meanings by collisions and reverberations. The meanings produced in this way tend to be ironic. Vinaver defines irony as: 'brutal discrepancy between what is expected and what happens' and maintains that its effect is like an electric shock in which a circuit is established and through which the current passes—'a current of meaning' (Vinaver, 1979: 74). These principles are particularly well illustrated in *A la renverse,* where the sun-tan cream firm is ruined because of a popular television programme in which the princess of Bourbon-Beaugency, dying of skin cancer, talks week by week of the progress of her illness and her former devotion to acquiring a sun-tan. For the 1980 production by Jacques Lassalle at the Chaillot theatre, a special television film was made, which was inserted into the stage performance using playback monitors. For the audience the experience was of two distinct discourses—the sentimentalised bravery of the dying princess and the desperate attempts to stimulate the market by the firm's executives—which completely failed to intersect but threw up richly comic ironies.

Because of their unusual form, the experience of watching these plays can at first be strange but it is not mystifying: 'after a few minutes' acclimatisation', wrote the critic Michel Cournot, 'the spectator-listener has the feeling that he holds within his grasp the multiple series of causes and effects contributing to a given event, whereas classic linear dialogue reduces these series to a single thread. From this grasp there arises, in the audience, a profound emotion, stemming no doubt from the fact that life itself seems to be captured in the fullness of its flux and all its mystery' (*Le Monde* 14 March 1980). Although all Vinaver's plays present moments of profound emotion, a mood of ironic humour is perhaps even more characteristic of them. In his view the role of the dramatist is to provoke cracks in the established order, to uncover the world in an unexpected light, and the method for doing this is ironic humour. He rejects the Romantic notion of the artist as a man with a mission, because if he presents a new vision he always ends up suppressed or censored by the established order. He claims instead the role of the fool, whose function is to say what nobody dares think and to confuse people's views (Vinaver, 1982: 316). His achievement is, as Sarrazac points out (1981), to have abandoned a theatre of *stories* for a theatre of *possibilities* which goes beyond the failure of the linear plot-line as explored, say, in *En attendant Godot*. In the fragmented structures of their plays in the sixties, writers such as Adamov and Gatti had already pointed towards this theatre of possibilities. Like Kalisky (see above p. 240), Gatti had invoked the need for different, parallel realities to be shown simultaneously on stage (Gatti, 1964: 15). Vinaver's plays represent a further refinement of similar ideas: he suggests that if it is impossible to make sense of our lives as linear sequences, then we must go back to each separate situation, and try out their possible combinations. In this way a new form of Epic theatre is created, opposed to the Aristotelian like Brecht's, and depending on the Modernist aesthetic of the tableau viewed kaleidoscopically from multiple viewpoints. Like Gatti and the other writers of the sixties, Vinaver and the writers of the *théâtre du quotidien* have been reaching for a *new way of seeing*; in so doing, they have helped to create a new dramatic form.

Jeanyves Guérin (essay date 1984)

SOURCE: Guérin, Jeanyves. "Is There Something Rotten in the State of French Theater?" In *Myths and Realities of Contemporary French Theater: Comparative Views*, edited by Patricia M. Hopkins and Wendell A. Aycock, pp. 13-35. Lubbock, TX: Texas Tech Press, 1984.

[*In the following essay, Guérin traces the development of French theater from the 1930s to the 1960s, noting that the non-establishment authors of the 1960s are now part of the established French literary scene and as such are focusing on experimentation that is based in realism and the use of traditional imagery.*]

During the nineteenth century, the French theater went through a long period of decline. Musset, Labiche, and later Giraudoux are like giant oaks called upon to hide a stunted forest. Strindberg, Ibsen, Chekhov, Pirandello and others had no French counterparts of their stature. But renewal came from the professionals in the theater. Louis Becq de Fouquières published *L'Art de la mise en scène* in 1884, and three years later André Antoine founded the *Théâtre libre*. After 1914, Jacques Copeau, one of the founders of *La Nouvelle Revue Française*, and the "Cartel"—Gaston Baty, Louis Jouvet, Charles Dullin, Georges Pitoeff—revived the classic repertory, introduced foreign masters to France, and encouraged poets to write for the theater. All of them relied on the intelligentsia and on an enlightened minority of the bourgeois audience, although most of the critics were hostile to them. Nevertheless these reformers were less radical than their German and Soviet contemporaries who were influenced by Expressionism. In 1945, in spite of Giraudoux, French drama lagged behind the novel, which enjoyed a particularly brilliant period between the two world wars, with Proust, Gide, Martin du Gard, Mauriac, Malraux, Bernanos, Giono and others. Competition with the cinema seemed to be fatal to the theater.

However, at the very moment when the leaders of the Cartel were dying off, there was an unexpected flourishing of authors. Philosophers such as Gabriel Marcel, Camus, and Sartre turned to the stage; to be sure, their plays have aged as quickly as the issues which they dealt with (although *Caligula* and *Huis clos* are still viable plays and the theme of *Les Justes* is as relevant today as it was then, for it questions the ideological roots of terrorism). Poets and/or novelists too began to write for the stage. While Claudel received belated but brilliant recognition, Francois Mauriac, Jean Genet, Jean Tardieu, Marcel Aymé, Audiberti, and Georges Schéhadé joined Montherlant whose *La Reine morte* made him a famous playwright. Lastly there was the Theater of the Absurd or "Anti-theater." Three expatriots—Samuel Beckett, Eugène Ionesco, Arthur Adamov—were the instigators of the most creative adventure in the contemporary stage; they were totally unexpected.

It is with a certain nostalgia that veteran critics remember a time when theatergoers could see *En attendant Godot, Les Chaises,* Audiberti's *Le mal court* and *La Hobereaute*, Genet's *Les Bonnes,* Jean Vauthier's *Capitaine Bada,* as well as Montherlant's *Port-Royal*, Jean Anouilh's *L'Alouette* and *Becket,* and Marcel Aymé's *La Tête des autres*. At the same time, Bertolt Brecht was being discovered, and nearly all of Ghelderode's plays were being performed. The range of new works had never been so wide. At that time there was a great interest in presenting new plays. Jean-Marie Serreau produced Ionesco as well as Brecht.

During that period, which today seems to have been a Golden Age, the *Comédie Française* was presenting its classical, neoclassical, and pseudo-classical repertory in a miserly fashion. But Jean Vilar drew the crowds to his *Théâtre National Populaire,* and Jean-Louis Barrault inspired a brilliant period at the *Théâtre Marigny* where he produced a great variety of French and foreign plays of classic, modern, and contemporary authors. Thanks to him, the avant-garde authors enjoyed a great success in the sixties. Meanwhile, on the Left Bank, a few brave souls organized communal theater groups which, in dire circumstances, produced the first avant-garde plays.

Jean Vilar was a disciple of Jacques Copeau and the heir of the Cartel. He owed much to Firmin Gémier, Romain Rolland, and the *Volksbühnen* too. His ideas on the theater were based on three principles which could not be dissociated: the democratization of the audience, a high-quality repertory, and the redefinition of stage directing. Vilar, who was less a Marxist than a humanist republican of the left influenced by the *Front Populaire,* longed for a theater open to everyone without restriction and operating as a public service.[1] Neither the *Comédie Française* nor the commercial theater fit that category. He took his ideas from the gathering of the Greek city at Epidaurus and from the medieval mysteries played in front of the cathedrals.

The *Théâtre National Populaire,* under the direction of Vilar, featured Shakespeare, Corneille, and Molière. According to Vilar, the works of the great classic writers are universal: "des oeuvres-mères d'où tout peut et doit sortir et qui appartiennent à tous."[2] Thirty years later, many people remember passionately how magnificent Gérard Philipe was as the Cid. Great masterpieces, Vilar said, are powerful enough to make any interpretative reading of them superfluous or redundant. The moral they state needs no commentary. His opinion that theater for the people is "le théâtre tout court"[3] did not prevent him from giving preference to certain recurrent themes, which, according to one critic, were, in simple terms, power, money, war, and peace.[4]

No writer was to Vilar what Chekhov had been to Stanislavsky, Giraudoux to Jouvet, and Claudel to Barrault. Yet he often expressed his ambition of bringing back the great tragic theater and of helping to establish poets. But his audience did not understand him when he presented Henri Pichette's *Nucléa* in 1952. The resounding failure of this play obliged Vilar to temper his ambitions. When he later mounted plays of Boris Vian, René de Obaldia, and Robert Pinget, their success was distinctly less than that to which he had been accustomed. Two major aims were in conflict: the sociological broadening of the audience and the presentation of new works. The regular followers of the *Théâtre National Populaire* condemned Vilar's successor when he favored new plays at the expense of the classics. Vilar had the unconditional support of many people, but he never earned the support of the state. To protect his experiments, he had to use the classics as a shield. That Shakespeare, Marlowe, Kleist, and Büchner were to him more modern than Sartre and Armand Salacrou cannot be contested. That the plays of Anouilh, Montherlant, and Ghelderode seemed reactionary to him is more than probable; he nevertheless mounted *Murder in the Cathedral* and *La Ville* despite the fact that he did not appreciate Eliot's and Claudel's conservative views at all. But that this lover of beautiful language did not dare to present Audiberti's *Le Cavalier seul* remains a mystery to me.

After 1954, Vilar found himself to be outflanked on the left. During his first season at the *Théâtre National Populaire*, he had produced Bertolt Brecht's *Mother Courage*. The coming of the *Berliner Ensemble* to the *Théâtre des Nations* was, for many people, the equivalent of a Copernican revolution. The review *Théâtre populaire*, which in the beginning had been as favorable to Vilar's point of view as the first *N.R.F.* had been to Copeau's, immediately turned into a Brechtian fortress. Roland Barthes played a decisive role at that moment. In the eighteenth issue of the journal, he formulated an essential premise of the new dogma, i.e., innovation is not simply a question of aesthetics but always implies a new consciousness of History. The concept of modernity is only pertinent if it is socially progressive. It was not enough for the theater to deal with politics, it had to be partisan.[5]

The first *Théâtre populaire* published Marlowe, Büchner, Kafka, Joyce, Ghelderode, and Audiberti and defended the avant-garde against its detractors. The second one published Sean O'Casey, Maxim Gorky, George Lukacs, Ernst Piscator, and, at great length, Brecht. Bernard Dort, key critic of the journal, sermonized to everyone, to Vilar as well as to the new playwrights. The critic, enlightened by Marx, knows; the writer, when non-Marxist, does not. One must reeducate simple people: every totalitarian state demands it. Few critics volunteer to do the job. "Nous voulons vous instruire," said the Molièresque Bartholomeus who parodied Dort in Ionesco's *L'Impromptu de l'Alma*.[6]

Thus the utopia of the People's Theater as a public service moved towards Communist politics and Marxist ideology. Logically indeed Roland Barthes defended Sartre's most Stalinist play, *Nekrassov*. In short, a sectarian aesthetic took root, which was based on an ideology as rigid as steel. After 1960, *Théâtre populaire* influenced deeply the T.N.P. whose repertory became more and more political. They performed not only Brecht's *Three Penny Opera*, *The Good Woman of Sezuan* and *Arturo Ui*, but also mediocre plays of paracommunist writers such as Sean O'Casey and Michel Vinaver, whom the Brechtomaniacs adored.

If Brecht's influence was so strong, it was because there was a great demand for it. The epic theater of which he is the champion surely represents progress if compared with the progressionist repertory of the fifties. Sartre after 1952 was content to politicize Bernstein.[7] *Le Colonel Foster plaidera coupable* is pure Stalinist propaganda. We now know that Roger Vailland had submitted his manuscript to the central committee of the Communist Party.[8] Brecht is not only a playwright but at the same time a writer, a theoretician, and a practitioner. He has no French counterpart. Furthermore, he is a Marxist. While the French Communist Party, which is by far the most Stalinist of the entire Western World, had lost many of its intellectuals between 1947 and 1956, the intelligentsia of the left became more and more involved in Marxism. One remembers Sartre's famous conversion to the Stalinist vulgate and Camus's isolation after *L'Homme révolté*. Raymond Aron resisted the collective movement but he was simply relegated to [his] readers of *Le Figaro* for his pains.

It is because French Marxist men of letters failed and were so deceptive that Brecht shone so brightly in contrast. His work was the only one that was able to unite ecumenically all sections of the left, i.e., orthodox Communists, fellow travelers, Marxists of every hue, and advanced socialists. Rare enough were those such as Eugène Ionesco and Audiberti whose voices did not enter into the Brechtian concert.[9] Jean-Louis Barrault remained indifferent to the new fashion, but, as André Malraux had appointed him as the head of the *Odéon*, he was reduced to being the favorite of the Gaullist regime.

So in the sixties, Brechtomania tended to operate as a professional ideology. A power network was formed and spread throughout reviews, universities, and so on. A new generation of stage directors who had not seen the Cartel's productions came to the fore and continued the work of these pioneers. Brecht was their god, Bernard Dort their chief prophet, and Roger Planchon their pope. Dort went on judging contemporary drama and directing by the standards of epic realism. Between 1958 and 1968, two million people saw three thousand performances of Brecht's twenty-three plays. Most of them were produced in the style of the *Berliner Ensemble*. Rags and drab colors were de rigueur.

Brecht influenced critics and stage directors more than writers. The latter resisted the advisers of the review *Théâtre populaire*; Eugène Ionesco often told how Dort wanted to teach him how to write epic plays. The Brechtians of the Left Bank felt that Adamov could become the French Brecht. He was first linked with Artaud, then with

Audiberti and Ionesco. Around 1955, he received Marxist illumination. Dort applauded *Paolo Paoli* for showing the author's rallying to a "réalisme historique supérieur." Adamov, he wrote, converted a "causalité fétichiste" into a "dialectique historique."[10] In fact, the playwright was totally incapable of articulating his persecution complex and his political commitment—quite to the contrary.[11]

The decentralized network of this People's Theater progressively closed the door to the authors of the avantgarde. If Beckett and even Ionesco were performed sometimes, Ghelderode, Audiberti, and Schéhadé endured a real political ostracism. Dort reproached them for not taking account of the audience. Their plays, he wrote, were "pur exercice littéraire," "création verbale toute formelle." Having accomplished their critical mission, they became simple "décorateurs de la scène bourgeoise,"[12] i.e., super-Anouilhs and super-Roussins. Now it was time, for them, to make the decisive choice, to give in or to give up. For the absurd is acceptable only if it is satirical, as it is with Max Frisch and Dürrenmatt. It must then be converted to socio-historical statements. If not, it is idealistic, metaphysical, and/or nihilist. In the same way that Sartre refused to antagonize Billancourt by criticizing Soviet totalitarianism, Antitheater, for Dort and company, had to be disposed of in the dustbin of literary history. Young playwrights were supposed to be more flexible. The "plaisir du jeu," Dort wrote, prevailed in Philippe Adrien's *La Baye*. Be careful, "Guignol est désarmant."[13] *L'Agression* was nothing but a moral play. Georges Michel, who was close to Sartre, did not apply the sacrosanct alienation effect: he could do better.[14]

The process expanded towards the end of the sixties. The merry month of May 1968 offered the rare show of an aborted revolution which was accompanied by a great party. Angry students took over the *Odéon Théâtre de France* and provoked Barrault's fall from grace. Almost all the theaters in France were on strike or were forced to close. Thirty directors of *Maisons de la Culture* and *Centres Dramatiques Nationaux* held a council in Villeurbanne, Planchon's bastion. They were seized with a frenzy of self-accusation: all they had done up until then was to pass on our culture to the happy few; the time had come to radicalize the general public. The conciliatory ideology of theater as a public service fell apart. Vilar himself confessed his failure. People did not appreciate his self-criticism. A host of hirsute protesters shouted him down in Avignon.

France entered the affluent society belatedly. A few intellectuals imagined they were still living in the China of the thirties and dreamed of stirring up class struggle which had grown soft with the years. Their reasoning was that if you explained that fact to the people, they would make the revolution themselves. So theater professionals, after 1968, chose to make the long march away from the institutions, which were perceived as being hypocritically repressive. Some of them went to the gates of factories and to working class suburbs where they questioned people and endlessly preached the revolutionary gospel to them.

Literature with a message generally appears in periods of pronounced political polarization, as in the thirties and during the Cold War. The paradox is that intellectuals and artists turned radical just after France had put an end to its colonial wars. Fortunately for them there remained the U.S. scapegoat: that meant their commitment was vicarious. So theater people addressed themselves principally to the faithful, i.e., to sects of subscribers to the same culture ("abonnés à la même culture qu'eux," as Rene Kalisky wrote).[15] They were convinced that, while discoursing eloquently about class struggle, they actually were taking part in it and were communicating to the real working class. Among the dramatic plots which were prevalent at the time, let us mention first the evolution of a character confronted with an event or a situation. The spectators were prompted to imitate this evolution when positive, and to reject it when negative. Another configuration: the antagonistic situation of which the prototype is the exemplary struggle between the valiant workers and their bad boss or between the heroic Viet Cong and the U.S. Army. Whether the good lose or win the battle is not important: the chosen people will win the war. "Ce n'est qu'un début, continuons le combat."

The degradation of the Brechtian model is obvious. These kinds of voluntary plays or childish sketches existed only for the interpretative and pragmatic statements (i.e., injunctions to act well) with which the playwright had larded them. In brief, we returned to *Proletkult* and to the *Cabaret rouge* or better to Guild Drama. The guerrilla theater or the street theater was showing things not as they really are or were but as the prevailing ideological code wished them to be. René Kalisky sees frankly nothing but an "univers paranoïaque climatisé"[16] in the Manichaean repertory that proliferated after 1968. Needless to say that *Geronimo, Sarcelles-sur-mer, Douze mois de la vie de Michel T., Histoire, vieille taupe, tu as bien travaillé, La Bécane, La Pastorale de Fos,* and other radical melodramas bombed pitifully. The simpler the thesis, the more perishable is the play (or the novel). One can see retrospectively how liberal the Democratic State was, which not only tolerated but often subsidized productions having openly subversive purposes. Malraux's successors, Edmond Michelet and Jacques Duhamel, defended young rebels whom the exasperated bourgeois elites longed to dismiss. The same institutions were, for some people, cultural supermarkets or museums and, for others, revolutionary centers. The main result of Brechtian dogmatism and of radical activism was that they weakened and discredited Vilar's work.

One would be wrong to view the Brechtian axiomatic as the exclusive *doxa* of the time. Bernard Dort himself admitted an impression of saturation. "Il est de fait," he wrote, "que nous avons le sentiment d'avoir fait le tour de Brecht."[17] The *poète maudit* Antonin Artaud, who just escaped from literary purgatory, was the hero of the young generation. Few (among whom Adamov, Barrault, and Roger Blin) were acquainted with him—in fact, *Le Théâtre et son double* was not published in paperback until 1966.

In the same way that the surrealist happening of May 1968 spoke the wooden Marxist language, although its spirit was profoundly libertarian, Artaud, who was the ultimate apolitical writer, was viewed as a radical guru of the same stature as Herbert Marcuse. People carried out his ideas more than they read his works. His scattered writings, which Jacques Derrida, Jean-François Lyotard, Michel Foucault, Gilles Deleuze, and Félix Guattari had commented on, were received as opening a part-mystical, part-libertarian path which hairy rebels rushed down.

These writings are too illusive and contradictory to breed any orthodoxy. Their deconstruction is easy: everyone may choose what he likes. *Le Théâtre et son double* justifies all sorts of things: collective creation, psychodrama, improvisation, happenings, sexual liberation, confrontation theater, etc. Conversational drama was replaced by a vociferous and gesticulating theater. Howling and groveling became the signs and testimonies of creativity. Dort sniffed out the danger: ". . . ainsi ce théâtre de participation physique devient-il théâtre de communion métaphysique; spectateurs et acteurs sont passés du constat à l'effusion. Le politique a été placé comme entre parenthèses; il est devenu le moyen d'une sorte d'extase collective. Le théâtre-choc est un théâtre d'autosatisfaction."[18]

The Living Theatre created a sensation and a scandal in Avignon. But Arrabal's "Théâtre panique" turned into commercial exhibitionism and the playwright reconverted himself into an antitotalitarian militant. Artaud's youngest adepts thought any institution had to be destroyed in order to free the creative and revolutionary energies that the actors' collectives contained. But nearly all self-managed communes failed in the seventies for want of professional competence. Fringe Theater became what Colette Godard called a "poubelle à ringards."[19] The *Théâtre du Soleil* and the *Grand Magic Circus,* from which the charismatic personalities of Ariane Mnouchkine and Jérôme Savary emerged, survived, for they had become institutions in themselves. The big loser after 1968 was the text. We shall come back to this point later.

The totemization of both Brecht and Artaud, like that of Marx and Freud, intensified their ideological competition, for syncretisms are always fragile. It ended in their mutual delegitimization. But if Brecht's decline was evident in the late seventies, it was mainly because his theoretical foundation had collapsed. The blows of the New Left destroyed the old Marxist paradigm and offered an alternative that combined libertarian anarchism and social democracy. The "new philosophers," all former radicals, vulgarized the theses of the New Left. (Their mistake was to claim the role of gurus; having done their job, Bernard-Henri Lévy and company lost all their credibility.) The taboo of being anti-communist disappeared when the last illusions about the East were torn apart in Prague. Ten years later, the most influential thinkers are Michel Foucault, René Girard, Cornelius Castoriadis, Alain Touraine, and André Glucksmann, who care little for the Marxist vulgate. The criticism of totalitarianism is the *doxa* of the eighties. Repented Maoists have turned into libertarians if not into liberals or conservatives. The change is so spectacular that the socialist spokesman of the government may plead in favor of individualistic values.[20] The French Left sold off the laws of History, the dictatorship of the proletariat, the cult of the state, the revolutionary eschatology, the class struggle, the belief in progress, the theory of dominant ideology, etc. New socialists developed a culture of government the base of which is pragmatism. François Mitterrand nowadays calls people to cooperate between social classes as eloquently as he once preached class struggle. The key words of the political vocabulary have changed: "reform," "contract," "negotiation," and "debate" have replaced "revolution," "struggle," "subversion," and "violence." The red flag and the brandished fist are today viewed as obsolete clichés. The intellectuals cherished them in the early seventies. The only Marx they now tolerate is called Groucho. So intellectuals and socialists on the one hand, the world of the theater on the other, have accomplished a long transmigration which has brought them from the Communist realm to the Socialist one. The real audience of the People's Theater, principally made up of white collars, teachers, and militants, made the same transmigration. Theater people fell into the spirit of the times, whether they liked it or not.

At the very moment when worn-out systems were falling apart, Brecht was the target of a violent frontal attack. When he was an eager young Stalinist, Guy Scarpetta published his inevitable article on Brecht and Artaud[21] in a cultural journal of the Communist Party. A few years later, brusquely awakened from his dogmatic somnolence, he reproached the German playwright for his archaic ideology, his simplistic economism, his narrow-minded rationalism, his allergy to metaphysics and to the sacred, his totalitarian disdain of ethics, his fetishization of dialectics, his detestation of non-aligned writers, his incapacity to understand Nazi barbarism, his minimization of Hitlerian anti-Semitism. Brecht, he added, praised Lyssenko, approved the trials and took part in the campaign against what Soviet propaganda called cosmopolitanism. In short, while he wanted to be popular with the people, he was only an apologist of the totalitarianism that died in Cambodia and in the Kolyma.[22] His discreet reservations in the fifties could not hide his stubborn approval of Stalinist crimes.

Eugène Ionesco had been saying these same things for twenty-five years, a voice crying in the wilderness. The main point is that Scarpetta, who had been Philippe Sollers's right-hand man since the sixties, spoke from an ultra-modernist position—*Tel Quel, Art Press*—where people viewed themselves as the authentic heirs and commentators of Joyce, Kafka, Artaud, and Beckett. Brecht, according to him, rejected the unconscious and what Georges Bataille called "la dépense improductive." He brutally radicalized the classics and reduced the *signifié* to a message as well as the *signifiant* to a militant rhetoric. Brechtism operated like a steamroller, a "machine à refoulement,"[23] whose purpose was to liquidate all that was alive in the contemporary French Theater. Neither Beckett nor Genet owes anything to an author who was unable to face the tragic side of History. Scarpetta also denied that Brecht was a renovator of the stage. His sole contribution was to be found in his rehashing of technical tricks which were as old as the theater. All he did was to make the wearisome realism of the nineteenth century didactic. To Scarpetta, the Living Theatre, Bob Wilson, Meyerhold, Artaud of course, and even Claudel are more important than Brecht. The logic inherent in his work was that of the totalitarian state enslaving intellectuals and crushing free thought. Between socialist realism and epic realism there are only nuances of minor importance. In both, the function of communication prevails over the function of poetry. Ambiguity is politically execrable and decoding must be unequivocal.

In short, cultural archaism keeps pace with totalitarian hardening. Scarpetta's lampoon laid the stress on Brecht's theoretical and political writings rather than on his plays, and among those he chose the worst, for instance, *Die Rundköpfe und die Spitzköpfe*. It could not have been written and published before; it operated as a fruitful ideological analyzer despite the exaggerations due to the polemic genre. A capital event occurred around 1975: the separation of aesthetic modernity and advanced political doctrines. In other words, Marxism and the adventure of contemporary art proved to be definitively incompatible. "C'est bien à l'élaboration d'une théorie marxiste de l'art que Brecht n'a cessé de travailler."[24] This argument of Bernard Dort is the boomerang that knocks down French Brechtians; the Marxist method, people think today, breeds a Marxist scholasticism which in turn breeds a Marxist academism. Those who kept insisting that Brecht's plays, theory, and professional practice could not be dissociated made it difficult to rescue their hero's work. The time was definitely over when Adamov claimed Brecht to be "de beaucoup le plus grand écrivain du XXe siècle."[25] Solzhenitsyn—the anti-Brecht—is by now the major reference for many disillusioned French intellectuals. Pity he does not write plays any longer.

Brecht ou le soldat mort gained the support of several reputed playwrights. A text signed by Ionesco, Arrabal, Schéhadé, Weingarten, Robert Pinget, and Roland Dubillard bears testimony to an obvious overdose of Brecht. "La figure de Brecht," they wrote, "sert chaque jour un peu plus d'emblème et d'alibi à tous ceux qui, sur le triple plan institutionnel, philosophique et esthétique, cherchent à freiner toute innovation formelle, toute aventure théâtrale non-conforme à leurs dogmes révolus."[26] It is rather significant that Marcel Maréchal, who is not allergic to Brecht at all, also incriminated French Brechtians, but with other arguments. "Dans la crise des auteurs," he declared, "il y a une sorte de terrorisme intellectuel qu'a exercé la classe brechtienne sur le théâtre . . . Les gens qui avaient une préoccupation politique donnaient une impression de grisaille, d'ennui, de stérilité, de didactisme . . . C'était vraiment la république des instituteurs."[27]

So Brecht at last is an ordinary playwright, no longer a demigod. In the seventies, *Herr Puntila und sein Knecht Matti* was even produced at the *Comédie Française*. While the haughtiest doctrinarians still cherished the Communist Bernard Sobel's serious productions, one could see less stilted, i.e., unorthodox shows. *Baal, Drommeln in der Nacht,* the expressionist plays of the younger Brecht, who was an anarchist, have been brought to light. Jean-Pierre Vincent and Jean Jourdheuil produced *Die Kleinbürger Hochzeit* sarcastically and without prohibiting the element of emotion. Others laid stress on Brecht's fascination with the lower depths, street punks, and hookers. His plays, to them, may be reworked as he himself did with Shakespeare's. Why not play Matti's pushiness and Puntila's homosexuality? Brecht is no longer totem and taboo.

Illumination henceforth came from elsewhere than grim East Germany. The demigods of the seventies were Grotowski, Peter Schulmann, Bob Wilson, Luca Ronconi, Peter Stein, and Richard Foreman, who are all stage directors. The review *Théâtre populaire* had been primarily concerned with texts; *Travail théâtral,* which took its place, favored the staging of plays. Parisian intellectuals remained ready to be dazzled and buoyantly rejected what they first applauded. On the other hand, Patrice Chéreau and Ariane Mnouchkine, the two star directors of the seventies, accomplished their own transmigration that brought them from politico-cultural radicalism to the direction of A.I.D.A. (*Association Internationale de Défense des Artistes*). Around 1968, everyone was obsessed with Vietnam. In 1982, A.I.D.A. called theater professionals to the aid of Vaclav Havel who was (and is) imprisoned in Prague; Samuel Beckett, Elie Wiesel, Arthur Miller et al. sent texts. Even Antoine Vitez, who was formerly the favorite director of the Communist Party, recently produced a play by the dissenter Aksionov and appointed a well-known militant of Solidarnosc to play Peter Handke's *Uber die Dörfer.* The whole cultural landscape has been reshaped.

No dominant view characterizes the present time. Not for decades have we been able to see such diversity in theatrical ideologies and stagings. From sectarianism we have arrived at reassuring eclecticism. There are no more polarizations such as Aristotelian drama versus epic drama or entertainment versus political theater. There are no more authorities who set ideological and aesthetic norms. No critics have an influence comparable to that of the conservative Jean-Jacques Gautier (*Le Figaro*), the radical Gilles Sandier (*Le Matin*), the liberal Bertrand Poirot-Delpech (*Le Monde*), and especially Jacques Lemarchand (*Combat, La Nouvelle Revue Française, Le Figaro littéraire*). Besides, journalists have less impact on the general public whose voice they are supposed to express than university theoreticians on the professionals. But the academic debate (what Ionesco called "la Théâtrologie") is more open than it was ten years ago.

The commercial theater just gets by. Small private enterprises envy state-subsidized companies. They put on hits; either they import international successes and adapt best sellers—the *Théâtre Marigny* entrusted Peter Shaffer's *Amadeus* to Roman Polanski and then mounted a stage version of *Gone With the Wind*; or they call on movie stars: in 1983-84, Isabelle Adjani was seen in *Miss Julie*, Jean-Claude Brialy in Sacha Guitry's *Désiré*, and Marcello Mastroianni in *Tchin Tchin*. The purveyors of commercial pap are still going strong. Yet no recent play of Marc Camoletti, Françoise Dorin, and Jean Poiret has scored the tremendous success of *Boeing Boeing* or *La Cage aux folles*. André Roussin seems to have retired. The aging Anouilh continues to harp on the same obsessions and resentments he nourished in the fifties. Sacha Guitry's comedies have been unearthed; when will Jean de Létraz's be? At the very moment when the *Boulevard* repertory was running out of steam, television was offering a mass audience its worn-out scripts of bourgeois adultery, social climbing, and the generation gap. The program "Au Théâtre ce soir" is one of the few whose success has been uninterrupted for years and years. In 1968, rebels wanted to move out of traditional proscenium theaters; TV installed its cameras in them. What if the general audience (Francis Jeanson's "non-public") was principally made up of TV viewers? Realism was absent at the Villeurbanne meeting. The best proof of the change may be found in the fact that the libertarian *Grand Magic Circus* is playing triumphantly new-romantic *Cyrano de Bergerac* at the *Théâtre Mogador*. What would Copeau and Vilar have said?

The treasures of the classical repertory, which were so abused in 1968, are being explored again. For instance, the *Comédie Française*, without neglecting *Cinna* and *L'Avare*, recently presented old Tristan l'Hermite's *La Mort de Sénèque*, Corneille's *Sertorius*, Diderot's *Est-il bon? est-il méchant?*, Victor Hugo's *Marie Tudor*, and Henri Becque's *Les Corbeaux*. The New Wave directors have been asked to stage them; their productions, however, have been uneven. Antoine Vitez directed Robert Garnier's *Hippolyte*, a sixteenth-century tragedy, and Jean-Louis Barrault unearthed *Angelo*, a rarely performed melodrama of Victor Hugo. One could find many other examples.

The internationalization of the classical repertory appears to represent a return to the twenties and to the time of Vilar. It is a good thing to play Marlowe, Calderón, Gozzi, Kleist, and others at the *Comédie Française*, the *Théâtre de la Ville* and the *Théâtre de l'Est Parisien*, theaters which now carry on the tradition of the former *Théâtre National Populaire*. It was only in 1982 that the baroque Calderón entered the repertory of the *Comédie Française*, which is the temple of classicism. The twentieth-century classics such as Chekhov, Pirandello, Giraudoux have been restored to favor too. "No more Claudel," the rebel students wrote on the walls of the Sorbonne. Ten years later, the most radical directors are competing to be the eleventh-hour Claudelians.[28] *L'Otage*, *Partage de midi*, *Tête d'or* are now produced even in the Communist suburbs of Paris. The same thing with Ionesco and Beckett. It is a sign of the times that the *Théâtre de l'Est Parisien* directed by Guy Rétoré presented *Tueur sans gages* and *Fin de partie* in the eighties and that Roger Planchon himself has just produced Ionesco's autobiographical drama.

What about the place of Antitheater nowadays? Adamov's plays are buried with him. But Ionesco's obstinacy has overcome his enemies. Although he does not hide his unprogressive likes and dislikes, neither his person nor his work provokes hostility anymore. Today, in February 1984, *Rhinocéros*, *Le Roi se meurt*, *La Cantatrice chauve*, and *La leçon* are being played in Paris. Doubtless the rise of individualism detected by sociologists[29] favors his plays which are no longer provocative, if of uneven quality. Ionesco, who openly distrusts "les scénocrates," likes to confide his works to stage directors such as Jacques Mauclair because he is sure they will respect his intentions. We should however mention two presentations which conform to the standards of the seventies: *La Cantatrice chauve* directed by Daniel Benoin and *Le Roi se meurt* by Jorge Lavelli.

Beckett is unanimously praised.[30] *Godot* is like the rock on which the waves of fashion crash. People go to see Madeleine Renaud in *Oh les beaux jours!* as formerly their great-grandparents went to see Sarah Bernhardt in *L'Aiglon*. His plays are produced everywhere, from the *Comédie Française* to the popes' palace in Avignon, from the *Cartoucherie de Vincennes* to Communist drama centers. The *Festival d'automne* pays yearly homage to his polysemous work. Nobody deplores his metaphysical pessimism any longer. As a matter of fact, *Godot* is read as an antitotalitarian text by Czech and Polish audiences to whom it has taught more on alienation than the complete works of Marx. The Beckettian character became the twin of the Solzhetsynian *zek* in *Catastrophe*. The text is so bare that it is indestructible. Roger Blin played *Fin de Partie* as an aborted *King Lear*. Today it is no longer viewed as a wretched variation on the absurd and incommunicability. Marcel Maréchal, for instance, made a colorful clownshow of it, as he also did with *King Lear*. It is significant that such an open work has recently given opportunities for great productions to directors as different as Otomar Krejca and Alan Schneider. To play the great Sam one must be rigorous and humble. Narcissists should not apply and they do not.

So the Antitheater of the fifties has become classic. The axiological revisions which were initiated by Apollinaire, Jarry, Roger Vitrac, and Ghelderode for a century were made acceptable by Ionesco, Beckett, and poets such as Audiberti and Genet. These playwrights undermined the relationships between the stage and the world, reality and fiction, the actor and his performance. In fact, they reduced the gap between the theater and the other arts, drama and the novel, or painting. Their creative logic is coherent but different from that which prevailed before. With these lucid innovators the theater cultivates its difference as theater. The "hyperthéâtralité"[31] of *Antithéâtre*, to quote Robert Abirached, relies on its subversive contestation of bourgeois theatricality, its quest for the sensorial shock, and the revival of former show traditions, all of which is not incompatible with a reaffirmed concern for the text—the text that is paradoxically based on connotation rather than on denotation. The writer remains "l'instigateur voire le maître de la théâtralité,"[32] as Abirached wrote.

These authors belong to a generation whose creative capacity is now exhausted. Vauthier only translates Shakespeare and the Elizabethans. Genet, Schéhadé, Aimé Césaire, and Weingarten seem to have abandoned the theater. Even in the sixties, Genet's *Les Paravents,* Roland Dubillard's *Naïves hirondelles,* Romain Weingarten's *L'Eté,* Obaldia's *Du Vent dans les branches de sassafras,* Marguerite Duras's *Des Journées entières dans les arbres,* Georges Michel's *La Promenade du dimanche* were presented. The new generation is regrettably deficient. Jean-Claude Grumberg (*En revenant de l'Expo, Dreyfus*), René Ehni (*Que ferons nous en novembre?*), Philippe Adrien (*La Baye*), Eric Westphal (*Toi et tes nuages*), René Kalisky (*Pique-nique à Claretta, Dave au bord de mer*), have not fulfilled the hopes raised by their first plays. Recently Jean-Christophe Bailly's *Les Céphéides,* Bernard Koltès's *Combat de nègre et de chien,* and especially Jean Audureau's *Félicité,* the first new play presented at the *Comédie Française* since 1966, flopped lamentably; their failures will probably discourage the search for new texts. Paris today imports Anglo-Saxon and German original plays. Where are the French Harold Pinters, Tom Stoppards, Edward Bonds, Peter Handkes, Botho Strausses, and Heiner Müllers?

If Brecht and occasionally his imitators are still produced, it is principally within the cultural empire of the Communist Party. A new realism appeared with the *Théâtre du quotidien,* the French equivalent of kitchen-sink drama. The process is to conduct a real investigation in the field, to hold a long dialogue with ordinary people, then to transcribe the collected materials. Works such as Jean-Paul Wenzel's *Loin d'Hagondange,* Jean-Pierre Vincent and others' *Palais de justice,* and Daniel Besnehard and others' *Clair d'usine* have no ideological bias that would lead to an insistent injunction to socio-political action. No more political centering, no more didactic commentary: *mimesis* prevails over *diegesis.* The microsociology of daily life relies on hyperrealism, i.e., on effects of reality. In fact, social subjects and history are dissociated.

These plays may be presented on proscenium stages without alienation effect nor stylization. In brief, they are a return to Antoine's "slice of life." As Daniel Besnehard wrote recently, "revisited and criticized naturalism" ("le naturalisme revisité et critiqué") may still be used as a style which carries theatricality ("un style porteur de Théâtralité"); a realism without ideological and political presupposition ("un réalisme sans présupposé idéologique et politique") is conceivable.[33] The purists reproach this verist drama for being static and equivocal, for hiding the cause and effect of social relationships, for reifying ideology, in short for not making social change imperative, as if that were not the job of trade unions and leftist politicians.[34] The popular success gained by *Clair d'usine* is the best response to their dogmatic statements.

The lack of new playwrights would appear to be a catastrophe, but the situation is explainable. For years and years, the authors have been "les Cendrillons,"[35] "le Lumpenprolétariat de l'entreprise théâtre."[36] One does not ill-treat *Sire le texte* with impunity. Molière was his own stage director. Corneille and Racine participated in the staging of their plays. We have already seen that stage directing became an autonomous and meaningful art with Antoine. The professionals of the stage henceforth took part in the reflexion on theater that was up until then the monopoly of literary men such as Aristotle, d'Aubignac, Corneille, Diderot, Victor Hugo, etc. Jouvet, Dullin, Copeau, Vilar, Barrault and others wrote books and articles. Throughout the twentieth century, there has been an increasing competition between the writer and the stage director.

"Qui est le créateur," Vilar asked, "l'auteur ou le metteur en scène?" He answered: "L'oeuvre du poète commande au metteur en scène."[37] For Charles Dullin, the stage director is the spiritual emissary of the author. From Copeau to Barrault, all directors were craftsmen who admitted the preeminence of the writers they respected profoundly. Their ideal was the collaboration between Giraudoux and Jouvet. Vilar denied stage directing as an end in itself. He rejected the show for the show's sake and what he called "la décoromanie."[38] When he noticed that "les créateurs des trente dernières années ne sont pas les auteurs mais les metteurs en scène," he deplored the fact; for in his mind, "le créateur c'est l'auteur."[39]

For a long time, the bourgeois and scholarly worship of the text meant that the show aspect of the production was disdained. Symbolist poets were so obsessed with writing that they forgot to be playwrights. Textocentrism (or logocentrism, if you prefer), when combined with a stubborn monosemism and with an arthritic stage code, leads to simple academism. For decades, the *Comédie Française* softened the strongest works of its classical repertory. Adolphe Appia, Gordon Craig, and Antonin Artaud made the opposite choice. For the latter, the work took on meaning only when produced. His followers made a pretext of the text. When Roger Planchon demanded power for artists, he was not thinking about writers at all; he was making himself the spokesman of directors confronted with narrow-minded technocrats.

The stage directors who appeared in the sixties were often subintellectuals educated in the Drama Department of the Sorbonne and/or people so intimidated by the superintellectuals that they imitated their mannerisms. "Maintenant," Marcel Maréchal declared sarcastically, "il naît tous les deux jours, à en croire la critique, des petits génies spontanés, généralement issus du mandarinat des profs."[40] Daniel Mesguich finds his inspiration in Jacques Derrida, Roland Barthes, Michel Foucault, and others. Most stage directors rely on philosophers, sociologists and psychoanalysts who hold the role of *dramaturg* (literary director). "Intellos du théâtre, maîtres à penser et / ou commissaires politiques,"[41] as Colette Godard wrote, they acquired a considerable importance. The coherence (or the incoherence) that they introduce in the reading of the play is that of their ideology or of their sexual fantasies. They surely cleaned up the text but only to bury it under heavy commentaries. The thick dossiers sold to spectators are typical testimonies of their arrogance.[42]

To improve *Hamlet,* Georges Lavaudant injected vitamins in the guise of quotations from Hélène Cixous and Jean-Luc Godard. Others used Marx, Lenin, Mao and, of course, all fashionable thinkers, Althusser, Lacan, and others. Collages and improvisation were de rigueur in the 70s. Everything was possible, everything was allowed. The text existed to be manipulated, adulterated, triturated. *Phèdre* took place in Galilee and Theseus spoke through a walkie-talkie. Dorine bit the hand of Tartuffe who was a Pasolinian punk. Alceste was an unknown mystic, etc. As Alfred Simon wrote, "on ne joue pas *Hamlet* mais le savoir moderne sur *Hamlet,*"[43] i.e., either the text and its story or the text and its various commentaries, or an immense intertext which includes several texts of the same author, or better of other authors, of which the coherence is thematic, didactic, or parodic. Daniel Mesguich wants to "show all the readings" ("montrer toutes les lectures").[44] Since the text was superfluous, there was no need to make it audible. Actors were asked to hoot, to bark, to mew, to shriek, or to whisper it. Shakespeare, Molière, and Racine had no way to express their disapproval. Claudel's family protested against Mesguich's staging of *Tête d'or.* Living authors took precautions.

"Il est impossible," Vauthier wrote, "que des parties d'une pièce soient laissées au bon gré d'un metteur en scène—ou sinon, il ne faut lui donner qu'un canevas et le charger d'écrire le texte aussi; le texte n'est d'ailleurs pas que dans les paroles. On n'a jamais vu que des moitiés de symphonies soient écrites par des exécutants."[45] Twenty-five years later, Eugène Ionesco used the same metaphor to express his hostility to those whom he called "les scénocrates." The stage director, he said, must be like an orchestra conductor, not like the composer.[46] His didascalia, which are addressed to the stage professionals, are more and more verbose and detailed. And so are those of Audiberti, Beckett, and Genet, as if these writers wanted not only to control the performance firmly, but also to prohibit any performance that would contradict their explicit will. We may notice that Jean Anouilh, Marguerite Duras, and Samuel Beckett are sometimes their own stage directors; they are more convincing as such than Roger Planchon is as a playwright.

We have jumped from a paranoiac over-politization to a schizophrenic depolitization. In 1968, people asserted the primacy of politics; ten years later, they wanted art above all. No more question of changing the world, society, life. Fanatics often turn into skeptics or cynics. Disillusioned stage directors became aesthetes. Since the end of the seventies, they have been interested in scenic display, in creating beautiful pictures. "L'image," one said, "si elle est belle et forte, dépoussière la mémoire, déclenche des sensations, d'autres images. Elle fabrique un théâtre à soi, ni bon ni mauvais, unique. Un théâtre sans images est l'image de la mort."[47] "La beauté," another one added, "est chère, hors de prix. La création n'a pas de prix, même si elle a un budget. C'est l'assemblage du luxe qui fait un beau spectacle, réussi ou non. Pas nécessairement un beau texte dont, par lassitude, nous disons que nous n'avons rien à foutre."[48] "L'image belle," Colette Godard comments, "est la dernière affirmation de la dignité humaine."[49]

The set designer tends to overshadow the literary director. He installs luxurious and expensive settings. He uses smoke, heavy machinery, sumptuous costumes, refined sound effects, and sophisticated lighting. The time is remote when Copeau and Vilar were content with the bare stage. The contemporary scene is a baroque one. Expense, waste, display, ostentation, and excess are values in themselves. Luchino Visconti, Jorge Lavelli, Luca Ronconi prepared the way for Patrice Chéreau, Georges Lavaudant, and Jean-Marie Patte. The increasing use of visual and spectacular effects is the indication that theatricality is getting out of hand. It is not surprising that star directors—Lavelli, Chéreau, Mesguich, Ariane Mnouchkine, and others—have been turning to the cinema and to opera.

Around 1980, the text was rehabilitated. Back from Bayreuth, Patrice Chéreau said that it was time to play the text, the whole text, and nothing but the text; for the theater was also text, if it was not entirely text. "On a traversé une période où le texte fut à deux doigts d'être éliminé, déconsidéré. Il faut travailler à renverser la vapeur. Il faut cesser de mettre au crédit du metteur en scène ce qui appartient à l'auteur."[50] The Chéreau who recently produced *Peer Gynt* and *Les Paravents* is no longer the one whose *Dom Juan* created a scandal. Having grown older, he is now a partisan of what Audiberti called the spoken opera,[51] which combines an imaginative performance and a respect for the text. The time of works in progress is over. As Raymond Jean wrote, "le déploiement du spectacle baroque au théâtre est inséparable du déploiement des mots."[52] But would the *Théâtre du Soleil* have mounted *Richard II* as a magnificent Japanese nô if it had not previously performed the astonishing *1789* which nobody will probably play again?

Marcel Maréchal holds a particular place among contemporary French professionals. To begin with, he has changed little in twenty years. The Trissotins of dramaturgy never impressed him. Secondly, he understood from the beginning that, to be popular, theater must be theater, and give pleasure to the audience. Rather than handing culture down to the masses, he wants to relate theater to popular culture. That is the reason why he addressed *Fracasse* and *Les Trois Mousquetaires* to people addicted to TV serials, making French Westerns and swashbucklers of these popular classics. But he also presented Audiberti's *Le Cavalier seul,* Louis Guilloux's *Cripure,* and Jean Vauthier's *Le Sang.* For he loves and knows how to find juicy texts. "Ce qu'il faut," he said, c'est mettre le texte à sa plus grande évidence. Le maître c'est le texte."[53] Marcel Maréchal works nowadays in Marseilles. Plays recently performed in Paris have been rarely characterized by the quality of their texts.

People make a virtue of necessity. Despite the fact that the socialist government has more than doubled the budget for cultural affairs, public grants are not unlimited. The crisis imposes severe measures, "la rigueur." The taxpayers refuse to subsidize arrogant narcissists whose productions would be played before empty houses. Put at the head of budget-greedy institutions, the angry young men of the seventies became, if not humble, at least pragmatic. They have to justify the money they receive and which the younger artists covet. The theatergoing public acts as an aware consumer. As we say in France, people vote with their feet: they boycott elitist or partisan productions.

There is an evident ebb of experimentation in the eighties. The same ebb can be found in fiction. The novelists of today turn their backs on the antinovel and rehabilitate readability, plot, characters, psychology, etc.[54] Not only the commercial theater but also an increasing part of subsidized theaters have chosen to be on the safe side. People favor well-made plays, especially when they are unsophisticatedly presented and played by intelligible actors. Success goes to whoever knows how to combine these ingredients, for instance Robert Hossein who, despite snobbish critics, filled the *Palais des sports* with his stage version of *Notre-Dame-de-Paris*.

There are no more certitudes. No ideological project, no aesthetic system is dominant. Bernard Dort's last book begins with a nostalgic variation on the theme "que sont mes amis devenus?" What happened to the *Berliner Ensemble*, the Living Theatre, the Bread and Puppet, Grotowski and Ronconi? Idols have fallen from their pedestals; gurus left without leaving their addresses. What we see is a counterattack on tradition—but a tradition which is more diversified than it ever was. In the same way that our classic repertory has annexed works which originally appeared to be rebellious, for instance those of Beckett and Brecht, institutions have absorbed free-lance professionals, fringe directors, and wandering companies to whom they have offered houses, grants, and audiences. The choice was to perish or to become an institution.

The general relativization of models concerns theater too, and it is a good thing. Are there any risks of a cultural regression? To me, a swing back is less probable in the theater than in the novel. It is comforting to notice that the revision of values has been principally to Beckett's advantage, not to Françoise Dorin's. Some attainments are irreversible: decentralization, the diversification of the audience, the rehabilitation of the spectacle, the adaptation of theater architectures, an acute consciousness of techniques, the importance given to the mask, make-up, gestures, etc. You cannot put the clock back; you cannot return to the stage of 1920 or 1950.

The realm of creativity seems to be equitably divided nowadays. Between the skimpy monosemism of the writer and that of the scholarly tradition, between the maniacal monosemism of some literary directors and the delirious polysemism of others which, in fact, becomes asemism, there is ample room available for the elaboration of the meaning of the text. The text does not belong to the author alone. He provides its first meaning, then the stage crew—director, *dramaturg*, designers, actors, etc.—takes charge of it and works on it within conditions stricter than those of the recent past. Let us hope the text will no longer be tortured. That is the condition which is necessary to the advent of new authors.

Notes

1. Jean Vilar, *Le théâtre, service public* (Paris: Gallimard, 1975), p. 46.

2. Jean Vilar, "Memorandum," *Théâtre populaire*, No. 40 (1960), p. 9.

3. "Memorandum," p. 5.

4. Guy Leclerc, Le *T.N.P.* de Jean Vilar (Paris: U.G.E. coll. 10/18, 1973), pp. 151-210. See also Philippa Wehle, *Le Théâtre populaire selon Jean Vilar* (Le Paradou, Actes Sud, 1981).

5. Roland Barthes, *Essais critiques* (Paris: Le Seuil, 1981), pp. 80-83.

6. Eugène Ionesco, *L'Impromptu de l'Alma* (Paris: Gallimard, coll. Folio, 1971), p. 112.

7. Alfred Simon, "Artaud chez Bernstein," *Esprit*, (July-August 1980), pp. 35-38.

8. Roger Vailland, *Ecrits intimes* (Paris: Gallimard, 1968), p. 319.

9. Jacques Audiberti, "Ecrans en vrac," *La Nouvelle N.R.F.,* 1 May 1957, 949-51; Ionesco, *Notes et Contre-notes* (Paris: Gallimard, coll. Idées, 1966), passim. See also Jeanyves Guérin, "Maîtres penseurs, maîtres censeurs, maîtres chanteurs," *La Nouvelle Revue Française*, 1 July 1978, pp. 102-110.

10. Bernard Dort, *Théâtre public* (Paris: Le Seuil, 1967), p. 262.

11. Jean Duvignaud and Jean Lagoutte, *Le Théâtre contemporain: culture et contre-culture* (Paris: Larousse, coll. Thèmes et textes, 1975), p. 49.

12. Dort, p. 244.

13. Bernard Dort, *Théâtre réel* (Paris: Le Seuil, 1971), p. 218.

14. *Théâtre réel*, p. 219.

15. René Kalisky, "Le théâtre climatisé," *Cahiers Renaud-Barrault*, No. 77 (1971), p. 114.

16. Kalisky, p. 115.

17. *Théâtre réel*, p. 165.

18. *Théâtre réel*, p. 284.

19. Colette Godard, *Le Théâtre depuis 1968* (Paris: Lattès, 1980), p. 25.

20. Max Gallo, *La Troisième Alliance* (Paris: Fayard, 1983). See Also Louis Dumont, *Essai sur les indi-*

vidualismes (Paris: Gallimard, 1983); Serge Lipovetsky, *L'Ere du vide* (Paris: Gallimard, 1983); Gérard Mendel, *Cinquante-quatre millions d'individus sans importance* (Paris: Robert Laffont, 1983).

21. Guy Scarpetta, "Brecht et Artaud," *La Nouvelle Critique* (May 1969), pp. 60-68.

22. Scarpetta, *Brecht ou le soldat mort* (Paris: Grasset, 1979), p. 12.

23. *Brecht ou le soldat mort*, pp. 63, 75.

24. Dort, *Théâtre réel*, p. 140.

25. Arthur Adamov, *Ici et maintenant* (Paris: Gallimard, 1964), p. 118.

26. "Ces intellectuels qui dénoncent un certain totalitarisme théâtral," *Les Nouvelles littéraires*, 15-21 November 1979, p. 28.

27. Marcel Maréchal, *La Mise en théâtre* (Paris: U.G.E. coll. 10/18, 1975), p. 62.

28. Jacqueline Veinstein, "Théâtrographie. Chronologie des créations dans l'oeuvre dramatique de Claudel," *Europe*, No. 635 (March 1982), pp. 100-113.

29. Jean Duvignaud, *La Planète des jeunes* (Paris: Stock, 1975).

30. See Alfred Simon, *Beckett* (Paris: Belfond, 1983), and its review by Bertrand Poirot-Delpech, "Job clergyman," *Le Monde*, 8 July 1983, p. 17. See also Bernard Dort, "Beckett populaire," *Le Monde-Dimanche*, 17 May 1981, p. xiv.

31. Robert Abirached, *La Crise du personnage dans le théâtre français* (Paris: Grasset, 1978), p. 417.

32. Abirached, p. 423.

33. Daniel Besnehard et al., "Notes sur une comédie ouvrière," *TEP-Actualité*, No. 149 (October 1983), pp. 2-3.

34. Patrice Pavis, *Dictionnaire du théâtre* (Paris: Editions Sociales, 1979), p. 293.

35. Bernard Dort, *Théâtre en jeu* (Paris: Le Seuil, 1979), p. 293.

36. Alfred Simon, *Le Théâtre à bout de souffle?* (Paris: Le Seuil, 1979), p. 19.

37. Jean Vilar, *De la Tradition théâtrale* (Paris: Gallimard, coll. Idées, 1963), pp. 36, 38.

38. *De la Tradition théâtrale*, p. 42.

39. *De la Tradition théâtrale*, pp. 77, 65.

40. *La Mise en théâtre*, p. 54. See also Alfred Simon, "Par les villages," *Esprit* (February 1984), pp. 171-172.

41. *Le Théâtre depuis 1968*, p. 11.

42. "Mettre en scène une pièce, c'est avant tout, et en fin de compte, *produire un discours*, et employer une part importante de l'argent à éditer ce discours. Discours savant, érudit, qui ne peut être saisi que par des lecteurs d'une technicité comparable. Conversation précieuse entre intimes, cependant que la quasi-totalité des spectateurs du théâtre, qui n'ont aucune pratique de ce langage, sont exclus du jeu. Il y a là quelque chose de réactionnaire, offensant," Michel Cournot, "Lointaine gare d'Austerlitz!" *Le Monde*, 8 February 1984, p. 15.

43. *Le Théâtre à bout de souffle?*, p. 55.

44. Daniel Mesguich, *Culture et communication* (December 1979), quoted by Godard, *Le Théâtre depuis 1968*, p. 229.

45. Jean Vauthier, "Lettre de Bordeaux," *Théâtre populaire*, No. 1 (1953), p. 52.

46. Eugène Ionesco, "Contre les metteurs en scène censeurs," in *Un Homme en question* (Paris: Gallimard, 1979), p. 169.

47. *Le Théâtre depuis 1968*, p. 198.

48. *Le Théâtre depuis 1968*, p. 199.

49. *Le Théâtre depuis 1968*, p. 173.

50. Quoted by the author in his review, "Le théâtre populaire à la croisée des chemins," *La Nouvelle Revue Française* (March 1982), pp. 108-109.

51. Audiberti, *Opéra parlé* in *Théâtre III* (Paris: Gallimard, 1956). See the author's "La philologie mène au rire," *Travaux de linguistique et de littérature*, XIX, 2 (1981), 219-231.

52. Raymond Jean, "Monsieur Molière et Monsieur Audiberti," *Sud*, Nos. 34-35 (1980), p. 20.

53. *La Mise en théâtre*, p. 83.

54. See the journal *Roman* and the novels of its key figure, Catherine Rihoit.

Bettina L. Knapp (essay date 1985)

SOURCE: Knapp, Bettina L. Introduction to *French Theater: 1918-1939*, pp. 1-14. London: Macmillan, 1985.

[*In the following essay, Knapp provides a brief history of French playwrights and directors during the years between the two world wars.*]

11 November 1918. The Armistice. The end of World War I. A spirit of intense joy swept over France. Jazz bands howled out their brash sounds and rhythmic beats; dancing became popular once again; parades filled the streets. Theatre flourished. Entertainment and excitement were the rule of the day. A counterpoise, certainly, to the harsh facts of war: one and a half million Frenchmen had died; count-

less had suffered in the trenches; still more had been permanently disabled, deprived of a normal future.

After the Armistice, Paris remained a composite of opposites. Its theatres seemed to satisfy the requirements of all classes, all types, all tastes. The classical and historical repertoire of the state subsidised Comédie-Française and Odéon offered the works of France's greats: Corneille, Molière, Marivaux, Musset, Beaumarchais, and so many others. Here young and old alike listened in rapt silence to the declamation of 'sacred' stanzas and monologues they had committed to memory in school.

Other people went to the theatre simply to be entertained and distracted. For these individuals, the so-called boulevard theatre answered their needs. Sacha Guitry (1885-1957) was perhaps the most popular dramatist actor of his day. In his stage works, which number one hundred and thirty, we find levity mingling with acrimony, flippancy with seriousness, love with hate, passion with rage, but always controlled, subtle, nuanced.

There were many playwrights who regaled, chilled, or cheered their audiences at this time. Jean-Jacques Bernard (1888-1972), for example, was a practitioner of what came to be known as 'the theatre of silence'. In *Martine* (1922) Bernard did away with psychological analyses, relying on gesture and pauses in the dialogue to emphasise the alteration of emotional situations and to underscore the agony of doubt. The protagonists in *The Cardboard Crown* (*La Couronne de carton,* 1920) and *Leopold the Well-Beloved* (*Léopold le bien-aimé,* 1927), by Jean Sarment (1898-1976), lived in an illusory world, a mirage-dominated realm. *Paquebot Tenacity* (1920) and *Madame Béliard* (1925), by Charles Vildrac, brought sensitive, withdrawn, and poetic people to the stage. The human tragedy inhabiting the lives of these eternal types was emphasised by externalising their deeply buried feelings through seemingly banal conversations.

The facile, supple, and humorous *Tovarich* (1934) of Jacques Deval (1894-1972), won the hearts of audiences the world over. The regional dramas of Marcel Pagnol (1895-1974)—*Marius* (1929), *Fanny* (1931), *Caesar* (1937)—were unforgettable for the reality of the characterisations and the poignant banter of the protagonists.

Violence, cruelty, and a psychoanalytical approach to drama also appeared in boulevard theatre. 'All my plays,' wrote H. R. Lenormand, 'attempt to elucidate the mystery of inner life, to unravel the enigma that man is to himself.' In *Time Is a Dream* (*Le Temps est un songe,* 1919), *The Eater of Dreams* (*Le Mangeur de rêves,* 1922), and *Man and his Phantoms* (*L'Homme et ses fantômes,* 1924), Lenormand (1882-1950) brings conflicted, antagonistic and anguished beings to the stage. These Freudian-oriented individuals are haunted by guilt, by repressed and obscure pulsations. Edouard Bourdet (1887-1945), who dug so incisively into the human psyche in *The Prisoner* (*La Prisonnière,* 1926) and *Difficult Times* (*Les Temps difficiles,* 1934), did away with theatrical conventions when he enacted pathological situations on the stage.

There were other playwrights and directors as well, who appeared shortly before World War I and whose creative breadth continued during the interwar period. Not as much appreciated by the majority as were the writers of the boulevard offerings, these highly creative and dedicated workers appealed more directly to an elite—an avant-garde. They questioned, disrupted, toppled the commercially oriented way of doing theatre, which they considered staid and uninspiring.

Jacques Copeau (1879-1949), one of these innovators, struggled valiantly against the business customs and practices of what he considered to be dishonest theatre. Artistry, integrity, and a spirit of renewal reigned in his newly formed theatre du Vieux-Colombier (1913-24)—a theatre he rebuilt from the bottom up along simple classic lines. He did away with the heavy ornamentation, gold plate, and rococo cut-glass chandeliers of the boulevard theatre. He let in clean air where there had been an accumulation of dust and stuffy ideas. He cleansed the theatrical *industry* of all he considered to be cheap and frustrating.

Copeau's Vieux-Colombier theatre was simple in conception and as harmonious as a Doric temple—at once functional, orderly, and beautiful: soft yellow wall panels, green curtains draped back on the side of the stage; indirect lighting soothing to the eyes; a bare stage permitting direct contact between audience and actors. Copeau embodied in the construction of his theatre all that he had assimilated and felt he could use of the ideas of Edward Gordon Craig (1872-1966), who believed the theatre to be an independent entity unto itself; a poetic and suggestive force capable of arresting the quintessential elements of an unfolding drama. From Constantin Stanislavsky (1863-1938), Copeau learned the techniques used in exteriorising a character's inner reality, in acting as an ensemble, and in coordinating every aspect of a production into a unified whole.

Copeau made finished and versatile actors out of the unleavened human talent at his disposal. Prior to the opening of the Vieux-Colombier theatre in Paris, he had his troupe come to the Limon, a country home he rented about an hour from the city by train. There his cast rehearsed out of doors. Stage settings were natural: a tree or flower. Copeau made every demand upon his actors, striving to create vigorous and graceful bodies, as physically adept as those of Elizabethan actors, able to fight, run, perform any arduous leap that a play might require. Louis Jouvet and Charles Dullin, who were members of Copeau's troupe, became masters of their bodies and voices, and of dramatic techniques. Productions of Thomas Heywood's *A Woman Killed with Kindness,* Molière's *The Miser,* Dostoyevky's *The Brothers Karamazov,* Shakespeare's *Twelfth Night,* Claudel's *The Exchange* were made memorable for their artistry and fresh conception. In *The Exchange,* for example, the decor consisted of one tree in the foreground and a black cloth representing the sky; emphasis was thereby focused on the actors' movements and gestures, and on lighting, voice, silences, enhancing the atmosphere of mystery and tension.

In the lengthening shadow of what seemed inevitable war, Jouvet was sent to the front; Copeau joined the auxiliary forces; Dullin, an infantryman, went to Lorraine. Lodged in wet, dirty barracks, often exposed to danger, the three managed to correspond. Copeau was brimming with new ideas. After his demobilisation (1915), Copeau went to Geneva, where he met Emile Jacques-Dalcroze (1865-1950), whose system of eurythmics was enjoying a great vogue. Dalcroze's philosophy was based on the firm belief that actors should learn rhythmic dancing so that they could coordinate bodily movements with speech. Dalcroze introduced Copeau to Adolphe Appia (1862-1928), who stressed the affinities between music and dialogue. Appia championed the creation of a three-dimensional stage; since actors are three-dimensional, he reasoned, so should be the backgrounds they inhabit; these reflect their needs, wants, and personalities and also link them to the time-space factor. Lighting was also vital to performance: it underscored dimensionality, showed up movement, attitude, and gesture. For Appia, lighting was a protagonist, and it became one for Copeau.

In 1917 Copeau and his troupe were sent to New York by the French Ministry of Fine Arts as France's unofficial cultural ambassador of good will. Jouvet and Dullin, both released from the army for medical reasons, joined him. After two arduous years in the United States, producing an incredible number of plays (by Brieux, Hervieu, Rostand, Donnay, Augier, Molière, and others), not always to receptive audiences, Copeau and his troupe returned to Paris. It was then that he founded his school, and, together with Jouvet, created his 'permanent set' at the Vieux-Colombier, the outcome of the work done at the Garrick Theatre in New York. The permanent set consisted of an architectural whole on the stage which was made up of several levels; there was an arch in the back, stairways on either side, and a projecting apron. It was on this incredibly versatile stage that Copeau created his important productions of plays by Corneille, Maeterlinck, Vildrac, Gide, Romains, Musset, Beaumarchais, Goldoni, and others.

Louis Jouvet (1887-1951) had remained with Copeau for ten years. He referred to himself at the end of this time as a 'valet of the theatre' because he had worked in so many different areas: lighting, staging, carpentry, costume design, and of course, as an actor. In 1923 he accepted the position of director of the Comédie des Champs-Elysées. He not only took over much of Copeau's repertoire, as well as his techniques, but he also added his own rich and inspired vision to the performing arts. His productions of Jules Romains' *Dr. Knock* (1923), Charles Vildrac's *Madame Béliard* (1925), Bernard Zimmer's *Bava the African* (1926), Jean Sarment's *Leopold the Well-Beloved* (1927), and Marcel Achard's *Jean of the Moon* (1929), to mention but a few, were at once poetic and arresting—simple in concept, a character's truth revealed through the word. Perhaps Jouvet's greatest contributions, however, were his productions of the works of Jean Giraudoux. Had it not been for their collaborative efforts, Giraudoux might have remained the novelist he had been prior to his meeting with Jouvet and not have become one of the most important dramatists of the twentieth century.

Jouvet, a master technician and craftsman, was objective, lucid in his approach to performance. He followed the dictates set forth by Diderot in his *Paradox of the Comedian*. Emotions must be controlled by the actor who incarnates them; they must be defined, delineated with breadth and exactness. A role has to be studied in all of its nuances: gestures, inflections, intonations articulated so that the text may emerge in all of its beauty and grandeur. Audiences are to be inspired by the *word,* the visual image on stage, the breathing they hear, and the emotions conveyed. An actor is to be on a par with the dramatist; that is, his interpretation must be creative. Yet, though fantasy and illusion are not banished from stage life, they must be mastered and directed. Nothing is to be left to chance. Sets, decors, sound effects, vocalisations, costume, lighting, are all to be set down prior to the performance. Like Copeau and Dullin, Jouvet considered the text—language—the play's most important asset. It is through language that great theatre is born. Dullin conveyed his passion for lucre through gesture and facial expression; through a voice that trembled and lips that salivated at the sight of riches; through eyes that glowed with lechery. Jean Vilard (1912-71) also participated in Dullin's troupe. He became director of the Théâtre National Populaire in 1950.

Jean-Louis Barrault (b. 1910) studied with Dullin for four years. He called him 'an aristocrat' of the theatre. From Dullin, Barrault learned the meaning of integrity; a scrupulous awareness of every facet of theatre—each important detail which goes into the creation of a production. It was in 1935, in a mime-drama based on William Faulkner's *As I Lay Dying,* that Barrault made his mark on the theatrical world. His powerful gestural performance, Antonin Artaud suggested, succeeded in organising stage space in an unforgettable manner. As Barrault moved forward on the proscenium, breaking in a wild horse, as he mimed a mother's death agony, controlling his breathing until it became raspy, he shot terror and admiration into the spectators' hearts.

Barrault, who joined the Comédie-Française in 1940, married Madeleine Renaud, already a member of this company, in 1936. Ten years later husband and wife realised a long-cherished dream: they founded their own company, the Théâtre Marigny. Passionate in their devotion to theatre, eclectic in their choice of dramatists, they mounted noteworthy productions of the works of such playwrights as Montherlant, Racine, Molière, Marivaux, Musset, Feydeau, Achard, Sartre, Vauthier, Anouilh, Gide, and Kafka. They also invited directors such as Roger Blin to direct works by Beckett and Genet. It was to Barrault that Claudel entrusted his most personal and poignant play, *Break* of Noon (*Partage de Midi*, 1948); a drama which until this time he had forbad all other directors to produce. Claudel knew that as Dullin's descendent, Barrault would ensure that faith and the work ethic prevailed in his theatre; no concessions to facilitate a production would be made.

Another creative force in the contemporary French theatre was George Pitoëff (1884-1939), the son of a theatrical director. Born and educated in Russia, he worked with Vsevolod Meyerhold (1874-1970) and the stage-set designer Leon Bakst (1866-1924), then with Stanislavsky. His production in St. Petersburg of Chekhov's *Three Sisters* (1912-14), was unforgettable: the decors consisted only of two screens, two lamps, several chairs, and a velvet curtain for a background. The rest of the burden fell upon the actors. In Paris, where he went to study mathematics, architecture, and law, he met his future wife, Ludmilla. Together they founded the Pitoëff Company (1918) and produced such works as Lenormand's *Eater of Dreams* (1922); plays by Claudel, Péguy, and Vitrac; Cocteau's *Orpheus* (1926); and Anouilh's *The Traveller without Luggage* (*Le Voyageur sans bagage*, 1937). Some compared Pitoëff's company to a League of Nations because of the many non-French playwrights that were invited to its stage: Gogol, Andreyev, Gorky, Pushkin, Tolstoy, Seneca, Turgenev, Chekhov, Shaw, Synge, Wilde, Strindberg, Goldoni, Pirandello, Ibsen.

Pitoëff never formulated his dramatic theories in a didactic manner. As was the case for Copeau, Jouvet, and Dullin, the text was uppermost for him. The mise-en-scène emerged directly from the written play and was designed to point up its greatness and concretise its verbal images and rhythms, thus filling the proscenium with electric charges. The director's goal, Pitoëff stated time and time again, was to attempt to understand those forces that had motivated the dramatist to create his work and empowered him to bring forth the creatures of his fantasy. It was on a bare stage, ascetic, monastic in quality, that poetic inspiration resided for Pitoëff—under the magic of the actor's play and the director's design. Influenced by Jacques-Dalcroze, as Copeau had been, Pitoëff accorded great importance to rhythm in fashioning a performance, in fleshing out characters and temperaments. Lighting was also used as a powerful evocative force, playing on backdrops of black, blue, or gray velvet curtains and geometrically conceived decors consisting mainly of a few essential pieces of furniture. A Pitoëff performance was a haunting experience.

Mention must also be made of Gaston Baty (1882-1952), an important director during the interwar period. Collaborator of Firmin Gémier, the actor who had incarnated King Ubu in Jarry's play by that name in 1896, Baty helped create plays by Lenormand, Claudel, Shaw, Crommelynck. In 1923 Baty founded his Compagnons de la Chimère. A disciple of Max Reinhardt (1873-1943), who specialised in mass effects, in mob scenes, using an entire auditorium to create atmosphere, frequently placing audiences within the action itself, Baty also enhanced the role and function of the theatrical director. 'A text cannot say everything,' he wrote. It can convey ideas and emotions, but only to a certain point. Beyond this another zone takes precedence, that of mystery, silence, creating a certain atmosphere and stage climate. The director's task is to bring a whole dimension of unknown forces onto the stage space, thus endowing it with renewed life and vigour. Unlike Copeau, Jouvet and Dullin, Baty attacked 'My Lord, the Word,' in his productions of plays by Musset, Lenormand, Goethe, Shakespeare, Gantillon, and Ansky. His adaptations of Flaubert's *Madame Bovary* (1936) underscored the dreamlike nature of the heroine by creating a flowering and sun-drenched arbour where she was seen walking arm in arm with her lover, enjoying a state of veritable rapture. When despair inundated her world, the lights grew weak and dim; the leaves and flowers, once so brilliant and alive, had withered. (In 1927 Dullin, Pitoëff, Jouvet, and Baty formed a cartel. In *Entr'acte*, the official organ of Jouvet's theatre, they expressed their ideas concerning their aims as directors.)

Michel Saint-Denis must also be included as one of Copeau's heirs. The director of the Compagnie des Quinze (made up of members of Copeau's former troupe), he approached theatre with the same seriousness and intensity as had his master. He imposed upon his troupe a rigorous course of studies which included dance, gymnastics, speech, improvisation, mime, and choral singing. The art of diction took on such musicality and depth that during certain performances it was imbued with unheard of incantatory qualities.

André Obey (1892-1975) offered his new play *Noah* to the Compagnie des Quinze as the opening fare for its first season in 1931 at the Vieux-Colombier. His spiritualised and humanised vision of Noah took on a universal dimension and the religious intensity of medieval miracle plays. Although Obey's Noah was a twentieth-century farmer whose domestic problems were great, his understanding of God and man was archetypal. When, for example, he talked on the phone to God, his metaphysical anguish was so acute that it flowed into the audience.

Dadaists and Surrealists were the descendants of experimental dramatists: Alfred Jarry (*King Ubu*, 1896) and Guillaume Apollinaire (*The Breasts of Tiresias*, *Les Mamelles de Teresias*, 1917), who had rejected the well-made psychological play as well as romantic and naturalistic dramas with their classical style, their evolving characters, dramatic climaxes, and shattering suspense scenes. Dadaists and Surrealists continued to subvert language and to destroy the logico-Cartesian approach to life and art; by giving precedence to the irrational domain. Tristan Tzara's *The Gas Heart* (*Le Coeur à gaz*, 1920) and Breton and Soupault's *If You Please* (*S'il vous plaît*, 1920), two highly charged and innovative works, conveyed the absurdity, the eroticism of life as they saw it, in cutting, imagistic, and discontinuous dialogue. The hypnotic power of words, the importance of the chance factor in the deployment of repressed emotions, were techniques used by those who sought to unleash unconscious impulses, until now imprisoned, repressed, crushed. The fantastic works of Georges Ribemont-Dessaignes, *The Hangman from Peru* (*Le Bourreau du Pérou*, 1926), Louis Aragon's spirited *The Mirror Wardrobe One Fine Evening* (*L'Armoire à glace un beau soir*, 1924), and Robert Desnos' fantastic *Place de l'Etoile* (1927) are living proof of the untapped and seemingly endless creative élan of these innovators. For Dadaists and Surrealists, dreams were truer than events lived out in the workaday world; and the word, when released automatically from the unconscious, incoherent though it may have seemed to the rationalist, unveiled a whole other dimension. It is this sphere that now took precedence over the cut-and-dry, the predictable and comprehensible workaday reality.

Antonin Artaud (1896-1949), also a Surrealist, was more of a theoretician of the theatre than he was a playwright. After breaking with Breton and his group (1926), he founded The Theatre Alfred Jarry, along with Roger Vitrac and Robert Aron. 'The spectator who comes to us', he wrote in his manifesto concerning his new theatre, 'knows that he has agreed to undergo a true operation, where not only his mind, but his senses and his flesh are going to come into play.' His productions of Vitrac's *The Mysteries of Love* (*Les Mystères de l'amour*, 1927) and *Victor* (1928), as well as some of his own works, made their mark on the avant-garde of his time. Later, in a series of essays he wrote between 1931 and 1935, published in volume form in *The Theatre and Its Double* (1938), he outlined his views concerning the creation of a Theatre of Cruelty. Artaud's seminal ideas did much to inspire later playwrights such as Ionesco, Genet, Beckett, Anouilh, and Arrabal.

The Flemish/Belgian dramatists Fernand Crommelynck and Michel de Ghelderode reacted powerfully to the provocative ideas of French playwrights and directors. Although they adhered, at least in name, to the basic theatrical conventions, Crommelynck and Ghelderode transcended them by allowing the domain of the irrational to burst forth onstage. Pain, passion, and rage erupted in all of their grotesque grandeur in such farces as Crommelynck's *The Magnificent Cuckold* (*Le Cocu magnifique*, 1921) and Ghelderode's *Escurial* (1927). The stark nature of these comedies—their violence, shrill antics, and savagely evoked joys and horrors as torrents of love and hatred pour forth from their characters—mark these works with a specially fearful quality, a madness, an expressionism perhaps unique in theatre. Audiences experienced a severe malaise when forced to face the hallucinatory world of Crommelynck and Ghelderode: delirious domains where burlesque and sensuality vie with the occult, sadomasochism walks arm in arm with heartfelt piety, and the macabre blends with the priapic.

More conventional than the works of the Dadaists and Surrealists or the Flemish/Belgian dramatists are the mythically oriented works of Cocteau, Giraudoux, Anouilh, and Claudel. Dramatising original experiences, often transcendental rather than personal, Cocteau's *Orpheus* (1926), Giraudoux's *Ondine* (1939) and *The Madwoman of Chaillot* (*La Folle de Chaillot*, 1945), Anouilh's *The Traveller without Luggage* (1937) and *The Thieves' Carnival* (*Le Bal des voleurs*, 1938), Claudel's *Break of Noon*, written in 1905, but officially performed only in 1948, are unsettling: they question, triturate, pain and render jubilant—but always in a subtle, nuanced, and sensitive manner. Their characters are recognisable; their sequences, relatively rational, certainly logical by comparison with the dramas of the Dadaists and Surrealists. Their dialogue, poetic, doleful, and poignant at times searing, speaks to the heart as well as the mind. Theirs is a theatre of all time, of all place, Everyman's.

Dramatists, directors, and actors between World Wars I and II gave form to what had existed in the vague no-man's-land of untried formulas. They brought integrity, sacrifice, and beauty to their artistic creations, gave eternity to a new brand of theatre. Each in his own way learned how to convey and instill raw pain and brutality as well as jubilation and tenderness—pointing up the serenity and poetry that accompany real love, and the grotesque and sublime in flights of fantasy or terror, be they deeply spiritual, sexual, or a fusion of both.

GENDER ISSUES AND FRENCH WOMEN WRITERS

Adele King (essay date 1989)

SOURCE: King, Adele. "Nathalie Sarraute." In *French Women Novelists: Defining a Female Style*, pp. 85-107. London: Macmillan, 1989.

[*In the following essay, King examines the works of Nathalie Sarraute, noting that the writer did not associate her strong sense of political feminism with her work.*]

> When I write, I am neither man nor woman, cat nor dog. I am not me. . . . I don't exist.
>
> (Rykiel, 1984, p. 40)

> I have never understood how some writers can display their life as they do. . . . What counts is the books.
>
> (Saporta, 1984, p. 23)

Nathalie Sarraute's strong 'political' feminism does not, she has said, have a direct relationship to her creative work. She does not think as a woman, she says, and one must not consider men and women as separate, for this leads to a 'destructive segregation'. Any definition of *l'écriture féminine* would include elements found in works by male authors, Proust, for example (Rykiel, 1984, p. 40). Women in her work are not militant feminists or even career oriented: 'These images of women that I have shown are images of feminine behaviour as you continue to see it everywhere. Many women accept playing the role that society imposes upon them' (Besser, 1976, p. 286). She also considers that her own life has no relevance to her work: 'You will find nothing there; or else you will be making arbitrary interpretations' (Saporta, 1984, p. 8). Sarraute's experiences as a Jew in occupied France, for example, have no overt relevance to her work. We are far from the autobiographical work of Colette or Marguerite Duras. Yet while granting the possible divorce between beliefs held and books written (easier to do, perhaps, than granting the divorce between personal experience and written work, as Sarraute also requests us to do), we may find underlying her work a vision of the world that reflects her position as a woman, a use of writing that shows a conscious or perhaps unconscious assumption of gender.

When Sarraute says that at the level of human behaviour and use of language with which she works there is no distinction of gender, she implies a fundamental human nature underlying any divisions. She denies not only gender, but also racial, national and class differences. Yet, in spite of her theory, Sarraute's characters have a certain number of external traits, among them sex. They are *il* or *elle,* not *on* (Brulotte, 1984, p. 45). Sarraute says that the use of *ils* or *elles* for a group is 'sometimes determined simply by a concern for the sound [*un souci de phonétique*] or by a desire to diversify' (Sarraute, 1972, p. 35). When she describes movements of consciousness before they exist in words, a level of 'pre-language', however, are not these movements to some extent based on perceptions that will vary according to what has been felt before? Will not the sensations she describes in some way reflect previous relations with other people and thus how one's gender is perceived by others? Sarraute is aware of how men and women are perceived differently, as can be seen in her reply to a critic who says she has an emotional relationship (*rapports affectifs*) to language: 'you would not look for emotion in Flaubert because he is not a woman' (p. 57). How could such awareness not be reflected in 'tropisms'?

Sarraute's works do not usually have female protagonists. She is seeking what is common to all human beings and is aware that women cannot, at least now, represent this communality. She refused, for example, to let an all-female cast perform one of her plays because 'Women can never, alas, represent the neuter'.¹ She seldom treats directly of what are considered typically feminine themes, such as maternal relations, sexual love, the female body. The lack of communication between individuals in her work, the impossibility of fully comprehending another individual, of which she speaks in *L'Ère du soupçon* (*The Age of Suspicion*), is not a result of a battle of the sexes, as in Colette. Where, then, should we look for possible indications of 'writing as a woman'?

Tropisms, as Sarraute herself defined them, are 'purely instinctive and are caused in us by other people or by the outer world and resemble the movements called tropisms by which living organisms expand or contract under certain influences, such as light, heat, and so on. These movements glide quickly round the border of our consciousness, they compose the small, rapid, and sometimes very complex dramas concealed beneath our actions, our gestures, the words we speak' (Sarraute, 1961, p. 428). These movements of approach and withdrawal, of contact and distance between individuals can be considered, according to Ellen W. Munley, as explorations of identity, as a process of alternative merger with or separation from other persons, a process particularly feminine, if we accept Nancy Chodorow's theory that 'women's sense of self is continuous with others', that women have 'more permeable ego boundaries'. In other words, the psychic reality underlying conscious thought—a reality which for Sarraute is shared by everyone—is nevertheless a reality of which women, because of their cultural conditioning, beginning with their experience of being mothered by women, may be especially aware (Munley, 1983).

In speaking of the *Nouveau Roman* as a possible literary movement, Sarraute makes an important distinction. What interests her is not objects themselves, which are merely 'catalysts', but rather 'the inner movements they release'. For Robbe-Grillet, on the contrary, what is important, she feels, is the 'play of surfaces'. A text is 'living' when its source is in 'a sensation', but it dies when it moves away from sensation to mere games, 'the "beauty" of language' (Saporta, 1984, pp. 21-3). As Valerie Minorgue has commented, Sarraute's work combines 'psychological realism with intense linguistic and literary reflexivity'; it is not concerned merely with the play of language, however, but aims at articulating 'human truths' (Minorgue, 1981, p. 18). Christiane Makward has observed that while 'l'écriture féminine', like the 'nouveau roman', does not distinguish between form and content, it nevertheless postulates 'a direct relation with non-linguistic, non-literary reality'. Sarraute's work is always concerned with this non-literary event.²

Sartre's definition of Sarraute's style in *Portrait d'un inconnu* (*Portrait of a Man Unknown,* 1948) may suggest a feminine approach, in the sense that the style is tentative, not aggressive; 'a style that approaches the object with reverent precautions, withdraws from it suddenly out of a sort of modesty, or through timidity before its complexity, then, when all is said and done, suddenly presents us with the drooling monster, almost without having touched it, through the magic of an image' (Sarraute, 1956, p. xiv, p. 14). Sarraute herself has described the importance she gives to the unfinished quality of her sentences, to the use of points of suspension: 'They give my sentences a certain rhythm, through which they breathe. And also they give my sentences this hesitating, groping aspect, as if they were trying to seize something that each minute escapes, slips away, comes back' (cited Brulotte, 1984, p. 51).

Sarraute's analysis of her style recalls some descriptions of *l'écriture féminine*: 'My sentences are unfinished, suspended, cut in pieces. Sometimes in defiance of strict grammar' (Besser, 1976, p. 285). Although this may appear opposed to the fluidity of which Cixous speaks, it is another means of depicting how sensations are not fixed, and is similar to Cixous's advocacy of a language in which rationality (here 'strict grammar') is sacrificed to the need to capture emotions unanalysable in terms of logic. Sarraute's use of separation and suspension might also be compared to the use of 'blank spaces' in the work of Marguerite Duras, for example. The lack of conclusion (the 'unfinished sentences') is allied to a lack of exciting intrigues, a refusal similar to Colette's to write of great themes, of the destiny of man. What is important is psychological states, an individual's response to events and other persons. More radically, Sarraute has suggested that she is not interested in events at all: 'In reality all my books are written on two levels. There is the level of the most banal external appearances . . . and then there is the invisible level, which interests me: the level of tropisms' (Rambures, 1972, p. 16). To read at the level of banal appearances is to read falsely. Sarraute defines her form as similar to that of other recent novelists, essentially a refusal of previous conventions of the novel: the character is only a *trompe-l'oeil* and is often part of a group, the plot is almost nonexistent, there is no chronological order, the dialogue is transformed (Sarraute, 1972, p. 26). She refuses any description of her characters; if one could say that a character was 'timid' or 'miserly', she feels, he would no longer be of interest, as he would be defined in conventional terms. If, after the appearance of tropisms, the reader is still interested in the character of Martereau, Sarraute is, she says, distressed (p. 53). Related to this refusal simply to tell a story with well-defined characters is the lack of a clear genre, another connection between Sarraute's work and various definitions of women's writing. Her books are hardly novels, but rather 'prose texts which are in a vaguely defined area between interior monologue, intimist theatre and Proustian introspection' (Arnette, 1976).

Sarraute's quest for tropisms has been described as a quest for spontaneity, for lucidity, a fight against conformism and the language of 'correct society':

> She comes to the defence of the madness and the passion that people want to lock up. She takes the side of rebels against conventional values . . . against 'One must not', 'That's not done', 'That's the way it is'. . . . For real contact. Against classifications, labels, definitions.
>
> (Brulotte, 1984, p. 40)

This, as well, is a link to *l'écriture féminine* in its refusal to accept the categories of thought and language prescribed by conventional (patriarchal) society. There are no absolute truths. In her defence of 'passion', of 'madness', Sarraute's work might be allied to that of Duras. It is not, of course, working with the same overt themes, is not concerned with the extreme traumas of love and passion that haunt Duras; but it is a similar rejection of the socially acceptable. Might not the narrator of *Portrait* in his voyeuristic obsession with the elderly father and his daughter be compared to Jacques Hold in *Le Ravissement de Lol V. Stein*? The self for Sarraute has been characterised as '*a space*, unstable and open to attack', a space without a language. The self without language occurs as well in Duras's work, but for Duras the self retreats into silence or madness. The self in Sarraute's novels often retreats rather into empty mechanisms and clichés. It is only the artist who seeks a language of truth, and the artist is sometimes equated with the 'mad prophet who denounces the established order' (Britton, 1982, p. 581).

Sarraute is always consciously concerned with the act of creation, how words influence our perceptions and emotions, how each human being organises his or her own world around clichés as well as individual experience. Narrators are thus, intrinsically, unrealiable. Narration may be a search for truth, but it is also 'an act of presumptuousness and even of aggression' (Minorgue, 1981, p. 23). The absence of the omniscient narrator is also the absence of an authority figure: 'We know that usually the narrator is presented as a projection of the old paternal role in the family. The father-narrator is installed as head of the story.' Sometimes Sarraute uses narrators who are limited, sometimes she multiplies the points of view. Often she invites a dialogue with the reader. The world of her novels is 'polymorphous and changing' (Brulotte, 1984, pp. 48-9).

Portrait d'un inconnu, Sarraute's first 'novel' which Sartre in his influential preface termed an 'anti-novel', is the story of a man watching an elderly father and his daughter. The narrator is very tentative in his approach, wary of what others may say to him, uncertain, incapable of reaching firm conclusions. He may, therefore, strike the reader as a 'marginal' individual, full of vague fears, lacking in aggression, or even in any self-confidence. He seems to want to be proved wrong. He cannot always control himself: 'I must keep my distance—but I couldn't stop myself. I felt already the attraction they still have for me, like a rush of air that draws everything along, a sort of dizziness, a plunge into the void' (Sarraute, 1956, p. 32, p. 31). He sees himself not as the seeker, but as the sought, the victim: 'Underneath his every action, even the apparently trivial and innocuous ones, there is a sort of wrong side, another facet, a hidden one, known only to us, and which is turned in my direction. It is through this, no doubt, that he attracts me and continues to have such a strong hold over me' (p. 91, pp. 92-3). His description of the old man recalls Claudine Herrmann's theory of the male who dominates his world: 'It is not only because of the look he has of waiting for his prey when he sits there withdrawn into himself, but also because of his position: in the center—he is in the center, he sits there in state, dominating everything—and the entire universe is like a web of his own weaving, which he drapes at will about himself' (p. 113, p. 116). The narrator has no such assurance. More radically, he knows that the old man has no such assurance. The feeling of domination that Herrmann ascribes to the male is an illusion in Sarraute's world. There are no essences: 'Above all, one must be aware of an impression of easy victory which he can give at times, when he accepts a little too willingly, for instance, a frontal attack, with a sort of motionlessness that is so different from the furtive leaps with which he usually escapes' (p. 117, p. 120). The narrator's role is to be the 'conducting rod through which all the currents that charged the atmosphere were passing' (p. 139, p. 144). We might consider that the narrator possesses what are often thought of as 'feminine' characteristics. (We can perhaps go this far, while remembering that for Sarraute there are no fixed personalities or characters.)

The narrator is looking for 'tropisms' initially, trying to catch the movements of the father and his daughter, not to reduce them to characters. He does not consider identity as fixed, but as fluid. He looks for

> the crack, the tiny crevice, the weak point, as delicate as a baby's fontanelle, at which I seem to see something that resembles a barely perceptible pulsation suddenly swell and begin to throb gently. I cling to it and press upon it. And then I feel a strange substance trickling from them in an endless stream, a substance as anonymous as lymph, or blood . . . And all that remains of the firm, rosy, velvety flesh of these 'live' persons is a shapeless gray covering.
>
> (Sarraute, 1956, p. 69, p. 72)

In so far as she accepts anything of herself entering into the novel, Sarraute would identify with this narrator, the seeker of tropisms: 'In fact, I am rather this observer, who is passionately interested in the still unknown that is happening between the father and the daughter. . . . What I would be in this story would be the "seeker of tropisms".' The narrator gives up: 'Then the *déjà vu* comes back. The traditional novel invades everything. A "normal" character, the fiancé, appears' (Saporta, 1984, pp. 6-7). When he creates an ordinary novel, he is dissatisfied with himself. The old man is not, he knows, 'the cheaply manufactured puppet, the dime-store trash intended for the common herd, but as he was in reality, indefinable, without outlines' (Sarraute, 1956, p. 203, p. 216). Finally, however, he accepts a place among those—in fact, the old women of the neighbourhood—who see life simply, as a series of clichés. Thus, he differs from Sarraute: 'He finally treats his obsession as madness. . . . I have never considered that I was mad' (Saporta, 1984, p. 7).

The unnamed narrator of *Portrait*, in refusing solidity to others, in hesitating to attribute to himself any authority, in his confusion of witnessed and imagined scenes (so that the reader is never sure what has 'in fact' taken place— was there a grand scene between the old man and his daughter or not?), undermines any sense of security. The world is fluid, language cannot seize it, the undercurrents of emotion are also unstable and often seem to emanate from a childish world of malevolent witches. Such a vision, appropriate to the 'age of suspicion' as Sarraute has defined it, may be considered feminine in its refusal of authority.

In *Martereau* (1953), according to Sarraute, there is a contrary movement to that of *Portrait*. Rather than tropisms being abandoned for a conventional view of the world, Martereau is initially seen as a conventional character and is gradually dissolved into an amorphous being:

> It's again a question of a literary experience, of a contrast between the monolithic character of Martereau as he fascinates the nephew at the beginning of their relationship and the same character as he is disintegrated by tropisms.
>
> (Saporta, 1984, p. 15)

The narrator of *Martereau* is another insecure, passive individual, who characterises himself as having an 'extreme self-effacement' (Sarraute, 1953, p. 2, p. 8). Like the narrator of *Portrait* he is thus in a good position to observe others and to discover what their behaviour may conceal beneath the surface. His lack of conventional aggressivity would seem to predispose him towards a less preconceived notion of other individuals, and also lead others more readily to drop their social masks, or at least, to be less than normally wary. Again, although Sarraute denies being interested in creating 'characters', 'personalities', she has chosen a narrator whose approach towards others leads him to a greater than normal ability to detect 'tropisms', a narrator who is conscious of what is

> expressed not in so many words, of course, as I am obliged to do now for lack of other means, not with real words like the ones we articulate distinctly out loud or in our thoughts, but suggested rather by certain sorts of very rapid signs . . . signs so brief and which slip so quickly through him and through me that I could never succeed in really understanding or seizing them, I can only recover them in bits and snatches and translate them awkwardly by the words these signs represent, fleeting impressions, thoughts, feelings, often forgotten.
>
> (Sarraute, 1953, p. 25, pp. 34-5)

The narrator's behaviour may often remind the reader of typically 'feminine' reactions:

> I try to make up for it, I should like to be forgiven. I resume our conversation in a slightly uneasy voice, I begin to ask questions.
>
> (p. 32, p. 42)

> I have often wondered what devil eggs me on at those moments . . . Some might say, a love of suffering . . . a morbid need to be humiliated, a vague desire to see that thing that has remained dangerously live under the ashes, finally burst into flame and devour me.
>
> (p. 33, p. 43)

> Always, even when I feel their teeth about to sink delicately into me, I am prepared to blame everything on myself.
>
> (p. 68, p. 83)

Indeed, he compares himself to a 'hysterical woman' (p. 77, p. 93). (Sarraute, of course, is not suggesting that either sex has a monopoly of hysteria, but rather that the narrator sees in a conventional way, and thus expects women to be more readily hysterical.)

In the narrator's aunt, Sarraute portrays typically feminine behaviour: pleasure in her appearance and how it is judged by others, pride in having accomplished things behind the scenes, while always remaining soft:

> 'Well, that little woman with her air of not lifting a finger, is all-powerful just now. That made your uncle very proud.' . . . It wouldn't need much to set her to twisting about with that simpering, falsely innocent manner that certain precocious little girls assume when they want to play the baby.
>
> (p. 4, pp. 10-11)

If no moral judgement is intended, according to Sarraute, it is still difficult not to read this opening scene of *Martereau* as a satire on a type of bourgeois woman, playing a role, or rather several roles, including that of the woman who gives up comfort to be independent. What is added, undoubtedly, to a typical portrait is the awareness of fluctuations, changes in sensations beneath the overt level of character.

The description of the relationship between the aunt and uncle, while showing the similar kinds of ploys for dominance, submission, role-playing engaged in by the two individuals, is also on one level a picture of the battle of the sexes. Sarraute's tropisms may be essentially identical for all individuals, but they still function with particular force in a marriage; *Martereau* is a fine portrayal of the tensions between man and wife in which, in spite of Sarraute's own comments, the differences in male and female reactions are evident. He is the wounded 'Samson' (p. 125, p. 149), she affects the '"Woman Reading" prose' (p. 90, p. 108). He wants to be 'Lord of creation' (p. 127, p. 151); she knows how to bring up topics, such as a letter from her brother, that will soothe him.

When he meets Martereau, the narrator already has a fixed image in his mind. Martereau is not like his aunt and uncle; there are no undercurrents in him: 'without the slightest crack through which anything whatsoever that was suspicious might seep, nothing but sincere solicitude, the frankest sort of good-heartedness' (p. 76, p. 92). Martereau's life seems to be summed up in a series of photos of contentment, with troubles only 'like big thick, heavy, blocks with clear outlines, clearly drawn . . . clear and clean, in one block, like Martereau himself. Worthy of him. Made to his measure' (pp. 83-4, p. 101). Thus the narrator believes that for Martereau the world and language are consistent: 'Words are not for him what they are for me—thin protective capsules that enclose noxious germs—but hard, solid objects, from one casting, it's useless to open them up, make cross-sections, examine them, we should find nothing' (p. 112, p. 133).

When his doubts about Martereau begin, they are immediately connected to a memory of his doubts as a child about his mother's generosity, doubts aroused by remarks of the servants concerning the poor bits of meat she leaves for them. (The incident is a memory of Sarraute herself, which she recalls in *Enfance*.) Thus the destruction of the narrator's confidence in stable personality is linked to a child's awareness that his parents are not perfect. The narrator initially swings from a vision of a perfect Martereau to a vision of a scoundrel. Maturity of vision, it is implied, means giving up notions of good and bad characters.

Martereau is a series of narrative constructions, in which the narrator shows alternative versions of various events from what he imagines to be the point of view of various individuals, or different alternatives that might have been experienced by a single consciousness. None of the versions is authoritative. Each individual, at least in his reconstruction (for we are always aware that the words are filtered through his perceptions), uses words and gestures, often commonplace expressions—clichés and literary stereotypes—to 'establish an approved version of himself and the surrounding world' (Minorgue, 1981, p. 66). The narrator—and here, at least, he can be seen as similar to Nathalie Sarraute, his creator—is aware that words are weapons in a dangerous game of attack, in the world of society and especially of the family. This realisation of the undercurrents of all social discourse is, I would argue, particularly acute in marginal people—such as the narrator, a sickly young man dependent upon the financial support of his uncle—and thus also of such members of marginal groups as women, for, in the society that Sarraute depicts, as indeed in most societies, women are usually dependent upon the financial support of men.

Sarraute is not making moral judgements about this society. In showing how human discourse is a kind of war, and in portraying the reactions of the most vulnerable participants in this war, she makes, however, a deeper analysis of the psychological dangers of the roles of the dominating and dominated (or of the sexes) than might be found in explicitly polemical work. By its ironic unmasking of conventional behaviour, stereotypes, verbal simplifications of emotions, the novel makes fun of any attempts to categorise social roles, thus mocking assigning women to roles as victims or men to roles as masters, and showing the fallacies both of accepting societal gender constructions and of doctrinaire attempts to deconstruct gender roles. This refusal of easy categorisation might well be seen as a more profoundly 'feminist' vision of the world—if we accept that 'feminism' can include the recognition of the essential similarities of all human psychological reactions—than more overt polemics.

Martereau is often very funny; Sarraute uses humour in her exploration of the war games of social relationships, a weapon perhaps too often avoided by explicitly feminist writers. Her sense of the ambiguities, the mutations in human relationships, and especially of how each of us plays various roles (often based on literary stereotypes), leads her to see the comedy as well as the deceptions of life. The world presented in *Martereau* may be more easily made comic because it is essentially, of course, a comfortable bourgeois world; in her fiction Sarraute avoids problems of economics and politics.

In *Le Planétarium* (*The Planetarium*, 1959) there is still a timid, self-conscious character, similar to the narrators of *Portrait* and *Martereau*. He is Alain Guimier, who first appears as a narrator at a social gathering, telling the story of his aunt's problems with her new door. In *Planétarium*, however, this character is not a first-person narrator, and is not the only narrative voice. Rather, we have a 'polyphonic narrative', a multiplicity of voices.[3] In the earlier novels, the unreliability and the self-interest of the narrative voices were evident in their partial points of view. In *Planétarium*, Sarraute takes her criticism of the single dependable narrative voice still further. The idea that the multi-voiced text is 'feminine' appears in many feminist theories. In Sarraute's work, polyphonic voicing is not overtly 'feminine', but might be considered as a formal stratagem particularly appropriate to expressing the view of the marginal individual—either a self-conscious, alienated person aware of a vague guilt, or a member of a subordinate group in the dominant culture.

There is very little 'action' in *Planétarium*, but rather, as in the earlier novels, a focus on the underlying struggles of the characters to create worlds (all whirling in a planetarium) in their own image. It is at this psychological level, beneath the rather banal surface, that Sarraute considers that her characters are all similar, not differentiated by sex, or age (in moments of stress, they all often revert to images from childhood). While she never portrays at any length characters from social classes other than the bourgeoisie, one must assume that such characters would also engage in similar struggles to impose their views, and in similar feelings of inadequacy, although their choice of clichés and images might be different. The creation of one's own world is basically a process of narration, thus a matter of words; these words are weapons of attack against the worlds created by others. While the surface of *Planétarium* is somewhat calmer than that of *Portrait*—there is no violence quite to equal that of the father's possible attack on his daughter—or of *Martereau*—there is no illegal behaviour equal to that of Martereau's possible attempt at appropriating the property of others—the in-fighting and the implicit domination are just as great.

Planétarium also includes, however, a use of words not developed in Sarraute's earlier work—words for explicitly literary creation. Alain wants to become a writer, and seeks the approval of an established writer, Germaine Lemaire. It is a theme that will be developed in some of Sarraute's later works—*Les Fruits d'or*, *Entre la vie et la mort*—where the creation and reception of a book are of primary importance, where the book itself becomes the main character (an obvious rejection of gender!). *Planétarium* is particularly rich because the two uses of words—in battles within the sphere of social relations, and in battles within the creator struggling to find the right word—are interrelated. Since Germaine Lemaire seems a rather conventional novelist (though how can we judge?) and since Alain is only aspiring to write, literary creation in this novel is not a more important theme than the social creation of a world through the use of words.

There are no fixed values, no stable characters, no certainties, no truths. Everyone's opinions of everyone else vacillate. It is a frightening world, in which each individual seeks an illusory security by establishing a fixed persona, or by the possession of objects. The anguish that Sarraute's characters feel, and seek to overcome, is comic, because expressed in terms of the insignificant—Aunt Berthe's obsession with the vulgar fingerplate installed on her door, for instance—but it is finally tragic, as it reveals the instability of all human projects. Alain worries about the impression he makes on others, feels people are laughing behind his back. His mother-in-law worries about being judged as a meddling old idiot. Gisèle is aware of 'the old sensation she used to have, her own peculiar fear, still the same, the terror that had never left her' (Sarraute, 1959, p. 65, p. 66). Even Germaine Lemaire, surrounded by admirers, is aware of the precariousness of her situation, of the need to 'watch herself. Try to understand. Each time she must make the effort to tilt over towards them' (p. 190, p. 201).

Within this fluctuating world, the relations between the sexes are obviously unstable. Gisèle's stereotyped view of a perfect marriage, beginning with a perfect wedding, crumbles quickly. She hears two 'wicked fairies' (p. 67, p. 69) talking at the wedding reception about Alain's small income. (Such images from childhood literature—evoking a world of the clearly good and clearly evil—are frequently used in Sarraute's work to point to the fixed values to which people cling, and which have little to do with real life.) Gisèle is increasingly aware that 'Complete fusion exists with no one' (p. 75, p. 77), a theme similar to that of Colette. Often Alain and Gisèle see each other in conventional roles. For her, men are 'strong, intelligent' (p. 127, p. 132); for him, she is one of the 'tender little children' who need protection (p. 140, p. 146). But such stereotyped emotions are not stable. Gisèle's admiration for her husband, like that he feels for Germaine Lemaire, is capable of quick reversal. Germaine Lemaire's experiences as a writer offer a parallel to those of characters involved in more commonplace activities. She too tries to impose order on her world, and finds that it is instable. Narrative, like reality, can never be ordered. Sometimes her writing seems to have caught a 'vivid impression of reality'; a moment later she sees it as 'congealed', 'frozen', 'hollow' (pp. 181-3, pp. 190-2).

To see the tragedy of life in terms of the everyday, the trivial, may be to see from the point of view of someone whose assigned world is the private rather than the political, but also of someone whose alienation is not so extreme as to seem to require radical solutions—in other words, someone in the situation of a woman, both inside and outside the social and political sphere. Sarraute herself suggested that her characters' anguish can be linked to that of Samuel Beckett's characters, but that her characters don't talk about it.[4] Sarraute's characters avoid the grand gesture, but also even speculations about identity and purpose. They wait, not for Godot, but for the repairman, or for the chance to establish themselves momentarily through a cutting judgement on one of their acquaintances. Sarraute comically allows a character to equate her preoccupations with more 'serious' events. Gisèle's words, as she tells her mother she would rather have a *bergère* than a pair of leather armchairs, 'like those that once revealed heresy and led directly to the stake, showed that evil was still there, as alive and strong as ever' (pp. 49-50, p. 51).

In *Planétarium*, the absence of a first-person narrator, combined with the prominence of scenes set in social groups, produces more frequent juxtapositions of various clichés and incomplete sentences than found in Sarraute's earlier fiction. The style is thus even more fluid, sustaining the theme of instability, but also creating a poetic effect:

> 'Good heavens, it's awful, we enjoy ourselves so much at your house that we forget how late it is . . .' Noise of chairs . . . and he, scowling in his corner, ignored, almost forgotten already. . . . 'It was delightful. So when shall I see you? Oh, very soon. Don't forget to let me hear from you. One of us will telephone at the beginning of next week. I'll count on you, then, surely?'
>
> (p. 41, p. 42)

'Grated carrots', 'tender', 'finely chopped', 'well seasoned' (p. 115, p. 120) become poetic leitmotifs in a conversation between Alain and his in-laws. Images are drawn frequently from fairy tales, children's games, stories of American Indians. Occasionally, however, a more sinister note intrudes:

> Escaped prisoners, members of the resistance, Jews hiding under false names, were lolling in the sun, chatting on village squares, seated about fountains, drinking together in bistros, as though nothing had happened, cunning, disquieting prey, cunningly forcing the others, the pure who had done nothing, the strong who had nothing to fear from anybody, into loathsome complicity . . . until one fine morning, a man got up—after all some one had to take it upon himself to do it—and hurried, slinking along the walls, to denounce them.
>
> (p. 220, p. 231)

This memory, or perhaps false memory, from Alain's childhood, which he recalls as he considers how to get Aunt Berthe's apartment, is as close as Sarraute comes to evoking her own experience of the war years in her fiction.

Entre la vie et la mort (*Between Life and Death*, 1968), which Sarraute considers her most important work, is a difficult book, a book about writing, the hesitations and uncertainties of the writer, the relation of the writer to the social milieu in which he or she lives, the possibility of producing a work that lives. What is 'between life and death' is not a person but a text. The writer, who is, along with 'his' work, the principal character of this novel, is a composite, not really an individual. What little we know about him is often contradictory. In what sense, even, beyond the use of the pronoun 'he', can we speak of this writer as male? He has no distinguishing characteristics, except that he has a mother before whom he feels shy and childish, is obviously middle class, and likes to drink tea. This writer, however, and what we can intuit about the way he works, bears striking resemblances to Sarraute herself and her method. He is, from an early age, aware of the power of words, an awareness which, initially, seems to him the mark of a poet, not 'someone who knows better than others how to look' but 'the man who knows how to make a poem out of words' (Sarraute, 1968, p. 26, p. 42). Later, however, he seems to consider that pure word-play may indicate a divorce from the real world, that what is important is capturing 'movements', neither images nor words, but what Sarraute terms 'tropisms'. Like Sarraute, the writer in *Entre la vie et la mort* is interested in platitudes, does not criticise but describes, rejects rigid forms. He is of a more than ordinarily 'porous' material, soaking up the world around him. When he comes to the moment of creation, he experiences great difficulties, working slowly, often feeling himself divided between creator and judge. In his attitudes towards the treatment of the writer by literary society, he is also like Sarraute. He rejects classification in any school, finds many of his readers insensitive to what he is doing, is annoyed by attempts to make him a public figure, denies that his work can be read as autobiographical. He even shares with Sarraute a similar memory of the joy of writing his first school composition on the death of an imaginary dog. Finally, what matters is whether the work itself is living: 'Nearer to me, but not too near . . . you my double, my witness . . . there, lean over with me . . . let's look together . . . does it emit, deposit . . . as on the mirror we hold before the mouth of the dying . . . a fine mist?' (p. 183, p. 204). *Entre la vie et la mort* is therefore a book about how Sarraute feels that the artist works, but a book in which not only the author herself, but also her fictitious writer, are of secondary importance.

If we try to find a feminine perspective in this text, it is perhaps necessary to speak of the modesty and the self-effacement of the author behind the text, as well as the shyness, uncertainty and social insecurity of the writer as character. The record of creativity, in which the artist's ego doesn't finally matter at all, in which the product is all that counts, is in contradiction, for example, to the Romantic impulse, an impulse that seems to many critics particularly masculine.[5] Stephen Heath suggests that Proust and Sarraute are similar in seeking what lies beneath the superficiality of conversation, but that Proust seeks what is individual beneath the surface, and Sarraute seeks what is shared (Heath, 1972, p. 50). Is Sarraute's concentration on what every person shares perhaps feminine in its reduction of human experience to fundamental emotions, in its refusal to attribute supreme importance to a 'romantic' individual sensibility? She is, of course, creating a picture of an 'ungendered' writer and work. In spite of her stated intention, however, the work, even the fictitious writer 'himself', may well seem to the reader 'feminine'. His world, like that of many of her earlier characters, is a world of fear and solitude, a world in which he feels out of place but would like to be accepted.

The basic preoccupation with states of consciousness and of awareness just below the level of consciousness, and of how such states are expressed or masked by words, exists in all Sarraute's writing from *Tropismes* through the novels to *L'Usage de la parole* (*The Use of Speech*, 1980), which combines elements of earlier works. It is in some ways closer to *Tropismes* as it dispenses with the sustained plot and characters of the novels; short sketches are related only in the most general thematic sense of showing how words are used. *L'Usage* also continues an examination of various themes from the novels. One theme is the recognition that beneath the surface meanings of conversation may lie words not used to communicate thoughts: words, for example, addressed to a friend 'so as to destroy those morbid cells in him in which his hostility, his hate proliferate' (Sarraute, 1980, p. 29, p. 32), words used to assert one's position, or to terrorise another. Another theme is an awareness of the impossibility of communication: 'he sees, facing him, his fellow man, endowed with an identical brain, capable of using an identical language. . . . Transformed . . . an unknown being' (pp. 40-41, p. 44). Our perceptions of others are always far from the indefinable reality; they are rather 'a roughly-sketched form, a crude diagram, a robot-portrait . . . a doll like the ones children cut out of cardboard' (p. 85, p. 85). The human personality, normally constructed according to social roles, is fragile and can crumble with terrifying results: 'a crevasse will open out between us . . . we'll be wrenched away from one another, ejected from our broken shells . . . two solitary souls errant' (p. 89, p. 88). Usually, however, the family tends to give individuals a socially constructed identity. This produces a loss of awareness of true individuality, but also a barrier against the terror of the void. In one family group we find: 'their soft, responsive contours melting and merging into one another, so that they no longer knew where one ended and the other began . . . they are a living ball . . . imbued with intimate, bland, sweet odours' (p. 51, p. 53). (So much for Plato's dream of the ball uniting lovers, a dream that, following Irigaray, we can see as an appropriation of the female into the male.)

If communication is impossible, it is both because of this unknown quality in any human being and also because of the vagueness of words, particularly abstract words: 'how rough and vague they are, how incapable of bringing out into the open and enabling us to see what might impel these people to take evasive action' (pp. 84-5, p. 84). Normally, however, we behave as if we understood others' language. The person who dares to say 'I don't understand' would break the hold 'of charlatanism, of terrorism, of conformism' (p. 150, p. 149). Such an action is perhaps only possible in a fairy-tale. Alexandra Sévin, writing in a politically radical magazine, uses Sarraute's work to attack the way the French Communist Party uses the language of power. She reads the *Je ne comprends pas* text, as the present-day revolt of women, since they are 'always dispossessed of the use of speech, reduced to repeating only words that are officially allowed'.[6] Perhaps she is too optimistic, since Sarraute talks of the fairy-tale ending of *Je ne comprends pas*; Sévin also finds a more overt political meaning than Sarraute's work would, I think, justify. Still, Sévin's article shows the extent to which Sarraute can appeal to militant feminist readers.

The language in *L'Usage* is more pared down and the perspective more readily comprehensible to the reader than in some of Sarraute's earlier work. The opening text, '*Ich sterbe*', for example, addresses the reader directly: 'You'll see; be patient' (p. 7, p. 11); and explains the meaning of words: 'they come back (as people say: "It's coming back to me")' (p. 7, p. 11). This narrator uses the first person, directs the reader, anticipates our questions: 'What is there to look for in these signs that are so easy to read?' (p. 19, p. 22); 'What's so surprising about that, then? Nothing in that, of course, but just a moment . . .' (p. 27, p. 30). The narrator tells the reader how to respond not only to the text, but to the words of the dying Chekhov that lie behind the text:

> All we have here, as you see, are a few slight eddies, a few brief ripples captured amongst the infinite number that these words produce. If some of you find this game diverting, they may—with patience and time—amuse themselves by discovering others. At all events they may be sure that they are not mistaken, for everything they may perceive is really there, in every one of us: circles that continue to increase when, propelled from such a distance and with such force, these words fall on us and shake us to the depths of our being: Ich sterbe.
>
> (p. 14, pp. 17-18)

Sarraute's suggestion that the reader cannot be mistaken might be seen as feminist, in so far as both reader-response theory and feminist theory reject the definitive, the authoritarian reading. Sarraute is, of course, speaking directly not of how to read her text, but of how to see the possible implications of Chekhov's last words—'I die'—and thus of the universality of the experience of death. But her words are also applicable to the level of awareness that her own texts strive to reach, a level at which authority, the voice of reason or established truth, is of less importance than the subconscious reactions of each individual. Our personal awareness cannot deceive us; each individual's examples have an equal validity:

> You could easily, if you agree, add to them; or substitute others you may find amongst those in your possession. . . . Which of us has not stockpiled some of them in the limitless reserve funds which we never have either the leisure or the desire to inspect, to inventory, but which nevertheless nourish our existence.
>
> (p. 35, p. 39)

Implicit in these appeals to the reader is a recognition that human beings, in spite of the difficulties of communication, share a common experience, that we are inseparable as well as separate.[7]

Each of the texts continues the appeal to the reader to enter into the creation of the experience, and gives this reader a clear orientation: 'We must observe that all the conditions are present that would justify us in assuming that we are witnessing a meeting of two friends' (pp. 20-1, p. 24); 'Here are two more interlocutors. . . . But here too, a little more patience is required' (p. 33, p. 37); 'and the whole of this story has been leading up to this dénouement' (p. 40, p. 43). *L'Usage de la parole* contains what Ellen Munley has termed a 'self-styled narrator-doctor of words who joins all of its loosely connected vignettes by virtue of her presence' (Munley, 1983, p. 238). There is even a certain tone of mockery, a suggestion that this narrator has written other, often misunderstood texts and that now, in a pedagogical fashion, she must clarify her intentions. Occasionally she mocks her own preoccupations, her own careful, meticulous examination of all facets of a word: 'no, don't be afraid, I'm not going to start again' (p. 110, p. 110); she realises that she herself might be the object of ridicule similar to that levelled at some of her characters. (If the narrator is a writer conscious of, and responding to, the criticisms sometimes levelled at Sarraute's work, we cannot, of course, identify the 'I' with Sarraute herself.)

In 'Ich sterbe', the description of Chekhov's last words, and therefore the text the furthest removed from the examination of minute movements between two unidentified speakers—the usual subject of these sketches—the narrator describes Chekhov as 'Wise. Modest. Reasonable. Always so undemanding' (p. 9, pp. 12-13), thus rather similar to the narrator of *L'Usage* in rejecting patriarchal authority. 'Ich sterbe' contains an implicit criticism of the ability of language to fix experience. 'The unsayable will be said', but only at the moment of death. All is vacillating, trembling, an 'infinite disorder' (p. 9, p. 13), until it is immobilised, tranquillised in the words '*Ich sterbe*', in which, finally, there is an order, but only the order of death. 'Ich sterbe' speaks as well of how, in saying that he is dying, Chekhov would choose foreign words, those most removed from previous experience, thus without the breath of any passion. Sarraute, for whom Russian is the *mother* language (the language of the mother whose rejection she felt so bitterly in her childhood), writes in French, perhaps also a way of retaining a certain distance from passion. Chekhov's words are addressed to the German doctor, not to Chekhov's wife, for, it is implied, at the moment of death there is no more 'we': 'No, not our sort of words, they are too light, too limp, they would never be able to cross what is now opening, yawning, between us . . . an immense chasm' (p. 12, p. 15). Perhaps in this rejection of the 'couple' there is another implicitly feminist theme.

The text most directly related to feminist concerns, however, is 'Your father. Your sister'. It is a strange piece, both in the uncertainty of the narrative tone and in the fluctuating perspective. The narrator wants to capture the force of the words 'Your father. Your sister' as indicating social roles, how the family is defined, how the mother, who speaks these words, sees herself as fixed within an identity. But the sentence chosen to embody these words—'If you go on like that, Armand, your father will prefer your sister'—suggests more, 'an unnatural mother', 'a vile, vulgar person' (p. 60, p. 61). The narrator insists that this other resonance in the sentence is of no interest, that the sentence could as well have been 'You know, Armand, your father will take your sister to the doctor's'. But finally, the narrator is uncertain that the words 'Your father. Your sister' have in themselves, without the rest of the sentence, the force attributed to them. The element of doubt here may be considered, I believe, as Sarraute's reflection on the possible feminist import of her work. She says she is interested in how fixed family roles are perceived and how they influence speech and conduct, how both the mother and the father are enclosed in certain patterns of behaviour, even if the woman may feel their force more fully. The possibility that the mother's setting of son and daughter against each other, her assumption that the father *should* prefer the son, might reflect the patriarchal bias of society has never, according to the narrator, been a consideration. (The narrator, of course, does not use such terms as 'patriarchal'.) And yet, she wonders if perhaps she has been wrong not to consider such issues.

Enfance (*Childhood,* 1983) is Sarraute's only autobiographical work, and the story stops when she enters the lycée. The implication is that the later life of the author, like that of the writer in *Entre la vie et la mort,* is only, really, the creation of her work. Occasionally in interviews Sarraute has referred to harrowing experiences, and indirectly to her own bravery as a Jew in occupied France during the war, but she has denied the relevance of personal experience to an interpretation of her work. Her childhood, however, she is willing to recount, while suggesting that such a project may be a sign of creative sterility.

Enfance is of interest to the reader of Sarraute's fiction, as it shows some of the personal emotions and experiences that underlie her work ('all the memories that she has killed, all the childhood that was stolen from her' [Cournot, 1986]), but are never allowed to surface. In this respect, she is rather like Marguerite Yourcenar (or Samuel Beckett) and in considerable contrast to those women novelists, such as Colette and Marguerite Duras, whose 'I' is often confounded with fictional characters. It is an attitude, I would suggest, that is also 'feminine' in its origins. Either the boundaries between the self and the other become blurred (which Chodorow would attribute to the role of the mother in a daughter's childhood), or the self is rigidly kept in the background. It is interesting, in this regard, to remember that Marguerite Yourcenar's mother died soon after giving birth to her daughter, and that Sarraute shows, in *Enfance,* the trauma of being rejected by a beautiful and inaccessible mother, who in a letter calls her daughter a 'monster of egotism' (Sarraute, 1983, p. 229, p. 240); Sarraute had to choose to stay with her father and her difficult, uncaring stepmother. We may also consider Sarraute's work as in some ways related to that of her mother, as a reaction to her mother. This does not appear as a theme in her work, cannot be analysed directly as in the work of Colette and Duras. Nevertheless, her comments on her mother's own writing show both similarities and contrasts:

> My mother wrote 'romans-fleuves', children's stories and short stories. She wrote, in contrast to me, with great ease and much joy. She used a very rich vocabulary. The stories often took place in peasant settings. She wrote under a masculine pseudonym and was rather proud that no one—critic or reader—realised that her work was written by a woman.
>
> (Cited in Saporta, 1984, p. 8)

If Nathalie Sarraute's style is very different from her mother's, there is a similar refusal to be identified by gender.

As a child, Sarraute is obsessed with the instability of her own family life, and attracted to those whose childhoods are spent with 'unified, fair and calm parents' (Sarraute, 1983, p. 233, p. 244). In spite of the traumas of her childhood, however, she often wants to assert, against the *alter ego* with whom she conducts her dialogue in *Enfance*, that she behaved 'in the same way as a lot of children do' (p. 16, p. 25). Even as a child, she rejected her own emotions, rejoiced when her mind seemed 'clean, flexible, healthy' (p. 119, p. 130). This control, this need to dominate the irrational, may explain to some degree Sarraute's insistence that she is writing about what all individuals share, and writing from an ungendered position, asserting a 'healthy' neutrality. *Enfance* also mentions another, more overt explanation for her refusal to consider her writing as feminine. In the intellectual discussions among her father's émigré friends in Paris, she is conscious that 'no one made the slightest distinction between men and women' (p. 177, p. 189). Her childhood world is thus one in which the sexes are united in intellectual pursuits, while widely differentiated in their expressions of emotion.

Enfance portrays a distrust of such abstract terms as 'happiness' and of emotional states—particularly irrational fear and sudden terror—that is shared by many of the characters in her novels. It also shares formal qualities with her fiction: a plurality of voices, with continual interruptions (there is Sarraute in dialogue with herself, and with her childhood self, who sometimes speaks directly in the present tense); a preoccupation with the need to find a word to pin down a feeling; a denial of any conventional interpretations. As a child Sarraute often read *The Prince and the Pauper*, important to her because of its theme of uncertain identity. While the book is obviously relevant to her own situation as a child without a clear sense of a 'home', it may also be seen as a prototype for the kind of fiction she creates in her maturity, in which characters have fluctuating, unstable qualities, and are haunted by fears of rejection.

An essential aim of Sarraute's work would seem to be to show a basic equality, the existence for both men and women of similarly banal conversations, a language filled with clichés, stereotyped reactions to the other sex, unstated emotions and sensations beneath the surface masks. The satiric element in her work thus functions finally toward a feminist end: a denial of any fundamental difference that might be used to prove the superiority of either sex. At the same time, these portraits of states of mind, because they exist within identifiable social situations, show the prejudices upon which relations between the sexes are based. There are no privileged characters in Sarraute's world. If women are not simply victims, neither are men naturally superior or inferior. Everyone is both aggressor and victim, just as everyone is unable to communicate with others.

What is the effect upon the reader of Sarraute's narrative technique and her preoccupations? First of all, it demands considerable co-operation from the reader, invites the reader to participate, in a manner that might be considered to undermine any air of authority, or any appearance of knowing the truth, on the part of the author. The reader is placed in a vacillating atmosphere where there are no rounded characters, no clearly discernible plot line, frequently no chronology. Expectations of stability in fiction are destroyed, and with them comes at least a questioning of stability in 'real life' beyond the novel.

Because of the very triviality of many of the situations, the reader may tend to find her or his own similarity to the reactions of the characters, see the fundamental common experiences that we all share, beneath our expectations of permanency, beneath our belief in such entities as 'love', 'respect'. This presumed reader is, finally, neither male nor female, but simply human. Sarraute's fiction describes a common store of human reactions underlying all gender determinations. Militants may discuss the political efficacy of such a vision in terms of political action, but in fiction it works as one way of breaking down categorisation, a method that may be as effective as either glorification of a female 'essence' or satire of socially imposed barriers.

Notes

1. Cited in Marion Scali, 'Sarraute, promenade', *Libération* (24 July 1986) p. 30.

2. Christiane Makward, 'Corps écrit, corps vécu', in Suzanne Lamy and Irene Pages (eds), *Féminité, subversion, écriture* (Quebec: Éditions du Remue-Ménage, 1983) pp. 127-38. Makward finds in Robbe-Grillet's work a great distance between the subject and the world, a distance which makes his work evolve towards sado-masochism, the contrary of 'l'écriture féminine'. See also Ann Jefferson, 'Representation in the Novels of Nathalie Sarraute', *Modern Language Review,* 73 (1978) pp. 513-24: 'the texts specifically deconstruct both the more traditional realist reading whereby the language of the text behaves as if it were a copy, and the more radical anti-representational reading implied by pure scriptural activity, in order to produce as much meaning as possible. In this respect Sarraute occupies a

somewhat anomalous position among her contemporaries' (p. 524). For a quite different reading of the contrast between Sarraute and Robbe-Grillet, see Lucien Goldmann, 'The *Nouveau Roman* and Reality', in *Towards a Sociology of the Novel*, trans. Alan Sheridan (London: Tavistock, 1975) pp. 132-51. Goldmann sees Sarraute as still believing in a human reality which writers can explore, whereas Robbe-Grillet fits into a later historical stage, accepting, as does Goldmann, the lack of any immutable reality. Goldmann's reading seems to accept the importance of the political and economic world, an importance that Sarraute, in fact, discounts. Perhaps this is another 'feminine' characteristic?

3. Minorgue suggests, however, that Alain is the narrator, who gives up the privileges of his role and displaces himself (Minorgue, 1981, pp. 87-8).

4. This is similar to Marguerite Duras's remark that a man would intervene, where she doesn't.

5. Dorothy Wordsworth, for example, wrote 'I should detest the idea of setting myself up as an Author'. See *The Letters of William and Dorothy Wordsworth, The Middle Years, 1806-1811*, ed. Ernest de Selincourt, rev. Mary Moorman (London: Clarendon Press, 1969) p. 454.

6. Alexandra Sévin, 'Nathalie Sarraute ou le piège des mots', *Elles voient rouge*, no. 4 (1980) esp. pp. 38-9.

7. Ellen Munley sees in *L'Usage de la parole* a positive message: 'With enough give and take, we can not only mutually understand but contribute to each other's development' (Munley, 1983, p. 246). This is perhaps overstating the case.

Adele King (essay date 1989)

SOURCE: King, Adele. "Marguerite Duras." In *French Women Novelists: Defining a Female Style*, pp. 134-63. London: Macmillan, 1989.

[*In the following essay, King presents an overview of Duras's writing, focusing mainly on her novels.*]

> Woman is desire.... We don't write at all from the same place as men. And when women don't write in the space of desire, they don't write.
>
> (Duras, 1977, p. 102)

Of all twentieth-century French women writers, it is Marguerite Duras who is most often cited as an example of a feminine author.[1] Hélène Cixous, for instance, does not see Nathalie Sarraute as 'feminine', places Monique Wittig a bit on the side, but finds that Marguerite Duras produces exemplary texts (Cixous, 1976a, p. 879). Duras has inspired, along with Cixous herself, the most overtly feminine critical readings, if we accept that in feminine readings the critic will be personally engaged, will not be primarily giving a detached explication.[2]

Duras's works lend themselves to feminist analysis in their themes (the emphasis on a passion that is all-powerful but never fulfilled, the search for self-definition, a 'madness' that rejects ordinary society, a consideration of politics in its relation to private life), in their formal structure (the paucity of events in the plot, the confusion of genres, the uncertainty of the narrative voice) and in their style (the use of the passive construction, the disjunction between what is said and 'objective' events, the confusion of pronouns, the silences, ellipses, paradoxes, the provisional nature of many of her sentences). She continually reworks certain obsessions; key stories and characters reappear from book to book, in different perspectives, creating the feeling that there is no *single* truth to be discovered about them. Her work also shows a progression towards greater modernism, in the sense of ambiguity, uncertainty, refusal of conventional plots—thus a modernism allied to a feminine aesthetic.

As Duras's work is vast, I can discuss only a few novels: *Un barrage contre le Pacifique* (*The Sea Wall*, 1950), *Moderato cantabile* (1958), *Le Ravissement de Lol V. Stein* (*The Ravishing of Lol Stein*, 1964), *Le Vice-consul* (*The Vice-Consul*, 1965), *L'Amante anglaise* (1967), *Détruire dit-elle* (*Destroy, She Said*, 1969), *L'Amour* (*Love*, 1971) and *L'Amant* (*The Lover*, 1984). *Un barrage* is an example of Duras's earlier, more realistic manner, and begins a story carried through thirty-four years later in *L'Amant*. *Moderato cantabile* is a turning point in her work, both in being balanced between a realistic plot and a poetic evocation of passion and, she has said, in representing a transition towards a greater sincerity, as she recognised that she lived the experience of the woman who wants to be killed (Duras, 1974, p. 59). *Le Ravissement de Lol V. Stein* and *Le Vice-consul* are her own preferences among her works: 'I am very happy when I read "Lol V. Stein", but the strongest and most violent joy is "Le Vice-consul"' (Blume, 1985, p. 7). *L'Amante anglaise* is a particularly striking example of Duras's use of a crime story to explore basic emotions—a frequent technique in her work—and of the deliberate, literary destruction of any ideal of 'truth' in fiction. *Détruire* and *L'Amour* are typical later works, moving beyond any comprehensible plot, demanding a new (perhaps more 'feminine'?) kind of reading. *L'Amour* is also a new exploration of the story of Lol V. Stein. *L'Amant,* one of Duras's more accessible and presumably more autobiographical works, takes up again the childhood she explored in her first works.

Un barrage contre le Pacifique appears largely based on Duras's own life in French Indo-China as a child, although she has said that 'while her family was still alive she wrote around, rather than about them' (Blume, 1985, p. 7). It is largely a realistic work, in the sense that the setting, characters and events are clearly described in detail, the narrative point of view is straightforward. It is a 'full' text, without the ellipses, uncertain dialogues and paradoxes of the later work. Yet, in spite of the realistic setting and the depiction of the corruption of French colonial power in Indo-China, the theme of the novel is the intensity and destructive effects of passion, the foundation of all Duras's later work. In *Barrage* the passion is *described* as it is seen by the young girl, Suzanne, in its observable effects: the mother's passion to save her compound from the floods, the sexual passion of her brother and that of the wealthy man who courts Suzanne. The novel is *about* passion, rather than an embodiment of desire itself. Suzanne, in fact, seems cynically detached from any passion. This detached point of view will change, gradually, in the later works, but the importance of an *observer* will remain.

In *Moderato cantabile* (1958), there is still a setting, identifiable characters, a series of events. The effect, however, is closer to the enactment of passion than a description of it. The organisation is, as Duras herself has noted, similar to that of a poem (Knapp, 1971, p. 655); the emotional intensity of the characters determines the style and the tone of the book. The title, *Moderato cantabile,* indicates two opposing themes: moderation, restraint, routine, the life of Anne Desbaresdes in her bourgeois family; and singing, freedom, escape from normality, Anne's relationship to her son. Anne Desbaresdes seeks to escape from the asphyxiation of her world into a world of passion that she can only equate with death. Duras has commented Anne wants to be killed, and does not love Chauvin; the story is not a love story, but a sexual story (Duras, 1974, p. 59), a story about the most basic emotional level of the individual's development. Much of the power of the novel comes from the *disproportion* between what she does and what she seeks. All she accomplishes, on an objective level, is to drink too much in the company of a man of whom she knows little except that socially he is very different from her, and to discuss, endlessly, a crime of passion of which in fact she knows almost nothing except what Chauvin invents. Until the penultimate scene, the dinner party, little happens. Emotion is expressed in inadequate words and inadequate gestures. Critics have noted the frequency of passive constructions in Duras's work. Anne is a creature of great desire, but very little will.

Anne's husband exists only as representative of convention. Her child, on the other hand, seems to have become, until she meets Chauvin, the only means through which she can express any desire to escape. Of Chauvin we know little except that he, like Anne, is caught in a desire which transcends his ability to express it and his capacity to act upon it. Like Anne, he seems fragmented, his body disintegrated. He appears motivated, however, by a desire to dominate Anne, to make her a character in his story. In his version of the story of the murder, the man has dominated the women, broken down her sense of her own identity.

Moderato cantabile is about language, to what extent language is of necessity a lie, to what extent it can express the deeper subjective level of emotion. Silences constitute an implicit criticism of rational language, not as specifically male-dominated, but as incapable of expressing passion. For Anne, what can express emotion is the scream, the scream of the dying woman, her own screams during the birth of her child. These are two events outside social norms, which cannot be expressed in socially sanctioned language. Trying to talk about the murder they have not witnessed, Anne and Chauvin invent a story, use words to interpret and to lie. What their words express is not an objective truth, or even their interpretation of an event, but their own emotions: his desire to dominate, hers to submit, to die. The ability to find a language which, under the surface, is capable of expressing the passions is aided by the use of alcohol, a frequent theme in Duras's work. The reader must be aware of the fact that Anne is often drunk to appreciate the silences, incongruities and repetitions in her speech. (In later works, Duras's characters often use such speech without being drunk, but in *Moderato cantabile* there is still some conventional realism.)

The central event which triggers the action of the novel is absent; the murder takes place 'offstage', and can only be reconstructed through the dialogue of Anne and Chauvin. *Moderato cantabile* has, none the less, a dramatic scene in the dinner party, skilfully intermingled with glimpses of Chauvin outside, a scene which could still be placed within the perspective of realistic fiction. It is also, however, a violent reversal of the narrative structure of the previous chapter, changing the system of focalisation and introducing an ironic narrative voice. Thus its 'realism' is undermined by its inappropriateness to the preceding narrative (Borgomano, 1985, p. 23). Increasingly Duras will avoid the dramatic, the striking social event, to get closer to to the heart of passion behind or beneath all surface objectivity.

The tension between the themes of *moderato* and *cantabile* cannot, it would seem, be resolved dialectically; there can only be return to ordinary life, or death after freedom. (We are reminded of analyses of nineteenth-century novels, in which the heroine must either submit to conventions or die because of an illicit passion.) Duras suggests in her own interpretation of the novel that there is a kind of resolution: 'Anne Desbaresdes is the middle-class woman who suddenly feels and sees something else. . . . The change she undergoes is irreversible, but nothing, afterwards, is proposed for her. Even her child has been taken away. She has nothing left. As for me, I think she will probably go towards madness' (Micciolo, 1978-9, p. 63).

Critics, however, have suggested what may be a more positive resolution:

> As she leaves the café, she has been able to transcend the opposition of *moderato/cantabile* and to accept an existence of *moderato cantabile*: she will neither continue her bourgeois life, nor has she succumbed to the deadly lure of passion. In her identification with the other woman, she has discovered the relational base of her own identity and has been able to transcend the separation imposed by the social roles of adult, of wife and mother.
>
> (Hirsch, 1982, p. 84)

Marianne Hirsch continues, however, to describe this resolution as an 'affirmation of death and destruction . . . as a mean to other lives which emerge after silence and emptiness have been reached'. In what sense this is a positive transcendence for Anne herself is unclear. George Moskos sees the murdered woman as a 'symbol of the violence done to women in a culture that depends for its existence (as subject) on their "elimination"'. Moskos sees Anne refusing to accept the fiction of domination that Chauvin has created, in order to be reborn 'in another place with another voice' (Moskos, 1984, p. 42, p. 51). Duras suggests, rather ambiguously, a possible social interpretation and a rebirth 'in another place':

> During the time of the book, Anne Desbaresdes is suspended between two worlds: that of pure annihilation, of madness, and that of the bourgeoisie, asphyxiation. It begins like that, the great mutation of humanity. . . . It is those who will come later who will go further than Anne Desbaresdes.
>
> (Micciolo, 1978-9, p. 63)

In what direction will they go, 'those who will come later'? Towards madness or towards asphyxiation? Or towards a world in which new possibilities will open? Duras said that Anne, caught in the stagnation common to most bourgeois women, could not get free through an intellectual or political experience, but only through her emotions. To some extent, *Moderato cantabile* has as a social theme a criticism of this bourgeois world, in which the salmon and the duck at the dinner party seem more alive than the people. There is in this novel and in other earlier Duras novels a suggestion of a possible amelioration of the human condition through political change, a suggestion found less and less frequently in her later work, or present there only in the sense that destruction can be a form of liberation.

If there is a dramatic event connected to *Le Ravissement de Lol V. Stein*, it is a *pre-text*, the story of Lol's abandonment by her fiancé years earlier. The novel itself is concerned not with that moment but with what it has produced later. (Often in Duras's work the echoes or repercussions of events are at least as important as the original events themselves.) Again, as in *Moderato cantabile*, the eroticism might be described as literary, since Lol's story is constructed, invented by the narrator, Jacques Hold, who informs his reader that he knows nothing, and yet who continues to tell his story, in which he is erotically involved: 'I know Lol Stein in the only way I can; through love' (Duras, 1985, p. 36, p. 46). His narration is not even logically consistent, as he often describes himself in the third person, sees himself from the outside, even sees Lol behind him. In this continual destruction of objective 'truth', this insistence that there can be no 'Oedipal' reading, lies the subversive element of *Le Ravissement* and perhaps of all Duras's later fiction.[3]

Lol is *par excellence* the female character without clear direction and individuation postulated by psychoanalysis. According to Michèle Montrelay: 'Lol no longer loves anyone. She has completely become love. She is "ravished", that is to say carried away in *jouissance* because suddenly her emptiness has been revealed to her' (Montrelay, 1977, pp. 15-16). She imitates 'the others, all the others, as many people as possible' (Duras, 1985, p. 24, p. 34). She is silent, or she lies. 'She thought that she had been cast into a mold, the identity of which was extremely vague and to which a variety of names might be given' (p. 32, p. 41). She seems only to have lived in the brief time when she was passionately in love with Michael Richardson; her identity, her life is thus dependent upon the existence of another. What is more, her life in the present of the novel is dependent upon Jacques Hold and his strange fascination with her story.

Lol's story is not that of the usual love triangle in which she loses a man to another woman, for, if we are to believe Jacques Hold (whose story is always, however, full of uncertainty) she does not suffer. Rather she enjoys the disintegration of her individuality, and reaches a kind of indifference. She then seems to reconstruct a situation like that of the ball where she was abandoned, by entering into a different triangular relationship with Jacques and his mistress Tatiana, by watching them make love, as she has dreamed of watching her fiancé Michael Richardson with Anne-Marie Stretter. The text suggests, however, that perhaps she sees nothing, when she is supposedly watching Jacques and Tatiana, that perhaps her knowledge of this scene comes from what Jacques tells her. Again, desire, eroticism, sensuality seem linked to a fiction, a creation of words, which, as always in Duras's work, signify to a large extent by showing what they cannot signify. Again, as well, desire seems to be mediated through the vision of another, just as Anne Desbaresdes needs Chauvin's version of the story of the murder victim.

After being abandoned by Michael Richardson, Lol stopped talking, she could not express the inexpressible:

> The only times she did speak was to say how impossible it was for her to express how boring and long it was, how interminable it was, to be Lol Stein. . . . The difficulty she experienced in searching for a single word seemed insurmountable.
>
> (p. 14, p. 24)

Later, she shows such detachment that Tatiana remarks that she speaks of her own life as if it were a book. Jacques Hold is aware of her lying: 'I desperately want to partake of the word which emerges from the lips of Lol Stein, I want to be a part of this lie which she has forged' (p. 97, p. 106). Lol describes to Jacques seeing Tatiana in the hotel room with him: 'naked beneath her dark hair, naked, naked, dark hair' (pp. 105-6, p. 115). The sentence, as Jacques hears it, conveys not information but emotion:

> The intensity of the sentence suddenly increases, the air around it has been rent, the sentence explodes, it blows the meaning apart. I hear it with a deafening roar, and I fail to understand it, I no longer even understand that it means nothing.
>
> (p. 106, p. 116)

If Lol cannot express in words the nothingness, the lack of a centre in her life, the language of the novel also does not try to find any clear meaning. Rather than constructing events, imagining 'obstacles, accidents', Jacques Hold prefers to open holes:

> To level the terrain, to dig down into it, to open the tombs wherein Lol is feigning death, seems to me fairer—given the necessity to fill in the missing links of Lol Stein's story—than to fabricate mountains.
>
> (p. 27, p. 37)

Rather than truth, his language conveys emotion.

At the end of the novel, Lol goes with Jacques to revisit the ballroom where the original traumatic scene of abandonment took place, only to discover that almost nothing remains:

> One trace remains, one. A single, indelible trace, at first we know not where. What? You don't know where? No trace, none, all has been buried, and Lol with it.
>
> (pp. 170-1, p. 181)

What is that single 'trace' that remains, and that a moment later becomes 'no trace'? An ambiguity subsists. Is there still something to discover? Lol earlier felt that if she could have discovered the right word, everything would have been changed at the end of the ball:

> that it would always have meant, for her mind as well as her body, both their greatest pain and their greatest joy, so commingled as to be undefinable, a single entity but unnamable for lack of a word. I like to believe—since I love her—that if Lol is silent in her daily life it is because, for a split second, she believed that this word might exist.
>
> (p. 38, p. 48)

Could this word have been found, and could the meaning of the single 'trace' have been identified? Or is there no word for feminine desire (Borgomano, 1984, p. 64)? Duras is capturing a level of uncertainty that underlies any indifference that Lol may achieve. After the visit to the Casino where Michael Richardson abandoned her, Lol still must see herself as double—as both Lol and Tatiana—and still must wait outside the Hôtel des Bois to watch when Jacques goes to meet Tatiana.

The language of *Le Ravissement de Lol V. Stein* gains intensity from the frequent repetitions, a certain monotony of rhythm, a deliberate simplicity. The sentences are often short, simple:

> [she] leads her toward the French doors which open onto the grounds. She opens it. I see what she wants. I move forward, Keeping to the wall. There. I'm at the corner of the house. From this point I can hear what they are saying.
>
> (p. 83, p. 92)

Or, alternatively, in attempting to catch the inexplicable, Jacques resorts to a convoluted syntax:

> It seemed as though she took everything for granted, and that the infinite weariness of being unable to escape from the state she was in was not something that had to be thought about, that she had become a desert into which some nomad-like faculty had propelled her, in the interminable search for what?
>
> (p. 14, p. 24)

The physical setting is not, as it still was to some extent in *Moderato cantabile,* a background against which the drama takes place. Rather Lol makes of her world an empty space, in which words and their referents convey nothingness. She arranges her house with great care and precision so that it has nothing to do with her. The house and gardens have a glacial order, operate on a strict schedule. There is no life, no vivacity. Lol's mistake in planning the garden is an evident symbol of her detachment from normal life:

> She wanted the garden paths to fan out evenly around the porch. But none of them intersected, and as a result they were unusable. John Bedford was much amused by the error.
>
> (p. 26, p. 35)

S. Tahla seems a place invented by a dreamer. Even the names—Hold, Tatiana, Lol, S. Tahla, U. Bridge—seem to refer to imaginary beings and places. This dream-like atmosphere is also conveyed through the many ambiguities, through the possibility that Jacques Hold is an unreliable narrator, especially through a structure in which the subject who orchestrates the dream-drama does not speak directly, is interpreted by another. Lol's story has been described as a 'wandering in space-time', in which nothing is fixed. Thus Lol doesn't grow older, and the novel doesn't end (Didier, 1981, pp. 281-2). Duras's work increasingly progresses towards a denial of any linear narrative.

In *Le Vice-consul* several stories are superimposed to create a poetic portrait of sorrow, desire, madness, alienation. First, there is the epic story of the beggar woman, chased from her home when she 'falls pregnant', who wanders across much of southeast Asia until she arrives in Calcutta. This woman is, like Lol, but in a more extreme fashion, a type of the indifference, the lack of individuation, of the female personality. She has no name, almost no physical attributes, no words beyond her plaintive song, which has been characterised as 'the cry of the woman perpetually out of relation to her maternal origin' (Willis, 1987, p. 103). She cannot speak. Thus it is not she, but a *man*, who tells her story. Peter Morgan, the narrator of her story, writes: 'How to put into words the things she never said? How to say what she will not say? How to describe the things that she does not know she has seen, the experiences that she does not know she has had? How to reconstruct the forgotten years?' (Duras, 1966, p. 55, p. 73). She is an embodiment of suffering. She is driven on by hunger, but also by a need to find her mother again, a mother whom she both loves and detests, and to whom she cannot return, a mother who has accepted social standards, for whom illegitimate pregnancy is a disgrace. In the extremity of her suffering, as she prostitutes herself for a bit of food, she is an epic figure of the sorrow of woman, for whom her mother and her own child are the only realities. She manages to give her child to a white woman, an act of unselfish love, but also a deliverance from an intolerable burden. In the description of her relation to her unborn child, Duras shows the ambiguity of maternal emotions: 'The child in her womb is growing more and more active. It is as though fish were snapping in her belly, or the insufferable infant were happily beating a drum' (p. 3, p. 12). As Monique Gosselin comments: 'Only a woman could write that or describe the resurrection of her own relationship to her mother when she experiences childbirth' (Gosselin, 1982, p. 159).

Another level of the story concerns the Vice-Consul, Jean-Marc de H., who presents a parallel to the beggar. His madness, however, takes the more active, masculine form of shooting at the lepers in Lahore, to call down the death he sees as the destiny of all humanity. While the beggar has had a number of children, unwanted products of her need to eat, he remains a virgin. Neither is able to reach any satisfaction of basic desires. His drama, like hers, is centred on his relationship to his mother, the basis, as Duras has noted, of all human emotion. In an interview she defines the movement of desire as an attempt to redress 'the definitive absence of this all-important presence, never replaced later, of my (the) mother' (quoted in Moskos, 1984, p. 37). The trauma of the child's inevitable separation from the mother is, perhaps, the central psychological event of human development, for children of both sexes. The beggar's mother has proved to be a cruel mother, forcing a second separation. Jean-Marc's mother abandoned him a second time when she remarried after her husband's death.

The Vice-Consul, who functions as an intermediary between the world of madness of the beggar woman and the world of the Europeans, is fascinated by Anne-Marie Stretter, wife of the French ambassador in Calcutta, and, incidently, the woman who seduced Michael Richardson away from Lol V. Stein in *Le Ravissement de Lol V. Stein*.[4] Anne-Marie Stretter recurs from one work to another; she is an obsession of Duras's; like the beggar, the character goes back to Duras's childhood. Anne-Marie Stretter was an adulterous woman, and someone had committed suicide because of her: 'for a long time she incarnated for me a sort of double power, a power of death and an everyday power'. Anne-Marie 'has gone beyond all prejudices . . . she is on a sure path to liberation'; 'she is an empty form . . . things are lodged in her'. 'Sometimes I tell myself that I have written because of her' (Duras and Porte, 1977, pp. 65-74).

Anne-Marie and the beggar are two faces of women: the desired, beautiful, rich woman with many lovers, mother of two daughters, whose life is nevertheless fundamentally empty; and the rejected, miserable outcast from a peasant family. Both are near madness and both, we learn, suffered from being rejected. Anne-Marie left her first husband: 'Even now, no one in Calcutta really knows whether she was living a life of shame or sunk in despair when he found her in Savannakhet' (Duras, 1966, p. 76, p. 99). Like the beggar, whom she met in Savannakhet, Anne-Marie is in exile in Calcutta after long wandering; unlike the beggar, she may have attempted suicide. The alternating scenes of the beggar's miserable existence and the luxury of embassy life finally suggest that beyond the social contrast lies a profound similarity between the lives of the two women, and also between them and the Vice-Consul.

We learn about these women through other voices, so that there is always a distancing. The technique emphasises the passive role of the two women. For Peter Morgan, the story is a way of throwing himself into the suffering of Calcutta, so that 'wisdom may start to grow out of bitter experience' (p. 18, p. 29). Although he learns about the beggar from Anne-Marie, he must substitute his own memories for those of the beggar to understand her madness.[5] The distancing narrative voice of Peter Morgan, and the uncertain narrative voices of the rest of the story, with which Morgan's tale is interspersed, permit the ambiguities, uncertainties at the heart of Duras's fiction. If we know that Peter Morgan must invent, we are not sure who is telling the story of Anne-Marie and the Vice-Consul. Perhaps Charles Rossett, a young attaché who has studied the Vice-Consul's dossier, and who is enamoured of Anne-Marie.

Peter Morgan's description of the wanderings of the beggar lends a legendary quality to her story, a story that becomes the opposite of a hero's search for his destiny:

> I need some signpost to lead me astray. Make your mind a blank. Refuse to recognize familiar land marks. Turn your steps towards the most hostile point on the horizon, towards the vast marshlands, bewilderingly criss-crossed by a thousand causeways.
>
> (p. 1, p. 9)

The language is, as often in Duras's work, full of repetitions, incomplete sentences, shifts from 'she' to 'I' in the middle of a paragraph. The characters are often unnamed, typical: *la dame, l'enfant blanche, la jeune fille*. Later *le directeur, les deux Anglais*, and so on, are used more often than proper names.

The scene of the dance at the embassy suggests a parallel to the never dramatised scene of Lol's abandonment at S. Tahla. It is in this artificial, conventional setting that the unconventional breaks through. Anne-Marie dances with the Vice-Consul. An indeterminate 'one', 'we', watches them dance, shocked at his social *faux pas*. Charles Rossett can only imagine that the pair are speaking of a new posting for the Vice-Consul, that he is using this opportunity to advance his shattered career. But in fact the conversation keeps turning around the edge of madness, around what cannot be expressed. Anne-Marie attempts to find 'the last word on the subject' (p. 96, p. 123). She wants to speak quickly, to avoid saying 'other quite different things, things much more remote, but which might just as well have been said. Why not? Don't you agree?' (p. 97, p. 124). He attempts a social conversation about leprosy because

> 'I have the feeling that if I tried to say what I really want to say to you, everything would crumble into dust'—he is trembling—'for what I want to say . . . to you . . . from me to you . . . there are no words. I should fumble . . . I should say something different from what I intended . . . one thing leads to another.'
>
> (p. 98, p. 125)

Then, finally, he arrives at the essence, why he shot at the lepers: 'One other thing I can tell you, if you will bear with me: Lahore was also, in a sense, hope. You do understand, don't you?' (p. 99, p. 126). And she, from the depths of her own alienation, understands. The scene is remarkable for catching an emotional undertone in a conversation made up mostly of hesitations, half-formed thoughts, an undertone that has, as it rarely does in Duras's work, no immediate erotic connotations.

L'Amante anglaise (the title is word play, *la menthe anglaise* or *en glaise,* English mint, or mint in clay) is Duras's reconstruction of a real crime in the form of fiction. Although it is called a novel, it is in fact a series of conversations supposedly taped by a male 'novelist' (again, the female figure does not speak directly) with the presumed murderer, Claire Lannes, her husband Pierre and Robert Lamy, the proprietor of the Balto Cafe where Claire was arrested. The 'novelist' also has, and transcribes, an earlier tape, made by the police at the time the murderer confessed. How the novelist obtained this tape is perhaps the least of the puzzles.

From the beginning we are aware that discrepancies and ambiguities will exist. In the first tape the speakers are not always clearly identified. Robert Lamy, the first interviewee, inquires: 'How about the difference between what I know and what I say—what will you do about that?' (Duras, 1967, p. 3, p. 9). The 'novelist' replies: 'That's the part of the book the reader has to supply for himself. It exists in any book' (p. 3, p. 10). Commenting on the conversation with the detective in the bar, the evening of Claire's arrest, Robert says 'We were inventing a crime, we and he between us' (p. 11, p. 21). We are never sure what is invented, what took place, within the fiction. (The ambiguity is, of course, compounded by the fact that *L'Amante anglaise* is based on a real event.) The 'novelist', whom we tend, in spite of his sex, to identify with Duras, is also not trustworthy. At one point he says he is not sure who is the murderer. Later he tells Pierre Lannes that there is proof in Claire's fingerprints found on the dismembered body. He denies wanting to impose any interpretation of the book that is being done (*le livre qui se fait*—the use of the passive construction here serves to keep the writer from taking personal responsibility for establishing any 'truth', any 'Oedipal' interpretation). In any case, 'that's just words' (p. 60, p. 99).

While borrowing elements from detective fiction, and containing a mystery to keep the reader in suspense (the victim's body was cut into pieces and thrown from a viaduct into passing trains, but the whereabouts of the head is not known), the book is really about typical Duras characters—the dispossessed, alienated, those on the edge of madness, those who are, as the murderer terms them, on 'my side', as opposed to 'the other side', that of conventional society. The themes therefore centre on the personalities of the main characters, the moment of destruction, what pushes Claire into killing her deaf-mute cousin, Marie-Thérèse Bousquet, who has served for seventeen years as her housekeeper.

Duras's interest in the moment of madness, of crime, is like that of Anne Desbaresdes in *Moderato cantabile*.[6] The Duras criminal, however, is not a romantic, Byronic figure, but rather almost a passive victim of emotions beyond his or her control. Before she is identified as the murderer, Claire queries what the difference is between a madman and a 'natural' person (the term is the detective's and seems to mean for him someone not a professional killer, though it also suggests someone not bound by convention). Violence against another is often a displaced suicide, an irrational gesture of escaping routine: 'Perhaps because they were together in a situation that was too static and had been in existence too long. Not necessarily an unhappy situation in itself, but stuck, no way out, if you see what I mean' (p. 18, p. 32). The 'novelist' suggests that Pierre let the police get Claire because he wanted to end an intolerable situation, and that his act is comparable to hers. For the 'novelist', Claire is not so much mad as someone who has never adapted to life (though later, he tells the imprisoned Claire that she is mad). Pierre suggests that he, that most people, are capable of a crime. Robert refuses to answer when asked whether he would have protected Claire from the police. It is from this group of basically non-aggressive, misfit characters that Duras's criminals come.

There are two figures of the alienated female personality: Claire and Marie-Thérèse. Both are natural victims and both resemble Lol V. Stein. Marie-Thérèse Bousquet is without a family, without friends, without a place in society, a marginal being. Her name suggests a connection to nature rather than normal society. (*Bosquet* means 'grove' in French.) The forest is a symbol, in much of Duras's work, for the frightening density of human sexuality: 'the forest is for the mad, you see. . . . I have been afraid of myself since puberty. In the forest, before puberty, I was not afraid' (Duras, 1977, pp. 27-8). Claire's most persistent memory of her cousin is as a child joyfully playing with a cat. For Pierre, Claire is an empty space: 'It was as if she was closed to everything and open to everything at one and the same time. You couldn't get anything into her to stay, she retained nothing. Like a place without any doors, where the wind blows through and sweeps everything away' (p. 55, pp. 90-1). Claire is unable to become involved in normal life, and indifferent to most of what society considers important. Her love affair before her marriage, with the policeman from Cahors (he is never given a name), gives a sense to all her life:

> I've never been separated from the happiness I had in Cahors, it overflowed on to all my life. You mustn't think it was just the happiness of a few years: it was a happiness to last forever. It still goes on now, when I'm asleep.
>
> (pp. 99-100, p. 159)[7]

Claire is unable to use words normally. Robert Lamy describes her speech: 'Ten different things at once. Floods of words. And then suddenly silence' (p. 32, p. 55). His description seems to conform to a feminist psychoanalytic theory about how women seek to relate, rather than separate, phenomena: 'Before you knew where you were she was off in all directions, everything would connect with everything else' (p. 33, p. 56). Like Lol, Claire cannot find the right words: 'If I'd been asked the right question I'd have found the right answer' (p. 103, p. 165). She wishes she could have found *n'importe qui* (anyone at all) to whom to write about her love. Her ideas, her thoughts cannot escape what she describes as a leaden cover over her head: 'they just fell back again and stayed under the lid, swarming, and it hurt so much that several times I thought of doing away with myself so as not to have to suffer any more' (p. 100, p. 160). But, unfortunately, as she realises, 'I wasn't intelligent enough for the intelligence that was in me' (p. 102, p. 163); she is a creature of strong feelings, without the rational use of language to explain them.

Pierre Lannes seems typically masculine in his attitudes. He invents an 'understandable' crime: a worker who kills a woman who refused to follow him into the forest to make love. He questions whether such a crime should be punished as another crime would be. Pierre is interested in women, has had many adventures, and has divorced his sexual activity from any love. He is mainly worried about growing old, not having the energy to look for women. He feels that Claire would have committed a crime with any man, anywhere, thus that he can have no responsibility. At the same time, however, he insists that she loved him, and refuses to place much importance on her previous love affair, which had led her to try to commit suicide. In his egotism, he seems to be more upset that his way of life has been altered, that he must find a new housekeeper, than that his wife has committed an extremely violent crime. At the end of the interview with Pierre, the 'novelist', who has tried to avoid interpretations, gives a clear one:

> I think you didn't only want to get rid of Claire—you wanted to get rid of Marie-Thérèse too. You wanted both of them to vanish out of your life so that you would be on your own again. I think you'd dreamed about the end of the world.
>
> (pp. 79-80, p. 129)

Thus *L'Amante anglaise*, a crime story, a psychological investigation, is based on a conflict between typically 'masculine' and 'feminine' personalities. There is, however, no resolution, no domination of the story.

In *Détruire, dit-elle*, the impulse towards destruction of *L'Amante anglaise* is given a more general, more political interpretation. The text of *Détruire* is a hybrid, moving between a novel or *récit* and a film script or play. It is a striking example of Duras's refusal to be limited to traditional genres. The three destroying characters—to some extent interchangeable—are Stein, Max Thor and Max's young wife, Alissa. Perhaps mad in the eyes of conventional society, they set out to destroy the bourgeois conventionalism of Elisabeth Alione and of her husband Bernard. The action takes place in a dream-like hotel which seems also to be a convalescent home, to which Elisabeth has come after losing a child at birth, but also after some unexplained relationship with her doctor. She is perhaps being isolated because of a moral transgression. The 'destruction' is subtle, at the level of gestures, small phrases, an invitation to Elisabeth to go into the 'forest' (an obvious symbol of the unconscious). The 'destruction' is also allied to 'love'. Alissa seems poised between loving and hating Elisabeth. At the conclusion, in spite of their attacks on the Aliones' way of life, the trio wants Bernard to stay with them, as they could love him. (This scene, Duras said, is the most important in the book.)

The life which they advocate is one in which Alissa can be loved by both the men, without jealousy, in which Alissa and Max leave the window open so that Stein can watch them make love (again the voyeur scene prominent in Duras's work), a world in which, as Alissa tells Elisabeth, one can act on one's own, not needing the advice of others, a world in which in the future there are only children. Max teaches a university course on the 'History of the future', where nothing is left, so that there is nothing to say, and the students can sleep. It is a world of innocence, of love without barriers, of a metaphysical breakdown of identity, a dream of 'revolution', symbolised by the music that enters in the final scene.

Détruire, dit-elle comes out of the events of May 1968. In an interview with *Cahiers du cinéma*, Duras speaks of the political implications of the work. It is a work about destruction of all police, all memory, all judgement; it is about falling in line with ignorance and perhaps with madness. Stein and Thor are 'German Jews' because 'We are all German Jews', all strangers to the systems of state and society (the slogan comes from May 1968). What Duras wants to encourage is a freedom at the level of the individual, a freedom that she relates to that of the 'hippie'. Duras realises that this may be a Utopian position; it is definitely one that the interviewers from *Cahiers du cinéma* cannot fully accept.

L'Amour takes up again, but in a very different manner, the basic situation of *Le Ravissement de Lol V. Stein*. It goes beneath or beyond descriptions or interpretations of the emptiness of lives such as Lol's (or Anne Desbaresdes's, Anne-Marie Stretter's, Claire's) to convey this emptiness poetically, largely through descriptions of light, sound, the sea, geometric movements. Scene, language, pure movement have practically replaced plot and character. The characters are: 'a man who watches' (the traveller: 'We will name this man the traveller—if by chance that is necessary' [Duras, 1972, pp. 13-14]), 'another man, who walks' (the prisoner/guardian), 'a woman', on a beach near a calm sea.[8] Their initial movements are described in a kind of balletic geometry, as they constitute three points of a shifting triangle. This triangle might be contrasted to the 'rectangle of sunlight' (p. 96) in the scene where the traveller says farewell to his wife and two children. *L'Amour* is thus a striking example of what Carol Murphy has described as Duras's later style: 'a *mise-en-œuvre* of the lack which is at the basis of all writing'; a 'pure musicality . . . replaces the verbal, logical and ordered narrative of traditional prose' (Murphy, 1982, p. 14, p. 143).

All this movement, because of its abstraction in *L'Amour,* leaves a naked emotion as the only certainty upon which the reader can focus. Yet the text itself is deliberately unemotional, restrained. There is a breakdown of individual identity, and a destruction of any social roles. Desire, linked to death, is all that remains. In *L'Amour* no one says 'I love you', no one takes responsibility for being a subject with desires. We are here in the presence of characters who are reduced to a level of reflecting the desires of others, whose life seems essentially without any normal supports. The quality of the novel is produced by a contrast between the emptiness, both the lack of emotion in the actual words, and their spacing on the page; and the intensity of the destructive impulses felt beneath the surface. Yet, in a sense, nothing happens; there is no moment of drama, no resolution. There is only a feeling of destruction, as if the only act of salvation is to go beyond identity or emotion.

Paradoxically, as the novel is less realistic than anything Duras wrote earlier, the physical setting is more important. It is not, however, a natural setting. The action takes place in S. Thala (the S. Tahla of *Le Ravissement*?), which extends, the woman says, as far as the stream. Later the prisoner agrees, but then adds that S. Thala also extends beyond the stream. One can neither go beyond S. Thala, nor enter S. Thala. It is thus, logically, an impossible place. Light in S. Thala grows, then suddenly 'stops'; there are noises of the sea and the seagulls, which also 'stop'. The seagulls 'devour the body of sand' (Duras, 1972, p. 23). There is a group of people in the background, whom the woman describes as 'my inhabitants of S. Thala' (p. 38). None of this is initially plausible. The atmosphere is poetic; S. Thala is a state of mind. Beyond is perhaps nothing, the end of the world (the world of Duras's play *Yes, peut-être*?): 'they were many: millions . . . everything is devastated' (p. 30). When the traveller asks the prisoner/guardian to say something about the story (or history), he replies: '—In my opinion, the island emerged first—he points to the sea—from there. S. Thala arrived afterwards, with the dust—he adds—you know? Time . . .' (p. 49). If there is a 'story' it is a kind of 'pre-history', of the beginning or the end of the universe.

The woman is hardly conscious of anything; her eyes are shut initially. She is 'looked at' (*elle est regardée,* p. 10), rather than 'looks', but is not aware of being 'looked at'. Her actions are the result of another's will: 'She advances moved by the will of the person who stopped behind her' (p. 34). When asked who she is, she replies 'The police have a number' (p. 39). She expects a child, but does not know who the father is. The prisoner/guardian says she is 'angry with God in general, it's nothing' (p. 46). She is 'an object of desire, she belongs to whoever wants her' (p. 50). All 'ego', all willpower has vanished. As for the prisoner/guardian 'the absence of his gaze is absolute' (p. 16). And the traveller is uncertain whether he has previously been in S. Thala. He writes, to some initially unidentified correspondent, not to come to S. Thala. But, for himself, he realises 'I have difficulty going away from her' (p. 47).

All this is mystery, initially, to the reader. We are told, however, that the story has begun before the arrival of the traveller. It is as if a series of movements, looks, disconnected bits of dialogue were the surface beneath which something is happening, beneath which there is a pattern that the reader must create. Gradually some events seem to become clarified as they relate to the past, to a story that seems to be that of Lol's abandonment during the ball, so that we can 'read' the woman on the beach as Lol after her second breakdown, as Lol when she has become mad. *L'Amour* thus depends on a *pre-text, Le Ravissement de Lol V. Stein.* The traveller goes into the entrance hall of a hotel, where the woman meets him; she recognises the place and the man, but initially this seems only because she saw him on the beach. Eventually, the woman and the traveller go together to the ballroom, where she remembers nothing, realises the futility of trying to recapture the past. What she can remember is her marriage to a musician, and her two children by him, but neither the ball when she was eighteen, nor the fathers of all her subsequent children. She remembers, in other words, the inessential, that which has no profound charge, no connection to her 'madness'.

The two men have also abandoned any projects in a rational world. The prisoner/guardian seems intent on destroying the world, on setting fire to S. Thala. He is the guardian of 'nothing' (p. 136). The traveller seems to have come to S. Thala because he is dying or wants to kill himself. There is a somewhat more realistic scene of his final encounter with his wife and children, in which he abandons them. The wife reacts emotionally. The children, perhaps more in tune with elemental truths, accept their father's action calmly. The traveller will remain with the woman. Is this because of love? Does he see in her a kind of madness, of openness to the irrational, that attracts him? Increasingly the reader becomes aware of the impossibility of establishing any clear sequence of events, of envisaging a setting for what is described that might conceivably exist in the normal world. Rather the world of S. Thala appears a world of the mad, who have abandoned any relationship to normal life, who live in an absolute state of primordial realities.

The style of the text is simplified to an extreme. Words and phrases are repeated; there seems to be no connection between sentences:

> He said:
> —Colour is disappearing.
> Colour disappears.
> Then, in turn, movement.
> The last sea gulls have left.
>
> (p. 26)

Yet this simplicity leads to no clarity. Rather, the discontinuity from one phrase to another suggests the world of the mad in which any analysable comprehensibility has vanished.[9] The point of view is that of the camera eye, recording movements, conversation, almost no connections between events. Descriptions often read as directions in a film script. The shifts in scene are a kind of *montage* from which any narrative continuity has been banished. Occasional references to the passing of time are simple ('Three days') and do not orient the reader within any normal chronological development.

The reader must construct the book. We are invited to enter a world in which what are considered normal drives, aggressions, will, even normal desires, even the 'love' of the title, have no meaning. *L'Amour* might thus be considered as the quintessence of the female mode, defined as receptivity to the natural world, denial of self-consciousness, negation of rationality. The woman, who cannot die, is said to 'go back into the dead dog' (p. 104). The traveller is also 'nothing' (p. 136). If the text could be compared to some of Beckett's work, it differs in that the woman, unlike Beckett's heroes, has no wish to consider, to think about, to remember, her situation. She accepts. To what extent are this reduction of fiction to the creation of an almost abstract atmosphere and this insistence on the need for destruction linked to something definable as a 'feminine' sensibility? Or are both the form and the theme expressions of Duras's individual sensibility, going beyond considerations of gender? In various interviews Duras has suggested that what she is doing is essentially feminine (although not, she would increasingly say, 'feminist'). Her distrust of traditional forms and rational language she has linked to being female, not part of a literary or cultural tradition:

> Men don't translate. They begin from a theoretical platform that is already in place, already elaborated. The writing of women is really translated from the unknown, like a new way of communicating rather than an already formed language. But to achieve that, we have to turn away from plagiarism.
>
> (Husserl-Kapit, 1975, p. 425)

Duras has suggested that she writes 'to lessen my importance. Let the book be important instead of me. To massacre myself, squander myself, *to be swallowed up in the parturition of the book*' (quoted in Gosselin, 1982, p. 167). This movement is particularly evident in *L'Amant*, another reworking, reliving of the past—the author's past and the past as described in earlier texts. *L'Amant* tells of Duras's love affair with the son of a rich Chinese businessman, when she was fifteen. It is incidentally about the racial tensions which this relationship provokes from both sides, but essentially it is about writing, sexual passion and desire, and how they are related.

The text exists in the interplay between past and present. The book begins by posing the question of why Duras's face became old suddenly, when she was eighteen. There is no strict chronological order; the narrative shifts from Duras's childhood to the death of her mother years later in France, or to her own experiences in wartime Paris, before returning again to childhood. There is, strictly, no past; what exists is not history, but a recreation. *L'Amant* is the past of Duras as she can recreate it only after having explored the essential emotions in her other works. While the girl's frankness, her admission that she needs money, her fear of her brother, may remind us of Suzanne in *Barrage*, the young girl differs in the intensity of her desire, in her need as well to be humiliated, insulted. *L'Amant*, Duras told an interviewer, 'is much closer to *Vice-consul* or *Lol V. Stein* than *Barrage*':[10]

> Before, I spoke of clear periods, those on which the light fell. Now I'm talking about the hidden stretches of that same youth, of certain facts, feelings, events that I buried. . . . if [writing] is not, each time, all things confounded into one through some inexpressible essence, then writing is nothing but advertisement.
>
> (Duras, 1984a, p. 8, pp. 14-15)

L'Amant, in other words, is an exploration of how Duras writes, of how she finds the essential, going to the depths, realising that the mystery of her relationship to her family will always remain hidden. 'I've never written, though I thought I wrote, never loved, though I thought I loved, never done anything but wait outside the closed door' (p. 25, p. 35).

Is there a logical contradiction when she claims now to be free from her family?

> Now I don't love them any more. I don't remember if I ever did. I've left them. . . . It's over, I don't remember. That's why I can write about her [the mother] so easily now, so long, so fully. She's become just something you write without difficulty, cursive writing.
>
> (pp. 28-9, p. 38)

One feels that in *L'Amant* Duras is saying everything she can, both her detachment, and the sense in which she is always still attached to the loved and hated mother, that the two contradictory attitudes exist together. She has described the book as a means of coming to terms with her mother:

I had written *Le Barrage* to tell the world about the injustice of which she was a victim. I had to write *L'Amant* to return her to ordinary humanity, and perhaps to expose her royalty to the promiscuity and the sexual pleasure of her child.

(Costaz, 1984, p. 28)

It is perhaps a measure of the difficulty of this task that the text shifts frequently between 'I' and 'she', as if admitting to having been the young girl enjoying sex with a Chinese businessman is still frightening, as if she sometimes is the girl, sometimes wants to distance herself.

L'Amant is about passion, sexual passion and the passions of life in the family. It is not about love. In an interview, Duras is explicit:

It was not a love which declared itself there. It was an entrance into desire. Violent, stronger than I was. . . . When I speak of lovers without love that's what I'm speaking about in the book. At the place where feelings don't enter, where happiness is the happiness of suffering, of humiliation.

(Costaz, 1984, p. 29)

As soon as she steps into the Chinese limousine, the young girl knows that she has made an essential choice. There is a feeling of fatality: 'It's as if this must be not only what she expects, but also what had to happen especially to her' (Duras, 1984, p. 36, p. 47). With her first sexual experience, she realises both the power her mother has held over the children and her mother's own ignorance of sexual pleasure. In its combination of thoughts about her family and her need for physical pleasure, the description of this first scene of love-making is of a rare directness and emotional power.

The conflict that she feels from the beginning between family and lover is especially intense because of her recognition of the power of her older brother over her, and of her power over him. A passionate desire to triumph over him, even to kill him, is also present. She blames him for the death of her younger brother, a death which changed her relationship to her mother:

Everything came to an end that day. I never asked her any more questions about our childhood, about herself. She died, for me, of my younger brother's death. So did my elder brother. I never got over the horror they inspired in me then. They don't mean anything to me any more.

(p. 28, p. 37)

Over and over again the text comes back to the constatation that the older son, who steals from the mother, gambles, tries to sell his sister, who later turns in Jews in occupied Paris, is the only loved child. *L'Amant* is as much an evocation of the power of the family as of the power of sexual desire:

I'm still part of the family, it's there I live, to the exclusion of everywhere else. It's in its aridity, its terrible harshness, its malignance, that I'm most deeply sure of myself, at the heart of my essential certainty, the certainty that later on I'll be a writer.

(p. 75, p. 93)

Family power is exercised as well by the Chinese father, who refuses his son's pleas to accept the white girl, who would prefer to see his son dead than with her.

The novel is filled with detailed indications of Duras's life at the age of fifteen, details which, she feels, make the reader see the young girl more clearly than any analysis. If the style is simpler than that of many of her novels, the structure is similar in its reliance on *montage*. Scenes of life with her mother and brothers are interspersed with scenes with her lover. Suddenly in the midst of the story of her early life, she moves to reminiscences about life in Paris during the war, about those she knew, both collaborators and resistance partisans. It is a world of shallow pretence in comparison to the world of her mother, brothers and lover.

Duras speaks of herself as a young white prostitute in the eyes of others, of her moral degeneracy, of her need to feel humiliated. Desire is accompanied by humiliation; it is also perverse. Of her friend, Hélène Lagonelle, more beautiful, more innocent, Duras says:

I'd like to give Hélène Lagonelle to the man who does that to me, so he may do it in turn to her. I want it to happen in my presence, I want her to do it as I wish. . . . It's via Hélène Lagonelle's body, through it, that the ultimate pleasure would pass from him to me. A pleasure unto death.

(p. 74, p. 92)

The voyeurism of Duras's work has an evident source here. In *L'Amant* she also describes the sources for two of the dominant female types in her novels and the reason for their prominence in her work. When she was eight years old she first encountered a mad woman, the source for the beggar of *Le Vice-consul*. She fears the mad woman because of the yet unacknowledged madness of her mother. Some years later, she realised that her mother's 'identity' might also disappear into madness. Is the beggar's abandoning of her children connected to Duras's feeling that her mother sacrificed her younger children to her eldest? A parallel is also suggested between the woman who served as a source for Anne-Marie Stretter and Duras herself; both cause the despair of their lovers, both are social outcasts. Perhaps the younger brother, whose death at twenty-seven made Duras feel she too was dead, is the source of the young, weak, unaggressive but sensitive men in her fiction: 'My younger brother had nothing to cry in the wilderness, he had nothing to say, here or anywhere, nothing. He was uneducated. . . . He was someone who didn't understand and was afraid' (p. 106, p. 129). Perhaps, as well, the attraction towards violence in her work has its source in her hatred of her elder brother. In its refusal to gloss over what may seem morally repugnant, in its denial of any excuses, as well as in its deep analysis of the relationship between mother and daughter, *L'Amant* may seem particularly feminine. There is no attempt at justification of a life, no moralising.

Duras's world is a difficult, almost unliveable world. Women are dispossessed, have no illusions, find that the slightest gesture requires an effort of will. Duras has said that all the women in her books have their source in Lol V. Stein, in a 'certain forgetting of themselves' (Duras, 1987, p. 32). They are always attracted towards love (often seem incapable of existing without a passionate attachment either in the present or, more often, in the past), yet love is linked to death. They are usually attracted to men who are also dispossessed, who are outside bourgeois conventionality—Chauvin, Monsieur Jo, the Vice-Consul—or share some feminine traits. Jacques Hold describes feeling, as he listens to Lol and Tatiana, 'similarly feminine voices which seem but one voice when they reach me' (Duras, 1985, p. 83, p. 92). As Xavière Gauthier has noted, there are hardly any fathers in all Duras's work, the exception being the father of Aurélia Steiner, and, as he is Jewish, he is 'marginal'.[11] Duras's families are filled with tensions, with a mixture of love and hatred. As she has said, 'There is always in relationships in the family something hateful. . . . We are not destined to live together' (Duras, 1984b, p. 93). As the novelist remarks in *L'Amante anglaise*, Claire and Marie-Thérèse got along well, without any quarrels for seventeen years, until Claire killed Marie-Thérèse.

The triangle set up by the three characters in *L'Amour*, which seems initially a spatial triangle, a series of balletic movements, is also a triangle of desire. Desire for Duras is almost always linked to the vision of another. In *Moderato cantabile* desire is mediated through the experience of another couple, but in the later novels desire is often expressed in a three-fold relationship: Lol, Michael Richardson and Anne-Marie Stretter, then Lol, Tatiana Karl and Jacques Hold; Anne-Marie Stretter, the Vice-Consul and Charles Rossett, or the beggar, Anne-Marie and Peter Morgan; Claire, Pierre and Alfonso, or Claire, Marie-Thérèse and the 'novelist'. There are, in other words, various permutations, but the emphasis is always on the need for one person's desire for another to be *seen, watched* by a third person. Perhaps the most explicitly erotic example is the narrator watching the man and the woman in *L'Homme assis dans le couloir* (*The Seated Man in the Passage*, 1980). The psychology involved is a curious kind of voyeurism, as well as exhibitionism. The most intense emotions described are often those of the third person.

Is the triangular desire in Duras's work related to the mediated desire described by René Girard? For Girard, desire is not direct and spontaneous, but always develops in response to a mediator. A (the subject) loves B (the object) because he knows that C (the mediator) loves B. If A and C are not too far separated by physical or temporal or social distance, A will see C as a rival: 'As the distance between mediator and subject decreases, the difference diminishes, the comprehension becomes more acute and the hatred more intense' (Girard, 1965, p. 73). The mediated desire that Girard examines, in various works by Proust and Stendhal, for instance, seems competitive, aggressive, masculine in essence. Romantic passion, for Girard, is a 'war waged by two rival vanities' (p. 108). The triangular desire of Duras's characters is different, and, we might argue, particularly feminine, whether the desiring character is, in fact, male or female. Lol does not want to recapture Michael Richardson from Anne-Marie Stretter, but wants to imagine their love-making, wants to share an identity. The rival is not actively hated; in so far as there is a destructive impulse it is directed at the self, not at the other. The desire is to *see* the mediator with the object of desire—an emotion having less to do with rivalry than with a losing of the self.

As Toril Moi has shown, Girard's mimetic triangle is based on a rivalry with the father, and is basically concerned with masculine desire. There is no place for the infant's pre-Oedipal desire for the mother (Moi, 1982). A reading of Duras's work, and her own reflections on her mother and their love/hate relationship, shows the difference in female desire from Girard's model. Rather than desire being mediated by a rival who is also in love with the object, desire is mediated, for Duras, by the mother who is not the rival, but the body with whom the lover desires reunion. The imitative desire of Duras's heroines seems finally to be an attempt to share the erotic experience with the maternal figure. In *L'Amant,* in spite of the professed detachment from the mother, the girl's affair with her Chinese lover is a way of making up to the mother, at least financially, for her suffering. She would like to share more with her mother: 'We looked at each other for some time, then she gave a sweet, slightly mocking smile, full of so deep a knowledge of her children and what awaited them later on that I almost told her about Cholon. But I didn't. I never did' (Duras, 1984, p. 93, p. 114). For Hélène Cixous, Duras's work is menacing in its sense of impotence, but this impotence is, she feels, allied to 'an extraordinary quantity of love' (Cixous and Foucault, 1975b, p. 19), a love which is above all tactile, not visual. Desire then becomes the need to touch, to join—a need which would seem the contrary of the visual triangle of Girard's mediated desire. Desire and destruction, eroticism and violence, are always linked. This may be the essential key to the feminine perspective of Duras's work. Her heroines are basically passive, willing victims of aggression. They want to lose their identity, to merge with another in a moment of desire which is also a moment of death.

Duras's position might be related to Derridean deconstruction in that she wants to examine polarities in order to reverse them: 'Reverse everything. Make women the point of departure in judging, make darkness the point of departure in judging what men call light, make obscurity the point of departure in judging what men call clarity' (Husserl-Kapit, 1975, p. 426). This is not, however, a revaluation that says 'intuition' and 'emotion' are good, but a redefinition of terms. In the interview, Susan Husserl-Kapit attempts to read Duras's novels in terms of conventional masculine and feminine qualities and says that Duras's female characters are more 'masculine' than her male characters because they are more 'active'. For Duras the distinction is on another plane: 'activity' has been 'redefined' to imply an ability to occupy space, a willingness to talk. 'Power' is not authority: women 'have a power that is almost involuntary. That's it, it isn't directed. It *is*. It's the difference between "being" and "appearing". It is power that operates directly, that functions directly. The women go straight into action without any programming' (p. 427). Creation, for Duras, is the use of this power, a power that is not analytic:

> everything shuts off—the analytic way of thinking, thinking inculcated by college, studies, reading, experience. I'm absolutely sure of what I'm telling you now. It's as if I were returning to a wild country. Nothing is concerted. Perhaps, before everything else, before being Duras, I am—simply—a woman.
>
> (p. 428)

The emphasis on remembering, on recreating the past, might also be seen as particularly feminine. Time does not progress in a linear fashion. but rather circles continually, is repetitive, spirals around a series of themes, of seminal events that cannot be recaptured. The need to *be seen* is also essentially feminine: the construction of the self as an object of desire for the gaze of the masculine other, a tactic used to gain material possessions by Suzanne in *Barrage,* becomes a way both of asserting a kind of identity and of merging that identity with the gaze of the other.

There is, at the *intradiegetic* level (where the narrator appears as narrator in the story) no female narrator in most of Duras's work: the detective in *L'Amante anglaise* is male, Peter Morgan tells the beggar's story in *Le Viceconsul,* Jacques Hold tells Lol's. Even the narrative *on* in several works (which is variously 'you', 'we', 'one') is unstable, fluctuating, does not allow us to place a narrator in authority. The first woman to write in Duras's work is Aurélia Steiner (whose mother is dead) (Borgomano, 1985, p. 83). The major exception to a male or an ungendered narrator, however, is *L'Amant,* where the narrative voice is variously Marguerite Duras as an older woman, Marguerite Duras as a fifteen-year-old, or an unidentifiable 'she'. It is as if she cannot fully assume the task of establishing an identity as narrator until *L'Amant* (after the death of her own mother, of course), and even here the voice shifts radically. If there is no clear narrative voice doing the telling, there is also no story prior to the *telling* of the story. We have not only the death of the author, but the death of the story. There is not even a setting. Duras says of the ball in *Le Ravissement de Lol V. Stein,* 'I see it occurring in two places'. If this is contradictory, 'What difference does it make?' (Duras, 1974, p. 130). All that remains is a voice, that may be interpreted as exposing the difficulty of a *woman's* entry into the realm of the dominant discourse, but also, more profoundly, as desconstructing any theatrical space, leaving only pure desire and pure horror.[12]

Duras has often spoken of her writing as allied to madness, to a loss of rationality: 'I never know very well where I am going: if I knew, I wouldn't write' (Duras, 1977, p. 37); 'When I write, I feel in an extreme state of concentration. I no longer possess myself, I am myself a strainer . . . there are things I don't recognise in what I write' (p. 98). She has identified madness as a particularly feminine experience. Madness is a withdrawal into an imagined past. Madness is also a desire for destruction, whether of the self or of another—often the two are linked. In some of the later works, the desire for destruction extends to the world. This madness is apparent in the style of her work, at least from *Moderato cantabile* onward. The settings become increasingly unrealistic; if S. Thala in *L'Amour* is a state of mind, so is the Vice-Consul's India. The return to a kind of realistic detail in *L'Amant* is continually subverted by the interplay of past and present, real and imaginary photos. 'Madness' as Duras uses the term seems to indicate particularly an openness to the world resulting from a progressive loss of personal identity. There are always 'holes', 'blank spaces' in the ego, which is not a unified personality. The deliberate simplicity of syntax, the eliminations of accumulated detail, the 'silence' of the texts seem an attempt to capture the irrational, to move into a realm where a word, a simple gesture is all that is left as a handle on normality.

In an interesting analysis of Duras's style, Dominique Noguez speaks of the use of 'parataxsis', a rhetorical device which is the opposite of ellipsis or resumé; every event is decomposed into a 'series of its phases, moment by moment'. Parataxsis, Noguez says is 'the sign of a slow conquest of what is uncertain', though perhaps with Duras we might add that the uncertain is never completely conquered. Duras writes 'narrative texts that refuse closure through the instability of their narrating agency'.[13]

In a *Cahiers du cinéma* interview concerning *Détruire, dit-elle,* Duras speaks of her creative activity after *Moderato cantabile* as proceeding from a deliberate emptying of thought, in a state close to fear. As a result, there are elements in her work which remain obscure to her, incapable of rational interpretation. This plunging into obscurity is, however, only one side of the story. She is also, on another level, conscious of using certain kinds of techniques, of, for instance, creating an openness in the text, multiple possible readings, so that the reader has a more important role. Her various comments on how she works suggest that the subject matter comes from unconscious depths, but that at the same time at least minimal formal decisions are made at a more rational level.[14] Her comments on politics are similarly divided: on the one hand she wants to reach a destruction of all systems, a kind of vacuum from which individual sensitivity can emerge; on the other hand, she speaks in more rational terms of what amounts to influencing the readers and spectators of her work towards a rejection of society. In other words, the work remains political, or anti-political, but in any case purposeful, even as it is also about doing away with purpose. Duras frequently speaks of her need to go beyond rational analysis in order to write; in some of her interviews, where she castigates 'male' reliance on abstraction, she seems to show an increasing distrust of the intellect. It is always, however, only the creative impulse that needs to be liberated from rationality. In terms of her own life, Duras seems to value rationality. When, for example, she speaks of the fascination she felt at one time for the Communist Party, she criticises it as a mistake. The militant is lost. 'When you have lost your ability to analyse, your perceptivity disappears, then your identity' (Costaz, 1984, p. 29).

There is not, however, finally, any attempt on Duras's part to find an essential feminine essence, but rather to give voice to a specific way of existing as a woman, her way, with its particularities. As she says in *Les Parleuses*, 'I cannot believe that Lol V. Stein is *Woman*' (Duras, 1974, p. 160). And in *La Vie matérielle*, 'I don't even write for women. I write about women in order to write about myself, about only myself throughout the centuries' (Duras, 1987, p. 53).[15]

Notes

1. Several years ago, at conferences in New Zealand and Australia, I read a paper on female style and asked the audience to try to identify the sex of the authors of four passages from French novels of the 1950s and 1960s, by Duras, Robbe-Grillet, LeClézio and Wittig. Only with Duras were readers to a large extent sure of the sex of the author.

2. See particularly Marcelle Marini, *Territoires du féminin* (Paris: Minuit, 1977).

3. See Susan Cohen, 'Phantasm and Narration in Marguerite Duras' *The Ravishing of Lol V. Stein*', *The Psychoanalytic Study of Literature*, ed. Joseph Reppen and Maurice Charney (Hillsdale, N.J.: Analytic Press, 1985) pp. 255-77.

4. It is not, however, completely certain that she is the same; the name of her lover is changed from Richardson to Richard. Anne-Marie Stretter reappears in *India Song*; the Vice-Consul whistles *Indiana's Song*, another link to *India Song*.

5. See Bal, 1977, esp. p. 68 for an analysis of how Peter Morgan's attempt to write the beggar's story questions not only the authenticity of literature but also the moral problem of whites in India. The beggar's story is subordinated to the story of European society.

6. Duras shocked many readers in France by her articles seeking to understand why 'le petit Grégory' was killed by his mother while the matter was *sub judice* in 1985.

7. There is an evident parallel here with the German lover in *Hiroshima, mon amour*.

8. As Christiane Makward has remarked, however, it is even impossible to say clearly how many female characters there are in the book. ('Structures du silence / du délire', *Poétique*, 25 (1978), p. 314. See Duras, 1974, pp. 68 and 199, where she first says she is not sure whether a 'woman in black' exists in *L'Amour*, and later says 'there are not two women in the novel'.) Of the woman whom the traveller is seeking it is said 'Where she goes, everything comes apart' and 'death becomes useless' (Duras, 1972, p. 81); this woman thus seems radically different from the woman with a cigarette in a bourgeois house. Duras said that *L'Amour* was written with what wasn't in *Le Ravissement* (quoted by Deborah Gaensbauer, 'Revolutionary Writing in Marguerite Duras' *L'Amour*', French Review, 55 (1982) pp. 633-9, esp. p. 634). It is impossible, however, to say that the woman is Lol, or that the prisoner is Jacques Hold, or that the traveller is Michael Richards (or Richardson).

9. Luce Irigaray's analysis of the language of schizophrenics, in *Parler n'est jamais neutre*, might well be applicable to the language of *L'Amour*, as well as to that of *Le Ravissement de Lol V. Stein*.

10. M.A., 'Duras à l'état sauvage', *Libération* (4 September 1984) pp. 28-9: 'Everything stops there, after the year of the lover. In writing, everything that I lived afterwards serves for nothing' (p. 29). Duras also said that *M.D.* (Paris: Edition de Minuit, 1983), a work by Yann Andréa describing Duras's battle with alcoholism, showed her clearly her own 'brutality' and 'savagery' and contributed to this return to herself that is *L'Amant*.

11. Xavière Gauthier, 'Marguerite Duras et la lutte des femmes', *Magazine littéraire*, 158 (1980) p. 19. One should, of course, add Monsieur Andesmas.

12. See Régis Durand, 'The Disposition of the Voice', in Michel Benamou and Charles Caramello (eds), *Performance in Postmodern Culture* (Milwaukee, Wis.: Center for Twentieth Century Studies, University of Wisconsin, 1977) pp. 99-110. In *La Vie matérielle* (1987), p. 14, Duras speaks of her distrust of theatre, of acting, which takes away from the text.

13. Dominique Noguez, 'La Gloire des mots', *L'Arc*, 98 (1985) pp. 26-9. Also Willis, 1987, p. 120. See also Pierre Fontanier, *Les Figures du discours* (Paris: Flammarion, 1968) p. 424, for a nineteenth-century discussion of *chronographie*, a rhetorical device to characterise time, that is basically similar to Noguez's parataxsis. Noguez's analysis of Duras's use of adjectives linking the abstract to the concrete ('colonial river', 'blond disorder') is also of interest.

14. 'Afterwards, when I reread my words, I reassemble them into sentences. I construct a sort of syntax, although a poor one' (Duras, 1986, p. 116).

15. See Kristeva, 1987, for an analysis of the particularity of Duras's vision. Also see Borgomano, 1985, for an interpretation of Duras's *fantasmes*.

Unfortunately, I cannot discuss here Duras's films, which suggest interesting comparisons to her novels. Some of the techniques of Duras's fiction, such as the cross-cutting between the dinner party and Chauvin in *Moderato cantabile*, are similar to those of more conventional cinema. Many of her films are, like her later fiction, deliberate reworkings of traditional genres to disrupt the normal responses of her reader or spectator. This is evident in the break between images and sound track in *India Song,* so that the characters appear on the screen without speaking and the voices commenting on the action seem to be offering only one possible interpretation. More radically, the sound track may be telling a story with no direct relation to the images, as in *Aurélia Steiner.* Another possibility is the reduction of the film to a reading of a film script, as in *Camion.* In each case, not only are the normal expectations of the audience disrupted, but the whole 'suspension of disbelief' on which most representational works of art have been based is subverted.

Elizabeth Fallaize (essay date 1990)

SOURCE: Fallaize, Elizabeth. "Resisting Romance: Simone de Beauvoir, '*The Woman Destroyed*' and the Romance Script." In *Contemporary French Fiction by Women: Feminist Perspectives,* edited by Margaret Atack and Phil Powrie, pp. 15-25. Manchester, England: Manchester University Press, 1990.

[*In the following essay, Fallaize examines de Beauvoir's ideology of romance in the context of* The Woman Destroyed.]

The feminist credentials of Simone de Beauvoir's fictional texts are sometimes assumed to be guaranteed by the fact that their author also produced *The Second Sex,* and indeed Beauvoir's fiction is most usually read against her essays (or Sartre's). However, more recently, there has been a tendency to judge the fiction—and to find it wanting in some respects—against the conventions of the romance plot.[1] It is indeed difficult to deny that elements of the romance plot are easily discernible in Beauvoir's early fiction: heterosexual couple formation plays a large part in the narrative, and within this couple the woman tends to be in what Rachel Blau Duplessis has called romantic thraldom (by which she means a totally defining love between apparent unequals—the lover has the power of conferring a sense of identity and purpose upon the loved one) to the often strongly gendered man.[2]

In the early fictional texts, published in the forties and fifties, the central women characters are on the whole rewarded by getting their man when they take the right turning after an initial period of bad faith—thus Françoise of *She Came to Stay* (1943) destroys the rival woman and is rewarded with the love and attention of both the central male characters; Hélène of *The Blood of Others* (1945) valorises love above all else and comes to merit the hero's love when she adopts his quest as her own; the central preoccupation of Anne of *The Mandarins* (1954) is her choice between two men. In more general terms it is quite clear that, despite the strong warnings she gives in *The Second Sex* about the dangers of love for women, Beau-voir herself valued love and the couple very highly. In the first volume of her autobiography, *Memoirs of a Dutiful Daughter,* she describes her anguish and fury as an adolescent at reading a novel in which a man and a woman 'made for each other' decide to sacrifice the possibility of a relationship in the interests of a cause: 'True love, from the moment it burst into passionate life, was irreplaceable (. . .). Daniel's career, the cause, and so on were all abstract things. I found it absurd and criminal that they should put them before love, happiness, life'.[3] Forty years later, in *Force of Circumstance,* she begins her summing-up of her life: 'There has been one undoubted success in my life: my relationship with Sartre'.[4] It is of course important to distinguish between placing a high value on love within the heterosexual couple on the one hand, and all the baggage of the romance ritual on the other, but maintaining the distinction between the two can be a slippery route.

However, the kind of observation which can be made of the extent to which the ideology of romance permeates Beauvoir's earlier fictional texts appears more difficult to make when we turn to her last two fictional texts, *Les Belles Images* (1966) and *The Woman Destroyed* (1968), written more than a decade after her earlier fiction and in a period of rapid transformation of the social roles of women. The thrust of both these texts is essentially a demystifying one, and though in *Les Belles Images,* Beauvoir's main attack is centred on the ideology of the technocratic bourgeoisie, the text also carries out a brutal dismantling of the ideology of the couple: the heroine finds that her husband and her lover are interchangeable and a whole series of romantic gestures and images—such as the sending of flowers, the gift of an expensive necklace, the romantic image of the handsome and elegant couple driving away in their Ferrari—are shown to be not just conventional and ritualistic but to conceal a materialism, a self-interest and even a violence sufficient to deter the most determined romantic heroine. The deconstruction of the romantic and the technocratic go hand in hand when the richest and most powerful male character of the text announces that he is to marry the daughter of his ex-mistress: 'No-one can rule their heart', he explains in self-satisfied justification.[5]

Nevertheless it is possible to ask whether this attack is really mounted on romantic ideology itself, or whether, on the contrary, it is not the characters' failure to meaningfully enact the amorous ritual which may be intended to signal the aridity and inhumanity of the bourgeoisie.[6] And this kind of doubt persists with 'The Woman Destroyed', the final story in the cycle of three short stories also entitled *The Woman Destroyed,* in which the problem of the romance plot becomes particularly acute. Before turning to the story itself, however, it is worth examining more closely the nature of the romance against which I propose to read the story. Blau Duplessis defines the romance plot as one which 'muffles the female character, represses female quest, valorises heterosexual ties, puts individuals into couples as a sign of their success. It evokes an aura around the couple itself and constructs couples based on an extreme of sexual difference'. Blau Duplessis accepts that 'narrative is a version of, or a special expression of, ideology: representations by which we construct and accept values and institutions'. But it does not appear that she gives an overwhelming force to this ideology since she assumes that women writers critical of androcentric culture can revise and restructure the romance plot, thus signalling 'a dissent from social norms as well as narrative forms'.[7]

In contrast to this position, Michelle Coquillat in her recent study of the *roman de gare* (popular romance) in France stresses heavily the ideological function of the romance plot, emphasising the way in which it renders 'natural' values which are actually socially determined and describing the *roman de gare* and its central code, romantic love, as a 'prodigious instrument' in our culture's persuasion process that to be real women we must seek our lives in love of our hero and in domesticity.[8] And Coquillat does not confine her conclusions to the more popular versions of literature: though the code can be perceived to be operating in its grossest form in the *roman de gare,* it is also to be discovered, she argues, albeit in more sophisticated wrappings, in the more elite reaches of literature.

The code that Coquillat discovers at work in the Harlequin series, in the novels of Guy des Cars, of Delly and other popular romance writers does in fact have much in common with Blau Duplessis's definition of the romance plot, despite the fact that Coquillat's model is based on reading 'popular' literature and Blau Duplessis's on 'higher' forms. However, both these studies focus on the separately published novel, and in the case of 'The Woman Destroyed', an even more relevant intertext is that of women's magazine fiction, since the first publication of 'The Woman Destroyed' was as serialised extracts in the prestigious French women's magazine *Elle.* Serialised over five issues, from 19 October to 16 November 1967, the text was accompanied by a series of illustrations of the story by Simone de Beauvoir's sister, Hélène de Beauvoir, and by large photographs of the author herself.[9] Both are important in making the story conform to the genre of women's magazine fiction since a series of illustrations of the heroine of the story are virtually *de rigueur.*

Jean Emelina has analysed other conventions of the women's magazine short story in France: like the *roman de gare,* the point of view of the narrative is that of a central female protagonist with whom the reader is encouraged to identify, and is usually a first-person account. There are various sub-genres, but in the 'true confession' type the tone is highly personal and intimate, revealing the connection between the story and the problems page of which the story is in some ways the prolongation. The setting is usually contemporary, the experience recounted always revolves around love and its problems, and there may be a considerable emphasis on the family (noticeably more so than in the English equivalent). The problems raised are always dealt with strictly on an individual level, as in most popular fiction, and not viewed as being related to any social, class or gender base—again, a feature of the *roman de gare* strongly emphasised by Coquillat.[10]

Turning now then to the story of 'The Woman Destroyed', we begin by identifying the features it shares with the women's magazine story in particular, and with romantic fiction in general. One of the most basic features of the women's magazine story is that it must be seen to be about women and for women, and this is much more true of all three stories of *The Woman Destroyed* than of any other of Simone de Beauvoir's fictional texts. In the case of the particular story with which we are concerned here, the central figure is Monique, a woman in her forties whose total energies in life are devoted to her husband and her children. Her diary constitutes the narrative and provides the woman-centred focus and confessional tone of the romance script. The central focus on the complications of love, also essential to the genre, is revealed as early as the sixth entry of the diary, where we find recorded the event which is to form the central crisis of the story: Monique's husband Maurice reveals that he is having an affair with another woman. The presence of the rival woman, virtually a *sine qua non* in Delly,[11] is used here as the stimulus to provoke Monique into examining her life with Maurice, past and present, and into trying out a number of remedies designed to win back her husband. Most of the remedies are more or less explicitly culled from reading agony and advice columns—after all, Monique's situation of being abandoned by her husband at forty when the children have left home constitutes a stock situation of such pages.

'This evening [writes Monique in her diary] I am going out with Maurice. The advice of Isabelle and of Miss Lonelihearts column—to get your husband back, be cheerful and elegant and go out with him, just the two of you.'[12] Advice also emerges from the female community, since Monique discusses her situation with a number of other women acquaintances. These other women are kept very shadowy, in keeping with another convention of the romance script, which is that the woman is always basically *alone*; other women are understood to be potential rivals rather than sources of support. From the women emerges a body of generalisations about men, of the kind: 'In Maurice, like most men, just beneath the surface slumbers an adolescent lacking in self-assurance'[13] and 'Men choose the easiest solution: it's easier to stay with your wife than to launch out into a new life'.[14] What these infantilising generalisations do is to compensate for the women's actual lack of power over men, and to construct in their attempts to guess at Maurice's likely motivations and behaviour a Maurice who is above all a *man,* above all, in other words, a member of another species. Maurice becomes the unknowable 'other' whose behaviour and remarks Monique must spend hours trying to decode. Here we have an almost pathological—and highly unexistential—construction of sexual difference, again an element crucial to the romantic code.[15]

On the basis of these suppositions about men and about the ground rules of the battle for men, Monique adopts what she calls the 'smile tactic'. Faced for example with the request that Maurice be allowed to spend the whole night out when he sees the other woman, Monique swallows hard and writes in her diary: 'No confrontations. If I ruin this affair for him it will look even more attractive to him from a distance, he'll feel he's missed out on something. If I let him go through with it properly he'll soon get tired of it. That's what Isabelle says'.[16] Bolstering herself with her tactic, Monique increasingly positions herself as a women's magazine reader, feeling optimistic the day that her stars tell her Sagittarians will be lucky in love this week and sending off examples of the handwriting of all three of them to be analysed—interestingly the results are made to be accurate, so that the text supports a belief in graphology, though Monique then has to lose her faith in it at this point in order to be able to avoid facing up to what the results tell her.

Monique's tactic, however, is not allowed to succeed, and in a reversal of the happy end of the genre, she is left alone at the end of the story without her husband. As she writes her diary, she begins to see that she has spent years constructing a mythology of the perfect couple, the perfect wife and mother, the perfect husband, and has refused all other perceptions. She comes, in a half-conscious kind of way, to blame herself for engineering a pregnancy in order to press Maurice into marriage and in order to give up a career in medicine which she found too demanding. She blames herself for having been too stifling as a mother, and Maurice accuses her of moulding one daughter into an exact replica of herself and forcing the other daughter to flee to the US to escape her attentions. In one sense the message of the text is clear and uncompromising—by making a career out of marriage and motherhood, Monique has made a mess of her life and possibly that of others.

So far so good—it is clear that Beauvoir's intention is to exploit the conventions of the romance to make them express different meanings, and to offer a salutary warning to the women reader. However, as Beauvoir writes in the last volume of her autobiography *All Said and Done*, it is dangerous to ask the reader to read between the lines.[17] We have already seen how closely the story mimics the genre. The ending does leave Monique on her own, but it also leaves her still in thraldom to the handsome Maurice, despite the lies he has told and the way in which he has used Monique as a domestic support (and in fact he has to be left looking like a nice sort of chap in order to allow the reader to focus on Monique's mistakes). Monique is thus left at the end of the story as the loser of the eternal female battle for the man. She does not feel that this particular man was not worth having. On the contrary, what she has learned is that her weapons in the battle were the wrong ones, and that her rival—who is a successful lawyer and takes care to follow Maurice's own career with eager interest—is using the right ones. Monique loses and her rival wins—the man remains the prize.

Even more problematically, perhaps, the use of the diary form and the individual confessional style of the narrative means that the text echoes the assumption of all romantic fiction, which is that Monique's situation is an individual matter. It is not absolutely impossible to squeeze out some social elements from the story, but we are a long way here from *Les Belles Images,* in which Simone de Beauvoir so strongly stresses the social forces contributing to the creation of the subject. In *Les Belles Images* the characters are seen to be constituted by the discourse of their group; in 'The Woman Destroyed' Monique is clearly held responsible for her refusal to go beyond the vocabulary of the romantic cliché, her insistence that phrases such as 'Two and two make four' and 'I love you, I love only you' have the same status.

The rules of romantic fiction, which Beauvoir tried to bend to her own purposes, turn out then to be insidiously recuperative. But the structures of the story are not the only thing working against Beauvoir's subversive enterprise. There is also the question of the readers. In *All Said and Done* Beauvoir describes how 'writers, students and teachers' wrote to her 'having fully appreciated my meaning', but after the serialisation in *Elle* she received shoals of a different kind of letter:

> I was overwhelmed with letters from women destroyed, half-destroyed or in the act of being destroyed. They identified themselves with the heroine; they attributed all possible virtues to her and they were astonished that she should remain attached to a man so unworthy of her. Their partiality made it evident that as far as their husbands, their rivals and they themselves were concerned, they shared Monique's blindness. Their reactions were based upon an immense incomprehension.[18]

But to be surprised by the reaction of the *Elle* readers is to fail to recognise the elements which the story has in common with the conventions of romance fiction, and to dismiss the implications of publishing in *Elle*. It is of course true that to publish in *Elle* was not at all the same thing as to publish in the more populist *presse du coeur* type of women's magazine like *Confidences* and *Intimité*. Evelyne Sullerot, in her study of French women's magazines carried out in the early 1960s, identifies *Elle* readers as having a level of education well above average, coming overwhelmingly from the middle classes and living almost exclusively in Paris or large towns. As a consequence, *Elle* readers of the sixties were far less conservative than the less well-educated, more rural and Catholic readers of the populist press, and *Elle,* which knew its readership well, was far more able to overstep limits and question conventions. It was the first French women's magazine to deal with issues of sexuality and contraception before even the advent of the sixties, and it had a highly distinctive agony column, reigned over by Marcelle Ségal. Her style was not the sympathetic, rather saccharine tone adopted by many of her peers in this period but was frequently abrasive and ironic, designed to shake her readers out of the somewhat narcissistic torpor into which many of her correspondents seemed sunk.[19]

However, despite this relatively energetic tone and the encouragement which *Elle* gave its readers to extend their interests outside the home, the *Elle* readership could not read Beauvoir's texts in the way that the 'writers, students and teachers' to whom Simone de Beauvoir refers in *All Said and Done* read it. Publishing in *Elle* meant entering the mass market—Sullerot estimates *Elle's* readership in the 1960s as in the order of three million women, the majority of whom were unlikely to have read any of Beauvoir's earlier fiction. What they would have had experience of, however, was the magazine fiction genre in which she appeared to be writing, and they clearly read it according to the conventions of the genre, identifying with the heroine whose comfortable middle-class Parisian lifestyle reflected the readers' own, and recognising the how-to-win-a-husband-back vocabulary which Monique clings to. This reading is encouraged by *Elle's* presentation of the text as 'an analysis of what happens in the mind, in the heart of a woman when the man she loves, and whom she trusts, deceives her'. The adultery of Maurice, understandable or even desirable perhaps in St Germain circles, was likely to be perceived primarily as a threat to domestic stability by the readers of a magazine which, for all its avant-garde reputation, devoted a considerable number of its pages to the domestic arts. The 1975 new law on divorce, replacing the 1889 Naquet law, was still more than six years in the future, and even the realist Marcelle Ségal advised her readers to stick with domestic fidelity and avoid breaking up the home.[20] The reaction of the *Elle* readers demonstrates that reading habits and expectations are not to be changed by a single text. When taken together with the other doubts about the text expressed by readers perfectly aware of Beauvoir's intentions, the difficulties of subverting a highly established and ideological script become evident.[21] However, the reaction of the *Elle* readership was not the only consequence for Beauvoir of the serialisation. In discussing the quality or rather lack of quality of the fiction published in magazines like *Elle* and *Marie-Claire*, relative to the quality of their other articles, Evelyne Sullerot points to the extreme reluctance of writers to sign work appearing in women's magazines, because of the damage to the author's literary reputation likely to ensue.[22] The reception of 'The Woman Destroyed' was heavily marked by its appearance in *Elle*. Bernard Pivot, at that time still a humble columnist for the *Figaro Littéraire*, wrote the book off as a 'shop-girls' romance with pink bows on it' on the strength of a single instalment.[23] Jacqueline Piatier in *Le Monde* was equally exultant to be able to damn the story as women's romance. Her review ends with the following line, in which she underlines the gulf between what she takes to be the philosophical pretensions of Simone de Beauvoir and the concerns of the story: 'Can it be that when philosophers start solving problems instead of posing them that they begin producing agony columns?'[24] No other fictional text by Beauvoir met with such a dismissive response on publication as *The Woman Destroyed*, despite the fact that the book quickly became a best-seller. It seems that Beauvoir may have underestimated the dangers of writing between the lines, especially when the lines are those of the romance script.

Most analysts of romantic fiction point to its ideological force, though opinions vary about the actual impact of this force on readers, just as, to look at the issue in a wider scope, commentators on ideology generally are divided about the extent to which it can be resisted. Janice Radway, for example, argues that despite its constant reworking of structures which confine women, romantic fiction can have an integrative and enabling effect on women's lives. Lennard Davis equally urges us to become resisting readers but is more inclined to the view that the novel is a form which 'by and large, is one that fundamentally resists change'.[25] Thus, even if we posit resisting readers, we are still left with the problem of the extent to which it is possible for the writer to subvert the conventions of such a strongly established genre.

To what extent can the writer carry out a demystifying task and become a critic of ideology, while attempting to work within the formal structures of that ideology? Is Beauvoir herself not bound by the very values which she perceives as destroying women? The demands of Beauvoir's own deeply-seated attachment to the value of the couple, the formal and ideological constraints of the genre and the habits of the readership seem, in the case of 'The Woman Destroyed', to have all weighed in the balance against this particular attempt to resist romance. Optimism about the scope for revising the romance plot and criticism of a writer on the grounds that she has apparently failed to rewrite the script have to be viewed in the context of these formidable odds.

Notes

1. See for example the chapter on relations between male and female characters in Mary Evans, *Simone de Beauvoir: A Feminist Mandarin* (London: Tavistock, 1985).

2. Rachel Blau Duplessis, *Writing Beyond the Ending. Narrative Strategies of Twentieth-Century Women Writers* (Bloomington: Indiana University Press, 1985), p. 5.

3. *Memoirs of a Dutiful Daughter*, trans. James Kirkup (Harmondsworth: Penguin, 1987), pp. 142-3.

4. *Force of Circumstance*, trans. Richard Howard (Harmondsworth: Penguin, 1985), p. 659.

5. *Les Belles Images*, trans. Patrick O'Brian (Harmondsworth: Penguin, 1983), p. 81; translation adapted.

6. In an article entitled 'What Love Is and Isn't' published in English in the American magazine *McCall* only the year before the publication of *Les Belles Images*, Beauvoir stressed what she describes as the revolutionary and liberating force of love and suggests that it is doubtful whether a person too much in harmony with society could experience love. From this perspective, the characters of *Les Belles Images* are clearly too other-directed and too anxious to conform to social pressures to allow themselves to expe-

rience a potentially revolutionary force. The article is reprinted in Claude Francis and Fernande Gontier, *Les Ecrits de Simone de Beauvoir* (Paris: Gallimard, 1979), pp. 413-21.

7. Blau Duplessis, *Writing Beyond,* p. 20.

8. Michelle Coquillat, *Romans d'amour* (Paris: Odile Jacob, 1989), pp. 10-12.

9. The photographs of Simone de Beauvoir are in fact much more prominent than the illustrations, an indication of the extent to which *Elle* was keen to promote the fact that it was publishing 'the greatest French woman writer of our day'. During the latter part of the sixties, circulation figures for women's magazines fell rapidly; Bonvoisin and Maignien attribute this fall in part to the radical changes taking place in French society affecting women's roles which magazines were unable to keep pace with. Perhaps *Elle* saw the publication of Beauvoir in its pages as a useful tactic at this stage, despite the conservative reaction of readers to earlier extracts from *The Prime of Life*. See Evelyne Sullerot, *La Presse féminine* (Paris: Armand Colin, 1963), p. 138; S-M. Bonvoisin and M. Maignien, *La Presse féminine* (Paris: Armand Colin, 1986), pp. 26-7.

10. Jean Emelina, 'La Nouvelle dans la presse du cœur: étude à partir d'un exemple', in *Hommage à Pierre Nardin* (Paris: Les Belles Lettres, 1977), pp. 291-303. I am grateful to Béatrice Damamme-Gilbert for drawing this article to my attention.

11. Coquillat, *Romans d'amour,* p. 34.

12. *The Woman Destroyed,* trans. Patrick O'Brian (Harmondsworth: Penguin, 1987), p. 117. All subsequent references are to this edition.

13. Ibid., p. 118; translation adapted.

14. Ibid., p. 165; translation adapted.

15. See Anne Barr Snitow, 'Mass Market Romance: Pornography for Women is Different' in Anne Snitow, Christine Stansell, Sharon Thompson (eds.), *Powers of Desire: The Politics of Sexuality* (New York: Monthly Review Press, 1983).

16. *Woman Destroyed,* pp. 121-2; translation adapted.

17. Beauvoir goes on in this paragraph to construct her imaginary reader as a detective: 'I hoped that people would read the books as a detective-story; here and there I scattered clues that would allow the reader to find the key to the mystery - but only if he tracked Monique down as one tracks down the guilty character', *All Said and Done,* trans. Patrick O'Brian (Harmondsworth: Penguin, 1987), p. 140. Subsequent references are to this edition. However, as Toril Moi points out, it is in fact Monique who actually becomes the detective in her frenzied quest for reliable knowledge. See Toril Moi, *Feminist Theory and Simone de Beauvoir* (Oxford: Blackwell, 1990), p. 80.

18. Ibid., p. 142.

19. See Sullerot, *Presse féminine,* pp. 193-5, and Bonvoisin and Maignien, *Presse féminine,* pp. 28-9.

20. A letter from 'Jacky' in the issue of 19 October in which serialisation of 'The Woman Destroyed' was begun, urges the reader to enjoy her lover on a temporary basis while hanging on to her husband. Marcelle Ségal replies: 'No, Jacky, this is not possible. My profession has its obligations, so does marriage, begging your pardon'.

21. See Toril Moi's excellent analysis of the rhetorical effects undermining authorial intentions in the story in *Feminist Theory and Simone de Beauvoir,* cited above.

22. Sullerot, *Presse féminine,* p. 129.

23. See Beauvoir, *All Said and Done,* p. 142.

24. Jacqueline Piatier, *Le Monde (des livres),* 24 janvier 1968, pp. I-II.

25. See Lennard J. Davis, *Resisting Novels: Ideology and Fiction* (London: Methuen, 1987), p. 227. Davis is particularly sceptical about the possibility of subverting romance fiction: 'It is unlikely that this major genre can have any radical political effect, crippled as it is by the weight of tradition and the demands of the audience' (p. 234).

Elizabeth A. Houlding (essay date 1997)

SOURCE: Houlding, Elizabeth A. "'L'Envers de la guerre': The Occupation of Violette Leduc." In *Gender and Fascism in Modern France,* edited by Melanie Hawthorne and Richard J. Golsan, pp. 83-100. Hanover, England: University Press of New England, 1997.

[*In the following essay, Houlding examines feminine and gender issues occupying French intellectuals during the war years based on an examination of Violette Leduc's* La Bâtarde.]

> At night I dreamed that the war was over, that the people with real ability had returned, that I was scurrying like a mangy dog to the refuge of an unemployment bureau. I would wake up soaked with sweat, convince myself with a stammering voice that it was a nightmare, then fall asleep again.[1]

Nightmarish images of the liberation of France from Nazi occupation recur frequently in Violette Leduc's autobiographical work, *La Bâtarde* (1964). At no point in this work does Leduc take part in her country's euphoric anticipation of Allied victory over the German occupying forces. Rather, for Violette Leduc, the liberation of France portends a dysphoric return to unemployment, despair, shame, and submission to those more able than herself. Who, we might ask, or what kind of woman would dread the end of Nazi domination and of history's most horrific international conflict? And, perhaps more scandalously, who would admit to such a thing in writing?

One might initially speculate that Leduc's fear of freedom is not entirely unusual, that it might, in fact, simply mirror the "articulation of female dread" identified by Susan Gubar in her important study of British women's literary responses to World War II.[2] Gubar defines this fear on the part of British women as an apprehension that "male vulnerability in wartime would result in violence against women" (230). Violette Leduc is of course French and not British; however, national differences matter little here since Leduc's specific and entirely personal fear is not fear of a backlash by men against women for taking their place during wartime, but is more like terror at the prospect of the community as a whole reverting to "normal" after a time of "gender disorder."

This fear of the consequences of a social backlash in which the masculine attempts to reassert itself would seem at least partly, however, to fit Leduc's near-despairing anxiety at the thought of a return a to prewar social order. According to Joan W. Scott, the return of peace does have the effect of spinning hard-won, often tenuous gains back in on themselves: "War is the ultimate disorder; peace thus implies a return to 'traditional' gender relationships, the familiar and natural order of families, men in public roles, women at home, and so on."[3] In Leduc's case, the gains at stake are her hard-won profits in the worlds of publishing and black-marketeering during the Occupation. Her fear of losing these becomes tangible in *La Bâtarde*, where her identification with other women and with socially defined gender roles is shot through with ambivalence. Whereas Gubar argues that "the literature women wrote about World War II needs to be understood as a documentation of women's sense that the war was a blitz on them," one can, in Leduc's case, offer a parallel but distinct revision of this interpretation by arguing that Leduc's autobiographical representation of the Occupation depicts the war as a blitz on herself alone. It remains uncomfortably but undeniably clear throughout *La Bâtarde* that Leduc prospered materially and socially under the conditions of "gender disorder" provoked by five years of war, national anxiety, and foreign occupation. As an example of French women's lives during wartime, Leduc resembles less the model wives of prisoners-of-war, the "women who wait" recently studied by Sarah Fishman, than the "outlaw" women into whose experience Miranda Pollard has called for further investigation, women whose tales offer marginal and "less respectable" narratives of Occupied France.[4]

La Bâtarde's representation of the war years is structured by a series of personal and intellectual moments, mostly concerning femininity, gender roles (especially the role of gender as manifested by Occupation discourse and activity), and discontent, which together elaborate a view of the effects of the Occupation on an "outlaw" French woman and her text. To be sure, Leduc provides an extreme example of the crisis in the social "place" and the self-definition of women during the Occupation. Her illegitimacy, psychological instability, class affiliations, and above all her bisexuality all come into play in her search for a stance that will most effectively distance her from the postwar desire for quiescence. But the fact that Leduc *is* unrepresentative, an "outlaw" to a prescribed concept of femininity as well as to social legitimacy, is conversely what makes *La Bâtarde* so important to a fuller understanding of the textual memory of the Occupation. Just as Leduc felt drawn to what she termed the "underside of the war"—"l'envers de la guerre," her text tells the story of the underside of gender relations of the time.[5]

In an argument related to that of Joan W. Scott, Denise Riley has claimed that "war throws gender into sharp relief."[6] Although the war between France and Germany officially ended in June 1940, certainly such a highlighting of gender systems obtained in occupied France. Vichy discourse surrounding the defeat is fraught with an anxious harking back to a distant past in which France had not yet fallen prey to the feminizing influences of the Third Republic. The National Revolution was described by Pétain as "a strongly human and virile reaction to a feminized republic, a republic of women and homosexuals."[7] Yet dedicated women were precisely what Pétain needed to launch this conservative social vision, since only they could bear the many French children desired by the grandfatherly leader. In the case of Violette Leduc, it is worth noting that there is no room in the discourse of Pétain's new nation for the woman who is *also* a homosexual ("une république de femmes *ou* d'invertis"). Vichy's aim was to shape the potentially troublesome "femme" into the warmer "épouse" and "mère."[8]

In her study of social policy concerning women in wartime and postwar Britain, Riley makes the following crucial observation: "Women *when named as a sex* by the formulations of social policy cannot escape being the incarnation of gender as strange or temporary workers; nor can they escape being seen as hovering on the edge of maternity" (260). If we apply Riley's remarks to the equally appropriate context of occupied France, we can argue that it would be virtually impossible not to recognize oneself *as* a woman under such extreme conditions, impossible to avoid what Riley terms "gendered self-consciousness."[9] If women are "the incarnation of gender," they are not subjects but signifiers within the social project. For Violette Leduc, bastard, bisexual, black-marketeer, the imposition of gendered self-consciousness represented both the greatest release of power and the most oppressive, nightmarish ambiguity.

Born in 1907, Violette Leduc arrived at the war years as an unmarried woman of mediocre health, with an unfinished high-school education, several badly ended love affairs (mostly, but not exclusively, with women), unresolved conflicts with her mother, and massive insecurities: in short, having successfully completed and passed through none of the traditional stages of a French woman's life of her generation. Leduc's particular brand of marginality was accompanied by a heightened awareness of the "norm," of the appropriate way of living a woman's life, of the ways of being and becoming a *jeune fille rangée*—Simone de Beauvoir's phrase for her own bourgeois Catholic upbringing. Leduc was constantly aware of her failure to follow the appropriate life plot. This pain of the *jeune fille dérangée*[10] acts as the ongoing leitmotif of her work: the pain of forever being the unacknowledged offspring of an illegitimate union, of bearing what she describes as an unforgivably ugly face from day to day, of her inability to establish satisfying relationships with others.

The product of a brief liaison between a young housemaid and the ne'er-do-well son in whose parents' household her mother, Berthe, worked, Leducnever received her legitimate name of the father or the kind affection of her mother. As the daughter of an abandoned, impoverished, and resentful woman, Leduc soon grew aware of the illegitimacy she eventually declared in the title of the work in question, a title that also bears the mark of gender in the English edition, *La Bâtarde*.[11] When *La Bâtarde* was published by Gallimard in 1964, it was accompanied by an important preface written by Simone de Beauvoir, literary protector, advisor, and friend of the less well-known Leduc. (Beauvoir was one of Gallimard's most distinguished authors by this point and was of course engaged in the writing of her own extremely successful autobiographical project.[12]) In introducing Leduc's first specifically autobiographical work to the reader, Beauvoir focused on Leduc's obsessive style and personality, and on what she termed her "scrupulous honesty" (xxiii) in telling the story of an unusual life.

Beauvoir also pointed out that Leduc did not hesitate to discuss in her work those topics that continually engaged her, regardless of their appropriateness as literary material for a woman of her generation. For example, Leduc in no way limited herself to a typically prescribed feminine *pudeur* (or modesty) when it came to revealing her obsessions with money, sexuality, psychological stability, and her physical appearance. On the other hand, this intensely personal writer remained, perhaps necessarily, disengaged from more public or ethical concerns, such as, for instance, the global historical significance of the war. I quote Beauvoir's preface here:

> [A]nything that does not touch her personally leaves her indifferent. She calls the Germans "the enemy" in order to make it clear that this borrowed notion has remained quite foreign to her. She does not owe allegiance to any camp. She has no sense of the universal, no sense of simultaneity; she is there where she is, with the weight of her past upon her shoulders.
>
> (xxiii)

In regard to the Occupation, then, we might well ask what it means to read the work of a writer who has, according to Beauvoir, "no sense of the universal." For Leduc is surely more than an existential author. Dealing with the political crisis of a country to which her own affiliations were inherently ambiguous, and feeling that she had been assigned at birth the role of "public enemy" within a society that now no longer knew who exactly the enemy was, Leduc filters this literal crisis of the nation through her own inescapable self.

That self, however, was hardly the most stable or trustworthy medium. Critics in general agree that Leduc never succeeded in creating a literary persona other than her troubled biographical self, a point with which Leduc concurred during an interview: "I told the story of my life as it happened, my books, my mistakes, my despair, in short, my life as a failed writer."[13] Although Leduc is not alone among women writers in suffering this critical fate, in her work the problem is perhaps more acute. Leduc's case, with its particular mix of ego and anomie, poses an interesting question in the problematics of autobiography and literary self-representation, namely, how does a flagrantly self-centered woman write about the outside world in her autobiographical work?[14] And more specifically, how does the historical event that was the Occupation enter Leduc's life and her text? It is her status as a witness, and the value of her testimony, that are at stake in these questions of Leduc's relationship to the universal.

In fact, the years of the Occupation are crucial to the development of both Leduc and *La Bâtarde*. The fact that Leduc chose to end her book with the closing moments of the Occupation of France in 1944 should not be overlooked; it is perhaps the most simple but also the most telling example of an important historical and textual coincidence. The co-terminiety of the book and the Occupation may at first seem surprising in a writer as obsessed by self and closed to the greater field of international politics and affairs, but *La Bâtarde* weaves life story and history together in ways that have previously been disregarded, but that are very telling in the larger context of the literary representation of the war years.

Like Beauvoir, Isabelle de Courtivron interprets Leduc's insistence upon italicizing the term "the enemy" to refer to the Germans within her work as symptomatic of Leduc's inability to identify with the social crisis around her. De Courtivron summarizes her view of Leduc's representation of the war in this way:

> Violette's reactions to the war are devoid of value judgment. The Germans, whom she feels obliged to label "the enemy," are invisible in her account. The tragedies she witnesses are told in a detached manner, exhibiting the same lack of concern with which Violette will later allude to the deportation of her Jewish neighbors. The world's catastrophes do not seem to affect her except insofar as they interfere with the course of her private world. An occasional allusion to the progression of the war, gleaned from dialogues of people who surround her, is the only marker of real time and events.[15]

Leduc's detachment from what is generally termed the "political" cannot be denied. There is no attempt made in the narrative of *La Bâtarde* to look back at the war years and analyze the politico-historical significance of events.

Yet I would argue that Leduc does indeed represent the Occupation. Indeed, to embrace the opposite point of view and focus on Leduc's subjectivity tends to deny the historical context and political content of Leduc's wartime text (and of women's texts in general). It is to do a disservice to all works of this period. To view Leduc's writing as apolitical in nature is to overlook precisely that which is historical and political about this work; it is to support the interpretation of women's writing as limited to the realm of the personal. To write that "the Germans are invisible" in Leduc's account, as though this were an unfortunate oversight on her part but one that bears confessing, is simply not to see where the Germans are in the text.

Leduc's refusal to comment directly upon the Germans or upon Nazi ideology does not mean they have no bearing in and on her text. The Germans are not invisible; like all aspects of the war and the Occupation, their presence is a fact, one with which Leduc copes in life and in language. But the war itself and the German "enemy" enter the text through an extremely partial, discontinuous discourse, through the men in Leduc's own life, and through the details of her daily life, as is the case with many other women of the time. The fragmented manner in which Leduc represents wartime and the intersections of the war and the Germans with her own life calls not for dismissal but rather for what I have termed a reading "between the lines."[16] To call for such internal reconstruction does not set us free to proffer our own version of what Leduc leaves unsaid by glossing her infelicities or supplementing her lack of political commentary. It is rather a reading that takes into account the indirectness of many women's experience of history, exemplified here by the oft-noted "fragmentary" nature of Leduc's narrative. In this way, we can account not only for the larger moments of international combat, the declarations of war, and the signing of peace treaties but also for the details of daily life, the private negotiation of food rationing, and the sexual politics of military occupation.

If Leduc does purposefully distance herself from the war through such tactics as the italicization of charged elements of public discourse or her refusal to include "value judgments" in her narrative of the time, these strategies tell us something important about the degree of Leduc's social alienation, and also about our expectations as readers of these wartime texts. Could it be that, unless War is represented monolithically, we tend to think that it is not present at all? Leduc's overriding concern with herself complicates, but certainly does not erase, her relationship to "real time and events." Given the critical commentary we have seen remarking upon Leduc's idiosyncrasies and limitations as an observer of her time, one might even be tempted to retitle her work *La Bâtarde or How Not To Write An Occupation Memoir*.[17]

We have already reached the midpoint of Leduc's six-hundred-page narrative when the possibility of war with Germany enters the text. Half of the book (or three hundred pages) is then devoted to the five years of World War II, a telling proportion in a story recounting the first thirty-seven years of Leduc's life. (The first half of *La Bâtarde* is an account of Leduc's unhappy childhood, adolescence, failed studies, and lesbian initiation, up to the age of thirty-two.) Immediately before the war, Leduc worked as a Girl Friday for Denise Batcheff, a film impresario. Leduc was constantly delighted by the contact with the bright lights of the Parisian artistic world this job afforded her. In addition to Maurice Sachs, by whose sophisticated banter and flirtatious attention she is attracted, Leduc mentions the office visits of Jean Gabin, Michèle Morgan, Jacques Prévert, and Robert Bresson, among others.

These were the early months of Leduc's friendship and fascination with Maurice Sachs, a writer and notorious member of the Parisian artistic world. Her frustrated love for Sachs was the first in a series of Leduc's attachments to homosexual men, Jean Genet among them. Although little known to today's readers, Maurice Sachs was a highly visible figure in Parisian literary circles between the two World Wars.[18] Through his association with Cocteau's "Boeuf sur le Toit" group in the 1920s, Sachs became known for his scandalous behavior, debauchery, and extravagance. Despite his sexual adventures and shady financial affairs, Sachs (who had been raised by his nonpracticing Jewish mother) underwent a very public conversion to Catholicism under the guidance of the Catholic intellectual Jacques Maritain and his wife Raïsa, with Jean Cocteau as his "godfather." His newfound piety and desire to become a priest ended in failure, however, when Sachs returned to his old ways and fell in love with a young man while on vacation at Juan-les-Pins. (Like Leduc, Sachs was also married for a brief time.) While Sachs adored celebrated writers such as Cocteau and Gide, Leduc was equally flattered by his attention and came to adore this profoundly dishonest and misogynistic character.

Shortly before the outbreak of war in 1939, Gabriel Mercier, an old friend of Leduc's and a potential lover, resurfaced after an absence of many years. At this point, Leduc's life seemed just about "complete." It was this precarious "almost" that the possibility of war threatened to destroy:

> I don't want the war to interrupt a new love affair and a new friendship. I had been a failure in everything: studies, piano, examinations, relationships, sleep, health, holidays, tranquillity of mind, gaiety, happiness, security, application at work. Now I was winning; I almost had a job, almost a lover, almost a friend with a position in Parisian society. They couldn't declare war, they couldn't take all that away from me. I shall never cease to insist on the terror of insecurity instilled into me as a child. One must always have a few sous in one's purse. The war would push me into the gutter.
>
> (289)

A failure at each and every duty of the daughters of her generation, Leduc feared that just as she was getting her feet on the ground, the war would sweep away all stability by removing both men, the friend (Sachs) and the lover

(Gabriel), from her side. Like many of her counterparts, including Simone de Beauvoir, Leduc's reaction when faced with the invasion of her private life by such things as history and war was to echo those common questions of selfish impatience: Why now, and why me?

As predicted, Leduc's job did indeed disappear with the declaration of war in September 1939. The men in her life received their postings (Sachs was sent to Caen as an interpreter, and Gabriel was assigned work as an office clerk), while Leduc found herself in Paris without a job, worried about money and her financial future. With both men away in the military, Leduc was concerned about their well-being and dutifully wrote both of them letters. Sachs did not remain in the military long, however, as he was discharged for "unacceptable sexual behavior" and soon returned to Paris.[19] Due to his complicated medical history, Gabriel was soon judged too weak to be sent to the front and was returned to Paris to take a job in the records department of the War Office.

As literary or indeed as memoir material, Leduc's relationships with Sachs and Gabriel are problematic. Clearly, neither of these men can serve as a traditional war hero. Indeed, in a conventional war narrative, the soldier's story should provide the plot. However, for a brief time at least, Gabriel's status as a soldier does propel Leduc's life story along a more conservative path. For, within weeks of the declaration of war between France and Germany, the lack of social stability drives Leduc to a previously unconsidered extreme: she announces a desire for the security of marriage to Gabriel, no matter how unorthodox their relationship has been up to this point. Therefore, what becomes important during the war and the Occupation is Leduc's surprising turn, after the two most serious lesbian relationships of her life, toward a visible heterosexual relationship and toward public acceptability.

. . . . .

When war invades women's private lives, even a life as unorthodox as Leduc's, the pressures brought to bear immediately center upon "a woman's place" in society. Leduc knew that as the legitimate bride of a French soldier she would be entitled to financial support from the state. And this woman wanted to be a bride as soon as possible: "Why weren't we both Americans? I longed for a runaway marriage like the heroine of a Western" (293). For the unmarried daughter of an unmarried mother, it was marriage above all that would place Leduc, for the first time in her life, in a legitimate position in society:

> My husband would be a soldier, I would be able to draw the allowance made to soldier's wives, I would have someone to love, and I would be saved . . . I had been in exile, and now I had come home again . . . My fourth finger feels uneasy, the poor thing needs a ring around it. You shall have your wedding ring, I promise you. It will shine, and when my marriage is glowing on my hand I shall know how to make the most of it.
>
> (293)

Exiled as a woman, repatriated as a wife, Leduc's legitimation proved, however, just as alienating as her original bastard state. Leduc does not make it entirely clear to her reader whether in fact she did benefit financially from becoming a war bride. Shortly after the wedding, Gabriel writes to tell her that she will not be able to draw an allowance from the army, but no reasons are given for this in the text, nor do we know if this was perhaps only a temporary delay due to French bureaucracy. From this point on, though, Leduc complains that her husband is an unsatisfactory provider: "The cards were down: Gabriel was not going to give me anything" (297). Within the convention of marriage, Leduc quickly finds herself in a familiar state of sexual frustration and financial uneasiness.

Simply stated, Leduc's feelings about sexual involvement with Gabriel were extremely conflicted. Gabriel's interest in Leduc appears to have been grounded more in friendship than in physical passion, with Leduc often dressing in masculine attire and adopting the role of Gabriel's "bonhomme." On their wedding night, when Gabriel declared, "Nothing is changed, you will be free, I shall be free" (296), Leduc was wounded by his indifference: "I admit it: I wanted to be attractive to Gabriel" (167). The chapter immediately following the euphoric wedding band passage opens with this evocative description: "It was an old marriage that smelt of napthalene" (294). Leduc's disappointment in marriage is perhaps predictable. Because of her marginality and lack of physical beauty, Leduc never felt that she could play the parts available to women of her time. Certainly she knew that her relationship with Gabriel did not conform to current heterosexual norms. Nonetheless, Leduc was no sooner in the marriage than she grew nostalgic for the life of the single woman, alone and independent. Pulled in both directions, Leduc wanted to have her wedding cake and eat it too.

. . . . .

In writing of this first winter of war and marriage, Leduc's representations of wartime experience center in great part on moments of gendered activity, moments that are grounded in Frenchwomen's experience of the time: waiting in line with other Parisian housewives for rationed food; waiting for letters from absent men; worrying about food and supplies. Leduc offers the following passage as an example of feminine conversation carried on to pass the time while waiting in line for vegetables. For both Leduc and the other women present, these exchanges constitute a veritable "orgy of platitudes" in which everyone participates. "All is not lost," one of the strong-minded ones whispered in my ear. 'All is not lost,' I would say to one weaker than myself. The enemy, our troops" (321). Leduc finds her place within the circularity of this exchange; she talks to the other women, commiserates, and for once she speaks the right language: "I chatted. I put myself in the others' shoes . . . I wanted to please them" (321). Leduc realizes that this sharing of common experience is largely a matter of manipulating the right vocabulary:

> So I talked: parcels to be packed for prisoners, letters received, letters sent, the advances, the defeats of our

enemies, a ray of hope, relatives in the country, relatives going short themselves in order to send a piece of bacon. Repetitions, twice-told tales, lamentations, threats. I imitated the other housewives.

(321)

Leduc takes satisfaction in her role as one of this group of women. She is eager to please and to identify with others, to get outside of herself by placing herself "in their shoes," or "in their skin," as expressed by the original French. Here at last is her link to Frenchness and to femininity, for as a newlywed she too has an enlisted husband and household worries. The identification with each other and with the nation comes through the domestic elements of their lives, literally through the home(front) which is their "lieu commun."

While these clichés place the speaker in a circuit of conversation, with the oppositional phrase "the enemy, our troops" functioning as a crucial password, it is not clear from Leduc's written account that information is actually exchanged. These words may prove to be merely skin deep, just another "formule de politesse" so beloved by the French, that is, a superficial means of establishing verbal contact that allows speakers to steer well clear of the unwelcome awkwardness of the private. What does appear to be essential here is the exclusionary rhetoric of "us" versus "them." While able to enter into this network of public exchange, Leduc is, however, unable to forget the conditions under which she personally enters the war: "This new vocabulary did nothing to help me in my war against Gabriel, nothing to prevent us from humiliating each other all the time. My defeat had merely coincided with the outbreak of war" (321). Leduc's private battles with her husband, Gabriel, with marriage, and with desire are not forgotten in the midst of war with Germany. But neither is the private seen to eclipse the public. The imagery here is one of mirroring and coincidence rather than exclusion. The war provides new ways for Leduc to visualize and articulate her domestic conflicts, by shifting her temporarily "outside" of herself, even by means of a seemingly trivial chat with other women about letters, packing string, and parcels.

While participating in these feminine exchanges in what she terms "good faith," Leduc admits in writing that she is "neutral" at best and, moreover, that she secretly desires the dramatic upheaval of the war for the personal opportunities an unstable environment may afford her:

> But in fact I was sincerely neutral. And what is more, I was hoping for world-wide disaster, I was hoping that when everyone in Paris had fled I would be promoted in their absence. I wanted bombs and mortar shells to shatter my past failures. The war would get me out of the rut I was in. (. . .) I was living in one squalid room; but all those luxury apartments with their signs "To Let"—they also belonged to me now. I breathed more freely in a Paris without people.

(321-22)

Although the "world-wide disaster" of war means exodus for many, it augurs liberation for Leduc, from her past, from social conventions and restraints, and, finally, from herself.

The structure of the confessional relationship with the reader that Leduc constructs in her text recalls very strongly a "window scene" in which de Courtivron locates the apotheosis of Leduc's obsessive relationship with her mentor Simone de Beauvoir. As de Courtivron notes in an analysis of *L'Affamée* (1948), a surrealistic account of Leduc's obsessive attachment to Beauvoir, Leduc's problem with "others," namely, her "failure to establish enduring relationships with other human beings," is one of miscalculated distance and skewed perception.[20] Conscious of this problem, Leduc herself creates a metaphor of binoculars, a device de Courtivron finds especially appropriate for describing Leduc's project of looking: "Binoculars cut you off from people by bringing you close to them. You close in on what's happening far from you but without participating in it."[21] Indeed, de Courtivron argues that the sole moment in *L'Affamée* during which Leduc manages to achieve the perfect distance from "Madame" (the Beauvoir figure), her constant object of observation, occurs when Leduc stands outside a café window and gazes in to watch Beauvoir as she reads peacefully on her own: "Separated by a glass pane, they are apart yet near."[22] Leduc's binocular gaze brings her relentlessly close to her objects of study, only to disappoint and disorient her when removed. Leduc's texts serve, then, as a window between herself and others. Through her texts, she manages to put herself into circulation, while guarding a self-protective distance.

In the moves between proximity and distance, Leduc establishes a cautious relationship with an imaginary "nous." Within the context of the Occupation, however, the stakes of proximity and distance are particularly meaningful. As a marginal member of French bourgeois society, Leduc often identifies *in writing* with victims of persecution under the Occupation, only to undermine this closeness through her acknowledged failure to make the slightest gesture of support to aid her Jewish neighbors, and through her profiteering on the black-market.

A telling example of Leduc's simultaneous identification with and distance from her "subjects" is found in her references to a young Jewish neighbor, Esther. This young girl, with whom Leduc does not appear to have a personal relationship, is referred to as her "friend on the other side of a windowpane" (320). Esther's second-floor room is directly across the courtyard from that of Violette and Gabriel. From their windows, Esther and Leduc serve as silent spectators of the other's life: "The visits we paid each other through our windowpanes were more real than any spoken greeting. I would appear, she would rush to see me; or she would be there, and I would hurtle to watch her" (321). Leduc observes Esther and comments upon her grace and beauty. In Leduc's terms, they know each other well: "Ours was a public idyll. We had nothing to say to one another, nothing to confide, nothing to offer" (321).

Both women are trapped within the lives they lead inside their respective rooms, Esther by the war, Leduc by her marriage. The actual terms of this relationship remain, however, undefined and entirely one-sided. Do the women truly have "nothing to say to one another" because their profound similarity and intimacy transcend speech? Or is it that Leduc is most comfortable with a relationship that remains unconsummated, seen through a window, or italicized, as it were?

When Gabriel announces that the Nazis have arrested Esther's father, Leduc admits that, at this point in her life, she cannot be seen as unlucky. Illegitimate daughters with failed professional and emotional lives remain insignificant and relatively secure citizens of occupied Paris:

> I didn't dare cry out that we were two monsters of indifference safe by our fireside. On my Aryan maiden's helmet there perched a parrot that would keep croaking: how lucky that we're not Jews, how lucky that we're not Jewish at this moment.
>
> (339)

Leduc takes a measure of pleasure in exposing her own indifference, cowardice, and anti-Semitism at this time: "Having been suppressed, reduced to zero at birth by members of the wealthy classes, I was by no means unhappy, now we were at war, to see the rich being forced to escape into the Unoccupied Zone" (339).

Leduc calls Esther into her narrative at different moments, much as the unnamed Jewish girl punctuates segments of Marguerite Duras's *La Douleur*.[23] As the Occupation progresses, Esther's family members are arrested; Esther herself is taken away in the middle of the night by the Germans:

> Next morning I was told that the enemy had come at five in the morning and taken Esther away. The neighbours had to tear the gas-pipe out of her mother's hands by brute force. Mme Lita and Mme Keller went out shopping as usual, with their yellow stars sewn on their bodices. They didn't dare mention Esther's disappearance.
>
> (352)

In this instance, the reader finds no ironic quotation marks around the words "the enemy," a choice we might attribute to Leduc's professed affection for Esther, and to her tendency to identify with victims rather than oppressors. However, each of these Jewish women, Esther, Mme Lita, and Mme Keller, remains forever silent in Leduc's text. The reader is left to wonder whether Mme Lita and Mme Keller did not dare mention the disappearance of Esther to Leduc in particular, or whether they chose, for their own reasons, not to communicate with their neighbor. And Leduc further clouds her identification with Esther by confessing that on the night of Esther's arrest she had been awakened by shouts and screams and had selfishly gone back to sleep "so as to escape the nightmare of a woman who was suffering" (352). Leduc had done nothing to intervene. In a disturbing admission, Leduc reveals to the reader that her nightmares of the period are conditioned not by fears of the present but by that future time at which the war and her good fortune will end: "At night I dreamed that the war was over, that the people with real ability had returned, that I was scurrying like a mangy dog to the refuge of an unemployment bureau. I would wake up soaked with sweat, convince myself with a stammering voice that it was a nightmare, then fall asleep again" (339).[24] Although one would in no way wish to defend Leduc—in fact, one could argue that she literally begs to be condemned by the reader for her cowardice and complicity with the Nazis and Vichy—it seems important to point out that here again, as in the representation of the Parisian housewives doing their marketing, the relationship with Esther is initially idealized (however offensively) as one of mirroring, harmony, and intimacy. Leduc's attraction to Esther and subsequent break with her suggest something quite different than the total "detachment" mentioned by de Courtivron. It is in no way the case that Jews or Germans are missing from Leduc's narrative; it is, rather, that Leduc refuses to describe her responses to Nazism and Vichy policy in more heroic, and thus, more readable, or more palatable terms of resistance.

The most striking examples of Leduc's simultaneous distance from and investment in femininity and the lifestyle of the good French housewife occur during her marriage to Gabriel and her active work life—a life that encompassed both licit and illicit forms of labor. Although worried about money, Leduc was never better employed than during the war years and the Occupation. Because of the exodus from Paris in the early months of the Occupation, there was a great shortage in the publishing business, and with the help of Maurice Sachs, Leduc was asked to write several short pieces for a women's magazine (311).[25] All the while she hid her marriage, her married name, and her much coveted wedding band from Sachs and her employers so that she would appear to be a "self-sufficient woman": "Invincible celibacy, I had hidden my wedding ring in my handbag before going into the magazine office . . . A self-sufficient woman must be single . . ." (312). The tension between the illegitimate daughter and the disappointed wife is now complicated by an additional, less conventional role, that of the outwardly single woman, the woman who writes.

For her second assignment, rather than "fiction," Leduc is asked to write several editorial articles, a kind of self-help column and morale booster for women separated by the war from the men they love. In her attempts to reproduce kernels of "common sense" about women's daily lives, Leduc's distance from the categories of "woman" and "wife" becomes painfully, and hilariously, clear. Blocked in the writing of these self-help columns, Leduc remarks of her female audience: "I had to inspire them with good humour, strength of mind, energy and health. Using the materials of their day-to-day existence I was supposed to provide a firm foundation for the women on the home front . . . My double life began" (323-24). In her narrative of this tension, Leduc brilliantly stages the contrast between the model life of the cheery French housewife and her own inability to live up to the apparently simple advice she is dispensing. As Judith Butler has observed, "[t]he injunction to *be* a given gender takes place through discursive routes: to be a good mother, to be a heterosexually desirable object, to be a fit worker, in sum, to signify a multiplicity of guarantees in response to a variety of different demands all at once."[26] The following cropped passage will serve as an example of Leduc's cutting analysis of the multiple binds of gender and identity during a time of war:

> I wrote several editorials.
>
> Get up early, I told my readers. I used to get up at eleven, screaming for Gabriel's sex inside me . . . I like begging, I like asking for things, being given things, getting something for nothing. Oh God, yes, oh God how magnificent it was, my mendicancy as I lay weeping on Gabriel's bare feet in front of the sink . . .
>
> And, above all, get out on the right side of the bed, I told my readers.
>
> I didn't give a damn about the right side of the bed. Exhausted by my privations, I collapsed limply on our divan. My tear-spattered hair rained down on my cheeks . . . Gabriel gave way because he couldn't kill me. Then he tore himself away from the room . . .
>
> Don't waste time: see that you're in a good temper when you get up. Put on your boxing gloves and face your everyday routine, Mesdames, Mesdemoiselles. Your difficulties will fly away, I told my readers.
>
> If I got up at the same time as Gabriel it was to argue about the two francs for the electricity, the three francs for the gas, the one franc for the coal, the hundred francs for the rent . . . Bizarre rivals in rapacity. We both lied about our earnings . . .
>
> Strength of mind above all else. Tend your nerves as though they were a precious garden. A sound mind in a sound body, the Greeks used to say. Not a moment to lose, breathe in breathe out, window wide open as soon as you get up, I told my readers.
>
> (326-27)

Not surprisingly, Leduc goes on to explain that she wrote only a few editorial articles for women and that they were not accepted for publication because she lacked the appropriate point of view: "What I did was meaningless, abortive, rejected. I couldn't see things through the readers' eyes" (331). In spite of this disclaimer concerning her unacceptable "way of seeing," Leduc indeed knew the appropriate clichés for the occasion. In this reader's eyes, this extended and willfully graphic passage represents a virtuoso redeployment on Leduc's part of the insipid discourses of femininity so prevalent in women's publications during the war. By obsessively dwelling on her failures, Leduc discloses the performative nature of gender and places herself and her readers soundly inside the gap between publicly constructed discourses of femininity and our private struggles with these received models. Indeed, Leduc makes clear to her reader that wherever she is located, the act of being a "woman" (a good mother, a good wife, a fit worker) lies, necessarily, somewhere else.

As a writer for fashion magazines and "la page féminine" of newspapers, Leduc was working in a woman's world. At the same time, she found that she was perceived as a woman more than ever before in her movements through occupied Paris. This was an extremely new and charged situation for Leduc, as she had not previously experienced such attention paid to the fact of her sex. Under the gaze of police enforcing the curfew, Leduc tries to make her way home one night after covering a cabaret act for a magazine. Desperate to get home to Gabriel, Leduc is allowed to pass without the required "ausweis," simply by virtue of being (dressed like) a woman. The French police officers on patrol warn her, nonetheless, that the clicking of her high-heeled shoes will make it more difficult for her to pass through the streets unnoticed:

> "You can try your luck if you want," he said, "but it's dangerous. All that way in those heels . . ."
>
> "They make a noise," I said miserably.
>
> "I'll bet they do," he replied. "Ah, women, women . . ."
>
> (346)

Interestingly, many women of the Resistance linked their ability to outsmart the Occupation forces to their manipulation of the prevailing stereotypes of femininity. In order to conceal illicit documents or material, women often hid them in one of the many feminine accessories typical of the time—shopping bags, hand bags, sewing bags, cosmetic bags, baby carriages, even in tubes of lipstick.[27] Leduc drew heavily and eagerly on these stereotypes during her black-market days in order to avoid arrest. After making it past the street patrol on this occasion, Leduc repeats the phrase "les femmes, les femmes" to herself like a mantric password to ward off danger as she runs through the unlit streets in her high heels toward her husband and home.

It was, however, in order to escape from the utterly real disappointments of domestic life with Gabriel that Leduc turned to the other principal male figure in her life at the time, Maurice Sachs. When Leduc first met Sachs, he moved within a world of writers, artists, and intellectuals but was not yet known as a writer himself. During the 1930s, Sachs worked for a time as a reader for the Gallimard publishing house. Yet, throughout his life, Sachs was drawn to illicit financial deals, and during the war this criminal activity escalated with his involvement in the trading of black-market jewelry and the trafficking of Jewish refugees into the Unoccupied Zone. For a time, Sachs also served as an informer for the Gestapo, but he was soon compromised on both sides of the law and opted to flee Paris in the fall of 1942. Leduc had separated from Gabriel by this time, and she chose to accompany Sachs in his flight to Normandy.

During their stay in the small town of Anceins, Sachs completed his autobiography *Le Sabbat* (1946) and brought about Leduc's "coming to writing"[28] by encouraging her to record her childhood memories. In Leduc's version of this pivotal episode, Sachs, exasperated by her incessant talk and complaints, turned to her and said: "Your unhappy childhood is beginning to bore me to distraction. This afternoon you will take your basket, a pen, and an exercise book, and you will go and sit under an apple tree. Then you will write down all the things you tell me" (403-404). And in fact, vexed but obedient, Leduc began to write the childhood memories that became her first book, *L'Asphyxie* (1946).[29] By subsequently abandoning Leduc in Normandy—to the world of fabulation and self-recreation, if you will—Sachs also set the conditions for Leduc's finally taking herself in hand, although not in the predictable way she had encouraged other women to do in her editorials. Only after Sachs's departure did Leduc wholeheartedly undertake the black-market dealing at which she proved to be extremely successful.

. . . . .

After mysteriously volunteering for work in a German factory in November 1942, Sachs disappeared while there and was presumed dead in 1945.[30] From Germany, Sachs made a desperate and perverse request of Leduc that clearly "named her as a sex" and, more precisely, as the mother of his (nonexistent) child. Here, too, we have only Leduc's version of his note to interpret:

> My love,
>
> You tell me that you are pregnant and that things are going badly for you.
>
> Would you like me to come and see you, would you feel better if I were by your side? Please answer. I kiss you my darling.
>
> Maurice
>
> (437)

Leduc's initial reaction was euphoric: "The miracle had taken place. I had a homosexual at my feet" (437). Although she immediately recognized the letter's urgent undertones and Sachs's wish to return to France, Leduc was tempted by the thought that there may be some truth to Sachs's vows of tenderness, and easily procured from her doctor a medical certificate verifying a (false) pregnancy. She never sent it.

Leduc explains to the reader her anger at Sachs's knowing manipulation of wartime policies and of her affections in this way: "'My love,' a mockery. 'My darling,' a mockery . . . There was no doubt that to Maurice my heart and his sperm were mere commodities of trade. I threw the certificate into the fire" (438). In later letters, Sachs claimed to have "found a way around his difficulties" and to bear Leduc no grudge. In the postwar years, Leduc remained haunted by her decision, by her refusal to indulge Sachs's physical and psychological requests, and by her failure, quite possibly, to save his life. It was, of course, not Leduc's heart that Sachs desired.[31]

Significantly, an earlier rejection of Vichy's powerful maternal model had also marked the end of Leduc's marriage to Gabriel. Having become pregnant, Leduc did not want to carry the pregnancy to term, and she informed Gabriel of her "visits to the so-called midwives" (356). Although Gabriel was by now living separately from Leduc, he offered to help her raise the child. After weeks of waiting for the mysterious procedures of the "so-called midwives" to take effect, Leduc finally aborted in the fifth month of pregnancy. As those who have seen Claude Chabrol's affecting film *Une Affaire de femmes* (1989) are aware, abortion was considered an illegal procedure under Vichy law, punishable by death as a form of treason against the French State.[32] After this final abortion attempt, an infection caused Leduc to fall gravely ill; she entered a clinic for treatment, and upon her release, spent several months convalescing at her mother's home (357).

La Bâtarde closes in 1944 with the depiction of Leduc's euphoria during a long walk from Paris back to the village in Normandy, in which she feels at home with her black-market colleagues:

> I reflect: my wealth and beauty in the paths of Normandy lay in the efforts I made. I kept going until I had what I wanted: I was existing at last. I was succeeding, and my courage led me astray. I toiled and I forgot myself.
>
> (468)

Finally a "self-sufficient woman," she has found her place in this village and in this "profession," just as she will find her place in the autobiographical text whose writing she has now begun. In transporting food into Paris to wealthy acquaintances of Sachs, Leduc experienced moments of personal danger and triumph. She is, paradoxically, most at peace when in motion, most successful and socially integrated when purposefully living in the margins and able to "forget herself." In her determination to enter into public circulation, both as a black-market dealer and as a writer, Leduc did not choose the most common routes. During the Occupation, this marginal woman proves that she is a survivor, although in ways that are much less heroic than we might wish. Leduc is eventually at her best during these years, productive, successful, and momentarily content.

Leduc chose to delay representation of the end of the war and the Liberation until the second volume of her autobiography, *La Folie en tête* (1970). We read there that, just as she had feared, the Liberation was a dysphoric and disturbing experience. Obsessed by fears of bankruptcy, Leduc was arrested in Normandy during the last winter of the war and taken in for questioning concerning her black-market trafficking. During her interrogation, she discovered that her notoriety among the local police had earned her the criminal name of "Paris-Beurre."[33] In turn, the police wanted Leduc to reveal the names of the farmers who acted as her suppliers during the Occupation. Rather than risk further punishment herself, Leduc chose to denounce the very individuals whom she had come to consider her allies. The end of the war signaled, then, the end of Leduc's positive associations with her friends in Normandy, and the end of her financial success and happiness. As France moved toward the postwar era, Leduc was thrown back into alienation and despair, caught between liberated Paris and a Normandy village whose inhabitants would no longer tolerate her presence: "Paris had been liberated, but I hadn't been liberated from my lust for profit . . . Paris had been liberated, and I was torn between a village in Normandy that no longer wanted anything to do with me and a city in which I had no wish to rot."[34] Unable to imagine a persona for herself in a world seeking to restore gender and social relations to a semblance of prewar order, Leduc surrenders to the anomie that had governed her life before the Occupation.

Although *La Bâtarde* was itself the object of great scandal and critical attention at the time of its publication in 1964, in recent years it had fallen out of print altogether. It has now been reissued by Gallimard.[35] Recognized as a work of great literary merit by many, *La Bâtarde* was considered as a candidate for the Goncourt and Fémina prizes but was rejected by both juries. The reason given for this by the Goncourt jury was that since the book was not, after all, a novel, it was not a legitimate contender for the prize. (Questions of genre, however, did not prevent Marguerite Duras's "autobiographical novel" *L'Amant* from receiving the Goncourt Prize twenty years later, in 1984.)

Often dismissed as a sordid lesbian exposé, it is worth considering to what extent *La Bâtarde*'s representation of the Occupation disclosed perhaps even more dangerous aspects of a woman's participation in social life. Although marginal, lesbianism holds its attractions as a literary subject. However, Leduc's blatant confession in *La Bâtarde* of complacency, hypocrisy, anti-Semitism, political inaction, greed, and black-market collaboration during the Occupation move the work into extremely volatile territory. What is more, *La Bâtarde*'s euphoric ending can be seen as daring to recast the narrative of a failed life in the form of a collaborator's wartime success story. Clearly, there are deeply troubling aspects of this work that have remained closeted, although Leduc defiantly placed them in plain sight. Dealing with a moment that was and was not a war, produced by a writer who felt that she was and was not a woman, Leduc's *La Bâtarde* offers today's readers a strangely legitimate way of looking at the still controversial, unclassifiable war years in France.

Notes

1. Violette Leduc, *La Bâtarde,* trans. Derek Coltman (London: Virago Press, 1985), 339. The original French edition of *La Bâtarde* was published by Gallimard in 1964. Subsequent references to the Coltman translation appear within the text. I would like to thank the members of my Reno reading group, Kathleen Boardman, Stacy Burton, Martha Hildreth, and Gaye Simmons, for the careful and insightful attention they brought to this article in draft form.

2. Susan Gubar, "'This Is My Rifle, This Is My Gun': World War II and the Blitz on Women," *Behind the Lines: Gender and the Two World Wars,* ed. Margaret Randolph Higonnet, Jane Jenson, Sonya Michel, and Margaret Collins Weitz (New Haven: Yale University Press, 1987), 227-59.

3. Joan W Scott, "Rewriting History," in Ibid., 27.

4. Sarah Fishman, *We Will Wait: Wives of French Prisoners of War, 1940-1945* (New Haven: Yale University Press, 1992). Like Fishman, Pollard is a feminist historian of Vichy France. Pollard's call for the study of "less respectable" narratives, those which allow us to imagine more marginal women's tales, appears in her review of Fishman's valuable book, "Forgotten Women," *The Women's Review of Books* 10.2 (November 1992): 21-22.

5. This expression appears on page 304 of the original French text (Paris: Gallimard, 1964). It is inexplicably missing from the Coltman translation and I have thus used my own translation here. In the passage in question, Leduc follows a German soldier as he walks through the streets of Paris hand-in-hand with a young French girl: "Le boulevard des Capucines me montraient l'envers de la guerre. Un guerrier promenait une jeune fille" (304). This is Leduc's first sighting of "an enemy in the street," and, significantly, this encounter introduces the Occupation to her reader as a conventional wartime drama with sexual connotations, conquests, and consequences for French women in which Leduc, a marginal figure, neither young nor beautiful, often adopts the role of voyeur.

6. Denise Riley, "Some Peculiarities of Social Policy concerning Women in Wartime and Postwar Britain," *Behind the Lines,* 260.

7. Quoted in Michèle Bordeaux, "Femmes hors d'Etat français, 1940-1944," *Femmes et fascismes,* ed. Rita Thalmann (Paris: Tierce, 1986), 138: "La Révolution nationale est une réaction très virilement humaine à une république féminisée, une république de femmes ou d'invertis."

8. For further analysis of these terms as manipulated within Vichy discourse, see Michèle Bordeaux, 138-39.

9. Denise Riley, *"Am I That Name?": Feminism and the Category of "Women" in History* (Minneapolis: University of Minnesota Press, 1988), 2.

10. I borrow this phrase from Jacqueline Piatier's review of *La Bâtarde* in *Le Monde,* 10 Oct. 1964: 13.

11. Leduc's first work, *L'Asphyxie,* chronicles her unhappy childhood and her troubled relationship with her mother (Paris: Gallimard, 1946).

12. Beauvoir began writing her autobiography in 1957. *Mémoires d'une jeune fille rangée* dates from 1958, *La Force de l'âge* from 1960. She concluded *La Force des choses*, the third volume of her autobiography, in March 1963. This volume was followed by an account of her mother's death, *Une Mort très douce* (1964). The final volume of Beauvoir's autobiography, *Tout compte fait*, appeared in 1972. Beauvoir encouraged Leduc to write an autobiography after witnessing the relative lack of popular success of Leduc's earlier works. According to Isabelle de Courtivron, Leduc spent four years writing *La Bâtarde*, from 1958 to 1962. *Violette Leduc* (Boston: Twayne, 1985), 29.

13. J. Piatier, *Le Monde*, 30 May 1972: 28, as quoted by Pièr Girard in *Œdipe masqué* (Paris: des femmes, 1986), 18: "J'ai raconté ma vie comme elle est arrivée, mes livres, mes erreurs, mes désespoirs, en somme ma vie d'écrivain raté" (my translation).

14. For further discussion of the question of autobiography and self-representation in Leduc's work, see Michèle Respaut, "Femme/ange, femme/monstre: *L'Affamée* de Violette Leduc," *Stanford French Review* 73 (Winter 1983): 365-74; Isabelle de Courtivron's ground-breaking critical overview, *Violette Leduc*, and her subsequent exploration of Leduc's relationship in life and writing with Simone de Beauvoir, "From Bastard to Pilgrim: Rites and Writing for Madame," *Yale French Studies* 72 (1986): 133-48; Pièr Girard's *Œdipe masqué*, a psychoanalytic reading of *L'Affamée* (Paris: des femmes, 1986); Martha Noel Evans's important chapter on Leduc in her book on twentieth-century French women writers, "Violette Leduc: The Bastard," *Masks of Tradition* (Ithaca: Cornell University Press, 1987); Shirley Neuman's "'An appearance walking in a forest the sexes burn': Autobiography and the Construction of the Feminine Body," *Signature* 2 (Winter 1989): 1-26; Eileen Boyd Sivert, "Permeable Boundaries and the Mother-Function in *L'Asphyxie*," *Tulsa Studies in Women's Literature* 11.2 (Fall 1992): 289-307. More recently, *Nord'*, a journal devoted to the literature of Northern France, published a special issue on Leduc's life and writing: *Nord'* 23 (June 1994).

15. De Courtivron, *Violette Leduc*, 32.

16. In my work in progress, *Between the Lines: Women, Witnessing, and the Occupation of France*, a study of literary testimony to the war years by Colette, Violette Leduc, Simone de Beauvoir, Marguerite Duras, Charlotte Delbo, and Elsa Triolet.

17. The term "anti-memoir" is only appropriate to the extent that Leduc clearly does not say "the right things" about the Nazis, about her Jewish neighbors, or about the war in general. Her refusal to do so should not be interpreted as a bald-faced rejection of the genre of autobiography or memoir, but as a provocation to literary convention and to social and readerly expectations.

18. For information concerning Maurice Sachs, I am drawing on Leduc's portrayal of him in *La Bâtarde*; Henri Raczymow's biography, *Maurice Sachs* (Paris: Gallimard, 1988); and Isabelle de Courtivron, *Violette Leduc*, 2-4.

19. De Courtivron, *Violette Leduc*, 3.

20. Isabelle de Courtivron, "From Bastard to Pilgrim," 136.

21. Violette Leduc, *La Folie en tête*, 231 (as translated and quoted by de Courtivron, "From Bastard to Pilgrim," 136).

22. De Courtivron, "From Bastard to Pilgrim," 138.

23. The final section of Duras's *La Douleur* focuses on a recurring Durassian figure, Aurélia Steiner, a young Jewish girl who, in this version, observes the world from her hiding-place window (Paris: P.O.L., 1985). Earlier in the work, however, within the diary "La Douleur," the girl remains unnamed.

24. In the original French, this reads quite differently: "La nuit je rêvais que la guerre était finie, que les valeurs rentraient . . ." (349). Leduc's fear of a return of social and moral "values" that condemn her lesbianism and criminality is, of course, less offensive than her anti-Semitism and her related conflation of Jews, among the "people of ability" to whom she has previously referred, with wealth (339).

25. Although the magazine is not named in *La Bâtarde*, it is identified in a later work as *Pour Elle* (*La Folie en tête*, 107). Dominique Veillon notes, in *La Mode sous l'Occupation*, that *Pour Elle* was a weekly women's magazine founded in August 1940 (with the approval of the German authorities) that lasted until March 1942 (Paris: Payot, 1990), 48.

26. Judith Butler, *Gender Trouble: Feminism and the Subversion of Identity* (New York: Routledge, 1990), 145.

27. Guylaine Guidez, *Femmes dans la guerre* (Paris: Perrin, 1989), 219.

28. My use of the phrase "coming to writing" relies on Nancy K. Miller's elaboration of the scenarios through which a woman "authorizes" herself, not only as a writer, but as a female/feminist subjectivity negotiating within the social. Whereas Leduc's previous journalistic writing had started her on the road to her vocation, I place her "coming to writing" at this later moment in which she begins writing for (her own) good. See Miller's *Subject to Change* (New York: Columbia University Press, 1988), 16, 158 n.3.

29. The circumstances of this "coming to writing" somewhat resemble those of Colette, who, famously, began to write her schoolgirl memoirs at the behest of her husband, Willy. Lest we be misled by Leduc's indirection, it should be noted that, once begun, her career as a writer was undertaken seriously over the

next thirty years until her death in 1972, and certainly not simply to please Maurice Sachs (or later, Simone de Beauvoir). Leduc continued writing in spite of the lack of success of her books: *L'Asphyxie* (1946), *L'Affamée* (1948), *Ravages* (1955), *La Vieille fille et le mort* (1958), *Trésors à prendre* (1960). Beauvoir insists that Leduc was an extremely disciplined writer, in spite of her lack of acceptance and her recurrent bouts of mental illness. It was not until the publication of *La Bâtarde* in 1964, written under the sign of total failure, that Leduc was to gain true critical and popular success. None of her subsequent books came remotely close to matching the bestseller status of this first volume of her autobiography: *Thérèse et Isabelle* (1965), *La Femme au petit renard* (1966), *La Folie en tête* (1970, vol. 2), *Le Taxi* (1971), *La Chasse à l'amour* (1973, vol. 3; posthumous publication edited by Beauvoir).

30. See Raczymow for the details surrounding Sachs's decision to go to Germany and the circumstances of his death there.

31. This was not the first time that Sachs had proposed motherhood to Leduc He had, in fact, asked if she would like to have a baby with him earlier in the war, after the collapse of her marriage to Gabriel. Leduc was flattered, sickened, and tempted by his ambiguous proposition: "Did he want to make me a mother in order to save me? It's not impossible" (353-54). This offer was also rejected.

32. Chabrol's film is loosely based on the life of Marie-Louise Giraud, a black-market abortionist convicted of treason by Vichy and guillotined on 29 July 1943. Giraud was the last woman to be executed within the French penal system. For an important analysis of Chabrol's film, see Rosemarie Scullion, "Family Fictions and Reproductive Realities in Occupied France: Claude Chabrol's *Une Affaire de femmes*," *L'Esprit Créateur* 33.1 (Spring 1993): 85-103. Concerning Vichy and abortion laws, see Miranda Pollard, "*Femme, Famille, France*: Vichy and the Politics of Gender," Ph.D. diss., Trinity College, Dublin, 263-89. Before writing *La Bâtarde*, Leduc had described the life-threatening illness caused by the abortion in her novel *Ravages* (1955).

33. Leduc had published fashion articles during the war in *Paris-Soir*.

34. Violette Leduc, *Mad in Pursuit*, trans. Derek Coltman (New York: Farrar, Straus and Giroux, 1971), 14-15.

35. The Gallimard re-edition dates from 1988 It is currently available in the "Blanche" and "Folio" editions, thereby rendering it a more likely candidate for classroom use.

IDEOLOGY AND POLITICS

Kirsteen H. R. Anderson (essay date January 2001)

SOURCE: Anderson, Kirsteen H. R. "Imagination and Ideology: Ethical Tensions in Twentieth-Century French Writing." *Modern Language Review* 96 (January 2001): 47-60.

[*In the following essay, Anderson traces the development of the French ethical imagination in the twentieth century, noting that as the century progressed, French intellectuals moved away from forms of thought that were morally accountable to their historical and cultural context.*]

Four prophetic presences could be taken to represent stages in the development of the French ethical imagination in the course of the twentieth century. Valéry's Hamlet, questioning the very ground on which European intellectual identity stands and the precariousness of its continuing existence (*La Crise de l'Esprit,* 1919); Camus's Clamence, denouncing yet simultaneously affirming the guilt-ridden hypocrisy of European bourgeois consciousness (*La Chute,* 1956); Tournier's Ogre, poised on the Franco-German frontier as he sifts the debris of Nazi totalitarianism for any redeeming shards of meaning (*Le Roi des Aulnes,* 1970); and Irigaray's Antigone, appealing ironically for rebirth from beneath centuries of phallogocentric rubble (*Ce Sexe qui n'en est pas un,* 1977).

Under their aegis I shall examine the tendency for imagination, as a concept implying subjective agency and accountability, to lose ground, as the century advances, to forms of thought that are no longer morally accountable to their cultural and historical context. This shift can be linked with a transition that occurs between two main senses of the term 'ideology'. Early- to mid-century readings interpret ideology mainly in its neutral sense, as systems of thought or belief, or symbolic systems, relating to social action or political practice. Mid- to late-century readings tend to understand ideology critically, as a state of false consciousness, as meaning in the service of power and as misrepresentation of reality.[1] The best French fictional writing exploits the tension between these two senses, refusing to relinquish a concern with consciousness as necessarily implicated in and responsible for its environment. Much theoretical discourse, in contrast, prefers to interpret ideology in its distorting sense, thus surrendering very willingly to a view of human consciousness and agency as impaired or impotent. These opposing attitudes to the subject's ethical and historical responsibility may be referred to, in shorthand, as imagination and ideology.

I focus on those authors whom I judge among the most influential in the period under discussion, and on the texts which will, in my view, stand the test of time: André

Gide's *L'Immoraliste* (1902), Albert Camus's *L'Étranger* (1942), Marguerite Yourcenar's *Mémoires d'Hadrien* (1951), Jean-Paul Sartre's *Les Mots* (1963) and Michel Tournier's *Le Roi des Aulnes* (1970).[2] I read these authors as memorialists of twentieth-century creative subjectivity or historians of the vicissitudes of the imagination responding to its cultural environment. Their texts chart the progress of a *conscience malheureuse* in crisis. As modernism and postmodernism fulfil themselves, through technological advance, the rationalization of economy and aesthetics and the methodological dehumanization of war and production line, consciousness is seduced into escaping into the false security of its own alienation. The failure of myth as culturally meaningful gives rise to myth as duplicity. Theoretical works also have their part to play here: Roland Barthes's *Mythologies* (Paris: Seuil, 1957), Alain Robbe-Grillet's *Pour un nouveau roman* (Paris: Minuit, 1963) and Michel Foucault's various writings on power (in the 1970s and 1980s) are relevant.

In attempting a genealogy of the creative consciousness in its relation to power and knowledge I retain the term 'imagination' deliberately, despite its long and problematic history, for the value that it attributes to human consciousness.[3] Broadly speaking, it has been defined in terms of two main functions: as reproductive, it is capable of imitating and representing reality, as creative, it is able to interpret and transform experience. Imagination emerges from nineteenth-century practice and debate as a definable if embattled phenomenon, potentially empowering and still largely attributable to human agency. It slips from critical sight in the course of the twentieth century, increasingly obscured in the French tradition behind interpretations of consciousness as unconsciously or collectively determined.[4] The postmodern undermining of the humanist imagination, perhaps an inevitable consequence of the 'death of God', denies its Promethean value as affirmative of the creative power of individual subjectivity. Many of the functions once attributed to the imagination are usurped by ideology.

Paradoxically, Nietzsche's effect, at least on his French devotees, has not led to an extension of human imaginative potential once freed from the shackles of Christian mythology and ethics. Instead, and his role here is paramount, it has encouraged a surrender of moral agency to a series of ambiguous fetishes.[5] To be clear, I am not claiming, with due respect to Sartre, that all writers should be ethically or historically responsible. Yet, surveying the extent to which much recent French theorizing is obsessed with fantasies implying power and control, while simultaneously arguing a position of powerlessness or paralysis for human consciousness, a question remains unanswered: why attribute so much authority and value to language (Barthes), form (Robbe-Grillet), ideology (Althusser), *écriture* (Tel Quel), the Symbolic Order (Lacan), or power (Foucault), but deny them to the critical consciousness of individual human subjects who remain, in my view, agents of their experience, to some extent at least?[6]

The power associated with these pseudo-deities, or developed as thematic in the work of, say, Jean Baudrillard, Foucault or Paul Virilio, does not imply empowerment, responsibility or resistance on the part of the creative imagination: subjectivity features as either outmoded, as the pawn of forces which transcend it, or as a 'possessed' entity riddled with the energies of a virtual reality.[7] Are we, as readers in retrospect of the twentieth-century French tradition, to conclude that its theoreticians have served it well through texts which, respectful of the mimetic paradigm, replicate the progressive paralysis of the moral will and faculty for interpretative response, and an ethically derelict reality?[8] Alternatively, should we conclude that they have betrayed the potential of human agency's imaginative responsibility in succumbing so readily (in a Vichy of the mind this time) to the persuasions of the negative that recent and contemporary experience are all too willing to offer?

A connected question, in this context of responsibility and empowerment, is why a number of influential French intellectuals should have allowed themselves, since the mid-century, an interlude from ethical involvement. Their retreat into theoretical impunity comes at a critical moment for European consciousness and identity, whose very survival depend on clarification, insight and understanding.[9] Reviewing the theoretical stance of some of the leading critical minds from the 1950s to the 1980s, one is struck by their withdrawal into a solitary, even solipsistic, attitude of distance from the community or of condemnation of the human.[10] Barthes depicts himself as outside the *polis*, relegated to the loneliness of a self-imposed exile deriving from his excessive lucidity. Sarcasm is his only mode of relation with his fellow man (*Mythologies*, p. 245). Robbe-Grillet's final solution fantasizes the purification of the landscape, moral, psychological and aesthetic, of all contaminating human meaning ('Nature, Humanisme, Tragédie' (1958) in *Pour un nouveau roman*.) Foucault, more brazenly, proclaims the 'death of man' (what place post-Holocaust fantasies here?) whose only access to subject status is through subjectification by power/knowledge strategies whose ultimate victory is incontestable.

Surely the principal lesson of the defeat of the Nazis in 1945 was precisely that resistance to the misuse of power is worthwhile and can be effective. Germany could easily have slipped back into an attitude of politico-cultural resentment in the immediate post-war period. Yet it is Habermas and the Frankfurt School who offer a critique of Foucaldian theories of power and the concomitant disempowerment of human agency; and an appeal for a more responsible subjectivity grounded in a renewed understanding of post-Enlightenment reason in history.[11] The perverse rejection of Enlightenment values, characteristic of certain contemporary French thinkers, has rightly been questioned.[12] An attempted explanation of the periodic retreat of the French critical mind into self-subjugation to the irrational in its most totalitarian forms points to the demoralizing ethical legacy of the Third Republic (Judt, *Past Im-*

perfect, pp. 15-25). To plead that we are all victims of the postmodern predicament is not convincing. Denying the efficacy of any human action on, or engagement with, a recalcitrant environment seems unduly negative. An alternative response would be to arouse the imagination to its maximum potential in demanding of it some contribution to the challenges of the present. Fictional writing does this better, I suggest, by persisting in exploiting the tension between humanist and postmodernist value systems whereas much theoretical discourse 'sells out' too fast to the 'death of man' scenario.

The key distinction here is between a form of thought that values symbolic richness (imaginative writing) and one that approximates to the clarity of scientific logic and abstraction (theory). The opposition of the mythical and the historical consciousness provides a supporting paradigm. Both myth and history may be read as narratives and thus, also, though in differing degrees, as symbolic modes of expression. Yet modern Western consciousness prefers to define itself as historical only, and uniquely in the sense of being differentiated, by scientific knowledge and analytical thinking, from mythical or symbolic thought, which is capable of synthesis and relates to archetypal configurations.[13] If imagination is taken as a metaphor for the condition of creativity then its relative eclipse in contemporary culture and philosophy is not surprising (Robinson and Rundell, *Rethinking Imagination,* p. 11). The predominance of structures of abstract thought which lack any connection to the lived reality of human experience is increasingly recognized as one of the regrettable by-products of a technology-driven culture of commodified consciousness. Similarly, so much of postmodern theory restricts itself uncourageously to the surface as though afraid to look deeper where meaning may also be found.[14] Parody and pastiche allow us to mark time but it is becoming urgent to move forward in cultural awareness rather than simply to repeat.[15]

Each of the fictional texts selected implies a burial or repression whether literal or metaphorical: of the old Adam (*L'Immoraliste*), of the mother (*L'Étranger*), of the child Poulou (*Les Mots*), of Antinoüs (*Mémoires d'Hadrien*), of Tiffauges alongside the Erl King (*Le Roi des Aulnes*). Each intuits that the depths contain value, should Western culture possess the means to decipher and recover it as meaning-bearing and not simply unconscious fantasy. Perhaps the step beyond our present postmodern predicament requires the resurrection of that buried other which contemporary thought thematizes variously as the expression of the body alienated in scientific discourse; as the image driven into disrepute by its misinterpretation in empiricist theories of knowledge; as creativity marginalized by predominantly rationalist, 'masculine' modes of consciousness, or as the murdered mother on whom patriarchal imperialism stands.[16] Evoking the same problem in different terms, perhaps Western culture must learn to see 'myth' and 'history' as complementary, not exclusive, ways of thinking; as, equally, narratives expressing the psychological or fantasy dimension of a culture. To restore cultural fertility demands a work of reintegration. We have to conceive of truth as embracing more than the strictly rational, and of power as empowerment rather than violence.

A partial gauge of the balance between imaginative empowerment and ideological impairment is the diminishing significance of guilt as a theme. The transition from imagination to ideology is accompanied, and perhaps in part accounted for, by the shift from a guilty (because responsible) consciousness, to a passive (because ethically drained) one. Such an emancipation of 'la conscience malheureuse' may be cause for rejoicing but is also a matter for concern: guilt at least indicates awareness of the other. Its disappearance from narrative and theoretical discourse is suggestive.[17] The loss of this significant other may have revealing gender implications. Imagination, unlike ideology, implies participant subjectivities: the subject defines itself in relation to an/the other. Perhaps the withdrawal of much masculine creative and theoretical vision into an attitude of megalomaniac power or abstraction is a response to an acute sense of infantile fear and rage at its vulnerability to its environment. Unable effectively to negotiate with the other, whether as human subjectivity, natural world or death, it tries to assert its control, over a context that it can neither understand nor master, by means of power envisaged as violence. When this strategy fails, it surrenders all responsibility for its context.[18]

Existentialism has no part in my discussion although it can be read as one of the last attempts at a secular ethics that the French tradition has offered. As generated in the 1930s and 1940s by De Beauvoir and Sartre, it was indeed an imaginative response to the demands of the other in a precise and extreme historical situation. It proffered a valid if arduous ideal in its vision of an individualized ethics. Its driving force was undoubtedly guilt as the obverse of responsibility. Yet I discount it for two reasons. Firstly, the fiction that it produced belongs too obviously to the *roman à thèse* category.[19] Secondly, it seems to me that Sartre abandoned the demands of his ideal (as too utopian or too demanding?) preferring the illusory promise of control over reality that reason, as encountered in Marxist theory, seemed to offer. He rejected negotiation with his context in favour of fantasies of power. He never completed his project for an ethics: much of the rest of his productive career was spent wrestling with the abstractions of the dialectic.[20] From an early and valid perception of the need for a consciousness rooted in ethics and of the potential of myth as having positive connotations, he moves to a reductive view of myth as history-induced alienation.

L'Immoraliste depicts an individual crisis, symptomatic of the crisis of European identity and of the ethical imagination assumed to be part of it. Nourished by humanist culture, alive to the resonances and implications of its history and myths, Michel fantasizes liberation from the burden of conscience and consciousness that this entails. The force of the text derives from the modernist dichotomy that inhabits it. It attempts, on the one hand, to restrain the protagonist within the stability of control—of his appetites, his intellectual allegiances, his physical and psychological potential, his narrative stance. Yet it reveals, on the other hand, the overwhelming attraction of the thrust to destroy all that structures his life—past, memory, culture. Power as authority rests exclusively with the male narrator: economically, intellectually and sexually, Michel dictates the course of events. This power is manifested principally as violence: in the wilful destruction of his earlier cultured self, of his material possessions, of his wife's health and life, and of his moral and spiritual integrity.

Yet, although it anticipates the bleak horizon of postmodernism's insights, the depiction of imaginative consciousness in *L'Immoraliste,* still infused with the memory if not the plenitude of myth, remains suspended between an attraction to ethical norms and surrender to nihilism. Its anchoring within an explicitly ethical problem provides the counterpoise to the lure of ideology: Michel voices the seductive influence of Nietzsche, Ménalque proposes a proto-existentialist ethic, Marceline pleads the cause of an averagely enfeebled human being. However ironically disguised, the text's lesson is clear. Michel's confession of masculine power's systematic destruction of the feminine other and of its own worth, although implicitly punctuated by the disingenuous querying of his own responsibility, calls unambiguously, by its very tone and structure, for moral judgment.

A number of fleeting and ambiguous images encapsulate the tension between plenitude and dereliction: the self as palimpsest, bearer of undeciphered potential; the attempted glory of baptism in the living water which somehow fails to purify; the desert as site of reduction and annihilation or purification and rebirth. Michel as moral agent may already have 'passed out of the major order and symmetries of Western civilisation' at the close of the narrative,[21] yet, and Steiner on the sinews of language as binding European culture into a recognizable continuity is valid here (pp. 87-88), the grip of his linguistic imagination has not faltered. (Contrast the bereftness and deficiency of Camus's *renégat* some fifty years later).

Forty years after *L'Immoraliste,* with the transition to Meursault's 'ce n'est pas de ma faute', the balance between individual agency and powerlessness is significantly altered. Meursault, already conveniently stripped of a European consciousness or humanist inheritance, pursuing Nietzschean logic through to its post-Gidean conclusion, succeeds Michel in the sands of North Africa. Like the latter, he wields the power of life and death. Comprehending his homelessness, for the condition of the absurd mind is to be deprived of the solace of contact with meaning, memory, others, continuity, he turns to violence. Perhaps the imagination has endured too much under the onslaught of its relegation to the present, of the inevitability of death and of the withdrawal of God. The pain of this mutilated consciousness rebuts comforting promises of lucidity, empowerment and creative transformation. Camus's own plea for the humanist imagination, 'il faut imaginer Sisyphe heureux', and his conviction of the urgent need for a myth appropriate to the contemporary moment are both admirable and implausible.[22] Yet *L'Étranger* as moral fable warns of the void deriving from existence unsupported by myth.

As Meursault loses control of any shape and purpose which his life might once have had while his mother was alive, he resorts to the only power he retains in an effort to overcome the fearful sense of vulnerability which abandonment to independent and unprotected existence induces. Masculine consciousness, simultaneously deprived of and rejecting its feminine other, reacts with violence: a violence of the sensibility which prevents him imagining Marie fully as empathetic other, perceiving her only as a means of punctual sexual satisfaction; violation of his own ethical being in his adoption of indifference, and violence at its most brutal in the climactic destruction of the Arab other which leads to his own execution and so to the abolition of the very possibility of imaginative or ethical agency. Meursault is as spiritually dead as Michel: there is no creative revolt in him. Yet Camus does not present him as entirely the pawn of linguistic terror (in contrast to Barthes's depiction of Dominici and Dupriez in *Mythologies*). Meursault constructs his narrative with a minimal but highly effective rhetoric. Linguistic cohesion, if not conventional meaning, still matters. Perhaps his imprisonment, a nourishing return to a foetal state of private and protected existence, has enabled him to resurrect, however briefly, the vestiges, if not the humanist core, of self. Thus *L'Étranger,* though to a lesser degree than *L'Immoraliste,* evokes a lingering remnant of linguistic if not moral empowerment.

Language and the linguistic imagination are important in the genealogy of the ideologized consciousness. In the 1930s and 1940s Camus and Sartre, amongst others, searching for a creative idiom that would be culturally and ethically empowering to contemporary society, focused on the possibility of reinventing myth, although their attempt was abandoned.[23] The evacuation of subjective responsibility for moral and historical involvement, discernible in some theoretical writing from the 1950s onwards, can be traced to the deification of language as successor to this dead myth: Barthes's vision of salvation through structure, which increasingly diverts him from the ethical difficulties encountered in relation to the linguistic sign; Robbe-Grillet's conception of a uniquely self-referential literary text functioning autonomously once unharnessed from the awkward complexities of authorial subjectivity; Tel Quel's proposal of a supposedly neutral 'textual production' to replace an inevitably ideological 'representation'; all these approaches operate by simultaneously advocating the power of creativity (as, for example, *écriture, forme, langage*) yet refusing to accept responsibility for it, to attribute it to an originating consciousness.

This ambiguous stance is questionable, possibly dangerous. It can be partially explained, if not justified, by the historical context: the fear of taking responsibility for conveying meaning in case it is the 'wrong' one may stem from the difficulties of making the 'right' choices during the war period, when only hindsight would reveal the 'truth' of right or wrong. Interpreting their stance more benignly, the fetishization of language may express an unconscious desire to retain the notion of value by attributing it to some force or presence in culture, while rescuing it from the ambiguities which arise if it is associated with human subjectivity.[24]

The question of value leads to two fictional texts exploiting the cultural problem of this same immediately postwar period: *Mémoires d'Hadrien* and *Les Mots* can be read as alternative models of imaginative response to the ethical and historical challenges facing the mid-century European consciousness. Yourcenar's text, so far removed in its classical serenity from contemporary taste, is often excluded from critical discussion on the grounds of its alleged post-colonial nostalgia for Empire, its vanished ideal of humanist self-confidence and its overtones of moral rearmament. It can be superficially sidelined as a utopian response to the urgency of postwar reconstruction of Europe ('Avoir vécu dans un monde qui se défait m'enseignait l'importance du Prince', *Carnet de notes* in *Mémoires d'Hadrien*, p. 329). Sartre's text, in contrast, chimes more satisfyingly with current critical canons in its narrative disruption, irony and overriding relativism. However, in any attempt to reinvigorate the imagination as an ethically empowering force, the real challenge and harder option may require a reassessment of the potential of the values to be found in Europe's past. It is perhaps precisely Hadrian's pre-Nietzschean secular morality, which, in providing an alternative to twentieth century atheisms, can offer the West a *ressourcement* drawing on, though not identical to, the Classical vision.[25]

To use the past in this way is not necessarily proof of the closure of the historical mind.[26] Such a judgment sees myth and history as oppositional. Yourcenar's interpretation of Hadrian, as an embodiment of power relevant to contemporary needs, can serve as a positive paradigm to twentieth-century historical consciousness, which stands in sharp contrast to the retreat into irony of Sartre's essentially nineteenth-century depiction.[27] So much unites yet separates these virtually contemporaneous fantasies of the subject in history. Two male narrators take stock of their lives in fictional memoirs (Hadrian) and fictionalized autobiography (Sartre). Yet the respective titles are already indicative of the contrasts I shall explore: memory, and the continuity of subjectivity and narrative, are paramount for Hadrian; language, as our defining though deceptive reality, for Sartre. Both are exemplars of a European identity, humanist versus postmodernist, yet are distinctively divided by their purpose and tone. Both meditate on power, the one within an expansionist reach towards the world of action, the other retreating into the apparent safety, yet ultimate suffocation, of self-condemning, word-based solipsism. Both are concerned with the possibility and meaning of freedom, one integrated realistically in the historical fabric of his era, the other at an uncomfortable remove from his contemporary moment.

What distinguishes them most profoundly is the fundamental difference in attitude of Yourcenar and Sartre towards the role of the creative imagination, in its relation to its context and to myth. The former conceives the value of imaginative empathy as enabling the subject in time to extend her understanding beyond the limitations of the now, towards the vitally enriching perspective of a past that inevitably informs the present. The latter, distrustful of imagination's powers, rationalizes it to the point of annihilation, criticising it both as a source of literature's enchantment and as an origin of ideology's nefarious influence. Hadrian, classically engendered, harmoniously structured as narrator, recalls his life-journey in the frame of the overarching metaphor of construction. Belief in the metanarrative still holds: the governing sense of his account is of a steady 'réalisation de soi', viewed spiritually as well as intellectually and psychologically, within the framework of the significance and expansion of the Roman Empire. Stability, strength, order, and endurance are qualities shared by man and Imperial domain. Hadrian's vision of existence, as worth deriving purpose from and endowing with meaning, is offered, by implication, as exemplary. He is not naive about the internal divisions and external disasters that mar the self's progress, but the mode of consciousness animating his beliefs, action and speech retains a basis in myth as valid.[28] His relation to both experience and language is one of *fiducia*. Power in its various manifestations, physical, cultural, spiritual, is shown as a balancing between success and failure. As an ideal of perfectibility and individual responsibility for self-creation, nothing could be further removed from Hadrian's self-portrait than the Sartrean formulation of subjectivity.

Poulou/Sartre, ironically self-defensive, flees reader and self in a prolonged game of stylistic sophistication and ontological sleight of hand. Progressively demolishing any ground on which his subjectivity might once have tried to stand, he refuses all myths of stability, certainty, security (family, childhood, reading, religion), and lies stranded at the close of his story in that uncertain no-man's land between past and present, success and failure, life and death. There is little to suggest any harnessing of ethical or spiritual potential in the uncreative environment depicted in *Les Mots*. Power in a variety of forms has shaped and produced the protagonist as a subject in the manner of Foucault: familial tradition, language, history as bourgeois ideology in nineteenth-century mould, are presented as delusory influences alienating the self from an implied 'truer' way of being. The Marxist metaphor of ideological inversion so fatally informs the narrative that even the potentially joyful energy of the linguistic imagination is transformed, in Sartre's masochistic fantasy, into a contaminating influence from which he can never free himself. Behind its ironic deflections *Les Mots,* with its revelation that neither imagination dethroned, nor ideology as *mythe* laid bare, can offer plenitude or solace, portrays a subjectivity filled with pain and deprived of forgiveness. Yet this is its strength: it emphasises the spiritual vacuum attendant on the destruction of the idols. Behind its postmodern wrappings *Les Mots* recounts the fall from an imaginative paradise into the disillusions of reality as myth, 'une énorme puissance collective' (p. 208).

One proposal to emerge from current efforts to generate a new role for the imagination suggests rethinking the relation between utopia and ideology. Instead of viewing them as oppositional imaginative practices, as in Sartre's text, Paul Ricœur argues that they could be thought of together, in their constructive, healthy aspect, as related figures of false consciousness.[29] These two poles are illustrated in the dramatic transition from the existentialist outlook of the 1940s and early 1950s, with its humanistic concept of self and of responsibility for experience, to Barthes's *Mythologies,* where a cynical analyst of mythical lies abandons his contemporary cultural wasteland as beyond redemption. For a new understanding of imagination to emerge, what belongs to myth, in its validating sense, may have to be brought back within the cognitive tradition of French thought which, thus far, has defined culturally valid knowledge almost exclusively in terms of a particular form of rationality.[30] Myth, in its most recent French forms, is almost exclusively negative in connotation.[31] A significant inflexion of its meaning, bending it towards the untrustworthy sense of political myth that Barthes will give it, comes in De Beauvoir's *Le Deuxième sexe* (2 vols Paris: Gallimard, 1949 and 1976). Starting from a neutral definition, 'Tout mythe implique un Sujet qui projette ses espoirs et ses craintes vers un ciel transcendant' (I, 235), she then develops a more political interpretation of myth as serving the interests of a specific social group ('le mythe s'explique en grande partie par l'usage que l'homme en fait' (I, 391) and 'les femmes ne se posant pas comme sujet [. . .] c'est encore à travers les rêves des hommes qu'elles rêvent' (I, 235). Women's alienation is demonstrated by the way in which they live out the projections which culture/men require of them. Myth has shifted closer to ideology as misrepresentation here, insofar as it is no longer the locus of values, serving an exemplary function for culture as a whole, but has instead become the expression of vested power interests.

Barthes's subsequent theory of myth develops further its ideological status as distortion of reality. In contrast to the purpose of De Beauvoir's critique of masculine myth, to stimulate women's critical reaction, on the assumption that they are capable of refusing collusion with patriarchal oppression by determining their own subjective agency, consciousness in consumer society according to Barthes is already ideologized beyond recall. *Mythologies* depicts its commodification as symptomatic of the postmodern condition. Imagination is never mentioned as such, though myth is defined, in implicit acknowledgement of Sartrean existentialism, as 'l'imaginaire de la mauvaise foi'. This can be nothing but a nostalgically decorative nod in the direction of ethical awareness since the individual consciousness, swamped by collective delusion, is stripped of all access to its constituent function as imagination. In Barthes's conception of culture as a mass of deluded consumers deprived of the capacity for self-analysis or ethical insight, there is no explicit acknowledgement of this crucial shift from an ethically empowered critical imagination to the collective anaesthetization of the fascinated consciousness.[32] Some critics interpret Barthes's myth-reading methodology as proof that his concern is with resistance to the paralysing effect of ideology.[33] Yet his depiction of the universalizing tendency of mystification, and his later admission that semioclasm is the only way to break its hold, permit the reader to doubt.[34]

Barthes's debased, or reductively political, variety of myth may be all that contemporary society is able to produce.[35] Assessing the multiple exclusions which afflict the mythologist (from politics, culture, history, the real), he faces an ethical impasse: 'ou bien, poser un réel entièrement perméable à l'histoire, et idéologiser; ou bien, à l'inverse, poser un réel finalement impénétrable, irréductible, et, dans ce cas, poétiser' (*Mythologies,* p. 247). It is perhaps impossible and undesirable to resurrect myth as culturally viable particularly in the light of the dubious applications of mythical thought in recent times. It may be that imaginative replenishment must come about in other ways. In the concluding section I shall argue that recent theories of metaphor, on the one hand, and new interpretations of rationality on the other, can perhaps point in the direction of an ethically and historically responsible consciousness to replace Western culture's problematic mythical inheritance. Tournier's fiction and Foucault's discourse on power provide a fertile context for assessing the risks and challenges of such a project.

Foucault's explicitly Nietzschean genealogies date from the 1970s; *Le Roi des Aulnes,* the most Germanocentric and Nietzschean in tonality of Tournier's texts, was published in 1970. Both writers lived in Germany, absorbed its cultural atmosphere and brought its intellectual influence to bear through their writings. As theorist and as novelist of postmodern subjectivity, each abstains from offering ethical guidance. Yet Tournier's dependence on the multivalency of literary symbolism inevitably engages the reader critically in contrast to the diminished role of individual subjectivity implied by Foucault's political and cultural pessimism. The undisputed impact of Tournier's writing derives largely from the resonance of his imagery and the cogency of his imaginative structures; his fictions are splendid proof of the semantic and iconic enhancement advocated by Ricœur as a means of extending imagination's reach into uncharted territory. The imaginative and historical consciousnesses are not, in the latter's view, separate but interdependent. The semantic innovation characteristic of metaphorical uses of language not only enhances our perception of experience by rendering it more vivid, it also opens up subjectivity to its context, whether as relatedness to the other or as interaction with history: 'The possibility of an historical experience in general lies in our ability to remain open to the effects of history [. . .]. We are affected by the effects of history, however, only to the extent that we are able to increase our capacity to be affected in this way. The imagination is the secret of this competence' (Robinson and Rundell, *Rethinking Imagination,* p. 129).

Tournier's texts hover between a postmodernist tendency to generate autonomously self-referential systems which, though symbolically rich, lack any consistent and convincing correspondence with reality, and an attitude of critique of just such an evacuated symbolism. This ambivalence can be read as a reminder of the responsibility which inventing new meaning for culture entails. His treatment of myth, power and history in *Le Roi des Aulnes* suggests that he is critical of their potential for misinterpretation; the text's openness to interpretation leaves scope for the reader's critical imagination. *Le Roi des Aulnes*, like *Mythologies*, can be read as a contemporary fable warning, by negative example, of the vital importance of interpreting accurately the signs of our culture, of selecting the 'right' myths by which to lead our lives, on pain of death. Tournier, like Yourcenar, selects a significant moment from Europe's past (the German Reich replaces the Roman Empire) to reveal, in striking counterpoint to Hadrian's validation of myth-empowered subjectivity, the disastrous effects of misunderstanding and abusing myth and symbolism. Blindness, not insight, characterize Tiffauges in his clumsy postmodern deciphering of his historical moment. Lacking the suppleness of the 'savage' or truly mythic mind, he is incapable of creative *bricolage*. His symptomatic borrowing of bits and pieces of inherited myth reveals the disempowered state of the contemporary consciousness, unable to synthesize the fragments of its experience.[36] Personal delusion and cultural catastrophe are the inevitable outcome of this untutored and undigested manipulation of structures of meaning whose subtlety and relevance elude him. Tournier experiments here with the possibility of myth providing nourishment, insight and value, yet, ultimately, seems to offer a powerful denunciation of the uselessness, and the danger to our contemporary predicament, of turning to 'broken' or unintegrated myth.

Tiffauges's fascinated consciousness, disempowered by the 'logic' of systems of meaning that transcend his grasp, cannot achieve a critical distance from experience. The unanchored symbolism of the Reich which, in a crucial passage in the text (pp. 320-24) is revealed as highly dangerous, can be interpreted on at least two levels: as the danger which follows when any sign is fetishized for its own internal logic; or as the risks incurred by any ideology, unharnessed from experience and released into abstraction. Both point to the cultural catastrophe which is inevitable when power, cut loose from responsible human agency, degenerates into terror. Though Tournier's retreat from history has been questioned, I would argue that, at least in this text, it serves a valuable purpose in universalizing the symbolic implications of his critique (similar to Camus's technique in *La Peste*).[37] Though the focus here is on ideology in one of its crudest forms as fascist or Nazi, the text is targeting by extension all such abuses of intelligence. Tournier may plead the aesthetic logic of the narrative to account for the impalement of the three boys, but the text does at least show how that logic leads to apocalypse as the outcome of irresponsible systematizing.[38]

The contrast with Foucault is revealing. His genealogies offer a critique of power in contemporary society. This is valid but problematic. Criticism implies truth-value, an issue that Foucault refuses to confront squarely. His writing thus embodies a fundamental contradiction: his depiction of power, though valuable in many respects, presents subjectivity as the product of power/knowledge strategies, yet argues for his own discourse some redemptive authority deriving from its freedom from such strategies.[39] Most major criticisms of his stance indicate how his sceptical freedom, detached irony and refusal to provide a positive characterization of the ethico-political position informing his critique lay it open to the 'danger of becoming empty—or, even worse, of withholding judgment from those catastrophic possibilities which have erupted or can erupt' (Bernstein, *New Constellation*, pp. 62-63). His vision of all-pervasive power resembles its representation in *Le Roi des Aulnes* as free-floating, dangerously detached from individual agency.

As a specific intellectual with some cultural authority, as he recognizes, his evasive stance is hard to justify. It is of a piece that his only contribution to ethics constitutes a retreat into aesthetics: his late interest in the self is essentially a rewriting of the Baudelairean dandy.[40] His ethics show no concern for the other as engaging responsibility. Tiffauges's obsessive concern with constructing a 'meaningful' self may be interpreted as a similar aestheticization of existence, yet Tournier's fictions at least offer the expression of a range of viewpoints. Foucault's discourse provides little potential for dialogue or diversity of interpretation: the reader is trapped within the monotone of an unchallenged 'reasoning' reminiscent of Camus's penitent judge or renegade priest.

Both these 'narratives' of postmodern subjectivity highlight Habermas's contention concerning the pathologies of modernity. If we are to move beyond a conception of reason as narrowly instrumental, a view which he criticizes as leading to the dehumanizing excesses of contemporary technocratic culture, then we must rethink the problem of rationality (Bernstein, *New Constellation*, p. 204). This, arguably, is what Foucault fails to do: though virulent in undermining Enlightenment reason, his conception of essentially victimized subjectivity (resistance occupies a limited place in his vision) provides no convincing alternative. Habermas's suspicion of some of the major trends in recent French intellectual life is understandable. Yet where theory speaks of closure, imaginative writing promises openness. Tournier's fictions suggest that the project of searching for better alternatives is worthwhile, just as Habermas emphasises that modernity is still an unfinished project. Tiffauges dies yet the child he fathers hints at a future that has yet to be imagined.

A new conception and practice of reason, integrated with rather than opposed to, imagination (and ironically it was Foucault who unearthed the damaging exclusions of this sort which undermine Western thought) could try to remain open to the other, to its own otherness. Both the French and the German traditions point in this direction. Ricœur's substantive reason giving way to procedural reason, or Habermas's instrumental rationality surrendering to dialogical rationality, both emphasize the cultural benefits of leaving behind an idea of reason as embodied in a world order, preferring a project of reason accomplished in intersubjective performance. Perhaps it was important that imagination should be dethroned, dusted and reflected upon. It may now be time to reinstate, if not imagination as it was once known, then at least a contemporary equivalent. Rather than juxtaposing fiction and theory, myth and history, unreason and reason in hostile tension, it could bring them into some kind of more fertile alignment. It is perhaps only in this way that an effective ethical consciousness, for which there can be no power without responsibility, can come into being.[41]

Notes

1. For definitions see Terry Eagleton, *Ideology: an introduction* (London: Verso, 1991) and John B. Thompson, *Ideology and Modern Culture: Critical Social Theory in the Era of Mass Communication* (Cambridge: Polity Press, 1990).

2. For the purposes of this article the editions referred to are: *L'Immoraliste* (Paris: Gallimard Folio, 1972); *L'Étranger* (Paris: Gallimard Folio, undated); *Mémoires d'Hadrien* (Paris: Gallimard Folio, 1974); *Les Mots*, ed by David Nott (London: Methuen, 1981); *Le Roi des Aulnes* (Paris: Gallimard Folio, 1976).

3. Key studies of the imagination include: Denis Donoghue, *The Sovereign Ghost: Studies in Imagination* (London: Faber & Faber, 1976); Richard Kearney, *The Wake of Imagination. Ideas of Creativity in Western Culture* (London: Hutchinson, 1988); Mary Warnock, *Imagination* (London: Faber & Faber, 1976).

4. The concept of the imaginary, with the increasing significance which it accords to the unconscious, occupies an ever more important position here. Developing out of the work of Gaston Bachelard and Sartre, it is central to Lacan and receives perhaps its most extensive recent theorization in the writings of Cornelius Castoriadis. For a range of perspectives on the future of the imagination, particularly concerning contemporary transformations of the concept of reason, see *Rethinking Imagination: Culture and Creativity*, ed. by Gillian Robinson and John Rundell (London: Routledge, 1994).

5. J. M. Cocking in *Imagination. A Study in the History of Ideas* (London: Routledge, 1991) identifies Nietzsche's *The Birth of Tragedy* as the greatest seminal influence on French theories of the imagination with his distinguishing of the conceptual language of knowledge from the imaginative language of fantasy (p. 76). Cocking argues, however, for imagination not separated from the logical and empirical.

6. Frank Füredi situates this passivity in the context of the current Western ethical and political crisis: anxiety about the future; nostalgic idealization of the past; the lack of any plausible vision of the common good as basis for a new consensus, and positive identification with society; the denigration of reason: all lead to a devaluation of consciousness as in charge of its destiny (*Mythical Past, Elusive Future. History and Society in an Anxious Age,* London: Pluto Press, 1992)

7. Arthur Kroker, *The Possessed Individual: Technology and Postmodernity* (London: Macmillan, 1992).

8. See Kearney's three paradigms in *The Wake of Imagination*: the Classical productive imagination, the Romantic mimetic imagination and the postmodern parodic imagination.

9. Julien Benda at least had the merit of identifying the importance of intellectual responsibility (*La Trahison des clercs,* 1927). More recently, the accountability to culture of the intellectual community in general has been a topic of concern: *The Political Responsibility of Intellectuals,* ed. by Ian Maclean and Alan Montefiori (Cambridge: Cambridge University Press, 1990). More specifically, reputable scholarship has revealed the recurrent attraction to the French mind of terrorist thought or totalitarian systematising which divorces reason and intellect from responsibly critical views of reality and moral answerability: Tony Judt, *Past Imperfect: French Intellectuals, 1944-1956* (Berkeley and Oxford: University of California Press, 1992); Christopher Norris, *Uncritical Theory. Postmodernism, Intellectuals and the Gulf War* (London: Lawrence & Wishart, 1992).

10. Nietzsche's exaltation of the exceptional individual is difficult to fit into any humanist ethical system: 'The Birth of Tragedy lays down the pattern of intellectual exploration by which the lone figure, removed from the human community and its ethical rules, is the privileged example of the philosopher' (Nicholas Hewitt, *Les Maladies du Siècle: The Image of Malaise in French Fiction and Thought in the Inter-War Years,* (Hull: Hull University Press, 1988) p. 68.

11. Jürgen Habermas, *The Philosophical Discourse of Modernity: Twelve Lectures,* trans. by Frederick Lawrence, Lectures 10 and 11, pp. 266-93 and 294-326 (Cambridge: Polity Press, 1987).

12. Terry Eagleton, *The Ideology of the Aesthetic* (Oxford: Blackwell, 1990), p. 396.

13. *Myth and the Crisis of Historical Consciousness,* ed. by Lee W. Gibbs and W. Taylor Stevenson (Scholars' Press, American Academy of Religion, 1975).

14. I discount the unconscious here on the grounds that, 'scientifically' legitimized by Freud, it has become a convenient but not always enlightening 'catch-all' term enabling us to avoid the necessity and difficulty of creating meaning.

15. A number of critics point in this direction: Zygmunt Bauman, *Postmodern Ethics* (Oxford: Blackwell, 1993); Richard Bernstein, *New Constellation: the*

ethical-political horizons of modernity/postmodernity (Cambridge: Polity Press, 1991); Christopher Norris, *Reclaiming Truth: contribution to a critique of cultural relativism* (London: Lawrence & Wishart, 1996).

16. It is worth noting that in Destutt de Tracy's coining of the term 'ideology' as, literally, the 'science of ideas', sensations, in other words the body, were a significant part of the equation (Thompson, *Ideology and the Modern Culture,* p. 30). See Eagleton's review of Western rationality as requiring reconnection with its somatic aspect through the aesthetic (*The Ideology of the Aesthetic*). Matricide is important in the ethics of Luce Irigaray and Julia Kristeva.

17. Judt notes that French thought, in following the worst of the Nietzschean heritage and opting for reason in its more totalitarian forms, lost a more moderate ethical vision to the States: 'Much central European (and Jewish) social and ethical theory went to the USA in exile—leaving France with Hegel, Nietzsche and Heidegger' (*Past Imperfect,* p. 77). Noteworthy here as a lost influence is Emmanuel Levinas whose concern for the other as the only valid basis for ethics is now being recovered.

18. The feminine vision, in contrast, apparently more attentive to otherness as inevitably part of human experience, maintains a negotiatory dialogue with the world. Irigaray attributes this sensitivity to the metaphorical as well as literal implications of the female organism's capacity to tolerate the other within itself during intercourse and pregnancy.

19. Susan Suleiman's *Authoritarian Fictions: the Ideological Novel as a Literary Genre* (New York: Columbia University Press, 1983) is valuable here. Alex Hughes provides a balanced assessment of *Le Sang des Autres* in this context in *Simone de Beauvoir: Le Sang des Autres,* Introductory Guides to French Literature, 28, (Glasgow: University of Glasgow French and German Publications, 1995).

20. See 'Notes for an Ethics' in Christina Howells, *Sartre: The Necessity of Freedom* (Cambridge: Cambridge University Press, 1988).

21. George Steiner, *In Bluebeard's Castle* (London: Faber & Faber, 1971), p. 48.

22. Camus, though condemned as naive, non-Parisian and not much of a systematic philosopher, nonetheless allowed his imagination to assess the rights and wrongs of Vichy, Resistance France and Cold War issues. Reason, in all its tortuous meanderings, never enabled Sartre to trust his imagination or to complete his lifelong project for an ethics. There is more than one reason for regarding *Les Mots* as the most honest because, ironically, it is the most imaginative work that he wrote.

23. Camus: *Le Mythe de Sisyphe* (Paris: Gallimard, 1942), Mediterranean thought and creative revolt in *L'Homme révolté* (Paris: Gallimard, 1951); Sartre: 'Forger des mythes' (1946) in *Un théâtre de situations,* ed. by Michel Contat and Michel Rybalka (Paris: Gallimard, 1973); and the entire existentialist project.

24. See Foucault's power as a '*deus absconditus* or religious creator' in David Hawkes, *Ideology* (London: Routledge, 1996), pp. 166-67.

25. Yourcenar cites Flaubert as detecting the potential of Hadrian's historical moment: 'Les dieux n'étant plus, et le Christ n'étant pas encore, il y a eu, de Cicéron à Marc Aurèle, un moment unique où l'homme seul a été' (*Carnet de notes,* p. 321).

26. Füredi's analysis contrasts historical thinking, critical and open to the future, with historical thought as idealizing the past, closed to any possibility of renewal, incapable of taking responsibility for creating the future.

27. Hayden White's *Metahistory: the Historical Imagination in Nineteenth-Century Europe* (Baltimore: Johns Hopkins University Press, 1973) surveys different forms of historical imagination acknowledging the fictive character of all historical reconstructions and analysing these in terms of narrative discourse. Sartre's fictionalized history of his emergent subjectivity lends itself well to this typology. White notes that 'much of the best historical reflection of the twentieth century has been concerned [. . .] to overcome the condition of irony into which the historical consciousness plunged in the late nineteenth century' (p. 433). Where Yourcenar's style of historical reflection belongs clearly to the twentieth century, Sartre's in *Les Mots* seems to echo the previous one.

28. 'Les réalités, non pas religeuses peut-être, mais mystiques me sont toujours apparues comme le seul axe de notre vie': Yourcenar in a letter to Charles Du Bos, quoted in *Le Sacré dans l'œuvre de Marguerite Yourcenar: Actes du colloque international de Bruxelles (26-28 mars 1992),* (Tours: Société Internationale d'Études Yourcenariennes, 1993), p. 99.

29. Paul Ricœur, 'Imagination in Discourse and Action' in Robinson and Rundell, *Rethinking Imagination,* Ch. 6, pp. 118-35. Ideology serves the function of social integration, utopia that of social subversion.

30. Johann Arnason, pointing to imagination's marginalization by reason in modern thought, calls for the hermeneutic transformation of both concepts insofar as both are crucial to the continuing self-interpretation of modernity (Robinson and Rundell, *Rethinking Imagination,* Ch. 8, pp. 155-70).

31. An exception here is the work of Claude Lévi-Strauss who arguably did most to return the concept of myth to centre-stage in France from the 1950s onwards. He interprets it in a way that makes it acceptable to the rationalist tradition. Developing his views mainly in opposition to Durkheimian thinking on myth, Lévi-

Strauss perceives the 'untamed' or 'multiconscious' mind of so-called 'primitive' man as better equipped to respond to his environment on many levels simultaneously (Terence Hawkes, *Structuralism and Semiotics*, New Idiom Series (London: Methuen, 1971), p. 52.) He defends it as being 'as rigorous as modern science' (p. 49); and identifies mythical thinking as formal and logical, quite distinct from the mystical and the sacred (Ivan Strenski, *Four Theories of Myth in Twentieth-Century History* (London: Macmillan, 1987), pp. 156-57).

32. It is acknowledged, by implication, when Barthes identifies his outsider status as mythologist as a moral position (*Mythologies*, p. 245). Thompson, in contrast, offers a positive reading of ideology in culture, contesting the myth of the passive recipient and arguing that the individual has a critical, appropriative role to play in the 'interpretative transformation of doxa' (pp. 25-26). It is nonetheless noteworthy that the term 'imagination' does not feature in his, admittedly, sociological and not literary study.

33. John Sturrock, 'Roland Barthes' in *Structuralism and Since*, ed. by John Sturrock (Oxford: Oxford University Press, 1979), p. 64.

34. 'Semioclasm' is the term used by Barthes in 'Change the Object Itself' to describe the destruction of the linguistic sign. (Roland Barthes, *Image-Music-Text*, ed. and trans. by Stephen Heath (London: Fontana, 1982), p. 167).

35. Christopher Flood, citing Ernst Cassirer in *The Myth of the State* (New Haven and London: Yale University Press, 1946) points to the tendency for this sort of myth, characterized as 'political', to emerge in times of cultural crisis (*Political Myth. A Theoretical Introduction,* New York and London: Garland Publishing, 1996, p. 74). Although he disqualifies Barthes's conception from his own schema, *Mythologies* may be read as an expression of the crisis in cultural values of the period.

36. Michael Worton examines the extent of his mythic borrowings in 'Myth-Reference in *Le Roi des Aulnes*', *Stanford French Review*, 36 (1981), 299-310. See also Tournier's comments on 'le mythe mort' in *Le Vent paraclet* (Paris: Gallimard, 1977), p. 188.

37. David Gascoigne provides a detailed discussion of the tension between history and archetypal symbolism in *Le Roi des Aulnes* in *Michel Tournier* (Oxford: Berg, 1996), pp. 183-206.

38. In *Le Vent paraclet* Tournier's own condemnation of the implosion of reason into unreason, 'la folie raisonneuse et systématique', is explicit (p. 113).

39. There is a good discussion of this point in the chapters on Foucault in Peter Dews, *Logics of Disintegration. Post-Structuralist Thought and the Claims of Critical Theory* (London: Verso, 1987).

40. Madan Sarup, *Identity, Culture and the Postmodern World* (Edinburgh: Edinburgh University Press, 1996), pp. 87-90.

41. Hans Jonas, *The Imperative of Responsibility. In Search of an Ethics for a Technological Age* (Chicago: University of Chicago Press, 1984).

MODERN FRENCH POETRY

Anna Balakian (essay date 1984)

SOURCE: Balakian, Anna. "From Mallarmé to Breton: Continuity and Discontinuity in the Poetics of Ambiguity." In *Writing in a Modern Temper: Essays on French Literature and Thought in Honor of Henri Peyre,* edited by Mary Ann Caws, pp. 118-34. Saratoga, CA: Amna Libri, 1984.

[*In the following essay, Balakian traces the path of modern French poetry with an examination of the works of Stéphane Mallarmé and André Breton.*]

Separated by half a century, Stéphane Mallarmé and André Breton follow each other like two milestones on the path of modern poetics, and their roles as heads of literary schools, symbolism and surrealism, invite comparison. Their positions as masters in the throes of the poetic activities of the avant-garde of their respective times had gained for them a cosmopolitan following in Paris, clusters of poets who were as much affected by the stature of their two personalities as by their pronouncements. By associating poetics with the processes in the other arts, such as music and dance in the case of Mallarmé and painting in the case of Breton, they succeeded in reducing the distance between poets and other categories of artists but also increased the gap between poetry and the other forms of literature, particularly in the dislike both expressed of the narrative form. At the end of their careers both reached advanced forms of writing, Mallarmé with his *Un Coup de dés jamais n'abolira le hasard,* Breton with his *Constellations,* surpassing the models they had first created and the variants adopted by those who had imitated them and followed in their paths.[1]

But the first level of the parallel between Breton and Mallarmé in its most obvious aspects stops here. Before looking in depth at other levels of connection, let us look at some obvious differences.

Mallarmé became a master among disciples who were some twenty years his juniors. Breton, on the other hand, became a leader among his contemporaries, despite the fact that he was identified as the "Pope" of surrealism. The concepts that constituted Mallarmé's *ars poetica* were handed down *a posteriori,* after he had practiced them in his poetry for some twenty years, after his aesthetics had been put to the test in his works, recognized and appreciated even if only by a limited number of readers. On the other hand, Breton had made his declarations of theory at an age when he had written little and proved nothing. His doctrines were chosen and pronounced *a priori* and accepted on faith. Mallarmé's manner was quiet, nondogmatic, his aspirations qualitative rather than quantitative. He had said that if he could catch the attention of one person in each city of France he would be quite satisfied. Breton's concepts took the form of Manifestoes, and like political manifestoes aimed to reach the many, with the firm conviction that poetry was a human necessity.

In a recent book called *Poetry and Repression,* the American critic, Harold Bloom, states—perhaps in reaction to the analytical studies of literature in isolated fragments—the importance of placing every writer in the current which reaches him.[2] Every act of poetic creativity, he insists, is actually a form of revision of previous poetic achievements, and consequently, there exists in literary history a flux and reflux in the course of literary phenomena and periods. This is, of course, another way of saying that the greatest influences are the negative, reactionary ones. Gide had made the same observation a while back. One can explain much about symbolism and surrealism on the basis of the theory of reactions. Although André Breton at age sixteen was writing Mallarmean sonnets, he was soon to attack the artifices of the symbolists, their withdrawal from the lifestream, their protracted introspections, their espousal of an ontology of fiction. The reaction of the surrealists to these postures is readily evident in the surrealist behavior and the revisionist character of the early poetry that ensued. The interiority of the poetic stance, which had become traditional, was reversed as the surrealists emerged from the expected shell to project themselves and their work into the concrete world and to try to transform it instead of turning their backs to it. The chamber is abandoned in favor of the street. Instead of withdrawing from exterior reality they wanted to come to grips with it and to manipulate it. One of the first poems of Breton is nothing more than a rebuttal of the symbolist mystique. Let me quote a few lines from the excellent translation of Kenneth White:

> Rather life than those prisms without depth even if the colors are purer
> Rather than that always clouded hour those terrible wagons of cold flame
> Than those soft stones
> Rather this triggered heart
> Than that murmuring mere
> And that white cloth singing in the air and in the earth
> That nuptial blessing linking my brow to the brow of absolute vanity
> Rather life
>
> *Clair de terre*[3]

On the level of symbols, the revision of the symbolist vision is also very obvious. The preponderant image of the symbolist lily is transformed into banal and common flowers, such as the wild rose and the sunflower. The swan is replaced by the high flying and more resilient egret or eagle (not yet considered an endangered species!), and if a certain difficulty of interpretation of discourse is preserved as we pass from symbolism to surrealism, it is no longer due to lexical rarefactions and semantic intricacies but to a vocabulary that is replete with words that have never been associated with each other before, which are innocent of previous poetic connotations, having been culled from the fields not of literature but botany and biology. Even in the choice of mythological figures, reaction to the standard choices brings back from the past some of the ones that have had less visibility in modern literature: Leda fades away; she was a favorite of the symbolists because she suggested to them the human being in whom divine seed is put by the embrace of a god. She is replaced by Melusine, suggesting on the contrary the divine being who aspires to become and to stay human in the interpretation of Breton. Hérodiade, Mallarmé's version of that fascinating Salome of the symbolists, is sterile in her static existence, and we know to what terrible violence her sickly narcissism was to lead her. The character of Esclarmonde in Breton's *Les Etats-Généraux* is a revolutionary heroine chosen from the medieval history of the religious wars of France; she is also violent but her violence is part of her martyrdom caused in the course of her quest for the common salvation of her people.

The examples could be multiplied to prove that reaction and revision were part of the passage from symbolism to surrealism, and this element has indeed been recognized in the commentaries of literary history. And on that level there is no need to comment further on differences already noted.

However, as soon as we detach Mallarmé from the symbolist framework, and Breton from the surrealist label, an analysis more closely applied to these two poets reveals elements that bring them closer together and which go beyond the purely aesthetic considerations to enter the field of ontological inquiry. What is poetry? What is its field of interaction? How is it a factor in the apprehension of reality? What is the nature of symbol?

Breton tells us in an article called "Fronton-Virage" that he was familiar with the cryptic sonnets of Mallarmé. And in his autobiographical *Entretiens* (published in the later years of his life) he explains in retrospective meditation that of course it was normal for an activist group like the surrealists to reject what came before them and free themselves from ancestors. But what surprised him, he said, was the fact that the official body of literary historians did not seem to recognize the fact that there was a chain of transmission that linked the two movements. How did they fail to notice that there were threads that knit together an underground tradition? an esoteric tradition that linked all across Europe from the early nineteenth century the poetic preoccupations of poets such as Novalis, Hoelderlin in Germany, Blake and Coleridge in England, Nerval and

Baudelaire in France, and reached a peak with Mallarmé?[4] In this hermetic tradition, the need for the marvelous and the imponderable remain constants among the variations in style related to passing literary schools, but the symbols changed, and certain natural phenomena took turns in functioning as mediations between human imagination and a reality which wavers behind certain common appearances. In this current which manifests successive foils for concealment and eventually reaches him, Breton recognizes the most fruitful indices of modern poetics. And in the case of Mallarmé, there had occurred a strange paradox. The agnostic little bourgeois that Mallarmé was in his personal life had carried on a sustained search for gnostic revelations and had made him dream of a future when "the instinct for heaven which resides in each human being" would be stirred by the poet who would have assumed the role of "mystagogue." But Mallarmé's mistake, according to Breton, was to have cultivated mystery for its own sake, simply to become difficult. Said Breton: "I know nothing so puerile as Mallarmé's compulsion not to let any text of his be read which might be too easily understood without injecting into it some shadow of mystification" (in "Le Merveilleux contre le mystère").[5] He found in this type of artificial mystification a form of weakness unworthy of Mallarmé and more characteristic of the minor symbolist poets. For this artificial mystery Breton wanted to substitute the marvelous, which is veiled only so that it may be unveiled, in the spirit of the operations of the alchemists who had found the same basic linguistic root in the word "veil" (*voile*) as in "revelation" and whose every effort for veiling carried in itself the clues to the unveiling and then to the reveiling of significations. Thus, the veil that in the eyes of the Romantic poets was the barrier between the real world and the supernal, and in the case of the symbolists "trembled" at the temple of Isis and became torn with Mallarmé and in Yeats; more and more permanent fissures became visible in the so-called impenetrable cloisters into which retreated the symbolists. The marvelous to which the symbolists sometimes yielded almost unconsciously became for Breton a form of reception, total and englobing, through which human beings could reach each other over and above the limitation of time and space.

Breton's criticism of Mallarmé is not altogether fair. If it is true that Mallarmé told the poets around him to work with mystery, he meant exactly the same thing as when Breton declared in his Second Manifesto that the surrealist must engage in deep occultation. Both meant that the poet had to work in silence and secrecy with the patience of an alchemist and be aware of the process of poetic creation. The admonition implied the difficulty of the process of writing poetry; it suggested that poetry required infinite care and undisturbed monitoring of the altered state. This awareness is manifest in all of Mallarmé's writings from the mysterious *Igitur*, the creation of which almost drove Mallarmé out of his mind, to the obsession he had in the last years of his life to write the Book, in the guise of a Magus and adept in the use of a magical language of hieroglyphics. In fact, this sense of a language of high power is the basis of the link between Mallarmé and Breton over and above the variety of poetic forms they adopt. Both feel that the mysterious powers of language enlarge consciousness and deepen the sense of existence. Mallarmé expressed this sense in his famous sentence: "The orphic explanation of the Earth, which is the only duty of the poet and the only literary play that counts."[6] This literary maneuver of language changes, according to both poets, the functioning of the logical, linear train of thought, and it is this change which distinguishes the new poetic form from all other forms of writing whether written in verse or prose. One of the most important propositions that Mallarmé made in the domain of poetics was that language was henceforth to be not a conveyer of thoughts but a container or thesaurus of poetic images whose disposition or precipitation or even tension with each other created poetic states or phenomena. Language thus became for him a pursuit and an end in itself. In his last poems as well as in his much studied last will and testament, *Un Coup de dés,* Mallarmé had discovered a secret inaccessible to most of his symbolist colleagues, and that he seems to have passed directly to Breton: that language contains in its sounds and words and in its morphological contours a great number of meanings that can be utilized simultaneously; this character of language was indeed the source of the ancient enigmas, or the rebus, or the oracle, and could be adapted to a polysemantic harmony in modern poetry. When we say that symbolism cultivated ambiguity in poetry, the word "ambiguity" is itself ambiguous. There is the kind of ambiguity you can find in the poetry of Verlaine, what he called "la chanson grise," the gray song, which creates a general sense of mystery inviting each reader to find his own interpretation of Verlaine's state of being, or substitute one of his own parallel to Verlaine's. The ambiguity of Mallarmé, which was to be passed on to Breton and to a few other surrealists is a systematic construction of associations of words which interplay, which create different states of meanings in synchronized structure, begin a series and suggest to the reader, through clues, how to continue the scale. It is a system which he called architectural and premeditated like the work of the alchemist to whom he compared himself. And contrary to the very spirit of this type of poetic construction, learned readers have been trying to decode a single meaning, to untangle the so-called difficulty, when the target of reader-critic should indeed be to discover and appreciate the *process* that creates a multiplicity of meanings. As early as 1923, when his own poetic writings were still ahead of him, Breton realized that there was much to be discovered about Mallarmé's poetics that was avant-garde and not to be confused with his conservative life-style. He also believed that it would take some time to sort out and understand his achievements: "It will be some time before Mallarmé will be discovered, the work of Mallarmé which the person of Mallarmé still hides from us, and eyes will be turned particularly in the direction of *Un Coup de dés* (letter of December 8, 1923). Breton meditated along the same lines as Mallarmé when he asked in his article on Raymond Roussel in "Fronton-Virage": how can one hide something in such a way as to invited possibilities of eventual deciphering? He came to the conclusion that this attitude which was of half-deceit, and at the same time somewhat engaging, was strictly conforming to the discourse of hermetic philosophers (*La Clé des champs*, p. 192). Both poets conclude in the same manner: that the occult does not reside principally in a particular philosophy but in the depths of language itself with its hide-and-seek quality, and if this quality is integral to language it means of course that the hermeticism is inherent in all thought that reaches beyond the surface of consciousness, the movement from the first layer of the self to the next is what Breton called the passage from the *moi* to the *soi*. The search for these facets of language was in fact for Breton, manifesting his belief in the *poetry of language over and above the language of poetry*, the guiding principle of his work from his first poems to the majestic ones of his mature period. Although he talked readily about the miracle of automatic writing, whatever psychic provocations he used were a means rather than an end, like finger exercises to the very structured poetics that combined with the aid of carefully chosen words and their fortuitous gravitations several registers of poetic states, generally one having to do with the immediacy of life, one on a mythological universal plane, and one digging into unconscious desire or dream, the synchronization suggesting a complex reality in the manner in which Mallarmé had evoked through the meditations of a Faun that unforgettable afternoon. And the timid school teacher that Mallarmé was, had crystallized desire, universal throughout the ages, through the miracle of a language that fused dream, fiction, and reality. He had pushed the art of the polysemantic much further on to a cosmic plane in the *Coup de dés*. For instance, the word that means in French pen and wing, *plume* brought together writing and flying, and the word veil and sail, *voile* associating sea and obstruction communicating human frailty and poetic power simultaneously, replaced linear thought with a system of analogical circularity going beyond allegory or even symbol.

Thus, poetry becomes a provocative guessing game, in principle inexhaustible, and in which the message that each person can pick up is apt to surpass the projections that the poet might have had in mind, creating an activity of the mind which can well illustrate the statement that the poet Aragon made in *Le Paysan de Paris*: that the very idea of limit is the only concept that is unacceptable to the human mind.[7]

But if both Mallarmé and Breton believed in the polysemantic character of language as a base for poetic activity, there is a basic difference in the search for the multiplicity of meaning. Mallarmé went about finding this multiplicity in a methodical manner, with etymological dictionaries, and relied on his knowledge of foreign languages—in his case English, his means of livelihood! Many of his findings (*trouvailles*) in polyvalence were put to use in a somewhat artificial manner and their hidden meanings were acceptable only in a fictitious world. Breton, however, thought etymological significations inert, unfunctional. He sought polyvalence in the subconscious functioning of language, such as in the speech of mediums or the deranged, on through the process of automatic writing, or dream transcription. That is why it is not paradoxical or contradictory to claim that Breton's poetry is both automatic and structured. Automatism is a state of grace for him, a state in which he can spontaneously make discoveries about language that hours of reflective study may fail to achieve. In retrospection he tells us this in his *Entretiens*: "Automatism, under whatever form you may want to envisage it, does not come upon demand." It is most likely to come, he says, to those who have an intimate relationship with the natural world; it is spontaneous, in the case of primitive societies, desired and sought by revolutionaries "who have believed in and who believe in the restoration of man in a world from which he has ceased to be alienated."[8]

In a short article called "Le La" Breton compared the role of the automatic phase to the "A" of the orchestra when it tunes up in preparation for performance.[9] For the poet, the "A" of automatism is the pure unmitigated data catalyzing the artistic work; this parallel between the musicians who prepare to perform and the poet who sharpens his imagination is a distinction which to my knowledge no one has shown except Breton and in a more subtle way Mallarmé before him in *Afternoon of a Faun*. In Breton's opinion it is the spontaneous process of automatism that breaks the shackles of inhibition and thereby permits the poet to collect the materials with which he will then *consciously* create his work of art. His essential work will consist of blending the spontaneous or fortuitous with the deliberate.

Meditating on the spontaneously creative power of words, Breton associated his efforts of course with those of Rimbaud, adventurer in poetics as in life-style. What Breton found noteworthy in the famous sonnet of the "Vowels" was not simply the polysemantic play with words and the discovery of their associations but the manner in which Rimbaud had "turned the word away from its duty to signify." This comment occurs in an early article entitled "Les Mots sans rides" in which Breton speculates about magnetic fields that make certain words gravitate toward others not only on the basis of associative meanings but by their spacial qualities and cognitive tensions. Words, he says, are creators of energy, and "the expression of an idea depends as much on the appearance of the words as on their meaning. There are words that work against the idea that they presume to express."[10] What he is saying is that once you have exploited the riches of meanings, once you have—in modern terminology—*deconstructed* their ordinary and mechanical connotations, you reach a point zero *but you don't stay there*—at least if you are a poet. You assign new significations to them. Mallarmé had had the same idea when he said that the "Aim of language is to become beautiful, and not to give preference to the expression of the beautiful over everything else."[11]

In "Les Mots sans rides," which was a work of his youth, Breton placed on the same level of theoretical conjecture what Mallarmé had already tried and tested concretely in his untitled sonnet "Le vierge, le vivace, et le bel aujourd'hui," in which the process he used is precisely to let the meaning of words and their analogical sonorities as well as morphological parallels spill on to each other and in a cumulative movement create the synthetic, virtual (as opposed to real) image of a swan, all the while crystallizing on the semantic register the physical and psychological state of the poet. This poem is the perfect example of Mallarmé's theory of the interaction of words in the creation of a substitute reality. He stated this notion in his preface to the theoretical work of a co-symbolist, René Ghil. He said in the preface to his *Traité du verbe*: "Contrary to a face value, easy and representative, as handled by the masses, Discourse is before anything else, a dream and song, which finds in the hands of the poet, because of the necessary constitution of an art dedicated to fictions, its own virtual image."[12] The dexterity needed to accomplish this feat of recreating the universe with the aid of language, Mallarmé characterizes it as a linguistic one attained through the cultivation of the possibilities of the interplay of words. His theoretical writings are widely interspersed with expressions such as "language in its play," "word play," "literary play." We might say that the game theory of language is at work, and that its work is a verbal play activity. When we come to Breton, however, "play" is too lowly a word to characterize what he considers the high mission of the destiny of language. The analogy is no longer confined to play but aims at *love*. Words make love with each other, subjected to all the traps and perils of chance, desire, attraction, copulation, and procreation. "From the moment when words are appreciated from a more and more emotional angle, from which we lend to their association, under certain forms, a power of deep, unique relationship, between one being and another, better still in which we dream thanks to them of reaching essence, it is clear that behavior in terms of language, will tend more and more to follow the pattern of behavior in love" (*La Clé des champs*, p. 12). The association of words includes the factor of the "emotional" here which is never mentioned in Mallarmé.

Onward from the major poem of his early period, "L'Union libre" to the series of love poems called *L'Air de l'eau*, and on and up to his last series of prose poems, *Constellations*, in which he departs completely from the verse line as Mallarmé had done in *Coup de dés*, the dominant pattern of Breton's poetry is that of verbal alliance paralleling intimate protoplasmic and cosmic alliances, with the broader structure of the erotic embrace. "Poetry is made in bed like love / Its rumpled sheets are the dawn of things" ("Sur la route de San Romano").[13] The mixing of metaphors is not a failing of rhetoric but a conscious effort to suggest the intermingling of spheres of human, natural, and cosmic activity such as human movement synchronized with snowing, soaring of birds, convulsion of earthquake: "Your flesh sprinkled with the flight of a thousand birds of paradise / Is a high flame lying in the snow."[14] Sometimes when the central word of the image has more than one meaning in French, it does not come off in English translation. The following lines in French do not carry across their double identity into English even in the expert hands of Kenneth White: "En partant j'ai mis le feu à une mèche de cheveux qui est celle d'une bombe / Et la mèche de cheveux creuse un tunnel sous Paris / Si seulement mon train entrait dans ce tunnel" rendered as "On leaving I set fire to a lock of hair which was the fuse of a bomb / And the lock of hair is hollowing out a tunnel under Paris / If only my train could enter that tunnel" (*Clair de terre*). The trouble is that the sensuality of hair and the explosive character of bomb which are integrated into the verbal polyvalence in French where "mèche" means both lock of hair and bomb, do not carry over into English and the hair-meaning cannot penetrate the bomb-meaning and vise versa although the translator can suggest a parallel on a linear level ("Aigrette"). The reason Breton loved the sunflower, "tournesol," so much is because his own poetic movements were like the physical ones of the sunflower and could be called "heliotropic." The words he chose gravitate like the sunflower toward fire (and explosion) whether of a human or cosmic nature. That is indeed the broad meaning of his last sentence in *Nadja*: "Beauty must be convulsive or not at all."

The dexterity Breton developed in making verbal alliances in close step with human concordances with the rhythms of nature, reached its peak with the prose poems called *Constellations*, and this structural pattern is evidenced in the number of words that are signifiers of conjunction and function as links in the interplay. The central character is a prestigitator whose success depends on the combination of dexterity and chance, the very attributes that Breton manipulates one against the other in the creation of poetry.

What is most significant in all this over and above common interests in language, is the fact that the problems of writing are directly associated both by Mallarmé and by Breton with the crucial problematics of life although the circumstance of life are not the same for the two poets. Above all the interest in the functioning of language is motivated by the thought that man finds his liberty in the use he makes of language; the other side of the coin is that if he does not find his liberty through language he may well risk finding his bondage in using language in the stilted way society can induce him to do. Breton moreover believes that there is a strong carry-over from man's effort to emancipate his language to that of emancipating his life. Thus is language in its poetic function integrally tied to the notion of existence in both poets in their awareness of the power of language to burgeon with thought rather than simply to express it. According to Breton, the last great French poet to have used language in its traditional way to convey thought rather than generate it was Baudelaire.

But despite this important parallel between Mallarmé and Breton in the composition of a poem and the central significance of language, we are obliged to recognize that distance between a poem of Mallarmé and one of Breton is not narrowed. If some of the means to the poetic objective are similar, if some of the techniques are handed down from the one to the other over the heads of a host of lesser poets of imitative nature, the objectives or intentions of the poetic activity envisaged, desired, reflect the differences both of their individual characters and the separate epochs in which they were nurtured. In their pursuit of liberty, both are obsessed by the forces of chance. Mallarmé spent a lifetime confronting and combatting chance in the context of the human will. Unable to cope with the struggle on the philosophical level, he posits it on the level of poetry. *Un Coup de dés* is the monument to the great battle he waged against chance. The artist/writer cannot abolish chance but in the very utterance of that statement he causes chance to stumble; in the spaces of the book even as in the spaces of the cosmos his presence and his effort to daunt the forces leading him to sure catastrophe compel him to engage with those forces and consider the possibility of survival through language. In the broad literature that emanates from symbolism, with which Mallarmé's name is so closely connected, I am aware only of two poets who tackle this cosmic problem, although many have used the exterior format of the *Coup de dés*. They are two Latin-American poets, Aldo Pellegrini of Argentina in *Distribución del silencio* and the Chilean Vincente Huidobro in *Altazor*.[15]

Breton was of an age that had had time to accept chance as a substitute for providence. Some of his contemporaries succumbed to that acceptance and developed an *écriture* that reflects not the struggle of Mallarmé but a diffidence and a begrudging imitation of the indifference with which chance strikes and passes. Theirs is the world of the absurd, as we all know. But Breton's stance is neither that of Mallarmé nor of the absurdists. Instead of thinking like Mallarmé that chance intrudes into the ordered scheme of the mind, he invites it with open arms; he sets out to seduce it, to court it, to appropriate its powers for his own ends whether along the lines of poetic discoveries or in questions of love as important to him as his poetics.

Both poets were rebels against the conditions of the society of their time, but they compensated for their dissatisfaction in quite different ways. Mallarmé turned his back on society, Breton attacked it with the notorious but symbolic revolver shot which he characterized as the typical surrealist attitude of alarm and anger in relation to the ills of society. Mallarmé's introverted rebellion reflected the spirit of decadence of the time. Writing became a refuge for him, an act of interiority, and the communication of a poem to others was likened by him to the dropping of a visiting card at someone's doorstep to say: "I came by but you were not there." The assumption was, of course, that symbolically speaking he was unlikely to be received by those on whose doors he knocked; that is to say, the poetic message would be subject to an absence of reception. But the retreat was not only vis-à-vis the readers, whom he assumed to be sparse. The withdrawal was also manifest in the kind of lexicon he chose, a lexicon which created for him a synthetic existence, a fictitious one, in which would flourish the flower absent from all bouquets, or that Hérodiade, enclosed in stone and tapestry, removed in time and space from any possibility of historical identification, a Salome intentionally misnamed to add a fictitious character beyond even legendary identification. With Mallarmé something new happened, and in this respect he was to have many followers into the modern world: he creates the fiction of the poet, ever more removed from reality than ever the fiction of the novelist was or has been, in which life itself finds a substitute in the undecipherable book (*le grimoire*). Biographers of Mallarmé have observed that he was sexually inhibited and repressed because of a very early marriage and a structured bourgeois life. That may be so; I am not here to dispute the conjectures of psychocriticism. But the sexual repression found vivid compensation in a language-oriented eroticism, in the *virtual* rather than real world, audacious and isolated, moving in the direction of the Septentrion, which he conceived as a dead star. There he can do all that he does not dare to do within the narrow confines of his life. Language in its liberty and generosity makes it possible for him to make love with two nymphs simultaneously, and if Beauty is on the wane in the real world, he shows us in that cryptic poem called "Prose pour Des Esseintes" a "Pulcherie" who survives thanks to the fictitious hyperbole of a gladiola too tall for this world but quite comfortable in "a world that did not exist."[16] In the pursuit of this fictitious world of new alliances of signifiers with signified his following is immense and international: Yeats, Valéry, Rilke, Stevens, to name some of the greatest.

André Breton's sense of the meaning of liberation was quite different. Here we have a philosophy of life which makes of man and the human experience of living a triumph over the artist, or, as he said it himself, makes art reversible to life. Rebellion, even as Mallarmé's refuge, is manifest in language which instead of crystallizing in a swan caught in ice, or a golden bird of Byzantium, plunges into natural phenomena to find there the hyperbole that surpasses the fictitious. Over and above all the exterior lables that his poetry has acquired, he characterized poetry as the result of "exceptional intensity of man before the spectacle of life."[17] He felt this as he viewed the activity of the Martiniquan poet, Aimé Césaire, in a country where the savage eye which Breton had sought to cultivate in his own Parisian environment had a much better chance to realize its potential. In a "Dialogue créole" which he conducted with his artist friend André Masson he observed: "One can wonder to what degree the poverty of European vegetation is responsible for the escape of the mind toward an imaginary flora. Should we not try to escape from that particular perception of what falls under our senses when we return to less favored places?"[18]

In conclusion, I will reiterate some of the points I have tried to make about the Mallarmé/Breton axis as they relate directly to current preoccupations with polysemantics, symbolization and writer/reader relationships. The impact of Mallarmé and Breton has been in three categories as we might conclude from my discussion, moving poetics toward a redefinition of the sacred, toward the reconsideration of the question of human relationship with nature, and the writer's relationship to the reader.

Mallarmé and Breton belonged to an era of philosophical transition, Mallarmé at its beginning, Breton at its closure. They were both intent on using poetry as an adjustment factor. In that respect, as they saw the divine being dislocated from its erstwhile association with the arts as a supernal presence, participating in the process of artistic creativity, they tried to preserve the notion of the sacred by appropriating its power.

Mallarmé's so-called "virtual reality" was such an attempt to capture the sacred. The artifact he created with high intellectual lucidity did not englobe him but was endowed with a certain autonomy from circumstantial strictures. Nothing is clearer than the analogy he makes in that early poem, "Le Don du poème," in which he compares the birth of a poem with the birth of a child. After difficult and prolonged labor, it is born and *given,* i.e., severed from the one who begot it. All we hear about the process is that it was "horrible" and if we look at the years Mallarmé spent correcting his works, we know that he was not exaggerating about the difficulties of creating. Lately he has been quoted repeatedly from *Crise de vers* where he says that his "I" disappeared into the poem.[19] In truth, it disappeared from the poem as well, leaving in its trace a multiplicity of potential "I"'s. The notion of the "sacred" surfaces in the manner in which a sacerdotal ritual is performed in the symbolization process whereby the earthly bread incorporates divine spirit. Mallarmé saw himself performing that type of ritual over and over again as he distilled material entities into ideations containing in their contours an infinite series of reidentifications. For Mallarmé, the word "Verbe" is sacred, as opposed to languages which are subjected to changing codes and mores. The poet is a mediator between the Verbe, with its integral meaning, and the languages of comprehension.

Breton also saw a desperate need in the modern world to preserve the notion of the sacred while rejecting its supernatural character. His solution was different although like Mallarmé he claimed a whole line of predecessors. He attached the creative process to that of analogical thinking which he found at the basis of all magical operations. But his major objective was not the production of an artifact endowed with a sacred character reinterpretable through the ages. For Breton, the process of creativity was more important than the ultimate product, and not something horribly difficult to do but rather supremely enjoyable. Influenced by the esoterism of the ages, and by contemporaries such as Pierre Mabille who was studying voodoo ritual, and Malcolm de Chazal engrossed in the rituals of Eastern cultures, he saw the transfer of the sacred into the notion of *volupté,* i.e., a vertiginous reception of physical reality and the effervescent participation of the poet in the universal intercourse amongst beings, things, animal, vegetable, mineral, human existences. Because this flow was evident not only in the primitive but in modern poetic perceptions—and he drew his examples from among the great poets of the nineteenth century in particular—he believed that it was a permanent manifestation which the polysemantic character of languages supported. The resulting artifact was part of the life experience, a provocation for other creative activity, i.e., everyman's rite of passage from surface reality to deeper levels where antinomies ceased to exist. The symbolization was not confined to the work of art but in the pool of language available to all. We proceed thus from the notion of poetry as an elitist activity to poetry for all. In this respect, the intentionality, so often the very subject of Breton's writings, is as important a text as the work of art that may arise to implement it. In fact, three of his major prose writings: *Nadja* (1928), *Les Vases communicants* (1932), and *L'Amour fou* (1937) are expressions of that intentionality. They are projects, instigations for works of greater proportion open to others. In these times, when the discussion of intentionality of the writer is frowned upon in critical circles, it is important to realize that in the case of surrealist writings it is at the heart of the matter and part of the transformational process of the work of art.

Like Mallarmé, Breton had that sense of delivery of the work of art to the reader except that for him the catalytic power (or sacred character) resided in the process of production rather than in the work produced. That is why sharing his intentions with the reader was so important. In the case of Mallarmé, the value of the work is to be judged empirically through the reception of the work itself; in the case of Breton it is the creator's communication of the altered state of apperception that has to be received along with the work itself, i.e., the transfer of emotion, of a sublimation.

What light do Mallarmé and Breton throw on the altered relationship of man with nature? In the case of Mallarmé, as I pointed out earlier, much of his work presents a rupture with the ordinary flow of natural states and phenomena. His garden is artificial, in a country that does not exist; his planet is dead except as it is cultivated by language creating artifacts on an empty and indifferent canvas. Nature in no way contributes to the sacralization of the poet's universe. He has deconstructed what was there before projecting his interiority onto a tangible exteriority. His negation of the gods involves also the negation of the principal sites where they had established correspondences. On this matter, he concurred with George W. Cox, whose work he rendered into French in his *Les Dieux antiques,* a work in which Cox had demythified ancient mythology by reducing the powers of the gods to natural movements of earth, sun, stars, etc.[20]

But the blank space, depopulated of its gods, does not thereby return to a void. Mallarmé does not deal in abstractions. His images are very concrete but the composite, derived from culling of physical images, no longer functions in its natural and original habitat. Instead, it is staged in a new space totally controlled by the stage directions of the poet. He is not alienated as a creator although he may well have been exiled as a human being.

Breton had the same preoccupation: how to revise modern man's relation with nature. Like Mallarmé, he considered his answer of primary importance to his role as poet. But his proposed solution was quite different. He made himself permeable to the larger and unpredictable movements of the physical world which work toward integration rather than separation of man in relation to nature. He could reach this sense of monistic integration by developing as we have already mentioned, the mental activity involved in establishing analogies. Every symbol created through analogy is integrated in a pool and only provisionally detached from the matrix where it correlates with an infinite number of others.

Now we might think that this resembles belief in a Swedenborgian network of correspondences except for the very important fact that nature is not viewed as a temple, intermediary between earth and an unknowable heaven; instead, we might say that it is a cauldron ever productive and attainable. The mission of the poet is not to make a break but to enter into the "synthetic comprehension of the world and to make man enter into this knowledge," as expressed by Pierre Mabille and quoted by Breton in one of his last essays, entitled "Pont Levis," which was published in the posthumous collection of Breton's prose, *Perspective cavalière*.[21] The fact of the matter is—and this is the basic quality of modernism as I see it—that correspondences are no longer recognized as preexisting to the artist's recognition of them; they are established by the artist himself, and their impact on human consciousness is strictly monitored by the artist. The aleatory character of natural and human phenomena is captured and vigilantly structured into the artifact.

To come to the third question: the relationship with the reader, Mallarmé and Breton united in their recognition of the writer's responsibility vis-à-vis the reader. Their position preempts that of modern hermeneutics in the assumption that interpretation is a creative activity and conducive to what Breton called "a perplexed lucidity." Both opened their works to the uncertainty and multiplicity of interpretation. Mallarmé based his polysemy on the strategic composition of the poem aimed at creating ambiguity. Breton relied on the inherent riches of the analogical content captured by both writer and reader through the practice of nonlinear reading. This procedure is not identifiable with modern poetics of criticism although the works of both poets have served as objects of the critical exercise in hermeneutics which decodes and recodes so-called "texts" through the practice of logical discourse. One of the basic distinctions Mallarmé and Breton made between poetry and other forms of writing was poetry's inherent hermeneutic function. In making this broad separation between *poésie* and prose, they had thought that they had liberated poetry from what Breton called the "yoke of Greco-Roman logistics." Poetry's subjection to methodologies applicable to expository writing would have struck them as paradoxical, indeed as a threat to the very survival of poetry.

Notes

1. Stéphane Mallarmé, *Un Coup de dés jamais n'abolira le hasard* in *Oeuvres complètes* (Editions de la Pléiade, 1956), pp. 455-77; hereafter abbreviated *OC*. André Breton, *Constellations* in *Signe ascendant* (Gallimard, 1968), pp. 127-71.

2. Harold Bloom, *Poetry and Repression* (New Haven, Conn.: Yale University Press, 1976).

3. André Breton, *Clair de terre*, tr. Kenneth White, *Selected Poems of André Breton* (London: Jonathan Cape, 1969), p. 19.

4. Breton, "Fronton-Virage" in *La Clé des champs* (Sagittaire, 1953) (written in 1948), and *Entretiens* (Gallimard, 1952), p. 78.

5. Breton, "Le Merveilleux contre le mystère," in *La Clé des champs* (Sagittaire, 1953), pp. 11-12 (written in 1936); the translation is mine.

6. Mallarmé, "Autobiographie," *OC*, p. 663; the translation is mine.

7. Louis Aragon, *Le Paysan de Paris* (Gallimard, 1926).

8. Breton, *Entretiens*, p. 257.

9. Breton, "Le La" in *Signe ascendant*, pp. 174-75 (written about 1960).

10. Breton, *Les Pas perdus* (Gallimard, 1924), p. 133.

11. Mallarmé, *Diptyque: Une Méthode, OC*, p. 853.

12. Mallarmé, *Traité de verbe, OC*, p. 858.

13. Breton, *Signe ascendant*, p. 122 (the translation is mine).

14. Breton, *L'Air de l'eau* in *Clair de terre* (Gallimard, 1966), p. 160 (original date of the poem 1934).

15. Aldo Pellegrini, *Distribución del silencio* (Buenos Aires: Ediciones "A partir de Cero," 1957), p. 27. Vicente Huidobro, *Altazor* in *Obras completas*, I (Zig-Zag, 1964).

16. Mallarmé, "Prose pour Des Esseintes," *OC*, p. 55.

17. Breton, "Un Grand Poète noir," in *Martinique, charmeuse de serpents* (Pauvert, 1972), p. 105.

18. Breton, "Dialogue créole," *ibid.,* pp. 18-19.

19. Mallarmé, *Crise de vers, OC*, p. 366.

20. Mallarmé, *Les Dieux antiques, OC,* pp. 1159-276.

21. *Perspective cavalière* (Gallimard, 1970), p. 201.

Michael Bishop (essay date 1985)

SOURCE: Bishop, Michael. "Yves Bonnefoy." In *The Contemporary Poetry of France: Eight Studies*, pp. 117-36. Amsterdam: Rodopi, 1985.

[*In the following essay, Bishop presents an overview of Bonnefoy's poetry, characterizing the poet as one of the most influential in modern French letters.*]

Les mots comme le ciel
Infini
Mais tout entier soudain dans la flaque brève[1]

From the publication in 1953 of his first major collection of poetry, *Du mouvement et de l'immobilité de Douve,* Yves Bonnefoy has exercised a fascination and influence in the realm of French letters that, having steadily grown, may now be said to have reached their point of full blossoming. His importance in the history of modern French literature is quite assured and may well be deemed ultimately even greater than those responsible for the 1983 *colloque de Cerisy* devoted to his work clearly already think. Author of fine translations of Shakespeare, eloquent and profound writings on the history and nature of art and poetry, Bonnefoy has allowed his poetic, and his creativity to develop away from the strict confines of literary schools and even broad contemporary intellectual trends, and rather in loose, though intimate contact with powerful and solitary voices of both the past—Baudelaire, Rimbaud, Mallarmé, Jouve, for example—and his own time: Jacques Dupin, Philippe Jaccottet, André Frénaud, André du Bouchet and others. His achievements in the realm of art criticism are, similarly, largely those of an inspired autodidact, and his recent appointment to the Collège de France bears witness not only to the brilliance of his enterprise but also to its dogged individuality. My aim here is to map the principal features of a poetics that has guided him both in his criticism and his creative writing from his earliest poetic utterances of *Anti-Platon* and even the *Traité du pianiste,* down through *Du mouvement et de l'immobilité de Douve* and the determining *proses* of *L'Improbable* and *Un Rêve fait à Mantoue,* to the essays of *Le Nuage rouge* and the sweeping, slow majesty of *Dans le leure du seuil.* Whilst a good deal of material cannot be touched upon, the general rigour and constancy of Bonnefoy's poetics will in this way come clearly into focus, as, it is hoped, will also the complexity and multifacetted nature of his thinking and approach. We shall thus have occasion to speak of aspects of Bonnefoy's poetics such as the distinction between presence and concept, the significance of death, ephemeralness and imperfection, hope and love, withdrawal and assent, language considered as problem and solution, and so on. Our final appreciation will reveal a poet working, both through the articulation of his poetics and his poetic praxis, at the intersection of the infinite and the briefest of illuminations.

The very early texts of *Anti-Platon,* dating back to 1947, still retain something of that air of enigma and obscurity that Bonnefoy himself is troubled to dispel in his reading, twenty years after their initial appearance, of the poems of *Hier régnant désert.* At the same time, however, they clearly mark out the principal obsessions and concerns that will be repeatedly elaborated and refined in his later work, both poetic and critical. The liminal poem of *Anti-Platon* (*D,* 9) stresses immediately the essential role that the particular, the specific, has to play in Bonnefoy's poetics, the inescapable importance—the importance we must not escape from—of the 'this-ness' of the world and our experience of it, set against the shimmering chimera of Idea:

Toutes choses d'ici, pays de l'osier, de la robe, de la pierre, c'est-à-dire: pays de l'eau sur les osiers et les pierres, pays des robes tachées. Ce rire couvert de sang, je vous le dis, trafiquants d'éternel, visages symétriques, absence du regard, pèse plus lourd dans la tête de l'homme que les parfaites Idées qui ne savent que déteindre sur sa bouche.

(*D,* 9)

What seems to matter, then, to Bonnefoy, and from the outset, is this thing, yet all things potentially, things here, 'stained', used, caught in the ebb and flow of life, not withdrawn beyond its actuality. And we, too, are not casual, detached observers, cannot be. Our laughter is inevitably to be 'bloodied' and this very admixture, of the comic and the tragic, the uplifting and the anguishing, has much greater ultimate significance and 'substance' for us than the 'perfect', the purely notional. What we need to assume, then, as Bonnefoy confirms in the closing text of this briefest of poetic sequences (cf. *D,* 17), is the very fragility, the precariousness, of our condition, in short the death that lies attendant upon us all, that is a consequence of the 'this-ness' of our being and whose message, paradoxically of fullness rather than banal finality, is central to Bonnefoy's poetics in general and especially, as we shall now see in our analysis of 'Les Tombeaux de Ravenne' and *Du mouvement et de l'immobilité de Douve,* the earlier expression of it.

The 1953 essay 'Les Tombeaux de Ravenne' (*D,* 19-39) presents Bonnefoy's fundamental thinking with respect to our being-in-the-world, opposing as it does the simplicity of human salvation through our acts of presence, to the perverseness and sophistry of our dismaying tendency to 'conceptualize' the world and our being in it. In this perspective Bonnefoy moves to show that the concept always involves 'un profond refus de la mort' (*D,* 22); it always entails evasion, *fuite,* a denial of human destiny, an effort to erase the ephemeralness and danger of existence and replace them with 'une demeure logique où les seuls principes qui vaillent sont de permanence et d'identité. Demeure faite de mots, mais éternelle' (*D,* 22). Where lucidness in the face of the openness, imperfection and sheer *hasard* of existence should prevail, a drugged 'idealism' sidesteps the world in order to remake it, force it to cohere, systematize itself comfortably, reassuringly. 'Y a-t-il un concept d'un pas venant dans la nuit', Bonnefoy pointedly asks, 'd'un cri, de l'ébranlement d'une pierre dans les broussailles? De l'impression que fait une maison vide? Mais non, rien n'a été gardé du réel que ce qui convient à notre repos' (*D,* 23). It is at this point that Bonnefoy evokes the Ravenna tombs. Initially impressed by their ornamentation, he is tempted to see in them, in this memorial locus of death, merely another, regrettably typical effort to refuse presence, here death, in an act of embellishment, abstraction, transcendence. Art in the face of death, would seem to flee the latter's 'truth'. And yet, Idea, embedding itself in stone, 'risks' itself (cf. *D,* 27), Bonnefoy soon realizes. The ornamentation of the tombs is denied evasion and transcendence by the truth, presence and particularness, 'this-ness', of an object that thus reaffirms passage, becoming, 'une liberté qui se lève' (*D*, 39), at the expense of (aesthetic) *angélisme*. Whereas conceptualization leads to an abandonment of what is, an abandonment that is 'ennui, angoisse, désespoir' in Bonnefoy's eyes, the Ravenna tombs provide an instance of insurrection of the world whereby 'comme par grâce tout le vif et le pur de l'être dans un instant est donné', and spirit and matter once more reach some precarious but joyous communion. In the place of the abstract generality of concept Bonnefoy offers us a 'universality' that always has its locus, its myriad loci, each depending upon our gaze, the use to which we put it (cf. *D*, 30), for the reciprocal exaltation and, as Reverdy would say, ontic 'consubstantiation' that self and world together can secure (cf. *D*, 31).[2] In place of absence, we are given presence, which puts us, at least fleetingly, in contact with that Baudelairean 'unité profonde de tout' (*D*, 34). And presence brings not the stupour of permanence and effete composure;[3] it is on the contrary the epitomy of fragmentation and dispersal—yet a fragmentation and a dispersal that *are*. 'O présence affermie dans l'éclatement déjà de toutes parts', Bonnefoy exlaims with fervour, 'dans la mesure où il est présent, l'objet ne cesse de disparaître. Dans la mesure où il disparaît, il impose, il crie sa présence' (*D*, 35). Ontic depth, 'toute la profondeur de ce qui est' (*D*, 36), is not, then, to be found in the sterilized illusions and veiled, feeble 'divinity' (cf. *D*, 38) of our conceptualization of the world, but rather is evidenced by breakage and wound, passingness and vulnerability. The 'immortality', the universality, the eternity that haunts Bonnefoy offers neither perfection nor any absolute, for they are steeped in time, marked by death: 'conjonction d'une immortalité impossible et d'une immortalité sentie', he argues, 'l'immortalité qu'il y a dans la présence du lierre est de l'éternel que l'on goûte, elle n'est pas la guérison de la mort' (*D*, 37).[4] It is important to stress, however, that in all of this, caught as he is in this essay in the abstractions of philosophical discourse, Bonnefoy's argument is restricted to this minimum. His ambition, his 'devoir absolu' (*D*, 32), is uncluttered, unpretentious, though utterly crucial: the affirmation of our being through a naming, a saying of presence. Poetry's function in this is serious, morally bound, privileged, uplifting. 'Voici le monde sensible', he declares, 'il faut que la parole, ce sixième et ce plus haut sens, se porte à sa rencontre et en déchiffre les signes. Pour moi je n'ai de goût qu'en cette tâche, recherche du secret que Kierkegaard n'avait plus' (*D*, 32). If there are obstacles in the path of such an ambition, as indeed there are in abundance,[5] there is equally the buoying or at least conpensatory thought that it is only in following this path that our starkly beautiful salvation may be found. 'L'acte de présence est en chaque instant la tragédie du monde et son dénouement', Bonnefoy tells us (*D*, 35). So, too, homologously, for *l'acte poétique*.

In the same year that 'Les Tombeaux de Ravenne' appeared, Bonnefoy published his remarkable *Du mouvement et de l'immobilité de Douve* and it is to an examination, firstly, of this determining and influential volume of poetry and, secondly, of that obscure but flickeringly brilliant subsequent collection, *Hier régnant désert*, that we now turn in order to see what, in actual poetic context, in the very *acte poétique* itself, continue to be the central obsessions, the fundamentals, of his poetics. The opening poems of *Du mouvement et de l'immobilité de Douve* establish in effect immediately and forcefully the primacy of the imagination of death in this collection. Everywhere Bonnefoy is appalled by its 'breakage', filled with horror at its 'musique affreuse' (*D*, 56), yet oddly resistant to the apparent finality of burial, strangely enthused even by the bizarre chemistry of disintegration he so powerfully evokes:

> Le ravin pénètre dans la bouche maintenant,
> Les cinq doigts se dispersent en hasards de forêt maintenant,
> La tête première coule entre les herbes maintenant,
> La gorge se farde de neige et de loups maintenant,
> Les yeux ventent sur quels passagers de la mort et c'est nous
> dans ce vent dans cette eau dans ce froid maintenant.
>
> (*D*, 61)

Everywhere, then, Bonnefoy is summoned by what flees, by what lies dark or is torn asunder (cf. *D*, 68) in death, by what he senses to be its problematic though centrally significant 'logic'. Bonnefoy's attitude to death is thus less confused, ambivalent, radically divided, than simply clear-eyed, lucidly aware of the essentially paradoxical nature of this logic. There are two related factors at play here. Death, despite its 'frightful', 'silly' orchestrations (cf. *D*, 56, 52), is felt, throughout these intense poems, to be doubly positive. It is the one phenomenon that, for Bonnefoy, flings us back towards our existence, our leaking yet potentially full being-in-the-world. It provides that very point of anchorage, that totally irreversible attachment to the earth that, viewed falsely, inauthentically, evasively, death itself ironically has so often deprived us of. In short, it is the 'bottom line', the very fundament, of our life. Furthermore, so many texts of *Du mouvement et de l'immobilité de Douve* succeed in bringing out what might, in fact, be thought of as a metaphor for this conception of death, but what may be equally regarded as an extension, an intimately related elaboration of it, namely the notions of continuity and cyclicalness that cling to this conception, death's 'complicity' with life. Douve may thus be 'blessée confuse dans les feuilles', but she remains 'prise par le sang de pistes qui se perdent, / Complice encore du vivre' (*D*, 51). (Douve's) being may be 'undone', but its undoneness is instantly reversed by an act of gathering initiated also by being this time construed as unconquerable: 'Etre défait que l'être invincible rassemble, / Présence ressaisie dans la torche du froid, / O guetteuse toujours je te découvre morte / Douve disant Phénix, je veille dans ce froid' (*D*, 53). Ravaged, insect-infested, caught in the dark process of earth's perpetuity, Douve thus still radiates joy (cf. *D*, 56), exults in her capacity for some stunning continuity and gritty illumination (cf. *D*, 56). Her precise, exact and still emanating presence is what strikes Bonnefoy, finally. Conveyor of the 'cold secret' of death she is, indubitably, essentially, yet there is an oddly crucial way in which Bonnefoy, in no spirit of false, empty, blind transcendence, it should be emphasized, sees this 'dead presence' as 'vivante, de ce sang qui renaît et s'accroît où se déchire le poème' (*D*, 62).[6] 'Il te faudra franchir la mort pour que tu vives', he declares in a later poem of the same volume, 'la plus pure présence est un sang répandu' (*D*, 76). Death in this perspective becomes the threshold of existence, our 'presence' being, reciprocally, paradoxically, most perfectly 'conveyed' by its dispersal, its act of loss. And, in consequence, a shimmering field of mirrored equivalences is set up between what appear to be mutually exclusive, contradictory, antagonistic phenomena: being and nothingness, presence and disappearance, disintegration and assembly. If death is, of necessity, still what it always has been, its meaning is not. For the poems of *Du mouvement et de l'immobilité de Douve* confirm, amongst other things I shall speak of later, not a frightened retreat from death but rather its firm, lucid embrace, its rooting of our being always in the movingness of existence, the rendering quasi-equivalent of the meaning of our true place of dwelling and the meaning of death's simultaneous 'ruination' and founding of this place.

Hier régnant désert appeared in 1958 and if certain of its poems inevitably echo the imaginative emphases of *Du mouvement et de l'immobilité de Douve,* other stresses emerge—albeit elliptically, bathed in a briefly flecked obscurity Bonnefoy himself is sensitive to[7]—to which we shall give out attention here. As with the purely 'theoretical' text of 'L'Acte et le lieu de la poésie' which was published in the same year and which will shortly be discussed in full, what always underpins the enigmatic discourse of this new collection is the role of language, of speech, poetry, in our existence. In one of the early poems Bonnefoy succinctly states the problem of language, its misuse, its purposelessness, its tendency always to be besides the point, and at the same time evokes allusively the healing we may bring to it:

> Et pourquoi disons-nous d'aussi vaines paroles,
> Allant et comme si la nuit n'existait pas?
> Mieux vaut marcher plus près de la ligne d'écume
> Et nous aventurer au seuil d'un autre froid.
>
> (*D*, 137)

(The) language (of poetry), as Bonnefoy generally sees it, is thus characterized by loss, unhappy orientation (cf. *D*, 147), it is turned away from those phenomena of our human condition that, only, can restore its authenticity, its value, opting at once for an indifference and sterility in the face of the world's streaming rawness, and for a beauty that, whilst thought transcendent, is, rather, empty in the idealizing harmonies it procures. Such a beauty, 'celle qui ruine l'être', must be discredited, Bonnefoy unflinchingly, unremittingly argues, 'déshonorée, dite coupable, faite sang. / Et cri, et nuit, de toute joie dépossédée' (*D*, 153). Moreover, it is within the framework of this destruction, this dismissal, that the 'inguérissable espoir' informing all of Bonnefoy' writing asserts itself. The 'torturing' of beauty, of the beauty of (the) language (of poetry), is not a wanton, gratuitous act; the 'blood' spilled, the 'scream' echoing in the night air, are, precisely, of infinitely greater (in)significance than the hollow, ringing perfection of anything we may articulate for the sake of, in (oblivious) praise of, its mere 'beauty'. 'L'imperfection est la cime', as the title of one of the poems of *Hier régnant désert* unambiguously affirms. The problem of language finds its solution in an unlikely fashion, for, essentially, it has arisen through a progressive perversion of its relation to being, experience, both the quotidian and the marvellous. Indeed the problem of language, and thus its solution, are profoundly ontological. And, in consequence, so many of the poems of this volume stress what we have seen already and shall continue to see throughout Yves Bonnefoy's writings, poetic or critical, namely the necessary imbrication of the logics of language and death (cf. *D*, 160), the turning of poetry's language away from its cosmetic effects back to the vital urgency of its elementary and elemental concerns, back to the frozen, broken simplicity of a nettle (cf. *D*, 158). Language's healing thus depends upon the birth of a new or renewed vision of its relation to presence, upon a new perception of the world as 'une terre d'aube' (*D*, 167), when, finally, 'l'inquiète voix consent d'aimer / La pierre simple' (*D*, 176). The second of the two poems presented under the title of 'L'Ordalie' delicately evokes much of this:

> Je ne sais pas si je suis vainqueur. Mais j'ai saisi
> D'un grand coeur l'arme enclose dans la pierre.
> J'ai parlé dans la nuit de l'arme, j'ai risqué
> Le sens et au delà du sens le monde froid.
>
> Un instant tout manqua,
> Le fer rouge de l'être ne troua plus
> La grisaille du verbe,
> Mais enfin le feu se leva,
> Le plus violent navire
> Entra au port.
>
> Aube d'un second jour,
> Je suis enfin venu dans ta maison brûlante
> Et j'ai rompu ce pain où l'eau lointaine coule.
>
> (*D*, 179)

In the face of continuing uncertainty the poet commits himself to an action that at least, risking all, meaning and world, 'risks' equally a seizing of something fundamentally human and crucial despite its otherness, its reclusion. Hiatus there no doubt is between being and language, but in the optic of Bonnefoy's poetics obstacle and setback are never held to be definitive. There dominates, rather, an atmosphere of possibility, accomplishment and reawakening. Speech, for Bonnefoy, can indeed enjoy its 'homecoming' and the simple communal gestures this affords.

If the poems of *Hier régnant désert* choose, as we would expect, a metaphorical mode of articulation of the message they seek to convey, the important essay 'L'Acte et le lieu de la poésie', whilst clearly more logically and cogently structured, often opts no less for an expression of its underlying principles that is poetically charged and most certainly at a remove from the dry linguistic or philosophic conceptualizations that abound today. Broadly, the essay moves from an assessment of the dangers besetting poetry to an affirmation of the latter's moral and ontological necessity—and feasibility, given certain things. The dangers that hem in poetry are constant, in Bonnefoy's view. Rooted in the past, they continue to plague the present. Essentially they are the dangers of hygiene and aesthetic, formalistic transcendence. Poetry thus may seek better to grasp satisfaction of the desire, the lack that inspires it,[8] by ridding itself of the world, of death, of imperfection—all those factors Bonnefoy deems so crucial to poetic, and existential, well-being. Mallarmé, despite his brilliance and exemplary dedication, is, in this respect, classically, and all too influentially, guilty. Of course, his ambition was noble, worthy and founded upon a hope, but for Bonnefoy it was an old, outmoded form of hope and his entire life and work in some paradoxically, ironically didactic way—if only we can be alert to the lesson—'a démontré l'échec de l'ancien mouvement d'espoir' (*D,* 189). In endeavouring to escape what he held to be the 'nothingness of everything'—a combination of words surely sufficient to make anyone, not just Bonnefoy, sit up and question one's thinking—Mallarmé placed all his trust in a phenomenon, language, poetry, that might save only 'l'amande même de l'être' (*D,* 188), but which, in fact, as he realizes himself only too well—and *teaches* us, despite all his other messages, Bonnefoy rightly stresses—cannot escape the nothingness, the exile that he would flee. Mallarmé may thus seek to be reborn in a higher plane, but his quest entails, in a sense disastrously, a poetry 'qui est l'existence vaincue, élan par élan, désir par désir' (*D,* 189). The danger of such a quest, for Bonnefoy, is in effect much graver than that thrown up by its failure, for only upon the recognition of such a failure can a new vigour flourish. 'Tous nous sommes rejetés hors du havre de la parole dans un pays de dangers; où des pressentiments, d'ailleurs, et l'insatisfaction de beaucoup de grands poètes, reprendront sens et autorité' (*D,* 190). This does not mean at all that the 'failure' of Mallarmé is all immediately sweetness and light for his heirs. On the contrary, a certain pessimism in his work, an avoidance of the 'lessons' of Baudelaire and Rimbaud, have prompted many to yield to 'le désir d'une discipline pour se retraire de ce qui est' (*D,* 199), to opt for une 'un acte de pure forme, . . . ce que je veux nommer la mauvaise mort' (*D,* 199). And it is here, precisely, in withdrawal from the 'alternative' dangers of existence—ephemeralness, precariousness, death—into a realm of false imaginary peace and harmony 'où tout n'est qu'ordre et beauté, / Luxe, calme et volupté', as Baudelaire himself all too temptingly portrayed it,[9] that the real danger, for the poet as for the (wo)man, manifests itself. Here, all is to be lost. In risking, in running the dangers of existence, all is to be gained. From such 'welcome' dangers everything may flow . . . once more. But for this new hope—articulated in contradistinction to 'l'ancien mouvement d'espoir', essentially misleading, inauthentic, evocative of the existentialist *mauvaise foi,* and doomed to failure—to prosper, the poet of the 'post-divine' age (cf. *D,* 187) must lucidly confront the human condition, ask the fundamental questions: what interests me, what do I really want, do I wish to 'avoid' death, a sense of loss, in the absent 'divinity' of some form, etc.?

If the answers to these questions are indeed not readily available, Bonnefoy uncompromisingly asserts: 'Mais je ne doute pas que la poésie moderne—la poésie sans les dieux—doive savoir ce qu'elle désire pour, en connaissance de cause, juger du pouvoir des mots' (*D,* 187). From lucidity only, then, Bonnefoy's essay argues, may flow a true hope, a hope that does indeed, as we have seen elsewhere, inspire his thought and direct his creative energies. From the opening lines of 'L'Acte et le lieu de la poésie', Bonnefoy's desire to restore hope to poetry, to render them identical even, is transparent (cf. *D,* 185). Moreover, the absolute availability of this hope, this possibility that is poetry, is, for Bonnefoy, blatantly evident, if only we can understand what we truly want and need. 'Comment ne pas reconnaître', he asks, quite rhetorically, 'au delà de ses bergeries, le goût de la poésie pour quelque chose d'errant et de livide qui semble sous des arbres éternels le spectre de la limite que l'on voudrait oublier?' (*D,* 130). The 'new' hope that we must 'reinvent' (cf. *D,* 202) does not thus float off into some into some thin, unbreathable ethereal atmosphere with its frozen crystalline forms; it anchors us, rather, in what may be thought of as the spirituality of our being-in-the-world, our limitless wandering among the leaden-hued limits of the earth. The poetry—the hope—that Bonnefoy proposes to us, offers us openness, future, movement, instead of congealment, past and sterility (cf. *D,* 213).[10] Very nearly '*un réalisme initiatique*' (*D,* 213) in the sense that it is 'au point de connaître, dans son durable exil, ce que peut ouvrir la *présence*' (*D,* 214), poetry, the poetry of Bonnefoy, the poetry 'to come', may thus finally attain to grace, truth, even beauty, providing it remains rooted in this fusion of hope and lucidness that Bonnefoy calls 'cette ardente mélancolie' (*D,* 213). Only within the bounds of this tensely interlocking relation can true poetry articulate itself. Only from the depths of his known poverty, his aware deprivation, can the crucial giving of a true poet come forth (cf. *D,* 213). Words themselves, as Bonnefoy argues Baudelaire came to understand, cannot constitute our salvation, which lies rather, as we saw in *Anti-Platon,* in our affirmation, and our love, of 'la seule réalité, irremplaçable, qui est telle chose ou tel être' (*D,* 195). Upon the ruins of such mortality there then appears, for poetry, for humanity, a loving and loved possibility (cf. *D,* 203). But here again it must be understood that no end, no ultimate solution, is implied. Openness prevails once more; poetry is open-ended in that it can only be movement towards, approach, means (cf. *D,* 199, 206). It can never, must never be what we want itself. It remains as search, never constituting in itself the object of our desire, 'la vérité de parole étant une proximité', as Bonnefoy puts it (*D,* 212), a continuing quest we assume as our moral, and ontological, duty.

In an effort to bring out at once the principal factors of the further elaboration of Yves Bonnefoy's poetics and the elements of constancy that always characterizes the latter, I shall now pass, over the critical pieces of *L'Improbable* with its penetrating and always personal discussion of *Les Fleurs du Mal*, and Bonnefoy's essay on Rimbaud, on to two other, somewhat later discursive pieces, both decidedly determining, 'La Seconde Simplicité and 'La Poésie française et le principe d'identité'. The first of these appeared in 1961 in the volume of that name, and later in 1967, in *Un rêve fait à Mantoue*, where the second essay was also published after its more or less simultaneous appearance that year with Maeght.[11]

'La Seconde Simplicité' is a short but strongly felt and powerfully eloquent essay on—or rather declaration of love for—'l'extravagance baroque' (RM, 25). This predilection may surprise, although it will be well understood by those who have had the pleasure of reading Bonnefoy's superb *Rome 1630: l'horizon du premier baroque* published in 1970, and at all events will be seen to lie at the centre of his poetics. What appeals in the baroque is, essentially, as Bonnefoy declares at the outset, 'la réaffirmation de l'objet sensible au coeur même, et combien vibrant, du vouloir propre des formes' (RM, 25). Where law, number, the music of form might seem still to reign, 'l'obscure gravitation charnelle' imposes its simple human magnetism in defiance of Renaissance classicism, purity, formal and spiritual idealism. In the face of doubt about the very reality of reality itself, our being here and now, the baroque, 'ce réalisme passionne!' (RM, 25), unambiguously asserts its, for Bonnefoy, crucial love for 'ce qui passe, ce qui est limité, ce qui meurt' (RM, 25). With the baroque the absolute crumbles, 'la joie imparfaite de la terre' as well as 'le tragique manque secret' shakily, precariously, yet triumphantly announce their return to the minds and hearts of people. What Bonnefoy particularly, and perhaps most significantly, likes in baroque art, however, are those paradoxical instances where what he terms, precisely, '*une simplicité seconde* se fait soudain dans l'agitation consumée' (RM, 25). Could it be that such instances denote a rearing of the all too beautiful head of abstraction and classicism, 'la trahison d'une cause, la dissociation, une fois de plus dans l'histoire humaine, du souci de construire et du sentiment de la mort' (RM, 26)? Bonnefoy opts finally for an optimistic view of things and prefers to see here, not a slippage, a retrograde hesitation, but on the contrary a supreme effort to marry idea and presence, perfection and imperfection, concept and death. 'C'est ce baroque plus simple', he proclaims, 'qui s'approche le plus, par lucidité ou sagesse, de l'impossible unité' (RM, 27). And it is this particular manifestation of the baroque that thus comes to represent for Bonnefoy that perhaps ideal and most legitimate conjunction of opposed, yet here mutually consenting, formal, aesthetic, spiritual 'law' and 'la précarité temporelle' or what he also calls 'cette présence absolue, sans répit, que nous aimons dans la pierre' (RM, 27).

The second of the two essays from *Un rêve fait à Mantoue* that will receive special attention here, 'La Poésie française et le principe d'identité', approaches, as might be expected, certain of the same haunting elements of his poetics we have heard Bonnefoy already articulate. But, once again, as with 'La Seconde Simplicité' new angles of observation open up enabling Bonnefoy to touch upon new factors and elaborate new stresses: the contrast, with respect to language, between its use and its 'madness', the logic of the invisible and the invisible in language, the distinction between analytical language and the language of desire, of integrity, and so on. One of the first observations Bonnefoy makes in fact—a central observation despite the rapid manner of his initial dealing with it—pertains to the nature and function of language in and out of poetry. The latter certainly does not entail a *use* of language. 'Peut-être une folie *dans* la langue', he suggests, 'mais qu'on ne peut comprendre en ce cas que par ses yeux de folie—que par sa façon à elle d'entendre et prendre les mots' (RM, 94). Essentially we find here, expressed in fresh terms, that decisive hiatus Bonnefoy sees yawning between the language of concept and that of presence. The former leads to the fragmentation of demonstration, the divisions and reifications of structure and reason; the latter offers a totality, an identity, a destiny that eschew all sectioning and reduction. The poetic act thus veers sharply away from assessment, analysis, even description, to become an *acte de présence* in, and through, words. Such 'madness' allows precisely for a gathering, 'dans une surabondance où je suis pris et sauvé', of a reality threatened with disassociation and disintegration (RM, 97). A restoration of place and unity thereby comes about which 'justifies' the world and operates a miraculous consubstantial ontological fusion, refusion, of self and world (cf. RM, 97).[12] From mere perception of the world—of '*une* salamandre', for example—as an analyzable, rational object of attention, we thus proceed to 'l'amour, qui est prescience de l'invisible qui est le vrai réel', the world, the salamander, become suddenly *visage, l'ange* (cf. RM, 98), 'la salamandre présente au coeur des autres présences' (RM, 98). It is in this poetico-ontological movement of language, the establishment of that unity that is, indeed, *présence,* that the confusion of category, concept and segregation yields to the sweet order of existence and wholeness. Beyond its conceptual aspects, then, Bonnefoy feels, language does in effect offer the same ontic unity as being renders available 'au delà des aspects qui ont fragmenté le sensible' (RM, 99). 'Tout langage', he goes on to maintain, 'est ainsi le champ pour l'élaboration d'une sorte d'ordre; pour la fondation d'un sacré dans le destin de celui qui parle; pour les efforts, au moins, d'une poésie'(RM, 99). Not that this 'order', this 'founding of a sacredness' imply, by some legerdemain, the reinstatement of the principles of perfection, structure, heterocosmicity (i.e. the poem as other world, as object apart). They most certainly do not. As far as Bonnefoy is concerned the poetic 'object' founded upon, and perceived in terms of, such factors, constitutes merely 'la dépouille . . . du poème', whereas what interests him, and what only, he argues, can matter and mean, are 'l'âme et le dessein du poème' (RM, 100), the fact that it finds its—our—salvation only in the display of its integralness, its vibrant oneness, its dynamic, loving joining together of world and self within itself.[13] This interlocking of self and world in some new consubstantial wholeness within the 'space' of the poem's language is, in effect, highly reminiscent of the poetics of Pierre Reverdy. And he, too, despite his earlier stress upon form, syntax and textual disposition, remains, like Bonnefoy, profoundly attached, finally, to the ontological and ethical criteria of the poem, rather than to the latter's aesthetic and structural essence. The vocabulary of the crucial passage closing the fifth part of Bonnefoy's 'La Poésie française et le principe d'identité' reflects this quite strongly: the poem offers justice, participation, consubstantiation, its most elevated moments allow us to glimpse a rare purity of evidence, to savour the liberation of the visible, to assume our—and the world's—true destiny (cf. *RM*, 100). Such a destiny, Bonnefoy declares, was constantly assumed by Rimbaud, whereas a Laforgue is torn between gravity, desire, and irony, between the compelling force of 'l'identité *intérieure* de la présence', as Bonnefoy says in his concluding lines (*RM*, 125), and the aspectual, reductive perspective that mar(k)s his work (cf. *RM*, 104-5). The great French poems of the Middle Ages, too, succeeded with utter simplicity and limpidness to 'élaborer un monde et, en se faisant transparents, nous concilier l'univers' (*RM*, 114), the 'identity' between poetic world and real world, *langue* and *terre*, attaining thereby to 'son degré le plus haut de saturation substantielle' (*RM*, 115), the invisible giving voice to the visible, the visible finding its true place of being beyond itself in the transparency of the invisible. The problem that exists now for the language and poetry—and the people—of France, a problem that has gradually worsened (cf. *RM*, passim, esp. 125), is that this 'identity principle', 'si intensément vécu comme axe de participation, comme évidence de l'être, dans la poésie médiévale' (*RM*, 116),[14] relies upon a capacity for intuition that runs against the grain of, and has indeed been almost forgotten by, our developing tradition of thinking and being in, and with, the world. There is, in consequence, and before it is too late, an 'order' to be reinstated, one that will allow for the poet—and humankind—to exchange conceptual essence for presence, aspectual hollowness for interior profundity. Only in the light of this reinstatement, Bonnefoy proclaims, can existence take up its true form, finiteness go beyond itself to embrace the unlimited, truth be conjured with *le sensible*. Only then, through our act of love, can we refuse, 'comme on purifie, ce qui fait le jeu du néant' (*RM*, 120). Whilst seeming to be vast, and of course in a sense it is, Bonnefoy's project can be realized by a significant switch in perspective, and by a concentration upon what, finally, radically matters in our lives.

In passing, lastly, to an appraisal of the imaginative inspiration of *Dans le leurre du seuil* in the context of the poetics under consideration, we pass to what, undoubtedly, is not only Bonnefoy's finest poetic creation to date but perhaps the finest he will ever produce, for it ranks amongst the most magnificent pieces of sustained poetry of the twentieth century.[15] It should be understood before proceeding to this necessarily compact account, that a number of other recent books and collections could equally well have merited and held our attention, especially given our present purposes: the somewhat earlier *Rome, 1630* (1970) or *L'Arrière-pays* (1972), the various essays of *Le Nuage rouge* and the *récits* of *Rue traversière,* both published in 1977, or the very recent *Entretiens sur la poésie* (1981) which gathers together material of the past fifteen years.[16] In choosing to conclude with a discussion of the 1975 *Dans le leurre du seuil,* then, we have opted, over the pressing merits of powerfully eloquent critical essays and intense shorter poetic *proses,* for the continuity and coherence of a great poem. Such a choice will, it is hoped, also remind us that, if Bonnefoy has written so much, so obsessively, *about* poetry, what matters ultimately is its practice from which its function may then flow. Moreover, in the case of this poem, as with *Du mouvement et de l'immobilité de Douve,* Bonnefoy offers us a superbly delicate imbrication of praxis and poetics, a self-reflexive creation whose passion embraces, and precisely according to his conception of 'la fonction du poème' (*NR,* 267) and the basic principles of his poetics, the interlocking, in a sense potentially equivalent, ontological natures of word and world.

The first part of *Dans le leurre du seuil,* entitled 'Le Fleuve' (*DLS,* 9-15), offers us an awakening, a suddenness of speech; it tells of a looking that is intent and imperative, at things no longer caught in some fictitious 'forever', 'cet à-jamais de silencieuse / Respiration nocturne', but flowing before the self and still signalling a possibility clearly crucial to Bonnefoy's poetics. Everywhere there is paradox, tension, 'choice', as we may like to think of it. Meaning may appear coagulated, somehow disastrously lost, blackly enigmatic, and yet the signs are still there. There is a fullness, even, a kind of perfection of form and substance in the world. There is, in short, equally, an evidence, and a feeling of certainty and joy that oddly persist. Here, Boris de Schloezer's death is, surprisingly, suddenly evoked, the bliss and illumination upon his face contrasted with those 'eaux brûlées d'énigme' that he left behind. The moment seems somehow to symbolize for Bonnefoy the jarring confrontation of a poetics of possible intuition and one of flat submission to the kaleidoscopic unfolding of incomprehensible acts and events upon 'l'amère terre nocturne'. 'Le Fleuve', however, is a poem of traversal, navigation and difficult continuity.

'Dans le leurre du seuil' is the title of the second part of Bonnefoy's long poem (*DLS,* 19-35). Its tone, too, is imperative, one of unambiguous moral compulsion and unremitting forcefulness. 'Heurte, / Heurte à jamais', Bonnefoy begins, 'Dans le leurre du seuil. // A la porte, scellée, / A la phrase, vide. / Dans le fer, n'éveillant / Que ces mots, le fer. // Dans le langage, noir'. The striking is, must be, persistent, an act of dogged continuity addressing itself to everything before us, world and word, in a effort to salvage *le célébrable* within. Bonnefoy is aware of the lateness of the gesture, certainly, but it is precisely this lateness that gives urgency to a gesture made against all the odds, often 'blindly' and in fatigue. It is important also to remain sensitive to the dual nature of the hammering, the 'striking' of the poet: it takes place in, upon, reality, primary experience, and in, upon, language, specific words. But, of course, these acts are essentially one and the same. Language may be holed, battered, devastated; the world's multiple 'faces tournées vers nous' may be plunged into silence. But, clearly, their separate healings are mutually dependent; the wholeness, the identity we have heard Bonnefoy speak of, can only come about through a therapeutic interaction or interpenetration whereby the sick and deprived heal one another. To achieve this cure, however, the necessity, the preciousness of the poet's/our continued listening and watching, Bonnefoy repeatedly writes, cannot be stressed enough. The empty noise of words, swept along in the wind, is, too, a constant anxiety in all of this. The time lived is not the time desired. It is still provisional, initiatory, transitional; a time, still, of hope and promise not yet—and indeed, Bonnefoy wonders, can it ever quite be?—beyond them. A time of striking 'dans le leurre du seuil'.

The following two sections of *Dans le leurre du seuil*, 'Deux couleurs' (*DLS*, 37-43) and 'Deux barques' (*DLS*, 45-55), continue to elaborate the fundamental themes at play in Bonnefoy's poetics, though, of course, there is no logical, systematic development of thought finely parcelled out into the illusory compartments of some overall thesis. What he initially affirms, in that style of shimmeringly coherent ellipses articulating themselves at the intersection of the unconscious and a sense of their *justesse,* is at once the difficulty of the (poetic/existential) gesture and a confidence that still clings firmly to it. The search Bonnefoy and the poem itself initiate, takes place so that 'la vie / De rien qu'un rêve' may be born. Their joint human and poetic intention would match being with ideal, existence with dream—an ideal and a dream that, whilst central, demanding a focussing of our entire attention, are, it is essential to underscore, in a sense also minimal, mere, *rien qu'un rêve,* a crucially significant goal oddly veined with the paradox of slightness and even a certain insignificance well known to poets such as Stéphane Mallarmé, André Frénaud or Michel Deguy.[17] Despite a muddiness clouding our view of the threshold, the place of access, 'l'arbre d'étoiles'is glimpsed, definitely there, moving in the water; and the sense—and the need, both ethical and aesthetic—of a birth, a new life welling up within us is urgent and real. Despite, too, the 'mauvais désir de l'infini' that continues to make itself felt, Bonnefoy gives confidence to that impulse that bids him 'consent' to the mortality of the world, to go forth into 'l'été mortel', joining with it, erasing all dualities, dissipating, being dissipated, miraculously realizing 'tard, l'inespéré, soudain'. In that movement, simple, crucial, access to an elusive yet briefly available peace and illumination becomes possible:

> Paix, sur l'eau éclairée. On dirait qu'une barque
> Passe, chargée de fruits; et qu'une vague
> De suffisance, ou d'immobilité,
> Soulève notre lieu et cette vie
> Comme une barque à peine autre, liée encore.
>
> (*DLS*, 51)

Bonnefoy's intuition, fleeting in itself, is of a fleeting yet sure phenomenon that speaks of plenitude and gentle adequacy. It is a phenomenon offering that quiet, almost inconspicuous transmutation of our experience, a transmutation edging us towards a sense of some marvellous otherness while maintaining an essential and firm attachment to substance and 'evident' reality—an experience, in short, of immediacy and transmutation, simultaneously.

The section of *Dans le leurre du seuil* that follows is entitled 'La Terre' (*DLS*, 57-75). It opens by picturing the poet shouting out his pressing, emotionally intense message to others, a message that urges them—all of us—to see the world, and the world, afresh, in the light of a simple though rich proximity that, rather than precluding an invisibility and a measure of eternity, on the contrary, and paradoxically, invites their collusion. In this new, or renewed, optic, 'rien n'a changé, / Ce sont les mêmes lieux et les mêmes choses, / Presque les mêmes mots, / Mais, vois, en toi, en moi / L'indivis, l'invisible se rassemblent'. What Bonnefoy calls the 'knotty', 'rent', 'forever earthy' side of the human condition thus embraces, and is in a sense simultaneous, synonymous with, 'la part impérissable de la vie', and he can henceforth speak with passion and conviction of 'l'à jamais de la fleur éphémère' without any sense of contradiction insinuating itself into his words. Life, the earth, is, then, once again seen as offering a conjunction, even a superimposition, of the forces of passing and consumption, and those of continuity and (re)incarnation. The earth itself—and of course the poet in his reading of its signs—is a place at once of dispersal and gathering, death and celebration of the dying. In its myriad fading and dying movements, the world leaps continually into incandescence, its insignificance suddenly—yet all the time—significant, 'toute une indifférence, illuminée'. And language, too, *parole*—that human, death-governed phenomenon—in passing, shines forth; in its brilliance, dies, but not without giving off its curiously persistent afterglow. The poet and the world—like all things and all people—in some freshly thought conformity with that *poétique de l'éclair* of René Char, thus conspire to be 'l'un pour l'autre comme la flamme / Quand elle se détache du flambeau, / La phrase de fumée un instant lisible / Avant de s'effacer dans l'air souverain'. What *already is,* then, may in this way be revealed anew, yet reaffirmed, as what we had never quite understood it to be. 'Oui', Bonnefoy goes on, 'toutes choses simples / Rétablies / Ici et là, sur leurs / Piliers de feu'. Everything, things and words, magnificently self-revealing at the moment of fiery farewell. What may be a source of anguish for others, the 'nothingness', as it were, of the being of world and word, thus remains a source of sober joy for Bonnefoy. His speech, his poetic utterance, may be a seemingly empty slobbering, 'la salive du rien', but, in the piercing purity of its articulation, it manages to bridge and heal and gladden.[18]

'Les Nuées' (*DLS*, 77-99) is the name given to the penultimate section of this long poem, with its obsessively voiced and criss-crossing lines of sense. It stresses, in a particularly important passage (*DLS*, 84-6), the need for faith and perseverance in the enterprise Bonnefoy proposes. Only if we show, despite all, what Sartre considered to be that clearly required faith in language, can meaning grow within our words and the earth be saved in that stunning process of birth and maturation whose reality and whose truth the poet dreams. Whilst, then, Bonnefoy never forgets 'la misère du sens', 'la tache noire dans l'image'—those elements that force his poetics to the brink of the tragic—he has still, and especially in *Dans le leurre du seuil*, that grittiness and air of suffused confidence that, though never seeking to abandon this sober perspective, see the world, and its language, as a kind of Mother Courage leading forth things and words in the midst of their evaporation, their 'woundedness', their imperfection. Consciously endeavouring to thrust aside 'la voix néante qui essaie de parler à travers la mienne', the conceits and idle satisfactions the latter alluringly proposes, Bonnefoy's poetic act nevertheless builds itself upon ontological and linguistic defect and incompletion[19] in a joyously impulsive movement towards the retention of this fleeting, maimed substance, in the lucid—and no longer simply 'childish'—hope of rendering, if not meaning itself, 'au moins l'idée du sens—à la lumière'. His poetics thus boldly, tragically and jubilantly, 'assumes' our insubstantialness, our cloud-like ephemeralness, our constant moving in and out of being/nothingness, in the intuition of a rock-bottom, minimal transcendence of the latter in that special place of conjuncture,

> Quand nous passons
> Déserts
> Dans la vitre embrasée de ce pays
> Qui ressemble au langage: illuminée
> Au loin, pierreux ici.
>
> (*DLS*, 98)

'L'Epars, l'indivisible', are the title words set before the closing pages of *Dans le leurre du seuil* (*DLS*, 101-21). They speak, as do so many texts of Michel Deguy or, again, Perse's last poem, *Chant pour un équinoxe*, of a scattering and division that are matched, even in a sense equated, with a special mode of unity and coherence that depend upon them. The text proper begins with an outburst of renewed affirmations which soon becomes a thrilling, restless, all-embracing litany of assent to the endless phenomena that gather their teeming diversity around, in and through, us, to constitute our being. In conformity with his poetics of an ephemeralness and death that illuminate, Bonnefoy seeks everywhere to confirm his approval and acceptance less of phenomena that seem to speak blatantly of fullness and wholeness than, for example, of that sun, that fire that lights up the world in its passingness, in its gleamingly traced and erased path through a world constantly giving fruit, giving birth at the moment of a death. 'Oui, par ce feu', he declares, 'par son reflet de feu sur l'eau paisible, / Par notre lieu, qui va, / Par le chemin de feu sous le fruit mûr'. Being and nothingness are hence tied together, constantly jostling and leap-frogging each other, creating an energy, a warmth, a light that permit what can be to be in an act and time that simultaneously burst into life and die (cf. *DLS*, 114). And of course the language to which the poet aspires will mould itself to this conception of things. Nothing will be total, totalizing, systemic, symphonic, perfected either formally or notionally. What will remain will be 'ces quelques mots que j'ai sauvés / Pour une bouche enfante'. Assent will be given to language, but only in its incompleteness, its imperfection: 'Oui, par les mots, / Quelques mots', he affirms. The gesture of poetry is not an All, an Absolute; it is merely—though crucially—a partial gesture, caught in time, even though straining beyond, better through, its particularness, towards some renewable, potentially (ever-)reborn meaning. This meaning, however, Bonnefoy repeats here, cannot be located in the closed space of a structure or what he likes to think of as an 'image'. Such meaning is to be dashed upon the rocks to the benefit of a meaning in flux, open, holed and more recessed, one that must be preserved: 'Et d'une main, / Certes, lever le fouet, injurier le sens, / Précipiter / Tout le charroi d'images dans les pierres /—De l'autre, plus profonde, retenir'. Moreover, in the key passage of 'L'Epars, l'indivisible' that immediately follows (cf. *DLS*, 116), Bonnefoy stresses the dangers of the imaginary heterocosm, the substitute, 'other' structure of the mind, in which we may erroneously seek refuge. No 'building' can truly occur, in effect; we must maintain, in simplicity and compassion, and yet profundity, a sense of 'la dérive majeure de la nuée', the deeply significant ephemeralness and 'informality' of it all—world and word. Pursuing 'dans l'orgueil le néant de quelque forme' is not, finally, worthy of humanity. Better, infinitely, to 'atteindre à la terre brève' and to ponder the sober yet profound lessons of its (in)significance. None of this implies that beauty lacks meaning (cf. *DLS*, 116-17). Despite death, beauty can gather the things of the world, in time; the 'minimalness' of being can be edged towards a simple yet spectacular maximum, as with André Frénaud. But it is not the beauty of what Bonnefoy thinks of as formal 'repose', the echoing empty chamber of words as form; but rather, through the 'violence' of the written act, a beauty affording peace with the world, yet ragged, raw, dying. Language, poetry, and the beauty and happiness they can offer, are yet, in all their illuminated ephemeralness, powerfully caught up in a sense Bonnefoy never loses and cares even at the close of his vastly majestic poem to underscore, of the endless process of reincarnation and continuity that complements that of death. His poetic assent thus affirms itself of necessity 'par la vie sans fin / . . . / Par hier réincarné, ce soir, demain / Oui, ici, là, ici, là-bas encore'. The 'wave' that is at once life and language, thus obeys and mimes this logic, gathering itself, swelling into shape and fullness, spending itself, breaking and crumbling, in a continuous process of discontinuous being and becoming. 'Les mots comme le ciel, / Aujourd'hui', Bonnefoy quietly but intensely proclaims as he bids us farewell, 'quelque chose qui s'assemble, qui se disperse. // Les mots comme le ciel / Infini / Mais tout entier soudain dans la flaque brève'. Language, poetry, like the world: breathing, rhythmically pulsing, mortal. But a mortality, a flashing briefness that reach, through their endless becoming, now, beyond themselves, towards an infinity bathed in the light of passing immediacy.

Notes

1. DLS, 121. The following abbreviations are used throughout: D: *Du mouvement et de l'immobilité de Douve* (Gallimard, 'Poésie', 1970); PE: *Pierre écrite* (Mercure de France, 1965 (1959); I: *L'Improbable* (Mercure de France, 1959); RM: *Un rêve fait à Mantoue* (Mercure de France, 1967); DLS: *Dans le leurre du seuil* (Mercure de France, 1975). Other books by Bonnefoy consulted include: *Arthur Rimbaud* (Seuil, 1961); *Rome, 1630* (Flammarion, 1970); *Rue traversière* (Mercure de France, 1977); *L'Ordalie* (Mercure de France, 1974); *Le Nuage rouge* (Mercure de France, 1977); *L'Arrière-pays* (Skira, 1972); *Entretiens sur la poésie* (A la baconnière, 1981); *L'Origine du langage,* George Nama, 1980; *La Présence et l'image,* Mercure de France, 1983. The main critical studies of Bonnefoy are John E. Jackson's essay in the Seghers volume, *Yves Bonnefoy* (1976), Jérôme Thelot's *Poétique d'Yves Bonnefoy* (Droz 1983) and John T. Naughton's *The Poetic of Yves Bonnefoy* (Univ. of Chicago, 1984), though I have not yet seen the last two. The shorter critical work of Jean-Pierre Richard, James Lawler, Richard Stamelman, Graham Martin, Philippe Jaccottet, B. Arndt, Sarah Lawall, Richard Vernier, Roger Munier, Alex Gordon, Mary Ann Caws again, and others, has in varying measure contributed to my growing appreciation of Bonnefoy. Some of these studies appear in the important special issues devoted to Bonnefoy, of *L'Arc* (1976) and *World Literature Today* (1979). The *actes* of the 1983 *colloque de Cerisy* will also appear soon with *SUD*.

2. The notion of the consubstantiality of self and world, through poetry or artistic creation, is, as I have shown in the context of other poets examined here, central to Reverdy's aesthetics, for, despite his stress upon poetic margin, *le poème-objet,* transmutation, etc., art/poetry remains, not apart, but for the world, for being, and its continuing validity depends not upon hygienic removal from reality but permanent osmotic contact with it. This and other related ideas are elaborated in my paper for the 1983 *colloque de Cerisy,* 'Bonnefoy et Reverdy', to be published with *SUD*.

3. Somewhat like André Frénaud, Bonnefoy perceives specific, heightened experiences of presence as attainment less of the *vrai lieu* proper, than of something corresponding to one's desire for the *vrai lieu,* as a series of places of halt and repose. But the quest is, finally, endless, caught up in, even equivalent to, one's human (and poetic) destiny.

4. Cf. D, 37: 'Qui tente la traversée de l'espace sensible rejoint une eau sacrée qui coule dans toute chose. Et pour peu qu'il y touche, il se sent immortel'. Saint-John Perse in so much of his work, and so splendidly in *Anabase,* is perhaps the one other modern poet who, in addition to Bonnefoy, so freely and deeply senses this imbrication of the sensible and the eternal, the changing, the dying, the imperfect, and the immortal, the immemorial that stares at us through the opaqueness of what is.

5. Cf. D,33: 'La pensée conceptuelle; mais aussi la notion d'un Dieu aux exigences morales; hors de l'esprit un pouvoir de nuit qui s'infiltre partout en objets truqués, en forces impures, en choses laides: tels sont les principaux obstacles sur le chemin du retour'.

6. Again one may think of Reverdy whose poetic equation permits a quasi-transcendence of the 'nothingness' of given being via the establishment of the 'true', 'real' locus of being in the poem. However, Bonnefoy's position is clearly different in certain respects (the primacy of the sensible, etc.) and his central argument leads elsewhere: he is endeavouring far less to argue poetic transcendence, the virtues of the poetic locus as place of survival, than the significance of death for our real, sentient, breathing being. To avoid this, to side-step it, is, indeed, to die, but before temporal death, i.e. futilely, unwittingly, in illusion.

7. Cf. Bonnefoy' own note, written in 1969 and appended to the 1970 Gallimard 'Poésie' edition: 'Toutefois, *Hier régnant désert* m'est maintenant obscur et, en quelques points, presque étranger Je l'ai un peu remanié par effort de le comprendre; et abrégé' (D, 222).

8. For Reverdy this lack, this desire, basing itself upon the very emptiness of primary being, could only be satisfied, briefly, in part, imperfectly, by the *bouche-abîme* of poetry, of art.

9. Cf. D, 214: 'Le repos de la forme n'est pas honnêtement acceptable'.

10. As Bonnefoy says, poetry, this hope, 'opère la transmutation de l'abouti en possible, du souvenir en attente, de l'espace désert en cheminement, en espoir. Et je pourrais dire qu'elle est un *réalisme initiatique* si elle nous donnait, au dénouement, le réel'. Here, in effect, Bonnefoy is manifestly closer to Reverdy in his reliance upon notions such as transmutation, the movement from the congealed, the dead, the incontrovertible, to the realm of a possibility, of renewed expectation, indeed of a poetic reality on the verge of mediating a consubstantiality, of allowing us to 'have', and truly to be with, primary reality.

11. Also in the *Revue d'esthétique,* juillet-décembre 1965.

12. 'Le mur est justifié', argues Bonnefoy in the same passage, 'et l'âtre, et l'olivier dehors et la terre. Et moi, redevenu tout cela, réveillé à ma profonde saveur—car cet espace se voûte en moi comme l'intérieur de mon existence' (RM, 97).

13. And not in the display, arrangement, organization, subtle expression of aspects of things and self, not in poetic objectification, reification, systematization, no matter how delicate, how intricate (cf. RM, 100).

14. Bonnefoy's essay on 'Les mots et la parole dans la *Chanson de Roland*', in *Le Nuage rouge,* is particularly illuminating in this regard (NR, 171-81).

15. This necessarily compact account of *Dans le leurre du seuil* is complemented by my forthcoming fuller assessment.

16. Or, indeed, the poems of *L'Origine du language* which, however, have as yet only appeared in the 1980 Georges Nama luxury edition, if one is to discount the translations of Susanna Lang appearing in the special number of *Sub-Stance* devoted to contemporary French poetry and edited by Philippe Denis (1979, 23/24, pp. 5-10).

17. I have endeavoured to show the importance of this shifting between these two extremes in the above studies of the work of Frénaud and Deguy in particular, and in an essay on Mallarmé (*Dalhousie Review,* 1982). With respect to Mallarmé, in particular, one might note Leo Bersani's contribution in his intelligent *The Death of Stéphane Mallarmé* (Cambridge U. P., 1982).

18. Cf. DLS, 73-4: 'N'étant que la puissance du rien, / La bouche, la salive du rien, / Je crie, // Et au-dessus de la vallée de toi, de moi / Demeure le cri de joie dans sa forme pure'.

19. Cf. DLS, 96: '. . . la parole / Etant inachevée comme l'être encore'.

RESISTANCE LITERATURE

Ian Higgins (essay date 1982)

SOURCE: Higgins, Ian. Introduction to *Anthology of Second World War French Poetry,* pp. 1-51. London: Methuen, 1982.

[*In the following excerpt from the introduction to* Anthology of Second World War French Poetry, *Higgins provides a critical analysis of French war poetry.*]

IV Poetry

A remarkable literary feature of the war was the sudden popularity of poetry. Many looked to it, both as readers and as writers, for a crystallization of their suffering and grief. The same was true, though less spectacularly, in Britain. But poetry also had practical advantages for *résistants* wanting maximum impact in clandestine publications. For instance, it need not take up much space—an important factor if you cannot get your hands on paper (which at that time was severely rationed). Another advantage is that rhythm and rhyme implant poetry more easily in the memory—an important factor when it was dangerous to carry compromising pieces of paper—and so many morale-boosting texts were spread by word of mouth. One of the most notable features of the Occupation, however, was the combination of legality with subversiveness in a kind of writing known as *contrebande*.

A lot of the poems in this anthology are of this type. *Contrebande* poetry has two themes: one on the surface—for example, love, nature, God—to which the authorities cannot take exception, and a hidden one, which will be seen by those who have eyes to see. Aragon, one of the most notable practitioners of *contrebande*, likened it to mediaeval troubadour poetry, in which the poet gets away with singing of his lover in the presence of her husband. Much of the most popular poetry of the war was of this kind. Some of these poets were in the Resistance, while others were not, but all were protesting against the Germans or Vichy. This poetry, since it was published legally, is clearly different from clandestine poetry: an illegal poem, anonymous or pseudonymous, has no need to pull its punches, but *contrebande* has to be more subtle.

Some of the focal points for the Resistance in the southern zone were literary magazines, notably *Confluences,* edited by René Tavernier in Lyon, *Fontaine,* edited by Max-Pol Fouchet in Algiers, and *Poésie,* edited by Pierre Seghers at Villeneuve-lès-Avignon. Seghers in particular is a good poet in his own right, and during the war produced poetry ranging from the vituperative, through *contrebande* to love poetry. He had set up as his own publisher in 1938, and then, before the defeat, he edited a soldiers' poetry magazine, *Poètes casqués* (usually abbreviated to *P.C.,* which means *poste de commandement* in military jargon). After the Armistice, this became *Poésie,* set up with the twin intention of promoting poetry and maintaining French resistance. As well as the review, Seghers published books of poems by some of the best-known poets of the war, and since the war he has been one of the most prolific publishers of poetry.

Publishing *contrebande* was fraught with risk. All three of the reviews mentioned here were threatened with closure by Vichy. Poets like Aragon and Masson eventually had to live completely in hiding and could not publish legally in France. Seghers was sought by the Germans from May 1944. In the northern zone, it was still more difficult, and one of the most resounding *contrebande* volumes, the 450-page *Domaine français,* put together by the editor of the review *Messages,* Jean Lescure, had to appear in Switzerland in 1943.

V The effect of the war

This brief sketch of the background to the poems is purely factual, but it is vital to realise that the war, for a French person, was not a set of dates and statistics. It was virtual famine, daily fear, perpetual distrust and confusion: who was right, the government or the 'terrorist' Resistance minority? The experience of the Resistance, for those seriously committed to it (as opposed to the hangers-on who joined at the time of the Liberation), was an exalting faith in the creation of a new, nobler humanity—a faith which was certainly undermined for many by the feuds and opportunism which inevitably followed the Liberation. But that faith, cemented by the danger and fear, and the experience of torture, imprisonment and the self-sacrifice of thousands of people, was a response to the depths of degradation to which humanity was showing it could sink—duplicity, self-interest, cowardice, a maniacal pursuit of prejudice, and a sick, obsessive, ingenious cruelty as degrading to torturer as to tortured. As Sartre said after the war, speaking of people under torture: 'Il ne s'agissait pas pour eux de croire en l'homme mais de le vouloir' (*Situations, II,* p. 248). That is, they had to 'will' man, to *prove* by their behaviour that there was something worth believing in man: it was impossible any longer to fall back on comforting notions like 'basic humanity'—and still less on ethnic or cultural superiority—because French and Germans alike had shown this undreamt-of capacity for degradation. The war, for the French, was to a great extent a civil war, and the dominant question was 'Will I get involved in this, and on which side?'

We in the 1980s have to remember two things above all. The first is that for everyone at the time, including all the poets in this anthology, history had not yet been written. Reading about the war now, we know, however vivid the account we read, that in the end, after a thousand setbacks, the Allies will win. The basic history of the Second World War is so like a classic adventure story that there is a grave danger of its becoming just that, a set of legends—The Few, El Alamein, Frenchmen derailing trains at night—with victory inevitable in the last reel. In fact, even more to the non-collaborationist French than to the British, the future had never looked blacker, with German victory seemingly certain, at least up to late 1942.

The second thing it is essential to remember is that the Second World War was not, and is not, simply a glorified football match with one side winning and the other losing. However often our televisions show us John Wayne zapping the Japs or Kenneth More the Jerries, that 'victory' does not cancel out the millions of people put to death for ideological reasons, nor the realization that mankind has as big a faculty for bigotry and depraved cruelty as for heroism. As some of these poets have variously said, Hitler in a sense won the war, because we are all impregnated with the evil it released.

Second World War French Poetry

The sudden vogue for poetry during the Occupation was welcomed by some critics as a *renouveau poétique,* with poets at long last addressing themselves passionately to ordinary people instead of to an intellectual élite; others deplored it as mere *poésie de circonstance.* The most talked-about poets at the time were nearly all, in different ways, associated with the Resistance. Consequently, if you mention Second World War poetry to most French people today, they immediately exclaim 'Resistance poetry'. Whatever the truth of the matter, 'Resistance poetry' has become firmly consecrated in popular mythology of the war, as durable and as incompletely understood in France as Dunkirk and the Battle of Britain are in the United Kingdom. Popularly, however, it is durable only as a myth, and not in its own right: for most people, even those who do not confuse war poetry with Resistance poetry, the term seems to mean patriotic propaganda in verse, an understandable aberration, useful in keeping up morale during the Occupation, but as ephemeral as the circumstances to which it refers.

These reactions raise important questions for the enjoyment and study of literature, and one function of this anthology is to enable readers to ask them in a profitable way. First, however, before suggesting what they are, one has to define war poetry.

There are many possible definitions of war poetry. For the purpose of this volume, I have chosen as war poetry those poems which, written during or immediately after the war, make reference to it or express a reaction to it. Virtually all, then, is wartime poetry; but not all wartime poetry is necessarily war poetry. Naturally, almost all poetry written at a given moment expresses a reaction to it, even if the reaction is to ignore it. If—for the sake of argument—we call this latter reaction 'indifferent', then the poems here have been chosen because they seem to express a 'concerned' reaction, which may, of course, be explicit or implicit. A poem expressing an 'indifferent' reaction—and there were plenty of those—will be a wartime poem, but not a war poem.

To British readers, the phrase 'war poetry' tends to evoke the anti-war poetry written in 1916-18 by Owen, Sassoon and others. French Second World War poetry is something very different—and different again from English Second World War poetry. The First World War English poets protested against war because of the futile slaughter of a war fought for no very clear reason other than nebulous ideas of national pride. The Second World War was a different affair. While the war-effort was largely sustained on patriotism, the enemy was much more clearly not simply another nation, but something evil: German territorial ambition was the expression of an inhuman ideology, which eventually could only be destroyed by war. English Second World War poetry, then, may mourn lost friends, describe a desert battle, or capture the atmosphere in a POW camp, but it lacks the passion of Owen's poetry, because the moral battle is taken for granted: Nazism is so self-evidently evil that propaganda and bullets unite in protest against it—what is left for the poet to protest against?

French Second World War poetry is more complicated than the English poetry of either war, or, indeed, than First World War French poetry. In 1914, the majority of French people actually welcomed the war, because it offered a chance of revenge for the Prussian victory of 1870. Further, the fighting was largely on French soil. Consequently, while the English poets protested against the senseless slaughter of millions, many French poets wrote sabre-rattling doggerel as crude as the chauvinism it expressed. Those poets who did eventually write against the war were prevented by censorship from publishing their work, while Apollinaire, the best-known French poet of the war, practised a kind of self-censorship in his published poetry, which was neither chauvinist nor anti-war.

In considering the differences between French and English Second World War poetry, it is essential to bear in mind the fact that, although the Blitz and the V-weapons brought the war on to British soil, they did not bring the Germans. France, on the other hand, was occupied, with two important consequences. First, the French had to come to terms with the everyday presence, in the streets and shops, and often in their houses, of soldiers who were the expression of Nazi ideology. Second, the press and radio, when not the official organs of the Germans or their French collaborators, were all subject to censorship, so that all legal information regarding politics and the course of the war was essentially pro-German. Another vital factor is the widespread sympathy to aspects of Nazism which had been apparent even before the war, and which fuelled collaboration with the Germans after the defeat of 1940. Chauvinism was impossible, because the enemy was not only this German soldier sitting at the next table, but also, perhaps, the French person sitting next to him. It therefore needed effort and courage to maintain a belief that Nazism was evil. For the British, on the other hand, it was in no sense a civil war. The evil which most British people saw themselves as fighting was, in a sense, simple and at a distance. They were fighting it in the straightforward way, with guns, and, except for the conscientious objectors, there was little option but to fight it. In France, the evil was more complicated, and omnipresent—even to speak against it was to risk death. It is not surprising that the poetry written in response to these conditions is different from the English poetry of either war.

What this French poetry does share with English First World War poetry, however, is the element of urgent moral protest. To a great extent, it may be this that gives Owen greater power than Sidney Keyes, and Emmanuel more than Edmond Rostand. For good poetry always seems to be essentially resistance, a denial or negation of the way the world is. When Baudelaire says of poetry that 'elle contredit sans cesse le fait, à peine de ne plus être' (*Curiosités esthétiques. L'Art romantique*, p. 565), he is calling for use of the imagination to take us beyond what it known into what is possible. This negation of the given is not something life-denying: two of the poets in this anthology, Éluard and Ponge, are among the most joyously affirmative of French poets, but only because they deeply deny the world as it is usually seen and expressed, and create it afresh. A simple pre-war example of this is an untitled poem by Éluard which begins 'La terre est bleue comme une orange' (*Œuvres complètes*, vol. I, p. 232). The reader's reaction to this line is to see blue and orange in vivid contrast with each other, and to reject the simile as impossible. The following line is 'Jamais une erreur les mots ne mentent pas', which drags the reader back to reconsider his rejection. Suddenly, the phrase becomes ambiguous, instead of nonsensical. Perhaps it is a way of saying that the earth is not blue? Perhaps it is orange, in sunlight? But when does the earth go blue? At night. This implies the revolving earth, the earth as a planet—and perhaps the sun as an orange: two spherical heavenly bodies. In any case, if you want to see a blue orange, it is easy: leave it to go mouldy, and it turns a splendid blue. The reader realises that his original puzzlement did not derive only from the visual contrast, but from two linguistic factors as well. First, the word 'comme' has a whole range of logical possibilities, but most are omitted in any given phrase in everyday discourse. An apparent perceptual contradiction is seen as a set of linguistic problems, Éluard forcing the reader to consider the structures of analogy, the meanings of a simple conjunction, and the question of whether 'une' means 'a particular' orange or 'any' orange. Second, because 'orange' is commonly used as an adjective, this restricts the reader's reaction to the noun 'orange': he instantly feels that the object has got to be orange. But why not round? or blue? Note that all these possibilities arise as questions: this is how the negation of perceptual and linguistic clichés is achieved. And later in the poem, with the imagery of sunrise, the questions are confirmed as the right ones, and in that way answered: this is how the negation is affirmative, as refreshing as a splash in the blue sea or a drink of orange-juice.

This example shows how apolitical peacetime poetry protests against accepted ways of looking at things by denying the world in its relation to language. But what about war poetry? It might be thought that, while poetry is a denial of the status quo, a poem protesting against, say, an invader, is no different from a political tract. In fact, the same is as true, in essence, of the passionate moral protest of war poetry as of the Éluard poem. A poem, to a far greater extent than a tract, actually draws attention to the relation between language and what it denotes. Sometimes it does this explicitly, but usually implicitly. The commonest ways of doing it are through imagery, syntactic deformation or ambiguity, and manipulation of sound and rhythm. Linguistic clichés are denied along with perceptual clichés, and language and world are renewed in terms of one another. The political tract, taking for granted the relation between the words and what they denote, preaches almost exclusively to the converted. A comparison of a tract with a politically orientated war poem will make the difference clear.

Here is a Communist tract—not because Communist tracts are any more crass than those of other parties, but because many of the best poets in this volume were Communists at the time: the reader will find it very instructive to contrast their poetry with the tract. This one is from late 1939, and refers to Armand Pillot, MP for the eighteenth *arrondissement* of Paris, who had broken with the party after the Soviet invasion of Finland (the italics are mine):

C'est au moment où, seul, le *Parti Communiste lutte courageusement* contre *les fauteurs de guerre* et la *réaction,* que Pillot abandonne sa place dans *le combat que mènent les travailleurs* contre les 15%, contre la vie chère, contre *les conditions ignobles de travail* que veulent leur imposer les *gros capitalistes fauteurs de guerre.*

(. . .)

Pour cacher sa peur de la répression, Pillot dit qu' 'il n'a pas compris les événements de Finlande'. Il n'a pas compris que l'U.R.S.S., *patrie des travailleurs du monde entier, sauvegardait la paix du monde* en signant la série de pactes avec les pays baltes. Pillot n'a pas compris que l'U.R.S.S. obligeait le *gouvernement fantôme* de Tanner à céder le pas à *l'armée et au gouvernement populaires* de Kuusinen. Et qu'ainsi l'U.R.S.S. garantissait aussi ses frontières au moment où tous *les pays capitalistes conspirent contre les grand Pays des Soviets* avec à sa tête *le génial Staline,* continuateur de Lénine.

Quelle différence entre la conduite de *ce rénégat* et la *courageuse attitude* de Maurice Thorez qui, malgré *la répression la plus impitoyable,* reste à son *poste de combat de soldat du Peuple.*

(. . .)

Les travailleurs du XVIIIème, *ardents combattants de la lutte anti-fasciste* et de Juin 36, *héritiers des Communards de 71,* chasseront celui qui renie tout ce passé et qui ne saurait conduire leur action pour *la défense de leur pain,* pour *les libertés démocratiques,* contre *la guerre impérialiste.*[1]

Most of the fears which underlie this tract were very well founded, but the text itself is yet another permutation of classic clichés (italicised here) and of traditional demagogic devices like cumulative repetition ('contre' three times, 'n'a pas compris' three times, 'pour . . . pour. . . . contre'), overstatement ('seul', 'monde entier', 'tous les pays capitalistes'), or rhetorical use of adjective before noun ('le génial Staline', 'la courageuse attitude'). Also typical of the style is the invocation of glorious precursors ('Communards de 71'), which is meant to confer on the present struggle the exemplary status of a precedent which has become legendary.

These clichés will have made no converts. They are a rallying-cry, a comforting and rousing reinforcement of the most cherished ideas of a party under great pressure. Now compare them with the last two stanzas of a poem from this anthology, Seghers' 'Octobre 41', which refers to the execution of the hostages at Châteaubriant and Bordeaux:

> Ils ressusciteront vêtus de feu dans nos écoles
> Arrachés aux bras de leurs enfants ils entendront
> Avec la guerre, l'exil et la fausse parole
>   D'autres enfants dire leurs noms
>
> Alors ils renaîtront à la fin de ce calvaire
> Malgré l'Octobre vert qui vit cent corps se plier
> Aux côtés de la Jeanne au visage de fer
>   Née de leur sang de fusillés.

Like the tract, these lines are a rallying-cry, a consoling affirmation of the age-old idea that dead martyrs will rise again, in the minds of the living. Like the tract, they invoke a legendary example, that of Joan of Arc, the French patriot *par excellence.* And they, too, use rhetorical repetition, with the three future tenses. Yet each of these devices is used quite differently in the poem, which differs fundamentally from the tract.

One of the simplest features of the poem is that most of the long lines have thirteen syllables, whereas traditional verse has twelve (see below, p. 34). The reader does not, of course, sit counting syllables as the poem is read, but to the French ear, familiar with traditional verse, the effect is inescapably one of a slightly clumsy imbalance, as if the speaker's emotion is so great that it cannot quite be fitted into an orthodox mould. The imbalance contrasts with the regular rhyme scheme, further drawing attention to this struggle to give words to the emotion. The reader is therefore made aware of the very processes of expression, which becomes part of what is expressed—a crucial difference between poem and tract. This theme is underlined by the reference to 'la fausse parole': the abuse of language by Vichy and the Germans contrasts with the use of language in the poem to create a new legend, the martyrs becoming a counter-myth to the myths fostered by Fascism. This process is explicit in the poem, whereas in the tract the parallel with the 1871 Commune is taken for granted. The very use made of rhymes, while straightforward, is a reminder that sound and meaning in language are interdependent. Having 'écoles' rhyme with 'parole' reinforces the theme that truth is language and legend, and so does the phonetic linking of the predictions of rebirth with the speaking of the martyrs' names, in 'ressuscite*ront* . . . ente*ndront* . . . *noms* . . . re*naîtront*'. These rhymes are emphasized rhythmically, because there is a pause after each one, and rhythm likewise plays a role in the revitalizing of the cliché 'calvaire' through its position in the rhyming chain 'guerre . . . calvaire . . . vert . . . fer'. It is, however, 'l'Octobre vert' that does most of the work here. Earlier in the poem there is a reference to 'Octobre, quand la vendange est faite dans le sang': the unsurprising reference to autumn as a time of death, and the implied blood-red vine leaves and wine, contrast strongly with the surprising spring-like green October. In fact, the green is an allusion to the colour of the German army uniform. The dominant sound of 'guerre', 'calvaire' and 'vert' then culminates in 'fer', Jeanne's grim, iron countenance throwing into relief the intangible spirituality of this paradoxical birth. Because the last line is short and rhymes with 'plier', it points up the contrast between spiritual birth and the bodily finality of 'qui vit cent corps se plier' (instead of, say, 'cent hommes mourir'), while the internal rhyme of 'Née' and 'fusillés' heightens the contrast still further. The new Jeanne—that is, a revitalized and purified France—is born *as* the minds of schoolchildren.

More could be said about these eight lines, but this should be enough to show the difference between the poem and the tract: whereas the tract simply takes existing linguistic usages for granted, in an attempt to reinforce the political doctrine, the poem actually presents the episode of the executed hostages in part as a challenge to expression, and is a response to that challenge. Although this example makes more or less explicit reference to it, this aspect of poetry is more usually implicit, in the relatively obtrusive nature of the language. It does indeed seem to be a feature of good poetry that, whatever else it communicates, it also conveys the struggle against inarticulateness—a gasp of ecstasy or a groan of misery may be very heartfelt, but they are even less inadequate as communication than as expression.

Poetry, then, contrasts with the political tract in so far as the tract, however subversive, exploits existing linguistic usage. Virtually all non-poetic political discourse is linguistically conservative. Poetry is more completely subversive, but its political effects may be very indirect or long term. However, although political poetry does run the risk of confirming received ideas, it does not have to do so. Indeed, for many of the poets in this anthology, the basic political struggle was itself a struggle to defend language. Philosophically, this is because language is the essential means by which man grasps the world and himself. During the Occupation, this became clear in the simplest ways, in the pressure put on single words. This is what Seghers calls 'la fausse parole' in 'Octobre 41'. For example, in the official view, *liberté* meant freedom to join in the Fascist crusade against Bolshevism; and to derail a German ammunition train was to commit a terrorist crime against freedom. The words *France* and *patrie* meant one thing to Vichy, and another to those who refused to collaborate. This is the burden of Aragon's anonymous preface to *L'Honneur des poètes II. Europe,* which he begins by linking Resistance poetry with that of the apolitical Symbolist Mallarmé:

> De tout temps, ce fut la mission des poètes, comme l'un d'entre eux un jour l'a définie, que de *Donner un sens plus pur aux mots de la tribu.*
>
> Il est bien que les poètes français aient su le faire, n'aient pas démissionné aux heures les plus sombres quand précisément le langage était détourné de son cours, les mots étaient dénaturés, pervertis par ces usurpateurs qui s'étaient emparés du vocable France lui-même . . .[2]

Jacques Gaucheron, in *La Poésie, la Résistance,* makes another simple, but vital point: at a time when the Germans seemed to have deprived the French people of practically everything, the French language itself was one of the most precious assets they had left: 'Parler français en présence d'Allemands qui ne comprennent rien est un plaisir. . . . Il suffit d'aller jusqu'au langage poétique, au point où ce qu'il y a de plus riche dans la langue n'est pas susceptible d'apprentissage, pour que l'expression poétique soit ressentie comme une parcelle de patrie' (p. 122). So while poetry may always be a form of resistance to the status quo, this became much more obvious through the circumstances of the Occupation than it often is in peacetime.

The relation between poetry and the circumstances in which it is written is the really important question raised by this poetry. The argument raged during and after the war, and has never died down. Many critics condemn war poetry as 'poetry of circumstance', and therefore ephemeral: comprehensible only to one part of one generation, it is not 'eternal', not real poetry. It is striking that this opinion was sometimes expressed even in some of the journals most actively opposed to collaboration.[3] 'Poetry of circumstance' used to mean simply poetry written to mark public events, like the Queen Mother's birthday, but, as used by these critics, the phrase means poetry which refers to social or political situations or events. 'Eternal' poetry is about things like love or death or nature, which are supposed to be always and everywhere the same and to elicit feelings which are accessible to introspection.

The most spectacular recent variant of this emphasis on introspection had been Surrealism, the dominant poetic movement of the inter-war period. It is notable that one of the most violent attacks on the so-called Resistance poets, *Le Déshonneur des poètes,* was the work of that most Surrealist of Surrealists, Benjamin Péret. Surrealism was strongly influenced by Freud's theory of the unconscious. Its goal was total revolution, through each individual's liberation from social, moral, political and aesthetic constraints. This was to be achieved by releasing from the unconscious all suppressed desire. The most extreme 'literary' means of doing this was automatic writing, in which words and phrases were written down as they welled up into the mind, without being subjected to any criticism or sifting. In the best Surrealism, the practice was different from the theory, and the aim was after all social subversion. Even so, the private imagery and the fierce rejection of constraint, including party political loyalty, do very often make this poetry look as if it was written in an ivory tower, by and for members of a middle-class intellectual élite uncaring of 'circumstances'.

The poets in this anthology, then, to a considerable extent represent a 'lost' generation, squeezed out of the reckoning by a combination of the élitist self-trumpeting of Surrealism and a woolly-minded, but equally élitist, suspicion that war poetry is poetry of circumstance, and that poetry of circumstance may be too limited in scope, or too easy, or too obscure, to be worth studying. Certainly, most war poetry is bad poetry. But open any literary magazine or any collection of poetry, and you find that most poetry is bad poetry anyway. Indeed, given the circumstances of deprivation, uncertainty and fear, it is perhaps amazing that so much Second World War French poetry should be so good. Clearly, the notion of 'circumstance' in this debate contains some confusion, which it is essential to disperse if the poetry is to be seen in anything like a just perspective.

As an example of a poem of circumstance in the traditional sense, here is Sir John Betjeman's poem for the Queen Mother on her eightieth birthday:

> We are your people
> Millions of us greet you

On this your birthday
Mother of our Queen.
Waves of good will go
Racing out to meet you
You who in peace and war
Our faithful friend have been.
You who have known the sadness of bereavement
The joyfulness of family jokes
And times when trust is tried,
Great was the day for our United Kingdoms
And God bless the Duke of York
Who chose you as his bride.[4]

If this is a poem at all, it must be as bad as any in English—not however, because it is a poem of circumstance, but because it looks like something written to order, in deference to the social and linguistic status quo, with no emotional or intellectual involvement on the part of the writer: world and language are not questioned in terms of one another.

As poems of circumstances in the current sense, one could take any of the poems in this anthology which refer to the war. Now if you know nothing about the Queen Mother or the war, your understanding of these poems will be limited. But if you know nothing about birch trees, or have never been in love, a poem about a birch tree or a lover will mean little to you. Birch trees and lovers are circumstances, like German soldiers or public celebrations. Circumstances are things around one, and a poem about a birch tree or a lover is a poem of circumstance, since it is a response to an external stimulus. Further, a poem about a birch tree written in 1930 is as much an expression of the circumstances of peace as a poem written about an execution in 1942 is an expression of the circumstances of war; and both—like a poem about a birch tree written in 1942—are as much expressions of the poet as they are of the circumstances. This is perhaps the reason why the question of poetry of circumstance has been so much discussed in the middle of the twentieth century: it is generally recognized that the mind only functions in response to things outside it, that feelings are not accessible to introspection, even the most intimate self-awareness only being possible in terms of things other than the self—that is, circumstances.

In this respect, it is noteworthy that some of the most politically committed poets in the anthology—for example, Aragon, Éluard or Masson—present the Occupation and intimate experience like sexual love in terms of one another. Indeed, it has to be said that the best Surrealist poetry of Breton (who does not figure in the anthology), Aragon, Desnos and Éluard implies this dialectic of circumstances and self. Éluard, in particular, was never a very orthodox Surrealist, because his poetry, however startling or fragmentary the imagery may sometimes be, more often seems to explore the relation between sensation and imagination than to plunge into the unconscious. Breton, the leader of the movement, no doubt had his own reasons for writing virtually no war poetry and leaving France in 1941; but it is not altogether surprising that the others should have turned to a less private poetry, more accessible to ordinary people. Certainly, most of the poets of the 'lost' generation pursue self-knowledge not through introspection but through investigating sensation—that is, the circumstances in which they experience emotion, whether this be love, or anger at oppression, or sorrow at the death of a comrade, or exultation on being released from captivity. One of the characteristics of the *renouveau poétique* of the war was that the poets wanted their work to be *à hauteur d'homme,* a term laughed at then and since by those who think that it simply means poetry which can be read widely, and that such poetry must be inferior. But poetry which is easy to approach does not have to be inferior. In any case, look at the poems in this anthology: some are immediately accessible, while others present an intellectual challenge; but they are all *poésie à hauteur d'homme,* because they express an emotional experience of the interdependence of self, language and circumstances, and do not ignore or deny this interdependence.

It is not, then, so much a question of whether the poet pays attention to circumstances or not, as of what circumstances are to the forefront of his emotional and intellectual attention at a given moment. In peacetime, the outside world changes relatively slowly, so the circumstances in terms of which a poet expresses his love may be little different from one generation to another. In the sunlit foliage of a tree, he may see his lover's hair, and a hundred years later we have little difficulty drawing analogies with our own experience of trees, sunshine and girls' hair. But the German Occupation changed the outside world drastically, so that even the most private feelings were likely to involve public affairs. With no food in the shops, with your best friends imprisoned or shot, with enemy soldiers and informers everywhere, you are as likely to be struck by the notices of executions pinned to the tree trunks as by the sunlight in the leaves. Poems like Desnos' 'Dans l'allée . . .' or Emmanuel's 'Cinq heures attachés . . .' are essentially neither more nor less poems of circumstance than Ronsard's 'Mignonne, allons voir si la rose . . .' or Baudelaire's 'Avec ses vêtements . . .'. True, if you do not know that there were twelve in a firing-squad, or that condemned *résistants* had been left tied to a stake before being shot, the Desnos and Emmanuel poems will be puzzling, just as Seghers' phrase 'Octobre vert' is puzzling if you do not know the colour of the German army uniform. But Ronsard's poem is odd if you do not know that sixteenth-century roses were as delicate and short-lived as dog-roses; Baudelaire's poem makes better sense if you know that dresses in the 1850s were ankle-length; and no matter how much you know about the Occupation, Ponge's 'Le platane' will mean little to you if you do not know what a plane tree is like.

An important corollary of this is that the reader's circumstances are as important to the meaning of a poem as the poet's. The reader of the 1980s, who has seen photographs taken from space showing the earth as a blue planet, is more likely than the reader of the 1930s to see Éluard's blue earth as an orange-shaped globe! But while it is true that the short-lived circumstances of the war make aspects of the war poetry obscure to us today, that does not in itself make it ephemeral, and is not a reason for not reading it. Ronsard and Baudelaire can be read with pleasure by those who know little about the linguistic and social conventions of the sixteenth and nineteenth centuries, but an annotated edition permits a different reading. Similarly, nearly all the poems in this anthology are accessible to a reader knowing nothing of the war, but the Introduction and Notes, changing the circumstances in which he reads the texts, will affect their meaning for him. Some of the best examples are the sonnets of Jean Cassou. These are fine poems in their own right, but their meaning may change when the reader learns that they were composed in prison; and when he then learns that Cassou made practically no intentional references to his imprisonment in these sonnets, their meaning may change again.

As may be clear by now, the criticism that this war poetry is poetry of circumstance usually hides a quite different criticism. Because so many poems of circumstance in the traditional sense are as bad as Betjeman's, it seems to be assumed that any poetry referring to social or political circumstances must also be written to order, and therefore 'committed', and therefore bad. By 'committed' poetry is meant poetry promoting a social or political cause, like the monarchy, or revolution, or liberation from Fascism. The mistake is to make an illogical series of assumptions: some war poetry is Resistance poetry, and some Resistance poetry is committed in this sense, so all Resistance poetry must be committed; so all war poetry must be committed. But the term 'Resistance poetry' is a vague one. Does it mean poetry about the Resistance, or poetry exhorting the reader to join the Resistance, or just poetry written by members of the Resistance? And while all poetry may be resistance, with a small 'r', half an hour's browsing in this anthology is enough to show that not all war poetry is Resistance poetry, with a capital 'R', in any of these three senses.

One has nevertheless to come to terms with the fact that there is no good poetry from the war years which was written by those with Fascist or *vichyste* sympathies. While poetry was being published in unprecedented quantities, the collaborationist weeklies and monthlies hardly ever printed poems, although they do abound in sarcastic references to the 'poètes-poètes' who have proliferated since 1940. One example of a poet who did find favour is Maurice Fombeure, of whose *À dos d'oiseau* M. Richard wrote, in *La Révolution nationale* for 19.12.42: 'Il y a plus de motifs d'espoirs français dans un livre comme celui-ci, plus de raisons d'optimisme que dans tous les discours des rhéteurs . . . Je retrouve, intactes, toutes les cordes de la voix de notre race dans celles de la lyre de Fombeure.' It is understandable that Fombeure's simple vignettes of a rustic life and homespun Christianity should have appealed to a *Vichyste* critic, when the parrotcry was that poetry should once more be 'nationale et traditionnelle'; and it is true that Fombeure, in his preface to Bérimont's *Lyre à feu*, argued that poets should go on writing as if there were no war, on the grounds that poetry is a private affair and has nothing to do with politics. But the sympathies of both Fombeure and Bérimont were unambiguously with the Resistance. Similarly, one looks in vain for collaborationist poetry in the wartime *La Nouvelle Revue française*, the prestigious literary monthly, whose editor, from 1941, was the Fascist Pierre Drieu la Rochelle. A variety of poets published under Drieu at first, but so far from the review being fed by collaborationist poetry, it folded up in 1943 for lack of contributions of any kind.

Without thorough study, it would be rash to suggest why collaboration should have produced virtually no poetry, and resistance or 'indifference' so much. Certainly, poets like Aragon and Masson were hostile to 'indifferent' poetry (in the sense defined above, p. 11), on the grounds that anything that did not promote the Resistance cause was in effect inimical to it, but one is hard put to it to find anything like explicit collaborationist poetry. The only collaborator of any note who wrote poetry seems to have been Robert Brasillach, the Fascist editor, for most of the war, of the anti-Semitic weekly *Je suis partout*. Brasillach's poetry perhaps gives a clue as to why there should have been so little collaborationist poetry. He published a collection in 1944, entitled *Poèmes*, which consists of poems written both before and during the war. It therefore encompasses the experience of phoney war, defeat, imprisonment in a POW camp, repatriation to resume the crusade against Jewry, and triumphant collaboration. Yet the extraordinary thing is this: while the Fascist ideology made a cult of strength, virility and suppression of the weak, and while French collaborationists were committed to the energetic creation of an *Ordre nouveau* in Europe, Brasillach's poetry, pre-war and wartime alike, is uniformly elegant, unoriginal, elegiac and completely toothless, consistently giving off an atmosphere of nostalgia and resignation.

Brasillach was arrested after the Liberation, and kept in Fresnes gaol until his trial and execution for treason. The poetry he wrote in Fresnes is collected in *Poèmes de Fresnes*: these have the same tone as the others, with an occasional bleat that if the other side had won, things would have been different. Now, it is true that if the Germans had won the war, history would have been written differently: the 'crusade for civilisation against Bolshevism' would have been successful, and the 'Judeo-Communist terrorists' of the Resistance would have been brought to 'justice'. Nevertheless, the fact remains that the losers—even those imprisoned in Fresnes or in fear for their lives—would have left an inspiring corpus of resilient, life-affirming, even ebullient poetry (see the anthology), while all the winners could have offered would have been Brasillach's flabby threnodies. Given the shortage of space here, it would have been perverse to include a selection of Brasillach's work, when so many better poets have had to be left out; but the contrast between his poetry and that chosen here, together with its freak status as the only instance of remotely collaborationist poetry, is extremely interesting, and perhaps gives support to the idea that good poetry is by definition protest and resistance, and cannot thrive on resignation or acceptance of the status quo.

In this respect, the case of Aragon—who was in the Resistance—is also important evidence. Ever since 1940, Aragon has waged a campaign for a 'national' poetry, returning to traditional popular forms so that it would be accessible to everybody. However, while this poetry is in this sense retrograde, he has an allied concern which theoretically prevents it being conservative, as the 'national and traditional' poetry dear to Vichy was presumably supposed to be. As he wrote in the preface to *Les Yeux d'Elsa*, a *contrebande* volume published in 1942, 'il n'y a poésie qu'autant qu'il y a méditation sur le langage, et à chaque pas réinvention de ce langage'. Aragon's poetry is very uneven in quality; the selection in this anthology probably suggests that the more it subverts linguistic usage, the more successful it is: like all good poets, and unlike Brasillach, Aragon at his best denies or resists the world in its relation to language.

Whatever meaning one gives to the term 'Resistance poetry', and however illogical the assumption that it is 'committed' poetry or its confusion with war poetry, there is a further question: why should poetry not be politically committed, anyway? The answer to this question frequently contains another confusion, between hostility to propaganda poetry and hostility to the cause for which a given poem is thought to be propaganda.

There are senses in which all literature can be said to be propaganda, and some propaganda has features which can also be found in poetry. But let us—for the sake of argument—use the generally accepted view of propaganda, and say that it attempts systematically to implant a political or social doctrine in people's minds. The tract quoted above is an example of propaganda. In so far as poetry is negation of the world in its relation to language, it is incompatible with propaganda, which depends on and reinforces political and linguistic clichés. However, as we have seen, different circumstances are likely to elicit different sorts of subject-matter in poetry. It would be surprising if, in the conditions of the Occupation, poetry hostile to Nazism had not moved some way along the spectrum of expression towards propaganda. For although the political situation was in some ways as complicated as it had been before the war, the really basic option was a simple one—whether to resist or not. Vichy repeatedly, and fruitlessly, called for political unity in the National Revolution—but it was the Resistance, a heterogeneous collection of beliefs, which for four years achieved the impossible, with Catholic and Communist, and many in between, united in a single struggle.

Political truth, then, was simple for the Resistance, which is why the Communist Aragon and the Catholic Emmanuel could both write poetry described as Resistance poetry. What lay behind much criticism of this 'commitment' was the fear that it was in fact a commitment to a Communist takeover after the war. Inevitably, many who had shared in the struggle against the Nazis and admired, say, Aragon's war poetry, were, after the Liberation—when circumstances changed and the struggle was a different one—unable to accept the principles typified in these lines from his 'Chanson du sixième hiver'.

> Rien n'est tout à fait à sa place
> Le cœur est encore en prison
> Les enfants ont des mains de glace
> Le toit n'est pas sur la maison
> Rien n'est tout à fait à sa place
> Le peuple ne commande pas.[5]

Aragon was not surprisingly constantly vilified in the collaborationist press because of his politics; others, like Emmanuel, who were not Communists, were still given that label. But if, for many people, war poetry was 'Communist poetry', the most widespread criticism of it, certainly since the war, and even at the time, has been that it is chauvinist doggerel, a modern version of the revanchist patriotic songs of Paul Déroulède (1846-1914).

The best way of judging this criticism is to look at an example of Déroulède's work. Here is an excerpt from one of his most famous poems, 'Le Clairon':

> L'air est pur, la route est large,
> Le Clairon sonne la charge,
> Les Zouaves vont chantant
> Et là-haut sur la colline,
> Dans la forêt qui domine,
> Le Prussien les attend.
> (. . .)
>
> À la première décharge,
> Le Clairon sonnant la charge,
> Tombe frappé sans recours;
> Mais, par un effort suprême,
> Menant le combat quand même
> Le Clairon sonne toujours.
> (. . .)
>
> Puis, dans la forêt pressée,
> Voyant la charge lancée,
> Et les Zouaves bondir,
> Alors le Clairon s'arrête
> Sa dernière tâche est faite,
> Il achève de mourir.[6]

Comparing this with the poems in the anthology will make it easy to see how absurd the charge of chauvinism is. Certainly, France figures by name in many of the poems: French heroes, the French Revolution, the French countryside, French culture, the French language, all are rallying-points for national pride. The concept of national pride is of course a hazy one, and can only mean anything in terms of the individual's experience of his relation to society. In the exceptional circumstances of invasion and occupation, many people's moral and political ideals, which are social ideals, not surprisingly crystallized round the brutal changes forced on their society by the invader. And, as we have seen, the phenomenon of collaboration meant that the meaning of the very word *France* was not as self-evident as it had been to people like Déroulède. The common cause in this war poetry was in fact not France, but Man. A Communist—to take one extreme—will think that man's best chance of moral regeneration lies in creating a socialist society. No wonder that French Communists, seeing the human degradation visited on the French by Fascism, concentrated their fight for a new humanity on France. A Catholic—to take the other extreme—may think that man's best chance of moral regeneration lies in a return to Christianity: French Catholics, too, however, concentrated their struggle on what they saw as a devilish ideology imposed on France by foreign military force. But, whether it was conceived politically or religiously, the moral regeneration was the end, and the patriotism the means. To use Sartre's term (see above, p. 9), all the poets in this volume, including those who invoke *la patrie,* are concerned to 'will' man, in full awareness that he cannot any longer be believed in or relied on, but has to be created, constantly, through his own efforts.

This view of man lays stress on circumstances: at any given moment a person is what he is in terms of the circumstances around him. It is no doubt in so far as it expresses this truth about human beings that the war poetry is 'eternal', even though the circumstances in which it was written have disappeared. Indeed, very often the universality has only become fully clear *because* the circumstances have changed. (This is something that has to be said in defence of those who, at the time, condemned this poetry as ephemeral: circumstances in the 1980s make it easier to see its 'eternal' quality than they did in the 1940s.) The various poems about Gabriel Péri are a good example (see Aragon's 'Ballade de celui qui chanta dans les supplices' and Notes). Péri was a Communist MP before the war. If you let this fact close your mind to the poems, because you are not a Communist, you throw the baby out with the bathwater. What makes each of these very different poems interesting is the theme of how the memory of a dead person plays an inspiring part in the present. This was as true when they were written as it is now: they are poems about the phenomenon of circumstance as much as they are 'poems of circumstance'. Because circumstances have changed since the Occupation, their impact will not be the same as it was then (although it may be as great), but that is an essential part of their themes. The same is true of Guillevic's 'Vercors' or Tardieu's 'Oradour', and it is as true of Auden's 'August 1968' or MacDiarmid's 'The skeleton of the future' as it is of Ronsard's 'Mignonne, allons voir . . .' or Agrippa d'Aubigné's 'Jugement', which was written in the early seventeenth century, and reprinted by Seghers in 1941 because of its contemporary relevance. We have not taken part in these conflicts or loved Marie, but we have been in love, remembered the dead, and hated tyranny in Chile and Kampuchea and Afghanistan and South Africa. The essence of the poems is not to tell us about the circumstances in which they were written, but, through expressing one person's passionate experience of it, to remind us about our relation to circumstance. As Éluard says in 'Faire vivre': 'Ceci est de tous les temps.'

Notes

1. The tract is reproduced in Guérin, A. *La Résistance,* Paris, Livre Club Diderot, 5 vols. (1973-76), vol. I, p. 326.

2. Quoted in Seghers, P. *La Résistance et ses poètes,* pp. 326-7.

3. See e.g. Henri Hell's 'Examen des revues' in *Fontaine,* 24 (1942), pp. 486-8.

4. Printed in *The Times,* 4.8.80, p. 2.

5. In *Les Lettres françaises,* 17.2.45, p. 3. Reprinted in *Le Musée Grévin. Les Poissons noirs et quelques poèmes inédits.*

6. Quoted from Dillaz, S. *La Chanson française de contestation.* Paris, Seghers, 1973, pp. 124-5.

Margaret Atack (essay date 1989)

SOURCE: Atack, Margaret. "Structures of Irony." In *Literature and the French Resistance: Cultural Politics and Narrative Forms, 1940-1950,* pp. 208-31. Manchester: Manchester University Press, 1989.

[*In the following essay, Atack examines postwar French literature.*]

'THE GAME OF WAR AND CHANCE'[1]

In *L'Univers concentrationnaire* (The Concentration Camp World), David Rousset places the concentration camps under the patronage of the modern masters of the grotesque, Jarry's Ubu, Kafka and Céline,[2] to present the incongruous juxtaposition of terror and bureaucratic order; but the discovery of the grotesque absurdity of this closed world is a key to survival, a sign of human resilience defying inhuman degradation. The post-war novel of the Occupation is paradoxically both less bleak and more pessimistic, burlesque or grotesque rather than tragic, as the incongruities of the human tragi-comedy are ironically highlighted by the narrator or by the structure of the narrative. All the novels of ambiguity accentuate to a greater or lesser extent the incoherence of the times, its failure to be accommodated within clear moral categories. The kaleidoscope of opinions and actions in *Les Epées* and *La Culbute* are reduced to appearing no more than absurd posturings as the main characters at the centre move between pro-Resistance, pro-Vichy and pro-German groups, cynically playing their part in each and being enthusiastically welcomed by all. In *Uranus* and *Mon Village à l'heure allemande* the presence in the narrative of a multiplicity of positions and attitudes inextricably linking political differences and personality clashes has a major role here, and combines with the episodic structure to create a disjointed effect, emphasising contingency at the expense of causality.

In *Les Forêts de la nuit* the role of the contingent is particularly important, taking the form of a primary disparity between intention and result which is the major theme of the Liberation scenes, but also structures minor episodes in the course of the novel. The fate of the letters Hélène de Balansun writes to Jean de Lavoncourt is a case in point. They all pass through many hands and most of them, for a variety of reasons ranging from fear of arrest to perverse bad temper, are destroyed. Two actually reach Spain, but Jean has already left for London when the second arrives and the man who has agreed to forward letters is arrested. So the letter not only fails to reach Jean, but ends up in the hands of a local concierge 'who had it translated by her daughter's lover, a journalist, and kept it carefully as a model of love literature'.[3] The irony of this passage is operating at several levels and can be categorised according to Robert Scholes's useful definitions of the diachronic and synchronic modes of narrative irony.[4] The diachronic mode, the disappointment of the protagonist's expectations, underlies the intentionally humorous manner in which the various letters fall by the wayside and frustrate Hélène's hope of communicating with Jean.[5] The fate of the final letter illustrates the synchronic mode, the disparity between the two codes; a letter inscribed within the code of interpersonal communication (involving both an intimate relationship and separation)[6] is reinscribed as an anthology piece within a literary code. As such it is a paradigm for the content of synchronic irony in the postwar novel, particularly, as will be seen, in relation to the Resistance: divorced from its original intention and context, it is turned into pure spectacle.

On the great day of the Liberation in Paris and Saint-Clar, expectations and intentions also fail to be realised, for its import lay in 'the gap between what should have been and what in fact was'.[7] The conflicts and moral confusions of the Occupation years concord to turn what should have been the culmination of the fight against the Germans and the beginning of a new era into an empty spectacle, the parochialism of which is particularly underlined in Saint-Clar: 'After the monstrous constraints of the Occupation years, after being plunged for so long in mud, blood and stupidity, one was entitled to expect a magnificent leap, exemplary punishments, ritual murder of the real culprits, the undamming of the lustral waters of joy and hope.' Instead they were treated to 'a speech in the good old electoral tradition and the farce of the head shaving'.[8] All that counts is the *appearance* of solidarity, in mass demonstrations of righteousness, and the narrative accumulates the incongruities which prove the point. Anyone who is prepared to fight is welcomed on the Parisian barricades and Philippe Arréguy, who has been hiding from the 'Gestapo française' since Francis's murder, reappears and joins the FFI for the love of a battle. In Saint-Clar too, the demonstrations of patriotic fervour at the public humiliation of its sacrificial victims like Cécile Delahaye have very shallow roots: 'Stupidity and hatred surged through this well fed, happy crowd of Saint Clar who had never suffered, for whom the war had been a Golconda and the Germans a blessing.'[9] The irony of these scenes belonging to the synchronic mode resides in the disparity between two moral codes; on the one hand the mass demonstrations of pro-Resistance anti-German feeling, on the other that constituted by the denunciations of the observers—Gérard Delahaye in Paris, Jacques Costellot in Saint-Clar, and the narrator—which underline it as a spectacular morality play for the benefit of the participants' consciences and manipulated by those orchestrating it. For Gérard, an *abbé* on a barricade is an actor overplaying his part of the 'curé combattant',[10] while the 'lynching' of a German corpse demonstrates that the darker aspects of the forests of the night are uncomfortably close. Jacques feels similar revulsion and disgust at the scenes in Saint-Clar. It falls to the narrator to highlight the absurdities arising from the public expression of Resistance fraternity on the part of those jockeying for political power, and especially Darricade, trying to outmanoeuvre the Socialists and Communists and remain on the right side of public opinion; avoiding any mention of the dead Francis because of the compromising expression of alliance with the bourgeoisie that might imply; publicly embracing *le capitaine* Figeac, the head of the local *maquis*,[11] whose prestige he sees as a personal threat. Figeac himself looks forward to the reimposition of a proper military hierarchy; he did not enjoy his subordinate role in the *maquis*, in a brigade commanded by a twenty-year-old Spaniard, nor the deplorable Resistance habit of being addressed in the intimate 'tu' form. One could multiply the examples, from the burlesque episodes of Fernande's public denunciations of Darricade's amoral behaviour during the Occupation, or M. de Balansun's discomfiture on realising the parade of young men he is smartly saluting is led by a well-known local tearaway, to his tragic intuitive realisation of the truth of Francis's death and its futility. As he oscillates between despair at this certainty and hope he may be wrong, his recurring phrase 'Francis has died for nothing' encapsulates the major theme of the novel, that the upheaval of the war has also been pointless, a temporary disturbance within the senseless human order.

A World In Chaos

The conclusions drawn by *Les Forêts de la nuit* go far beyond the confines of one small town in south-west France. It is explicitly stated that the Occupation has drawn Saint-Clar into the wider conflict: 'The town was directly involved in History (. . .) Its destiny was linked to that of the entire planet, and it was vaguely (obscurément) aware of the fact.'[12] That the novel is seeking to elucidate a truth about the Occupation which is not a purely local truth is, however, primarily borne by the structuration of the characters, which is dependent on producing the gamut of possible figures—collaboration, Resistance, indifference, profiteer, support for Vichy and le Maréchal, occupying forces (pro-Nazi and anti-Nazi). In other words, the novel presents a political and social cross-section which enables Saint-Clar to be both a particular town in the south-west close to the demarcation line and typical of France as a whole.[13] This exemplary typicality which is the basis for the generalising comments in the text also surfaces at the time of the Liberation, in relation to the disappointing return to the status quo which characterised the celebrations: 'But was Saint-Clar perhaps an exceptional town in

France? Would we perhaps, also, soon learn that the greatness and sacrifice of a handful of the French had easily redeemed the spineless behaviour of the pallid, weary mass? Would it perhaps be fitting to wait for a few days, a few months, to see the true face of the country form and shine forth once more?'[14] But nothing in the post-war section of the *Epilogues* either contradicts the pessimistic judgements made, or restricts them to the particular circumstances and conditions prevailing in Saint-Clar.

A similar political and social cross-section conferring typicality on the events and conflicts of the novel is found in *Mon Village à l'heure allemande* and *Uranus*. Jumainville is described as 'just a typical French village, no more, no less'.[15] Georges Brassens comments in his 1965 preface to *Banlieue sud-est*: 'Most French towns were in the same boat at the time, and the book became universal. It was a tourist guide through our adolescence for all of us',[16] which is fully confirmed by the range of characters and events and by the frequent general descriptions of 'the youth of the Occupation'. Even the extremely small cast of main characters in *Les Chiens de paille* which is, furthermore, set in an isolated part of the north-western coast of France, includes a Communist, a Gaullist, a collaborator and a black marketeer, fulfilling the function of metonymically representing France and thus supporting the general comments of the detached observer Constant. *La Culbute* and *Les Epées* also ensure that the attitudes and actions of the main protagonist-narrator are not read as purely personal idiosyncracies by relating his vision of the world to the general state of France.[17] The tripartite structure most clearly in evidence in *La Peste*—the particular setting and events constituting the 'narrative real', which metonymically relates to the general situation of France under the Occupation, and in turn supports wider considerations of the nature of existence in the world—is in fact a characteristic feature of the novel of ambiguity.

The social and political chaos of the Occupation and its aftermath is often echoing that of the world, or is shown to have universal implications for the nature of human endeavour, and this ensures the *thematic* coherence of the different levels. The impossibility of effecting a transition to peace after the war is also frequently emphasised. The planet Uranus of whose bleak desolation Watrin dreams, corresponding to the devastation of Blémont after the bombing, articulates the descriptions of the town with wider, quasi-metaphysical considerations. In *La Culbute* and *Les Epées* it is the absurdity of life which is exemplified in the grotesque farce of the Occupation, and particularly in any attitude of moral seriousness, whereas *La Peste* and *L'Education européenne,* equally concerned to demonstrate the limitations of human endeavour in the face of the absurd, highlight the moral qualities of that endeavour as the true source of human dignity. What is emerging from all these novels is not a local but a universal truth.[18]

Both the novels of unity and the novels of ambiguity operate within a moral framework, but the relation of the ethical to the narrative event is very different in each. In Resistance fiction the relation is one of continuity: the perception of the war as a cultural event means that the transcendent values of humanism which are being defended form both the context and the purpose of the events of the narrative, whereas in the post-war novel, although the values of justice, fraternity, reason, and of right and wrong are still present, the narrative event is in contradiction with the ethical, which is variously encoded by these very events as unrealisable, inappropriate, or belonging to the past. But if it is not the event which produces the ethical reading of the world, then the major question is where the latter comes from. In the novels of irresponsibility (*La Culbute, Les Epées* and to a certain extent *Banlieue sud-est*), deliberate transgression constitutes the identity of the main characters, and this sustains the presence of the ethical. The knowledge that the world is flouting what are presented as previously acceptable moral categories is borne in *Uranus* by the educators (Archambaud, one of the main characters, in his role as father, Didier a local teacher) who have to prepare the younger generation for contemporary reality, though their observations are subordinated to those of the 'super-educator' of the text, *le professeur* Watrin. For *Mon Village à l'heure allemande* the relation between ethics and the world is hypothetical, unresolved, consisting in the interrogations of what the future will bring—'a human jungle or a return to beauty, truth and all the tralala'.[19] *Les Forêts de la nuit* encodes justice and purity as unrealisable in the repeated use of the past conditional 'should have', which functions as an unfulfilled imperative. Janek of *L'Education européene* and Rieux of *La Peste* both transmit what they have learnt through experience: the disparity between human aspirations to justice, meaning and truth and the reality of the human condition.

In every case, the structural disparity between the 'narrative real' and the extradiegetic commentary means that what will emerge as the knowledge to be transmitted is not inherent in individual actions or events, but is centred on the figure of the narrator or those who assume the narrator's function as observers or instructors. The novels of ambiguity are no less didactic than the novels of unity, but the fact that knowledge is structured hierarchically, belonging to the narrator and his surrogates rather than the characters, to the observer rather than the observed, means that the reader is now invited to share the narrator's view of the spectacle of the human comedy.

The Narrator and the Hidden God

Francis Jeanson devotes a section of his famous review of *L'Homme révolté*: 'Albert Camus ou l'âme révoltée' (Albert Camus or the soul in revolt) to *La Peste* which he describes as 'a transcendental chronicle': '*La Peste* related events seen from on high, by a subjectivity outside the situation which was not living them itself and was content to look on.'[20] Camus protested strongly at this interpretation, as the narator Rieux is one of the main actors of the drama of the plague and the evolution from *L'Etranger* to *La Peste* 'was a movement towards solidarity and participation'.[21] But Jeanson is surely right to insist that the impersonal style of narration cannot be dismissed as being of no matter, and that the narrator and the doctor are different textual figures, situated at different levels of the narrative.[22] As extradiegetic narrator of the plague Rieux enjoys the omniscience characteristic of the subject of the *énonciation* in relation to the events and characters being narrated, stemming from his superior knowledge and moral authority, for the narration of the plague is governed by the message it is to produce, that the disease is only a symptom revealing a capricious creation hostile to men. And it is to this that Jeanson takes exception: 'For anyone looking on from on high, the agitation of people down on the earth's surface could well appear pretty meaningless.'[23] The all-encompassing vision inherent in Rieux's position as narrator is also embodied diegetically, when the character Rieux installs himself on the terrace, firstly with Tarrou, but finally alone, and it is from a position of dominance above the town that he decides to write his chronicle.

This 'view from above' is found in all the novels of ambiguity, establishing the *structural* coherence of the three levels of the narrative, for they all seek to deduce a moral lesson from the particular events of the Occupation which they narrate. Though the modalities vary, from a sombre realisation of the absurd contingency of existence, as in *La Peste*, to a now lighthearted, now vituperative presentation of the absurdities of life, the marriage of technique and metaphysics which Jeanson described as a 'resolutely absurdist stylistic procedure'[24] could apply to them all. The epilogue of *L'Education européenne* ends with Janek Twardowski rising to a position of absolute ascendancy over the events he has lived, by means of an image giving an unwittingly literal interpretation of 'agitation on the earth's surface'. He is now the sub-lieutenant Twardowski, revisiting the forest hideouts and recalling the past, and specifically the last moments of his friend Dobranski, when Janek promised, though convinced of its futility, to finish the novel Dobranski had wanted to write. Inserted into this dialogue is an image of columns of tiny, busy ants, each dragging a small blade of grass, each impelled by the great importance of their difficult task. As Janek was convinced that men would not heed the message of the book to mend their ways, so ants now crawl straight over the copy of *L'Education européenne* which lieutenant Twardowski has placed on the ground. The distance between Janek and the ants is then transformed into that between Janek-narrator and men in a final vision of creation itself: 'The world where men suffer and die is the same one where ants suffer and die: a cruel incomprehensible world, where the only thing that counts is to carry ever further an absurd twig (. . .) without ever stopping to rest or to ask why. . . .'[25] The superior knowledge underpinning the authority of the narrator is revealed in both *La Peste* and *L'Education européenne* to lie in the recognition of the limitations of human endeavour, a truth which informs the narration of events and of which the majority of characters are ignorant. A similar disparity in knowledge lies at the heart of the irony in all the novels of ambiguity, which operates primarily with the narrator displaying his knowledge at the characters' expense. Of course in practice this cannot be separated from the content of that knowledge, that human actions are taking place in a world of lost or unattainable values; incapable of fulfilling their own expectations, they can only demonstrate the validity of the narrator's.

There are many variations on this common schema. I shall concentrate here on *Uranus, Les Chiens de paille* and *Les Forêts de la nuit*, which exemplify the absurdist implications of the 'view from above' within a traditionally realist form, before turning to the novels of irresponsibility where the irony extends to the very mode of writing.

Watrin and Archambaud are the two major sources of moral commentary on the social and human experience of the Liberation period as it is presented in *Uranus*. Archambaud consistently underlines the manner in which all pay lip-service to the Resistance, whose prestige is backed up by the military terror of the FFI. The jockeying for power between the Communists and the Socialists, each trying to exploit their Resistance credentials, is shown to reinforce the simplistic equation between the Resistance and moral purity which overrides all other considerations. In this sense too, Blémont exemplifies France: 'Going beyond the town's limits, Archambaud considered the question at the level of the *département*, then at the level of the entire nation. The hypocrites now numbered millions. In all the provinces of France, in the villages, in the large towns and the small towns, he saw two-faced people proliferating.'[26] The end of the Occupation has produced a complete about-turn which is aiming to efface the past, and specifically the support for Vichy and the Maréchal, in line with the new morality. Preparing for the celebrations to welcome home the town's prisoners, Archambaud recalls the Maréchal's visit to Blémont. The same crowd is now going to applaud the insults which he expects the speakers to heap on Pétain; but there is no suggestion that the 'grande clameur de tendresse (great noise of affection)'[27] which had greeted Pétain was itself in any way forced: there is nothing inherently hypocritical about public manifestations or political opinions. Archambaud is articulating the socio-political thesis of the book, that the criminalisation of support for Vichy by the politicians[28] has installed a general fear dictating public obeisance of the new morality, precisely because support for the Maréchal was universal and sincere. (And it is worth opening a lengthy parenthesis here to note how common, not to say banal, is the scenario of 'the crowds welcoming de Gaulle after having welcomed Pétain', from the post-war novel to *Le Chagrin et la pitié* and beyond, in critical and imaginative writing. As with *Uranus*, there is always an anti-'résistantialisme'—or even, it might occasionally be recognised, anti-Resistance—axe to grind, which has a certain ironic charm, given the frequency of the statements on collaborationist turncoats and sudden espousal of less compromising causes as Germany's star wanes, in the clandestine Resistance press.)

Watrin completely agrees with Archambaud on his analysis of contemporary manners but puts a very different gloss on it; since the bombardment of Blémont he has been transported in dreams to the bleak horror of the planet Uranus where he experiences the anguish of the absence of all hope, and the Earth now appears to him in a different light. From these interplanetary heights the rich diversity of all forms of life is a source of poetry and wonder:

> One cannot conceive of anything finer or gentler than men. No, Archambaud, don't say anything. I know. But their wars, their concentration camps, their works of justice, I see them as impishness and ebullient behaviour. Don't they have songs for suffering? Don't talk to me of selfishness or hypocrisy. The selfishness of man is as adorable as that of a butterfly or a squirrel.[29]

This zoological vision of the planet excludes a moral attitude to social, political and moral conflicts which are inscribed within the natural order of things.

The narrator espouses the points of view of both his surrogate observers. There is never any suggestion that Archambaud's analysis or reason for indignation are either unreliable or criticisable. The case of Watrin is more complex. He is a rather burlesque figure, both in his lyrically effusive manner and the somewhat ridiculous exaggeration that the human jungle is as much a source of wonder as any other, which is in direct contradiction to the Archambaud position and also refuted by some of the scenes of the novel. The identification of the ruins of Blémont and the planet Uranus is strong enough for the alternative reading of the Earth as source of despair and anguish to be sustained. Where Archambaud and Watrin agree is that men are far more complex creatures than political and intellectual systems of thought, which deal in moral abstractions, allow. Throughout the novel the Communist Jourdan is a particular butt for irony, in the caricaturally limited nature of the fixed ideas and stereotypes of good and evil he is shown to believe in.

Archambaud's perception of an absurd attempt to engineer a national *volte-face* also relies on a disparity between human experience and simplistic ideas imposed from elsewhere, and his interest leads directly into the substance of the narrative: 'He watched for the difficulties such a situation could create in everyday life, and the moral or psychological abnormalities which resulted.'[30] Concentrating on the social and personal aspects of daily life under the Liberation, the narrative ironies, conveying variously amusement or indignation, present life in Blémont as an ultimately meaningless variety of clashes and conflicts, or an unsustainable morality play imposed by a powerful few. The very choice of the central situation illustrates this. Because of the shortage of accommodation, the Archambaud family (father, mother and Marie-Anne their daughter) has to house Watrin and the Gaigneux family (parents and four children). Into this household comes Maxime Loin, whom Archambaud discovers one night hiding from the FFI and agrees to shelter. All the possibilities afforded by such a situation are exploited—arguments in the kitchen between the two wives; amorous intrigues involving Loin, Gaigneux, Marie-Anne and Mme Archambaud; the need to keep Loin's presence from Gaigneux and Jourdan, a frequent visitor. And there are innumerable examples of particular remarks, or episodes which, displaying all the extravagances of a farce to amuse rather than engage the emotions, exemplify Watrin's indulgence towards the endearing habits and the resilience of the human animal whom it is impossible to take seriously however seriously he takes himself. One example would be characterisation of Léopold, the larger-than-life alcoholic café proprietor, who is the only true enthusiast for Racine in the classes which now have to be held in his café and who finally turns his hand to composing alexandrines, but in inappropriate contemporary slang. On the other hand, that Léopold is shot by *gendarmes* who come to arrest him acting on the orders of those protecting Monglat is not given the same tonality at all. Nor is the public beating-up of Gallien, a Maréchaliste ex-prisoner of war, at the welcoming ceremony at the station. Only Watrin goes forward to help him-Archambaud cannot find the courage to join him, and a doctor refuses to see to him. Watrin is finally escorted away by the police, leaving the wounded man on the ground as the speeches continue: '"Delivered from its enemies, from all its enemies, a young, ardent France, led by an elite whose intelligence, vision and humanity are the admiration of the whole world . . ." proclaimed the speaker.'[31] If, as Jean Cathelin argues, Aymé is concerned to present 'part of the recent history of France which greatly resembles the Shakespearian definition of life: "A tale told by an idiot, full of sound and fury"',[32] he achieves it as much as anything through the distancing effect of this farcical juxtaposition of characters and incidents.

None of the characters is in overall control in *Uranus*. The Communists think they are, politically, but in fact they are manipulated by Monglat as he uses his powerful friends in Paris. Only the narrator and the reader are aware of the foibles and the private dramas of all the characters, of the true facts behind the sequence of events. The same is even more true of *Les Forêts de la nuit*. The ignorance of the characters, each of whom has only partial knowledge of the events of the novel and the motivations of those concerned, is a major factor sustaining the importance of contingency, one of the bases for the technique of incongruous juxtaposition which is fully exploited, both to underline their ignorance and make a mockery of their actions and hopes which are always necessarily off target. By the end of the novel little can be taken at face value. Mme Costellot's mention of the efforts she made to intervene on Francis's behalf with von Brackner and the German authorities, Darricade's rise to fame with the image of Francis the Resistance martyr in tow, have ironic depths by virtue of the reader's superior knowledge. In all this the narrator is very evident—in the generalising scenes looking down on the town and its inhabitants, in the characterisation which, as in *Uranus,* is constituted by the thoughts of the characters and the narrator's judgements, and particularly in the Liberation scenes, where the disappointment that the events do not match what should have been is to be located in the extradiegetic discourse of the *énonciation*.

The narration of the Occupation years in *Les Forêts de la nuit* is constituted to a great extent by political and personal clashes between the French and within the Resistance, and therefore the hopes expressed on the great Liberation day, for a 'purifying wind (souffle)', a 'magnificent leap' which would change the face of France, appear virtually from nowhere, just as the working-class masses, the *maquisards* and the FFI do. The only Resistance character committed to the fight against social injustice was *le Mohican*, but he equally underlined the class differences opposing him to Francis, and the provisional nature of their common cause, and predicted, after an extremely sarcastic description of the defeat of the Germans and the nation in unison celebrating its victory with freedom restored: 'It will all just be starting.'[33] His judgement is fully confirmed—indeed, operates as a virtual *annonce*—by the Liberation scenes where the mass celebrations are at the same time the proof that nothing has changed. For the voice enunciating the judgement on these scenes, the possibility of change is already past, they are excluding what *should have* happened. But in the past of the novel which has been enunciated, everything tends to precisely the cynical victory being described. In other words, this is one of the 'moments de décrochage' (literally 'unhooking'), in Claude Duchet's terms, revealing the *hors-texte*, by which he means the implicit knowledge and codes of the text[34] which is constituted here by the Resistance discourse of heroism, grandeur and social renewal. With a mechanism recalling *Drôle de jeu*, this discourse is deliberately set aside in the *Avertissement*: 'Many books, since the end of the war, have shown and celebrated those whose fight saved honour and contributed to victory. I would have added nothing to these works', and the diegetic development specifically disproves it. This reveals the historical gap between the *énonciation*, which is post-Occupation, and the *énoncé*, for in all novels where the final battles for Liberation and the immediate post-Liberation period form the conclusion to the narrative,[35] the Occupation is thereby produced as an historically dated phenomenon, belonging to the time of the *énoncé*. From the point of view of the analysis of the temporal structures of the narrative levels, Resistance and Occupation could be said to occupy a similar position to that of the pre-war history in the Resistance novels, where questions or predictions concerning the future can also be classed as ignorant or knowledgeable in relation to later narrative developments which constitute the historical present of the *énonciation*. In *Les Forêts de la nuit* irony is the major expression of the tension between the *énoncé* and the *énonciation*, proving that human and social reality will defeat the Resistance coding of it as potentially noble, and also operating at the expense of the town's inhabitants who collectively exemplify, in greater or lesser degrees of stupidity and selfishness, the limitations of human endeavour.

Drieu la Rochelle composed *Les Chiens de paille* about the same time as his article 'Bilan', summing up his achievements and failures at the *NRF*,[36] and the political thesis of the novel is very similar to the arguments set out there, that the world is entering a new phase in its history in the battle between the two empires of America and Russia, and France is prevented by its own decadence, which Vichy has proved incapable of countering, from saving itself from foreign occupation. The political activists in the country are all hitched to the bandwagon of one or another foreign power. In the article, however, Drieu comes down firmly on the side of Hitler as the only man in a position to safeguard Europe against foreign domination—England is seen as no more than a puppet of the United States—and specifically against Russia which is identified as the greatest threat. In the novel Germany does not enjoy this prestige, and the collaborator Bardy represents just one of several options alongside the Gaullist Préault, the Communist Salis, and Cormont, the believer in 'the wretched and derisory myth of "France standing alone"'.[37] The intrigues between these various characters, especially for the control of a secret arms depot, is narrated from Constant's point of view, who is both character and commentator on the cast of characters. He is further set apart from the other characters both on the level of characterisation—he is the adventurer with a truly global knowledge of the cultures of the world and all possible experiences, and who is now going beyond adventurism—and through his metaphysical interest in Eastern, Christian and Nietzchean philosophies which underlies the political perception of the upheavals taking place in the world as constituting yet another clash between decadence and barbarity to engender a new world order. The figure of the traitor is again central here, linking the metaphysical, the political and finally the diegetic as Constant, deciding that Cormont on the one hand and the internationalists on the other are locked in a static battle beyond which they cannot progress, takes on the role of Judas to sacrifice the Christ-like figure of Cormont and accomplish the destiny of France.

The distance between humanity and Constant, who variously espouses the point of view of the gods, of God and of non-being which is beyond any individual creator, is more pertinent than the differences opposing the various factions. As in the other novels of ambiguity, the 'view from above' accompanies the absence of any figure of the enemy. Gaullists and collaborators, for example, are marked by resemblance, not difference;[38] men are creatures governed by passions which enslave them for they fail to recognise the futile nature of their passions, of all existence, which would save them.[39] But if Constant if omniscient, he is certainly not omnipotent and is himself at the mercy of the extradiegetic narrator who is as elusive as any hidden God, appearing primarily to deliver the thunderbolt of the final paragraph, in the shape of an English plane which drops a bomb on the house where Constant is about to blow up Cormont, Susini the black marketeer and himself.[40] The historical gap between *énonciation* and *énoncé* is also revealed. Constant reflects that the divisions and conflicts opposing Gaullists and Communists, Gaullists and Gaullists, Gaullists, Communists and collaborators, form a kind of dance whose rules are understood and respected by all, but which would still erupt into violent explosions: 'which break with all half-measures. (. . .) But France, in 1942, had *not yet* reached that point; deaths by violence were *still only* counted in tens.'[41]

Jeanson accused Camus of writing a metaphysical novel which should have been called 'the human condition': 'The real scene is not this town, but the world; and the real characters were not those men and women of Oran but all humanity, not that disease but absolute Evil',[42] a statement which, allowing for the different metaphysical content, might have been made of any of the novels under consideration here. In *La Peste* evil in the world is both alien to man and elided with the human condition. In the other novels of ambiguity, it is the nature of man himself which explains the irrational absurd world which confronts the individual. Both perspectives reveal the ahistorical character of the 'view from above', of the heights from which the narrative subject, excentric to the world, can thereby seize it as a totality: the particular conditions under the Occupation are a manifestation of the infernal cycle of human action in the world,[43] which is thus intimately bound up with the essentialist view of human nature: 'Men were always the same',[44] reflects Rieux. The unbridgeable gap between the realities of the Occupation and straightforward moral judgements of right and wrong is underpinned by the absolute knowledge that value cannot be produced by action in the world. The common thread linking these novels is that the world is inauthentic.

If irony can generally be said to reside in a discrepancy between a statement and contextual information,[45] then the latter is revealed in the whole range of narrative ironies deployed at the expense of characters who rely on their actions being meaningful or on being able to behave in accordance with well-defined codes of behaviour. But this can be further refined. Robert Scholes isolates three kinds of irony in narrative, two of which[46] are extremely pertinent here: the irony that needs 'no authoritative discourse to focus it but draws upon simple principles of value and a clear social consensus',[47] and the irony that is 'controllable only at the price of introducing a highly coercive and manipulative discourse'.[48] Both kinds are to be found in the novels of ambiguity, the former presenting the spectacle of the Occupation and Liberation as an enactment of the well-known adage: 'Plus ça change, plus c'est la même chose' (the more things change, the more they stay the same), the latter directed at any discourse which asserts that value can be grounded in man's action in the world, and primarily at Resistance discourse whose central value is man himself. We have already see the manner in which this refutation operates in *Les Forêts de la nuit*. *Uranus* is concerned to demonstrate that any social renewal produced by a Communist-Socialist dominated Resistance is a moral sham, not least because the ideas which inspire it are insubstantial abstract doctrines bearing no relation to reality. *Les Chiens de paille* seeks to demonstrate the hollow nature of all transcendence in that it is always a sign of decadence. France is said to have entered a phase of decadence and is thus in this latest battle realigning the forces of civilisation and barbarity, re-enacting the destiny of the Jews overrun by foreign troops. Political and metaphysical theses converge at this point, for in spite of the general language, and its anti-semitism, it is Resistance discourse which is being pinpointed, and particularly its concern with the absolute and the universal:

> The Jews were now only intellectuals and men of letters, not even men of letters, but kinds of priests, frenetic monks, vain, hideous, grotesque, and who, in the middle of Greek philosophers and athletes, of Roman aristocrats and soldiers, continued to make speeches about the supremacy of Jewish genius, naturally a 'purely intellectual', entirely spiritual supremacy! Having had their arses kicked and kicked again, they spoke of the supremacy of their arses over the boot that was doing the kicking.[49]

It is here that a connection can perhaps be established between the novels of ambiguity and the crisis of humanism which becomes so insistent by the end of the war, for what is denied by the overriding vision of the superior narrative viewpoint is the possibility of transcendence. Human actions in the world, caught in the realm of the contingent and the relative, cannot fulfil aspirations to the absolute, whereas in the Resistance fiction action in the world undeniably founds the values of humanism, and there is an unbroken continuity between the narrative event and the values it incarnates. The impossibility of transcendence takes two forms in the novels of ambiguity. The first could be called the tragic mode, registering the crisis of values but not completely rejecting them as such. Vercors and Camus both illustrate this.[50] The more usual form lies in the convergence between the knowledge of the meaninglessness of human existence, and the socio-political thesis on the nature of Resistance morality (or more accurately, of 'résistantialisme') which is accordingly seen as inappropriate. Both concord in the use of irony to demonstrate absurdity, and in the appeal to the hidden God.

Lucien Goldmann, whose work *Le Dieu caché*[51] is being explicitly recalled here, shows that the figure of the hidden God, both present and absent, is essential to the seventeenth-century 'tragic consciousness', the perception of the divorce between the absolute values of God and the impossibility of realising them in the world. Jeanson brings out the importance of the ever-absent, ever-present God in Camus's work: 'Camus is certainly not an atheist, but a passive antideist. He does not deny God's existence (because he accuses him of injustice), (. . .) all he wants is to challenge him',[52] and Sartre talks of man in Camus's world of eternal injustice, demanding meaning from a God who is eternally silent.[53] Camus himself has Rieux refer to God 'in that sky where he says nothing'.[54] In this, as in so many other ways, *La Peste* is typical of the post-war novel of the Occupation, for they all use references to God, a signal that human action is being judged in reference to a transcendent absolute. But rather than the impassive, silent interlocutor of Camus's man in revolt, God is merely a figure in the cosmology, an ironic or anguished observer mirroring the stance of the God-like narrator.[55]

In spite of the importance of this particular *vision du monde* for a realisation of the loss of value in human existence, to agree with Jeanson that *La Peste*—and by extension any of these novels—is *really* (and therefore only) a metaphysical novel would be tantamount to saying the 'narrative real' can be effaced from the text. On the contrary, the frequency of the mechanism of the character-turned-author should alert us to the very specific structures of these novels. Edwin Moses writes: 'To have an external narrator tell the story of an enclosed city which is a symbol of the whole world would be ridiculous on the face of it: it would make the narrator into God.'[56] However much the identification of Rieux as narrator fudges the presence of an implicit, non-individualised narrator, however much Rieux enjoys a God-like omniscience, Moses is making an essential point[57] that Rieux as narrator is structurally tied to the diegetic development of the plague. In these novels, action in the world—which *is* the diegetic development of the Occupation and Liberation periods—is constitutive of the knowledge of the text, that no action can found value, and it is the function of the narrator, who is both of this world and not of it, to *realise* the contradiction.[58]

'In the country of the Ironic, Omniscience itself appears absurd': thus Scholes sums up his third category of irony,[59] that of the self-conscious narrative consistently using the ironic mode to draw attention to its own artifices. It is perhaps not surprising that a constant juggling with the *énonciation* and the *énoncé* is most apparent in novels such as *La Culbute*, *Les Epées* and *Banlieue sud-est* which portray the Occupation years as a grandiose melodrama of contradictory scripts earnestly acted out by a large cast of ham actors,[60] where the narrator emerges primarily as scriptwriter *extraordinaire*. Gone is the absolute assurance of *La Peste* and *L'Education européenne*, where the seriousness of the account of the character-narrator is never questioned. In none of these novels is the perception of the absurdity of life, of which the Occupation is a particularly acute manifestation, at all in doubt; what is destroyed in *La Culbute*, *Les Epées* and *Banlieue sud-est* is the possibility of the narrative detachment from that realisation which sustains the 'view from above', and therefore the implicit assumption that the project of writing is not itself subordinated to the order of the absurd.

The suicide letter of the young François Sanders in the first chapter of *Les Epées* serves as a paradigm of the kind of shifts deployed to signal the literary status of the writing. After a portrait of himself and his family he continues: 'I think nothing has been forgotten. I have just reread what I have written. It is a very good piece of homework and I think I would get a high mark if the subject of the essay had been: what are your thoughts on the eve of your suicide? Express them in the most touching way you can, in a letter to a stranger. Make a plan.'[61] All the irony resides in the clash of two incompatible kinds of writing—part of a narrative development marking the precocious cynicism and authority of this fifteen-year-old fourth-former, or a no less cynical parody of essay writing and its belletristic pretentions—and the concomitant doubt as to how the preceding pages should have been read. Similarly, the Stendhalien footnotes,[62] the café Lafcadio situate the narration within a tradition of literary irony, and also, by these ironic signals of the presence of the narrator, place to the fore the irredeemably literary nature of the narrative event and its relation to the narration.

Banlieue sud-est uses a whole range of devices to call attention to the narrative: imitation of documents, ironic headlines used particularly for the generalising images typical of the 'view from above',[63] footnotes, descriptive passages striking a deliberately false lyrical note and parodying the designation 'literature',[64] the appearance of M. René Fallet, firstly as character,[65] and, in the final pages, as author.[66] Moreover, the first chapter of the novel has a most ambiguous status. Given that the second chapter begins with the main character suddenly waking up, it could be read as his extravagant dreams; narrated by a disembodied 'I', each paragraph describes a different identity, 'I am the bloke who possesses love', 'I am a large rock in the forest of Fontainebleau', 'I am a woman.' But it would be more in keeping with a narrative which refuses to take its own narration seriously to read it as an amusing display of the omniscience and omnipotence of the narrator who, outside diegetic time, is truly outside time: 'I am the master of the universe. I am immortal',[67] for whom literally anything is possible: 'I am the greatest cycling champion the Earth has ever seen. Same as for the "Love-Me"; here, I say "I win", and it's done'.[68] and who, in the very accumulation of narrative identities, in fact has none.

If the ironic devices in *Banlieue sud-est* and *Les Epées* are concerned above all to recall that there is no transcendence of the written, this is an even more central concern of *La Culbute*, which sustains a constant tension between the will to omnipotence of the self as narrator and his subordination to elements beyond his control, between freedom and destiny.[69] Bearing particularly on writing and signification, *La Culbute* can therefore be placed in a long tradition of reflection, from *Jacques le Fataliste* to *Djinn*, on the nature of narrative, its tendencies to absolute contingency and absolute necessity, and its relation to reality. Georges Renaut realises that, as far as writing is concerned, omnipotence is on the side of necessity: by adopting the handle 'de la Motte', having a card printed with his new name, he is his own creation.[70] The project of the diary is to subordinate the formlessness of existence to necessity, and it is in this light that one can understand his letters of denunciation, which are so many attempts to write other people into his narrative. M. Fouilloux in the flat upstairs is arrested, Renaut having denounced him for listening to English radio, and he hears the family acting out the scene he has written for them (Fouilloux's brave words as he is taken from his family, his wife's cries of 'My husband, my husband'); unbeknownst to them, others are players in the film he is directing. His superiority lies in his knowledge: 'I am acting in *My Life* (. . .) A realist film, made by destiny.'[71] But he is constantly in danger of falling into the void of absolute freedom: 'And I am also acting in a second story (. . .) a fantasy film. I do not know its title—I am looking in vain for the director's team and the producer.'[72] His drama does not lie in trying to choose the ordered laws of narrative over reality, but in a veritable crisis of signification. For the world of reality and objects is also ruled by the tyranny of signs:

> It is not life which imitates life, just like that, gratuitously. Art is needed as an intermediary. Life imitates the imitation that art creates of life. We have heard the sound effects people on the radio substituting spoons for the sea too often (. . .) and we no longer know, always supposing they exist, what natural sounds are like. The bed and the lift are play-acting at imitating life, they are making theatre with life, they are sound effects. We can suspect them of being as cruel as men.[73]

It is also governed by their anarchic proliferation. There are so many images labelled 'Laval' circulating in the world that the question *who is Laval?* becomes particularly hard to answer: 'Is Laval the man smiling nicely at Hitler or the man saving France by the sweat of his brow?'[74] and, as with Pétain, Churchill or Hitler, the possibility of affixing value of unique truth to one image rather than another is undermined by the very indeterminacy of the sign which cannot be fixed to one original essence. From that point of view, however, they resist the order and logic of narrative: 'They have lost their being. Having acted so much they have produced too many individuals under their own skin and they are no more than a haunted stage. Mystery, nasty mystery. How then can history be written?'[75] A similar disparity underlies his reactions to the enigmatic phrases of the English radio; at first he celebrates their freedom and opacity, and then realises they might be obeying a logic, encoding his own death sentence. His project to impose his own script (although he is often tempted by the total freedom, and nihilation, of signification) is constantly threatened by the fear of being written into someone else's 'film'.

The insistence in *La Culbute* on the irremediable facticity of human existence can thus be said to echo the impossibility of transcendence characteristic of the other novels of ambiguity. Similarly the narrative games and strategies in *Banlieue sud-est*, *Les Epées* and *La Culbute* around the omniscience of the narrator-author also serve to construct this figure as both diegetic and extradiegetic, recalling *La Peste* and *L'Education européenne*, and it is here that one can elucidate the essential ambiguity at the heart of the structures of irony, an ambiguity which might be summed up as variations on the famous phrase 'loser takes all'. Georges Renaut, for example, goes to the rendezvous which he fears contains the hidden sentence of death, but his diary remains, permanently inscribing his disappearance within the order of the narrative: like the narrator of *Banlieue sud-est*, on the level of the *énonciation* Georges Renaut is indestructible. In all these novels, however painful the knowledge, however dramatic the defeat which recognition of the futility of action in the world entails, it is nonetheless the key to narrative survival.

Notes

1. 'Le jeu de la guerre et du hasard', *La Culbute*, p.11.
2. Paris, 1971, pp.10-11, p.43.
3. *Les Forêts*, p. 151.
4. *Semiotics and Interpretation*, New Haven and London, p.75.
5. This passage is preparing for the episode when Hélène sends her last letter to Jean breaking off the relationship. 'That kind of letter always arrives', she reflects (p.230). And it does, provoking Jean's suicide. Given the difficulties of communication as proved by these earlier letters, one could say that her expectations are ironically *fulfilled*.
6. One of Hélène's other letters is given in full on pp.149-50 and serves as an illustration of the type.
7. P.475.
8. P.469.
9. *Ibid.*
10. P.450.
11. '"Le baiser de Lamourette" était de rigueur cejour-là', comments the narrator. p.456.
12. P.307.
13. It also relies on the classic Paris/province opposition of the provincial novel.
14. P.476.
15. P.18.
16. P.8.
17. See *La Culbute*, p.103, pp. 195-6 and *Les Epées*, p.100.
18. 'Truth' here being used in the sense of what the narrative presents as true.
19. P.309.
20. *Les Temps modernes*, vol.7, no.79, mai 1952, p.2072.
21. 'Lettre au directeur des *Temps modernes*', *Les Temps modernes*, vol.8, no.82, août 1952, p.321.
22. See in the same volume, 'Pour tout vous dire . . .', p.355.
23. 'Albert Camus ou l'âme révoltée', pp.2073-4
24. 'Albert Camus ou l'âme révoltée', p.2073. S.B. John also comments on the importance of the omniscient narrator in post-war fiction, in 'The Ambiguous Invader'.
25. P.175 (1946).
26. P.35.

27. P.319.

28. Antagonism to political parties being itself a Vichy theme, that Pétain appealed directly to the French, and not as a politician. There is no mention in *Uranus* of a similar guilt generated by support for Laval. Nor any hint that a pro-Vichy attitude might have conceivably been misplaced. On the contrary, the 'bouclier' theme is extended to include collaboration, when Archambaud debates whether to shelter Loin the fascist: 'He did not feel any sense of solidarity with this man and resented him having seen collaboration as a means of subjugating France, whereas for Archambaud himself it was a means of defence'(p.42).

29. P.236.

30. P.36.

31. P.340.

32. *Marcel Aymé ou la paysan de Paris*, p.119.

33. P.36. And his views are echoed, from the other side of the political fence, by the 'Resister' Darricade: 'For Darricade, the real fight had begun at dawn that day' (p.459).

34. 'Le hors-texte reste plus ou moins perceptible tout au long de la chaîne narrative, notamment aux moments de décrochage entre discours et récit, entre énonciation et énoncé, entre le je et le on, entre la parole rapportée et son support textuel', 'Réflexions sur les rapports du roman et de la société', *Roman et société*, p.71.

35. A variation on this occurs in *Le Chemin des écoliers*, by Marcel Aymé, which does end during the Occupation, but where the post-war fates of many of the characters are given in footnotes. The time of the *énonciation* is again post-Occupation.

36. *NRF*, janvier-juin 1943, pp.103-11. In the Preface to *Les Chiens de paille*, he says the novel was written in the spring of 1943.

37. P.186.

38. P.39.

39. P.53.

40. Thus confirming the quotations placed as an epigraph, on the absolute indifference of creation towards men.

41. Pp.193-4 Emphasis added.

42. 'Albert Camus ou l'âme révoltée', p.2073.

43. Cf. *Les Forêts*, the scenes of the crowd jeering at Balansun and Cécile 'were *exactly* the same as the hallucinating images of pogroms in Nazi Germany, which the French newspapers were publishing in 39-40' (p.469). Emphasis added.

44. P.1473.

45. Helmut Bonheim, *The Narrative Modes*, Cambridge, 1982, p.156.

46. The third will be discussed later in this chapter.

47. *Semiotics and Interpretation*, p.86.

48. *Ibid*.

49. Pp.149-150.

50. Vercors, for example, writes of the degradation imposed by the Nazis, and also, in *Les Lettres françaises*, denounces the failure of the *épuration* (i.e. the failure to reject those in Resistance eyes guilty of collaboration) as immoral ('La Gangrène', *LF*, no.39, 30 janvier 1945, p.1.

51. Paris, 1955.

52. Jeanson, 'Albert Camus ou l'âme révoltée', p.2085.

53. Sartre, 'Réponse à Albert Camus', p.346.

54. P.1323.

55. See particularly *Les Chiens de paille*, pp. 34-5; *Uranus*, p.195.

56. 'Functional Complexity: the Narrative Techniques of *The Plague*', *Modern Fiction Studies*, vol.20, no.3, autumn 1974, p.423.

57. Although he does discuss Rieux as sole narrator, and is therefore confusing Rieux, extradiegetic narrator of the plague, and the extradiegetic narrator of the *text*, who is responsible for example for the substitution plague/Occupation (which Moses does not discuss at all).

58. A good example at the level of narrative description would be Watrin's reaction to Gaigneux's defence of the extremely unsavoury Rochard, who has landed Léopold in prison: 'The professor gave him a smile that was both discouraged and amused' (p.161), 'discouraged' in so far as Watrin is genuinely hoping Gaigneux will help obtain Léopold's release; 'amused' by yet another picturesque example of the human 'jungle'.

59. *Semiotics and Interpretation*, p.86.

60. Echoes of which occur in other novels. Cf. p.396 above, re the abbé on the barricades.

61. P.13.

62. P.104: 'C'est un milicien qui parle'; p.106: 'C'est une âme sans idéal qui parle.'

63. 'PANORAMIQUE' (p.340), 'FIN DU PANORAMIQUE' (p.341), 'REPRISE DU PANORAMIQUE' (p.347), 'RE-FIN DU PANORAMIQUE' (p.351).

64. Pp.127-9.

65. Pp.284-5.
66. Pp.381-2.
67. P.12.
68. *Ibid.*
69. P.19.
70. P.15.
71. P.77.
72. *Ibid.*
73. P.19.
74. P.121. Jean Duffy makes a not dissimilar point in relation to Claude Simon's novel *La Corde raide,* in 'The Subversion of Historical Representation in Claude Simon', *French Studies,* Volume XVI No.4 October 1987, pp.422-3.
75. P.122.

FURTHER READING

Criticism

Britton, Celia. *The Nouveau Roman: Fiction, Theory, and Politics.* New York: St. Martin's Press, 1992, 231 p.
    Focuses on the nouveau roman style of novel-writing in France, leading into a discussion of the counter-reaction to this style of writing during the 1980s.

Hamer, Kathyryn. "Cultural (Pre)Occupation: *Comoedia* and French Identity, 1941-44." *Literature and History* 10 (spring 2001): 42-53.
    A discussion of literary activity in France during the second world war.

Kaplan, Alice Yaeger. *Reproductions of Banality: Fascism, Literature, and French Intellectual Life.* Minneapolis: University of Minnesota Press, 1986, 214 p.
    Study of the effect of fascism on French literary and intellectual activity.

Marcel Proust: The Critical Heritage, edited by Leighton Hodson. London and New York: Routledge, 1989, 421 p.
    Selected essays from a conference focusing on the exploration of the relationship between aspects of history, literature, and film.

A New History of French Literature, edited by Denis Hollier. Cambridge, MA, and London: Harvard University Press, 1989, 1150 p.
    A detailed history of French literature, from 778 A.D. to the present day.

Poster, Mark. *Existential Marxism in Postwar France: From Sartre to Althusser. Princeton.* Princeton, NJ: Princeton University Press, 1975, 415 p.
    Examines the relationship between Marxism and existentialism as a dominant theme of French intellectual thought in postwar France.

Scott, Malcolm. *The Struggle for the Soul of the French Novel: French Catholic and Realist Novelists, 1850-1970.* London: Macmillan, 1989, 294 p.
    Traces the relationship between religious influence and the development of the novel in French literature.

Scriven, Michael. *Paul Nizan: Communist Novelist.* London: Macmillan Press, 1988, 200 p.
    A detailed examination of Nizan's work, including his novels.

How to Use This Index

The main references

> **Calvino, Italo**
> 1923-1985 .... CLC 5, 8, 11, 22, 33, 39,
> 73; SSC 3

list all author entries in the following Gale Literary Criticism series:

    BLC = *Black Literature Criticism*
    CLC = *Contemporary Literary Criticism*
    CLR = *Children's Literature Review*
    CMLC = *Classical and Medieval Literature Criticism*
    DA = *DISCovering Authors*
    DAB = *DISCovering Authors: British*
    DAC = *DISCovering Authors: Canadian*
    DAM = *DISCovering Authors: Modules*
          DRAM: *Dramatists Module;* **MST:** *Most-Studied Authors Module;*
          MULT: *Multicultural Authors Module;* **NOV:** *Novelists Module;*
          POET: *Poets Module;* **POP:** *Popular Fiction and Genre Authors Module*
    DC = *Drama Criticism*
    HLC = *Hispanic Literature Criticism*
    LC = *Literature Criticism from 1400 to 1800*
    NCLC = *Nineteenth-Century Literature Criticism*
    NNAL = *Native North American Literature*
    PC = *Poetry Criticism*
    SSC = *Short Story Criticism*
    TCLC = *Twentieth-Century Literary Criticism*
    WLC = *World Literature Criticism, 1500 to the Present*

The cross-references

> See also CANR 23; CA 85-88;
> obituary CA116

list all author entries in the following Gale biographical and literary sources:

    AAYA = *Authors & Artists for Young Adults*
    AITN = *Authors in the News*
    BEST = *Bestsellers*
    BW = *Black Writers*
    CA = *Contemporary Authors*
    CAAS = *Contemporary Authors Autobiography Series*
    CABS = *Contemporary Authors Bibliographical Series*
    CANR = *Contemporary Authors New Revision Series*
    CAP = *Contemporary Authors Permanent Series*
    CDALB = *Concise Dictionary of American Literary Biography*
    CDBLB = *Concise Dictionary of British Literary Biography*
    DLB = *Dictionary of Literary Biography*
    DLBD = *Dictionary of Literary Biography Documentary Series*
    DLBY = *Dictionary of Literary Biography Yearbook*
    HW = *Hispanic Writers*
    JRDA = *Junior DISCovering Authors*
    MAICYA = *Major Authors and Illustrators for Children and Young Adults*
    MTCW = *Major 20th-Century Writers*
    SAAS = *Something about the Author Autobiography Series*
    SATA = *Something about the Author*
    YABC = *Yesterday's Authors of Books for Children*

Literary Criticism Series
Cumulative Author Index

20/1631
See Upward, Allen
A/C Cross
See Lawrence, T(homas) E(dward)
Abasiyanik, Sait Faik 1906-1954
See Sait Faik
See also CA 123
Abbey, Edward 1927-1989 .... **CLC 36, 59**
See also ANW; CA 45-48; 128; CANR 2, 41; DA3; DLB 256; MTCW 2; TCWW 2
Abbott, Lee K(ittredge) 1947- .... **CLC 48**
See also CA 124; CANR 51, 101; DLB 130
Abe, Kobo 1924-1993 .... **CLC 8, 22, 53, 81**
See also CA 65-68; 140; CANR 24, 60; DAM NOV; DFS 14; DLB 182; MJW; MTCW 1, 2; SFW 4; TCLC 121
Abe Kobo
See Abe, Kobo
Abelard, Peter c. 1079-c. 1142 ...... **CMLC 11**
See also DLB 115, 208
Abell, Kjeld 1901-1961 .... **CLC 15**
See also CA 191; 111; DLB 214
Abish, Walter 1931- .... **CLC 22; SSC 44**
See also CA 101; CANR 37; CN 7; DLB 130, 227
Abrahams, Peter (Henry) 1919- .... **CLC 4**
See also AFW; BW 1; CA 57-60; CANR 26; CDWLB 3; CN 7; DLB 117, 225; MTCW 1, 2; RGEL 2; WLIT 2
Abrams, M(eyer) H(oward) 1912- ... **CLC 24**
See also CA 57-60; CANR 13, 33; DLB 67
Abse, Dannie 1923- .... **CLC 7, 29**
See also CA 53-56; CAAS 1; CANR 4, 46, 74; CBD; CP 7; DAB; DAM POET; DLB 27, 245; MTCW 1
Abutsu 1222(?)-1283 .... **CMLC 46**
See also Abutsu-ni
Abutsu-ni
See Abutsu
See also DLB 203
Achebe, (Albert) Chinua(lumogu)
1930- ...... **CLC 1, 3, 5, 7, 11, 26, 51, 75, 127, 152; BLC 1; WLC**
See also AAYA 15; AFW; BPFB 1; BW 2, 3; CA 1-4R; CANR 6, 26, 47; CDWLB 3; CLR 20; CN 7; CP 7; CWRI 5; DA; DA3; DAB; DAC; DAM MST, MULT, NOV; DLB 117; DNFS 1; EXPN; EXPS; LAIT 2; MAICYA 1, 2; MTCW 1, 2; NFS 2; RGEL 2; RGSF 2; SATA 38, 40; SATA-Brief 38; SSFS 3, 13; WLIT 2
Acker, Kathy 1948-1997 .... **CLC 45, 111**
See also CA 117; 122; 162; CANR 55; CN 7
Ackroyd, Peter 1949- .... **CLC 34, 52, 140**
See also BRWS 6; CA 123; 127; CANR 51, 74, 99; CN 7; DLB 155, 231; HGG; INT 127; MTCW 1; RHW

Acorn, Milton 1923-1986 .... **CLC 15**
See also CA 103; CCA 1; DAC; DLB 53; INT 103
Adamov, Arthur 1908-1970 .... **CLC 4, 25**
See also CA 17-18; 25-28R; CAP 2; DAM DRAM; GFL 1789 to the Present; MTCW 1; RGWL 2
Adams, Alice (Boyd) 1926-1999 .. **CLC 6, 13, 46; SSC 24**
See also CA 81-84; 179; CANR 26, 53, 75, 88; CN 7; CSW; DLB 234; DLBY 1986; INT CANR-26; MTCW 1, 2; SSFS 14
Adams, Andy 1859-1935 .... **TCLC 56**
See also TCWW 2; YABC 1
Adams, Brooks 1848-1927 .... **TCLC 80**
See also CA 123; DLB 47
Adams, Douglas (Noel) 1952-2001 .. **CLC 27, 60**
See also AAYA 4, 33; BEST 89:3; BYA 14; CA 106; 197; CANR 34, 64; CPW; DA3; DAM POP; DLBY 1983; JRDA; MTCW 1; NFS 7; SATA 116; SATA-Obit 128; SFW 4
Adams, Francis 1862-1893 .... **NCLC 33**
Adams, Henry (Brooks)
1838-1918 .... **TCLC 4, 52**
See also AMW; CA 104; 133; CANR 77; DA; DAB; DAC; DAM MST; DLB 12, 47, 189; MTCW 1; NCFS 1
Adams, John 1735-1826 .... **NCLC 106**
See also DLB 31, 183
Adams, Richard (George) 1920- ... **CLC 4, 5, 18**
See also AAYA 16; AITN 1, 2; BPFB 1; BYA 5; CA 49-52; CANR 3, 35; CLR 20; CN 7; DAM NOV; FANT; JRDA; LAIT 5; MAICYA 1, 2; MTCW 1, 2; NFS 11; SATA 7, 69; YAW
Adamson, Joy(-Friederike Victoria)
1910-1980 .... **CLC 17**
See also CA 69-72; 93-96; CANR 22; MTCW 1; SATA 11; SATA-Obit 22
Adcock, Fleur 1934- .... **CLC 41**
See also CA 25-28R, 182; CAAE 182; CAAS 23; CANR 11, 34, 69, 101; CP 7; CWP; DLB 40; FW
Addams, Charles (Samuel)
1912-1988 .... **CLC 30**
See also CA 61-64; 126; CANR 12, 79
Addams, Jane 1860-1945 .... **TCLC 76**
See also AMWS 1; FW
Addison, Joseph 1672-1719 .... **LC 18**
See also BRW 3; CDBLB 1660-1789; DLB 101; RGEL 2; WLIT 3
Adler, Alfred (F.) 1870-1937 .... **TCLC 61**
See also CA 119; 159

Adler, C(arole) S(chwerdtfeger)
1932- .... **CLC 35**
See also AAYA 4, 41; CA 89-92; CANR 19, 40, 101; CLR 78; JRDA; MAICYA 1, 2; SAAS 15; SATA 26, 63, 102, 126; YAW
Adler, Renata 1938- .... **CLC 8, 31**
See also CA 49-52; CANR 95; CN 7; MTCW 1
Adorno, Theodor W(iesengrund)
1903-1969 .... **TCLC 111**
See also CA 89-92; 25-28R; CANR 89; DLB 242
Ady, Endre 1877-1919 .... **TCLC 11**
See also CA 107; CDWLB 4; DLB 215; EW 9
A.E. .... **TCLC 3, 10**
See also Russell, George William
See also DLB 19
Aelfric c. 955-c. 1010 .... **CMLC 46**
See also DLB 146
Aeschines c. 390B.C.-c. 320B.C. ..... **CMLC 47**
See also DLB 176
Aeschylus 525(?)B.C.-456(?)B.C. .. **CMLC 11, 51; DC 8; WLCS**
See also AW 1; CDWLB 1; DA; DAB; DAC; DAM DRAM, MST; DFS 5, 10; DLB 176; RGWL 2
Aesop 620(?)B.C.-560(?)B.C. .... **CMLC 24**
See also CLR 14; MAICYA 1, 2; SATA 64
Affable Hawk
See MacCarthy, Sir (Charles Otto) Desmond
Africa, Ben
See Bosman, Herman Charles
Afton, Effie
See Harper, Frances Ellen Watkins
Agapida, Fray Antonio
See Irving, Washington
Agee, James (Rufus) 1909-1955 ...... **TCLC 1, 19**
See also AITN 1; AMW; CA 108; 148; CDALB 1941-1968; DAM NOV; DLB 2, 26, 152; DLBY 1989; LAIT 3; MTCW 1; RGAL 4
Aghill, Gordon
See Silverberg, Robert
Agnon, S(hmuel) Y(osef Halevi)
1888-1970 .... **CLC 4, 8, 14; SSC 30**
See also CA 17-18; 25-28R; CANR 60, 102; CAP 2; MTCW 1, 2; RGSF 2; RGWL 2
Agrippa von Nettesheim, Henry Cornelius
1486-1535 .... **LC 27**
Aguilera Malta, Demetrio 1909-1981
See also CA 111; 124; CANR 87; DAM MULT, NOV; DLB 145; HLCS 1; HW 1
Agustini, Delmira 1886-1914
See also CA 166; HLCS 1; HW 1, 2; LAW

Aherne, Owen
See Cassill, R(onald) V(erlin)
Ai 1947- .... **CLC 4, 14, 69**
See also CA 85-88; CAAS 13; CANR 70; DLB 120
Aickman, Robert (Fordyce)
1914-1981 .... **CLC 57**
See also CA 5-8R; CANR 3, 72, 100; HGG; SUFW
Aiken, Conrad (Potter) 1889-1973 .... **CLC 1, 3, 5, 10, 52; PC 26; SSC 9**
See also AMW; CA 5-8R; 45-48; CANR 4, 60; CDALB 1929-1941; DAM NOV, POET; DLB 9, 45, 102; EXPS; HGG; MTCW 1, 2; RGAL 4; RGSF 2; SATA 3, 30; SSFS 8
Aiken, Joan (Delano) 1924- .... **CLC 35**
See also AAYA 1, 25; CA 9-12R, 182; CAAE 182; CANR 4, 23, 34, 64; CLR 1, 19; DLB 161; FANT; HGG; JRDA; MAICYA 1, 2; MTCW 1; RHW; SAAS 1; SATA 2, 30, 73; SATA-Essay 109; WYA; YAW
Ainsworth, William Harrison
1805-1882 .... **NCLC 13**
See also DLB 21; HGG; RGEL 2; SATA 24; SUFW
Aitmatov, Chingiz (Torekulovich)
1928- .... **CLC 71**
See also CA 103; CANR 38; MTCW 1; RGSF 2; SATA 56
Akers, Floyd
See Baum, L(yman) Frank
Akhmadulina, Bella Akhatovna
1937- .... **CLC 53**
See also CA 65-68; CWP; CWW 2; DAM POET
Akhmatova, Anna 1888-1966 ..... **CLC 11, 25, 64, 126; PC 2**
See also CA 19-20; 25-28R; CANR 35; CAP 1; DA3; DAM POET; EW 10; MTCW 1, 2; RGWL 2
Aksakov, Sergei Timofeyvich
1791-1859 .... **NCLC 2**
See also DLB 198
Aksenov, Vassily
See Aksyonov, Vassily (Pavlovich)
Akst, Daniel 1956- .... **CLC 109**
See also CA 161
Aksyonov, Vassily (Pavlovich)
1932- .... **CLC 22, 37, 101**
See also CA 53-56; CANR 12, 48, 77; CWW 2
Akutagawa Ryunosuke
1892-1927 .... **TCLC 16; SSC 44**
See also CA 117; 154; DLB 180; MJW; RGSF 2; RGWL 2
Alain 1868-1951 .... **TCLC 41**
See also CA 163; GFL 1789 to the Present
Alain-Fournier .... **TCLC 6**
See Fournier, Henri Alban
See also DLB 65; GFL 1789 to the Present; RGWL 2
Alarcon, Pedro Antonio de
1833-1891 .... **NCLC 1**
Alas (y Urena), Leopoldo (Enrique Garcia)
1852-1901 .... **TCLC 29**
See also CA 113; 131; HW 1; RGSF 2
Albee, Edward (Franklin III) 1928- . **CLC 1, 2, 3, 5, 9, 11, 13, 25, 53, 86, 113; DC 11; WLC**
See also AITN 1; AMW; CA 5-8R; CABS 3; CAD; CANR 8, 54, 74; CD 5; CDALB 1941-1968; DA; DA3; DAB; DAC; DAM DRAM, MST; DFS 2, 3, 8, 10, 13, 14; DLB 7; INT CANR-8; LAIT 4; MTCW 1, 2; RGAL 4; TUS
Alberti, Rafael 1902-1999 .... **CLC 7**
See also CA 85-88; 185; CANR 81; DLB 108; HW 2; RGWL 2

Albert the Great 1193(?)-1280 ...... **CMLC 16**
See also DLB 115
Alcala-Galiano, Juan Valera y
See Valera y Alcala-Galiano, Juan
Alcayaga, Lucila Godoy
See Godoy Alcayaga, Lucila
Alcott, Amos Bronson 1799-1888 .... **NCLC 1**
See also DLB 1, 223
Alcott, Louisa May 1832-1888 . **NCLC 6, 58, 83; SSC 27; WLC**
See also AAYA 20; AMWS 1; BPFB 1; BYA 2; CDALB 1865-1917; CLR 1, 38; DA; DA3; DAB; DAC; DAM MST, NOV; DLB 1, 42, 79, 223, 239, 242; DLBD 14; FW; JRDA; LAIT 2; MAICYA 1, 2; NFS 12; RGAL 4; SATA 100; WCH; WYA; YABC 1; YAW
Aldanov, M. A.
See Aldanov, Mark (Alexandrovich)
Aldanov, Mark (Alexandrovich)
1886(?)-1957 .... **TCLC 23**
See also CA 118; 181
Aldington, Richard 1892-1962 .... **CLC 49**
See also CA 85-88; CANR 45; DLB 20, 36, 100, 149; RGEL 2
Aldiss, Brian W(ilson) 1925- . **CLC 5, 14, 40; SSC 36**
See also AAYA 42; CA 5-8R; CAAE 190; CAAS 2; CANR 5, 28, 64; CN 7; DAM NOV; DLB 14; MTCW 1, 2; SATA 34; SFW 4
Alegria, Claribel 1924- .... **CLC 75; HLCS 1; PC 26**
See also CA 131; CAAS 15; CANR 66, 94; CWW 2; DAM MULT; DLB 145; HW 1; MTCW 1
Alegria, Fernando 1918- .... **CLC 57**
See also CA 9-12R; CANR 5, 32, 72; HW 1, 2
Aleichem, Sholom .... **TCLC 1, 35; SSC 33**
See also Rabinovitch, Sholem
Aleixandre, Vicente 1898-1984 ... **TCLC 113; HLCS 1**
See also CANR 81; DLB 108; HW 2; RGWL 2
Alencon, Marguerite d'
See de Navarre, Marguerite
Alepoudelis, Odysseus
See Elytis, Odysseus
See also CWW 2
Aleshkovsky, Joseph 1929-
See Aleshkovsky, Yuz
See also CA 121; 128
Aleshkovsky, Yuz .... **CLC 44**
See also Aleshkovsky, Joseph
Alexander, Lloyd (Chudley) 1924- ... **CLC 35**
See also AAYA 1, 27; BPFB 1; BYA 5, 6, 7, 9, 10, 11; CA 1-4R; CANR 1, 24, 38, 55; CLR 1, 5, 48; CWRI 5; DLB 52; FANT; JRDA; MAICYA 1, 2; MAICYAS 1; MTCW 1; SAAS 19; SATA 3, 49, 81, 129; SUFW; WYA; YAW
Alexander, Meena 1951- .... **CLC 121**
See also CA 115; CANR 38, 70; CP 7; CWP; FW
Alexander, Samuel 1859-1938 .... **TCLC 77**
Alexie, Sherman (Joseph, Jr.)
1966- .... **CLC 96, 154**
See also AAYA 28; CA 138; CANR 95; DA3; DAM MULT; DLB 175, 206; MTCW 1; NNAL
Alfau, Felipe 1902-1999 .... **CLC 66**
See also CA 137
Alfieri, Vittorio 1749-1803 .... **NCLC 101**
See also EW 4; RGWL 2
Alfred, Jean Gaston
See Ponge, Francis

Alger, Horatio, Jr. 1832-1899 .... **NCLC 8, 83**
See also DLB 42; LAIT 2; RGAL 4; SATA 16; TUS
Al-Ghazali, Muhammad ibn Muhammad
1058-1111 .... **CMLC 50**
See also DLB 115
Algren, Nelson 1909-1981 ..... **CLC 4, 10, 33; SSC 33**
See also AMWS 9; BPFB 1; CA 13-16R; 103; CANR 20, 61; CDALB 1941-1968; DLB 9; DLBY 1981, 1982, 2000; MTCW 1, 2; RGAL 4; RGSF 2
Ali, Ahmed 1908-1998 .... **CLC 69**
See also CA 25-28R; CANR 15, 34
Alighieri, Dante
See Dante
Allan, John B.
See Westlake, Donald E(dwin)
Allan, Sidney
See Hartmann, Sadakichi
Allan, Sydney
See Hartmann, Sadakichi
Allard, Janet .... **CLC 59**
Allen, Edward 1948- .... **CLC 59**
Allen, Fred 1894-1956 .... **TCLC 87**
Allen, Paula Gunn 1939- .... **CLC 84**
See also AMWS 4; CA 112; 143; CANR 63; CWP; DA3; DAM MULT; DLB 175; FW; MTCW 1; NNAL; RGAL 4
Allen, Roland
See Ayckbourn, Alan
Allen, Sarah A.
See Hopkins, Pauline Elizabeth
Allen, Sidney H.
See Hartmann, Sadakichi
Allen, Woody 1935- .... **CLC 16, 52**
See also AAYA 10; CA 33-36R; CANR 27, 38, 63; DAM POP; DLB 44; MTCW 1
Allende, Isabel 1942- . **CLC 39, 57, 97; HLC 1; WLCS**
See also AAYA 18; CA 125; 130; CANR 51, 74; CDWLB 3; CWW 2; DA3; DAM MULT, NOV; DLB 145; DNFS 1; FW; HW 1, 2; INT CA-130; LAIT 5; LAWS 1; MTCW 1, 2; NCFS 1; NFS 6; RGSF 2; SSFS 11; WLIT 1
Alleyn, Ellen
See Rossetti, Christina (Georgina)
Alleyne, Carla D. .... **CLC 65**
Allingham, Margery (Louise)
1904-1966 .... **CLC 19**
See also CA 5-8R; 25-28R; CANR 4, 58; CMW 4; DLB 77; MSW; MTCW 1, 2
Allingham, William 1824-1889 .... **NCLC 25**
See also DLB 35; RGEL 2
Allison, Dorothy E. 1949- .... **CLC 78, 153**
See also CA 140; CANR 66, 107; CSW; DA3; FW; MTCW 1; NFS 11; RGAL 4
Alloula, Malek .... **CLC 65**
Allston, Washington 1779-1843 .... **NCLC 2**
See also DLB 1, 235
Almedingen, E. M. .... **CLC 12**
See also Almedingen, Martha Edith von
See also SATA 3
Almedingen, Martha Edith von 1898-1971
See Almedingen, E. M.
See also CA 1-4R; CANR 1
Almodovar, Pedro 1949(?)- .... **CLC 114; HLCS 1**
See also CA 133; CANR 72; HW 2
Almqvist, Carl Jonas Love
1793-1866 .... **NCLC 42**
Alonso, Damaso 1898-1990 .... **CLC 14**
See also CA 110; 131; 130; CANR 72; DLB 108; HW 1, 2
Alov
See Gogol, Nikolai (Vasilyevich)

Alta 1942- .... **CLC 19**
See also CA 57-60
Alter, Robert B(ernard) 1935- .... **CLC 34**
See also CA 49-52; CANR 1, 47, 100
Alther, Lisa 1944- .... **CLC 7, 41**
See also BPFB 1; CA 65-68; CAAS 30; CANR 12, 30, 51; CN 7; CSW; GLL 2; MTCW 1
Althusser, L.
See Althusser, Louis
Althusser, Louis 1918-1990 .... **CLC 106**
See also CA 131; 132; CANR 102; DLB 242
Altman, Robert 1925- .... **CLC 16, 116**
See also CA 73-76; CANR 43
Alurista
See Urista, Alberto H.
See also DLB 82; HLCS 1
Alvarez, A(lfred) 1929- .... **CLC 5, 13**
See also CA 1-4R; CANR 3, 33, 63, 101; CN 7; CP 7; DLB 14, 40
Alvarez, Alejandro Rodriguez 1903-1965
See Casona, Alejandro
See also CA 131; 93-96; HW 1
Alvarez, Julia 1950- .... **CLC 93; HLCS 1**
See also AAYA 25; AMWS 7; CA 147; CANR 69, 101; CN 7; DA3; MTCW 1; NFS 5, 9; SATA 129; WLIT 1
Alvaro, Corrado 1896-1956 .... **TCLC 60**
See also CA 163
Amado, Jorge 1912-2001 ... **CLC 13, 40, 106; HLC 1**
See also CA 77-80; CANR 35, 74; DAM MULT, NOV; DLB 113; HW 2; LAW; LAWS 1; MTCW 1, 2; RGWL 2; WLIT 1
Ambler, Eric 1909-1998 .... **CLC 4, 6, 9**
See also BRWS 4; CA 9-12R; 171; CANR 7, 38, 74; CMW 4; CN 7; DLB 77; MSW; MTCW 1, 2
Ambrose, Stephen E(dward) 1936- .... **CLC 145**
See also CA 1-4R; CANR 3, 43, 57, 83, 105; NCFS 2; SATA 40
Amichai, Yehuda 1924-2000 .. **CLC 9, 22, 57, 116; PC 38**
See also CA 85-88; 189; CANR 46, 60, 99; CWW 2; MTCW 1
Amichai, Yehudah
See Amichai, Yehuda
Amiel, Henri Frederic 1821-1881 .... **NCLC 4**
See also DLB 217
Amis, Kingsley (William) 1922-1995 ...... **CLC 1, 2, 3, 5, 8, 13, 40, 44, 129**
See also AITN 2; BPFB 1; BRWS 2; CA 9-12R; 150; CANR 8, 28, 54; CDBLB 1945-1960; CN 7; CP 7; DA; DA3; DAB; DAC; DAM MST, NOV; DLB 15, 27, 100, 139; DLBY 1996; HGG; INT CANR-8; MTCW 1, 2; RGEL 2; RGSF 2; SFW 4
Amis, Martin (Louis) 1949- .... **CLC 4, 9, 38, 62, 101**
See also BEST 90:3; BRWS 4; CA 65-68; CANR 8, 27, 54, 73, 95; CN 7; DA3; DLB 14, 194; INT CANR-27; MTCW 1
Ammons, A(rchie) R(andolph) 1926-2001 ...... **CLC 2, 3, 5, 8, 9, 25, 57, 108; PC 16**
See also AITN 1; AMWS 7; CA 9-12R; 193; CANR 6, 36, 51, 73, 107; CP 7; CSW; DAM POET; DLB 5, 165; MTCW 1, 2; RGAL 4
Amo, Tauraatua i
See Adams, Henry (Brooks)
Amory, Thomas 1691(?)-1788 .... **LC 48**
See also DLB 39

Anand, Mulk Raj 1905- .... **CLC 23, 93**
See also CA 65-68; CANR 32, 64; CN 7; DAM NOV; MTCW 1, 2; RGSF 2
Anatol
See Schnitzler, Arthur
Anaximander c. 611B.C.-c. 546B.C. .... **CMLC 22**
Anaya, Rudolfo A(lfonso) 1937- ...... **CLC 23, 148; HLC 1**
See also AAYA 20; BYA 13; CA 45-48; CAAS 4; CANR 1, 32, 51; CN 7; DAM MULT, NOV; DLB 82, 206; HW 1; LAIT 4; MTCW 1, 2; NFS 12; RGAL 4; RGSF 2; WLIT 1
Andersen, Hans Christian 1805-1875 ... **NCLC 7, 79; SSC 6; WLC**
See also CLR 6; DA; DA3; DAB; DAC; DAM MST, POP; EW 6; MAICYA 1, 2; RGSF 2; RGWL 2; SATA 100; WCH; YABC 1
Anderson, C. Farley
See Mencken, H(enry) L(ouis); Nathan, George Jean
Anderson, Jessica (Margaret) Queale 1916- .... **CLC 37**
See also CA 9-12R; CANR 4, 62; CN 7
Anderson, Jon (Victor) 1940- .... **CLC 9**
See also CA 25-28R; CANR 20; DAM POET
Anderson, Lindsay (Gordon) 1923-1994 .... **CLC 20**
See also CA 125; 128; 146; CANR 77
Anderson, Maxwell 1888-1959 .... **TCLC 2**
See also CA 105; 152; DAM DRAM; DLB 7, 228; MTCW 2; RGAL 4
Anderson, Poul (William) 1926-2001 .... **CLC 15**
See also AAYA 5, 34; BPFB 1; BYA 6, 8, 9; CA 1-4R, 181; 199; CAAE 181; CAAS 2; CANR 2, 15, 34, 64; CLR 58; DLB 8; FANT; INT CANR-15; MTCW 1, 2; SATA 90; SATA-Brief 39; SATA-Essay 106; SCFW 2; SFW 4; SUFW
Anderson, Robert (Woodruff) 1917- .... **CLC 23**
See also AITN 1; CA 21-24R; CANR 32; DAM DRAM; DLB 7; LAIT 5
Anderson, Roberta Joan
See Mitchell, Joni
Anderson, Sherwood 1876-1941 ..... **TCLC 1, 10, 24; SSC 1, 46; WLC**
See also AAYA 30; AMW; BPFB 1; CA 104; 121; CANR 61; CDALB 1917-1929; DA; DA3; DAB; DAC; DAM MST, NOV; DLB 4, 9, 86; DLBD 1; EXPS; GLL 2; MTCW 1, 2; NFS 4; RGAL 4; RGSF 2; SSFS 4, 10, 11
Andier, Pierre
See Desnos, Robert
Andouard
See Giraudoux, Jean(-Hippolyte)
Andrade, Carlos Drummond de ..... **CLC 18**
See also Drummond de Andrade, Carlos
See also RGWL 2
Andrade, Mario de .... **TCLC 43**
See also de Andrade, Mario
See also LAW; RGWL 2; WLIT 1
Andreae, Johann V(alentin) 1586-1654 .... **LC 32**
See also DLB 164
Andreas Capellanus fl. c. 1185- .... **CMLC 45**
See also DLB 208
Andreas-Salome, Lou 1861-1937 ... **TCLC 56**
See also CA 178; DLB 66
Andress, Lesley
See Sanders, Lawrence
Andrewes, Lancelot 1555-1626 .... **LC 5**
See also DLB 151, 172

Andrews, Cicily Fairfield
See West, Rebecca
Andrews, Elton V.
See Pohl, Frederik
Andreyev, Leonid (Nikolaevich) 1871-1919 .... **TCLC 3**
See also CA 104; 185
Andric, Ivo 1892-1975 .... **CLC 8; SSC 36**
See also CA 81-84; 57-60; CANR 43, 60; CDWLB 4; DLB 147; EW 11; MTCW 1; RGSF 2; RGWL 2
Androvar
See Prado (Calvo), Pedro
Angelique, Pierre
See Bataille, Georges
Angell, Roger 1920- .... **CLC 26**
See also CA 57-60; CANR 13, 44, 70; DLB 171, 185
Angelou, Maya 1928- ..... **CLC 12, 35, 64, 77, 155; BLC 1; PC 32; WLCS**
See also AAYA 7, 20; AMWS 4; BPFB 1; BW 2, 3; BYA 2; CA 65-68; CANR 19, 42, 65; CDALBS; CLR 53; CP 7; CPW; CSW; CWP; DA; DA3; DAB; DAC; DAM MST, MULT, POET, POP; DLB 38; EXPN; EXPP; LAIT 4; MAICYA 2; MAICYAS 1; MAWW; MTCW 1, 2; NCFS 2; NFS 2; PFS 2, 3; RGAL 4; SATA 49; WYA; YAW
Angouleme, Marguerite d'
See de Navarre, Marguerite
Anna Comnena 1083-1153 .... **CMLC 25**
Annensky, Innokenty (Fyodorovich) 1856-1909 .... **TCLC 14**
See also CA 110; 155
Annunzio, Gabriele d'
See D'Annunzio, Gabriele
Anodos
See Coleridge, Mary E(lizabeth)
Anon, Charles Robert
See Pessoa, Fernando (Antonio Nogueira)
Anouilh, Jean (Marie Lucien Pierre) 1910-1987 . **CLC 1, 3, 8, 13, 40, 50; DC 8**
See also CA 17-20R; 123; CANR 32; DAM DRAM; DFS 9, 10; EW 13; GFL 1789 to the Present; MTCW 1, 2; RGWL 2
Anthony, Florence
See Ai
Anthony, John
See Ciardi, John (Anthony)
Anthony, Peter
See Shaffer, Anthony (Joshua); Shaffer, Peter (Levin)
Anthony, Piers 1934- .... **CLC 35**
See also AAYA 11; BYA 7; CA 21-24R; CAAE 200; CANR 28, 56, 73, 102; CPW; DAM POP; DLB 8; FANT; MAICYA 2; MAICYAS 1; MTCW 1, 2; SAAS 22; SATA 84; SATA-Essay 129; SFW 4; SUFW; YAW
Anthony, Susan B(rownell) 1820-1906 .... **TCLC 84**
See also FW
Antoine, Marc
See Proust, (Valentin-Louis-George-Eugene-)Marcel
Antoninus, Brother
See Everson, William (Oliver)
Antonioni, Michelangelo 1912- .... **CLC 20, 144**
See also CA 73-76; CANR 45, 77
Antschel, Paul 1920-1970
See Celan, Paul
See also CA 85-88; CANR 33, 61; MTCW 1
Anwar, Chairil 1922-1949 .... **TCLC 22**
See also CA 121

Anzaldua, Gloria (Evanjelina) 1942-
See also CA 175; CSW; CWP; DLB 122; FW; HLCS 1; RGAL 4
Apess, William 1798-1839(?) .... **NCLC 73**
See also DAM MULT; DLB 175, 243; NNAL
Apollinaire, Guillaume 1880-1918 .. **TCLC 3, 8, 51; PC 7**
See also CA 152; DAM POET; DLB 258; EW 9; GFL 1789 to the Present; MTCW 1; RGWL 2; WP
Apollonius of Rhodes
See Apollonius Rhodius
See also AW 1; RGWL 2
Apollonius Rhodius c. 300B.C.-c. 220B.C. .... **CMLC 28**
See also Apollonius of Rhodes
See also DLB 176
Appelfeld, Aharon 1932- ... **CLC 23, 47; SSC 42**
See also CA 112; 133; CANR 86; CWW 2; RGSF 2
Apple, Max (Isaac) 1941- .... **CLC 9, 33; SSC 50**
See also CA 81-84; CANR 19, 54; DLB 130
Appleman, Philip (Dean) 1926- .... **CLC 51**
See also CA 13-16R; CAAS 18; CANR 6, 29, 56
Appleton, Lawrence
See Lovecraft, H(oward) P(hillips)
Apteryx
See Eliot, T(homas) S(tearns)
Apuleius, (Lucius Madaurensis) 125(?)-175(?) .... **CMLC 1**
See also AW 2; CDWLB 1; DLB 211; RGWL 2; SUFW
Aquin, Hubert 1929-1977 .... **CLC 15**
See also CA 105; DLB 53
Aquinas, Thomas 1224(?)-1274 ..... **CMLC 33**
See also DLB 115; EW 1
Aragon, Louis 1897-1982 .... **CLC 3, 22**
See also CA 69-72; 108; CANR 28, 71; DAM NOV, POET; DLB 72, 258; EW 11; GFL 1789 to the Present; GLL 2; MTCW 1, 2; RGWL 2
Arany, Janos 1817-1882 .... **NCLC 34**
Aranyos, Kakay 1847-1910
See Mikszath, Kalman
Arbuthnot, John 1667-1735 .... **LC 1**
See also DLB 101
Archer, Herbert Winslow
See Mencken, H(enry) L(ouis)
Archer, Jeffrey (Howard) 1940- .... **CLC 28**
See also AAYA 16; BEST 89:3; BPFB 1; CA 77-80; CANR 22, 52, 95; CPW; DA3; DAM POP; INT CANR-22
Archer, Jules 1915- .... **CLC 12**
See also CA 9-12R; CANR 6, 69; SAAS 5; SATA 4, 85
Archer, Lee
See Ellison, Harlan (Jay)
Archilochus c. 7th cent. B.C.- .... **CMLC 44**
See also DLB 176
Arden, John 1930- .... **CLC 6, 13, 15**
See also BRWS 2; CA 13-16R; CAAS 4; CANR 31, 65, 67; CBD; CD 5; DAM DRAM; DFS 9; DLB 13, 245; MTCW 1
Arenas, Reinaldo 1943-1990 .. **CLC 41; HLC 1**
See also CA 124; 128; 133; CANR 73, 106; DAM MULT; DLB 145; GLL 2; HW 1; LAW; LAWS 1; MTCW 1; RGSF 2; WLIT 1
Arendt, Hannah 1906-1975 .... **CLC 66, 98**
See also CA 17-20R; 61-64; CANR 26, 60; DLB 242; MTCW 1, 2
Aretino, Pietro 1492-1556 .... **LC 12**
See also RGWL 2

Arghezi, Tudor -1967 .... **CLC 80**
See also Theodorescu, Ion N.
See also CA 167; CDWLB 4; DLB 220
Arguedas, Jose Maria 1911-1969 .... **CLC 10, 18; HLCS 1**
See also CA 89-92; CANR 73; DLB 113; HW 1; LAW; RGWL 2; WLIT 1
Argueta, Manlio 1936- .... **CLC 31**
See also CA 131; CANR 73; CWW 2; DLB 145; HW 1
Arias, Ron(ald Francis) 1941-
See also CA 131; CANR 81; DAM MULT; DLB 82; HLC 1; HW 1, 2; MTCW 2
Ariosto, Ludovico 1474-1533 .... **LC 6**
See also EW 2; RGWL 2
Aristides
See Epstein, Joseph
Aristophanes 450B.C.-385B.C. .... **CMLC 4, 51; DC 2; WLCS**
See also AW 1; CDWLB 1; DA; DA3; DAB; DAC; DAM DRAM, MST; DFS 10; DLB 176; RGWL 2
Aristotle 384B.C.-322B.C. .... **CMLC 31; WLCS**
See also AW 1; CDWLB 1; DA; DA3; DAB; DAC; DAM MST; DLB 176; RGEL 2
Arlt, Roberto (Godofredo Christophersen) 1900-1942 .... **TCLC 29; HLC 1**
See also CA 123; 131; CANR 67; DAM MULT; HW 1, 2; LAW
Armah, Ayi Kwei 1939- .... **CLC 5, 33, 136; BLC 1**
See also AFW; BW 1; CA 61-64; CANR 21, 64; CDWLB 3; CN 7; DAM MULT, POET; DLB 117; MTCW 1; WLIT 2
Armatrading, Joan 1950- .... **CLC 17**
See also CA 114; 186
Arnette, Robert
See Silverberg, Robert
Arnim, Achim von (Ludwig Joachim von Arnim) 1781-1831 ..... **NCLC 5; SSC 29**
See also DLB 90
Arnim, Bettina von 1785-1859 .... **NCLC 38**
See also DLB 90; RGWL 2
Arnold, Matthew 1822-1888 ..... **NCLC 6, 29, 89; PC 5; WLC**
See also BRW 5; CDBLB 1832-1890; DA; DAB; DAC; DAM MST, POET; DLB 32, 57; EXPP; PAB; PFS 2; WP
Arnold, Thomas 1795-1842 .... **NCLC 18**
See also DLB 55
Arnow, Harriette (Louisa) Simpson 1908-1986 .... **CLC 2, 7, 18**
See also BPFB 1; CA 9-12R; 118; CANR 14; DLB 6; FW; MTCW 1, 2; RHW; SATA 42; SATA-Obit 47
Arouet, Francois-Marie
See Voltaire
Arp, Hans
See Arp, Jean
Arp, Jean 1887-1966 .... **CLC 5**
See also CA 81-84; 25-28R; CANR 42, 77; EW 10; TCLC 115
Arrabal
See Arrabal, Fernando
Arrabal, Fernando 1932- ... **CLC 2, 9, 18, 58**
See also CA 9-12R; CANR 15
Arreola, Juan Jose 1918-2001 .... **CLC 147; HLC 1; SSC 38**
See also CA 113; 131; 200; CANR 81; DAM MULT; DLB 113; DNFS 2; HW 1, 2; LAW; RGSF 2
Arrian c. 89(?)-c. 155(?) .... **CMLC 43**
See also DLB 176
Arrick, Fran .... **CLC 30**
See also Gaberman, Judie Angell
See also BYA 6

Artaud, Antonin (Marie Joseph) 1896-1948 .... **TCLC 3, 36; DC 14**
See also CA 104; 149; DA3; DAM DRAM; DLB 258; EW 11; GFL 1789 to the Present; MTCW 1; RGWL 2
Arthur, Ruth M(abel) 1905-1979 ..... **CLC 12**
See also CA 9-12R; 85-88; CANR 4; CWRI 5; SATA 7, 26
Artsybashev, Mikhail (Petrovich) 1878-1927 .... **TCLC 31**
See also CA 170
Arundel, Honor (Morfydd) 1919-1973 .... **CLC 17**
See also CA 21-22; 41-44R; CAP 2; CLR 35; CWRI 5; SATA 4; SATA-Obit 24
Arzner, Dorothy 1900-1979 .... **CLC 98**
Asch, Sholem 1880-1957 .... **TCLC 3**
See also CA 105; GLL 2
Ash, Shalom
See Asch, Sholem
Ashbery, John (Lawrence) 1927- .. **CLC 2, 3, 4, 6, 9, 13, 15, 25, 41, 77, 125; PC 26**
See also Berry, Jonas
See also AMWS 3; CA 5-8R; CANR 9, 37, 66, 102; CP 7; DA3; DAM POET; DLB 5, 165; DLBY 1981; INT CANR-9; MTCW 1, 2; PAB; PFS 11; RGAL 4; WP
Ashdown, Clifford
See Freeman, R(ichard) Austin
Ashe, Gordon
See Creasey, John
Ashton-Warner, Sylvia (Constance) 1908-1984 .... **CLC 19**
See also CA 69-72; 112; CANR 29; MTCW 1, 2
Asimov, Isaac 1920-1992 ..... **CLC 1, 3, 9, 19, 26, 76, 92**
See also AAYA 13; BEST 90:2; BPFB 1; BYA 4, 6, 7, 9; CA 1-4R; 137; CANR 2, 19, 36, 60; CLR 12, 79; CMW 4; CPW; DA3; DAM POP; DLB 8; DLBY 1992; INT CANR-19; JRDA; LAIT 5; MAICYA 1, 2; MTCW 1, 2; RGAL 4; SATA 1, 26, 74; SCFW 2; SFW 4; YAW
Assis, Joaquim Maria Machado de
See Machado de Assis, Joaquim Maria
Astell, Mary 1666-1731 .... **LC 68**
See also DLB 252; FW
Astley, Thea (Beatrice May) 1925- .. **CLC 41**
See also CA 65-68; CANR 11, 43, 78; CN 7
Astley, William 1855-1911
See Warung, Price
Aston, James
See White, T(erence) H(anbury)
Asturias, Miguel Angel 1899-1974 .... **CLC 3, 8, 13; HLC 1**
See also CA 25-28; 49-52; CANR 32; CAP 2; CDWLB 3; DA3; DAM MULT, NOV; DLB 113; HW 1; LAW; MTCW 1, 2; RGWL 2; WLIT 1
Atares, Carlos Saura
See Saura (Atares), Carlos
Athanasius c. 295-c. 373 .... **CMLC 48**
Atheling, William
See Pound, Ezra (Weston Loomis)
Atheling, William, Jr.
See Blish, James (Benjamin)
Atherton, Gertrude (Franklin Horn) 1857-1948 .... **TCLC 2**
See also CA 104; 155; DLB 9, 78, 186; HGG; RGAL 4; SUFW; TCWW 2
Atherton, Lucius
See Masters, Edgar Lee
Atkins, Jack
See Harris, Mark
Atkinson, Kate .... **CLC 99**
See also CA 166; CANR 101

364

Attaway, William (Alexander)
1911-1986 .... **CLC 92; BLC 1**
See also BW 2, 3; CA 143; CANR 82; DAM MULT; DLB 76

Atticus
See Fleming, Ian (Lancaster); Wilson, (Thomas) Woodrow

Atwood, Margaret (Eleanor) 1939- ... **CLC 2, 3, 4, 8, 13, 15, 25, 44, 84, 135; PC 8; SSC 2, 46; WLC**
See also AAYA 12; BEST 89:2; BPFB 1; CA 49-52; CANR 3, 24, 33, 59, 95; CN 7; CP 7; CPW; CWP; DA; DA3; DAB; DAC; DAM MST, NOV, POET; DLB 53, 251; EXPN; FW; INT CANR-24; LAIT 5; MTCW 1, 2; NFS 4, 12, 13, 14; PFS 7; RGSF 2; SATA 50; SSFS 3, 13; YAW

Aubigny, Pierre d'
See Mencken, H(enry) L(ouis)

Aubin, Penelope 1685-1731(?) .... **LC 9**
See also DLB 39

Auchincloss, Louis (Stanton) 1917- .. **CLC 4, 6, 9, 18, 45; SSC 22**
See also AMWS 4; CA 1-4R; CANR 6, 29, 55, 87; CN 7; DAM NOV; DLB 2, 244; DLBY 1980; INT CANR-29; MTCW 1; RGAL 4

Auden, W(ystan) H(ugh) 1907-1973 . **CLC 1, 2, 3, 4, 6, 9, 11, 14, 43, 123; PC 1; WLC**
See also AAYA 18; AMWS 2; BRW 7; BRWR 1; CA 9-12R; 45-48; CANR 5, 61, 105; CDBLB 1914-1945; DA; DA3; DAB; DAC; DAM DRAM, MST, POET; DLB 10, 20; EXPP; MTCW 1, 2; PAB; PFS 1, 3, 4, 10; WP

Audiberti, Jacques 1900-1965 .... **CLC 38**
See also CA 25-28R; DAM DRAM

Audubon, John James 1785-1851 . **NCLC 47**
See also ANW; DLB 248

Auel, Jean M(arie) 1936- .... **CLC 31, 107**
See also AAYA 7; BEST 90:4; BPFB 1; CA 103; CANR 21, 64; CPW; DA3; DAM POP; INT CANR-21; NFS 11; RHW; SATA 91

Auerbach, Erich 1892-1957 .... **TCLC 43**
See also CA 118; 155

Augier, Emile 1820-1889 .... **NCLC 31**
See also DLB 192; GFL 1789 to the Present

August, John
See De Voto, Bernard (Augustine)

Augustine, St. 354-430 .... **CMLC 6; WLCS**
See also DA; DA3; DAB; DAC; DAM MST; DLB 115; EW 1; RGWL 2

Aunt Belinda
See Braddon, Mary Elizabeth

Aunt Weedy
See Alcott, Louisa May

Aurelius
See Bourne, Randolph S(illiman)

Aurelius, Marcus 121-180 .... **CMLC 45**
See also Marcus Aurelius
See also RGWL 2

Aurobindo, Sri
See Ghose, Aurabinda

Austen, Jane 1775-1817 ...... **NCLC 1, 13, 19, 33, 51, 81, 95; WLC**
See also AAYA 19; BRW 4; BRWR 2; BYA 3; CDBLB 1789-1832; DA; DA3; DAB; DAC; DAM MST, NOV; DLB 116; EXPN; LAIT 2; NFS 1, 14; WLIT 3; WYAS 1

Auster, Paul 1947- .... **CLC 47, 131**
See also CA 69-72; CANR 23, 52, 75; CMW 4; CN 7; DA3; DLB 227; MTCW 1

Austin, Frank
See Faust, Frederick (Schiller)
See also TCWW 2

Austin, Mary (Hunter) 1868-1934 . **TCLC 25**
See also Stairs, Gordon
See also CA 109; 178; DLB 9, 78, 206, 221; FW; TCWW 2

Averroes 1126-1198 .... **CMLC 7**
See also DLB 115

Avicenna 980-1037 .... **CMLC 16**
See also DLB 115

Avison, Margaret 1918- .... **CLC 2, 4, 97**
See also CA 17-20R; CP 7; DAC; DAM POET; DLB 53; MTCW 1

Axton, David
See Koontz, Dean R(ay)

Ayckbourn, Alan 1939- ...... **CLC 5, 8, 18, 33, 74; DC 13**
See also BRWS 5; CA 21-24R; CANR 31, 59; CBD; CD 5; DAB; DAM DRAM; DFS 7; DLB 13, 245; MTCW 1, 2

Aydy, Catherine
See Tennant, Emma (Christina)

Ayme, Marcel (Andre) 1902-1967 ... **CLC 11; SSC 41**
See also CA 89-92; CANR 67; CLR 25; DLB 72; EW 12; GFL 1789 to the Present; RGSF 2; RGWL 2; SATA 91

Ayrton, Michael 1921-1975 .... **CLC 7**
See also CA 5-8R; 61-64; CANR 9, 21

Azorin .... **CLC 11**
See also Martinez Ruiz, Jose
See also EW 9

Azuela, Mariano 1873-1952 .. **TCLC 3; HLC 1**
See also CA 104; 131; CANR 81; DAM MULT; HW 1, 2; LAW; MTCW 1, 2

Baastad, Babbis Friis
See Friis-Baastad, Babbis Ellinor

Bab
See Gilbert, W(illiam) S(chwenck)

Babbis, Eleanor
See Friis-Baastad, Babbis Ellinor

Babel, Isaac
See Babel, Isaak (Emmanuilovich)
See also EW 11; SSFS 10

Babel, Isaak (Emmanuilovich)
1894-1941(?) .... **TCLC 2, 13; SSC 16**
See also CA 104; 155; MTCW 1; RGSF 2; RGWL 2

Babits, Mihaly 1883-1941 .... **TCLC 14**
See also CA 114; CDWLB 4; DLB 215

Babur 1483-1530 .... **LC 18**

Babylas 1898-1962
See Ghelderode, Michel de

Baca, Jimmy Santiago 1952-
See also CA 131; CANR 81, 90; CP 7; DAM MULT; DLB 122; HLC 1; HW 1, 2

Bacchelli, Riccardo 1891-1985 .... **CLC 19**
See also CA 29-32R; 117

Bach, Richard (David) 1936- .... **CLC 14**
See also AITN 1; BEST 89:2; BPFB 1; BYA 5; CA 9-12R; CANR 18, 93; CPW; DAM NOV, POP; FANT; MTCW 1; SATA 13

Bache, Benjamin Franklin
1769-1798 .... **LC 74**
See also DLB 43

Bachman, Richard
See King, Stephen (Edwin)

Bachmann, Ingeborg 1926-1973 .... **CLC 69**
See also CA 93-96; 45-48; CANR 69; DLB 85; RGWL 2

Bacon, Francis 1561-1626 .... **LC 18, 32**
See also BRW 1; CDBLB Before 1660; DLB 151, 236, 252; RGEL 2

Bacon, Roger 1214(?)-1294 .... **CMLC 14**
See also DLB 115

Bacovia, George 1881-1957 .... **TCLC 24**
See also Vasiliu, Gheorghe
See also CDWLB 4; DLB 220

Badanes, Jerome 1937- .... **CLC 59**

Bagehot, Walter 1826-1877 .... **NCLC 10**
See also DLB 55

Bagnold, Enid 1889-1981 .... **CLC 25**
See also BYA 2; CA 5-8R; 103; CANR 5, 40; CBD; CWD; CWRI 5; DAM DRAM; DLB 13, 160, 191, 245; FW; MAICYA 1, 2; RGEL 2; SATA 1, 25

Bagritsky, Eduard 1895-1934 .... **TCLC 60**

Bagrjana, Elisaveta
See Belcheva, Elisaveta Lyubomirova

Bagryana, Elisaveta -1991 .... **CLC 10**
See also Belcheva, Elisaveta Lyubomirova
See also CA 178; CDWLB 4; DLB 147

Bailey, Paul 1937- .... **CLC 45**
See also CA 21-24R; CANR 16, 62; CN 7; DLB 14; GLL 2

Baillie, Joanna 1762-1851 .... **NCLC 71**
See also DLB 93; RGEL 2

Bainbridge, Beryl (Margaret) 1934- . **CLC 4, 5, 8, 10, 14, 18, 22, 62, 130**
See also BRWS 6; CA 21-24R; CANR 24, 55, 75, 88; CN 7; DAM NOV; DLB 14, 231; MTCW 1, 2

Baker, Carlos (Heard)
1909-1987 .... **TCLC 119**
See also CA 5-8R; 122; CANR 3, 63; DLB 103

Baker, Elliott 1922- .... **CLC 8**
See also CA 45-48; CANR 2, 63; CN 7

Baker, Jean H. .... **TCLC 3, 10**
See also Russell, George William

Baker, Nicholson 1957- .... **CLC 61**
See also CA 135; CANR 63; CN 7; CPW; DA3; DAM POP; DLB 227

Baker, Ray Stannard 1870-1946 .... **TCLC 47**
See also CA 118

Baker, Russell (Wayne) 1925- .... **CLC 31**
See also BEST 89:4; CA 57-60; CANR 11, 41, 59; MTCW 1, 2

Bakhtin, M.
See Bakhtin, Mikhail Mikhailovich

Bakhtin, M. M.
See Bakhtin, Mikhail Mikhailovich

Bakhtin, Mikhail
See Bakhtin, Mikhail Mikhailovich

Bakhtin, Mikhail Mikhailovich
1895-1975 .... **CLC 83**
See also CA 128; 113; DLB 242

Bakshi, Ralph 1938(?)- .... **CLC 26**
See also CA 112; 138; IDFW 3

Bakunin, Mikhail (Alexandrovich)
1814-1876 .... **NCLC 25, 58**

Baldwin, James (Arthur) 1924-1987 . **CLC 1, 2, 3, 4, 5, 8, 13, 15, 17, 42, 50, 67, 90, 127; BLC 1; DC 1; SSC 10, 33; WLC**
See also AAYA 4, 34; AFAW 1, 2; AMWS 1; BW 1; CA 1-4R; 124; CABS 1; CAD; CANR 3, 24; CDALB 1941-1968; CPW; DA; DA3; DAB; DAC; DAM MST, MULT, NOV, POP; DFS 11; DLB 2, 7, 33, 249; DLBY 1987; EXPS; LAIT 5; MTCW 1, 2; NFS 4; RGAL 4; RGSF 2; SATA 9; SATA-Obit 54; SSFS 2

Bale, John 1495-1563 .... **LC 62**
See also DLB 132; RGEL 2

Ball, Hugo 1886-1927 .... **TCLC 104**

Ballard, J(ames) G(raham) 1930- . **CLC 3, 6, 14, 36, 137; SSC 1**
See also AAYA 3; BRWS 5; CA 5-8R; CANR 15, 39, 65, 107; CN 7; DA3; DAM NOV, POP; DLB 14, 207; HGG; MTCW 1, 2; NFS 8; RGEL 2; RGSF 2; SATA 93; SFW 4

Balmont, Konstantin (Dmitriyevich)
1867-1943 .... **TCLC 11**
See also CA 109; 155

Baltausis, Vincas 1847-1910
See Mikszath, Kalman

Balzac, Honore de 1799-1850 ... NCLC **5, 35, 53**; SSC **5**; WLC
See also DA; DA3; DAB; DAC; DAM MST, NOV; DLB 119; EW 5; GFL 1789 to the Present; RGSF 2; RGWL 2; SSFS 10; SUFW

Bambara, Toni Cade 1939-1995 ...... CLC **19, 88**; BLC **1**; SSC **35**; WLCS
See also AAYA 5; AFAW 1, 2; BW 2, 3; BYA 12, 14; CA 29-32R; 150; CANR 24, 49, 81; CDALBS; DA; DA3; DAC; DAM MST, MULT; DLB 38, 218; EXPS; MTCW 1, 2; RGAL 4; RGSF 2; SATA 112; SSFS 4, 7, 12; TCLC 116

Bamdad, A.
See Shamlu, Ahmad

Banat, D. R.
See Bradbury, Ray (Douglas)

Bancroft, Laura
See Baum, L(yman) Frank

Banim, John 1798-1842 .... NCLC **13**
See also DLB 116, 158, 159; RGEL 2

Banim, Michael 1796-1874 .... NCLC **13**
See also DLB 158, 159

Banjo, The
See Paterson, A(ndrew) B(arton)

Banks, Iain
See Banks, Iain M(enzies)

Banks, Iain M(enzies) 1954- .... CLC **34**
See also CA 123; 128; CANR 61, 106; DLB 194; HGG; INT 128; SFW 4

Banks, Lynne Reid .... CLC **23**
See also Reid Banks, Lynne
See also AAYA 6; BYA 7

Banks, Russell 1940- .... CLC **37, 72**; SSC **42**
See also AMWS 5; CA 65-68; CAAS 15; CANR 19, 52, 73; CN 7; DLB 130; NFS 13

Banville, John 1945- .... CLC **46, 118**
See also CA 117; 128; CANR 104; CN 7; DLB 14; INT 128

Banville, Theodore (Faullain) de 1832-1891 .... NCLC **9**
See also DLB 217; GFL 1789 to the Present

Baraka, Amiri 1934- . CLC **1, 2, 3, 5, 10, 14, 33, 115**; BLC **1**; DC **6**; PC **4**; WLCS
See also Jones, LeRoi
See also AFAW 1, 2; AMWS 2; BW 2, 3; CA 21-24R; CABS 3; CAD; CANR 27, 38, 61; CD 5; CDALB 1941-1968; CP 7; CPW; DA; DA3; DAC; DAM MST, MULT, POET, POP; DFS 3, 11; DLB 5, 7, 16, 38; DLBD 8; MTCW 1, 2; PFS 9; RGAL 4; WP

Baratynsky, Evgenii Abramovich 1800-1844 .... NCLC **103**
See also DLB 205

Barbauld, Anna Laetitia 1743-1825 .... NCLC **50**
See also DLB 107, 109, 142, 158; RGEL 2

Barbellion, W. N. P. .... TCLC **24**
See also Cummings, Bruce F(rederick)

Barber, Benjamin R. 1939- .... CLC **141**
See also CA 29-32R; CANR 12, 32, 64

Barbera, Jack (Vincent) 1945- .... CLC **44**
See also CA 110; CANR 45

Barbey d'Aurevilly, Jules-Amedee 1808-1889 .... NCLC **1**; SSC **17**
See also DLB 119; GFL 1789 to the Present

Barbour, John c. 1316-1395 .... CMLC **33**
See also DLB 146

Barbusse, Henri 1873-1935 .... TCLC **5**
See also CA 105; 154; DLB 65; RGWL 2

Barclay, Bill
See Moorcock, Michael (John)

Barclay, William Ewert
See Moorcock, Michael (John)

Barea, Arturo 1897-1957 .... TCLC **14**
See also CA 111

Barfoot, Joan 1946- .... CLC **18**
See also CA 105

Barham, Richard Harris 1788-1845 .... NCLC **77**
See also DLB 159

Baring, Maurice 1874-1945 .... TCLC **8**
See also CA 105; 168; DLB 34; HGG

Baring-Gould, Sabine 1834-1924 ... TCLC **88**
See also DLB 156, 190

Barker, Clive 1952- .... CLC **52**
See also AAYA 10; BEST 90:3; BPFB 1; CA 121; 129; CANR 71; CPW; DA3; DAM POP; HGG; INT 129; MTCW 1, 2

Barker, George Granville 1913-1991 .... CLC **8, 48**
See also CA 9-12R; 135; CANR 7, 38; DAM POET; DLB 20; MTCW 1

Barker, Harley Granville
See Granville-Barker, Harley
See also DLB 10

Barker, Howard 1946- .... CLC **37**
See also CA 102; CBD; CD 5; DLB 13, 233

Barker, Jane 1652-1732 .... LC **42**
See also DLB 39, 131

Barker, Pat(ricia) 1943- ...... CLC **32, 94, 146**
See also BRWS 4; CA 117; 122; CANR 50, 101; CN 7; INT 122

Barlach, Ernst (Heinrich) 1870-1938 .... TCLC **84**
See also CA 178; DLB 56, 118

Barlow, Joel 1754-1812 .... NCLC **23**
See also AMWS 2; DLB 37; RGAL 4

Barnard, Mary (Ethel) 1909- .... CLC **48**
See also CA 21-22; CAP 2

Barnes, Djuna 1892-1982 .... CLC **3, 4, 8, 11, 29, 127**; SSC **3**
See also Steptoe, Lydia
See also AMWS 3; CA 9-12R; 107; CAD; CANR 16, 55; CWD; DLB 4, 9, 45; GLL 1; MTCW 1, 2; RGAL 4

Barnes, Julian (Patrick) 1946- . CLC **42, 141**
See also BRWS 4; CA 102; CANR 19, 54; CN 7; DAB; DLB 194; DLBY 1993; MTCW 1

Barnes, Peter 1931- .... CLC **5, 56**
See also CA 65-68; CAAS 12; CANR 33, 34, 64; CBD; CD 5; DFS 6; DLB 13, 233; MTCW 1

Barnes, William 1801-1886 .... NCLC **75**
See also DLB 32

Baroja (y Nessi), Pio 1872-1956 ..... TCLC **8**; HLC **1**
See also CA 104; EW 9

Baron, David
See Pinter, Harold

Baron Corvo
See Rolfe, Frederick (William Serafino Austin Lewis Mary)

Barondess, Sue K(aufman) 1926-1977 .... CLC **8**
See also Kaufman, Sue
See also CA 1-4R; 69-72; CANR 1

Baron de Teive
See Pessoa, Fernando (Antonio Nogueira)

Baroness Von S.
See Zangwill, Israel

Barres, (Auguste-)Maurice 1862-1923 .... TCLC **47**
See also CA 164; DLB 123; GFL 1789 to the Present

Barreto, Afonso Henrique de Lima
See Lima Barreto, Afonso Henrique de

Barrett, Andrea 1954- .... CLC **150**
See also CA 156; CANR 92

Barrett, Michele .... CLC **65**

Barrett, (Roger) Syd 1946- .... CLC **35**

Barrett, William (Christopher) 1913-1992 .... CLC **27**
See also CA 13-16R; 139; CANR 11, 67; INT CANR-11

Barrie, J(ames) M(atthew) 1860-1937 .... TCLC **2**
See also BRWS 3; BYA 4, 5; CA 104; 136; CANR 77; CDBLB 1890-1914; CLR 16; CWRI 5; DA3; DAB; DAM DRAM; DFS 7; DLB 10, 141, 156; FANT; MAICYA 1, 2; MTCW 1; SATA 100; SUFW; WCH; WLIT 4; YABC 1

Barrington, Michael
See Moorcock, Michael (John)

Barrol, Grady
See Bograd, Larry

Barry, Mike
See Malzberg, Barry N(athaniel)

Barry, Philip 1896-1949 .... TCLC **11**
See also CA 109; 199; DFS 9; DLB 7, 228; RGAL 4

Bart, Andre Schwarz
See Schwarz-Bart, Andre

Barth, John (Simmons) 1930- ... CLC **1, 2, 3, 5, 7, 9, 10, 14, 27, 51, 89**; SSC **10**
See also AITN 1, 2; AMW; AMWS 1; CA 1-4R; CABS 1; CANR 5, 23, 49, 64; CN 7; DAM NOV; DLB 2, 227; FANT; MTCW 1; RGAL 4; RGSF 2; RHW; SSFS 6

Barthelme, Donald 1931-1989 ... CLC **1, 2, 3, 5, 6, 8, 13, 23, 46, 59, 115**; SSC **2**
See also AMWS 4; BPFB 1; CA 21-24R; 129; CANR 20, 58; DA3; DAM NOV; DLB 2, 234; DLBY 1980, 1989; FANT; MTCW 1, 2; RGAL 4; RGSF 2; SATA 7; SATA-Obit 62; SSFS 3

Barthelme, Frederick 1943- ...... CLC **36, 117**
See also CA 114; 122; CANR 77; CN 7; CSW; DLB 244; DLBY 1985; INT CA-122

Barthes, Roland (Gerard) 1915-1980 .... CLC **24, 83**
See also CA 130; 97-100; CANR 66; EW 13; GFL 1789 to the Present; MTCW 1, 2

Barzun, Jacques (Martin) 1907- ...... CLC **51, 145**
See also CA 61-64; CANR 22, 95

Bashevis, Isaac
See Singer, Isaac Bashevis

Bashkirtseff, Marie 1859-1884 .... NCLC **27**

Basho, Matsuo
See Matsuo Basho
See also RGWL 2; WP

Basil of Caesaria c. 330-379 .... CMLC **35**

Bass, Kingsley B., Jr.
See Bullins, Ed

Bass, Rick 1958- .... CLC **79, 143**
See also ANW; CA 126; CANR 53, 93; CSW; DLB 212

Bassani, Giorgio 1916-2000 .... CLC **9**
See also CA 65-68; 190; CANR 33; CWW 2; DLB 128, 177; MTCW 1; RGWL 2

Bastian, Ann .... CLC **70**

Bastos, Augusto (Antonio) Roa
See Roa Bastos, Augusto (Antonio)

Bataille, Georges 1897-1962 .... CLC **29**
See also CA 101; 89-92

Bates, H(erbert) E(rnest) 1905-1974 .... CLC **46**; SSC **10**
See also CA 93-96; 45-48; CANR 34; DA3; DAB; DAM POP; DLB 162, 191; EXPS; MTCW 1, 2; RGSF 2; SSFS 7

Bauchart
See Camus, Albert

Baudelaire, Charles 1821-1867 . **NCLC 6, 29, 55; PC 1; SSC 18; WLC**
See also DA; DA3; DAB; DAC; DAM MST, POET; DLB 217; EW 7; GFL 1789 to the Present; RGWL 2

Baudouin, Marcel
See Peguy, Charles (Pierre)

Baudouin, Pierre
See Peguy, Charles (Pierre)

Baudrillard, Jean 1929- .... **CLC 60**

Baum, L(yman) Frank 1856-1919 ... **TCLC 7**
See also CA 108; 133; CLR 15; CWRI 5; DLB 22; FANT; JRDA; MAICYA 1, 2; MTCW 1, 2; NFS 13; RGAL 4; SATA 18, 100; WCH

Baum, Louis F.
See Baum, L(yman) Frank

Baumbach, Jonathan 1933- .... **CLC 6, 23**
See also CA 13-16R; CAAS 5; CANR 12, 66; CN 7; DLBY 1980; INT CANR-12; MTCW 1

Bausch, Richard (Carl) 1945- .... **CLC 51**
See also AMWS 7; CA 101; CAAS 14; CANR 43, 61, 87; CSW; DLB 130

Baxter, Charles (Morley) 1947- . **CLC 45, 78**
See also CA 57-60; CANR 40, 64, 104; CPW; DAM POP; DLB 130; MTCW 2

Baxter, George Owen
See Faust, Frederick (Schiller)

Baxter, James K(eir) 1926-1972 .... **CLC 14**
See also CA 77-80

Baxter, John
See Hunt, E(verette) Howard, (Jr.)

Bayer, Sylvia
See Glassco, John

Baynton, Barbara 1857-1929 .... **TCLC 57**
See also DLB 230; RGSF 2

Beagle, Peter S(oyer) 1939- .... **CLC 7, 104**
See also BPFB 1; BYA 9, 10; CA 9-12R; CANR 4, 51, 73; DA3; DLBY 1980; FANT; INT CANR-4; MTCW 1; SATA 60, 130; SUFW; YAW

Bean, Normal
See Burroughs, Edgar Rice

Beard, Charles A(ustin) 1874-1948 .... **TCLC 15**
See also CA 115; 189; DLB 17; SATA 18

Beardsley, Aubrey 1872-1898 .... **NCLC 6**

Beattie, Ann 1947- ..... **CLC 8, 13, 18, 40, 63, 146; SSC 11**
See also AMWS 5; BEST 90:2; BPFB 1; CA 81-84; CANR 53, 73; CN 7; CPW; DA3; DAM NOV, POP; DLB 218; DLBY 1982; MTCW 1, 2; RGAL 4; RGSF 2; SSFS 9

Beattie, James 1735-1803 .... **NCLC 25**
See also DLB 109

Beauchamp, Kathleen Mansfield 1888-1923
See Mansfield, Katherine
See also CA 104; 134; DA; DA3; DAC; DAM MST; MTCW 2

Beaumarchais, Pierre-Augustin Caron de 1732-1799 .... **LC 61; DC 4**
See also DAM DRAM; DFS 14; EW 4; GFL Beginnings to 1789; RGWL 2

Beaumont, Francis 1584(?)-1616 .... **LC 33; DC 6**
See also BRW 2; CDBLB Before 1660; DLB 58

Beauvoir, Simone (Lucie Ernestine Marie Bertrand) de 1908-1986 .... **CLC 1, 2, 4, 8, 14, 31, 44, 50, 71, 124; SSC 35; WLC**
See also BPFB 1; CA 9-12R; 118; CANR 28, 61; DA; DA3; DAB; DAC; DAM MST, NOV; DLB 72; DLBY 1986; EW 12; FW; GFL 1789 to the Present; MTCW 1, 2; RGSF 2; RGWL 2

Becker, Carl (Lotus) 1873-1945 ..... **TCLC 63**
See also CA 157; DLB 17

Becker, Jurek 1937-1997 .... **CLC 7, 19**
See also CA 85-88; 157; CANR 60; CWW 2; DLB 75

Becker, Walter 1950- .... **CLC 26**

Beckett, Samuel (Barclay) 1906-1989 .. **CLC 1, 2, 3, 4, 6, 9, 10, 11, 14, 18, 29, 57, 59, 83; SSC 16; WLC**
See also BRWR 1; BRWS 1; CA 5-8R; 130; CANR 33, 61; CBD; CDBLB 1945-1960; DA; DA3; DAB; DAC; DAM DRAM, MST, NOV; DFS 2, 7; DLB 13, 15, 233; DLBY 1990; GFL 1789 to the Present; MTCW 1, 2; RGSF 2; RGWL 2; WLIT 4

Beckford, William 1760-1844 .... **NCLC 16**
See also BRW 3; DLB 39, 213; HGG; SUFW

Beckman, Gunnel 1910- .... **CLC 26**
See also CA 33-36R; CANR 15; CLR 25; MAICYA 1, 2; SAAS 9; SATA 6

Becque, Henri 1837-1899 .... **NCLC 3**
See also DLB 192; GFL 1789 to the Present

Becquer, Gustavo Adolfo 1836-1870 .... **NCLC 106; HLCS 1**
See also DAM MULT

Beddoes, Thomas Lovell 1803-1849 .... **NCLC 3; DC 15**
See also DLB 96

Bede c. 673-735 .... **CMLC 20**
See also DLB 146

Bedford, Donald F.
See Fearing, Kenneth (Flexner)

Beecher, Catharine Esther 1800-1878 .... **NCLC 30**
See also DLB 1, 243

Beecher, John 1904-1980 .... **CLC 6**
See also AITN 1; CA 5-8R; 105; CANR 8

Beer, Johann 1655-1700 .... **LC 5**
See also DLB 168

Beer, Patricia 1924- .... **CLC 58**
See also CA 61-64; 183; CANR 13, 46; CP 7; CWP; DLB 40; FW

Beerbohm, Max
See Beerbohm, (Henry) Max(imilian)

Beerbohm, (Henry) Max(imilian) 1872-1956 .... **TCLC 1, 24**
See also BRWS 2; CA 104; 154; CANR 79; DLB 34, 100; FANT

Beer-Hofmann, Richard 1866-1945 .... **TCLC 60**
See also CA 160; DLB 81

Beg, Shemus
See Stephens, James

Begiebing, Robert J(ohn) 1946- .... **CLC 70**
See also CA 122; CANR 40, 88

Behan, Brendan 1923-1964 ...... **CLC 1, 8, 11, 15, 79**
See also BRWS 2; CA 73-76; CANR 33; CBD; CDBLB 1945-1960; DAM DRAM; DFS 7; DLB 13, 233; MTCW 1, 2

Behn, Aphra 1640(?)-1689 .... **LC 1, 30, 42; DC 4; PC 13; WLC**
See also BRWS 3; DA; DA3; DAB; DAC; DAM DRAM, MST, NOV, POET; DLB 39, 80, 131; FW; WLIT 3

Behrman, S(amuel) N(athaniel) 1893-1973 .... **CLC 40**
See also CA 13-16; 45-48; CAD; CAP 1; DLB 7, 44; IDFW 3; RGAL 4

Belasco, David 1853-1931 .... **TCLC 3**
See also CA 104; 168; DLB 7; RGAL 4

Belcheva, Elisaveta Lyubomirova 1893-1991 .... **CLC 10**
See also Bagryana, Elisaveta

Beldone, Phil "Cheech"
See Ellison, Harlan (Jay)

Beleno
See Azuela, Mariano

Belinski, Vissarion Grigoryevich 1811-1848 .... **NCLC 5**
See also DLB 198

Belitt, Ben 1911- .... **CLC 22**
See also CA 13-16R; CAAS 4; CANR 7, 77; CP 7; DLB 5

Bell, Gertrude (Margaret Lowthian) 1868-1926 .... **TCLC 67**
See also CA 167; DLB 174

Bell, J. Freeman
See Zangwill, Israel

Bell, James Madison 1826-1902 ... **TCLC 43; BLC 1**
See also BW 1; CA 122; 124; DAM MULT; DLB 50

Bell, Madison Smartt 1957- ...... **CLC 41, 102**
See also AMWS 10; BPFB 1; CA 111, 183; CAAE 183; CANR 28, 54, 73; CN 7; CSW; DLB 218; MTCW 1

Bell, Marvin (Hartley) 1937- .... **CLC 8, 31**
See also CA 21-24R; CAAS 14; CANR 59, 102; CP 7; DAM POET; DLB 5; MTCW 1

Bell, W. L. D.
See Mencken, H(enry) L(ouis)

Bellamy, Atwood C.
See Mencken, H(enry) L(ouis)

Bellamy, Edward 1850-1898 ...... **NCLC 4, 86**
See also DLB 12; RGAL 4; SFW 4

Belli, Gioconda 1949-
See also CA 152; CWW 2; HLCS 1

Bellin, Edward J.
See Kuttner, Henry

Belloc, (Joseph) Hilaire (Pierre Sebastien Rene Swanton) 1870-1953 ...... **TCLC 7, 18; PC 24**
See also CA 106; 152; CWRI 5; DAM POET; DLB 19, 100, 141, 174; MTCW 1; SATA 112; WCH; YABC 1

Belloc, Joseph Peter Rene Hilaire
See Belloc, (Joseph) Hilaire (Pierre Sebastien Rene Swanton)

Belloc, Joseph Pierre Hilaire
See Belloc, (Joseph) Hilaire (Pierre Sebastien Rene Swanton)

Belloc, M. A.
See Lowndes, Marie Adelaide (Belloc)

Bellow, Saul 1915- . **CLC 1, 2, 3, 6, 8, 10, 13, 15, 25, 33, 34, 63, 79; SSC 14; WLC**
See also AITN 2; AMW; BEST 89:3; BPFB 1; CA 5-8R; CABS 1; CANR 29, 53, 95; CDALB 1941-1968; CN 7; DA; DA3; DAB; DAC; DAM MST, NOV, POP; DLB 2, 28; DLBD 3; DLBY 1982; MTCW 1, 2; NFS 4, 14; RGAL 4; RGSF 2; SSFS 12

Belser, Reimond Karel Maria de 1929-
See Ruyslinck, Ward
See also CA 152

Bely, Andrey .... **TCLC 7; PC 11**
See also Bugayev, Boris Nikolayevich
See also EW 9; MTCW 1

Belyi, Andrei
See Bugayev, Boris Nikolayevich
See also RGWL 2

Benary, Margot
See Benary-Isbert, Margot

Benary-Isbert, Margot 1889-1979 .... **CLC 12**
See also CA 5-8R; 89-92; CANR 4, 72; CLR 12; MAICYA 1, 2; SATA 2; SATA-Obit 21

Benavente (y Martinez), Jacinto 1866-1954 .... **TCLC 3; HLCS 1**
See also CA 106; 131; CANR 81; DAM DRAM, MULT; GLL 2; HW 1, 2; MTCW 1, 2

Benchley, Peter (Bradford) 1940- .. **CLC 4, 8**
See also AAYA 14; AITN 2; BPFB 1; CA 17-20R; CANR 12, 35, 66; CPW; DAM NOV, POP; HGG; MTCW 1, 2; SATA 3, 89

Benchley, Robert (Charles)
1889-1945 .... **TCLC 1, 55**
See also CA 105; 153; DLB 11; RGAL 4

Benda, Julien 1867-1956 .... **TCLC 60**
See also CA 120; 154; GFL 1789 to the Present

Benedict, Ruth (Fulton)
1887-1948 .... **TCLC 60**
See also CA 158; DLB 246

Benedikt, Michael 1935- .... **CLC 4, 14**
See also CA 13-16R; CANR 7; CP 7; DLB 5

Benet, Juan 1927-1993 .... **CLC 28**
See also CA 143

Benet, Stephen Vincent 1898-1943 . **TCLC 7; SSC 10**
See also CA 104; 152; DA3; DAM POET; DLB 4, 48, 102, 249; DLBY 1997; HGG; MTCW 1; RGAL 4; RGSF 2; SUFW; WP; YABC 1

Benet, William Rose 1886-1950 ..... **TCLC 28**
See also CA 118; 152; DAM POET; DLB 45; RGAL 4

Benford, Gregory (Albert) 1941- ..... **CLC 52**
See also BPFB 1; CA 69-72, 175; CAAE 175; CAAS 27; CANR 12, 24, 49, 95; CSW; DLBY 1982; SCFW 2; SFW 4

Bengtsson, Frans (Gunnar)
1894-1954 .... **TCLC 48**
See also CA 170

Benjamin, David
See Slavitt, David R(ytman)

Benjamin, Lois
See Gould, Lois

Benjamin, Walter 1892-1940 .... **TCLC 39**
See also CA 164; DLB 242; EW 11

Benn, Gottfried 1886-1956 .. **TCLC 3; PC 35**
See also CA 106; 153; DLB 56; RGWL 2

Bennett, Alan 1934- .... **CLC 45, 77**
See also CA 103; CANR 35, 55, 106; CBD; CD 5; DAB; DAM MST; MTCW 1, 2

Bennett, (Enoch) Arnold
1867-1931 .... **TCLC 5, 20**
See also BRW 6; CA 106; 155; CDBLB 1890-1914; DLB 10, 34, 98, 135; MTCW 2

Bennett, Elizabeth
See Mitchell, Margaret (Munnerlyn)

Bennett, George Harold 1930-
See Bennett, Hal
See also BW 1; CA 97-100; CANR 87

Bennett, Hal .... **CLC 5**
See also Bennett, George Harold
See also DLB 33

Bennett, Jay 1912- .... **CLC 35**
See also AAYA 10; CA 69-72; CANR 11, 42, 79; JRDA; SAAS 4; SATA 41, 87; SATA-Brief 27; WYA; YAW

Bennett, Louise (Simone) 1919- ...... **CLC 28; BLC 1**
See also BW 2, 3; CA 151; CDWLB 3; CP 7; DAM MULT; DLB 117

Benson, E(dward) F(rederic)
1867-1940 .... **TCLC 27**
See also CA 114; 157; DLB 135, 153; HGG; SUFW

Benson, Jackson J. 1930- .... **CLC 34**
See also CA 25-28R; DLB 111

Benson, Sally 1900-1972 .... **CLC 17**
See also CA 19-20; 37-40R; CAP 1; SATA 1, 35; SATA-Obit 27

Benson, Stella 1892-1933 .... **TCLC 17**
See also CA 117; 155; DLB 36, 162; FANT

Bentham, Jeremy 1748-1832 .... **NCLC 38**
See also DLB 107, 158, 252

Bentley, E(dmund) C(lerihew)
1875-1956 .... **TCLC 12**
See also CA 108; DLB 70; MSW

Bentley, Eric (Russell) 1916- .... **CLC 24**
See also CA 5-8R; CAD; CANR 6, 67; CBD; CD 5; INT CANR-6

Beranger, Pierre Jean de
1780-1857 .... **NCLC 34**

Berdyaev, Nicolas
See Berdyaev, Nikolai (Aleksandrovich)

Berdyaev, Nikolai (Aleksandrovich)
1874-1948 .... **TCLC 67**
See also CA 120; 157

Berdyayev, Nikolai (Aleksandrovich)
See Berdyaev, Nikolai (Aleksandrovich)

Berendt, John (Lawrence) 1939- ...... **CLC 86**
See also CA 146; CANR 75, 93; DA3; MTCW 1

Beresford, J(ohn) D(avys)
1873-1947 .... **TCLC 81**
See also CA 112; 155; DLB 162, 178, 197; SFW 4; SUFW

Bergelson, David 1884-1952 .... **TCLC 81**

Berger, Colonel
See Malraux, (Georges-)Andre

Berger, John (Peter) 1926- .... **CLC 2, 19**
See also BRWS 4; CA 81-84; CANR 51, 78; CN 7; DLB 14, 207

Berger, Melvin H. 1927- .... **CLC 12**
See also CA 5-8R; CANR 4; CLR 32; SAAS 2; SATA 5, 88; SATA-Essay 124

Berger, Thomas (Louis) 1924- .. **CLC 3, 5, 8, 11, 18, 38**
See also BPFB 1; CA 1-4R; CANR 5, 28, 51; CN 7; DAM NOV; DLB 2; DLBY 1980; FANT; INT CANR-28; MTCW 1, 2; RHW; TCWW 2

Bergman, (Ernst) Ingmar 1918- ...... **CLC 16, 72**
See also CA 81-84; CANR 33, 70; DLB 257; MTCW 2

Bergson, Henri(-Louis) 1859-1941 . **TCLC 32**
See also CA 164; EW 8; GFL 1789 to the Present

Bergstein, Eleanor 1938- .... **CLC 4**
See also CA 53-56; CANR 5

Berkeley, George 1685-1753 .... **LC 65**
See also DLB 101, 252

Berkoff, Steven 1937- .... **CLC 56**
See also CA 104; CANR 72; CBD; CD 5

Berlin, Isaiah 1909-1997 .... **TCLC 105**
See also CA 85-88; 162

Bermant, Chaim (Icyk) 1929-1998 ... **CLC 40**
See also CA 57-60; CANR 6, 31, 57, 105; CN 7

Bern, Victoria
See Fisher, M(ary) F(rances) K(ennedy)

Bernanos, (Paul Louis) Georges
1888-1948 .... **TCLC 3**
See also CA 104; 130; DLB 72; GFL 1789 to the Present; RGWL 2

Bernard, April 1956- .... **CLC 59**
See also CA 131

Berne, Victoria
See Fisher, M(ary) F(rances) K(ennedy)

Bernhard, Thomas 1931-1989 ..... **CLC 3, 32, 61; DC 14**
See also CA 85-88; 127; CANR 32, 57; CDWLB 2; DLB 85, 124; MTCW 1; RGWL 2

Bernhardt, Sarah (Henriette Rosine)
1844-1923 .... **TCLC 75**
See also CA 157

Bernstein, Charles 1950- .... **CLC 142,**
See also CA 129; CAAS 24; CANR 90; CP 7; DLB 169

Berriault, Gina 1926-1999 .... **CLC 54, 109; SSC 30**
See also CA 116; 129; 185; CANR 66; DLB 130; SSFS 7,11

Berrigan, Daniel 1921- .... **CLC 4**
See also CA 33-36R; CAAE 187; CAAS 1; CANR 11, 43, 78; CP 7; DLB 5

Berrigan, Edmund Joseph Michael, Jr.
1934-1983
See Berrigan, Ted
See also CA 61-64; 110; CANR 14, 102

Berrigan, Ted .... **CLC 37**
See also Berrigan, Edmund Joseph Michael, Jr.
See also DLB 5, 169; WP

Berry, Charles Edward Anderson 1931-
See Berry, Chuck
See also CA 115

Berry, Chuck .... **CLC 17**
See also Berry, Charles Edward Anderson

Berry, Jonas
See Ashbery, John (Lawrence)
See also GLL 1

Berry, Wendell (Erdman) 1934- ... **CLC 4, 6, 8, 27, 46; PC 28**
See also AITN 1; AMWS 10; ANW; CA 73-76; CANR 50, 73, 101; CP 7; CSW; DAM POET; DLB 5, 6, 234; MTCW 1

Berryman, John 1914-1972 ... **CLC 1, 2, 3, 4, 6, 8, 10, 13, 25, 62**
See also AMW; CA 13-16; 33-36R; CABS 2; CANR 35; CAP 1; CDALB 1941-1968; DAM POET; DLB 48; MTCW 1, 2; PAB; RGAL 4; WP

Bertolucci, Bernardo 1940- ...... **CLC 16, 157**
See also CA 106

Berton, Pierre (Francis Demarigny)
1920- .... **CLC 104**
See also CA 1-4R; CANR 2, 56; CPW; DLB 68; SATA 99

Bertrand, Aloysius 1807-1841 .... **NCLC 31**
See also Bertrand, Louis oAloysiusc

Bertrand, Louis oAloysiusc
See Bertrand, Aloysius
See also DLB 217

Bertran de Born c. 1140-1215 .... **CMLC 5**

Besant, Annie (Wood) 1847-1933 ..... **TCLC 9**
See also CA 105; 185

Bessie, Alvah 1904-1985 .... **CLC 23**
See also CA 5-8R; 116; CANR 2, 80; DLB 26

Bethlen, T. D.
See Silverberg, Robert

Beti, Mongo .... **CLC 27; BLC 1**
See also Biyidi, Alexandre
See also AFW; CANR 79; DAM MULT; WLIT 2

Betjeman, John 1906-1984 ...... **CLC 2, 6, 10, 34, 43**
See also BRW 7; CA 9-12R; 112; CANR 33, 56; CDBLB 1945-1960; DA3; DAB; DAM MST, POET; DLB 20; DLBY 1984; MTCW 1, 2

Bettelheim, Bruno 1903-1990 .... **CLC 79**
See also CA 81-84; 131; CANR 23, 61; DA3; MTCW 1, 2

Betti, Ugo 1892-1953 .... **TCLC 5**
See also CA 104; 155; RGWL 2

Betts, Doris (Waugh) 1932- ...... **CLC 3, 6, 28; SSC 45**
See also CA 13-16R; CANR 9, 66, 77; CN 7; CSW; DLB 218; DLBY 1982; INT CANR-9; RGAL 4

Bevan, Alistair
See Roberts, Keith (John Kingston)

Bey, Pilaff
See Douglas, (George) Norman

Bialik, Chaim Nachman
1873-1934 .... **TCLC 25**
See also CA 170

Bickerstaff, Isaac
See Swift, Jonathan

Bidart, Frank 1939- .... **CLC 33**
See also CA 140; CANR 106; CP 7

Bienek, Horst 1930- .... **CLC 7, 11**
See also CA 73-76; DLB 75

Bierce, Ambrose (Gwinett)
1842-1914(?) ..... **TCLC 1, 7, 44; SSC 9; WLC**
See also AMW; BYA 11; CA 104; 139; CANR 78; CDALB 1865-1917; DA; DA3; DAC; DAM MST; DLB 11, 12, 23, 71, 74, 186; EXPS; HGG; LAIT 2; RGAL 4; RGSF 2; SSFS 9; SUFW

Biggers, Earl Derr 1884-1933 .... **TCLC 65**
See also CA 108; 153

Billings, Josh
See Shaw, Henry Wheeler

Billington, (Lady) Rachel (Mary)
1942- .... **CLC 43**
See also AITN 2; CA 33-36R; CANR 44; CN 7

Binchy, Maeve 1940- .... **CLC 153**
See also BEST 90:1; BPFB 1; CA 127; 134; CANR 50, 96; CN 7; CPW; DA3; DAM POP; INT CA-134; MTCW 1; RHW

Binyon, T(imothy) J(ohn) 1936- .... **CLC 34**
See also CA 111; CANR 28

Bion 335B.C.-245B.C. .... **CMLC 39**

Bioy Casares, Adolfo 1914-1999 ... **CLC 4, 8, 13, 88; HLC 1; SSC 17**
See also Casares, Adolfo Bioy; Miranda, Javier; Sacastru, Martin
See also CA 29-32R; 177; CANR 19, 43, 66; DAM MULT; DLB 113; HW 1, 2; LAW; MTCW 1, 2

Birch, Allison .... **CLC 65**

Bird, Cordwainer
See Ellison, Harlan (Jay)

Bird, Robert Montgomery
1806-1854 .... **NCLC 1**
See also DLB 202; RGAL 4

Birkerts, Sven 1951- .... **CLC 116**
See also CA 128; 133, 176; CAAE 176; CAAS 29; INT 133

Birney, (Alfred) Earle 1904-1995 .. **CLC 1, 4, 6, 11**
See also CA 1-4R; CANR 5, 20; CP 7; DAC; DAM MST, POET; DLB 88; MTCW 1; PFS 8; RGEL 2

Biruni, al 973-1048(?) .... **CMLC 28**

Bishop, Elizabeth 1911-1979 ..... **CLC 1, 4, 9, 13, 15, 32; PC 3, 34**
See also AMWS 1; CA 5-8R; 89-92; CABS 2; CANR 26, 61, 108; CDALB 1968-1988; DA; DA3; DAC; DAM MST, POET; DLB 5, 169; GLL 2; MAWW; MTCW 1, 2; PAB; PFS 6, 12; RGAL 4; SATA-Obit 24; TCLC 121; WP

Bishop, John 1935- .... **CLC 10**
See also CA 105

Bishop, John Peale 1892-1944 ..... **TCLC 103**
See also CA 107; 155; DLB 4, 9, 45; RGAL 4

Bissett, Bill 1939- .... **CLC 18; PC 14**
See also CA 69-72; CAAS 19; CANR 15; CCA 1; CP 7; DLB 53; MTCW 1

Bissoondath, Neil (Devindra)
1955- .... **CLC 120**
See also CA 136; CN 7; DAC

Bitov, Andrei (Georgievich) 1937- ... **CLC 57**
See also CA 142

Biyidi, Alexandre 1932-
See Beti, Mongo
See also BW 1, 3; CA 114; 124; CANR 81; DA3; MTCW 1, 2

Bjarme, Brynjolf
See Ibsen, Henrik (Johan)

Bjoernson, Bjoernstjerne (Martinius)
1832-1910 .... **TCLC 7, 37**
See also CA 104

Black, Robert
See Holdstock, Robert P.

Blackburn, Paul 1926-1971 .... **CLC 9, 43**
See also CA 81-84; 33-36R; CANR 34; DLB 16; DLBY 1981

Black Elk 1863-1950 .... **TCLC 33**
See also CA 144; DAM MULT; MTCW 1; NNAL; WP

Black Hobart
See Sanders, (James) Ed(ward)

Blacklin, Malcolm
See Chambers, Aidan

Blackmore, R(ichard) D(oddridge)
1825-1900 .... **TCLC 27**
See also CA 120; DLB 18; RGEL 2

Blackmur, R(ichard) P(almer)
1904-1965 .... **CLC 2, 24**
See also AMWS 2; CA 11-12; 25-28R; CANR 71; CAP 1; DLB 63

Black Tarantula
See Acker, Kathy

Blackwood, Algernon (Henry)
1869-1951 .... **TCLC 5**
See also CA 105; 150; DLB 153, 156, 178; HGG; SUFW

Blackwood, Caroline 1931-1996 .... **CLC 6, 9, 100**
See also CA 85-88; 151; CANR 32, 61, 65; CN 7; DLB 14, 207; HGG; MTCW 1

Blade, Alexander
See Hamilton, Edmond; Silverberg, Robert

Blaga, Lucian 1895-1961 .... **CLC 75**
See also CA 157; DLB 220

Blair, Eric (Arthur) 1903-1950
See Orwell, George
See also CA 104; 132; DA; DA3; DAB; DAC; DAM MST, NOV; MTCW 1, 2; SATA 29

Blair, Hugh 1718-1800 .... **NCLC 75**

Blais, Marie-Claire 1939- .... **CLC 2, 4, 6, 13, 22**
See also CA 21-24R; CAAS 4; CANR 38, 75, 93; DAC; DAM MST; DLB 53; FW; MTCW 1, 2

Blaise, Clark 1940- .... **CLC 29**
See also AITN 2; CA 53-56; CAAS 3; CANR 5, 66, 106; CN 7; DLB 53; RGSF 2

Blake, Fairley
See De Voto, Bernard (Augustine)

Blake, Nicholas
See Day Lewis, C(ecil)
See also DLB 77; MSW

Blake, William 1757-1827 .... **NCLC 13, 37, 57; PC 12; WLC**
See also BRW 3; BRWR 1; CDBLB 1789-1832; CLR 52; DA; DA3; DAB; DAC; DAM MST, POET; DLB 93, 163; EXPP; MAICYA 1, 2; PAB; PFS 2, 12; SATA 30; WCH; WLIT 3; WP

Blanchot, Maurice 1907- .... **CLC 135**
See also CA 117; 144; DLB 72

Blasco Ibanez, Vicente 1867-1928 . **TCLC 12**
See also BPFB 1; CA 110; 131; CANR 81; DA3; DAM NOV; EW 8; HW 1, 2; MTCW 1

Blatty, William Peter 1928- .... **CLC 2**
See also CA 5-8R; CANR 9; DAM POP; HGG

Bleeck, Oliver
See Thomas, Ross (Elmore)

Blessing, Lee 1949- .... **CLC 54**
See also CAD; CD 5

Blight, Rose
See Greer, Germaine

Blish, James (Benjamin) 1921-1975 . **CLC 14**
See also BPFB 1; CA 1-4R; 57-60; CANR 3; DLB 8; MTCW 1; SATA 66; SCFW 2; SFW 4

Bliss, Reginald
See Wells, H(erbert) G(eorge)

Blixen, Karen (Christentze Dinesen)
1885-1962
See Dinesen, Isak
See also CA 25-28; CANR 22, 50; CAP 2; DA3; DLB 214; MTCW 1, 2; SATA 44

Bloch, Robert (Albert) 1917-1994 .... **CLC 33**
See also AAYA 29; CA 5-8R, 179; 146; CAAE 179; CAAS 20; CANR 5, 78; DA3; DLB 44; HGG; INT CANR-5; MTCW 1; SATA 12; SATA-Obit 82; SFW 4; SUFW

Blok, Alexander (Alexandrovich)
1880-1921 .... **TCLC 5; PC 21**
See also CA 104; 183; EW 9; RGWL 2

Blom, Jan
See Breytenbach, Breyten

Bloom, Harold 1930- .... **CLC 24, 103**
See also CA 13-16R; CANR 39, 75, 92; DLB 67; MTCW 1; RGAL 4

Bloomfield, Aurelius
See Bourne, Randolph S(illiman)

Blount, Roy (Alton), Jr. 1941- .... **CLC 38**
See also CA 53-56; CANR 10, 28, 61; CSW; INT CANR-28; MTCW 1, 2

Bloy, Leon 1846-1917 .... **TCLC 22**
See also CA 121; 183; DLB 123; GFL 1789 to the Present

Bluggage, Oranthy
See Alcott, Louisa May

Blume, Judy (Sussman) 1938- .... **CLC 12, 30**
See also AAYA 3, 26; BYA 1, 8, 12; CA 29-32R; CANR 13, 37, 66; CLR 2, 15, 69; CPW; DA3; DAM NOV, POP; DLB 52; JRDA; MAICYA 1, 2; MAICYAS 1; MTCW 1, 2; SATA 2, 31, 79; WYA; YAW

Blunden, Edmund (Charles)
1896-1974 .... **CLC 2, 56**
See also BRW 6; CA 17-18; 45-48; CANR 54; CAP 2; DLB 20, 100, 155; MTCW 1; PAB

Bly, Robert (Elwood) 1926- .... **CLC 1, 2, 5, 10, 15, 38, 128; PC 39**
See also AMWS 4; CA 5-8R; CANR 41, 73; CP 7; DA3; DAM POET; DLB 5; MTCW 1, 2; RGAL 4

Boas, Franz 1858-1942 .... **TCLC 56**
See also CA 115; 181

Bobette
See Simenon, Georges (Jacques Christian)

Boccaccio, Giovanni 1313-1375 ... **CMLC 13; SSC 10**
See also EW 2; RGSF 2; RGWL 2

Bochco, Steven 1943- .... **CLC 35**
See also AAYA 11; CA 124; 138

Bode, Sigmund
See O'Doherty, Brian

Bodel, Jean 1167(?)-1210 .... **CMLC 28**

Bodenheim, Maxwell 1892-1954 .... **TCLC 44**
See also CA 110; 187; DLB 9, 45; RGAL 4

Bodker, Cecil 1927- .... **CLC 21**
See also CA 73-76; CANR 13, 44; CLR 23; MAICYA 1, 2; SATA 14

Bodker, Cecil 1927-
See Bodker, Cecil

Boell, Heinrich (Theodor)
1917-1985 ..... **CLC 2, 3, 6, 9, 11, 15, 27, 32, 72; SSC 23; WLC**
See also Boll, Heinrich
See also CA 21-24R; 116; CANR 24; DA; DA3; DAB; DAC; DAM MST, NOV; DLB 69; DLBY 1985; MTCW 1, 2

Boerne, Alfred
See Doeblin, Alfred
Boethius c. 480-c. 524 .... **CMLC 15**
See also DLB 115; RGWL 2
Boff, Leonardo (Genezio Darci)
1938- .... **CLC 70; HLC 1**
See also CA 150; DAM MULT; HW 2
Bogan, Louise 1897-1970 .... **CLC 4, 39, 46, 93; PC 12**
See also AMWS 3; CA 73-76; 25-28R; CANR 33, 82; DAM POET; DLB 45, 169; MAWW; MTCW 1, 2; RGAL 4
Bogarde, Dirk
See Van Den Bogarde, Derek Jules Gaspard Ulric Niven
See also DLB 14
Bogosian, Eric 1953- .... **CLC 45, 141**
See also CA 138; CAD; CANR 102; CD 5
Bograd, Larry 1953- .... **CLC 35**
See also CA 93-96; CANR 57; SAAS 21; SATA 33, 89; WYA
Boiardo, Matteo Maria 1441-1494 .... **LC 6**
Boileau-Despreaux, Nicolas 1636-1711 . **LC 3**
See also EW 3; GFL Beginnings to 1789; RGWL 2
Bojer, Johan 1872-1959 .... **TCLC 64**
See also CA 189
Bok, Edward W. 1863-1930 .... **TCLC 101**
See also DLB 91; DLBD 16
Boland, Eavan (Aisling) 1944- .. **CLC 40, 67, 113**
See also BRWS 5; CA 143; CANR 61; CP 7; CWP; DAM POET; DLB 40; FW; MTCW 2; PFS 12
Boll, Heinrich
See Boell, Heinrich (Theodor)
See also BPFB 1; CDWLB 2; EW 13; RGSF 2; RGWL 2
Bolt, Lee
See Faust, Frederick (Schiller)
Bolt, Robert (Oxton) 1924-1995 .... **CLC 14**
See also CA 17-20R; 147; CANR 35, 67; CBD; DAM DRAM; DFS 2; DLB 13, 233; LAIT 1; MTCW 1
Bombal, Maria Luisa 1910-1980 ...... **SSC 37; HLCS 1**
See also CA 127; CANR 72; HW 1; LAW; RGSF 2
Bombet, Louis-Alexandre-Cesar
See Stendhal
Bomkauf
See Kaufman, Bob (Garnell)
Bonaventura .... **NCLC 35**
See also DLB 90
Bond, Edward 1934- .... **CLC 4, 6, 13, 23**
See also BRWS 1; CA 25-28R; CANR 38, 67, 106; CBD; CD 5; DAM DRAM; DFS 3,8; DLB 13; MTCW 1
Bonham, Frank 1914-1989 .... **CLC 12**
See also AAYA 1; BYA 1, 3; CA 9-12R; CANR 4, 36; JRDA; MAICYA 1, 2; SAAS 3; SATA 1, 49; SATA-Obit 62; TCWW 2; YAW
Bonnefoy, Yves 1923- .... **CLC 9, 15, 58**
See also CA 85-88; CANR 33, 75, 97; CWW 2; DAM MST, POET; DLB 258; GFL 1789 to the Present; MTCW 1, 2
Bontemps, Arna(ud Wendell)
1902-1973 .... **CLC 1, 18; BLC 1**
See also BW 1; CA 1-4R; 41-44R; CANR 4, 35; CLR 6; CWRI 5; DA3; DAM MULT, NOV, POET; DLB 48, 51; JRDA; MAICYA 1, 2; MTCW 1, 2; SATA 2, 44; SATA-Obit 24; WCH; WP
Booth, Martin 1944- .... **CLC 13**
See also CA 93-96; CAAE 188; CAAS 2; CANR 92

Booth, Philip 1925- .... **CLC 23**
See also CA 5-8R; CANR 5, 88; CP 7; DLBY 1982
Booth, Wayne C(layson) 1921- .... **CLC 24**
See also CA 1-4R; CAAS 5; CANR 3, 43; DLB 67
Borchert, Wolfgang 1921-1947 .... **TCLC 5**
See also CA 104; 188; DLB 69, 124
Borel, Petrus 1809-1859 .... **NCLC 41**
See also DLB 119; GFL 1789 to the Present
Borges, Jorge Luis 1899-1986 ... **CLC 1, 2, 3, 4, 6, 8, 9, 10, 13, 19, 44, 48, 83; HLC 1; PC 22, 32; SSC 4, 41; WLC**
See also AAYA 26; BPFB 1; CA 21-24R; CANR 19, 33, 75, 105; CDWLB 3; DA; DA3; DAB; DAC; DAM MST, MULT; DLB 113; DLBY 1986; DNFS 1, 2; HW 1, 2; LAW; MSW; MTCW 1, 2; RGSF 2; RGWL 2; SFW 4; SSFS 4, 9; TCLC 109; WLIT 1
Borowski, Tadeusz 1922-1951 .... **TCLC 9; SSC 48**
See also CA 106; 154; CDWLB 4, 4; DLB 215; RGSF 2; SSFS 13
Borrow, George (Henry)
1803-1881 .... **NCLC 9**
See also DLB 21, 55, 166
Bosch (Gavino), Juan 1909-2001
See also CA 151; DAM MST, MULT; DLB 145; HLCS 1; HW 1, 2
Bosman, Herman Charles
1905-1951 .... **TCLC 49**
See also Malan, Herman
See also CA 160; DLB 225; RGSF 2
Bosschere, Jean de 1878(?)-1953 ... **TCLC 19**
See also CA 115; 186
Boswell, James 1740-1795 ... **LC 4, 50; WLC**
See also BRW 3; CDBLB 1660-1789; DA; DAB; DAC; DAM MST; DLB 104, 142; WLIT 3
Bottomley, Gordon 1874-1948 ..... **TCLC 107**
See also CA 120; 192; DLB 10
Bottoms, David 1949- .... **CLC 53**
See also CA 105; CANR 22; CSW; DLB 120; DLBY 1983
Boucicault, Dion 1820-1890 .... **NCLC 41**
Boucolon, Maryse
See Conde, Maryse
Bourget, Paul (Charles Joseph)
1852-1935 .... **TCLC 12**
See also CA 107; 196; DLB 123; GFL 1789 to the Present
Bourjaily, Vance (Nye) 1922- .... **CLC 8, 62**
See also CA 1-4R; CAAS 1; CANR 2, 72; CN 7; DLB 2, 143
Bourne, Randolph S(illiman)
1886-1918 .... **TCLC 16**
See also CA 117; 155; DLB 63
Bova, Ben(jamin William) 1932- .... **CLC 45**
See also AAYA 16; CA 5-8R; CAAS 18; CANR 11, 56, 94; CLR 3; DLBY 1981; INT CANR-11; MAICYA 1, 2; MTCW 1; SATA 6, 68; SFW 4
Bowen, Elizabeth (Dorothea Cole)
1899-1973 . **CLC 1, 3, 6, 11, 15, 22, 118; SSC 3, 28**
See also BRWS 2; CA 17-18; 41-44R; CANR 35, 105; CAP 2; CDBLB 1945-1960; DA3; DAM NOV; DLB 15, 162; EXPS; FW; HGG; MTCW 1, 2; NFS 13; RGSF 2; SSFS 5; SUFW; WLIT 4
Bowering, George 1935- .... **CLC 15, 47**
See also CA 21-24R; CAAS 16; CANR 10; CP 7; DLB 53
Bowering, Marilyn R(uthe) 1949- .... **CLC 32**
See also CA 101; CANR 49; CP 7; CWP
Bowers, Edgar 1924-2000 .... **CLC 9**
See also CA 5-8R; 188; CANR 24; CP 7; CSW; DLB 5

Bowie, David .... **CLC 17**
See also Jones, David Robert
Bowles, Jane (Sydney) 1917-1973 ..... **CLC 3, 68**
See also CA 19-20; 41-44R; CAP 2
Bowles, Paul (Frederick) 1910-1999 . **CLC 1, 2, 19, 53; SSC 3**
See also AMWS 4; CA 1-4R; 186; CAAS 1; CANR 1, 19, 50, 75; CN 7; DA3; DLB 5, 6, 218; MTCW 1, 2; RGAL 4
Bowles, William Lisle 1762-1850 . **NCLC 103**
See also DLB 93
Box, Edgar
See Vidal, Gore
See also GLL 1
Boyd, James 1888-1944 .... **TCLC 115**
See also CA 186; DLB 9; DLBD 16; RGAL 4; RHW
Boyd, Nancy
See Millay, Edna St. Vincent
See also GLL 1
Boyd, Thomas (Alexander)
1898-1935 .... **TCLC 111**
See also CA 111; 183; DLB 9; DLBD 16
Boyd, William 1952- .... **CLC 28, 53, 70**
See also CA 114; 120; CANR 51, 71; CN 7; DLB 231
Boyle, Kay 1902-1992 .... **CLC 1, 5, 19, 58, 121; SSC 5**
See also CA 13-16R; 140; CAAS 1; CANR 29, 61; DLB 4, 9, 48, 86; DLBY 1993; MTCW 1, 2; RGAL 4; RGSF 2; SSFS 10, 13, 14
Boyle, Mark
See Kienzle, William X(avier)
Boyle, Patrick 1905-1982 .... **CLC 19**
See also CA 127
Boyle, T. C.
See Boyle, T(homas) Coraghessan
See also AMWS 8
Boyle, T(homas) Coraghessan
1948- .... **CLC 36, 55, 90; SSC 16**
See also Boyle, T. C.
See also BEST 90:4; BPFB 1; CA 120; CANR 44, 76, 89; CN 7; CPW; DA3; DAM POP; DLB 218; DLBY 1986; MTCW 2; SSFS 13
Boz
See Dickens, Charles (John Huffam)
Brackenridge, Hugh Henry
1748-1816 .... **NCLC 7**
See also DLB 11, 37; RGAL 4
Bradbury, Edward P.
See Moorcock, Michael (John)
See also MTCW 2
Bradbury, Malcolm (Stanley)
1932-2000 .... **CLC 32, 61**
See also CA 1-4R; CANR 1, 33, 91, 98; CN 7; DA3; DAM NOV; DLB 14, 207; MTCW 1, 2
Bradbury, Ray (Douglas) 1920- .... **CLC 1, 3, 10, 15, 42, 98; SSC 29; WLC**
See also AAYA 15; AITN 1, 2; AMWS 4; BPFB 1; BYA 4, 5, 11; CA 1-4R; CANR 2, 30, 75; CDALB 1968-1988; CN 7; CPW; DA; DA3; DAB; DAC; DAM MST, NOV, POP; DLB 2, 8; EXPN; EXPS; HGG; LAIT 3, 5; MTCW 1, 2; NFS 1; RGAL 4; RGSF 2; SATA 11, 64, 123; SCFW 2; SFW 4; SSFS 1; SUFW; YAW
Braddon, Mary Elizabeth
1837-1915 .... **TCLC 111**
See also Aunt Belinda
See also CA 108; 179; CMW 4; DLB 18, 70, 156; HGG
Bradford, Gamaliel 1863-1932 .... **TCLC 36**
See also CA 160; DLB 17
Bradford, William 1590-1657 .... **LC 64**
See also DLB 24, 30; RGAL 4

Bradley, David (Henry), Jr. 1950- ... **CLC 23, 118; BLC 1**
See also BW 1, 3; CA 104; CANR 26, 81; CN 7; DAM MULT; DLB 33

Bradley, John Ed(mund, Jr.) 1958- . **CLC 55**
See also CA 139; CANR 99; CN 7; CSW

Bradley, Marion Zimmer 1930-1999 .... **CLC 30**
See also Chapman, Lee; Dexter, John; Gardner, Miriam; Ives, Morgan; Rivers, Elfrida
See also AAYA 40; BPFB 1; CA 57-60; 185; CAAS 10; CANR 7, 31, 51, 75, 107; CPW; DA3; DAM POP; DLB 8; FANT; FW; MTCW 1, 2; SATA 90; SATA-Obit 116; SFW 4; YAW

Bradshaw, John 1933- .... **CLC 70**
See also CA 138; CANR 61

Bradstreet, Anne 1612(?)-1672 .... **LC 4, 30; PC 10**
See also AMWS 1; CDALB 1640-1865; DA; DA3; DAB; DAC; DAM MST, POET; DLB 24; EXPP; FW; PFS 6; RGAL 4; WP

Brady, Joan 1939- .... **CLC 86**
See also CA 141

Bragg, Melvyn 1939- .... **CLC 10**
See also BEST 89:3; CA 57-60; CANR 10, 48, 89; CN 7; DLB 14; RHW

Brahe, Tycho 1546-1601 .... **LC 45**

Braine, John (Gerard) 1922-1986 . **CLC 1, 3, 41**
See also CA 1-4R; 120; CANR 1, 33; CDBLB 1945-1960; DLB 15; DLBY 1986; MTCW 1

Bramah, Ernest 1868-1942 .... **TCLC 72**
See also CA 156; CMW 4; DLB 70; FANT

Brammer, William 1930(?)-1978 ...... **CLC 31**
See also CA 77-80

Brancati, Vitaliano 1907-1954 .... **TCLC 12**
See also CA 109

Brancato, Robin F(idler) 1936- .... **CLC 35**
See also AAYA 9; BYA 6; CA 69-72; CANR 11, 45; CLR 32; JRDA; MAICYAS 1; SAAS 9; SATA 97; WYA; YAW

Brand, Max
See Faust, Frederick (Schiller)
See also BPFB 1; TCWW 2

Brand, Millen 1906-1980 .... **CLC 7**
See also CA 21-24R; 97-100; CANR 72

Branden, Barbara .... **CLC 44**
See also CA 148

Brandes, Georg (Morris Cohen) 1842-1927 .... **TCLC 10**
See also CA 105; 189

Brandys, Kazimierz 1916-2000 .... **CLC 62**

Branley, Franklyn M(ansfield) 1915- .... **CLC 21**
See also CA 33-36R; CANR 14, 39; CLR 13; MAICYA 1, 2; SAAS 16; SATA 4, 68

Brathwaite, Edward Kamau 1930- . **CLC 11; BLCS**
See also BW 2, 3; CA 25-28R; CANR 11, 26, 47, 107; CDWLB 3; CP 7; DAM POET; DLB 125

Brathwaite, Kamau
See Brathwaite, Edward Kamau

Brautigan, Richard (Gary) 1935-1984 ..... **CLC 1, 3, 5, 9, 12, 34, 42**
See also BPFB 1; CA 53-56; 113; CANR 34; DA3; DAM NOV; DLB 2, 5, 206; DLBY 1980, 1984; FANT; MTCW 1; RGAL 4; SATA 56

Brave Bird, Mary
See Crow Dog, Mary (Ellen)
See also NNAL

Braverman, Kate 1950- .... **CLC 67**
See also CA 89-92

Brecht, (Eugen) Bertolt (Friedrich) 1898-1956 ..... **TCLC 1, 6, 13, 35; DC 3; WLC**
See also CA 104; 133; CANR 62; CDWLB 2; DA; DA3; DAB; DAC; DAM DRAM, MST; DFS 4, 5, 9; DLB 56, 124; EW 11; IDTP; MTCW 1, 2; RGWL 2

Brecht, Eugen Berthold Friedrich
See Brecht, (Eugen) Bertolt (Friedrich)

Bremer, Fredrika 1801-1865 .... **NCLC 11**
See also DLB 254

Brennan, Christopher John 1870-1932 .... **TCLC 17**
See also CA 117; 188; DLB 230

Brennan, Maeve 1917-1993 .... **CLC 5**
See also CA 81-84; CANR 72, 100

Brent, Linda
See Jacobs, Harriet A(nn)

Brentano, Clemens (Maria) 1778-1842 .... **NCLC 1**
See also DLB 90; RGWL 2

Brent of Bin Bin
See Franklin, (Stella Maria Sarah) Miles (Lampe)

Brenton, Howard 1942- .... **CLC 31**
See also CA 69-72; CANR 33, 67; CBD; CD 5; DLB 13; MTCW 1

Breslin, James 1930-
See Breslin, Jimmy
See also CA 73-76; CANR 31, 75; DAM NOV; MTCW 1, 2

Breslin, Jimmy .... **CLC 4, 43**
See also Breslin, James
See also AITN 1; DLB 185; MTCW 2

Bresson, Robert 1901(?)-1999 .... **CLC 16**
See also CA 110; 187; CANR 49

Breton, Andre 1896-1966 .. **CLC 2, 9, 15, 54; PC 15**
See also CA 19-20; 25-28R; CANR 40, 60; CAP 2; DLB 65, 258; EW 11; GFL 1789 to the Present; MTCW 1, 2; RGWL 2; WP

Breytenbach, Breyten 1939(?)- .. **CLC 23, 37, 126**
See also CA 113; 129; CANR 61; CWW 2; DAM POET; DLB 225

Bridgers, Sue Ellen 1942- .... **CLC 26**
See also AAYA 8; BYA 7, 8; CA 65-68; CANR 11, 36; CLR 18; DLB 52; JRDA; MAICYA 1, 2; SAAS 1; SATA 22, 90; SATA-Essay 109; WYA; YAW

Bridges, Robert (Seymour) 1844-1930 .... **TCLC 1; PC 28**
See also BRW 6; CA 104; 152; CDBLB 1890-1914; DAM POET; DLB 19, 98

Bridie, James .... **TCLC 3**
See also Mavor, Osborne Henry
See also DLB 10

Brin, David 1950- .... **CLC 34**
See also AAYA 21; CA 102; CANR 24, 70; INT CANR-24; SATA 65; SCFW 2; SFW 4

Brink, Andre (Philippus) 1935- . **CLC 18, 36, 106**
See also AFW; BRWS 6; CA 104; CANR 39, 62, 109; CN 7; DLB 225; INT CA-103; MTCW 1, 2; WLIT 2

Brinsmead, H(esba) F(ay) 1922- .... **CLC 21**
See also CA 21-24R; CANR 10; CLR 47; CWRI 5; MAICYA 1, 2; SAAS 5; SATA 18, 78

Brittain, Vera (Mary) 1893(?)-1970 . **CLC 23**
See also CA 13-16; 25-28R; CANR 58; CAP 1; DLB 191; FW; MTCW 1, 2

Broch, Hermann 1886-1951 .... **TCLC 20**
See also CA 117; CDWLB 2; DLB 85, 124; EW 10; RGWL 2

Brock, Rose
See Hansen, Joseph
See also GLL 1

Brod, Max 1884-1968 .... **TCLC 115**
See also CA 5-8R; 25-28R; CANR 7; DLB 81

Brodkey, Harold (Roy) 1930-1996 ... **CLC 56**
See also CA 111; 151; CANR 71; CN 7; DLB 130

Brodskii, Iosif
See Brodsky, Joseph
See also RGWL 2

Brodsky, Iosif Alexandrovich 1940-1996
See Brodsky, Joseph
See also AITN 1; CA 41-44R; 151; CANR 37, 106; DA3; DAM POET; MTCW 1, 2

Brodsky, Joseph . **CLC 4, 6, 13, 36, 100; PC 9**
See also Brodsky, Iosif Alexandrovich
See also AMWS 8; CWW 2; MTCW 1

Brodsky, Michael (Mark) 1948- .... **CLC 19**
See also CA 102; CANR 18, 41, 58; DLB 244

Brodzki, Bella ed. .... **CLC 65**

Brome, Richard 1590(?)-1652 .... **LC 61**
See also DLB 58

Bromell, Henry 1947- .... **CLC 5**
See also CA 53-56; CANR 9

Bromfield, Louis (Brucker) 1896-1956 .... **TCLC 11**
See also CA 107; 155; DLB 4, 9, 86; RGAL 4; RHW

Broner, E(sther) M(asserman) 1930- .... **CLC 19**
See also CA 17-20R; CANR 8, 25, 72; CN 7; DLB 28

Bronk, William (M.) 1918-1999 .... **CLC 10**
See also CA 89-92; 177; CANR 23; CP 7; DLB 165

Bronstein, Lev Davidovich
See Trotsky, Leon

Bronte, Anne 1820-1849 ..... **NCLC 4, 71, 102**
See also BRW 5; BRWR 1; DA3; DLB 21, 199

Bronte, (Patrick) Branwell 1817-1848 .... **NCLC 109**

Bronte, Charlotte 1816-1855 ...... **NCLC 3, 8, 33, 58, 105; WLC**
See also AAYA 17; BRW 5; BRWR 1; BYA 2; CDBLB 1832-1890; DA; DA3; DAB; DAC; DAM MST, NOV; DLB 21, 159, 199; EXPN; LAIT 2; NFS 4; WLIT 4

Bronte, Emily (Jane) 1818-1848 ... **NCLC 16, 35; PC 8; WLC**
See also AAYA 17; BPFB 1; BRW 5; BRWR 1; BYA 3; CDBLB 1832-1890; DA; DA3; DAB; DAC; DAM MST, NOV, POET; DLB 21, 32, 199; EXPN; LAIT 1; WLIT 3

Brontes
See Bronte, Anne; Bronte, Charlotte; Bronte, Emily (Jane)

Brooke, Frances 1724-1789 .... **LC 6, 48**
See also DLB 39, 99

Brooke, Henry 1703(?)-1783 .... **LC 1**
See also DLB 39

Brooke, Rupert (Chawner) 1887-1915 ..... **TCLC 2, 7; PC 24; WLC**
See also BRWS 3; CA 104; 132; CANR 61; CDBLB 1914-1945; DA; DAB; DAC; DAM MST, POET; DLB 19, 216; EXPP; GLL 2; MTCW 1, 2; PFS 7

Brooke-Haven, P.
See Wodehouse, P(elham) G(renville)

Brooke-Rose, Christine 1926(?)- ...... **CLC 40**
See also BRWS 4; CA 13-16R; CANR 58; CN 7; DLB 14, 231; SFW 4

Brookner, Anita 1928- .. **CLC 32, 34, 51, 136**
See also BRWS 4; CA 114; 120; CANR 37, 56, 87; CN 7; CPW; DA3; DAB; DAM POP; DLB 194; DLBY 1987; MTCW 1, 2

Brooks, Cleanth 1906-1994 . **CLC 24, 86, 110**
See also CA 17-20R; 145; CANR 33, 35; CSW; DLB 63; DLBY 1994; INT CANR-35; MTCW 1, 2

Brooks, George
See Baum, L(yman) Frank

Brooks, Gwendolyn (Elizabeth) 1917-2000 .. **CLC 1, 2, 4, 5, 15, 49, 125; BLC 1; PC 7; WLC**
See also AAYA 20; AFAW 1, 2; AITN 1; AMWS 3; BW 2, 3; CA 1-4R; 190; CANR 1, 27, 52, 75; CDALB 1941-1968; CLR 27; CP 7; CWP; DA; DA3; DAC; DAM MST, MULT, POET; DLB 5, 76, 165; EXPP; MAWW; MTCW 1, 2; PFS 1, 2, 4, 6; RGAL 4; SATA 6; SATA-Obit 123; WP

Brooks, Mel .... **CLC 12**
See also Kaminsky, Melvin
See also AAYA 13; DLB 26

Brooks, Peter (Preston) 1938- .... **CLC 34**
See also CA 45-48; CANR 1, 107

Brooks, Van Wyck 1886-1963 .... **CLC 29**
See also AMW; CA 1-4R; CANR 6; DLB 45, 63, 103

Brophy, Brigid (Antonia) 1929-1995 .... **CLC 6, 11, 29, 105**
See also CA 5-8R; CAAS 4; CANR 25, 53; CBD; CN 7; CWD; DA3; DLB 14; MTCW 1, 2

Brosman, Catharine Savage 1934- ..... **CLC 9**
See also CA 61-64; CANR 21, 46

Brossard, Nicole 1943- .... **CLC 115**
See also CA 122; CAAS 16; CCA 1; CWP; CWW 2; DLB 53; FW; GLL 2

Brother Antoninus
See Everson, William (Oliver)

The Brothers Quay
See Quay, Stephen; Quay, Timothy

Broughton, T(homas) Alan 1936- ...... **CLC 19**
See also CA 45-48; CANR 2, 23, 48

Broumas, Olga 1949- .... **CLC 10, 73**
See also CA 85-88; CANR 20, 69; CP 7; CWP; GLL 2

Broun, Heywood 1888-1939 .... **TCLC 104**
See also DLB 29, 171

Brown, Alan 1950- .... **CLC 99**
See also CA 156

Brown, Charles Brockden 1771-1810 .... **NCLC 22, 74**
See also AMWS 1; CDALB 1640-1865; DLB 37, 59, 73; FW; HGG; RGAL 4

Brown, Christy 1932-1981 .... **CLC 63**
See also BYA 13; CA 105; 104; CANR 72; DLB 14

Brown, Claude 1937-2002 ... **CLC 30; BLC 1**
See also AAYA 7; BW 1, 3; CA 73-76; CANR 81; DAM MULT

Brown, Dee (Alexander) 1908- ... **CLC 18, 47**
See also AAYA 30; CA 13-16R; CAAS 6; CANR 11, 45, 60; CPW; CSW; DA3; DAM POP; DLBY 1980; LAIT 2; MTCW 1, 2; SATA 5, 110; TCWW 2

Brown, George
See Wertmueller, Lina

Brown, George Douglas 1869-1902 .... **TCLC 28**
See also Douglas, George
See also CA 162

Brown, George Mackay 1921-1996 ... **CLC 5, 48, 100**
See also BRWS 6; CA 21-24R; 151; CAAS 6; CANR 12, 37, 67; CN 7; CP 7; DLB 14, 27, 139; MTCW 1; RGSF 2; SATA 35

Brown, (William) Larry 1951- .... **CLC 73**
See also CA 130; 134; CSW; DLB 234; INT 133

Brown, Moses
See Barrett, William (Christopher)

Brown, Rita Mae 1944- .... **CLC 18, 43, 79**
See also BPFB 1; CA 45-48; CANR 2, 11, 35, 62, 95; CN 7; CPW; CSW; DA3; DAM NOV, POP; FW; INT CANR-11; MTCW 1, 2; NFS 9; RGAL 4

Brown, Roderick (Langmere) Haig-
See Haig-Brown, Roderick (Langmere)

Brown, Rosellen 1939- .... **CLC 32**
See also CA 77-80; CAAS 10; CANR 14, 44, 98; CN 7

Brown, Sterling Allen 1901-1989 ...... **CLC 1, 23, 59; BLC 1**
See also AFAW 1, 2; BW 1, 3; CA 85-88; 127; CANR 26; DA3; DAM MULT, POET; DLB 48, 51, 63; MTCW 1, 2; RGAL 4; WP

Brown, Will
See Ainsworth, William Harrison

Brown, William Wells 1815-1884 ... **NCLC 2, 89; BLC 1; DC 1**
See also DAM MULT; DLB 3, 50, 183, 248; RGAL 4

Browne, (Clyde) Jackson 1948(?)- ... **CLC 21**
See also CA 120

Browning, Elizabeth Barrett 1806-1861 ... **NCLC 1, 16, 61, 66; PC 6; WLC**
See also BRW 4; CDBLB 1832-1890; DA; DA3; DAB; DAC; DAM MST, POET; DLB 32, 199; EXPP; PAB; PFS 2; WLIT 4; WP

Browning, Robert 1812-1889 . **NCLC 19, 79; PC 2; WLCS**
See also BRW 4; BRWR 2; CDBLB 1832-1890; DA; DA3; DAB; DAC; DAM MST, POET; DLB 32, 163; EXPP; PAB; PFS 1; RGEL 2; TEA; WLIT 4; WP; YABC 1

Browning, Tod 1882-1962 .... **CLC 16**
See also CA 141; 117

Brownson, Orestes Augustus 1803-1876 .... **NCLC 50**
See also DLB 1, 59, 73, 243

Bruccoli, Matthew J(oseph) 1931- ... **CLC 34**
See also CA 9-12R; CANR 7, 87; DLB 103

Bruce, Lenny .... **CLC 21**
See also Schneider, Leonard Alfred

Bruin, John
See Brutus, Dennis

Brulard, Henri
See Stendhal

Brulls, Christian
See Simenon, Georges (Jacques Christian)

Brunner, John (Kilian Houston) 1934-1995 .... **CLC 8, 10**
See also CA 1-4R; 149; CAAS 8; CANR 2, 37; CPW; DAM POP; MTCW 1, 2; SCFW 2; SFW 4

Bruno, Giordano 1548-1600 .... **LC 27**
See also RGWL 2

Brutus, Dennis 1924- ... **CLC 43; BLC 1; PC 24**
See also AFW; BW 2, 3; CA 49-52; CAAS 14; CANR 2, 27, 42, 81; CDWLB 3; CP 7; DAM MULT, POET; DLB 117, 225

Bryan, C(ourtlandt) D(ixon) B(arnes) 1936- .... **CLC 29**
See also CA 73-76; CANR 13, 68; DLB 185; INT CANR-13

Bryan, Michael
See Moore, Brian
See also CCA 1

Bryan, William Jennings 1860-1925 .... **TCLC 99**

Bryant, William Cullen 1794-1878 . **NCLC 6, 46; PC 20**
See also AMWS 1; CDALB 1640-1865; DA; DAB; DAC; DAM MST, POET; DLB 3, 43, 59, 189, 250; EXPP; PAB; RGAL 4

Bryusov, Valery Yakovlevich 1873-1924 .... **TCLC 10**
See also CA 107; 155; SFW 4

Buchan, John 1875-1940 .... **TCLC 41**
See also CA 108; 145; CMW 4; DAB; DAM POP; DLB 34, 70, 156; HGG; MSW; MTCW 1; RGEL 2; RHW; YABC 2

Buchanan, George 1506-1582 .... **LC 4**
See also DLB 132

Buchanan, Robert 1841-1901 .... **TCLC 107**
See also CA 179; DLB 18, 35

Buchheim, Lothar-Guenther 1918- .... **CLC 6**
See also CA 85-88

Buchner, (Karl) Georg 1813-1837 . **NCLC 26**
See also CDWLB 2; DLB 133; EW 6; RGSF 2; RGWL 2

Buchwald, Art(hur) 1925- .... **CLC 33**
See also AITN 1; CA 5-8R; CANR 21, 67, 107; MTCW 1, 2; SATA 10

Buck, Pearl S(ydenstricker) 1892-1973 .... **CLC 7, 11, 18, 127**
See also AAYA 42; AITN 1; AMWS 2; BPFB 1; CA 1-4R; 41-44R; CANR 1, 34; CDALBS; DA; DA3; DAB; DAC; DAM MST, NOV; DLB 9, 102; LAIT 3; MTCW 1, 2; RGAL 4; RHW; SATA 1, 25

Buckler, Ernest 1908-1984 .... **CLC 13**
See also CA 11-12; 114; CAP 1; CCA 1; DAC; DAM MST; DLB 68; SATA 47

Buckley, Vincent (Thomas) 1925-1988 .... **CLC 57**
See also CA 101

Buckley, William F(rank), Jr. 1925- . **CLC 7, 18, 37**
See also AITN 1; BPFB 1; CA 1-4R; CANR 1, 24, 53, 93; CMW 4; CPW; DA3; DAM POP; DLB 137; DLBY 1980; INT CANR-24; MTCW 1, 2; TUS

Buechner, (Carl) Frederick 1926- . **CLC 2, 4, 6, 9**
See also BPFB 1; CA 13-16R; CANR 11, 39, 64; CN 7; DAM NOV; DLBY 1980; INT CANR-11; MTCW 1, 2

Buell, John (Edward) 1927- .... **CLC 10**
See also CA 1-4R; CANR 71; DLB 53

Buero Vallejo, Antonio 1916-2000 ... **CLC 15, 46, 139**
See also CA 106; 189; CANR 24, 49, 75; DFS 11; HW 1; MTCW 1, 2

Bufalino, Gesualdo 1920(?)-1990 ...... **CLC 74**
See also CWW 2; DLB 196

Bugayev, Boris Nikolayevich 1880-1934 .... **TCLC 7; PC 11**
See also Bely, Andrey; Belyi, Andrei
See also CA 104; 165; MTCW 1

Bukowski, Charles 1920-1994 ... **CLC 2, 5, 9, 41, 82, 108; PC 18; SSC 45**
See also CA 17-20R; 144; CANR 40, 62, 105; CPW; DA3; DAM NOV, POET; DLB 5, 130, 169; MTCW 1, 2

Bulgakov, Mikhail (Afanas'evich) 1891-1940 .... **TCLC 2, 16; SSC 18**
See also BPFB 1; CA 105; 152; DAM DRAM, NOV; NFS 8; RGSF 2; RGWL 2; SFW 4

Bulgya, Alexander Alexandrovich 1901-1956 .... **TCLC 53**
See also Fadeyev, Alexander
See also CA 117; 181

Bullins, Ed 1935- ... **CLC 1, 5, 7; BLC 1; DC 6**
See also BW 2, 3; CA 49-52; CAAS 16; CAD; CANR 24, 46, 73; CD 5; DAM DRAM, MULT; DLB 7, 38, 249; MTCW 1, 2; RGAL 4

Bulwer-Lytton, Edward (George Earle Lytton) 1803-1873 .... **NCLC 1, 45**
See also DLB 21; RGEL 2; SFW 4; SUFW

Bunin, Ivan Alexeyevich
1870-1953 .... **TCLC 6; SSC 5**
See also CA 104; RGSF 2; RGWL 2

Bunting, Basil 1900-1985 ...... **CLC 10, 39, 47**
See also BRWS 7; CA 53-56; 115; CANR 7; DAM POET; DLB 20; RGEL 2

Bunuel, Luis 1900-1983 ... **CLC 16, 80; HLC 1**
See also CA 101; 110; CANR 32, 77; DAM MULT; HW 1

Bunyan, John 1628-1688 ..... **LC 4, 69; WLC**
See also BRW 2; BYA 5; CDBLB 1660-1789; DA; DAB; DAC; DAM MST; DLB 39; RGEL 2; WCH; WLIT 3

Buravsky, Alexandr .... **CLC 59**

Burckhardt, Jacob (Christoph)
1818-1897 .... **NCLC 49**
See also EW 6

Burford, Eleanor
See Hibbert, Eleanor Alice Burford

Burgess, Anthony . **CLC 1, 2, 4, 5, 8, 10, 13, 15, 22, 40, 62, 81, 94**
See also Wilson, John (Anthony) Burgess
See also AAYA 25; AITN 1; BRWS 1; CDBLB 1960 to Present; DAB; DLB 14, 194; DLBY 1998; MTCW 1; RGEL 2; RHW; SFW 4; YAW

Burke, Edmund 1729(?)-1797 .... **LC 7, 36; WLC**
See also BRW 3; DA; DA3; DAB; DAC; DAM MST; DLB 104, 252; RGEL 2

Burke, Kenneth (Duva) 1897-1993 ... **CLC 2, 24**
See also AMW; CA 5-8R; 143; CANR 39, 74; DLB 45, 63; MTCW 1, 2; RGAL 4

Burke, Leda
See Garnett, David

Burke, Ralph
See Silverberg, Robert

Burke, Thomas 1886-1945 .... **TCLC 63**
See also CA 113; 155; CMW 4; DLB 197

Burney, Fanny 1752-1840 .... **NCLC 12, 54, 107**
See also BRWS 3; DLB 39; RGEL 2

Burney, Frances
See Burney, Fanny

Burns, Robert 1759-1796 ... **LC 3, 29, 40; PC 6; WLC**
See also BRW 3; CDBLB 1789-1832; DA; DA3; DAB; DAC; DAM MST, POET; DLB 109; EXPP; PAB; RGEL 2; WP

Burns, Tex
See L'Amour, Louis (Dearborn)
See also TCWW 2

Burnshaw, Stanley 1906- .... **CLC 3, 13, 44**
See also CA 9-12R; CP 7; DLB 48; DLBY 1997

Burr, Anne 1937- .... **CLC 6**
See also CA 25-28R

Burroughs, Edgar Rice 1875-1950 . **TCLC 2, 32**
See also AAYA 11; BPFB 1; BYA 4, 9; CA 104; 132; DA3; DAM NOV; DLB 8; FANT; MTCW 1, 2; RGAL 4; SATA 41; SCFW 2; SFW 4; YAW

Burroughs, William S(eward)
1914-1997 .. **CLC 1, 2, 5, 15, 22, 42, 75, 109; WLC**
See also Lee, William; Lee, Willy
See also AITN 2; AMWS 3; BPFB 1; CA 9-12R; 160; CANR 20, 52, 104; CN 7; CPW; DA; DA3; DAB; DAC; DAM MST, NOV, POP; DLB 2, 8, 16, 152, 237; DLBY 1981, 1997; HGG; MTCW 1, 2; RGAL 4; SFW 4; TCLC 121

Burton, Sir Richard F(rancis)
1821-1890 .... **NCLC 42**
See also DLB 55, 166, 184

Burton, Robert 1577-1640 .... **LC 74**
See also DLB 151; RGEL 2

Busch, Frederick 1941- ..... **CLC 7, 10, 18, 47**
See also CA 33-36R; CAAS 1; CANR 45, 73, 92; CN 7; DLB 6, 218

Bush, Ronald 1946- .... **CLC 34**
See also CA 136

Bustos, F(rancisco)
See Borges, Jorge Luis

Bustos Domecq, H(onorio)
See Bioy Casares, Adolfo; Borges, Jorge Luis

Butler, Octavia E(stelle) 1947- .... **CLC 38, 121; BLCS**
See also AAYA 18; AFAW 2; BPFB 1; BW 2, 3; CA 73-76; CANR 12, 24, 38, 73; CLR 65; CPW; DA3; DAM MULT, POP; DLB 33; MTCW 1, 2; NFS 8; SATA 84; SCFW 2; SFW 4; SSFS 6; YAW

Butler, Robert Olen, (Jr.) 1945- .... **CLC 81**
See also BPFB 1; CA 112; CANR 66; CSW; DAM POP; DLB 173; INT CA-112; MTCW 1; SSFS 11

Butler, Samuel 1612-1680 .... **LC 16, 43**
See also DLB 101, 126; RGEL 2

Butler, Samuel 1835-1902 .... **TCLC 1, 33; WLC**
See also BRWS 2; CA 143; CDBLB 1890-1914; DA; DA3; DAB; DAC; DAM MST, NOV; DLB 18, 57, 174; RGEL 2; SFW 4; TEA

Butler, Walter C.
See Faust, Frederick (Schiller)

Butor, Michel (Marie Francois)
1926- .... **CLC 1, 3, 8, 11, 15**
See also CA 9-12R; CANR 33, 66; DLB 83; EW 13; GFL 1789 to the Present; MTCW 1, 2

Butts, Mary 1890(?)-1937 .... **TCLC 77**
See also CA 148; DLB 240

Buxton, Ralph
See Silverstein, Alvin; Silverstein, Virginia B(arbara Opshelor)

Buzo, Alexander (John) 1944- .... **CLC 61**
See also CA 97-100; CANR 17, 39, 69; CD 5

Buzzati, Dino 1906-1972 .... **CLC 36**
See also CA 160; 33-36R; DLB 177; RGWL 2; SFW 4

Byars, Betsy (Cromer) 1928- .... **CLC 35**
See also AAYA 19; BYA 3; CA 33-36R, 183; CAAE 183; CANR 18, 36, 57, 102; CLR 1, 16, 72; DLB 52; INT CANR-18; JRDA; MAICYA 1, 2; MAICYAS 1; MTCW 1; SAAS 1; SATA 4, 46, 80; SATA-Essay 108; WYA; YAW

Byatt, A(ntonia) S(usan Drabble)
1936- .... **CLC 19, 65, 136**
See also BPFB 1; BRWS 4; CA 13-16R; CANR 13, 33, 50, 75, 96; DA3; DAM NOV, POP; DLB 14, 194; MTCW 1, 2; RGSF 2; RHW

Byrne, David 1952- .... **CLC 26**
See also CA 127

Byrne, John Keyes 1926-
See Leonard, Hugh
See also CA 102; CANR 78; INT CA-102

Byron, George Gordon (Noel)
1788-1824 ..... **NCLC 2, 12, 109; PC 16; WLC**
See also BRW 4; CDBLB 1789-1832; DA; DA3; DAB; DAC; DAM MST, POET; DLB 96, 110; EXPP; PAB; PFS 1, 14; RGEL 2; WLIT 3; WP

Byron, Robert 1905-1941 .... **TCLC 67**
See also CA 160; DLB 195

C. 3. 3.
See Wilde, Oscar (Fingal O'Flahertie Wills)

Caballero, Fernan 1796-1877 .... **NCLC 10**

Cabell, Branch
See Cabell, James Branch

Cabell, James Branch 1879-1958 .... **TCLC 6**
See also CA 105; 152; DLB 9, 78; FANT; MTCW 1; RGAL 4; SUFW

Cabeza de Vaca, Alvar Nunez
1490-1557(?) .... **LC 61**

Cable, George Washington
1844-1925 .... **TCLC 4; SSC 4**
See also CA 104; 155; DLB 12, 74; DLBD 13; RGAL 4

Cabral de Melo Neto, Joao
1920-1999 .... **CLC 76**
See also CA 151; DAM MULT; LAW; LAWS 1

Cabrera Infante, G(uillermo) 1929- . **CLC 5, 25, 45, 120; HLC 1; SSC 39**
See also CA 85-88; CANR 29, 65; CDWLB 3; DA3; DAM MULT; DLB 113; HW 1, 2; LAW; LAWS 1; MTCW 1, 2; RGSF 2; WLIT 1

Cade, Toni
See Bambara, Toni Cade

Cadmus and Harmonia
See Buchan, John

Caedmon fl. 658-680 .... **CMLC 7**
See also DLB 146

Caeiro, Alberto
See Pessoa, Fernando (Antonio Nogueira)

Caesar, Julius .... **CMLC 47**
See also Julius Caesar
See also AW 1; RGWL 2

Cage, John (Milton, Jr.) 1912-1992 . **CLC 41**
See also CA 13-16R; 169; CANR 9, 78; DLB 193; INT CANR-9

Cahan, Abraham 1860-1951 .... **TCLC 71**
See also CA 108; 154; DLB 9, 25, 28; RGAL 4

Cain, G.
See Cabrera Infante, G(uillermo)

Cain, Guillermo
See Cabrera Infante, G(uillermo)

Cain, James M(allahan) 1892-1977 .. **CLC 3, 11, 28**
See also AITN 1; BPFB 1; CA 17-20R; 73-76; CANR 8, 34, 61; CMW 4; DLB 226; MSW; MTCW 1; RGAL 4

Caine, Hall 1853-1931 .... **TCLC 97**
See also RHW

Caine, Mark
See Raphael, Frederic (Michael)

Calasso, Roberto 1941- .... **CLC 81**
See also CA 143; CANR 89

Calderon de la Barca, Pedro
1600-1681 .... **LC 23; DC 3; HLCS 1**
See also EW 2; RGWL 2

Caldwell, Erskine (Preston)
1903-1987 .... **CLC 1, 8, 14, 50, 60; SSC 19**
See also AITN 1; AMW; BPFB 1; CA 1-4R; 121; CAAS 1; CANR 2, 33; DA3; DAM NOV; DLB 9, 86; MTCW 1, 2; RGAL 4; RGSF 2; TCLC 117

Caldwell, (Janet Miriam) Taylor (Holland)
1900-1985 .... **CLC 2, 28, 39**
See also BPFB 1; CA 5-8R; 116; CANR 5; DA3; DAM NOV, POP; DLBD 17; RHW

Calhoun, John Caldwell
1782-1850 .... **NCLC 15**
See also DLB 3, 248

Calisher, Hortense 1911- ..... **CLC 2, 4, 8, 38, 134; SSC 15**
See also CA 1-4R; CANR 1, 22, 67; CN 7; DA3; DAM NOV; DLB 2, 218; INT CANR-22; MTCW 1, 2; RGAL 4; RGSF 2

Callaghan, Morley Edward
1903-1990 .... **CLC 3, 14, 41, 65**
See also CA 9-12R; 132; CANR 33, 73; DAC; DAM MST; DLB 68; MTCW 1, 2; RGEL 2; RGSF 2

Callimachus c. 305B.C.-c. 240B.C. .... **CMLC 18**
See also AW 1; DLB 176; RGWL 2

Calvin, Jean
See Calvin, John
See also GFL Beginnings to 1789

Calvin, John 1509-1564 .... **LC 37**
See also Calvin, Jean

Calvino, Italo 1923-1985 .... **CLC 5, 8, 11, 22, 33, 39, 73; SSC 3, 48**
See also CA 85-88; 116; CANR 23, 61; DAM NOV; DLB 196; EW 13; MTCW 1, 2; RGSF 2; RGWL 2; SFW 4; SSFS 12

Camden, William 1551-1623 .... **LC 77**
See also DLB 172

Cameron, Carey 1952- .... **CLC 59**
See also CA 135

Cameron, Peter 1959- .... **CLC 44**
See also CA 125; CANR 50; DLB 234; GLL 2

Camoens, Luis Vaz de 1524(?)-1580
See also EW 2; HLCS 1

Camoes, Luis de 1524(?)-1580 .... **LC 62; HLCS 1; PC 31**
See also RGWL 2

Campana, Dino 1885-1932 .... **TCLC 20**
See also CA 117; DLB 114

Campanella, Tommaso 1568-1639 .... **LC 32**
See also RGWL 2

Campbell, John W(ood, Jr.)
1910-1971 .... **CLC 32**
See also CA 21-22; 29-32R; CANR 34; CAP 2; DLB 8; MTCW 1; SCFW; SFW 4

Campbell, Joseph 1904-1987 .... **CLC 69**
See also AAYA 3; BEST 89:2; CA 1-4R; 124; CANR 3, 28, 61, 107; DA3; MTCW 1, 2

Campbell, Maria 1940- .... **CLC 85**
See also CA 102; CANR 54; CCA 1; DAC; NNAL

Campbell, Paul N. 1923-
See hooks, bell
See also CA 21-24R

Campbell, (John) Ramsey 1946- .... **CLC 42; SSC 19**
See also CA 57-60; CANR 7, 102; HGG; INT CANR-7; SUFW

Campbell, (Ignatius) Roy (Dunnachie)
1901-1957 .... **TCLC 5**
See also AFW; CA 104; 155; DLB 20, 225; MTCW 2; RGEL 2

Campbell, Thomas 1777-1844 .... **NCLC 19**
See also DLB 93, 144; RGEL 2

Campbell, Wilfred .... **TCLC 9**
See also Campbell, William

Campbell, William 1858(?)-1918
See Campbell, Wilfred
See also CA 106; DLB 92

Campion, Jane .... **CLC 95**
See also AAYA 33; CA 138; CANR 87

Camus, Albert 1913-1960 ...... **CLC 1, 2, 4, 9, 11, 14, 32, 63, 69, 124; DC 2; SSC 9; WLC**
See also AAYA 36; AFW; BPFB 1; CA 89-92; DA; DA3; DAB; DAC; DAM DRAM, MST, NOV; DLB 72; EW 13; EXPN; EXPS; GFL 1789 to the Present; MTCW 1, 2; NFS 6; RGSF 2; RGWL 2; SSFS 4; WLC

Canby, Vincent 1924-2000 .... **CLC 13**
See also CA 81-84; 191

Cancale
See Desnos, Robert

Canetti, Elias 1905-1994 .. **CLC 3, 14, 25, 75, 86**
See also CA 21-24R; 146; CANR 23, 61, 79; CDWLB 2; CWW 2; DA3; DLB 85, 124; EW 12; MTCW 1, 2; RGWL 2

Canfield, Dorothea F.
See Fisher, Dorothy (Frances) Canfield

Canfield, Dorothea Frances
See Fisher, Dorothy (Frances) Canfield

Canfield, Dorothy
See Fisher, Dorothy (Frances) Canfield

Canin, Ethan 1960- .... **CLC 55**
See also CA 131; 135

Cankar, Ivan 1876-1918 .... **TCLC 105**
See also CDWLB 4; DLB 147

Cannon, Curt
See Hunter, Evan

Cao, Lan 1961- .... **CLC 109**
See also CA 165

Cape, Judith
See Page, P(atricia) K(athleen)
See also CCA 1

Capek, Karel 1890-1938 .... **TCLC 6, 37; DC 1; SSC 36; WLC**
See also CA 104; 140; CDWLB 4; DA; DA3; DAB; DAC; DAM DRAM, MST, NOV; DFS 7, 11 !**; DLB 215; EW 10; MTCW 1; RGSF 2; RGWL 2; SCFW 2; SFW 4

Capote, Truman 1924-1984 . **CLC 1, 3, 8, 13, 19, 34, 38, 58; SSC 2, 47; WLC**
See also AMWS 3; BPFB 1; CA 5-8R; 113; CANR 18, 62; CDALB 1941-1968; CPW; DA; DA3; DAB; DAC; DAM MST, NOV, POP; DLB 2, 185, 227; DLBY 1980, 1984; EXPS; GLL 1; LAIT 3; MTCW 1, 2; NCFS 2; RGAL 4; RGSF 2; SATA 91; SSFS 2

Capra, Frank 1897-1991 .... **CLC 16**
See also CA 61-64; 135

Caputo, Philip 1941- .... **CLC 32**
See also CA 73-76; CANR 40; YAW

Caragiale, Ion Luca 1852-1912 ...... **TCLC 76**
See also CA 157

Card, Orson Scott 1951- .... **CLC 44, 47, 50**
See also AAYA 11, 42; BPFB 1; BYA 5, 8; CA 102; CANR 27, 47, 73, 102, 106; CPW; DA3; DAM POP; FANT; INT CANR-27; MTCW 1, 2; NFS 5; SATA 83, 127; SCFW 2; SFW 4; YAW

Cardenal, Ernesto 1925- ... **CLC 31; HLC 1; PC 22**
See also CA 49-52; CANR 2, 32, 66; CWW 2; DAM MULT, POET; HW 1, 2; LAWS 1; MTCW 1, 2; RGWL 2

Cardozo, Benjamin N(athan)
1870-1938 .... **TCLC 65**
See also CA 117; 164

Carducci, Giosue (Alessandro Giuseppe)
1835-1907 .... **TCLC 32**
See also CA 163; EW 7; RGWL 2

Carew, Thomas 1595(?)-1640 . **LC 13; PC 29**
See also BRW 2; DLB 126; PAB; RGEL 2

Carey, Ernestine Gilbreth 1908- ...... **CLC 17**
See also CA 5-8R; CANR 71; SATA 2

Carey, Peter 1943- .... **CLC 40, 55, 96**
See also CA 123; 127; CANR 53, 76; CN 7; INT CA-127; MTCW 1, 2; RGSF 2; SATA 94

Carleton, William 1794-1869 .... **NCLC 3**
See also DLB 159; RGEL 2; RGSF 2

Carlisle, Henry (Coffin) 1926- .... **CLC 33**
See also CA 13-16R; CANR 15, 85

Carlsen, Chris
See Holdstock, Robert P.

Carlson, Ron(ald F.) 1947- .... **CLC 54**
See also CA 105; CAAE 189; CANR 27; DLB 244

Carlyle, Thomas 1795-1881 ..... **NCLC 22, 70**
See also BRW 4; CDBLB 1789-1832; DA; DAB; DAC; DAM MST; DLB 55, 144, 254; RGEL 2

Carman, (William) Bliss
1861-1929 .... **TCLC 7; PC 34**
See also CA 104; 152; DAC; DLB 92; RGEL 2

Carnegie, Dale 1888-1955 .... **TCLC 53**

Carossa, Hans 1878-1956 .... **TCLC 48**
See also CA 170; DLB 66

Carpenter, Don(ald Richard)
1931-1995 .... **CLC 41**
See also CA 45-48; 149; CANR 1, 71

Carpenter, Edward 1844-1929 .... **TCLC 88**
See also CA 163; GLL 1

Carpentier (y Valmont), Alejo
1904-1980 . **CLC 8, 11, 38, 110; HLC 1; SSC 35**
See also CA 65-68; 97-100; CANR 11, 70; CDWLB 3; DAM MULT; DLB 113; HW 1, 2; LAW; RGSF 2; RGWL 2; WLIT 1

Carr, Caleb 1955(?)- .... **CLC 86**
See also CA 147; CANR 73; DA3

Carr, Emily 1871-1945 .... **TCLC 32**
See also CA 159; DLB 68; FW; GLL 2

Carr, John Dickson 1906-1977 .... **CLC 3**
See also Fairbairn, Roger
See also CA 49-52; 69-72; CANR 3, 33, 60; CMW 4; MSW; MTCW 1, 2

Carr, Philippa
See Hibbert, Eleanor Alice Burford

Carr, Virginia Spencer 1929- .... **CLC 34**
See also CA 61-64; DLB 111

Carrere, Emmanuel 1957- .... **CLC 89**

Carrier, Roch 1937- .... **CLC 13, 78**
See also CA 130; CANR 61; CCA 1; DAC; DAM MST; DLB 53; SATA 105

Carroll, James P. 1943(?)- .... **CLC 38**
See also CA 81-84; CANR 73; MTCW 1

Carroll, Jim 1951- .... **CLC 35, 143**
See also AAYA 17; CA 45-48; CANR 42

Carroll, Lewis ... **NCLC 2, 53; PC 18; WLC**
See also Dodgson, Charles Lutwidge
See also AAYA 39; BRW 5; BYA 5, 13; CDBLB 1832-1890; CLR 2, 18; DLB 18, 163, 178; DLBY 1998; EXPN; EXPP; FANT; JRDA; LAIT 1; NFS 7; PFS 11; RGEL 2; SUFW; WCH

Carroll, Paul Vincent 1900-1968 ...... **CLC 10**
See also CA 9-12R; 25-28R; DLB 10; RGEL 2

Carruth, Hayden 1921- ..... **CLC 4, 7, 10, 18, 84; PC 10**
See also CA 9-12R; CANR 4, 38, 59; CP 7; DLB 5, 165; INT CANR-4; MTCW 1, 2; SATA 47

Carson, Rachel Louise 1907-1964 .... **CLC 71**
See also AMWS 9; ANW; CA 77-80; CANR 35; DA3; DAM POP; FW; LAIT 4; MTCW 1, 2; NCFS 1; SATA 23

Carter, Angela (Olive) 1940-1992 .... **CLC 5, 41, 76; SSC 13**
See also BRWS 3; CA 53-56; 136; CANR 12, 36, 61, 106; DA3; DLB 14, 207; EXPS; FANT; FW; MTCW 1, 2; RGSF 2; SATA 66; SATA-Obit 70; SFW 4; SSFS 4, 12; WLIT 4

Carter, Nick
See Smith, Martin Cruz

Carver, Raymond 1938-1988 ..... **CLC 22, 36, 53, 55, 126; SSC 8, 51**
See also AMWS 3; BPFB 1; CA 33-36R; 126; CANR 17, 34, 61, 103; CPW; DA3; DAM NOV; DLB 130; DLBY 1984, 1988; MTCW 1, 2; RGAL 4; RGSF 2; SSFS 3, 6, 12, 13; TCWW 2

Cary, Elizabeth, Lady Falkland
1585-1639 .... **LC 30**

Cary, (Arthur) Joyce (Lunel)
1888-1957 .... **TCLC 1, 29**
See also BRW 7; CA 104; 164; CDBLB 1914-1945; DLB 15, 100; MTCW 2; RGEL 2

Casanova de Seingalt, Giovanni Jacopo
1725-1798 .... **LC 13**

Casares, Adolfo Bioy
See Bioy Casares, Adolfo
See also RGSF 2

Casas, Bartolome de las 1474-1566
See Las Casas, Bartolome de
See also WLIT 1

Casely-Hayford, J(oseph) E(phraim)
1866-1903 .... **TCLC 24; BLC 1**
See also BW 2; CA 123; 152; DAM MULT

Casey, John (Dudley) 1939- .... **CLC 59**
See also BEST 90:2; CA 69-72; CANR 23, 100

Casey, Michael 1947- .... **CLC 2**
See also CA 65-68; CANR 109; DLB 5

Casey, Patrick
See Thurman, Wallace (Henry)

Casey, Warren (Peter) 1935-1988 .... **CLC 12**
See also CA 101; 127; INT 101

Casona, Alejandro .... **CLC 49**
See also Alvarez, Alejandro Rodriguez

Cassavetes, John 1929-1989 .... **CLC 20**
See also CA 85-88; 127; CANR 82

Cassian, Nina 1924- .... **PC 17**
See also CWP; CWW 2

Cassill, R(onald) V(erlin) 1919- ... **CLC 4, 23**
See also CA 9-12R; CAAS 1; CANR 7, 45; CN 7; DLB 6, 218

Cassiodorus, Flavius Magnus c. 490(?)-c. 583(?) .... **CMLC 43**

Cassirer, Ernst 1874-1945 .... **TCLC 61**
See also CA 157

Cassity, (Allen) Turner 1929- .... **CLC 6, 42**
See also CA 17-20R; CAAS 8; CANR 11; CSW; DLB 105

Castaneda, Carlos (Cesar Aranha)
1931(?)-1998 .... **CLC 12, 119**
See also CA 25-28R; CANR 32, 66, 105; DNFS 1; HW 1; MTCW 1

Castedo, Elena 1937- .... **CLC 65**
See also CA 132

Castedo-Ellerman, Elena
See Castedo, Elena

Castellanos, Rosario 1925-1974 .... **CLC 66; HLC 1; SSC 39**
See also CA 131; 53-56; CANR 58; CDWLB 3; DAM MULT; DLB 113; FW; HW 1; LAW; MTCW 1; RGSF 2; RGWL 2

Castelvetro, Lodovico 1505-1571 .... **LC 12**

Castiglione, Baldassare 1478-1529 ...... **LC 12**
See also Castiglione, Baldesar
See also RGWL 2

Castiglione, Baldesar
See Castiglione, Baldassare
See also EW 2

Castillo, Ana (Hernandez Del)
1953- .... **CLC 151**
See also AAYA 42; CA 131; CANR 51, 86; CWP; DLB 122, 227; DNFS 2; FW; HW 1

Castle, Robert
See Hamilton, Edmond

Castro (Ruz), Fidel 1926(?)-
See also CA 110; 129; CANR 81; DAM MULT; HLC 1; HW 2

Castro, Guillen de 1569-1631 .... **LC 19**

Castro, Rosalia de 1837-1885 .... **NCLC 3, 78**
See also DAM MULT

Cather, Willa (Sibert) 1873-1947 .... **TCLC 1, 11, 31, 99; SSC 2, 50; WLC**
See also AAYA 24; AMW; AMWR 1; BPFB 1; CA 104; 128; CDALB 1865-1917; DA; DA3; DAB; DAC; DAM MST, NOV; DLB 9, 54, 78, 256; DLBD 1; EXPN; EXPS; LAIT 3; MAWW; MTCW 1, 2; NFS 2; RGAL 4; RGSF 2; RHW; SATA 30; SSFS 2, 7; TCWW 2

Catherine II
See Catherine the Great
See also DLB 150

Catherine the Great 1729-1796 .... **LC 69**
See also Catherine II

Cato, Marcus Porcius
234B.C.-149B.C. .... **CMLC 21**
See also Cato the Elder

Cato the Elder
See Cato, Marcus Porcius
See also DLB 211

Catton, (Charles) Bruce 1899-1978 . **CLC 35**
See also AITN 1; CA 5-8R; 81-84; CANR 7, 74; DLB 17; SATA 2; SATA-Obit 24

Catullus c. 84B.C.-54B.C. .... **CMLC 18**
See also AW 2; CDWLB 1; DLB 211; RGWL 2

Cauldwell, Frank
See King, Francis (Henry)

Caunitz, William J. 1933-1996 .... **CLC 34**
See also BEST 89:3; CA 125; 130; 152; CANR 73; INT 130

Causley, Charles (Stanley) 1917- .... **CLC 7**
See also CA 9-12R; CANR 5, 35, 94; CLR 30; CWRI 5; DLB 27; MTCW 1; SATA 3, 66

Caute, (John) David 1936- .... **CLC 29**
See also CA 1-4R; CAAS 4; CANR 1, 33, 64; CBD; CD 5; CN 7; DAM NOV; DLB 14, 231

Cavafy, C(onstantine) P(eter) ... **TCLC 2, 7; PC 36**
See also Kavafis, Konstantinos Petrou
See also CA 148; DA3; DAM POET; EW 8; MTCW 1; RGWL 2; WP

Cavallo, Evelyn
See Spark, Muriel (Sarah)

Cavanna, Betty .... **CLC 12**
See also Harrison, Elizabeth (Allen) Cavanna
See also JRDA; MAICYA 1; SAAS 4; SATA 1, 30

Cavendish, Margaret Lucas
1623-1673 .... **LC 30**
See also DLB 131, 252; RGEL 2

Caxton, William 1421(?)-1491(?) .... **LC 17**
See also DLB 170

Cayer, D. M.
See Duffy, Maureen

Cayrol, Jean 1911- .... **CLC 11**
See also CA 89-92; DLB 83

Cela, Camilo Jose 1916-2002 .... **CLC 4, 13, 59, 122; HLC 1**
See also BEST 90:2; CA 21-24R; CAAS 10; CANR 21, 32, 76; DAM MULT; DLBY 1989; EW 13; HW 1; MTCW 1, 2; RGSF 2; RGWL 2

Celan, Paul -1970 .... **CLC 10, 19, 53, 82; PC 10**
See also Antschel, Paul
See also CDWLB 2; DLB 69; RGWL 2

Celine, Louis-Ferdinand .. **CLC 1, 3, 4, 7, 9, 15, 47, 124**
See also Destouches, Louis-Ferdinand
See also DLB 72; EW 11; GFL 1789 to the Present; RGWL 2

Cellini, Benvenuto 1500-1571 .... **LC 7**

Cendrars, Blaise .... **CLC 18, 106**
See also Sauser-Hall, Frederic
See also DLB 258; GFL 1789 to the Present; RGWL 2; WP

Centlivre, Susanna 1669(?)-1723 .... **LC 65**
See also DLB 84; RGEL 2

Cernuda (y Bidon), Luis 1902-1963 . **CLC 54**
See also CA 131; 89-92; DAM POET; DLB 134; GLL 1; HW 1; RGWL 2

Cervantes, Lorna Dee 1954- .... **PC 35**
See also CA 131; CANR 80; CWP; DLB 82; EXPP; HLCS 1; HW 1

Cervantes (Saavedra), Miguel de
1547-1616 .... **LC 6, 23; HLCS; SSC 12; WLC**
See also BYA 1, 14; DA; DAB; DAC; DAM MST, NOV; EW 2; LAIT 1; NFS 8; RGSF 2; RGWL 2

Cesaire, Aime (Fernand) 1913- . **CLC 19, 32, 112; BLC 1; PC 25**
See also BW 2, 3; CA 65-68; CANR 24, 43, 81; DA3; DAM MULT, POET; GFL 1789 to the Present; MTCW 1, 2; WP

Chabon, Michael 1963- .... **CLC 55, 149**
See also CA 139; CANR 57, 96

Chabrol, Claude 1930- .... **CLC 16**
See also CA 110

Challans, Mary 1905-1983
See Renault, Mary
See also CA 81-84; 111; CANR 74; DA3; MTCW 2; SATA 23; SATA-Obit 36

Challis, George
See Faust, Frederick (Schiller)
See also TCWW 2

Chambers, Aidan 1934- .... **CLC 35**
See also AAYA 27; CA 25-28R; CANR 12, 31, 58; JRDA; MAICYA 1, 2; SAAS 12; SATA 1, 69, 108; WYA; YAW

Chambers, James 1948-
See Cliff, Jimmy
See also CA 124

Chambers, Jessie
See Lawrence, D(avid) H(erbert Richards)
See also GLL 1

Chambers, Robert W(illiam)
1865-1933 .... **TCLC 41**
See also CA 165; DLB 202; HGG; SATA 107; SUFW

Chamisso, Adelbert von
1781-1838 .... **NCLC 82**
See also DLB 90; RGWL 2; SUFW

Chandler, Raymond (Thornton)
1888-1959 .... **TCLC 1, 7; SSC 23**
See also AAYA 25; AMWS 4; BPFB 1; CA 104; 129; CANR 60, 107; CDALB 1929-1941; CMW 4; DA3; DLB 226, 253; DLBD 6; MSW; MTCW 1, 2; RGAL 4

Chang, Eileen 1921-1995 .... **SSC 28**
See also CA 166; CWW 2

Chang, Jung 1952- .... **CLC 71**
See also CA 142

Chang Ai-Ling
See Chang, Eileen

Channing, William Ellery
1780-1842 .... **NCLC 17**
See also DLB 1, 59, 235; RGAL 4

Chao, Patricia 1955- .... **CLC 119**
See also CA 163

Chaplin, Charles Spencer
1889-1977 .... **CLC 16**
See also Chaplin, Charlie
See also CA 81-84; 73-76

Chaplin, Charlie
See Chaplin, Charles Spencer
See also DLB 44

Chapman, George 1559(?)-1634 .... **LC 22**
See also BRW 1; DAM DRAM; DLB 62, 121; RGEL 2

Chapman, Graham 1941-1989 .... **CLC 21**
See also Monty Python
See also CA 116; 129; CANR 35, 95

Chapman, John Jay 1862-1933 .... **TCLC 7**
See also CA 104; 191

Chapman, Lee
See Bradley, Marion Zimmer
See also GLL 1

Chapman, Walker
See Silverberg, Robert

Chappell, Fred (Davis) 1936- ..... **CLC 40, 78**
See also CA 5-8R; CAAE 198; CAAS 4; CANR 8, 33, 67; CN 7; CP 7; CSW; DLB 6, 105; HGG

Char, Rene(-Emile) 1907-1988 .... **CLC 9, 11, 14, 55**
See also CA 13-16R; 124; CANR 32; DAM POET; DLB 258; GFL 1789 to the Present; MTCW 1, 2; RGWL 2

Charby, Jay
See Ellison, Harlan (Jay)

Chardin, Pierre Teilhard de
See Teilhard de Chardin, (Marie Joseph) Pierre

Chariton fl. 1st cent. (?)- .... **CMLC 49**

Charlemagne 742-814 .... **CMLC 37**

Charles I 1600-1649 .... **LC 13**

Charriere, Isabelle de 1740-1805 .. **NCLC 66**

Chartier, Emile-Auguste
See Alain

Charyn, Jerome 1937- .... **CLC 5, 8, 18**
See also CA 5-8R; CAAS 1; CANR 7, 61, 101; CMW 4; CN 7; DLBY 1983; MTCW 1

Chase, Adam
See Marlowe, Stephen

Chase, Mary (Coyle) 1907-1981 .... **DC 1**
See also CA 77-80; 105; CAD; CWD; DFS 11; DLB 228; SATA 17; SATA-Obit 29

Chase, Mary Ellen 1887-1973 .... **CLC 2**
See also CA 13-16; 41-44R; CAP 1; SATA 10

Chase, Nicholas
See Hyde, Anthony
See also CCA 1

Chateaubriand, Francois Rene de 1768-1848 .... **NCLC 3**
See also DLB 119; EW 5; GFL 1789 to the Present; RGWL 2

Chatterje, Sarat Chandra 1876-1936(?)
See Chatterji, Saratchandra
See also CA 109

Chatterji, Bankim Chandra 1838-1894 .... **NCLC 19**

Chatterji, Saratchandra .... **TCLC 13**
See also Chatterje, Sarat Chandra
See also CA 186

Chatterton, Thomas 1752-1770 .... **LC 3, 54**
See also DAM POET; DLB 109; RGEL 2

Chatwin, (Charles) Bruce 1940-1989 .... **CLC 28, 57, 59**
See also AAYA 4; BEST 90:1; BRWS 4; CA 85-88; 127; CPW; DAM POP; DLB 194, 204

Chaucer, Daniel
See Ford, Ford Madox
See also RHW

Chaucer, Geoffrey 1340(?)-1400 .. **LC 17, 56; PC 19; WLCS**
See also BRW 1; BRWR 2; CDBLB Before 1660; DA; DA3; DAB; DAC; DAM MST, POET; DLB 146; LAIT 1; PAB; PFS 14; RGEL 2; WLIT 3; WP

Chavez, Denise (Elia) 1948-
See also CA 131; CANR 56, 81; DAM MULT; DLB 122; FW; HLC 1; HW 1, 2; MTCW 2

Chaviaras, Strates 1935-
See Haviaras, Stratis
See also CA 105

Chayefsky, Paddy .... **CLC 23**
See also Chayefsky, Sidney
See also CAD; DLB 7, 44; DLBY 1981; RGAL 4

Chayefsky, Sidney 1923-1981
See Chayefsky, Paddy
See also CA 9-12R; 104; CANR 18; DAM DRAM

Chedid, Andree 1920- .... **CLC 47**
See also CA 145; CANR 95

Cheever, John 1912-1982 ..... **CLC 3, 7, 8, 11, 15, 25, 64; SSC 1, 38; WLC**
See also AMWS 1; BPFB 1; CA 5-8R; 106; CABS 1; CANR 5, 27, 76; CDALB 1941-1968; CPW; DA; DA3; DAB; DAC; DAM MST, NOV, POP; DLB 2, 102, 227; DLBY 1980, 1982; EXPS; INT CANR-5; MTCW 1, 2; RGAL 4; RGSF 2; SSFS 2, 14

Cheever, Susan 1943- .... **CLC 18, 48**
See also CA 103; CANR 27, 51, 92; DLBY 1982; INT CANR-27

Chekhonte, Antosha
See Chekhov, Anton (Pavlovich)

Chekhov, Anton (Pavlovich) 1860-1904 . **TCLC 3, 10, 31, 55, 96; DC 9; SSC 2, 28, 41, 51; WLC**
See also BYA 14; CA 104; 124; DA; DA3; DAB; DAC; DAM DRAM, MST; DFS 1, 5, 10, 12; EW 7; EXPS; LAIT 3; RGSF 2; RGWL 2; SATA 90; SSFS 5, 13, 14

Cheney, Lynne V. 1941- .... **CLC 70**
See also CA 89-92; CANR 58

Chernyshevsky, Nikolai Gavrilovich
See Chernyshevsky, Nikolay Gavrilovich
See also DLB 238

Chernyshevsky, Nikolay Gavrilovich 1828-1889 .... **NCLC 1**
See also Chernyshevsky, Nikolai Gavrilovich

Cherry, Carolyn Janice 1942-
See Cherryh, C. J.
See also CA 65-68; CANR 10

Cherryh, C. J. .... **CLC 35**
See also Cherry, Carolyn Janice
See also AAYA 24; BPFB 1; DLBY 1980; FANT; SATA 93; SCFW 2; SFW 4; YAW

Chesnutt, Charles W(addell) 1858-1932 . **TCLC 5, 39; BLC 1; SSC 7**
See also AFAW 1; BW 1, 3; CA 106; 125; CANR 76; DAM MULT; DLB 12, 50, 78; MTCW 1, 2; RGAL 4; RGSF 2; SSFS 11

Chester, Alfred 1929(?)-1971 .... **CLC 49**
See also CA 196; 33-36R; DLB 130

Chesterton, G(ilbert) K(eith) 1874-1936 . **TCLC 1, 6, 64; PC 28; SSC 1, 46**
See also BRW 6; CA 104; 132; CANR 73; CDBLB 1914-1945; CMW 4; DAM NOV, POET; DLB 10, 19, 34, 70, 98, 149, 178; FANT; MSW; MTCW 1, 2; RGEL 2; RGSF 2; SATA 27; SUFW

Chiang, Pin-chin 1904-1986
See Ding Ling
See also CA 118

Ch'ien, Chung-shu 1910-1998 .... **CLC 22**
See also CA 130, CANR 73, MTCW 1, 2

Chikamatsu Monzaemon 1653-1724 ... **LC 66**
See also RGWL 2

Child, L. Maria
See Child, Lydia Maria

Child, Lydia Maria 1802-1880 .. **NCLC 6, 73**
See also DLB 1, 74, 243; RGAL 4; SATA 67

Child, Mrs.
See Child, Lydia Maria

Child, Philip 1898-1978 .... **CLC 19, 68**
See also CA 13-14; CAP 1; DLB 68; RHW; SATA 47

Childers, (Robert) Erskine 1870-1922 .... **TCLC 65**
See also CA 113; 153; DLB 70

Childress, Alice 1920-1994 .. **CLC 12, 15, 86, 96; BLC 1; DC 4**
See also AAYA 8; BW 2, 3; BYA 2; CA 45-48; 146; CAD; CANR 3, 27, 50, 74; CLR 14; CWD; DA3; DAM DRAM, MULT, NOV; DFS 2, 8, 14; DLB 7, 38, 249; JRDA; LAIT 5; MAICYA 1, 2; MAICYAS 1; MTCW 1, 2; RGAL 4; SATA 7, 48, 81; TCLC 116; WYA; YAW

Chin, Frank (Chew, Jr.) 1940- ...... **CLC 135; DC 7**
See also CA 33-36R; CANR 71; CD 5; DAM MULT; DLB 206; LAIT 5; RGAL 4

Chin, Marilyn (Mei Ling) 1955- .... **PC 40**
See also CA 129; CANR 70; CWP

Chislett, (Margaret) Anne 1943- ...... **CLC 34**
See also CA 151

Chitty, Thomas Willes 1926- .... **CLC 11**
See also Hinde, Thomas
See also CA 5-8R; CN 7

Chivers, Thomas Holley 1809-1858 .... **NCLC 49**
See also DLB 3, 248; RGAL 4

Choi, Susan .... **CLC 119**

Chomette, Rene Lucien 1898-1981
See Clair, Rene
See also CA 103

Chomsky, (Avram) Noam 1928- ..... **CLC 132**
See also CA 17-20R; CANR 28, 62; DA3; DLB 246; MTCW 1, 2

Chopin, Kate .. **TCLC 5, 14; SSC 8; WLCS**
See also Chopin, Katherine
See also AAYA 33; AMWS 1; CDALB 1865-1917; DA; DAB; DLB 12, 78; EXPN; EXPS; FW; LAIT 3; MAWW; NFS 3; RGAL 4; RGSF 2; SSFS 2, 13

Chopin, Katherine 1851-1904
See Chopin, Kate
See also CA 104; 122; DA3; DAC; DAM MST, NOV

Chretien de Troyes c. 12th cent. - . **CMLC 10**
See also DLB 208; EW 1; RGWL 2

Christie
See Ichikawa, Kon

Christie, Agatha (Mary Clarissa) 1890-1976 .. **CLC 1, 6, 8, 12, 39, 48, 110**
See also AAYA 9; AITN 1, 2; BPFB 1; BRWS 2; CA 17-20R; 61-64; CANR 10, 37, 108; CBD; CDBLB 1914-1945; CMW 4; CPW; CWD; DA3; DAB; DAC; DAM NOV; DFS 2; DLB 13, 77, 245; MSW; MTCW 1, 2; NFS 8; RGEL 2; RHW; SATA 36; YAW

Christie, (Ann) Philippa .... **CLC 21**
See also Pearce, Philippa
See also BYA 5; CANR 109; CLR 9; DLB 161; MAICYA 1; SATA 1, 67, 129

Christine de Pizan 1365(?)-1431(?) .... **LC 9**
See also DLB 208; RGWL 2

Chubb, Elmer
See Masters, Edgar Lee

Chulkov, Mikhail Dmitrievich 1743-1792 .... **LC 2**
See also DLB 150

Churchill, Caryl 1938- .... **CLC 31, 55, 157; DC 5**
See also BRWS 4; CA 102; CANR 22, 46, 108; CBD; CWD; DFS 12; DLB 13; FW; MTCW 1; RGEL 2

Churchill, Charles 1731-1764 .... **LC 3**
See also DLB 109; RGEL 2
Churchill, Sir Winston (Leonard Spencer)
1874-1965 .... **TCLC 113**
See also BRW 6; CA 97-100; CDBLB
1890-1914; DA3; DLB 100; DLBD 16;
LAIT 4; MTCW 1, 2
Chute, Carolyn 1947- .... **CLC 39**
See also CA 123
Ciardi, John (Anthony) 1916-1986 . **CLC 10, 40, 44, 129**
See also CA 5-8R; 118; CAAS 2; CANR 5,
33; CLR 19; CWRI 5; DAM POET; DLB
5; DLBY 1986; INT CANR-5; MAICYA
1, 2; MTCW 1, 2; RGAL 4; SAAS 26;
SATA 1, 65; SATA-Obit 46
Cibber, Colley 1671-1757 .... **LC 66**
See also DLB 84; RGEL 2
Cicero, Marcus Tullius
106B.C.-43B.C. .... **CMLC 3**
See also AW 1; CDWLB 1; DLB 211;
RGWL 2
Cimino, Michael 1943- .... **CLC 16**
See also CA 105
Cioran, E(mil) M. 1911-1995 .... **CLC 64**
See also CA 25-28R; 149; CANR 91; DLB
220
Cisneros, Sandra 1954- .. **CLC 69, 118; HLC 1; SSC 32**
See also AAYA 9; AMWS 7; CA 131;
CANR 64; CWP; DA3; DAM MULT;
DLB 122, 152; EXPN; FW; HW 1, 2;
LAIT 5; MAICYA 2; MTCW 2; NFS 2;
RGAL 4; RGSF 2; SSFS 3, 13; WLIT 1;
YAW
Cixous, Helene 1937- .... **CLC 92**
See also CA 126; CANR 55; CWW 2; DLB
83, 242; FW; GLL 2; MTCW 1, 2
Clair, Rene .... **CLC 20**
See also Chomette, Rene Lucien
Clampitt, Amy 1920-1994 .... **CLC 32; PC 19**
See also AMWS 9; CA 110; 146; CANR
29, 79; DLB 105
Clancy, Thomas L., Jr. 1947-
See Clancy, Tom
See also CA 125; 131; CANR 62, 105;
DA3; INT CA-131; MTCW 1, 2
Clancy, Tom .... **CLC 45, 112**
See also Clancy, Thomas L., Jr.
See also AAYA 9; BEST 89:1, 90:1; BPFB
1; BYA 10, 11; CMW 4; CPW; DAM
NOV, POP; DLB 227
Clare, John 1793-1864 .. **NCLC 9, 86; PC 23**
See also DAB; DAM POET; DLB 55, 96;
RGEL 2
Clarin
See Alas (y Urena), Leopoldo (Enrique
Garcia)
Clark, Al C.
See Goines, Donald
Clark, (Robert) Brian 1932- .... **CLC 29**
See also CA 41-44R; CANR 67; CBD; CD
5
Clark, Curt
See Westlake, Donald E(dwin)
Clark, Eleanor 1913-1996 .... **CLC 5, 19**
See also CA 9-12R; 151; CANR 41; CN 7;
DLB 6
Clark, J. P.
See Clark Bekedermo, J(ohnson) P(epper)
See also CDWLB 3; DLB 117
Clark, John Pepper
See Clark Bekedermo, J(ohnson) P(epper)
See also AFW; CD 5; CP 7; RGEL 2
Clark, M. R.
See Clark, Mavis Thorpe

Clark, Mavis Thorpe 1909-1999 ...... **CLC 12**
See also CA 57-60; CANR 8, 37, 107; CLR
30; CWRI 5; MAICYA 1, 2; SAAS 5;
SATA 8, 74
Clark, Walter Van Tilburg
1909-1971 .... **CLC 28**
See also CA 9-12R; 33-36R; CANR 63;
DLB 9, 206; LAIT 2; RGAL 4; SATA 8
Clark Bekedermo, J(ohnson) P(epper)
1935- .... **CLC 38; BLC 1; DC 5**
See also Clark, J. P.; Clark, John Pepper
See also BW 1; CA 65-68; CANR 16, 72;
DAM DRAM, MULT; DFS 13; MTCW 1
Clarke, Arthur C(harles) 1917- .... **CLC 1, 4, 13, 18, 35, 136; SSC 3**
See also AAYA 4, 33; BPFB 1; BYA 13;
CA 1-4R; CANR 2, 28, 55, 74; CN 7;
CPW; DA3; DAM POP; JRDA; LAIT 5;
MAICYA 1, 2; MTCW 1, 2; SATA 13,
70, 115; SCFW; SFW 4; SSFS 4; YAW
Clarke, Austin 1896-1974 .... **CLC 6, 9**
See also CA 29-32; 49-52; CAP 2; DAM
POET; DLB 10, 20; RGEL 2
Clarke, Austin C(hesterfield) 1934- .. **CLC 8, 53; BLC 1; SSC 45**
See also BW 1; CA 25-28R; CAAS 16;
CANR 14, 32, 68; CN 7; DAC; DAM
MULT; DLB 53, 125; DNFS 2; RGSF 2
Clarke, Gillian 1937- .... **CLC 61**
See also CA 106; CP 7; CWP; DLB 40
Clarke, Marcus (Andrew Hislop)
1846-1881 .... **NCLC 19**
See also DLB 230; RGEL 2; RGSF 2
Clarke, Shirley 1925-1997 .... **CLC 16**
See also CA 189
Clash, The
See Headon, (Nicky) Topper; Jones, Mick;
Simonon, Paul; Strummer, Joe
Claudel, Paul (Louis Charles Marie)
1868-1955 .... **TCLC 2, 10**
See also CA 104; 165; DLB 192, 258; EW
8; GFL 1789 to the Present; RGWL 2
Claudian 370(?)-404(?) .... **CMLC 46**
See also RGWL 2
Claudius, Matthias 1740-1815 .... **NCLC 75**
See also DLB 97
Clavell, James (duMaresq)
1925-1994 .... **CLC 6, 25, 87**
See also BPFB 1; CA 25-28R; 146; CANR
26, 48; CPW; DA3; DAM NOV, POP;
MTCW 1, 2; NFS 10; RHW
Clayman, Gregory .... **CLC 65**
Cleaver, (Leroy) Eldridge
1935-1998 .... **CLC 30, 119; BLC 1**
See also BW 1, 3; CA 21-24R; 167; CANR
16, 75; DA3; DAM MULT; MTCW 2;
YAW
Cleese, John (Marwood) 1939- .... **CLC 21**
See also Monty Python
See also CA 112; 116; CANR 35; MTCW 1
Cleishbotham, Jebediah
See Scott, Sir Walter
Cleland, John 1710-1789 .... **LC 2, 48**
See also DLB 39; RGEL 2
Clemens, Samuel Langhorne 1835-1910
See Twain, Mark
See also CA 104; 135; CDALB 1865-1917;
DA; DA3; DAB; DAC; DAM MST, NOV;
DLB 12, 23, 64, 74, 186, 189; JRDA;
MAICYA 1, 2; SATA 100; YABC 2
Clement of Alexandria
150(?)-215(?) .... **CMLC 41**
Cleophil
See Congreve, William
Clerihew, E.
See Bentley, E(dmund) C(lerihew)
Clerk, N. W.
See Lewis, C(live) S(taples)

Cliff, Jimmy .... **CLC 21**
See also Chambers, James
See also CA 193
Cliff, Michelle 1946- .... **CLC 120; BLCS**
See also BW 2; CA 116; CANR 39, 72; CD-
WLB 3; DLB 157; FW; GLL 2
Clifford, Lady Anne 1590-1676 .... **LC 76**
See also DLB 151
Clifton, (Thelma) Lucille 1936- .... **CLC 19, 66; BLC 1; PC 17**
See also AFAW 2; BW 2, 3; CA 49-52;
CANR 2, 24, 42, 76, 97; CLR 5; CP 7;
CSW; CWP; CWRI 5; DA3; DAM MULT,
POET; DLB 5, 41; EXPP; MAICYA 1, 2;
MTCW 1, 2; PFS 1, 14; SATA 20, 69,
128; WP
Clinton, Dirk
See Silverberg, Robert
Clough, Arthur Hugh 1819-1861 ... **NCLC 27**
See also BRW 5; DLB 32; RGEL 2
Clutha, Janet Paterson Frame 1924-
See Frame, Janet
See also CA 1-4R; CANR 2, 36, 76; MTCW
1, 2; SATA 119
Clyne, Terence
See Blatty, William Peter
Cobalt, Martin
See Mayne, William (James Carter)
Cobb, Irvin S(hrewsbury)
1876-1944 .... **TCLC 77**
See also CA 175; DLB 11, 25, 86
Cobbett, William 1763-1835 .... **NCLC 49**
See also DLB 43, 107, 158; RGEL 2
Coburn, D(onald) L(ee) 1938- .... **CLC 10**
See also CA 89-92
Cocteau, Jean (Maurice Eugene Clement)
1889-1963 ...... **CLC 1, 8, 15, 16, 43; DC 17; WLC**
See also CA 25-28; CANR 40; CAP 2; DA;
DA3; DAB; DAC; DAM DRAM, MST,
NOV; DLB 65, 258; EW 10; GFL 1789 to
the Present; MTCW 1, 2; RGWL 2; TCLC
119
Codrescu, Andrei 1946- .... **CLC 46, 121**
See also CA 33-36R; CAAS 19; CANR 13,
34, 53, 76; DA3; DAM POET; MTCW 2
Coe, Max
See Bourne, Randolph S(illiman)
Coe, Tucker
See Westlake, Donald E(dwin)
Coen, Ethan 1958- .... **CLC 108**
See also CA 126; CANR 85
Coen, Joel 1955- .... **CLC 108**
See also CA 126
The Coen Brothers
See Coen, Ethan; Coen, Joel
Coetzee, J(ohn) M(ichael) 1940- ...... **CLC 23, 33, 66, 117**
See also AAYA 37; AFW; BRWS 6; CA 77-
80; CANR 41, 54, 74; CN 7; DA3; DAM
NOV; DLB 225; MTCW 1, 2; WLIT 2
Coffey, Brian
See Koontz, Dean R(ay)
Coffin, Robert P(eter) Tristram
1892-1955 .... **TCLC 95**
See also CA 123; 169; DLB 45
Cohan, George M(ichael)
1878-1942 .... **TCLC 60**
See also CA 157; DLB 249; RGAL 4
Cohen, Arthur A(llen) 1928-1986 ...... **CLC 7, 31**
See also CA 1-4R; 120; CANR 1, 17, 42;
DLB 28
Cohen, Leonard (Norman) 1934- ...... **CLC 3, 38**
See also CA 21-24R; CANR 14, 69; CN 7;
CP 7; DAC; DAM MST; DLB 53;
MTCW 1

Cohen, Matt(hew) 1942-1999 .... **CLC 19**
See also CA 61-64; 187; CAAS 18; CANR 40; CN 7; DAC; DLB 53
Cohen-Solal, Annie 19(?)- .... **CLC 50**
Colegate, Isabel 1931- .... **CLC 36**
See also CA 17-20R; CANR 8, 22, 74; CN 7; DLB 14, 231; INT CANR-22; MTCW 1
Coleman, Emmett
See Reed, Ishmael
Coleridge, Hartley 1796-1849 .... **NCLC 90**
See also DLB 96
Coleridge, M. E.
See Coleridge, Mary E(lizabeth)
Coleridge, Mary E(lizabeth)
1861-1907 .... **TCLC 73**
See also CA 116; 166; DLB 19, 98
Coleridge, Samuel Taylor
1772-1834 ...... **NCLC 9, 54, 99, 111; PC 11, 39; WLC**
See also BRW 4; BRWR 2; BYA 4; CDBLB 1789-1832; DA; DA3; DAB; DAC; DAM MST, POET; DLB 93, 107; EXPP; PAB; PFS 4, 5; RGEL 2; WLIT 3; WP
Coleridge, Sara 1802-1852 .... **NCLC 31**
See also DLB 199
Coles, Don 1928- .... **CLC 46**
See also CA 115; CANR 38; CP 7
Coles, Robert (Martin) 1929- .... **CLC 108**
See also CA 45-48; CANR 3, 32, 66, 70; INT CANR-32; SATA 23
Colette, (Sidonie-Gabrielle)
1873-1954 .... **TCLC 1, 5, 16; SSC 10**
See also Willy, Colette
See also CA 104; 131; DA3; DAM NOV; DLB 65; EW 9; GFL 1789 to the Present; MTCW 1, 2; RGWL 2
Collett, (Jacobine) Camilla (Wergeland)
1813-1895 .... **NCLC 22**
Collier, Christopher 1930- .... **CLC 30**
See also AAYA 13; BYA 2; CA 33-36R; CANR 13, 33, 102; JRDA; MAICYA 1, 2; SATA 16, 70; WYA; YAW 1
Collier, James Lincoln 1928- .... **CLC 30**
See also AAYA 13; BYA 2; CA 9-12R; CANR 4, 33, 60, 102; CLR 3; DAM POP; JRDA; MAICYA 1, 2; SAAS 21; SATA 8, 70; WYA; YAW 1
Collier, Jeremy 1650-1726 .... **LC 6**
Collier, John 1901-1980 .... **SSC 19**
See also CA 65-68; 97-100; CANR 10; DLB 77, 255; FANT; SUFW
Collingwood, R(obin) G(eorge)
1889(?)-1943 .... **TCLC 67**
See also CA 117; 155
Collins, Hunt
See Hunter, Evan
Collins, Linda 1931- .... **CLC 44**
See also CA 125
Collins, (William) Wilkie
1824-1889 .... **NCLC 1, 18, 93**
See also BRWS 6; CDBLB 1832-1890; CMW 4; DLB 18, 70, 159; MSW; RGEL 2; RGSF 2; SUFW; WLIT 4
Collins, William 1721-1759 .... **LC 4, 40**
See also BRW 3; DAM POET; DLB 109; RGEL 2
Collodi, Carlo .... **NCLC 54**
See also Lorenzini, Carlo
See also CLR 5; WCH
Colman, George
See Glassco, John
Colonna, Vittoria 1492-1547 .... **LC 71**
See also RGWL 2
Colt, Winchester Remington
See Hubbard, L(afayette) Ron(ald)
Colter, Cyrus 1910-2002 .... **CLC 58**
See also BW 1; CA 65-68; CANR 10, 66; CN 7; DLB 33

Colton, James
See Hansen, Joseph
See also GLL 1
Colum, Padraic 1881-1972 .... **CLC 28**
See also BYA 4; CA 73-76; 33-36R; CANR 35; CLR 36; CWRI 5; DLB 19; MAICYA 1, 2; MTCW 1; RGEL 2; SATA 15; WCH
Colvin, James
See Moorcock, Michael (John)
Colwin, Laurie (E.) 1944-1992 .... **CLC 5, 13, 23, 84**
See also CA 89-92; 139; CANR 20, 46; DLB 218; DLBY 1980; MTCW 1
Comfort, Alex(ander) 1920-2000 .... **CLC 7**
See also CA 1-4R; 190; CANR 1, 45; CP 7; DAM POP; MTCW 1
Comfort, Montgomery
See Campbell, (John) Ramsey
Compton-Burnett, I(vy)
1892(?)-1969 .... **CLC 1, 3, 10, 15, 34**
See also BRW 7; CA 1-4R; 25-28R; CANR 4; DAM NOV; DLB 36; MTCW 1; RGEL 2
Comstock, Anthony 1844-1915 ...... **TCLC 13**
See also CA 110; 169
Comte, Auguste 1798-1857 .... **NCLC 54**
Conan Doyle, Arthur
See Doyle, Sir Arthur Conan
See also BPFB 1; BYA 4, 5, 11
Conde (Abellan), Carmen 1901-1996
See also CA 177; DLB 108; HLCS 1; HW 2
Conde, Maryse 1937- ..... **CLC 52, 92; BLCS**
See also BW 2, 3; CA 110; CAAE 190; CANR 30, 53, 76; CWW 2; DAM MULT; MTCW 1
Condillac, Etienne Bonnot de
1714-1780 .... **LC 26**
Condon, Richard (Thomas)
1915-1996 .... **CLC 4, 6, 8, 10, 45, 100**
See also BEST 90:3; BPFB 1; CA 1-4R; 151; CAAS 1; CANR 2, 23; CMW 4; CN 7; DAM NOV; INT CANR-23; MTCW 1, 2
Confucius 551B.C.-479B.C. .... **CMLC 19; WLCS**
See also DA; DA3; DAB; DAC; DAM MST
Congreve, William 1670-1729 . **LC 5, 21; DC 2; WLC**
See also BRW 2; CDBLB 1660-1789; DA; DAB; DAC; DAM DRAM, MST, POET; DFS 14; DLB 39, 84; RGEL 2; WLIT 3
Connell, Evan S(helby), Jr. 1924- . **CLC 4, 6, 45**
See also AAYA 7; CA 1-4R; CAAS 2; CANR 2, 39, 76, 97; CN 7; DAM NOV; DLB 2; DLBY 1981; MTCW 1, 2
Connelly, Marc(us Cook) 1890-1980 . **CLC 7**
See also CA 85-88; 102; CANR 30; DFS 12; DLB 7; DLBY 1980; RGAL 4; SATA-Obit 25
Connor, Ralph .... **TCLC 31**
See also Gordon, Charles William
See also DLB 92; TCWW 2
Conrad, Joseph 1857-1924 ... **TCLC 1, 6, 13, 25, 43, 57; SSC 9; WLC**
See also AAYA 26; BPFB 1; BRW 6; BRWR 2; BYA 2; CA 104; 131; CANR 60; CDBLB 1890-1914; DA; DA3; DAB; DAC; DAM MST, NOV; DLB 10, 34, 98, 156; EXPN; EXPS; LAIT 2; MTCW 1, 2; NFS 2; RGEL 2; RGSF 2; SATA 27; SSFS 1, 12; WLIT 4
Conrad, Robert Arnold
See Hart, Moss

Conroy, (Donald) Pat(rick) 1945- ... **CLC 30, 74**
See also AAYA 8; AITN 1; BPFB 1; CA 85-88; CANR 24, 53; CPW; CSW; DA3; DAM NOV, POP; DLB 6; LAIT 5; MTCW 1, 2
Constant (de Rebecque), (Henri) Benjamin
1767-1830 .... **NCLC 6**
See also DLB 119; EW 4; GFL 1789 to the Present
Conway, Jill K(er) 1934- .... **CLC 152**
See also CA 130; CANR 94
Conybeare, Charles Augustus
See Eliot, T(homas) S(tearns)
Cook, Michael 1933-1994 .... **CLC 58**
See also CA 93-96; CANR 68; DLB 53
Cook, Robin 1940- .... **CLC 14**
See also AAYA 32; BEST 90:2; BPFB 1; CA 108; 111; CANR 41, 90, 109; CPW; DA3; DAM POP; HGG; INT CA-111
Cook, Roy
See Silverberg, Robert
Cooke, Elizabeth 1948- .... **CLC 55**
See also CA 129
Cooke, John Esten 1830-1886 .... **NCLC 5**
See also DLB 3, 248; RGAL 4
Cooke, John Estes
See Baum, L(yman) Frank
Cooke, M. E.
See Creasey, John
Cooke, Margaret
See Creasey, John
Cooke, Rose Terry 1827-1892 ...... **NCLC 110**
See also DLB 12, 74
Cook-Lynn, Elizabeth 1930- .... **CLC 93**
See also CA 133; DAM MULT; DLB 175; NNAL
Cooney, Ray .... **CLC 62**
See also CBD
Cooper, Douglas 1960- .... **CLC 86**
Cooper, Henry St. John
See Creasey, John
Cooper, J(oan) California (?)- .... **CLC 56**
See also AAYA 12; BW 1; CA 125; CANR 55; DAM MULT; DLB 212
Cooper, James Fenimore
1789-1851 .... **NCLC 1, 27, 54**
See also AAYA 22; AMW; BPFB 1; CDALB 1640-1865; DA3; DLB 3, 183, 250, 254; LAIT 1; NFS 9; RGAL 4; SATA 19; WCH
Coover, Robert (Lowell) 1932- ...... **CLC 3, 7, 15, 32, 46, 87; SSC 15**
See also AMWS 5; BPFB 1; CA 45-48; CANR 3, 37, 58; CN 7; DAM NOV; DLB 2, 227; DLBY 1981; MTCW 1, 2; RGAL 4; RGSF 2
Copeland, Stewart (Armstrong)
1952- .... **CLC 26**
Copernicus, Nicolaus 1473-1543 .... **LC 45**
Coppard, A(lfred) E(dgar)
1878-1957 .... **TCLC 5; SSC 21**
See also CA 114; 167; DLB 162; HGG; RGEL 2; RGSF 2; SUFW; YABC 1
Coppee, Francois 1842-1908 .... **TCLC 25**
See also CA 170; DLB 217
Coppola, Francis Ford 1939- ... **CLC 16, 126**
See also AAYA 39; CA 77-80; CANR 40, 78; DLB 44
Corbiere, Tristan 1845-1875 .... **NCLC 43**
See also DLB 217; GFL 1789 to the Present
Corcoran, Barbara (Asenath)
1911- .... **CLC 17**
See also AAYA 14; CA 21-24R; CAAE 191; CAAS 2; CANR 11, 28, 48; CLR 50; DLB 52; JRDA; MAICYA 2; MAICYAS 1; RHW; SAAS 20; SATA 3, 77, 125
Cordelier, Maurice
See Giraudoux, Jean(-Hippolyte)

Corelli, Marie .... **TCLC 51**
See also Mackay, Mary
See also DLB 34, 156; RGEL 2; SUFW

Corman, Cid .... **CLC 9**
See also Corman, Sidney
See also CAAS 2; DLB 5, 193

Corman, Sidney 1924-
See Corman, Cid
See also CA 85-88; CANR 44; CP 7; DAM POET

Cormier, Robert (Edmund) 1925-2000 .... **CLC 12, 30**
See also AAYA 3, 19; BYA 1, 2, 6, 8, 9; CA 1-4R; CANR 5, 23, 76, 93; CDALB 1968-1988; CLR 12, 55; DA; DAB; DAC; DAM MST, NOV; DLB 52; EXPN; INT CANR-23; JRDA; LAIT 5; MAICYA 1, 2; MTCW 1, 2; NFS 2; SATA 10, 45, 83; SATA-Obit 122; WYA; YAW

Corn, Alfred (DeWitt III) 1943- .... **CLC 33**
See also CA 179; CAAE 179; CAAS 25; CANR 44; CP 7; CSW; DLB 120; DLBY 1980

Corneille, Pierre 1606-1684 .... **LC 28**
See also DAB; DAM MST; EW 3; GFL Beginnings to 1789; RGWL 2

Cornwell, David (John Moore) 1931- .... **CLC 9, 15**
See also le Carre, John
See also CA 5-8R; CANR 13, 33, 59, 107; DA3; DAM POP; MTCW 1, 2

Cornwell, Patricia (Daniels) 1956- . **CLC 155**
See also AAYA 16; BPFB 1; CA 134; CANR 53; CMW 4; CPW; CSW; DAM POP; MSW; MTCW 1

Corso, (Nunzio) Gregory 1930-2001 . **CLC 1, 11; PC 33**
See also CA 5-8R; 193; CANR 41, 76; CP 7; DA3; DLB 5, 16, 237; MTCW 1, 2; WP

Cortazar, Julio 1914-1984 ... **CLC 2, 3, 5, 10, 13, 15, 33, 34, 92; HLC 1; SSC 7**
See also BPFB 1; CA 21-24R; CANR 12, 32, 81; CDWLB 3; DA3; DAM MULT, NOV; DLB 113; EXPS; HW 1, 2; LAW; MTCW 1, 2; RGSF 2; RGWL 2; SSFS 3; WLIT 1

Cortes, Hernan 1485-1547 .... **LC 31**

Corvinus, Jakob
See Raabe, Wilhelm (Karl)

Corvo, Baron
See Rolfe, Frederick (William Serafino Austin Lewis Mary)
See also GLL 1; RGEL 2

Corwin, Cecil
See Kornbluth, C(yril) M.

Cosic, Dobrica 1921- .... **CLC 14**
See also CA 122; 138; CDWLB 4; CWW 2; DLB 181

Costain, Thomas B(ertram) 1885-1965 .... **CLC 30**
See also BYA 3; CA 5-8R; 25-28R; DLB 9; RHW

Costantini, Humberto 1924(?)-1987 . **CLC 49**
See also CA 131; 122; HW 1

Costello, Elvis 1955- .... **CLC 21**

Costenoble, Philostene 1898-1962
See Ghelderode, Michel de

Costenoble, Philostene 1898-1962
See Ghelderode, Michel de

Cotes, Cecil V.
See Duncan, Sara Jeannette

Cotter, Joseph Seamon Sr. 1861-1949 .... **TCLC 28; BLC 1**
See also BW 1; CA 124; DAM MULT; DLB 50

Couch, Arthur Thomas Quiller
See Quiller-Couch, Sir Arthur (Thomas)

Coulton, James
See Hansen, Joseph

Couperus, Louis (Marie Anne) 1863-1923 .... **TCLC 15**
See also CA 115; RGWL 2

Coupland, Douglas 1961- .... **CLC 85, 133**
See also AAYA 34; CA 142; CANR 57, 90; CCA 1; CPW; DAC; DAM POP

Court, Wesli
See Turco, Lewis (Putnam)

Courtenay, Bryce 1933- .... **CLC 59**
See also CA 138; CPW

Courtney, Robert
See Ellison, Harlan (Jay)

Cousteau, Jacques-Yves 1910-1997 .. **CLC 30**
See also CA 65-68; 159; CANR 15, 67; MTCW 1; SATA 38, 98

Coventry, Francis 1725-1754 .... **LC 46**

Coverdale, Miles c. 1487-1569 .... **LC 77**
See also DLB 167

Cowan, Peter (Walkinshaw) 1914- .... **SSC 28**
See also CA 21-24R; CANR 9, 25, 50, 83; CN 7; RGSF 2

Coward, Noel (Peirce) 1899-1973 . **CLC 1, 9, 29, 51**
See also AITN 1; BRWS 2; CA 17-18; 41-44R; CANR 35; CAP 2; CBD; CDBLB 1914-1945; DA3; DAM DRAM; DFS 3, 6; DLB 10, 245; IDFW 3, 4; MTCW 1, 2; RGEL 2

Cowley, Abraham 1618-1667 .... **LC 43**
See also BRW 2; DLB 131, 151; PAB; RGEL 2

Cowley, Malcolm 1898-1989 .... **CLC 39**
See also AMWS 2; CA 5-8R; 128; CANR 3, 55; DLB 4, 48; DLBY 1981, 1989; MTCW 1, 2

Cowper, William 1731-1800 ..... **NCLC 8, 94; PC 40**
See also BRW 3; DA3; DAM POET; DLB 104, 109; RGEL 2

Cox, William Trevor 1928-
See Trevor, William
See also CA 9-12R; CANR 4, 37, 55, 76, 102; DAM NOV; INT CANR-37; MTCW 1, 2

Coyne, P. J.
See Masters, Hilary

Cozzens, James Gould 1903-1978 . **CLC 1, 4, 11, 92**
See also AMW; BPFB 1; CA 9-12R; 81-84; CANR 19; CDALB 1941-1968; DLB 9; DLBD 2; DLBY 1984, 1997; MTCW 1, 2; RGAL 4

Crabbe, George 1754-1832 .... **NCLC 26**
See also BRW 3; DLB 93; RGEL 2

Crace, Jim 1946- .... **CLC 157**
See also CA 128; 135; CANR 55, 70; CN 7; DLB 231; INT CA-135

Craddock, Charles Egbert
See Murfree, Mary Noailles

Craig, A. A.
See Anderson, Poul (William)

Craik, Mrs.
See Craik, Dinah Maria (Mulock)
See also RGEL 2

Craik, Dinah Maria (Mulock) 1826-1887 .... **NCLC 38**
See also Craik, Mrs.; Mulock, Dinah Maria
See also DLB 35, 163; MAICYA 1, 2; SATA 34

Cram, Ralph Adams 1863-1942 ..... **TCLC 45**
See also CA 160

Crane, (Harold) Hart 1899-1932 .... **TCLC 2, 5, 80; PC 3; WLC**
See also AMW; CA 104; 127; CDALB 1917-1929; DA; DA3; DAB; DAC; DAM MST, POET; DLB 4, 48; MTCW 1, 2; RGAL 4

Crane, R(onald) S(almon) 1886-1967 .... **CLC 27**
See also CA 85-88; DLB 63

Crane, Stephen (Townley) 1871-1900 ...... **TCLC 11, 17, 32; SSC 7; WLC**
See also AAYA 21; AMW; BPFB 1; BYA 3; CA 109; 140; CANR 84; CDALB 1865-1917; DA; DA3; DAB; DAC; DAM MST, NOV, POET; DLB 12, 54, 78; EXPN; EXPS; LAIT 2; NFS 4; PFS 9; RGAL 4; RGSF 2; SSFS 4; WYA; YABC 2

Cranshaw, Stanley
See Fisher, Dorothy (Frances) Canfield

Crase, Douglas 1944- .... **CLC 58**
See also CA 106

Crashaw, Richard 1612(?)-1649 .... **LC 24**
See also BRW 2; DLB 126; PAB; RGEL 2

Craven, Margaret 1901-1980 .... **CLC 17**
See also BYA 2; CA 103; CCA 1; DAC; LAIT 5

Crawford, F(rancis) Marion 1854-1909 .... **TCLC 10**
See also CA 107; 168; DLB 71; HGG; RGAL 4; SUFW

Crawford, Isabella Valancy 1850-1887 .... **NCLC 12**
See also DLB 92; RGEL 2

Crayon, Geoffrey
See Irving, Washington

Creasey, John 1908-1973 .... **CLC 11**
See also Marric, J. J.
See also CA 5-8R; 41-44R; CANR 8, 59; CMW 4; DLB 77; MTCW 1

Crebillon, Claude Prosper Jolyot de (fils) 1707-1777 .... **LC 1, 28**
See also GFL Beginnings to 1789

Credo
See Creasey, John

Credo, Alvaro J. de
See Prado (Calvo), Pedro

Creeley, Robert (White) 1926- .. **CLC 1, 2, 4, 8, 11, 15, 36, 78**
See also AMWS 4; CA 1-4R; CAAS 10; CANR 23, 43, 89; CP 7; DA3; DAM POET; DLB 5, 16, 169; DLBD 17; MTCW 1, 2; RGAL 4; WP

Crevecoeur, Hector St. John de
See Crevecoeur, Michel Guillaume Jean de
See also ANW

Crevecoeur, Michel Guillaume Jean de 1735-1813 .... **NCLC 105**
See also Crevecoeur, Hector St. John de
See also AMWS 1; DLB 37

Crevel, Rene 1900-1935 .... **TCLC 112**
See also GLL 2

Crews, Harry (Eugene) 1935- ..... **CLC 6, 23, 49**
See also AITN 1; BPFB 1; CA 25-28R; CANR 20, 57; CN 7; CSW; DA3; DLB 6, 143, 185; MTCW 1, 2; RGAL 4

Crichton, (John) Michael 1942- .... **CLC 2, 6, 54, 90**
See also AAYA 10; AITN 2; BPFB 1; CA 25-28R; CANR 13, 40, 54, 76; CMW 4; CN 7; CPW; DA3; DAM NOV, POP; DLBY 1981; INT CANR-13; JRDA; MTCW 1, 2; SATA 9, 88; SFW 4; YAW

Crispin, Edmund .... **CLC 22**
See also Montgomery, (Robert) Bruce
See also DLB 87; MSW

Cristofer, Michael 1945(?)- .... **CLC 28**
See also CA 110; 152; CAD; CD 5; DAM DRAM; DLB 7

Croce, Benedetto 1866-1952 .... **TCLC 37**
See also CA 120; 155; EW 8

Crockett, David 1786-1836 .... **NCLC 8**
See also DLB 3, 11, 183, 248

Crockett, Davy
See Crockett, David
Crofts, Freeman Wills 1879-1957 .. **TCLC 55**
See also CA 115; 195; CMW 4; DLB 77; MSW
Croker, John Wilson 1780-1857 .... **NCLC 10**
See also DLB 110
Crommelynck, Fernand 1885-1970 .. **CLC 75**
See also CA 189; 89-92
Cromwell, Oliver 1599-1658 .... **LC 43**
Cronenberg, David 1943- .... **CLC 143**
See also CA 138; CCA 1
Cronin, A(rchibald) J(oseph)
1896-1981 .... **CLC 32**
See also BPFB 1; CA 1-4R; 102; CANR 5; DLB 191; SATA 47; SATA-Obit 25
Cross, Amanda
See Heilbrun, Carolyn G(old)
See also BPFB 1; CMW; CPW; MSW
Crothers, Rachel 1878-1958 .... **TCLC 19**
See also CA 113; 194; CAD; CWD; DLB 7; RGAL 4
Croves, Hal
See Traven, B.
Crow Dog, Mary (Ellen) (?)- .... **CLC 93**
See also Brave Bird, Mary
See also CA 154
Crowfield, Christopher
See Stowe, Harriet (Elizabeth) Beecher
Crowley, Aleister .... **TCLC 7**
See also Crowley, Edward Alexander
See also GLL 1
Crowley, Edward Alexander 1875-1947
See Crowley, Aleister
See also CA 104; HGG
Crowley, John 1942- .... **CLC 57**
See also BPFB 1; CA 61-64; CANR 43, 98; DLBY 1982; SATA 65; SFW 4
Crud
See Crumb, R(obert)
Crumarums
See Crumb, R(obert)
Crumb, R(obert) 1943- .... **CLC 17**
See also CA 106; CANR 107
Crumbum
See Crumb, R(obert)
Crumski
See Crumb, R(obert)
Crum the Bum
See Crumb, R(obert)
Crunk
See Crumb, R(obert)
Crustt
See Crumb, R(obert)
Crutchfield, Les
See Trumbo, Dalton
Cruz, Victor Hernandez 1949- .... **PC 37**
See also BW 2; CA 65-68; CAAS 17; CANR 14, 32, 74; CP 7; DAM MULT, POET; DLB 41; DNFS 1; EXPP; HLC 1; HW 1, 2; MTCW 1; WP
Cryer, Gretchen (Kiger) 1935- .... **CLC 21**
See also CA 114; 123
Csath, Geza 1887-1919 .... **TCLC 13**
See also CA 111
Cudlip, David R(ockwell) 1933- .... **CLC 34**
See also CA 177
Cullen, Countee 1903-1946 .... **TCLC 4, 37; BLC 1; PC 20; WLCS**
See also AFAW 2; AMWS 4; BW 1; CA 108; 124; CDALB 1917-1929; DA; DA3; DAC; DAM MST, MULT, POET; DLB 4, 48, 51; EXPP; MTCW 1, 2; PFS 3; RGAL 4; SATA 18; WP
Cum, R.
See Crumb, R(obert)

Cummings, Bruce F(rederick) 1889-1919
See Barbellion, W. N. P.
See also CA 123
Cummings, E(dward) E(stlin)
1894-1962 .. **CLC 1, 3, 8, 12, 15, 68; PC 5; WLC**
See also AAYA 41; AMW; CA 73-76; CANR 31; CDALB 1929-1941; DA; DA3; DAB; DAC; DAM MST, POET; DLB 4, 48; EXPP; MTCW 1, 2; PAB; PFS 1, 3, 12, 13; RGAL 4; WP
Cunha, Euclides (Rodrigues Pimenta) da
1866-1909 .... **TCLC 24**
See also CA 123; LAW; WLIT 1
Cunningham, E. V.
See Fast, Howard (Melvin)
Cunningham, J(ames) V(incent)
1911-1985 .... **CLC 3, 31**
See also CA 1-4R; 115; CANR 1, 72; DLB 5
Cunningham, Julia (Woolfolk)
1916- .... **CLC 12**
See also CA 9-12R; CANR 4, 19, 36; CWRI 5; JRDA; MAICYA 1, 2; SAAS 2; SATA 1, 26
Cunningham, Michael 1952- .... **CLC 34**
See also CA 136; CANR 96; GLL 2
Cunninghame Graham, R. B.
See Cunninghame Graham, Robert (Gallnigad) Bontine
Cunninghame Graham, Robert (Gallnigad) Bontine 1852-1936 .... **TCLC 19**
See also Graham, R(obert) B(ontine) Cunninghame
See also CA 119; 184
Currie, Ellen 19(?)- .... **CLC 44**
Curtin, Philip
See Lowndes, Marie Adelaide (Belloc)
Curtis, Price
See Ellison, Harlan (Jay)
Cutrate, Joe
See Spiegelman, Art
Cynewulf c. 770- .... **CMLC 23**
See also DLB 146; RGEL 2
Cyrano de Bergerac, Savinien de
1619-1655 .... **LC 65**
See also GFL Beginnings to 1789; RGWL 2
Czaczkes, Shmuel Yosef Halevi
See Agnon, S(hmuel) Y(osef Halevi)
Dabrowska, Maria (Szumska)
1889-1965 .... **CLC 15**
See also CA 106; CDWLB 4; DLB 215
Dabydeen, David 1955- .... **CLC 34**
See also BW 1; CA 125; CANR 56, 92; CN 7; CP 7
Dacey, Philip 1939- .... **CLC 51**
See also CA 37-40R; CAAS 17; CANR 14, 32, 64; CP 7; DLB 105
Dagerman, Stig (Halvard)
1923-1954 .... **TCLC 17**
See also CA 117; 155; DLB 259
D'Aguiar, Fred 1960- .... **CLC 145**
See also CA 148; CANR 83, 101; CP 7; DLB 157
Dahl, Roald 1916-1990 .... **CLC 1, 6, 18, 79**
See also AAYA 15; BPFB 1; BRWS 4; BYA 5; CA 1-4R; 133; CANR 6, 32, 37, 62; CLR 1, 7, 41; CPW; DA3; DAB; DAC; DAM MST, NOV, POP; DLB 139, 255; HGG; JRDA; MAICYA 1, 2; MTCW 1, 2; RGSF 2; SATA 1, 26, 73; SATA-Obit 65; SSFS 4; YAW
Dahlberg, Edward 1900-1977 .. **CLC 1, 7, 14**
See also CA 9-12R; 69-72; CANR 31, 62; DLB 48; MTCW 1; RGAL 4
Daitch, Susan 1954- .... **CLC 103**
See also CA 161

Dale, Colin .... **TCLC 18**
See also Lawrence, T(homas) E(dward)
Dale, George E.
See Asimov, Isaac
Dalton, Roque 1935-1975(?) .... **PC 36**
See also CA 176; HLCS 1; HW 2
Daly, Elizabeth 1878-1967 .... **CLC 52**
See also CA 23-24; 25-28R; CANR 60; CAP 2; CMW 4
Daly, Maureen 1921- .... **CLC 17**
See also AAYA 5; BYA 6; CANR 37, 83, 108; JRDA; MAICYA 1, 2; SAAS 1; SATA 2, 129; WYA; YAW
Damas, Leon-Gontran 1912-1978 .... **CLC 84**
See also BW 1; CA 125; 73-76
Dana, Richard Henry Sr.
1787-1879 .... **NCLC 53**
Daniel, Samuel 1562(?)-1619 .... **LC 24**
See also DLB 62; RGEL 2
Daniels, Brett
See Adler, Renata
Dannay, Frederic 1905-1982 .... **CLC 11**
See also Queen, Ellery
See also CA 1-4R; 107; CANR 1, 39; CMW 4; DAM POP; DLB 137; MTCW 1
D'Annunzio, Gabriele 1863-1938 ... **TCLC 6, 40**
See also CA 104; 155; EW 8; RGWL 2
Danois, N. le
See Gourmont, Remy(-Marie-Charles) de
Dante 1265-1321 .... **CMLC 3, 18, 39; PC 21; WLCS**
See also DA; DA3; DAB; DAC; DAM MST, POET; EFS 1; EW 1; LAIT 1; RGWL 2; WP
d'Antibes, Germain
See Simenon, Georges (Jacques Christian)
Danticat, Edwidge 1969- .... **CLC 94, 139**
See also AAYA 29; CA 152; CAAE 192; CANR 73; DNFS 1; EXPS; MTCW 1; SSFS 1; YAW
Danvers, Dennis 1947- .... **CLC 70**
Danziger, Paula 1944- .... **CLC 21**
See also AAYA 4, 36; BYA 6, 7, 14; CA 112; 115; CANR 37, 102; CLR 20; JRDA; MAICYA 1, 2; SATA 36, 63, 102; SATA-Brief 30; WYA; YAW
Da Ponte, Lorenzo 1749-1838 .... **NCLC 50**
Dario, Ruben 1867-1916 ... **TCLC 4; HLC 1; PC 15**
See also CA 131; CANR 81; DAM MULT; HW 1, 2; LAW; MTCW 1, 2; RGWL 2
Darley, George 1795-1846 .... **NCLC 2**
See also DLB 96; RGEL 2
Darrow, Clarence (Seward)
1857-1938 .... **TCLC 81**
See also CA 164
Darwin, Charles 1809-1882 .... **NCLC 57**
See also BRWS 7; DLB 57, 166; RGEL 2; WLIT 4
Darwin, Erasmus 1731-1802 .... **NCLC 106**
See also DLB 93; RGEL 2
Daryush, Elizabeth 1887-1977 ...... **CLC 6, 19**
See also CA 49-52; CANR 3, 81; DLB 20
Dasgupta, Surendranath
1887-1952 .... **TCLC 81**
See also CA 157
Dashwood, Edmee Elizabeth Monica de la Pasture 1890-1943
See Delafield, E. M.
See also CA 119; 154
Daudet, (Louis Marie) Alphonse
1840-1897 .... **NCLC 1**
See also DLB 123; GFL 1789 to the Present; RGSF 2
Daumal, Rene 1908-1944 .... **TCLC 14**
See also CA 114
Davenant, William 1606-1668 .... **LC 13**
See also DLB 58, 126; RGEL 2

Davenport, Guy (Mattison, Jr.)
1927- .... **CLC 6, 14, 38; SSC 16**
See also CA 33-36R; CANR 23, 73; CN 7; CSW; DLB 130

David, Robert
See Nezval, Vitezslav

Davidson, Avram (James) 1923-1993
See Queen, Ellery
See also CA 101; 171; CANR 26; DLB 8; FANT; SFW 4; SUFW

Davidson, Donald (Grady)
1893-1968 .... **CLC 2, 13, 19**
See also CA 5-8R; 25-28R; CANR 4, 84; DLB 45

Davidson, Hugh
See Hamilton, Edmond

Davidson, John 1857-1909 .... **TCLC 24**
See also CA 118; DLB 19; RGEL 2

Davidson, Sara 1943- .... **CLC 9**
See also CA 81-84; CANR 44, 68; DLB 185

Davie, Donald (Alfred) 1922-1995 .... **CLC 5, 8, 10, 31; PC 29**
See also BRWS 6; CA 1-4R; 149; CAAS 3; CANR 1, 44; CP 7; DLB 27; MTCW 1; RGEL 2

Davie, Elspeth 1919-1995 .... **SSC 52**
See also CA 120; 126; 150; DLB 139

Davies, Ray(mond Douglas) 1944- ... **CLC 21**
See also CA 116; 146; CANR 92

Davies, Rhys 1901-1978 .... **CLC 23**
See also CA 9-12R; 81-84; CANR 4; DLB 139, 191

Davies, (William) Robertson
1913-1995 .... **CLC 2, 7, 13, 25, 42, 75, 91; WLC**
See also Marchbanks, Samuel
See also BEST 89:2; BPFB 1; CA 33-36R; 150; CANR 17, 42, 103; CN 7; CPW; DA; DA3; DAB; DAC; DAM MST, NOV, POP; DLB 68; HGG; INT CANR-17; MTCW 1, 2; RGEL 2

Davies, Walter C.
See Kornbluth, C(yril) M.

Davies, William Henry 1871-1940 ... **TCLC 5**
See also CA 104; 179; DLB 19, 174; RGEL 2

Da Vinci, Leonardo 1452-1519 ..... **LC 12, 57, 60**
See also AAYA 40

Davis, Angela (Yvonne) 1944- .... **CLC 77**
See also BW 2, 3; CA 57-60; CANR 10, 81; CSW; DA3; DAM MULT; FW

Davis, B. Lynch
See Bioy Casares, Adolfo; Borges, Jorge Luis

Davis, Gordon
See Hunt, E(verette) Howard, (Jr.)

Davis, H(arold) L(enoir) 1896-1960 . **CLC 49**
See also ANW; CA 178; 89-92; DLB 9, 206; SATA 114

Davis, Rebecca (Blaine) Harding
1831-1910 .... **TCLC 6; SSC 38**
See also CA 104; 179; DLB 74, 239; FW; NFS 14; RGAL 4

Davis, Richard Harding
1864-1916 .... **TCLC 24**
See also CA 114; 179; DLB 12, 23, 78, 79, 189; DLBD 13; RGAL 4

Davison, Frank Dalby 1893-1970 ..... **CLC 15**
See also CA 116

Davison, Lawrence H.
See Lawrence, D(avid) H(erbert Richards)

Davison, Peter (Hubert) 1928- .... **CLC 28**
See also CA 9-12R; CAAS 4; CANR 3, 43, 84; CP 7; DLB 5

Davys, Mary 1674-1732 .... **LC 1, 46**
See also DLB 39

Dawson, Fielding 1930-2002 .... **CLC 6**
See also CA 85-88; CANR 108; DLB 130

Dawson, Peter
See Faust, Frederick (Schiller)
See also TCWW 2, 2

Day, Clarence (Shepard, Jr.)
1874-1935 .... **TCLC 25**
See also CA 108; DLB 11

Day, John 1574(?)-1640(?) .... **LC 70**
See also DLB 62, 170; RGEL 2

Day, Thomas 1748-1789 .... **LC 1**
See also DLB 39; YABC 1

Day Lewis, C(ecil) 1904-1972 . **CLC 1, 6, 10; PC 11**
See also Blake, Nicholas
See also BRWS 3; CA 13-16; 33-36R; CANR 34; CAP 1; CWRI 5; DAM POET; DLB 15, 20; MTCW 1, 2; RGEL 2

Dazai Osamu .... **TCLC 11; SSC 41**
See also Tsushima, Shuji
See also CA 164; DLB 182; MJW; RGSF 2; RGWL 2

de Andrade, Carlos Drummond
See Drummond de Andrade, Carlos

de Andrade, Mario 1892-1945
See Andrade, Mario de
See also CA 178; HW 2

Deane, Norman
See Creasey, John

Deane, Seamus (Francis) 1940- ...... **CLC 122**
See also CA 118; CANR 42

de Beauvoir, Simone (Lucie Ernestine Marie Bertrand)
See Beauvoir, Simone (Lucie Ernestine Marie Bertrand) de

de Beer, P.
See Bosman, Herman Charles

de Brissac, Malcolm
See Dickinson, Peter (Malcolm)

de Campos, Alvaro
See Pessoa, Fernando (Antonio Nogueira)

de Chardin, Pierre Teilhard
See Teilhard de Chardin, (Marie Joseph) Pierre

Dee, John 1527-1608 .... **LC 20**
See also DLB 136, 213

Deer, Sandra 1940- .... **CLC 45**
See also CA 186

De Ferrari, Gabriella 1941- .... **CLC 65**
See also CA 146

Defoe, Daniel 1660(?)-1731 .. **LC 1, 42; WLC**
See also AAYA 27; BRW 3; BRWR 1; BYA 4; CDBLB 1660-1789; CLR 61; DA; DA3; DAB; DAC; DAM MST, NOV; DLB 39, 95, 101; JRDA; LAIT 1; MAICYA 1, 2; NFS 9, 13; RGEL 2; SATA 22; WCH; WLIT 3

de Gourmont, Remy(-Marie-Charles)
See Gourmont, Remy(-Marie-Charles) de

de Hartog, Jan 1914- .... **CLC 19**
See also CA 1-4R; CANR 1; DFS 12

de Hostos, E. M.
See Hostos (y Bonilla), Eugenio Maria de

de Hostos, Eugenio M.
See Hostos (y Bonilla), Eugenio Maria de

Deighton, Len .... **CLC 4, 7, 22, 46**
See also Deighton, Leonard Cyril
See also AAYA 6; BEST 89:2; BPFB 1; CDBLB 1960 to Present; CMW 4; CN 7; CPW; DLB 87

Deighton, Leonard Cyril 1929-
See Deighton, Len
See also CA 9-12R; CANR 19, 33, 68; DA3; DAM NOV, POP; MTCW 1, 2

Dekker, Thomas 1572(?)-1632 ..... **LC 22; DC 12**
See also CDBLB Before 1660; DAM DRAM; DLB 62, 172; RGEL 2

Delafield, E. M. .... **TCLC 61**
See also Dashwood, Edmee Elizabeth Monica de la Pasture
See also DLB 34; RHW

de la Mare, Walter (John)
1873-1956 . **TCLC 4, 53; SSC 14; WLC**
See also CA 163; CDBLB 1914-1945; CLR 23; CWRI 5; DA3; DAB; DAC; DAM MST, POET; DLB 19, 153, 162, 255; EXPP; HGG; MAICYA 1, 2; MTCW 1; RGEL 2; RGSF 2; SATA 16; SUFW; WCH

Delaney, Franey
See O'Hara, John (Henry)

Delaney, Shelagh 1939- .... **CLC 29**
See also CA 17-20R; CANR 30, 67; CBD; CD 5; CDBLB 1960 to Present; CWD; DAM DRAM; DFS 7; DLB 13; MTCW 1

Delany, Martin Robison
1812-1885 .... **NCLC 93**
See also DLB 50; RGAL 4

Delany, Mary (Granville Pendarves)
1700-1788 .... **LC 12**

Delany, Samuel R(ay), Jr. 1942- . **CLC 8, 14, 38, 141; BLC 1**
See also AAYA 24; AFAW 2; BPFB 1; BW 2, 3; CA 81-84; CANR 27, 43; DAM MULT; DLB 8, 33; MTCW 1, 2; RGAL 4; SCFW

De La Ramee, (Marie) Louise 1839-1908
See Ouida
See also SATA 20

de la Roche, Mazo 1879-1961 .... **CLC 14**
See also CA 85-88; CANR 30; DLB 68; RGEL 2; RHW; SATA 64

De La Salle, Innocent
See Hartmann, Sadakichi

Delbanco, Nicholas (Franklin)
1942- .... **CLC 6, 13**
See also CA 17-20R; CAAE 189; CAAS 2; CANR 29, 55; DLB 6, 234

del Castillo, Michel 1933- .... **CLC 38**
See also CA 109; CANR 77

Deledda, Grazia (Cosima)
1875(?)-1936 .... **TCLC 23**
See also CA 123; RGWL 2

Deleuze, Gilles 1925-1995 .... **TCLC 116**

Delgado, Abelardo (Lalo) B(arrientos) 1930-
See also CA 131; CAAS 15; CANR 90; DAM MST, MULT; DLB 82; HLC 1; HW 1, 2

Delibes, Miguel .... **CLC 8, 18**
See also Delibes Setien, Miguel

Delibes Setien, Miguel 1920-
See Delibes, Miguel
See also CA 45-48; CANR 1, 32; HW 1; MTCW 1

DeLillo, Don 1936- ..... **CLC 8, 10, 13, 27, 39, 54, 76, 143**
See also AMWS 6; BEST 89:1; BPFB 1; CA 81-84; CANR 21, 76, 92; CN 7; CPW; DA3; DAM NOV, POP; DLB 6, 173; MTCW 1, 2; RGAL 4

de Lisser, H. G.
See De Lisser, H(erbert) G(eorge)
See also DLB 117

De Lisser, H(erbert) G(eorge)
1878-1944 .... **TCLC 12**
See also de Lisser, H. G.
See also BW 2; CA 109; 152

Deloire, Pierre
See Peguy, Charles (Pierre)

Deloney, Thomas 1543(?)-1600 .... **LC 41**
See also DLB 167; RGEL 2

Deloria, Vine (Victor), Jr. 1933- ...... **CLC 21, 122**
See also CA 53-56; CANR 5, 20, 48, 98; DAM MULT; DLB 175; MTCW 1; NNAL; SATA 21

Del Vecchio, John M(ichael) 1947- .. **CLC 29**
See also CA 110; DLBD 9

de Man, Paul (Adolph Michel)
1919-1983 .... **CLC 55**
See also CA 128; 111; CANR 61; DLB 67; MTCW 1, 2

DeMarinis, Rick 1934- .... **CLC 54**
See also CA 57-60, 184; CAAE 184; CAAS 24; CANR 9, 25, 50; DLB 218

Dembry, R. Emmet
See Murfree, Mary Noailles

Demby, William 1922- .... **CLC 53; BLC 1**
See also BW 1, 3; CA 81-84; CANR 81; DAM MULT; DLB 33

de Menton, Francisco
See Chin, Frank (Chew, Jr.)

Demetrius of Phalerum c.
307B.C.- .... **CMLC 34**

Demijohn, Thom
See Disch, Thomas M(ichael)

Deming, Richard 1915-1983
See Queen, Ellery
See also CA 9-12R; CANR 3, 94; SATA 24

Democritus c. 460B.C.-c. 370B.C. . **CMLC 47**

de Montherlant, Henry (Milon)
See Montherlant, Henry (Milon) de

Demosthenes 384B.C.-322B.C. ...... **CMLC 13**
See also AW 1; DLB 176; RGWL 2

de Natale, Francine
See Malzberg, Barry N(athaniel)

de Navarre, Marguerite 1492-1549 ..... **LC 61**
See also Marguerite d'Angouleme; Marguerite de Navarre

Denby, Edwin (Orr) 1903-1983 .... **CLC 48**
See also CA 138; 110

Denham, John 1615-1669 .... **LC 73**
See also DLB 58, 126; RGEL 2

Denis, Julio
See Cortazar, Julio

Denmark, Harrison
See Zelazny, Roger (Joseph)

Dennis, John 1658-1734 .... **LC 11**
See also DLB 101; RGEL 2

Dennis, Nigel (Forbes) 1912-1989 ...... **CLC 8**
See also CA 25-28R; 129; DLB 13, 15, 233; MTCW 1

Dent, Lester 1904(?)-1959 .... **TCLC 72**
See also CA 112; 161; CMW 4; SFW 4

De Palma, Brian (Russell) 1940- ...... **CLC 20**
See also CA 109

De Quincey, Thomas 1785-1859 ..... **NCLC 4, 87**
See also BRW 4; CDBLB 1789-1832; DLB 110, 144; RGEL 2

Deren, Eleanora 1908(?)-1961
See Deren, Maya
See also CA 192; 111

Deren, Maya .... **CLC 16, 102**
See also Deren, Eleanora

Derleth, August (William)
1909-1971 .... **CLC 31**
See also BPFB 1; BYA 9, 10; CA 1-4R; 29-32R; CANR 4; CMW 4; DLB 9; DLBD 17; HGG; SATA 5; SUFW

Der Nister 1884-1950 .... **TCLC 56**

de Routisie, Albert
See Aragon, Louis

Derrida, Jacques 1930- .... **CLC 24, 87**
See also CA 124; 127; CANR 76, 98; DLB 242; MTCW 1

Derry Down Derry
See Lear, Edward

Dersonnes, Jacques
See Simenon, Georges (Jacques Christian)

Desai, Anita 1937- .... **CLC 19, 37, 97**
See also BRWS 5; CA 81-84; CANR 33, 53, 95; CN 7; CWRI 5; DA3; DAB; DAM NOV; DNFS 2; FW; MTCW 1, 2; SATA 63, 126

Desai, Kiran 1971- .... **CLC 119**
See also CA 171

de Saint-Luc, Jean
See Glassco, John

de Saint Roman, Arnaud
See Aragon, Louis

Desbordes-Valmore, Marceline
1786-1859 .... **NCLC 97**
See also DLB 217

Descartes, Rene 1596-1650 .... **LC 20, 35**
See also EW 3; GFL Beginnings to 1789

De Sica, Vittorio 1901(?)-1974 .... **CLC 20**
See also CA 117

Desnos, Robert 1900-1945 .... **TCLC 22**
See also CA 121; 151; CANR 107; DLB 258

Destouches, Louis-Ferdinand
1894-1961 .... **CLC 9, 15**
See also Celine, Louis-Ferdinand
See also CA 85-88; CANR 28; MTCW 1

de Tolignac, Gaston
See Griffith, D(avid Lewelyn) W(ark)

Deutsch, Babette 1895-1982 .... **CLC 18**
See also BYA 3; CA 1-4R; 108; CANR 4, 79; DLB 45; SATA 1; SATA-Obit 33

Devenant, William 1606-1649 .... **LC 13**

Devkota, Laxmiprasad 1909-1959 . **TCLC 23**
See also CA 123

De Voto, Bernard (Augustine)
1897-1955 .... **TCLC 29**
See also CA 113; 160; DLB 9, 256

De Vries, Peter 1910-1993 ..... **CLC 1, 2, 3, 7, 10, 28, 46**
See also CA 17-20R; 142; CANR 41; DAM NOV; DLB 6; DLBY 1982; MTCW 1, 2

Dewey, John 1859-1952 .... **TCLC 95**
See also CA 114; 170; DLB 246; RGAL 4

Dexter, John
See Bradley, Marion Zimmer
See also GLL 1

Dexter, Martin
See Faust, Frederick (Schiller)
See also TCWW 2

Dexter, Pete 1943- .... **CLC 34, 55**
See also BEST 89:2; CA 127; 131; CPW; DAM POP; INT 131; MTCW 1

Diamano, Silmang
See Senghor, Leopold Sedar

Diamond, Neil 1941- .... **CLC 30**
See also CA 108

Diaz del Castillo, Bernal 1496-1584 .. **LC 31; HLCS 1**
See also LAW

di Bassetto, Corno
See Shaw, George Bernard

Dick, Philip K(indred) 1928-1982 ... **CLC 10, 30, 72**
See also AAYA 24; BPFB 1; BYA 11; CA 49-52; 106; CANR 2, 16; CPW; DA3; DAM NOV, POP; DLB 8; MTCW 1, 2; NFS 5; SCFW; SFW 4

Dickens, Charles (John Huffam)
1812-1870 ..... **NCLC 3, 8, 18, 26, 37, 50, 86, 105; SSC 17, 49; WLC**
See also AAYA 23; BRW 5; BYA 1, 2, 3, 13, 14; CDBLB 1832-1890; CMW 4; DA; DA3; DAB; DAC; DAM MST, NOV; DLB 21, 55, 70, 159, 166; EXPN; HGG; JRDA; LAIT 1, 2; MAICYA 1, 2; NFS 4, 5, 10, 14; RGEL 2; RGSF 2; SATA 15; SUFW; WCH; WLIT 4; WYA

Dickey, James (Lafayette)
1923-1997 .... **CLC 1, 2, 4, 7, 10, 15, 47, 109; PC 40**
See also AITN 1, 2; AMWS 4; BPFB 1; CA 9-12R; 156; CABS 2; CANR 10, 48, 61, 105; CDALB 1968-1988; CP 7; CPW; CSW; DA3; DAM NOV, POET, POP; DLB 5, 193; DLBD 7; DLBY 1982, 1993, 1996, 1997, 1998; INT CANR-10; MTCW 1, 2; NFS 9; PFS 6, 11; RGAL 4

Dickey, William 1928-1994 .... **CLC 3, 28**
See also CA 9-12R; 145; CANR 24, 79; DLB 5

Dickinson, Charles 1951- .... **CLC 49**
See also CA 128

Dickinson, Emily (Elizabeth)
1830-1886 ... **NCLC 21, 77; PC 1; WLC**
See also AAYA 22; AMW; AMWR 1; CDALB 1865-1917; DA; DA3; DAB; DAC; DAM MST, POET; DLB 1, 243; EXPP; MAWW; PAB; PFS 1, 2, 3, 4, 5, 6, 8, 10, 11, 13; RGAL 4; SATA 29; WP; WYA

Dickinson, Mrs. Herbert Ward
See Phelps, Elizabeth Stuart

Dickinson, Peter (Malcolm) 1927- .. **CLC 12, 35**
See also AAYA 9; BYA 5; CA 41-44R; CANR 31, 58, 88; CLR 29; CMW 4; DLB 87, 161; JRDA; MAICYA 1, 2; SATA 5, 62, 95; SFW 4; WYA; YAW

Dickson, Carr
See Carr, John Dickson

Dickson, Carter
See Carr, John Dickson

Diderot, Denis 1713-1784 .... **LC 26**
See also EW 4; GFL Beginnings to 1789; RGWL 2

Didion, Joan 1934- . **CLC 1, 3, 8, 14, 32, 129**
See also AITN 1; AMWS 4; CA 5-8R; CANR 14, 52, 76; CDALB 1968-1988; CN 7; DA3; DAM NOV; DLB 2, 173, 185; DLBY 1981, 1986; MAWW; MTCW 1, 2; NFS 3; RGAL 4; TCWW 2

Dietrich, Robert
See Hunt, E(verette) Howard, (Jr.)

Difusa, Pati
See Almodovar, Pedro

Dillard, Annie 1945- .... **CLC 9, 60, 115**
See also AAYA 6, 43; AMWS 6; ANW; CA 49-52; CANR 3, 43, 62, 90; DA3; DAM NOV; DLBY 1980; LAIT 4, 5; MTCW 1, 2; NCFS 1; RGAL 4; SATA 10

Dillard, R(ichard) H(enry) W(ilde)
1937- .... **CLC 5**
See also CA 21-24R; CAAS 7; CANR 10; CP 7; CSW; DLB 5, 244

Dillon, Eilis 1920-1994 .... **CLC 17**
See also CA 9-12R, 182; 147; CAAE 182; CAAS 3; CANR 4, 38, 78; CLR 26; MAICYA 1, 2; MAICYAS 1; SATA 2, 74; SATA-Essay 105; SATA-Obit 83; YAW

Dimont, Penelope
See Mortimer, Penelope (Ruth)

Dinesen, Isak .... **CLC 10, 29, 95; SSC 7**
See also Blixen, Karen (Christentze Dinesen)
See also EW 10; EXPS; FW; HGG; LAIT 3; MTCW 1; NCFS 2; NFS 9; RGSF 2; RGWL 2; SSFS 3, 6, 13; WLIT 2

Ding Ling .... **CLC 68**
See also Chiang, Pin-chin

Diphusa, Patty
See Almodovar, Pedro

Disch, Thomas M(ichael) 1940- ... **CLC 7, 36**
See also AAYA 17; BPFB 1; CA 21-24R; CAAS 4; CANR 17, 36, 54, 89; CLR 18; CP 7; DA3; DLB 8; HGG; MAICYA 1, 2; MTCW 1, 2; SAAS 15; SATA 92; SCFW; SFW 4

Disch, Tom
See Disch, Thomas M(ichael)

d'Isly, Georges
See Simenon, Georges (Jacques Christian)

Disraeli, Benjamin 1804-1881 ... **NCLC 2, 39, 79**
See also BRW 4; DLB 21, 55; RGEL 2

Ditcum, Steve
See Crumb, R(obert)

Dixon, Paige
See Corcoran, Barbara (Asenath)

Dixon, Stephen 1936- .... **CLC 52; SSC 16**
See also CA 89-92; CANR 17, 40, 54, 91; CN 7; DLB 130

Doak, Annie
See Dillard, Annie

Dobell, Sydney Thompson 1824-1874 .... **NCLC 43**
See also DLB 32; RGEL 2

Doblin, Alfred .... **TCLC 13**
See also Doeblin, Alfred
See also CDWLB 2; RGWL 2

Dobrolyubov, Nikolai Alexandrovich 1836-1861 .... **NCLC 5**

Dobson, Austin 1840-1921 .... **TCLC 79**
See also DLB 35, 144

Dobyns, Stephen 1941- .... **CLC 37**
See also CA 45-48; CANR 2, 18, 99; CMW 4; CP 7

Doctorow, E(dgar) L(aurence) 1931- .... **CLC 6, 11, 15, 18, 37, 44, 65, 113**
See also AAYA 22; AITN 2; AMWS 4; BEST 89:3; BPFB 1; CA 45-48; CANR 2, 33, 51, 76, 97; CDALB 1968-1988; CN 7; CPW; DA3; DAM NOV, POP; DLB 2, 28, 173; DLBY 1980; LAIT 3; MTCW 1, 2; NFS 6; RGAL 4; RHW

Dodgson, Charles Lutwidge 1832-1898
See Carroll, Lewis
See also CLR 2; DA; DA3; DAB; DAC; DAM MST, NOV, POET; MAICYA 1, 2; SATA 100; YABC 2

Dodson, Owen (Vincent) 1914-1983 .... **CLC 79; BLC 1**
See also BW 1; CA 65-68; 110; CANR 24; DAM MULT; DLB 76

Doeblin, Alfred 1878-1957 .... **TCLC 13**
See also Doblin, Alfred
See also CA 110; 141; DLB 66

Doerr, Harriet 1910- .... **CLC 34**
See also CA 117; 122; CANR 47; INT 122

Domecq, H(onorio Bustos)
See Bioy Casares, Adolfo

Domecq, H(onorio) Bustos
See Bioy Casares, Adolfo; Borges, Jorge Luis

Domini, Rey
See Lorde, Audre (Geraldine)
See also GLL 1

Dominique
See Proust, (Valentin-Louis-George-Eugene-)Marcel

Don, A
See Stephen, Sir Leslie

Donaldson, Stephen R(eeder) 1947- .... **CLC 46, 138**
See also AAYA 36; BPFB 1; CA 89-92; CANR 13, 55, 99; CPW; DAM POP; FANT; INT CANR-13; SATA 121; SFW 4; SUFW

Donleavy, J(ames) P(atrick) 1926- .... **CLC 1, 4, 6, 10, 45**
See also AITN 2; BPFB 1; CA 9-12R; CANR 24, 49, 62, 80; CBD; CD 5; CN 7; DLB 6, 173; INT CANR-24; MTCW 1, 2; RGAL 4

Donne, John 1572-1631 ..... **LC 10, 24; PC 1; WLC**
See also BRW 1; BRWR 2; CDBLB Before 1660; DA; DAB; DAC; DAM MST, POET; DLB 121, 151; EXPP; PAB; PFS 2, 11; RGEL 2; WLIT 3; WP

Donnell, David 1939(?)- .... **CLC 34**
See also CA 197

Donoghue, P. S.
See Hunt, E(verette) Howard, (Jr.)

Donoso (Yanez), Jose 1924-1996 ... **CLC 4, 8, 11, 32, 99; HLC 1; SSC 34**
See also CA 81-84; 155; CANR 32, 73; CDWLB 3; DAM MULT; DLB 113; HW 1, 2; LAW; LAWS 1; MTCW 1, 2; RGSF 2; WLIT 1

Donovan, John 1928-1992 .... **CLC 35**
See also AAYA 20; CA 97-100; 137; CLR 3; MAICYA 1, 2; SATA 72; SATA-Brief 29; YAW

Don Roberto
See Cunninghame Graham, Robert (Gallnigad) Bontine

Doolittle, Hilda 1886-1961 . **CLC 3, 8, 14, 31, 34, 73; PC 5; WLC**
See also H. D.
See also AMWS 1; CA 97-100; CANR 35; DA; DAC; DAM MST, POET; DLB 4, 45; FW; GLL 1; MAWW; MTCW 1, 2; PFS 6; RGAL 4

Doppo, Kunikida .... **TCLC 99**
See also Kunikida Doppo

Dorfman, Ariel 1942- .... **CLC 48, 77; HLC 1**
See also CA 124; 130; CANR 67, 70; CWW 2; DAM MULT; DFS 4; HW 1, 2; INT CA-130; WLIT 1

Dorn, Edward (Merton) 1929-1999 .... **CLC 10, 18**
See also CA 93-96; 187; CANR 42, 79; CP 7; DLB 5; INT 93-96; WP

Dor-Ner, Zvi .... **CLC 70**

Dorris, Michael (Anthony) 1945-1997 .... **CLC 109**
See also AAYA 20; BEST 90:1; BYA 12; CA 102; 157; CANR 19, 46, 75; CLR 58; DA3; DAM MULT, NOV; DLB 175; LAIT 5; MTCW 2; NFS 3; NNAL; RGAL 4; SATA 75; SATA-Obit 94; TCWW 2; YAW

Dorris, Michael A.
See Dorris, Michael (Anthony)

Dorsan, Luc
See Simenon, Georges (Jacques Christian)

Dorsange, Jean
See Simenon, Georges (Jacques Christian)

Dos Passos, John (Roderigo) 1896-1970 ... **CLC 1, 4, 8, 11, 15, 25, 34, 82; WLC**
See also AMW; BPFB 1; CA 1-4R; 29-32R; CANR 3; CDALB 1929-1941; DA; DA3; DAB; DAC; DAM MST, NOV; DLB 4, 9; DLBD 1, 15; DLBY 1996; MTCW 1, 2; NFS 14; RGAL 4

Dossage, Jean
See Simenon, Georges (Jacques Christian)

Dostoevsky, Fedor Mikhailovich 1821-1881 . **NCLC 2, 7, 21, 33, 43; SSC 2, 33, 44; WLC**
See also Dostoevsky, Fyodor
See also AAYA 40; DA; DA3; DAB; DAC; DAM MST, NOV; EW 7; EXPN; NFS 3, 8; RGSF 2; RGWL 2; SSFS 8

Dostoevsky, Fyodor
See Dostoevsky, Fedor Mikhailovich
See also DLB 238

Doughty, Charles M(ontagu) 1843-1926 .... **TCLC 27**
See also CA 115; 178; DLB 19, 57, 174

Douglas, Ellen .... **CLC 73**
See also Haxton, Josephine Ayres; Williamson, Ellen Douglas
See also CN 7; CSW

Douglas, Gavin 1475(?)-1522 .... **LC 20**
See also DLB 132; RGEL 2

Douglas, George
See Brown, George Douglas
See also RGEL 2

Douglas, Keith (Castellain) 1920-1944 .... **TCLC 40**
See also BRW 7; CA 160; DLB 27; PAB; RGEL 2

Douglas, Leonard
See Bradbury, Ray (Douglas)

Douglas, Michael
See Crichton, (John) Michael

Douglas, (George) Norman 1868-1952 .... **TCLC 68**
See also BRW 6; CA 119; 157; DLB 34, 195; RGEL 2

Douglas, William
See Brown, George Douglas

Douglass, Frederick 1817(?)-1895 .. **NCLC 7, 55; BLC 1; WLC**
See also AFAW 1, 2; AMWS 3; CDALB 1640-1865; DA; DA3; DAC; DAM MST, MULT; DLB 1, 43, 50, 79, 243; FW; LAIT 2; NCFS 2; RGAL 4; SATA 29

Dourado, (Waldomiro Freitas) Autran 1926- .... **CLC 23, 60**
See also CA 25-28R, 179; CANR 34, 81; DLB 145; HW 2

Dourado, Waldomiro Autran
See Dourado, (Waldomiro Freitas) Autran
See also CA 179

Dove, Rita (Frances) 1952- .... **CLC 50, 81; BLCS; PC 6**
See also AMWS 4; BW 2; CA 109; CAAS 19; CANR 27, 42, 68, 76, 97; CDALBS; CP 7; CSW; CWP; DA3; DAM MULT, POET; DLB 120; EXPP; MTCW 1; PFS 1; RGAL 4

Doveglion
See Villa, Jose Garcia

Dowell, Coleman 1925-1985 .... **CLC 60**
See also CA 25-28R; 117; CANR 10; DLB 130; GLL 2

Dowson, Ernest (Christopher) 1867-1900 .... **TCLC 4**
See also CA 105; 150; DLB 19, 135; RGEL 2

Doyle, A. Conan
See Doyle, Sir Arthur Conan

Doyle, Sir Arthur Conan 1859-1930 .... **TCLC 7; SSC 12; WLC**
See also Conan Doyle, Arthur
See also AAYA 14; BRWS 2; CA 104; 122; CDBLB 1890-1914; CMW 4; DA; DA3; DAB; DAC; DAM MST, NOV; DLB 18, 70, 156, 178; EXPS; HGG; LAIT 2; MSW; MTCW 1, 2; RGEL 2; RGSF 2; RHW; SATA 24; SCFW 2; SFW 4; SSFS 2; WCH; WLIT 4; WYA; YAW

Doyle, Conan
See Doyle, Sir Arthur Conan

Doyle, John
See Graves, Robert (von Ranke)

Doyle, Roddy 1958(?)- .... **CLC 81**
See also AAYA 14; BRWS 5; CA 143; CANR 73; CN 7; DA3; DLB 194

Doyle, Sir A. Conan
See Doyle, Sir Arthur Conan

Dr. A
See Asimov, Isaac; Silverstein, Alvin; Silverstein, Virginia B(arbara Opshelor)

Drabble, Margaret 1939- ...... **CLC 2, 3, 5, 8, 10, 22, 53, 129**
See also BRWS 4; CA 13-16R; CANR 18, 35, 63; CDBLB 1960 to Present; CN 7; CPW; DA3; DAB; DAC; DAM MST, NOV, POP; DLB 14, 155, 231; FW; MTCW 1, 2; RGEL 2; SATA 48

Drapier, M. B.
See Swift, Jonathan

Drayham, James
See Mencken, H(enry) L(ouis)

Drayton, Michael 1563-1631 .... **LC 8**
See also DAM POET; DLB 121; RGEL 2

Dreadstone, Carl
See Campbell, (John) Ramsey

Dreiser, Theodore (Herman Albert) 1871-1945 .... **TCLC 10, 18, 35, 83; SSC 30; WLC**
See also AMW; CA 106; 132; CDALB 1865-1917; DA; DA3; DAC; DAM MST, NOV; DLB 9, 12, 102, 137; DLBD 1; LAIT 2; MTCW 1, 2; NFS 8; RGAL 4

Drexler, Rosalyn 1926- .... **CLC 2, 6**
See also CA 81-84; CAD; CANR 68; CD 5; CWD

Dreyer, Carl Theodor 1889-1968 ...... **CLC 16**
See also CA 116

Drieu la Rochelle, Pierre(-Eugene) 1893-1945 .... **TCLC 21**
See also CA 117; DLB 72; GFL 1789 to the Present

Drinkwater, John 1882-1937 .... **TCLC 57**
See also CA 109; 149; DLB 10, 19, 149; RGEL 2

Drop Shot
See Cable, George Washington

Droste-Hulshoff, Annette Freiin von 1797-1848 .... **NCLC 3**
See also CDWLB 2; DLB 133; RGSF 2; RGWL 2

Drummond, Walter
See Silverberg, Robert

Drummond, William Henry 1854-1907 .... **TCLC 25**
See also CA 160; DLB 92

Drummond de Andrade, Carlos 1902-1987 .... **CLC 18**
See also Andrade, Carlos Drummond de
See also CA 132; 123; LAW

Drury, Allen (Stuart) 1918-1998 .... **CLC 37**
See also CA 57-60; 170; CANR 18, 52; CN 7; INT CANR-18

Dryden, John 1631-1700 ..... **LC 3, 21; DC 3; PC 25; WLC**
See also BRW 2; CDBLB 1660-1789; DA; DAB; DAC; DAM DRAM, MST, POET; DLB 80, 101, 131; EXPP; IDTP; RGEL 2; TEA; WLIT 3

Duberman, Martin (Bauml) 1930- ..... **CLC 8**
See also CA 1-4R; CAD; CANR 2, 63; CD 5

Dubie, Norman (Evans) 1945- .... **CLC 36**
See also CA 69-72; CANR 12; CP 7; DLB 120; PFS 12

Du Bois, W(illiam) E(dward) B(urghardt) 1868-1963 ... **CLC 1, 2, 13, 64, 96; BLC 1; WLC**
See also AAYA 40; AFAW 1, 2; AMWS 2; BW 1, 3; CA 85-88; CANR 34, 82; CDALB 1865-1917; DA; DA3; DAC; DAM MST, MULT, NOV; DLB 47, 50, 91, 246; EXPP; LAIT 2; MTCW 1, 2; NCFS 1; PFS 13; RGAL 4; SATA 42

Dubus, Andre 1936-1999 ..... **CLC 13, 36, 97; SSC 15**
See also AMWS 7; CA 21-24R; 177; CANR 17; CN 7; CSW; DLB 130; INT CANR-17; RGAL 4; SSFS 10

Duca Minimo
See D'Annunzio, Gabriele

Ducharme, Rejean 1941- .... **CLC 74**
See also CA 165; DLB 60

Duchen, Claire .... **CLC 65**

Duclos, Charles Pinot- 1704-1772 .... **LC 1**
See also GFL Beginnings to 1789

Dudek, Louis 1918- .... **CLC 11, 19**
See also CA 45-48; CAAS 14; CANR 1; CP 7; DLB 88

Duerrenmatt, Friedrich 1921-1990 ... **CLC 1, 4, 8, 11, 15, 43, 102**
See also Durrenmatt, Friedrich
See also CA 17-20R; CANR 33; CMW 4; DAM DRAM; DLB 69, 124; MTCW 1, 2

Duffy, Bruce 1953(?)- .... **CLC 50**
See also CA 172

Duffy, Maureen 1933- .... **CLC 37**
See also CA 25-28R; CANR 33, 68; CBD; CN 7; CP 7; CWD; CWP; DLB 14; FW; MTCW 1

Du Fu
See Tu Fu
See also RGWL 2

Dugan, Alan 1923- .... **CLC 2, 6**
See also CA 81-84; CP 7; DLB 5; PFS 10

du Gard, Roger Martin
See Martin du Gard, Roger

Duhamel, Georges 1884-1966 .... **CLC 8**
See also CA 81-84; 25-28R; CANR 35; DLB 65; GFL 1789 to the Present; MTCW 1

Dujardin, Edouard (Emile Louis) 1861-1949 .... **TCLC 13**
See also CA 109; DLB 123

Dulles, John Foster 1888-1959 .... **TCLC 72**
See also CA 115; 149

Dumas, Alexandre (pere) 1802-1870 .... **NCLC 11, 71; WLC**
See also AAYA 22; BYA 3; DA; DA3; DAB; DAC; DAM MST, NOV; DLB 119, 192; EW 6; GFL 1789 to the Present; LAIT 1, 2; NFS 14; RGWL 2; SATA 18; WCH

Dumas, Alexandre (fils) 1824-1895 .... **NCLC 9; DC 1**
See also DLB 192; GFL 1789 to the Present; RGWL 2

Dumas, Claudine
See Malzberg, Barry N(athaniel)

Dumas, Henry L. 1934-1968 .... **CLC 6, 62**
See also BW 1; CA 85-88; DLB 41; RGAL 4

du Maurier, Daphne 1907-1989 .. **CLC 6, 11, 59; SSC 18**
See also AAYA 37; BPFB 1; BRWS 3; CA 5-8R; 128; CANR 6, 55; CMW 4; CPW; DA3; DAB; DAC; DAM MST, POP; DLB 191; HGG; LAIT 3; MSW; MTCW 1, 2; NFS 12; RGEL 2; RGSF 2; RHW; SATA 27; SATA-Obit 60; SSFS 14

Du Maurier, George 1834-1896 ...... **NCLC 86**
See also DLB 153, 178; RGEL 2

Dunbar, Paul Laurence 1872-1906 . **TCLC 2, 12; BLC 1; PC 5; SSC 8; WLC**
See also AFAW 1, 2; AMWS 2; BW 1, 3; CA 104; 124; CANR 79; CDALB 1865-1917; DA; DA3; DAC; DAM MST, MULT, POET; DLB 50, 54, 78; EXPP; RGAL 4; SATA 34

Dunbar, William 1460(?)-1520(?) .... **LC 20**
See also DLB 132, 146; RGEL 2

Duncan, Dora Angela
See Duncan, Isadora

Duncan, Isadora 1877(?)-1927 .... **TCLC 68**
See also CA 118; 149

Duncan, Lois 1934- .... **CLC 26**
See also AAYA 4, 34; BYA 6, 8; CA 1-4R; CANR 2, 23, 36; CLR 29; JRDA; MAICYA 1, 2; MAICYAS 1; SAAS 2; SATA 1, 36, 75; WYA; YAW

Duncan, Robert (Edward) 1919-1988 .... **CLC 1, 2, 4, 7, 15, 41, 55; PC 2**
See also CA 9-12R; 124; CANR 28, 62; DAM POET; DLB 5, 16, 193; MTCW 1, 2; PFS 13; RGAL 4; WP

Duncan, Sara Jeannette 1861-1922 .... **TCLC 60**
See also CA 157; DLB 92

Dunlap, William 1766-1839 .... **NCLC 2**
See also DLB 30, 37, 59; RGAL 4

Dunn, Douglas (Eaglesham) 1942- .... **CLC 6, 40**
See also CA 45-48; CANR 2, 33; CP 7; DLB 40; MTCW 1

Dunn, Katherine (Karen) 1945- .... **CLC 71**
See also CA 33-36R; CANR 72; HGG; MTCW 1

Dunn, Stephen (Elliott) 1939- .... **CLC 36**
See also CA 33-36R; CANR 12, 48, 53, 105; CP 7; DLB 105

Dunne, Finley Peter 1867-1936 ...... **TCLC 28**
See also CA 108; 178; DLB 11, 23; RGAL 4

Dunne, John Gregory 1932- .... **CLC 28**
See also CA 25-28R; CANR 14, 50; CN 7; DLBY 1980

Dunsany, Lord .... **TCLC 2, 59**
See also Dunsany, Edward John Moreton Drax Plunkett
See also DLB 77, 153, 156, 255; FANT; IDTP; RGEL 2; SFW 4; SUFW

Dunsany, Edward John Moreton Drax Plunkett 1878-1957
See Dunsany, Lord
See also CA 104; 148; DLB 10; MTCW 1

du Perry, Jean
See Simenon, Georges (Jacques Christian)

Durang, Christopher (Ferdinand) 1949- .... **CLC 27, 38**
See also CA 105; CAD; CANR 50, 76; CD 5; MTCW 1

Duras, Marguerite 1914-1996 . **CLC 3, 6, 11, 20, 34, 40, 68, 100; SSC 40**
See also BPFB 1; CA 25-28R; 151; CANR 50; CWW 2; DLB 83; GFL 1789 to the Present; IDFW 4; MTCW 1, 2; RGWL 2

Durban, (Rosa) Pam 1947- .... **CLC 39**
See also CA 123; CANR 98; CSW

Durcan, Paul 1944- .... **CLC 43, 70**
See also CA 134; CP 7; DAM POET

Durkheim, Emile 1858-1917 .... **TCLC 55**

Durrell, Lawrence (George) 1912-1990 ..... **CLC 1, 4, 6, 8, 13, 27, 41**
See also BPFB 1; BRWS 1; CA 9-12R; 132; CANR 40, 77; CDBLB 1945-1960; DAM NOV; DLB 15, 27, 204; DLBY 1990; MTCW 1, 2; RGEL 2; SFW 4

Durrenmatt, Friedrich
See Duerrenmatt, Friedrich
See also CDWLB 2; EW 13; RGWL 2

Dutt, Toru 1856-1877 .... **NCLC 29**
See also DLB 240

Dwight, Timothy 1752-1817 .... **NCLC 13**
See also DLB 37; RGAL 4

Dworkin, Andrea 1946- .... **CLC 43, 123**
See also CA 77-80; CAAS 21; CANR 16, 39, 76, 96; FW; GLL 1; INT CANR-16; MTCW 1, 2

Dwyer, Deanna
See Koontz, Dean R(ay)

Dwyer, K. R.
See Koontz, Dean R(ay)

Dwyer, Thomas A. 1923- .... **CLC 114**
See also CA 115

Dybek, Stuart 1942- .... **CLC 114**
See also CA 97-100; CANR 39; DLB 130

Dye, Richard
See De Voto, Bernard (Augustine)

Dyer, Geoff 1958- .... **CLC 149**
See also CA 125; CANR 88

Dylan, Bob 1941- .... **CLC 3, 4, 6, 12, 77; PC 37**
See also CA 41-44R; CANR 108; CP 7; DLB 16

Dyson, John 1943- .... **CLC 70**
See also CA 144

E. V. L.
See Lucas, E(dward) V(errall)

Eagleton, Terence (Francis) 1943- .. **CLC 63, 132**
See also CA 57-60; CANR 7, 23, 68; DLB 242; MTCW 1, 2

Eagleton, Terry
See Eagleton, Terence (Francis)

Early, Jack
See Scoppettone, Sandra
See also GLL 1

East, Michael
See West, Morris L(anglo)

Eastaway, Edward
See Thomas, (Philip) Edward

Eastlake, William (Derry) 1917-1997 .... **CLC 8**
See also CA 5-8R; 158; CAAS 1; CANR 5, 63; CN 7; DLB 6, 206; INT CANR-5; TCWW 2

Eastman, Charles A(lexander) 1858-1939 .... **TCLC 55**
See also CA 179; CANR 91; DAM MULT; DLB 175; NNAL; YABC 1

Eberhart, Richard (Ghormley) 1904- .... **CLC 3, 11, 19, 56**
See also AMW; CA 1-4R; CANR 2; CDALB 1941-1968; CP 7; DAM POET; DLB 48; MTCW 1; RGAL 4

Eberstadt, Fernanda 1960- .... **CLC 39**
See also CA 136; CANR 69

Echegaray (y Eizaguirre), Jose (Maria Waldo) 1832-1916 .... **TCLC 4; HLCS 1**
See also CA 104; CANR 32; HW 1; MTCW 1

Echeverria, (Jose) Esteban (Antonino) 1805-1851 .... **NCLC 18**
See also LAW

Echo
See Proust, (Valentin-Louis-George-Eugene-)Marcel

Eckert, Allan W. 1931- .... **CLC 17**
See also AAYA 18; BYA 2; CA 13-16R; CANR 14, 45; INT CANR-14; MAICYA 2; MAICYAS 1; SAAS 21; SATA 29, 91; SATA-Brief 27

Eckhart, Meister 1260(?)-1327(?) ... **CMLC 9**
See also DLB 115

Eckmar, F. R.
See de Hartog, Jan

Eco, Umberto 1932- .... **CLC 28, 60, 142**
See also BEST 90:1; BPFB 1; CA 77-80; CANR 12, 33, 55; CPW; CWW 2; DA3; DAM NOV, POP; DLB 196, 242; MSW; MTCW 1, 2

Eddison, E(ric) R(ucker) 1882-1945 .... **TCLC 15**
See also CA 109; 156; DLB 255; FANT; SFW 4; SUFW

Eddy, Mary (Ann Morse) Baker 1821-1910 .... **TCLC 71**
See also CA 113; 174

Edel, (Joseph) Leon 1907-1997 .. **CLC 29, 34**
See also CA 1-4R; 161; CANR 1, 22; DLB 103; INT CANR-22

Eden, Emily 1797-1869 .... **NCLC 10**

Edgar, David 1948- .... **CLC 42**
See also CA 57-60; CANR 12, 61; CBD; CD 5; DAM DRAM; DLB 13, 233; MTCW 1

Edgerton, Clyde (Carlyle) 1944- ...... **CLC 39**
See also AAYA 17; CA 118; 134; CANR 64; CSW; INT 134; YAW

Edgeworth, Maria 1768-1849 .... **NCLC 1, 51**
See also BRWS 3; DLB 116, 159, 163; FW; RGEL 2; SATA 21; WLIT 3

Edmonds, Paul
See Kuttner, Henry

Edmonds, Walter D(umaux) 1903-1998 .... **CLC 35**
See also BYA 2; CA 5-8R; CANR 2; CWRI 5; DLB 9; LAIT 1; MAICYA 1, 2; RHW; SAAS 4; SATA 1, 27; SATA-Obit 99

Edmondson, Wallace
See Ellison, Harlan (Jay)

Edson, Russell 1935- .... **CLC 13**
See also CA 33-36R; DLB 244; WP

Edwards, Bronwen Elizabeth
See Rose, Wendy

Edwards, G(erald) B(asil) 1899-1976 .... **CLC 25**
See also CA 110

Edwards, Gus 1939- .... **CLC 43**
See also CA 108; INT 108

Edwards, Jonathan 1703-1758 .... **LC 7, 54**
See also AMW; DA; DAC; DAM MST; DLB 24; RGAL 4

Efron, Marina Ivanovna Tsvetaeva
See Tsvetaeva (Efron), Marina (Ivanovna)

Egoyan, Atom 1960- .... **CLC 151**
See also CA 157

Ehle, John (Marsden, Jr.) 1925- .... **CLC 27**
See also CA 9-12R; CSW

Ehrenbourg, Ilya (Grigoryevich)
See Ehrenburg, Ilya (Grigoryevich)

Ehrenburg, Ilya (Grigoryevich) 1891-1967 .... **CLC 18, 34, 62**
See also CA 102; 25-28R

Ehrenburg, Ilyo (Grigoryevich)
See Ehrenburg, Ilya (Grigoryevich)

Ehrenreich, Barbara 1941- .... **CLC 110**
See also BEST 90:4; CA 73-76; CANR 16, 37, 62; DLB 246; FW; MTCW 1, 2

Eich, Guenter 1907-1972 .... **CLC 15**
See also Eich, Gunter
See also CA 111; 93-96; DLB 69, 124

Eich, Gunter
See Eich, Guenter
See also RGWL 2

Eichendorff, Joseph 1788-1857 .... **NCLC 8**
See also DLB 90; RGWL 2

Eigner, Larry .... **CLC 9**
See also Eigner, Laurence (Joel)
See also CAAS 23; DLB 5; WP

Eigner, Laurence (Joel) 1927-1996
See Eigner, Larry
See also CA 9-12R; 151; CANR 6, 84; CP 7; DLB 193

Einhard c. 770-840 .... **CMLC 50**
See also DLB 148

Einstein, Albert 1879-1955 .... **TCLC 65**
See also CA 121; 133; MTCW 1, 2

Eiseley, Loren Corey 1907-1977 .... **CLC 7**
See also AAYA 5; ANW; CA 1-4R; 73-76; CANR 6; DLBD 17

Eisenstadt, Jill 1963- .... **CLC 50**
See also CA 140

Eisenstein, Sergei (Mikhailovich) 1898-1948 .... **TCLC 57**
See also CA 114; 149

Eisner, Simon
See Kornbluth, C(yril) M.

Ekeloef, (Bengt) Gunnar 1907-1968 .... **CLC 27; PC 23**
See also Ekelof, (Bengt) Gunnar
See also CA 123; 25-28R; DAM POET

Ekelof, (Bengt) Gunnar 1907-1968
See Ekeloef, (Bengt) Gunnar
See also DLB 259; EW 12

Ekelund, Vilhelm 1880-1949 .... **TCLC 75**
See also CA 189

Ekwensi, C. O. D.
See Ekwensi, Cyprian (Odiatu Duaka)

Ekwensi, Cyprian (Odiatu Duaka) 1921- .... **CLC 4; BLC 1**
See also AFW; BW 2, 3; CA 29-32R; CANR 18, 42, 74; CDWLB 3; CN 7; CWRI 5; DAM MULT; DLB 117; MTCW 1, 2; RGEL 2; SATA 66; WLIT 2

Elaine .... **TCLC 18**
See also Leverson, Ada

El Crummo
See Crumb, R(obert)

Elder, Lonne III 1931-1996 .... **DC 8**
See also BLC 1; BW 1, 3; CA 81-84; 152; CAD; CANR 25; DAM MULT; DLB 7, 38, 44

Eleanor of Aquitaine 1122-1204 ... **CMLC 39**

Elia
See Lamb, Charles

Eliade, Mircea 1907-1986 .... **CLC 19**
See also CA 65-68; 119; CANR 30, 62; CDWLB 4; DLB 220; MTCW 1; SFW 4

Eliot, A. D.
See Jewett, (Theodora) Sarah Orne

Eliot, Alice
See Jewett, (Theodora) Sarah Orne

Eliot, Dan
See Silverberg, Robert

Eliot, George 1819-1880 ...... **NCLC 4, 13, 23, 41, 49, 89; PC 20; WLC**
See also BRW 5; BRWR 2; CDBLB 1832-1890; CN 7; CPW; DA; DA3; DAB; DAC; DAM MST, NOV; DLB 21, 35, 55; RGEL 2; RGSF 2; SSFS 8; WLIT 3

Eliot, John 1604-1690 .... **LC 5**
See also DLB 24

Eliot, T(homas) S(tearns) 1888-1965 ...... **CLC 1, 2, 3, 6, 9, 10, 13, 15, 24, 34, 41, 55, 57, 113; PC 5, 31; WLC**
See also AAYA 28; AMW; AMWR 1; BRW 7; BRWR 2; CA 5-8R; 25-28R; CANR 41; CDALB 1929-1941; DA; DA3; DAB; DAC; DAM DRAM, MST, POET; DFS 4, 13; DLB 7, 10, 45, 63, 245; DLBY 1988; EXPP; LAIT 3; MTCW 1, 2; PAB; PFS 1, 7; RGAL 4; RGEL 2; WLIT 4; WP

Elizabeth 1866-1941 .... **TCLC 41**

Elkin, Stanley L(awrence) 1930-1995 .. **CLC 4, 6, 9, 14, 27, 51, 91; SSC 12**
See also AMWS 6; BPFB 1; CA 9-12R; 148; CANR 8, 46; CN 7; CPW; DAM NOV, POP; DLB 2, 28, 218; DLBY 1980; INT CANR-8; MTCW 1, 2; RGAL 4

Elledge, Scott .... **CLC 34**

Elliot, Don
See Silverberg, Robert

Elliott, Don
See Silverberg, Robert

Elliott, George P(aul) 1918-1980 .... **CLC 2**
See also CA 1-4R; 97-100; CANR 2; DLB 244

Elliott, Janice 1931-1995 .... **CLC 47**
See also CA 13-16R; CANR 8, 29, 84; CN 7; DLB 14; SATA 119

Elliott, Sumner Locke 1917-1991 ..... **CLC 38**
See also CA 5-8R; 134; CANR 2, 21

Elliott, William
See Bradbury, Ray (Douglas)
Ellis, A. E. .... **CLC 7**
Ellis, Alice Thomas .... **CLC 40**
See also Haycraft, Anna (Margaret)
See also DLB 194; MTCW 1
Ellis, Bret Easton 1964- ...... **CLC 39, 71, 117**
See also AAYA 2, 43; CA 118; 123; CANR 51, 74; CN 7; CPW; DA3; DAM POP; HGG; INT CA-123; MTCW 1; NFS 11
Ellis, (Henry) Havelock
1859-1939 .... **TCLC 14**
See also CA 109; 169; DLB 190
Ellis, Landon
See Ellison, Harlan (Jay)
Ellis, Trey 1962- .... **CLC 55**
See also CA 146; CANR 92
Ellison, Harlan (Jay) 1934- ... **CLC 1, 13, 42, 139; SSC 14**
See also AAYA 29; BPFB 1; BYA 14; CA 5-8R; CANR 5, 46; CPW; DAM POP; DLB 8; HGG; INT CANR-5; MTCW 1, 2; SCFW 2; SFW 4; SSFS 13, 14; SUFW
Ellison, Ralph (Waldo) 1914-1994 .... **CLC 1, 3, 11, 54, 86, 114; BLC 1; SSC 26; WLC**
See also AAYA 19; AFAW 1, 2; AMWS; BPFB 1; BW 1, 3; BYA 2; CA 9-12R; 145; CANR 24, 53; CDALB 1941-1968; CSW; DA; DA3; DAB; DAC; DAM MST, MULT, NOV; DLB 2, 76, 227; DLBY 1994; EXPN; EXPS; LAIT 4; MTCW 1, 2; NCFS 3; NFS 2; RGAL 4; RGSF 2; SSFS 1, 11; YAW
Ellmann, Lucy (Elizabeth) 1956- ..... **CLC 61**
See also CA 128
Ellmann, Richard (David)
1918-1987 .... **CLC 50**
See also BEST 89:2; CA 1-4R; 122; CANR 2, 28, 61; DLB 103; DLBY 1987; MTCW 1, 2
Elman, Richard (Martin)
1934-1997 .... **CLC 19**
See also CA 17-20R; 163; CAAS 3; CANR 47
Elron
See Hubbard, L(afayette) Ron(ald)
Eluard, Paul .... **TCLC 7, 41; PC 38**
See also Grindel, Eugene
See also GFL 1789 to the Present; RGWL 2
Elyot, Thomas 1490(?)-1546 .... **LC 11**
See also DLB 136; RGEL 2
Elytis, Odysseus 1911-1996 .... **CLC 15, 49, 100; PC 21**
See also Alepoudelis, Odysseus
See also CA 102; 151; CANR 94; CWW 2; DAM POET; EW 13; MTCW 1, 2; RGWL 2
Emecheta, (Florence Onye) Buchi
1944- .... **CLC 14, 48, 128; BLC 2**
See also AFW; BW 2, 3; CA 81-84; CANR 27, 81; CDWLB 3; CN 7; CWRI 5; DA3; DAM MULT; DLB 117; FW; MTCW 1, 2; NFS 12, 14; SATA 66; WLIT 2
Emerson, Mary Moody
1774-1863 .... **NCLC 66**
Emerson, Ralph Waldo 1803-1882 . **NCLC 1, 38, 98; PC 18; WLC**
See also AMW; ANW; CDALB 1640-1865; DA; DA3; DAB; DAC; DAM MST, POET; DLB 1, 59, 73, 183, 223; EXPP; LAIT 2; NCFS 3; PFS 4; RGAL 4; WP
Eminescu, Mihail 1850-1889 .... **NCLC 33**
Empedocles 5th cent. B.C.- .... **CMLC 50**
See also DLB 176
Empson, William 1906-1984 ... **CLC 3, 8, 19, 33, 34**
See also BRWS 2; CA 17-20R; 112; CANR 31, 61; DLB 20; MTCW 1, 2; RGEL 2

Enchi, Fumiko (Ueda) 1905-1986 ..... **CLC 31**
See also Enchi Fumiko
See also CA 129; 121; FW; MJW
Enchi Fumiko
See Enchi, Fumiko (Ueda)
See also DLB 182
Ende, Michael (Andreas Helmuth)
1929-1995 .... **CLC 31**
See also BYA 5; CA 118; 124; 149; CANR 36; CLR 14; DLB 75; MAICYA 1, 2; MAICYAS 1; SATA 61, 130; SATA-Brief 42; SATA-Obit 86
Endo, Shusaku 1923-1996 ..... **CLC 7, 14, 19, 54, 99; SSC 48**
See also Endo Shusaku
See also CA 29-32R; 153; CANR 21, 54; DA3; DAM NOV; MTCW 1, 2; RGSF 2; RGWL 2
Endo Shusaku
See Endo, Shusaku
See also DLB 182
Engel, Marian 1933-1985 .... **CLC 36**
See also CA 25-28R; CANR 12; DLB 53; FW; INT CANR-12
Engelhardt, Frederick
See Hubbard, L(afayette) Ron(ald)
Engels, Friedrich 1820-1895 .... **NCLC 85**
See also DLB 129
Enright, D(ennis) J(oseph) 1920- .. **CLC 4, 8, 31**
See also CA 1-4R; CANR 1, 42, 83; CP 7; DLB 27; SATA 25
Enzensberger, Hans Magnus
1929- .... **CLC 43; PC 28**
See also CA 116; 119; CANR 103
Ephron, Nora 1941- .... **CLC 17, 31**
See also AAYA 35; AITN 2; CA 65-68; CANR 12, 39, 83
Epicurus 341B.C.-270B.C. .... **CMLC 21**
See also DLB 176
Epsilon
See Betjeman, John
Epstein, Daniel Mark 1948- .... **CLC 7**
See also CA 49-52; CANR 2, 53, 90
Epstein, Jacob 1956- .... **CLC 19**
See also CA 114
Epstein, Jean 1897-1953 .... **TCLC 92**
Epstein, Joseph 1937- .... **CLC 39**
See also CA 112; 119; CANR 50, 65
Epstein, Leslie 1938- .... **CLC 27**
See also CA 73-76; CAAS 12; CANR 23, 69
Equiano, Olaudah 1745(?)-1797 .... **LC 16; BLC 2**
See also AFAW 1, 2; CDWLB 3; DAM MULT; DLB 37, 50; WLIT 2
Erasmus, Desiderius 1469(?)-1536 .... **LC 16**
See also DLB 136; EW 2; RGWL 2
Erdman, Paul E(mil) 1932- .... **CLC 25**
See also AITN 1; CA 61-64; CANR 13, 43, 84
Erdrich, Louise 1954- .... **CLC 39, 54, 120**
See also AAYA 10; AMWS 4; BEST 89:1; BPFB 1; CA 114; CANR 41, 62; CDALBS; CN 7; CP 7; CPW; CWP; DA3; DAM MULT, NOV, POP; DLB 152, 175, 206; EXPP; LAIT 5; MTCW 1; NFS 5; NNAL; PFS 14; RGAL 4; SATA 94; SSFS 14; TCWW 2
Erenburg, Ilya (Grigoryevich)
See Ehrenburg, Ilya (Grigoryevich)
Erickson, Stephen Michael 1950-
See Erickson, Steve
See also CA 129; SFW 4
Erickson, Steve .... **CLC 64**
See also Erickson, Stephen Michael
See also CANR 60, 68
Ericson, Walter
See Fast, Howard (Melvin)

Eriksson, Buntel
See Bergman, (Ernst) Ingmar
Ernaux, Annie 1940- .... **CLC 88**
See also CA 147; CANR 93; NCFS 3
Erskine, John 1879-1951 .... **TCLC 84**
See also CA 112; 159; DLB 9, 102; FANT
Eschenbach, Wolfram von
See Wolfram von Eschenbach
Eseki, Bruno
See Mphahlele, Ezekiel
Esenin, Sergei (Alexandrovich)
1895-1925 .... **TCLC 4**
See also CA 104; RGWL 2
Eshleman, Clayton 1935- .... **CLC 7**
See also CA 33-36R; CAAS 6; CANR 93; CP 7; DLB 5
Espriella, Don Manuel Alvarez
See Southey, Robert
Espriu, Salvador 1913-1985 .... **CLC 9**
See also CA 154; 115; DLB 134
Espronceda, Jose de 1808-1842 ..... **NCLC 39**
Esquivel, Laura 1951(?)- ... **CLC 141; HLCS 1**
See also AAYA 29; CA 143; CANR 68; DA3; DNFS 2; LAIT 3; MTCW 1; NFS 5; WLIT 1
Esse, James
See Stephens, James
Esterbrook, Tom
See Hubbard, L(afayette) Ron(ald)
Estleman, Loren D. 1952- .... **CLC 48**
See also AAYA 27; CA 85-88; CANR 27, 74; CMW 4; CPW; DA3; DAM NOV, POP; DLB 226; INT CANR-27; MTCW 1, 2
Euclid 306B.C.-283B.C. .... **CMLC 25**
Eugenides, Jeffrey 1960(?)- .... **CLC 81**
See also CA 144
Euripides c. 484B.C.-406B.C. .... **CMLC 23, 51; DC 4; WLCS**
See also AW 1; CDWLB 1; DA; DA3; DAB; DAC; DAM DRAM, MST; DFS 1, 4, 6; DLB 176; LAIT 1; RGWL 2
Evan, Evin
See Faust, Frederick (Schiller)
Evans, Caradoc 1878-1945 ... **TCLC 85; SSC 43**
See also DLB 162
Evans, Evan
See Faust, Frederick (Schiller)
See also TCWW 2
Evans, Marian
See Eliot, George
Evans, Mary Ann
See Eliot, George
Evarts, Esther
See Benson, Sally
Everett, Percival
See Everett, Percival L.
See also CSW
Everett, Percival L. 1956- .... **CLC 57**
See also Everett, Percival
See also BW 2; CA 129; CANR 94
Everson, R(onald) G(ilmour)
1903-1992 .... **CLC 27**
See also CA 17-20R; DLB 88
Everson, William (Oliver)
1912-1994 .... **CLC 1, 5, 14**
See also CA 9-12R; 145; CANR 20; DLB 5, 16, 212; MTCW 1
Evtushenko, Evgenii Aleksandrovich
See Yevtushenko, Yevgeny (Alexandrovich)
See also RGWL 2
Ewart, Gavin (Buchanan)
1916-1995 .... **CLC 13, 46**
See also BRWS 7; CA 89-92; 150; CANR 17, 46; CP 7; DLB 40; MTCW 1

Ewers, Hanns Heinz 1871-1943 ..... **TCLC 12**
See also CA 109; 149

Ewing, Frederick R.
See Sturgeon, Theodore (Hamilton)

Exley, Frederick (Earl) 1929-1992 .... **CLC 6, 11**
See also AITN 2; BPFB 1; CA 81-84; 138; DLB 143; DLBY 1981

Eynhardt, Guillermo
See Quiroga, Horacio (Sylvestre)

Ezekiel, Nissim 1924- .... **CLC 61**
See also CA 61-64; CP 7

Ezekiel, Tish O'Dowd 1943- .... **CLC 34**
See also CA 129

Fadeyev, A.
See Bulgya, Alexander Alexandrovich

Fadeyev, Alexander .... **TCLC 53**
See also Bulgya, Alexander Alexandrovich

Fagen, Donald 1948- .... **CLC 26**

Fainzilberg, Ilya Arnoldovich 1897-1937
See Ilf, Ilya
See also CA 120; 165

Fair, Ronald L. 1932- .... **CLC 18**
See also BW 1; CA 69-72; CANR 25; DLB 33

Fairbairn, Roger
See Carr, John Dickson

Fairbairns, Zoe (Ann) 1948- .... **CLC 32**
See also CA 103; CANR 21, 85; CN 7

Fairfield, Flora
See Alcott, Louisa May

Fairman, Paul W. 1916-1977
See Queen, Ellery
See also CA 114; SFW 4

Falco, Gian
See Papini, Giovanni

Falconer, James
See Kirkup, James

Falconer, Kenneth
See Kornbluth, C(yril) M.

Falkland, Samuel
See Heijermans, Herman

Fallaci, Oriana 1930- .... **CLC 11, 110**
See also CA 77-80; CANR 15, 58; FW; MTCW 1

Faludi, Susan 1959- .... **CLC 140**
See also CA 138; FW; MTCW 1; NCFS 3

Faludy, George 1913- .... **CLC 42**
See also CA 21-24R

Faludy, Gyoergy
See Faludy, George

Fanon, Frantz 1925-1961 .... **CLC 74; BLC 2**
See also BW 1; CA 116; 89-92; DAM MULT; WLIT 2

Fanshawe, Ann 1625-1680 .... **LC 11**

Fante, John (Thomas) 1911-1983 ..... **CLC 60**
See also CA 69-72; 109; CANR 23, 104; DLB 130; DLBY 1983

Farah, Nuruddin 1945- .. **CLC 53, 137; BLC 2**
See also AFW; BW 2, 3; CA 106; CANR 81; CDWLB 3; CN 7; DAM MULT; DLB 125; WLIT 2

Fargue, Leon-Paul 1876(?)-1947 .... **TCLC 11**
See also CA 109; CANR 107; DLB 258

Farigoule, Louis
See Romains, Jules

Farina, Richard 1936(?)-1966 .... **CLC 9**
See also CA 81-84; 25-28R

Farley, Walter (Lorimer) 1915-1989 .... **CLC 17**
See also BYA 14; CA 17-20R; CANR 8, 29, 84; DLB 22; JRDA; MAICYA 1, 2; SATA 2, 43; YAW

Farmer, Philip Jose 1918- .... **CLC 1, 19**
See also AAYA 28; BPFB 1; CA 1-4R; CANR 4, 35; DLB 8; MTCW 1; SATA 93; SCFW 2; SFW 4

Farquhar, George 1677-1707 .... **LC 21**
See also BRW 2; DAM DRAM; DLB 84; RGEL 2

Farrell, J(ames) G(ordon) 1935-1979 .... **CLC 6**
See also CA 73-76; 89-92; CANR 36; DLB 14; MTCW 1; RGEL 2; RHW; WLIT 4

Farrell, James T(homas) 1904-1979 . **CLC 1, 4, 8, 11, 66; SSC 28**
See also AMW; BPFB 1; CA 5-8R; 89-92; CANR 9, 61; DLB 4, 9, 86; DLBD 2; MTCW 1, 2; RGAL 4

Farrell, Warren (Thomas) 1943- ...... **CLC 70**
See also CA 146

Farren, Richard J.
See Betjeman, John

Farren, Richard M.
See Betjeman, John

Fassbinder, Rainer Werner 1946-1982 .... **CLC 20**
See also CA 93-96; 106; CANR 31

Fast, Howard (Melvin) 1914- ... **CLC 23, 131**
See also AAYA 16; BPFB 1; CA 1-4R; 181; CAAE 181; CAAS 18; CANR 1, 33, 54, 75, 98; CMW 4; CN 7; CPW; DAM NOV; DLB 9; INT CANR-33; MTCW 1; RHW; SATA 7; SATA-Essay 107; TCWW 2; YAW

Faulcon, Robert
See Holdstock, Robert P.

Faulkner, William (Cuthbert) 1897-1962 .... **CLC 1, 3, 6, 8, 9, 11, 14, 18, 28, 52, 68; SSC 1, 35, 42; WLC**
See also AAYA 7; AMW; AMWR 1; BPFB 1; BYA 5; CA 81-84; CANR 33; CDALB 1929-1941; DA; DA3; DAB; DAC; DAM MST, NOV; DLB 9, 11, 44, 102; DLBD 2; DLBY 1986, 1997; EXPN; EXPS; LAIT 2; MTCW 1, 2; NFS 4, 8, 13; RGAL 4; RGSF 2; SSFS 2, 5, 6, 12

Fauset, Jessie Redmon 1882(?)-1961 .... **CLC 19, 54; BLC 2**
See also AFAW 2; BW 1; CA 109; CANR 83; DAM MULT; DLB 51; FW; MAWW

Faust, Frederick (Schiller) 1892-1944(?) .... **TCLC 49**
See also Austin, Frank; Brand, Max; Challis, George; Dawson, Peter; Dexter, Martin; Evans, Evan; Frederick, John; Frost, Frederick; Manning, David; Silver, Nicholas
See also CA 108; 152; DAM POP; DLB 256

Fawkes, Guy
See Benchley, Robert (Charles)

Fearing, Kenneth (Flexner) 1902-1961 .... **CLC 51**
See also CA 93-96; CANR 59; CMW 4; DLB 9; RGAL 4

Fecamps, Elise
See Creasey, John

Federman, Raymond 1928- .... **CLC 6, 47**
See also CA 17-20R; CAAS 8; CANR 10, 43, 83, 108; CN 7; DLBY 1980

Federspiel, J(uerg) F. 1931- .... **CLC 42**
See also CA 146

Feiffer, Jules (Ralph) 1929- ...... **CLC 2, 8, 64**
See also AAYA 3; CA 17-20R; CAD; CANR 30, 59; CD 5; DAM DRAM; DLB 7, 44; INT CANR-30; MTCW 1; SATA 8, 61, 111

Feige, Hermann Albert Otto Maximilian
See Traven, B.

Feinberg, David B. 1956-1994 .... **CLC 59**
See also CA 135; 147

Feinstein, Elaine 1930- .... **CLC 36**
See also CA 69-72; CAAS 1; CANR 31, 68; CN 7; CP 7; CWP; DLB 14, 40; MTCW 1

Feke, Gilbert David .... **CLC 65**

Feldman, Irving (Mordecai) 1928- ..... **CLC 7**
See also CA 1-4R; CANR 1; CP 7; DLB 169

Felix-Tchicaya, Gerald
See Tchicaya, Gerald Felix

Fellini, Federico 1920-1993 .... **CLC 16, 85**
See also CA 65-68; 143; CANR 33

Felsen, Henry Gregor 1916-1995 ..... **CLC 17**
See also CA 1-4R; 180; CANR 1; SAAS 2; SATA 1

Felski, Rita .... **CLC 65**

Fenno, Jack
See Calisher, Hortense

Fenollosa, Ernest (Francisco) 1853-1908 .... **TCLC 91**

Fenton, James Martin 1949- .... **CLC 32**
See also CA 102; CANR 108; CP 7; DLB 40; PFS 11

Ferber, Edna 1887-1968 .... **CLC 18, 93**
See also AITN 1; CA 5-8R; 25-28R; CANR 68, 105; DLB 9, 28, 86; MTCW 1, 2; RGAL 4; RHW; SATA 7; TCWW 2

Ferdowsi, Abu'l Qasem 940-1020 . **CMLC 43**
See also RGWL 2

Ferguson, Helen
See Kavan, Anna

Ferguson, Niall 1964- .... **CLC 134**
See also CA 190

Ferguson, Samuel 1810-1886 .... **NCLC 33**
See also DLB 32; RGEL 2

Fergusson, Robert 1750-1774 .... **LC 29**
See also DLB 109; RGEL 2

Ferling, Lawrence
See Ferlinghetti, Lawrence (Monsanto)

Ferlinghetti, Lawrence (Monsanto) 1919(?)- ..... **CLC 2, 6, 10, 27, 111; PC 1**
See also CA 5-8R; CANR 3, 41, 73; CDALB 1941-1968; CP 7; DA3; DAM POET; DLB 5, 16; MTCW 1, 2; RGAL 4; WP

Fern, Fanny
See Parton, Sara Payson Willis

Fernandez, Vicente Garcia Huidobro
See Huidobro Fernandez, Vicente Garcia

Fernandez-Armesto, Felipe .... **CLC 70**

Fernandez de Lizardi, Jose Joaquin
See Lizardi, Jose Joaquin Fernandez de

Ferre, Rosario 1942- ...... **CLC 139; HLCS 1; SSC 36**
See also CA 131; CANR 55, 81; CWW 2; DLB 145; HW 1, 2; LAWS 1; MTCW 1; WLIT 1

Ferrer, Gabriel (Francisco Victor) Miro
See Miro (Ferrer), Gabriel (Francisco Victor)

Ferrier, Susan (Edmonstone) 1782-1854 .... **NCLC 8**
See also DLB 116; RGEL 2

Ferrigno, Robert 1948(?)- .... **CLC 65**
See also CA 140

Ferron, Jacques 1921-1985 .... **CLC 94**
See also CA 117; 129; CCA 1; DAC; DLB 60

Feuchtwanger, Lion 1884-1958 .... **TCLC 3**
See also CA 104; 187; DLB 66

Feuillet, Octave 1821-1890 .... **NCLC 45**
See also DLB 192

Feydeau, Georges (Leon Jules Marie) 1862-1921 .... **TCLC 22**
See also CA 113; 152; CANR 84; DAM DRAM; DLB 192; GFL 1789 to the Present; RGWL 2

Fichte, Johann Gottlieb 1762-1814 .... **NCLC 62**
See also DLB 90

Ficino, Marsilio 1433-1499 .... **LC 12**
Fiedeler, Hans
See Doeblin, Alfred
Fiedler, Leslie A(aron) 1917- .. **CLC 4, 13, 24**
See also CA 9-12R; CANR 7, 63; CN 7; DLB 28, 67; MTCW 1, 2; RGAL 4
Field, Andrew 1938- .... **CLC 44**
See also CA 97-100; CANR 25
Field, Eugene 1850-1895 .... **NCLC 3**
See also DLB 23, 42, 140; DLBD 13; MAICYA 1, 2; RGAL 4; SATA 16
Field, Gans T.
See Wellman, Manly Wade
Field, Michael 1915-1971 .... **TCLC 43**
See also CA 29-32R
Field, Peter
See Hobson, Laura Z(ametkin)
See also TCWW 2
Fielding, Helen 1959(?)- .... **CLC 146**
See also CA 172; DLB 231
Fielding, Henry 1707-1754 .. **LC 1, 46; WLC**
See also BRW 3; BRWR 1; CDBLB 1660-1789; DA; DA3; DAB; DAC; DAM DRAM, MST, NOV; DLB 39, 84, 101; RGEL 2; WLIT 3
Fielding, Sarah 1710-1768 .... **LC 1, 44**
See also DLB 39; RGEL 2
Fields, W. C. 1880-1946 .... **TCLC 80**
See also DLB 44
Fierstein, Harvey (Forbes) 1954- ..... **CLC 33**
See also CA 123; 129; CAD; CD 5; CPW; DA3; DAM DRAM, POP; DFS 6; GLL
Figes, Eva 1932- .... **CLC 31**
See also CA 53-56; CANR 4, 44, 83; CN 7; DLB 14; FW
Finch, Anne 1661-1720 .... **LC 3; PC 21**
See also DLB 95
Finch, Robert (Duer Claydon)
1900-1995 .... **CLC 18**
See also CA 57-60; CANR 9, 24, 49; CP 7; DLB 88
Findley, Timothy 1930- .... **CLC 27, 102**
See also CA 25-28R; CANR 12, 42, 69, 109; CCA 1; CN 7; DAC; DAM MST; DLB 53; FANT; RHW
Fink, William
See Mencken, H(enry) L(ouis)
Firbank, Louis 1942-
See Reed, Lou
See also CA 117
Firbank, (Arthur Annesley) Ronald
1886-1926 .... **TCLC 1**
See also BRWS 2; CA 104; 177; DLB 36; RGEL 2
Fish, Stanley
See Fish, Stanley Eugene
Fish, Stanley E.
See Fish, Stanley Eugene
Fish, Stanley Eugene 1938- .... **CLC 142**
See also CA 112; 132; CANR 90; DLB 67
Fisher, Dorothy (Frances) Canfield
1879-1958 .... **TCLC 87**
See also CA 114; 136; CANR 80; CLR 71,; CWRI 5; DLB 9, 102; MAICYA 1, 2; YABC 1
Fisher, M(ary) F(rances) K(ennedy)
1908-1992 .... **CLC 76, 87**
See also CA 77-80; 138; CANR 44; MTCW 1
Fisher, Roy 1930- .... **CLC 25**
See also CA 81-84; CAAS 10; CANR 16; CP 7; DLB 40
Fisher, Rudolph 1897-1934 .. **TCLC 11; BLC 2; SSC 25**
See also BW 1, 3; CA 107; 124; CANR 80; DAM MULT; DLB 51, 102
Fisher, Vardis (Alvero) 1895-1968 ...... **CLC 7**
See also CA 5-8R; 25-28R; CANR 68; DLB 9, 206; RGAL 4; TCWW 2

Fiske, Tarleton
See Bloch, Robert (Albert)
Fitch, Clarke
See Sinclair, Upton (Beall)
Fitch, John IV
See Cormier, Robert (Edmund)
Fitzgerald, Captain Hugh
See Baum, L(yman) Frank
FitzGerald, Edward 1809-1883 .... **NCLC 9**
See also BRW 4; DLB 32; RGEL 2
Fitzgerald, F(rancis) Scott (Key)
1896-1940 . **TCLC 1, 6, 14, 28, 55; SSC 6, 31; WLC**
See also AAYA 24; AITN 1; AMW; AMWR 1; BPFB 1; CA 110; 123; CDALB 1917-1929; DA; DA3; DAB; DAC; DAM MST, NOV; DLB 4, 9, 86, 219; DLBD 1, 15, 16; DLBY 1981, 1996; EXPN; EXPS; LAIT 3; MTCW 1, 2; NFS 2; RGAL 4; RGSF 2; SSFS 4
Fitzgerald, Penelope 1916-2000 . **CLC 19, 51, 61, 143**
See also BRWS 5; CA 85-88; 190; CAAS 10; CANR 56, 86; CN 7; DLB 14, 194; MTCW 2
Fitzgerald, Robert (Stuart)
1910-1985 .... **CLC 39**
See also CA 1-4R; 114; CANR 1; DLBY 1980
FitzGerald, Robert D(avid)
1902-1987 .... **CLC 19**
See also CA 17-20R; RGEL 2
Fitzgerald, Zelda (Sayre)
1900-1948 .... **TCLC 52**
See also AMWS 9; CA 117; 126; DLBY 1984
Flanagan, Thomas (James Bonner)
1923- .... **CLC 25, 52**
See also CA 108; CANR 55; CN 7; DLBY 1980; INT 108; MTCW 1; RHW
Flaubert, Gustave 1821-1880 .... **NCLC 2, 10, 19, 62, 66; SSC 11; WLC**
See also DA; DA3; DAB; DAC; DAM MST, NOV; DLB 119; EW 7; EXPS; GFL 1789 to the Present; LAIT 2; NFS 14; RGSF 2; RGWL 2; SSFS 6
Flavius Josephus
See Josephus, Flavius
Flecker, Herman Elroy
See Flecker, (Herman) James Elroy
Flecker, (Herman) James Elroy
1884-1915 .... **TCLC 43**
See also CA 109; 150; DLB 10, 19; RGEL 2
Fleming, Ian (Lancaster) 1908-1964 . **CLC 3, 30**
See also AAYA 26; BPFB 1; CA 5-8R; CANR 59; CDBLB 1945-1960; CMW 4; CPW; DA3; DAM POP; DLB 87, 201; MSW; MTCW 1, 2; RGEL 2; SATA 9; YAW
Fleming, Thomas (James) 1927- ...... **CLC 37**
See also CA 5-8R; CANR 10, 102; INT CANR-10; SATA 8
Fletcher, John 1579-1625 .... **LC 33; DC 6**
See also BRW 2; CDBLB Before 1660; DLB 58; RGEL 2
Fletcher, John Gould 1886-1950 .... **TCLC 35**
See also CA 107; 167; DLB 4, 45; RGAL 4
Fleur, Paul
See Pohl, Frederik
Flooglebuckle, Al
See Spiegelman, Art
Flora, Fletcher 1914-1969
See Queen, Ellery
See also CA 1-4R; CANR 3, 85
Flying Officer X
See Bates, H(erbert) E(rnest)

Fo, Dario 1926- .... **CLC 32, 109; DC 10**
See also CA 116; 128; CANR 68; CWW 2; DA3; DAM DRAM; DLBY 1997; MTCW 1, 2
Fogarty, Jonathan Titulescu Esq.
See Farrell, James T(homas)
Follett, Ken(neth Martin) 1949- .... **CLC 18**
See also AAYA 6; BEST 89:4; BPFB 1; CA 81-84; CANR 13, 33, 54, 102; CMW 4; CPW; DA3; DAM NOV, POP; DLB 87; DLBY 1981; INT CANR-33; MTCW 1
Fontane, Theodor 1819-1898 .... **NCLC 26**
See also CDWLB 2; DLB 129; EW 6; RGWL 2
Fontenot, Chester .... **CLC 65**
Foote, Horton 1916- .... **CLC 51, 91**
See also CA 73-76; CAD; CANR 34, 51; CD 5; CSW; DA3; DAM DRAM; DLB 26; INT CANR-34
Foote, Mary Hallock 1847-1938 .. **TCLC 108**
See also DLB 186, 188, 202, 221
Foote, Shelby 1916- .... **CLC 75**
See also AAYA 40; CA 5-8R; CANR 3, 45, 74; CN 7; CPW; CSW; DA3; DAM NOV, POP; DLB 2, 17; MTCW 2; RHW
Forbes, Cosmo
See Lewton, Val
Forbes, Esther 1891-1967 .... **CLC 12**
See also AAYA 17; BYA 2; CA 13-14; 25-28R; CAP 1; CLR 27; DLB 22; JRDA; MAICYA 1, 2; RHW; SATA 2, 100; YAW
Forche, Carolyn (Louise) 1950- .... **CLC 25, 83, 86; PC 10**
See also CA 109; 117; CANR 50, 74; CP 7; CWP; DA3; DAM POET; DLB 5, 193; INT CA-117; MTCW 1; RGAL 4
Ford, Elbur
See Hibbert, Eleanor Alice Burford
Ford, Ford Madox 1873-1939 ... **TCLC 1, 15, 39, 57**
See also Chaucer, Daniel
See also BRW 6; CA 104; 132; CANR 74; CDBLB 1914-1945; DA3; DAM NOV; DLB 34, 98, 162; MTCW 1, 2; RGEL 2
Ford, Henry 1863-1947 .... **TCLC 73**
See also CA 115; 148
Ford, John 1586-1639 .... **LC 68; DC 8**
See also BRW 2; CDBLB Before 1660; DA3; DAM DRAM; DFS 7; DLB 58; IDTP; RGEL 2
Ford, John 1895-1973 .... **CLC 16**
See also CA 187; 45-48
Ford, Richard 1944- .... **CLC 46, 99**
See also AMWS 5; CA 69-72; CANR 11, 47, 86; CN 7; CSW; DLB 227; MTCW 1; RGAL 4; RGSF 2
Ford, Webster
See Masters, Edgar Lee
Foreman, Richard 1937- .... **CLC 50**
See also CA 65-68; CAD; CANR 32, 63; CD 5
Forester, C(ecil) S(cott) 1899-1966 ... **CLC 35**
See also CA 73-76; 25-28R; CANR 83; DLB 191; RGEL 2; RHW; SATA 13
Forez
See Mauriac, Francois (Charles)
Forman, James Douglas 1932- .... **CLC 21**
See also AAYA 17; CA 9-12R; CANR 4, 19, 42; JRDA; MAICYA 1; SATA 8, 70; YAW
Fornes, Maria Irene 1930- . **CLC 39, 61; DC 10; HLCS 1**
See also CA 25-28R; CAD; CANR 28, 81; CD 5; CWD; DLB 7; HW 1, 2; INT CANR-28; MTCW 1; RGAL 4

Forrest, Leon (Richard) 1937-1997 .. **CLC 4; BLCS**
See also AFAW 2; BW 2; CA 89-92; 162; CAAS 7; CANR 25, 52, 87; CN 7; DLB 33

Forster, E(dward) M(organ)
1879-1970 ...... **CLC 1, 2, 3, 4, 9, 10, 13, 15, 22, 45, 77; SSC 27; WLC**
See also AAYA 2, 37; BRW 6; BRWR 2; CA 13-14; 25-28R; CANR 45; CAP 1; CDBLB 1914-1945; DA; DA3; DAB; DAC; DAM MST, NOV; DLB 34, 98, 162, 178, 195; DLBD 10; EXPN; LAIT 3; MTCW 1, 2; NCFS 1; NFS 3, 10, 11; RGEL 2; RGSF 2; SATA 57; SUFW; WLIT 4

Forster, John 1812-1876 .... **NCLC 11**
See also DLB 144, 184

Forster, Margaret 1938- .... **CLC 149**
See also CA 133; CANR 62; CN 7; DLB 155

Forsyth, Frederick 1938- .... **CLC 2, 5, 36**
See also BEST 89:4; CA 85-88; CANR 38, 62; CMW 4; CN 7; CPW; DAM NOV, POP; DLB 87; MTCW 1, 2

Forten, Charlotte L. 1837-1914 .... **TCLC 16; BLC 2**
See also Grimke, Charlotte L(ottie) Forten
See also DLB 50, 239

Foscolo, Ugo 1778-1827 .... **NCLC 8, 97**
See also EW 5

Fosse, Bob .... **CLC 20**
See also Fosse, Robert Louis

Fosse, Robert Louis 1927-1987
See Fosse, Bob
See also CA 110; 123

Foster, Hannah Webster
1758-1840 .... **NCLC 99**
See also DLB 37, 200; RGAL 4

Foster, Stephen Collins
1826-1864 .... **NCLC 26**
See also RGAL 4

Foucault, Michel 1926-1984 . **CLC 31, 34, 69**
See also CA 105; 113; CANR 34; DLB 242; EW 13; GFL 1789 to the Present; GLL 1; MTCW 1, 2

Fouque, Friedrich (Heinrich Karl) de la Motte 1777-1843 .... **NCLC 2**
See also DLB 90; RGWL 2; SUFW

Fourier, Charles 1772-1837 .... **NCLC 51**

Fournier, Henri Alban 1886-1914
See Alain-Fournier
See also CA 104; 179

Fournier, Pierre 1916- .... **CLC 11**
See Gascar, Pierre
See also CA 89-92; CANR 16, 40

Fowles, John (Robert) 1926- . **CLC 1, 2, 3, 4, 6, 9, 10, 15, 33, 87; SSC 33**
See also BPFB 1; BRWS 1; CA 5-8R; CANR 25, 71, 103; CDBLB 1960 to Present; CN 7; DA3; DAB; DAC; DAM MST; DLB 14, 139, 207; HGG; MTCW 1, 2; RGEL 2; RHW; SATA 22; WLIT 4

Fox, Paula 1923- .... **CLC 2, 8, 121**
See also AAYA 3, 37; BYA 3; CA 73-76; CANR 20, 36, 62, 105; CLR 1, 44; DLB 52; JRDA; MAICYA 1, 2; MTCW 1; NFS 12; SATA 17, 60, 120; WYA; YAW

Fox, William Price (Jr.) 1926- .... **CLC 22**
See also CA 17-20R; CANR 11; CSW; DLB 2; DLBY 1981

Foxe, John 1517(?)-1587 .... **LC 14**
See also DLB 132

Frame, Janet .. **CLC 2, 3, 6, 22, 66, 96; SSC 29**
See also Clutha, Janet Paterson Frame
See also CN 7; CWP; RGEL 2; RGSF 2

France, Anatole .... **TCLC 9**
See also Thibault, Jacques Anatole Francois
See also DLB 123; GFL 1789 to the Present; MTCW 1; RGWL 2; SUFW

Francis, Claude .... **CLC 50**
See also CA 192

Francis, Dick 1920- .... **CLC 2, 22, 42, 102**
See also AAYA 5, 21; BEST 89:3; BPFB 1; CA 5-8R; CANR 9, 42, 68, 100; CDBLB 1960 to Present; CMW 4; CN 7; DA3; DAM POP; DLB 87; INT CANR-9; MSW; MTCW 1, 2

Francis, Robert (Churchill)
1901-1987 .... **CLC 15; PC 34**
See also AMWS 9; CA 1-4R; 123; CANR 1; EXPP; PFS 12

Francis, Lord Jeffrey
See Jeffrey, Francis
See also DLB 107

Frank, Anne(lies Marie)
1929-1945 .... **TCLC 17; WLC**
See also AAYA 12; BYA 1; CA 113; 133; CANR 68; DA; DA3; DAB; DAC; DAM MST; LAIT 4; MAICYA 2; MAICYAS 1; MTCW 1, 2; NCFS 2; SATA 87; SATA-Brief 42; WYA; YAW

Frank, Bruno 1887-1945 .... **TCLC 81**
See also CA 189; DLB 118

Frank, Elizabeth 1945- .... **CLC 39**
See also CA 121; 126; CANR 78; INT 126

Frankl, Viktor E(mil) 1905-1997 ...... **CLC 93**
See also CA 65-68; 161

Franklin, Benjamin
See Hasek, Jaroslav (Matej Frantisek)

Franklin, Benjamin 1706-1790 .... **LC 25; WLCS**
See also AMW; CDALB 1640-1865; DA; DA3; DAB; DAC; DAM MST; DLB 24, 43, 73, 183; LAIT 1; RGAL 4; TUS

Franklin, (Stella Maria Sarah) Miles (Lampe) 1879-1954 .... **TCLC 7**
See also CA 104; 164; DLB 230; FW; MTCW 2; RGEL 2; TWA

Fraser, George MacDonald 1925- ...... **CLC 7**
See also CA 45-48, 180; CAAE 180; CANR 2, 48, 74; MTCW 1; RHW

Fraser, Sylvia 1935- .... **CLC 64**
See also CA 45-48; CANR 1, 16, 60; CCA 1

Frayn, Michael 1933- .... **CLC 3, 7, 31, 47**
See also BRWS 7; CA 5-8R; CANR 30, 69; CBD; CD 5; CN 7; DAM DRAM, NOV; DLB 13, 14, 194, 245; FANT; MTCW 1, 2; SFW 4

Fraze, Candida (Merrill) 1945- .... **CLC 50**
See also CA 126

Frazer, Andrew
See Marlowe, Stephen

Frazer, J(ames) G(eorge)
1854-1941 .... **TCLC 32**
See also BRWS 3; CA 118

Frazer, Robert Caine
See Creasey, John

Frazer, Sir James George
See Frazer, J(ames) G(eorge)

Frazier, Charles 1950- .... **CLC 109**
See also AAYA 34; CA 161; CSW

Frazier, Ian 1951- .... **CLC 46**
See also CA 130; CANR 54, 93

Frederic, Harold 1856-1898 .... **NCLC 10**
See also AMW; DLB 12, 23; DLBD 13; RGAL 4

Frederick, John
See Faust, Frederick (Schiller)
See also TCWW 2

Frederick the Great 1712-1786 .... **LC 14**

Fredro, Aleksander 1793-1876 .... **NCLC 8**

Freeling, Nicolas 1927- .... **CLC 38**
See also CA 49-52; CAAS 12; CANR 1, 17, 50, 84; CMW 4; CN 7; DLB 87

Freeman, Douglas Southall
1886-1953 .... **TCLC 11**
See also CA 109; 195; DLB 17; DLBD 17

Freeman, Judith 1946- .... **CLC 55**
See also CA 148; DLB 256

Freeman, Mary E(leanor) Wilkins
1852-1930 .... **TCLC 9; SSC 1, 47**
See also CA 106; 177; DLB 12, 78, 221; EXPS; FW; HGG; MAWW; RGAL 4; RGSF 2; SSFS 4, 8; SUFW; TUS

Freeman, R(ichard) Austin
1862-1943 .... **TCLC 21**
See also CA 113; CANR 84; CMW 4; DLB 70

French, Albert 1943- .... **CLC 86**
See also BW 3; CA 167

French, Marilyn 1929- .... **CLC 10, 18, 60**
See also BPFB 1; CA 69-72; CANR 3, 31; CN 7; CPW; DAM DRAM, NOV, POP; FW; INT CANR-31; MTCW 1, 2

French, Paul
See Asimov, Isaac

Freneau, Philip Morin 1752-1832 .. **NCLC 1, 111**
See also AMWS 2; DLB 37, 43; RGAL 4

Freud, Sigmund 1856-1939 .... **TCLC 52**
See also CA 115; 133; CANR 69; EW 8; MTCW 1, 2; NCFS 3

Freytag, Gustav 1816-1895 .... **NCLC 109**
See also DLB 129

Friedan, Betty (Naomi) 1921- .... **CLC 74**
See also CA 65-68; CANR 18, 45, 74; DLB 246; FW; MTCW 1, 2

Friedlander, Saul 1932- .... **CLC 90**
See also CA 117; 130; CANR 72

Friedman, B(ernard) H(arper)
1926- .... **CLC 7**
See also CA 1-4R; CANR 3, 48

Friedman, Bruce Jay 1930- ...... **CLC 3, 5, 56**
See also CA 9-12R; CAD; CANR 25, 52, 101; CD 5; CN 7; DLB 2, 28, 244; INT CANR-25

Friel, Brian 1929- .... **CLC 5, 42, 59, 115; DC 8**
See also BRWS 5; CA 21-24R; CANR 33, 69; CBD; CD 5; DFS 11; DLB 13; MTCW 1; RGEL 2

Friis-Baastad, Babbis Ellinor
1921-1970 .... **CLC 12**
See also CA 17-20R; 134; SATA 7

Frisch, Max (Rudolf) 1911-1991 ... **CLC 3, 9, 14, 18, 32, 44**
See also CA 85-88; 134; CANR 32, 74; CD-WLB 2; DAM DRAM, NOV; DLB 69, 124; EW 13; MTCW 1, 2; RGWL 2; TCLC 121

Fromentin, Eugene (Samuel Auguste)
1820-1876 .... **NCLC 10**
See also DLB 123; GFL 1789 to the Present

Frost, Frederick
See Faust, Frederick (Schiller)
See also TCWW 2

Frost, Robert (Lee) 1874-1963 .. **CLC 1, 3, 4, 9, 10, 13, 15, 26, 34, 44; PC 1, 39; WLC**
See also AAYA 21; AMW; AMWR 1; CA 89-92; CANR 33; CDALB 1917-1929; CLR 67; DA; DA3; DAB; DAC; DAM MST, POET; DLB 54; DLBD 7; EXPP; MTCW 1, 2; PAB; PFS 1, 2, 3, 4, 5, 6, 7, 10, 13; RGAL 4; SATA 14; WP; WYA

Froude, James Anthony
1818-1894 .... **NCLC 43**
See also DLB 18, 57, 144

Froy, Herald
See Waterhouse, Keith (Spencer)

Fry, Christopher 1907- .... **CLC 2, 10, 14**
See also BRWS 3; CA 17-20R; CAAS 23; CANR 9, 30, 74; CBD; CD 5; CP 7; DAM DRAM; DLB 13; MTCW 1, 2; RGEL 2; SATA 66

Frye, (Herman) Northrop
1912-1991 .... **CLC 24, 70**
See also CA 5-8R; 133; CANR 8, 37; DLB 67, 68, 246; MTCW 1, 2; RGAL 4

Fuchs, Daniel 1909-1993 .... **CLC 8, 22**
See also CA 81-84; 142; CAAS 5; CANR 40; DLB 9, 26, 28; DLBY 1993

Fuchs, Daniel 1934- .... **CLC 34**
See also CA 37-40R; CANR 14, 48

Fuentes, Carlos 1928- .. **CLC 3, 8, 10, 13, 22, 41, 60, 113; HLC 1; SSC 24; WLC**
See also AAYA 4; AITN 2; BPFB 1; CA 69-72; CANR 10, 32, 68, 104; CDWLB 3; CWW 2; DA; DA3; DAB; DAC; DAM MST, MULT, NOV; DLB 113; DNFS 2; HW 1, 2; LAIT 3; LAW; LAWS 1; MTCW 1, 2; NFS 8; RGSF 2; RGWL 2; WLIT 1

Fuentes, Gregorio Lopez y
See Lopez y Fuentes, Gregorio

Fuertes, Gloria 1918-1998 .... **PC 27**
See also CA 178, 180; DLB 108; HW 2; SATA 115

Fugard, (Harold) Athol 1932- . **CLC 5, 9, 14, 25, 40, 80; DC 3**
See also AAYA 17; AFW; CA 85-88; CANR 32, 54; CD 5; DAM DRAM; DFS 3, 6, 10; DLB 225; DNFS 1, 2; MTCW 1; RGEL 2; WLIT 2

Fugard, Sheila 1932- .... **CLC 48**
See also CA 125

Fukuyama, Francis 1952- .... **CLC 131**
See also CA 140; CANR 72

Fuller, Charles (H., Jr.) 1939- .... **CLC 25; BLC 2; DC 1**
See also BW 2; CA 108; 112; CAD; CANR 87; CD 5; DAM DRAM, MULT; DFS 8; DLB 38; INT CA-112; MTCW 1

Fuller, Henry Blake 1857-1929 .... **TCLC 103**
See also CA 108; 177; DLB 12; RGAL 4

Fuller, John (Leopold) 1937- .... **CLC 62**
See also CA 21-24R; CANR 9, 44; CP 7; DLB 40

Fuller, Margaret
See Ossoli, Sarah Margaret (Fuller)
See also AMWS 2; DLB 183, 223, 239

Fuller, Roy (Broadbent) 1912-1991 ... **CLC 4, 28**
See also BRWS 7; CA 5-8R; 135; CAAS 10; CANR 53, 83; CWRI 5; DLB 15, 20; RGEL 2; SATA 87

Fuller, Sarah Margaret
See Ossoli, Sarah Margaret (Fuller)

Fuller, Sarah Margaret
See Ossoli, Sarah Margaret (Fuller)
See also DLB 1, 59, 73

Fulton, Alice 1952- .... **CLC 52**
See also CA 116; CANR 57, 88; CP 7; CWP; DLB 193

Furphy, Joseph 1843-1912 .... **TCLC 25**
See also CA 163; DLB 230; RGEL 2

Fuson, Robert H(enderson) 1927- .... **CLC 70**
See also CA 89-92; CANR 103

Fussell, Paul 1924- .... **CLC 74**
See also BEST 90:1; CA 17-20R; CANR 8, 21, 35, 69; INT CANR-21; MTCW 1, 2

Futabatei, Shimei 1864-1909 .... **TCLC 44**
See also Futabatei Shimei
See also CA 162; MJW

Futabatei Shimei
See Futabatei, Shimei
See also DLB 180

Futrelle, Jacques 1875-1912 .... **TCLC 19**
See also CA 113; 155; CMW 4

Gaboriau, Emile 1835-1873 .... **NCLC 14**
See also CMW 4; MSW

Gadda, Carlo Emilio 1893-1973 .... **CLC 11**
See also CA 89-92; DLB 177

Gaddis, William 1922-1998 ... **CLC 1, 3, 6, 8, 10, 19, 43, 86**
See also AMWS 4; BPFB 1; CA 17-20R; 172; CANR 21, 48; CN 7; DLB 2; MTCW 1, 2; RGAL 4

Gaelique, Moruen le
See Jacob, (Cyprien-)Max

Gage, Walter
See Inge, William (Motter)

Gaines, Ernest J(ames) 1933- ...... **CLC 3, 11, 18, 86; BLC 2**
See also AAYA 18; AFAW 1, 2; AITN 1; BPFB 2; BW 2, 3; BYA 6; CA 9-12R; CANR 6, 24, 42, 75; CDALB 1968-1988; CLR 62; CN 7; CSW; DA3; DAM MULT; DLB 2, 33, 152; DLBY 1980; EXPN; LAIT 5; MTCW 1, 2; NFS 5, 7; RGAL 4; RGSF 2; RHW; SATA 86; SSFS 5; YAW

Gaitskill, Mary 1954- .... **CLC 69**
See also CA 128; CANR 61; DLB 244

Galdos, Benito Perez
See Perez Galdos, Benito
See also EW 7

Gale, Zona 1874-1938 .... **TCLC 7**
See also CA 105; 153; CANR 84; DAM DRAM; DLB 9, 78, 228; RGAL 4

Galeano, Eduardo (Hughes) 1940- . **CLC 72; HLCS 1**
See also CA 29-32R; CANR 13, 32, 100; HW 1

Galiano, Juan Valera y Alcala
See Valera y Alcala-Galiano, Juan

Galilei, Galileo 1564-1642 .... **LC 45**

Gallagher, Tess 1943- .... **CLC 18, 63; PC 9**
See also CA 106; CP 7; CWP; DAM POET; DLB 120, 212, 244

Gallant, Mavis 1922- . **CLC 7, 18, 38; SSC 5**
See also CA 69-72; CANR 29, 69; CCA 1; CN 7; DAC; DAM MST; DLB 53; MTCW 1, 2; RGEL 2; RGSF 2

Gallant, Roy A(rthur) 1924- .... **CLC 17**
See also CA 5-8R; CANR 4, 29, 54; CLR 30; MAICYA 1, 2; SATA 4, 68, 110

Gallico, Paul (William) 1897-1976 ..... **CLC 2**
See also AITN 1; CA 5-8R; 69-72; CANR 23; DLB 9, 171; FANT; MAICYA 1, 2; SATA 13

Gallo, Max Louis 1932- .... **CLC 95**
See also CA 85-88

Gallois, Lucien
See Desnos, Robert

Gallup, Ralph
See Whitemore, Hugh (John)

Galsworthy, John 1867-1933 .... **TCLC 1, 45; SSC 22; WLC**
See also BRW 6; CA 104; 141; CANR 75; CDBLB 1890-1914; DA; DA3; DAB; DAC; DAM DRAM, MST, NOV; DLB 10, 34, 98, 162; DLBD 16; MTCW 1; RGEL 2; SSFS 3

Galt, John 1779-1839 .... **NCLC 1, 110**
See also DLB 99, 116, 159; RGEL 2; RGSF 2

Galvin, James 1951- .... **CLC 38**
See also CA 108; CANR 26

Gamboa, Federico 1864-1939 .... **TCLC 36**
See also CA 167; HW 2; LAW

Gandhi, M. K.
See Gandhi, Mohandas Karamchand

Gandhi, Mahatma
See Gandhi, Mohandas Karamchand

Gandhi, Mohandas Karamchand
1869-1948 .... **TCLC 59**
See also CA 121; 132; DA3; DAM MULT; MTCW 1, 2

Gann, Ernest Kellogg 1910-1991 ..... **CLC 23**
See also AITN 1; BPFB 2; CA 1-4R; 136; CANR 1, 83; RHW

Garber, Eric 1943(?)-
See Holleran, Andrew
See also CANR 89

Garcia, Cristina 1958- .... **CLC 76**
See also CA 141; CANR 73; DNFS 1; HW 2

Garcia Lorca, Federico 1898-1936 . **TCLC 1, 7, 49; DC 2; HLC 2; PC 3; WLC**
See also Lorca, Federico Garcia
See also CA 104; 131; CANR 81; DA; DA3; DAB; DAC; DAM DRAM, MST, MULT, POET; DFS 10; DLB 108; HW 1, 2; MTCW 1, 2

Garcia Marquez, Gabriel (Jose)
1928- ..... **CLC 2, 3, 8, 10, 15, 27, 47, 55, 68; HLC 1; SSC 8; WLC**
See also AAYA 3, 33; BEST 89:1, 90:4; BPFB 2; BYA 12; CA 33-36R; CANR 10, 28, 50, 75, 82; CDWLB 3; CPW; DA; DA3; DAB; DAC; DAM MST, MULT, NOV, POP; DLB 113; DNFS 1, 2; EXPN; EXPS; HW 1, 2; LAIT 2; LAW; LAWS 1; MTCW 1, 2; NCFS 3; NFS 1, 5, 10; RGSF 2; RGWL 2; SSFS 1, 6; WLIT 1

Garcilaso de la Vega, El Inca 1503-1536
See also HLCS 1; LAW

Gard, Janice
See Latham, Jean Lee

Gard, Roger Martin du
See Martin du Gard, Roger

Gardam, Jane (Mary) 1928- .... **CLC 43**
See also CA 49-52; CANR 2, 18, 33, 54, 106; CLR 12; DLB 14, 161, 231; MAICYA 1, 2; MTCW 1; SAAS 9; SATA 39, 76, 130; SATA-Brief 28; YAW

Gardner, Herb(ert) 1934- .... **CLC 44**
See also CA 149; CAD; CD 5

Gardner, John (Champlin), Jr.
1933-1982 .... **CLC 2, 3, 5, 7, 8, 10, 18, 28, 34; SSC 7**
See also AITN 1; AMWS 6; BPFB 2; CA 65-68; 107; CANR 33, 73; CDALBS; CPW; DA3; DAM NOV, POP; DLB 2; DLBY 1982; FANT; MTCW 1; NFS 3; RGAL 4; RGSF 2; SATA 40; SATA-Obit 31; SSFS 8

Gardner, John (Edmund) 1926- .... **CLC 30**
See also CA 103; CANR 15, 69; CMW 4; CPW; DAM POP; MTCW 1

Gardner, Miriam
See Bradley, Marion Zimmer
See also GLL 1

Gardner, Noel
See Kuttner, Henry

Gardons, S. S.
See Snodgrass, W(illiam) D(e Witt)

Garfield, Leon 1921-1996 .... **CLC 12**
See also AAYA 8; BYA 1, 3; CA 17-20R; 152; CANR 38, 41, 78; CLR 21; DLB 161; JRDA; MAICYA 1, 2; MAICYAS 1; SATA 1, 32, 76; SATA-Obit 90; WYA; YAW

Garland, (Hannibal) Hamlin
1860-1940 .... **TCLC 3; SSC 18**
See also CA 104; DLB 12, 71, 78, 186; RGAL 4; RGSF 2; TCWW 2

Garneau, (Hector de) Saint-Denys
1912-1943 .... **TCLC 13**
See also CA 111; DLB 88

Garner, Alan 1934- .... **CLC 17**
See also AAYA 18; BYA 3, 5; CA 73-76; 178; CAAE 178; CANR 15, 64; CLR 20; CPW; DAB; DAM POP; DLB 161;

FANT; MAICYA 1, 2; MTCW 1, 2; SATA 18, 69; SATA-Essay 108; SUFW; YAW

Garner, Hugh 1913-1979 .... **CLC 13**
See also Warwick, Jarvis
See also CA 69-72; CANR 31; CCA 1; DLB 68

Garnett, David 1892-1981 .... **CLC 3**
See also CA 5-8R; 103; CANR 17, 79; DLB 34; FANT; MTCW 2; RGEL 2; SFW 4; SUFW

Garos, Stephanie
See Katz, Steve

Garrett, George (Palmer) 1929- .. **CLC 3, 11, 51; SSC 30**
See also AMWS 7; BPFB 2; CA 1-4R; CAAS 5; CANR 1, 42, 67, 109; CN 7; CP 7; CSW; DLB 2, 5, 130, 152; DLBY 1983

Garrick, David 1717-1779 .... **LC 15**
See also DAM DRAM; DLB 84, 213; RGEL 2

Garrigue, Jean 1914-1972 .... **CLC 2, 8**
See also CA 5-8R; 37-40R; CANR 20

Garrison, Frederick
See Sinclair, Upton (Beall)

Garro, Elena 1920(?)-1998
See also CA 131; 169; CWW 2; DLB 145; HLCS 1; HW 1; LAWS 1; WLIT 1

Garth, Will
See Hamilton, Edmond; Kuttner, Henry

Garvey, Marcus (Moziah, Jr.) 1887-1940 .... **TCLC 41; BLC 2**
See also BW 1; CA 120; 124; CANR 79; DAM MULT

Gary, Romain .... **CLC 25**
See Kacew, Romain
See also DLB 83

Gascar, Pierre .... **CLC 11**
See also Fournier, Pierre

Gascoyne, David (Emery) 1916-2001 .... **CLC 45**
See also CA 65-68; 200; CANR 10, 28, 54; CP 7; DLB 20; MTCW 1; RGEL 2

Gaskell, Elizabeth Cleghorn 1810-1865 .... **NCLC 5, 70, 97; SSC 25**
See also BRW 5; CDBLB 1832-1890; DAB; DAM MST; DLB 21, 144, 159; RGEL 2; RGSF 2

Gass, William H(oward) 1924- . **CLC 1, 2, 8, 11, 15, 39, 132; SSC 12**
See also AMWS 6; CA 17-20R; CANR 30, 71, 100; CN 7; DLB 2, 227; MTCW 1, 2; RGAL 4

Gassendi, Pierre 1592-1655 .... **LC 54**
See also GFL Beginnings to 1789

Gasset, Jose Ortega y
See Ortega y Gasset, Jose

Gates, Henry Louis, Jr. 1950- .... **CLC 65; BLCS**
See also BW 2, 3; CA 109; CANR 25, 53, 75; CSW; DA3; DAM MULT; DLB 67; MTCW 1; RGAL 4

Gautier, Theophile 1811-1872 .. **NCLC 1, 59; PC 18; SSC 20**
See also DAM POET; DLB 119; EW 6; GFL 1789 to the Present; RGWL 2; SUFW

Gawsworth, John
See Bates, H(erbert) E(rnest)

Gay, John 1685-1732 .... **LC 49**
See also BRW 3; DAM DRAM; DLB 84, 95; RGEL 2; WLIT 3

Gay, Oliver
See Gogarty, Oliver St. John

Gay, Peter (Jack) 1923- .... **CLC 158**
See also CA 13-16R; CANR 18, 41, 77; INT CANR-18

Gaye, Marvin (Pentz, Jr.) 1939-1984 .... **CLC 26**
See also CA 195; 112

Gebler, Carlo (Ernest) 1954- .... **CLC 39**
See also CA 119; 133; CANR 96

Gee, Maggie (Mary) 1948- .... **CLC 57**
See also CA 130; CN 7; DLB 207

Gee, Maurice (Gough) 1931- .... **CLC 29**
See also AAYA 42; CA 97-100; CANR 67; CLR 56; CN 7; CWRI 5; MAICYA 2; RGSF 2; SATA 46, 101

Gelbart, Larry (Simon) 1928- .... **CLC 21, 61**
See also Gelbart, Larry
See also CA 73-76; CANR 45, 94

Gelbart, Larry 1928-
See Gelbart, Larry (Simon)
See also CAD; CD 5

Gelber, Jack 1932- .... **CLC 1, 6, 14, 79**
See also CA 1-4R; CAD; CANR 2; DLB 7, 228

Gellhorn, Martha (Ellis) 1908-1998 .... **CLC 14, 60**
See also CA 77-80; 164; CANR 44; CN 7; DLBY 1982, 1998

Genet, Jean 1910-1986 .. **CLC 1, 2, 5, 10, 14, 44, 46**
See also CA 13-16R; CANR 18; DA3; DAM DRAM; DFS 10; DLB 72; DLBY 1986; EW 13; GFL 1789 to the Present; GLL 1; MTCW 1, 2; RGWL 2

Gent, Peter 1942- .... **CLC 29**
See also AITN 1; CA 89-92; DLBY 1982

Gentile, Giovanni 1875-1944 .... **TCLC 96**
See also CA 119

Gentlewoman in New England, A
See Bradstreet, Anne

Gentlewoman in Those Parts, A
See Bradstreet, Anne

Geoffrey of Monmouth c. 1100-1155 .... **CMLC 44**
See also DLB 146

George, Jean
See George, Jean Craighead

George, Jean Craighead 1919- .... **CLC 35**
See also AAYA 8; BYA 2, 4; CA 5-8R; CANR 25; CLR 1; DLB 52; JRDA; MAICYA 1, 2; SATA 2, 68, 124; WYA; YAW

George, Stefan (Anton) 1868-1933 . **TCLC 2, 14**
See also CA 104; 193; EW 8

Georges, Georges Martin
See Simenon, Georges (Jacques Christian)

Gerhardi, William Alexander
See Gerhardie, William Alexander

Gerhardie, William Alexander 1895-1977 .... **CLC 5**
See also CA 25-28R; 73-76; CANR 18; DLB 36; RGEL 2

Gerson, Jean 1363-1429 .... **LC 77**
See also DLB 208

Gersonides 1288-1344 .... **CMLC 49**
See also DLB 115

Gerstler, Amy 1956- .... **CLC 70**
See also CA 146; CANR 99

Gertler, T. .... **CLC 134**
See also CA 116; 121

Ghalib .... **NCLC 39, 78**
See also Ghalib, Asadullah Khan

Ghalib, Asadullah Khan 1797-1869
See Ghalib
See also DAM POET; RGWL 2

Ghelderode, Michel de 1898-1962 ..... **CLC 6, 11; DC 15**
See also CA 85-88; CANR 40, 77; DAM DRAM; EW 11

Ghiselin, Brewster 1903-2001 .... **CLC 23**
See also CA 13-16R; CAAS 10; CANR 13; CP 7

Ghose, Aurabinda 1872-1950 .... **TCLC 63**
See also CA 163

Ghose, Zulfikar 1935- .... **CLC 42**
See also CA 65-68; CANR 67; CN 7; CP 7

Ghosh, Amitav 1956- .... **CLC 44, 153**
See also CA 147; CANR 80; CN 7

Giacosa, Giuseppe 1847-1906 .... **TCLC 7**
See also CA 104

Gibb, Lee
See Waterhouse, Keith (Spencer)

Gibbon, Lewis Grassic .... **TCLC 4**
See also Mitchell, James Leslie
See also RGEL 2

Gibbons, Kaye 1960- .... **CLC 50, 88, 145**
See also AAYA 34; AMWS 10; CA 151; CANR 75; CSW; DA3; DAM POP; MTCW 1; NFS 3; RGAL 4; SATA 117

Gibran, Kahlil 1883-1931 . **TCLC 1, 9; PC 9**
See also CA 104; 150; DA3; DAM POET, POP; MTCW 2

Gibran, Khalil
See Gibran, Kahlil

Gibson, William 1914- .... **CLC 23**
See also CA 9-12R; CAD 2; CANR 9, 42, 75; CD 5; DA; DAB; DAC; DAM DRAM, MST; DFS 2; DLB 7; LAIT 2; MTCW 2; SATA 66; YAW

Gibson, William (Ford) 1948- ... **CLC 39, 63; SSC 52**
See also AAYA 12; BPFB 2; CA 126; 133; CANR 52, 90, 106; CN 7; CPW; DA3; DAM POP; DLB 251; MTCW 2; SCFW 2; SFW 4

Gide, Andre (Paul Guillaume) 1869-1951 ..... **TCLC 5, 12, 36; SSC 13; WLC**
See also CA 104; 124; DA; DA3; DAB; DAC; DAM MST, NOV; DLB 65; EW 8; GFL 1789 to the Present; MTCW 1, 2; RGSF 2; RGWL 2

Gifford, Barry (Colby) 1946- .... **CLC 34**
See also CA 65-68; CANR 9, 30, 40, 90

Gilbert, Frank
See De Voto, Bernard (Augustine)

Gilbert, W(illiam) S(chwenck) 1836-1911 .... **TCLC 3**
See also CA 104; 173; DAM DRAM, POET; RGEL 2; SATA 36

Gilbreth, Frank B(unker), Jr. 1911-2001 .... **CLC 17**
See also CA 9-12R; SATA 2

Gilchrist, Ellen (Louise) 1935- .. **CLC 34, 48, 143; SSC 14**
See also BPFB 2; CA 113; 116; CANR 41, 61, 104; CN 7; CPW; CSW; DAM POP; DLB 130; EXPS; MTCW 1, 2; RGAL 4; RGSF 2; SSFS 9

Giles, Molly 1942- .... **CLC 39**
See also CA 126; CANR 98

Gill, Eric 1882-1940 .... **TCLC 85**

Gill, Patrick
See Creasey, John

Gillette, Douglas .... **CLC 70**

Gilliam, Terry (Vance) 1940- .... **CLC 21, 141**
See also Monty Python
See also AAYA 19; CA 108; 113; CANR 35; INT 113

Gillian, Jerry
See Gilliam, Terry (Vance)

Gilliatt, Penelope (Ann Douglass) 1932-1993 .... **CLC 2, 10, 13, 53**
See also AITN 2; CA 13-16R; 141; CANR 49; DLB 14

Gilman, Charlotte (Anna) Perkins (Stetson) 1860-1935 ..... **TCLC 9, 37, 117; SSC 13**
See also BYA 11; CA 106; 150; DLB 221; EXPS; FW; HGG; LAIT 2; MAWW; MTCW 1; RGAL 4; RGSF 2; SFW 4; SSFS 1

391

Gilmour, David 1946- .... **CLC 35**

Gilpin, William 1724-1804 .... **NCLC 30**

Gilray, J. D.
See Mencken, H(enry) L(ouis)

Gilroy, Frank D(aniel) 1925- .... **CLC 2**
See also CA 81-84; CAD; CANR 32, 64, 86; CD 5; DLB 7

Gilstrap, John 1957(?)- .... **CLC 99**
See also CA 160; CANR 101

Ginsberg, Allen 1926-1997 .... **CLC 1, 2, 3, 4, 6, 13, 36, 69, 109; PC 4; WLC**
See also AAYA 33; AITN 1; AMWS 2; CA 1-4R; 157; CANR 2, 41, 63, 95; CDALB 1941-1968; CP 7; DA; DA3; DAB; DAC; DAM MST, POET; DLB 5, 16, 169, 237; GLL 1; MTCW 1, 2; PAB; PFS 5; RGAL 4; TCLC 120; WP

Ginzburg, Eugenia .... **CLC 59**

Ginzburg, Natalia 1916-1991 .... **CLC 5, 11, 54, 70**
See also CA 85-88; 135; CANR 33; DFS 14; DLB 177; EW 13; MTCW 1, 2; RGWL 2

Giono, Jean 1895-1970 .... **CLC 4, 11**
See also CA 45-48; 29-32R; CANR 2, 35; DLB 72; GFL 1789 to the Present; MTCW 1; RGWL 2

Giovanni, Nikki 1943- .... **CLC 2, 4, 19, 64, 117; BLC 2; PC 19; WLCS**
See also AAYA 22; AITN 1; BW 2, 3; CA 29-32R; CAAS 6; CANR 18, 41, 60, 91; CDALBS; CLR 6, 73; CP 7; CSW; CWP; CWRI 5; DA; DA3; DAB; DAC; DAM MST, MULT, POET; DLB 5, 41; EXPP; INT CANR-18; MAICYA 1, 2; MTCW 1, 2; RGAL 4; SATA 24, 107; YAW

Giovene, Andrea 1904-1998 .... **CLC 7**
See also CA 85-88

Gippius, Zinaida (Nikolayevna) 1869-1945
See Hippius, Zinaida
See also CA 106

Giraudoux, Jean(-Hippolyte) 1882-1944 .... **TCLC 2, 7**
See also CA 104; 196; DAM DRAM; DLB 65; EW 9; GFL 1789 to the Present; RGWL 2

Gironella, Jose Maria 1917-1991 ..... **CLC 11**
See also CA 101; RGWL 2

Gissing, George (Robert) 1857-1903 .... **TCLC 3, 24, 47; SSC 37**
See also BRW 5; CA 105; 167; DLB 18, 135, 184; RGEL 2

Giurlani, Aldo
See Palazzeschi, Aldo

Gladkov, Fyodor (Vasilyevich) 1883-1958 .... **TCLC 27**
See also CA 170

Glanville, Brian (Lester) 1931- .... **CLC 6**
See also CA 5-8R; CAAS 9; CANR 3, 70; CN 7; DLB 15, 139; SATA 42

Glasgow, Ellen (Anderson Gholson) 1873-1945 .... **TCLC 2, 7; SSC 34**
See also AMW; CA 104; 164; DLB 9, 12; MAWW; MTCW 2; RGAL 4; RHW; SSFS 9

Glaspell, Susan 1882(?)-1948 . **TCLC 55; DC 10; SSC 41**
See also AMWS 3; CA 110; 154; DFS 8; DLB 7, 9, 78, 228; MAWW; RGAL 4; SSFS 3; TCWW 2; YABC 2

Glassco, John 1909-1981 .... **CLC 9**
See also CA 13-16R; 102; CANR 15; DLB 68

Glasscock, Amnesia
See Steinbeck, John (Ernst)

Glasser, Ronald J. 1940(?)- .... **CLC 37**

Glassman, Joyce
See Johnson, Joyce

Gleick, James (W.) 1954- .... **CLC 147**
See also CA 131; 137; CANR 97; INT CA-137

Glendinning, Victoria 1937- .... **CLC 50**
See also CA 120; 127; CANR 59, 89; DLB 155

Glissant, Edouard 1928- .... **CLC 10, 68**
See also CA 153; CWW 2; DAM MULT

Gloag, Julian 1930- .... **CLC 40**
See also AITN 1; CA 65-68; CANR 10, 70; CN 7

Glowacki, Aleksander
See Prus, Boleslaw

Gluck, Louise (Elisabeth) 1943- .. **CLC 7, 22, 44, 81; PC 16**
See also AMWS 5; CA 33-36R; CANR 40, 69, 108; CP 7; CWP; DA3; DAM POET; DLB 5; MTCW 2; PFS 5; RGAL 4

Glyn, Elinor 1864-1943 .... **TCLC 72**
See also DLB 153; RHW

Gobineau, Joseph-Arthur 1816-1882 .... **NCLC 17**
See also DLB 123; GFL 1789 to the Present

Godard, Jean-Luc 1930- .... **CLC 20**
See also CA 93-96

Godden, (Margaret) Rumer 1907-1998 .... **CLC 53**
See also AAYA 6; BPFB 2; BYA 2, 5; CA 5-8R; 172; CANR 4, 27, 36, 55, 80; CLR 20; CN 7; CWRI 5; DLB 161; MAICYA 1, 2; RHW; SAAS 12; SATA 3, 36; SATA-Obit 109

Godoy Alcayaga, Lucila 1899-1957 .... **TCLC 2; HLC 2; PC 32**
See also Mistral, Gabriela
See also BW 2; CA 104; 131; CANR 81; DAM MULT; DNFS; HW 1, 2; MTCW 1, 2

Godwin, Gail (Kathleen) 1937- ..... **CLC 5, 8, 22, 31, 69, 125**
See also BPFB 2; CA 29-32R; CANR 15, 43, 69; CN 7; CPW; CSW; DA3; DAM POP; DLB 6, 234; INT CANR-15; MTCW 1, 2

Godwin, William 1756-1836 .... **NCLC 14**
See also CDBLB 1789-1832; CMW 4; DLB 39, 104, 142, 158, 163; HGG; RGEL 2

Goebbels, Josef
See Goebbels, (Paul) Joseph

Goebbels, (Paul) Joseph 1897-1945 .... **TCLC 68**
See also CA 115; 148

Goebbels, Joseph Paul
See Goebbels, (Paul) Joseph

Goethe, Johann Wolfgang von 1749-1832 ... **NCLC 4, 22, 34, 90; PC 5; SSC 38; WLC**
See also CDWLB 2; DA; DA3; DAB; DAC; DAM DRAM, MST, POET; DLB 94; EW 5; RGWL 2

Gogarty, Oliver St. John 1878-1957 .... **TCLC 15**
See also CA 109; 150; DLB 15, 19; RGEL 2

Gogol, Nikolai (Vasilyevich) 1809-1852 .... **NCLC 5, 15, 31; DC 1; SSC 4, 29, 52; WLC**
See also DA; DAB; DAC; DAM DRAM, MST; DFS 12; DLB 198; EW 6; EXPS; RGSF 2; RGWL 2; SSFS 7

Goines, Donald 1937(?)-1974 . **CLC 80; BLC 2**
See also AITN 1; BW 1, 3; CA 124; 114; CANR 82; CMW 4; DA3; DAM MULT, POP; DLB 33

Gold, Herbert 1924- ... **CLC 4, 7, 14, 42, 152**
See also CA 9-12R; CANR 17, 45; CN 7; DLB 2; DLBY 1981

Goldbarth, Albert 1948- .... **CLC 5, 38**
See also CA 53-56; CANR 6, 40; CP 7; DLB 120

Goldberg, Anatol 1910-1982 .... **CLC 34**
See also CA 131; 117

Goldemberg, Isaac 1945- .... **CLC 52**
See also CA 69-72; CAAS 12; CANR 11, 32; HW 1; WLIT 1

Golding, William (Gerald) 1911-1993 ...... **CLC 1, 2, 3, 8, 10, 17, 27, 58, 81; WLC**
See also AAYA 5; BPFB 2; BRWR 1; BRWS 1; BYA 2; CA 5-8R; 141; CANR 13, 33, 54; CDBLB 1945-1960; DA; DA3; DAB; DAC; DAM MST, NOV; DLB 15, 100, 255; EXPN; HGG; LAIT 4; MTCW 1, 2; NFS 2; RGEL 2; RHW; SFW 4; WLIT 4; YAW

Goldman, Emma 1869-1940 .... **TCLC 13**
See also CA 110; 150; DLB 221; FW; RGAL 4

Goldman, Francisco 1954- .... **CLC 76**
See also CA 162

Goldman, William (W.) 1931- ...... **CLC 1, 48**
See also BPFB 2; CA 9-12R; CANR 29, 69, 106; CN 7; DLB 44; FANT; IDFW 3, 4

Goldmann, Lucien 1913-1970 .... **CLC 24**
See also CA 25-28; CAP 2

Goldoni, Carlo 1707-1793 .... **LC 4**
See also DAM DRAM; EW 4; RGWL 2

Goldsberry, Steven 1949- .... **CLC 34**
See also CA 131

Goldsmith, Oliver 1730-1774 .. **LC 2, 48; DC 8; WLC**
See also BRW 3; CDBLB 1660-1789; DA; DAB; DAC; DAM DRAM, MST, NOV, POET; DFS 1; DLB 39, 89, 104, 109, 142; IDTP; RGEL 2; SATA 26; TEA; WLIT 3

Goldsmith, Peter
See Priestley, J(ohn) B(oynton)

Gombrowicz, Witold 1904-1969 .... **CLC 4, 7, 11, 49**
See also CA 19-20; 25-28R; CANR 105; CAP 2; CDWLB 4; DAM DRAM; DLB 215; EW 12; RGWL 2

Gomez de Avellaneda, Gertrudis 1814-1873 .... **NCLC 111**
See also LAW

Gomez de la Serna, Ramon 1888-1963 .... **CLC 9**
See also CA 153; 116; CANR 79; HW 1, 2

Goncharov, Ivan Alexandrovich 1812-1891 .... **NCLC 1, 63**
See also DLB 238; EW 6; RGWL 2

Goncourt, Edmond (Louis Antoine Huot) de 1822-1896 .... **NCLC 7**
See also DLB 123; EW 7; GFL 1789 to the Present; RGWL 2

Goncourt, Jules (Alfred Huot) de 1830-1870 .... **NCLC 7**
See also DLB 123; EW 7; GFL 1789 to the Present; RGWL 2

Gongora (y Argote), Luis de 1561-1627 .... **LC 72**
See also RGWL 2

Gontier, Fernande 19(?)- .... **CLC 50**

Gonzalez Martinez, Enrique 1871-1952 .... **TCLC 72**
See also CA 166; CANR 81; HW 1, 2

Goodison, Lorna 1947- .... **PC 36**
See also CA 142; CANR 88; CP 7; CWP; DLB 157

Goodman, Paul 1911-1972 ..... **CLC 1, 2, 4, 7**
See also CA 19-20; 37-40R; CAD; CANR 34; CAP 2; DLB 130, 246; MTCW 1; RGAL 4

Gordimer, Nadine 1923- ...... **CLC 3, 5, 7, 10, 18, 33, 51, 70, 123; SSC 17; WLCS**
See also AAYA 39; AFW; BRWS 2; CA 5-8R; CANR 3, 28, 56, 88; CN 7; DA; DA3; DAB; DAC; DAM MST, NOV; DLB 225; EXPS; INT CANR-28; MTCW 1, 2; NFS 4; RGEL 2; RGSF 2; SSFS 2, 14; WLIT 2; YAW

Gordon, Adam Lindsay 1833-1870 .... **NCLC 21**
See also DLB 230

Gordon, Caroline 1895-1981 . **CLC 6, 13, 29, 83; SSC 15**
See also AMW; CA 11-12; 103; CANR 36; CAP 1; DLB 4, 9, 102; DLBD 17; DLBY 1981; MTCW 1, 2; RGAL 4; RGSF 2

Gordon, Charles William 1860-1937
See Connor, Ralph
See also CA 109

Gordon, Mary (Catherine) 1949- .... **CLC 13, 22, 128**
See also AMWS 4; BPFB 2; CA 102; CANR 44, 92; CN 7; DLB 6; DLBY 1981; FW; INT CA-102; MTCW 1

Gordon, N. J.
See Bosman, Herman Charles

Gordon, Sol 1923- .... **CLC 26**
See also CA 53-56; CANR 4; SATA 11

Gordone, Charles 1925-1995 .. **CLC 1, 4; DC 8**
See also BW 1, 3; CA 93-96, 180; 150; CAAE 180; CAD; CANR 55; DAM DRAM; DLB 7; INT 93-96; MTCW 1

Gore, Catherine 1800-1861 .... **NCLC 65**
See also DLB 116; RGEL 2

Gorenko, Anna Andreevna
See Akhmatova, Anna

Gorky, Maxim .... **TCLC 8; SSC 28; WLC**
See also Peshkov, Alexei Maximovich
See also DAB; DFS 9; EW 8; MTCW 2

Goryan, Sirak
See Saroyan, William

Gosse, Edmund (William) 1849-1928 .... **TCLC 28**
See also CA 117; DLB 57, 144, 184; RGEL 2

Gotlieb, Phyllis Fay (Bloom) 1926- .. **CLC 18**
See also CA 13-16R; CANR 7; DLB 88, 251; SFW 4

Gottesman, S. D.
See Kornbluth, C(yril) M.; Pohl, Frederik

Gottfried von Strassburg fl. c. 1170-1215 .... **CMLC 10**
See also CDWLB 2; DLB 138; EW 1; RGWL 2

Gould, Lois .... **CLC 4, 10**
See also CA 77-80; CANR 29; MTCW 1

Gourmont, Remy(-Marie-Charles) de 1858-1915 .... **TCLC 17**
See also CA 109; 150; GFL 1789 to the Present; MTCW 2

Govier, Katherine 1948- .... **CLC 51**
See also CA 101; CANR 18, 40; CCA 1

Gower, John c. 1330-1408 .... **LC 76**
See also BRW 1; DLB 146; RGEL 2

Goyen, (Charles) William 1915-1983 .... **CLC 5, 8, 14, 40**
See also AITN 2; CA 5-8R; 110; CANR 6, 71; DLB 2, 218; DLBY 1983; INT CANR-6

Goytisolo, Juan 1931- .... **CLC 5, 10, 23, 133; HLC 1**
See also CA 85-88; CANR 32, 61; CWW 2; DAM MULT; GLL 2; HW 1, 2; MTCW 1, 2

Gozzano, Guido 1883-1916 .... **PC 10**
See also CA 154; DLB 114

Gozzi, (Conte) Carlo 1720-1806 .... **NCLC 23**

Grabbe, Christian Dietrich 1801-1836 .... **NCLC 2**
See also DLB 133; RGWL 2

Grace, Patricia Frances 1937- .... **CLC 56**
See also CA 176; CN 7; RGSF 2

Gracian y Morales, Baltasar 1601-1658 .... **LC 15**

Gracq, Julien .... **CLC 11, 48**
See also Poirier, Louis
See also CWW 2; DLB 83; GFL 1789 to the Present

Grade, Chaim 1910-1982 .... **CLC 10**
See also CA 93-96; 107

Graduate of Oxford, A
See Ruskin, John

Grafton, Garth
See Duncan, Sara Jeannette

Graham, John
See Phillips, David Graham

Graham, Jorie 1951- .... **CLC 48, 118**
See also CA 111; CANR 63; CP 7; CWP; DLB 120; PFS 10

Graham, R(obert) B(ontine) Cunninghame
See Cunninghame Graham, Robert (Gallnigad) Bontine
See also DLB 98, 135, 174; RGEL 2; RGSF 2

Graham, Robert
See Haldeman, Joe (William)

Graham, Tom
See Lewis, (Harry) Sinclair

Graham, W(illiam) S(idney) 1918-1986 .... **CLC 29**
See also BRWS 7; CA 73-76; 118; DLB 20; RGEL 2

Graham, Winston (Mawdsley) 1910- .... **CLC 23**
See also CA 49-52; CANR 2, 22, 45, 66; CMW 4; CN 7; DLB 77; RHW

Grahame, Kenneth 1859-1932 .... **TCLC 64**
See also BYA 5; CA 108; 136; CANR 80; CLR 5; CWRI 5; DA3; DAB; DLB 34, 141, 178; FANT; MAICYA 1, 2; MTCW 2; RGEL 2; SATA 100; WCH; YABC 1

Granger, Darius John
See Marlowe, Stephen

Granin, Daniil .... **CLC 59**

Granovsky, Timofei Nikolaevich 1813-1855 .... **NCLC 75**
See also DLB 198

Grant, Skeeter
See Spiegelman, Art

Granville-Barker, Harley 1877-1946 .... **TCLC 2**
See also Barker, Harley Granville
See also CA 104; DAM DRAM; RGEL 2

Granzotto, Gianni
See Granzotto, Giovanni Battista

Granzotto, Giovanni Battista 1914-1985 .... **CLC 70**
See also CA 166

Grass, Guenter (Wilhelm) 1927- ... **CLC 1, 2, 4, 6, 11, 15, 22, 32, 49, 88; WLC**
See also BPFB 2; CA 13-16R; CANR 20, 75, 93; CDWLB 2; DA; DA3; DAB; DAC; DAM MST, NOV; DLB 75, 124; EW 13; MTCW 1, 2; RGWL 2

Gratton, Thomas
See Hulme, T(homas) E(rnest)

Grau, Shirley Ann 1929- .... **CLC 4, 9, 146; SSC 15**
See also CA 89-92; CANR 22, 69; CN 7; CSW; DLB 2, 218; INT CA-89-92, CANR-22; MTCW 1

Gravel, Fern
See Hall, James Norman

Graver, Elizabeth 1964- .... **CLC 70**
See also CA 135; CANR 71

Graves, Richard Perceval 1895-1985 .... **CLC 44**
See also CA 65-68; CANR 9, 26, 51

Graves, Robert (von Ranke) 1895-1985 .. **CLC 1, 2, 6, 11, 39, 44, 45; PC 6**
See also BPFB 2; BRW 7; BYA 4; CA 5-8R; 117; CANR 5, 36; CDBLB 1914-1945; DA3; DAB; DAC; DAM MST, POET; DLB 20, 100, 191; DLBD 18; DLBY 1985; MTCW 1, 2; NCFS 2; RGEL 2; RHW; SATA 45

Graves, Valerie
See Bradley, Marion Zimmer

Gray, Alasdair (James) 1934- .... **CLC 41**
See also CA 126; CANR 47, 69, 106; CN 7; DLB 194; HGG; INT CA-126; MTCW 1, 2; RGSF 2

Gray, Amlin 1946- .... **CLC 29**
See also CA 138

Gray, Francine du Plessix 1930- ..... **CLC 22, 153**
See also BEST 90:3; CA 61-64; CAAS 2; CANR 11, 33, 75, 81; DAM NOV; INT CANR-11; MTCW 1, 2

Gray, John (Henry) 1866-1934 ...... **TCLC 19**
See also CA 119; 162; RGEL 2

Gray, Simon (James Holliday) 1936- .... **CLC 9, 14, 36**
See also AITN 1; CA 21-24R; CAAS 3; CANR 32, 69; CD 5; DLB 13; MTCW 1; RGEL 2

Gray, Spalding 1941- ..... **CLC 49, 112; DC 7**
See also CA 128; CAD; CANR 74; CD 5; CPW; DAM POP; MTCW 2

Gray, Thomas 1716-1771 .... **LC 4, 40; PC 2; WLC**
See also BRW 3; CDBLB 1660-1789; DA; DA3; DAB; DAC; DAM MST; DLB 109; EXPP; PAB; PFS 9; RGEL 2; WP

Grayson, David
See Baker, Ray Stannard

Grayson, Richard (A.) 1951- .... **CLC 38**
See also CA 85-88; CANR 14, 31, 57; DLB 234

Greeley, Andrew M(oran) 1928- ...... **CLC 28**
See also BPFB 2; CA 5-8R; CAAS 7; CANR 7, 43, 69, 104; CMW 4; CPW; DA3; DAM POP; MTCW 1, 2

Green, Anna Katharine 1846-1935 .... **TCLC 63**
See also CA 112; 159; CMW 4; DLB 202, 221; MSW

Green, Brian
See Card, Orson Scott

Green, Hannah
See Greenberg, Joanne (Goldenberg)

Green, Hannah 1927(?)-1996 .... **CLC 3**
See also CA 73-76; CANR 59, 93; NFS 10

Green, Henry .... **CLC 2, 13, 97**
See also Yorke, Henry Vincent
See also BRWS 2; CA 175; DLB 15; RGEL 2

Green, Julian (Hartridge) 1900-1998
See Green, Julien
See also CA 21-24R; 169; CANR 33, 87; DLB 4, 72; MTCW 1

Green, Julien .... **CLC 3, 11, 77**
See also Green, Julian (Hartridge)
See also GFL 1789 to the Present; MTCW 2

Green, Paul (Eliot) 1894-1981 .... **CLC 25**
See also AITN 1; CA 5-8R; 103; CANR 3; DAM DRAM; DLB 7, 9, 249; DLBY 1981; RGAL 4

Greenberg, Ivan 1908-1973
See Rahv, Philip
See also CA 85-88

Greenberg, Joanne (Goldenberg) 1932- .... **CLC 7, 30**
See also AAYA 12; CA 5-8R; CANR 14, 32, 69; CN 7; SATA 25; YAW

Greenberg, Richard 1959(?)- .... **CLC 57**
See also CA 138; CAD; CD 5

Greenblatt, Stephen J(ay) 1943- ...... **CLC 70**
See also CA 49-52

Greene, Bette 1934- .... **CLC 30**
See also AAYA 7; BYA 3; CA 53-56; CANR 4; CLR 2; CWRI 5; JRDA; LAIT 4; MAICYA 1, 2; NFS 10; SAAS 16; SATA 8, 102; WYA; YAW

Greene, Gael .... **CLC 8**
See also CA 13-16R; CANR 10

Greene, Graham (Henry) 1904-1991 .... **CLC 1, 3, 6, 9, 14, 18, 27, 37, 70, 72, 125; SSC 29; WLC**
See also AITN 2; BPFB 2; BRWR 2; BRWS 1; BYA 3; CA 13-16R; 133; CANR 35, 61; CBD; CDBLB 1945-1960; CMW 4; DA; DA3; DAB; DAC; DAM MST, NOV, DLB 13, 15, 77, 100, 162, 201, 204; DLBY 1991; MSW; MTCW 1, 2; RGEL 2; SATA 20; SSFS 14; WLIT 4

Greene, Robert 1558-1592 .... **LC 41**
See also DLB 62, 167; IDTP; RGEL 2; TEA

Greer, Germaine 1939- .... **CLC 131**
See also AITN 1; CA 81-84; CANR 33, 70; FW; MTCW 1, 2

Greer, Richard
See Silverberg, Robert

Gregor, Arthur 1923- .... **CLC 9**
See also CA 25-28R; CAAS 10; CANR 11; CP 7; SATA 36

Gregor, Lee
See Pohl, Frederik

Gregory, Lady Isabella Augusta (Persse) 1852-1932 .... **TCLC 1**
See also BRW 6; CA 104; 184; DLB 10; IDTP; RGEL 2

Gregory, J. Dennis
See Williams, John A(lfred)

Grekova, I. .... **CLC 59**

Grendon, Stephen
See Derleth, August (William)

Grenville, Kate 1950- .... **CLC 61**
See also CA 118; CANR 53, 93

Grenville, Pelham
See Wodehouse, P(elham) G(renville)

Greve, Felix Paul (Berthold Friedrich) 1879-1948
See Grove, Frederick Philip
See also CA 104; 141, 175; CANR 79; DAC; DAM MST

Grey, Zane 1872-1939 .... **TCLC 6**
See also BPFB 2; CA 104; 132; DA3; DAM POP; DLB 9, 212; MTCW 1, 2; RGAL 4; TCWW 2

Grieg, (Johan) Nordahl (Brun) 1902-1943 .... **TCLC 10**
See also CA 107; 189

Grieve, C(hristopher) M(urray) 1892-1978 .... **CLC 11, 19**
See also MacDiarmid, Hugh; Pteleon
See also CA 5-8R; 85-88; CANR 33, 107; DAM POET; MTCW 1; RGEL 2

Griffin, Gerald 1803-1840 .... **NCLC 7**
See also DLB 159; RGEL 2

Griffin, John Howard 1920-1980 ..... **CLC 68**
See also AITN 1; CA 1-4R; 101; CANR 2

Griffin, Peter 1942- .... **CLC 39**
See also CA 136

Griffith, D(avid) L(ewelyn) W(ark) 1875(?)-1948 .... **TCLC 68**
See also CA 119; 150; CANR 80

Griffith, Lawrence
See Griffith, D(avid) L(ewelyn) W(ark)

Griffiths, Trevor 1935- .... **CLC 13, 52**
See also CA 97-100; CANR 45; CBD; CD 5; DLB 13, 245

Griggs, Sutton (Elbert) 1872-1930 .... **TCLC 77**
See also CA 123; 186; DLB 50

Grigson, Geoffrey (Edward Harvey) 1905-1985 .... **CLC 7, 39**
See also CA 25-28R; 118; CANR 20, 33; DLB 27; MTCW 1, 2

Grillparzer, Franz 1791-1872 . **NCLC 1, 102; DC 14; SSC 37**
See also CDWLB 2; DLB 133; EW 5; RGWL 2

Grimble, Reverend Charles James
See Eliot, T(homas) S(tearns)

Grimke, Charlotte L(ottie) Forten 1837(?)-1914
See Forten, Charlotte L.
See also BW 1; CA 117; 124; DAM MULT, POET

Grimm, Jacob Ludwig Karl 1785-1863 .... **NCLC 3, 77; SSC 36**
See also DLB 90; MAICYA 1, 2; RGSF 2; RGWL 2; SATA 22; WCH

Grimm, Wilhelm Karl 1786-1859 .. **NCLC 3, 77; SSC 36**
See also CDWLB 2; DLB 90; MAICYA 1, 2; RGSF 2; RGWL 2; SATA 22; WCH

Grimmelshausen, Hans Jakob Christoffel von
See Grimmelshausen, Johann Jakob Christoffel von
See also RGWL 2

Grimmelshausen, Johann Jakob Christoffel von 1621-1676 .... **LC 6**
See also Grimmelshausen, Hans Jakob Christoffel von
See also CDWLB 2; DLB 168

Grindel, Eugene 1895-1952
See Eluard, Paul
See also CA 104; 193

Grisham, John 1955- .... **CLC 84**
See also AAYA 14; BPFB 2; CA 138; CANR 47, 69; CMW 4; CN 7; CPW; CSW; DA3; DAM POP; MSW; MTCW 2

Grossman, David 1954- .... **CLC 67**
See also CA 138; CWW 2

Grossman, Vasily (Semenovich) 1905-1964 .... **CLC 41**
See also CA 124; 130; MTCW 1

Grove, Frederick Philip .... **TCLC 4**
See also Greve, Felix Paul (Berthold Friedrich)
See also DLB 92; RGEL 2

Grubb
See Crumb, R(obert)

Grumbach, Doris (Isaac) 1918- . **CLC 13, 22, 64**
See also CA 5-8R; CAAS 2; CANR 9, 42, 70; CN 7; INT CANR-9; MTCW 2

Grundtvig, Nicolai Frederik Severin 1783-1872 .... **NCLC 1**

Grunge
See Crumb, R(obert)

Grunwald, Lisa 1959- .... **CLC 44**
See also CA 120

Guare, John 1938- .... **CLC 8, 14, 29, 67**
See also CA 73-76; CAD; CANR 21, 69; CD 5; DAM DRAM; DFS 8, 13; DLB 7, 249; MTCW 1, 2; RGAL 4

Gubar, Susan (David) 1944- .... **CLC 145**
See also CA 108; CANR 45, 70; FW; MTCW 1; RGAL 4

Gudjonsson, Halldor Kiljan 1902-1998
See Laxness, Halldor
See also CA 103; 164; CWW 2

Guenter, Erich
See Eich, Guenter

Guest, Barbara 1920- .... **CLC 34**
See also CA 25-28R; CANR 11, 44, 84; CP 7; CWP; DLB 5, 193

Guest, Edgar A(lbert) 1881-1959 ... **TCLC 95**
See also CA 112; 168

Guest, Judith (Ann) 1936- .... **CLC 8, 30**
See also AAYA 7; CA 77-80; CANR 15, 75; DA3; DAM NOV, POP; EXPN; INT CANR-15; LAIT 5; MTCW 1, 2; NFS 1

Guevara, Che .... **CLC 87; HLC 1**
See also Guevara (Serna), Ernesto

Guevara (Serna), Ernesto 1928-1967 .... **CLC 87; HLC 1**
See also Guevara, Che
See also CA 127; 111; CANR 56; DAM MULT; HW 1

Guicciardini, Francesco 1483-1540 ..... **LC 49**

Guild, Nicholas M. 1944- .... **CLC 33**
See also CA 93-96

Guillemin, Jacques
See Sartre, Jean-Paul

Guillen, Jorge 1893-1984 . **CLC 11; HLCS 1; PC 35**
See also CA 89-92; 112; DAM MULT, POET; DLB 108; HW 1; RGWL 2

Guillen, Nicolas (Cristobal) 1902-1989 .... **CLC 48, 79; BLC 2; HLC 1; PC 23**
See also BW 2; CA 116; 125; 129; CANR 84; DAM MST, MULT, POET; HW 1; LAW; RGWL 2; WP

Guillen y Alavarez, Jorge
See Guillen, Jorge

Guillevic, (Eugene) 1907-1997 .... **CLC 33**
See also CA 93-96; CWW 2

Guillois
See Desnos, Robert

Guillois, Valentin
See Desnos, Robert

Guimaraes Rosa, Joao
See Rosa, Joao Guimaraes
See also LAW

Guimaraes Rosa, Joao 1908-1967
See also CA 175; HLCS 2; LAW; RGSF 2; RGWL 2

Guiney, Louise Imogen 1861-1920 .... **TCLC 41**
See also CA 160; DLB 54; RGAL 4

Guinizelli, Guido c. 1230-1276 ...... **CMLC 49**

Guiraldes, Ricardo (Guillermo) 1886-1927 .... **TCLC 39**
See also CA 131; HW 1; LAW; MTCW 1

Gumilev, Nikolai (Stepanovich) 1886-1921 .... **TCLC 60**
See also CA 165

Gunesekera, Romesh 1954- .... **CLC 91**
See also CA 159; CN 7

Gunn, Bill .... **CLC 5**
See also Gunn, William Harrison
See also DLB 38

Gunn, Thom(son William) 1929- .. **CLC 3, 6, 18, 32, 81; PC 26**
See also BRWS 4; CA 17-20R; CANR 9, 33; CDBLB 1960 to Present; CP 7; DAM POET; DLB 27; INT CANR-33; MTCW 1; PFS 9; RGEL 2

Gunn, William Harrison 1934(?)-1989
See Gunn, Bill
See also AITN 1; BW 1, 3; CA 13-16R; 128; CANR 12, 25, 76

Gunn Allen, Paula
See Allen, Paula Gunn

Gunnars, Kristjana 1948- .... **CLC 69**
See also CA 113; CCA 1; CP 7; CWP; DLB 60

Gurdjieff, G(eorgei) I(vanovich) 1877(?)-1949 .... **TCLC 71**
See also CA 157

Gurganus, Allan 1947- .... **CLC 70**
See also BEST 90:1; CA 135; CN 7; CPW; CSW; DAM POP; GLL 1

Gurney, A(lbert) R(amsdell), Jr.
1930- .... **CLC 32, 50, 54**
See also AMWS 5; CA 77-80; CAD; CANR 32, 64; CD 5; DAM DRAM

Gurney, Ivor (Bertie) 1890-1937 ... **TCLC 33**
See also BRW 6; CA 167; PAB; RGEL 2

Gurney, Peter
See Gurney, A(lbert) R(amsdell), Jr.

Guro, Elena 1877-1913 .... **TCLC 56**

Gustafson, James M(oody) 1925- ... **CLC 100**
See also CA 25-28R; CANR 37

Gustafson, Ralph (Barker)
1909-1995 .... **CLC 36**
See also CA 21-24R; CANR 8, 45, 84; CP 7; DLB 88; RGEL 2

Gut, Gom
See Simenon, Georges (Jacques Christian)

Guterson, David 1956- .... **CLC 91**
See also CA 132; CANR 73; MTCW 2; NFS 13

Guthrie, A(lfred) B(ertram), Jr.
1901-1991 .... **CLC 23**
See also CA 57-60; 134; CANR 24; DLB 6, 212; SATA 62; SATA-Obit 67

Guthrie, Isobel
See Grieve, C(hristopher) M(urray)

Guthrie, Woodrow Wilson 1912-1967
See Guthrie, Woody
See also CA 113; 93-96

Guthrie, Woody .... **CLC 35**
See also Guthrie, Woodrow Wilson
See also LAIT 3

Gutierrez Najera, Manuel 1859-1895
See also HLCS 2; LAW

Guy, Rosa (Cuthbert) 1928- .... **CLC 26**
See also AAYA 4, 37; BW 2; CA 17-20R; CANR 14, 34, 83; CLR 13; DLB 33; DNFS 1; JRDA; MAICYA 1; SATA 14, 62, 122; YAW

Gwendolyn
See Bennett, (Enoch) Arnold

H. D. .... **CLC 3, 8, 14, 31, 34, 73; PC 5**
See also Doolittle, Hilda

H. de V.
See Buchan, John

Haavikko, Paavo Juhani 1931- .. **CLC 18, 34**
See also CA 106

Habbema, Koos
See Heijermans, Herman

Habermas, Juergen 1929- .... **CLC 104**
See also CA 109; CANR 85; DLB 242

Habermas, Jurgen
See Habermas, Juergen

Hacker, Marilyn 1942- . **CLC 5, 9, 23, 72, 91**
See also CA 77-80; CANR 68; CP 7; CWP; DAM POET; DLB 120; FW; GLL 2

Haeckel, Ernst Heinrich (Philipp August)
1834-1919 .... **TCLC 83**
See also CA 157

Hafiz c. 1326-1389(?) .... **CMLC 34**
See also RGWL 2

Haggard, H(enry) Rider
1856-1925 .... **TCLC 11**
See also BRWS 3; BYA 4, 5; CA 108; 148; DLB 70, 156, 174, 178; FANT; MTCW 2; RGEL 2; RHW; SATA 16; SCFW; SFW 4; SUFW; WLIT 4

Hagiosy, L.
See Larbaud, Valery (Nicolas)

Hagiwara, Sakutaro 1886-1942 .... **TCLC 60; PC 18**
See also CA 154

Haig, Fenil
See Ford, Ford Madox

Haig-Brown, Roderick (Langmere)
1908-1976 .... **CLC 21**
See also CA 5-8R; 69-72; CANR 4, 38, 83; CLR 31; CWRI 5; DLB 88; MAICYA 1, 2; SATA 12

Hailey, Arthur 1920- .... **CLC 5**
See also AITN 2; BEST 90:3; BPFB 2; CA 1-4R; CANR 2, 36, 75; CCA 1; CN 7; CPW; DAM NOV, POP; DLB 88; DLBY 1982; MTCW 1, 2

Hailey, Elizabeth Forsythe 1938- .... **CLC 40**
See also CA 93-96; CAAE 188; CAAS 1; CANR 15, 48; INT CANR-15

Haines, John (Meade) 1924- .... **CLC 58**
See also CA 17-20R; CANR 13, 34; CSW; DLB 5, 212

Hakluyt, Richard 1552-1616 .... **LC 31**
See also DLB 136; RGEL 2

Haldeman, Joe (William) 1943- .... **CLC 61**
See also Graham, Robert
See also AAYA 38; CA 53-56, 179; CAAE 179; CAAS 25; CANR 6, 70, 72; DLB 8; INT CANR-6; SCFW 2; SFW 4

Hale, Sarah Josepha (Buell)
1788-1879 .... **NCLC 75**
See also DLB 1, 42, 73, 243

Halevy, Elie 1870-1937 .... **TCLC 104**

Haley, Alex(ander Murray Palmer)
1921-1992 .... **CLC 8, 12, 76; BLC 2**
See also AAYA 26; BPFB 2; BW 2, 3; CA 77-80; 136; CANR 61; CDALBS; CPW; CSW; DA; DA3; DAB; DAC; DAM MST, MULT, POP; DLB 38; LAIT 5; MTCW 1, 2; NFS 9

Haliburton, Thomas Chandler
1796-1865 .... **NCLC 15**
See also DLB 11, 99; RGEL 2; RGSF 2

Hall, Donald (Andrew, Jr.) 1928- .... **CLC 1, 13, 37, 59, 151**
See also CA 5-8R; CAAS 7; CANR 2, 44, 64, 106; CP 7; DAM POET; DLB 5; MTCW 1; RGAL 4; SATA 23, 97

Hall, Frederic Sauser
See Sauser-Hall, Frederic

Hall, James
See Kuttner, Henry

Hall, James Norman 1887-1951 ..... **TCLC 23**
See also CA 123; 173; LAIT 1; RHW 1; SATA 21

Hall, (Marguerite) Radclyffe
1880-1943 .... **TCLC 12**
See also BRWS 6; CA 110; 150; CANR 83; DLB 191; MTCW 2; RGEL 2; RHW

Hall, Rodney 1935- .... **CLC 51**
See also CA 109; CANR 69; CN 7; CP 7

Hallam, Arthur Henry
1811-1833 .... **NCLC 110**
See also DLB 32

Halleck, Fitz-Greene 1790-1867 .... **NCLC 47**
See also DLB 3, 250; RGAL 4

Halliday, Michael
See Creasey, John

Halpern, Daniel 1945- .... **CLC 14**
See also CA 33-36R; CANR 93; CP 7

Hamburger, Michael (Peter Leopold)
1924- .... **CLC 5, 14**
See also CA 5-8R; CAAE 196; CAAS 4; CANR 2, 47; CP 7; DLB 27

Hamill, Pete 1935- .... **CLC 10**
See also CA 25-28R; CANR 18, 71

Hamilton, Alexander
1755(?)-1804 .... **NCLC 49**
See also DLB 37

Hamilton, Clive
See Lewis, C(live) S(taples)

Hamilton, Edmond 1904-1977 .... **CLC 1**
See also CA 1-4R; CANR 3, 84; DLB 8; SATA 118; SFW 4

Hamilton, Eugene (Jacob) Lee
See Lee-Hamilton, Eugene (Jacob)

Hamilton, Franklin
See Silverberg, Robert

Hamilton, Gail
See Corcoran, Barbara (Asenath)

Hamilton, Mollie
See Kaye, M(ary) M(argaret)

Hamilton, (Anthony Walter) Patrick
1904-1962 .... **CLC 51**
See also CA 176; 113; DLB 10, 191

Hamilton, Virginia (Esther)
1936-2002 .... **CLC 26**
See also AAYA 2, 21; BW 2, 3; BYA 1, 2, 8; CA 25-28R; CANR 20, 37, 73; CLR 1, 11, 40; DAM MULT; DLB 33, 52; DLBY 01; INT CANR-20; JRDA; LAIT 5; MAICYA 1, 2; MAICYAS 1; MTCW 1, 2; SATA 4, 56, 79, 123; WYA; YAW

Hammett, (Samuel) Dashiell
1894-1961 .... **CLC 3, 5, 10, 19, 47; SSC 17**
See also AITN 1; AMWS 4; BPFB 2; CA 81-84; CANR 42; CDALB 1929-1941; CMW 4; DA3; DLB 226; DLBD 6; DLBY 1996; LAIT 3; MSW; MTCW 1, 2; RGAL 4; RGSF 2

Hammon, Jupiter 1720(?)-1800(?) . **NCLC 5; BLC 2; PC 16**
See also DAM MULT, POET; DLB 31, 50

Hammond, Keith
See Kuttner, Henry

Hamner, Earl (Henry), Jr. 1923- ...... **CLC 12**
See also AITN 2; CA 73-76; DLB 6

Hampton, Christopher (James)
1946- .... **CLC 4**
See also CA 25-28R; CD 5; DLB 13; MTCW 1

Hamsun, Knut .... **TCLC 2, 14, 49**
See also Pedersen, Knut
See also EW 8; RGWL 2

Handke, Peter 1942- .... **CLC 5, 8, 10, 15, 38, 134; DC 17**
See also CA 77-80; CANR 33, 75, 104; CWW 2; DAM DRAM, NOV; DLB 85, 124; MTCW 1, 2

Handy, W(illiam) C(hristopher)
1873-1958 .... **TCLC 97**
See also BW 3; CA 121; 167

Hanley, James 1901-1985 ...... **CLC 3, 5, 8, 13**
See also CA 73-76; 117; CANR 36; CBD; DLB 191; MTCW 1; RGEL 2

Hannah, Barry 1942- .... **CLC 23, 38, 90**
See also BPFB 2; CA 108; 110; CANR 43, 68; CN 7; CSW; DLB 6, 234; INT CA-110; MTCW 1; RGSF 2

Hannon, Ezra
See Hunter, Evan

Hansberry, Lorraine (Vivian)
1930-1965 ... **CLC 17, 62; BLC 2; DC 2**
See also AAYA 25; AFAW 1, 2; AMWS 4; BW 1, 3; CA 109; 25-28R; CABS 3; CANR 58; CDALB 1941-1968; DA; DA3; DAB; DAC; DAM DRAM, MST, MULT; DFS 2; DLB 7, 38; FW; LAIT 4; MTCW 1, 2; RGAL 4

Hansen, Joseph 1923- .... **CLC 38**
See also Brock, Rose; Colton, James
See also BPFB 2; CA 29-32R; CAAS 17; CANR 16, 44, 66; CMW 4; DLB 226; GLL 1; INT CANR-16

Hansen, Martin A(lfred)
1909-1955 .... **TCLC 32**
See also CA 167; DLB 214

Hansen and Philipson eds. .... **CLC 65**

Hanson, Kenneth O(stlin) 1922- .... **CLC 13**
See also CA 53-56; CANR 7

Hardwick, Elizabeth (Bruce) 1916- . **CLC 13**
See also AMWS 3; CA 5-8R; CANR 3, 32, 70, 100; CN 7; CSW; DA3; DAM NOV; DLB 6; MAWW; MTCW 1, 2

Hardy, Thomas 1840-1928 .. **TCLC 4, 10, 18, 32, 48, 53, 72; PC 8; SSC 2; WLC**
See also BRW 6; BRWR 1; CA 104; 123; CDBLB 1890-1914; DA; DA3; DAB; DAC; DAM MST, NOV, POET; DLB 18, 19, 135; EXPN; EXPP; LAIT 2; MTCW 1, 2; NFS 3, 11; PFS 3, 4; RGEL 2; RGSF 2; WLIT 4

Hare, David 1947- .... **CLC 29, 58, 136**
See also BRWS 4; CA 97-100; CANR 39, 91; CBD; CD 5; DFS 4, 7; DLB 13; MTCW 1

Harewood, John
See Van Druten, John (William)

Harford, Henry
See Hudson, W(illiam) H(enry)

Hargrave, Leonie
See Disch, Thomas M(ichael)

Harjo, Joy 1951- .... **CLC 83; PC 27**
See also CA 114; CANR 35, 67, 91; CP 7; CWP; DAM MULT; DLB 120, 175; MTCW 2; NNAL; RGAL 4

Harlan, Louis R(udolph) 1922- .... **CLC 34**
See also CA 21-24R; CANR 25, 55, 80

Harling, Robert 1951(?)- .... **CLC 53**
See also CA 147

Harmon, William (Ruth) 1938- .... **CLC 38**
See also CA 33-36R; CANR 14, 32, 35; SATA 65

Harper, F. E. W.
See Harper, Frances Ellen Watkins

Harper, Frances E. W.
See Harper, Frances Ellen Watkins

Harper, Frances E. Watkins
See Harper, Frances Ellen Watkins

Harper, Frances Ellen
See Harper, Frances Ellen Watkins

Harper, Frances Ellen Watkins
1825-1911 ..... **TCLC 14; BLC 2; PC 21**
See also AFAW 1, 2; BW 1, 3; CA 111; 125; CANR 79; DAM MULT, POET; DLB 50, 221; MAWW; RGAL 4

Harper, Michael S(teven) 1938- ... **CLC 7, 22**
See also AFAW 2; BW 1; CA 33-36R; CANR 24, 108; CP 7; DLB 41; RGAL 4

Harper, Mrs. F. E. W.
See Harper, Frances Ellen Watkins

Harris, Christie (Lucy) Irwin
1907- .... **CLC 12**
See also CA 5-8R; CANR 6, 83; CLR 47; DLB 88; JRDA; MAICYA 1, 2; SAAS 10; SATA 6, 74; SATA-Essay 116

Harris, Frank 1856-1931 .... **TCLC 24**
See also CA 109; 150; CANR 80; DLB 156, 197; RGEL 2

Harris, George Washington
1814-1869 .... **NCLC 23**
See also DLB 3, 11, 248; RGAL 4

Harris, Joel Chandler 1848-1908 ... **TCLC 2; SSC 19**
See also CA 104; 137; CANR 80; CLR 49; DLB 11, 23, 42, 78, 91; LAIT 2; MAICYA 1, 2; RGSF 2; SATA 100; WCH; YABC 1

Harris, John (Wyndham Parkes Lucas) Beynon 1903-1969
See Wyndham, John
See also CA 102; 89-92; CANR 84; SATA 118; SFW 4

Harris, MacDonald .... **CLC 9**
See also Heiney, Donald (William)

Harris, Mark 1922- .... **CLC 19**
See also CA 5-8R; CAAS 3; CANR 2, 55, 83; CN 7; DLB 2; DLBY 1980

Harris, Norman .... **CLC 65**

Harris, (Theodore) Wilson 1921- ...... **CLC 25**
See also BRWS 5; BW 2, 3; CA 65-68; CAAS 16; CANR 11, 27, 69; CDWLB 3; CN 7; CP 7; DLB 117; MTCW 1; RGEL 2

Harrison, Barbara Grizzuti 1934- . **CLC 144**
See also CA 77-80; CANR 15, 48; INT CANR-15

Harrison, Elizabeth (Allen) Cavanna 1909-2001
See Cavanna, Betty
See also CA 9-12R; 200; CANR 6, 27, 85, 104; MAICYA 2; YAW

Harrison, Harry (Max) 1925- .... **CLC 42**
See also CA 1-4R; CANR 5, 21, 84; DLB 8; SATA 4; SCFW 2; SFW 4

Harrison, James (Thomas) 1937- ...... **CLC 6, 14, 33, 66, 143; SSC 19**
See also Harrison, Jim
See also CA 13-16R; CANR 8, 51, 79; CN 7; CP 7; DLBY 1982; INT CANR-8

Harrison, Jim
See Harrison, James (Thomas)
See also AMWS 8; RGAL 4; TCWW 2

Harrison, Kathryn 1961- .... **CLC 70, 151**
See also CA 144; CANR 68

Harrison, Tony 1937- .... **CLC 43, 129**
See also BRWS 5; CA 65-68; CANR 44, 98; CBD; CD 5; CP 7; DLB 40, 245; MTCW 1; RGEL 2

Harriss, Will(ard Irvin) 1922- .... **CLC 34**
See also CA 111

Harson, Sley
See Ellison, Harlan (Jay)

Hart, Ellis
See Ellison, Harlan (Jay)

Hart, Josephine 1942(?)- .... **CLC 70**
See also CA 138; CANR 70; CWP; DAM POP

Hart, Moss 1904-1961 .... **CLC 66**
See also CA 109; 89-92; CANR 84; DAM DRAM; DFS 1; DLB 7; RGAL 4

Harte, (Francis) Bret(t)
1836(?)-1902 .... **TCLC 1, 25; SSC 8; WLC**
See also AMWS 2; CA 104; 140; CANR 80; CDALB 1865-1917; DA; DA3; DAC; DAM MST; DLB 12, 64, 74, 79, 186; EXPS; LAIT 2; RGAL 4; RGSF 2; SATA 26; SSFS 3

Hartley, L(eslie) P(oles) 1895-1972 ... **CLC 2, 22**
See also BRWS 7; CA 45-48; 37-40R; CANR 33; DLB 15, 139; HGG; MTCW 1, 2; RGEL 2; RGSF 2; SUFW

Hartman, Geoffrey H. 1929- .... **CLC 27**
See also CA 117; 125; CANR 79; DLB 67

Hartmann, Sadakichi 1869-1944 ...... **TCLC 73**
See also CA 157; DLB 54

Hartmann von Aue c. 1170-c. 1210 .... **CMLC 15**
See also CDWLB 2; DLB 138; RGWL 2

Haruf, Kent 1943- .... **CLC 34**
See also CA 149; CANR 91

Harwood, Ronald 1934- .... **CLC 32**
See also CA 1-4R; CANR 4, 55; CBD; CD 5; DAM DRAM, MST; DLB 13

Hasegawa Tatsunosuke
See Futabatei, Shimei

Hasek, Jaroslav (Matej Frantisek)
1883-1923 .... **TCLC 4**
See also CA 104; 129; CDWLB 4; DLB 215; EW 9; MTCW 1, 2; RGSF 2; RGWL 2

Hass, Robert 1941- ... **CLC 18, 39, 99; PC 16**
See also AMWS 6; CA 111; CANR 30, 50, 71; CP 7; DLB 105, 206; RGAL 4; SATA 94

Hastings, Hudson
See Kuttner, Henry

Hastings, Selina .... **CLC 44**

Hathorne, John 1641-1717 .... **LC 38**

Hatteras, Amelia
See Mencken, H(enry) L(ouis)

Hatteras, Owen .... **TCLC 18**
See also Mencken, H(enry) L(ouis); Nathan, George Jean

Hauptmann, Gerhart (Johann Robert)
1862-1946 .... **TCLC 4; SSC 37**
See also CA 104; 153; CDWLB 2; DAM DRAM; DLB 66, 118; EW 8; RGSF 2; RGWL 2

Havel, Vaclav 1936- ..... **CLC 25, 58, 65, 123; DC 6**
See also CA 104; CANR 36, 63; CDWLB 4; CWW 2; DA3; DAM DRAM; DFS 10; DLB 232; MTCW 1, 2

Haviaras, Stratis .... **CLC 33**
See also Chaviaras, Strates

Hawes, Stephen 1475(?)-1529(?) .... **LC 17**
See also DLB 132; RGEL 2

Hawkes, John (Clendennin Burne, Jr.)
1925-1998 .. **CLC 1, 2, 3, 4, 7, 9, 14, 15, 27, 49**
See also BPFB 2; CA 1-4R; 167; CANR 2, 47, 64; CN 7; DLB 2, 7, 227; DLBY 1980, 1998; MTCW 1, 2; RGAL 4

Hawking, S. W.
See Hawking, Stephen W(illiam)

Hawking, Stephen W(illiam) 1942- . **CLC 63, 105**
See also AAYA 13; BEST 89:1; CA 126; 129; CANR 48; CPW; DA3; MTCW 2

Hawkins, Anthony Hope
See Hope, Anthony

Hawthorne, Julian 1846-1934 .... **TCLC 25**
See also CA 165; HGG

Hawthorne, Nathaniel 1804-1864 ... **NCLC 2, 10, 17, 23, 39, 79, 95; SSC 3, 29, 39; WLC**
See also AAYA 18; AMW; AMWR 1; BPFB 2; BYA 3; CDALB 1640-1865; DA; DA3; DAB; DAC; DAM MST, NOV; DLB 1, 74, 183, 223; EXPN; EXPS; HGG; LAIT 1; NFS 1; RGAL 4; RGSF 2; SSFS 1, 7, 11; SUFW; WCH; YABC 2

Haxton, Josephine Ayres 1921-
See Douglas, Ellen
See also CA 115; CANR 41, 83

Hayaseca y Eizaguirre, Jorge
See Echegaray (y Eizaguirre), Jose (Maria Waldo)

Hayashi, Fumiko 1904-1951 .... **TCLC 27**
See also Hayashi Fumiko
See also CA 161

Hayashi Fumiko
See Hayashi, Fumiko
See also DLB 180

Haycraft, Anna (Margaret) 1932-
See Ellis, Alice Thomas
See also CA 122; CANR 85, 90; MTCW 2

Hayden, Robert E(arl) 1913-1980 . **CLC 5, 9, 14, 37; BLC 2; PC 6**
See also AFAW 1, 2; AMWS 2; BW 1, 3; CA 69-72; 97-100; CABS 2; CANR 24, 75, 82; CDALB 1941-1968; DA; DAC; DAM MST, MULT, POET; DLB 5, 76; EXPP; MTCW 1, 2; PFS 1; RGAL 4; SATA 19; SATA-Obit 26; WP

Hayek, F(riedrich) A(ugust von)
1899-1992 .... **TCLC 109**
See also CA 93-96; 137; CANR 20; MTCW 1, 2

Hayford, J(oseph) E(phraim) Casely
See Casely-Hayford, J(oseph) E(phraim)

Hayman, Ronald 1932- .... **CLC 44**
See also CA 25-28R; CANR 18, 50, 88; CD 5; DLB 155

Hayne, Paul Hamilton 1830-1886 . **NCLC 94**
See also DLB 3, 64, 79, 248; RGAL 4

Haywood, Eliza (Fowler) 1693(?)-1756 .... **LC 1, 44**
See also DLB 39; RGEL 2

Hazlitt, William 1778-1830 ...... **NCLC 29, 82**
See also BRW 4; DLB 110, 158; RGEL 2

Hazzard, Shirley 1931- .... **CLC 18**
See also CA 9-12R; CANR 4, 70; CN 7; DLBY 1982; MTCW 1

Head, Bessie 1937-1986 .... **CLC 25, 67; BLC 2; SSC 52**
See also AFW; BW 2, 3; CA 29-32R; 119; CANR 25, 82; CDWLB 3; DA3; DAM MULT; DLB 117, 225; EXPS; FW; MTCW 1, 2; RGSF 2; SSFS 5, 13; WLIT 2

Headon, (Nicky) Topper 1956(?)- ...... **CLC 30**

Heaney, Seamus (Justin) 1939- ..... **CLC 5, 7, 14, 25, 37, 74, 91; PC 18; WLCS**
See also BRWR 1; BRWS 2; CA 85-88; CANR 25, 48, 75, 91; CDBLB 1960 to Present; CP 7; DA3; DAB; DAM POET; DLB 40; DLBY 1995; EXPP; MTCW 1, 2; PAB; PFS 2, 5, 8; RGEL 2; WLIT 4

Hearn, (Patricio) Lafcadio (Tessima Carlos) 1850-1904 .... **TCLC 9**
See also CA 105; 166; DLB 12, 78, 189; HGG; RGAL 4

Hearne, Vicki 1946- .... **CLC 56**
See also CA 139

Hearon, Shelby 1931- .... **CLC 63**
See also AITN 2; AMWS 8; CA 25-28R; CANR 18, 48, 103; CSW

Heat-Moon, William Least .... **CLC 29**
See also Trogdon, William (Lewis)
See also AAYA 9

Hebbel, Friedrich 1813-1863 .... **NCLC 43**
See also CDWLB 2; DAM DRAM; DLB 129; EW 6; RGWL 2

Hebert, Anne 1916-2000 .... **CLC 4, 13, 29**
See also CA 85-88; 187; CANR 69; CCA 1; CWP; CWW 2; DA3; DAC; DAM MST, POET; DLB 68; GFL 1789 to the Present; MTCW 1, 2

Hecht, Anthony (Evan) 1923- ...... **CLC 8, 13, 19**
See also AMWS 10; CA 9-12R; CANR 6, 108; CP 7; DAM POET; DLB 5, 169; PFS 6; WP

Hecht, Ben 1894-1964 .... **CLC 8**
See also CA 85-88; DFS 9; DLB 7, 9, 25, 26, 28, 86; FANT; IDFW 3, 4; RGAL 4; TCLC 101

Hedayat, Sadeq 1903-1951 .... **TCLC 21**
See also CA 120; RGSF 2

Hegel, Georg Wilhelm Friedrich 1770-1831 .... **NCLC 46**
See also DLB 90

Heidegger, Martin 1889-1976 .... **CLC 24**
See also CA 81-84; 65-68; CANR 34; MTCW 1, 2

Heidenstam, (Carl Gustaf) Verner von 1859-1940 .... **TCLC 5**
See also CA 104

Heifner, Jack 1946- .... **CLC 11**
See also CA 105; CANR 47

Heijermans, Herman 1864-1924 .... **TCLC 24**
See also CA 123

Heilbrun, Carolyn G(old) 1926- .... **CLC 25**
See also Cross, Amanda
See also CA 45-48; CANR 1, 28, 58, 94; FW

Hein, Christoph 1944- .... **CLC 154**
See also CA 158; CANR 108; CDWLB 2; CWW 2; DLB 124

Heine, Heinrich 1797-1856 .... **NCLC 4, 54; PC 25**
See also CDWLB 2; DLB 90; EW 5; RGWL 2

Heinemann, Larry (Curtiss) 1944- .. **CLC 50**
See also CA 110; CAAS 21; CANR 31, 81; DLBD 9; INT CANR-31

Heiney, Donald (William) 1921-1993
See Harris, MacDonald
See also CA 1-4R; 142; CANR 3, 58; FANT

Heinlein, Robert A(nson) 1907-1988 . **CLC 1, 3, 8, 14, 26, 55**
See also AAYA 17; BPFB 2; BYA 4, 13; CA 1-4R; 125; CANR 1, 20, 53; CLR 75; CPW; DA3; DAM POP; DLB 8; EXPS; JRDA; LAIT 5; MAICYA 1, 2; MTCW 1, 2; RGAL 4; SATA 9, 69; SATA-Obit 56; SCFW; SFW 4; SSFS 7; YAW

Helforth, John
See Doolittle, Hilda

Hellenhofferu, Vojtech Kapristian z
See Hasek, Jaroslav (Matej Frantisek)

Heller, Joseph 1923-1999 . **CLC 1, 3, 5, 8, 11, 36, 63; WLC**
See also AAYA 24; AITN 1; AMWS 4; BPFB 1; BYA 1; CA 5-8R; 187; CABS 1; CANR 8, 42, 66; CN 7; CPW; DA; DA3; DAB; DAC; DAM MST, NOV, POP; DLB 2, 28, 227; DLBY 1980; EXPN; INT CANR-8; LAIT 4; MTCW 1, 2; NFS 1; RGAL 4; YAW

Hellman, Lillian (Florence) 1906-1984 .. **CLC 2, 4, 8, 14, 18, 34, 44, 52; DC 1**
See also AITN 1, 2; AMWS 1; CA 13-16R; 112; CAD; CANR 33; CWD; DA3; DAM DRAM; DFS 1, 3, 14; DLB 7, 228; DLBY 1984; FW; LAIT 3; MAWW; MTCW 1, 2; RGAL 4; TCLC 119

Helprin, Mark 1947- .... **CLC 7, 10, 22, 32**
See also CA 81-84; CANR 47, 64; CDALBS; CPW; DA3; DAM NOV, POP; DLBY 1985; FANT; MTCW 1, 2

Helvetius, Claude-Adrien 1715-1771 .. **LC 26**

Helyar, Jane Penelope Josephine 1933-
See Poole, Josephine
See also CA 21-24R; CANR 10, 26; CWRI 5; SATA 82

Hemans, Felicia 1793-1835 .... **NCLC 29, 71**
See also DLB 96; RGEL 2

Hemingway, Ernest (Miller) 1899-1961 .... **CLC 1, 3, 6, 8, 10, 13, 19, 30, 34, 39, 41, 44, 50, 61, 80; SSC 1, 25, 36, 40; WLC**
See also AAYA 19; AMW; AMWR 1; BPFB 2; BYA 2, 3, 13; CA 77-80; CANR 34; CDALB 1917-1929; DA; DA3; DAB; DAC; DAM MST, NOV; DLB 4, 9, 102, 210; DLBD 1, 15, 16; DLBY 1981, 1987, 1996, 1998; EXPN; EXPS; LAIT 3, 4; MTCW 1, 2; NFS 1, 5, 6, 14; RGAL 4; RGSF 2; SSFS 1, 6, 8, 9, 11; TCLC 115; WYA

Hempel, Amy 1951- .... **CLC 39**
See also CA 118; 137; CANR 70; DA3; DLB 218; EXPS; MTCW 2; SSFS 2

Henderson, F. C.
See Mencken, H(enry) L(ouis)

Henderson, Sylvia
See Ashton-Warner, Sylvia (Constance)

Henderson, Zenna (Chlarson) 1917-1983 .... **SSC 29**
See also CA 1-4R; 133; CANR 1, 84; DLB 8; SATA 5; SFW 4

Henkin, Joshua .... **CLC 119**
See also CA 161

Henley, Beth .... **CLC 23; DC 6, 14**
See also Henley, Elizabeth Becker
See also CABS 3; CAD; CD 5; CSW; CWD; DFS 2; DLBY 1986; FW

Henley, Elizabeth Becker 1952-
See Henley, Beth
See also CA 107; CANR 32, 73; DA3; DAM DRAM, MST; MTCW 1, 2

Henley, William Ernest 1849-1903 .. **TCLC 8**
See also CA 105; DLB 19; RGEL 2

Hennissart, Martha
See Lathen, Emma
See also CA 85-88; CANR 64

Henry VIII 1491-1547 .... **LC 10**
See also DLB 132

Henry, O. .... **TCLC 1, 19; SSC 5, 49; WLC**
See also Porter, William Sydney
See also AAYA 41; AMWS 2; EXPS; RGAL 4; RGSF 2; SSFS 2

Henry, Patrick 1736-1799 .... **LC 25**
See also LAIT 1

Henryson, Robert 1430(?)-1506(?) ...... **LC 20**
See also BRWS 7; DLB 146; RGEL 2

Henschke, Alfred
See Klabund

Hentoff, Nat(han Irving) 1925- .... **CLC 26**
See also AAYA 4, 42; BYA 6; CA 1-4R; CAAS 6; CANR 5, 25, 77; CLR 1, 52; INT CANR-25; JRDA; MAICYA 1, 2; SATA 42, 69; SATA-Brief 27; WYA; YAW

Heppenstall, (John) Rayner 1911-1981 .... **CLC 10**
See also CA 1-4R; 103; CANR 29

Heraclitus c. 540B.C.-c. 450B.C. ... **CMLC 22**
See also DLB 176

Herbert, Frank (Patrick) 1920-1986 .... **CLC 12, 23, 35, 44, 85**
See also AAYA 21; BPFB 2; BYA 4, 14; CA 53-56; 118; CANR 5, 43; CDALBS; CPW; DAM POP; DLB 8; INT CANR-5; LAIT 5; MTCW 1, 2; SATA 9, 37; SATA-Obit 47; SCFW 2; SFW 4; YAW

Herbert, George 1593-1633 .... **LC 24; PC 4**
See also BRW 1; BRWR 2; CDBLB Before 1660; DAB; DAM POET; DLB 126; EXPP; RGEL 2; WP

Herbert, Zbigniew 1924-1998 .... **CLC 9, 43**
See also CA 89-92; 169; CANR 36, 74; CDWLB 4; CWW 2; DAM POET; DLB 232; MTCW 1

Herbst, Josephine (Frey) 1897-1969 .... **CLC 34**
See also CA 5-8R; 25-28R; DLB 9

Herder, Johann Gottfried von 1744-1803 .... **NCLC 8**
See also DLB 97; EW 4

Heredia, Jose Maria 1803-1839
See also HLCS 2; LAW

Hergesheimer, Joseph 1880-1954 ... **TCLC 11**
See also CA 109; 194; DLB 102, 9; RGAL 4

Herlihy, James Leo 1927-1993 .... **CLC 6**
See also CA 1-4R; 143; CAD; CANR 2

Hermogenes fl. c. 175- .... **CMLC 6**

Hernandez, Jose 1834-1886 .... **NCLC 17**
See also LAW; RGWL 2; WLIT 1

Herodotus c. 484B.C.-c. 420B.C. .. **CMLC 17**
See also AW 1; CDWLB 1; DLB 176; RGWL 2

Herrick, Robert 1591-1674 .... **LC 13; PC 9**
See also BRW 2; DA; DAB; DAC; DAM MST, POP; DLB 126; EXPP; PFS 13; RGAL 4; RGEL 2; WP

Herring, Guilles
See Somerville, Edith Oenone

Herriot, James -1995 .... **CLC 12**
See also Wight, James Alfred
See also AAYA 1; BPFB 2; CA 148; CANR 40; CPW; DAM POP; LAIT 3; MAICYA 2; MAICYAS 1; MTCW 2; SATA 86; YAW

Herris, Violet
See Hunt, Violet

Herrmann, Dorothy 1941- .... **CLC 44**
See also CA 107

Herrmann, Taffy
See Herrmann, Dorothy

Hersey, John (Richard) 1914-1993 .... **CLC 1, 2, 7, 9, 40, 81, 97**
See also AAYA 29; BPFB 2; CA 17-20R; 140; CANR 33; CDALBS; CPW; DAM POP; DLB 6, 185; MTCW 1, 2; SATA 25; SATA-Obit 76

Herzen, Aleksandr Ivanovich 1812-1870 .... **NCLC 10, 61**

Herzl, Theodor 1860-1904 .... **TCLC 36**
See also CA 168

Herzog, Werner 1942- .... **CLC 16**
See also CA 89-92

Hesiod c. 8th cent. B.C.- .... **CMLC 5**
See also AW 1; DLB 176; RGWL 2

Hesse, Hermann 1877-1962 ... **CLC 1, 2, 3, 6, 11, 17, 25, 69; SSC 9, 49; WLC**
See also AAYA 43; BPFB 2; CA 17-18; CAP 2; CDWLB 2; DA; DA3; DAB; DAC; DAM MST, NOV; DLB 66; EW 9; EXPN; LAIT 1; MTCW 1, 2; NFS 6; RGWL 2; SATA 50

Hewes, Cady
See De Voto, Bernard (Augustine)

Heyen, William 1940- .... **CLC 13, 18**
See also CA 33-36R; CAAS 9; CANR 98; CP 7; DLB 5

Heyerdahl, Thor 1914-2002 .... **CLC 26**
See also CA 5-8R; CANR 5, 22, 66, 73; LAIT 4; MTCW 1, 2; SATA 2, 52

Heym, Georg (Theodor Franz Arthur) 1887-1912 .... **TCLC 9**
See also CA 106; 181

Heym, Stefan 1913- .... **CLC 41**
See also CA 9-12R; CANR 4; CWW 2; DLB 69

Heyse, Paul (Johann Ludwig von) 1830-1914 .... **TCLC 8**
See also CA 104; DLB 129

Heyward, (Edwin) DuBose 1885-1940 .... **TCLC 59**
See also CA 108; 157; DLB 7, 9, 45, 249; SATA 21

Heywood, John 1497(?)-1580(?) .... **LC 65**
See also DLB 136; RGEL 2

Hibbert, Eleanor Alice Burford 1906-1993 .... **CLC 7**
See also Holt, Victoria
See also BEST 90:4; CA 17-20R; 140; CANR 9, 28, 59; CMW 4; CPW; DAM POP; MTCW 2; RHW; SATA 2; SATA-Obit 74

Hichens, Robert (Smythe) 1864-1950 .... **TCLC 64**
See also CA 162; DLB 153; HGG; RHW; SUFW

Higgins, George V(incent) 1939-1999 .... **CLC 4, 7, 10, 18**
See also BPFB 2; CA 77-80; 186; CAAS 5; CANR 17, 51, 89, 96; CMW 4; CN 7; DLB 2; DLBY 1981, 1998; INT CANR-17; MSW; MTCW 1

Higginson, Thomas Wentworth 1823-1911 .... **TCLC 36**
See also CA 162; DLB 1, 64, 243

Higgonet, Margaret ed. .... **CLC 65**

Highet, Helen
See MacInnes, Helen (Clark)

Highsmith, (Mary) Patricia 1921-1995 .... **CLC 2, 4, 14, 42, 102**
See also Morgan, Claire
See also BRWS 5; CA 1-4R; 147; CANR 1, 20, 48, 62, 108; CMW 4; CPW; DA3; DAM NOV, POP; MSW; MTCW 1, 2

Highwater, Jamake (Mamake) 1942(?)-2001 .... **CLC 12**
See also AAYA 7; BPFB 2; BYA 4; CA 65-68; 199; CAAS 7; CANR 10, 34, 84; CLR 17; CWRI 5; DLB 52; DLBY 1985; JRDA; MAICYA 1, 2; SATA 32, 69; SATA-Brief 30

Highway, Tomson 1951- .... **CLC 92**
See also CA 151; CANR 75; CCA 1; CD 5; DAC; DAM MULT; DFS 2; MTCW 2; NNAL

Hijuelos, Oscar 1951- .... **CLC 65; HLC 1**
See also AAYA 25; AMWS 8; BEST 90:1; CA 123; CANR 50, 75; CPW; DA3; DAM MULT, POP; DLB 145; HW 1, 2; MTCW 2; RGAL 4; WLIT 1

Hikmet, Nazim 1902(?)-1963 .... **CLC 40**
See also CA 141; 93-96

Hildegard von Bingen 1098-1179 . **CMLC 20**
See also DLB 148

Hildesheimer, Wolfgang 1916-1991 .. **CLC 49**
See also CA 101; 135; DLB 69, 124

Hill, Geoffrey (William) 1932- ...... **CLC 5, 8, 18, 45**
See also BRWS 5; CA 81-84; CANR 21, 89; CDBLB 1960 to Present; CP 7; DAM POET; DLB 40; MTCW 1; RGEL 2

Hill, George Roy 1921- .... **CLC 26**
See also CA 110; 122

Hill, John
See Koontz, Dean R(ay)

Hill, Susan (Elizabeth) 1942- ...... **CLC 4, 113**
See also CA 33-36R; CANR 29, 69; CN 7; DAB; DAM MST, NOV; DLB 14, 139; HGG; MTCW 1; RHW

Hillard, Asa G. III .... **CLC 70**

Hillerman, Tony 1925- .... **CLC 62**
See also AAYA 40; BEST 89:1; BPFB 2; CA 29-32R; CANR 21, 42, 65, 97; CMW 4; CPW; DA3; DAM POP; DLB 206; MSW; RGAL 4; SATA 6; TCWW 2; YAW

Hillesum, Etty 1914-1943 .... **TCLC 49**
See also CA 137

Hilliard, Noel (Harvey) 1929-1996 ... **CLC 15**
See also CA 9-12R; CANR 7, 69; CN 7

Hillis, Rick 1956- .... **CLC 66**
See also CA 134

Hilton, James 1900-1954 .... **TCLC 21**
See also CA 108; 169; DLB 34, 77; FANT; SATA 34

Himes, Chester (Bomar) 1909-1984 .. **CLC 2, 4, 7, 18, 58, 108; BLC 2**
See also AFAW 2; BPFB 2; BW 2; CA 25-28R; 114; CANR 22, 89; CMW 4; DAM MULT; DLB 2, 76, 143, 226; MSW; MTCW 1, 2; RGAL 4

Hinde, Thomas .... **CLC 6, 11**
See also Chitty, Thomas Willes

Hine, (William) Daryl 1936- .... **CLC 15**
See also CA 1-4R; CAAS 15; CANR 1, 20; CP 7; DLB 60

Hinkson, Katharine Tynan
See Tynan, Katharine

Hinojosa(-Smith), Rolando (R.) 1929-
See also CA 131; CAAS 16; CANR 62; DAM MULT; DLB 82; HLC 1; HW 1, 2; MTCW 2; RGAL 4

Hinton, S(usan) E(loise) 1950- .. **CLC 30, 111**
See also AAYA 2, 33; BPFB 2; BYA 2, 3; CA 81-84; CANR 32, 62, 92; CDALBS; CLR 3, 23; CPW; DA; DA3; DAB; DAC; DAM MST, NOV; JRDA; LAIT 5; MAICYA 1, 2; MTCW 1, 2; NFS 5, 9; SATA 19, 58, 115; WYA; YAW

Hippius, Zinaida .... **TCLC 9**
See also Gippius, Zinaida (Nikolayevna)

Hiraoka, Kimitake 1925-1970
See Mishima, Yukio
See also CA 97-100; 29-32R; DA3; DAM DRAM; MTCW 1, 2

Hirsch, E(ric) D(onald), Jr. 1928- .... **CLC 79**
See also CA 25-28R; CANR 27, 51; DLB 67; INT CANR-27; MTCW 1

Hirsch, Edward 1950- .... **CLC 31, 50**
See also CA 104; CANR 20, 42, 102; CP 7; DLB 120

Hitchcock, Alfred (Joseph) 1899-1980 .... **CLC 16**
See also AAYA 22; CA 159; 97-100; SATA 27; SATA-Obit 24

Hitchens, Christopher (Eric) 1949- .... **CLC 157**
See also CA 149; CANR 89

Hitler, Adolf 1889-1945 .... **TCLC 53**
See also CA 117; 147

Hoagland, Edward 1932- .... **CLC 28**
See also ANW; CA 1-4R; CANR 2, 31, 57, 107; CN 7; DLB 6; SATA 51; TCWW 2

Hoban, Russell (Conwell) 1925- ... **CLC 7, 25**
See also BPFB 2; CA 5-8R; CANR 23, 37, 66; CLR 3, 69; CN 7; CWRI 5; DAM NOV; DLB 52; FANT; MAICYA 1, 2; MTCW 1, 2; SATA 1, 40, 78; SFW 4

Hobbes, Thomas 1588-1679 .... **LC 36**
See also DLB 151, 252; RGEL 2

Hobbs, Perry
See Blackmur, R(ichard) P(almer)

Hobson, Laura Z(ametkin) 1900-1986 .... **CLC 7, 25**
See also Field, Peter
See also BPFB 2; CA 17-20R; 118; CANR 55; DLB 28; SATA 52

Hoccleve, Thomas c. 1368-c. 1437 ...... **LC 75**
See also DLB 146; RGEL 2

Hoch, Edward D(entinger) 1930-
See Queen, Ellery
See also CA 29-32R; CANR 11, 27, 51, 97; CMW 4; SFW 4

Hochhuth, Rolf 1931- .... **CLC 4, 11, 18**
See also CA 5-8R; CANR 33, 75; CWW 2; DAM DRAM; DLB 124; MTCW 1, 2

Hochman, Sandra 1936- .... **CLC 3, 8**
See also CA 5-8R; DLB 5

Hochwaelder, Fritz 1911-1986 .... **CLC 36**
See also Hochwalder, Fritz
See also CA 29-32R; 120; CANR 42; DAM DRAM; MTCW 1

Hochwalder, Fritz
See Hochwaelder, Fritz
See also RGWL 2

Hocking, Mary (Eunice) 1921- .... **CLC 13**
See also CA 101; CANR 18, 40

Hodgins, Jack 1938- .... **CLC 23**
See also CA 93-96; CN 7; DLB 60

Hodgson, William Hope 1877(?)-1918 .... **TCLC 13**
See also CA 111; 164; CMW 4; DLB 70, 153, 156, 178; HGG; MTCW 2; SFW 4; SUFW

Hoeg, Peter 1957- .... **CLC 95, 156**
See also CA 151; CANR 75; CMW 4; DA3; DLB 214; MTCW 2

Hoffman, Alice 1952- .... **CLC 51**
See also AAYA 37; AMWS 10; CA 77-80; CANR 34, 66, 100; CN 7; CPW; DAM NOV; MTCW 1, 2

Hoffman, Daniel (Gerard) 1923- . **CLC 6, 13, 23**
See also CA 1-4R; CANR 4; CP 7; DLB 5

Hoffman, Stanley 1944- .... **CLC 5**
See also CA 77-80

Hoffman, William 1925- .... **CLC 141**
See also CA 21-24R; CANR 9, 103; CSW; DLB 234

Hoffman, William M(oses) 1939- ..... **CLC 40**
See also CA 57-60; CANR 11, 71

Hoffmann, E(rnst) T(heodor) A(madeus)
1776-1822 .... **NCLC 2; SSC 13**
See also CDWLB 2; DLB 90; EW 5; RGSF 2; RGWL 2; SATA 27; SUFW; WCH

Hofmann, Gert 1931- .... **CLC 54**
See also CA 128

Hofmannsthal, Hugo von
1874-1929 .... **TCLC 11; DC 4**
See also CA 106; 153; CDWLB 2; DAM DRAM; DFS 12; DLB 81, 118; EW 9; RGWL 2

Hogan, Linda 1947- .... **CLC 73; PC 35**
See also AMWS 4; ANW; BYA 12; CA 120; CANR 45, 73; CWP; DAM MULT; DLB 175; NNAL; TCWW 2

Hogarth, Charles
See Creasey, John

Hogarth, Emmett
See Polonsky, Abraham (Lincoln)

Hogg, James 1770-1835 .... **NCLC 4, 109**
See also DLB 93, 116, 159; HGG; RGEL 2; SUFW

Holbach, Paul Henri Thiry Baron
1723-1789 .... **LC 14**

Holberg, Ludvig 1684-1754 .... **LC 6**
See also RGWL 2

Holcroft, Thomas 1745-1809 .... **NCLC 85**
See also DLB 39, 89, 158; RGEL 2

Holden, Ursula 1921- .... **CLC 18**
See also CA 101; CAAS 8; CANR 22

Holderlin, (Johann Christian) Friedrich
1770-1843 .... **NCLC 16; PC 4**
See also CDWLB 2; DLB 90; EW 5; RGWL 2

Holdstock, Robert
See Holdstock, Robert P.

Holdstock, Robert P. 1948- .... **CLC 39**
See also CA 131; CANR 81; FANT; HGG; SFW 4

Holinshed, Raphael fl. 1580- .... **LC 69**
See also DLB 167; RGEL 2

Holland, Isabelle 1920- .... **CLC 21**
See also AAYA 11; CA 21-24R; 181; CAAE 181; CANR 10, 25, 47; CLR 57; CWRI 5; JRDA; LAIT 4; MAICYA 1, 2; SATA 8, 70; SATA-Essay 103; WYA

Holland, Marcus
See Caldwell, (Janet Miriam) Taylor (Holland)

Hollander, John 1929- .... **CLC 2, 5, 8, 14**
See also CA 1-4R; CANR 1, 52; CP 7; DLB 5; SATA 13

Hollander, Paul
See Silverberg, Robert

Holleran, Andrew 1943(?)- .... **CLC 38**
See Garber, Eric
See also CA 144; GLL 1

Holley, Marietta 1836(?)-1926 .... **TCLC 99**
See also CA 118; DLB 11

Hollinghurst, Alan 1954- .... **CLC 55, 91**
See also CA 114; CN 7; DLB 207; GLL 1

Hollis, Jim
See Summers, Hollis (Spurgeon, Jr.)

Holly, Buddy 1936-1959 .... **TCLC 65**

Holmes, Gordon
See Shiel, M(atthew) P(hipps)

Holmes, John
See Souster, (Holmes) Raymond

Holmes, John Clellon 1926-1988 ...... **CLC 56**
See also CA 9-12R; 125; CANR 4; DLB 16, 237

Holmes, Oliver Wendell, Jr.
1841-1935 .... **TCLC 77**
See also CA 114; 186

Holmes, Oliver Wendell
1809-1894 .... **NCLC 14, 81**
See also AMWS 1; CDALB 1640-1865; DLB 1, 189, 235; EXPP; RGAL 4; SATA 34

Holmes, Raymond
See Souster, (Holmes) Raymond

Holt, Victoria
See Hibbert, Eleanor Alice Burford
See also BPFB 2

Holub, Miroslav 1923-1998 .... **CLC 4**
See also CA 21-24R; 169; CANR 10; CDWLB 4; CWW 2; DLB 232

Homer c. 8th cent. B.C.- .... **CMLC 1, 16; PC 23; WLCS**
See also AW 1; CDWLB 1; DA; DA3; DAB; DAC; DAM MST, POET; DLB 176; EFS 1; LAIT 1; RGWL 2; WP

Hongo, Garrett Kaoru 1951- .... **PC 23**
See also CA 133; CAAS 22; CP 7; DLB 120; EXPP; RGAL 4

Honig, Edwin 1919- .... **CLC 33**
See also CA 5-8R; CAAS 8; CANR 4, 45; CP 7; DLB 5

Hood, Hugh (John Blagdon) 1928- . **CLC 15, 28; SSC 42**
See also CA 49-52; CAAS 17; CANR 1, 33, 87; CN 7; DLB 53; RGSF 2

Hood, Thomas 1799-1845 .... **NCLC 16**
See also BRW 4; DLB 96; RGEL 2

Hooker, (Peter) Jeremy 1941- .... **CLC 43**
See also CA 77-80; CANR 22; CP 7; DLB 40

hooks, bell .... **CLC 94**
See Watkins, Gloria Jean
See also DLB 246

Hope, A(lec) D(erwent) 1907-2000 .... **CLC 3, 51**
See also BRWS 7; CA 21-24R; 188; CANR 33, 74; MTCW 1, 2; PFS 8; RGEL 2

Hope, Anthony 1863-1933 .... **TCLC 83**
See also CA 157; DLB 153, 156; RGEL 2; RHW

Hope, Brian
See Creasey, John

Hope, Christopher (David Tully)
1944- .... **CLC 52**
See also AFW; CA 106; CANR 47, 101; CN 7; DLB 225; SATA 62

Hopkins, Gerard Manley
1844-1889 .... **NCLC 17; PC 15; WLC**
See also BRW 5; BRWR 2; CDBLB 1890-1914; DA; DA3; DAB; DAC; DAM MST, POET; DLB 35, 57; EXPP; PAB; RGEL 2; WP

Hopkins, John (Richard) 1931-1998 .. **CLC 4**
See also CA 85-88; 169; CBD; CD 5

Hopkins, Pauline Elizabeth
1859-1930 .... **TCLC 28; BLC 2**
See also AFAW 2; BW 2, 3; CA 141; CANR 82; DAM MULT; DLB 50

Hopkinson, Francis 1737-1791 .... **LC 25**
See also DLB 31; RGAL 4

Hopley-Woolrich, Cornell George 1903-1968
See Woolrich, Cornell
See also CA 13-14; CANR 58; CAP 1; CMW 4; DLB 226; MTCW 2

Horace 65B.C.-8B.C. .... **CMLC 39**
See also AW 2; CDWLB 1; DLB 211; RGWL 2

Horatio
See Proust, (Valentin-Louis-George-Eugene-)Marcel

Horgan, Paul (George Vincent O'Shaughnessy) 1903-1995 .. **CLC 9, 53**
See also BPFB 2; CA 13-16R; 147; CANR 9, 35; DAM NOV; DLB 102, 212; DLBY 1985; INT CANR-9; MTCW 1, 2; SATA 13; SATA-Obit 84; TCWW 2

Horn, Peter
See Kuttner, Henry

Hornem, Horace Esq.
See Byron, George Gordon (Noel)

Horney, Karen (Clementine Theodore Danielsen) 1885-1952 .... **TCLC 71**
See also CA 114; 165; DLB 246; FW

Hornung, E(rnest) W(illiam)
1866-1921 .... **TCLC 59**
See also CA 108; 160; CMW 4; DLB 70

Horovitz, Israel (Arthur) 1939- .... **CLC 56**
See also CA 33-36R; CAD; CANR 46, 59; CD 5; DAM DRAM; DLB 7

Horton, George Moses
1797(?)-1883(?) .... **NCLC 87**
See also DLB 50

Horvath, Odon von 1901-1938 .... **TCLC 45**
See also von Horvath, Oedoen
See also CA 118; 194; DLB 85, 124; RGWL 2

Horvath, Oedoen von -1938
See Horvath, Odon von

Horwitz, Julius 1920-1986 .... **CLC 14**
See also CA 9-12R; 119; CANR 12

Hospital, Janette Turner 1942- .... **CLC 42, 145**
See also CA 108; CANR 48; CN 7; RGSF 2

Hostos, E. M. de
See Hostos (y Bonilla), Eugenio Maria de

Hostos, Eugenio M. de
See Hostos (y Bonilla), Eugenio Maria de

Hostos, Eugenio Maria
See Hostos (y Bonilla), Eugenio Maria de

Hostos (y Bonilla), Eugenio Maria de
1839-1903 .... **TCLC 24**
See also CA 123; 131; HW 1

Houdini
See Lovecraft, H(oward) P(hillips)

Hougan, Carolyn 1943- .... **CLC 34**
See also CA 139

Household, Geoffrey (Edward West)
1900-1988 .... **CLC 11**
See also CA 77-80; 126; CANR 58; CMW 4; DLB 87; SATA 14; SATA-Obit 59

Housman, A(lfred) E(dward)
1859-1936 ... **TCLC 1, 10; PC 2; WLCS**
See also BRW 6; CA 104; 125; DA; DA3; DAB; DAC; DAM MST, POET; DLB 19; EXPP; MTCW 1, 2; PAB; PFS 4, 7; RGEL 2; WP

Housman, Laurence 1865-1959 .... **TCLC 7**
See also CA 106; 155; DLB 10; FANT; RGEL 2; SATA 25

Howard, Elizabeth Jane 1923- ..... **CLC 7, 29**
See also CA 5-8R; CANR 8, 62; CN 7

Howard, Maureen 1930- .... **CLC 5, 14, 46, 151**
See also CA 53-56; CANR 31, 75; CN 7; DLBY 1983; INT CANR-31; MTCW 1, 2

Howard, Richard 1929- .... **CLC 7, 10, 47**
See also AITN 1; CA 85-88; CANR 25, 80; CP 7; DLB 5; INT CANR-25

Howard, Robert E(rvin)
1906-1936 .... **TCLC 8**
See also BPFB 2; BYA 5; CA 105; 157; FANT; SUFW

Howard, Warren F.
See Pohl, Frederik

Howe, Fanny (Quincy) 1940- .... **CLC 47**
See also CA 117; CAAE 187; CAAS 27; CANR 70; CP 7; CWP; SATA-Brief 52

Howe, Irving 1920-1993 .... **CLC 85**
See also AMWS 6; CA 9-12R; 141; CANR 21, 50; DLB 67; MTCW 1, 2

Howe, Julia Ward 1819-1910 .... **TCLC 21**
See also CA 117; 191; DLB 1, 189, 235; FW

Howe, Susan 1937- .... **CLC 72, 152**
See also AMWS 4; CA 160; CP 7; CWP; DLB 120; FW; RGAL 4

Howe, Tina 1937- .... **CLC 48**
See also CA 109; CAD; CD 5; CWD

Howell, James 1594(?)-1666 .... **LC 13**
See also DLB 151

Howells, W. D.
See Howells, William Dean

Howells, William D.
See Howells, William Dean

Howells, William Dean 1837-1920 .. **TCLC 7, 17, 41; SSC 36**
See also AMW; CA 104; 134; CDALB 1865-1917; DLB 12, 64, 74, 79, 189; MTCW 2; RGAL 4

Howes, Barbara 1914-1996 .... **CLC 15**
See also CA 9-12R; 151; CAAS 3; CANR 53; CP 7; SATA 5

Hrabal, Bohumil 1914-1997 .... **CLC 13, 67**
See also CA 106; 156; CAAS 12; CANR 57; CWW 2; DLB 232; RGSF 2

Hrotsvit of Gandersheim c. 935-c. 1000 .... **CMLC 29**
See also DLB 148

Hsi, Chu 1130-1200 .... **CMLC 42**

Hsun, Lu
See Lu Hsun

Hubbard, L(afayette) Ron(ald) 1911-1986 .... **CLC 43**
See also CA 77-80; 118; CANR 52; CPW; DA3; DAM POP; FANT; MTCW 2; SFW 4

Huch, Ricarda (Octavia) 1864-1947 .... **TCLC 13**
See also CA 111; 189; DLB 66

Huddle, David 1942- .... **CLC 49**
See also CA 57-60; CAAS 20; CANR 89; DLB 130

Hudson, Jeffrey
See Crichton, (John) Michael

Hudson, W(illiam) H(enry) 1841-1922 .... **TCLC 29**
See also CA 115; 190; DLB 98, 153, 174; RGEL 2; SATA 35

Hueffer, Ford Madox
See Ford, Ford Madox

Hughart, Barry 1934- .... **CLC 39**
See also CA 137; FANT; SFW 4

Hughes, Colin
See Creasey, John

Hughes, David (John) 1930- .... **CLC 48**
See also CA 116; 129; CN 7; DLB 14

Hughes, Edward James
See Hughes, Ted
See also DA3; DAM MST, POET

Hughes, (James) Langston 1902-1967 .... **CLC 1, 5, 10, 15, 35, 44, 108; BLC 2; DC 3; PC 1; SSC 6; WLC**
See also AAYA 12; AFAW 1, 2; AMWR 1; AMWS 1; BW 1, 3; CA 1-4R; 25-28R; CANR 1, 34, 82; CDALB 1929-1941; CLR 17; DA; DA3; DAB; DAC; DAM DRAM, MST, MULT, POET; DLB 4, 7, 48, 51, 86, 228; EXPP; EXPS; JRDA; LAIT 3; MAICYA 1, 2; MTCW 1, 2; PAB; PFS 1, 3, 6, 10; RGAL 4; RGSF 2; SATA 4, 33; SSFS 4, 7; WCH; WP; YAW

Hughes, Richard (Arthur Warren) 1900-1976 .... **CLC 1, 11**
See also CA 5-8R; 65-68; CANR 4; DAM NOV; DLB 15, 161; MTCW 1; RGEL 2; SATA 8; SATA-Obit 25

Hughes, Ted 1930-1998 . **CLC 2, 4, 9, 14, 37, 119; PC 7**
See also Hughes, Edward James
See also BRWR 2; BRWS 1; CA 1-4R; 171; CANR 1, 33, 66, 108; CLR 3; CP 7; DAB; DAC; DLB 40, 161; EXPP; MAI-CYA 1, 2; MTCW 1, 2; PAB; PFS 4; RGEL 2; SATA 49; SATA-Brief 27; SATA-Obit 107; YAW

Hugo, Richard
See Hugo, Richard F(ranklin)

Hugo, Richard F(ranklin) 1923-1982 .... **CLC 6, 18, 32**
See also AMWS 6; CA 49-52; 108; CANR 3; DAM POET; DLB 5, 206; RGAL 4

Hugo, Victor (Marie) 1802-1885 .... **NCLC 3, 10, 21; PC 17; WLC**
See also AAYA 28; DA; DA3; DAB; DAC; DAM DRAM, MST, NOV, POET; DLB 119, 192, 217; EFS 2; EW 6; EXPN; GFL 1789 to the Present; LAIT 1, 2; NFS 5; RGWL 2; SATA 47

Huidobro, Vicente
See Huidobro Fernandez, Vicente Garcia
See also LAW

Huidobro Fernandez, Vicente Garcia 1893-1948 .... **TCLC 31**
See also CA 131; HW 1

Hulme, Keri 1947- .... **CLC 39, 130**
See also CA 125; CANR 69; CN 7; CP 7; CWP; FW; INT 125

Hulme, T(homas) E(rnest) 1883-1917 .... **TCLC 21**
See also BRWS 6; CA 117; DLB 19

Hume, David 1711-1776 .... **LC 7, 56**
See also BRWS 3; DLB 104, 252

Humphrey, William 1924-1997 .... **CLC 45**
See also AMWS 9; CA 77-80; 160; CANR 68; CN 7; CSW; DLB 6, 212, 234; TCWW 2

Humphreys, Emyr Owen 1919- .... **CLC 47**
See also CA 5-8R; CANR 3, 24; CN 7; DLB 15

Humphreys, Josephine 1945- ..... **CLC 34, 57**
See also CA 121; 127; CANR 97; CSW; INT 127

Huneker, James Gibbons 1860-1921 .... **TCLC 65**
See also CA 193; DLB 71; RGAL 4

Hungerford, Hesba Fay
See Brinsmead, H(esba) F(ay)

Hungerford, Pixie
See Brinsmead, H(esba) F(ay)

Hunt, E(verette) Howard, (Jr.) 1918- .... **CLC 3**
See also AITN 1; CA 45-48; CANR 2, 47, 103; CMW 4

Hunt, Francesca
See Holland, Isabelle

Hunt, Howard
See Hunt, E(verette) Howard, (Jr.)

Hunt, Kyle
See Creasey, John

Hunt, (James Henry) Leigh 1784-1859 .... **NCLC 1, 70**
See also DAM POET; DLB 96, 110, 144; RGEL 2; TEA

Hunt, Marsha 1946- .... **CLC 70**
See also BW 2, 3; CA 143; CANR 79

Hunt, Violet 1866(?)-1942 .... **TCLC 53**
See also CA 184; DLB 162, 197

Hunter, E. Waldo
See Sturgeon, Theodore (Hamilton)

Hunter, Evan 1926- .... **CLC 11, 31**
See also McBain, Ed
See also AAYA 39; BPFB 2; CA 5-8R; CANR 5, 38, 62, 97; CMW 4; CN 7; CPW; DAM POP; DLBY 1982; INT CANR-5; MSW; MTCW 1; SATA 25; SFW 4

Hunter, Kristin (Eggleston) 1931-
See Lattany, Kristin (Hunter)

Hunter, Mary
See Austin, Mary (Hunter)

Hunter, Mollie 1922- .... **CLC 21**
See also McIlwraith, Maureen Mollie Hunter
See also AAYA 13; BYA 6; CANR 37, 78; CLR 25; DLB 161; JRDA; MAICYA 1, 2; SAAS 7; SATA 54, 106; WYA; YAW

Hunter, Robert (?)-1734 .... **LC 7**

Hurston, Zora Neale 1891-1960 .. **CLC 7, 30, 61; BLC 2; DC 12; SSC 4; WLCS**
See also AAYA 15; AFAW 1, 2; AMWS 6; BW 1, 3; BYA 12; CA 85-88; CANR 61; CDALBS; DA; DA3; DAC; DAM MST, MULT, NOV; DFS 6; DLB 51, 86; EXPN; EXPS; FW; LAIT 3; MAWW; MTCW 1, 2; NFS 3; RGAL 4; RGSF 2; SSFS 1, 6, 11; TCLC 121; YAW

Husserl, E. G.
See Husserl, Edmund (Gustav Albrecht)

Husserl, Edmund (Gustav Albrecht) 1859-1938 .... **TCLC 100**
See also CA 116; 133

Huston, John (Marcellus) 1906-1987 .... **CLC 20**
See also CA 73-76; 123; CANR 34; DLB 26

Hustvedt, Siri 1955- .... **CLC 76**
See also CA 137

Hutten, Ulrich von 1488-1523 .... **LC 16**
See also DLB 179

Huxley, Aldous (Leonard) 1894-1963 .... **CLC 1, 3, 4, 5, 8, 11, 18, 35, 79; SSC 39; WLC**
See also AAYA 11; BPFB 2; BRW 7; CA 85-88; CANR 44, 99; CDBLB 1914-1945; DA; DA3; DAB; DAC; DAM MST, NOV; DLB 36, 100, 162, 195, 255; EXPN; LAIT 5; MTCW 1, 2; NFS 6; RGEL 2; SATA 63; SCFW 2; SFW 4; YAW

Huxley, T(homas) H(enry) 1825-1895 .... **NCLC 67**
See also DLB 57

Huysmans, Joris-Karl 1848-1907 ... **TCLC 7, 69**
See also CA 104; 165; DLB 123; EW 7; GFL 1789 to the Present; RGWL 2

Hwang, David Henry 1957- .. **CLC 55; DC 4**
See also CA 127; 132; CAD; CANR 76; CD 5; DA3; DAM DRAM; DFS 11; DLB 212, 228; INT CA-132; MTCW 2; RGAL 4

Hyde, Anthony 1946- .... **CLC 42**
See also Chase, Nicholas
See also CA 136; CCA 1

Hyde, Margaret O(ldroyd) 1917- ...... **CLC 21**
See also CA 1-4R; CANR 1, 36; CLR 23; JRDA; MAICYA 1, 2; SAAS 8; SATA 1, 42, 76

Hynes, James 1956(?)- .... **CLC 65**
See also CA 164; CANR 105

Hypatia c. 370-415 .... **CMLC 35**

Ian, Janis 1951- .... **CLC 21**
See also CA 105; 187

Ibanez, Vicente Blasco
See Blasco Ibanez, Vicente

Ibarbourou, Juana de 1895-1979
See also HLCS 2; HW 1; LAW

Ibarguengoitia, Jorge 1928-1983 .... **CLC 37**
See also CA 124; 113; HW 1

Ibsen, Henrik (Johan) 1828-1906 ... **TCLC 2, 8, 16, 37, 52; DC 2; WLC**
See also CA 104; 141; DA; DA3; DAB; DAC; DAM DRAM, MST; DFS 1, 6, 8, 10, 11; EW 7; LAIT 2; RGWL 2

Ibuse, Masuji 1898-1993 .... **CLC 22**
See also Ibuse Masuji
See also CA 127; 141; MJW

Ibuse Masuji
See Ibuse, Masuji
See also DLB 180

Ichikawa, Kon 1915- .... **CLC 20**
See also CA 121

Ichiyo, Higuchi 1872-1896 .... **NCLC 49**
See also MJW

Idle, Eric 1943-2000 .... **CLC 21**
See also Monty Python
See also CA 116; CANR 35, 91

Ignatow, David 1914-1997 .... **CLC 4, 7, 14, 40; PC 34**
See also CA 9-12R; 162; CAAS 3; CANR 31, 57, 96; CP 7; DLB 5

Ignotus
See Strachey, (Giles) Lytton

Ihimaera, Witi 1944- .... **CLC 46**
See also CA 77-80; CN 7; RGSF 2

Ilf, Ilya .... **TCLC 21**
See also Fainzilberg, Ilya Arnoldovich

Illyes, Gyula 1902-1983 .... **PC 16**
See also CA 114; 109; CDWLB 4; DLB 215; RGWL 2

Immermann, Karl (Lebrecht) 1796-1840 .... **NCLC 4, 49**
See also DLB 133

Ince, Thomas H. 1882-1924 .... **TCLC 89**
See also IDFW 3, 4

Inchbald, Elizabeth 1753-1821 ...... **NCLC 62**
See also DLB 39, 89; RGEL 2

Inclan, Ramon (Maria) del Valle
See Valle-Inclan, Ramon (Maria) del

Infante, G(uillermo) Cabrera
See Cabrera Infante, G(uillermo)

Ingalls, Rachel (Holmes) 1940- .... **CLC 42**
See also CA 123; 127

Ingamells, Reginald Charles
See Ingamells, Rex

Ingamells, Rex 1913-1955 .... **TCLC 35**
See also CA 167

Inge, William (Motter) 1913-1973 ..... **CLC 1, 8, 19**
See also CA 9-12R; CDALB 1941-1968; DA3; DAM DRAM; DFS 1, 5, 8; DLB 7, 249; MTCW 1, 2; RGAL 4

Ingelow, Jean 1820-1897 .... **NCLC 39, 107**
See also DLB 35, 163; FANT; SATA 33

Ingram, Willis J.
See Harris, Mark

Innaurato, Albert (F.) 1948(?)- ... **CLC 21, 60**
See also CA 115; 122; CAD; CANR 78; CD 5; INT CA-122

Innes, Michael
See Stewart, J(ohn) I(nnes) M(ackintosh)
See also MSW

Innis, Harold Adams 1894-1952 .... **TCLC 77**
See also CA 181; DLB 88

Ionesco, Eugene 1912-1994 ... **CLC 1, 4, 6, 9, 11, 15, 41, 86; DC 12; WLC**
See also CA 9-12R; 144; CANR 55; CWW 2; DA; DA3; DAB; DAC; DAM DRAM, MST; DFS 4, 9; EW 13; GFL 1789 to the Present; MTCW 1, 2; RGWL 2; SATA 7; SATA-Obit 79

Iqbal, Muhammad 1877-1938 .... **TCLC 28**

Ireland, Patrick
See O'Doherty, Brian

Irenaeus St. 130- .... **CMLC 42**

Iron, Ralph
See Schreiner, Olive (Emilie Albertina)

Irving, John (Winslow) 1942- ... **CLC 13, 23, 38, 112**
See also AAYA 8; AMWS 6; BEST 89:3; BPFB 2; CA 25-28R; CANR 28, 73; CN 7; CPW; DA3; DAM NOV, POP; DLB 6; DLBY 1982; MTCW 1, 2; NFS 12, 14; RGAL 4

Irving, Washington 1783-1859 . **NCLC 2, 19, 95; SSC 2, 37; WLC**
See also AMW; CDALB 1640-1865; DA; DA3; DAB; DAC; DAM MST; DLB 3, 11, 30, 59, 73, 74, 183, 186, 250, 254; EXPS; LAIT 1; RGAL 4; RGSF 2; SSFS 1, 8; SUFW; WCH; YABC 2

Irwin, P. K.
See Page, P(atricia) K(athleen)

Isaacs, Jorge Ricardo 1837-1895 ... **NCLC 70**
See also LAW

Isaacs, Susan 1943- .... **CLC 32**
See also BEST 89:1; BPFB 2; CA 89-92; CANR 20, 41, 65; CPW; DA3; DAM POP; INT CANR-20; MTCW 1, 2

Isherwood, Christopher (William Bradshaw) 1904-1986 .... **CLC 1, 9, 11, 14, 44**
See also AMWS 14; BRW 7; CA 13-16R; 117; CANR 35, 97; DA3; DAM DRAM, NOV; DLB 15, 195; DLBY 1986; IDTP; MTCW 1, 2; RGAL 4; RGEL 2; WLIT 4

Ishiguro, Kazuo 1954- .. **CLC 27, 56, 59, 110**
See also BEST 90:2; BPFB 2; BRWS 4; CA 120; CANR 49, 95; CN 7; DA3; DAM NOV; DLB 194; MTCW 1, 2; NFS 13; WLIT 4

Ishikawa, Hakuhin
See Ishikawa, Takuboku

Ishikawa, Takuboku 1886(?)-1912 .... **TCLC 15; PC 10**
See also CA 113; 153; DAM POET

Iskander, Fazil 1929- .... **CLC 47**
See also CA 102

Isler, Alan (David) 1934- .... **CLC 91**
See also CA 156; CANR 105

Ivan IV 1530-1584 .... **LC 17**

Ivanov, Vyacheslav Ivanovich 1866-1949 .... **TCLC 33**
See also CA 122

Ivask, Ivar Vidrik 1927-1992 .... **CLC 14**
See also CA 37-40R; 139; CANR 24

Ives, Morgan
See Bradley, Marion Zimmer
See also GLL 1

Izumi Shikibu c. 973-c. 1034 .... **CMLC 33**

J .... **CLC 8**
See also CA 33-36R; CANR 28, 67; CN 7; DLB 2, 28, 218; DLBY 1980

J. R. S.
See Gogarty, Oliver St. John

Jabran, Kahlil
See Gibran, Kahlil

Jabran, Khalil
See Gibran, Kahlil

Jackson, Daniel
See Wingrove, David (John)

Jackson, Helen Hunt 1830-1885 .... **NCLC 90**
See also DLB 42, 47, 186, 189; RGAL 4

Jackson, Jesse 1908-1983 .... **CLC 12**
See also BW 1; CA 25-28R; 109; CANR 27; CLR 28; CWRI 5; MAICYA 1, 2; SATA 2, 29; SATA-Obit 48

Jackson, Laura (Riding) 1901-1991
See Riding, Laura
See also CA 65-68; 135; CANR 28, 89; DLB 48

Jackson, Sam
See Trumbo, Dalton

Jackson, Sara
See Wingrove, David (John)

Jackson, Shirley 1919-1965 . **CLC 11, 60, 87; SSC 9, 39; WLC**
See also AAYA 9; AMWS 9; BPFB 2; CA 1-4R; 25-28R; CANR 4, 52; CDALB 1941-1968; DA; DA3; DAC; DAM MST; DLB 6, 234; HGG; LAIT 4; MTCW 2; RGAL 4; SATA 2; SSFS 1; SUFW

Jacob, (Cyprien-)Max 1876-1944 .... **TCLC 6**
See also CA 104; 193; GFL 1789 to the Present; GLL 2; RGWL 2

Jacobs, Harriet A(nn) 1813(?)-1897 .... **NCLC 67**
See also AFAW 1, 2; DLB 239; FW; LAIT 2; RGAL 4

Jacobs, Jim 1942- .... **CLC 12**
See also CA 97-100; INT 97-100

Jacobs, W(illiam) W(ymark) 1863-1943 .... **TCLC 22**
See also CA 121; 167; DLB 135; EXPS; HGG; RGEL 2; RGSF 2; SSFS 2; SUFW

Jacobsen, Jens Peter 1847-1885 ..... **NCLC 34**

Jacobsen, Josephine 1908- .... **CLC 48, 102**
See also CA 33-36R; CAAS 18; CANR 23, 48; CCA 1; CP 7; DLB 244

Jacobson, Dan 1929- .... **CLC 4, 14**
See also AFW; CA 1-4R; CANR 2, 25, 66; CN 7; DLB 14, 207, 225; MTCW 1; RGSF 2

Jacqueline
See Carpentier (y Valmont), Alejo

Jagger, Mick 1944- .... **CLC 17**

Jahiz, al- c. 780-c. 869 .... **CMLC 25**

Jakes, John (William) 1932- .... **CLC 29**
See also AAYA 32; BEST 89:4; BPFB 2; CA 57-60; CANR 10, 43, 66; CPW; CSW; DA3; DAM NOV, POP; DLBY 1983; FANT; INT CANR-10; MTCW 1, 2; RHW; SATA 62; SFW 4; TCWW 2

James I 1394-1437 .... **LC 20**
See also RGEL 2

James, Andrew
See Kirkup, James

James, C(yril) L(ionel) R(obert) 1901-1989 .... **CLC 33; BLCS**
See also BW 2; CA 117; 125; 128; CANR 62; DLB 125; MTCW 1

James, Daniel (Lewis) 1911-1988
See Santiago, Danny
See also CA 174; 125

James, Dynely
See Mayne, William (James Carter)

James, Henry Sr. 1811-1882 .... **NCLC 53**

James, Henry 1843-1916 ..... **TCLC 2, 11, 24, 40, 47, 64; SSC 8, 32, 47; WLC**
See also AMW; AMWR 1; BPFB 2; BRW 6; CA 104; 132; CDALB 1865-1917; DA; DA3; DAB; DAC; DAM MST, NOV; DLB 12, 71, 74, 189; DLBD 13; EXPS; HGG; LAIT 2; MTCW 1, 2; NFS 12; RGAL 4; RGEL 2; RGSF 2; SSFS 9; SUFW

James, M. R.
See James, Montague (Rhodes)
See also DLB 156, 201

James, Montague (Rhodes) 1862-1936 .... **TCLC 6; SSC 16**
See also James, M. R.
See also CA 104; HGG; RGEL 2; RGSF 2; SUFW

James, P. D. .... **CLC 18, 46, 122**
See also White, Phyllis Dorothy James
See also BEST 90:2; BPFB 2; BRWS 4; CDBLB 1960 to Present; DLB 87; DLBD 17; MSW

James, Philip
See Moorcock, Michael (John)

James, Samuel
See Stephens, James

James, Seumas
See Stephens, James

James, Stephen
See Stephens, James

James, William 1842-1910 .... **TCLC 15, 32**
See also AMW; CA 109; 193; RGAL 4

Jameson, Anna 1794-1860 .... **NCLC 43**
See also DLB 99, 166

Jameson, Fredric (R.) 1934- .... **CLC 142**
See also CA 196; DLB 67

Jami, Nur al-Din 'Abd al-Rahman
1414-1492 .... **LC 9**

Jammes, Francis 1868-1938 .... **TCLC 75**
See also CA 198; GFL 1789 to the Present

Jandl, Ernst 1925-2000 .... **CLC 34**
See also CA 200

Janowitz, Tama 1957- .... **CLC 43, 145**
See also CA 106; CANR 52, 89; CN 7; CPW; DAM POP

Japrisot, Sebastien 1931- .... **CLC 90**
See also Rossi, Jean Baptiste
See also CMW 4

Jarrell, Randall 1914-1965 .... **CLC 1, 2, 6, 9, 13, 49**
See also AMW; BYA 5; CA 5-8R; 25-28R; CABS 2; CANR 6, 34; CDALB 1941-1968; CLR 6; CWRI 5; DAM POET; DLB 48, 52; EXPP; MAICYA 1, 2; MTCW 1, 2; PAB; PFS 2; RGAL 4; SATA 7

Jarry, Alfred 1873-1907 .... **TCLC 2, 14; SSC 20**
See also CA 104; 153; DA3; DAM DRAM; DFS 8; DLB 192, 258; EW 9; GFL 1789 to the Present; RGWL 2

Jawien, Andrzej
See John Paul II, Pope

Jaynes, Roderick
See Coen, Ethan

Jeake, Samuel, Jr.
See Aiken, Conrad (Potter)

Jean Paul 1763-1825 .... **NCLC 7**

Jefferies, (John) Richard
1848-1887 .... **NCLC 47**
See also DLB 98, 141; RGEL 2; SATA 16; SFW 4

Jeffers, (John) Robinson 1887-1962 .. **CLC 2, 3, 11, 15, 54; PC 17; WLC**
See also AMWS 2; CA 85-88; CANR 35; CDALB 1917-1929; DA; DAC; DAM MST, POET; DLB 45, 212; MTCW 1, 2; PAB; PFS 3, 4; RGAL 4

Jefferson, Janet
See Mencken, H(enry) L(ouis)

Jefferson, Thomas 1743-1826 . **NCLC 11, 103**
See also ANW; CDALB 1640-1865; DA3; DLB 31, 183; LAIT 1; RGAL 4

Jeffrey, Francis 1773-1850 .... **NCLC 33**
See also Francis, Lord Jeffrey

Jelakowitch, Ivan
See Heijermans, Herman

Jellicoe, (Patricia) Ann 1927- .... **CLC 27**
See also CA 85-88; CBD; CD 5; CWD; CWRI 5; DLB 13, 233; FW

Jemyma
See Holley, Marietta

Jen, Gish .... **CLC 70**
See also Jen, Lillian

Jen, Lillian 1956(?)-
See Jen, Gish
See also CA 135; CANR 89

Jenkins, (John) Robin 1912- .... **CLC 52**
See also CA 1-4R; CANR 1; CN 7; DLB 14

Jennings, Elizabeth (Joan)
1926-2001 .... **CLC 5, 14, 131**
See also BRWS 5; CA 61-64; 200; CAAS 5; CANR 8, 39, 66; CP 7; CWP; DLB 27; MTCW 1; SATA 66

Jennings, Waylon 1937- .... **CLC 21**

Jensen, Johannes V. 1873-1950 ...... **TCLC 41**
See also CA 170; DLB 214

Jensen, Laura (Linnea) 1948- .... **CLC 37**
See also CA 103

Jerome, Jerome K(lapka)
1859-1927 .... **TCLC 23**
See also CA 119; 177; DLB 10, 34, 135; RGEL 2

Jerrold, Douglas William
1803-1857 .... **NCLC 2**
See also DLB 158, 159; RGEL 2

Jewett, (Theodora) Sarah Orne
1849-1909 .... **TCLC 1, 22; SSC 6, 44**
See also AMW; CA 108; 127; CANR 71; DLB 12, 74, 221; EXPS; FW; MAWW; RGAL 4; RGSF 2; SATA 15; SSFS 4

Jewsbury, Geraldine (Endsor)
1812-1880 .... **NCLC 22**
See also DLB 21

Jhabvala, Ruth Prawer 1927- . **CLC 4, 8, 29, 94, 138**
See also BRWS 5; CA 1-4R; CANR 2, 29, 51, 74, 91; CN 7; DAB; DAM NOV; DLB 139, 194; IDFW 3, 4; INT CANR-29; MTCW 1, 2; RGSF 2; RGWL 2; RHW

Jibran, Kahlil
See Gibran, Kahlil

Jibran, Khalil
See Gibran, Kahlil

Jiles, Paulette 1943- .... **CLC 13, 58**
See also CA 101; CANR 70; CWP

Jimenez (Mantecon), Juan Ramon
1881-1958 .... **TCLC 4; HLC 1; PC 7**
See also CA 104; 131; CANR 74; DAM MULT, POET; DLB 134; EW 9; HW 1; MTCW 1, 2; RGWL 2

Jimenez, Ramon
See Jimenez (Mantecon), Juan Ramon

Jimenez Mantecon, Juan
See Jimenez (Mantecon), Juan Ramon

Jin, Ha .... **CLC 109**
See also Jin, Xuefei
See also CA 152; DLB 244

Jin, Xuefei 1956-
See Jin, Ha
See also CANR 91

Joel, Billy .... **CLC 26**
See also Joel, William Martin

Joel, William Martin 1949-
See Joel, Billy
See also CA 108

John, Saint 107th cent. -100 .... **CMLC 27**

John of the Cross, St. 1542-1591 .... **LC 18**
See also RGWL 2

John Paul II, Pope 1920- .... **CLC 128**
See also CA 106; 133

Johnson, B(ryan) S(tanley William)
1933-1973 .... **CLC 6, 9**
See also CA 9-12R; 53-56; CANR 9; DLB 14, 40; RGEL 2

Johnson, Benj. F. of Boo
See Riley, James Whitcomb

Johnson, Benjamin F. of Boo
See Riley, James Whitcomb

Johnson, Charles (Richard) 1948- .... **CLC 7, 51, 65; BLC 2**
See also AFAW 2; AMWS 6; BW 2, 3; CA 116; CAAS 18; CANR 42, 66, 82; CN 7; DAM MULT; DLB 33; MTCW 2; RGAL 4

Johnson, Denis 1949- .... **CLC 52**
See also CA 117; 121; CANR 71, 99; CN 7; DLB 120

Johnson, Diane 1934- .... **CLC 5, 13, 48**
See also BPFB 2; CA 41-44R; CANR 17, 40, 62, 95; CN 7; DLBY 1980; INT CANR-17; MTCW 1

Johnson, Eyvind (Olof Verner)
1900-1976 .... **CLC 14**
See also CA 73-76; 69-72; CANR 34, 101; DLB 259; EW 12

Johnson, J. R.
See James, C(yril) L(ionel) R(obert)

Johnson, James Weldon
1871-1938 . **TCLC 3, 19; BLC 2; PC 24**
See also AFAW 1, 2; BW 1, 3; CA 104; 125; CANR 82; CDALB 1917-1929; CLR 32; DA3; DAM MULT, POET; DLB 51; EXPP; MTCW 1, 2; PFS 1; RGAL 4; SATA 31

Johnson, Joyce 1935- .... **CLC 58**
See also CA 125; 129; CANR 102

Johnson, Judith (Emlyn) 1936- .... **CLC 7, 15**
See also Sherwin, Judith Johnson
See also CA 25-28R; 153; CANR 34

Johnson, Lionel (Pigot)
1867-1902 .... **TCLC 19**
See also CA 117; DLB 19; RGEL 2

Johnson, Marguerite (Annie)
See Angelou, Maya

Johnson, Mel
See Malzberg, Barry N(athaniel)

Johnson, Pamela Hansford
1912-1981 .... **CLC 1, 7, 27**
See also CA 1-4R; 104; CANR 2, 28; DLB 15; MTCW 1, 2; RGEL 2

Johnson, Paul (Bede) 1928- .... **CLC 147**
See also BEST 89:4; CA 17-20R; CANR 34, 62, 100

Johnson, Robert .... **CLC 70**

Johnson, Robert 1911(?)-1938 .... **TCLC 69**
See also BW 3; CA 174

Johnson, Samuel 1709-1784 .... **LC 15, 52; WLC**
See also BRW 3; BRWR 1; CDBLB 1660-1789; DA; DAB; DAC; DAM MST; DLB 39, 95, 104, 142, 213; RGEL 2; TEA

Johnson, Uwe 1934-1984 .. **CLC 5, 10, 15, 40**
See also CA 1-4R; 112; CANR 1, 39; CDWLB 2; DLB 75; MTCW 1; RGWL 2

Johnston, George (Benson) 1913- .... **CLC 51**
See also CA 1-4R; CANR 5, 20; CP 7; DLB 88

Johnston, Jennifer (Prudence)
1930- .... **CLC 7, 150**
See also CA 85-88; CANR 92; CN 7; DLB 14

Joinville, Jean de 1224(?)-1317 ..... **CMLC 38**

Jolley, (Monica) Elizabeth 1923- ..... **CLC 46; SSC 19**
See also CA 127; CAAS 13; CANR 59; CN 7; RGSF 2

Jones, Arthur Llewellyn 1863-1947
See Machen, Arthur
See also CA 104; 179; HGG

Jones, D(ouglas) G(ordon) 1929- ..... **CLC 10**
See also CA 29-32R; CANR 13, 90; CP 7; DLB 53

Jones, David (Michael) 1895-1974 .... **CLC 2, 4, 7, 13, 42**
See also BRW 6; BRWS 7; CA 9-12R; 53-56; CANR 28; CDBLB 1945-1960; DLB 20, 100; MTCW 1; PAB; RGEL 2

Jones, David Robert 1947-
See Bowie, David
See also CA 103; CANR 104

Jones, Diana Wynne 1934- .... **CLC 26**
See also AAYA 12; BYA 6, 7, 9, 11, 13; CA 49-52; CANR 4, 26, 56; CLR 23; DLB 161; FANT; JRDA; MAICYA 1, 2; SAAS 7; SATA 9, 70, 108; SFW 4; YAW

Jones, Edward P. 1950- .... **CLC 76**
See also BW 2, 3; CA 142; CANR 79; CSW

Jones, Gayl 1949- ...... **CLC 6, 9, 131; BLC 2**
See also AFAW 1, 2; BW 2, 3; CA 77-80; CANR 27, 66; CN 7; CSW; DA3; DAM MULT; DLB 33; MTCW 1, 2; RGAL 4

Jones, James 1931-1978 ...... **CLC 1, 3, 10, 39**
See also AITN 1, 2; BPFB 2; CA 1-4R; 69-72; CANR 6; DLB 2, 143; DLBD 17; DLBY 1998; MTCW 1; RGAL 4

Jones, John J.
See Lovecraft, H(oward) P(hillips)

Jones, LeRoi .... **CLC 1, 2, 3, 5, 10, 14**
See also Baraka, Amiri
See also MTCW 2

Jones, Louis B. 1953- .... **CLC 65**
See also CA 141; CANR 73
Jones, Madison (Percy, Jr.) 1925- ...... **CLC 4**
See also CA 13-16R; CAAS 11; CANR 7, 54, 83; CN 7; CSW; DLB 152
Jones, Mervyn 1922- .... **CLC 10, 52**
See also CA 45-48; CAAS 5; CANR 1, 91; CN 7; MTCW 1
Jones, Mick 1956(?)- .... **CLC 30**
Jones, Nettie (Pearl) 1941- .... **CLC 34**
See also BW 2; CA 137; CAAS 20; CANR 88
Jones, Preston 1936-1979 .... **CLC 10**
See also CA 73-76; 89-92; DLB 7
Jones, Robert F(rancis) 1934- .... **CLC 7**
See also CA 49-52; CANR 2, 61
Jones, Rod 1953- .... **CLC 50**
See also CA 128
Jones, Terence Graham Parry
1942- .... **CLC 21**
See also Jones, Terry; Monty Python
See also CA 112; 116; CANR 35, 93; INT 116; SATA 127
Jones, Terry
See Jones, Terence Graham Parry
See also SATA 67; SATA-Brief 51
Jones, Thom (Douglas) 1945(?)- ...... **CLC 81**
See also CA 157; CANR 88; DLB 244
Jong, Erica 1942- .... **CLC 4, 6, 8, 18, 83**
See also AITN 1; AMWS 5; BEST 90:2; BPFB 2; CA 73-76; CANR 26, 52, 75; CN 7; CP 7; CPW; DA3; DAM NOV, POP; DLB 2, 5, 28, 152; FW; INT CANR-26; MTCW 1, 2
Jonson, Ben(jamin) 1572(?)-1637 .. **LC 6, 33; DC 4; PC 17; WLC**
See also BRW 1; BRWR 1; CDBLB Before 1660; DA; DAB; DAC; DAM DRAM, MST, POET; DFS 4, 10; DLB 62, 121; RGEL 2; WLIT 3
Jordan, June 1936- .... **CLC 5, 11, 23, 114; BLCS; PC 38**
See also Meyer, June
See also AAYA 2; AFAW 1, 2; BW 2, 3; CA 33-36R; CANR 25, 70; CLR 10; CP 7; CWP; DAM MULT, POET; DLB 38; GLL 2; LAIT 5; MAICYA 1, 2; MTCW 1; SATA 4; YAW
Jordan, Neil (Patrick) 1950- .... **CLC 110**
See also CA 124; 130; CANR 54; CN 7; GLL 2; INT 130
Jordan, Pat(rick M.) 1941- .... **CLC 37**
See also CA 33-36R
Jorgensen, Ivar
See Ellison, Harlan (Jay)
Jorgenson, Ivar
See Silverberg, Robert
Joseph, George Ghevarughese .... **CLC 70**
Josephson, Mary
See O'Doherty, Brian
Josephus, Flavius c. 37-100 .... **CMLC 13**
See also AW 2; DLB 176
Josiah Allen's Wife
See Holley, Marietta
Josipovici, Gabriel (David) 1940- ...... **CLC 6, 43, 153**
See also CA 37-40R; CAAS 8; CANR 47, 84; CN 7; DLB 14
Joubert, Joseph 1754-1824 .... **NCLC 9**
Jouve, Pierre Jean 1887-1976 .... **CLC 47**
See also CA 65-68; DLB 258
Jovine, Francesco 1902-1950 .... **TCLC 79**
Joyce, James (Augustine Aloysius)
1882-1941 ... **TCLC 3, 8, 16, 35, 52; DC 16; PC 22; SSC 3, 26, 44; WLC**
See also AAYA 42; BRW 7; BRWR 1; BYA 11, 13; CA 104; 126; CDBLB 1914-1945; DA; DA3; DAB; DAC; DAM MST, NOV, POET; DLB 10, 19, 36, 162, 247; EXPN;

EXPS; LAIT 3; MTCW 1, 2; NFS 7; RGSF 2; SSFS 1; WLIT 4
Jozsef, Attila 1905-1937 .... **TCLC 22**
See also CA 116; CDWLB 4; DLB 215
Juana Ines de la Cruz, Sor
1651(?)-1695 ...... **LC 5; HLCS 1; PC 24**
See also FW; LAW; RGWL 2; WLIT 1
Juana Inez de La Cruz, Sor
See Juana Ines de la Cruz, Sor
Judd, Cyril
See Kornbluth, C(yril) M.; Pohl, Frederik
Juenger, Ernst 1895-1998 .... **CLC 125**
See also Junger, Ernst
See also CA 101; 167; CANR 21, 47, 106; DLB 56
Julian of Norwich 1342(?)-1416(?) . **LC 6, 52**
See also DLB 146
Julius Caesar 100B.C.-44B.C.
See Caesar, Julius
See also CDWLB 1; DLB 211
Junger, Ernst
See Juenger, Ernst
See also CDWLB 2; RGWL 2
Junger, Sebastian 1962- .... **CLC 109**
See also AAYA 28; CA 165
Juniper, Alex
See Hospital, Janette Turner
Junius
See Luxemburg, Rosa
Just, Ward (Swift) 1935- .... **CLC 4, 27**
See also CA 25-28R; CANR 32, 87; CN 7; INT CANR-32
Justice, Donald (Rodney) 1925- .. **CLC 6, 19, 102**
See also AMWS 7; CA 5-8R; CANR 26, 54, 74; CP 7; CSW; DAM POET; DLBY 1983; INT CANR-26; MTCW 2; PFS 14
Juvenal c. 60-c. 130 .... **CMLC 8**
See also AW 2; CDWLB 1; DLB 211; RGWL 2
Juvenis
See Bourne, Randolph S(illiman)
Kabakov, Sasha .... **CLC 59**
Kacew, Romain 1914-1980
See Gary, Romain
See also CA 108; 102
Kadare, Ismail 1936- .... **CLC 52**
See also CA 161
Kadohata, Cynthia .... **CLC 59, 122**
See also CA 140
Kafka, Franz 1883-1924 . **TCLC 2, 6, 13, 29, 47, 53, 112; SSC 5, 29, 35; WLC**
See also AAYA 31; BPFB 2; CA 105; 126; CDWLB 2; DA; DA3; DAB; DAC; DAM MST, NOV; DLB 81; EW 9; EXPS; MTCW 1, 2; NFS 7; RGSF 2; RGWL 2; SFW 4; SSFS 3, 7, 12
Kahanovitsch, Pinkhes
See Der Nister
Kahn, Roger 1927- .... **CLC 30**
See also CA 25-28R; CANR 44, 69; DLB 171; SATA 37
Kain, Saul
See Sassoon, Siegfried (Lorraine)
Kaiser, Georg 1878-1945 .... **TCLC 9**
See also CA 106; 190; CDWLB 2; DLB 124; RGWL 2
Kaledin, Sergei .... **CLC 59**
Kaletski, Alexander 1946- .... **CLC 39**
See also CA 118; 143
Kalidasa fl. c. 400-455 .... **CMLC 9; PC 22**
See also RGWL 2
Kallman, Chester (Simon)
1921-1975 .... **CLC 2**
See also CA 45-48; 53-56; CANR 3
Kaminsky, Melvin 1926-
See Brooks, Mel
See also CA 65-68; CANR 16

Kaminsky, Stuart M(elvin) 1934- ..... **CLC 59**
See also CA 73-76; CANR 29, 53, 89; CMW 4
Kandinsky, Wassily 1866-1944 .... **TCLC 92**
See also CA 118; 155
Kane, Francis
See Robbins, Harold
Kane, Henry 1918-
See Queen, Ellery
See also CA 156; CMW 4
Kane, Paul
See Simon, Paul (Frederick)
Kanin, Garson 1912-1999 .... **CLC 22**
See also AITN 1; CA 5-8R; 177; CAD; CANR 7, 78; DLB 7; IDFW 3, 4
Kaniuk, Yoram 1930- .... **CLC 19**
See also CA 134
Kant, Immanuel 1724-1804 ..... **NCLC 27, 67**
See also DLB 94
Kantor, MacKinlay 1904-1977 .... **CLC 7**
See also CA 61-64; 73-76; CANR 60, 63; DLB 9, 102; MTCW 2; RHW; TCWW 2
Kanze Motokiyo
See Zeami
Kaplan, David Michael 1946- .... **CLC 50**
See also CA 187
Kaplan, James 1951- .... **CLC 59**
See also CA 135
Karageorge, Michael
See Anderson, Poul (William)
Karamzin, Nikolai Mikhailovich
1766-1826 .... **NCLC 3**
See also DLB 150; RGSF 2
Karapanou, Margarita 1946- .... **CLC 13**
See also CA 101
Karinthy, Frigyes 1887-1938 .... **TCLC 47**
See also CA 170; DLB 215
Karl, Frederick R(obert) 1927- .... **CLC 34**
See also CA 5-8R; CANR 3, 44
Kastel, Warren
See Silverberg, Robert
Kataev, Evgeny Petrovich 1903-1942
See Petrov, Evgeny
See also CA 120
Kataphusin
See Ruskin, John
Katz, Steve 1935- .... **CLC 47**
See also CA 25-28R; CAAS 14, 64; CANR 12; CN 7; DLBY 1983
Kauffman, Janet 1945- .... **CLC 42**
See also CA 117; CANR 43, 84; DLB 218; DLBY 1986
Kaufman, Bob (Garnell) 1925-1986 . **CLC 49**
See also BW 1; CA 41-44R; 118; CANR 22; DLB 16, 41
Kaufman, George S. 1889-1961 .... **CLC 38; DC 17**
See also CA 108; 93-96; DAM DRAM; DFS 1, 10; DLB 7; INT CA-108; MTCW 2; RGAL 4
Kaufman, Sue .... **CLC 3, 8**
See also Barondess, Sue K(aufman)
Kavafis, Konstantinos Petrou 1863-1933
See Cavafy, C(onstantine) P(eter)
See also CA 104
Kavan, Anna 1901-1968 .... **CLC 5, 13, 82**
See also BRWS 7; CA 5-8R; CANR 6, 57; DLB 255; MTCW 1; RGEL 2; SFW 4
Kavanagh, Dan
See Barnes, Julian (Patrick)
Kavanagh, Julie 1952- .... **CLC 119**
See also CA 163
Kavanagh, Patrick (Joseph)
1904-1967 .... **CLC 22; PC 33**
See also BRWS 7; CA 123; 25-28R; DLB 15, 20; MTCW 1; RGEL 2

Kawabata, Yasunari 1899-1972 ..... **CLC 2, 5, 9, 18, 107; SSC 17**
See also Kawabata Yasunari
See also CA 93-96; 33-36R; CANR 88; DAM MULT; MJW; MTCW 2; RGSF 2; RGWL 2

Kawabata Yasunari
See Kawabata, Yasunari
See also DLB 180

Kaye, M(ary) M(argaret) 1909- .... **CLC 28**
See also CA 89-92; CANR 24, 60, 102; MTCW 1, 2; RHW; SATA 62

Kaye, Mollie
See Kaye, M(ary) M(argaret)

Kaye-Smith, Sheila 1887-1956 .... **TCLC 20**
See also CA 118; DLB 36

Kaymor, Patrice Maguilene
See Senghor, Leopold Sedar

Kazakov, Yuri Pavlovich 1927-1982 . **SSC 43**
See also CA 5-8R; CANR 36; MTCW 1; RGSF 2

Kazan, Elia 1909- .... **CLC 6, 16, 63**
See also CA 21-24R; CANR 32, 78

Kazantzakis, Nikos 1883(?)-1957 .... **TCLC 2, 5, 33**
See also BPFB 2; CA 105; 132; DA3; EW 9; MTCW 1, 2; RGWL 2

Kazin, Alfred 1915-1998 ..... **CLC 34, 38, 119**
See also AMWS 8; CA 1-4R; CAAS 7; CANR 1, 45, 79; DLB 67

Keane, Mary Nesta (Skrine) 1904-1996
See Keane, Molly
See also CA 108; 114; 151; CN 7; RHW

Keane, Molly .... **CLC 31**
See also Keane, Mary Nesta (Skrine)
See also INT 114

Keates, Jonathan 1946(?)- .... **CLC 34**
See also CA 163

Keaton, Buster 1895-1966 .... **CLC 20**
See also CA 194

Keats, John 1795-1821 ... **NCLC 8, 73; PC 1; WLC**
See also BRW 4; BRWR 1; CDBLB 1789-1832; DA; DA3; DAB; DAC; DAM MST, POET; DLB 96, 110; EXPP; PAB; PFS 1, 2, 3, 9; RGEL 2; WLIT 3; WP

Keble, John 1792-1866 .... **NCLC 87**
See also DLB 32, 55; RGEL 2

Keene, Donald 1922- .... **CLC 34**
See also CA 1-4R; CANR 5

Keillor, Garrison .... **CLC 40, 115**
See also Keillor, Gary (Edward)
See also AAYA 2; BEST 89:3; BPFB 2; DLBY 1987; SATA 58

Keillor, Gary (Edward) 1942-
See Keillor, Garrison
See also CA 111; 117; CANR 36, 59; CPW; DA3; DAM POP; MTCW 1, 2

Keith, Carlos
See Lewton, Val

Keith, Michael
See Hubbard, L(afayette) Ron(ald)

Keller, Gottfried 1819-1890 .... **NCLC 2; SSC 26**
See also CDWLB 2; DLB 129; EW; RGSF 2; RGWL 2

Keller, Nora Okja 1965- .... **CLC 109**
See also CA 187

Kellerman, Jonathan 1949- .... **CLC 44**
See also AAYA 35; BEST 90:1; CA 106; CANR 29, 51; CMW 4; CPW; DA3; DAM POP; INT CANR 29

Kelley, William Melvin 1937- .... **CLC 22**
See also BW 1; CA 77-80; CANR 27, 83; CN 7; DLB 33

Kellogg, Marjorie 1922- .... **CLC 2**
See also CA 81-84

Kellow, Kathleen
See Hibbert, Eleanor Alice Burford

Kelly, M(ilton) T(errence) 1947- ...... **CLC 55**
See also CA 97-100; CAAS 22; CANR 19, 43, 84; CN 7

Kelly, Robert 1935- .... **SSC 50**
See also CA 17-20R; CAAS 19; CANR 47; CP 7; DLB 5, 130, 165

Kelman, James 1946- .... **CLC 58, 86**
See also BRWS 5; CA 148; CANR 85; CN 7; DLB 194; RGSF 2; WLIT 4

Kemal, Yashar 1923- .... **CLC 14, 29**
See also CA 89-92; CANR 44; CWW 2

Kemble, Fanny 1809-1893 .... **NCLC 18**
See also DLB 32

Kemelman, Harry 1908-1996 .... **CLC 2**
See also AITN 1; BPFB 2; CA 9-12R; 155; CANR 6, 71; CMW 4; DLB 28

Kempe, Margery 1373(?)-1440(?) ... **LC 6, 56**
See also DLB 146; RGEL 2

Kempis, Thomas a 1380-1471 .... **LC 11**

Kendall, Henry 1839-1882 .... **NCLC 12**
See also DLB 230

Keneally, Thomas (Michael) 1935- ... **CLC 5, 8, 10, 14, 19, 27, 43, 117**
See also BRWS 4; CA 85-88; CANR 10, 50, 74; CN 7; CPW; DA3; DAM NOV; MTCW 1, 2; RGEL 2; RHW

Kennedy, Adrienne (Lita) 1931- ..... **CLC 66; BLC 2; DC 5**
See also AFAW 2; BW 2, 3; CA 103; CAAS 20; CABS 3; CANR 26, 53, 82; CD 5; DAM MULT; DFS 9; DLB 38; FW

Kennedy, John Pendleton 1795-1870 .... **NCLC 2**
See also DLB 3, 248, 254; RGAL 4

Kennedy, Joseph Charles 1929-
See Kennedy, X. J.
See also CA 1-4R; CANR 4, 30, 40; CP 7; CWRI 5; MAICYA 2; MAICYAS 1; SATA 14, 86; SATA-Essay 130

Kennedy, William 1928- ... **CLC 6, 28, 34, 53**
See also AAYA 1; AMWS 7; BPFB 2; CA 85-88; CANR 14, 31, 76; CN 7; DA3; DAM NOV; DLB 143; DLBY 1985; INT CANR-31; MTCW 1, 2; SATA 57

Kennedy, X. J. .... **CLC 8, 42**
See also Kennedy, Joseph Charles
See also CAAS 9; CLR 27; DLB 5; SAAS 22

Kenny, Maurice (Francis) 1929- .... **CLC 87**
See also CA 144; CAAS 22; DAM MULT; DLB 175; NNAL

Kent, Kelvin
See Kuttner, Henry

Kenton, Maxwell
See Southern, Terry

Kenyon, Robert O.
See Kuttner, Henry

Kepler, Johannes 1571-1630 .... **LC 45**

Ker, Jill
See Conway, Jill K(er)

Kerkow, H. C.
See Lewton, Val

Kerouac, Jack 1922-1969 ...... **CLC 1, 2, 3, 5, 14, 29, 61; WLC**
See also Kerouac, Jean-Louis Lebris de
See also AAYA 25; AMWS 3; BPFB 2; CDALB 1941-1968; CPW; DLB 2, 16, 237; DLBD 3; DLBY 1995; GLL 1; MTCW 2; NFS 8; RGAL 4; TCLC 117; WP

Kerouac, Jean-Louis Lebris de 1922-1969
See Kerouac, Jack
See also AITN 1; CA 5-8R; 25-28R; CANR 26, 54, 95; DA; DA3; DAB; DAC; DAM MST, NOV, POET, POP; MTCW 1, 2

Kerr, Jean 1923- .... **CLC 22**
See also CA 5-8R; CANR 7; INT CANR-7

Kerr, M. E. .... **CLC 12, 35**
See also Meaker, Marijane (Agnes)
See also AAYA 2, 23; BYA 1, 7, 8; CLR 29; SAAS 1; WYA

Kerr, Robert .... **CLC 55**

Kerrigan, (Thomas) Anthony 1918- .. **CLC 4, 6**
See also CA 49-52; CAAS 11; CANR 4

Kerry, Lois
See Duncan, Lois

Kesey, Ken (Elton) 1935-2001 ... **CLC 1, 3, 6, 11, 46, 64; WLC**
See also AAYA 25; BPFB 2; CA 1-4R; CANR 22, 38, 66; CDALB 1968-1988; CN 7; CPW; DA; DA3; DAB; DAC; DAM MST, NOV, POP; DLB 2, 16, 206; EXPN; LAIT 4; MTCW 1, 2; NFS 2; RGAL 4; SATA 66; SATA-Obit 131; YAW

Kesselring, Joseph (Otto) 1902-1967 .... **CLC 45**
See also CA 150; DAM DRAM, MST

Kessler, Jascha (Frederick) 1929- ...... **CLC 4**
See also CA 17-20R; CANR 8, 48

Kettelkamp, Larry (Dale) 1933- .... **CLC 12**
See also CA 29-32R; CANR 16; SAAS 3; SATA 2

Key, Ellen (Karolina Sofia) 1849-1926 .... **TCLC 65**
See also DLB 259

Keyber, Conny
See Fielding, Henry

Keyes, Daniel 1927- .... **CLC 80**
See also AAYA 23; BYA 11; CA 17-20R, 181; CAAE 181; CANR 10, 26, 54, 74; DA; DA3; DAC; DAM MST, NOV; EXPN; LAIT 4; MTCW 1; NFS 2; SATA 37; SFW 4

Keynes, John Maynard 1883-1946 .... **TCLC 64**
See also CA 114; 162, 163; DLBD 10; MTCW 2

Khanshendel, Chiron
See Rose, Wendy

Khayyam, Omar 1048-1131 ... **CMLC 11; PC 8**
See also Omar Khayyam
See also DA3; DAM POET

Kherdian, David 1931- .... **CLC 6, 9**
See also AAYA 42; CA 21-24R; CAAE 192; CAAS 2; CANR 39, 78; CLR 24; JRDA; LAIT 3; MAICYA 1, 2; SATA 16, 74; SATA-Essay 125

Khlebnikov, Velimir .... **TCLC 20**
See also Khlebnikov, Viktor Vladimirovich
See also EW 10; RGWL 2

Khlebnikov, Viktor Vladimirovich 1885-1922
See Khlebnikov, Velimir
See also CA 117

Khodasevich, Vladislav (Felitsianovich) 1886-1939 .... **TCLC 15**
See also CA 115

Kielland, Alexander Lange 1849-1906 .... **TCLC 5**
See also CA 104

Kiely, Benedict 1919- .... **CLC 23, 43**
See also CA 1-4R; CANR 2, 84; CN 7; DLB 15

Kienzle, William X(avier) 1928- .... **CLC 25**
See also CA 93-96; CAAS 1; CANR 9, 31, 59; CMW 4; DA3; DAM POP; INT CANR-31; MSW; MTCW 1, 2

Kierkegaard, Soren 1813-1855 ..... **NCLC 34, 78**
See also EW 6

Kieslowski, Krzysztof 1941-1996 .... **CLC 120**
See also CA 147; 151

Killens, John Oliver 1916-1987 .... **CLC 10**
See also BW 2; CA 77-80; 123; CAAS 2; CANR 26; DLB 33

Killigrew, Anne 1660-1685 .... **LC 4, 73**
See also DLB 131

Killigrew, Thomas 1612-1683 .... **LC 57**
See also DLB 58; RGEL 2

Kim
See Simenon, Georges (Jacques Christian)

Kincaid, Jamaica 1949- ..... **CLC 43, 68, 137; BLC 2**
See also AAYA 13; AFAW 2; AMWS 7; BRWS 7; BW 2, 3; CA 125; CANR 47, 59, 95; CDALBS; CDWLB 3; CLR 63; CN 7; DA3; DAM MULT, NOV; DLB 157, 227; DNFS 1; EXPS; FW; MTCW 2; NCFS 1; NFS 3; SSFS 5, 7; YAW

King, Francis (Henry) 1923- .... **CLC 8, 53, 145**
See also CA 1-4R; CANR 1, 33, 86; CN 7; DAM NOV; DLB 15, 139; MTCW 1

King, Kennedy
See Brown, George Douglas

King, Martin Luther, Jr. 1929-1968 .... **CLC 83; BLC 2; WLCS**
See also BW 2, 3; CA 25-28; CANR 27, 44; CAP 2; DA; DA3; DAB; DAC; DAM MST, MULT; LAIT 5; MTCW 1, 2; SATA 14

King, Stephen (Edwin) 1947- .... **CLC 12, 26, 37, 61, 113; SSC 17**
See also AAYA 1, 17; AMWS 5; BEST 90:1; BPFB 2; CA 61-64; CANR 1, 30, 52, 76; CPW; DA3; DAM NOV, POP; DLB 143; DLBY 1980; HGG; JRDA; LAIT 5; MTCW 1, 2; RGAL 4; SATA 9, 55; SUFW; WYAS 1; YAW

King, Steve
See King, Stephen (Edwin)

King, Thomas 1943- .... **CLC 89**
See also CA 144; CANR 95; CCA 1; CN 7; DAC; DAM MULT; DLB 175; NNAL; SATA 96

Kingman, Lee .... **CLC 17**
See also Natti, (Mary) Lee
See also CWRI 5; SAAS 3; SATA 1, 67

Kingsley, Charles 1819-1875 .... **NCLC 35**
See also CLR 77; DLB 21, 32, 163, 178, 190; FANT; MAICYA 2; MAICYAS 1; RGEL 2; WCH; YABC 2

Kingsley, Henry 1830-1876 .... **NCLC 107**
See also DLB 21, 230; RGEL 2

Kingsley, Sidney 1906-1995 .... **CLC 44**
See also CA 85-88; 147; CAD; DFS 14; DLB 7; RGAL 4

Kingsolver, Barbara 1955- . **CLC 55, 81, 130**
See also AAYA 15; AMWS 7; CA 129; 134; CANR 60, 96; CDALBS; CPW; CSW; DA3; DAM POP; DLB 206; INT CA-134; LAIT 5; MTCW 2; NFS 5, 10, 12; RGAL 4

Kingston, Maxine (Ting Ting) Hong 1940- .... **CLC 12, 19, 58, 121; AAL; WLCS**
See also AAYA 8; AMWS 5; BPFB 2; CA 69-72; CANR 13, 38, 74, 87; CDALBS; CN 7; DA3; DAM MULT, NOV; DLB 173, 212; DLBY 1980; FW; INT CANR-13; LAIT 5; MAWW; MTCW 1, 2; NFS 6; RGAL 4; SATA 53; SSFS 3

Kinnell, Galway 1927- ..... **CLC 1, 2, 3, 5, 13, 29, 129; PC 26**
See also AMWS 3; CA 9-12R; CANR 10, 34, 66; CP 7; DLB 5; DLBY 1987; INT CANR-34; MTCW 1, 2; PAB; PFS 9; RGAL 4; WP

Kinsella, Thomas 1928- .... **CLC 4, 19, 138**
See also BRWS 5; CA 17-20R; CANR 15; CP 7; DLB 27; MTCW 1, 2; RGEL 2

Kinsella, W(illiam) P(atrick) 1935- . **CLC 27, 43**
See also AAYA 7; BPFB 2; CA 97-100; CAAS 7; CANR 21, 35, 66, 75; CN 7; CPW; DAC; DAM NOV, POP; FANT; INT CANR-21; LAIT 5; MTCW 1, 2; RGSF 2

Kinsey, Alfred C(harles) 1894-1956 .... **TCLC 91**
See also CA 115; 170; MTCW 2

Kipling, (Joseph) Rudyard 1865-1936 .. **TCLC 8, 17; PC 3; SSC 5; WLC**
See also AAYA 32; BRW 6; BYA 4; CA 105; 120; CANR 33; CDBLB 1890-1914; CLR 39, 65; CWRI 5; DA; DA3; DAB; DAC; DAM MST, POET; DLB 19, 34, 141, 156; EXPS; FANT; LAIT 3; MAICYA 1, 2; MTCW 1, 2; RGEL 2; RGSF 2; SATA 100; SFW 4; SSFS 8; SUFW; WCH; WLIT 4; YABC 2

Kirk, Russell (Amos) 1918-1994 .. **TCLC 119**
See also AITN 1; CA 1-4R; 145; CAAS 9; CANR 1, 20, 60; HGG; INT CANR-20; MTCW 1, 2

Kirkland, Caroline M. 1801-1864 . **NCLC 85**
See also DLB 3, 73, 74, 250, 254; DLBD 13

Kirkup, James 1918- .... **CLC 1**
See also CA 1-4R; CAAS 4; CANR 2; CP 7; DLB 27; SATA 12

Kirkwood, James 1930(?)-1989 .... **CLC 9**
See also AITN 2; CA 1-4R; 128; CANR 6, 40; GLL 2

Kirshner, Sidney
See Kingsley, Sidney

Kis, Danilo 1935-1989 .... **CLC 57**
See also CA 109; 118; 129; CANR 61; CDWLB 4; DLB 181; MTCW 1; RGSF 2; RGWL 2

Kissinger, Henry A(lfred) 1923- ..... **CLC 137**
See also CA 1-4R; CANR 2, 33, 66, 109; MTCW 1

Kivi, Aleksis 1834-1872 .... **NCLC 30**

Kizer, Carolyn (Ashley) 1925- ... **CLC 15, 39, 80**
See also CA 65-68; CAAS 5; CANR 24, 70; CP 7; CWP; DAM POET; DLB 5, 169; MTCW 2

Klabund 1890-1928 .... **TCLC 44**
See also CA 162; DLB 66

Klappert, Peter 1942- .... **CLC 57**
See also CA 33-36R; CSW; DLB 5

Klein, A(braham) M(oses) 1909-1972 .... **CLC 19**
See also CA 101; 37-40R; DAB; DAC; DAM MST; DLB 68; RGEL 2

Klein, Joe
See Klein, Joseph

Klein, Joseph 1946- .... **CLC 154**
See also CA 85-88; CANR 55

Klein, Norma 1938-1989 .... **CLC 30**
See also AAYA 2, 35; BPFB 2; BYA 6, 7, 8; CA 41-44R; 128; CANR 15, 37; CLR 2, 19; INT CANR-15; JRDA; MAICYA 1, 2; SAAS 1; SATA 7, 57; WYA; YAW

Klein, T(heodore) E(ibon) D(onald) 1947- .... **CLC 34**
See also CA 119; CANR 44, 75; HGG

Kleist, Heinrich von 1777-1811 .... **NCLC 2, 37; SSC 22**
See also CDWLB 2; DAM DRAM; DLB 90; EW 5; RGSF 2; RGWL 2

Klima, Ivan 1931- .... **CLC 56**
See also CA 25-28R; CANR 17, 50, 91; CDWLB 4; CWW 2; DAM NOV; DLB 232

Klimentov, Andrei Platonovich 1899-1951 .... **TCLC 14; SSC 42**
See also CA 108

Klinger, Friedrich Maximilian von 1752-1831 .... **NCLC 1**
See also DLB 94

Klingsor the Magician
See Hartmann, Sadakichi

Klopstock, Friedrich Gottlieb 1724-1803 .... **NCLC 11**
See also DLB 97; EW 4; RGWL 2

Knapp, Caroline 1959-2002 .... **CLC 99**
See also CA 154

Knebel, Fletcher 1911-1993 .... **CLC 14**
See also AITN 1; CA 1-4R; 140; CAAS 3; CANR 1, 36; SATA 36; SATA-Obit 75

Knickerbocker, Diedrich
See Irving, Washington

Knight, Etheridge 1931-1991 . **CLC 40; BLC 2; PC 14**
See also BW 1, 3; CA 21-24R; 133; CANR 23, 82; DAM POET; DLB 41; MTCW 2; RGAL 4

Knight, Sarah Kemble 1666-1727 .... **LC 7**
See also DLB 24, 200

Knister, Raymond 1899-1932 .... **TCLC 56**
See also CA 186; DLB 68; RGEL 2

Knowles, John 1926-2001 ... **CLC 1, 4, 10, 26**
See also AAYA 10; BPFB 2; BYA 3; CA 17-20R; CANR 40, 74, 76; CDALB 1968-1988; CN 7; DA; DAC; DAM MST, NOV; DLB 6; EXPN; MTCW 1, 2; NFS 2; RGAL 4; SATA 8, 89; YAW

Knox, Calvin M.
See Silverberg, Robert

Knox, John c. 1505-1572 .... **LC 37**
See also DLB 132

Knye, Cassandra
See Disch, Thomas M(ichael)

Koch, C(hristopher) J(ohn) 1932- .... **CLC 42**
See also CA 127; CANR 84; CN 7

Koch, Christopher
See Koch, C(hristopher) J(ohn)

Koch, Kenneth 1925- .... **CLC 5, 8, 44**
See also CA 1-4R; CAD; CANR 6, 36, 57, 97; CD 5; CP 7; DAM POET; DLB 5; INT CANR-36; MTCW 2; SATA 65; WP

Kochanowski, Jan 1530-1584 .... **LC 10**
See also RGWL 2

Kock, Charles Paul de 1794-1871 . **NCLC 16**

Koda Rohan
See Koda Shigeyuki

Koda Rohan
See Koda Shigeyuki
See also DLB 180

Koda Shigeyuki 1867-1947 .... **TCLC 22**
See also Koda Rohan
See also CA 121; 183

Koestler, Arthur 1905-1983 ... **CLC 1, 3, 6, 8, 15, 33**
See also BRWS 1; CA 1-4R; 109; CANR 1, 33; CDBLB 1945-1960; DLBY 1983; MTCW 1, 2; RGEL 2

Kogawa, Joy Nozomi 1935- .... **CLC 78, 129**
See also CA 101; CANR 19, 62; CN 7; CWP; DAC; DAM MST, MULT; FW; MTCW 2; NFS 3; SATA 99

Kohout, Pavel 1928- .... **CLC 13**
See also CA 45-48; CANR 3

Koizumi, Yakumo
See Hearn, (Patricio) Lafcadio (Tessima Carlos)

Kolmar, Gertrud 1894-1943 .... **TCLC 40**
See also CA 167

Komunyakaa, Yusef 1947- .... **CLC 86, 94; BLCS**
See also AFAW 2; CA 147; CANR 83; CP 7; CSW; DLB 120; PFS 5; RGAL 4

Konrad, George
See Konrad, Gyorgy
See also CWW 2

Konrad, Gyorgy 1933- .... **CLC 4, 10, 73**
See also Konrad, George
See also CA 85-88; CANR 97; CDWLB 4; CWW 2; DLB 232

Konwicki, Tadeusz 1926- .... **CLC 8, 28, 54, 117**
See also CA 101; CAAS 9; CANR 39, 59; CWW 2; DLB 232; IDFW 3; MTCW 1

Koontz, Dean R(ay) 1945- .... **CLC 78**
See also AAYA 9, 31; BEST 89:3, 90:2; CA 108; CANR 19, 36, 52, 95; CMW 4; CPW; DA3; DAM NOV, POP; HGG; MTCW 1; SATA 92; SFW 4; YAW

Kopernik, Mikolaj
See Copernicus, Nicolaus

Kopit, Arthur (Lee) 1937- ...... **CLC 1, 18, 33**
See also AITN 1; CA 81-84; CABS 3; CD 5; DAM DRAM; DFS 7, 14; DLB 7; MTCW 1; RGAL 4

Kops, Bernard 1926- .... **CLC 4**
See also CA 5-8R; CANR 84; CBD; CN 7; CP 7; DLB 13

Kornbluth, C(yril) M. 1923-1958 .... **TCLC 8**
See also CA 105; 160; DLB 8; SFW 4

Korolenko, V. G.
See Korolenko, Vladimir Galaktionovich

Korolenko, Vladimir
See Korolenko, Vladimir Galaktionovich

Korolenko, Vladimir G.
See Korolenko, Vladimir Galaktionovich

Korolenko, Vladimir Galaktionovich 1853-1921 .... **TCLC 22**
See also CA 121

Korzybski, Alfred (Habdank Skarbek) 1879-1950 .... **TCLC 61**
See also CA 123; 160

Kosinski, Jerzy (Nikodem) 1933-1991 .... **CLC 1, 2, 3, 6, 10, 15, 53, 70**
See also AMWS 7; BPFB 2; CA 17-20R; 134; CANR 9, 46; DA3; DAM NOV; DLB 2; DLBY 1982; HGG; MTCW 1, 2; NFS 12; RGAL 4

Kostelanetz, Richard (Cory) 1940- .. **CLC 28**
See also CA 13-16R; CAAS 8; CANR 38, 77; CN 7; CP 7

Kotlowitz, Robert 1924- .... **CLC 4**
See also CA 33-36R; CANR 36

Kotzebue, August (Friedrich Ferdinand) von 1761-1819 .... **NCLC 25**
See also DLB 94

Kotzwinkle, William 1938- ..... **CLC 5, 14, 35**
See also BPFB 2; CA 45-48; CANR 3, 44, 84; CLR 6; DLB 173; FANT; MAICYA 1, 2; SATA 24, 70; SFW 4; YAW

Kowna, Stancy
See Szymborska, Wislawa

Kozol, Jonathan 1936- .... **CLC 17**
See also CA 61-64; CANR 16, 45, 96

Kozoll, Michael 1940(?)- .... **CLC 35**

Kramer, Kathryn 19(?)- .... **CLC 34**

Kramer, Larry 1935- .... **CLC 42; DC 8**
See also CA 124; 126; CANR 60; DAM POP; DLB 249; GLL 1

Krasicki, Ignacy 1735-1801 .... **NCLC 8**

Krasinski, Zygmunt 1812-1859 .... **NCLC 4**
See also RGWL 2

Kraus, Karl 1874-1936 .... **TCLC 5**
See also CA 104; DLB 118

Kreve (Mickevicius), Vincas 1882-1954 .... **TCLC 27**
See also CA 170; DLB 220

Kristeva, Julia 1941- .... **CLC 77, 140**
See also CA 154; CANR 99; DLB 242; FW

Kristofferson, Kris 1936- .... **CLC 26**
See also CA 104

Krizanc, John 1956- .... **CLC 57**
See also CA 187

Krleza, Miroslav 1893-1981 .... **CLC 8, 114**
See also CA 97-100; 105; CANR 50; CDWLB 4; DLB 147; EW 11; RGWL 2

Kroetsch, Robert 1927- .. **CLC 5, 23, 57, 132**
See also CA 17-20R; CANR 8, 38; CCA 1; CN 7; CP 7; DAC; DAM POET; DLB 53; MTCW 1

Kroetz, Franz
See Kroetz, Franz Xaver

Kroetz, Franz Xaver 1946- .... **CLC 41**
See also CA 130

Kroker, Arthur (W.) 1945- .... **CLC 77**
See also CA 161

Kropotkin, Peter (Aleksieevich) 1842-1921 .... **TCLC 36**
See also CA 119

Krotkov, Yuri 1917-1981 .... **CLC 19**
See also CA 102

Krumb
See Crumb, R(obert)

Krumgold, Joseph (Quincy) 1908-1980 .... **CLC 12**
See also BYA 1, 2; CA 9-12R; 101; CANR 7; MAICYA 1, 2; SATA 1, 48; SATA-Obit 23; YAW

Krumwitz
See Crumb, R(obert)

Krutch, Joseph Wood 1893-1970 ..... **CLC 24**
See also ANW; CA 1-4R; 25-28R; CANR 4; DLB 63, 206

Krutzch, Gus
See Eliot, T(homas) S(tearns)

Krylov, Ivan Andreevich 1768(?)-1844 .... **NCLC 1**
See also DLB 150

Kubin, Alfred (Leopold Isidor) 1877-1959 .... **TCLC 23**
See also CA 112; 149; CANR 104; DLB 81

Kubrick, Stanley 1928-1999 .... **CLC 16**
See also AAYA 30; CA 81-84; 177; CANR 33; DLB 26; TCLC 112

Kueng, Hans 1928-
See Kung, Hans
See also CA 53-56; CANR 66; MTCW 1, 2

Kumin, Maxine (Winokur) 1925- ..... **CLC 5, 13, 28; PC 15**
See also AITN 2; AMWS 4; ANW; CA 1-4R; CAAS 8; CANR 1, 21, 69; CP 7; CWP; DA3; DAM POET; DLB 5; EXPP; MTCW 1, 2; PAB; SATA 12

Kundera, Milan 1929- . **CLC 4, 9, 19, 32, 68, 115, 135; SSC 24**
See also AAYA 2; BPFB 2; CA 85-88; CANR 19, 52, 74; CDWLB 4; CWW 2; DA3; DAM NOV; DLB 232; EW 13; MTCW 1, 2; RGSF 2; SSFS 10

Kunene, Mazisi (Raymond) 1930- ... **CLC 85**
See also BW 1, 3; CA 125; CANR 81; CP 7; DLB 117

Kung, Hans .... **CLC 130**
See also Kueng, Hans

Kunikida Doppo 1869(?)-1908
See Doppo, Kunikida
See also DLB 180

Kunitz, Stanley (Jasspon) 1905- .. **CLC 6, 11, 14, 148; PC 19**
See also AMWS 3; CA 41-44R; CANR 26, 57, 98; CP 7; DA3; DLB 48; INT CANR-26; MTCW 1, 2; PFS 11; RGAL 4

Kunze, Reiner 1933- .... **CLC 10**
See also CA 93-96; CWW 2; DLB 75

Kuprin, Aleksander Ivanovich 1870-1938 .... **TCLC 5**
See also CA 104; 182

Kureishi, Hanif 1954(?)- .... **CLC 64, 135**
See also CA 139; CBD; CD 5; CN 7; DLB 194, 245; GLL 2; IDFW 4; WLIT 4

Kurosawa, Akira 1910-1998 ..... **CLC 16, 119**
See also AAYA 11; CA 101; 170; CANR 46; DAM MULT

Kushner, Tony 1957(?)- .... **CLC 81; DC 10**
See also AMWS 9; CA 144; CAD; CANR 74; CD 5; DA3; DAM DRAM; DFS 5; DLB 228; GLL 1; LAIT 5; MTCW 2; RGAL 4

Kuttner, Henry 1915-1958 .... **TCLC 10**
See also CA 107; 157; DLB 8; FANT; SCFW 2; SFW 4

Kuzma, Greg 1944- .... **CLC 7**
See also CA 33-36R; CANR 70

Kuzmin, Mikhail 1872(?)-1936 ...... **TCLC 40**
See also CA 170

Kyd, Thomas 1558-1594 .... **LC 22; DC 3**
See also BRW 1; DAM DRAM; DLB 62; IDTP; RGEL 2; TEA; WLIT 3

Kyprianos, Iossif
See Samarakis, Antonis

Labrunie, Gerard
See Nerval, Gerard de

La Bruyere, Jean de 1645-1696 .... **LC 17**
See also EW 3; GFL Beginnings to 1789

Lacan, Jacques (Marie Emile) 1901-1981 .... **CLC 75**
See also CA 121; 104

Laclos, Pierre Ambroise Francois 1741-1803 .... **NCLC 4, 87**
See also EW 4; GFL Beginnings to 1789; RGWL 2

Lacolere, Francois
See Aragon, Louis

La Colere, Francois
See Aragon, Louis

La Deshabilleuse
See Simenon, Georges (Jacques Christian)

Lady Gregory
See Gregory, Lady Isabella Augusta (Persse)

Lady of Quality, A
See Bagnold, Enid

La Fayette, Marie-(Madelaine Pioche de la Vergne) 1634-1693 .... **LC 2**
See also GFL Beginnings to 1789; RGWL 2

Lafayette, Rene
See Hubbard, L(afayette) Ron(ald)

La Fontaine, Jean de 1621-1695 .... **LC 50**
See also EW 3; GFL Beginnings to 1789; MAICYA 1, 2; RGWL 2; SATA 18

Laforgue, Jules 1860-1887 . **NCLC 5, 53; PC 14; SSC 20**
See also DLB 217; EW 7; GFL 1789 to the Present; RGWL 2

Layamon
See Layamon
See also DLB 146

Lagerkvist, Paer (Fabian) 1891-1974 .... **CLC 7, 10, 13, 54**
See also Lagerkvist, Par
See also CA 85-88; 49-52; DA3; DAM DRAM, NOV; MTCW 1, 2

Lagerkvist, Par .... **SSC 12**
See also Lagerkvist, Paer (Fabian)
See also DLB 259; EW 10; MTCW 2; RGSF 2; RGWL 2

Lagerloef, Selma (Ottiliana Lovisa) 1858-1940 .... **TCLC 4, 36**
See also Lagerlof, Selma (Ottiliana Lovisa)
See also CA 108; MTCW 2; SATA 15

Lagerlof, Selma (Ottiliana Lovisa)
See Lagerloef, Selma (Ottiliana Lovisa)
See also CLR 7; SATA 15

La Guma, (Justin) Alex(ander) 1925-1985 .... **CLC 19; BLCS**
See also AFW; BW 1, 3; CA 49-52; 118; CANR 25, 81; CDWLB 3; DAM NOV; DLB 117, 225; MTCW 1, 2; WLIT 2

Laidlaw, A. K.
See Grieve, C(hristopher) M(urray)

Lainez, Manuel Mujica
See Mujica Lainez, Manuel
See also HW 1

Laing, R(onald) D(avid) 1927-1989 . **CLC 95**
See also CA 107; 129; CANR 34; MTCW 1

Lamartine, Alphonse (Marie Louis Prat) de 1790-1869 .... **NCLC 11; PC 16**
See also DAM POET; DLB 217; GFL 1789 to the Present; RGWL 2

Lamb, Charles 1775-1834 .. **NCLC 10; WLC**
See also BRW 4; CDBLB 1789-1832; DA; DAB; DAC; DAM MST; DLB 93, 107, 163; RGEL 2; SATA 17

Lamb, Lady Caroline 1785-1828 ... **NCLC 38**
See also DLB 116

Lamming, George (William) 1927- ... **CLC 2, 4, 66, 144; BLC 2**
See also BW 2, 3; CA 85-88; CANR 26, 76; CDWLB 3; CN 7; DAM MULT; DLB 125; MTCW 1, 2; RGEL 2

L'Amour, Louis (Dearborn) 1908-1988 .... **CLC 25, 55**
See also Burns, Tex; Mayo, Jim
See also AAYA 16; AITN 2; BEST 89:2; BPFB 2; CA 1-4R; 125; CANR 3, 25, 40; CPW; DA3; DAM NOV, POP; DLB 206; DLBY 1980; MTCW 1, 2; RGAL 4

Lampedusa, Giuseppe (Tomasi) di .... **TCLC 13**
See also Tomasi di Lampedusa, Giuseppe
See also CA 164; EW 11; MTCW 2; RGWL 2

Lampman, Archibald 1861-1899 ... **NCLC 25**
See also DLB 92; RGEL 2

Lancaster, Bruce 1896-1963 .... **CLC 36**
See also CA 9-10; CANR 70; CAP 1; SATA 9

Lanchester, John .... **CLC 99**
See also CA 194

Landau, Mark Alexandrovich
See Aldanov, Mark (Alexandrovich)

Landau-Aldanov, Mark Alexandrovich
See Aldanov, Mark (Alexandrovich)

Landis, Jerry
See Simon, Paul (Frederick)

Landis, John 1950- .... **CLC 26**
See also CA 112; 122

Landolfi, Tommaso 1908-1979 .... **CLC 11, 49**
See also CA 127; 117; DLB 177

Landon, Letitia Elizabeth 1802-1838 .... **NCLC 15**
See also DLB 96

Landor, Walter Savage 1775-1864 .... **NCLC 14**
See also BRW 4; DLB 93, 107; RGEL 2

Landwirth, Heinz 1927-
See Lind, Jakov
See also CA 9-12R; CANR 7

Lane, Patrick 1939- .... **CLC 25**
See also CA 97-100; CANR 54; CP 7; DAM POET; DLB 53; INT 97-100

Lang, Andrew 1844-1912 .... **TCLC 16**
See also CA 114; 137; CANR 85; DLB 98, 141, 184; FANT; MAICYA 1, 2; RGEL 2; SATA 16; WCH

Lang, Fritz 1890-1976 .... **CLC 20, 103**
See also CA 77-80; 69-72; CANR 30

Lange, John
See Crichton, (John) Michael

Langer, Elinor 1939- .... **CLC 34**
See also CA 121

Langland, William 1332(?)-1400(?) ...... **LC 19**
See also BRW 1; DA; DAB; DAC; DAM MST, POET; DLB 146; RGEL 2; WLIT 3

Langstaff, Launcelot
See Irving, Washington

Lanier, Sidney 1842-1881 .... **NCLC 6**
See also AMWS 1; DAM POET; DLB 64; DLBD 13; EXPP; MAICYA 1; PFS 14; RGAL 4; SATA 18

Lanyer, Aemilia 1569-1645 .... **LC 10, 30**
See also DLB 121

Lao-Tzu
See Lao Tzu

Lao Tzu c. 6th cent. B.C.-3rd cent. B.C. .... **CMLC 7**

Lapine, James (Elliot) 1949- .... **CLC 39**
See also CA 123; 130; CANR 54; INT 130

Larbaud, Valery (Nicolas) 1881-1957 .... **TCLC 9**
See also CA 106; 152; GFL 1789 to the Present

Lardner, Ring
See Lardner, Ring(gold) W(ilmer)
See also BPFB 2; CDALB 1917-1929; DLB 11, 25, 86, 171; DLBD 16; RGAL 4; RGSF 2

Lardner, Ring W., Jr.
See Lardner, Ring(gold) W(ilmer)

Lardner, Ring(gold) W(ilmer) 1885-1933 .... **TCLC 2, 14; SSC 32**
See also Lardner, Ring
See also AMW; CA 104; 131; MTCW 1, 2

Laredo, Betty
See Codrescu, Andrei

Larkin, Maia
See Wojciechowska, Maia (Teresa)

Larkin, Philip (Arthur) 1922-1985 ... **CLC 3, 5, 8, 9, 13, 18, 33, 39, 64; PC 21**
See also BRWS 1; CA 5-8R; 117; CANR 24, 62; CDBLB 1960 to Present; DA3; DAB; DAM MST, POET; DLB 27; MTCW 1, 2; PFS 3, 4, 12; RGEL 2

Larra (y Sanchez de Castro), Mariano Jose de 1809-1837 .... **NCLC 17**

Larsen, Eric 1941- .... **CLC 55**
See also CA 132

Larsen, Nella 1893-1963 ...... **CLC 37; BLC 2**
See also AFAW 1, 2; BW 1; CA 125; CANR 83; DAM MULT; DLB 51; FW

Larson, Charles R(aymond) 1938- ... **CLC 31**
See also CA 53-56; CANR 4

Larson, Jonathan 1961-1996 .... **CLC 99**
See also AAYA 28; CA 156

Las Casas, Bartolome de 1474-1566 . **LC 31; HLCS**
See also Casas, Bartolome de las
See also LAW

Lasch, Christopher 1932-1994 .... **CLC 102**
See also CA 73-76; 144; CANR 25; DLB 246; MTCW 1, 2

Lasker-Schueler, Else 1869-1945 ... **TCLC 57**
See also CA 183; DLB 66, 124

Laski, Harold J(oseph) 1893-1950 . **TCLC 79**
See also CA 188

Latham, Jean Lee 1902-1995 .... **CLC 12**
See also AITN 1; BYA 1; CA 5-8R; CANR 7, 84; CLR 50; MAICYA 1, 2; SATA 2, 68; YAW

Latham, Mavis
See Clark, Mavis Thorpe

Lathen, Emma .... **CLC 2**
See also Hennissart, Martha; Latsis, Mary J(ane)
See also BPFB 2; CMW 4

Lathrop, Francis
See Leiber, Fritz (Reuter, Jr.)

Latsis, Mary J(ane) 1927(?)-1997
See Lathen, Emma
See also CA 85-88; 162; CMW 4

Lattany, Kristin (Hunter) 1931- .... **CLC 35**
See also AITN 1; BW 1; BYA 3; CA 13-16R; CANR 13, 108; CLR 3; CN 7; DLB 33; INT CANR-13; MAICYA 1; SAAS 10; SATA 12; YAW

Lattimore, Richmond (Alexander) 1906-1984 .... **CLC 3**
See also CA 1-4R; 112; CANR 1

Laughlin, James 1914-1997 .... **CLC 49**
See also CA 21-24R; 162; CAAS 22; CANR 9, 47; CP 7; DLB 48; DLBY 1996, 1997

Laurence, (Jean) Margaret (Wemyss) 1926-1987 . **CLC 3, 6, 13, 50, 62; SSC 7**
See also BYA 13; CA 5-8R; 121; CANR 33; DAC; DAM MST; DLB 53; FW; MTCW 1, 2; NFS 11; RGEL 2; RGSF 2; SATA-Obit 50; TCWW 2

Laurent, Antoine 1952- .... **CLC 50**

Lauscher, Hermann
See Hesse, Hermann

Lautreamont 1846-1870 .. **NCLC 12; SSC 14**
See also Lautreamont, Isidore Lucien Ducasse
See also GFL 1789 to the Present; RGWL 2

Lautreamont, Isidore Lucien Ducasse
See Lautreamont
See also DLB 217

Laverty, Donald
See Blish, James (Benjamin)

Lavin, Mary 1912-1996 . **CLC 4, 18, 99; SSC 4**
See also CA 9-12R; 151; CANR 33; CN 7; DLB 15; FW; MTCW 1; RGEL 2; RGSF 2

Lavond, Paul Dennis
See Kornbluth, C(yril) M.; Pohl, Frederik

Lawler, Raymond Evenor 1922- .... **CLC 58**
See also CA 103; CD 5; RGEL 2

Lawrence, D(avid) H(erbert Richards) 1885-1930 .... **TCLC 2, 9, 16, 33, 48, 61, 93; SSC 4, 19; WLC**
See also Chambers, Jessie
See also BPFB 2; BRW 7; BRWR 2; CA 104; 121; CDBLB 1914-1945; DA; DA3; DAB; DAC; DAM MST, NOV, POET; DLB 10, 19, 36, 98, 162, 195; EXPP; EXPS; LAIT 2, 3; MTCW 1, 2; PFS 6; RGEL 2; RGSF 2; SSFS 2, 6; WLIT 4; WP

Lawrence, T(homas) E(dward) 1888-1935 .... **TCLC 18**
See also Dale, Colin
See also BRWS 2; CA 115; 167; DLB 195

Lawrence of Arabia
See Lawrence, T(homas) E(dward)

Lawson, Henry (Archibald Hertzberg) 1867-1922 .... **TCLC 27; SSC 18**
See also CA 120; 181; DLB 230; RGEL 2; RGSF 2

Lawton, Dennis
See Faust, Frederick (Schiller)

Laxness, Halldor .... **CLC 25**
See also Gudjonsson, Halldor Kiljan
See also EW 12; RGWL 2

Layamon fl. c. 1200- .... **CMLC 10**
See also Layamon
See also RGEL 2

Laye, Camara 1928-1980 ... **CLC 4, 38; BLC 2**
See also AFW; BW 1; CA 85-88; 97-100; CANR 25; DAM MULT; MTCW 1, 2; WLIT 2

Layton, Irving (Peter) 1912- .... **CLC 2, 15**
See also CA 1-4R; CANR 2, 33, 43, 66; CP 7; DAC; DAM MST, POET; DLB 88; MTCW 1, 2; PFS 12; RGEL 2

Lazarus, Emma 1849-1887 ...... **NCLC 8, 109**

Lazarus, Felix
See Cable, George Washington

Lazarus, Henry
See Slavitt, David R(ytman)

Lea, Joan
See Neufeld, John (Arthur)

Leacock, Stephen (Butler)
1869-1944 .... **TCLC 2; SSC 39**
See also CA 104; 141; CANR 80; DAC; DAM MST; DLB 92; MTCW 2; RGEL 2; RGSF 2

Lead, Jane Ward 1623-1704 .... **LC 72**
See also DLB 131

Lear, Edward 1812-1888 .... **NCLC 3**
See also BRW 5; CLR 1, 75; DLB 32, 163, 166; MAICYA 1, 2; RGEL 2; SATA 18, 100; WCH; WP

Lear, Norman (Milton) 1922- .... **CLC 12**
See also CA 73-76

Leautaud, Paul 1872-1956 .... **TCLC 83**
See also DLB 65; GFL 1789 to the Present

Leavis, F(rank) R(aymond)
1895-1978 .... **CLC 24**
See also BRW 7; CA 21-24R; 77-80; CANR 44; DLB 242; MTCW 1, 2; RGEL 2

Leavitt, David 1961- .... **CLC 34**
See also CA 116; 122; CANR 50, 62, 101; CPW; DA3; DAM POP; DLB 130; GLL 1; INT 122; MTCW 2

Leblanc, Maurice (Marie Emile)
1864-1941 .... **TCLC 49**
See also CA 110; CMW 4

Lebowitz, Fran(ces Ann) 1951(?)- ... **CLC 11, 36**
See also CA 81-84; CANR 14, 60, 70; INT CANR-14; MTCW 1

Lebrecht, Peter
See Tieck, (Johann) Ludwig

le Carre, John .... **CLC 3, 5, 9, 15, 28**
See also Cornwell, David (John Moore)
See also AAYA 16; BEST 89:4; BPFB 2; BRWS 2; CDBLB 1960 to Present; CMW 4; CN 7; CPW; DLB 87; MSW; MTCW 2; RGEL 2

Le Clezio, J(ean) M(arie) G(ustave)
1940- .... **CLC 31, 155**
See also CA 116; 128; DLB 83; GFL 1789 to the Present; RGSF 2

Leconte de Lisle, Charles-Marie-Rene
1818-1894 .... **NCLC 29**
See also DLB 217; EW 6; GFL 1789 to the Present

Le Coq, Monsieur
See Simenon, Georges (Jacques Christian)

Leduc, Violette 1907-1972 .... **CLC 22**
See also CA 13-14; 33-36R; CANR 69; CAP 1; GFL 1789 to the Present; GLL 1

Ledwidge, Francis 1887(?)-1917 .... **TCLC 23**
See also CA 123; DLB 20

Lee, Andrea 1953- .... **CLC 36; BLC 2**
See also BW 1, 3; CA 125; CANR 82; DAM MULT

Lee, Andrew
See Auchincloss, Louis (Stanton)

Lee, Chang-rae 1965- .... **CLC 91**
See also CA 148; CANR 89

Lee, Don L. .... **CLC 2**
See also Madhubuti, Haki R.

Lee, George W(ashington)
1894-1976 .... **CLC 52; BLC 2**
See also BW 1; CA 125; CANR 83; DAM MULT; DLB 51

Lee, (Nelle) Harper 1926- .... **CLC 12, 60; WLC**
See also AAYA 13; AMWS 8; BPFB 2; BYA 3; CA 13-16R; CANR 51; CDALB 1941-1968; CSW; DA; DA3; DAB; DAC; DAM MST, NOV; DLB 6; EXPN; LAIT 3; MTCW 1, 2; NFS 2; SATA 11; WYA; YAW

Lee, Helen Elaine 1959(?)- .... **CLC 86**
See also CA 148

Lee, John .... **CLC 70**

Lee, Julian
See Latham, Jean Lee

Lee, Larry
See Lee, Lawrence

Lee, Laurie 1914-1997 .... **CLC 90**
See also CA 77-80; 158; CANR 33, 73; CP 7; CPW; DAB; DAM POP; DLB 27; MTCW 1; RGEL 2

Lee, Lawrence 1941-1990 .... **CLC 34**
See also CA 131; CANR 43

Lee, Li-Young 1957- .... **PC 24**
See also CA 153; CP 7; DLB 165; PFS 11

Lee, Manfred B(ennington)
1905-1971 .... **CLC 11**
See also Queen, Ellery
See also CA 1-4R; 29-32R; CANR 2; CMW 4; DLB 137

Lee, Shelton Jackson 1957(?)- .... **CLC 105; BLCS**
See also Lee, Spike
See also BW 2, 3; CA 125; CANR 42; DAM MULT

Lee, Spike
See Lee, Shelton Jackson
See also AAYA 4, 29

Lee, Stan 1922- .... **CLC 17**
See also AAYA 5; CA 108; 111; INT 111

Lee, Tanith 1947- .... **CLC 46**
See also AAYA 15; CA 37-40R; CANR 53, 102; FANT; SATA 8, 88; SFW 4; SUFW; YAW

Lee, Vernon .... **TCLC 5; SSC 33**
See also Paget, Violet
See also DLB 57, 153, 156, 174, 178; GLL 1; SUFW

Lee, William
See Burroughs, William S(eward)
See also GLL 1

Lee, Willy
See Burroughs, William S(eward)
See also GLL 1

Lee-Hamilton, Eugene (Jacob)
1845-1907 .... **TCLC 22**
See also CA 117

Leet, Judith 1935- .... **CLC 11**
See also CA 187

Le Fanu, Joseph Sheridan
1814-1873 .... **NCLC 9, 58; SSC 14**
See also CMW 4; DA3; DAM POP; DLB 21, 70, 159, 178; HGG; RGEL 2; RGSF 2; SUFW

Leffland, Ella 1931- .... **CLC 19**
See also CA 29-32R; CANR 35, 78, 82; DLBY 1984; INT CANR-35; SATA 65

Leger, Alexis
See Leger, (Marie-Rene Auguste) Alexis Saint-Leger

**Leger, (Marie-Rene Auguste) Alexis
Saint-Leger** 1887-1975 .. **CLC 4, 11, 46; PC 23**
See also Perse, Saint-John; Saint-John Perse
See also CA 13-16R; 61-64; CANR 43; DAM POET; MTCW 1

Leger, Saintleger
See Leger, (Marie-Rene Auguste) Alexis Saint-Leger

Le Guin, Ursula K(roeber) 1929- ..... **CLC 8, 13, 22, 45, 71, 136; SSC 12**
See also AAYA 9, 27; AITN 1; BPFB 2; BYA 5, 8, 11, 14; CA 21-24R; CANR 9, 32, 52, 74; CDALB 1968-1988; CLR 3, 28; CN 7; CPW; DA3; DAB; DAC; DAM MST, POP; DLB 8, 52, 256; EXPS; FANT; FW; INT CANR-32; JRDA; LAIT 5; MAICYA 1, 2; MTCW 1, 2; NFS 6, 9; SATA 4, 52, 99; SCFW; SFW 4; SSFS 2; SUFW; WYA; YAW

Lehmann, Rosamond (Nina)
1901-1990 .... **CLC 5**
See also CA 77-80; 131; CANR 8, 73; DLB 15; MTCW 2; RGEL 2; RHW

Leiber, Fritz (Reuter, Jr.)
1910-1992 .... **CLC 25**
See also BPFB 2; CA 45-48; 139; CANR 2, 40, 86; DLB 8; FANT; HGG; MTCW 1, 2; SATA 45; SATA-Obit 73; SCFW 2; SFW 4; SUFW

Leibniz, Gottfried Wilhelm von
1646-1716 .... **LC 35**
See also DLB 168

Leimbach, Martha 1963-
See Leimbach, Marti
See also CA 130

Leimbach, Marti .... **CLC 65**
See also Leimbach, Martha

Leino, Eino .... **TCLC 24**
See also Loennbohm, Armas Eino Leopold

Leiris, Michel (Julien) 1901-1990 ..... **CLC 61**
See also CA 119; 128; 132; GFL 1789 to the Present

Leithauser, Brad 1953- .... **CLC 27**
See also CA 107; CANR 27, 81; CP 7; DLB 120

Lelchuk, Alan 1938- .... **CLC 5**
See also CA 45-48; CAAS 20; CANR 1, 70; CN 7

Lem, Stanislaw 1921- ...... **CLC 8, 15, 40, 149**
See also CA 105; CAAS 1; CANR 32; CWW 2; MTCW 1; SCFW 2; SFW 4

Lemann, Nancy 1956- .... **CLC 39**
See also CA 118; 136

Lemonnier, (Antoine Louis) Camille
1844-1913 .... **TCLC 22**
See also CA 121

Lenau, Nikolaus 1802-1850 .... **NCLC 16**

L'Engle, Madeleine (Camp Franklin)
1918- .... **CLC 12**
See also AAYA 28; AITN 2; BPFB 2; BYA 2, 4, 5, 7; CA 1-4R; CANR 3, 21, 39, 66, 107; CLR 1, 14, 57; CPW; CWRI 5; DA3; DAM POP; DLB 52; JRDA; MAICYA 1, 2; MTCW 1, 2; SAAS 15; SATA 1, 27, 75, 128; SFW 4; WYA; YAW

Lengyel, Jozsef 1896-1975 .... **CLC 7**
See also CA 85-88; 57-60; CANR 71; RGSF 2

Lenin 1870-1924
See Lenin, V. I.
See also CA 121; 168

Lenin, V. I. .... **TCLC 67**
See also Lenin

Lennon, John (Ono) 1940-1980 .. **CLC 12, 35**
See also CA 102; SATA 114

Lennox, Charlotte Ramsay
1729(?)-1804 .... **NCLC 23**
See also DLB 39; RGEL 2

Lentricchia, Frank, (Jr.) 1940- .... **CLC 34**
See also CA 25-28R; CANR 19, 106; DLB 246

Lenz, Gunter .... **CLC 65**

Lenz, Siegfried 1926- .... **CLC 27; SSC 33**
See also CA 89-92; CANR 80; CWW 2; DLB 75; RGSF 2; RGWL 2

Leon, David
See Jacob, (Cyprien-)Max

Leonard, Elmore (John, Jr.) 1925- . **CLC 28, 34, 71, 120**
See also AAYA 22; AITN 1; BEST 89:1, 90:4; BPFB 2; CA 81-84; CANR 12, 28, 53, 76, 96; CMW 4; CN 7; CPW; DA3; DAM POP; DLB 173, 226; INT CANR-28; MSW; MTCW 1, 2; RGAL 4; TCWW 2

Leonard, Hugh .... **CLC 19**
See also Byrne, John Keyes
See also CBD; CD 5; DFS 13; DLB 13

Leonov, Leonid (Maximovich)
1899-1994 .... **CLC 92**
See also CA 129; CANR 74, 76; DAM NOV; MTCW 1, 2

Leopardi, (Conte) Giacomo
1798-1837 .... **NCLC 22; PC 37**
See also EW 5; RGWL 2; WP

Le Reveler
See Artaud, Antonin (Marie Joseph)

Lerman, Eleanor 1952- .... **CLC 9**
See also CA 85-88; CANR 69

Lerman, Rhoda 1936- .... **CLC 56**
See also CA 49-52; CANR 70

Lermontov, Mikhail Iur'evich
See Lermontov, Mikhail Yuryevich
See also DLB 205

Lermontov, Mikhail Yuryevich
1814-1841 .... **NCLC 5, 47; PC 18**
See also Lermontov, Mikhail Iur'evich
See also EW 6; RGWL 2

Leroux, Gaston 1868-1927 .... **TCLC 25**
See also CA 108; 136; CANR 69; CMW 4; SATA 65

Lesage, Alain-Rene 1668-1747 .... **LC 2, 28**
See also EW 3; GFL Beginnings to 1789; RGWL 2

Leskov, N(ikolai) S(emenovich) 1831-1895
See Leskov, Nikolai (Semyonovich)

Leskov, Nikolai (Semyonovich)
1831-1895 .... **NCLC 25; SSC 34**
See also Leskov, Nikolai Semenovich

Leskov, Nikolai Semenovich
See Leskov, Nikolai (Semyonovich)
See also DLB 238

Lesser, Milton
See Marlowe, Stephen

Lessing, Doris (May) 1919- ... **CLC 1, 2, 3, 6, 10, 15, 22, 40, 94; SSC 6; WLCS**
See also AFW; BRWS 1; CA 9-12R; CAAS 14; CANR 33, 54, 76; CDBLB 1960 to Present; CN 7; DA; DA3; DAB; DAC; DAM MST, NOV; DLB 15, 139; DLBY 1985; EXPS; FW; LAIT 4; MTCW 1, 2; RGEL 2; RGSF 2; SFW 4; SSFS 1, 12; WLIT 2, 4

Lessing, Gotthold Ephraim 1729-1781 . **LC 8**
See also CDWLB 2; DLB 97; EW 4; RGWL 2

Lester, Richard 1932- .... **CLC 20**

Levenson, Jay .... **CLC 70**

Lever, Charles (James)
1806-1872 .... **NCLC 23**
See also DLB 21; RGEL 2

Leverson, Ada 1865(?)-1936(?) .... **TCLC 18**
See also Elaine
See also CA 117; DLB 153; RGEL 2

Levertov, Denise 1923-1997 .. **CLC 1, 2, 3, 5, 8, 15, 28, 66; PC 11**
See also AMWS 3; CA 1-4R; 178; 163; CAAE 178; CAAS 19; CANR 3, 29, 50, 108; CDALBS; CP 7; CWP; DAM POET; DLB 5, 165; EXPP; FW; INT CANR-29; MTCW 1, 2; PAB; PFS 7; RGAL 4; WP

Levi, Jonathan .... **CLC 76**
See also CA 197

Levi, Peter (Chad Tigar)
1931-2000 .... **CLC 41**
See also CA 5-8R; 187; CANR 34, 80; CP 7; DLB 40

Levi, Primo 1919-1987 . **CLC 37, 50; SSC 12**
See also CA 13-16R; 122; CANR 12, 33, 61, 70; DLB 177; MTCW 1, 2; RGWL 2; TCLC 109

Levin, Ira 1929- .... **CLC 3, 6**
See also CA 21-24R; CANR 17, 44, 74; CMW 4; CN 7; CPW; DA3; DAM POP; HGG; MTCW 1, 2; SATA 66; SFW 4

Levin, Meyer 1905-1981 .... **CLC 7**
See also AITN 1; CA 9-12R; 104; CANR 15; DAM POP; DLB 9, 28; DLBY 1981; SATA 21; SATA-Obit 27

Levine, Norman 1924- .... **CLC 54**
See also CA 73-76; CAAS 23; CANR 14, 70; DLB 88

Levine, Philip 1928- .. **CLC 2, 4, 5, 9, 14, 33, 118; PC 22**
See also AMWS 5; CA 9-12R; CANR 9, 37, 52; CP 7; DAM POET; DLB 5; PFS 8

Levinson, Deirdre 1931- .... **CLC 49**
See also CA 73-76; CANR 70

Levi-Strauss, Claude 1908- .... **CLC 38**
See also CA 1-4R; CANR 6, 32, 57; DLB 242; GFL 1789 to the Present; MTCW 1, 2

Levitin, Sonia (Wolff) 1934- .... **CLC 17**
See also AAYA 13; CA 29-32R; CANR 14, 32, 79; CLR 53; JRDA; MAICYA 1, 2; SAAS 2; SATA 4, 68, 119; SATA-Essay 131; YAW

Levon, O. U.
See Kesey, Ken (Elton)

Levy, Amy 1861-1889 .... **NCLC 59**
See also DLB 156, 240

Lewes, George Henry 1817-1878 ... **NCLC 25**
See also DLB 55, 144

Lewis, Alun 1915-1944 .... **TCLC 3; SSC 40**
See also BRW 7; CA 104; 188; DLB 20, 162; PAB; RGEL 2

Lewis, C. Day
See Day Lewis, C(ecil)

Lewis, C(live) S(taples) 1898-1963 .... **CLC 1, 3, 6, 14, 27, 124; WLC**
See also AAYA 3, 39; BPFB 2; BRWS 3; CA 81-84; CANR 33, 71; CDBLB 1945-1960; CLR 3, 27; CWRI 5; DA; DA3; DAB; DAC; DAM MST, NOV, POP; DLB 15, 100, 160, 255; FANT; JRDA; MAICYA 1, 2; MTCW 1, 2; RGEL 2; SATA 13, 100; SCFW; SFW 4; SUFW; WCH; WYA; YAW

Lewis, Cecil Day
See Day Lewis, C(ecil)

Lewis, Janet 1899-1998 .... **CLC 41**
See also Winters, Janet Lewis
See also CA 9-12R; 172; CANR 29, 63; CAP 1; CN 7; DLBY 1987; RHW; TCWW 2

Lewis, Matthew Gregory
1775-1818 .... **NCLC 11, 62**
See also DLB 39, 158, 178; HGG; RGEL 2; SUFW

Lewis, (Harry) Sinclair 1885-1951 . **TCLC 4, 13, 23, 39; WLC**
See also AMW; BPFB 2; CA 104; 133; CDALB 1917-1929; DA; DA3; DAB; DAC; DAM MST, NOV; DLB 9, 102; DLBD 1; LAIT 3; MTCW 1, 2; RGAL 4

Lewis, (Percy) Wyndham
1884(?)-1957 .. **TCLC 2, 9, 104; SSC 34**
See also BRW 7; CA 104; 157; DLB 15; FANT; MTCW 2; RGEL 2

Lewisohn, Ludwig 1883-1955 .... **TCLC 19**
See also CA 107; DLB 4, 9, 28, 102

Lewton, Val 1904-1951 .... **TCLC 76**
See also CA 199; IDFW 3, 4

Leyner, Mark 1956- .... **CLC 92**
See also CA 110; CANR 28, 53; DA3; MTCW 2

Lezama Lima, Jose 1910-1976 .... **CLC 4, 10, 101; HLCS 2**
See also CA 77-80; CANR 71; DAM MULT; DLB 113; HW 1, 2; LAW; RGWL 2

L'Heureux, John (Clarke) 1934- .... **CLC 52**
See also CA 13-16R; CANR 23, 45, 88; DLB 244

Liddell, C. H.
See Kuttner, Henry

Lie, Jonas (Lauritz Idemil)
1833-1908(?) .... **TCLC 5**
See also CA 115

Lieber, Joel 1937-1971 .... **CLC 6**
See also CA 73-76; 29-32R

Lieber, Stanley Martin
See Lee, Stan

Lieberman, Laurence (James)
1935- .... **CLC 4, 36**
See also CA 17-20R; CANR 8, 36, 89; CP 7

Lieh Tzu fl. 7th cent. B.C.-5th cent. B.C. .... **CMLC 27**

Lieksman, Anders
See Haavikko, Paavo Juhani

Li Fei-kan 1904-
See Pa Chin
See also CA 105

Lifton, Robert Jay 1926- .... **CLC 67**
See also CA 17-20R; CANR 27, 78; INT CANR-27; SATA 66

Lightfoot, Gordon 1938- .... **CLC 26**
See also CA 109

Lightman, Alan P(aige) 1948- .... **CLC 81**
See also CA 141; CANR 63, 105

Ligotti, Thomas (Robert) 1953- ...... **CLC 44; SSC 16**
See also CA 123; CANR 49; HGG

Li Ho 791-817 .... **PC 13**

Liliencron, (Friedrich Adolf Axel) Detlev von 1844-1909 .... **TCLC 18**
See also CA 117

Lilly, William 1602-1681 .... **LC 27**

Lima, Jose Lezama
See Lezama Lima, Jose

Lima Barreto, Afonso Henrique de
1881-1922 .... **TCLC 23**
See also CA 117; 181; LAW

Lima Barreto, Afonso Henriques de
See Lima Barreto, Afonso Henrique de

Limonov, Edward 1944- .... **CLC 67**
See also CA 137

Lin, Frank
See Atherton, Gertrude (Franklin Horn)

Lincoln, Abraham 1809-1865 .... **NCLC 18**
See also LAIT 2

Lind, Jakov .... **CLC 1, 2, 4, 27, 82**
See also Landwirth, Heinz
See also CAAS 4

Lindbergh, Anne (Spencer) Morrow
1906-2001 .... **CLC 82**
See also BPFB 2; CA 17-20R; 193; CANR 16, 73; DAM NOV; MTCW 1, 2; SATA 33; SATA-Obit 125

Lindsay, David 1878(?)-1945 .... **TCLC 15**
See also CA 113; 187; DLB 255; FANT; SFW 4; SUFW

Lindsay, (Nicholas) Vachel
1879-1931 .... **TCLC 17; PC 23; WLC**
See also AMWS 1; CA 114; 135; CANR 79; CDALB 1865-1917; DA; DA3; DAC; DAM MST, POET; DLB 54; EXPP; RGAL 4; SATA 40; WP

Linke-Poot
See Doeblin, Alfred

Linney, Romulus 1930- .... **CLC 51**
See also CA 1-4R; CAD; CANR 40, 44, 79; CD 5; CSW; RGAL 4

Linton, Eliza Lynn 1822-1898 .... **NCLC 41**
See also DLB 18

Li Po 701-763 .... **CMLC 2; PC 29**
See also WP

Lipsius, Justus 1547-1606 .... **LC 16**

Lipsyte, Robert (Michael) 1938- .... **CLC 21**
See also AAYA 7; CA 17-20R; CANR 8, 57; CLR 23, 76; DA; DAC; DAM MST, NOV; JRDA; LAIT 5; MAICYA 1, 2; SATA 5, 68, 113; WYA; YAW

Lish, Gordon (Jay) 1934- ... **CLC 45; SSC 18**
See also CA 113; 117; CANR 79; DLB 130; INT 117

Lispector, Clarice 1925(?)-1977 .... **CLC 43; HLCS 2; SSC 34**
See also CA 139; 116; CANR 71; CDWLB 3; DLB 113; DNFS 1; FW; HW 2; LAW; RGSF 2; RGWL 2; WLIT 1

Littell, Robert 1935(?)- .... **CLC 42**
See also CA 109; 112; CANR 64; CMW 4

Little, Malcolm 1925-1965
See Malcolm X
See also BW 1, 3; CA 125; 111; CANR 82; DA; DA3; DAB; DAC; DAM MST, MULT; MTCW 1, 2; NCFS 3

Littlewit, Humphrey Gent.
See Lovecraft, H(oward) P(hillips)

Litwos
See Sienkiewicz, Henryk (Adam Alexander Pius)

Liu, E. 1857-1909 .... **TCLC 15**
See also CA 115; 190

Lively, Penelope (Margaret) 1933- .. **CLC 32, 50**
See also BPFB 2; CA 41-44R; CANR 29, 67, 79; CLR 7; CN 7; CWRI 5; DAM NOV; DLB 14, 161, 207; FANT; JRDA; MAICYA 1, 2; MTCW 1, 2; SATA 7, 60, 101

Livesay, Dorothy (Kathleen) 1909-1996 .... **CLC 4, 15, 79**
See also AITN 2; CA 25-28R; CAAS 8; CANR 36, 67; DAC; DAM MST, POET; DLB 68; FW; MTCW 1; RGEL 2

Livy c. 59B.C.-c. 12 .... **CMLC 11**
See also AW 2; CDWLB 1; DLB 211; RGWL 2

Lizardi, Jose Joaquin Fernandez de 1776-1827 .... **NCLC 30**
See also LAW

Llewellyn, Richard
See Llewellyn Lloyd, Richard Dafydd Vivian
See also DLB 15

Llewellyn Lloyd, Richard Dafydd Vivian 1906-1983 .... **CLC 7, 80**
See also Llewellyn, Richard
See also CA 53-56; 111; CANR 7, 71; SATA 11; SATA-Obit 37

Llosa, (Jorge) Mario (Pedro) Vargas
See Vargas Llosa, (Jorge) Mario (Pedro)

Lloyd, Manda
See Mander, (Mary) Jane

Lloyd Webber, Andrew 1948-
See Webber, Andrew Lloyd
See also AAYA 1, 38; CA 116; 149; DAM DRAM; SATA 56

Llull, Ramon c. 1235-c. 1316 .... **CMLC 12**

Lobb, Ebenezer
See Upward, Allen

Locke, Alain (Le Roy) 1886-1954 . **TCLC 43; BLCS**
See also BW 1, 3; CA 106; 124; CANR 79; RGAL 4

Locke, John 1632-1704 .... **LC 7, 35**
See also DLB 101, 213, 252; RGEL 2; WLIT 3

Locke-Elliott, Sumner
See Elliott, Sumner Locke

Lockhart, John Gibson 1794-1854 .. **NCLC 6**
See also DLB 110, 116, 144

Lockridge, Ross (Franklin), Jr. 1914-1948 .... **TCLC 111**
See also CA 108; 145; CANR 79; DLB 143; DLBY 1980; RGAL 4; RHW

Lodge, David (John) 1935- .... **CLC 36, 141**
See also BEST 90:1; BRWS 4; CA 17-20R; CANR 19, 53, 92; CN 7; CPW; DAM POP; DLB 14, 194; INT CANR-19; MTCW 1, 2

Lodge, Thomas 1558-1625 .... **LC 41**
See also DLB 172; RGEL 2

Loewinsohn, Ron(ald William) 1937- .... **CLC 52**
See also CA 25-28R; CANR 71

Logan, Jake
See Smith, Martin Cruz

Logan, John (Burton) 1923-1987 .... **CLC 5**
See also CA 77-80; 124; CANR 45; DLB 5

Lo Kuan-chung 1330(?)-1400(?) .... **LC 12**

Lombard, Nap
See Johnson, Pamela Hansford

Lomotey (editor), Kofi .... **CLC 70**

London, Jack 1876-1916 ..... **TCLC 9, 15, 39; SSC 4, 49; WLC**
See also London, John Griffith
See also AAYA 13; AITN 2; AMW; BPFB 2; BYA 4, 13; CDALB 1865-1917; DLB 8, 12, 78, 212; EXPS; LAIT 3; NFS 8; RGAL 4; RGSF 2; SATA 18; SFW 4; SSFS 7; TCWW 2; TUS; WYA; YAW

London, John Griffith 1876-1916
See London, Jack
See also CA 110; 119; CANR 73; DA; DA3; DAB; DAC; DAM MST, NOV; JRDA; MAICYA 1, 2; MTCW 1, 2

Long, Emmett
See Leonard, Elmore (John, Jr.)

Longbaugh, Harry
See Goldman, William (W.)

Longfellow, Henry Wadsworth 1807-1882 ..... **NCLC 2, 45, 101, 103; PC 30; WLCS**
See also AMW; CDALB 1640-1865; DA; DA3; DAB; DAC; DAM MST, POET; DLB 1, 59, 235; EXPP; PAB; PFS 2, 7; RGAL 4; SATA 19; WP

Longinus c. 1st cent. - .... **CMLC 27**
See also AW 2; DLB 176

Longley, Michael 1939- .... **CLC 29**
See also CA 102; CP 7; DLB 40

Longus fl. c. 2nd cent. - .... **CMLC 7**

Longway, A. Hugh
See Lang, Andrew

Lonnrot, Elias 1802-1884 .... **NCLC 53**
See also EFS 1

Lonsdale, Roger ed. .... **CLC 65**

Lopate, Phillip 1943- .... **CLC 29**
See also CA 97-100; CANR 88; DLBY 1980; INT 97-100

Lopez, Barry (Holstun) 1945- .... **CLC 70**
See also AAYA 9; ANW; CA 65-68; CANR 7, 23, 47, 68, 92; DLB 256; INT CANR-7, -23; MTCW 1; RGAL 4; SATA 67

Lopez Portillo (y Pacheco), Jose 1920- .... **CLC 46**
See also CA 129; HW 1

Lopez y Fuentes, Gregorio 1897(?)-1966 .... **CLC 32**
See also CA 131; HW 1

Lorca, Federico Garcia
See Garcia Lorca, Federico
See also DFS 4; EW 11; RGWL 2; WP

Lord, Bette Bao 1938- .... **CLC 23; AAL**
See also BEST 90:3; BPFB 2; CA 107; CANR 41, 79; INT CA-107; SATA 58

Lord Auch
See Bataille, Georges

Lord Byron
See Byron, George Gordon (Noel)

Lorde, Audre (Geraldine) 1934-1992 .. **CLC 18, 71; BLC 2; PC 12**
See also Domini, Rey
See also AFAW 1, 2; BW 1, 3; CA 25-28R; 142; CANR 16, 26, 46, 82; DA3; DAM MULT, POET; DLB 41; FW; MTCW 1, 2; RGAL 4

Lord Houghton
See Milnes, Richard Monckton

Lord Jeffrey
See Jeffrey, Francis

Loreaux, Nichol .... **CLC 65**

Lorenzini, Carlo 1826-1890
See Collodi, Carlo
See also MAICYA 1, 2; SATA 29, 100

Lorenzo, Heberto Padilla
See Padilla (Lorenzo), Heberto

Loris
See Hofmannsthal, Hugo von

Loti, Pierre .... **TCLC 11**
See also Viaud, (Louis Marie) Julien
See also DLB 123; GFL 1789 to the Present

Lou, Henri
See Andreas-Salome, Lou

Louie, David Wong 1954- .... **CLC 70**
See also CA 139

Louis, Father M.
See Merton, Thomas

Lovecraft, H(oward) P(hillips) 1890-1937 .... **TCLC 4, 22; SSC 3, 52**
See also AAYA 14; BPFB 2; CA 104; 133; CANR 106; DA3; DAM POP; HGG; MTCW 1, 2; RGAL 4; SCFW; SFW 4; SUFW

Lovelace, Earl 1935- .... **CLC 51**
See also BW 2; CA 77-80; CANR 41, 72; CD 5; CDWLB 3; CN 7; DLB 125; MTCW 1

Lovelace, Richard 1618-1657 .... **LC 24**
See also BRW 2; DLB 131; EXPP; PAB; RGEL 2

Lowell, Amy 1874-1925 ... **TCLC 1, 8; PC 13**
See also AMW; CA 104; 151; DAM POET; DLB 54, 140; EXPP; MAWW; MTCW 2; RGAL 4

Lowell, James Russell 1819-1891 ... **NCLC 2, 90**
See also AMWS 1; CDALB 1640-1865; DLB 1, 11, 64, 79, 189, 235; RGAL 4

Lowell, Robert (Traill Spence, Jr.) 1917-1977 ..... **CLC 1, 2, 3, 4, 5, 8, 9, 11, 15, 37, 124; PC 3; WLC**
See also AMW; CA 9-12R; 73-76; CABS 2; CANR 26, 60; CDALBS; DA; DA3; DAB; DAC; DAM MST, NOV; DLB 5, 169; MTCW 1, 2; PAB; PFS 6, 7; RGAL 4; WP

Lowenthal, Michael (Francis) 1969- .... **CLC 119**
See also CA 150

Lowndes, Marie Adelaide (Belloc) 1868-1947 .... **TCLC 12**
See also CA 107; CMW 4; DLB 70; RHW

Lowry, (Clarence) Malcolm 1909-1957 .... **TCLC 6, 40; SSC 31**
See also BPFB 2; BRWS 3; CA 105; 131; CANR 62, 105; CDBLB 1945-1960; DLB 15; MTCW 1, 2; RGEL 2

Lowry, Mina Gertrude 1882-1966
See Loy, Mina
See also CA 113

Loxsmith, John
See Brunner, John (Kilian Houston)

Loy, Mina .... **CLC 28; PC 16**
See also Lowry, Mina Gertrude
See also DAM POET; DLB 4, 54

Loyson-Bridet
See Schwob, Marcel (Mayer Andre)

Lucan 39-65 .... **CMLC 33**
See also AW 2; DLB 211; EFS 2; RGWL 2
Lucas, Craig 1951- .... **CLC 64**
See also CA 137; CAD; CANR 71, 109; CD 5; GLL 2
Lucas, E(dward) V(errall)
1868-1938 .... **TCLC 73**
See also CA 176; DLB 98, 149, 153; SATA 20
Lucas, George 1944- .... **CLC 16**
See also AAYA 1, 23; CA 77-80; CANR 30; SATA 56
Lucas, Hans
See Godard, Jean-Luc
Lucas, Victoria
See Plath, Sylvia
Lucian c. 125-c. 180 .... **CMLC 32**
See also AW 2; DLB 176; RGWL 2
Lucretius c. 94B.C.-c. 49B.C. .... **CMLC 48**
See also AW 2; CDWLB 1; DLB 211; EFS 2; RGWL 2
Ludlam, Charles 1943-1987 .... **CLC 46, 50**
See also CA 85-88; 122; CAD; CANR 72, 86
Ludlum, Robert 1927-2001 .... **CLC 22, 43**
See also AAYA 10; BEST 89:1, 90:3; BPFB 2; CA 33-36R; 195; CANR 25, 41, 68, 105; CMW 4; CPW; DA3; DAM NOV, POP; DLBY 1982; MSW; MTCW 1, 2
Ludwig, Ken .... **CLC 60**
See also CA 195; CAD
Ludwig, Otto 1813-1865 .... **NCLC 4**
See also DLB 129
Lugones, Leopoldo 1874-1938 ...... **TCLC 15; HLCS 2**
See also CA 116; 131; CANR 104; HW 1; LAW
Lu Hsun .... **TCLC 3; SSC 20**
See also Shu-Jen, Chou
Lukacs, George .... **CLC 24**
See also Lukacs, Gyorgy (Szegeny von)
Lukacs, Gyorgy (Szegeny von) 1885-1971
See Lukacs, George
See also CA 101; 29-32R; CANR 62; CDWLB 4; DLB 215, 242; EW 10; MTCW 2
Luke, Peter (Ambrose Cyprian)
1919-1995 .... **CLC 38**
See also CA 81-84; 147; CANR 72; CBD; CD 5; DLB 13
Lunar, Dennis
See Mungo, Raymond
Lurie, Alison 1926- .... **CLC 4, 5, 18, 39**
See also BPFB 2; CA 1-4R; CANR 2, 17, 50, 88; CN 7; DLB 2; MTCW 1; SATA 46, 112
Lustig, Arnost 1926- .... **CLC 56**
See also AAYA 3; CA 69-72; CANR 47, 102; CWW 2; DLB 232; SATA 56
Luther, Martin 1483-1546 .... **LC 9, 37**
See also CDWLB 2; DLB 179; EW 2; RGWL 2
Luxemburg, Rosa 1870(?)-1919 ..... **TCLC 63**
See also CA 118
Luzi, Mario 1914- .... **CLC 13**
See also CA 61-64; CANR 9, 70; CWW 2; DLB 128
L'vov, Arkady .... **CLC 59**
Lyly, John 1554(?)-1606 .... **LC 41; DC 7**
See also BRW 1; DAM DRAM; DLB 62, 167; RGEL 2
L'Ymagier
See Gourmont, Remy(-Marie-Charles) de
Lynch, B. Suarez
See Borges, Jorge Luis
Lynch, David (K.) 1946- .... **CLC 66**
See also CA 124; 129
Lynch, James
See Andreyev, Leonid (Nikolaevich)

Lyndsay, Sir David 1485-1555 .... **LC 20**
See also RGEL 2
Lynn, Kenneth S(chuyler)
1923-2001 .... **CLC 50**
See also CA 1-4R; 196; CANR 3, 27, 65
Lynx
See West, Rebecca
Lyons, Marcus
See Blish, James (Benjamin)
Lyotard, Jean-Francois
1924-1998 .... **TCLC 103**
See also DLB 242
Lyre, Pinchbeck
See Sassoon, Siegfried (Lorraine)
Lytle, Andrew (Nelson) 1902-1995 ... **CLC 22**
See also CA 9-12R; 150; CANR 70; CN 7; CSW; DLB 6; DLBY 1995; RGAL 4; RHW
Lyttelton, George 1709-1773 .... **LC 10**
See also RGEL 2
Lytton of Knebworth, Baron
See Bulwer-Lytton, Edward (George Earle Lytton)
Maas, Peter 1929-2001 .... **CLC 29**
See also CA 93-96; INT CA-93-96; MTCW 2
Macaulay, Catherine 1731-1791 .... **LC 64**
See also DLB 104
Macaulay, (Emilie) Rose
1881(?)-1958 .... **TCLC 7, 44**
See also CA 104; DLB 36; RGEL 2; RHW
Macaulay, Thomas Babington
1800-1859 .... **NCLC 42**
See also BRW 4; CDBLB 1832-1890; DLB 32, 55; RGEL 2
MacBeth, George (Mann)
1932-1992 .... **CLC 2, 5, 9**
See also CA 25-28R; 136; CANR 61, 66; DLB 40; MTCW 1; PFS 8; SATA 4; SATA-Obit 70
MacCaig, Norman (Alexander)
1910-1996 .... **CLC 36**
See also BRWS 6; CA 9-12R; CANR 3, 34; CP 7; DAB; DAM POET; DLB 27; RGEL 2
MacCarthy, Sir (Charles Otto) Desmond
1877-1952 .... **TCLC 36**
See also CA 167
MacDiarmid, Hugh .... **CLC 2, 4, 11, 19, 63; PC 9**
See also Grieve, C(hristopher) M(urray)
See also CDBLB 1945-1960; DLB 20; RGEL 2
MacDonald, Anson
See Heinlein, Robert A(nson)
Macdonald, Cynthia 1928- .... **CLC 13, 19**
See also CA 49-52; CANR 4, 44; DLB 105
MacDonald, George 1824-1905 .... **TCLC 9, 113**
See also BYA 5; CA 106; 137; CANR 80; CLR 67; DLB 18, 163, 178; FANT; MAICYA 1, 2; RGEL 2; SATA 33, 100; SFW 4; SUFW; WCH
Macdonald, John
See Millar, Kenneth
MacDonald, John D(ann)
1916-1986 .... **CLC 3, 27, 44**
See also BPFB 2; CA 1-4R; 121; CANR 1, 19, 60; CMW 4; CPW; DAM NOV, POP; DLB 8; DLBY 1986; MSW; MTCW 1, 2; SFW 4
Macdonald, John Ross
See Millar, Kenneth
Macdonald, Ross ..... **CLC 1, 2, 3, 14, 34, 41**
See also Millar, Kenneth
See also AMWS 4; BPFB 2; DLBD 6; MSW; RGAL 4
MacDougal, John
See Blish, James (Benjamin)

MacDougal, John
See Blish, James (Benjamin)
MacDowell, John
See Parks, Tim(othy Harold)
MacEwen, Gwendolyn (Margaret)
1941-1987 .... **CLC 13, 55**
See also CA 9-12R; 124; CANR 7, 22; DLB 53, 251; SATA 50; SATA-Obit 55
Macha, Karel Hynek 1810-1846 .... **NCLC 46**
Machado (y Ruiz), Antonio
1875-1939 .... **TCLC 3**
See also CA 104; 174; DLB 108; EW 9; HW 2; RGWL 2
Machado de Assis, Joaquim Maria
1839-1908 ..... **TCLC 10; BLC 2; HLCS 2; SSC 24**
See also CA 107; 153; CANR 91; LAW; RGSF 2; RGWL 2; WLIT 1
Machen, Arthur .... **TCLC 4; SSC 20**
See also Jones, Arthur Llewellyn
See also CA 179; DLB 156, 178; RGEL 2; SUFW
Machiavelli, Niccolo 1469-1527 ..... **LC 8, 36; DC 16; WLCS**
See also DA; DAB; DAC; DAM MST; EW 2; LAIT 1; NFS 9; RGWL 2
MacInnes, Colin 1914-1976 .... **CLC 4, 23**
See also CA 69-72; 65-68; CANR 21; DLB 14; MTCW 1, 2; RGEL 2; RHW
MacInnes, Helen (Clark)
1907-1985 .... **CLC 27, 39**
See also BPFB 2; CA 1-4R; 117; CANR 1, 28, 58; CMW 4; CPW; DAM POP; DLB 87; MSW; MTCW 1, 2; SATA 22; SATA-Obit 44
Mackay, Mary 1855-1924
See Corelli, Marie
See also CA 118; 177; FANT; RHW
Mackenzie, Compton (Edward Montague)
1883-1972 .... **CLC 18**
See also CA 21-22; 37-40R; CAP 2; DLB 34, 100; RGEL 2; TCLC 116
Mackenzie, Henry 1745-1831 .... **NCLC 41**
See also DLB 39; RGEL 2
Mackintosh, Elizabeth 1896(?)-1952
See Tey, Josephine
See also CA 110; CMW 4
MacLaren, James
See Grieve, C(hristopher) M(urray)
Mac Laverty, Bernard 1942- .... **CLC 31**
See also CA 116; 118; CANR 43, 88; CN 7; INT CA-118; RGSF 2
MacLean, Alistair (Stuart)
1922(?)-1987 .... **CLC 3, 13, 50, 63**
See also CA 57-60; 121; CANR 28, 61; CMW 4; CPW; DAM POP; MTCW 1; SATA 23; SATA-Obit 50; TCWW 2
Maclean, Norman (Fitzroy)
1902-1990 .... **CLC 78; SSC 13**
See also CA 102; 132; CANR 49; CPW; DAM POP; DLB 206; TCWW 2
MacLeish, Archibald 1892-1982 ... **CLC 3, 8, 14, 68**
See also AMW; CA 9-12R; 106; CAD; CANR 33, 63; CDALBS; DAM POET; DLB 4, 7, 45; DLBY 1982; EXPP; MTCW 1, 2; PAB; PFS 5; RGAL 4
MacLennan, (John) Hugh
1907-1990 .... **CLC 2, 14, 92**
See also CA 5-8R; 142; CANR 33; DAC; DAM MST; DLB 68; MTCW 1, 2; RGEL 2
MacLeod, Alistair 1936- .... **CLC 56**
See also CA 123; CCA 1; DAC; DAM MST; DLB 60; MTCW 2; RGSF 2
Macleod, Fiona
See Sharp, William
See also RGEL 2; SUFW

MacNeice, (Frederick) Louis
1907-1963 .... **CLC 1, 4, 10, 53**
See also BRW 7; CA 85-88; CANR 61; DAB; DAM POET; DLB 10, 20; MTCW 1, 2; RGEL 2

MacNeill, Dand
See Fraser, George MacDonald

Macpherson, James 1736-1796 .... **LC 29**
See also Ossian
See also DLB 109; RGEL 2

Macpherson, (Jean) Jay 1931- .... **CLC 14**
See also CA 5-8R; CANR 90; CP 7; CWP; DLB 53

Macrobius fl. 430- .... **CMLC 48**

MacShane, Frank 1927-1999 .... **CLC 39**
See also CA 9-12R; 186; CANR 3, 33; DLB 111

Macumber, Mari
See Sandoz, Mari(e Susette)

Madach, Imre 1823-1864 .... **NCLC 19**

Madden, (Jerry) David 1933- .... **CLC 5, 15**
See also CA 1-4R; CAAS 3; CANR 4, 45; CN 7; CSW; DLB 6; MTCW 1

Maddern, Al(an)
See Ellison, Harlan (Jay)

Madhubuti, Haki R. 1942- . **CLC 6, 73; BLC 2; PC 5**
See also Lee, Don L.
See also BW 2, 3; CA 73-76; CANR 24, 51, 73; CP 7; CSW; DAM MULT, POET; DLB 5, 41; DLBD 8; MTCW 2; RGAL 4

Maepenn, Hugh
See Kuttner, Henry

Maepenn, K. H.
See Kuttner, Henry

Maeterlinck, Maurice 1862-1949 ..... **TCLC 3**
See also CA 104; 136; CANR 80; DAM DRAM; DLB 192; EW 8; GFL 1789 to the Present; RGWL 2; SATA 66

Maginn, William 1794-1842 .... **NCLC 8**
See also DLB 110, 159

Mahapatra, Jayanta 1928- .... **CLC 33**
See also CA 73-76; CAAS 9; CANR 15, 33, 66, 87; CP 7; DAM MULT

Mahfouz, Naguib (Abdel Aziz Al-Sabilgi)
1911(?)- .... **CLC 153**
See also Mahfuz, Najib (Abdel Aziz al-Sabilgi)
See also BEST 89:2; CA 128; CANR 55, 101; CWW 2; DA3; DAM NOV; MTCW 1, 2; RGWL 2; SSFS 9

Mahfuz, Najib (Abdel Aziz al-Sabilgi)
.... **CLC 52, 55**
See also Mahfouz, Naguib (Abdel Aziz Al-Sabilgi)
See also AFW; DLBY 1988; RGSF 2; WLIT 2

Mahon, Derek 1941- .... **CLC 27**
See also BRWS 6; CA 113; 128; CANR 88; CP 7; DLB 40

Maiakovskii, Vladimir
See Mayakovski, Vladimir (Vladimirovich)
See also IDTP; RGWL 2

Mailer, Norman 1923- ... **CLC 1, 2, 3, 4, 5, 8, 11, 14, 28, 39, 74, 111**
See also AAYA 31; AITN 2; AMW; BPFB 2; CA 9-12R; CABS 1; CANR 28, 74, 77; CDALB 1968-1988; CN 7; CPW; DA; DA3; DAB; DAC; DAM MST, NOV, POP; DLB 2, 16, 28, 185; DLBD 3; DLBY 1980, 1983; MTCW 1, 2; NFS 10; RGAL 4

Maillet, Antonine 1929- .... **CLC 54, 118**
See also CA 115; 120; CANR 46, 74, 77; CCA 1; CWW 2; DAC; DLB 60; INT 120; MTCW 2

Mais, Roger 1905-1955 .... **TCLC 8**
See also BW 1, 3; CA 105; 124; CANR 82; CDWLB 3; DLB 125; MTCW 1; RGEL 2

Maistre, Joseph 1753-1821 .... **NCLC 37**
See also GFL 1789 to the Present

Maitland, Frederic William
1850-1906 .... **TCLC 65**

Maitland, Sara (Louise) 1950- .... **CLC 49**
See also CA 69-72; CANR 13, 59; FW

Major, Clarence 1936- . **CLC 3, 19, 48; BLC 2**
See also AFAW 2; BW 2, 3; CA 21-24R; CAAS 6; CANR 13, 25, 53, 82; CN 7; CP 7; CSW; DAM MULT; DLB 33; MSW

Major, Kevin (Gerald) 1949- .... **CLC 26**
See also AAYA 16; CA 97-100; CANR 21, 38; CLR 11; DAC; DLB 60; INT CANR-21; JRDA; MAICYA 1, 2; MAICYAS 1; SATA 32, 82; WYA; YAW

Maki, James
See Ozu, Yasujiro

Malabaila, Damiano
See Levi, Primo

Malamud, Bernard 1914-1986 .. **CLC 1, 2, 3, 5, 8, 9, 11, 18, 27, 44, 78, 85; SSC 15; WLC**
See also AAYA 16; AMWS 1; BPFB 2; CA 5-8R; 118; CABS 1; CANR 28, 62; CDALB 1941-1968; CPW; DA; DA3; DAB; DAC; DAM MST, NOV, POP; DLB 2, 28, 152; DLBY 1980, 1986; EXPS; LAIT 4; MTCW 1, 2; NFS 4, 9; RGAL 4; RGSF 2; SSFS 8, 13

Malan, Herman
See Bosman, Herman Charles; Bosman, Herman Charles

Malaparte, Curzio 1898-1957 .... **TCLC 52**

Malcolm, Dan
See Silverberg, Robert

Malcolm X .... **CLC 82, 117; BLC 2; WLCS**
See also Little, Malcolm
See also LAIT 5

Malherbe, Francois de 1555-1628 .... **LC 5**
See also GFL Beginnings to 1789

Mallarme, Stephane 1842-1898 ...... **NCLC 4, 41; PC 4**
See also DAM POET; DLB 217; EW 7; GFL 1789 to the Present; RGWL 2

Mallet-Joris, Francoise 1930- .... **CLC 11**
See also CA 65-68; CANR 17; DLB 83; GFL 1789 to the Present

Malley, Ern
See McAuley, James Phillip

Mallowan, Agatha Christie
See Christie, Agatha (Mary Clarissa)

Maloff, Saul 1922- .... **CLC 5**
See also CA 33-36R

Malone, Louis
See MacNeice, (Frederick) Louis

Malone, Michael (Christopher)
1942- .... **CLC 43**
See also CA 77-80; CANR 14, 32, 57

Malory, Sir Thomas 1410(?)-1471(?) . **LC 11; WLCS**
See also BRW 1; BRWR 2; CDBLB Before 1660; DA; DAB; DAC; DAM MST; DLB 146; EFS 2; RGEL 2; SATA 59; SATA-Brief 33; WLIT 3

Malouf, (George Joseph) David
1934- .... **CLC 28, 86**
See also CA 124; CANR 50, 76; CN 7; CP 7; MTCW 2

Malraux, (Georges-)Andre
1901-1976 .... **CLC 1, 4, 9, 13, 15, 57**
See also BPFB 2; CA 21-22; 69-72; CANR 34, 58; CAP 2; DA3; DAM NOV; DLB 72; EW 12; GFL 1789 to the Present; MTCW 1, 2; RGWL 2

Malzberg, Barry N(athaniel) 1939- ... **CLC 7**
See also CA 61-64; CAAS 4; CANR 16; CMW 4; DLB 8; SFW 4

Mamet, David (Alan) 1947- .. **CLC 9, 15, 34, 46, 91; DC 4**
See also AAYA 3; CA 81-84; CABS 3; CANR 15, 41, 67, 72; CD 5; DA3; DAM DRAM; DFS 2, 3, 6, 12; DLB 7; IDFW 4; MTCW 1, 2; RGAL 4

Mamoulian, Rouben (Zachary)
1897-1987 .... **CLC 16**
See also CA 25-28R; 124; CANR 85

Mandelshtam, Osip
See Mandelstam, Osip (Emilievich)
See also EW 10; RGWL 2

Mandelstam, Osip (Emilievich)
1891(?)-1943(?) .... **TCLC 2, 6; PC 14**
See also Mandelshtam, Osip
See also CA 104; 150; MTCW 2

Mander, (Mary) Jane 1877-1949 ... **TCLC 31**
See also CA 162; RGEL 2

Mandeville, Sir John fl. 1350- ...... **CMLC 19**
See also DLB 146

Mandiargues, Andre Pieyre de .... **CLC 41**
See also Pieyre de Mandiargues, Andre
See also DLB 83

Mandrake, Ethel Belle
See Thurman, Wallace (Henry)

Mangan, James Clarence
1803-1849 .... **NCLC 27**
See also RGEL 2

Maniere, J.-E.
See Giraudoux, Jean(-Hippolyte)

Mankiewicz, Herman (Jacob)
1897-1953 .... **TCLC 85**
See also CA 120; 169; DLB 26; IDFW 3, 4

Manley, (Mary) Delariviere
1672(?)-1724 .... **LC 1, 42**
See also DLB 39, 80; RGEL 2

Mann, Abel
See Creasey, John

Mann, Emily 1952- .... **DC 7**
See also CA 130; CAD; CANR 55; CD 5; CWD

Mann, (Luiz) Heinrich 1871-1950 ... **TCLC 9**
See also CA 106; 164, 181; DLB 66, 118; EW 8; RGWL 2

Mann, (Paul) Thomas 1875-1955 ... **TCLC 2, 8, 14, 21, 35, 44, 60; SSC 5; WLC**
See also BPFB 2; CA 104; 128; CDWLB 2; DA; DA3; DAB; DAC; DAM MST, NOV; DLB 66; EW 9; GLL 1; MTCW 1, 2; RGSF 2; RGWL 2; SSFS 4, 9

Mannheim, Karl 1893-1947 .... **TCLC 65**

Manning, David
See Faust, Frederick (Schiller)
See also TCWW 2

Manning, Frederic 1887(?)-1935 ... **TCLC 25**
See also CA 124

Manning, Olivia 1915-1980 .... **CLC 5, 19**
See also CA 5-8R; 101; CANR 29; FW; MTCW 1; RGEL 2

Mano, D. Keith 1942- .... **CLC 2, 10**
See also CA 25-28R; CAAS 6; CANR 26, 57; DLB 6

Mansfield, Katherine .... **TCLC 2, 8, 39; SSC 9, 23, 38; WLC**
See also Beauchamp, Kathleen Mansfield
See also BPFB 2; BRW 7; DAB; DLB 162; EXPS; FW; GLL 1; RGEL 2; RGSF 2; SSFS 2, 8, 10, 11

Manso, Peter 1940- .... **CLC 39**
See also CA 29-32R; CANR 44

Mantecon, Juan Jimenez
See Jimenez (Mantecon), Juan Ramon

Mantel, Hilary (Mary) 1952- .... **CLC 144**
See also CA 125; CANR 54, 101; CN 7; RHW

Manton, Peter
See Creasey, John

Man Without a Spleen, A
See Chekhov, Anton (Pavlovich)

Manzoni, Alessandro 1785-1873 ... **NCLC 29, 98**
See also EW 5; RGWL 2
Map, Walter 1140-1209 .... **CMLC 32**
Mapu, Abraham (ben Jekutiel)
1808-1867 .... **NCLC 18**
Mara, Sally
See Queneau, Raymond
Marat, Jean Paul 1743-1793 .... **LC 10**
Marcel, Gabriel Honore 1889-1973 . **CLC 15**
See also CA 102; 45-48; MTCW 1, 2
March, William 1893-1954 .... **TCLC 96**
Marchbanks, Samuel
See Davies, (William) Robertson
See also CCA 1
Marchi, Giacomo
See Bassani, Giorgio
Marcus Aurelius
See Aurelius, Marcus
See also AW 2
Marguerite
See de Navarre, Marguerite
Marguerite d'Angouleme
See de Navarre, Marguerite
See also GFL Beginnings to 1789
Marguerite de Navarre
See de Navarre, Marguerite
See also RGWL 2
Margulies, Donald 1954- .... **CLC 76**
See also CA 200; DFS 13; DLB 228
Marie de France c. 12th cent. - ..... **CMLC 8; PC 22**
See also DLB 208; FW; RGWL 2
Marie de l'Incarnation 1599-1672 ...... **LC 10**
Marier, Captain Victor
See Griffith, D(avid Lewelyn) W(ark)
Mariner, Scott
See Pohl, Frederik
Marinetti, Filippo Tommaso
1876-1944 .... **TCLC 10**
See also CA 107; DLB 114; EW 9
Marivaux, Pierre Carlet de Chamblain de
1688-1763 .... **LC 4; DC 7**
See also GFL Beginnings to 1789; RGWL 2
Markandaya, Kamala .... **CLC 8, 38**
See also Taylor, Kamala (Purnaiya)
See also BYA 13; CN 7
Markfield, Wallace 1926- .... **CLC 8**
See also CA 69-72; CAAS 3; CN 7; DLB 2, 28
Markham, Edwin 1852-1940 .... **TCLC 47**
See also CA 160; DLB 54, 186; RGAL 4
Markham, Robert
See Amis, Kingsley (William)
Marks, J
See Highwater, Jamake (Mamake)
Marks, J.
See Highwater, Jamake (Mamake)
Marks-Highwater, J
See Highwater, Jamake (Mamake)
Marks-Highwater, J.
See Highwater, Jamake (Mamake)
Markson, David M(errill) 1927- .... **CLC 67**
See also CA 49-52; CANR 1, 91; CN 7
Marley, Bob .... **CLC 17**
See also Marley, Robert Nesta
Marley, Robert Nesta 1945-1981
See Marley, Bob
See also CA 107; 103
Marlowe, Christopher 1564-1593 ...... **LC 22, 47; DC 1; WLC**
See also BRW 1; BRWR 1; CDBLB Before 1660; DA; DA3; DAB; DAC; DAM DRAM, MST; DFS 1, 5, 13; DLB 62; EXPP; RGEL 2; WLIT 3

Marlowe, Stephen 1928- .... **CLC 70**
See also Queen, Ellery
See also CA 13-16R; CANR 6, 55; CMW 4; SFW 4
Marmontel, Jean-Francois 1723-1799 .. **LC 2**
Marquand, John P(hillips)
1893-1960 .... **CLC 2, 10**
See also AMW; BPFB 2; CA 85-88; CANR 73; CMW 4; DLB 9, 102; MTCW 2; RGAL 4
Marques, Rene 1919-1979 .. **CLC 96; HLC 2**
See also CA 97-100; 85-88; CANR 78; DAM MULT; DLB 113; HW 1, 2; LAW; RGSF 2
Marquez, Gabriel (Jose) Garcia
See Garcia Marquez, Gabriel (Jose)
Marquis, Don(ald Robert Perry)
1878-1937 .... **TCLC 7**
See also CA 104; 166; DLB 11, 25; RGAL 4
Marric, J. J.
See Creasey, John
See also MSW
Marryat, Frederick 1792-1848 .... **NCLC 3**
See also DLB 21, 163; RGEL 2; WCH
Marsden, James
See Creasey, John
Marsh, Edward 1872-1953 .... **TCLC 99**
Marsh, (Edith) Ngaio 1899-1982 .. **CLC 7, 53**
See also CA 9-12R; CANR 6, 58; CMW 4; CPW; DAM POP; DLB 77; MSW; MTCW 1, 2; RGEL 2
Marshall, Garry 1934- .... **CLC 17**
See also AAYA 3; CA 111; SATA 60
Marshall, Paule 1929- .. **CLC 27, 72; BLC 3; SSC 3**
See also AFAW 1, 2; BPFB 2; BW 2, 3; CA 77-80; CANR 25, 73; CN 7; DA3; DAM MULT; DLB 33, 157, 227; MTCW 1, 2; RGAL 4
Marshallik
See Zangwill, Israel
Marsten, Richard
See Hunter, Evan
Marston, John 1576-1634 .... **LC 33**
See also BRW 2; DAM DRAM; DLB 58, 172; RGEL 2
Martha, Henry
See Harris, Mark
Marti (y Perez), Jose (Julian)
1853-1895 .... **NCLC 63; HLC 2**
See also DAM MULT; HW 2; LAW; RGWL 2; WLIT 1
Martial c. 40-c. 104 .... **CMLC 35; PC 10**
See also AW 2; CDWLB 1; DLB 211; RGWL 2
Martin, Ken
See Hubbard, L(afayette) Ron(ald)
Martin, Richard
See Creasey, John
Martin, Steve 1945- .... **CLC 30**
See also CA 97-100; CANR 30, 100; MTCW 1
Martin, Valerie 1948- .... **CLC 89**
See also BEST 90:2; CA 85-88; CANR 49, 89
Martin, Violet Florence
1862-1915 .... **TCLC 51**
Martin, Webber
See Silverberg, Robert
Martindale, Patrick Victor
See White, Patrick (Victor Martindale)
Martin du Gard, Roger
1881-1958 .... **TCLC 24**
See also CA 118; CANR 94; DLB 65; GFL 1789 to the Present; RGWL 2
Martineau, Harriet 1802-1876 .... **NCLC 26**
See also DLB 21, 55, 159, 163, 166, 190; FW; RGEL 2; YABC 2

Martines, Julia
See O'Faolain, Julia
Martinez, Enrique Gonzalez
See Gonzalez Martinez, Enrique
Martinez, Jacinto Benavente y
See Benavente (y Martinez), Jacinto
Martinez de la Rosa, Francisco de Paula
1787-1862 .... **NCLC 102**
Martinez Ruiz, Jose 1873-1967
See Azorin; Ruiz, Jose Martinez
See also CA 93-96; HW 1
Martinez Sierra, Gregorio
1881-1947 .... **TCLC 6**
See also CA 115
Martinez Sierra, Maria (de la O'LeJarraga)
1874-1974 .... **TCLC 6**
See also CA 115
Martinsen, Martin
See Follett, Ken(neth Martin)
Martinson, Harry (Edmund)
1904-1978 .... **CLC 14**
See also CA 77-80; CANR 34; DLB 259
Martyn, Edward 1859-1923 .... **TCLC 121**
See also CA 179; DLB 10; RGEL 2
Marut, Ret
See Traven, B.
Marut, Robert
See Traven, B.
Marvell, Andrew 1621-1678 .... **LC 4, 43; PC 10; WLC**
See also BRW 2; BRWR 2; CDBLB 1660-1789; DA; DAB; DAC; DAM MST, POET; DLB 131; EXPP; PFS 5; RGEL 2; WP
Marx, Karl (Heinrich) 1818-1883 . **NCLC 17**
See also DLB 129
Masaoka, Shiki .... **TCLC 18**
See also Masaoka, Tsunenori
Masaoka, Tsunenori 1867-1902
See Masaoka, Shiki
See also CA 117; 191
Masefield, John (Edward)
1878-1967 .... **CLC 11, 47**
See also CA 19-20; 25-28R; CANR 33; CAP 2; CDBLB 1890-1914; DAM POET; DLB 10, 19, 153, 160; EXPP; FANT; MTCW 1, 2; PFS 5; RGEL 2; SATA 19
Maso, Carole 19(?)- .... **CLC 44**
See also CA 170; GLL 2; RGAL 4
Mason, Bobbie Ann 1940- ... **CLC 28, 43, 82, 154; SSC 4**
See also AAYA 5, 42; AMWS 8; BPFB 2; CA 53-56; CANR 11, 31, 58, 83; CDALBS; CN 7; CSW; DA3; DLB 173; DLBY 1987; EXPS; INT CANR-31; MTCW 1, 2; NFS 4; RGAL 4; RGSF 2; SSFS 3,8; YAW
Mason, Ernst
See Pohl, Frederik
Mason, Hunni B.
See Sternheim, (William Adolf) Carl
Mason, Lee W.
See Malzberg, Barry N(athaniel)
Mason, Nick 1945- .... **CLC 35**
Mason, Tally
See Derleth, August (William)
Mass, Anna .... **CLC 59**
Mass, William
See Gibson, William
Massinger, Philip 1583-1640 .... **LC 70**
See also DLB 58; RGEL 2
Master Lao
See Lao Tzu
Masters, Edgar Lee 1868-1950 .... **TCLC 2, 25; PC 1, 36; WLCS**
See also AMWS 1; CA 104; 133; CDALB 1865-1917; DA; DAC; DAM MST, POET; DLB 54; EXPP; MTCW 1, 2; RGAL 4; WP

Masters, Hilary 1928- .... **CLC 48**
See also CA 25-28R; CANR 13, 47, 97; CN 7; DLB 244

Mastrosimone, William 19(?)- .... **CLC 36**
See also CA 186; CAD; CD 5

Mathe, Albert
See Camus, Albert

Mather, Cotton 1663-1728 .... **LC 38**
See also AMWS 2; CDALB 1640-1865; DLB 24, 30, 140; RGAL 4

Mather, Increase 1639-1723 .... **LC 38**
See also DLB 24

Matheson, Richard (Burton) 1926- .. **CLC 37**
See also AAYA 31; CA 97-100; CANR 88, 99; DLB 8, 44; HGG; INT 97-100; SCFW 2; SFW 4

Mathews, Harry 1930- .... **CLC 6, 52**
See also CA 21-24R; CAAS 6; CANR 18, 40, 98; CN 7

Mathews, John Joseph 1894-1979 .... **CLC 84**
See also CA 19-20; 142; CANR 45; CAP 2; DAM MULT; DLB 175; NNAL

Mathias, Roland (Glyn) 1915- .... **CLC 45**
See also CA 97-100; CANR 19, 41; CP 7; DLB 27

Matsuo Basho 1644-1694 .... **LC 62; PC 3**
See also Basho, Matsuo
See also DAM POET; PFS 2, 7

Mattheson, Rodney
See Creasey, John

Matthews, (James) Brander
1852-1929 .... **TCLC 95**
See also DLB 71, 78; DLBD 13

Matthews, Greg 1949- .... **CLC 45**
See also CA 135

Matthews, William (Procter III)
1942-1997 .... **CLC 40**
See also AMWS 9; CA 29-32R; 162; CAAS 18; CANR 12, 57; CP 7; DLB 5

Matthias, John (Edward) 1941- .... **CLC 9**
See also CA 33-36R; CANR 56; CP 7

Matthiessen, F(rancis) O(tto)
1902-1950 .... **TCLC 100**
See also CA 185; DLB 63

Matthiessen, Peter 1927- ... **CLC 5, 7, 11, 32, 64**
See also AAYA 6, 40; AMWS 5; ANW; BEST 90:4; BPFB 2; CA 9-12R; CANR 21, 50, 73, 100; CN 7; DA3; DAM NOV; DLB 6, 173; MTCW 1, 2; SATA 27

Maturin, Charles Robert
1780(?)-1824 .... **NCLC 6**
See also DLB 178; HGG; RGEL 2; SUFW

Matute (Ausejo), Ana Maria 1925- .. **CLC 11**
See also CA 89-92; MTCW 1; RGSF 2

Maugham, W. S.
See Maugham, W(illiam) Somerset

Maugham, W(illiam) Somerset
1874-1965 .. **CLC 1, 11, 15, 67, 93; SSC 8; WLC**
See also BPFB 2; BRW 6; CA 5-8R; 25-28R; CANR 40; CDBLB 1914-1945; CMW 4; DA; DA3; DAB; DAC; DAM DRAM, MST, NOV; DLB 10, 36, 77, 100, 162, 195; LAIT 3; MTCW 1, 2; RGEL 2; RGSF 2; SATA 54

Maugham, William Somerset
See Maugham, W(illiam) Somerset

Maupassant, (Henri Rene Albert) Guy de
1850-1893 .... **NCLC 1, 42, 83; SSC 1; WLC**
See also BYA 14; DA; DA3; DAB; DAC; DAM MST; DLB 123; EW 7; EXPS; GFL 1789 to the Present; LAIT 2; RGSF 2; RGWL 2; SSFS 4; SUFW; TWA

Maupin, Armistead (Jones, Jr.)
1944- .... **CLC 95**
See also CA 125; 130; CANR 58, 101; CPW; DA3; DAM POP; GLL 1; INT 130; MTCW 2

Maurhut, Richard
See Traven, B.

Mauriac, Claude 1914-1996 .... **CLC 9**
See also CA 89-92; 152; CWW 2; DLB 83; GFL 1789 to the Present

Mauriac, Francois (Charles)
1885-1970 .... **CLC 4, 9, 56; SSC 24**
See also CA 25-28; CAP 2; DLB 65; EW 10; GFL 1789 to the Present; MTCW 1, 2; RGWL 2

Mavor, Osborne Henry 1888-1951
See Bridie, James
See also CA 104

Maxwell, William (Keepers, Jr.)
1908-2000 .... **CLC 19**
See also AMWS 8; CA 93-96; 189; CANR 54, 95; CN 7; DLB 218; DLBY 1980; INT CA-93-96; SATA-Obit 128

May, Elaine 1932- .... **CLC 16**
See also CA 124; 142; CAD; CWD; DLB 44

Mayakovski, Vladimir (Vladimirovich)
1893-1930 .... **TCLC 4, 18**
See also Maiakovskii, Vladimir; Mayakovsky, Vladimir
See also CA 104; 158; MTCW 2; SFW 4

Mayakovsky, Vladimir
See Mayakovski, Vladimir (Vladimirovich)
See also EW 11; WP

Mayhew, Henry 1812-1887 .... **NCLC 31**
See also DLB 18, 55, 190

Mayle, Peter 1939(?)- .... **CLC 89**
See also CA 139; CANR 64, 109

Maynard, Joyce 1953- .... **CLC 23**
See also CA 111; 129; CANR 64

Mayne, William (James Carter)
1928- .... **CLC 12**
See also AAYA 20; CA 9-12R; CANR 37, 80, 100; CLR 25; FANT; JRDA; MAICYA 1, 2; MAICYAS 1; SAAS 11; SATA 6, 68, 122; YAW

Mayo, Jim
See L'Amour, Louis (Dearborn)
See also TCWW 2

Maysles, Albert 1926- .... **CLC 16**
See also CA 29-32R

Maysles, David 1932-1987 .... **CLC 16**
See also CA 191

Mazer, Norma Fox 1931- .... **CLC 26**
See also AAYA 5, 36; BYA 1, 8; CA 69-72; CANR 12, 32, 66; CLR 23; JRDA; MAICYA 1, 2; SAAS 1; SATA 24, 67, 105; WYA; YAW

Mazzini, Guiseppe 1805-1872 .... **NCLC 34**

McAlmon, Robert (Menzies)
1895-1956 .... **TCLC 97**
See also CA 107; 168; DLB 4, 45; DLBD 15; GLL 1

McAuley, James Phillip 1917-1976 .. **CLC 45**
See also CA 97-100; RGEL 2

McBain, Ed
See Hunter, Evan
See also MSW

McBrien, William (Augustine)
1930- .... **CLC 44**
See also CA 107; CANR 90

McCabe, Patrick 1955- .... **CLC 133**
See also CA 130; CANR 50, 90; CN 7; DLB 194

McCaffrey, Anne (Inez) 1926- .... **CLC 17**
See also AAYA 6, 34; AITN 2; BEST 89:2; BPFB 2; BYA 5; CA 25-28R; CANR 15, 35, 55, 96; CLR 49; CPW; DA3; DAM NOV, POP; DLB 8; JRDA; MAICYA 1, 2; MTCW 1, 2; SAAS 11; SATA 8, 70, 116; SFW 4; WYA; YAW

McCall, Nathan 1955(?)- .... **CLC 86**
See also BW 3; CA 146; CANR 88

McCann, Arthur
See Campbell, John W(ood, Jr.)

McCann, Edson
See Pohl, Frederik

McCarthy, Charles, Jr. 1933-
See McCarthy, Cormac
See also CANR 42, 69, 101; CN 7; CPW; CSW; DA3; DAM POP; MTCW 2

McCarthy, Cormac .... **CLC 4, 57, 59, 101**
See also McCarthy, Charles, Jr.
See also AAYA 41; AMWS 8; BPFB 2; CA 13-16R; CANR 10; DLB 6, 143, 256; TCWW 2

McCarthy, Mary (Therese)
1912-1989 .. **CLC 1, 3, 5, 14, 24, 39, 59; SSC 24**
See also AMW; BPFB 2; CA 5-8R; 129; CANR 16, 50, 64; DA3; DLB 2; DLBY 1981; FW; INT CANR-16; MAWW; MTCW 1, 2; RGAL 4

McCartney, (James) Paul 1942- . **CLC 12, 35**
See also CA 146

McCauley, Stephen (D.) 1955- .... **CLC 50**
See also CA 141

McClaren, Peter .... **CLC 70**

McClure, Michael (Thomas) 1932- ... **CLC 6, 10**
See also CA 21-24R; CAD; CANR 17, 46, 77; CD 5; CP 7; DLB 16; WP

McCorkle, Jill (Collins) 1958- .... **CLC 51**
See also CA 121; CSW; DLB 234; DLBY 1987

McCourt, Frank 1930- .... **CLC 109**
See also CA 157; CANR 97; NCFS 1

McCourt, James 1941- .... **CLC 5**
See also CA 57-60; CANR 98

McCourt, Malachy 1932- .... **CLC 119**
See also SATA 126

McCoy, Horace (Stanley)
1897-1955 .... **TCLC 28**
See also CA 108; 155; CMW 4; DLB 9

McCrae, John 1872-1918 .... **TCLC 12**
See also CA 109; DLB 92; PFS 5

McCreigh, James
See Pohl, Frederik

McCullers, (Lula) Carson (Smith)
1917-1967 .... **CLC 1, 4, 10, 12, 48, 100; SSC 9, 24; WLC**
See also AAYA 21; AMW; BPFB 2; CA 5-8R; 25-28R; CABS 1, 3; CANR 18; CDALB 1941-1968; DA; DA3; DAB; DAC; DAM MST, NOV; DFS 5; DLB 2, 7, 173, 228; EXPS; FW; GLL 1; LAIT 3, 4; MAWW; MTCW 1, 2; NFS 6, 13; RGAL 4; RGSF 2; SATA 27; SSFS 5; YAW

McCulloch, John Tyler
See Burroughs, Edgar Rice

McCullough, Colleen 1938(?)- .. **CLC 27, 107**
See also AAYA 36; BPFB 2; CA 81-84; CANR 17, 46, 67, 98; CPW; DA3; DAM NOV, POP; MTCW 1, 2; RHW

McDermott, Alice 1953- .... **CLC 90**
See also CA 109; CANR 40, 90

McElroy, Joseph 1930- .... **CLC 5, 47**
See also CA 17-20R; CN 7

McEwan, Ian (Russell) 1948- ...... **CLC 13, 66**
See also BEST 90:4; BRWS 4; CA 61-64; CANR 14, 41, 69, 87; CN 7; DAM NOV; DLB 14, 194; HGG; MTCW 1, 2; RGSF 2

McFadden, David 1940- .... **CLC 48**
See also CA 104; CP 7; DLB 60; INT 104

McFarland, Dennis 1950- .... **CLC 65**
See also CA 165

McGahern, John 1934- ... **CLC 5, 9, 48, 156; SSC 17**
See also CA 17-20R; CANR 29, 68; CN 7; DLB 14, 231; MTCW 1

McGinley, Patrick (Anthony) 1937- . **CLC 41**
See also CA 120; 127; CANR 56; INT 127

McGinley, Phyllis 1905-1978 .... **CLC 14**
See also CA 9-12R; 77-80; CANR 19; CWRI 5; DLB 11, 48; PFS 9, 13; SATA 2, 44; SATA-Obit 24

McGinniss, Joe 1942- .... **CLC 32**
See also AITN 2; BEST 89:2; CA 25-28R; CANR 26, 70; CPW; DLB 185; INT CANR-26

McGivern, Maureen Daly
See Daly, Maureen

McGrath, Patrick 1950- .... **CLC 55**
See also CA 136; CANR 65; CN 7; DLB 231; HGG

McGrath, Thomas (Matthew) 1916-1990 .... **CLC 28, 59**
See also AMWS 10; CA 9-12R; 132; CANR 6, 33, 95; DAM POET; MTCW 1; SATA 41; SATA-Obit 66

McGuane, Thomas (Francis III) 1939- .... **CLC 3, 7, 18, 45, 127**
See also AITN 2; BPFB 2; CA 49-52; CANR 5, 24, 49, 94; CN 7; DLB 2, 212; DLBY 1980; INT CANR-24; MTCW 1; TCWW 2

McGuckian, Medbh 1950- ... **CLC 48; PC 27**
See also BRWS 5; CA 143; CP 7; CWP; DAM POET; DLB 40

McHale, Tom 1942(?)-1982 .... **CLC 3, 5**
See also AITN 1; CA 77-80; 106

McIlvanney, William 1936- .... **CLC 42**
See also CA 25-28R; CANR 61; CMW 4; DLB 14, 207

McIlwraith, Maureen Mollie Hunter
See Hunter, Mollie
See also SATA 2

McInerney, Jay 1955- .... **CLC 34, 112**
See also AAYA 18; BPFB 2; CA 116; 123; CANR 45, 68; CN 7; CPW; DA3; DAM POP; INT 123; MTCW 2

McIntyre, Vonda N(eel) 1948- .... **CLC 18**
See also CA 81-84; CANR 17, 34, 69; MTCW 1; SFW 4; YAW

McKay, Claude .... **TCLC 7, 41; BLC 3; PC 2; WLC**
See also McKay, Festus Claudius
See also AFAW 1, 2; AMWS 10; DAB; DLB 4, 45, 51, 117; EXPP; GLL 2; LAIT 3; PAB; PFS 4; RGAL 4; WP

McKay, Festus Claudius 1889-1948
See McKay, Claude
See also BW 1, 3; CA 104; 124; CANR 73; DA; DAC; DAM MST, MULT, NOV, POET; MTCW 1, 2

McKuen, Rod 1933- .... **CLC 1, 3**
See also AITN 1; CA 41-44R; CANR 40

McLoughlin, R. B.
See Mencken, H(enry) L(ouis)

McLuhan, (Herbert) Marshall 1911-1980 .... **CLC 37, 83**
See also CA 9-12R; 102; CANR 12, 34, 61; DLB 88; INT CANR-12; MTCW 1, 2

McMillan, Terry (L.) 1951- .... **CLC 50, 61, 112; BLCS**
See also AAYA 21; BPFB 2; BW 2, 3; CA 140; CANR 60, 104; CPW; DA3; DAM MULT, NOV, POP; MTCW 2; RGAL 4; YAW

McMurtry, Larry (Jeff) 1936- .. **CLC 2, 3, 7, 11, 27, 44, 127**
See also AAYA 15; AITN 2; AMWS 5; BEST 89:2; BPFB 2; CA 5-8R; CANR 19, 43, 64, 103; CDALB 1968-1988; CN 7; CPW; CSW; DA3; DAM NOV, POP; DLB 2, 143, 256; DLBY 1980, 1987; MTCW 1, 2; RGAL 4; TCWW 2

McNally, T. M. 1961- .... **CLC 82**

McNally, Terrence 1939- .... **CLC 4, 7, 41, 91**
See also CA 45-48; CAD; CANR 2, 56; CD 5; DA3; DAM DRAM; DLB 7, 249; GLL 1; MTCW 2

McNamer, Deirdre 1950- .... **CLC 70**

McNeal, Tom .... **CLC 119**

McNeile, Herman Cyril 1888-1937
See Sapper
See also CA 184; CMW 4; DLB 77

McNickle, (William) D'Arcy 1904-1977 .... **CLC 89**
See also CA 9-12R; 85-88; CANR 5, 45; DAM MULT; DLB 175, 212; NNAL; RGAL 4; SATA-Obit 22

McPhee, John (Angus) 1931- .... **CLC 36**
See also AMWS 3; ANW; BEST 90:1; CA 65-68; CANR 20, 46, 64, 69; CPW; DLB 185; MTCW 1, 2

McPherson, James Alan 1943- .. **CLC 19, 77; BLCS**
See also BW 1, 3; CA 25-28R; CAAS 17; CANR 24, 74; CN 7; CSW; DLB 38, 244; MTCW 1, 2; RGAL 4; RGSF 2

McPherson, William (Alexander) 1933- .... **CLC 34**
See also CA 69-72; CANR 28; INT CANR-28

McTaggart, J. McT. Ellis
See McTaggart, John McTaggart Ellis

McTaggart, John McTaggart Ellis 1866-1925 .... **TCLC 105**
See also CA 120

Mead, George Herbert 1873-1958 . **TCLC 89**

Mead, Margaret 1901-1978 .... **CLC 37**
See also AITN 1; CA 1-4R; 81-84; CANR 4; DA3; FW; MTCW 1, 2; SATA-Obit 20

Meaker, Marijane (Agnes) 1927-
See Kerr, M. E.
See also CA 107; CANR 37, 63; INT 107; JRDA; MAICYA 1, 2; MAICYAS 1; MTCW 1; SATA 20, 61, 99; SATA-Essay 111; YAW

Medoff, Mark (Howard) 1940- .... **CLC 6, 23**
See also AITN 1; CA 53-56; CAD; CANR 5; CD 5; DAM DRAM; DFS 4; DLB 7; INT CANR-5

Medvedev, P. N.
See Bakhtin, Mikhail Mikhailovich

Meged, Aharon
See Megged, Aharon

Meged, Aron
See Megged, Aharon

Megged, Aharon 1920- .... **CLC 9**
See also CA 49-52; CAAS 13; CANR 1

Mehta, Ved (Parkash) 1934- .... **CLC 37**
See also CA 1-4R; CANR 2, 23, 69; MTCW 1

Melanter
See Blackmore, R(ichard) D(oddridge)

Melies, Georges 1861-1938 .... **TCLC 81**

Melikow, Loris
See Hofmannsthal, Hugo von

Melmoth, Sebastian
See Wilde, Oscar (Fingal O'Flahertie Wills)

Meltzer, Milton 1915- .... **CLC 26**
See also AAYA 8; BYA 2, 6; CA 13-16R; CANR 38, 92, 107; CLR 13; DLB 61; JRDA; MAICYA 1, 2; SAAS 1; SATA 1, 50, 80, 128; SATA-Essay 124; WYA; YAW

Melville, Herman 1819-1891 ..... **NCLC 3, 12, 29, 45, 49, 91, 93; SSC 1, 17, 46; WLC**
See also AAYA 25; AMW; AMWR 1; CDALB 1640-1865; DA; DA3; DAB; DAC; DAM MST, NOV; DLB 3, 74, 250, 254; EXPN; EXPS; LAIT 1, 2; NFS 7, 9; RGAL 4; RGSF 2; SATA 59; SSFS 3

Members, Mark
See Powell, Anthony (Dymoke)

Membreno, Alejandro .... **CLC 59**

Menander c. 342B.C.-c. 293B.C. .... **CMLC 9, 51; DC 3**
See also AW 1; CDWLB 1; DAM DRAM; DLB 176; RGWL 2

Menchu, Rigoberta 1959-
See also CA 175; DNFS 1; HLCS 2; WLIT 1

Mencken, H(enry) L(ouis) 1880-1956 .... **TCLC 13**
See also AMW; CA 105; 125; CDALB 1917-1929; DLB 11, 29, 63, 137, 222; MTCW 1, 2; RGAL 4

Mendelsohn, Jane 1965- .... **CLC 99**
See also CA 154; CANR 94

Mercer, David 1928-1980 .... **CLC 5**
See also CA 9-12R; 102; CANR 23; CBD; DAM DRAM; DLB 13; MTCW 1; RGEL 2

Merchant, Paul
See Ellison, Harlan (Jay)

Meredith, George 1828-1909 ... **TCLC 17, 43**
See also CA 117; 153; CANR 80; CDBLB 1832-1890; DAM POET; DLB 18, 35, 57, 159; RGEL 2

Meredith, William (Morris) 1919- .... **CLC 4, 13, 22, 55; PC 28**
See also CA 9-12R; CAAS 14; CANR 6, 40; CP 7; DAM POET; DLB 5

Merezhkovsky, Dmitry Sergeyevich 1865-1941 .... **TCLC 29**
See also CA 169

Merimee, Prosper 1803-1870 ... **NCLC 6, 65; SSC 7**
See also DLB 119, 192; EW 6; EXPS; GFL 1789 to the Present; RGSF 2; RGWL 2; SSFS 8; SUFW

Merkin, Daphne 1954- .... **CLC 44**
See also CA 123

Merlin, Arthur
See Blish, James (Benjamin)

Merrill, James (Ingram) 1926-1995 .. **CLC 2, 3, 6, 8, 13, 18, 34, 91; PC 28**
See also AMWS 3; CA 13-16R; 147; CANR 10, 49, 63, 108; DA3; DAM POET; DLB 5, 165; DLBY 1985; INT CANR-10; MTCW 1, 2; PAB; RGAL 4

Merriman, Alex
See Silverberg, Robert

Merriman, Brian 1747-1805 .... **NCLC 70**

Merritt, E. B.
See Waddington, Miriam

Merton, Thomas 1915-1968 ..... **CLC 1, 3, 11, 34, 83; PC 10**
See also AMWS 8; CA 5-8R; 25-28R; CANR 22, 53; DA3; DLB 48; DLBY 1981; MTCW 1, 2

Merwin, W(illiam) S(tanley) 1927- ... **CLC 1, 2, 3, 5, 8, 13, 18, 45, 88**
See also AMWS 3; CA 13-16R; CANR 15, 51; CP 7; DA3; DAM POET; DLB 5, 169; INT CANR-15; MTCW 1, 2; PAB; PFS 5; RGAL 4

Metcalf, John 1938- .... **CLC 37; SSC 43**
See also CA 113; CN 7; DLB 60; RGSF 2

Metcalf, Suzanne
See Baum, L(yman) Frank

Mew, Charlotte (Mary) 1870-1928 .. **TCLC 8**
See also CA 105; 189; DLB 19, 135; RGEL 2

Mewshaw, Michael 1943- .... **CLC 9**
See also CA 53-56; CANR 7, 47; DLBY 1980

Meyer, Conrad Ferdinand
1825-1905 .... **NCLC 81**
See also DLB 129; EW; RGWL 2
Meyer, Gustav 1868-1932
See Meyrink, Gustav
See also CA 117; 190
Meyer, June
See Jordan, June
See also GLL 2
Meyer, Lynn
See Slavitt, David R(ytman)
Meyers, Jeffrey 1939- .... **CLC 39**
See also CA 73-76; CAAE 186; CANR 54, 102; DLB 111
Meynell, Alice (Christina Gertrude Thompson) 1847-1922 .... **TCLC 6**
See also CA 104; 177; DLB 19, 98; RGEL 2
Meyrink, Gustav .... **TCLC 21**
See also Meyer, Gustav
See also DLB 81
Michaels, Leonard 1933- .... **CLC 6, 25; SSC 16**
See also CA 61-64; CANR 21, 62; CN 7; DLB 130; MTCW 1
Michaux, Henri 1899-1984 .... **CLC 8, 19**
See also CA 85-88; 114; DLB 258; GFL 1789 to the Present; RGWL 2
Micheaux, Oscar (Devereaux)
1884-1951 .... **TCLC 76**
See also BW 3; CA 174; DLB 50; TCWW 2
Michelangelo 1475-1564 .... **LC 12**
See also AAYA 43
Michelet, Jules 1798-1874 .... **NCLC 31**
See also EW 5; GFL 1789 to the Present
Michels, Robert 1876-1936 .... **TCLC 88**
Michener, James A(lbert)
1907(?)-1997 .. **CLC 1, 5, 11, 29, 60, 109**
See also AAYA 27; AITN 1; BEST 90:1; BPFB 2; CA 5-8R; 161; CANR 21, 45, 68; CN 7; CPW; DA3; DAM NOV, POP; DLB 6; MTCW 1, 2; RHW
Mickiewicz, Adam 1798-1855 . **NCLC 3, 101; PC 38**
See also EW 5; RGWL 2
Middleton, Christopher 1926- .... **CLC 13**
See also CA 13-16R; CANR 29, 54; CP 7; DLB 40
Middleton, Richard (Barham)
1882-1911 .... **TCLC 56**
See also CA 187; DLB 156; HGG
Middleton, Stanley 1919- .... **CLC 7, 38**
See also CA 25-28R; CAAS 23; CANR 21, 46, 81; CN 7; DLB 14
Middleton, Thomas 1580-1627 .... **LC 33; DC 5**
See also BRW 2; DAM DRAM, MST; DLB 58; RGEL 2
Migueis, Jose Rodrigues 1901- .... **CLC 10**
Mikszath, Kalman 1847-1910 .... **TCLC 31**
See also CA 170
Miles, Jack .... **CLC 100**
See also CA 200
Miles, John Russiano
See Miles, Jack
Miles, Josephine (Louise)
1911-1985 .... **CLC 1, 2, 14, 34, 39**
See also CA 1-4R; 116; CANR 2, 55; DAM POET; DLB 48
Militant
See Sandburg, Carl (August)
Mill, Harriet (Hardy) Taylor
1807-1858 .... **NCLC 102**
See also FW
Mill, John Stuart 1806-1873 .... **NCLC 11, 58**
See also CDBLB 1832-1890; DLB 55, 190; FW 1; RGEL 2

Millar, Kenneth 1915-1983 .... **CLC 14**
See also Macdonald, Ross
See also CA 9-12R; 110; CANR 16, 63, 107; CMW 4; CPW; DA3; DAM POP; DLB 2, 226; DLBD 6; DLBY 1983; MTCW 1, 2
Millay, E. Vincent
See Millay, Edna St. Vincent
Millay, Edna St. Vincent
1892-1950 ... **TCLC 4, 49; PC 6; WLCS**
See also Boyd, Nancy
See also AMW; CA 104; 130; CDALB 1917-1929; DA; DA3; DAB; DAC; DAM MST, POET; DLB 45, 249; EXPP; MAWW; MTCW 1, 2; PAB; PFS 3; RGAL 4; WP
Miller, Arthur 1915- ...... **CLC 1, 2, 6, 10, 15, 26, 47, 78; DC 1; WLC**
See also AAYA 15; AITN 1; AMW; CA 1-4R; CABS 3; CAD; CANR 2, 30, 54, 76; CD 5; CDALB 1941-1968; DA; DA3; DAB; DAC; DAM DRAM, MST; DFS 1, 3; DLB 7; LAIT 4; MTCW 1, 2; RGAL 4; WYAS 1
Miller, Henry (Valentine)
1891-1980 .... **CLC 1, 2, 4, 9, 14, 43, 84; WLC**
See also AMW; BPFB 2; CA 9-12R; 97-100; CANR 33, 64; CDALB 1929-1941; DA; DA3; DAB; DAC; DAM MST, NOV; DLB 4, 9; DLBY 1980; MTCW 1, 2; RGAL 4
Miller, Jason 1939(?)-2001 .... **CLC 2**
See also AITN 1; CA 73-76; 197; CAD; DFS 12; DLB 7
Miller, Sue 1943- .... **CLC 44**
See also BEST 90:3; CA 139; CANR 59, 91; DA3; DAM POP; DLB 143
Miller, Walter M(ichael, Jr.)
1923-1996 .... **CLC 4, 30**
See also BPFB 2; CA 85-88; CANR 108; DLB 8; SCFW; SFW 4
Millett, Kate 1934- .... **CLC 67**
See also AITN 1; CA 73-76; CANR 32, 53, 76; DA3; DLB 246; FW; GLL 1; MTCW 1, 2
Millhauser, Steven (Lewis) 1943- .... **CLC 21, 54, 109**
See also CA 110; 111; CANR 63; CN 7; DA3; DLB 2; FANT; INT CA-111; MTCW 2
Millin, Sarah Gertrude 1889-1968 ... **CLC 49**
See also CA 102; 93-96; DLB 225
Milne, A(lan) A(lexander)
1882-1956 .... **TCLC 6, 88**
See also BRWS 5; CA 104; 133; CLR 1, 26; CMW 4; CWRI 5; DA3; DAB; DAC; DAM MST; DLB 10, 77, 100, 160; FANT; MAICYA 1, 2; MTCW 1, 2; RGEL 2; SATA 100; WCH; YABC 1
Milner, Ron(ald) 1938- .... **CLC 56; BLC 3**
See also AITN 1; BW 1; CA 73-76; CAD; CANR 24, 81; CD 5; DAM MULT; DLB 38; MTCW 1
Milnes, Richard Monckton
1809-1885 .... **NCLC 61**
See also DLB 32, 184
Milosz, Czeslaw 1911- ...... **CLC 5, 11, 22, 31, 56, 82; PC 8; WLCS**
See also CA 81-84; CANR 23, 51, 91; CD-WLB 4; CWW 2; DA3; DAM MST, POET; DLB 215; EW 13; MTCW 1, 2; RGWL 2
Milton, John 1608-1674 ..... **LC 9, 43; PC 19, 29; WLC**
See also BRW 2; BRWR 2; CDBLB 1660-1789; DA; DA3; DAB; DAC; DAM MST, POET; DLB 131, 151; EFS 1; EXPP; LAIT 1; PAB; PFS 3; RGEL 2; WLIT 3; WP

Min, Anchee 1957- .... **CLC 86**
See also CA 146; CANR 94
Minehaha, Cornelius
See Wedekind, (Benjamin) Frank(lin)
Miner, Valerie 1947- .... **CLC 40**
See also CA 97-100; CANR 59; FW; GLL 2
Minimo, Duca
See D'Annunzio, Gabriele
Minot, Susan 1956- .... **CLC 44**
See also AMWS 6; CA 134; CN 7
Minus, Ed 1938- .... **CLC 39**
See also CA 185
Miranda, Javier
See Bioy Casares, Adolfo
See also CWW 2
Mirbeau, Octave 1848-1917 .... **TCLC 55**
See also DLB 123, 192; GFL 1789 to the Present
Miro (Ferrer), Gabriel (Francisco Victor)
1879-1930 .... **TCLC 5**
See also CA 104; 185
Misharin, Alexandr .... **CLC 59**
Mishima, Yukio ... **CLC 2, 4, 6, 9, 27; DC 1; SSC 4**
See also Hiraoka, Kimitake
See also BPFB 2; DLB 182; GLL 1; MJW; MTCW 2; RGSF 2; RGWL 2; SSFS 5, 12
Mistral, Frederic 1830-1914 .... **TCLC 51**
See also CA 122; GFL 1789 to the Present
Mistral, Gabriela
See Godoy Alcayaga, Lucila
See also DNFS 1; LAW; RGWL 2; WP
Mistry, Rohinton 1952- .... **CLC 71**
See also CA 141; CANR 86; CCA 1; CN 7; DAC; SSFS 6
Mitchell, Clyde
See Ellison, Harlan (Jay); Silverberg, Robert
Mitchell, James Leslie 1901-1935
See Gibbon, Lewis Grassic
See also CA 104; 188; DLB 15
Mitchell, Joni 1943- .... **CLC 12**
See also CA 112; CCA 1
Mitchell, Joseph (Quincy)
1908-1996 .... **CLC 98**
See also CA 77-80; 152; CANR 69; CN 7; CSW; DLB 185; DLBY 1996
Mitchell, Margaret (Munnerlyn)
1900-1949 .... **TCLC 11**
See also AAYA 23; BPFB 2; BYA 1; CA 109; 125; CANR 55, 94; CDALBS; DA3; DAM NOV, POP; DLB 9; LAIT 2; MTCW 1, 2; NFS 9; RGAL 4; RHW; WYAS 1; YAW
Mitchell, Peggy
See Mitchell, Margaret (Munnerlyn)
Mitchell, S(ilas) Weir 1829-1914 .... **TCLC 36**
See also CA 165; DLB 202; RGAL 4
Mitchell, W(illiam) O(rmond)
1914-1998 .... **CLC 25**
See also CA 77-80; 165; CANR 15, 43; CN 7; DAC; DAM MST; DLB 88
Mitchell, William 1879-1936 .... **TCLC 81**
Mitford, Mary Russell 1787-1855 .... **NCLC 4**
See also DLB 110, 116; RGEL 2
Mitford, Nancy 1904-1973 .... **CLC 44**
See also CA 9-12R; DLB 191; RGEL 2
Miyamoto, (Chujo) Yuriko
1899-1951 .... **TCLC 37**
See also Miyamoto Yuriko
See also CA 170, 174
Miyamoto Yuriko
See Miyamoto, (Chujo) Yuriko
See also DLB 180
Miyazawa, Kenji 1896-1933 .... **TCLC 76**
See also CA 157
Mizoguchi, Kenji 1898-1956 .... **TCLC 72**
See also CA 167

Mo, Timothy (Peter) 1950(?)- ... **CLC 46, 134**
See also CA 117; CN 7; DLB 194; MTCW 1; WLIT 4

Modarressi, Taghi (M.) 1931-1997 ... **CLC 44**
See also CA 121; 134; INT 134

Modiano, Patrick (Jean) 1945- .... **CLC 18**
See also CA 85-88; CANR 17, 40; CWW 2; DLB 83

Mofolo, Thomas (Mokopu) 1875(?)-1948 .... **TCLC 22; BLC 3**
See also AFW; CA 121; 153; CANR 83; DAM MULT; DLB 225; MTCW 2; WLIT 2

Mohr, Nicholasa 1938- .... **CLC 12; HLC 2**
See also AAYA 8; CA 49-52; CANR 1, 32, 64; CLR 22; DAM MULT; DLB 145; HW 1, 2; JRDA; LAIT 5; MAICYA 2; MAICYAS 1; RGAL 4; SAAS 8; SATA 8, 97; SATA-Essay 113; WYA; YAW

Mojtabai, A(nn) G(race) 1938- ..... **CLC 5, 9, 15, 29**
See also CA 85-88; CANR 88

Moliere 1622-1673 ..... **LC 10, 28, 64; DC 13; WLC**
See also DA; DA3; DAB; DAC; DAM DRAM, MST; DFS 13; EW 3; GFL Beginnings to 1789; RGWL 2

Molin, Charles
See Mayne, William (James Carter)

Molnar, Ferenc 1878-1952 .... **TCLC 20**
See also CA 109; 153; CANR 83; CDWLB 4; DAM DRAM; DLB 215; RGWL 2

Momaday, N(avarre) Scott 1934- ...... **CLC 2, 19, 85, 95; PC 25; WLCS**
See also AAYA 11; AMWS 4; ANW; BPFB 2; CA 25-28R; CANR 14, 34, 68; CDALBS; CN 7; CPW; DA; DA3; DAB; DAC; DAM MST, MULT, NOV, POP; DLB 143, 175, 256; EXPP; INT CANR-14; LAIT 4; MTCW 1, 2; NFS 10; NNAL; PFS 2, 11; RGAL 4; SATA 48; SATA-Brief 30; WP; YAW

Monette, Paul 1945-1995 .... **CLC 82**
See also AMWS 10; CA 139; 147; CN 7; GLL 1

Monroe, Harriet 1860-1936 .... **TCLC 12**
See also CA 109; DLB 54, 91

Monroe, Lyle
See Heinlein, Robert A(nson)

Montagu, Elizabeth 1720-1800 .... **NCLC 7**
See also FW

Montagu, Mary (Pierrepont) Wortley 1689-1762 .... **LC 9, 57; PC 16**
See also DLB 95, 101; RGEL 2

Montagu, W. H.
See Coleridge, Samuel Taylor

Montague, John (Patrick) 1929- ..... **CLC 13, 46**
See also CA 9-12R; CANR 9, 69; CP 7; DLB 40; MTCW 1; PFS 12; RGEL 2

Montaigne, Michel (Eyquem) de 1533-1592 .... **LC 8; WLC**
See also DA; DAB; DAC; DAM MST; EW 2; GFL Beginnings to 1789; RGWL 2

Montale, Eugenio 1896-1981 ... **CLC 7, 9, 18; PC 13**
See also CA 17-20R; 104; CANR 30; DLB 114; EW 11; MTCW 1; RGWL 2

Montesquieu, Charles-Louis de Secondat 1689-1755 .... **LC 7, 69**
See also EW 3; GFL Beginnings to 1789

Montessori, Maria 1870-1952 ...... **TCLC 103**
See also CA 115; 147

Montgomery, (Robert) Bruce 1921(?)-1978
See Crispin, Edmund
See also CA 179; 104; CMW 4

Montgomery, L(ucy) M(aud) 1874-1942 .... **TCLC 51**
See also AAYA 12; BYA 1; CA 108; 137; CLR 8; DA3; DAC; DAM MST; DLB 92; DLBD 14; JRDA; MAICYA 1, 2; MTCW 2; RGEL 2; SATA 100; WCH; WYA; YABC 1

Montgomery, Marion H., Jr. 1925- .... **CLC 7**
See also AITN 1; CA 1-4R; CANR 3, 48; CSW; DLB 6

Montgomery, Max
See Davenport, Guy (Mattison, Jr.)

Montherlant, Henry (Milon) de 1896-1972 .... **CLC 8, 19**
See also CA 85-88; 37-40R; DAM DRAM; DLB 72; EW 11; GFL 1789 to the Present; MTCW 1

Monty Python
See Chapman, Graham; Cleese, John (Marwood); Gilliam, Terry (Vance); Idle, Eric; Jones, Terence Graham Parry; Palin, Michael (Edward)
See also AAYA 7

Moodie, Susanna (Strickland) 1803-1885 .... **NCLC 14**
See also DLB 99

Moody, Hiram F. III 1961-
See Moody, Rick
See also CA 138; CANR 64

Moody, Minerva
See Alcott, Louisa May

Moody, Rick .... **CLC 147**
See also Moody, Hiram F. III

Moody, William Vaughan 1869-1910 .... **TCLC 105**
See also CA 110; 178; DLB 7, 54; RGAL 4

Mooney, Edward 1951-
See Mooney, Ted
See also CA 130

Mooney, Ted .... **CLC 25**
See also Mooney, Edward

Moorcock, Michael (John) 1939- ...... **CLC 5, 27, 58**
See also Bradbury, Edward P.
See also AAYA 26; CA 45-48; CAAS 5; CANR 2, 17, 38, 64; CN 7; DLB 14, 231; FANT; MTCW 1, 2; SATA 93; SFW 4; SUFW

Moore, Brian 1921-1999 ... **CLC 1, 3, 5, 7, 8, 19, 32, 90**
See also Bryan, Michael
See also CA 1-4R; 174; CANR 1, 25, 42, 63; CCA 1; CN 7; DAB; DAC; DAM MST; DLB 251; FANT; MTCW 1, 2; RGEL 2

Moore, Edward
See Muir, Edwin
See also RGEL 2

Moore, G. E. 1873-1958 .... **TCLC 89**

Moore, George Augustus 1852-1933 .... **TCLC 7; SSC 19**
See also BRW 6; CA 104; 177; DLB 10, 18, 57, 135; RGEL 2; RGSF 2

Moore, Lorrie .... **CLC 39, 45, 68**
See also Moore, Marie Lorena
See also AMWS 10; DLB 234

Moore, Marianne (Craig) 1887-1972 .... **CLC 1, 2, 4, 8, 10, 13, 19, 47; PC 4; WLCS**
See also AMW; CA 1-4R; 33-36R; CANR 3, 61; CDALB 1929-1941; DA; DA3; DAB; DAC; DAM MST, POET; DLB 45; DLBD 7; EXPP; MAWW; MTCW 1, 2; PAB; PFS 14; RGAL 4; SATA 20; WP

Moore, Marie Lorena 1957-
See Moore, Lorrie
See also CA 116; CANR 39, 83; CN 7; DLB 234

Moore, Thomas 1779-1852 .... **NCLC 6, 110**
See also DLB 96, 144; RGEL 2

Moorhouse, Frank 1938- .... **SSC 40**
See also CA 118; CANR 92; CN 7; RGSF 2

Mora, Pat(ricia) 1942-
See also CA 129; CANR 57, 81; CLR 58; DAM MULT; DLB 209; HLC 2; HW 1, 2; MAICYA 2; SATA 92

Moraga, Cherrie 1952- .... **CLC 126**
See also CA 131; CANR 66; DAM MULT; DLB 82, 249; FW; GLL 1

Morand, Paul 1888-1976 .... **CLC 41; SSC 22**
See also CA 184; 69-72; DLB 65

Morante, Elsa 1918-1985 .... **CLC 8, 47**
See also CA 85-88; 117; CANR 35; DLB 177; MTCW 1, 2; RGWL 2

Moravia, Alberto .... **CLC 2, 7, 11, 27, 46; SSC 26**
See also Pincherle, Alberto
See also DLB 177; EW 12; MTCW 2; RGSF 2; RGWL 2

More, Hannah 1745-1833 .... **NCLC 27**
See also DLB 107, 109, 116, 158; RGEL 2

More, Henry 1614-1687 .... **LC 9**
See also DLB 126, 252

More, Sir Thomas 1478(?)-1535 .... **LC 10, 32**
See also BRWS 7; DLB 136; RGEL 2

Moreas, Jean .... **TCLC 18**
See also Papadiamantopoulos, Johannes
See also GFL 1789 to the Present

Morgan, Berry 1919- .... **CLC 6**
See also CA 49-52; DLB 6

Morgan, Claire
See Highsmith, (Mary) Patricia
See also GLL 1

Morgan, Edwin (George) 1920- .... **CLC 31**
See also CA 5-8R; CANR 3, 43, 90; CP 7; DLB 27

Morgan, (George) Frederick 1922- .. **CLC 23**
See also CA 17-20R; CANR 21; CP 7

Morgan, Harriet
See Mencken, H(enry) L(ouis)

Morgan, Jane
See Cooper, James Fenimore

Morgan, Janet 1945- .... **CLC 39**
See also CA 65-68

Morgan, Lady 1776(?)-1859 .... **NCLC 29**
See also DLB 116, 158; RGEL 2

Morgan, Robin (Evonne) 1941- .... **CLC 2**
See also CA 69-72; CANR 29, 68; FW; GLL 2; MTCW 1; SATA 80

Morgan, Scott
See Kuttner, Henry

Morgan, Seth 1949(?)-1990 .... **CLC 65**
See also CA 185; 132

Morgenstern, Christian (Otto Josef Wolfgang) 1871-1914 .... **TCLC 8**
See also CA 105; 191

Morgenstern, S.
See Goldman, William (W.)

Mori, Rintaro
See Mori Ogai
See also CA 110

Moricz, Zsigmond 1879-1942 .... **TCLC 33**
See also CA 165; DLB 215

Morike, Eduard (Friedrich) 1804-1875 .... **NCLC 10**
See also DLB 133; RGWL 2

Mori Ogai
See Mori Ogai
See also DLB 180

Mori Ogai 1862-1922 .... **TCLC 14**
See also Mori Ogai; Ogai
See also CA 164; TWA

Moritz, Karl Philipp 1756-1793 .... **LC 2**
See also DLB 94

Morland, Peter Henry
See Faust, Frederick (Schiller)

Morley, Christopher (Darlington)
1890-1957 .... **TCLC 87**
See also CA 112; DLB 9; RGAL 4

Morren, Theophil
See Hofmannsthal, Hugo von

Morris, Bill 1952- .... **CLC 76**

Morris, Julian
See West, Morris L(anglo)

Morris, Steveland Judkins 1950(?)-
See Wonder, Stevie
See also CA 111

Morris, William 1834-1896 .... **NCLC 4**
See also BRW 5; CDBLB 1832-1890; DLB 18, 35, 57, 156, 178, 184; FANT; RGEL 2; SFW 4; SUFW

Morris, Wright 1910-1998 .. **CLC 1, 3, 7, 18, 37**
See also AMW; CA 9-12R; 167; CANR 21, 81; CN 7; DLB 2, 206, 218; DLBY 1981; MTCW 1, 2; RGAL 4; TCLC 107; TCWW 2

Morrison, Arthur 1863-1945 .... **TCLC 72; SSC 40**
See also CA 120; 157; CMW 4; DLB 70, 135, 197; RGEL 2

Morrison, Chloe Anthony Wofford
See Morrison, Toni

Morrison, James Douglas 1943-1971
See Morrison, Jim
See also CA 73-76; CANR 40

Morrison, Jim .... **CLC 17**
See also Morrison, James Douglas

Morrison, Toni 1931- . **CLC 4, 10, 22, 55, 81, 87; BLC 3**
See also AAYA 1, 22; AFAW 1, 2; AMWS 3; BPFB 2; BW 2, 3; CA 29-32R; CANR 27, 42, 67; CDALB 1968-1988; CN 7; CPW; DA; DA3; DAB; DAC; DAM MST, MULT, NOV, POP; DLB 6, 33, 143; DLBY 1981; EXPN; FW; LAIT 2, 4; MAWW; MTCW 1, 2; NFS 1, 6, 8, 14; RGAL 4; RHW; SATA 57; SSFS 5; YAW

Morrison, Van 1945- .... **CLC 21**
See also CA 116; 168

Morrissy, Mary 1958- .... **CLC 99**

Mortimer, John (Clifford) 1923- ..... **CLC 28, 43**
See also CA 13-16R; CANR 21, 69, 109; CD 5; CDBLB 1960 to Present; CMW 4; CN 7; CPW; DA3; DAM DRAM, POP; DLB 13, 245; INT CANR-21; MSW; MTCW 1, 2; RGEL 2

Mortimer, Penelope (Ruth)
1918-1999 .... **CLC 5**
See also CA 57-60; 187; CANR 45, 88; CN 7

Mortimer, Sir John
See Mortimer, John (Clifford)

Morton, Anthony
See Creasey, John

Morton, Thomas 1579(?)-1647(?) .... **LC 72**
See also DLB 24; RGEL 2

Mosca, Gaetano 1858-1941 .... **TCLC 75**

Mosher, Howard Frank 1943- .... **CLC 62**
See also CA 139; CANR 65

Mosley, Nicholas 1923- .... **CLC 43, 70**
See also CA 69-72; CANR 41, 60, 108; CN 7; DLB 14, 207

Mosley, Walter 1952- .... **CLC 97; BLCS**
See also AAYA 17; BPFB 2; BW 2; CA 142; CANR 57, 92; CMW 4; CPW; DA3; DAM MULT, POP; MSW; MTCW 2

Moss, Howard 1922-1987 . **CLC 7, 14, 45, 50**
See also CA 1-4R; 123; CANR 1, 44; DAM POET; DLB 5

Mossgiel, Rab
See Burns, Robert

Motion, Andrew (Peter) 1952- .... **CLC 47**
See also BRWS 7; CA 146; CANR 90; CP 7; DLB 40

Motley, Willard (Francis)
1912-1965 .... **CLC 18**
See also BW 1; CA 117; 106; CANR 88; DLB 76, 143

Motoori, Norinaga 1730-1801 .... **NCLC 45**

Mott, Michael (Charles Alston)
1930- .... **CLC 15, 34**
See also CA 5-8R; CAAS 7; CANR 7, 29

Mountain Wolf Woman 1884-1960 ... **CLC 92**
See also CA 144; CANR 90; NNAL

Moure, Erin 1955- .... **CLC 88**
See also CA 113; CP 7; CWP; DLB 60

Mowat, Farley (McGill) 1921- .... **CLC 26**
See also AAYA 1; BYA 2; CA 1-4R; CANR 4, 24, 42, 68, 108; CLR 20; CPW; DAC; DAM MST; DLB 68; INT CANR-24; JRDA; MAICYA 1; MTCW 1, 2; SATA 3, 55; YAW

Mowatt, Anna Cora 1819-1870 ..... **NCLC 74**
See also RGAL 4

Moyers, Bill 1934- .... **CLC 74**
See also AITN 2; CA 61-64; CANR 31, 52

Mphahlele, Es'kia
See Mphahlele, Ezekiel
See also AFW; CDWLB 3; DLB 125, 225; RGSF 2; SSFS 11

Mphahlele, Ezekiel 1919- .... **CLC 25, 133; BLC 3**
See also Mphahlele, Es'kia
See also BW 2, 3; CA 81-84; CANR 26, 76; CN 7; DA3; DAM MULT; MTCW 2; SATA 119

Mqhayi, S(amuel) E(dward) K(rune Loliwe)
1875-1945 .... **TCLC 25; BLC 3**
See also CA 153; CANR 87; DAM MULT

Mrozek, Slawomir 1930- .... **CLC 3, 13**
See also CA 13-16R; CAAS 10; CANR 29; CDWLB 4; CWW 2; DLB 232; MTCW 1

Mrs. Belloc-Lowndes
See Lowndes, Marie Adelaide (Belloc)

M'Taggart, John M'Taggart Ellis
See McTaggart, John McTaggart Ellis

Mtwa, Percy (?)- .... **CLC 47**

Mueller, Lisel 1924- .... **CLC 13, 51; PC 33**
See also CA 93-96; CP 7; DLB 105; PFS 9, 13

Muggeridge, Malcolm (Thomas)
1903-1990 .... **TCLC 120**
See also AITN 1; CA 101; CANR 33, 63; MTCW 1, 2

Muir, Edwin 1887-1959 .... **TCLC 2, 87**
See also Moore, Edward
See also BRWS 6; CA 104; 193; DLB 20, 100, 191; RGEL 2

Muir, John 1838-1914 .... **TCLC 28**
See also AMWS 9; ANW; CA 165; DLB 186

Mujica Lainez, Manuel 1910-1984 ... **CLC 31**
See also Lainez, Manuel Mujica
See also CA 81-84; 112; CANR 32; HW 1

Mukherjee, Bharati 1940- .... **CLC 53, 115; AAL; SSC 38**
See also BEST 89:2; CA 107; CANR 45, 72; CN 7; DAM NOV; DLB 60, 218; DNFS 1, 2; FW; MTCW 1, 2; RGAL 4; RGSF 2; SSFS 7

Muldoon, Paul 1951- .... **CLC 32, 72**
See also BRWS 4; CA 113; 129; CANR 52, 91; CP 7; DAM POET; DLB 40; INT 129; PFS 7

Mulisch, Harry 1927- .... **CLC 42**
See also CA 9-12R; CANR 6, 26, 56

Mull, Martin 1943- .... **CLC 17**
See also CA 105

Muller, Wilhelm .... **NCLC 73**

Mulock, Dinah Maria
See Craik, Dinah Maria (Mulock)
See also RGEL 2

Munford, Robert 1737(?)-1783 .... **LC 5**
See also DLB 31

Mungo, Raymond 1946- .... **CLC 72**
See also CA 49-52; CANR 2

Munro, Alice 1931- .... **CLC 6, 10, 19, 50, 95; SSC 3; WLCS**
See also AITN 2; BPFB 2; CA 33-36R; CANR 33, 53, 75; CCA 1; CN 7; DA3; DAC; DAM MST, NOV; DLB 53; MTCW 1, 2; RGEL 2; RGSF 2; SATA 29; SSFS 5, 13

Munro, H(ector) H(ugh) 1870-1916
See Saki
See also CA 104; 130; CANR 104; CDBLB 1890-1914; DA; DA3; DAB; DAC; DAM MST, NOV; DLB 34, 162; EXPS; MTCW 1, 2; RGEL 2; WLC

Murakami, Haruki 1949- .... **CLC 150**
See also Murakami Haruki
See also CA 165; CANR 102; MJW; SFW 4

Murakami Haruki
See Murakami, Haruki
See also DLB 182

Murasaki, Lady
See Murasaki Shikibu

Murasaki Shikibu 978(?)-1026(?) ... **CMLC 1**
See also EFS 2; RGWL 2

Murdoch, (Jean) Iris 1919-1999 ... **CLC 1, 2, 3, 4, 6, 8, 11, 15, 22, 31, 51**
See also BRWS 1; CA 13-16R; 179; CANR 8, 43, 68, 103; CDBLB 1960 to Present; CN 7; DA3; DAB; DAC; DAM MST, NOV; DLB 14, 194, 233; INT CANR-8; MTCW 1, 2; RGEL 2; WLIT 4

Murfree, Mary Noailles 1850-1922 ... **SSC 22**
See also CA 122; 176; DLB 12, 74; RGAL 4

Murnau, Friedrich Wilhelm
See Plumpe, Friedrich Wilhelm

Murphy, Richard 1927- .... **CLC 41**
See also BRWS 5; CA 29-32R; CP 7; DLB 40

Murphy, Sylvia 1937- .... **CLC 34**
See also CA 121

Murphy, Thomas (Bernard) 1935- ... **CLC 51**
See also CA 101

Murray, Albert L. 1916- .... **CLC 73**
See also BW 2; CA 49-52; CANR 26, 52, 78; CSW; DLB 38

Murray, James Augustus Henry
1837-1915 .... **TCLC 117**

Murray, Judith Sargent
1751-1820 .... **NCLC 63**
See also DLB 37, 200

Murray, Les(lie Allan) 1938- .... **CLC 40**
See also BRWS 7; CA 21-24R; CANR 11, 27, 56, 103; CP 7; DAM POET; DLBY 01; RGEL 2

Murry, J. Middleton
See Murry, John Middleton

Murry, John Middleton
1889-1957 .... **TCLC 16**
See also CA 118; DLB 149

Musgrave, Susan 1951- .... **CLC 13, 54**
See also CA 69-72; CANR 45, 84; CCA 1; CP 7; CWP

Musil, Robert (Edler von)
1880-1942 .... **TCLC 12, 68; SSC 18**
See also CA 109; CANR 55, 84; CDWLB 2; DLB 81, 124; EW 9; MTCW 2; RGSF 2; RGWL 2

Muske, Carol .... **CLC 90**
See also Muske-Dukes, Carol (Anne)

Muske-Dukes, Carol (Anne) 1945-
See Muske, Carol
See also CA 65-68; CANR 32, 70; CWP

Musset, (Louis Charles) Alfred de
1810-1857 .... **NCLC 7**
See also DLB 192, 217; EW 6; GFL 1789 to the Present; RGWL 2; TWA

Mussolini, Benito (Amilcare Andrea)
1883-1945 .... **TCLC 96**
See also CA 116

My Brother's Brother
See Chekhov, Anton (Pavlovich)

Myers, L(eopold) H(amilton)
1881-1944 .... **TCLC 59**
See also CA 157; DLB 15; RGEL 2

Myers, Walter Dean 1937- .. **CLC 35; BLC 3**
See also AAYA 4, 23; BW 2; BYA 6, 8, 11; CA 33-36R; CANR 20, 42, 67, 108; CLR 4, 16, 35; DAM MULT, NOV; DLB 33; INT CANR-20; JRDA; LAIT 5; MAICYA 1, 2; MAICYAS 1; MTCW 2; SAAS 2; SATA 41, 71, 109; SATA-Brief 27; WYA; YAW

Myers, Walter M.
See Myers, Walter Dean

Myles, Symon
See Follett, Ken(neth Martin)

Nabokov, Vladimir (Vladimirovich)
1899-1977 .... **CLC 1, 2, 3, 6, 8, 11, 15, 23, 44, 46, 64; SSC 11; WLC**
See also AMW; AMWR 1; BPFB 2; CA 5-8R; 69-72; CANR 20, 102; CDALB 1941-1968; DA; DA3; DAB; DAC; DAM MST, NOV; DLB 2, 244; DLBD 3; DLBY 1980, 1991; EXPS; MTCW 1, 2; NFS 9; RGAL 4; RGSF 2; SSFS 6; TCLC 108

Naevius c. 265B.C.-201B.C. .... **CMLC 37**
See also DLB 211

Nagai, Kafu .... **TCLC 51**
See also Nagai, Sokichi
See also DLB 180

Nagai, Sokichi 1879-1959
See Nagai, Kafu
See also CA 117

Nagy, Laszlo 1925-1978 .... **CLC 7**
See also CA 129; 112

Naidu, Sarojini 1879-1949 .... **TCLC 80**
See also RGEL 2

Naipaul, Shiva(dhar Srinivasa)
1945-1985 .... **CLC 32, 39**
See also CA 110; 112; 116; CANR 33; DA3; DAM NOV; DLB 157; DLBY 1985; MTCW 1, 2

Naipaul, V(idiadhar) S(urajprasad)
1932- .... **CLC 4, 7, 9, 13, 18, 37, 105; SSC 38**
See also BPFB 2; BRWS 1; CA 1-4R; CANR 1, 33, 51, 91; CDBLB 1960 to Present; CDWLB 3; CN 7; DA3; DAB; DAC; DAM MST, NOV; DLB 125, 204, 207; DLBY 1985, 2001; MTCW 1, 2; RGEL 2; RGSF 2; WLIT 4

Nakos, Lilika 1899(?)- .... **CLC 29**

Narayan, R(asipuram) K(rishnaswami)
1906-2001 . **CLC 7, 28, 47, 121; SSC 25**
See also BPFB 2; CA 81-84; 196; CANR 33, 61; CN 7; DA3; DAM NOV; DNFS 1; MTCW 1, 2; RGEL 2; RGSF 2; SATA 62; SSFS 5

Nash, (Frediric) Ogden 1902-1971 . **CLC 23; PC 21**
See also CA 13-14; 29-32R; CANR 34, 61; CAP 1; DAM POET; DLB 11; MAICYA 1, 2; MTCW 1, 2; RGAL 4; SATA 2, 46; TCLC 109; WP

Nashe, Thomas 1567-1601(?) .... **LC 41**
See also DLB 167; RGEL 2

Nathan, Daniel
See Dannay, Frederic

Nathan, George Jean 1882-1958 .... **TCLC 18**
See also Hatteras, Owen
See also CA 114; 169; DLB 137

Natsume, Kinnosuke
See Natsume, Soseki

Natsume, Soseki 1867-1916 .... **TCLC 2, 10**
See also Natsume Soseki; Soseki
See also CA 104; 195; RGWL 2

Natsume Soseki
See Natsume, Soseki
See also DLB 180

Natti, (Mary) Lee 1919-
See Kingman, Lee
See also CA 5-8R; CANR 2

Navarre, Marguerite de
See de Navarre, Marguerite

Naylor, Gloria 1950- . **CLC 28, 52, 156; BLC 3; WLCS**
See also AAYA 6, 39; AFAW 1, 2; AMWS 8; BW 2, 3; CA 107; CANR 27, 51, 74; CN 7; CPW; DA; DA3; DAC; DAM MST, MULT, NOV, POP; DLB 173; FW; MTCW 1, 2; NFS 4, 7; RGAL 4

Neff, Debra .... **CLC 59**

Neihardt, John Gneisenau
1881-1973 .... **CLC 32**
See also CA 13-14; CANR 65; CAP 1; DLB 9, 54, 256; LAIT 2

Nekrasov, Nikolai Alekseevich
1821-1878 .... **NCLC 11**

Nelligan, Emile 1879-1941 .... **TCLC 14**
See also CA 114; DLB 92

Nelson, Willie 1933- .... **CLC 17**
See also CA 107

Nemerov, Howard (Stanley)
1920-1991 .... **CLC 2, 6, 9, 36; PC 24**
See also AMW; CA 1-4R; 134; CABS 2; CANR 1, 27, 53; DAM POET; DLB 5, 6; DLBY 1983; INT CANR-27; MTCW 1, 2; PFS 10, 14; RGAL 4

Neruda, Pablo 1904-1973 .. **CLC 1, 2, 5, 7, 9, 28, 62; HLC 2; PC 4; WLC**
See also CA 19-20; 45-48; CAP 2; DA; DA3; DAB; DAC; DAM MST, MULT, POET; DNFS 2; HW 1; LAW; MTCW 1, 2; PFS 11; RGWL 2; WLIT 1; WP

Nerval, Gerard de 1808-1855 ... **NCLC 1, 67; PC 13; SSC 18**
See also DLB 217; EW 6; GFL 1789 to the Present; RGSF 2; RGWL 2

Nervo, (Jose) Amado (Ruiz de)
1870-1919 .... **TCLC 11; HLCS 2**
See also CA 109; 131; HW 1; LAW

Nesbit, Malcolm
See Chester, Alfred

Nessi, Pio Baroja y
See Baroja (y Nessi), Pio

Nestroy, Johann 1801-1862 .... **NCLC 42**
See also DLB 133; RGWL 2

Netterville, Luke
See O'Grady, Standish (James)

Neufeld, John (Arthur) 1938- .... **CLC 17**
See also AAYA 11; CA 25-28R; CANR 11, 37, 56; CLR 52; MAICYA 1, 2; SAAS 3; SATA 6, 81; SATA-Essay 131; YAW

Neumann, Alfred 1895-1952 .... **TCLC 100**
See also CA 183; DLB 56

Neumann, Ferenc
See Molnar, Ferenc

Neville, Emily Cheney 1919- .... **CLC 12**
See also BYA 2; CA 5-8R; CANR 3, 37, 85; JRDA; MAICYA 1, 2; SAAS 2; SATA 1; YAW

Newbound, Bernard Slade 1930-
See Slade, Bernard
See also CA 81-84; CANR 49; CD 5; DAM DRAM

Newby, P(ercy) H(oward)
1918-1997 .... **CLC 2, 13**
See also CA 5-8R; 161; CANR 32, 67; CN 7; DAM NOV; DLB 15; MTCW 1; RGEL 2

Newcastle
See Cavendish, Margaret Lucas

Newlove, Donald 1928- .... **CLC 6**
See also CA 29-32R; CANR 25

Newlove, John (Herbert) 1938- .... **CLC 14**
See also CA 21-24R; CANR 9, 25; CP 7

Newman, Charles 1938- .... **CLC 2, 8**
See also CA 21-24R; CANR 84; CN 7

Newman, Edwin (Harold) 1919- ...... **CLC 14**
See also AITN 1; CA 69-72; CANR 5

Newman, John Henry 1801-1890 . **NCLC 38, 99**
See also BRWS 7; DLB 18, 32, 55; RGEL 2

Newton, (Sir) Isaac 1642-1727 ...... **LC 35, 53**
See also DLB 252

Newton, Suzanne 1936- .... **CLC 35**
See also BYA 7; CA 41-44R; CANR 14; JRDA; SATA 5, 77

New York Dept. of Ed. .... **CLC 70**

Nexo, Martin Andersen
1869-1954 .... **TCLC 43**
See also DLB 214

Nezval, Vitezslav 1900-1958 .... **TCLC 44**
See also CA 123; CDWLB 4; DLB 215

Ng, Fae Myenne 1957(?)- .... **CLC 81**
See also CA 146

Ngema, Mbongeni 1955- .... **CLC 57**
See also BW 2; CA 143; CANR 84; CD 5

Ngugi, James T(hiong'o) .... **CLC 3, 7, 13**
See also Ngugi wa Thiong'o

Ngugi wa Thiong'o
See Ngugi wa Thiong'o
See also DLB 125

Ngugi wa Thiong'o 1938- .... **CLC 36; BLC 3**
See also Ngugi, James T(hiong'o); Ngugi wa Thiong'o
See also AFW; BW 2; CA 81-84; CANR 27, 58; CDWLB 3; DAM MULT, NOV; DNFS 2; MTCW 1, 2; RGEL 2

Nichol, B(arrie) P(hillip) 1944-1988 . **CLC 18**
See also CA 53-56; DLB 53; SATA 66

Nichols, John (Treadwell) 1940- .... **CLC 38**
See also CA 9-12R; CAAE 190; CAAS 2; CANR 6, 70; DLBY 1982; TCWW 2

Nichols, Leigh
See Koontz, Dean R(ay)

Nichols, Peter (Richard) 1927- .... **CLC 5, 36, 65**
See also CA 104; CANR 33, 86; CBD; CD 5; DLB 13, 245; MTCW 1

Nicholson, Linda ed. .... **CLC 65**

Ni Chuilleanain, Eilean 1942- .... **PC 34**
See also CA 126; CANR 53, 83; CP 7; CWP; DLB 40

Nicolas, F. R. E.
See Freeling, Nicolas

Niedecker, Lorine 1903-1970 ...... **CLC 10, 42**
See also CA 25-28; CAP 2; DAM POET; DLB 48

Nietzsche, Friedrich (Wilhelm)
1844-1900 .... **TCLC 10, 18, 55**
See also CA 107; 121; CDWLB 2; DLB 129; EW 7; RGWL 2

Nievo, Ippolito 1831-1861 .... **NCLC 22**

Nightingale, Anne Redmon 1943-
See Redmon, Anne
See also CA 103

Nightingale, Florence 1820-1910 ... **TCLC 85**
See also CA 188; DLB 166

Nijo Yoshimoto 1320-1388 .... **CMLC 49**
See also DLB 203

Nik. T. O.
See Annensky, Innokenty (Fyodorovich)

Nin, Anais 1903-1977 ..... **CLC 1, 4, 8, 11, 14, 60, 127; SSC 10**
See also AITN 2; AMWS 10; BPFB 2; CA 13-16R; 69-72; CANR 22, 53; DAM NOV, POP; DLB 2, 4, 152; GLL 2; MAWW; MTCW 1, 2; RGAL 4; RGSF 2

Nisbet, Robert A(lexander) 1913-1996 .... **TCLC 117**
See also CA 25-28R; 153; CANR 17; INT CANR-17

Nishida, Kitaro 1870-1945 .... **TCLC 83**

Nishiwaki, Junzaburo 1894-1982 .... **PC 15**
See also Nishiwaki, Junzaburo
See also CA 194; 107; MJW

Nishiwaki, Junzaburo 1894-1982
See Nishiwaki, Junzaburo
See also CA 194

Nissenson, Hugh 1933- .... **CLC 4, 9**
See also CA 17-20R; CANR 27, 108; CN 7; DLB 28

Niven, Larry .... **CLC 8**
See also Niven, Laurence Van Cott
See also AAYA 27; BPFB 2; BYA 10; DLB 8; SCFW 2

Niven, Laurence Van Cott 1938-
See Niven, Larry
See also CA 21-24R; CAAS 12; CANR 14, 44, 66; CPW; DAM POP; MTCW 1, 2; SATA 95; SFW 4

Nixon, Agnes Eckhardt 1927- .... **CLC 21**
See also CA 110

Nizan, Paul 1905-1940 .... **TCLC 40**
See also CA 161; DLB 72; GFL 1789 to the Present

Nkosi, Lewis 1936- .... **CLC 45; BLC 3**
See also BW 1, 3; CA 65-68; CANR 27, 81; CBD; CD 5; DAM MULT; DLB 157, 225

Nodier, (Jean) Charles (Emmanuel) 1780-1844 .... **NCLC 19**
See also DLB 119; GFL 1789 to the Present

Noguchi, Yone 1875-1947 .... **TCLC 80**

Nolan, Christopher 1965- .... **CLC 58**
See also CA 111; CANR 88

Noon, Jeff 1957- .... **CLC 91**
See also CA 148; CANR 83; SFW 4

Norden, Charles
See Durrell, Lawrence (George)

Nordhoff, Charles (Bernard) 1887-1947 .... **TCLC 23**
See also CA 108; DLB 9; LAIT 1; RHW 1; SATA 23

Norfolk, Lawrence 1963- .... **CLC 76**
See also CA 144; CANR 85; CN 7

Norman, Marsha 1947- .... **CLC 28; DC 8**
See also CA 105; CABS 3; CAD; CANR 41; CD 5; CSW; CWD; DAM DRAM; DFS 2; DLBY 1984; FW

Normyx
See Douglas, (George) Norman

Norris, (Benjamin) Frank(lin, Jr.) 1870-1902 .... **TCLC 24; SSC 28**
See also AMW; BPFB 2; CA 110; 160; CDALB 1865-1917; DLB 12, 71, 186; NFS 12; RGAL 4; TCWW 2; TUS

Norris, Leslie 1921- .... **CLC 14**
See also CA 11-12; CANR 14; CAP 1; CP 7; DLB 27, 256

North, Andrew
See Norton, Andre

North, Anthony
See Koontz, Dean R(ay)

North, Captain George
See Stevenson, Robert Louis (Balfour)

North, Milou
See Erdrich, Louise

Northrup, B. A.
See Hubbard, L(afayette) Ron(ald)

North Staffs
See Hulme, T(homas) E(rnest)

Northup, Solomon 1808-1863 ...... **NCLC 105**

Norton, Alice Mary
See Norton, Andre
See also MAICYA 1; SATA 1, 43

Norton, Andre 1912- .... **CLC 12**
See also Norton, Alice Mary
See also AAYA 14; BPFB 2; BYA 4, 10, 12; CA 1-4R; CANR 68; CLR 50; DLB 8, 52; JRDA; MAICYA 2; MTCW 1; SATA 91; SUFW; YAW

Norton, Caroline 1808-1877 .... **NCLC 47**
See also DLB 21, 159, 199

Norway, Nevil Shute 1899-1960
See Shute, Nevil
See also CA 102; 93-96; CANR 85; MTCW 2

Norwid, Cyprian Kamil 1821-1883 .... **NCLC 17**

Nosille, Nabrah
See Ellison, Harlan (Jay)

Nossack, Hans Erich 1901-1978 .... **CLC 6**
See also CA 93-96; 85-88; DLB 69

Nostradamus 1503-1566 .... **LC 27**

Nosu, Chuji
See Ozu, Yasujiro

Notenburg, Eleanora (Genrikhovna) von
See Guro, Elena

Nova, Craig 1945- .... **CLC 7, 31**
See also CA 45-48; CANR 2, 53

Novak, Joseph
See Kosinski, Jerzy (Nikodem)

Novalis 1772-1801 .... **NCLC 13**
See also CDWLB 2; DLB 90; EW 5; RGWL 2

Novis, Emile
See Weil, Simone (Adolphine)

Nowlan, Alden (Albert) 1933-1983 ... **CLC 15**
See also CA 9-12R; CANR 5; DAC; DAM MST; DLB 53; PFS 12

Noyes, Alfred 1880-1958 ...... **TCLC 7; PC 27**
See also CA 104; 188; DLB 20; EXPP; FANT; PFS 4; RGEL 2

Nunn, Kem .... **CLC 34**
See also CA 159

Nwapa, Flora 1931-1993 .... **CLC 133; BLCS**
See also BW 2; CA 143; CANR 83; CDWLB 3; CWRI 5; DLB 125; WLIT 2

Nye, Robert 1939- .... **CLC 13, 42**
See also CA 33-36R; CANR 29, 67, 107; CN 7; CP 7; CWRI 5; DAM NOV; DLB 14; FANT; HGG; MTCW 1; RHW; SATA 6

Nyro, Laura 1947-1997 .... **CLC 17**
See also CA 194

Oates, Joyce Carol 1938- .. **CLC 1, 2, 3, 6, 9, 11, 15, 19, 33, 52, 108, 134; SSC 6; WLC**
See also AAYA 15; AITN 1; AMWS 2; BEST 89:2; BPFB 2; BYA 11; CA 5-8R; CANR 25, 45, 74; CDALB 1968-1988; CN 7; CP 7; CPW; CWP; DA; DA3; DAB; DAC; DAM MST, NOV, POP; DLB 2, 5, 130; DLBY 1981; EXPS; FW; HGG; INT CANR-25; LAIT 4; MAWW; MTCW 1, 2; NFS 8; RGAL 4; RGSF 2; SSFS 1, 8

O'Brian, Patrick 1914-2000 .... **CLC 152**
See also CA 144; 187; CANR 74; CPW; MTCW 2; RHW

O'Brien, Darcy 1939-1998 .... **CLC 11**
See also CA 21-24R; 167; CANR 8, 59

O'Brien, E. G.
See Clarke, Arthur C(harles)

O'Brien, Edna 1936- ..... **CLC 3, 5, 8, 13, 36, 65, 116; SSC 10**
See also BRWS 5; CA 1-4R; CANR 6, 41, 65, 102; CDBLB 1960 to Present; CN 7; DA3; DAM NOV; DLB 14, 231; FW; MTCW 1, 2; RGSF 2; WLIT 4

O'Brien, Fitz-James 1828-1862 ..... **NCLC 21**
See also DLB 74; RGAL 4; SUFW

O'Brien, Flann .... **CLC 1, 4, 5, 7, 10, 47**
See also O Nuallain, Brian
See also BRWS 2; DLB 231; RGEL 2

O'Brien, Richard 1942- .... **CLC 17**
See also CA 124

O'Brien, (William) Tim(othy) 1946- . **CLC 7, 19, 40, 103**
See also AAYA 16; AMWS 5; CA 85-88; CANR 40, 58; CDALBS; CN 7; CPW; DA3; DAM POP; DLB 152; DLBD 9; DLBY 1980; MTCW 2; RGAL 4; SSFS 5

Obstfelder, Sigbjoern 1866-1900 .... **TCLC 23**
See also CA 123

O'Casey, Sean 1880-1964 ..... **CLC 1, 5, 9, 11, 15, 88; DC 12; WLCS**
See also BRW 7; CA 89-92; CANR 62; CBD; CDBLB 1914-1945; DA3; DAB; DAC; DAM DRAM, MST; DLB 10; MTCW 1, 2; RGEL 2; WLIT 4

O'Cathasaigh, Sean
See O'Casey, Sean

Occom, Samson 1723-1792 .... **LC 60**
See also DLB 175; NNAL

Ochs, Phil(ip David) 1940-1976 .... **CLC 17**
See also CA 185; 65-68

O'Connor, Edwin (Greene) 1918-1968 .... **CLC 14**
See also CA 93-96; 25-28R

O'Connor, (Mary) Flannery 1925-1964 .... **CLC 1, 2, 3, 6, 10, 13, 15, 21, 66, 104; SSC 1, 23; WLC**
See also AAYA 7; AMW; BPFB 3; CA 1-4R; CANR 3, 41; CDALB 1941-1968; DA; DA3; DAB; DAC; DAM MST, NOV; DLB 2, 152; DLBD 12; DLBY 1980; EXPS; LAIT 5; MAWW; MTCW 1, 2; NFS 3; RGAL 4; RGSF 2; SSFS 2, 7, 10

O'Connor, Frank .... **CLC 23; SSC 5**
See also O'Donovan, Michael John
See also DLB 162; RGSF 2; SSFS 5

O'Dell, Scott 1898-1989 .... **CLC 30**
See also AAYA 3; BPFB 3; BYA 1, 2, 3, 5; CA 61-64; 129; CANR 12, 30; CLR 1, 16; DLB 52; JRDA; MAICYA 1, 2; SATA 12, 60; WYA; YAW

Odets, Clifford 1906-1963 ...... **CLC 2, 28, 98; DC 6**
See also AMWS 2; CA 85-88; CAD; CANR 62; DAM DRAM; DFS 3; DLB 7, 26; MTCW 1, 2; RGAL 4

O'Doherty, Brian 1928- .... **CLC 76**
See also CA 105; CANR 108

O'Donnell, K. M.
See Malzberg, Barry N(athaniel)

O'Donnell, Lawrence
See Kuttner, Henry

O'Donovan, Michael John 1903-1966 .... **CLC 14**
See also O'Connor, Frank
See also CA 93-96; CANR 84

Oe, Kenzaburo 1935- .. **CLC 10, 36, 86; SSC 20**
See also Oe Kenzaburo
See also CA 97-100; CANR 36, 50, 74; DA3; DAM NOV; DLBY 1994; MTCW 1, 2

Oe Kenzaburo
See Oe, Kenzaburo
See also CWW 2; DLB 182; EWL 3; MJW; RGSF 2; RGWL 2

O'Faolain, Julia 1932- .... **CLC 6, 19, 47, 108**
See also CA 81-84; CAAS 2; CANR 12, 61; CN 7; DLB 14, 231; FW; MTCW 1; RHW

O'Faolain, Sean 1900-1991 ...... **CLC 1, 7, 14, 32, 70; SSC 13**
See also CA 61-64; 134; CANR 12, 66; DLB 15, 162; MTCW 1, 2; RGEL 2; RGSF 2

O'Flaherty, Liam 1896-1984 .... **CLC 5, 34; SSC 6**
See also CA 101; 113; CANR 35; DLB 36, 162; DLBY 1984; MTCW 1, 2; RGEL 2; RGSF 2; SSFS 5

Ogai
See Mori Ogai
See also MJW

Ogilvy, Gavin
See Barrie, J(ames) M(atthew)

O'Grady, Standish (James) 1846-1928 .... **TCLC 5**
See also CA 104; 157

O'Grady, Timothy 1951- .... **CLC 59**
See also CA 138

O'Hara, Frank 1926-1966 .. **CLC 2, 5, 13, 78**
See also CA 9-12R; 25-28R; CANR 33; DA3; DAM POET; DLB 5, 16, 193; MTCW 1, 2; PFS 8; 12; RGAL 4; WP

O'Hara, John (Henry) 1905-1970 . **CLC 1, 2, 3, 6, 11, 42; SSC 15**
See also AMW; BPFB 3; CA 5-8R; 25-28R; CANR 31, 60; CDALB 1929-1941; DAM NOV; DLB 9, 86; DLBD 2; MTCW 1, 2; NFS 11; RGAL 4; RGSF 2

O Hehir, Diana 1922- .... **CLC 41**
See also CA 93-96

Ohiyesa 1858-1939
See Eastman, Charles A(lexander)

Okigbo, Christopher (Ifeanyichukwu) 1932-1967 .... **CLC 25, 84; BLC 3; PC 7**
See also AFW; BW 1, 3; CA 77-80; CANR 74; CDWLB 3; DAM MULT, POET; DLB 125; MTCW 1, 2; RGEL 2

Okri, Ben 1959- .... **CLC 87**
See also AFW; BRWS 5; BW 2; CA 130; 138; CANR 65; CN 7; DLB 157, 231; INT CA-138; MTCW 2; RGSF 2; WLIT 2

Olds, Sharon 1942- .. **CLC 32, 39, 85; PC 22**
See also AMWS 10; CA 101; CANR 18, 41, 66, 98; CP 7; CPW; CWP; DAM POET; DLB 120; MTCW 2

Oldstyle, Jonathan
See Irving, Washington

Olesha, Iurii
See Olesha, Yuri (Karlovich)
See also RGWL 2

Olesha, Yuri (Karlovich) 1899-1960 .. **CLC 8**
See also Olesha, Iurii
See also CA 85-88; EW 11

Oliphant, Mrs.
See Oliphant, Margaret (Oliphant Wilson)
See also SUFW

Oliphant, Laurence 1829(?)-1888 .. **NCLC 47**
See also DLB 18, 166

Oliphant, Margaret (Oliphant Wilson) 1828-1897 .... **NCLC 11, 61; SSC 25**
See also Oliphant, Mrs.
See also DLB 18, 159, 190; HGG; RGEL 2; RGSF 2

Oliver, Mary 1935- .... **CLC 19, 34, 98**
See also AMWS 7; CA 21-24R; CANR 9, 43, 84, 92; CP 7; CWP; DLB 5, 193

Olivier, Laurence (Kerr) 1907-1989 . **CLC 20**
See also CA 111; 150; 129

Olsen, Tillie 1912- ... **CLC 4, 13, 114; SSC 11**
See also BYA 11; CA 1-4R; CANR 1, 43, 74; CDALBS; CN 7; DA; DA3; DAB; DAC; DAM MST; DLB 28, 206; DLBY 1980; EXPS; FW; MTCW 1, 2; RGAL 4; RGSF 2; SSFS 1

Olson, Charles (John) 1910-1970 .. **CLC 1, 2, 5, 6, 9, 11, 29; PC 19**
See also AMWS 2; CA 13-16; 25-28R; CABS 2; CANR 35, 61; CAP 1; DAM POET; DLB 5, 16, 193; MTCW 1, 2; RGAL 4; WP

Olson, Toby 1937- .... **CLC 28**
See also CA 65-68; CANR 9, 31, 84; CP 7

Olyesha, Yuri
See Olesha, Yuri (Karlovich)

Omar Khayyam
See Khayyam, Omar
See also RGWL 2

Ondaatje, (Philip) Michael 1943- .... **CLC 14, 29, 51, 76; PC 28**
See also CA 77-80; CANR 42, 74, 109; CN 7; CP 7; DA3; DAB; DAC; DAM MST; DLB 60; MTCW 2; PFS 8

Oneal, Elizabeth 1934-
See Oneal, Zibby
See also CA 106; CANR 28, 84; MAICYA 1, 2; SATA 30, 82; YAW

Oneal, Zibby .... **CLC 30**
See also Oneal, Elizabeth
See also AAYA 5, 41; BYA 13; CLR 13; JRDA; WYA

O'Neill, Eugene (Gladstone) 1888-1953 ...... **TCLC 1, 6, 27, 49; WLC**
See also AITN 1; AMW; CA 110; 132; CAD; CDALB 1929-1941; DA; DA3; DAB; DAC; DAM DRAM, MST; DFS 9, 11, 12; DLB 7; LAIT 3; MTCW 1, 2; RGAL 4

Onetti, Juan Carlos 1909-1994 ... **CLC 7, 10; HLCS 2; SSC 23**
See also CA 85-88; 145; CANR 32, 63; CDWLB 3; DAM MULT, NOV; DLB 113; HW 1, 2; LAW; MTCW 1, 2; RGSF 2

O Nuallain, Brian 1911-1966
See O'Brien, Flann
See also CA 21-22; 25-28R; CAP 2; DLB 231; FANT

Ophuls, Max 1902-1957 .... **TCLC 79**
See also CA 113

Opie, Amelia 1769-1853 .... **NCLC 65**
See also DLB 116, 159; RGEL 2

Oppen, George 1908-1984 ..... **CLC 7, 13, 34; PC 35**
See also CA 13-16R; 113; CANR 8, 82; DLB 5, 165; TCLC 107

Oppenheim, E(dward) Phillips 1866-1946 .... **TCLC 45**
See also CA 111; CMW 4; DLB 70

Opuls, Max
See Ophuls, Max

Origen c. 185-c. 254 .... **CMLC 19**

Orlovitz, Gil 1918-1973 .... **CLC 22**
See also CA 77-80; 45-48; DLB 2, 5

Orris
See Ingelow, Jean

Ortega y Gasset, Jose 1883-1955 ... **TCLC 9; HLC 2**
See also CA 106; 130; DAM MULT; EW 9; HW 1, 2; MTCW 1, 2

Ortese, Anna Maria 1914- .... **CLC 89**
See also DLB 177

Ortiz, Simon J(oseph) 1941- ..... **CLC 45; PC 17**
See also AMWS 4; CA 134; CANR 69; CP 7; DAM MULT, POET; DLB 120, 175, 256; EXPP; NNAL; PFS 4; RGAL 4

Orton, Joe .... **CLC 4, 13, 43; DC 3**
See also Orton, John Kingsley
See also BRWS 5; CBD; CDBLB 1960 to Present; DFS 3, 6; DLB 13; GLL 1; MTCW 2; RGEL 2; WLIT 4

Orton, John Kingsley 1933-1967
See Orton, Joe
See also CA 85-88; CANR 35, 66; DAM DRAM; MTCW 1, 2

Orwell, George .... **TCLC 2, 6, 15, 31, 51; WLC**
See also Blair, Eric (Arthur)
See also BPFB 3; BRW 7; BYA 5; CDBLB 1945-1960; CLR 68; DAB; DLB 15, 98, 195, 255; EXPN; LAIT 4, 5; NFS 3, 7; RGEL 2; SCFW 2; SFW 4; SSFS 4; WLIT 4; YAW

Osborne, David
See Silverberg, Robert

Osborne, George
See Silverberg, Robert

Osborne, John (James) 1929-1994 .... **CLC 1, 2, 5, 11, 45; WLC**
See also BRWS 1; CA 13-16R; 147; CANR 21, 56; CDBLB 1945-1960; DA; DAB; DAC; DAM DRAM, MST; DFS 4; DLB 13; MTCW 1, 2; RGEL 2

Osborne, Lawrence 1958- .... **CLC 50**
See also CA 189

Osbourne, Lloyd 1868-1947 .... **TCLC 93**

Oshima, Nagisa 1932- .... **CLC 20**
See also CA 116; 121; CANR 78

Oskison, John Milton 1874-1947 ... **TCLC 35**
See also CA 144; CANR 84; DAM MULT; DLB 175; NNAL

Ossian c. 3rd cent. - .... **CMLC 28**
See also Macpherson, James

Ossoli, Sarah Margaret (Fuller) 1810-1850 .... **NCLC 5, 50**
See also Fuller, Margaret; Fuller, Sarah Margaret
See also CDALB 1640-1865; FW; SATA 25

Ostriker, Alicia (Suskin) 1937- .... **CLC 132**
See also CA 25-28R; CAAS 24; CANR 10, 30, 62, 99; CWP; DLB 120; EXPP

Ostrovsky, Alexander 1823-1886 .. **NCLC 30, 57**

Otero, Blas de 1916-1979 .... **CLC 11**
See also CA 89-92; DLB 134

Otto, Rudolf 1869-1937 .... **TCLC 85**

Otto, Whitney 1955- .... **CLC 70**
See also CA 140

Ouida .... **TCLC 43**
See also De La Ramee, (Marie) Louise
See also DLB 18, 156; RGEL 2

Ouologuem, Yambo 1940- .... **CLC 146**
See also CA 111; 176

Ousmane, Sembene 1923- ... **CLC 66; BLC 3**
See also Sembene, Ousmane
See also BW 1, 3; CA 117; 125; CANR 81; CWW 2; MTCW 1

Ovid 43B.C.-17 .... **CMLC 7; PC 2**
See also AW 2; CDWLB 1; DA3; DAM POET; DLB 211; RGWL 2; WP

Owen, Hugh
See Faust, Frederick (Schiller)

Owen, Wilfred (Edward Salter) 1893-1918 ... **TCLC 5, 27; PC 19; WLC**
See also BRW 6; CA 104; 141; CDBLB 1914-1945; DA; DAB; DAC; DAM MST, POET; DLB 20; EXPP; MTCW 2; PFS 10; RGEL 2; WLIT 4

Owens, Rochelle 1936- .... **CLC 8**
See also CA 17-20R; CAAS 2; CAD; CANR 39; CD 5; CP 7; CWD; CWP

Oz, Amos 1939- .... **CLC 5, 8, 11, 27, 33, 54**
See also CA 53-56; CANR 27, 47, 65; CWW 2; DAM NOV; MTCW 1, 2; RGSF 2

Ozick, Cynthia 1928- .... **CLC 3, 7, 28, 62, 155; SSC 15**
See also AMWS 5; BEST 90:1; CA 17-20R; CANR 23, 58; CN 7; CPW; DA3; DAM NOV, POP; DLB 28, 152; DLBY 1982;

EXPS; INT CANR-23; MTCW 1, 2; RGAL 4; RGSF 2; SSFS 3, 12

Ozu, Yasujiro 1903-1963 .... **CLC 16**
See also CA 112

Pacheco, C.
See Pessoa, Fernando (Antonio Nogueira)

Pacheco, Jose Emilio 1939-
See also CA 111; 131; CANR 65; DAM MULT; HLC 2; HW 1, 2; RGSF 2

Pa Chin .... **CLC 18**
See also Li Fei-kan

Pack, Robert 1929- .... **CLC 13**
See also CA 1-4R; CANR 3, 44, 82; CP 7; DLB 5; SATA 118

Padgett, Lewis
See Kuttner, Henry

Padilla (Lorenzo), Heberto
1932-2000 .... **CLC 38**
See also AITN 1; CA 123; 131; 189; HW 1

Page, Jimmy 1944- .... **CLC 12**

Page, Louise 1955- .... **CLC 40**
See also CA 140; CANR 76; CBD; CD 5; CWD; DLB 233

Page, P(atricia) K(athleen) 1916- ...... **CLC 7, 18; PC 12**
See also Cape, Judith
See also CA 53-56; CANR 4, 22, 65; CP 7; DAC; DAM MST; DLB 68; MTCW 1; RGEL 2

Page, Stanton
See Fuller, Henry Blake

Page, Stanton
See Fuller, Henry Blake

Page, Thomas Nelson 1853-1922 .... **SSC 23**
See also CA 118; 177; DLB 12, 78; DLBD 13; RGAL 4

Pagels, Elaine Hiesey 1943- .... **CLC 104**
See also CA 45-48; CANR 2, 24, 51; FW

Paget, Violet 1856-1935
See Lee, Vernon
See also CA 104; 166; GLL 1; HGG

Paget-Lowe, Henry
See Lovecraft, H(oward) P(hillips)

Paglia, Camille (Anna) 1947- .... **CLC 68**
See also CA 140; CANR 72; CPW; FW; GLL 2; MTCW 2

Paige, Richard
See Koontz, Dean R(ay)

Paine, Thomas 1737-1809 .... **NCLC 62**
See also AMWS 1; CDALB 1640-1865; DLB 31, 43, 73, 158; LAIT 1; RGAL 4; RGEL 2

Palamas, Kostes 1859-1943 .... **TCLC 5**
See also CA 105; 190; RGWL 2

Palazzeschi, Aldo 1885-1974 .... **CLC 11**
See also CA 89-92; 53-56; DLB 114

Pales Matos, Luis 1898-1959
See Pales Matos, Luis
See also HLCS 2; HW 1; LAW

Paley, Grace 1922- .. **CLC 4, 6, 37, 140; SSC 8**
See also AMWS 6; CA 25-28R; CANR 13, 46, 74; CN 7; CPW; DA3; DAM POP; DLB 28, 218; EXPS; FW; INT CANR-13; MAWW; MTCW 1, 2; RGAL 4; RGSF 2; SSFS 3

Palin, Michael (Edward) 1943- .... **CLC 21**
See also Monty Python
See also CA 107; CANR 35, 109; SATA 67

Palliser, Charles 1947- .... **CLC 65**
See also CA 136; CANR 76; CN 7

Palma, Ricardo 1833-1919 .... **TCLC 29**
See also CA 168; LAW

Pancake, Breece Dexter 1952-1979
See Pancake, Breece D'J
See also CA 123; 109

Pancake, Breece D'J .... **CLC 29**
See also Pancake, Breece Dexter
See also DLB 130

Panchenko, Nikolai .... **CLC 59**

Pankhurst, Emmeline (Goulden)
1858-1928 .... **TCLC 100**
See also CA 116; FW

Panko, Rudy
See Gogol, Nikolai (Vasilyevich)

Papadiamantis, Alexandros
1851-1911 .... **TCLC 29**
See also CA 168

Papadiamantopoulos, Johannes 1856-1910
See Moreas, Jean
See also CA 117

Papini, Giovanni 1881-1956 .... **TCLC 22**
See also CA 121; 180

Paracelsus 1493-1541 .... **LC 14**
See also DLB 179

Parasol, Peter
See Stevens, Wallace

Pardo Bazan, Emilia 1851-1921 .... **SSC 30**
See also FW; RGSF 2; RGWL 2

Pareto, Vilfredo 1848-1923 .... **TCLC 69**
See also CA 175

Paretsky, Sara 1947- .... **CLC 135**
See also AAYA 30; BEST 90:3; CA 125; 129; CANR 59, 95; CMW 4; CPW; DA3; DAM POP; INT CA-129; MSW; RGAL 4

Parfenie, Maria
See Codrescu, Andrei

Parini, Jay (Lee) 1948- .... **CLC 54, 133**
See also CA 97-100; CAAS 16; CANR 32, 87

Park, Jordan
See Kornbluth, C(yril) M.; Pohl, Frederik

Park, Robert E(zra) 1864-1944 ..... **TCLC 73**
See also CA 122; 165

Parker, Bert
See Ellison, Harlan (Jay)

Parker, Dorothy (Rothschild)
1893-1967 .. **CLC 15, 68; PC 28; SSC 2**
See also AMWS 9; CA 19-20; 25-28R; CAP 2; DA3; DAM POET; DLB 11, 45, 86; EXPP; FW; MAWW; MTCW 1, 2; RGAL 4; RGSF 2

Parker, Robert B(rown) 1932- .... **CLC 27**
See also AAYA 28; BEST 89:4; BPFB 3; CA 49-52; CANR 1, 26, 52, 89; CMW 4; CPW; DAM NOV, POP; INT CANR-26; MSW; MTCW 1

Parkin, Frank 1940- .... **CLC 43**
See also CA 147

Parkman, Francis, Jr. 1823-1893 .. **NCLC 12**
See also AMWS 2; DLB 1, 30, 183, 186, 235; RGAL 4

Parks, Gordon (Alexander Buchanan)
1912- .... **CLC 1, 16; BLC 3**
See also AAYA 36; AITN 2; BW 2, 3; CA 41-44R; CANR 26, 66; DA3; DAM MULT; DLB 33; MTCW 2; SATA 8, 108

Parks, Tim(othy Harold) 1954- ...... **CLC 147**
See also CA 126; 131; CANR 77; DLB 231; INT CA-131

Parmenides c. 515B.C.-c.
450B.C. .... **CMLC 22**
See also DLB 176

Parnell, Thomas 1679-1718 .... **LC 3**
See also DLB 95; RGEL 2

Parra, Nicanor 1914- ... **CLC 2, 102; HLC 2; PC 39**
See also CA 85-88; CANR 32; CWW 2; DAM MULT; HW 1; LAW; MTCW 1

Parra Sanojo, Ana Teresa de la 1890-1936
See de la Parra, (Ana) Teresa (Sonojo)
See also HLCS 2; LAW

Parrish, Mary Frances
See Fisher, M(ary) F(rances) K(ennedy)

Parshchikov, Aleksei .... **CLC 59**

Parson, Professor
See Coleridge, Samuel Taylor

Parson Lot
See Kingsley, Charles

Parton, Sara Payson Willis
1811-1872 .... **NCLC 86**
See also DLB 43, 74, 239

Partridge, Anthony
See Oppenheim, E(dward) Phillips

Pascal, Blaise 1623-1662 .... **LC 35**
See also EW 3; GFL Beginnings to 1789; RGWL 2

Pascoli, Giovanni 1855-1912 .... **TCLC 45**
See also CA 170; EW 7

Pasolini, Pier Paolo 1922-1975 .. **CLC 20, 37, 106; PC 17**
See also CA 93-96; 61-64; CANR 63; DLB 128, 177; MTCW 1; RGWL 2

Pasquini
See Silone, Ignazio

Pastan, Linda (Olenik) 1932- .... **CLC 27**
See also CA 61-64; CANR 18, 40, 61; CP 7; CSW; CWP; DAM POET; DLB 5; PFS 8

Pasternak, Boris (Leonidovich)
1890-1960 ...... **CLC 7, 10, 18, 63; PC 6; SSC 31; WLC**
See also BPFB 3; CA 127; 116; DA; DA3; DAB; DAC; DAM MST, NOV, POET; EW 10; MTCW 1, 2; RGSF 2; RGWL 2; WP

Patchen, Kenneth 1911-1972 .... **CLC 1, 2, 18**
See also CA 1-4R; 33-36R; CANR 3, 35; DAM POET; DLB 16, 48; MTCW 1; RGAL 4

Pater, Walter (Horatio) 1839-1894 . **NCLC 7, 90**
See also BRW 5; CDBLB 1832-1890; DLB 57, 156; RGEL 2

Paterson, A(ndrew) B(arton)
1864-1941 .... **TCLC 32**
See also CA 155; DLB 230; RGEL 2; SATA 97

Paterson, Katherine (Womeldorf)
1932- .... **CLC 12, 30**
See also AAYA 1, 31; BYA 1, 2, 7; CA 21-24R; CANR 28, 59; CLR 7, 50; CWRI 5; DLB 52; JRDA; LAIT 4; MAICYA 1, 2; MAICYAS 1; MTCW 1; SATA 13, 53, 92; WYA; YAW

Patmore, Coventry Kersey Dighton
1823-1896 .... **NCLC 9**
See also DLB 35, 98; RGEL 2

Paton, Alan (Stewart) 1903-1988 .... **CLC 4, 10, 25, 55, 106; WLC**
See also AAYA 26; AFW; BPFB 3; BRWS 2; BYA 1; CA 13-16; 125; CANR 22; CAP 1; DA; DA3; DAB; DAC; DAM MST, NOV; DLB 225; DLBD 17; EXPN; LAIT 4; MTCW 1, 2; NFS 3, 12; RGEL 2; SATA 11; SATA-Obit 56; WLIT 2

Paton Walsh, Gillian 1937- .... **CLC 35**
See also Paton Walsh, Jill; Walsh, Jill Paton
See also AAYA 11; CANR 38, 83; CLR 2, 65; DLB 161; JRDA; MAICYA 1, 2; SAAS 3; SATA 4, 72, 109; YAW

Paton Walsh, Jill
See Paton Walsh, Gillian
See also BYA 1, 8

Patton, George S(mith), Jr.
1885-1945 .... **TCLC 79**
See also CA 189

Paulding, James Kirke 1778-1860 ... **NCLC 2**
See also DLB 3, 59, 74, 250; RGAL 4

Paulin, Thomas Neilson 1949-
See Paulin, Tom
See also CA 123; 128; CANR 98; CP 7

Paulin, Tom .... **CLC 37**
See also Paulin, Thomas Neilson
See also DLB 40

Pausanias c. 1st cent. - .... **CMLC 36**
Paustovsky, Konstantin (Georgievich)
  1892-1968 .... **CLC 40**
  See also CA 93-96; 25-28R
Pavese, Cesare 1908-1950 .. **TCLC 3; PC 13; SSC 19**
  See also CA 104; 169; DLB 128, 177; EW 12; RGSF 2; RGWL 2
Pavic, Milorad 1929- .... **CLC 60**
  See also CA 136; CDWLB 4; CWW 2; DLB 181
Pavlov, Ivan Petrovich 1849-1936 . **TCLC 91**
  See also CA 118; 180
Payne, Alan
  See Jakes, John (William)
Paz, Gil
  See Lugones, Leopoldo
Paz, Octavio 1914-1998 . **CLC 3, 4, 6, 10, 19, 51, 65, 119; HLC 2; PC 1; WLC**
  See also CA 73-76; 165; CANR 32, 65, 104; CWW 2; DA; DA3; DAB; DAC; DAM MST, MULT, POET; DLBY 1990, 1998; DNFS 1; HW 1, 2; LAW; LAWS 1; MTCW 1, 2; RGWL 2; SSFS 13; WLIT 1
p'Bitek, Okot 1931-1982 ..... **CLC 96; BLC 3**
  See also AFW; BW 2, 3; CA 124; 107; CANR 82; DAM MULT; DLB 125; MTCW 1, 2; RGEL 2; WLIT 2
Peacock, Molly 1947- .... **CLC 60**
  See also CA 103; CAAS 21; CANR 52, 84; CP 7; CWP; DLB 120
Peacock, Thomas Love
  1785-1866 .... **NCLC 22**
  See also BRW 4; DLB 96, 116; RGEL 2; RGSF 2
Peake, Mervyn 1911-1968 .... **CLC 7, 54**
  See also CA 5-8R; 25-28R; CANR 3; DLB 15, 160, 255; FANT; MTCW 1; RGEL 2; SATA 23; SFW 4
Pearce, Philippa
  See Christie, (Ann) Philippa
  See also CA 5-8R; CANR 4, 109; CWRI 5; FANT; MAICYA 2
Pearl, Eric
  See Elman, Richard (Martin)
Pearson, T(homas) R(eid) 1956- .... **CLC 39**
  See also CA 120; 130; CANR 97; CSW; INT 130
Peck, Dale 1967- .... **CLC 81**
  See also CA 146; CANR 72; GLL 2
Peck, John (Frederick) 1941- .... **CLC 3**
  See also CA 49-52; CANR 3, 100; CP 7
Peck, Richard (Wayne) 1934- .... **CLC 21**
  See also AAYA 1, 24; BYA 1, 6, 8, 11; CA 85-88; CANR 19, 38; CLR 15; INT CANR-19; JRDA; MAICYA 1, 2; SAAS 2; SATA 18, 55, 97; SATA-Essay 110; WYA; YAW
Peck, Robert Newton 1928- .... **CLC 17**
  See also AAYA 3, 43; BYA 1, 6; CA 81-84, 182; CAAE 182; CANR 31, 63; CLR 45; DA; DAC; DAM MST; JRDA; LAIT 3; MAICYA 1, 2; SAAS 1; SATA 21, 62, 111; SATA-Essay 108; WYA; YAW
Peckinpah, (David) Sam(uel)
  1925-1984 .... **CLC 20**
  See also CA 109; 114; CANR 82
Pedersen, Knut 1859-1952
  See Hamsun, Knut
  See also CA 104; 119; CANR 63; MTCW 1, 2
Peeslake, Gaffer
  See Durrell, Lawrence (George)
Peguy, Charles (Pierre)
  1873-1914 .... **TCLC 10**
  See also CA 107; 193; DLB 258; GFL 1789 to the Present

Peirce, Charles Sanders
  1839-1914 .... **TCLC 81**
  See also CA 194
Pellicer, Carlos 1900(?)-1977
  See also CA 153; 69-72; HLCS 2; HW 1
Pena, Ramon del Valle y
  See Valle-Inclan, Ramon (Maria) del
Pendennis, Arthur Esquir
  See Thackeray, William Makepeace
Penn, William 1644-1718 .... **LC 25**
  See also DLB 24
PEPECE
  See Prado (Calvo), Pedro
Pepys, Samuel 1633-1703 ... **LC 11, 58; WLC**
  See also BRW 2; CDBLB 1660-1789; DA; DA3; DAB; DAC; DAM MST; DLB 101, 213; RGEL 2; WLIT 3
Percy, Thomas 1729-1811 .... **NCLC 95**
  See also DLB 104
Percy, Walker 1916-1990 .... **CLC 2, 3, 6, 8, 14, 18, 47, 65**
  See also AMWS 3; BPFB 3; CA 1-4R; 131; CANR 1, 23, 64; CPW; CSW; DA3; DAM NOV, POP; DLB 2; DLBY 1980, 1990; MTCW 1, 2; RGAL 4
Percy, William Alexander
  1885-1942 .... **TCLC 84**
  See also CA 163; MTCW 2
Perec, Georges 1936-1982 .... **CLC 56, 116**
  See also CA 141; DLB 83; GFL 1789 to the Present
Pereda (y Sanchez de Porrua), Jose Maria de 1833-1906 .... **TCLC 16**
  See also CA 117
Pereda y Porrua, Jose Maria de
  See Pereda (y Sanchez de Porrua), Jose Maria de
Peregoy, George Weems
  See Mencken, H(enry) L(ouis)
Perelman, S(idney) J(oseph)
  1904-1979 .. **CLC 3, 5, 9, 15, 23, 44, 49; SSC 32**
  See also AITN 1, 2; BPFB 3; CA 73-76; 89-92; CANR 18; DAM DRAM; DLB 11, 44; MTCW 1, 2; RGAL 4
Peret, Benjamin 1899-1959 .... **TCLC 20; PC 33**
  See also CA 117; 186; GFL 1789 to the Present
Peretz, Isaac Loeb 1851(?)-1915 ... **TCLC 16; SSC 26**
  See also CA 109
Peretz, Yitzkhok Leibush
  See Peretz, Isaac Loeb
Perez Galdos, Benito 1843-1920 ... **TCLC 27; HLCS 2**
  See also Galdos, Benito Perez
  See also CA 125; 153; HW 1; RGWL 2
Peri Rossi, Cristina 1941- .. **CLC 156; HLCS 2**
  See also CA 131; CANR 59, 81; DLB 145; HW 1, 2
Perlata
  See Peret, Benjamin
Perloff, Marjorie G(abrielle)
  1931- .... **CLC 137**
  See also CA 57-60; CANR 7, 22, 49, 104
Perrault, Charles 1628-1703 ... **LC 2, 56; DC 12**
  See also BYA 4; CLR 79; GFL Beginnings to 1789; MAICYA 1, 2; RGWL 2; SATA 25; WCH
Perry, Anne 1938- .... **CLC 126**
  See also CA 101; CANR 22, 50, 84; CMW 4; CN 7; CPW
Perry, Brighton
  See Sherwood, Robert E(mmet)

Perse, St.-John
  See Leger, (Marie-Rene Auguste) Alexis Saint-Leger
Perse, Saint-John
  See Leger, (Marie-Rene Auguste) Alexis Saint-Leger
  See also DLB 258
Perutz, Leo(pold) 1882-1957 .... **TCLC 60**
  See also CA 147; DLB 81
Peseenz, Tulio F.
  See Lopez y Fuentes, Gregorio
Pesetsky, Bette 1932- .... **CLC 28**
  See also CA 133; DLB 130
Peshkov, Alexei Maximovich 1868-1936
  See Gorky, Maxim
  See also CA 105; 141; CANR 83; DA; DAC; DAM DRAM, MST, NOV; MTCW 2
Pessoa, Fernando (Antonio Nogueira)
  1898-1935 ..... **TCLC 27; HLC 2; PC 20**
  See also CA 125; 183; DAM MULT; EW 10; RGWL 2; WP
Peterkin, Julia Mood 1880-1961 ...... **CLC 31**
  See also CA 102; DLB 9
Peters, Joan K(aren) 1945- .... **CLC 39**
  See also CA 158; CANR 109
Peters, Robert L(ouis) 1924- .... **CLC 7**
  See also CA 13-16R; CAAS 8; CP 7; DLB 105
Petofi, Sandor 1823-1849 .... **NCLC 21**
  See also RGWL 2
Petrakis, Harry Mark 1923- .... **CLC 3**
  See also CA 9-12R; CANR 4, 30, 85; CN 7
Petrarch 1304-1374 .... **CMLC 20; PC 8**
  See also DA3; DAM POET; EW 2; RGWL 2
Petronius c. 20-66 .... **CMLC 34**
  See also AW 2; CDWLB 1; DLB 211; RGWL 2
Petrov, Evgeny .... **TCLC 21**
  See also Kataev, Evgeny Petrovich
Petry, Ann (Lane) 1908-1997 ... **CLC 1, 7, 18**
  See also AFAW 1, 2; BPFB 3; BW 1, 3; BYA 2; CA 5-8R; 157; CAAS 6; CANR 4, 46; CLR 12; CN 7; DLB 76; JRDA; LAIT 1; MAICYA 1, 2; MAICYAS 1; MTCW 1; RGAL 4; SATA 5; SATA-Obit 94; TCLC 112
Petursson, Halligrimur 1614-1674 .... **LC 8**
Peychinovich
  See Vazov, Ivan (Minchov)
Phaedrus c. 15B.C.-c. 50 .... **CMLC 25**
  See also DLB 211
Phelps (Ward), Elizabeth Stuart
  See Phelps, Elizabeth Stuart
  See also FW
Phelps, Elizabeth Stuart
  1844-1911 .... **TCLC 113**
  See also Phelps (Ward), Elizabeth Stuart
  See also DLB 74
Philips, Katherine 1632-1664 . **LC 30; PC 40**
  See also DLB 131; RGEL 2
Philipson, Morris H. 1926- .... **CLC 53**
  See also CA 1-4R; CANR 4
Phillips, Caryl 1958- .... **CLC 96; BLCS**
  See also BRWS 5; BW 2; CA 141; CANR 63, 104; CBD; CD 5; CN 7; DA3; DAM MULT; DLB 157; MTCW 2; WLIT 4
Phillips, David Graham
  1867-1911 .... **TCLC 44**
  See also CA 108; 176; DLB 9, 12; RGAL 4
Phillips, Jack
  See Sandburg, Carl (August)
Phillips, Jayne Anne 1952- .... **CLC 15, 33, 139; SSC 16**
  See also BPFB 3; CA 101; CANR 24, 50, 96; CN 7; CSW; DLBY 1980; INT CANR-24; MTCW 1, 2; RGAL 4; RGSF 2; SSFS 4

Phillips, Richard
See Dick, Philip K(indred)
Phillips, Robert (Schaeffer) 1938- .... **CLC 28**
See also CA 17-20R; CAAS 13; CANR 8; DLB 105
Phillips, Ward
See Lovecraft, H(oward) P(hillips)
Piccolo, Lucio 1901-1969 .... **CLC 13**
See also CA 97-100; DLB 114
Pickthall, Marjorie L(owry) C(hristie)
1883-1922 .... **TCLC 21**
See also CA 107; DLB 92
Pico della Mirandola, Giovanni
1463-1494 .... **LC 15**
Piercy, Marge 1936- .... **CLC 3, 6, 14, 18, 27, 62, 128; PC 29**
See also BPFB 3; CA 21-24R; CAAE 187; CAAS 1; CANR 13, 43, 66; CN 7; CP 7; CWP; DLB 120, 227; EXPP; FW; MTCW 1, 2; PFS 9; SFW 4
Piers, Robert
See Anthony, Piers
Pieyre de Mandiargues, Andre 1909-1991
See Mandiargues, Andre Pieyre de
See also CA 103; 136; CANR 22, 82; GFL 1789 to the Present
Pilnyak, Boris 1894-1938 . **TCLC 23; SSC 48**
See also Vogau, Boris Andreyevich
Pinchback, Eugene
See Toomer, Jean
Pincherle, Alberto 1907-1990 ...... **CLC 11, 18**
See also Moravia, Alberto
See also CA 25-28R; 132; CANR 33, 63; DAM NOV; MTCW 1
Pinckney, Darryl 1953- .... **CLC 76**
See also BW 2, 3; CA 143; CANR 79
Pindar 518(?)B.C.-438(?)B.C. .... **CMLC 12; PC 19**
See also AW 1; CDWLB 1; DLB 176; RGWL 2
Pineda, Cecile 1942- .... **CLC 39**
See also CA 118; DLB 209
Pinero, Arthur Wing 1855-1934 .... **TCLC 32**
See also CA 110; 153; DAM DRAM; DLB 10; RGEL 2
Pinero, Miguel (Antonio Gomez)
1946-1988 .... **CLC 4, 55**
See also CA 61-64; 125; CAD; CANR 29, 90; HW 1
Pinget, Robert 1919-1997 .... **CLC 7, 13, 37**
See also CA 85-88; 160; CWW 2; DLB 83; GFL 1789 to the Present
Pink Floyd
See Barrett, (Roger) Syd; Gilmour, David; Mason, Nick; Waters, Roger; Wright, Rick
Pinkney, Edward 1802-1828 .... **NCLC 31**
See also DLB 248
Pinkwater, Daniel Manus 1941- .... **CLC 35**
See also AAYA 1; BYA 9; CA 29-32R; CANR 12, 38, 89; CLR 4; CSW; FANT; JRDA; MAICYA 1, 2; SAAS 3; SATA 8, 46, 76, 114; SFW 4; YAW
Pinkwater, Manus
See Pinkwater, Daniel Manus
Pinsky, Robert 1940- .... **CLC 9, 19, 38, 94, 121; PC 27**
See also AMWS 6; CA 29-32R; CAAS 4; CANR 58, 97; CP 7; DA3; DAM POET; DLBY 1982, 1998; MTCW 2; RGAL 4
Pinta, Harold
See Pinter, Harold
Pinter, Harold 1930- .. **CLC 1, 3, 6, 9, 11, 15, 27, 58, 73; DC 15; WLC**
See also BRWR 1; BRWS 1; CA 5-8R; CANR 33, 65; CBD; CD 5; CDBLB 1960 to Present; DA; DA3; DAB; DAC; DAM DRAM, MST; DFS 3, 5, 7, 14; DLB 13; IDFW 3, 4; MTCW 1, 2; RGEL 2

Piozzi, Hester Lynch (Thrale)
1741-1821 .... **NCLC 57**
See also DLB 104, 142
Pirandello, Luigi 1867-1936 ...... **TCLC 4, 29; DC 5; SSC 22; WLC**
See also CA 104; 153; CANR 103; DA; DA3; DAB; DAC; DAM DRAM, MST; DFS 4, 9; EW 8; MTCW 2; RGSF 2; RGWL 2
Pirsig, Robert M(aynard) 1928- ... **CLC 4, 6, 73**
See also CA 53-56; CANR 42, 74; CPW 1; DA3; DAM POP; MTCW 1, 2; SATA 39
Pisarev, Dmitry Ivanovich
1840-1868 .... **NCLC 25**
Pix, Mary (Griffith) 1666-1709 .... **LC 8**
See also DLB 80
Pixerecourt, (Rene Charles) Guilbert de
1773-1844 .... **NCLC 39**
See also DLB 192; GFL 1789 to the Present
Plaatje, Sol(omon) T(shekisho)
1878-1932 .... **TCLC 73; BLCS**
See also BW 2, 3; CA 141; CANR 79; DLB 125, 225
Plaidy, Jean
See Hibbert, Eleanor Alice Burford
Planche, James Robinson
1796-1880 .... **NCLC 42**
See also RGEL 2
Plant, Robert 1948- .... **CLC 12**
Plante, David (Robert) 1940- . **CLC 7, 23, 38**
See also CA 37-40R; CANR 12, 36, 58, 82; CN 7; DAM NOV; DLBY 1983; INT CANR-12; MTCW 1
Plath, Sylvia 1932-1963 ..... **CLC 1, 2, 3, 5, 9, 11, 14, 17, 50, 51, 62, 111; PC 1, 37; WLC**
See also AAYA 13; AMWS 1; BPFB 3; CA 19-20; CANR 34, 101; CAP 2; CDALB 1941-1968; DA; DA3; DAB; DAC; DAM MST, POET; DLB 5, 6, 152; EXPN; EXPP; FW; LAIT 4; MAWW; MTCW 1, 2; NFS 1; PAB; PFS 1; RGAL 4; SATA 96; WP; YAW
Plato c. 428B.C.-347B.C. ... **CMLC 8; WLCS**
See also AW 1; CDWLB 1; DA; DA3; DAB; DAC; DAM MST; DLB 176; LAIT 1; RGWL 2
Platonov, Andrei
See Klimentov, Andrei Platonovich
Platt, Kin 1911- .... **CLC 26**
See also AAYA 11; CA 17-20R; CANR 11; JRDA; SAAS 17; SATA 21, 86; WYA
Plautus c. 254B.C.-c. 184B.C. .... **CMLC 24; DC 6**
See also AW 1; CDWLB 1; DLB 211; RGWL 2
Plick et Plock
See Simenon, Georges (Jacques Christian)
Plieksans, Janis
See Rainis, Janis
Plimpton, George (Ames) 1927- .... **CLC 36**
See also AITN 1; CA 21-24R; CANR 32, 70, 103; DLB 185, 241; MTCW 1, 2; SATA 10
Pliny the Elder c. 23-79 .... **CMLC 23**
See also DLB 211
Plomer, William Charles Franklin
1903-1973 .... **CLC 4, 8**
See also AFW; CA 21-22; CANR 34; CAP 2; DLB 20, 162, 191, 225; MTCW 1; RGEL 2; RGSF 2; SATA 24
Plotinus 204-270 .... **CMLC 46**
See also CDWLB 1; DLB 176
Plowman, Piers
See Kavanagh, Patrick (Joseph)
Plum, J.
See Wodehouse, P(elham) G(renville)

Plumly, Stanley (Ross) 1939- .... **CLC 33**
See also CA 108; 110; CANR 97; CP 7; DLB 5, 193; INT 110
Plumpe, Friedrich Wilhelm
1888-1931 .... **TCLC 53**
See also CA 112
Po Chu-i 772-846 .... **CMLC 24**
Poe, Edgar Allan 1809-1849 ..... **NCLC 1, 16, 55, 78, 94, 97; PC 1; SSC 1, 22, 34, 35; WLC**
See also AAYA 14; AMW; BPFB 3; BYA 5, 11; CDALB 1640-1865; CMW 4; DA; DA3; DAB; DAC; DAM MST, POET; DLB 3, 59, 73, 74, 248, 254; EXPP; EXPS; HGG; LAIT 2; MSW; PAB; PFS 1, 3, 9; RGAL 4; RGSF 2; SATA 23; SCFW 2; SFW 4; SSFS 2, 4, 7, 8; SUFW; WP; WYA
Poet of Titchfield Street, The
See Pound, Ezra (Weston Loomis)
Pohl, Frederik 1919- .... **CLC 18; SSC 25**
See also AAYA 24; CA 61-64; CAAE 188; CAAS 1; CANR 11, 37, 81; CN 7; DLB 8; INT CANR-11; MTCW 1, 2; SATA 24; SCFW 2; SFW 4
Poirier, Louis 1910-
See Gracq, Julien
See also CA 122; 126; CWW 2
Poitier, Sidney 1927- .... **CLC 26**
See also BW 1; CA 117; CANR 94
Polanski, Roman 1933- .... **CLC 16**
See also CA 77-80
Poliakoff, Stephen 1952- .... **CLC 38**
See also CA 106; CBD; CD 5; DLB 13
Police, The
See Copeland, Stewart (Armstrong); Summers, Andrew James; Sumner, Gordon Matthew
Polidori, John William 1795-1821 . **NCLC 51**
See also DLB 116; HGG
Pollitt, Katha 1949- .... **CLC 28, 122**
See also CA 120; 122; CANR 66, 108; MTCW 1, 2
Pollock, (Mary) Sharon 1936- .... **CLC 50**
See also CA 141; CD 5; CWD; DAC; DAM DRAM, MST; DFS 3; DLB 60; FW
Polo, Marco 1254-1324 .... **CMLC 15**
Polonsky, Abraham (Lincoln)
1910-1999 .... **CLC 92**
See also CA 104; 187; DLB 26; INT 104
Polybius c. 200B.C.-c. 118B.C. .... **CMLC 17**
See also AW 1; DLB 176; RGWL 2
Pomerance, Bernard 1940- .... **CLC 13**
See also CA 101; CAD; CANR 49; CD 5; DAM DRAM; DFS 9; LAIT 2
Ponge, Francis 1899-1988 .... **CLC 6, 18**
See also CA 85-88; 126; CANR 40, 86; DAM POET; GFL 1789 to the Present; RGWL 2
Poniatowska, Elena 1933- . **CLC 140; HLC 2**
See also CA 101; CANR 32, 66, 107; CDWLB 3; DAM MULT; DLB 113; HW 1, 2; LAWS 1; WLIT 1
Pontoppidan, Henrik 1857-1943 .... **TCLC 29**
See also CA 170
Poole, Josephine .... **CLC 17**
See also Helyar, Jane Penelope Josephine
See also SAAS 2; SATA 5
Popa, Vasko 1922-1991 .... **CLC 19**
See also CA 112; 148; CDWLB 4; DLB 181; RGWL 2
Pope, Alexander 1688-1744 ...... **LC 3, 58, 60, 64; PC 26; WLC**
See also BRW 3; BRWR 1; CDBLB 1660-1789; DA; DA3; DAB; DAC; DAM MST, POET; DLB 95, 101, 213; EXPP; PAB; PFS 12; RGEL 2; WLIT 3; WP

Popov, Yevgeny .... **CLC 59**
See also BW 2, 3; CA 142; CANR 90, 109; SATA 81, 129

Porter, Connie (Rose) 1959(?)- .... **CLC 70**
See also BW 2, 3; CA 142; CANR 90, 109; SATA 81, 129

Porter, Gene(va Grace) Stratton .. **TCLC 21**
See also Stratton-Porter, Gene(va Grace)
See also BPFB 3; CA 112; CWRI 5; RHW

Porter, Katherine Anne 1890-1980 .. **CLC 1, 3, 7, 10, 13, 15, 27, 101; SSC 4, 31, 43**
See also AAYA 42; AITN 2; AMW; BPFB 3; CA 1-4R; 101; CANR 1, 65; CDALBS; DA; DA3; DAB; DAC; DAM MST, NOV; DLB 4, 9, 102; DLBD 12; DLBY 1980; EXPS; LAIT 3; MAWW; MTCW 1, 2; NFS 14; RGAL 4; RGSF 2; SATA 39; SATA-Obit 23; SSFS 1, 8, 11

Porter, Peter (Neville Frederick) 1929- .... **CLC 5, 13, 33**
See also CA 85-88; CP 7; DLB 40

Porter, William Sydney 1862-1910
See Henry, O.
See also CA 104; 131; CDALB 1865-1917; DA; DA3; DAB; DAC; DAM MST; DLB 12, 78, 79; MTCW 1, 2; YABC 2

Portillo (y Pacheco), Jose Lopez
See Lopez Portillo (y Pacheco), Jose

Portillo Trambley, Estela 1927-1998
See Trambley, Estela Portillo
See also CANR 32; DAM MULT; DLB 209; HLC 2; HW 1

Posse, Abel .... **CLC 70**

Post, Melville Davisson 1869-1930 .... **TCLC 39**
See also CA 110; CMW 4

Potok, Chaim 1929- .... **CLC 2, 7, 14, 26, 112**
See also AAYA 15; AITN 1, 2; BPFB 3; BYA 1; CA 17-20R; CANR 19, 35, 64, 98; CN 7; DA3; DAM NOV; DLB 28, 152; EXPN; INT CANR-19; LAIT 4; MTCW 1, 2; NFS 4; SATA 33, 106; YAW

Potter, Dennis (Christopher George) 1935-1994 .... **CLC 58, 86, 123**
See also CA 107; 145; CANR 33, 61; CBD; DLB 233; MTCW 1

Pound, Ezra (Weston Loomis) 1885-1972 .. **CLC 1, 2, 3, 4, 5, 7, 10, 13, 18, 34, 48, 50, 112; PC 4; WLC**
See also AMW; AMWR 1; CA 5-8R; 37-40R; CANR 40; CDALB 1917-1929; DA; DA3; DAB; DAC; DAM MST, POET; DLB 4, 45, 63; DLBD 15; EFS 2; EXPP; MTCW 1, 2; PAB; PFS 2, 8; RGAL 4; WP

Povod, Reinaldo 1959-1994 .... **CLC 44**
See also CA 136; 146; CANR 83

Powell, Adam Clayton, Jr. 1908-1972 .... **CLC 89; BLC 3**
See also BW 1, 3; CA 102; 33-36R; CANR 86; DAM MULT

Powell, Anthony (Dymoke) 1905-2000 .... **CLC 1, 3, 7, 9, 10, 31**
See also BRW 7; CA 1-4R; 189; CANR 1, 32, 62, 107; CDBLB 1945-1960; CN 7; DLB 15; MTCW 1, 2; RGEL 2

Powell, Dawn 1896(?)-1965 .... **CLC 66**
See also CA 5-8R; DLBY 1997

Powell, Padgett 1952- .... **CLC 34**
See also CA 126; CANR 63, 101; CSW; DLB 234; DLBY 01

Powell, (Oval) Talmage 1920-2000
See Queen, Ellery
See also CA 5-8R; CANR 2, 80

Power, Susan 1961- .... **CLC 91**
See also BYA 14; CA 160; NFS 11

Powers, J(ames) F(arl) 1917-1999 ..... **CLC 1, 4, 8, 57; SSC 4**
See also CA 1-4R; 181; CANR 2, 61; CN 7; DLB 130; MTCW 1; RGAL 4; RGSF 2

Powers, John J(ames) 1945-
See Powers, John R.
See also CA 69-72

Powers, John R. .... **CLC 66**
See also Powers, John J(ames)

Powers, Richard (S.) 1957- .... **CLC 93**
See also AMWS 9; BPFB 3; CA 148; CANR 80; CN 7

Pownall, David 1938- .... **CLC 10**
See also CA 89-92, 180; CAAS 18; CANR 49, 101; CBD; CD 5; CN 7; DLB 14

Powys, John Cowper 1872-1963 ... **CLC 7, 9, 15, 46, 125**
See also CA 85-88; CANR 106; DLB 15, 255; FANT; MTCW 1, 2; RGEL 2; SUFW

Powys, T(heodore) F(rancis) 1875-1953 .... **TCLC 9**
See also CA 106; 189; DLB 36, 162; FANT; RGEL 2; SUFW

Prado (Calvo), Pedro 1886-1952 ... **TCLC 75**
See also CA 131; HW 1; LAW

Prager, Emily 1952- .... **CLC 56**

Pratt, E(dwin) J(ohn) 1883(?)-1964 . **CLC 19**
See also CA 141; 93-96; CANR 77; DAC; DAM POET; DLB 92; RGEL 2

Premchand .... **TCLC 21**
See also Srivastava, Dhanpat Rai

Preussler, Otfried 1923- .... **CLC 17**
See also CA 77-80; SATA 24

Prevert, Jacques (Henri Marie) 1900-1977 .... **CLC 15**
See also CA 77-80; 69-72; CANR 29, 61; DLB 258; GFL 1789 to the Present; IDFW 3, 4; MTCW 1; RGWL 2; SATA-Obit 30

Prevost, (Antoine Francois) 1697-1763 .... **LC 1**
See also EW 4; GFL Beginnings to 1789; RGWL 2

Price, (Edward) Reynolds 1933- ... **CLC 3, 6, 13, 43, 50, 63; SSC 22**
See also AMWS 6; CA 1-4R; CANR 1, 37, 57, 87; CN 7; CSW; DAM NOV; DLB 2, 218; INT CANR-37

Price, Richard 1949- .... **CLC 6, 12**
See also CA 49-52; CANR 3; DLBY 1981

Prichard, Katharine Susannah 1883-1969 .... **CLC 46**
See also CA 11-12; CANR 33; CAP 1; MTCW 1; RGEL 2; RGSF 2; SATA 66

Priestley, J(ohn) B(oynton) 1894-1984 .... **CLC 2, 5, 9, 34**
See also BRW 7; CA 9-12R; 113; CANR 33; CDBLB 1914-1945; DA3; DAM DRAM, NOV; DLB 10, 34, 77, 100, 139; DLBY 1984; MTCW 1, 2; RGEL 2; SFW 4

Prince 1958(?)- .... **CLC 35**

Prince, F(rank) T(empleton) 1912- .. **CLC 22**
See also CA 101; CANR 43, 79; CP 7; DLB 20

Prince Kropotkin
See Kropotkin, Peter (Alekseievich)

Prior, Matthew 1664-1721 .... **LC 4**
See also DLB 95; RGEL 2

Prishvin, Mikhail 1873-1954 .... **TCLC 75**

Pritchard, William H(arrison) 1932- .... **CLC 34**
See also CA 65-68; CANR 23, 95; DLB 111

Pritchett, V(ictor) S(awdon) 1900-1997 ... **CLC 5, 13, 15, 41; SSC 14**
See also BPFB 3; BRWS 3; CA 61-64; 157; CANR 31, 63; CN 7; DA3; DAM NOV; DLB 15, 139; MTCW 1, 2; RGEL 2; RGSF 2

Private 19022
See Manning, Frederic

Probst, Mark 1925- .... **CLC 59**
See also CA 130

Prokosch, Frederic 1908-1989 ...... **CLC 4, 48**
See also CA 73-76; 128; CANR 82; DLB 48; MTCW 2

Propertius, Sextus c. 50B.C.-c. 16B.C. .... **CMLC 32**
See also AW 2; CDWLB 1; DLB 211; RGWL 2

Prophet, The
See Dreiser, Theodore (Herman Albert)

Prose, Francine 1947- .... **CLC 45**
See also CA 109; 112; CANR 46, 95; DLB 234; SATA 101

Proudhon
See Cunha, Euclides (Rodrigues Pimenta) da

Proulx, Annie
See Proulx, E(dna) Annie

Proulx, E(dna) Annie 1935- ...... **CLC 81, 158**
See also AMWS 7; BPFB 3; CA 145; CANR 65; CN 7; CPW 1; DA3; DAM POP; MTCW 2

Proust, (Valentin-Louis-George-Eugene-)Marcel 1871-1922 .... **TCLC 7, 13, 33; WLC**
See also BPFB 3; CA 104; 120; DA; DA3; DAB; DAC; DAM MST, NOV; DLB 65; EW 8; GFL 1789 to the Present; MTCW 1, 2; RGWL 2

Prowler, Harley
See Masters, Edgar Lee

Prus, Boleslaw 1845-1912 .... **TCLC 48**
See also RGWL 2

Pryor, Richard (Franklin Lenox Thomas) 1940- .... **CLC 26**
See also CA 122; 152

Przybyszewski, Stanislaw 1868-1927 .... **TCLC 36**
See also CA 160; DLB 66

Pteleon
See Grieve, C(hristopher) M(urray)
See also DAM POET

Puckett, Lute
See Masters, Edgar Lee

Puig, Manuel 1932-1990 .... **CLC 3, 5, 10, 28, 65, 133; HLC 2**
See also BPFB 3; CA 45-48; CANR 2, 32, 63; CDWLB 3; DA3; DAM MULT; DLB 113; DNFS 1; GLL 1; HW 1, 2; LAW; MTCW 1, 2; RGWL 2; WLIT 1

Pulitzer, Joseph 1847-1911 .... **TCLC 76**
See also CA 114; DLB 23

Purchas, Samuel 1577(?)-1626 .... **LC 70**
See also DLB 151

Purdy, A(lfred) W(ellington) 1918-2000 .... **CLC 3, 6, 14, 50**
See also CA 81-84; 189; CAAS 17; CANR 42, 66; CP 7; DAC; DAM MST, POET; DLB 88; PFS 5; RGEL 2

Purdy, James (Amos) 1923- .... **CLC 2, 4, 10, 28, 52**
See also AMWS 7; CA 33-36R; CAAS 1; CANR 19, 51; CN 7; DLB 2, 218; INT CANR-19; MTCW 1; RGAL 4

Pure, Simon
See Swinnerton, Frank Arthur

Pushkin, Aleksandr Sergeevich
See Pushkin, Alexander (Sergeyevich)
See also DLB 205

Pushkin, Alexander (Sergeyevich) 1799-1837 .... **NCLC 3, 27, 83; PC 10; SSC 27; WLC**
See also DA; DA3; DAB; DAC; DAM DRAM, MST, POET; EW 5; EXPS; RGSF 2; RGWL 2; SATA 61; SSFS 9

P'u Sung-ling 1640-1715 .... **LC 49; SSC 31**

Putnam, Arthur Lee
See Alger, Horatio, Jr.

Puzo, Mario 1920-1999 .... **CLC 1, 2, 6, 36, 107**
See also BPFB 3; CA 65-68; 185; CANR 4, 42, 65, 99; CN 7; CPW; DA3; DAM NOV, POP; DLB 6; MTCW 1, 2; RGAL 4

Pygge, Edward
See Barnes, Julian (Patrick)

Pyle, Ernest Taylor 1900-1945
See Pyle, Ernie
See also CA 115; 160

Pyle, Ernie .... **TCLC 75**
See also Pyle, Ernest Taylor
See also DLB 29; MTCW 2

Pyle, Howard 1853-1911 .... **TCLC 81**
See also BYA 2, 4; CA 109; 137; CLR 22; DLB 42, 188; DLBD 13; LAIT 1; MAICYA 1, 2; SATA 16, 100; WCH; YAW

Pym, Barbara (Mary Crampton) 1913-1980 .... **CLC 13, 19, 37, 111**
See also BPFB 3; BRWS 2; CA 13-14; 97-100; CANR 13, 34; CAP 1; DLB 14, 207; DLBY 1987; MTCW 1, 2; RGEL 2

Pynchon, Thomas (Ruggles, Jr.) 1937- ...... **CLC 2, 3, 6, 9, 11, 18, 33, 62, 72, 123; SSC 14; WLC**
See also AMWS 2; BEST 90:2; BPFB 3; CA 17-20R; CANR 22, 46, 73; CN 7; CPW 1; DA; DA3; DAB; DAC; DAM MST, NOV, POP; DLB 2, 173; MTCW 1, 2; RGAL 4; SFW 4; TUS

Pythagoras c. 582B.C.-c. 507B.C. . **CMLC 22**
See also DLB 176

Q
See Quiller-Couch, Sir Arthur (Thomas)

Qian, Chongzhu
See Ch'ien, Chung-shu

Qian Zhongshu
See Ch'ien, Chung-shu

Qroll
See Dagerman, Stig (Halvard)

Quarrington, Paul (Lewis) 1953- ..... **CLC 65**
See also CA 129; CANR 62, 95

Quasimodo, Salvatore 1901-1968 ..... **CLC 10**
See also CA 13-16; 25-28R; CAP 1; DLB 114; EW 12; MTCW 1; RGWL 2

Quay, Stephen 1947- .... **CLC 95**
See also CA 189

Quay, Timothy 1947- .... **CLC 95**
See also CA 189

Queen, Ellery .... **CLC 3, 11**
See also Dannay, Frederic; Davidson, Avram (James); Deming, Richard; Fairman, Paul W.; Flora, Fletcher; Hoch, Edward D(entinger); Kane, Henry; Lee, Manfred B(ennington); Marlowe, Stephen; Powell, (Oval) Talmage; Sheldon, Walter J(ames); Sturgeon, Theodore (Hamilton); Tracy, Don(ald Fiske); Vance, John Holbrook
See also BPFB 3; CMW 4; MSW; RGAL 4

Queen, Ellery, Jr.
See Dannay, Frederic; Lee, Manfred B(ennington)

Queneau, Raymond 1903-1976 ..... **CLC 2, 5, 10, 42**
See also CA 77-80; 69-72; CANR 32; DLB 72, 258; EW 12; GFL 1789 to the Present; MTCW 1, 2; RGWL 2

Quevedo, Francisco de 1580-1645 .... **LC 23**

Quiller-Couch, Sir Arthur (Thomas) 1863-1944 .... **TCLC 53**
See also CA 118; 166; DLB 135, 153, 190; HGG; RGEL 2; SUFW

Quin, Ann (Marie) 1936-1973 .... **CLC 6**
See also CA 9-12R; 45-48; DLB 14, 231

Quinn, Martin
See Smith, Martin Cruz

Quinn, Peter 1947- .... **CLC 91**
See also CA 197

Quinn, Simon
See Smith, Martin Cruz

Quintana, Leroy V. 1944- .... **PC 36**
See also CA 131; CANR 65; DAM MULT; DLB 82; HLC 2; HW 1, 2

Quiroga, Horacio (Sylvestre) 1878-1937 .... **TCLC 20; HLC 2**
See also CA 117; 131; DAM MULT; HW 1; LAW; MTCW 1; RGSF 2; WLIT 1

Quoirez, Francoise 1935- .... **CLC 9**
See also Sagan, Francoise
See also CA 49-52; CANR 6, 39, 73; CWW 2; MTCW 1, 2

Raabe, Wilhelm (Karl) 1831-1910 . **TCLC 45**
See also CA 167; DLB 129

Rabe, David (William) 1940- .. **CLC 4, 8, 33; DC 16**
See also CA 85-88; CABS 3; CAD; CANR 59; CD 5; DAM DRAM; DFS 3, 8, 13; DLB 7, 228

Rabelais, Francois 1494-1553 .... **LC 5, 60; WLC**
See also DA; DAB; DAC; DAM MST; EW 2; GFL Beginnings to 1789; RGWL 2

Rabinovitch, Sholem 1859-1916
See Aleichem, Sholom
See also CA 104

Rabinyan, Dorit 1972- .... **CLC 119**
See also CA 170

Rachilde
See Vallette, Marguerite Eymery

Racine, Jean 1639-1699 .... **LC 28**
See also DA3; DAB; DAM MST; EW 3; GFL Beginnings to 1789; RGWL 2

Radcliffe, Ann (Ward) 1764-1823 ... **NCLC 6, 55, 106**
See also DLB 39, 178; HGG; RGEL 2; SUFW; WLIT 3

Radclyffe-Hall, Marguerite
See Hall, (Marguerite) Radclyffe

Radiguet, Raymond 1903-1923 ...... **TCLC 29**
See also CA 162; DLB 65; GFL 1789 to the Present; RGWL 2

Radnoti, Miklos 1909-1944 .... **TCLC 16**
See also CA 118; CDWLB 4; DLB 215; RGWL 2

Rado, James 1939- .... **CLC 17**
See also CA 105

Radvanyi, Netty 1900-1983
See Seghers, Anna
See also CA 85-88; 110; CANR 82

Rae, Ben
See Griffiths, Trevor

Raeburn, John (Hay) 1941- .... **CLC 34**
See also CA 57-60

Ragni, Gerome 1942-1991 .... **CLC 17**
See also CA 105; 134

Rahv, Philip .... **CLC 24**
See also Greenberg, Ivan
See also DLB 137

Raimund, Ferdinand Jakob 1790-1836 .... **NCLC 69**
See also DLB 90

Raine, Craig (Anthony) 1944- .. **CLC 32, 103**
See also CA 108; CANR 29, 51, 103; CP 7; DLB 40; PFS 7

Raine, Kathleen (Jessie) 1908- ..... **CLC 7, 45**
See also CA 85-88; CANR 46, 109; CP 7; DLB 20; MTCW 1; RGEL 2

Rainis, Janis 1865-1929 .... **TCLC 29**
See also CA 170; CDWLB 4; DLB 220

Rakosi, Carl .... **CLC 47**
See also Rawley, Callman
See also CAAS 5; CP 7; DLB 193

Ralegh, Sir Walter
See Raleigh, Sir Walter
See also BRW 1; RGEL 2; WP

Raleigh, Richard
See Lovecraft, H(oward) P(hillips)

Raleigh, Sir Walter 1554(?)-1618 .... **LC 31, 39; PC 31**
See also Ralegh, Sir Walter
See also CDBLB Before 1660; DLB 172; EXPP; PFS 14; TEA

Rallentando, H. P.
See Sayers, Dorothy L(eigh)

Ramal, Walter
See de la Mare, Walter (John)

Ramana Maharshi 1879-1950 .... **TCLC 84**

Ramoacn y Cajal, Santiago 1852-1934 .... **TCLC 93**

Ramon, Juan
See Jimenez (Mantecon), Juan Ramon

Ramos, Graciliano 1892-1953 .... **TCLC 32**
See also CA 167; HW 2; LAW; WLIT 1

Rampersad, Arnold 1941- .... **CLC 44**
See also BW 2, 3; CA 127; 133; CANR 81; DLB 111; INT 133

Rampling, Anne
See Rice, Anne
See also GLL 2

Ramsay, Allan 1686(?)-1758 .... **LC 29**
See also DLB 95; RGEL 2

Ramsay, Jay
See Campbell, (John) Ramsey

Ramuz, Charles-Ferdinand 1878-1947 .... **TCLC 33**
See also CA 165

Rand, Ayn 1905-1982 ...... **CLC 3, 30, 44, 79; WLC**
See also AAYA 10; AMWS 4; BPFB 3; BYA 12; CA 13-16R; 105; CANR 27, 73; CDALBS; CPW; DA; DA3; DAC; DAM MST, NOV, POP; DLB 227; MTCW 1, 2; NFS 10; RGAL 4; SFW 4; YAW

Randall, Dudley (Felker) 1914-2000 . **CLC 1, 135; BLC 3**
See also BW 1, 3; CA 25-28R; 189; CANR 23, 82; DAM MULT; DLB 41; PFS 5

Randall, Robert
See Silverberg, Robert

Ranger, Ken
See Creasey, John

Rank, Otto 1884-1939 .... **TCLC 115**

Ransom, John Crowe 1888-1974 .. **CLC 2, 4, 5, 11, 24**
See also AMW; CA 5-8R; 49-52; CANR 6, 34; CDALBS; DA3; DAM POET; DLB 45, 63; EXPP; MTCW 1, 2; RGAL 4

Rao, Raja 1909- .... **CLC 25, 56**
See also CA 73-76; CANR 51; CN 7; DAM NOV; MTCW 1, 2; RGEL 2; RGSF 2

Raphael, Frederic (Michael) 1931- ... **CLC 2, 14**
See also CA 1-4R; CANR 1, 86; CN 7; DLB 14

Ratcliffe, James P.
See Mencken, H(enry) L(ouis)

Rathbone, Julian 1935- .... **CLC 41**
See also CA 101; CANR 34, 73

Rattigan, Terence (Mervyn) 1911-1977 .... **CLC 7**
See also BRWS 7; CA 85-88; 73-76; CBD; CDBLB 1945-1960; DAM DRAM; DFS 8; DLB 13; IDFW 3, 4; MTCW 1, 2; RGEL 2

Ratushinskaya, Irina 1954- .... **CLC 54**
See also CA 129; CANR 68; CWW 2

Raven, Simon (Arthur Noel) 1927-2001 .... **CLC 14**
See also CA 81-84; 197; CANR 86; CN 7

Ravenna, Michael
See Welty, Eudora (Alice)

Rawley, Callman 1903-
See Rakosi, Carl
See also CA 21-24R; CANR 12, 32, 91

Rawlings, Marjorie Kinnan
1896-1953 .... **TCLC 4**
See also AAYA 20; AMWS 10; ANW; BPFB 3; BYA 3; CA 104; 137; CANR 74; CLR 63; DLB 9, 22, 102; DLBD 17; JRDA; MAICYA 1, 2; MTCW 2; RGAL 4; SATA 100; WCH; YABC 1; YAW

Ray, Satyajit 1921-1992 .... **CLC 16, 76**
See also CA 114; 137; DAM MULT

Read, Herbert Edward 1893-1968 ..... **CLC 4**
See also BRW 6; CA 85-88; 25-28R; DLB 20, 149; PAB; RGEL 2

Read, Piers Paul 1941- .... **CLC 4, 10, 25**
See also CA 21-24R; CANR 38, 86; CN 7; DLB 14; SATA 21

Reade, Charles 1814-1884 .... **NCLC 2, 74**
See also DLB 21; RGEL 2

Reade, Hamish
See Gray, Simon (James Holliday)

Reading, Peter 1946- .... **CLC 47**
See also CA 103; CANR 46, 96; CP 7; DLB 40

Reaney, James 1926- .... **CLC 13**
See also CA 41-44R; CAAS 15; CANR 42; CD 5; CP 7; DAC; DAM MST; DLB 68; RGEL 2; SATA 43

Rebreanu, Liviu 1885-1944 .... **TCLC 28**
See also CA 165; DLB 220

Rechy, John (Francisco) 1934- ...... **CLC 1, 7, 14, 18, 107; HLC 2**
See also CA 5-8R; CAAE 195; CAAS 4; CANR 6, 32, 64; CN 7; DAM MULT; DLB 122; DLBY 1982; HW 1, 2; INT CANR-6; RGAL 4

Redcam, Tom 1870-1933 .... **TCLC 25**

Reddin, Keith .... **CLC 67**
See also CAD

Redgrove, Peter (William) 1932- . **CLC 6, 41**
See also BRWS 6; CA 1-4R; CANR 3, 39, 77; CP 7; DLB 40

Redmon, Anne .... **CLC 22**
See also Nightingale, Anne Redmon
See also DLBY 1986

Reed, Eliot
See Ambler, Eric

Reed, Ishmael 1938- .. **CLC 2, 3, 5, 6, 13, 32, 60; BLC 3**
See also AFAW 1, 2; AMWS 10; BPFB 3; BW 2, 3; CA 21-24R; CANR 25, 48, 74; CN 7; CP 7; CSW; DA3; DAM MULT; DLB 2, 5, 33, 169, 227; DLBD 8; MSW; MTCW 1, 2; PFS 6; RGAL 4; TCWW 2

Reed, John (Silas) 1887-1920 .... **TCLC 9**
See also CA 106; 195

Reed, Lou .... **CLC 21**
See also Firbank, Louis

Reese, Lizette Woodworth 1856-1935 . **PC 29**
See also CA 180; DLB 54

Reeve, Clara 1729-1807 .... **NCLC 19**
See also DLB 39; RGEL 2

Reich, Wilhelm 1897-1957 .... **TCLC 57**
See also CA 199

Reid, Christopher (John) 1949- .... **CLC 33**
See also CA 140; CANR 89; CP 7; DLB 40

Reid, Desmond
See Moorcock, Michael (John)

Reid Banks, Lynne 1929-
See Banks, Lynne Reid
See also CA 1-4R; CANR 6, 22, 38, 87; CLR 24; CN 7; JRDA; MAICYA 1, 2; SATA 22, 75, 111; YAW

Reilly, William K.
See Creasey, John

Reiner, Max
See Caldwell, (Janet Miriam) Taylor (Holland)

Reis, Ricardo
See Pessoa, Fernando (Antonio Nogueira)

Remarque, Erich Maria 1898-1970 . **CLC 21**
See also AAYA 27; BPFB 3; CA 77-80; 29-32R; CDWLB 2; DA; DA3; DAB; DAC; DAM MST, NOV; DLB 56; EXPN; LAIT 3; MTCW 1, 2; NFS 4; RGWL 2

Remington, Frederic 1861-1909 ..... **TCLC 89**
See also CA 108; 169; DLB 12, 186, 188; SATA 41

Remizov, A.
See Remizov, Aleksei (Mikhailovich)

Remizov, A. M.
See Remizov, Aleksei (Mikhailovich)

Remizov, Aleksei (Mikhailovich)
1877-1957 .... **TCLC 27**
See also CA 125; 133

Renan, Joseph Ernest 1823-1892 .. **NCLC 26**
See also GFL 1789 to the Present

Renard, Jules 1864-1910 .... **TCLC 17**
See also CA 117; GFL 1789 to the Present

Renault, Mary .... **CLC 3, 11, 17**
See also Challans, Mary
See also BPFB 3; BYA 2; DLBY 1983; GLL 1; LAIT 1; MTCW 2; RGEL 2; RHW

Rendell, Ruth (Barbara) 1930- .. **CLC 28, 48**
See also Vine, Barbara
See also BPFB 3; CA 109; CANR 32, 52, 74; CN 7; CPW; DAM POP; DLB 87; INT CANR-32; MSW; MTCW 1, 2

Renoir, Jean 1894-1979 .... **CLC 20**
See also CA 129; 85-88

Resnais, Alain 1922- .... **CLC 16**

Reverdy, Pierre 1889-1960 .... **CLC 53**
See also CA 97-100; 89-92; DLB 258; GFL 1789 to the Present

Rexroth, Kenneth 1905-1982 .... **CLC 1, 2, 6, 11, 22, 49, 112; PC 20**
See also CA 5-8R; 107; CANR 14, 34, 63; CDALB 1941-1968; DAM POET; DLB 16, 48, 165, 212; DLBY 1982; INT CANR-14; MTCW 1, 2; RGAL 4

Reyes, Alfonso 1889-1959 .. **TCLC 33; HLCS 2**
See also CA 131; HW 1; LAW

Reyes y Basoalto, Ricardo Eliecer Neftali
See Neruda, Pablo

Reymont, Wladyslaw (Stanislaw)
1868(?)-1925 .... **TCLC 5**
See also CA 104

Reynolds, Jonathan 1942- .... **CLC 6, 38**
See also CA 65-68; CANR 28

Reynolds, Joshua 1723-1792 .... **LC 15**
See also DLB 104

Reynolds, Michael S(hane)
1937-2000 .... **CLC 44**
See also CA 65-68; 189; CANR 9, 89, 97

Reznikoff, Charles 1894-1976 .... **CLC 9**
See also CA 33-36; 61-64; CAP 2; DLB 28, 45; WP

Rezzori (d'Arezzo), Gregor von
1914-1998 .... **CLC 25**
See also CA 122; 136; 167

Rhine, Richard
See Silverstein, Alvin; Silverstein, Virginia B(arbara Opshelor)

Rhodes, Eugene Manlove
1869-1934 .... **TCLC 53**
See also CA 198; DLB 256

R'hoone, Lord
See Balzac, Honore de

Rhys, Jean 1894(?)-1979 .... **CLC 2, 4, 6, 14, 19, 51, 124; SSC 21**
See also BRWS 2; CA 25-28R; 85-88; CANR 35, 62; CDBLB 1945-1960; CDWLB 3; DA3; DAM NOV; DLB 36, 117, 162; DNFS 2; MTCW 1, 2; RGEL 2; RGSF 2; RHW

Ribeiro, Darcy 1922-1997 .... **CLC 34**
See also CA 33-36R; 156

Ribeiro, Joao Ubaldo (Osorio Pimentel)
1941- .... **CLC 10, 67**
See also CA 81-84

Ribman, Ronald (Burt) 1932- .... **CLC 7**
See also CA 21-24R; CAD; CANR 46, 80; CD 5

Ricci, Nino 1959- .... **CLC 70**
See also CA 137; CCA 1

Rice, Anne 1941- .... **CLC 41, 128**
See also Rampling, Anne
See also AAYA 9; AMWS 7; BEST 89:2; BPFB 3; CA 65-68; CANR 12, 36, 53, 74, 100; CN 7; CPW; CSW; DA3; DAM POP; GLL 2; HGG; MTCW 2; YAW

Rice, Elmer (Leopold) 1892-1967 ...... **CLC 7, 49**
See also CA 21-22; 25-28R; CAP 2; DAM DRAM; DFS 12; DLB 4, 7; MTCW 1, 2; RGAL 4

Rice, Tim(othy Miles Bindon)
1944- .... **CLC 21**
See also CA 103; CANR 46; DFS 7

Rich, Adrienne (Cecile) 1929- ... **CLC 3, 6, 7, 11, 18, 36, 73, 76, 125; PC 5**
See also AMWS 1; CA 9-12R; CANR 20, 53, 74; CDALBS; CP 7; CSW; CWP; DA3; DAM POET; DLB 5, 67; EXPP; FW; MAWW; MTCW 1, 2; PAB; RGAL 4; WP

Rich, Barbara
See Graves, Robert (von Ranke)

Rich, Robert
See Trumbo, Dalton

Richard, Keith .... **CLC 17**
See also Richards, Keith

Richards, David Adams 1950- .... **CLC 59**
See also CA 93-96; CANR 60; DAC; DLB 53

Richards, I(vor) A(rmstrong)
1893-1979 .... **CLC 14, 24**
See also BRWS 2; CA 41-44R; 89-92; CANR 34, 74; DLB 27; MTCW 2; RGEL 2

Richards, Keith 1943-
See Richard, Keith
See also CA 107; CANR 77

Richardson, Anne
See Roiphe, Anne (Richardson)

Richardson, Dorothy Miller
1873-1957 .... **TCLC 3**
See also CA 104; 192; DLB 36; FW; RGEL 2

Richardson (Robertson), Ethel Florence Lindesay 1870-1946
See Richardson, Henry Handel
See also CA 105; 190; DLB 230; RHW

Richardson, Henry Handel .... **TCLC 4**
See also Richardson (Robertson), Ethel Florence Lindesay
See also DLB 197; RGEL 2; RGSF 2

Richardson, John 1796-1852 .... **NCLC 55**
See also CCA 1; DAC; DLB 99

Richardson, Samuel 1689-1761 ...... **LC 1, 44; WLC**
See also BRW 3; CDBLB 1660-1789; DA; DAB; DAC; DAM MST, NOV; DLB 39; RGEL 2; WLIT 3

Richler, Mordecai 1931-2001 .... **CLC 3, 5, 9, 13, 18, 46, 70**
See also AITN 1; CA 65-68; CANR 31, 62; CCA 1; CLR 17; CWRI 5; DAC; DAM MST, NOV; DLB 53; MAICYA 1, 2; MTCW 1, 2; RGEL 2; SATA 44, 98; SATA-Brief 27

Richter, Conrad (Michael)
1890-1968 .... **CLC 30**
See also AAYA 21; BYA 2; CA 5-8R; 25-28R; CANR 23; DLB 9, 212; LAIT 1; MTCW 1, 2; RGAL 4; SATA 3; TCWW 2; YAW

Ricostranza, Tom
See Ellis, Trey

Riddell, Charlotte 1832-1906 .... **TCLC 40**
See also Riddell, Mrs. J. H.
See also CA 165; DLB 156

Riddell, Mrs. J. H.
See Riddell, Charlotte
See also HGG; SUFW

Ridge, John Rollin 1827-1867 .... **NCLC 82**
See also CA 144; DAM MULT; DLB 175; NNAL

Ridgeway, Jason
See Marlowe, Stephen

Ridgway, Keith 1965- .... **CLC 119**
See also CA 172

Riding, Laura .... **CLC 3, 7**
See also Jackson, Laura (Riding)
See also RGAL 4

Riefenstahl, Berta Helene Amalia 1902-
See Riefenstahl, Leni
See also CA 108

Riefenstahl, Leni .... **CLC 16**
See also Riefenstahl, Berta Helene Amalia

Riffe, Ernest
See Bergman, (Ernst) Ingmar

Riggs, (Rolla) Lynn 1899-1954 .... **TCLC 56**
See also CA 144; DAM MULT; DLB 175; NNAL

Riis, Jacob A(ugust) 1849-1914 ..... **TCLC 80**
See also CA 113; 168; DLB 23

Riley, James Whitcomb
1849-1916 .... **TCLC 51**
See also CA 118; 137; DAM POET; MAICYA 1, 2; RGAL 4; SATA 17

Riley, Tex
See Creasey, John

Rilke, Rainer Maria 1875-1926 .. **TCLC 1, 6, 19; PC 2**
See also CA 104; 132; CANR 62, 99; CDWLB 2; DA3; DAM POET; DLB 81; EW 9; MTCW 1, 2; RGWL 2; WP

Rimbaud, (Jean Nicolas) Arthur
1854-1891 .... **NCLC 4, 35, 82; PC 3; WLC**
See also DA; DA3; DAB; DAC; DAM MST, POET; DLB 217; EW 7; GFL 1789 to the Present; RGWL 2; TWA; WP

Rinehart, Mary Roberts
1876-1958 .... **TCLC 52**
See also BPFB 3; CA 108; 166; RGAL 4; RHW

Ringmaster, The
See Mencken, H(enry) L(ouis)

Ringwood, Gwen(dolyn Margaret) Pharis
1910-1984 .... **CLC 48**
See also CA 148; 112; DLB 88

Rio, Michel 19(?)- .... **CLC 43**

Ritsos, Giannes
See Ritsos, Yannis

Ritsos, Yannis 1909-1990 .... **CLC 6, 13, 31**
See also CA 77-80; 133; CANR 39, 61; EW 12; MTCW 1; RGWL 2

Ritter, Erika 1948(?)- .... **CLC 52**
See also CD 5; CWD

Rivera, Jose Eustasio 1889-1928 ... **TCLC 35**
See also CA 162; HW 1, 2; LAW

Rivera, Tomas 1935-1984
See also CA 49-52; CANR 32; DLB 82; HLCS 2; HW 1; RGAL 4; TCWW 2; WLIT 1

Rivers, Conrad Kent 1933-1968 .... **CLC 1**
See also BW 1; CA 85-88; DLB 41

Rivers, Elfrida
See Bradley, Marion Zimmer
See also GLL 1

Riverside, John
See Heinlein, Robert A(nson)

Rizal, Jose 1861-1896 .... **NCLC 27**

Roa Bastos, Augusto (Antonio)
1917- .... **CLC 45; HLC 2**
See also CA 131; DAM MULT; DLB 113; HW 1; LAW; RGSF 2; WLIT 1

Robbe-Grillet, Alain 1922- .... **CLC 1, 2, 4, 6, 8, 10, 14, 43, 128**
See also BPFB 3; CA 9-12R; CANR 33, 65; DLB 83; EW 13; GFL 1789 to the Present; IDFW 3, 4; MTCW 1, 2; RGWL 2

Robbins, Harold 1916-1997 .... **CLC 5**
See also BPFB 3; CA 73-76; 162; CANR 26, 54; DA3; DAM NOV; MTCW 1, 2

Robbins, Thomas Eugene 1936-
See Robbins, Tom
See also CA 81-84; CANR 29, 59, 95; CN 7; CPW; CSW; DA3; DAM NOV, POP; MTCW 1, 2

Robbins, Tom .... **CLC 9, 32, 64**
See also Robbins, Thomas Eugene
See also AAYA 32; AMWS 10; BEST 90:3; BPFB 3; DLBY 1980; MTCW 2

Robbins, Trina 1938- .... **CLC 21**
See also CA 128

Roberts, Charles G(eorge) D(ouglas)
1860-1943 .... **TCLC 8**
See also CA 105; 188; CLR 33; CWRI 5; DLB 92; RGEL 2; RGSF 2; SATA 88; SATA-Brief 29

Roberts, Elizabeth Madox
1886-1941 .... **TCLC 68**
See also CA 111; 166; CWRI 5; DLB 9, 54, 102; RGAL 4; RHW; SATA 33; SATA-Brief 27; WCH

Roberts, Kate 1891-1985 .... **CLC 15**
See also CA 107; 116

Roberts, Keith (John Kingston)
1935-2000 .... **CLC 14**
See also CA 25-28R; CANR 46; SFW 4

Roberts, Kenneth (Lewis)
1885-1957 .... **TCLC 23**
See also CA 109; 199; DLB 9; RGAL 4; RHW

Roberts, Michele (Brigitte) 1949- ..... **CLC 48**
See also CA 115; CANR 58; CN 7; DLB 231; FW

Robertson, Ellis
See Ellison, Harlan (Jay); Silverberg, Robert

Robertson, Thomas William
1829-1871 .... **NCLC 35**
See also Robertson, Tom
See also DAM DRAM

Robertson, Tom
See Robertson, Thomas William
See also RGEL 2

Robeson, Kenneth
See Dent, Lester

Robinson, Edwin Arlington
1869-1935 .... **TCLC 5, 101; PC 1, 35**
See also AMW; CA 104; 133; CDALB 1865-1917; DA; DAC; DAM MST, POET; DLB 54; EXPP; MTCW 1, 2; PAB; PFS 4; RGAL 4; WP

Robinson, Henry Crabb
1775-1867 .... **NCLC 15**
See also DLB 107

Robinson, Jill 1936- .... **CLC 10**
See also CA 102; INT 102

Robinson, Kim Stanley 1952- .... **CLC 34**
See also AAYA 26; CA 126; CN 7; SATA 109; SCFW 2; SFW 4

Robinson, Lloyd
See Silverberg, Robert

Robinson, Marilynne 1944- .... **CLC 25**
See also CA 116; CANR 80; CN 7; DLB 206

Robinson, Smokey .... **CLC 21**
See also Robinson, William, Jr.

Robinson, William, Jr. 1940-
See Robinson, Smokey
See also CA 116

Robison, Mary 1949- .... **CLC 42, 98**
See also CA 113; 116; CANR 87; CN 7; DLB 130; INT 116; RGSF 2

Rochester
See Wilmot, John
See also RGEL 2

Rod, Edouard 1857-1910 .... **TCLC 52**

Roddenberry, Eugene Wesley 1921-1991
See Roddenberry, Gene
See also CA 110; 135; CANR 37; SATA 45; SATA-Obit 69

Roddenberry, Gene .... **CLC 17**
See also Roddenberry, Eugene Wesley
See also AAYA 5; SATA-Obit 69

Rodgers, Mary 1931- .... **CLC 12**
See also BYA 5; CA 49-52; CANR 8, 55, 90; CLR 20; CWRI 5; INT CANR-8; JRDA; MAICYA 1, 2; SATA 8, 130

Rodgers, W(illiam) R(obert)
1909-1969 .... **CLC 7**
See also CA 85-88; DLB 20; RGEL 2

Rodman, Eric
See Silverberg, Robert

Rodman, Howard 1920(?)-1985 .... **CLC 65**
See also CA 118

Rodman, Maia
See Wojciechowska, Maia (Teresa)

Rodo, Jose Enrique 1871(?)-1917
See also CA 178; HLCS 2; HW 2; LAW

Rodolph, Utto
See Ouologuem, Yambo

Rodriguez, Claudio 1934-1999 .... **CLC 10**
See also CA 188; DLB 134

Rodriguez, Richard 1944- .... **CLC 155; HLC 2**
See also CA 110; CANR 66; DAM MULT; DLB 82, 256; HW 1, 2; LAIT 5; NCFS 3; WLIT 1

Roelvaag, O(le) E(dvart) 1876-1931
See Rolvaag, O(le) E(dvart)
See also CA 117; 171

Roethke, Theodore (Huebner)
1908-1963 .... **CLC 1, 3, 8, 11, 19, 46, 101; PC 15**
See also AMW; CA 81-84; CABS 2; CDALB 1941-1968; DA3; DAM POET; DLB 5, 206; EXPP; MTCW 1, 2; PAB; PFS 3; RGAL 4; WP

Rogers, Samuel 1763-1855 .... **NCLC 69**
See also DLB 93; RGEL 2

Rogers, Thomas Hunton 1927- .... **CLC 57**
See also CA 89-92; INT 89-92

Rogers, Will(iam Penn Adair)
1879-1935 .... **TCLC 8, 71**
See also CA 105; 144; DA3; DAM MULT; DLB 11; MTCW 2; NNAL

Rogin, Gilbert 1929- .... **CLC 18**
See also CA 65-68; CANR 15

Rohan, Koda
See Koda Shigeyuki

Rohlfs, Anna Katharine Green
See Green, Anna Katharine

Rohmer, Eric .... **CLC 16**
See also Scherer, Jean-Marie Maurice

Rohmer, Sax .... **TCLC 28**
See also Ward, Arthur Henry Sarsfield
See also DLB 70; MSW; SUFW

Roiphe, Anne (Richardson) 1935- .. **CLC 3, 9**
See also CA 89-92; CANR 45, 73; DLBY 1980; INT 89-92

Rojas, Fernando de 1475-1541 .... **LC 23; HLCS 1**
See also RGWL 2

Rojas, Gonzalo 1917-
See also CA 178; HLCS 2; HW 2; LAWS 1

Rolfe, Frederick (William Serafino Austin Lewis Mary) 1860-1913 .... **TCLC 12**
See Corvo, Baron
See also CA 107; DLB 34, 156; RGEL 2

Rolland, Romain 1866-1944 .... **TCLC 23**
See also CA 118; 197; DLB 65; GFL 1789 to the Present; RGWL 2

Rolle, Richard c. 1300-c. 1349 ...... **CMLC 21**
See also DLB 146; RGEL 2

Rolvaag, O(le) E(dvart) .... **TCLC 17**
See also Roelvaag, O(le) E(dvart)
See also DLB 9, 212; NFS 5; RGAL 4

Romain Arnaud, Saint
See Aragon, Louis

Romains, Jules 1885-1972 .... **CLC 7**
See also CA 85-88; CANR 34; DLB 65; GFL 1789 to the Present; MTCW 1

Romero, Jose Ruben 1890-1952 .... **TCLC 14**
See also CA 114; 131; HW 1; LAW

Ronsard, Pierre de 1524-1585 . **LC 6, 54; PC 11**
See also EW 2; GFL Beginnings to 1789; RGWL 2

Rooke, Leon 1934- .... **CLC 25, 34**
See also CA 25-28R; CANR 23, 53; CCA 1; CPW; DAM POP

Roosevelt, Franklin Delano 1882-1945 .... **TCLC 93**
See also CA 116; 173; LAIT 3

Roosevelt, Theodore 1858-1919 ..... **TCLC 69**
See also CA 115; 170; DLB 47, 186

Roper, William 1498-1578 .... **LC 10**

Roquelaure, A. N.
See Rice, Anne

Rosa, Joao Guimaraes 1908-1967 ... **CLC 23; HLCS 1**
See also Guimaraes Rosa, Joao
See also CA 89-92; DLB 113; WLIT 1

Rose, Wendy 1948- .... **CLC 85; PC 13**
See also CA 53-56; CANR 5, 51; CWP; DAM MULT; DLB 175; NNAL; PFS 13; RGAL 4; SATA 12

Rosen, R. D.
See Rosen, Richard (Dean)

Rosen, Richard (Dean) 1949- .... **CLC 39**
See also CA 77-80; CANR 62; CMW 4; INT CANR-30

Rosenberg, Isaac 1890-1918 .... **TCLC 12**
See also BRW 6; CA 107; 188; DLB 20, 216; PAB; RGEL 2

Rosenblatt, Joe .... **CLC 15**
See also Rosenblatt, Joseph

Rosenblatt, Joseph 1933-
See Rosenblatt, Joe
See also CA 89-92; CP 7; INT 89-92

Rosenfeld, Samuel
See Tzara, Tristan

Rosenstock, Sami
See Tzara, Tristan

Rosenstock, Samuel
See Tzara, Tristan

Rosenthal, M(acha) L(ouis) 1917-1996 .... **CLC 28**
See also CA 1-4R; 152; CAAS 6; CANR 4, 51; CP 7; DLB 5; SATA 59

Ross, Barnaby
See Dannay, Frederic

Ross, Bernard L.
See Follett, Ken(neth Martin)

Ross, J. H.
See Lawrence, T(homas) E(dward)

Ross, John Hume
See Lawrence, T(homas) E(dward)

Ross, Martin 1862-1915
See Martin, Violet Florence
See also DLB 135; GLL 2; RGEL 2; RGSF 2

Ross, (James) Sinclair 1908-1996 ... **CLC 13; SSC 24**
See also CA 73-76; CANR 81; CN 7; DAC; DAM MST; DLB 88; RGEL 2; RGSF 2; TCWW 2

Rossetti, Christina (Georgina) 1830-1894 .... **NCLC 2, 50, 66; PC 7; WLC**
See also BRW 5; BYA 4; DA; DA3; DAB; DAC; DAM MST, POET; DLB 35, 163, 240; EXPP; MAICYA 1, 2; PFS 10, 14; RGEL 2; SATA 20; WCH

Rossetti, Dante Gabriel 1828-1882 . **NCLC 4, 77; WLC**
See also BRW 5; CDBLB 1832-1890; DA; DAB; DAC; DAM MST, POET; DLB 35; EXPP; RGEL 2

Rossi, Cristina Peri
See Peri Rossi, Cristina

Rossi, Jean Baptiste 1931-
See Japrisot, Sebastien

Rossner, Judith (Perelman) 1935- . **CLC 6, 9, 29**
See also AITN 2; BEST 90:3; BPFB 3; CA 17-20R; CANR 18, 51, 73; CN 7; DLB 6; INT CANR-18; MTCW 1, 2

Rostand, Edmond (Eugene Alexis) 1868-1918 .... **TCLC 6, 37; DC 10**
See also CA 104; 126; DA; DA3; DAB; DAC; DAM DRAM, MST; DFS 1; DLB 192; LAIT 1; MTCW 1; RGWL 2

Roth, Henry 1906-1995 ..... **CLC 2, 6, 11, 104**
See also AMWS 9; CA 11-12; 149; CANR 38, 63; CAP 1; CN 7; DA3; DLB 28; MTCW 1, 2; RGAL 4

Roth, (Moses) Joseph 1894-1939 ... **TCLC 33**
See also CA 160; DLB 85; RGWL 2

Roth, Philip (Milton) 1933- ... **CLC 1, 2, 3, 4, 6, 9, 15, 22, 31, 47, 66, 86, 119; SSC 26; WLC**
See also AMWS 3; BEST 90:3; BPFB 3; CA 1-4R; CANR 1, 22, 36, 55, 89; CDALB 1968-1988; CN 7; CPW 1; DA; DA3; DAB; DAC; DAM MST, NOV, POP; DLB 2, 28, 173; DLBY 1982; MTCW 1, 2; RGAL 4; RGSF 2; SSFS 12

Rothenberg, Jerome 1931- .... **CLC 6, 57**
See also CA 45-48; CANR 1, 106; CP 7; DLB 5, 193

Rotter, Pat ed. .... **CLC 65**

Roumain, Jacques (Jean Baptiste) 1907-1944 .... **TCLC 19; BLC 3**
See also BW 1; CA 117; 125; DAM MULT

Rourke, Constance (Mayfield) 1885-1941 .... **TCLC 12**
See also CA 107; YABC 1

Rousseau, Jean-Baptiste 1671-1741 ...... **LC 9**

Rousseau, Jean-Jacques 1712-1778 .... **LC 14, 36; WLC**
See also DA; DA3; DAB; DAC; DAM MST; EW 4; GFL Beginnings to 1789; RGWL 2

Roussel, Raymond 1877-1933 .... **TCLC 20**
See also CA 117; GFL 1789 to the Present

Rovit, Earl (Herbert) 1927- .... **CLC 7**
See also CA 5-8R; CANR 12

Rowe, Elizabeth Singer 1674-1737 ..... **LC 44**
See also DLB 39, 95

Rowe, Nicholas 1674-1718 .... **LC 8**
See also DLB 84; RGEL 2

Rowlandson, Mary 1637(?)-1678 .... **LC 66**
See also DLB 24, 200; RGAL 4

Rowley, Ames Dorrance
See Lovecraft, H(oward) P(hillips)

Rowling, J(oanne) K(athleen) 1966(?)- .... **CLC 137**
See also AAYA 34; BYA 13, 14; CA 173; CLR 66, 80; SATA 109

Rowson, Susanna Haswell 1762(?)-1824 .... **NCLC 5, 69**
See also DLB 37, 200; RGAL 4

Roy, Arundhati 1960(?)- .... **CLC 109**
See also CA 163; CANR 90; DLBY 1997

Roy, Gabrielle 1909-1983 .... **CLC 10, 14**
See also CA 53-56; 110; CANR 5, 61; CCA 1; DAB; DAC; DAM MST; DLB 68; MTCW 1; RGWL 2; SATA 104

Royko, Mike 1932-1997 .... **CLC 109**
See also CA 89-92; 157; CANR 26; CPW

Rozanov, Vassili 1856-1919 .... **TCLC 104**

Rozewicz, Tadeusz 1921- ...... **CLC 9, 23, 139**
See also CA 108; CANR 36, 66; CWW 2; DA3; DAM POET; DLB 232; MTCW 1, 2

Ruark, Gibbons 1941- .... **CLC 3**
See also CA 33-36R; CAAS 23; CANR 14, 31, 57; DLB 120

Rubens, Bernice (Ruth) 1923- .... **CLC 19, 31**
See also CA 25-28R; CANR 33, 65; CN 7; DLB 14, 207; MTCW 1

Rubin, Harold
See Robbins, Harold

Rudkin, (James) David 1936- .... **CLC 14**
See also CA 89-92; CBD; CD 5; DLB 13

Rudnik, Raphael 1933- .... **CLC 7**
See also CA 29-32R

Ruffian, M.
See Hasek, Jaroslav (Matej Frantisek)

Ruiz, Jose Martinez .... **CLC 11**
See also Martinez Ruiz, Jose

Rukeyser, Muriel 1913-1980 . **CLC 6, 10, 15, 27; PC 12**
See also AMWS 6; CA 5-8R; 93-96; CANR 26, 60; DA3; DAM POET; DLB 48; FW; GLL 2; MTCW 1, 2; PFS 10; RGAL 4; SATA-Obit 22

Rule, Jane (Vance) 1931- .... **CLC 27**
See also CA 25-28R; CAAS 18; CANR 12, 87; CN 7; DLB 60; FW

Rulfo, Juan 1918-1986 .. **CLC 8, 80; HLC 2; SSC 25**
See also CA 85-88; 118; CANR 26; CDWLB 3; DAM MULT; DLB 113; HW 1, 2; LAW; MTCW 1, 2; RGSF 2; RGWL 2; WLIT 1

Rumi, Jalal al-Din 1207-1273 .... **CMLC 20**
See also RGWL 2; WP

Runeberg, Johan 1804-1877 .... **NCLC 41**

Runyon, (Alfred) Damon 1884(?)-1946 .... **TCLC 10**
See also CA 107; 165; DLB 11, 86, 171; MTCW 2; RGAL 4

Rush, Norman 1933- .... **CLC 44**
See also CA 121; 126; INT 126

Rushdie, (Ahmed) Salman 1947- .... **CLC 23, 31, 55, 100; WLCS**
See also BEST 89:3; BPFB 3; BRWS 4; CA 108; 111; CANR 33, 56, 108; CN 7; CPW 1; DA3; DAB; DAC; DAM MST, NOV, POP; DLB 194; FANT; INT CA-111; MTCW 1, 2; RGEL 2; RGSF 2; WLIT 4

Rushforth, Peter (Scott) 1945- .... **CLC 19**
See also CA 101

Ruskin, John 1819-1900 .... **TCLC 63**
See also BRW 5; BYA 5; CA 114; 129; CDBLB 1832-1890; DLB 55, 163, 190; RGEL 2; SATA 24; WCH

Russ, Joanna 1937- .... **CLC 15**
See also BPFB 3; CA 5-28R; CANR 11, 31, 65; CN 7; DLB 8; FW; GLL 1; MTCW 1; SCFW 2; SFW 4

Russell, George William 1867-1935
See A.E.; Baker, Jean H.
See also CA 104; 153; CDBLB 1890-1914; DAM POET; RGEL 2

Russell, Jeffrey Burton 1934- .... **CLC 70**
See also CA 25-28R; CANR 11, 28, 52

Russell, (Henry) Ken(neth Alfred)
1927- .... **CLC 16**
See also CA 105

Russell, William Martin 1947-
See Russell, Willy
See also CA 164; CANR 107

Russell, Willy .... **CLC 60**
See Russell, William Martin
See also CBD; CD 5; DLB 233

Rutherford, Mark .... **TCLC 25**
See also White, William Hale
See also DLB 18; RGEL 2

Ruyslinck, Ward .... **CLC 14**
See also Belser, Reimond Karel Maria de

Ryan, Cornelius (John) 1920-1974 ..... **CLC 7**
See also CA 69-72; 53-56; CANR 38

Ryan, Michael 1946- .... **CLC 65**
See also CA 49-52; CANR 109; DLBY 1982

Ryan, Tim
See Dent, Lester

Rybakov, Anatoli (Naumovich)
1911-1998 .... **CLC 23, 53**
See also CA 126; 135; 172; SATA 79; SATA-Obit 108

Ryder, Jonathan
See Ludlum, Robert

Ryga, George 1932-1987 .... **CLC 14**
See also CA 101; 124; CANR 43, 90; CCA 1; DAC; DAM MST; DLB 60

S. H.
See Hartmann, Sadakichi

S. S.
See Sassoon, Siegfried (Lorraine)

Saba, Umberto 1883-1957 .... **TCLC 33**
See also CA 144; CANR 79; DLB 114; RGWL 2

Sabatini, Rafael 1875-1950 .... **TCLC 47**
See also BPFB 3; CA 162; RHW

Sabato, Ernesto (R.) 1911- .... **CLC 10, 23; HLC 2**
See also CA 97-100; CANR 32, 65; CDWLB 3; DAM MULT; DLB 145; HW 1, 2; LAW; MTCW 1, 2

Sa-Carniero, Mario de 1890-1916 . **TCLC 83**

Sacastru, Martin
See Bioy Casares, Adolfo
See also CWW 2

Sacher-Masoch, Leopold von
1836(?)-1895 .... **NCLC 31**

Sachs, Marilyn (Stickle) 1927- .... **CLC 35**
See also AAYA 2; BYA 6; CA 17-20R; CANR 13, 47; CLR 2; JRDA; MAICYA 1, 2; SAAS 2; SATA 3, 68; SATA-Essay 110; WYA; YAW

Sachs, Nelly 1891-1970 .... **CLC 14, 98**
See also CA 17-18; 25-28R; CANR 87; CAP 2; MTCW 2; RGWL 2

Sackler, Howard (Oliver)
1929-1982 .... **CLC 14**
See also CA 61-64; 108; CAD; CANR 30; DLB 7

Sacks, Oliver (Wolf) 1933- .... **CLC 67**
See also CA 53-56; CANR 28, 50, 76; CPW; DA3; INT CANR-28; MTCW 1, 2

Sadakichi
See Hartmann, Sadakichi

Sade, Donatien Alphonse Francois
1740-1814 .... **NCLC 3, 47**
See also EW 4; GFL Beginnings to 1789; RGWL 2

Sadoff, Ira 1945- .... **CLC 9**
See also CA 53-56; CANR 5, 21, 109; DLB 120

Saetone
See Camus, Albert

Safire, William 1929- .... **CLC 10**
See also CA 17-20R; CANR 31, 54, 91

Sagan, Carl (Edward) 1934-1996 .... **CLC 30, 112**
See also AAYA 2; CA 25-28R; 155; CANR 11, 36, 74; CPW; DA3; MTCW 1, 2; SATA 58; SATA-Obit 94

Sagan, Francoise .... **CLC 3, 6, 9, 17, 36**
See also Quoirez, Francoise
See also CWW 2; DLB 83; GFL 1789 to the Present; MTCW 2

Sahgal, Nayantara (Pandit) 1927- ..... **CLC 41**
See also CA 9-12R; CANR 11, 88; CN 7

Said, Edward W. 1935- .... **CLC 123**
See also CA 21-24R; CANR 45, 74, 107; DLB 67; MTCW 2

Saint, H(arry) F. 1941- .... **CLC 50**
See also CA 127

St. Aubin de Teran, Lisa 1953-
See Teran, Lisa St. Aubin de
See also CA 118; 126; CN 7; INT 126

Saint Birgitta of Sweden c. 1303-1373 .... **CMLC 24**

Sainte-Beuve, Charles Augustin
1804-1869 .... **NCLC 5**
See also DLB 217; EW 6; GFL 1789 to the Present

Saint-Exupery, Antoine (Jean Baptiste Marie Roger) de 1900-1944 .... **TCLC 2, 56; WLC**
See also BPFB 3; BYA 3; CA 108; 132; CLR 10; DA3; DAM NOV; DLB 72; EW 12; GFL 1789 to the Present; LAIT 3; MAICYA 1; MTCW 1, 2; RGWL 2; SATA 20

St. John, David
See Hunt, E(verette) Howard, (Jr.)

St. John, J. Hector
See Crevecoeur, Michel Guillaume Jean de

Saint-John Perse
See Leger, (Marie-Rene Auguste) Alexis Saint-Leger
See also EW 10; GFL 1789 to the Present; RGWL 2

Saintsbury, George (Edward Bateman)
1845-1933 .... **TCLC 31**
See also CA 160; DLB 57, 149

Sait Faik .... **TCLC 23**
See also Abasiyanik, Sait Faik

Saki .... **TCLC 3; SSC 12**
See also Munro, H(ector) H(ugh)
See also BRWS 6; LAIT 2; MTCW 2; RGEL 2; SSFS 1; SUFW

Sakutaro, Hagiwara
See Hagiwara, Sakutaro

Sala, George Augustus 1828-1895 . **NCLC 46**

Saladin 1138-1193 .... **CMLC 38**

Salama, Hannu 1936- .... **CLC 18**

Salamanca, J(ack) R(ichard) 1922- .. **CLC 4, 15**
See also CA 25-28R; CAAE 193

Salas, Floyd Francis 1931-
See also CA 119; CAAS 27; CANR 44, 75, 93; DAM MULT; DLB 82; HLC 2; HW 1, 2; MTCW 2

Sale, J. Kirkpatrick
See Sale, Kirkpatrick

Sale, Kirkpatrick 1937- .... **CLC 68**
See also CA 13-16R; CANR 10

Salinas, Luis Omar 1937- ... **CLC 90; HLC 2**
See also CA 131; CANR 81; DAM MULT; DLB 82; HW 1, 2

Salinas (y Serrano), Pedro
1891(?)-1951 .... **TCLC 17**
See also CA 117; DLB 134

Salinger, J(erome) D(avid) 1919- .. **CLC 1, 3, 8, 12, 55, 56, 138; SSC 2, 28; WLC**
See also AAYA 2, 36; AMW; BPFB 3; CA 5-8R; CANR 39; CDALB 1941-1968; CLR 18; CN 7; CPW 1; DA; DA3; DAB; DAC; DAM MST, NOV, POP; DLB 2, 102, 173; EXPN; LAIT 4; MAICYA 1, 2; MTCW 1, 2; NFS 1; RGAL 4; RGSF 2; SATA 67; WYA; YAW

Salisbury, John
See Caute, (John) David

Salter, James 1925- .... **CLC 7, 52, 59**
See also AMWS 9; CA 73-76; CANR 107; DLB 130

Saltus, Edgar (Everton) 1855-1921 . **TCLC 8**
See also CA 105; DLB 202; RGAL 4

Saltykov, Mikhail Evgrafovich
1826-1889 .... **NCLC 16**
See also DLB 238:

Saltykov-Shchedrin, N.
See Saltykov, Mikhail Evgrafovich

Samarakis, Antonis 1919- .... **CLC 5**
See also CA 25-28R; CAAS 16; CANR 36

Sanchez, Florencio 1875-1910 .... **TCLC 37**
See also CA 153; HW 1; LAW

Sanchez, Luis Rafael 1936- .... **CLC 23**
See also CA 128; DLB 145; HW 1; WLIT 1

Sanchez, Sonia 1934- .... **CLC 5, 116; BLC 3; PC 9**
See also BW 2, 3; CA 33-36R; CANR 24, 49, 74; CLR 18; CP 7; CSW; CWP; DA3; DAM MULT; DLB 41; DLBD 8; MAICYA 1, 2; MTCW 1, 2; SATA 22; WP

Sand, George 1804-1876 ..... **NCLC 2, 42, 57; WLC**
See also DA; DA3; DAB; DAC; DAM MST, NOV; DLB 119, 192; EW 6; FW; GFL 1789 to the Present; RGWL 2

Sandburg, Carl (August) 1878-1967 . **CLC 1, 4, 10, 15, 35; PC 2; WLC**
See also AAYA 24; AMW; BYA 1, 3; CA 5-8R; 25-28R; CANR 35; CDALB 1865-1917; CLR 67; DA; DA3; DAB; DAC; DAM MST, POET; DLB 17, 54; EXPP; LAIT 2; MAICYA 1, 2; MTCW 1, 2; PAB; PFS 3, 6, 12; RGAL 4; SATA 8; WCH; WP; WYA

Sandburg, Charles
See Sandburg, Carl (August)

Sandburg, Charles A.
See Sandburg, Carl (August)

Sanders, (James) Ed(ward) 1939- .... **CLC 53**
See also Sanders, Edward
See also CA 13-16R; CAAS 21; CANR 13, 44, 78; CP 7; DAM POET; DLB 16, 244

Sanders, Edward
See Sanders, (James) Ed(ward)
See also DLB 244

Sanders, Lawrence 1920-1998 .... **CLC 41**
See also BEST 89:4; BPFB 3; CA 81-84; 165; CANR 33, 62; CMW 4; CPW; DA3; DAM POP; MTCW 1

Sanders, Noah
See Blount, Roy (Alton), Jr.

Sanders, Winston P.
See Anderson, Poul (William)

Sandoz, Mari(e Susette) 1900-1966 .. **CLC 28**
See also CA 1-4R; 25-28R; CANR 17, 64; DLB 9, 212; LAIT 2; MTCW 1, 2; SATA 5; TCWW 2

Saner, Reg(inald Anthony) 1931- .... **CLC 9**
See also CA 65-68; CP 7

Sankara 788-820 .... **CMLC 32**

Sannazaro, Jacopo 1456(?)-1530 .... **LC 8**
See also RGWL 2

Sansom, William 1912-1976 . **CLC 2, 6; SSC 21**
See also CA 5-8R; 65-68; CANR 42; DAM NOV; DLB 139; MTCW 1; RGEL 2; RGSF 2

Santayana, George 1863-1952 .... **TCLC 40**
See also AMW; CA 115; 194; DLB 54, 71, 246; DLBD 13; RGAL 4

Santiago, Danny .... **CLC 33**
See also James, Daniel (Lewis)
See also DLB 122

Santmyer, Helen Hooven
1895-1986 .... **CLC 33**
See also CA 1-4R; 118; CANR 15, 33; DLBY 1984; MTCW 1; RHW

Santoka, Taneda 1882-1940 .... **TCLC 72**

Santos, Bienvenido N(uqui)
1911-1996 .... **CLC 22**
See also CA 101; 151; CANR 19, 46; DAM MULT; RGAL 4

Sapir, Edward 1884-1939 .... **TCLC 108**
See also DLB 92

Sapper .... **TCLC 44**
See also McNeile, Herman Cyril

Sapphire
See Sapphire, Brenda

Sapphire, Brenda 1950- .... **CLC 99**

Sappho fl. 625?-6th cent. B.C.- ... **CMLC 3; PC 5**
See also CDWLB 1; DA3; DAM POET; DLB 176; RGWL 2; WP

Saramago, Jose 1922- ..... **CLC 119; HLCS 1**
See also CA 153; CANR 96

Sarduy, Severo 1937-1993 .... **CLC 6, 97; HLCS 2**
See also CA 89-92; 142; CANR 58, 81; CWW 2; DLB 113; HW 1, 2; LAW

Sargeson, Frank 1903-1982 .... **CLC 31**
See also CA 25-28R; 106; CANR 38, 79; GLL 2; RGEL 2; RGSF 2

Sarmiento, Domingo Faustino 1811-1888
See also HLCS 2; LAW; WLIT 1

Sarmiento, Felix Ruben Garcia
See Dario, Ruben

Saro-Wiwa, Ken(ule Beeson)
1941-1995 .... **CLC 114**
See also BW 2; CA 142; 150; CANR 60; DLB 157

Saroyan, William 1908-1981 ... **CLC 1, 8, 10, 29, 34, 56; SSC 21; WLC**
See also CA 5-8R; 103; CAD; CANR 30; CDALBS; DA; DA3; DAB; DAC; DAM DRAM, MST, NOV; DLB 7, 9, 86; DLBY 1981; LAIT 4; MTCW 1, 2; RGAL 4; RGSF 2; SATA 23; SATA-Obit 24; SSFS 14

Sarraute, Nathalie 1900-1999 .... **CLC 1, 2, 4, 8, 10, 31, 80**
See also BPFB 3; CA 9-12R; 187; CANR 23, 66; CWW 2; DLB 83; EW 12; GFL 1789 to the Present; MTCW 1, 2; RGWL 2

Sarton, (Eleanor) May 1912-1995 ..... **CLC 4, 14, 49, 91; PC 39**
See also AMWS 8; CA 1-4R; 149; CANR 1, 34, 55; CN 7; CP 7; DAM POET; DLB 48; DLBY 1981; FW; INT CANR-34; MTCW 1, 2; RGAL 4; SATA 36; SATA-Obit 86; TCLC 120

Sartre, Jean-Paul 1905-1980 . **CLC 1, 4, 7, 9, 13, 18, 24, 44, 50, 52; DC 3; SSC 32; WLC**
See also CA 9-12R; 97-100; CANR 21; DA; DA3; DAB; DAC; DAM DRAM, MST, NOV; DFS 5; DLB 72; EW 12; GFL 1789 to the Present; MTCW 1, 2; RGSF 2; RGWL 2; SSFS 9

Sassoon, Siegfried (Lorraine)
1886-1967 .... **CLC 36, 130; PC 12**
See also BRW 6; CA 104; 25-28R; CANR 36; DAB; DAM MST, NOV, POET; DLB 20, 191; DLBD 18; MTCW 1, 2; PAB; RGEL 2

Satterfield, Charles
See Pohl, Frederik

Satyremont
See Peret, Benjamin

Saul, John (W. III) 1942- .... **CLC 46**
See also AAYA 10; BEST 90:4; CA 81-84; CANR 16, 40, 81; CPW; DAM NOV, POP; HGG; SATA 98

Saunders, Caleb
See Heinlein, Robert A(nson)

Saura (Atares), Carlos 1932-1998 .... **CLC 20**
See also CA 114; 131; CANR 79; HW 1

Sauser-Hall, Frederic 1887-1961 ...... **CLC 18**
See also Cendrars, Blaise
See also CA 102; 93-96; CANR 36, 62; MTCW 1

Saussure, Ferdinand de
1857-1913 .... **TCLC 49**
See also DLB 242

Savage, Catharine
See Brosman, Catharine Savage

Savage, Thomas 1915- .... **CLC 40**
See also CA 126; 132; CAAS 15; CN 7; INT 132; TCWW 2

Savan, Glenn (?)- .... **CLC 50**

Sayers, Dorothy L(eigh)
1893-1957 .... **TCLC 2, 15**
See also BPFB 3; BRWS 3; CA 104; 119; CANR 60; CDBLB 1914-1945; CMW 4; DAM POP; DLB 10, 36, 77, 100; MSW; MTCW 1, 2; RGEL 2; SSFS 12

Sayers, Valerie 1952- .... **CLC 50, 122**
See also CA 134; CANR 61; CSW

Sayles, John (Thomas) 1950- . **CLC 7, 10, 14**
See also CA 57-60; CANR 41, 84; DLB 44

Scammell, Michael 1935- .... **CLC 34**
See also CA 156

Scannell, Vernon 1922- .... **CLC 49**
See also CA 5-8R; CANR 8, 24, 57; CP 7; CWRI 5; DLB 27; SATA 59

Scarlett, Susan
See Streatfeild, (Mary) Noel

Scarron 1847-1910
See Mikszath, Kalman

Schaeffer, Susan Fromberg 1941- ...... **CLC 6, 11, 22**
See also CA 49-52; CANR 18, 65; CN 7; DLB 28; MTCW 1, 2; SATA 22

Schama, Simon (Michael) 1945- ..... **CLC 150**
See also BEST 89:4; CA 105; CANR 39, 91

Schary, Jill
See Robinson, Jill

Schell, Jonathan 1943- .... **CLC 35**
See also CA 73-76; CANR 12

Schelling, Friedrich Wilhelm Joseph von
1775-1854 .... **NCLC 30**
See also DLB 90

Scherer, Jean-Marie Maurice 1920-
See Rohmer, Eric
See also CA 110

Schevill, James (Erwin) 1920- .... **CLC 7**
See also CA 5-8R; CAAS 12; CAD; CD 5

Schiller, Friedrich von
1759-1805 .... **NCLC 39, 69; DC 12**
See also CDWLB 2; DAM DRAM; DLB 94; EW 5; RGWL 2

Schisgal, Murray (Joseph) 1926- .... **CLC 6**
See also CA 21-24R; CAD; CANR 48, 86; CD 5

Schlee, Ann 1934- .... **CLC 35**
See also CA 101; CANR 29, 88; SATA 44; SATA-Brief 36

Schlegel, August Wilhelm von
1767-1845 .... **NCLC 15**
See also DLB 94; RGWL 2

Schlegel, Friedrich 1772-1829 .... **NCLC 45**
See also DLB 90; EW 5; RGWL 2

Schlegel, Johann Elias (von)
1719(?)-1749 .... **LC 5**

Schleiermacher, Friedrich
1768-1834 .... **NCLC 107**
See also DLB 90

Schlesinger, Arthur M(eier), Jr.
1917- .... **CLC 84**
See also AITN 1; CA 1-4R; CANR 1, 28, 58, 105; DLB 17; INT CANR-28; MTCW 1, 2; SATA 61

Schmidt, Arno (Otto) 1914-1979 ...... **CLC 56**
See also CA 128; 109; DLB 69

Schmitz, Aron Hector 1861-1928
See Svevo, Italo
See also CA 104; 122; MTCW 1

Schnackenberg, Gjertrud (Cecelia)
1953- .... **CLC 40**
See also CA 116; CANR 100; CP 7; CWP; DLB 120; PFS 13

Schneider, Leonard Alfred 1925-1966
See Bruce, Lenny
See also CA 89-92

Schnitzler, Arthur 1862-1931 ... **TCLC 4; DC 17; SSC 15**
See also CA 104; CDWLB 2; DLB 81, 118; EW 8; RGSF 2; RGWL 2

Schoenberg, Arnold Franz Walter
1874-1951 .... **TCLC 75**
See also CA 109; 188

Schonberg, Arnold
See Schoenberg, Arnold Franz Walter

Schopenhauer, Arthur 1788-1860 .. **NCLC 51**
See also DLB 90; EW 5

Schor, Sandra (M.) 1932(?)-1990 ..... **CLC 65**
See also CA 132

Schorer, Mark 1908-1977 .... **CLC 9**
See also CA 5-8R; 73-76; CANR 7; DLB 103

Schrader, Paul (Joseph) 1946- .... **CLC 26**
See also CA 37-40R; CANR 41; DLB 44

Schreiner, Olive (Emilie Albertina)
1855-1920 .... **TCLC 9**
See also AFW; BRWS 2; CA 105; 154; DLB 18, 156, 190, 225; FW; RGEL 2; WLIT 2

Schulberg, Budd (Wilson) 1914- .. **CLC 7, 48**
See also BPFB 3; CA 25-28R; CANR 19, 87; CN 7; DLB 6, 26, 28; DLBY 1981, 2001

Schulman, Arnold
See Trumbo, Dalton

Schulz, Bruno 1892-1942 .. **TCLC 5, 51; SSC 13**
See also CA 115; 123; CANR 86; CDWLB 4; DLB 215; MTCW 2; RGSF 2; RGWL 2

Schulz, Charles M(onroe)
1922-2000 .... **CLC 12**
See also AAYA 39; CA 9-12R; 187; CANR 6; INT CANR-6; SATA 10; SATA-Obit 118

Schumacher, E(rnst) F(riedrich)
1911-1977 .... **CLC 80**
See also CA 81-84; 73-76; CANR 34, 85

Schuyler, James Marcus 1923-1991 .. **CLC 5, 23**
See also CA 101; 134; DAM POET; DLB 5, 169; INT 101; WP

Schwartz, Delmore (David)
1913-1966 ... **CLC 2, 4, 10, 45, 87; PC 8**
See also AMWS 2; CA 17-18; 25-28R; CANR 35; CAP 2; DLB 28, 48; MTCW 1, 2; PAB; RGAL 4

Schwartz, Ernst
See Ozu, Yasujiro
Schwartz, John Burnham 1965- .... **CLC 59**
See also CA 132
Schwartz, Lynne Sharon 1939- .... **CLC 31**
See also CA 103; CANR 44, 89; DLB 218; MTCW 2
Schwartz, Muriel A.
See Eliot, T(homas) S(tearns)
Schwarz-Bart, Andre 1928- .... **CLC 2, 4**
See also CA 89-92; CANR 109
Schwarz-Bart, Simone 1938- . **CLC 7; BLCS**
See also BW 2; CA 97-100
Schwitters, Kurt (Hermann Edward Karl Julius) 1887-1948 .... **TCLC 95**
See also CA 158
Schwob, Marcel (Mayer Andre) 1867-1905 .... **TCLC 20**
See also CA 117; 168; DLB 123; GFL 1789 to the Present
Sciascia, Leonardo 1921-1989 .. **CLC 8, 9, 41**
See also CA 85-88; 130; CANR 35; DLB 177; MTCW 1; RGWL 2
Scoppettone, Sandra 1936- .... **CLC 26**
See also Early, Jack
See also AAYA 11; BYA 8; CA 5-8R; CANR 41, 73; GLL 1; MAICYA 2; MAICYAS 1; SATA 9, 92; WYA; YAW
Scorsese, Martin 1942- .... **CLC 20, 89**
See also AAYA 38; CA 110; 114; CANR 46, 85
Scotland, Jay
See Jakes, John (William)
Scott, Duncan Campbell 1862-1947 .... **TCLC 6**
See also CA 104; 153; DAC; DLB 92; RGEL 2
Scott, Evelyn 1893-1963 .... **CLC 43**
See also CA 104; 112; CANR 64; DLB 9, 48; RHW
Scott, F(rancis) R(eginald) 1899-1985 .... **CLC 22**
See also CA 101; 114; CANR 87; DLB 88; INT CA-101; RGEL 2
Scott, Frank
See Scott, F(rancis) R(eginald)
Scott, Joan .... **CLC 65**
Scott, Joanna 1960- .... **CLC 50**
See also CA 126; CANR 53, 92
Scott, Paul (Mark) 1920-1978 ...... **CLC 9, 60**
See also BRWS 1; CA 81-84; 77-80; CANR 33; DLB 14, 207; MTCW 1; RGEL 2; RHW
Scott, Sarah 1723-1795 .... **LC 44**
See also DLB 39
Scott, Sir Walter 1771-1832 .... **NCLC 15, 69, 110; PC 13; SSC 32; WLC**
See also AAYA 22; BRW 4; BYA 2; CDBLB 1789-1832; DA; DAB; DAC; DAM MST, NOV, POET; DLB 93, 107, 116, 144, 159; HGG; LAIT 1; RGEL 2; RGSF 2; SSFS 10; SUFW; WLIT 3; YABC 2
Scribe, (Augustin) Eugene 1791-1861 .... **NCLC 16; DC 5**
See also DAM DRAM; DLB 192; GFL 1789 to the Present; RGWL 2
Scrum, R.
See Crumb, R(obert)
Scudery, Georges de 1601-1667 .... **LC 75**
See also GFL Beginnings to 1789
Scudery, Madeleine de 1607-1701 .. **LC 2, 58**
See also GFL Beginnings to 1789
Scum
See Crumb, R(obert)
Scumbag, Little Bobby
See Crumb, R(obert)
Seabrook, John
See Hubbard, L(afayette) Ron(ald)

Sealy, I(rwin) Allan 1951- .... **CLC 55**
See also CA 136; CN 7
Search, Alexander
See Pessoa, Fernando (Antonio Nogueira)
Sebastian, Lee
See Silverberg, Robert
Sebastian Owl
See Thompson, Hunter S(tockton)
Sebestyen, Ouida 1924- .... **CLC 30**
See also AAYA 8; BYA 7; CA 107; CANR 40; CLR 17; JRDA; MAICYA 1, 2; SAAS 10; SATA 39; WYA; YAW
Secundus, H. Scriblerus
See Fielding, Henry
Sedges, John
See Buck, Pearl S(ydenstricker)
Sedgwick, Catharine Maria 1789-1867 .... **NCLC 19, 98**
See also DLB 1, 74, 183, 239, 243, 254; RGAL 4
Seelye, John (Douglas) 1931- .... **CLC 7**
See also CA 97-100; CANR 70; INT 97-100; TCWW 2
Seferiades, Giorgos Stylianou 1900-1971
See Seferis, George
See also CA 5-8R; 33-36R; CANR 5, 36; MTCW 1
Seferis, George .... **CLC 5, 11**
See also Seferiades, Giorgos Stylianou
See also EW 12; RGWL 2
Segal, Erich (Wolf) 1937- .... **CLC 3, 10**
See also BEST 89:1; BPFB 3; CA 25-28R; CANR 20, 36, 65; CPW; DAM POP; DLBY 1986; INT CANR-20; MTCW 1
Seger, Bob 1945- .... **CLC 35**
Seghers, Anna -1983 .... **CLC 7**
See also Radvanyi, Netty
See also CDWLB 2; DLB 69
Seidel, Frederick (Lewis) 1936- .... **CLC 18**
See also CA 13-16R; CANR 8, 99; CP 7; DLBY 1984
Seifert, Jaroslav 1901-1986 .. **CLC 34, 44, 93**
See also CA 127; CDWLB 4; DLB 215; MTCW 1, 2
Sei Shonagon c. 966-1017(?) .... **CMLC 6**
Sejour, Victor 1817-1874 .... **DC 10**
See also DLB 50
Sejour Marcou et Ferrand, Juan Victor
See Sejour, Victor
Selby, Hubert, Jr. 1928- .... **CLC 1, 2, 4, 8; SSC 20**
See also CA 13-16R; CANR 33, 85; CN 7; DLB 2, 227
Selzer, Richard 1928- .... **CLC 74**
See also CA 65-68; CANR 14, 106
Sembene, Ousmane
See Ousmane, Sembene
See also AFW; CWW 2; WLIT 2
Senancour, Etienne Pivert de 1770-1846 .... **NCLC 16**
See also DLB 119; GFL 1789 to the Present
Sender, Ramon (Jose) 1902-1982 ...... **CLC 8; HLC 2**
See also CA 5-8R; 105; CANR 8; DAM MULT; HW 1; MTCW 1; RGWL 2
Seneca, Lucius Annaeus c. 4B.C.-c. 65 .... **CMLC 6; DC 5**
See also AW 2; CDWLB 1; DAM DRAM; DLB 211; RGWL 2
Senghor, Leopold Sedar 1906-2001 . **CLC 54, 130; BLC 3; PC 25**
See also AFW; BW 2; CA 116; 125; CANR 47, 74; DAM MULT, POET; DNFS 2; GFL 1789 to the Present; MTCW 1, 2
Senna, Danzy 1970- .... **CLC 119**
See also CA 169

Serling, (Edward) Rod(man) 1924-1975 .... **CLC 30**
See also AAYA 14; AITN 1; CA 162; 57-60; DLB 26; SFW 4
Serna, Ramon Gomez de la
See Gomez de la Serna, Ramon
Serpieres
See Guillevic, (Eugene)
Service, Robert
See Service, Robert W(illiam)
See also BYA 4; DAB; DLB 92
Service, Robert W(illiam) 1874(?)-1958 .... **TCLC 15; WLC**
See also Service, Robert
See also CA 115; 140; CANR 84; DA; DAC; DAM MST, POET; PFS 10; RGEL 2; SATA 20
Seth, Vikram 1952- .... **CLC 43, 90**
See also CA 121; 127; CANR 50, 74; CN 7; CP 7; DA3; DAM MULT; DLB 120; INT 127; MTCW 2
Seton, Cynthia Propper 1926-1982 .. **CLC 27**
See also CA 5-8R; 108; CANR 7
Seton, Ernest (Evan) Thompson 1860-1946 .... **TCLC 31**
See also ANW; BYA 3; CA 109; CLR 59; DLB 92; DLBD 13; JRDA; SATA 18
Seton-Thompson, Ernest
See Seton, Ernest (Evan) Thompson
Settle, Mary Lee 1918- .... **CLC 19, 61**
See also BPFB 3; CA 89-92; CAAS 1; CANR 44, 87; CN 7; CSW; DLB 6; INT 89-92
Seuphor, Michel
See Arp, Jean
Sevigne, Marie (de Rabutin-Chantal) 1626-1696 .... **LC 11**
See also GFL Beginnings to 1789
Sewall, Samuel 1652-1730 .... **LC 38**
See also DLB 24; RGAL 4
Sexton, Anne (Harvey) 1928-1974 ..... **CLC 2, 4, 6, 8, 10, 15, 53, 123; PC 2; WLC**
See also AMWS 2; CA 1-4R; 53-56; CABS 2; CANR 3, 36; CDALB 1941-1968; DA; DA3; DAB; DAC; DAM MST, POET; DLB 5, 169; EXPP; FW; MAWW; MTCW 1, 2; PAB; PFS 4, 14; RGAL 4; SATA 10
Shaara, Jeff 1952- .... **CLC 119**
See also CA 163; CANR 109
Shaara, Michael (Joseph, Jr.) 1929-1988 .... **CLC 15**
See also AITN 1; BPFB 3; CA 102; 125; CANR 52, 85; DAM POP; DLBY 1983
Shackleton, C. C.
See Aldiss, Brian W(ilson)
Shacochis, Bob .... **CLC 39**
See also Shacochis, Robert G.
Shacochis, Robert G. 1951-
See Shacochis, Bob
See also CA 119; 124; CANR 100; INT 124
Shaffer, Anthony (Joshua) 1926-2001 .... **CLC 19**
See also CA 110; 116; 200; CBD; CD 5; DAM DRAM; DFS 13; DLB 13
Shaffer, Peter (Levin) 1926- .. **CLC 5, 14, 18, 37, 60; DC 7**
See also BRWS 1; CA 25-28R; CANR 25, 47, 74; CBD; CD 5; CDBLB 1960 to Present; DA3; DAB; DAM DRAM, MST; DFS 5, 13; DLB 13, 233; MTCW 1, 2; RGEL 2
Shakey, Bernard
See Young, Neil
Shalamov, Varlam (Tikhonovich) 1907(?)-1982 .... **CLC 18**
See also CA 129; 105; RGSF 2
Shamlu, Ahmad 1925-2000 .... **CLC 10**
See also CWW 2

Shammas, Anton 1951- .... **CLC 55**
See also CA 199

Shandling, Arline
See Berriault, Gina

Shange, Ntozake 1948- .... **CLC 8, 25, 38, 74, 126; BLC 3; DC 3**
See also AAYA 9; AFAW 1, 2; BW 2; CA 85-88; CABS 3; CAD; CANR 27, 48, 74; CD 5; CP 7; CWD; CWP; DA3; DAM DRAM, MULT; DFS 2, 11; DLB 38, 249; FW; LAIT 5; MTCW 1, 2; NFS 11; RGAL 4; YAW

Shanley, John Patrick 1950- .... **CLC 75**
See also CA 128; 133; CAD; CANR 83; CD 5

Shapcott, Thomas W(illiam) 1935- .. **CLC 38**
See also CA 69-72; CANR 49, 83, 103; CP 7

Shapiro, Jane 1942- .... **CLC 76**
See also CA 196

Shapiro, Karl (Jay) 1913-2000 ...... **CLC 4, 8, 15, 53; PC 25**
See also AMWS 2; CA 1-4R; 188; CAAS 6; CANR 1, 36, 66; CP 7; DLB 48; EXPP; MTCW 1, 2; PFS 3; RGAL 4

Sharp, William 1855-1905 .... **TCLC 39**
See also Macleod, Fiona
See also CA 160; DLB 156; RGEL 2

Sharpe, Thomas Ridley 1928-
See Sharpe, Tom
See also CA 114; 122; CANR 85; INT CA-122

Sharpe, Tom .... **CLC 36**
See also Sharpe, Thomas Ridley
See also CN 7; DLB 14, 231

Shatrov, Mikhail .... **CLC 59**

Shaw, Bernard
See Shaw, George Bernard
See also DLB 190

Shaw, G. Bernard
See Shaw, George Bernard

Shaw, George Bernard 1856-1950 .. **TCLC 3, 9, 21, 45; WLC**
See also Shaw, Bernard
See also BRW 6; BRWR 2; CA 104; 128; CDBLB 1914-1945; DA; DA3; DAB; DAC; DAM DRAM, MST; DFS 1, 3, 6, 11; DLB 10, 57; LAIT 3; MTCW 1, 2; RGEL 2; WLIT 4

Shaw, Henry Wheeler 1818-1885 .. **NCLC 15**
See also DLB 11; RGAL 4

Shaw, Irwin 1913-1984 .... **CLC 7, 23, 34**
See also AITN 1; BPFB 3; CA 13-16R; 112; CANR 21; CDALB 1941-1968; CPW; DAM DRAM, POP; DLB 6, 102; DLBY 1984; MTCW 1, 21

Shaw, Robert 1927-1978 .... **CLC 5**
See also AITN 1; CA 1-4R; 81-84; CANR 4; DLB 13, 14

Shaw, T. E.
See Lawrence, T(homas) E(dward)

Shawn, Wallace 1943- .... **CLC 41**
See also CA 112; CAD; CD 5

Shchedrin, N.
See Saltykov, Mikhail Evgrafovich

Shea, Lisa 1953- .... **CLC 86**
See also CA 147

Sheed, Wilfrid (John Joseph) 1930- . **CLC 2, 4, 10, 53**
See also CA 65-68; CANR 30, 66; CN 7; DLB 6; MTCW 1, 2

Sheldon, Alice Hastings Bradley 1915(?)-1987
See Tiptree, James, Jr.
See also CA 108; 122; CANR 34; INT 108; MTCW 1

Sheldon, John
See Bloch, Robert (Albert)

Sheldon, Walter J(ames) 1917-1996
See Queen, Ellery
See also AITN 1; CA 25-28R; CANR 10

Shelley, Mary Wollstonecraft (Godwin) 1797-1851 ...... **NCLC 14, 59, 103; WLC**
See also AAYA 20; BPFB 3; BRW 3; BRWS 3; BYA 5; CDBLB 1789-1832; DA; DA3; DAB; DAC; DAM MST, NOV; DLB 110, 116, 159, 178; EXPN; HGG; LAIT 1; NFS 1; RGEL 2; SATA 29; SCFW; SFW 4; WLIT 3

Shelley, Percy Bysshe 1792-1822 .. **NCLC 18, 93; PC 14; WLC**
See also BRW 4; BRWR 1; CDBLB 1789-1832; DA; DA3; DAB; DAC; DAM MST, POET; DLB 96, 110, 158; EXPP; PAB; PFS 2; RGEL 2; WLIT 3; WP

Shepard, Jim 1956- .... **CLC 36**
See also CA 137; CANR 59, 104; SATA 90

Shepard, Lucius 1947- .... **CLC 34**
See also CA 128; 141; CANR 81; HGG; SCFW 2; SFW 4

Shepard, Sam 1943- .... **CLC 4, 6, 17, 34, 41, 44; DC 5**
See also AAYA 1; AMWS 3; CA 69-72; CABS 3; CAD; CANR 22; CD 5; DA3; DAM DRAM; DFS 3, 6, 7, 14; DLB 7, 212; IDFW 3, 4; MTCW 1, 2; RGAL 4

Shepherd, Michael
See Ludlum, Robert

Sherburne, Zoa (Lillian Morin) 1912-1995 .... **CLC 30**
See also AAYA 13; CA 1-4R; 176; CANR 3, 37; MAICYA 1, 2; SAAS 18; SATA 3; YAW

Sheridan, Frances 1724-1766 .... **LC 7**
See also DLB 39, 84

Sheridan, Richard Brinsley 1751-1816 .... **NCLC 5, 91; DC 1; WLC**
See also BRW 3; CDBLB 1660-1789; DA; DAB; DAC; DAM DRAM, MST; DFS 4, 14; DLB 89; RGEL 2; WLIT 3

Sherman, Jonathan Marc .... **CLC 55**

Sherman, Martin 1941(?)- .... **CLC 19**
See also CA 116; 123; CANR 86

Sherwin, Judith Johnson
See Johnson, Judith (Emlyn)
See also CANR 85; CP 7; CWP

Sherwood, Frances 1940- .... **CLC 81**
See also CA 146

Sherwood, Robert E(mmet) 1896-1955 .... **TCLC 3**
See also CA 104; 153; CANR 86; DAM DRAM; DFS 11; DLB 7, 26, 249; IDFW 3, 4; RGAL 4

Shestov, Lev 1866-1938 .... **TCLC 56**

Shevchenko, Taras 1814-1861 .... **NCLC 54**

Shiel, M(atthew) P(hipps) 1865-1947 .... **TCLC 8**
See also Holmes, Gordon
See also CA 106; 160; DLB 153; HGG; MTCW 2; SFW 4; SUFW

Shields, Carol 1935- .... **CLC 91, 113**
See also AMWS 7; CA 81-84; CANR 51, 74, 98; CCA 1; CN 7; CPW; DA3; DAC; MTCW 2

Shields, David 1956- .... **CLC 97**
See also CA 124; CANR 48, 99

Shiga, Naoya 1883-1971 ..... **CLC 33; SSC 23**
See also Shiga Naoya
See also CA 101; 33-36R; MJW

Shiga Naoya
See Shiga, Naoya
See also DLB 180

Shilts, Randy 1951-1994 .... **CLC 85**
See also AAYA 19; CA 115; 127; 144; CANR 45; DA3; GLL 1; INT 127; MTCW 2

Shimazaki, Haruki 1872-1943
See Shimazaki Toson
See also CA 105; 134; CANR 84

Shimazaki Toson .... **TCLC 5**
See also Shimazaki, Haruki
See also DLB 180

Sholokhov, Mikhail (Aleksandrovich) 1905-1984 .... **CLC 7, 15**
See also CA 101; 112; MTCW 1, 2; RGWL 2; SATA-Obit 36

Shone, Patric
See Hanley, James

Shreve, Susan Richards 1939- .... **CLC 23**
See also CA 49-52; CAAS 5; CANR 5, 38, 69, 100; MAICYA 1, 2; SATA 46, 95; SATA-Brief 41

Shue, Larry 1946-1985 .... **CLC 52**
See also CA 145; 117; DAM DRAM; DFS 7

Shu-Jen, Chou 1881-1936
See Lu Hsun
See also CA 104

Shulman, Alix Kates 1932- .... **CLC 2, 10**
See also CA 29-32R; CANR 43; FW; SATA 7

Shusaku, Endo
See Endo, Shusaku

Shuster, Joe 1914-1992 .... **CLC 21**

Shute, Nevil .... **CLC 30**
See also Norway, Nevil Shute
See also BPFB 3; DLB 255; NFS 9; RHW; SFW 4

Shuttle, Penelope (Diane) 1947- .... **CLC 7**
See also CA 93-96; CANR 39, 84, 92, 108; CP 7; CWP; DLB 14, 40

Sidney, Mary 1561-1621 .... **LC 19, 39**
See also Sidney Herbert, Mary

Sidney, Sir Philip 1554-1586 . **LC 19, 39; PC 32**
See also BRW 1; BRWR 2; CDBLB Before 1660; DA; DA3; DAB; DAC; DAM MST, POET; DLB 167; EXPP; PAB; RGEL 2; TEA; WP

Sidney Herbert, Mary
See Sidney, Mary
See also DLB 167

Siegel, Jerome 1914-1996 .... **CLC 21**
See also CA 116; 169; 151

Siegel, Jerry
See Siegel, Jerome

Sienkiewicz, Henryk (Adam Alexander Pius) 1846-1916 .... **TCLC 3**
See also CA 104; 134; CANR 84; RGSF 2; RGWL 2

Sierra, Gregorio Martinez
See Martinez Sierra, Gregorio

Sierra, Maria (de la O'LeJarraga) Martinez
See Martinez Sierra, Maria (de la O'LeJarraga)

Sigal, Clancy 1926- .... **CLC 7**
See also CA 1-4R; CANR 85; CN 7

Sigourney, Lydia H.
See Sigourney, Lydia Howard (Huntley)
See also DLB 73, 183

Sigourney, Lydia Howard (Huntley) 1791-1865 .... **NCLC 21, 87**
See also Sigourney, Lydia H.; Sigourney, Lydia Huntley
See also DLB 1

Sigourney, Lydia Huntley
See Sigourney, Lydia Howard (Huntley)
See also DLB 42, 239, 243

Siguenza y Gongora, Carlos de 1645-1700 .... **LC 8; HLCS 2**
See also LAW

Sigurjonsson, Johann 1880-1919 ... **TCLC 27**
See also CA 170

Sikelianos, Angelos 1884-1951 ...... **TCLC 39; PC 29**
See also RGWL 2

Silkin, Jon 1930-1997 .... **CLC 2, 6, 43**
See also CA 5-8R; CAAS 5; CANR 89; CP 7; DLB 27

Silko, Leslie (Marmon) 1948- .... **CLC 23, 74, 114; SSC 37; WLCS**
See also AAYA 14; AMWS 4; ANW; BYA 12; CA 115; 122; CANR 45, 65; CN 7; CP 7; CPW 1; CWP; DA; DA3; DAC; DAM MST, MULT, POP; DLB 143, 175, 256; EXPP; EXPS; LAIT 4; MTCW 2; NFS 4; NNAL; PFS 9; RGAL 4; RGSF 2; SSFS 4, 8, 10, 11

Sillanpaa, Frans Eemil 1888-1964 ... **CLC 19**
See also CA 129; 93-96; MTCW 1

Sillitoe, Alan 1928- .. **CLC 1, 3, 6, 10, 19, 57, 148**
See also AITN 1; BRWS 5; CA 9-12R; CAAE 191; CAAS 2; CANR 8, 26, 55; CDBLB 1960 to Present; CN 7; DLB 14, 139; MTCW 1, 2; RGEL 2; RGSF 2; SATA 61

Silone, Ignazio 1900-1978 .... **CLC 4**
See also CA 25-28; 81-84; CANR 34; CAP 2; EW 12; MTCW 1; RGSF 2; RGWL 2

Silone, Ignazione
See Silone, Ignazio

Silver, Joan Micklin 1935- .... **CLC 20**
See also CA 114; 121; INT 121

Silver, Nicholas
See Faust, Frederick (Schiller)
See also TCWW 2

Silverberg, Robert 1935- .... **CLC 7, 140**
See also AAYA 24; BPFB 3; BYA 7, 9; CA 1-4R; 186; CAAE 186; CAAS 3; CANR 1, 20, 36, 85; CLR 59; CN 7; CPW; DAM POP; DLB 8; INT CANR-20; MAICYA 1, 2; MTCW 1, 2; SATA 13, 91; SATA-Essay 104; SCFW 2; SFW 4

Silverstein, Alvin 1933- .... **CLC 17**
See also CA 49-52; CANR 2; CLR 25; JRDA; MAICYA 1, 2; SATA 8, 69, 124

Silverstein, Virginia B(arbara Opshelor) 1937- .... **CLC 17**
See also CA 49-52; CANR 2; CLR 25; JRDA; MAICYA 1; SATA 8, 69, 124

Sim, Georges
See Simenon, Georges (Jacques Christian)

Simak, Clifford D(onald) 1904-1988 . **CLC 1, 55**
See also CA 1-4R; 125; CANR 1, 35; DLB 8; MTCW 1; SATA-Obit 56; SFW 4

Simenon, Georges (Jacques Christian) 1903-1989 .... **CLC 1, 2, 3, 8, 18, 47**
See also BPFB 3; CA 85-88; 129; CANR 35; CMW 4; DA3; DAM POP; DLB 72; DLBY 1989; EW 12; GFL 1789 to the Present; MSW; MTCW 1, 2; RGWL 2

Simic, Charles 1938- .... **CLC 6, 9, 22, 49, 68, 130**
See also AMWS 8; CA 29-32R; CAAS 4; CANR 12, 33, 52, 61, 96; CP 7; DA3; DAM POET; DLB 105; MTCW 2; PFS 7; RGAL 4; WP

Simmel, Georg 1858-1918 .... **TCLC 64**
See also CA 157

Simmons, Charles (Paul) 1924- .... **CLC 57**
See also CA 89-92; INT 89-92

Simmons, Dan 1948- .... **CLC 44**
See also AAYA 16; CA 138; CANR 53, 81; CPW; DAM POP; HGG

Simmons, James (Stewart Alexander) 1933- .... **CLC 43**
See also CA 105; CAAS 21; CP 7; DLB 40

Simms, William Gilmore 1806-1870 .... **NCLC 3**
See also DLB 3, 30, 59, 73, 248, 254; RGAL 4

Simon, Carly 1945- .... **CLC 26**
See also CA 105

Simon, Claude 1913-1984 ... **CLC 4, 9, 15, 39**
See also CA 89-92; CANR 33; DAM NOV; DLB 83; EW 13; GFL 1789 to the Present; MTCW 1

Simon, Myles
See Follett, Ken(neth Martin)

Simon, (Marvin) Neil 1927- ... **CLC 6, 11, 31, 39, 70; DC 14**
See also AAYA 32; AITN 1; AMWS 4; CA 21-24R; CANR 26, 54, 87; CD 5; DA3; DAM DRAM; DFS 2, 6, 12; DLB 7; LAIT 4; MTCW 1, 2; RGAL 4

Simon, Paul (Frederick) 1941(?)- ..... **CLC 17**
See also CA 116; 153

Simonon, Paul 1956(?)- .... **CLC 30**

Simonson, Rick ed. .... **CLC 70**

Simpson, Harriette
See Arnow, Harriette (Louisa) Simpson

Simpson, Louis (Aston Marantz) 1923- .... **CLC 4, 7, 9, 32, 149**
See also AMWS 9; CA 1-4R; CAAS 4; CANR 1, 61; CP 7; DAM POET; DLB 5; MTCW 1, 2; PFS 7, 11, 14; RGAL 4

Simpson, Mona (Elizabeth) 1957- ... **CLC 44, 146**
See also CA 122; 135; CANR 68, 103; CN 7

Simpson, N(orman) F(rederick) 1919- .... **CLC 29**
See also CA 13-16R; CBD; DLB 13; RGEL 2

Sinclair, Andrew (Annandale) 1935- . **CLC 2, 14**
See also CA 9-12R; CAAS 5; CANR 14, 38, 91; CN 7; DLB 14; FANT; MTCW 1

Sinclair, Emil
See Hesse, Hermann

Sinclair, Iain 1943- .... **CLC 76**
See also CA 132; CANR 81; CP 7; HGG

Sinclair, Iain MacGregor
See Sinclair, Iain

Sinclair, Irene
See Griffith, D(avid Lewelyn) W(ark)

Sinclair, Mary Amelia St. Clair 1865(?)-1946
See Sinclair, May
See also CA 104; HGG; RHW

Sinclair, May .... **TCLC 3, 11**
See also Sinclair, Mary Amelia St. Clair
See also CA 166; DLB 36, 135; RGEL 2; SUFW

Sinclair, Roy
See Griffith, D(avid Lewelyn) W(ark)

Sinclair, Upton (Beall) 1878-1968 ..... **CLC 1, 11, 15, 63; WLC**
See also AMWS 5; BPFB 3; BYA 2; CA 5-8R; 25-28R; CANR 7; CDALB 1929-1941; DA; DA3; DAB; DAC; DAM MST, NOV; DLB 9; INT CANR-7; LAIT 3; MTCW 1, 2; NFS 6; RGAL 4; SATA 9; YAW

Singer, Isaac
See Singer, Isaac Bashevis

Singer, Isaac Bashevis 1904-1991 .. **CLC 1, 3, 6, 9, 11, 15, 23, 38, 69, 111; SSC 3; WLC**
See also AAYA 32; AITN 1, 2; AMW; BPFB 3; BYA 1, 4; CA 1-4R; 134; CANR 1, 39, 106; CDALB 1941-1968; CLR 1; CWRI 5; DA; DA3; DAB; DAC; DAM MST, NOV; DLB 6, 28, 52; DLBY 1991; EXPS; HGG; JRDA; LAIT 3; MAICYA 1, 2; MTCW 1, 2; RGAL 4; RGSF 2; SATA 3, 27; SATA-Obit 68; SSFS 2, 12

Singer, Israel Joshua 1893-1944 .... **TCLC 33**
See also CA 169

Singh, Khushwant 1915- .... **CLC 11**
See also CA 9-12R; CAAS 9; CANR 6, 84; CN 7; RGEL 2

Singleton, Ann
See Benedict, Ruth (Fulton)

Singleton, John 1968(?)- .... **CLC 156**
See also BW 2, 3; CA 138; CANR 67, 82; DAM MULT

Sinjohn, John
See Galsworthy, John

Sinyavsky, Andrei (Donatevich) 1925-1997 .... **CLC 8**
See also Tertz, Abram
See also CA 85-88; 159

Sirin, V.
See Nabokov, Vladimir (Vladimirovich)

Sissman, L(ouis) E(dward) 1928-1976 .... **CLC 9, 18**
See also CA 21-24R; 65-68; CANR 13; DLB 5

Sisson, C(harles) H(ubert) 1914- .... **CLC 8**
See also CA 1-4R; CAAS 3; CANR 3, 48, 84; CP 7; DLB 27

Sitwell, Dame Edith 1887-1964 ... **CLC 2, 9, 67; PC 3**
See also BRW 7; CA 9-12R; CANR 35; CDBLB 1945-1960; DAM POET; DLB 20; MTCW 1, 2; RGEL 2

Siwaarmill, H. P.
See Sharp, William

Sjoewall, Maj 1935- .... **CLC 7**
See also Sjowall, Maj
See also CA 65-68; CANR 73

Sjowall, Maj
See Sjoewall, Maj
See also BPFB 3; CMW 4; MSW

Skelton, John 1460(?)-1529 ..... **LC 71; PC 25**
See also BRW 1; DLB 136; RGEL 2

Skelton, Robin 1925-1997 .... **CLC 13**
See also Zuk, Georges
See also AITN 2; CA 5-8R; 160; CAAS 5; CANR 28, 89; CCA 1; CP 7; DLB 27, 53

Skolimowski, Jerzy 1938- .... **CLC 20**
See also CA 128

Skram, Amalie (Bertha) 1847-1905 .... **TCLC 25**
See also CA 165

Skvorecky, Josef (Vaclav) 1924- ...... **CLC 15, 39, 69, 152**
See also CA 61-64; CAAS 1; CANR 10, 34, 63, 108; CDWLB 4; DA3; DAC; DAM NOV; DLB 232; MTCW 1, 2

Slade, Bernard .... **CLC 11, 46**
See also Newbound, Bernard Slade
See also CAAS 9; CCA 1; DLB 53

Slaughter, Carolyn 1946- .... **CLC 56**
See also CA 85-88; CANR 85; CN 7

Slaughter, Frank G(ill) 1908-2001 ... **CLC 29**
See also AITN 2; CA 5-8R; 197; CANR 5, 85; INT CANR-5; RHW

Slavitt, David R(ytman) 1935- ...... **CLC 5, 14**
See also CA 21-24R; CAAS 3; CANR 41, 83; CP 7; DLB 5, 6

Slesinger, Tess 1905-1945 .... **TCLC 10**
See also CA 107; 199; DLB 102

Slessor, Kenneth 1901-1971 .... **CLC 14**
See also CA 102; 89-92; RGEL 2

Slowacki, Juliusz 1809-1849 .... **NCLC 15**

Smart, Christopher 1722-1771 . **LC 3; PC 13**
See also DAM POET; DLB 109; RGEL 2

Smart, Elizabeth 1913-1986 .... **CLC 54**
See also CA 81-84; 118; DLB 88

Smiley, Jane (Graves) 1949- ...... **CLC 53, 76, 144**
See also AMWS 6; BPFB 3; CA 104; CANR 30, 50, 74, 96; CN 7; CPW 1; DA3; DAM POP; DLB 227, 234; INT CANR-30

Smith, A(rthur) J(ames) M(arshall)
1902-1980 .... **CLC 15**
See also CA 1-4R; 102; CANR 4; DAC; DLB 88; RGEL 2

Smith, Adam 1723(?)-1790 .... **LC 36**
See also DLB 104, 252; RGEL 2

Smith, Alexander 1829-1867 .... **NCLC 59**
See also DLB 32, 55

Smith, Anna Deavere 1950- .... **CLC 86**
See also CA 133; CANR 103; CD 5; DFS 2

Smith, Betty (Wehner) 1904-1972 .... **CLC 19**
See also BPFB 3; BYA 3; CA 5-8R; 33-36R; DLBY 1982; LAIT 3; RGAL 4; SATA 6

Smith, Charlotte (Turner)
1749-1806 .... **NCLC 23**
See also DLB 39, 109; RGEL 2

Smith, Clark Ashton 1893-1961 .... **CLC 43**
See also CA 143; CANR 81; FANT; HGG; MTCW 2; SCFW 2; SFW 4; SUFW

Smith, Dave .... **CLC 22, 42**
See also Smith, David (Jeddie)
See also CAAS 7; DLB 5

Smith, David (Jeddie) 1942-
See Smith, Dave
See also CA 49-52; CANR 1, 59; CP 7; CSW; DAM POET

Smith, Florence Margaret 1902-1971
See Smith, Stevie
See also CA 17-18; 29-32R; CANR 35; CAP 2; DAM POET; MTCW 1, 2

Smith, Iain Crichton 1928-1998 .... **CLC 64**
See also CA 21-24R; 171; CN 7; CP 7; DLB 40, 139; RGSF 2

Smith, John 1580(?)-1631 .... **LC 9**
See also DLB 24, 30; TUS

Smith, Johnston
See Crane, Stephen (Townley)

Smith, Joseph, Jr. 1805-1844 .... **NCLC 53**

Smith, Lee 1944- .... **CLC 25, 73**
See also CA 114; 119; CANR 46; CSW; DLB 143; DLBY 1983; INT CA-119; RGAL 4

Smith, Martin
See Smith, Martin Cruz

Smith, Martin Cruz 1942- .... **CLC 25**
See also BEST 89:4; BPFB 3; CA 85-88; CANR 6, 23, 43, 65; CMW 4; CPW; DAM MULT, POP; HGG; INT CANR-23; MTCW 2; NNAL; RGAL 4

Smith, Mary-Ann Tirone 1944- .... **CLC 39**
See also CA 118; 136

Smith, Patti 1946- .... **CLC 12**
See also CA 93-96; CANR 63

Smith, Pauline (Urmson)
1882-1959 .... **TCLC 25**
See also DLB 225

Smith, Rosamond
See Oates, Joyce Carol

Smith, Sheila Kaye
See Kaye-Smith, Sheila

Smith, Stevie .... **CLC 3, 8, 25, 44; PC 12**
See also Smith, Florence Margaret
See also BRWS 2; DLB 20; MTCW 2; PAB; PFS 3; RGEL 2

Smith, Wilbur (Addison) 1933- .... **CLC 33**
See also CA 13-16R; CANR 7, 46, 66; CPW; MTCW 1, 2

Smith, William Jay 1918- .... **CLC 6**
See also CA 5-8R; CANR 44, 106; CP 7; CSW; CWRI 5; DLB 5; MAICYA 1, 2; SAAS 22; SATA 2, 68

Smith, Woodrow Wilson
See Kuttner, Henry

Smith, Zadie 1976- .... **CLC 158**
See also CA 193

Smolenskin, Peretz 1842-1885 .... **NCLC 30**

Smollett, Tobias (George) 1721-1771 ... **LC 2, 46**
See also BRW 3; CDBLB 1660-1789; DLB 39, 104; RGEL 2

Snodgrass, W(illiam) D(e Witt)
1926- .... **CLC 2, 6, 10, 18, 68**
See also AMWS 6; CA 1-4R; CANR 6, 36, 65, 85; CP 7; DAM POET; DLB 5; MTCW 1, 2; RGAL 4

Snow, C(harles) P(ercy) 1905-1980 ... **CLC 1, 4, 6, 9, 13, 19**
See also BRW 7; CA 5-8R; 101; CANR 28; CDBLB 1945-1960; DAM NOV; DLB 15, 77; DLBD 17; MTCW 1, 2; RGEL 2

Snow, Frances Compton
See Adams, Henry (Brooks)

Snyder, Gary (Sherman) 1930- . **CLC 1, 2, 5, 9, 32, 120; PC 21**
See also AMWS 8; ANW; CA 17-20R; CANR 30, 60; CP 7; DA3; DAM POET; DLB 5, 16, 165, 212, 237; MTCW 2; PFS 9; RGAL 4; WP

Snyder, Zilpha Keatley 1927- .... **CLC 17**
See also AAYA 15; BYA 1; CA 9-12R; CANR 38; CLR 31; JRDA; MAICYA 1, 2; SAAS 2; SATA 1, 28, 75, 110; SATA-Essay 112; YAW

Soares, Bernardo
See Pessoa, Fernando (Antonio Nogueira)

Sobh, A.
See Shamlu, Ahmad

Sobol, Joshua 1939- .... **CLC 60**
See also Sobol, Yehoshua
See also CA 200; CWW 2

Sobol, Yehoshua 1939-
See Sobol, Joshua
See also CWW 2

Socrates 470B.C.-399B.C. .... **CMLC 27**

Soderberg, Hjalmar 1869-1941 ...... **TCLC 39**
See also DLB 259; RGSF 2

Soderbergh, Steven 1963- .... **CLC 154**
See also AAYA 43

Sodergran, Edith (Irene)
See Soedergran, Edith (Irene)
See also DLB 259; EW 11; RGWL 2

Soedergran, Edith (Irene)
1892-1923 .... **TCLC 31**
See also Sodergran, Edith (Irene)

Softly, Edgar
See Lovecraft, H(oward) P(hillips)

Softly, Edward
See Lovecraft, H(oward) P(hillips)

Sokolov, Raymond 1941- .... **CLC 7**
See also CA 85-88

Sokolov, Sasha .... **CLC 59**

Solo, Jay
See Ellison, Harlan (Jay)

Sologub, Fyodor .... **TCLC 9**
See also Teternikov, Fyodor Kuzmich

Solomons, Ikey Esquir
See Thackeray, William Makepeace

Solomos, Dionysios 1798-1857 .... **NCLC 15**

Solwoska, Mara
See French, Marilyn

Solzhenitsyn, Aleksandr I(sayevich)
1918- .. **CLC 1, 2, 4, 7, 9, 10, 18, 26, 34, 78, 134; SSC 32; WLC**
See also AITN 1; BPFB 3; CA 69-72; CANR 40, 65; DA; DA3; DAB; DAC; DAM MST, NOV; EW 13; EXPS; LAIT 4; MTCW 1, 2; NFS 6; RGSF 2; RGWL 2; SSFS 9

Somers, Jane
See Lessing, Doris (May)

Somerville, Edith Oenone
1858-1949 .... **TCLC 51**
See also CA 196; DLB 135; RGEL 2; RGSF 2

Somerville & Ross
See Martin, Violet Florence; Somerville, Edith Oenone

Sommer, Scott 1951- .... **CLC 25**
See also CA 106

Sondheim, Stephen (Joshua) 1930- . **CLC 30, 39, 147**
See also AAYA 11; CA 103; CANR 47, 67; DAM DRAM; LAIT 4

Song, Cathy 1955- .... **PC 21**
See also CA 154; CWP; DLB 169; EXPP; FW; PFS 5

Sontag, Susan 1933- .... **CLC 1, 2, 10, 13, 31, 105**
See also AMWS 3; CA 17-20R; CANR 25, 51, 74, 97; CN 7; CPW; DA3; DAM POP; DLB 2, 67; MAWW; MTCW 1, 2; RGAL 4; RHW; SSFS 10

Sophocles 496(?)B.C.-406(?)B.C. .... **CMLC 2, 47, 51; DC 1; WLCS**
See also AW 1; CDWLB 1; DA; DA3; DAB; DAC; DAM DRAM, MST; DFS 1, 4, 8; DLB 176; LAIT 1; RGWL 2

Sordello 1189-1269 .... **CMLC 15**

Sorel, Georges 1847-1922 .... **TCLC 91**
See also CA 118; 188

Sorel, Julia
See Drexler, Rosalyn

Sorokin, Vladimir .... **CLC 59**

Sorrentino, Gilbert 1929- .. **CLC 3, 7, 14, 22, 40**
See also CA 77-80; CANR 14, 33; CN 7; CP 7; DLB 5, 173; DLBY 1980; INT CANR-14

Soseki
See Natsume, Soseki
See also MJW

Soto, Gary 1952- ... **CLC 32, 80; HLC 2; PC 28**
See also AAYA 10, 37; BYA 11; CA 119; 125; CANR 50, 74, 107; CLR 38; CP 7; DAM MULT; DLB 82; EXPP; HW 1, 2; INT CA-125; JRDA; MAICYA 2; MAICYAS 1; MTCW 2; PFS 7; RGAL 4; SATA 80, 120; WYA; YAW

Soupault, Philippe 1897-1990 .... **CLC 68**
See also CA 116; 147; 131; GFL 1789 to the Present

Souster, (Holmes) Raymond 1921- .... **CLC 5, 14**
See also CA 13-16R; CAAS 14; CANR 13, 29, 53; CP 7; DA3; DAC; DAM POET; DLB 88; RGEL 2; SATA 63

Southern, Terry 1924(?)-1995 .... **CLC 7**
See also BPFB 3; CA 1-4R; 150; CANR 1, 55, 107; CN 7; DLB 2; IDFW 3, 4

Southey, Robert 1774-1843 .... **NCLC 8, 97**
See also BRW 4; DLB 93, 107, 142; RGEL 2; SATA 54

Southworth, Emma Dorothy Eliza Nevitte
1819-1899 .... **NCLC 26**
See also DLB 239

Souza, Ernest
See Scott, Evelyn

Soyinka, Wole 1934- .... **CLC 3, 5, 14, 36, 44; BLC 3; DC 2; WLC**
See also AFW; BW 2, 3; CA 13-16R; CANR 27, 39, 82; CD 5; CDWLB 3; CN 7; CP 7; DA; DA3; DAB; DAC; DAM DRAM, MST, MULT; DFS 10; DLB 125; MTCW 1, 2; RGEL 2; WLIT 2

Spackman, W(illiam) M(ode)
1905-1990 .... **CLC 46**
See also CA 81-84; 132

Spacks, Barry (Bernard) 1931- .... **CLC 14**
See also CA 154; CANR 33, 109; CP 7; DLB 105

Spanidou, Irini 1946- .... **CLC 44**
See also CA 185

Spark, Muriel (Sarah) 1918- ..... **CLC 2, 3, 5, 8, 13, 18, 40, 94; SSC 10**
See also BRWS 1; CA 5-8R; CANR 12, 36, 76, 89; CDBLB 1945-1960; CN 7; CP 7; DA3; DAB; DAC; DAM MST, NOV; DLB 15, 139; FW; INT CANR-12; LAIT 4; MTCW 1, 2; RGEL 2; WLIT 4; YAW

Spaulding, Douglas
See Bradbury, Ray (Douglas)

Spaulding, Leonard
See Bradbury, Ray (Douglas)

Spelman, Elizabeth .... **CLC 65**

Spence, J. A. D.
See Eliot, T(homas) S(tearns)

Spencer, Elizabeth 1921- .... **CLC 22**
See also CA 13-16R; CANR 32, 65, 87; CN 7; CSW; DLB 6, 218; MTCW 1; RGAL 4; SATA 14

Spencer, Leonard G.
See Silverberg, Robert

Spencer, Scott 1945- .... **CLC 30**
See also CA 113; CANR 51; DLBY 1986

Spender, Stephen (Harold) 1909-1995 .... **CLC 1, 2, 5, 10, 41, 91**
See also BRWS 2; CA 9-12R; 149; CANR 31, 54; CDBLB 1945-1960; CP 7; DA3; DAM POET; DLB 20; MTCW 1, 2; PAB; RGEL 2

Spengler, Oswald (Arnold Gottfried) 1880-1936 .... **TCLC 25**
See also CA 118; 189

Spenser, Edmund 1552(?)-1599 ..... **LC 5, 39; PC 8; WLC**
See also BRW 1; CDBLB Before 1660; DA; DA3; DAB; DAC; DAM MST, POET; DLB 167; EFS 2; EXPP; PAB; RGEL 2; WLIT 3; WP

Spicer, Jack 1925-1965 .... **CLC 8, 18, 72**
See also CA 85-88; DAM POET; DLB 5, 16, 193; GLL 1; WP

Spiegelman, Art 1948- .... **CLC 76**
See also AAYA 10; CA 125; CANR 41, 55, 74; MTCW 2; SATA 109; YAW

Spielberg, Peter 1929- .... **CLC 6**
See also CA 5-8R; CANR 4, 48; DLBY 1981

Spielberg, Steven 1947- .... **CLC 20**
See also AAYA 8, 24; CA 77-80; CANR 32; SATA 32

Spillane, Frank Morrison 1918-
See Spillane, Mickey
See also CA 25-28R; CANR 28, 63; DA3; MTCW 1, 2; SATA 66

Spillane, Mickey .... **CLC 3, 13**
See also Spillane, Frank Morrison
See also BPFB 3; CMW 4; DLB 226; MSW; MTCW 2

Spinoza, Benedictus de 1632-1677 .. **LC 9, 58**

Spinrad, Norman (Richard) 1940- ... **CLC 46**
See also BPFB 3; CA 37-40R; CAAS 19; CANR 20, 91; DLB 8; INT CANR-20; SFW 4

Spitteler, Carl (Friedrich Georg) 1845-1924 .... **TCLC 12**
See also CA 109; DLB 129

Spivack, Kathleen (Romola Drucker) 1938- .... **CLC 6**
See also CA 49-52

Spoto, Donald 1941- .... **CLC 39**
See also CA 65-68; CANR 11, 57, 93

Springsteen, Bruce (F.) 1949- .... **CLC 17**
See also CA 111

Spurling, Hilary 1940- .... **CLC 34**
See also CA 104; CANR 25, 52, 94

Spyker, John Howland
See Elman, Richard (Martin)

Squires, (James) Radcliffe 1917-1993 .... **CLC 51**
See also CA 1-4R; 140; CANR 6, 21

Srivastava, Dhanpat Rai 1880(?)-1936
See Premchand
See also CA 118; 197

Stacy, Donald
See Pohl, Frederik

Stael
See Stael-Holstein, Anne Louise Germaine Necker
See also EW 5; RGWL 2

Stael, Germaine de
See Stael-Holstein, Anne Louise Germaine Necker
See also DLB 119, 192; FW; GFL 1789 to the Present; TWA

Stael-Holstein, Anne Louise Germaine Necker 1766-1817 .... **NCLC 3, 91**
See also Stael; Stael, Germaine de

Stafford, Jean 1915-1979 .. **CLC 4, 7, 19, 68; SSC 26**
See also CA 1-4R; 85-88; CANR 3, 65; DLB 2, 173; MTCW 1, 2; RGAL 4; RGSF 2; SATA-Obit 22; TCWW 2

Stafford, William (Edgar) 1914-1993 .... **CLC 4, 7, 29**
See also CA 5-8R; 142; CANR 5; CANR 22; DAM POET; DLB 5, 206; EXPP; INT CANR-22; PFS 2, 8; RGAL 4; WP

Stagnelius, Eric Johan 1793-1823 . **NCLC 61**

Staines, Trevor
See Brunner, John (Kilian Houston)

Stairs, Gordon
See Austin, Mary (Hunter)
See also TCWW 2

Stairs, Gordon 1868-1934
See Austin, Mary (Hunter)

Stalin, Joseph 1879-1953 .... **TCLC 92**

Stancykowna
See Szymborska, Wislawa

Stannard, Martin 1947- .... **CLC 44**
See also CA 142; DLB 155

Stanton, Elizabeth Cady 1815-1902 .... **TCLC 73**
See also CA 171; DLB 79; FW

Stanton, Maura 1946- .... **CLC 9**
See also CA 89-92; CANR 15; DLB 120

Stanton, Schuyler
See Baum, L(yman) Frank

Stapledon, (William) Olaf 1886-1950 .... **TCLC 22**
See also CA 111; 162; DLB 15, 255; SFW 4

Starbuck, George (Edwin) 1931-1996 .... **CLC 53**
See also CA 21-24R; 153; CANR 23; DAM POET

Stark, Richard
See Westlake, Donald E(dwin)

Staunton, Schuyler
See Baum, L(yman) Frank

Stead, Christina (Ellen) 1902-1983 ... **CLC 2, 5, 8, 32, 80**
See also BRWS 4; CA 13-16R; 109; CANR 33, 40; FW; MTCW 1, 2; RGEL 2; RGSF 2

Stead, William Thomas 1849-1912 .... **TCLC 48**
See also CA 167

Stebnitsky, M.
See Leskov, Nikolai (Semyonovich)

Steele, Sir Richard 1672-1729 .... **LC 18**
See also BRW 3; CDBLB 1660-1789; DLB 84, 101; RGEL 2; WLIT 3

Steele, Timothy (Reid) 1948- .... **CLC 45**
See also CA 93-96; CANR 16, 50, 92; CP 7; DLB 120

Steffens, (Joseph) Lincoln 1866-1936 .... **TCLC 20**
See also CA 117

Stegner, Wallace (Earle) 1909-1993 .. **CLC 9, 49, 81; SSC 27**
See also AITN 1; AMWS 4; ANW; BEST 90:3; BPFB 3; CA 1-4R; 141; CAAS 9; CANR 1, 21, 46; DAM NOV; DLB 9, 206; DLBY 1993; MTCW 1, 2; RGAL 4; TCWW 2

Stein, Gertrude 1874-1946 .... **TCLC 1, 6, 28, 48; PC 18; SSC 42; WLC**
See also AMW; CA 104; 132; CANR 108; CDALB 1917-1929; DA; DA3; DAB; DAC; DAM MST, NOV, POET; DLB 4, 54, 86, 228; DLBD 15; EXPS; GLL 1; MAWW; MTCW 1, 2; RGAL 4; RGSF 2; SSFS 5; WP

Steinbeck, John (Ernst) 1902-1968 ... **CLC 1, 5, 9, 13, 21, 34, 45, 75, 124; SSC 11, 37; WLC**
See also AAYA 12; AMW; BPFB 3; BYA 2, 3, 13; CA 1-4R; 25-28R; CANR 1, 35; CDALB 1929-1941; DA; DA3; DAB; DAC; DAM DRAM, MST, NOV; DLB 7, 9, 212; DLBD 2; EXPS; LAIT 3; MTCW 1, 2; NFS 1, 5, 7; RGAL 4; RGSF 2; RHW; SATA 9; SSFS 3, 6; TCWW 2; WYA; YAW

Steinem, Gloria 1934- .... **CLC 63**
See also CA 53-56; CANR 28, 51; DLB 246; FW; MTCW 1, 2

Steiner, George 1929- .... **CLC 24**
See also CA 73-76; CANR 31, 67, 108; DAM NOV; DLB 67; MTCW 1, 2; SATA 62

Steiner, K. Leslie
See Delany, Samuel R(ay), Jr.

Steiner, Rudolf 1861-1925 .... **TCLC 13**
See also CA 107

Stendhal 1783-1842 .. **NCLC 23, 46; SSC 27; WLC**
See also DA; DA3; DAB; DAC; DAM MST, NOV; DLB 119; EW 5; GFL 1789 to the Present; RGWL 2

Stephen, Adeline Virginia
See Woolf, (Adeline) Virginia

Stephen, Sir Leslie 1832-1904 .... **TCLC 23**
See also BRW 5; CA 123; DLB 57, 144, 190

Stephen, Sir Leslie
See Stephen, Sir Leslie

Stephen, Virginia
See Woolf, (Adeline) Virginia

Stephens, James 1882(?)-1950 .... **TCLC 4; SSC 50**
See also CA 104; 192; DLB 19, 153, 162; FANT; RGEL 2; SUFW

Stephens, Reed
See Donaldson, Stephen R(eeder)

Steptoe, Lydia
See Barnes, Djuna
See also GLL 1

Sterchi, Beat 1949- .... **CLC 65**

Sterling, Brett
See Bradbury, Ray (Douglas); Hamilton, Edmond

Sterling, Bruce 1954- .... **CLC 72**
See also CA 119; CANR 44; SCFW 2; SFW 4

Sterling, George 1869-1926 .... **TCLC 20**
See also CA 117; 165; DLB 54

Stern, Gerald 1925- .... **CLC 40, 100**
See also AMWS 9; CA 81-84; CANR 28, 94; CP 7; DLB 105; RGAL 4

Stern, Richard (Gustave) 1928- ... **CLC 4, 39**
See also CA 1-4R; CANR 1, 25, 52; CN 7; DLB 218; DLBY 1987; INT CANR-25

Sternberg, Josef von 1894-1969 .... **CLC 20**
See also CA 81-84

Sterne, Laurence 1713-1768 .... **LC 2, 48;**
WLC
See also BRW 3; CDBLB 1660-1789; DA;
DAB; DAC; DAM MST, NOV; DLB 39;
RGEL 2

Sternheim, (William Adolf) Carl
1878-1942 .... **TCLC 8**
See also CA 105; 193; DLB 56, 118; RGWL 2

Stevens, Mark 1951- .... **CLC 34**
See also CA 122

Stevens, Wallace 1879-1955 ...... **TCLC 3, 12, 45; PC 6; WLC**
See also AMW; AMWR 1; CA 104; 124;
CDALB 1929-1941; DA; DA3; DAB;
DAC; DAM MST, POET; DLB 54; EXPP;
MTCW 1, 2; PAB; PFS 13; RGAL 4; WP

Stevenson, Anne (Katharine) 1933- .. **CLC 7, 33**
See also BRWS 6; CA 17-20R; CAAS 9;
CANR 9, 33; CP 7; CWP; DLB 40;
MTCW 1; RHW

Stevenson, Robert Louis (Balfour)
1850-1894 ...... **NCLC 5, 14, 63; SSC 11, 51; WLC**
See also AAYA 24; BPFB 3; BRW 5;
BRWR 1; BYA 1, 2, 4, 13; CDBLB 1890-
1914; CLR 10, 11; DA; DA3; DAB;
DAC; DAM MST, NOV; DLB 18, 57,
141, 156, 174; DLBD 13; HGG; JRDA;
LAIT 1, 3; MAICYA 1, 2; NFS 11; RGEL
2; RGSF 2; SATA 100; SUFW; WCH;
WLIT 4; WYA; YABC 2; YAW

Stewart, J(ohn) I(nnes) M(ackintosh)
1906-1994 .... **CLC 7, 14, 32**
See also Innes, Michael
See also CA 85-88; 147; CAAS 3; CANR
47; CMW 4; MTCW 1, 2

Stewart, Mary (Florence Elinor)
1916- .... **CLC 7, 35, 117**
See also AAYA 29; BPFB 3; CA 1-4R;
CANR 1, 59; CMW 4; CPW; DAB;
FANT; RHW; SATA 12; YAW

Stewart, Mary Rainbow
See Stewart, Mary (Florence Elinor)

Stifle, June
See Campbell, Maria

Stifter, Adalbert 1805-1868 .. **NCLC 41; SSC 28**
See also CDWLB 2; DLB 133; RGSF 2;
RGWL 2

Still, James 1906-2001 .... **CLC 49**
See also CA 65-68; 195; CAAS 17; CANR
10, 26; CSW; DLB 9; DLBY 01; SATA
29; SATA-Obit 127

Sting 1951-
See Sumner, Gordon Matthew
See also CA 167

Stirling, Arthur
See Sinclair, Upton (Beall)

Stitt, Milan 1941- .... **CLC 29**
See also CA 69-72

Stockton, Francis Richard 1834-1902
See Stockton, Frank R.
See also CA 108; 137; MAICYA 1, 2; SATA 44; SFW 4

Stockton, Frank R. .... **TCLC 47**
See also Stockton, Francis Richard
See also BYA 4, 13; DLB 42, 74; DLBD
13; EXPS; SATA-Brief 32; SSFS 3;
SUFW; WCH

Stoddard, Charles
See Kuttner, Henry

Stoker, Abraham 1847-1912
See Stoker, Bram
See also CA 105; 150; DA; DA3; DAC;
DAM MST, NOV; HGG; SATA 29

Stoker, Bram .... **TCLC 8; WLC**
See also Stoker, Abraham
See also AAYA 23; BPFB 3; BRWS 3; BYA
5; CDBLB 1890-1914; DAB; DLB 36, 70,
178; RGEL 2; SUFW; WLIT 4

Stolz, Mary (Slattery) 1920- .... **CLC 12**
See also AAYA 8; AITN 1; CA 5-8R;
CANR 13, 41; JRDA; MAICYA 1, 2;
SAAS 3; SATA 10, 71; YAW

Stone, Irving 1903-1989 .... **CLC 7**
See also AITN 1; BPFB 3; CA 1-4R; 129;
CAAS 3; CANR 1, 23; CPW; DA3; DAM
POP; INT CANR-23; MTCW 1, 2; RHW;
SATA 3; SATA-Obit 64

Stone, Oliver (William) 1946- .... **CLC 73**
See also AAYA 15; CA 110; CANR 55

Stone, Robert (Anthony) 1937- ... **CLC 5, 23, 42**
See also AMWS 5; BPFB 3; CA 85-88;
CANR 23, 66, 95; CN 7; DLB 152; INT
CANR-23; MTCW 1

Stone, Zachary
See Follett, Ken(neth Martin)

Stoppard, Tom 1937- ... **CLC 1, 3, 4, 5, 8, 15, 29, 34, 63, 91; DC 6; WLC**
See also BRWR 2; BRWS 1; CA 81-84;
CANR 39, 67; CBD; CD 5; CDBLB 1960
to Present; DA; DA3; DAB; DAC; DAM
DRAM, MST; DFS 2, 5, 8, 11, 13; DLB
13, 233; DLBY 1985; MTCW 1, 2; RGEL
2; WLIT 4

Storey, David (Malcolm) 1933- . **CLC 2, 4, 5, 8**
See also BRWS 1; CA 81-84; CANR 36;
CBD; CD 5; CN 7; DAM DRAM; DLB
13, 14, 207, 245; MTCW 1; RGEL 2

Storm, Hyemeyohsts 1935- .... **CLC 3**
See also CA 81-84; CANR 45; DAM
MULT; NNAL

Storm, (Hans) Theodor (Woldsen)
1817-1888 .... **NCLC 1; SSC 27**
See also DLB 129; EW

Storm, Theodor 1817-1888 .... **SSC 27**
See also CDWLB 2; RGSF 2; RGWL 2

Storni, Alfonsina 1892-1938 .. **TCLC 5; HLC 2; PC 33**
See also CA 104; 131; DAM MULT; HW
1; LAW

Stoughton, William 1631-1701 .... **LC 38**
See also DLB 24

Stout, Rex (Todhunter) 1886-1975 ..... **CLC 3**
See also AITN 2; BPFB 3; CA 61-64;
CANR 71; CMW 4; MSW; RGAL 4

Stow, (Julian) Randolph 1935- ... **CLC 23, 48**
See also CA 13-16R; CANR 33; CN 7;
MTCW 1; RGEL 2

Stowe, Harriet (Elizabeth) Beecher
1811-1896 .... **NCLC 3, 50; WLC**
See also AMWS 1; CDALB 1865-1917;
DA; DA3; DAB; DAC; DAM MST, NOV;
DLB 1, 12, 42, 74, 189, 239, 243; EXPN;
JRDA; LAIT 2; MAICYA 1, 2; NFS 6;
RGAL 4; YABC 1

Strabo c. 64B.C.-c. 25 .... **CMLC 37**
See also DLB 176

Strachey, (Giles) Lytton
1880-1932 .... **TCLC 12**
See also BRWS 2; CA 110; 178; DLB 149;
DLBD 10; MTCW 2

Strand, Mark 1934- .... **CLC 6, 18, 41, 71**
See also AMWS 4; CA 21-24R; CANR 40,
65, 100; CP 7; DAM POET; DLB 5; PAB;
PFS 9; RGAL 4; SATA 41

Stratton-Porter, Gene(va Grace) 1863-1924
See Porter, Gene(va Grace) Stratton
See also ANW; CA 137; DLB 221; DLBD
14; MAICYA 1, 2; SATA 15

Straub, Peter (Francis) 1943- ... **CLC 28, 107**
See also BEST 89:1; BPFB 3; CA 85-88;
CANR 28, 65, 109; CPW; DAM POP;
DLBY 1984; HGG; MTCW 1, 2

Strauss, Botho 1944- .... **CLC 22**
See also CA 157; CWW 2; DLB 124

Streatfeild, (Mary) Noel
1897(?)-1986 .... **CLC 21**
See also CA 81-84; 120; CANR 31; CLR
17; CWRI 5; DLB 160; MAICYA 1, 2;
SATA 20; SATA-Obit 48

Stribling, T(homas) S(igismund)
1881-1965 .... **CLC 23**
See also CA 189; 107; CMW 4; DLB 9;
RGAL 4

Strindberg, (Johan) August
1849-1912 ...... **TCLC 1, 8, 21, 47; WLC**
See also CA 104; 135; DA; DA3; DAB;
DAC; DAM DRAM, MST; DFS 4, 9;
DLB 259; EW 7; IDTP; MTCW 2; RGWL 2

Stringer, Arthur 1874-1950 .... **TCLC 37**
See also CA 161; DLB 92

Stringer, David
See Roberts, Keith (John Kingston)

Stroheim, Erich von 1885-1957 ..... **TCLC 71**

Strugatskii, Arkadii (Natanovich)
1925-1991 .... **CLC 27**
See also CA 106; 135; SFW 4

Strugatskii, Boris (Natanovich)
1933- .... **CLC 27**
See also CA 106; SFW 4

Strummer, Joe 1953(?)- .... **CLC 30**

Strunk, William, Jr. 1869-1946 ...... **TCLC 92**
See also CA 118; 164

Stryk, Lucien 1924- .... **PC 27**
See also CA 13-16R; CANR 10, 28, 55; CP 7

Stuart, Don A.
See Campbell, John W(ood, Jr.)

Stuart, Ian
See MacLean, Alistair (Stuart)

Stuart, Jesse (Hilton) 1906-1984 ... **CLC 1, 8, 11, 14, 34; SSC 31**
See also CA 5-8R; 112; CANR 31; DLB 9,
48, 102; DLBY 1984; SATA 2; SATA-
Obit 36

Stubblefield, Sally
See Trumbo, Dalton

Sturgeon, Theodore (Hamilton)
1918-1985 .... **CLC 22, 39**
See also Queen, Ellery
See also BPFB 3; BYA 9, 10; CA 81-84;
116; CANR 32, 103; DLB 8; DLBY 1985;
HGG; MTCW 1, 2; SCFW; SFW 4;
SUFW

Sturges, Preston 1898-1959 .... **TCLC 48**
See also CA 114; 149; DLB 26

Styron, William 1925- ... **CLC 1, 3, 5, 11, 15, 60; SSC 25**
See also AMW; BEST 90:4; BPFB 3; CA
5-8R; CANR 6, 33, 74; CDALB 1968-
1988; CN 7; CPW; CSW; DA3; DAM
NOV, POP; DLB 2, 143; DLBY 1980;
INT CANR-6; LAIT 2; MTCW 1, 2;
NCFS 1; RGAL 4; RHW

Su, Chien 1884-1918
See Su Man-shu
See also CA 123

Suarez Lynch, B.
See Bioy Casares, Adolfo; Borges, Jorge
Luis

Suassuna, Ariano Vilar 1927-
See also CA 178; HLCS 1; HW 2; LAW

Suckling, Sir John 1609-1642 . **LC 75; PC 30**
See also BRW 2; DAM POET; DLB 58,
126; EXPP; PAB; RGEL 2

Suckow, Ruth 1892-1960 .... **SSC 18**
See also CA 193; 113; DLB 9, 102; RGAL 4; TCWW 2

Sudermann, Hermann 1857-1928 .. **TCLC 15**
See also CA 107; DLB 118

Sue, Eugene 1804-1857 .... **NCLC 1**
See also DLB 119

Sueskind, Patrick 1949- .... **CLC 44**
See also Suskind, Patrick

Sukenick, Ronald 1932- .... **CLC 3, 4, 6, 48**
See also CA 25-28R; CAAS 8; CANR 32, 89; CN 7; DLB 173; DLBY 1981

Suknaski, Andrew 1942- .... **CLC 19**
See also CA 101; CP 7; DLB 53

Sullivan, Vernon
See Vian, Boris

Sully Prudhomme, Rene-Francois-Armand 1839-1907 .... **TCLC 31**
See also GFL 1789 to the Present

Su Man-shu .... **TCLC 24**
See also Su, Chien

Summerforest, Ivy B.
See Kirkup, James

Summers, Andrew James 1942- .... **CLC 26**

Summers, Andy
See Summers, Andrew James

Summers, Hollis (Spurgeon, Jr.) 1916- .... **CLC 10**
See also CA 5-8R; CANR 3; DLB 6

Summers, (Alphonsus Joseph-Mary Augustus) Montague 1880-1948 .... **TCLC 16**
See also CA 118; 163

Sumner, Gordon Matthew .... **CLC 26**
See also Police, The; Sting

Surtees, Robert Smith 1805-1864 .. **NCLC 14**
See also DLB 21; RGEL 2

Susann, Jacqueline 1921-1974 .... **CLC 3**
See also AITN 1; BPFB 3; CA 65-68; 53-56; MTCW 1, 2

Su Shi
See Su Shih
See also RGWL 2

Su Shih 1036-1101 .... **CMLC 15**
See also Su Shi

Suskind, Patrick
See Sueskind, Patrick
See also BPFB 3; CA 145; CWW 2

Sutcliff, Rosemary 1920-1992 .... **CLC 26**
See also AAYA 10; BYA 1, 4; CA 5-8R; 139; CANR 37; CLR 1, 37; CPW; DAB; DAC; DAM MST, POP; JRDA; MAICYA 1, 2; MAICYAS 1; RHW; SATA 6, 44, 78; SATA-Obit 73; WYA; YAW

Sutro, Alfred 1863-1933 .... **TCLC 6**
See also CA 105; 185; DLB 10; RGEL 2

Sutton, Henry
See Slavitt, David R(ytman)

Suzuki, D. T.
See Suzuki, Daisetz Teitaro

Suzuki, Daisetz T.
See Suzuki, Daisetz Teitaro

Suzuki, Daisetz Teitaro 1870-1966 .... **TCLC 109**
See also CA 121; 111; MTCW 1, 2

Suzuki, Teitaro
See Suzuki, Daisetz Teitaro

Svevo, Italo .... **TCLC 2, 35; SSC 25**
See also Schmitz, Aron Hector
See also EW 8; RGWL 2

Swados, Elizabeth (A.) 1951- .... **CLC 12**
See also CA 97-100; CANR 49; INT 97-100

Swados, Harvey 1920-1972 .... **CLC 5**
See also CA 5-8R; 37-40R; CANR 6; DLB 2

Swan, Gladys 1934- .... **CLC 69**
See also CA 101; CANR 17, 39

Swanson, Logan
See Matheson, Richard (Burton)

Swarthout, Glendon (Fred) 1918-1992 .... **CLC 35**
See also CA 1-4R; 139; CANR 1, 47; LAIT 5; SATA 26; TCWW 2; YAW

Sweet, Sarah C.
See Jewett, (Theodora) Sarah Orne

Swenson, May 1919-1989 ...... **CLC 4, 14, 61, 106; PC 14**
See also AMWS 4; CA 5-8R; 130; CANR 36, 61; DA; DAB; DAC; DAM MST, POET; DLB 5; EXPP; GLL 2; MTCW 1, 2; SATA 15; WP

Swift, Augustus
See Lovecraft, H(oward) P(hillips)

Swift, Graham (Colin) 1949- .... **CLC 41, 88**
See also BRWS 5; CA 117; 122; CANR 46, 71; CN 7; DLB 194; MTCW 2; RGSF 2

Swift, Jonathan 1667-1745 .. **LC 1, 42; PC 9; WLC**
See also AAYA 41; BRW 3; BRWR 1; BYA 5, 14; CDBLB 1660-1789; CLR 53; DA; DA3; DAB; DAC; DAM MST, NOV, POET; DLB 39, 95, 101; EXPN; LAIT 1; NFS 6; RGEL 2; SATA 19; WCH; WLIT 3

Swinburne, Algernon Charles 1837-1909 ... **TCLC 8, 36; PC 24; WLC**
See also BRW 5; CA 105; 140; CDBLB 1832-1890; DA; DA3; DAB; DAC; DAM MST, POET; DLB 35, 57; PAB; RGEL 2

Swinfen, Ann .... **CLC 34**

Swinnerton, Frank Arthur 1884-1982 .... **CLC 31**
See also CA 108; DLB 34

Swithen, John
See King, Stephen (Edwin)

Sylvia
See Ashton-Warner, Sylvia (Constance)

Symmes, Robert Edward
See Duncan, Robert (Edward)

Symonds, John Addington 1840-1893 .... **NCLC 34**
See also DLB 57, 144

Symons, Arthur 1865-1945 .... **TCLC 11**
See also CA 107; 189; DLB 19, 57, 149; RGEL 2

Symons, Julian (Gustave) 1912-1994 .... **CLC 2, 14, 32**
See also CA 49-52; 147; CAAS 3; CANR 3, 33, 59; CMW 4; DLB 87, 155; DLBY 1992; MSW; MTCW 1

Synge, (Edmund) J(ohn) M(illington) 1871-1909 .... **TCLC 6, 37; DC 2**
See also BRW 6; BRWR 1; CA 104; 141; CDBLB 1890-1914; DAM DRAM; DLB 10, 19; RGEL 2; WLIT 4

Syruc, J.
See Milosz, Czeslaw

Szirtes, George 1948- .... **CLC 46**
See also CA 109; CANR 27, 61; CP 7

Szymborska, Wislawa 1923- .... **CLC 99**
See also CA 154; CANR 91; CDWLB 4; CWP; CWW 2; DA3; DLB 232; DLBY 1996; MTCW 2

T. O., Nik
See Annensky, Innokenty (Fyodorovich)

Tabori, George 1914- .... **CLC 19**
See also CA 49-52; CANR 4, 69; CBD; CD 5; DLB 245

Tagore, Rabindranath 1861-1941 ... **TCLC 3, 53; PC 8; SSC 48**
See also CA 104; 120; DA3; DAM DRAM, POET; MTCW 1, 2; RGEL 2; RGSF 2; RGWL 2

Taine, Hippolyte Adolphe 1828-1893 .... **NCLC 15**
See also EW 7; GFL 1789 to the Present

Talese, Gay 1932- .... **CLC 37**
See also AITN 1; CA 1-4R; CANR 9, 58; DLB 185; INT CANR-9; MTCW 1, 2

Tallent, Elizabeth (Ann) 1954- .... **CLC 45**
See also CA 117; CANR 72; DLB 130

Tally, Ted 1952- .... **CLC 42**
See also CA 120; 124; CAD; CD 5; INT 124

Talvik, Heiti 1904-1947 .... **TCLC 87**

Tamayo y Baus, Manuel 1829-1898 .... **NCLC 1**

Tammsaare, A(nton) H(ansen) 1878-1940 .... **TCLC 27**
See also CA 164; CDWLB 4; DLB 220

Tam'si, Tchicaya U
See Tchicaya, Gerald Felix

Tan, Amy (Ruth) 1952- .... **CLC 59, 120, 151; AAL**
See also AAYA 9; AMWS 10; BEST 89:3; BPFB 3; CA 136; CANR 54, 105; CDALBS; CN 7; CPW 1; DA3; DAM MULT, NOV, POP; DLB 173; EXPN; FW; LAIT 3, 5; MTCW 2; NFS 1, 13; RGAL 4; SATA 75; SSFS 9; YAW

Tandem, Felix
See Spitteler, Carl (Friedrich Georg)

Tanizaki, Jun'ichiro 1886-1965 ... **CLC 8, 14, 28; SSC 21**
See also Tanizaki Jun'ichiro
See also CA 93-96; 25-28R; MJW; MTCW 2; RGSF 2; RGWL 2

Tanizaki Jun'ichiro
See Tanizaki, Jun'ichiro
See also DLB 180

Tanner, William
See Amis, Kingsley (William)

Tao Lao
See Storni, Alfonsina

Tarantino, Quentin (Jerome) 1963- .... **CLC 125**
See also CA 171

Tarassoff, Lev
See Troyat, Henri

Tarbell, Ida M(inerva) 1857-1944 . **TCLC 40**
See also CA 122; 181; DLB 47

Tarkington, (Newton) Booth 1869-1946 .... **TCLC 9**
See also BPFB 3; BYA 3; CA 110; 143; CWRI 5; DLB 9, 102; MTCW 2; RGAL 4; SATA 17

Tarkovsky, Andrei (Arsenyevich) 1932-1986 .... **CLC 75**
See also CA 127

Tartt, Donna 1964(?)- .... **CLC 76**
See also CA 142

Tasso, Torquato 1544-1595 .... **LC 5**
See also EFS 2; EW 2; RGWL 2

Tate, (John Orley) Allen 1899-1979 .. **CLC 2, 4, 6, 9, 11, 14, 24**
See also AMW; CA 5-8R; 85-88; CANR 32, 108; DLB 4, 45, 63; DLBD 17; MTCW 1, 2; RGAL 4; RHW

Tate, Ellalice
See Hibbert, Eleanor Alice Burford

Tate, James (Vincent) 1943- ...... **CLC 2, 6, 25**
See also CA 21-24R; CANR 29, 57; CP 7; DLB 5, 169; PFS 10; RGAL 4; WP

Tauler, Johannes c. 1300-1361 .... **CMLC 37**
See also DLB 179

Tavel, Ronald 1940- .... **CLC 6**
See also CA 21-24R; CAD; CANR 33; CD 5

Taviani, Paolo 1931- .... **CLC 70**
See also CA 153

Taylor, Bayard 1825-1878 .... **NCLC 89**
See also DLB 3, 189, 250, 254; RGAL 4

Taylor, C(ecil) P(hilip) 1929-1981 .... **CLC 27**
See also CA 25-28R; 105; CANR 47; CBD

Taylor, Edward 1642(?)-1729 .... **LC 11**
See also AMW; DA; DAB; DAC; DAM MST, POET; DLB 24; EXPP; RGAL 4

Taylor, Eleanor Ross 1920- .... **CLC 5**
See also CA 81-84; CANR 70

Taylor, Elizabeth 1932-1975 ..... **CLC 2, 4, 29**
See also CA 13-16R; CANR 9, 70; DLB 139; MTCW 1; RGEL 2; SATA 13

Taylor, Frederick Winslow
1856-1915 .... **TCLC 76**
See also CA 188

Taylor, Henry (Splawn) 1942- .... **CLC 44**
See also CA 33-36R; CAAS 7; CANR 31; CP 7; DLB 5; PFS 10

Taylor, Kamala (Purnaiya) 1924-
See Markandaya, Kamala
See also CA 77-80; NFS 13

Taylor, Mildred D(elois) 1943- .... **CLC 21**
See also AAYA 10; BW 1; BYA 3, 8; CA 85-88; CANR 25; CLR 9, 59; CSW; DLB 52; JRDA; LAIT 3; MAICYA 1, 2; SAAS 5; SATA 15, 70; WYA; YAW

Taylor, Peter (Hillsman) 1917-1994 .. **CLC 1, 4, 18, 37, 44, 50, 71; SSC 10**
See also AMWS 5; BPFB 3; CA 13-16R; 147; CANR 9, 50; CSW; DLB 218; DLBY 1981, 1994; EXPS; INT CANR-9; MTCW 1, 2; RGSF 2; SSFS 9

Taylor, Robert Lewis 1912-1998 .... **CLC 14**
See also CA 1-4R; 170; CANR 3, 64; SATA 10

Tchekhov, Anton
See Chekhov, Anton (Pavlovich)

Tchicaya, Gerald Felix 1931-1988 .. **CLC 101**
See also CA 129; 125; CANR 81

Tchicaya U Tam'si
See Tchicaya, Gerald Felix

Teasdale, Sara 1884-1933 .... **TCLC 4; PC 31**
See also CA 104; 163; DLB 45; GLL 1; PFS 14; RGAL 4; SATA 32

Tegner, Esaias 1782-1846 .... **NCLC 2**

Teilhard de Chardin, (Marie Joseph) Pierre
1881-1955 .... **TCLC 9**
See also CA 105; GFL 1789 to the Present

Temple, Ann
See Mortimer, Penelope (Ruth)

Tennant, Emma (Christina) 1937- .. **CLC 13, 52**
See also CA 65-68; CAAS 9; CANR 10, 38, 59, 88; CN 7; DLB 14; SFW 4

Tenneshaw, S. M.
See Silverberg, Robert

Tennyson, Alfred 1809-1892 ... **NCLC 30, 65; PC 6; WLC**
See also BRW 4; CDBLB 1832-1890; DA; DA3; DAB; DAC; DAM MST, POET; DLB 32; EXPP; PAB; PFS 1, 2, 4, 11; RGEL 2; WLIT 4; WP

Teran, Lisa St. Aubin de .... **CLC 36**
See also St. Aubin de Teran, Lisa

Terence c. 184B.C.-c. 159B.C. .... **CMLC 14; DC 7**
See also AW 1; CDWLB 1; DLB 211; RGWL 2

Teresa de Jesus, St. 1515-1582 .... **LC 18**

Terkel, Louis 1912-
See Terkel, Studs
See also CA 57-60; CANR 18, 45, 67; DA3; MTCW 1, 2

Terkel, Studs .... **CLC 38**
See also Terkel, Louis
See also AAYA 32; AITN 1; MTCW 2

Terry, C. V.
See Slaughter, Frank G(ill)

Terry, Megan 1932- .... **CLC 19; DC 13**
See also CA 77-80; CABS 3; CAD; CANR 43; CD 5; CWD; DLB 7, 249; GLL 2

Tertullian c. 155-c. 245 .... **CMLC 29**

Tertz, Abram
See Sinyavsky, Andrei (Donatevich)
See also CWW 2; RGSF 2

Tesich, Steve 1943(?)-1996 .... **CLC 40, 69**
See also CA 105; 152; CAD; DLBY 1983

Tesla, Nikola 1856-1943 .... **TCLC 88**

Teternikov, Fyodor Kuzmich 1863-1927
See Sologub, Fyodor
See also CA 104

Tevis, Walter 1928-1984 .... **CLC 42**
See also CA 113; SFW 4

Tey, Josephine .... **TCLC 14**
See also Mackintosh, Elizabeth
See also DLB 77; MSW

Thackeray, William Makepeace
1811-1863 .... **NCLC 5, 14, 22, 43; WLC**
See also BRW 5; CDBLB 1832-1890; DA; DA3; DAB; DAC; DAM MST, NOV; DLB 21, 55, 159, 163; NFS 13; RGEL 2; SATA 23; WLIT 3

Thakura, Ravindranatha
See Tagore, Rabindranath

Thames, C. H.
See Marlowe, Stephen

Tharoor, Shashi 1956- .... **CLC 70**
See also CA 141; CANR 91; CN 7

Thelwell, Michael Miles 1939- .... **CLC 22**
See also BW 2; CA 101

Theobald, Lewis, Jr.
See Lovecraft, H(oward) P(hillips)

Theocritus c. 310B.C.- .... **CMLC 45**
See also AW 1; DLB 176; RGWL 2

Theodorescu, Ion N. 1880-1967
See Arghezi, Tudor
See also CA 116

Theriault, Yves 1915-1983 .... **CLC 79**
See also CA 102; CCA 1; DAC; DAM MST; DLB 88

Theroux, Alexander (Louis) 1939- .... **CLC 2, 25**
See also CA 85-88; CANR 20, 63; CN 7

Theroux, Paul (Edward) 1941- ...... **CLC 5, 8, 11, 15, 28, 46**
See also AAYA 28; AMWS 8; BEST 89:4; BPFB 3; CA 33-36R; CANR 20, 45, 74; CDALBS; CN 7; CPW 1; DA3; DAM POP; DLB 2, 218; HGG; MTCW 1, 2; RGAL 4; SATA 44, 109

Thesen, Sharon 1946- .... **CLC 56**
See also CA 163; CP 7; CWP

Thespis fl. 6th cent. B.C.- .... **CMLC 51**

Thevenin, Denis
See Duhamel, Georges

Thibault, Jacques Anatole Francois
1844-1924
See France, Anatole
See also CA 106; 127; DA3; DAM NOV; MTCW 1, 2

Thiele, Colin (Milton) 1920- .... **CLC 17**
See also CA 29-32R; CANR 12, 28, 53, 105; CLR 27; MAICYA 1, 2; SAAS 2; SATA 14, 72, 125; YAW

Thomas, Audrey (Callahan) 1935- .... **CLC 7, 13, 37, 107; SSC 20**
See also AITN 2; CA 21-24R; CAAS 19; CANR 36, 58; CN 7; DLB 60; MTCW 1; RGSF 2

Thomas, Augustus 1857-1934 .... **TCLC 97**

Thomas, D(onald) M(ichael) 1935- . **CLC 13, 22, 31, 132**
See also BPFB 3; BRWS 4; CA 61-64; CAAS 11; CANR 17, 45, 75; CDBLB 1960 to Present; CN 7; CP 7; DA3; DLB 40, 207; HGG; INT CANR-17; MTCW 1, 2; SFW 4

Thomas, Dylan (Marlais)
1914-1953 ... **TCLC 1, 8, 45, 105; PC 2; SSC 3, 44; WLC**
See also BRWS 1; CA 104; 120; CANR 65; CDBLB 1945-1960; DA; DA3; DAB; DAC; DAM DRAM, MST, POET; DLB 13, 20, 139; EXPP; LAIT 3; MTCW 1, 2; PAB; PFS 1, 3, 8; RGEL 2; RGSF 2; SATA 60; WLIT 4; WP

Thomas, (Philip) Edward
1878-1917 .... **TCLC 10**
See also BRW 6; BRWS 3; CA 106; 153; DAM POET; DLB 19, 98, 156, 216; PAB; RGEL 2

Thomas, Joyce Carol 1938- .... **CLC 35**
See also AAYA 12; BW 2, 3; CA 113; 116; CANR 48; CLR 19; DLB 33; INT CA-116; JRDA; MAICYA 1, 2; MTCW 1, 2; SAAS 7; SATA 40, 78, 123; WYA; YAW

Thomas, Lewis 1913-1993 .... **CLC 35**
See also ANW; CA 85-88; 143; CANR 38, 60; MTCW 1, 2

Thomas, M. Carey 1857-1935 .... **TCLC 89**
See also FW

Thomas, Paul
See Mann, (Paul) Thomas

Thomas, Piri 1928- .... **CLC 17; HLCS 2**
See also CA 73-76; HW 1

Thomas, R(onald) S(tuart)
1913-2000 .... **CLC 6, 13, 48**
See also CA 89-92; 189; CAAS 4; CANR 30; CDBLB 1960 to Present; CP 7; DAB; DAM POET; DLB 27; MTCW 1; RGEL 2

Thomas, Ross (Elmore) 1926-1995 .. **CLC 39**
See also CA 33-36R; 150; CANR 22, 63; CMW 4

Thompson, Francis (Joseph)
1859-1907 .... **TCLC 4**
See also BRW 5; CA 104; 189; CDBLB 1890-1914; DLB 19; RGEL 2; TEA

Thompson, Francis Clegg
See Mencken, H(enry) L(ouis)

Thompson, Hunter S(tockton)
1939- .... **CLC 9, 17, 40, 104**
See also BEST 89:1; BPFB 3; CA 17-20R; CANR 23, 46, 74, 77; CPW; CSW; DA3; DAM POP; DLB 185; MTCW 1, 2

Thompson, James Myers
See Thompson, Jim (Myers)

Thompson, Jim (Myers)
1906-1977(?) .... **CLC 69**
See also BPFB 3; CA 140; CMW 4; CPW; DLB 226; MSW

Thompson, Judith .... **CLC 39**
See also CWD

Thomson, James 1700-1748 ..... **LC 16, 29, 40**
See also BRWS 3; DAM POET; DLB 95; RGEL 2

Thomson, James 1834-1882 .... **NCLC 18**
See also DAM POET; DLB 35; RGEL 2

Thoreau, Henry David 1817-1862 .. **NCLC 7, 21, 61; PC 30; WLC**
See also AAYA 42; AMW; ANW; BYA 3; CDALB 1640-1865; DA; DA3; DAB; DAC; DAM MST; DLB 1, 183, 223; LAIT 2; NCFS 3; RGAL 4

Thorndike, E. L.
See Thorndike, Edward L(ee)

Thorndike, Edward L(ee)
1874-1949 .... **TCLC 107**
See also CA 121

Thornton, Hall
See Silverberg, Robert

Thucydides c. 455B.C.-c. 395B.C. .. **CMLC 17**
See also AW 1; DLB 176; RGWL 2

Thumboo, Edwin Nadason 1933- .... **PC 30**
See also CA 194

Thurber, James (Grover)
1894-1961 .. **CLC 5, 11, 25, 125; SSC 1, 47**
See also AMWS 1; BPFB 3; BYA 5; CA 73-76; CANR 17, 39; CDALB 1929-1941; CWRI 5; DA; DA3; DAB; DAC; DAM DRAM, MST, NOV; DLB 4, 11, 22, 102; EXPS; FANT; LAIT 3; MAICYA 1, 2; MTCW 1, 2; RGAL 4; RGSF 2; SATA 13; SSFS 1, 10; SUFW

Thurman, Wallace (Henry)
1902-1934 .... **TCLC 6; BLC 3**
See also BW 1, 3; CA 104; 124; CANR 81; DAM MULT; DLB 51

Tibullus c. 54B.C.-c. 18B.C. .... **CMLC 36**
See also AW 2; DLB 211; RGWL 2

Ticheburn, Cheviot
See Ainsworth, William Harrison

Tieck, (Johann) Ludwig
1773-1853 .... **NCLC 5, 46; SSC 31**
See also CDWLB 2; DLB 90; EW 5; IDTP; RGSF 2; RGWL 2; SUFW

Tiger, Derry
See Ellison, Harlan (Jay)

Tilghman, Christopher 1948(?)- .... **CLC 65**
See also CA 159; CSW; DLB 244

Tillich, Paul (Johannes)
1886-1965 .... **CLC 131**
See also CA 5-8R; 25-28R; CANR 33; MTCW 1, 2

Tillinghast, Richard (Williford)
1940- .... **CLC 29**
See also CA 29-32R; CAAS 23; CANR 26, 51, 96; CP 7; CSW

Timrod, Henry 1828-1867 .... **NCLC 25**
See also DLB 3, 248; RGAL 4

Tindall, Gillian (Elizabeth) 1938- ...... **CLC 7**
See also CA 21-24R; CANR 11, 65, 107; CN 7

Tiptree, James, Jr. .... **CLC 48, 50**
See also Sheldon, Alice Hastings Bradley
See also DLB 8; SCFW; SFW 4

Tirso de Molina
See Tirso de Molina
See also RGWL 2

Tirso de Molina 1580(?)-1648 ..... **LC 73; DC 13; HLCS 2**
See also Tirso de Molina

Titmarsh, Michael Angelo
See Thackeray, William Makepeace

Tocqueville, Alexis (Charles Henri Maurice Clerel Comte) de 1805-1859 .. **NCLC 7, 63**
See also EW 6; GFL 1789 to the Present

Tolkien, J(ohn) R(onald) R(euel)
1892-1973 .... **CLC 1, 2, 3, 8, 12, 38; WLC**
See also AAYA 10; AITN 1; BPFB 3; BRWS 2; CA 17-18; 45-48; CANR 36; CAP 2; CDBLB 1914-1945; CLR 56; CPW 1; CWRI 5; DA; DA3; DAB; DAC; DAM MST, NOV, POP; DLB 15, 160, 255; EFS 2; FANT; JRDA; LAIT 1; MAICYA 1, 2; MTCW 1, 2; NFS 8; RGEL 2; SATA 2, 32, 100; SATA-Obit 24; SFW 4; SUFW; WCH; WYA; YAW

Toller, Ernst 1893-1939 .... **TCLC 10**
See also CA 107; 186; DLB 124; RGWL 2

Tolson, M. B.
See Tolson, Melvin B(eaunorus)

Tolson, Melvin B(eaunorus)
1898(?)-1966 .... **CLC 36, 105; BLC 3**
See also AFAW 1, 2; BW 1, 3; CA 124; 89-92; CANR 80; DAM MULT, POET; DLB 48, 76; RGAL 4

Tolstoi, Aleksei Nikolaevich
See Tolstoy, Alexey Nikolaevich

Tolstoi, Lev
See Tolstoy, Leo (Nikolaevich)
See also RGSF 2; RGWL 2

Tolstoy, Alexey Nikolaevich
1882-1945 .... **TCLC 18**
See also CA 107; 158; SFW 4

Tolstoy, Leo (Nikolaevich)
1828-1910 .. **TCLC 4, 11, 17, 28, 44, 79; SSC 9, 30, 45; WLC**
See also Tolstoi, Lev
See also CA 104; 123; DA; DA3; DAB; DAC; DAM MST, NOV; DLB 238; EFS 2; EW 7; EXPS; IDTP; LAIT 2; NFS 10; SATA 26; SSFS 5

Tolstoy, Count Leo
See Tolstoy, Leo (Nikolaevich)

Tomasi di Lampedusa, Giuseppe 1896-1957
See Lampedusa, Giuseppe (Tomasi) di
See also CA 111; DLB 177

Tomlin, Lily .... **CLC 17**
See also Tomlin, Mary Jean

Tomlin, Mary Jean 1939(?)-
See Tomlin, Lily
See also CA 117

Tomlinson, (Alfred) Charles 1927- .... **CLC 2, 4, 6, 13, 45; PC 17**
See also CA 5-8R; CANR 33; CP 7; DAM POET; DLB 40

Tomlinson, H(enry) M(ajor)
1873-1958 .... **TCLC 71**
See also CA 118; 161; DLB 36, 100, 195

Tonson, Jacob
See Bennett, (Enoch) Arnold

Toole, John Kennedy 1937-1969 ..... **CLC 19, 64**
See also BPFB 3; CA 104; DLBY 1981; MTCW 2

Toomer, Eugene
See Toomer, Jean

Toomer, Eugene Pinchback
See Toomer, Jean

Toomer, Jean 1892-1967 .... **CLC 1, 4, 13, 22; BLC 3; PC 7; SSC 1, 45; WLCS**
See also AFAW 1, 2; AMWS 3, 9; BW 1; CA 85-88; CDALB 1917-1929; DA3; DAM MULT; DLB 45, 51; EXPP; EXPS; MTCW 1, 2; NFS 11; RGAL 4; RGSF 2; SSFS 5

Toomer, Nathan Jean
See Toomer, Jean

Toomer, Nathan Pinchback
See Toomer, Jean

Torley, Luke
See Blish, James (Benjamin)

Tornimparte, Alessandra
See Ginzburg, Natalia

Torre, Raoul della
See Mencken, H(enry) L(ouis)

Torrence, Ridgely 1874-1950 .... **TCLC 97**
See also DLB 54, 249

Torrey, E(dwin) Fuller 1937- .... **CLC 34**
See also CA 119; CANR 71

Torsvan, Ben Traven
See Traven, B.

Torsvan, Benno Traven
See Traven, B.

Torsvan, Berick Traven
See Traven, B.

Torsvan, Berwick Traven
See Traven, B.

Torsvan, Bruno Traven
See Traven, B.

Torsvan, Traven
See Traven, B.

Tourneur, Cyril 1575(?)-1626 .... **LC 66**
See also BRW 2; DAM DRAM; DLB 58; RGEL 2

Tournier, Michel (Edouard) 1924- .... **CLC 6, 23, 36, 95**
See also CA 49-52; CANR 3, 36, 74; DLB 83; GFL 1789 to the Present; MTCW 1, 2; SATA 23

Tournimparte, Alessandra
See Ginzburg, Natalia

Towers, Ivar
See Kornbluth, C(yril) M.

Towne, Robert (Burton) 1936(?)- ...... **CLC 87**
See also CA 108; DLB 44; IDFW 3, 4

Townsend, Sue .... **CLC 61**
See also Townsend, Susan Elaine
See also AAYA 28; CBD; CWD; SATA 55, 93; SATA-Brief 48

Townsend, Susan Elaine 1946-
See Townsend, Sue
See also CA 119; 127; CANR 65, 107; CD 5; CPW; DAB; DAC; DAM MST; INT 127; YAW

Townshend, Peter (Dennis Blandford)
1945- .... **CLC 17, 42**
See also CA 107

Tozzi, Federigo 1883-1920 .... **TCLC 31**
See also CA 160

Tracy, Don(ald Fiske) 1905-1970(?)
See Queen, Ellery
See also CA 1-4R; 176; CANR 2

Trafford, F. G.
See Riddell, Charlotte

Traill, Catharine Parr 1802-1899 .. **NCLC 31**
See also DLB 99

Trakl, Georg 1887-1914 .... **TCLC 5; PC 20**
See also CA 104; 165; EW 10; MTCW 2; RGWL 2

Transtroemer, Tomas (Goesta)
1931- .... **CLC 52, 65**
See also Transtromer, Tomas
See also CA 117; 129; CAAS 17; DAM POET

Transtromer, Tomas
See Transtroemer, Tomas (Goesta)
See also DLB 257

Transtromer, Tomas Gosta
See Transtroemer, Tomas (Goesta)

Traven, B. 1882(?)-1969 .... **CLC 8, 11**
See also CA 19-20; 25-28R; CAP 2; DLB 9, 56; MTCW 1; RGAL 4

Trediakovsky, Vasilii Kirillovich
1703-1769 .... **LC 68**
See also DLB 150

Treitel, Jonathan 1959- .... **CLC 70**

Trelawny, Edward John
1792-1881 .... **NCLC 85**
See also DLB 110, 116, 144

Tremain, Rose 1943- .... **CLC 42**
See also CA 97-100; CANR 44, 95; CN 7; DLB 14; RGSF 2; RHW

Tremblay, Michel 1942- .... **CLC 29, 102**
See also CA 116; 128; CCA 1; CWW 2; DAC; DAM MST; DLB 60; GLL 1; MTCW 1, 2

Trevanian .... **CLC 29**
See also Whitaker, Rod(ney)

Trevor, Glen
See Hilton, James

Trevor, William .. **CLC 7, 9, 14, 25, 71, 116; SSC 21**
See also Cox, William Trevor
See also BRWS 4; CBD; CD 5; CN 7; DLB 14, 139; MTCW 2; RGEL 2; RGSF 2; SSFS 10

Trifonov, Iurii (Valentinovich)
See Trifonov, Yuri (Valentinovich)
See also RGWL 2

Trifonov, Yuri (Valentinovich)
1925-1981 .... **CLC 45**
See also Trifonov, Iurii (Valentinovich)
See also CA 126; 103; MTCW 1

Trilling, Diana (Rubin) 1905-1996 . **CLC 129**
See also CA 5-8R; 154; CANR 10, 46; INT CANR-10; MTCW 1, 2

Trilling, Lionel 1905-1975 .... **CLC 9, 11, 24**
See also AMWS 3; CA 9-12R; 61-64; CANR 10, 105; DLB 28, 63; INT CANR-10; MTCW 1, 2; RGAL 4

Trimball, W. H.
See Mencken, H(enry) L(ouis)

Tristan
See Gomez de la Serna, Ramon

Tristram
See Housman, A(lfred) E(dward)

Trogdon, William (Lewis) 1939-
See Heat-Moon, William Least
See also CA 115; 119; CANR 47, 89; CPW; INT CA-119

Trollope, Anthony 1815-1882 .... **NCLC 6, 33, 101; SSC 28; WLC**
See also BRW 5; CDBLB 1832-1890; DA; DA3; DAB; DAC; DAM MST, NOV; DLB 21, 57, 159; RGEL 2; RGSF 2; SATA 22

Trollope, Frances 1779-1863 .... **NCLC 30**
See also DLB 21, 166

Trotsky, Leon 1879-1940 .... **TCLC 22**
See also CA 118; 167

Trotter (Cockburn), Catharine
1679-1749 .... **LC 8**
See also DLB 84, 252

Trotter, Wilfred 1872-1939 .... **TCLC 97**

Trout, Kilgore
See Farmer, Philip Jose

Trow, George W. S. 1943- .... **CLC 52**
See also CA 126; CANR 91

Troyat, Henri 1911- .... **CLC 23**
See also CA 45-48; CANR 2, 33, 67; GFL 1789 to the Present; MTCW 1

Trudeau, G(arretson) B(eekman) 1948-
See Trudeau, Garry B.
See also CA 81-84; CANR 31; SATA 35

Trudeau, Garry B. .... **CLC 12**
See also Trudeau, G(arretson) B(eekman)
See also AAYA 10; AITN 2

Truffaut, Francois 1932-1984 ... **CLC 20, 101**
See also CA 81-84; 113; CANR 34

Trumbo, Dalton 1905-1976 .... **CLC 19**
See also CA 21-24R; 69-72; CANR 10; DLB 26; IDFW 3, 4; YAW

Trumbull, John 1750-1831 .... **NCLC 30**
See also DLB 31; RGAL 4

Trundlett, Helen B.
See Eliot, T(homas) S(tearns)

Truth, Sojourner 1797(?)-1883 .... **NCLC 94**
See also DLB 239; FW; LAIT 2

Tryon, Thomas 1926-1991 .... **CLC 3, 11**
See also AITN 1; BPFB 3; CA 29-32R; 135; CANR 32, 77; CPW; DA3; DAM POP; HGG; MTCW 1

Tryon, Tom
See Tryon, Thomas

Ts'ao Hsueh-ch'in 1715(?)-1763 .... **LC 1**

Tsushima, Shuji 1909-1948
See Dazai Osamu
See also CA 107

Tsvetaeva (Efron), Marina (Ivanovna)
1892-1941 .... **TCLC 7, 35; PC 14**
See also CA 104; 128; CANR 73; EW 11; MTCW 1, 2; RGWL 2

Tuck, Lily 1938- .... **CLC 70**
See also CA 139; CANR 90

Tu Fu 712-770 .... **PC 9**
See also Du Fu
See also DAM MULT; WP

Tunis, John R(oberts) 1889-1975 ..... **CLC 12**
See also BYA 1; CA 61-64; CANR 62; DLB 22, 171; JRDA; MAICYA 1, 2; SATA 37; SATA-Brief 30; YAW

Tuohy, Frank .... **CLC 37**
See also Tuohy, John Francis
See also DLB 14, 139

Tuohy, John Francis 1925-
See Tuohy, Frank
See also CA 5-8R; 178; CANR 3, 47; CN 7

Turco, Lewis (Putnam) 1934- ..... **CLC 11, 63**
See also CA 13-16R; CAAS 22; CANR 24, 51; CP 7; DLBY 1984

Turgenev, Ivan (Sergeevich)
1818-1883 .... **NCLC 21, 37; DC 7; SSC 7; WLC**
See also DA; DAB; DAC; DAM MST, NOV; DFS 6; DLB 238; EW 6; RGSF 2; RGWL 2

Turgot, Anne-Robert-Jacques
1727-1781 .... **LC 26**

Turner, Frederick 1943- .... **CLC 48**
See also CA 73-76; CAAS 10; CANR 12, 30, 56; DLB 40

Turton, James
See Crace, Jim

Tutu, Desmond M(pilo) 1931- .... **CLC 80; BLC 3**
See also BW 1, 3; CA 125; CANR 67, 81; DAM MULT

Tutuola, Amos 1920-1997 ...... **CLC 5, 14, 29; BLC 3**
See also AFW; BW 2, 3; CA 9-12R; 159; CANR 27, 66; CDWLB 3; CN 7; DA3; DAM MULT; DLB 125; DNFS 2; MTCW 1, 2; RGEL 2; WLIT 2

Twain, Mark .... **TCLC 6, 12, 19, 36, 48, 59; SSC 34; WLC**
See also Clemens, Samuel Langhorne
See also AAYA 20; AMW; BPFB 3; BYA 2, 3, 11, 14; CLR 58, 60, 66; DLB 11; EXPN; EXPS; FANT; LAIT 2; NFS 1, 6; RGAL 4; RGSF 2; SFW 4; SSFS 1, 7; SUFW; WCH; WYA; YAW

Tyler, Anne 1941- . **CLC 7, 11, 18, 28, 44, 59, 103**
See also AAYA 18; AMWS 4; BEST 89:1; BPFB 3; BYA 12; CA 9-12R; CANR 11, 33, 53, 109; CDALBS; CN 7; CPW; CSW; DAM NOV, POP; DLB 6, 143; DLBY 1982; EXPN; MAWW; MTCW 1, 2; NFS 2, 7, 10; RGAL 4; SATA 7, 90; YAW

Tyler, Royall 1757-1826 .... **NCLC 3**
See also DLB 37; RGAL 4

Tynan, Katharine 1861-1931 .... **TCLC 3**
See also CA 104; 167; DLB 153, 240; FW

Tyutchev, Fyodor 1803-1873 .... **NCLC 34**

Tzara, Tristan 1896-1963 ..... **CLC 47; PC 27**
See also CA 153; 89-92; DAM POET; MTCW 2

Uhry, Alfred 1936- .... **CLC 55**
See also CA 127; 133; CAD; CD 5; CSW; DA3; DAM DRAM, POP; DFS 11; INT CA-133

Ulf, Haerved
See Strindberg, (Johan) August

Ulf, Harved
See Strindberg, (Johan) August

Ulibarri, Sabine R(eyes) 1919- .... **CLC 83; HLCS 2**
See also CA 131; CANR 81; DAM MULT; DLB 82; HW 1, 2; RGSF 2

Unamuno (y Jugo), Miguel de
1864-1936 . **TCLC 2, 9; HLC 2; SSC 11**
See also CA 104; 131; CANR 81; DAM MULT, NOV; DLB 108; EW 8; HW 1, 2; MTCW 1, 2; RGSF 2; RGWL 2

Undercliffe, Errol
See Campbell, (John) Ramsey

Underwood, Miles
See Glassco, John

Undset, Sigrid 1882-1949 ..... **TCLC 3; WLC**
See also CA 104; 129; DA; DA3; DAB; DAC; DAM MST, NOV; EW 9; FW; MTCW 1, 2; RGWL 2

Ungaretti, Giuseppe 1888-1970 ... **CLC 7, 11, 15**
See also CA 19-20; 25-28R; CAP 2; DLB 114; EW 10; RGWL 2

Unger, Douglas 1952- .... **CLC 34**
See also CA 130; CANR 94

Unsworth, Barry (Forster) 1930- .... **CLC 76, 127**
See also BRWS 7; CA 25-28R; CANR 30, 54; CN 7; DLB 194

Updike, John (Hoyer) 1932- . **CLC 1, 2, 3, 5, 7, 9, 13, 15, 23, 34, 43, 70, 139; SSC 13, 27; WLC**
See also AAYA 36; AMW; AMWR 1; BPFB 3; BYA 12; CA 1-4R; CABS 1; CANR 4, 33, 51, 94; CDALB 1968-1988; CN 7; CP 7; CPW 1; DA; DA3; DAB; DAC; DAM MST, NOV, POET, POP; DLB 2, 5, 143, 218, 227; DLBD 3; DLBY 1980, 1982, 1997; EXPP; HGG; MTCW 1, 2; NFS 12; RGAL 4; RGSF 2; SSFS 3

Upshaw, Margaret Mitchell
See Mitchell, Margaret (Munnerlyn)

Upton, Mark
See Sanders, Lawrence

Upward, Allen 1863-1926 .... **TCLC 85**
See also CA 117; 187; DLB 36

Urdang, Constance (Henriette)
1922-1996 .... **CLC 47**
See also CA 21-24R; CANR 9, 24; CP 7; CWP

Uriel, Henry
See Faust, Frederick (Schiller)

Uris, Leon (Marcus) 1924- .... **CLC 7, 32**
See also AITN 1, 2; BEST 89:2; BPFB 3; CA 1-4R; CANR 1, 40, 65; CN 7; CPW 1; DA3; DAM NOV, POP; MTCW 1, 2; SATA 49

Urista, Alberto H. 1947- .... **PC 34**
See also Alurista
See also CA 45-48, 182; CANR 2, 32; HLCS 1; HW 1

Urmuz
See Codrescu, Andrei

Urquhart, Guy
See McAlmon, Robert (Menzies)

Urquhart, Jane 1949- .... **CLC 90**
See also CA 113; CANR 32, 68; CCA 1; DAC

Usigli, Rodolfo 1905-1979
See also CA 131; HLCS 1; HW 1; LAW

Ustinov, Peter (Alexander) 1921- .... **CLC 1**
See also AITN 1; CA 13-16R; CANR 25, 51; CBD; CD 5; DLB 13; MTCW 2

U Tam'si, Gerald Felix Tchicaya
See Tchicaya, Gerald Felix

U Tam'si, Tchicaya
See Tchicaya, Gerald Felix

Vachss, Andrew (Henry) 1942- .... **CLC 106**
See also CA 118; CANR 44, 95; CMW 4

Vachss, Andrew H.
See Vachss, Andrew (Henry)

Vaculik, Ludvik 1926- .... **CLC 7**
See also CA 53-56; CANR 72; CWW 2; DLB 232

Vaihinger, Hans 1852-1933 .... **TCLC 71**
See also CA 116; 166

Valdez, Luis (Miguel) 1940- ..... **CLC 84; DC 10; HLC 2**
See also CA 101; CAD; CANR 32, 81; CD 5; DAM MULT; DFS 5; DLB 122; HW 1; LAIT 4

Valenzuela, Luisa 1938- .... **CLC 31, 104; HLCS 2; SSC 14**
See also CA 101; CANR 32, 65; CDWLB 3; CWW 2; DAM MULT; DLB 113; FW; HW 1, 2; LAW; RGSF 2

Valera y Alcala-Galiano, Juan 1824-1905 .... **TCLC 10**
See also CA 106

Valery, (Ambroise) Paul (Toussaint Jules) 1871-1945 .... **TCLC 4, 15; PC 9**
See also CA 104; 122; DA3; DAM POET; DLB 258; EW 8; GFL 1789 to the Present; MTCW 1, 2; RGWL 2

Valle-Inclan, Ramon (Maria) del 1866-1936 .... **TCLC 5; HLC 2**
See also CA 106; 153; CANR 80; DAM MULT; DLB 134; EW 8; HW 2; RGSF 2; RGWL 2

Vallejo, Antonio Buero
See Buero Vallejo, Antonio

Vallejo, Cesar (Abraham) 1892-1938 .... **TCLC 3, 56; HLC 2**
See also CA 105; 153; DAM MULT; HW 1; LAW; RGWL 2

Valles, Jules 1832-1885 .... **NCLC 71**
See also DLB 123; GFL 1789 to the Present

Vallette, Marguerite Eymery 1860-1953 .... **TCLC 67**
See also CA 182; DLB 123, 192

Valle Y Pena, Ramon del
See Valle-Inclan, Ramon (Maria) del

Van Ash, Cay 1918- .... **CLC 34**

Vanbrugh, Sir John 1664-1726 .... **LC 21**
See also BRW 2; DAM DRAM; DLB 80; IDTP; RGEL 2

Van Campen, Karl
See Campbell, John W(ood, Jr.)

Vance, Gerald
See Silverberg, Robert

Vance, Jack .... **CLC 35**
See also Vance, John Holbrook
See also DLB 8; FANT; SCFW 2; SFW 4; SUFW

Vance, John Holbrook 1916-
See Queen, Ellery; Vance, Jack
See also CA 29-32R; CANR 17, 65; CMW 4; MTCW 1

Van Den Bogarde, Derek Jules Gaspard Ulric Niven 1921-1999 .... **CLC 14**
See also Bogarde, Dirk
See also CA 77-80; 179

Vandenburgh, Jane .... **CLC 59**
See also CA 168

Vanderhaeghe, Guy 1951- .... **CLC 41**
See also BPFB 3; CA 113; CANR 72

van der Post, Laurens (Jan) 1906-1996 .... **CLC 5**
See also AFW; CA 5-8R; 155; CANR 35; CN 7; DLB 204; RGEL 2

van de Wetering, Janwillem 1931- ... **CLC 47**
See also CA 49-52; CANR 4, 62, 90; CMW 4

Van Dine, S. S. .... **TCLC 23**
See also Wright, Willard Huntington
See also MSW

Van Doren, Carl (Clinton) 1885-1950 .... **TCLC 18**
See also CA 111; 168

Van Doren, Mark 1894-1972 .... **CLC 6, 10**
See also CA 1-4R; 37-40R; CANR 3; DLB 45; MTCW 1, 2; RGAL 4

Van Druten, John (William) 1901-1957 .... **TCLC 2**
See also CA 104; 161; DLB 10; RGAL 4

Van Duyn, Mona (Jane) 1921- ...... **CLC 3, 7, 63, 116**
See also CA 9-12R; CANR 7, 38, 60; CP 7; CWP; DAM POET; DLB 5

Van Dyne, Edith
See Baum, L(yman) Frank

van Itallie, Jean-Claude 1936- .... **CLC 3**
See also CA 45-48; CAAS 2; CAD; CANR 1, 48; CD 5; DLB 7

Van Loot, Cornelius Obenchain
See Roberts, Kenneth (Lewis)

van Ostaijen, Paul 1896-1928 .... **TCLC 33**
See also CA 163

Van Peebles, Melvin 1932- .... **CLC 2, 20**
See also BW 2, 3; CA 85-88; CANR 27, 67, 82; DAM MULT

van Schendel, Arthur(-Francois-Emile) 1874-1946 .... **TCLC 56**

Vansittart, Peter 1920- .... **CLC 42**
See also CA 1-4R; CANR 3, 49, 90; CN 7; RHW

Van Vechten, Carl 1880-1964 .... **CLC 33**
See also AMWS 2; CA 183; 89-92; DLB 4, 9; RGAL 4

van Vogt, A(lfred) E(lton) 1912-2000 . **CLC 1**
See also BPFB 3; BYA 13, 14; CA 21-24R; 190; CANR 28; DLB 8, 251; SATA 14; SATA-Obit 124; SCFW; SFW 4

Varda, Agnes 1928- .... **CLC 16**
See also CA 116; 122

Vargas Llosa, (Jorge) Mario (Pedro) 1936- .... **CLC 3, 6, 9, 10, 15, 31, 42, 85; HLC 2**
See also Llosa, (Jorge) Mario (Pedro) Vargas
See also BPFB 3; CA 73-76; CANR 18, 32, 42, 67; CDWLB 3; DA; DA3; DAB; DAC; DAM MST, MULT, NOV; DLB 145; DNFS 2; HW 1, 2; LAIT 5; LAW; LAWS 1; MTCW 1, 2; RGWL 2; SSFS 14; WLIT 1

Vasiliu, George
See Bacovia, George

Vasiliu, Gheorghe
See Bacovia, George
See also CA 123; 189

Vassa, Gustavus
See Equiano, Olaudah

Vassilikos, Vassilis 1933- .... **CLC 4, 8**
See also CA 81-84; CANR 75

Vaughan, Henry 1621-1695 .... **LC 27**
See also BRW 2; DLB 131; PAB; RGEL 2

Vaughn, Stephanie .... **CLC 62**

Vazov, Ivan (Minchov) 1850-1921 . **TCLC 25**
See also CA 121; 167; CDWLB 4; DLB 147

Veblen, Thorstein B(unde) 1857-1929 .... **TCLC 31**
See also AMWS 1; CA 115; 165; DLB 246

Vega, Lope de 1562-1635 ...... **LC 23; HLCS 2**
See also EW 2; RGWL 2

Vendler, Helen (Hennessy) 1933- - ... **CLC 138**
See also CA 41-44R; CANR 25, 72; MTCW 1, 2

Venison, Alfred
See Pound, Ezra (Weston Loomis)

Verdi, Marie de
See Mencken, H(enry) L(ouis)

Verdu, Matilde
See Cela, Camilo Jose

Verga, Giovanni (Carmelo) 1840-1922 .... **TCLC 3; SSC 21**
See also CA 104; 123; CANR 101; EW 7; RGSF 2; RGWL 2

Vergil 70B.C.-19B.C. .... **CMLC 9, 40; PC 12; WLCS**
See also Virgil
See also AW 2; DA; DA3; DAB; DAC; DAM MST, POET; EFS 1

Verhaeren, Emile (Adolphe Gustave) 1855-1916 .... **TCLC 12**
See also CA 109; GFL 1789 to the Present

Verlaine, Paul (Marie) 1844-1896 .. **NCLC 2, 51; PC 2, 32**
See also DAM POET; DLB 217; EW 7; GFL 1789 to the Present; RGWL 2

Verne, Jules (Gabriel) 1828-1905 ... **TCLC 6, 52**
See also AAYA 16; BYA 4; CA 110; 131; DA3; DLB 123; GFL 1789 to the Present; JRDA; LAIT 2; MAICYA 1, 2; RGWL 2; SATA 21; SCFW; SFW 4; WCH

Verus, Marcus Annius
See Aurelius, Marcus

Very, Jones 1813-1880 .... **NCLC 9**
See also DLB 1, 243; RGAL 4

Vesaas, Tarjei 1897-1970 .... **CLC 48**
See also CA 190; 29-32R; EW 11

Vialis, Gaston
See Simenon, Georges (Jacques Christian)

Vian, Boris 1920-1959 .... **TCLC 9**
See also CA 106; 164; DLB 72; GFL 1789 to the Present; MTCW 2; RGWL 2

Viaud, (Louis Marie) Julien 1850-1923
See Loti, Pierre
See also CA 107

Vicar, Henry
See Felsen, Henry Gregor

Vicker, Angus
See Felsen, Henry Gregor

Vidal, Gore 1925- ...... **CLC 2, 4, 6, 8, 10, 22, 33, 72, 142**
See also Box, Edgar
See also AITN 1; AMWS 4; BEST 90:2; BPFB 3; CA 5-8R; CAD; CANR 13, 45, 65, 100; CD 5; CDALBS; CN 7; CPW; DA3; DAM NOV, POP; DFS 2; DLB 6, 152; INT CANR-13; MTCW 1, 2; RGAL 4; RHW

Viereck, Peter (Robert Edwin) 1916- .... **CLC 4; PC 27**
See also CA 1-4R; CANR 1, 47; CP 7; DLB 5; PFS 9, 14

Vigny, Alfred (Victor) de 1797-1863 .... **NCLC 7, 102; PC 26**
See also DAM POET; DLB 119, 192, 217; EW 5; GFL 1789 to the Present; RGWL 2

Vilakazi, Benedict Wallet 1906-1947 .... **TCLC 37**
See also CA 168

Villa, Jose Garcia 1914-1997 .... **PC 22**
See also AAL; CA 25-28R; CANR 12; EXPP

Villarreal, Jose Antonio 1924-
See also CA 133; CANR 93; DAM MULT; DLB 82; HLC 2; HW 1; LAIT 4; RGAL 4

Villaurrutia, Xavier 1903-1950 ...... **TCLC 80**
See also CA 192; HW 1; LAW

Villehardouin, Geoffroi de 1150(?)-1218(?) .... **CMLC 38**

Villiers de l'Isle Adam, Jean Marie Mathias Philippe Auguste 1838-1889 ... **NCLC 3; SSC 14**
See also DLB 123, 192; GFL 1789 to the Present; RGSF 2

Villon, Francois 1431-1463(?) . **LC 62; PC 13**
See also DLB 208; EW 2; RGWL 2

Vine, Barbara .... **CLC 50**
See also Rendell, Ruth (Barbara)
See also BEST 90:4

Vinge, Joan (Carol) D(ennison) 1948- .... **CLC 30; SSC 24**
See also AAYA 32; BPFB 3; CA 93-96; CANR 72; SATA 36, 113; SFW 4; YAW

Viola, Herman J(oseph) 1938- .... **CLC 70**
See also CA 61-64; CANR 8, 23, 48, 91; SATA 126

Violis, G.
See Simenon, Georges (Jacques Christian)

Viramontes, Helena Maria 1954-
See also CA 159; DLB 122; HLCS 2; HW 2
Virgil
See Vergil
See also CDWLB 1; DLB 211; LAIT 1; RGWL 2; WP
Visconti, Luchino 1906-1976 .... **CLC 16**
See also CA 81-84; 65-68; CANR 39
Vittorini, Elio 1908-1966 .... **CLC 6, 9, 14**
See also CA 133; 25-28R; EW 12; RGWL 2
Vivekananda, Swami 1863-1902 .... **TCLC 88**
Vizenor, Gerald Robert 1934- .... **CLC 103**
See also CA 13-16R; CAAS 22; CANR 5, 21, 44, 67; DAM MULT; DLB 175, 227; MTCW 2; NNAL; TCWW 2
Vizinczey, Stephen 1933- .... **CLC 40**
See also CA 128; CCA 1; INT 128
Vliet, R(ussell) G(ordon)
1929-1984 .... **CLC 22**
See also CA 37-40R; 112; CANR 18
Vogau, Boris Andreyevich 1894-1937(?)
See Pilnyak, Boris
See also CA 123
Vogel, Paula A(nne) 1951- .... **CLC 76**
See also CA 108; CAD; CD 5; CWD; DFS 14; RGAL 4
Voigt, Cynthia 1942- .... **CLC 30**
See also AAYA 3, 30; BYA 1, 3, 6, 7, 8; CA 106; CANR 18, 37, 40, 94; CLR 13, 48; INT CANR-18; JRDA; LAIT 5; MAICYA 1, 2; MAICYAS 1; SATA 48, 79, 116; SATA-Brief 33; WYA; YAW
Voigt, Ellen Bryant 1943- .... **CLC 54**
See also CA 69-72; CANR 11, 29, 55; CP 7; CSW; CWP; DLB 120
Voinovich, Vladimir (Nikolaevich)
1932- .... **CLC 10, 49, 147**
See also CA 81-84; CAAS 12; CANR 33, 67; MTCW 1
Vollmann, William T. 1959- .... **CLC 89**
See also CA 134; CANR 67; CPW; DA3; DAM NOV, POP; MTCW 2
Voloshinov, V. N.
See Bakhtin, Mikhail Mikhailovich
Voltaire 1694-1778 ..... **LC 14; SSC 12; WLC**
See also BYA 13; DA; DA3; DAB; DAC; DAM DRAM, MST; EW 4; GFL Beginnings to 1789; NFS 7; RGWL 2
von Aschendrof, Baron Ignatz 1873-1939
See Ford, Ford Madox
von Daeniken, Erich 1935- .... **CLC 30**
See also AITN 1; CA 37-40R; CANR 17, 44
von Daniken, Erich
See von Daeniken, Erich
von Hartmann, Eduard
1842-1906 .... **TCLC 96**
von Hayek, Friedrich August
See Hayek, F(riedrich) A(ugust von)
von Heidenstam, (Carl Gustaf) Verner
See Heidenstam, (Carl Gustaf) Verner von
von Heyse, Paul (Johann Ludwig)
See Heyse, Paul (Johann Ludwig von)
von Hofmannsthal, Hugo
See Hofmannsthal, Hugo von
von Horvath, Odon
See Horvath, Odon von
von Horvath, Odon
See Horvath, Odon von
von Horvath, Oedoen
See Horvath, Odon von
See also CA 184
von Liliencron, (Friedrich Adolf Axel) Detlev
See Liliencron, (Friedrich Adolf Axel) Detlev von

Vonnegut, Kurt, Jr. 1922- . **CLC 1, 2, 3, 4, 5, 8, 12, 22, 40, 60, 111; SSC 8; WLC**
See also AAYA 6; AITN 1; AMWS 2; BEST 90:4; BPFB 3; BYA 3, 14; CA 1-4R; CANR 1, 25, 49, 75, 92; CDALB 1968-1988; CN 7; CPW 1; DA; DA3; DAB; DAC; DAM MST, NOV, POP; DLB 2, 8, 152; DLBD 3; DLBY 1980; EXPN; EXPS; LAIT 4; MTCW 1, 2; NFS 3; RGAL 4; SCFW; SFW 4; SSFS 5; TUS; YAW
Von Rachen, Kurt
See Hubbard, L(afayette) Ron(ald)
von Rezzori (d'Arezzo), Gregor
See Rezzori (d'Arezzo), Gregor von
von Sternberg, Josef
See Sternberg, Josef von
Vorster, Gordon 1924- .... **CLC 34**
See also CA 133
Vosce, Trudie
See Ozick, Cynthia
Voznesensky, Andrei (Andreievich)
1933- .... **CLC 1, 15, 57**
See also CA 89-92; CANR 37; CWW 2; DAM POET; MTCW 1
Waddington, Miriam 1917- .... **CLC 28**
See also CA 21-24R; CANR 12, 30; CCA 1; CP 7; DLB 68
Wagman, Fredrica 1937- .... **CLC 7**
See also CA 97-100; INT 97-100
Wagner, Linda W.
See Wagner-Martin, Linda (C.)
Wagner, Linda Welshimer
See Wagner-Martin, Linda (C.)
Wagner, Richard 1813-1883 .... **NCLC 9**
See also DLB 129; EW 6
Wagner-Martin, Linda (C.) 1936- .... **CLC 50**
See also CA 159
Wagoner, David (Russell) 1926- .... **CLC 3, 5, 15; PC 33**
See also AMWS 9; CA 1-4R; CAAS 3; CANR 2, 71; CN 7; CP 7; DLB 5, 256; SATA 14; TCWW 2
Wah, Fred(erick James) 1939- .... **CLC 44**
See also CA 107; 141; CP 7; DLB 60
Wahloo, Per 1926-1975 .... **CLC 7**
See also BPFB 3; CA 61-64; CANR 73; CMW 4; MSW
Wahloo, Peter
See Wahloo, Per
Wain, John (Barrington) 1925-1994 . **CLC 2, 11, 15, 46**
See also CA 5-8R; 145; CAAS 4; CANR 23, 54; CDBLB 1960 to Present; DLB 15, 27, 139, 155; MTCW 1, 2
Wajda, Andrzej 1926- .... **CLC 16**
See also CA 102
Wakefield, Dan 1932- .... **CLC 7**
See also CA 21-24R; CAAS 7; CN 7
Wakefield, Herbert Russell
1888-1965 .... **TCLC 120**
See also CA 5-8R; CANR 77; HGG; SUFW
Wakoski, Diane 1937- .... **CLC 2, 4, 7, 9, 11, 40; PC 15**
See also CA 13-16R; CAAS 1; CANR 9, 60, 106; CP 7; CWP; DAM POET; DLB 5; INT CANR-9; MTCW 2
Wakoski-Sherbell, Diane
See Wakoski, Diane
Walcott, Derek (Alton) 1930- .... **CLC 2, 4, 9, 14, 25, 42, 67, 76; BLC 3; DC 7**
See also BW 2; CA 89-92; CANR 26, 47, 75, 80; CBD; CD 5; CDWLB 3; CP 7; DA3; DAB; DAC; DAM MST, MULT, POET; DLB 117; DLBY 1981; DNFS 1; EFS 1; MTCW 1, 2; PFS 6; RGEL 2
Waldman, Anne (Lesley) 1945- .... **CLC 7**
See also CA 37-40R; CAAS 17; CANR 34, 69; CP 7; CWP; DLB 16

Waldo, E. Hunter
See Sturgeon, Theodore (Hamilton)
Waldo, Edward Hamilton
See Sturgeon, Theodore (Hamilton)
Walker, Alice (Malsenior) 1944- ... **CLC 5, 6, 9, 19, 27, 46, 58, 103; BLC 3; PC 30; SSC 5; WLCS**
See also AAYA 3, 33; AFAW 1, 2; AMWS 3; BEST 89:4; BPFB 3; BW 2, 3; CA 37-40R; CANR 9, 27, 49, 66, 82; CDALB 1968-1988; CN 7; CPW; CSW; DA; DA3; DAB; DAC; DAM MST, MULT, NOV, POET, POP; DLB 6, 33, 143; EXPN; EXPS; FW; INT CANR-27; LAIT 3; MAWW; MTCW 1, 2; NFS 5; RGAL 4; RGSF 2; SATA 31; SSFS 2, 11; YAW
Walker, David Harry 1911-1992 ...... **CLC 14**
See also CA 1-4R; 137; CANR 1; CWRI 5; SATA 8; SATA-Obit 71
Walker, Edward Joseph 1934-
See Walker, Ted
See also CA 21-24R; CANR 12, 28, 53; CP 7
Walker, George F. 1947- .... **CLC 44, 61**
See also CA 103; CANR 21, 43, 59; CD 5; DAB; DAC; DAM MST; DLB 60
Walker, Joseph A. 1935- .... **CLC 19**
See also BW 1, 3; CA 89-92; CAD; CANR 26; CD 5; DAM DRAM, MST; DFS 12; DLB 38
Walker, Margaret (Abigail)
1915-1998 .... **CLC 1, 6; BLC; PC 20**
See also AFAW 1, 2; BW 2, 3; CA 73-76; 172; CANR 26, 54, 76; CN 7; CP 7; CSW; DAM MULT; DLB 76, 152; EXPP; FW; MTCW 1, 2; RGAL 4; RHW
Walker, Ted .... **CLC 13**
See also Walker, Edward Joseph
See also DLB 40
Wallace, David Foster 1962- ...... **CLC 50, 114**
See also AMWS 10; CA 132; CANR 59; DA3; MTCW 2
Wallace, Dexter
See Masters, Edgar Lee
Wallace, (Richard Horatio) Edgar
1875-1932 .... **TCLC 57**
See also CA 115; CMW 4; DLB 70; MSW; RGEL 2
Wallace, Irving 1916-1990 .... **CLC 7, 13**
See also AITN 1; BPFB 3; CA 1-4R; 132; CAAS 1; CANR 1, 27; CPW; DAM NOV, POP; INT CANR-27; MTCW 1, 2
Wallant, Edward Lewis 1926-1962 ... **CLC 5, 10**
See also CA 1-4R; CANR 22; DLB 2, 28, 143; MTCW 1, 2; RGAL 4
Wallas, Graham 1858-1932 .... **TCLC 91**
Walley, Byron
See Card, Orson Scott
Walpole, Horace 1717-1797 .... **LC 2, 49**
See also BRW 3; DLB 39, 104, 213; HGG; RGEL 2; SUFW
Walpole, Hugh (Seymour)
1884-1941 .... **TCLC 5**
See also CA 104; 165; DLB 34; HGG; MTCW 2; RGEL 2; RHW
Walser, Martin 1927- .... **CLC 27**
See also CA 57-60; CANR 8, 46; CWW 2; DLB 75, 124
Walser, Robert 1878-1956 .... **TCLC 18; SSC 20**
See also CA 118; 165; CANR 100; DLB 66
Walsh, Gillian Paton
See Paton Walsh, Gillian
Walsh, Jill Paton .... **CLC 35**
See also Paton Walsh, Gillian
See also CLR 2, 65; WYA
Walter, Villiam Christian
See Andersen, Hans Christian

Walton, Izaak 1593-1683 .... **LC 72**
See also BRW 2; CDBLB Before 1660; DLB 151, 213; RGEL 2
Wambaugh, Joseph (Aloysius, Jr.)
1937- .... **CLC 3, 18**
See also AITN 1; BEST 89:3; BPFB 3; CA 33-36R; CANR 42, 65; CMW 4; CPW 1; DA3; DAM NOV, POP; DLB 6; DLBY 1983; MSW; MTCW 1, 2
Wang Wei 699(?)-761(?) .... **PC 18**
Ward, Arthur Henry Sarsfield 1883-1959
See Rohmer, Sax
See also CA 108; 173; CMW 4; HGG
Ward, Douglas Turner 1930- .... **CLC 19**
See also BW 1; CA 81-84; CAD; CANR 27; CD 5; DLB 7, 38
Ward, E. D.
See Lucas, E(dward) V(errall)
Ward, Mrs. Humphry 1851-1920
See Ward, Mary Augusta
See also RGEL 2
Ward, Mary Augusta 1851-1920 ... **TCLC 55**
See also Ward, Mrs. Humphry
See also DLB 18
Ward, Peter
See Faust, Frederick (Schiller)
Warhol, Andy 1928(?)-1987 .... **CLC 20**
See also AAYA 12; BEST 89:4; CA 89-92; 121; CANR 34
Warner, Francis (Robert le Plastrier)
1937- .... **CLC 14**
See also CA 53-56; CANR 11
Warner, Marina 1946- .... **CLC 59**
See also CA 65-68; CANR 21, 55; CN 7; DLB 194
Warner, Rex (Ernest) 1905-1986 ...... **CLC 45**
See also CA 89-92; 119; DLB 15; RGEL 2; RHW
Warner, Susan (Bogert)
1819-1885 .... **NCLC 31**
See also DLB 3, 42, 239, 250, 254
Warner, Sylvia (Constance) Ashton
See Ashton-Warner, Sylvia (Constance)
Warner, Sylvia Townsend
1893-1978 .... **CLC 7, 19; SSC 23**
See also BRWS 7; CA 61-64; 77-80; CANR 16, 60, 104; DLB 34, 139; FANT; FW; MTCW 1, 2; RGEL 2; RGSF 2; RHW
Warren, Mercy Otis 1728-1814 ..... **NCLC 13**
See also DLB 31, 200; RGAL 4
Warren, Robert Penn 1905-1989 .. **CLC 1, 4, 6, 8, 10, 13, 18, 39, 53, 59; PC 37; SSC 4; WLC**
See also AITN 1; AMW; BPFB 3; BYA 1; CA 13-16R; 129; CANR 10, 47; CDALB 1968-1988; DA; DA3; DAB; DAC; DAM MST, NOV, POET; DLB 2, 48, 152; DLBY 1980, 1989; INT CANR-10; MTCW 1, 2; NFS 13; RGAL 4; RGSF 2; RHW; SATA 46; SATA-Obit 63; SSFS 8
Warshofsky, Isaac
See Singer, Isaac Bashevis
Warton, Thomas 1728-1790 .... **LC 15**
See also DAM POET; DLB 104, 109; RGEL 2
Waruk, Kona
See Harris, (Theodore) Wilson
Warung, Price .... **TCLC 45**
See also Astley, William
See also DLB 230; RGEL 2
Warwick, Jarvis
See Garner, Hugh
See also CCA 1
Washington, Alex
See Harris, Mark
Washington, Booker T(aliaferro)
1856-1915 .... **TCLC 10; BLC 3**
See also BW 1; CA 114; 125; DA3; DAM MULT; LAIT 2; RGAL 4; SATA 28

Washington, George 1732-1799 .... **LC 25**
See also DLB 31
Wassermann, (Karl) Jakob
1873-1934 .... **TCLC 6**
See also CA 104; 163; DLB 66
Wasserstein, Wendy 1950- .. **CLC 32, 59, 90; DC 4**
See also CA 121; 129; CABS 3; CAD; CANR 53, 75; CD 5; CWD; DA3; DAM DRAM; DFS 5; DLB 228; FW; INT CA-129; MTCW 2; SATA 94
Waterhouse, Keith (Spencer) 1929- .. **CLC 47**
See also CA 5-8R; CANR 38, 67, 109; CBD; CN 7; DLB 13, 15; MTCW 1, 2
Waters, Frank (Joseph) 1902-1995 .. **CLC 88**
See also CA 5-8R; 149; CAAS 13; CANR 3, 18, 63; DLB 212; DLBY 1986; RGAL 4; TCWW 2
Waters, Mary C. .... **CLC 70**
Waters, Roger 1944- .... **CLC 35**
Watkins, Frances Ellen
See Harper, Frances Ellen Watkins
Watkins, Gerrold
See Malzberg, Barry N(athaniel)
Watkins, Gloria Jean 1952(?)-
See hooks, bell
See also BW 2; CA 143; CANR 87; MTCW 2; SATA 115
Watkins, Paul 1964- .... **CLC 55**
See also CA 132; CANR 62, 98
Watkins, Vernon Phillips
1906-1967 .... **CLC 43**
See also CA 9-10; 25-28R; CAP 1; DLB 20; RGEL 2
Watson, Irving S.
See Mencken, H(enry) L(ouis)
Watson, John H.
See Farmer, Philip Jose
Watson, Richard F.
See Silverberg, Robert
Waugh, Auberon (Alexander)
1939-2001 .... **CLC 7**
See also CA 45-48; 192; CANR 6, 22, 92; DLB 14, 194
Waugh, Evelyn (Arthur St. John)
1903-1966 .. **CLC 1, 3, 8, 13, 19, 27, 44, 107; SSC 41; WLC**
See also BPFB 3; BRW 7; CA 85-88; 25-28R; CANR 22; CDBLB 1914-1945; DA; DA3; DAB; DAC; DAM MST, NOV, POP; DLB 15, 162, 195; MTCW 1, 2; NFS 13; RGEL 2; RGSF 2; WLIT 4
Waugh, Harriet 1944- .... **CLC 6**
See also CA 85-88; CANR 22
Ways, C. R.
See Blount, Roy (Alton), Jr.
Waystaff, Simon
See Swift, Jonathan
Webb, Beatrice (Martha Potter)
1858-1943 .... **TCLC 22**
See also CA 117; 162; DLB 190; FW
Webb, Charles (Richard) 1939- .... **CLC 7**
See also CA 25-28R
Webb, James H(enry), Jr. 1946- ...... **CLC 22**
See also CA 81-84
Webb, Mary Gladys (Meredith)
1881-1927 .... **TCLC 24**
See also CA 182; 123; DLB 34; FW
Webb, Mrs. Sidney
See Webb, Beatrice (Martha Potter)
Webb, Phyllis 1927- .... **CLC 18**
See also CA 104; CANR 23; CCA 1; CP 7; CWP; DLB 53
Webb, Sidney (James) 1859-1947 .. **TCLC 22**
See also CA 117; 163; DLB 190
Webber, Andrew Lloyd .... **CLC 21**
See also Lloyd Webber, Andrew
See also DFS 7

Weber, Lenora Mattingly
1895-1971 .... **CLC 12**
See also CA 19-20; 29-32R; CAP 1; SATA 2; SATA-Obit 26
Weber, Max 1864-1920 .... **TCLC 69**
See also CA 109; 189
Webster, John 1580(?)-1634(?) .... **LC 33; DC 2; WLC**
See also BRW 2; CDBLB Before 1660; DA; DAB; DAC; DAM DRAM, MST; DLB 58; IDTP; RGEL 2; WLIT 3
Webster, Noah 1758-1843 .... **NCLC 30**
See also DLB 1, 37, 42, 43, 73, 243
Wedekind, (Benjamin) Frank(lin)
1864-1918 .... **TCLC 7**
See also CA 104; 153; CDWLB 2; DAM DRAM; DLB 118; EW 8; RGWL 2
Wehr, Demaris .... **CLC 65**
Weidman, Jerome 1913-1998 .... **CLC 7**
See also AITN 2; CA 1-4R; 171; CAD; CANR 1; DLB 28
Weil, Simone (Adolphine)
1909-1943 .... **TCLC 23**
See also CA 117; 159; EW 12; FW; GFL 1789 to the Present; MTCW 2
Weininger, Otto 1880-1903 .... **TCLC 84**
Weinstein, Nathan
See West, Nathanael
Weinstein, Nathan von Wallenstein
See West, Nathanael
Weir, Peter (Lindsay) 1944- .... **CLC 20**
See also CA 113; 123
Weiss, Peter (Ulrich) 1916-1982 .. **CLC 3, 15, 51**
See also CA 45-48; 106; CANR 3; DAM DRAM; DFS 3; DLB 69, 124; RGWL 2
Weiss, Theodore (Russell) 1916- ... **CLC 3, 8, 14**
See also CA 9-12R; CAAE 189; CAAS 2; CANR 46, 94; CP 7; DLB 5
Welch, (Maurice) Denton
1915-1948 .... **TCLC 22**
See also CA 121; 148; RGEL 2
Welch, James 1940- .... **CLC 6, 14, 52**
See also CA 85-88; CANR 42, 66, 107; CN 7; CP 7; CPW; DAM MULT, POP; DLB 175, 256; NNAL; RGAL 4; TCWW 2
Weldon, Fay 1931- . **CLC 6, 9, 11, 19, 36, 59, 122**
See also BRWS 4; CA 21-24R; CANR 16, 46, 63, 97; CDBLB 1960 to Present; CN 7; CPW; DAM POP; DLB 14, 194; FW; HGG; INT CANR-16; MTCW 1, 2; RGEL 2; RGSF 2
Wellek, Rene 1903-1995 .... **CLC 28**
See also CA 5-8R; 150; CAAS 7; CANR 8; DLB 63; INT CANR-8
Weller, Michael 1942- .... **CLC 10, 53**
See also CA 85-88; CAD; CD 5
Weller, Paul 1958- .... **CLC 26**
Wellershoff, Dieter 1925- .... **CLC 46**
See also CA 89-92; CANR 16, 37
Welles, (George) Orson 1915-1985 .. **CLC 20, 80**
See also AAYA 40; CA 93-96; 117
Wellman, John McDowell 1945-
See Wellman, Mac
See also CA 166; CD 5
Wellman, Mac .... **CLC 65**
See also Wellman, John McDowell; Wellman, John McDowell
See also CAD; RGAL 4
Wellman, Manly Wade 1903-1986 ... **CLC 49**
See also CA 1-4R; 118; CANR 6, 16, 44; FANT; SATA 6; SATA-Obit 47; SFW 4; SUFW
Wells, Carolyn 1869(?)-1942 .... **TCLC 35**
See also CA 113; 185; CMW 4; DLB 11

Wells, H(erbert) G(eorge)
1866-1946 .... **TCLC 6, 12, 19; SSC 6; WLC**
See also AAYA 18; BPFB 3; BRW 6; CA 110; 121; CDBLB 1914-1945; CLR 64; DA; DA3; DAB; DAC; DAM MST, NOV; DLB 34, 70, 156, 178; EXPS; HGG; LAIT 3; MTCW 1, 2; RGEL 2; RGSF 2; SATA 20; SCFW; SFW 4; SSFS 3; SUFW; WCH; WLIT 4; YAW

Wells, Rosemary 1943- .... **CLC 12**
See also AAYA 13; BYA 7, 8; CA 85-88; CANR 48; CLR 16, 69; CWRI 5; MAICYA 1, 2; SAAS 1; SATA 18, 69, 114; YAW

Welsh, Irvine 1958- .... **CLC 144**
See also CA 173

Welty, Eudora (Alice) 1909-2001 .. **CLC 1, 2, 5, 14, 22, 33, 105; SSC 1, 27, 51; WLC**
See also AMW; AMWR 1; BPFB 3; CA 9-12R; 199; CABS 1; CANR 32, 65; CDALB 1941-1968; CN 7; CSW; DA; DA3; DAB; DAC; DAM MST, NOV; DLB 2, 102, 143; DLBD 12; DLBY 1987, 2001; EXPS; HGG; LAIT 3; MAWW; MTCW 1, 2; NFS 13; RGAL 4; RGSF 2; RHW; SSFS 2, 10

Wen I-to 1899-1946 .... **TCLC 28**

Wentworth, Robert
See Hamilton, Edmond

Werfel, Franz (Viktor) 1890-1945 ... **TCLC 8**
See also CA 104; 161; DLB 81, 124; RGWL 2

Wergeland, Henrik Arnold
1808-1845 .... **NCLC 5**

Wersba, Barbara 1932- .... **CLC 30**
See also AAYA 2, 30; BYA 6, 12, 13; CA 29-32R, 182; CAAE 182; CANR 16, 38; CLR 3, 78; DLB 52; JRDA; MAICYA 1, 2; SAAS 2; SATA 1, 58; SATA-Essay 103; WYA; YAW

Wertmueller, Lina 1928- .... **CLC 16**
See also CA 97-100; CANR 39, 78

Wescott, Glenway 1901-1987 .. **CLC 13; SSC 35**
See also CA 13-16R; 121; CANR 23, 70; DLB 4, 9, 102; RGAL 4

Wesker, Arnold 1932- .... **CLC 3, 5, 42**
See also CA 1-4R; CAAS 7; CANR 1, 33; CBD; CD 5; CDBLB 1960 to Present; DAB; DAM DRAM; DLB 13; MTCW 1; RGEL 2

Wesley, Richard (Errol) 1945- .... **CLC 7**
See also BW 1; CA 57-60; CAD; CANR 27; CD 5; DLB 38

Wessel, Johan Herman 1742-1785 .... **LC 7**

West, Anthony (Panther)
1914-1987 .... **CLC 50**
See also CA 45-48; 124; CANR 3, 19; DLB 15

West, C. P.
See Wodehouse, P(elham) G(renville)

West, Cornel (Ronald) 1953- .... **CLC 134; BLCS**
See also CA 144; CANR 91; DLB 246

West, Delno C(loyde), Jr. 1936- .... **CLC 70**
See also CA 57-60

West, Dorothy 1907-1998 .... **TCLC 108**
See also BW 2; CA 143; 169; DLB 76

West, (Mary) Jessamyn 1902-1984 ... **CLC 7, 17**
See also CA 9-12R; 112; CANR 27; DLB 6; DLBY 1984; MTCW 1, 2; RHW; SATA-Obit 37; YAW

West, Morris L(anglo) 1916-1999 ..... **CLC 6, 33**
See also BPFB 3; CA 5-8R; 187; CANR 24, 49, 64; CN 7; CPW; MTCW 1, 2

West, Nathanael 1903-1940 .... **TCLC 1, 14, 44; SSC 16**
See also AMW; BPFB 3; CA 104; 125; CDALB 1929-1941; DA3; DLB 4, 9, 28; MTCW 1, 2; RGAL 4

West, Owen
See Koontz, Dean R(ay)

West, Paul 1930- .... **CLC 7, 14, 96**
See also CA 13-16R; CAAS 7; CANR 22, 53, 76, 89; CN 7; DLB 14; INT CANR-22; MTCW 2

West, Rebecca 1892-1983 ... **CLC 7, 9, 31, 50**
See also BPFB 3; BRWS 3; CA 5-8R; 109; CANR 19; DLB 36; DLBY 1983; FW; MTCW 1, 2; RGEL 2

Westall, Robert (Atkinson)
1929-1993 .... **CLC 17**
See also AAYA 12; BYA 2, 6, 7, 8, 9; CA 69-72; 141; CANR 18, 68; CLR 13; FANT; JRDA; MAICYA 1, 2; MAICYAS 1; SAAS 2; SATA 23, 69; SATA-Obit 75; WYA; YAW

Westermarck, Edward 1862-1939 . **TCLC 87**

Westlake, Donald E(dwin) 1933- .. **CLC 7, 33**
See also BPFB 3; CA 17-20R; CAAS 13; CANR 16, 44, 65, 94; CMW 4; CPW; DAM POP; INT CANR-16; MSW; MTCW 2

Westmacott, Mary
See Christie, Agatha (Mary Clarissa)

Weston, Allen
See Norton, Andre

Wetcheek, J. L.
See Feuchtwanger, Lion

Wetering, Janwillem van de
See van de Wetering, Janwillem

Wetherald, Agnes Ethelwyn
1857-1940 .... **TCLC 81**
See also DLB 99

Wetherell, Elizabeth
See Warner, Susan (Bogert)

Whale, James 1889-1957 .... **TCLC 63**

Whalen, Philip 1923- .... **CLC 6, 29**
See also CA 9-12R; CANR 5, 39; CP 7; DLB 16; WP

Wharton, Edith (Newbold Jones)
1862-1937 ... **TCLC 3, 9, 27, 53; SSC 6; WLC**
See also AAYA 25; AMW; AMWR 1; BPFB 3; CA 104; 132; CDALB 1865-1917; DA; DA3; DAB; DAC; DAM MST, NOV; DLB 4, 9, 12, 78, 189; DLBD 13; EXPS; HGG; LAIT 2, 3; MAWW; MTCW 1, 2; NFS 5, 11; RGAL 4; RGSF 2; RHW; SSFS 6, 7; SUFW

Wharton, James
See Mencken, H(enry) L(ouis)

Wharton, William (a pseudonym) . **CLC 18, 37**
See also CA 93-96; DLBY 1980; INT 93-96

Wheatley (Peters), Phillis
1753(?)-1784 ... **LC 3, 50; BLC 3; PC 3; WLC**
See also AFAW 1, 2; CDALB 1640-1865; DA; DA3; DAC; DAM MST, MULT, POET; DLB 31, 50; EXPP; PFS 13; RGAL 4

Wheelock, John Hall 1886-1978 .... **CLC 14**
See also CA 13-16R; 77-80; CANR 14; DLB 45

White, Babington
See Braddon, Mary Elizabeth

White, E(lwyn) B(rooks)
1899-1985 .... **CLC 10, 34, 39**
See also AITN 2; AMWS 1; CA 13-16R; 116; CANR 16, 37; CDALBS; CLR 1, 21; CPW; DA3; DAM POP; DLB 11, 22; FANT; MAICYA 1, 2; MTCW 1, 2; RGAL 4; SATA 2, 29, 100; SATA-Obit 44

White, Edmund (Valentine III)
1940- .... **CLC 27, 110**
See also AAYA 7; CA 45-48; CANR 3, 19, 36, 62, 107; CN 7; DA3; DAM POP; DLB 227; MTCW 1, 2

White, Hayden V. 1928- .... **CLC 148**
See also CA 128; DLB 246

White, Patrick (Victor Martindale)
1912-1990 .... **CLC 3, 4, 5, 7, 9, 18, 65, 69; SSC 39**
See also BRWS 1; CA 81-84; 132; CANR 43; MTCW 1; RGEL 2; RGSF 2; RHW

White, Phyllis Dorothy James 1920-
See James, P. D.
See also CA 21-24R; CANR 17, 43, 65; CMW 4; CN 7; CPW; DA3; DAM POP; MTCW 1, 2

White, T(erence) H(anbury)
1906-1964 .... **CLC 30**
See also AAYA 22; BPFB 3; BYA 4, 5; CA 73-76; CANR 37; DLB 160; FANT; JRDA; LAIT 1; MAICYA 1, 2; RGEL 2; SATA 12; SUFW; YAW

White, Terence de Vere 1912-1994 ... **CLC 49**
See also CA 49-52; 145; CANR 3

White, Walter
See White, Walter F(rancis)

White, Walter F(rancis)
1893-1955 .... **TCLC 15; BLC 3**
See also BW 1; CA 115; 124; DAM MULT; DLB 51

White, William Hale 1831-1913
See Rutherford, Mark
See also CA 121; 189

Whitehead, Alfred North
1861-1947 .... **TCLC 97**
See also CA 117; 165; DLB 100

Whitehead, E(dward) A(nthony)
1933- .... **CLC 5**
See also CA 65-68; CANR 58; CBD; CD 5

Whitehead, Ted
See Whitehead, E(dward) A(nthony)

Whitemore, Hugh (John) 1936- .... **CLC 37**
See also CA 132; CANR 77; CBD; CD 5; INT CA-132

Whitman, Sarah Helen (Power)
1803-1878 .... **NCLC 19**
See also DLB 1, 243

Whitman, Walt(er) 1819-1892 .. **NCLC 4, 31, 81; PC 3; WLC**
See also AAYA 42; AMW; AMWR 1; CDALB 1640-1865; DA; DA3; DAB; DAC; DAM MST, POET; DLB 3, 64, 224, 250; EXPP; LAIT 2; PAB; PFS 2, 3, 13; RGAL 4; SATA 20; WP; WYAS 1

Whitney, Phyllis A(yame) 1903- .... **CLC 42**
See also AAYA 36; AITN 2; BEST 90:3; CA 1-4R; CANR 3, 25, 38, 60; CLR 59; CMW 4; CPW; DA3; DAM POP; JRDA; MAICYA 1, 2; MTCW 2; RHW; SATA 1, 30; YAW

Whittemore, (Edward) Reed (Jr.)
1919- .... **CLC 4**
See also CA 9-12R; CAAS 8; CANR 4; CP 7; DLB 5

Whittier, John Greenleaf
1807-1892 .... **NCLC 8, 59**
See also AMWS 1; DLB 1, 243; RGAL 4

Whittlebot, Hernia
See Coward, Noel (Peirce)

Wicker, Thomas Grey 1926-
See Wicker, Tom
See also CA 65-68; CANR 21, 46

Wicker, Tom .... **CLC 7**
See also Wicker, Thomas Grey

Wideman, John Edgar 1941- ...... **CLC 5, 34, 36, 67, 122; BLC 3**
See also AFAW 1, 2; AMWS 10; BPFB 4; BW 2, 3; CA 85-88; CANR 14, 42, 67,

109; CN 7; DAM MULT; DLB 33, 143; MTCW 2; RGAL 4; RGSF 2; SSFS 6, 12

Wiebe, Rudy (Henry) 1934- .. **CLC 6, 11, 14, 138**
See also CA 37-40R; CANR 42, 67; CN 7; DAC; DAM MST; DLB 60; RHW

Wieland, Christoph Martin 1733-1813 .... **NCLC 17**
See also DLB 97; EW 4; RGWL 2

Wiene, Robert 1881-1938 .... **TCLC 56**

Wieners, John 1934- .... **CLC 7**
See also CA 13-16R; CP 7; DLB 16; WP

Wiesel, Elie(zer) 1928- .... **CLC 3, 5, 11, 37; WLCS**
See also AAYA 7; AITN 1; CA 5-8R; CAAS 4; CANR 8, 40, 65; CDALBS; DA; DA3; DAB; DAC; DAM MST, NOV; DLB 83; DLBY 1987; INT CANR-8; LAIT 4; MTCW 1, 2; NFS 4; SATA 56; YAW

Wiggins, Marianne 1947- .... **CLC 57**
See also BEST 89:3; CA 130; CANR 60

Wiggs, Susan .... **CLC 70**

Wight, James Alfred 1916-1995
See Herriot, James
See also CA 77-80; SATA 55; SATA-Brief 44

Wilbur, Richard (Purdy) 1921- ..... **CLC 3, 6, 9, 14, 53, 110**
See also AMWS 3; CA 1-4R; CABS 2; CANR 2, 29, 76, 93; CDALBS; CP 7; DA; DAB; DAC; DAM MST, POET; DLB 5, 169; EXPP; INT CANR-29; MTCW 1, 2; PAB; PFS 11, 12; RGAL 4; SATA 9, 108; WP

Wild, Peter 1940- .... **CLC 14**
See also CA 37-40R; CP 7; DLB 5

Wilde, Oscar (Fingal O'Flahertie Wills) 1854(?)-1900 ..... **TCLC 1, 8, 23, 41; DC 17; SSC 11; WLC**
See also BRW 5; BRWR 2; CA 104; 119; CDBLB 1890-1914; DA; DA3; DAB; DAC; DAM DRAM, MST, NOV; DFS 4, 8, 9; DLB 10, 19, 34, 57, 141, 156, 190; EXPS; FANT; RGEL 2; RGSF 2; SATA 24; SSFS 7; SUFW; TEA; WCH; WLIT 4

Wilder, Billy .... **CLC 20**
See also Wilder, Samuel
See also DLB 26

Wilder, Samuel 1906-2002
See Wilder, Billy
See also CA 89-92

Wilder, Stephen
See Marlowe, Stephen

Wilder, Thornton (Niven) 1897-1975 .. **CLC 1, 5, 6, 10, 15, 35, 82; DC 1; WLC**
See also AAYA 29; AITN 2; AMW; CA 13-16R; 61-64; CAD; CANR 40; CDALBS; DA; DA3; DAB; DAC; DAM DRAM, MST, NOV; DFS 1, 4; DLB 4, 7, 9, 228; DLBY 1997; LAIT 3; MTCW 1, 2; RGAL 4; RHW; WYAS 1

Wilding, Michael 1942- ...... **CLC 73; SSC 50**
See also CA 104; CANR 24, 49, 106; CN 7; RGSF 2

Wiley, Richard 1944- .... **CLC 44**
See also CA 121; 129; CANR 71

Wilhelm, Kate .... **CLC 7**
See also Wilhelm, Katie (Gertrude)
See also AAYA 20; CAAS 5; DLB 8; INT CANR-17; SCFW 2

Wilhelm, Katie (Gertrude) 1928-
See Wilhelm, Kate
See also CA 37-40R; CANR 17, 36, 60, 94; MTCW 1; SFW 4

Wilkins, Mary
See Freeman, Mary E(leanor) Wilkins

Willard, Nancy 1936- .... **CLC 7, 37**
See also BYA 5; CA 89-92; CANR 10, 39, 68, 107; CLR 5; CWP; CWRI 5; DLB 5, 52; FANT; MAICYA 1, 2; MTCW 1; SATA 37, 71, 127; SATA-Brief 30

William of Ockham 1290-1349 ..... **CMLC 32**

Williams, Ben Ames 1889-1953 ...... **TCLC 89**
See also CA 183; DLB 102

Williams, C(harles) K(enneth) 1936- .... **CLC 33, 56, 148**
See also CA 37-40R; CAAS 26; CANR 57, 106; CP 7; DAM POET; DLB 5

Williams, Charles
See Collier, James Lincoln

Williams, Charles (Walter Stansby) 1886-1945 .... **TCLC 1, 11**
See also CA 104; 163; DLB 100, 153, 255; FANT; RGEL 2; SUFW

Williams, (George) Emlyn 1905-1987 .... **CLC 15**
See also CA 104; 123; CANR 36; DAM DRAM; DLB 10, 77; MTCW 1

Williams, Hank 1923-1953 .... **TCLC 81**

Williams, Hugo 1942- .... **CLC 42**
See also CA 17-20R; CANR 45; CP 7; DLB 40

Williams, J. Walker
See Wodehouse, P(elham) G(renville)

Williams, John A(lfred) 1925- ..... **CLC 5, 13; BLC 3**
See also AFAW 2; BW 2, 3; CA 53-56; CAAE 195; CAAS 3; CANR 6, 26, 51; CN 7; CSW; DAM MULT; DLB 2, 33; INT CANR-6; RGAL 4; SFW 4

Williams, Jonathan (Chamberlain) 1929- .... **CLC 13**
See also CA 9-12R; CAAS 12; CANR 8, 108; CP 7; DLB 5

Williams, Joy 1944- .... **CLC 31**
See also CA 41-44R; CANR 22, 48, 97

Williams, Norman 1952- .... **CLC 39**
See also CA 118

Williams, Sherley Anne 1944-1999 . **CLC 89; BLC 3**
See also AFAW 2; BW 2, 3; CA 73-76; 185; CANR 25, 82; DAM MULT, POET; DLB 41; INT CANR-25; SATA 78; SATA-Obit 116

Williams, Shirley
See Williams, Sherley Anne

Williams, Tennessee 1911-1983 . **CLC 1, 2, 5, 7, 8, 11, 15, 19, 30, 39, 45, 71, 111; DC 4; WLC**
See also AAYA 31; AITN 1, 2; AMW; CA 5-8R; 108; CABS 3; CAD; CANR 31; CDALB 1941-1968; DA; DA3; DAB; DAC; DAM DRAM, MST; DFS 1, 3, 7, 12; DLB 7; DLBD 4; DLBY 1983; GLL 1; LAIT 4; MTCW 1, 2; RGAL 4

Williams, Thomas (Alonzo) 1926-1990 .... **CLC 14**
See also CA 1-4R; 132; CANR 2

Williams, William C.
See Williams, William Carlos

Williams, William Carlos 1883-1963 .... **CLC 1, 2, 5, 9, 13, 22, 42, 67; PC 7; SSC 31**
See also AMW; AMWR 1; CA 89-92; CANR 34; CDALB 1917-1929; DA; DA3; DAB; DAC; DAM MST, POET; DLB 4, 16, 54, 86; EXPP; MTCW 1, 2; PAB; PFS 1, 6, 11; RGAL 4; RGSF 2; WP

Williamson, David (Keith) 1942- ..... **CLC 56**
See also CA 103; CANR 41; CD 5

Williamson, Ellen Douglas 1905-1984
See Douglas, Ellen
See also CA 17-20R; 114; CANR 39

Williamson, Jack .... **CLC 29**
See also Williamson, John Stewart
See also CAAS 8; DLB 8; SCFW 2

Williamson, John Stewart 1908-
See Williamson, Jack
See also CA 17-20R; CANR 23, 70; SFW 4

Willie, Frederick
See Lovecraft, H(oward) P(hillips)

Willingham, Calder (Baynard, Jr.) 1922-1995 .... **CLC 5, 51**
See also CA 5-8R; 147; CANR 3; CSW; DLB 2, 44; IDFW 3, 4; MTCW 1

Willis, Charles
See Clarke, Arthur C(harles)

Willy
See Colette, (Sidonie-Gabrielle)

Willy, Colette
See Colette, (Sidonie-Gabrielle)
See also GLL 1

Wilmot, John 1647-1680 .... **LC 75**
See also Rochester
See also BRW 2; DLB 131; PAB

Wilson, A(ndrew) N(orman) 1950- .. **CLC 33**
See also BRWS 6; CA 112; 122; CN 7; DLB 14, 155, 194; MTCW 2

Wilson, Angus (Frank Johnstone) 1913-1991 . **CLC 2, 3, 5, 25, 34; SSC 21**
See also BRWS 1; CA 5-8R; 134; CANR 21; DLB 15, 139, 155; MTCW 1, 2; RGEL 2; RGSF 2

Wilson, August 1945- ..... **CLC 39, 50, 63, 118; BLC 3; DC 2; WLCS**
See also AAYA 16; AFAW 2; AMWS 8; BW 2, 3; CA 115; 122; CAD; CANR 42, 54, 76; CD 5; DA; DA3; DAB; DAC; DAM DRAM, MST, MULT; DFS 3, 7; DLB 228; LAIT 4; MTCW 1, 2; RGAL 4

Wilson, Brian 1942- .... **CLC 12**

Wilson, Colin 1931- .... **CLC 3, 14**
See also CA 1-4R; CAAS 5; CANR 1, 22, 33, 77; CMW 4; CN 7; DLB 14, 194; HGG; MTCW 1; SFW 4

Wilson, Dirk
See Pohl, Frederik

Wilson, Edmund 1895-1972 .. **CLC 1, 2, 3, 8, 24**
See also AMW; CA 1-4R; 37-40R; CANR 1, 46; DLB 63; MTCW 1, 2; RGAL 4

Wilson, Ethel Davis (Bryant) 1888(?)-1980 .... **CLC 13**
See also CA 102; DAC; DAM POET; DLB 68; MTCW 1; RGEL 2

Wilson, Harriet
See Wilson, Harriet E. Adams
See also DLB 239

Wilson, Harriet E. Adams 1827(?)-1863(?) .... **NCLC 78; BLC 3**
See also Wilson, Harriet
See also DLB 50, 243

Wilson, John 1785-1854 .... **NCLC 5**

Wilson, John (Anthony) Burgess 1917-1993
See Burgess, Anthony
See also CA 1-4R; 143; CANR 2, 46; DA3; DAC; DAM NOV; MTCW 1, 2

Wilson, Lanford 1937- .... **CLC 7, 14, 36**
See also CA 17-20R; CABS 3; CAD; CANR 45, 96; CD 5; DAM DRAM; DFS 4, 9, 12; DLB 7

Wilson, Robert M. 1944- .... **CLC 7, 9**
See also CA 49-52; CAD; CANR 2, 41, CD 5; MTCW 1

Wilson, Robert McLiam 1964- .... **CLC 59**
See also CA 132

Wilson, Sloan 1920- .... **CLC 32**
See also CA 1-4R; CANR 1, 44; CN 7

Wilson, Snoo 1948- .... **CLC 33**
See also CA 69-72; CBD; CD 5

Wilson, William S(mith) 1932- .... **CLC 49**
See also CA 81-84

Wilson, (Thomas) Woodrow
1856-1924 .... **TCLC 79**
See also CA 166; DLB 47

Wilson and Warnke eds. .... **CLC 65**

Winchilsea, Anne (Kingsmill) Finch
1661-1720
See Finch, Anne
See also RGEL 2

Windham, Basil
See Wodehouse, P(elham) G(renville)

Wingrove, David (John) 1954- .... **CLC 68**
See also CA 133; SFW 4

Winnemucca, Sarah 1844-1891 ..... **NCLC 79**
See also DAM MULT; DLB 175; NNAL;
RGAL 4

Winstanley, Gerrard 1609-1676 .... **LC 52**

Wintergreen, Jane
See Duncan, Sara Jeannette

Winters, Janet Lewis .... **CLC 41**
See also Lewis, Janet
See also DLBY 1987

Winters, (Arthur) Yvor 1900-1968 .... **CLC 4, 8, 32**
See also AMWS 2; CA 11-12; 25-28R; CAP 1; DLB 48; MTCW 1; RGAL 4

Winterson, Jeanette 1959- .... **CLC 64, 158**
See also BRWS 4; CA 136; CANR 58; CN 7; CPW; DA3; DAM POP; DLB 207; FANT; FW; GLL 1; MTCW 2; RHW

Winthrop, John 1588-1649 .... **LC 31**
See also DLB 24, 30

Wirth, Louis 1897-1952 .... **TCLC 92**

Wiseman, Frederick 1930- .... **CLC 20**
See also CA 159

Wister, Owen 1860-1938 .... **TCLC 21**
See also BPFB 3; CA 108; 162; DLB 9, 78, 186; RGAL 4; SATA 62; TCWW 2

Witkacy
See Witkiewicz, Stanislaw Ignacy

Witkiewicz, Stanislaw Ignacy
1885-1939 .... **TCLC 8**
See also CA 105; 162; CDWLB 4; DLB 215; EW 10; RGWL 2; SFW 4

Wittgenstein, Ludwig (Josef Johann)
1889-1951 .... **TCLC 59**
See also CA 113; 164; MTCW 2

Wittig, Monique 1935(?)- .... **CLC 22**
See also CA 116; 135; CWW 2; DLB 83;
FW; GLL 1

Wittlin, Jozef 1896-1976 .... **CLC 25**
See also CA 49-52; 65-68; CANR 3

Wodehouse, P(elham) G(renville)
1881-1975 ... **CLC 1, 2, 5, 10, 22; SSC 2**
See also AITN 2; BRWS 3; CA 45-48; 57-60; CANR 3, 33; CDBLB 1914-1945;
CPW 1; DA3; DAB; DAC; DAM NOV;
DLB 34, 162; MTCW 1, 2; RGEL 2;
RGSF 2; SATA 22; SSFS 10; TCLC 108

Woiwode, L.
See Woiwode, Larry (Alfred)

Woiwode, Larry (Alfred) 1941- ... **CLC 6, 10**
See also CA 73-76; CANR 16, 94; CN 7;
DLB 6; INT CANR-16

Wojciechowska, Maia (Teresa)
1927- .... **CLC 26**
See also AAYA 8; BYA 3; CA 9-12R, 183;
CAAE 183; CANR 4, 41; CLR 1; JRDA;
MAICYA 1, 2; SAAS 1; SATA 1, 28, 83;
SATA-Essay 104; YAW

Wojtyla, Karol
See John Paul II, Pope

Wolf, Christa 1929- .... **CLC 14, 29, 58, 150**
See also CA 85-88; CANR 45; CDWLB 2;
CWW 2; DLB 75; FW; MTCW 1; RGWL 2; SSFS 14

Wolf, Naomi 1962- .... **CLC 157**
See also CA 141; FW

Wolfe, Gene (Rodman) 1931- .... **CLC 25**
See also AAYA 35; CA 57-60; CAAS 9;
CANR 6, 32, 60; CPW; DAM POP; DLB 8; FANT; MTCW 2; SATA 118; SCFW 2;
SFW 4

Wolfe, George C. 1954- .... **CLC 49; BLCS**
See also CA 149; CAD; CD 5

Wolfe, Thomas (Clayton)
1900-1938 ...... **TCLC 4, 13, 29, 61; SSC 33; WLC**
See also AMW; BPFB 3; CA 104; 132;
CANR 102; CDALB 1929-1941; DA;
DA3; DAB; DAC; DAM MST, NOV;
DLB 9, 102, 229; DLBD 2, 16; DLBY 1985, 1997; MTCW 1, 2; RGAL 4

Wolfe, Thomas Kennerly, Jr.
1930- .... **CLC 147**
See also Wolfe, Tom
See also CA 13-16R; CANR 9, 33, 70, 104;
DA3; DAM POP; DLB 185; INT CANR-9; MTCW 1, 2; TUS

Wolfe, Tom .... **CLC 1, 2, 9, 15, 35, 51**
See also Wolfe, Thomas Kennerly, Jr.
See also AAYA 8; AITN 2; AMWS 3; BEST 89:1; BPFB 3; CN 7; CPW; CSW; DLB 152; LAIT 5; RGAL 4

Wolff, Geoffrey (Ansell) 1937- .... **CLC 41**
See also CA 29-32R; CANR 29, 43, 78

Wolff, Sonia
See Levitin, Sonia (Wolff)

Wolff, Tobias (Jonathan Ansell)
1945- .... **CLC 39, 64**
See also AAYA 16; AMWS 7; BEST 90:2;
BYA 12; CA 114; 117; CAAS 22; CANR 54, 76, 96; CN 7; CSW; DA3; DLB 130;
INT CA-117; MTCW 2; RGAL 4; RGSF 2; SSFS 4, 11

Wolfram von Eschenbach c. 1170-c.
1220 .... **CMLC 5**
See also CDWLB 2; DLB 138; EW 1;
RGWL 2

Wolitzer, Hilma 1930- .... **CLC 17**
See also CA 65-68; CANR 18, 40; INT CANR-18; SATA 31; YAW

Wollstonecraft, Mary 1759-1797 ..... **LC 5, 50**
See also BRWS 3; CDBLB 1789-1832;
DLB 39, 104, 158, 252; FW; LAIT 1;
RGEL 2; WLIT 3

Wonder, Stevie .... **CLC 12**
See also Morris, Steveland Judkins

Wong, Jade Snow 1922- .... **CLC 17**
See also CA 109; CANR 91; SATA 112

Woodberry, George Edward
1855-1930 .... **TCLC 73**
See also CA 165; DLB 71, 103

Woodcott, Keith
See Brunner, John (Kilian Houston)

Woodruff, Robert W.
See Mencken, H(enry) L(ouis)

Woolf, (Adeline) Virginia
1882-1941 .. **TCLC 1, 5, 20, 43, 56, 101; SSC 7; WLC**
See also BPFB 3; BRW 7; BRWR 1; CA 104; 130; CANR 64; CDBLB 1914-1945;
DA; DA3; DAB; DAC; DAM MST, NOV;
DLB 36, 100, 162; DLBD 10; EXPS; FW;
LAIT 4; MTCW 1, 2; NCFS 2; NFS 8, 12; RGEL 2; RGSF 2; SSFS 4, 12; WLIT 4

Woollcott, Alexander (Humphreys)
1887-1943 .... **TCLC 5**
See also CA 105; 161; DLB 29

Woolrich, Cornell .... **CLC 77**
See also Hopley-Woolrich, Cornell George
See also MSW

Woolson, Constance Fenimore
1840-1894 .... **NCLC 82**
See also DLB 12, 74, 189, 221; RGAL 4

Wordsworth, Dorothy 1771-1855 .. **NCLC 25**
See also DLB 107

Wordsworth, William 1770-1850 .. **NCLC 12, 38, 111; PC 4; WLC**
See also BRW 4; CDBLB 1789-1832; DA;
DA3; DAB; DAC; DAM MST, POET;
DLB 93, 107; EXPP; PAB; PFS 2; RGEL 2; WLIT 3; WP

Wotton, Sir Henry 1568-1639 .... **LC 68**
See also DLB 121; RGEL 2

Wouk, Herman 1915- .... **CLC 1, 9, 38**
See also BPFB 2, 3; CA 5-8R; CANR 6, 33, 67; CDALBS; CN 7; CPW; DA3;
DAM NOV, POP; DLBY 1982; INT CANR-6; LAIT 4; MTCW 1, 2; NFS 7

Wright, Charles (Penzel, Jr.) 1935- .. **CLC 6, 13, 28, 119, 146**
See also AMWS 5; CA 29-32R; CAAS 7;
CANR 23, 36, 62, 88; CP 7; DLB 165;
DLBY 1982; MTCW 1, 2; PFS 10

Wright, Charles Stevenson 1932- ... **CLC 49; BLC 3**
See also BW 1; CA 9-12R; CANR 26; CN 7; DAM MULT, POET; DLB 33

Wright, Frances 1795-1852 .... **NCLC 74**
See also DLB 73

Wright, Frank Lloyd 1867-1959 .... **TCLC 95**
See also AAYA 33; CA 174

Wright, Jack R.
See Harris, Mark

Wright, James (Arlington)
1927-1980 .... **CLC 3, 5, 10, 28; PC 36**
See also AITN 2; AMWS 3; CA 49-52; 97-100; CANR 4, 34, 64; CDALBS; DAM POET; DLB 5, 169; EXPP; MTCW 1, 2;
PFS 7, 8; RGAL 4; WP

Wright, Judith (Arundell)
1915-2000 .... **CLC 11, 53; PC 14**
See also CA 13-16R; 188; CANR 31, 76, 93; CP 7; CWP; MTCW 1, 2; PFS 8;
RGEL 2; SATA 14; SATA-Obit 121

Wright, L(aurali) R. 1939- .... **CLC 44**
See also CA 138; CMW 4

Wright, Richard (Nathaniel)
1908-1960 .... **CLC 1, 3, 4, 9, 14, 21, 48, 74; BLC 3; SSC 2; WLC**
See also AAYA 5, 42; AFAW 1, 2; AMW;
BPFB 3; BW 1; BYA 2; CA 108; CANR 64; CDALB 1929-1941; DA; DA3; DAB;
DAC; DAM MST, MULT, NOV; DLB 76, 102; DLBD 2; EXPN; LAIT 3, 4; MTCW 1, 2; NCFS 1; NFS 1, 7; RGAL 4; RGSF 2; SSFS 3, 9; YAW

Wright, Richard B(ruce) 1937- .... **CLC 6**
See also CA 85-88; DLB 53

Wright, Rick 1945- .... **CLC 35**

Wright, Rowland
See Wells, Carolyn

Wright, Stephen 1946- .... **CLC 33**

Wright, Willard Huntington 1888-1939
See Van Dine, S. S.
See also CA 115; 189; CMW 4; DLBD 16

Wright, William 1930- .... **CLC 44**
See also CA 53-56; CANR 7, 23

Wroth, Lady Mary 1587-1653(?) .... **LC 30; PC 38**
See also DLB 121

Wu Ch'eng-en 1500(?)-1582(?) .... **LC 7**

Wu Ching-tzu 1701-1754 .... **LC 2**

Wurlitzer, Rudolph 1938(?)- .... **CLC 2, 4, 15**
See also CA 85-88; CN 7; DLB 173

Wyatt, Sir Thomas c. 1503-1542 . **LC 70; PC 27**
See also BRW 1; DLB 132; EXPP; RGEL 2; TEA

Wycherley, William 1640-1716 .... **LC 8, 21**
See also BRW 2; CDBLB 1660-1789; DAM DRAM; DLB 80; RGEL 2

Wylie, Elinor (Morton Hoyt)
1885-1928 .... **TCLC 8; PC 23**
See also AMWS 1; CA 105; 162; DLB 9, 45; EXPP; RGAL 4

Wylie, Philip (Gordon) 1902-1971 ... **CLC 43**
See also CA 21-22; 33-36R; CAP 2; DLB 9; SFW 4

Wyndham, John .... **CLC 19**
See also Harris, John (Wyndham Parkes Lucas) Beynon
See also DLB 255; SCFW 2

Wyss, Johann David Von
1743-1818 .... **NCLC 10**
See also JRDA; MAICYA 1, 2; SATA 29; SATA-Brief 27

Xenophon c. 430B.C.-c. 354B.C. ... **CMLC 17**
See also AW 1; DLB 176; RGWL 2

Yakumo Koizumi
See Hearn, (Patricio) Lafcadio (Tessima Carlos)

Yamamoto, Hisaye 1921- .... **SSC 34; AAL**
See also DAM MULT; LAIT 4; SSFS 14

Yanez, Jose Donoso
See Donoso (Yanez), Jose

Yanovsky, Basile S.
See Yanovsky, V(assily) S(emenovich)

Yanovsky, V(assily) S(emenovich)
1906-1989 .... **CLC 2, 18**
See also CA 97-100; 129

Yates, Richard 1926-1992 .... **CLC 7, 8, 23**
See also CA 5-8R; 139; CANR 10, 43; DLB 2, 234; DLBY 1981, 1992; INT CANR-10

Yeats, W. B.
See Yeats, William Butler

Yeats, William Butler 1865-1939 .... **TCLC 1, 11, 18, 31, 93, 116; PC 20; WLC**
See also BRW 6; BRWR 1; CA 104; 127; CANR 45; CDBLB 1890-1914; DA; DA3; DAB; DAC; DAM DRAM, MST, POET; DLB 10, 19, 98, 156; EXPP; MTCW 1, 2; NCFS 3; PAB; PFS 1, 2, 5, 7, 13; RGEL 2; WLIT 4; WP

Yehoshua, A(braham) B. 1936- .. **CLC 13, 31**
See also CA 33-36R; CANR 43, 90; RGSF 2

Yellow Bird
See Ridge, John Rollin

Yep, Laurence Michael 1948- .... **CLC 35**
See also AAYA 5, 31; BYA 7; CA 49-52; CANR 1, 46, 92; CLR 3, 17, 54; DLB 52; FANT; JRDA; MAICYA 1, 2; MAICYAS 1; SATA 7, 69, 123; WYA; YAW

Yerby, Frank G(arvin) 1916-1991 . **CLC 1, 7, 22; BLC 3**
See also BPFB 3; BW 1, 3; CA 9-12R; 136; CANR 16, 52; DAM MULT; DLB 76; INT CANR-16; MTCW 1; RGAL 4; RHW

Yesenin, Sergei Alexandrovich
See Esenin, Sergei (Alexandrovich)

Yevtushenko, Yevgeny (Alexandrovich)
1933- ...... **CLC 1, 3, 13, 26, 51, 126; PC 40**
See also Evtushenko, Evgenii Aleksandrovich
See also CA 81-84; CANR 33, 54; CWW 2; DAM POET; MTCW 1

Yezierska, Anzia 1885(?)-1970 .... **CLC 46**
See also CA 126; 89-92; DLB 28, 221; FW; MTCW 1; RGAL 4

Yglesias, Helen 1915- .... **CLC 7, 22**
See also CA 37-40R; CAAS 20; CANR 15, 65, 95; CN 7; INT CANR-15; MTCW 1

Yokomitsu, Riichi 1898-1947 .... **TCLC 47**
See also CA 170

Yonge, Charlotte (Mary)
1823-1901 .... **TCLC 48**
See also CA 109; 163; DLB 18, 163; RGEL 2; SATA 17; WCH

York, Jeremy
See Creasey, John

York, Simon
See Heinlein, Robert A(nson)

Yorke, Henry Vincent 1905-1974 ..... **CLC 13**
See also Green, Henry
See also CA 85-88; 49-52

Yosano Akiko 1878-1942 .... **TCLC 59; PC 11**
See also CA 161

Yoshimoto, Banana .... **CLC 84**
See also Yoshimoto, Mahoko
See also NFS 7

Yoshimoto, Mahoko 1964-
See Yoshimoto, Banana
See also CA 144; CANR 98

Young, Al(bert James) 1939- . **CLC 19; BLC 3**
See also BW 2, 3; CA 29-32R; CANR 26, 65, 109; CN 7; CP 7; DAM MULT; DLB 33

Young, Andrew (John) 1885-1971 ...... **CLC 5**
See also CA 5-8R; CANR 7, 29; RGEL 2

Young, Collier
See Bloch, Robert (Albert)

Young, Edward 1683-1765 .... **LC 3, 40**
See also DLB 95; RGEL 2

Young, Marguerite (Vivian)
1909-1995 .... **CLC 82**
See also CA 13-16; 150; CAP 1; CN 7

Young, Neil 1945- .... **CLC 17**
See also CA 110; CCA 1

Young Bear, Ray A. 1950- .... **CLC 94**
See also CA 146; DAM MULT; DLB 175; NNAL

Yourcenar, Marguerite 1903-1987 ... **CLC 19, 38, 50, 87**
See also BPFB 3; CA 69-72; CANR 23, 60, 93; DAM NOV; DLB 72; DLBY 1988; EW 12; GFL 1789 to the Present; GLL 1; MTCW 1, 2; RGWL 2

Yuan, Chu 340(?)B.C.-278(?)B.C. . **CMLC 36**

Yurick, Sol 1925- .... **CLC 6**
See also CA 13-16R; CANR 25; CN 7

Zabolotsky, Nikolai Alekseevich
1903-1958 .... **TCLC 52**
See also CA 116; 164

Zagajewski, Adam 1945- .... **PC 27**
See also CA 186; DLB 232

Zalygin, Sergei -2000 .... **CLC 59**

Zamiatin, Evgenii
See Zamyatin, Evgeny Ivanovich
See also RGSF 2; RGWL 2

Zamiatin, Yevgenii
See Zamyatin, Evgeny Ivanovich

Zamora, Bernice (B. Ortiz) 1938- .. **CLC 89; HLC 2**
See also CA 151; CANR 80; DAM MULT; DLB 82; HW 1, 2

Zamyatin, Evgeny Ivanovich
1884-1937 .... **TCLC 8, 37**
See also Zamiatin, Evgenii
See also CA 105; 166; EW 10; SFW 4

Zangwill, Israel 1864-1926 ... **TCLC 16; SSC 44**
See also CA 109; 167; CMW 4; DLB 10, 135, 197; RGEL 2

Zappa, Francis Vincent, Jr. 1940-1993
See Zappa, Frank
See also CA 108; 143; CANR 57

Zappa, Frank .... **CLC 17**
See also Zappa, Francis Vincent, Jr.

Zaturenska, Marya 1902-1982 ..... **CLC 6, 11**
See also CA 13-16R; 105; CANR 22

Zeami 1363-1443 .... **DC 7**
See also DLB 203; RGWL 2

Zelazny, Roger (Joseph) 1937-1995 . **CLC 21**
See also AAYA 7; BPFB 3; CA 21-24R; 148; CANR 26, 60; CN 7; DLB 8; FANT; MTCW 1, 2; SATA 57; SATA-Brief 39; SCFW; SFW 4; SUFW

Zhdanov, Andrei Alexandrovich
1896-1948 .... **TCLC 18**
See also CA 117; 167

Zhukovsky, Vasilii Andreevich
See Zhukovsky, Vasily (Andreevich)
See also DLB 205

Zhukovsky, Vasily (Andreevich)
1783-1852 .... **NCLC 35**
See also Zhukovsky, Vasilii Andreevich

Ziegenhagen, Eric .... **CLC 55**

Zimmer, Jill Schary
See Robinson, Jill

Zimmerman, Robert
See Dylan, Bob

Zindel, Paul 1936- .... **CLC 6, 26; DC 5**
See also AAYA 2, 37; BYA 2, 3, 8, 11, 14; CA 73-76; CAD; CANR 31, 65, 108; CD 5; CDALBS; CLR 3, 45; DA; DA3; DAB; DAC; DAM DRAM, MST, NOV; DFS 12; DLB 7, 52; JRDA; LAIT 5; MAICYA 1, 2; MTCW 1, 2; NFS 14; SATA 16, 58, 102; WYA; YAW

Zinov'Ev, A. A.
See Zinoviev, Alexander (Aleksandrovich)

Zinoviev, Alexander (Aleksandrovich)
1922- .... **CLC 19**
See also CA 116; 133; CAAS 10

Zoilus
See Lovecraft, H(oward) P(hillips)

Zola, Emile (Edouard Charles Antoine)
1840-1902 ...... **TCLC 1, 6, 21, 41; WLC**
See also CA 104; 138; DA; DA3; DAB; DAC; DAM MST, NOV; DLB 123; EW 7; GFL 1789 to the Present; IDTP; RGWL 2

Zoline, Pamela 1941- .... **CLC 62**
See also CA 161; SFW 4

Zoroaster 628(?)B.C.-551(?)B.C. ... **CMLC 40**

Zorrilla y Moral, Jose 1817-1893 .... **NCLC 6**

Zoshchenko, Mikhail (Mikhailovich)
1895-1958 .... **TCLC 15; SSC 15**
See also CA 115; 160; RGSF 2

Zuckmayer, Carl 1896-1977 .... **CLC 18**
See also CA 69-72; DLB 56, 124; RGWL 2

Zuk, Georges
See Skelton, Robin
See also CCA 1

Zukofsky, Louis 1904-1978 ... **CLC 1, 2, 4, 7, 11, 18; PC 11**
See also AMWS 3; CA 9-12R; 77-80; CANR 39; DAM POET; DLB 5, 165; MTCW 1; RGAL 4

Zweig, Paul 1935-1984 .... **CLC 34, 42**
See also CA 85-88; 113

Zweig, Stefan 1881-1942 .... **TCLC 17**
See also CA 112; 170; DLB 81, 118

Zwingli, Huldreich 1484-1531 .... **LC 37**
See also DLB 179

Literary Criticism Series
Cumulative Topic Index

This index lists all topic entries in Gale's *Classical and Medieval Literature Criticism, Contemporary Literary Criticism, Drama Criticism, Literature Criticism from 1400 to 1800, Nineteenth-Century Literature Criticism,* and *Twentieth-Century Literary Criticism.*

The Aesopic Fable LC 51: 1-100
the British Aesopic Fable, 1-54
the Aesopic tradition in non-English-speaking cultures, 55-66
political uses of the Aesopic fable, 67-88
the evolution of the Aesopic fable, 89-99

Age of Johnson LC 15: 1-87
Johnson's London, 3-15
aesthetics of neoclassicism, 15-36
"age of prose and reason," 36-45
clubmen and bluestockings, 45-56
printing technology, 56-62
periodicals: "a map of busy life," 62-74
transition, 74-86

Age of Spenser LC 39: 1-70
overviews and general studies, 2-21
literary style, 22-34
poets and the crown, 34-70

AIDS in Literature CLC 81: 365-416

Alcohol and Literature TCLC 70: 1-58
overview, 2-8
fiction, 8-48
poetry and drama, 48-58

American Abolitionism NCLC 44: 1-73
overviews and general studies, 2-26
abolitionist ideals, 26-46
the literature of abolitionism, 46-72

American Autobiography TCLC 86: 1-115
overviews and general studies, 3-36
American authors and autobiography, 36-82
African-American autobiography, 82-114

American Black Humor Fiction TCLC 54: 1-85
characteristics of black humor, 2-13
origins and development, 13-38
black humor distinguished from related literary trends, 38-60
black humor and society, 60-75
black humor reconsidered, 75-83

American Civil War in Literature NCLC 32: 1-109
overviews and general studies, 2-20
regional perspectives, 20-54
fiction popular during the war, 54-79
the historical novel, 79-108

American Frontier in Literature NCLC 28: 1-103
definitions, 2-12
development, 12-17
nonfiction writing about the frontier, 17-30
frontier fiction, 30-45
frontier protagonists, 45-66
portrayals of Native Americans, 66-86
feminist readings, 86-98
twentieth-century reaction against frontier literature, 98-100

American Humor Writing NCLC 52: 1-59
overviews and general studies, 2-12
the Old Southwest, 12-42
broader impacts, 42-5
women humorists, 45-58

American Mercury, The TCLC 74: 1-80

American Popular Song, Golden Age of TCLC 42: 1-49
background and major figures, 2-34
the lyrics of popular songs, 34-47

American Proletarian Literature TCLC 54: 86-175
overviews and general studies, 87-95
American proletarian literature and the American Communist Party, 95-111
ideology and literary merit, 111-7
novels, 117-36
Gastonia, 136-48
drama, 148-54
journalism, 154-9
proletarian literature in the United States, 159-74

American Romanticism NCLC 44: 74-138
overviews and general studies, 74-84
sociopolitical influences, 84-104
Romanticism and the American frontier, 104-15
thematic concerns, 115-37

American Western Literature TCLC 46: 1-100
definition and development of American Western literature, 2-7
characteristics of the Western novel, 8-23
Westerns as history and fiction, 23-34
critical reception of American Western literature, 34-41
the Western hero, 41-73
women in Western fiction, 73-91
later Western fiction, 91-9

American Writers in Paris TCLC 98: 1-156
overviews and general studies, 2-155

Anarchism NCLC 84: 1-97
overviews and general studies, 2-23
the French anarchist tradition, 23-56
Anglo-American anarchism, 56-68
anarchism: incidents and issues, 68-97

Animals in Literature TCLC 106: 1-120
overviews and general studies, 2-8
animals in American literature, 8-45
animals in Canadian literature, 45-57
animals in European literature, 57-100
animals in Latin American literature, 100-06
animals in women's literature, 106-20

Antebellum South, Literature of the NCLC 112:1-188
overviews, 4-55
culture of the Old South, 55-68
antebellum fiction: pastoral and heroic romance, 68-120
role of women: a subdued rebellion, 120-59
slavery and the slave narrative, 159-85

The Apocalyptic Movement TCLC 106: 121-69

Aristotle CMLC 31:1-397
philosophy, 3-100
poetics, 101-219
rhetoric, 220-301
science, 302-397

Art and Literature TCLC 54: 176-248
overviews and general studies, 176-93
definitions, 193-219
influence of visual arts on literature, 219-31
spatial form in literature, 231-47

Arthurian Literature CMLC 10: 1-127
historical context and literary beginnings, 2-27
development of the legend through Malory, 27-64
development of the legend from Malory to the Victorian Age, 65-81
themes and motifs, 81-95
principal characters, 95-125

Arthurian Revival NCLC 36: 1-77
overviews and general studies, 2-12
Tennyson and his influence, 12-43
other leading figures, 43-73
the Arthurian legend in the visual arts, 73-6

Australian Literature TCLC 50: 1-94
origins and development, 2-21

CUMULATIVE TOPIC INDEX

characteristics of Australian literature, 21-33
historical and critical perspectives, 33-41
poetry, 41-58
fiction, 58-76
drama, 76-82
Aboriginal literature, 82-91

Beat Generation, Literature of the TCLC 42: 50-102
overviews and general studies, 51-9
the Beat generation as a social phenomenon, 59-62
development, 62-5
Beat literature, 66-96
influence, 97-100

The Bell Curve Controversy CLC 91: 281-330

***Bildungsroman* in Nineteenth-Century Literature** NCLC 20: 92-168
surveys, 93-113
in Germany, 113-40
in England, 140-56
female *Bildungsroman*, 156-67

Bloomsbury Group TCLC 34: 1-73
history and major figures, 2-13
definitions, 13-7
influences, 17-27
thought, 27-40
prose, 40-52
and literary criticism, 52-4
political ideals, 54-61
response to, 61-71

The Blues in Literature TCLC 82: 1-71

Bly, Robert, *Iron John: A Book about Men and Men's Work* CLC 70: 414-62

The Book of J CLC 65: 289-311

British Ephemeral Literature LC 59: 1-70
overviews and general studies, 1-9
broadside ballads, 10-40
chapbooks, jestbooks, pamphlets, and newspapers, 40-69

Buddhism and Literature TCLC 70: 59-164
eastern literature, 60-113
western literature, 113-63

Businessman in American Literature TCLC 26: 1-48
portrayal of the businessman, 1-32
themes and techniques in business fiction, 32-47

The Calendar LC 55: 1-92
overviews and general studies, 2-19
measuring time, 19-28
calendars and culture, 28-60
calendar reform, 60-92

Catholicism in Nineteenth-Century American Literature NCLC 64: 1-58
3-14
polemical literature, 14-46
Catholicism in literature, 47-57

Celtic Mythology CMLC 26: 1-111
overviews and general studies, 2-22
Celtic myth as literature and history, 22-48
Celtic religion: Druids and divinities, 48-80
Fionn MacCuhaill and the Fenian cycle, 80-111

Celtic Twilight See **Irish Literary Renaissance**

Chartist Movement and Literature, The NCLC 60: 1-84
overview: nineteenth-century working-class fiction, 2-19
Chartist fiction and poetry, 19-73
the Chartist press, 73-84

Child Labor in Nineteenth-Century Literature NCLC 108: 1-133
overviews, 3-10
climbing boys and chimney sweeps, 10-16
the international traffic in children, 16-45
critics and reformers, 45-82
fictional representations of child laborers, 83-132

Children's Literature, Nineteenth-Century NCLC 52: 60-135
overviews and general studies, 61-72
moral tales, 72-89
fairy tales and fantasy, 90-119
making men/making women, 119-34

Christianity in Twentieth-Century Literature TCLC 110: 1-79
overviews and general studies, 2-31
Christianity in twentieth-century fiction, 31-78

The City and Literature TCLC 90: 1-124
overviews and general studies, 2-9
the city in American literature, 9-86
the city in European literature, 86-124

Civic Critics, Russian NCLC 20: 402-46
principal figures and background, 402-9
and Russian Nihilism, 410-6
aesthetic and critical views, 416-45

The Cockney School NCLC 68: 1-64
overview, 2-7
Blackwood's Magazine and the contemporary critical response, 7-24
the political and social import of the Cockneys and their critics, 24-63

Colonial America: The Intellectual Background LC 25: 1-98
overviews and general studies, 2-17
philosophy and politics, 17-31
early religious influences in Colonial America, 31-60
consequences of the Revolution, 60-78
religious influences in post-revolutionary America, 78-87
colonial literary genres, 87-97

Colonialism in Victorian English Literature NCLC 56: 1-77
overviews and general studies, 2-34
colonialism and gender, 34-51
monsters and the occult, 51-76

Columbus, Christopher, Books on the Quincentennial of His Arrival in the New World CLC 70: 329-60

Comic Books TCLC 66: 1-139
historical and critical perspectives, 2-48
superheroes, 48-67
underground comix, 67-88
comic books and society, 88-122
adult comics and graphic novels, 122-36

Connecticut Wits NCLC 48: 1-95
overviews and general studies, 2-40
major works, 40-76
intellectual context, 76-95

Crime in Literature TCLC 54: 249-307
evolution of the criminal figure in literature, 250-61
crime and society, 261-77
literary perspectives on crime and punishment, 277-88
writings by criminals, 288-306

The Crusades CMLC 38: 1-144
history of the Crusades, 3-60
literature of the Crusades, 60-116
the Crusades and the people: attitudes and influences, 116-44

Cyberpunk TCLC 106: 170-366
overviews and general studies, 171-88
feminism and cyberpunk, 188-230
history and cyberpunk, 230-70
sexuality and cyberpunk, 270-98
social issues and cyberpunk, 299-366

Czechoslovakian Literature of the Twentieth Century TCLC 42:103-96
through World War II, 104-35
de-Stalinization, the Prague Spring, and contemporary literature, 135-72
Slovak literature, 172-85
Czech science fiction, 185-93

Dadaism TCLC 46: 101-71
background and major figures, 102-16
definitions, 116-26
manifestos and commentary by Dadaists, 126-40
theater and film, 140-58
nature and characteristics of Dadaist writing, 158-70

Darwinism and Literature NCLC 32: 110-206
background, 110-31
direct responses to Darwin, 131-71
collateral effects of Darwinism, 171-205

Death in American Literature NCLC 92: 1-170
overviews and general studies, 2-32
death in the works of Emily Dickinson, 32-72
death in the works of Herman Melville, 72-101
death in the works of Edgar Allan Poe, 101-43
death in the works of Walt Whitman, 143-70

Death in Nineteenth-Century British Literature NCLC 68: 65-142
overviews and general studies, 66-92
responses to death, 92-102
feminist perspectives, 103-17
striving for immortality, 117-41

Death in Literature TCLC 78:1-183
fiction, 2-115
poetry, 115-46
drama, 146-81

de Man, Paul, Wartime Journalism of CLC 55: 382-424

Detective Fiction, Nineteenth-Century NCLC 36: 78-148
origins of the genre, 79-100
history of nineteenth-century detective fiction, 101-33
significance of nineteenth-century detective fiction, 133-46

Detective Fiction, Twentieth-Century TCLC 38: 1-96
genesis and history of the detective story, 3-22
defining detective fiction, 22-32
evolution and varieties, 32-77
the appeal of detective fiction, 77-90

Dime Novels NCLC 84: 98-168
overviews and general studies, 99-123
popular characters, 123-39
major figures and influences, 139-52
socio-political concerns, 152-167

Disease and Literature TCLC 66: 140-283
overviews and general studies, 141-65
disease in nineteenth-century literature, 165-81
tuberculosis and literature, 181-94
women and disease in literature, 194-221
plague literature, 221-53
AIDS in literature, 253-82

El Dorado, The Legend of See **Legend of El Dorado, The**

The Double in Nineteenth-Century Literature NCLC 40: 1-95
genesis and development of the theme, 2-15
the double and Romanticism, 16-27
sociological views, 27-52
psychological interpretations, 52-87

philosophical considerations, 87-95
Dramatic Realism NCLC 44: 139-202
  overviews and general studies, 140-50
  origins and definitions, 150-66
  impact and influence, 166-93
  realist drama and tragedy, 193-201
Drugs and Literature TCLC 78: 184-282
  overviews and general studies, 185-201
  pre-twentieth-century literature, 201-42
  twentieth-century literature, 242-82
Eastern Mythology CMLC 26: 112-92
  heroes and kings, 113-51
  cross-cultural perspective, 151-69
  relations to history and society, 169-92
Eighteenth-Century British Periodicals LC 63: 1-123
  rise of periodicals, 2-31
  impact and influence of periodicals, 31-64
  periodicals and society, 64-122
Eighteenth-Century Travel Narratives LC 77: 252-355
  overviews and general studies, 254-79
  eighteenth-century European travel narratives, 279-334
  non-European eighteenth-century travel narratives, 334-55
Electronic "Books": Hypertext and Hyperfiction CLC 86: 367-404
  books vs. CD-ROMS, 367-76
  hypertext and hyperfiction, 376-95
  implications for publishing, libraries, and the public, 395-403
Eliot, T. S., Centenary of Birth CLC 55: 345-75
Elizabethan Drama LC 22: 140-240
  origins and influences, 142-67
  characteristics and conventions, 167-83
  theatrical production, 184-200
  histories, 200-12
  comedy, 213-20
  tragedy, 220-30
Elizabethan Prose Fiction LC 41: 1-70
  overviews and general studies, 1-15
  origins and influences, 15-43
  style and structure, 43-69
Enclosure of the English Common NCLC 88: 1-57
  overviews and general studies, 1-12
  early reaction to enclosure, 12-23
  nineteenth-century reaction to enclosure, 23-56
The Encyclopedists LC 26: 172-253
  overviews and general studies, 173-210
  intellectual background, 210-32
  views on esthetics, 232-41
  views on women, 241-52
English Caroline Literature LC 13: 221-307
  background, 222-41
  evolution and varieties, 241-62
  the Cavalier mode, 262-75
  court and society, 275-91
  politics and religion, 291-306
English Decadent Literature of the 1890s NCLC 28: 104-200
  fin de siècle: the Decadent period, 105-19
  definitions, 120-37
  major figures: "the tragic generation," 137-50
  French literature and English literary Decadence, 150-7
  themes, 157-61
  poetry, 161-82
  periodicals, 182-96
English Essay, Rise of the LC 18: 238-308
  definitions and origins, 236-54
  influence on the essay, 254-69
  historical background, 269-78
  the essay in the seventeenth century, 279-93
  the essay in the eighteenth century, 293-307
English Mystery Cycle Dramas LC 34: 1-88
  overviews and general studies, 1-27
  the nature of dramatic performances, 27-42
  the medieval worldview and the mystery cycles, 43-67
  the doctrine of repentance and the mystery cycles, 67-76
  the fall from grace in the mystery cycles, 76-88
The English Realist Novel, 1740-1771 LC 51: 102-98
  overviews and general studies, 103-22
  from Romanticism to Realism, 123-58
  women and the novel, 159-175
  the novel and other literary forms, 176-197
English Revolution, Literature of the LC 43: 1-58
  overviews and general studies, 2-24
  pamphlets of the English Revolution, 24-38
  political sermons of the English Revolution, 38-48
  poetry of the English Revolution, 48-57
English Romantic Hellenism NCLC 68: 143-250
  overviews and general studies, 144-69
  historical development of English Romantic Hellenism, 169-91
  influence of Greek mythology on the Romantics, 191-229
  influence of Greek literature, art, and culture on the Romantics, 229-50
English Romantic Poetry NCLC 28: 201-327
  overviews and reputation, 202-37
  major subjects and themes, 237-67
  forms of Romantic poetry, 267-78
  politics, society, and Romantic poetry, 278-99
  philosophy, religion, and Romantic poetry, 299-324
The Epistolary Novel LC 59: 71-170
  overviews and general studies, 72-96
  women and the Epistolary novel, 96-138
  principal figures: Britain, 138-53
  principal figures: France, 153-69
Espionage Literature TCLC 50: 95-159
  overviews and general studies, 96-113
  espionage fiction/formula fiction, 113-26
  spies in fact and fiction, 126-38
  the female spy, 138-44
  social and psychological perspectives, 144-58
European Debates on the Conquest of the Americas LC 67: 1-129
  overviews and general studies, 3-56
  major Spanish figures, 56-98
  English perceptions of Native Americans, 98-129
European Romanticism NCLC 36: 149-284
  definitions, 149-77
  origins of the movement, 177-82
  Romantic theory, 182-200
  themes and techniques, 200-23
  Romanticism in Germany, 223-39
  Romanticism in France, 240-61
  Romanticism in Italy, 261-4
  Romanticism in Spain, 264-8
  impact and legacy, 268-82
Exile in Literature TCLC 122: 1-129
  overviews and general studies, 2-33
  exile in fiction, 33-92
  German literature in exile, 92-129
Existentialism and Literature TCLC 42: 197-268
  overviews and definitions, 198-209
  history and influences, 209-19
  Existentialism critiqued and defended, 220-35
  philosophical and religious perspectives, 235-41
  Existentialist fiction and drama, 241-67
Familiar Essay NCLC 48: 96-211
  definitions and origins, 97-130
  overview of the genre, 130-43
  elements of form and style, 143-59
  elements of content, 159-73
  the Cockneys: Hazlitt, Lamb, and Hunt, 173-91
  status of the genre, 191-210
The Faust Legend LC 47: 1-117
Fear in Literature TCLC 74: 81-258
  overviews and general studies, 81
  pre-twentieth-century literature, 123
  twentieth-century literature, 182
Feminism in the 1990s: Commentary on Works by Naomi Wolf, Susan Faludi, and Camille Paglia CLC 76: 377-415
Feminist Criticism in 1990 CLC 65: 312-60
Fifteenth-Century English Literature LC 17: 248-334
  background, 249-72
  poetry, 272-315
  drama, 315-23
  prose, 323-33
Film and Literature TCLC 38: 97-226
  overviews and general studies, 97-119
  film and theater, 119-34
  film and the novel, 134-45
  the art of the screenplay, 145-66
  genre literature/genre film, 167-79
  the writer and the film industry, 179-90
  authors on film adaptations of their works, 190-200
  fiction into film: comparative essays, 200-23
Finance and Money as Represented in Nineteenth-Century Literature NCLC 76: 1-69
  historical perspectives, 2-20
  the image of money, 20-37
  the dangers of money, 37-50
  women and money, 50-69
Folklore and Literature TCLC 86: 116-293
  overviews and general studies, 118-144
  Native American literature, 144-67
  African-American literature, 167-238
  folklore and the American West, 238-57
  modern and postmodern literature, 257-91
Food in Literature TCLC 114: 1-133
  food and children's literature, 2-14
  food as a literary device, 14-32
  rituals invloving food, 33-45
  food and social and ethnic identity, 45-90
  women's relationship with food, 91-132
Food in Nineteenth-Century Literature NCLC 108: 134-288
  overviews, 136-74
  food and social class, 174-85
  food and gender, 185-219
  food and love, 219-31
  food and sex, 231-48
  eating disorders, 248-70
  vegetarians, carnivores, and cannibals, 270-87
French Drama in the Age of Louis XIV LC 28: 94-185
  overview, 95-127
  tragedy, 127-46

comedy, 146-66
tragicomedy, 166-84

French Enlightenment LC 14: 81-145
the question of definition, 82-9
le siècle des lumières, 89-94
women and the salons, 94-105
censorship, 105-15
the philosophy of reason, 115-31
influence and legacy, 131-44

French New Novel TCLC 98: 158-234
overviews and general studies, 158-92
influences, 192-213
themes, 213-33

French Realism NCLC 52: 136-216
origins and definitions, 137-70
issues and influence, 170-98
realism and representation, 198-215

French Revolution and English Literature NCLC 40: 96-195
history and theory, 96-123
romantic poetry, 123-50
the novel, 150-81
drama, 181-92
children's literature, 192-5

Futurism, Italian TCLC 42: 269-354
principles and formative influences, 271-9
manifestos, 279-88
literature, 288-303
theater, 303-19
art, 320-30
music, 330-6
architecture, 336-9
and politics, 339-46
reputation and significance, 346-51

Gaelic Revival See Irish Literary Renaissance

Gates, Henry Louis, Jr., and African-American Literary Criticism CLC 65: 361-405

Gay and Lesbian Literature CLC 76: 416-39

German Exile Literature TCLC 30: 1-58
the writer and the Nazi state, 1-10
definition of, 10-4
life in exile, 14-32
surveys, 32-50
Austrian literature in exile, 50-2
German publishing in the United States, 52-7

German Expressionism TCLC 34: 74-160
history and major figures, 76-85
aesthetic theories, 85-109
drama, 109-26
poetry, 126-38
film, 138-42
painting, 142-7
music, 147-53
and politics, 153-8

The Gilded Age NCLC 84: 169-271
popular themes, 170-90
Realism, 190-208
Aestheticism, 208-26
socio-political concerns, 226-70

***Glasnost* and Contemporary Soviet Literature** CLC 59: 355-97

Gothic Novel NCLC 28: 328-402
development and major works, 328-34
definitions, 334-50
themes and techniques, 350-78
in America, 378-85
in Scotland, 385-91
influence and legacy, 391-400

The Governess in Nineteenth-Century Literature NCLC 104: 1-131
overviews and general studies, 3-28
social roles and economic conditions, 28-86
fictional governesses, 86-131

Graphic Narratives CLC 86: 405-32
history and overviews, 406-21
the "Classics Illustrated" series, 421-2
reviews of recent works, 422-32

Graveyard Poets LC 67: 131-212
origins and development, 131-52
major figures, 152-75
major works, 175-212

Greek Historiography CMLC 17: 1-49

Greek Mythology CMLC 26: 193-320
overviews and general studies, 194-209
origins and development of Greek mythology, 209-29
cosmogonies and divinities in Greek mythology, 229-54
heroes and heroines in Greek mythology, 254-80
women in Greek mythology, 280-320

Greek Theater CMLC 51: 1-58
criticism, 2-58

Hard-Boiled Fiction TCLC 118: 1-109
overviews and general studies, 2-39
major authors, 39-76
women and hard-boiled fiction, 76-109

Harlem Renaissance TCLC 26: 49-125
principal issues and figures, 50-67
the literature and its audience, 67-74
theme and technique in poetry, fiction, and drama, 74-115
and American society, 115-21
achievement and influence, 121-2

Havel, Václav, Playwright and President CLC 65: 406-63

Historical Fiction, Nineteenth-Century NCLC 48: 212-307
definitions and characteristics, 213-36
Victorian historical fiction, 236-65
American historical fiction, 265-88
realism in historical fiction, 288-306

Hollywood and Literature TCLC 118: 110-251
overviews and general studies, 111-20
adaptations, 120-65
socio-historical and cultural impact, 165-206
theater and hollywood, 206-51

Holocaust and the Atomic Bomb: Fifty Years Later CLC 91: 331-82
the Holocaust remembered, 333-52
Anne Frank revisited, 352-62
the atomic bomb and American memory, 362-81

Holocaust Denial Literature TCLC 58: 1-110
overviews and general studies, 1-30
Robert Faurisson and Noam Chomsky, 30-52
Holocaust denial literature in America, 52-71
library access to Holocaust denial literature, 72-5
the authenticity of Anne Frank's diary, 76-90
David Irving and the "normalization" of Hitler, 90-109

Holocaust, Literature of the TCLC 42: 355-450
historical overview, 357-61
critical overview, 361-70
diaries and memoirs, 370-95
novels and short stories, 395-425
poetry, 425-41
drama, 441-8

Homosexuality in Nineteenth-Century Literature NCLC 56: 78-182
defining homosexuality, 80-111
Greek love, 111-44
trial and danger, 144-81

Hungarian Literature of the Twentieth Century TCLC 26: 126-88
surveys of, 126-47
Nyugat and early twentieth-century literature, 147-56
mid-century literature, 156-68
and politics, 168-78
since the 1956 revolt, 178-87

Hysteria in Nineteenth-Century Literature NCLC 64: 59-184
the history of hysteria, 60-75
the gender of hysteria, 75-103
hysteria and women's narratives, 103-57
hysteria in nineteenth-century poetry, 157-83

Imagism TCLC 74: 259-454
history and development, 260
major figures, 288
sources and influences, 352
Imagism and other movements, 397
influence and legacy, 431

Immigrants in Nineteenth-Century Literature, Representation of NCLC 112: 188-298
overview, 189-99
immigrants in America, 199-223
immigrants and labor, 223-60
immigrants in England, 260-97

Incest in Nineteenth-Century American Literature NCLC 76: 70-141
overview, 71-88
the concern for social order, 88-117
authority and authorship, 117-40

Incest in Victorian Literature NCLC 92: 172-318
overviews and general studies, 173-85
novels, 185-276
plays, 276-84
poetry, 284-318

Indian Literature in English TCLC 54: 308-406
overview, 309-13
origins and major figures, 313-25
the Indo-English novel, 325-55
Indo-English poetry, 355-67
Indo-English drama, 367-72
critical perspectives on Indo-English literature, 372-80
modern Indo-English literature, 380-9
Indo-English authors on their work, 389-404

The Industrial Revolution in Literature NCLC 56: 183-273
historical and cultural perspectives, 184-201
contemporary reactions to the machine, 201-21
themes and symbols in literature, 221-73

The Irish Famine as Represented in Nineteenth-Century Literature NCLC 64: 185-261
overviews and general studies, 187-98
historical background, 198-212
famine novels, 212-34
famine poetry, 234-44
famine letters and eye-witness accounts, 245-61

Irish Literary Renaissance TCLC 46: 172-287
overview, 173-83
development and major figures, 184-202
influence of Irish folklore and mythology, 202-22
Irish poetry, 222-34
Irish drama and the Abbey Theatre, 234-56
Irish fiction, 256-86

Irish Nationalism and Literature NCLC 44: 203-73
 the Celtic element in literature, 203-19
 anti-Irish sentiment and the Celtic response, 219-34
 literary ideals in Ireland, 234-45
 literary expressions, 245-73

Irish Novel, The NCLC 80: 1-130
 overviews and general studies, 3-9
 principal figures, 9-22
 peasant and middle class Irish novelists, 22-76
 aristocratic Irish and Anglo-Irish novelists, 76-129

Israeli Literature TCLC 94: 1-137
 overviews and general studies, 2-18
 Israeli fiction, 18-33
 Israeli poetry, 33-62
 Israeli drama, 62-91
 women and Israeli literature, 91-112
 Arab characters in Israeli literature, 112-36

Italian Futurism See Futurism, Italian

Italian Humanism LC 12: 205-77
 origins and early development, 206-18
 revival of classical letters, 218-23
 humanism and other philosophies, 224-39
 humanism and humanists, 239-46
 the plastic arts, 246-57
 achievement and significance, 258-76

Italian Romanticism NCLC 60: 85-145
 origins and overviews, 86-101
 Italian Romantic theory, 101-25
 the language of Romanticism, 125-45

Jacobean Drama LC 33: 1-37
 the Jacobean worldview: an era of transition, 2-14
 the moral vision of Jacobean drama, 14-22
 Jacobean tragedy, 22-3
 the Jacobean masque, 23-36

Jazz and Literature TCLC 102: 3-124

Jewish-American Fiction TCLC 62: 1-181
 overviews and general studies, 2-24
 major figures, 24-48
 Jewish writers and American life, 48-78
 Jewish characters in American fiction, 78-108
 themes in Jewish-American fiction, 108-43
 Jewish-American women writers, 143-59
 the Holocaust and Jewish-American fiction, 159-81

Jews in Literature TCLC 118: 252-417
 overviews and general studies, 253-97
 representing the Jew in literature, 297-351
 the Holocaust in literature, 351-416

Journals of Lewis and Clark, The NCLC 100: 1-88
 overviews and general studies, 4-30
 journal-keeping methods, 30-46
 Fort Mandan, 46-51
 the Clark journal, 51-65
 the journals as literary texts, 65-87

Kabuki LC 73: 118-232
 overviews and general studies, 120-40
 the development of Kabuki, 140-65
 major works, 165-95
 Kabuki and society, 195-231

Kit-Kat Club, The LC 71: 66-112
 overviews and general studies, 67-88
 major figures, 88-107
 attacks on the Kit-Kat Club, 107-12

Knickerbocker Group, The NCLC 56: 274-341
 overviews and general studies, 276-314
 Knickerbocker periodicals, 314-26
 writers and artists, 326-40

Lake Poets, The NCLC 52: 217-304
 characteristics of the Lake Poets and their works, 218-27
 literary influences and collaborations, 227-66
 defining and developing Romantic ideals, 266-84
 embracing Conservatism, 284-303

Larkin, Philip, Controversy CLC 81: 417-64

Latin American Literature, Twentieth-Century TCLC 58: 111-98
 historical and critical perspectives, 112-36
 the novel, 136-45
 the short story, 145-9
 drama, 149-60
 poetry, 160-7
 the writer and society, 167-86
 Native Americans in Latin American literature, 186-97

Legend of El Dorado, The LC 74: 248-350
 overviews, 249-308
 major explorations for El Dorado, 308-50

The Levellers LC 51: 200-312
 overviews and general studies, 201-29
 principal figures, 230-86
 religion, political philosophy, and pamphleteering, 287-311

Literary Prizes TCLC 122: 130-203
 overviews and general studies, 131-34
 the Nobel Prize in Literature, 135-83
 the Pulitzer Prize, 183-203

Literature and Millenial Lists CLC 119: 431-67
 The Modern Library list, 433
 The Waterstone list, 438-439

Literature of the American Cowboy NCLC 96: 1-60
 overview, 3-20
 cowboy fiction, 20-36
 cowboy poetry and songs, 36-59

Literature of the California Gold Rush NCLC 92: 320-85
 overviews and general studies, 322-24
 early California Gold Rush fiction, 324-44
 Gold Rush folklore and legend, 344-51
 the rise of Western local color, 351-60
 social relations and social change, 360-385

Living Theatre, The DC 16: 154-214

Madness in Nineteenth-Century Literature NCLC 76: 142-284
 overview, 143-54
 autobiography, 154-68
 poetry, 168-215
 fiction, 215-83

Madness in Twentieth-Century Literature TCLC 50: 160-225
 overviews and general studies, 161-71
 madness and the creative process, 171-86
 suicide, 186-91
 madness in American literature, 191-207
 madness in German literature, 207-13
 madness and feminist artists, 213-24

Magic Realism TCLC 110: 80-327
 overviews and general studies, 81-94
 magic realism in African literature, 95-110
 magic realism in American literature, 110-32
 magic realism in Canadian literature, 132-46
 magic realism in European literature, 146-66
 magic realism in Asian literature, 166-79
 magic realism in Latin-American literature, 179-223
 magic realism in Israeli literature and the novels of Salman Rushdie, 223-38
 magic realism in literature written by women, 239-326

The Masque LC 63: 124-265
 development of the masque, 125-62
 sources and structure, 162-220
 race and gender in the masque, 221-64

Medical Writing LC 55: 93-195
 colonial America, 94-110
 enlightenment, 110-24
 medieval writing, 124-40
 sexuality, 140-83
 vernacular, 185-95

Memoirs of Trauma CLC 109: 419-466
 overview, 420
 criticism, 429

Metaphysical Poets LC 24: 356-439
 early definitions, 358-67
 surveys and overviews, 367-92
 cultural and social influences, 392-406
 stylistic and thematic variations, 407-38

Missionaries in the Nineteenth-Century, Literature of NCLC 112: 299-392
 history and development, 300-16
 uses of ethnography, 316-31
 sociopolitical concerns, 331-82
 David Livingstone, 382-91

Modern Essay, The TCLC 58: 199-273
 overview, 200-7
 the essay in the early twentieth century, 207-19
 characteristics of the modern essay, 219-32
 modern essayists, 232-45
 the essay as a literary genre, 245-73

Modern French Literature TCLC 122: 205-359
 overviews and general studies, 207-43
 French theater, 243-77
 gender issues and French women writers, 277-315
 ideology and politics, 315-24
 modern French poetry, 324-41
 resistance literature, 341-58

Modern Irish Literature TCLC 102: 125-321
 overview, 129-44
 dramas, 144-70
 fiction, 170-247
 poetry, 247-321

Modern Japanese Literature TCLC 66: 284-389
 poetry, 285-305
 drama, 305-29
 fiction, 329-61
 western influences, 361-87

Modernism TCLC 70: 165-275
 definitions, 166-184
 Modernism and earlier influences, 184-200
 stylistic and thematic traits, 200-229
 poetry and drama, 229-242
 redefining Modernism, 242-275

Muckraking Movement in American Journalism TCLC 34: 161-242
 development, principles, and major figures, 162-70
 publications, 170-9
 social and political ideas, 179-86
 targets, 186-208
 fiction, 208-19
 decline, 219-29
 impact and accomplishments, 229-40

Multiculturalism in Literature and Education CLC 70: 361-413

Music and Modern Literature TCLC 62: 182-329
 overviews and general studies, 182-211
 musical form/literary form, 211-32
 music in literature, 232-50
 the influence of music on literature, 250-73
 literature and popular music, 273-303
 jazz and poetry, 303-28

Native American Literature CLC 76: 440-76

Natural School, Russian NCLC 24: 205-40
 history and characteristics, 205-25
 contemporary criticism, 225-40

Naturalism NCLC 36: 285-382
 definitions and theories, 286-305
 critical debates on Naturalism, 305-16
 Naturalism in theater, 316-32
 European Naturalism, 332-61
 American Naturalism, 361-72
 the legacy of Naturalism, 372-81

Negritude TCLC 50: 226-361
 origins and evolution, 227-56
 definitions, 256-91
 Negritude in literature, 291-343
 Negritude reconsidered, 343-58

New Criticism TCLC 34: 243-318
 development and ideas, 244-70
 debate and defense, 270-99
 influence and legacy, 299-315

The New World in Renaissance Literature LC 31: 1-51
 overview, 1-18
 utopia vs. terror, 18-31
 explorers and Native Americans, 31-51

New York Intellectuals and *Partisan Review* TCLC 30: 117-98
 development and major figures, 118-28
 influence of Judaism, 128-39
 Partisan Review, 139-57
 literary philosophy and practice, 157-75
 political philosophy, 175-87
 achievement and significance, 187-97

The New Yorker TCLC 58: 274-357
 overviews and general studies, 274-95
 major figures, 295-304
 New Yorker style, 304-33
 fiction, journalism, and humor at *The New Yorker*, 333-48
 the new *New Yorker*, 348-56

Newgate Novel NCLC 24: 166-204
 development of Newgate literature, 166-73
 Newgate Calendar, 173-7
 Newgate fiction, 177-95
 Newgate drama, 195-204

Nigerian Literature of the Twentieth Century TCLC 30: 199-265
 surveys of, 199-227
 English language and African life, 227-45
 politics and the Nigerian writer, 245-54
 Nigerian writers and society, 255-62

Nihilism and Literature TCLC 110: 328-93
 overviews and general studies, 328-44
 European and Russian nihilism, 344-73
 nihilism in the works of Albert Camus, Franz Kafka, and John Barth, 373-92

Nineteenth-Century Captivity Narratives NCLC 80:131-218
 overview, 132-37
 the political significance of captivity narratives, 137-67
 images of gender, 167-96
 moral instruction, 197-217

Nineteenth-Century Euro-American Literary Representations of Native Americans NCLC 104: 132-264
 overviews and general studies, 134-53
 Native American history, 153-72
 the Indians of the Northeast, 172-93
 the Indians of the Southeast, 193-212
 the Indians of the West, 212-27
 Indian-hater fiction, 227-43
 the Indian as exhibit, 243-63

Nineteenth-Century Native American Autobiography NCLC 64: 262-389
 overview, 263-8
 problems of authorship, 268-81
 the evolution of Native American autobiography, 281-304
 political issues, 304-15
 gender and autobiography, 316-62
 autobiographical works during the turn of the century, 362-88

Norse Mythology CMLC 26: 321-85
 history and mythological tradition, 322-44
 Eddic poetry, 344-74
 Norse mythology and other traditions, 374-85

Northern Humanism LC 16: 281-356
 background, 282-305
 precursor of the Reformation, 305-14
 the Brethren of the Common Life, the Devotio Moderna, and education, 314-40
 the impact of printing, 340-56

Novel of Manners, The NCLC 56: 342-96
 social and political order, 343-53
 domestic order, 353-73
 depictions of gender, 373-83
 the American novel of manners, 383-95

Novels of the Ming and Early Ch'ing Dynasties LC 76: 213-356
 overviews and historical development, 214-45
 major works—overview, 245-85
 genre studies, 285-325
 cultural and social themes, 325-55

Nuclear Literature: Writings and Criticism in the Nuclear Age TCLC 46: 288-390
 overviews and general studies, 290-301
 fiction, 301-35
 poetry, 335-8
 nuclear war in Russo-Japanese literature, 338-55
 nuclear war and women writers, 355-67
 the nuclear referent and literary criticism, 367-88

Occultism in Modern Literature TCLC 50: 362-406
 influence of occultism on literature, 363-72
 occultism, literature, and society, 372-87
 fiction, 387-96
 drama, 396-405

Opium and the Nineteenth-Century Literary Imagination NCLC 20:250-301
 original sources, 250-62
 historical background, 262-71
 and literary society, 271-9
 and literary creativity, 279-300

Orientalism NCLC 96: 149-364
 overviews and general studies, 150-98
 Orientalism and imperialism, 198-229
 Orientalism and gender, 229-59
 Orientalism and the nineteenth-century novel, 259-321
 Orientalism in nineteenth-century poetry, 321-63

The Oxford Movement NCLC 72: 1-197
 overviews and general studies, 2-24
 background, 24-59
 and education, 59-69
 religious responses, 69-128
 literary aspects, 128-178
 political implications, 178-196

The Parnassian Movement NCLC 72: 198-241
 overviews and general studies, 199-231
 and epic form, 231-38
 and positivism, 238-41

Pastoral Literature of the English Renaissance LC 59: 171-282
 overviews and general studies, 172-214
 principal figures of the Elizabethan period, 214-33
 principal figures of the later Renaissance, 233-50
 pastoral drama, 250-81

Periodicals, Nineteenth-Century British NCLC 24: 100-65
 overviews and general studies, 100-30
 in the Romantic Age, 130-41
 in the Victorian era, 142-54
 and the reviewer, 154-64

Plath, Sylvia, and the Nature of Biography CLC 86: 433-62
 the nature of biography, 433-52
 reviews of *The Silent Woman*, 452-61

Political Theory from the 15th to the 18th Century LC 36: 1-55
 overview, 1-26
 natural law, 26-42
 empiricism, 42-55

Polish Romanticism NCLC 52: 305-71
 overviews and general studies, 306-26
 major figures, 326-40
 Polish Romantic drama, 340-62
 influences, 362-71

Politics and Literature TCLC 94: 138-61
 overviews and general studies, 139-96
 Europe, 196-226
 Latin America, 226-48
 Africa and the Caribbean, 248-60

Popular Literature TCLC 70: 279-382
 overviews and general studies, 280-324
 "formula" fiction, 324-336
 readers of popular literature, 336-351
 evolution of popular literature, 351-382

The Portrayal of Jews in Nineteenth-Century English Literature NCLC 72: 242-368
 overviews and general studies, 244-77
 Anglo-Jewish novels, 277-303
 depictions by non-Jewish writers, 303-44
 Hebraism versus Hellenism, 344-67

The Portrayal of Mormonism NCLC 96: 61-148
 overview, 63-72
 early Mormon literature, 72-100
 Mormon periodicals and journals, 100-10
 women writers, 110-22
 Mormonism and nineteenth-century literature, 122-42
 Mormon poetry, 142-47

Postcolonialism TCLC 114: 134-239
 overviews and general studies, 135-153
 African postcolonial writing, 153-72
 Asian/Pacific literature, 172-78
 postcolonial literary theory, 178-213
 postcolonial women's writing, 213-38

Postmodernism TCLC 90:125-307
 overview, 126-166
 criticism, 166-224
 fiction, 224-282
 poetry, 282-300
 drama, 300-307

Pre-Raphaelite Movement NCLC 20: 302-401
 overview, 302-4
 genesis, 304-12
 Germ and *Oxford and Cambridge Magazine*, 312-20
 Robert Buchanan and the "Fleshly School of Poetry," 320-31

satires and parodies, 331-4
surveys, 334-51
aesthetics, 351-75
sister arts of poetry and painting, 375-94
influence, 394-9

Pre-romanticism LC 40: 1-56
overviews and general studies, 2-14
defining the period, 14-23
new directions in poetry and prose, 23-45
the focus on the self, 45-56

Pre-Socratic Philosophy CMLC 22: 1-56
overviews and general studies, 3-24
the Ionians and the Pythagoreans, 25-35
Heraclitus, the Eleatics, and the Atomists, 36-47
the Sophists, 47-55

Protestant Reformation, Literature of the LC 37: 1-83
overviews and general studies, 1-49
humanism and scholasticism, 49-69
the reformation and literature, 69-82

Psychoanalysis and Literature TCLC 38: 227-338
overviews and general studies, 227-46
Freud on literature, 246-51
psychoanalytic views of the literary process, 251-61
psychoanalytic theories of response to literature, 261-88
psychoanalysis and literary criticism, 288-312
psychoanalysis as literature/literature as psychoanalysis, 313-34

The Quarrel between the Ancients and the Moderns LC 63: 266-381
overviews and general studies, 267-301
Renaissance origins, 301-32
Quarrel between the Ancients and the Moderns in France, 332-58
Battle of the Books in England, 358-80

Rap Music CLC 76: 477-50

Renaissance Natural Philosophy LC 27: 201-87
cosmology, 201-28
astrology, 228-54
magic, 254-86

Representations of the Devil in Nineteenth-Century Literature NCLC 100: 89-223
overviews and general studies, 90-115
the Devil in American fiction, 116-43
English Romanticism: the satanic school, 143-89
Luciferian discourse in European literature, 189-222

Restoration Drama LC 21: 184-275
general overviews and general studies, 185-230
Jeremy Collier stage controversy, 230-9
other critical interpretations, 240-75

Revenge Tragedy LC 71: 113-242
overviews and general studies, 113-51
Elizabethan attitudes toward revenge, 151-88
the morality of revenge, 188-216
reminders and remembrance, 217-41

Revising the Literary Canon CLC 81: 465-509

Revising the Literary Canon TCLC 114: 240-84
overviews and general studies, 241-85
canon change in American literature, 285-339
gender and the literary canon, 339-59
minority and third-world literature and the canon, 359-84

Revolutionary Astronomers LC 51: 314-65
overviews and general studies, 316-25
principal figures, 325-51
Revolutionary astronomical models, 352-64

Robin Hood, Legend of LC 19: 205-58
origins and development of the Robin Hood legend, 206-20
representations of Robin Hood, 220-44
Robin Hood as hero, 244-56

Rushdie, Salman, *Satanic Verses* **Controversy** CLC 55: 214-63; 59:404-56

Russian Nihilism NCLC 28: 403-47
definitions and overviews, 404-17
women and Nihilism, 417-27
literature as reform: the Civic Critics, 427-33
Nihilism and the Russian novel: Turgenev and Dostoevsky, 433-47

Russian Thaw TCLC 26: 189-247
literary history of the period, 190-206
theoretical debate of socialist realism, 206-11
Novy Mir, 211-7
Literary Moscow, 217-24
Pasternak, *Zhivago,* and the Nobel prize, 224-7
poetry of liberation, 228-31
Brodsky trial and the end of the Thaw, 231-6
achievement and influence, 236-46

Salem Witch Trials LC 38: 1-145
overviews and general studies, 2-30
historical background, 30-65
judicial background, 65-78
the search for causes, 78-115
the role of women in the trials, 115-44

Salinger, J. D., Controversy Surrounding *In Search of J. D. Salinger* CLC 55: 325-44

Science and Modern Literature TCLC 90: 308-419
overviews and general studies, 295-333
fiction, 333-95
poetry, 395-405
drama, 405-19

Science in Nineteenth-Century Literature NCLC 100: 224-366
overviews and general studies, 225-65
major figures, 265-336
sociopolitical concerns, 336-65

Science Fiction, Nineteenth-Century NCLC 24: 241-306
background, 242-50
definitions of the genre, 251-56
representative works and writers, 256-75
themes and conventions, 276-305

Scottish Chaucerians LC 20: 363-412

Scottish Poetry, Eighteenth-Century LC 29: 95-167
overviews and general studies, 96-114
the Scottish Augustans, 114-28
the Scots Vernacular Revival, 132-63
Scottish poetry after Burns, 163-66

Sea in Literature, The TCLC 82: 72-191
drama, 73-9
poetry, 79-119
fiction, 119-91

Sea in Nineteenth-Century English and American Literature, The NCLC 104: 265-362
overviews and general studies, 267-306
major figures in American sea fiction—Cooper and Melville, 306-29
American sea poetry and short stories, 329-45
English sea literature, 345-61

Sensation Novel, The NCLC 80: 219-330
overviews and general studies, 221-46
principal figures, 246-62
nineteenth-century reaction, 262-91
feminist criticism, 291-329

Sentimental Novel, The NCLC 60: 146-245
overviews and general studies, 147-58
the politics of domestic fiction, 158-79
a literature of resistance and repression, 179-212
the reception of sentimental fiction, 213-44

Sex and Literature TCLC 82: 192-434
overviews and general studies, 193-216
drama, 216-63
poetry, 263-87
fiction, 287-431

Sherlock Holmes Centenary TCLC 26: 248-310
Doyle's life and the composition of the Holmes stories, 248-59
life and character of Holmes, 259-78
method, 278-79
Holmes and the Victorian world, 279-92
Sherlockian scholarship, 292-301
Doyle and the development of the detective story, 301-07
Holmes's continuing popularity, 307-09

The Silver Fork Novel NCLC 88: 58-140
criticism, 59-139

Slave Narratives, American NCLC 20: 1-91
background, 2-9
overviews and general studies, 9-24
contemporary responses, 24-7
language, theme, and technique, 27-70
historical authenticity, 70-5
antecedents, 75-83
role in development of Black American literature, 83-8

The Slave Trade in British and American Literature LC 59: 283-369
overviews and general studies, 284-91
depictions by white writers, 291-331
depictions by former slaves, 331-67

Social Conduct Literature LC 55: 196-298
overviews and general studies, 196-223
prescriptive ideology in other literary forms, 223-38
role of the press, 238-63
impact of conduct literature, 263-87
conduct literature and the perception of women, 287-96
women writing for women, 296-98

Socialism NCLC 88: 141-237
origins, 142-54
French socialism, 154-83
Anglo-American socialism, 183-205
Socialist-Feminism, 205-36

Southern Literature of the Reconstruction NCLC 108: 289-369
overview, 290-91
reconstruction literature: the consequences of war, 291-321
old south to new: continuities in southern culture, 321-68

Spanish Civil War Literature TCLC 26: 311-85
topics in, 312-33
British and American literature, 333-59
French literature, 359-62
Spanish literature, 362-73

German literature, 373-75
political idealism and war literature, 375-83

Spanish Golden Age Literature LC 23: 262-332
overviews and general studies, 263-81
verse drama, 281-304
prose fiction, 304-19
lyric poetry, 319-31

Spasmodic School of Poetry NCLC 24: 307-52
history and major figures, 307-21
the Spasmodics on poetry, 321-7
Firmilian and critical disfavor, 327-39
theme and technique, 339-47
influence, 347-51

Sports in Literature TCLC 86: 294-445
overviews and general studies, 295-324
major writers and works, 324-402
sports, literature, and social issues, 402-45

Steinbeck, John, Fiftieth Anniversary of *The Grapes of Wrath* CLC 59: 311-54

Sturm und Drang NCLC 40: 196-276
definitions, 197-238
poetry and poetics, 238-58
drama, 258-75

Supernatural Fiction in the Nineteenth Century NCLC 32: 207-87
major figures and influences, 208-35
the Victorian ghost story, 236-54
the influence of science and occultism, 254-66
supernatural fiction and society, 266-86

Supernatural Fiction, Modern TCLC 30: 59-116
evolution and varieties, 60-74
"decline" of the ghost story, 74-86
as a literary genre, 86-92
technique, 92-101
nature and appeal, 101-15

Surrealism TCLC 30: 334-406
history and formative influences, 335-43
manifestos, 343-54
philosophic, aesthetic, and political principles, 354-75
poetry, 375-81
novel, 381-6
drama, 386-92
film, 392-8
painting and sculpture, 398-403
achievement, 403-5

Symbolism, Russian TCLC 30: 266-333
doctrines and major figures, 267-92
theories, 293-8
and French Symbolism, 298-310
themes in poetry, 310-4
theater, 314-20
and the fine arts, 320-32

Symbolist Movement, French NCLC 20: 169-249
background and characteristics, 170-86
principles, 186-91
attacked and defended, 191-7
influences and predecessors, 197-211
and Decadence, 211-6
theater, 216-26
prose, 226-33
decline and influence, 233-47

Television and Literature TCLC 78: 283-426
television and literacy, 283-98
reading vs. watching, 298-341
adaptations, 341-62
literary genres and television, 362-90

television genres and literature, 390-410
children's literature/children's television, 410-25

Theater of the Absurd TCLC 38: 339-415
"The Theater of the Absurd," 340-7
major plays and playwrights, 347-58
and the concept of the absurd, 358-86
theatrical techniques, 386-94
predecessors of, 394-402
influence of, 402-13

Tin Pan Alley See **American Popular Song, Golden Age of**

Tobacco Culture LC 55: 299-366
social and economic attitudes toward tobacco, 299-344
tobacco trade between the old world and the new world, 344-55
tobacco smuggling in Great Britain, 355-66

Transcendentalism, American NCLC 24: 1-99
overviews and general studies, 3-23
contemporary documents, 23-41
theological aspects of, 42-52
and social issues, 52-74
literature of, 74-96

Travel Writing in the Nineteenth Century NCLC 44: 274-392
the European grand tour, 275-303
the Orient, 303-47
North America, 347-91

Travel Writing in the Twentieth Century TCLC 30: 407-56
conventions and traditions, 407-27
and fiction writing, 427-43
comparative essays on travel writers, 443-54

Tristan and Isolde Legend CMLC 42: 311-404

True-Crime Literature CLC 99: 333-433
history and analysis, 334-407
reviews of true-crime publications, 407-23
writing instruction, 424-29
author profiles, 429-33

Ulysses and the Process of Textual Reconstruction TCLC 26: 386-416
evaluations of the new *Ulysses,* 386-94
editorial principles and procedures, 394-401
theoretical issues, 401-16

Utilitarianism NCLC 84: 272-340
J. S. Mill's Utilitarianism: liberty, equality, justice, 273-313
Jeremy Bentham's Utilitarianism: the science of happiness, 313-39

Utopianism NCLC 88: 238-346
overviews: Utopian literature, 239-59
Utopianism in American literature, 259-99
Utopianism in British literature, 299-311
Utopianism and Feminism, 311-45

Utopian Literature, Nineteenth-Century NCLC 24: 353-473
definitions, 354-74
overviews and general studies, 374-88
theory, 388-408
communities, 409-26
fiction, 426-53
women and fiction, 454-71

Utopian Literature, Renaissance LC 32: 1-63
overviews and general studies, 2-25
classical background, 25-33
utopia and the social contract, 33-9
origins in mythology, 39-48

utopia and the Renaissance country house, 48-52
influence of millenarianism, 52-62

Vampire in Literature TCLC 46: 391-454
origins and evolution, 392-412
social and psychological perspectives, 413-44
vampire fiction and science fiction, 445-53

Vernacular Bibles LC 67: 214-388
overviews and general studies, 215-59
the English Bible, 259-355
the German Bible, 355-88

Victorian Autobiography NCLC 40: 277-363
development and major characteristics, 278-88
themes and techniques, 289-313
the autobiographical tendency in Victorian prose and poetry, 313-47
Victorian women's autobiographies, 347-62

Victorian Fantasy Literature NCLC 60: 246-384
overviews and general studies, 247-91
major figures, 292-366
women in Victorian fantasy literature, 366-83

Victorian Hellenism NCLC 68: 251-376
overviews and general studies, 252-78
the meanings of Hellenism, 278-335
the literary influence, 335-75

Victorian Novel NCLC 32: 288-454
development and major characteristics, 290-310
themes and techniques, 310-58
social criticism in the Victorian novel, 359-97
urban and rural life in the Victorian novel, 397-406
women in the Victorian novel, 406-25
Mudie's Circulating Library, 425-34
the late-Victorian novel, 434-51

Vietnamese Literature TCLC 102: 322-386

Vietnam War in Literature and Film CLC 91: 383-437
overview, 384-8
prose, 388-412
film and drama, 412-24
poetry, 424-35

Violence in Literature TCLC 98: 235-358
overviews and general studies, 236-74
violence in the works of modern authors, 274-358

Vorticism TCLC 62: 330-426
Wyndham Lewis and Vorticism, 330-8
characteristics and principles of Vorticism, 338-65
Lewis and Pound, 365-82
Vorticist writing, 382-416
Vorticist painting, 416-26

Well-Made Play, The NCLC 80: 331-370
overviews and general studies, 332-45
Scribe's style, 345-56
the influence of the well-made play, 356-69

Women's Autobiography, Nineteenth Century NCLC 76: 285-368
overviews and general studies, 287-300
autobiographies concerned with religious and political issues, 300-15
autobiographies by women of color, 315-38
autobiographies by women pioneers, 338-51
autobiographies by women of letters, 351-68

Women's Diaries, Nineteenth-Century NCLC 48: 308-54
    overview, 308-13
    diary as history, 314-25
    sociology of diaries, 325-34
    diaries as psychological scholarship, 334-43
    diary as autobiography, 343-8
    diary as literature, 348-53

Women in Modern Literature TCLC 94: 262-425
    overviews and general studies, 263-86
    American literature, 286-304
    other national literatures, 304-33
    fiction, 333-94
    poetry, 394-407
    drama, 407-24

Women Writers, Seventeenth-Century LC 30: 2-58
    overview, 2-15
    women and education, 15-9
    women and autobiography, 19-31
    women's diaries, 31-9
    early feminists, 39-58

World War I Literature TCLC 34: 392-486
    overview, 393-403
    English, 403-27
    German, 427-50
    American, 450-66
    French, 466-74
    and modern history, 474-82

Yellow Journalism NCLC 36: 383-456
    overviews and general studies, 384-96
    major figures, 396-413

Young Playwrights Festival
    1988 CLC 55: 376-81
    1989 CLC 59: 398-403
    1990 CLC 65: 444-8

TCLC Cumulative Nationality Index

AMERICAN

Adams, Andy **56**
Adams, Brooks **80**
Adams, Henry (Brooks) **4, 52**
Addams, Jane **76**
Agee, James (Rufus) **1, 19**
Allen, Fred **87**
Anderson, Maxwell **2**
Anderson, Sherwood **1, 10, 24**
Anthony, Susan B(rownell) **84**
Atherton, Gertrude (Franklin Horn) **2**
Austin, Mary (Hunter) **25**
Baker, Ray Stannard **47**
Baker, Carlos (Heard) **119**
Bambara, Toni Cade **116**
Barry, Philip **11**
Baum, L(yman) Frank **7**
Beard, Charles A(ustin) **15**
Becker, Carl (Lotus) **63**
Belasco, David **3**
Bell, James Madison **43**
Benchley, Robert (Charles) **1, 55**
Benedict, Ruth (Fulton) **60**
Benét, Stephen Vincent **7**
Benét, William Rose **28**
Bierce, Ambrose (Gwinett) **1, 7, 44**
Biggers, Earl Derr **65**
Bishop, Elizabeth **121**
Bishop, John Peale **103**
Black Elk **33**
Boas, Franz **56**
Bodenheim, Maxwell **44**
Bok, Edward W. **101**
Bourne, Randolph S(illiman) **16**
Boyd, James **115**
Boyd, Thomas (Alexander) **111**
Bradford, Gamaliel **36**
Brennan, Christopher John **17**
Bromfield, Louis (Brucker) **11**
Broun, Heywood **104**
Bryan, William Jennings **99**
Burroughs, Edgar Rice **2, 32**
Burroughs, William S(eward) **121**
Cabell, James Branch **6**
Cable, George Washington **4**
Cahan, Abraham **71**
Caldwell, Erskine (Preston) **117**
Cardozo, Benjamin N(athan) **65**
Carnegie, Dale **53**
Cather, Willa (Sibert) **1, 11, 31, 99**
Chambers, Robert W(illiam) **41**
Chandler, Raymond (Thornton) **1, 7**
Chapman, John Jay **7**
Chesnutt, Charles W(addell) **5, 39**
Childress, Alice **116**
Cobb, Irvin S(hrewsbury) **77**
Coffin, Robert P(eter) Tristram **95**
Cohan, George M(ichael) **60**
Comstock, Anthony **13**
Cotter, Joseph Seamon Sr. **28**
Cram, Ralph Adams **45**
Crane, (Harold) Hart **2, 5, 80**

Crane, Stephen (Townley) **11, 17, 32**
Crawford, F(rancis) Marion **10**
Crothers, Rachel **19**
Cullen, Countée **4, 37**
Darrow, Clarence (Seward) **81**
Davis, Rebecca (Blaine) Harding **6**
Davis, Richard Harding **24**
Day, Clarence (Shepard Jr.) **25**
Dent, Lester **72**
De Voto, Bernard (Augustine) **29**
Dewey, John **95**
Dreiser, Theodore (Herman Albert) **10, 18, 35, 83**
Dulles, John Foster **72**
Dunbar, Paul Laurence **2, 12**
Duncan, Isadora **68**
Dunne, Finley Peter **28**
Eastman, Charles A(lexander) **55**
Eddy, Mary (Ann Morse) Baker **71**
Einstein, Albert **65**
Erskine, John **84**
Faust, Frederick (Schiller) **49**
Fenollosa, Ernest (Francisco) **91**
Fields, W. C. **80**
Fisher, Dorothy (Frances) Canfield **87**
Fisher, Rudolph **11**
Fitzgerald, F(rancis) Scott (Key) **1, 6, 14, 28, 55**
Fitzgerald, Zelda (Sayre) **52**
Fletcher, John Gould **35**
Foote, Mary Hallock **108**
Ford, Henry **73**
Forten, Charlotte L. **16**
Freeman, Douglas Southall **11**
Freeman, Mary E(leanor) Wilkins **9**
Fuller, Henry Blake **103**
Futrelle, Jacques **19**
Gale, Zona **7**
Garland, (Hannibal) Hamlin **3**
Gilman, Charlotte (Anna) Perkins (Stetson) **9, 37, 117**
Ginsberg, Allen **120**
Glasgow, Ellen (Anderson Gholson) **2, 7**
Glaspell, Susan **55**
Goldman, Emma **13**
Green, Anna Katharine **63**
Grey, Zane **6**
Griffith, D(avid Lewelyn) W(ark) **68**
Griggs, Sutton (Elbert) **77**
Guest, Edgar A(lbert) **95**
Guiney, Louise Imogen **41**
Hall, James Norman **23**
Handy, W(illiam) C(hristopher) **97**
Harper, Frances Ellen Watkins **14**
Harris, Joel Chandler **2**
Harte, (Francis) Bret(t) **1, 25**
Hartmann, Sadakichi **73**
Hatteras, Owen **18**
Hawthorne, Julian **25**
Hearn, (Patricio) Lafcadio (Tessima Carlos) **9**
Hecht, Ben **101**
Hellman, Lillian (Florence) **119**
Hemingway, Ernest (Miller) **115**

Henry, O. **1, 19**
Hergesheimer, Joseph **11**
Heyward, (Edwin) DuBose **59**
Higginson, Thomas Wentworth **36**
Holley, Marietta **99**
Holly, Buddy **65**
Holmes, Oliver Wendell Jr. **77**
Hopkins, Pauline Elizabeth **28**
Horney, Karen (Clementine Theodore Danielsen) **71**
Howard, Robert E(rvin) **8**
Howe, Julia Ward **21**
Howells, William Dean **7, 17, 41**
Huneker, James Gibbons **65**
Hurston, Zora Neale **121**
Ince, Thomas H. **89**
James, Henry **2, 11, 24, 40, 47, 64**
James, William **15, 32**
Jewett, (Theodora) Sarah Orne **1, 22**
Johnson, James Weldon **3, 19**
Johnson, Robert **69**
Kerouac, Jack **117**
Kinsey, Alfred C(harles) **91**
Kirk, Russell (Amos) **119**
Kornbluth, C(yril) M. **8**
Korzybski, Alfred (Habdank Skarbek) **61**
Kubrick, Stanley **112**
Kuttner, Henry **10**
Lardner, Ring(gold) W(ilmer) **2, 14**
Lewis, (Harry) Sinclair **4, 13, 23, 39**
Lewisohn, Ludwig **19**
Lewton, Val **76**
Lindsay, (Nicholas) Vachel **17**
Locke, Alain (Le Roy) **43**
Lockridge, Ross (Franklin) Jr. **111**
London, Jack **9, 15, 39**
Lovecraft, H(oward) P(hillips) **4, 22**
Lowell, Amy **1, 8**
Mankiewicz, Herman (Jacob) **85**
March, William **96**
Markham, Edwin **47**
Marquis, Don(ald Robert Perry) **7**
Masters, Edgar Lee **2, 25**
Matthews, (James) Brander **95**
Matthiessen, F(rancis) O(tto) **100**
McAlmon, Robert (Menzies) **97**
McCoy, Horace (Stanley) **28**
Mead, George Herbert **89**
Mencken, H(enry) L(ouis) **13**
Micheaux, Oscar (Devereaux) **76**
Millay, Edna St. Vincent **4, 49**
Mitchell, Margaret (Munnerlyn) **11**
Mitchell, S(ilas) Weir **36**
Mitchell, William **81**
Monroe, Harriet **12**
Moody, William Vaughan **105**
Morley, Christopher (Darlington) **87**
Morris, Wright **107**
Muir, John **28**
Nash, (Fredric) Ogden **109**
Nathan, George Jean **18**
Neumann, Alfred **100**
Nisbet, Robert A(lexander) **117**

Nordhoff, Charles (Bernard) 23
Norris, (Benjamin) Frank(lin Jr.) 24
O'Neill, Eugene (Gladstone) 1, 6, 27, 49
Oppen, George 107
Osbourne, Lloyd 93
Oskison, John Milton 35
Park, Robert E(zra) 73
Patton, George S(mith) Jr. 79
Peirce, Charles Sanders 81
Percy, William Alexander 84
Petry, Ann (Lane) 112
Phelps, Elizabeth Stuart 113
Phillips, David Graham 44
Post, Melville Davisson 39
Pulitzer, Joseph 76
Pyle, Ernie 75
Pyle, Howard 81
Rawlings, Marjorie Kinnan 4
Reed, John (Silas) 9
Reich, Wilhelm 57
Remington, Frederic 89
Rhodes, Eugene Manlove 53
Riggs, (Rolla) Lynn 56
Riis, Jacob A(ugust) 80
Riley, James Whitcomb 51
Rinehart, Mary Roberts 52
Roberts, Elizabeth Madox 68
Roberts, Kenneth (Lewis) 23
Robinson, Edwin Arlington 5, 101
Rogers, Will(iam Penn Adair) 8, 71
Roosevelt, Franklin Delano 93
Roosevelt, Theodore 69
Rourke, Constance (Mayfield) 12
Runyon, (Alfred) Damon 10
Saltus, Edgar (Everton) 8
Santayana, George 40
Sapir, Edward 108
Schoenberg, Arnold Franz Walter 75
Sherwood, Robert E(mmet) 3
Slesinger, Tess 10
Stanton, Elizabeth Cady 73
Steffens, (Joseph) Lincoln 20
Stein, Gertrude 1, 6, 28, 48
Sterling, George 20
Stevens, Wallace 3, 12, 45
Stockton, Frank R. 47
Stroheim, Erich von 71
Strunk, William Jr. 92
Sturges, Preston 48
Tarbell, Ida M(inerva) 40
Tarkington, (Newton) Booth 9
Taylor, Frederick Winslow 76
Teasdale, Sara 4
Tesla, Nikola 88
Thomas, Augustus 97
Thomas, M. Carey 89
Thorndike, Edward L(ee) 107
Thurman, Wallace (Henry) 6
Torrence, Ridgely 97
Twain, Mark 6, 12, 19, 36, 48, 59
Van Doren, Carl (Clinton) 18
Veblen, Thorstein B(unde) 31
Washington, Booker T(aliaferro) 10
Wells, Carolyn 35
West, Dorothy 108
West, Nathanael 1, 14, 44
Whale, James 63
Wharton, Edith (Newbold Jones) 3, 9, 27, 53
White, Walter F(rancis) 15
Williams, Ben Ames 89
Williams, Hank 81
Wilson, (Thomas) Woodrow 79
Wirth, Louis 92
Wister, Owen 21
Wolfe, Thomas (Clayton) 4, 13, 29, 61
Woodberry, George Edward 73
Woollcott, Alexander (Humphreys) 5
Wright, Frank Lloyd 95
Wylie, Elinor (Morton Hoyt) 8

ARGENTINIAN

Arlt, Roberto (Godofredo Christophersen) 29
Borges, Jorge Luis 109
Güiraldes, Ricardo (Guillermo) 39
Hudson, W(illiam) H(enry) 29
Lugones, Leopoldo 15
Storni, Alfonsina 5

AUSTRALIAN

Baynton, Barbara 57
Franklin, (Stella Maria Sarah) Miles (Lampe) 7
Furphy, Joseph 25
Ingamells, Rex 35
Lawson, Henry (Archibald Hertzberg) 27
Paterson, A(ndrew) B(arton) 32
Warung, Price 45

AUSTRIAN

Beer-Hofmann, Richard 60
Broch, Hermann 20
Brod, Max 115
Freud, Sigmund 52
Hayek, F(riedrich) A(ugust von) 109
Hofmannsthal, Hugo von 11
Kafka, Franz 2, 6, 13, 29, 47, 53, 112
Kraus, Karl 5
Kubin, Alfred (Leopold Isidor) 23
Meyrink, Gustav 21
Musil, Robert (Edler von) 12, 68
Perutz, Leo(pold) 60
Rank, Otto 115
Roth, (Moses) Joseph 33
Schnitzler, Arthur 4
Steiner, Rudolf 13
Stroheim, Erich von 71
Trakl, Georg 5
Weininger, Otto 84
Werfel, Franz (Viktor) 8
Zweig, Stefan 17

BELGIAN

Bosschere, Jean de 19
Lemonnier, (Antoine Louis) Camille 22
Maeterlinck, Maurice 3
Sarton, May (Eleanor) 120
van Ostaijen, Paul 33
Verhaeren, Émile (Adolphe Gustave) 12

BRAZILIAN

Cunha, Euclides (Rodrigues Pimenta) da 24
Lima Barreto, Afonso Henrique de 23
Machado de Assis, Joaquim Maria 10
Ramos, Graciliano 32

BULGARIAN

Vazov, Ivan (Minchov) 25

CANADIAN

Campbell, Wilfred 9
Carman, (William) Bliss 7
Carr, Emily 32
Connor, Ralph 31
Drummond, William Henry 25
Duncan, Sara Jeannette 60
Garneau, (Hector de) Saint-Denys 13
Innis, Harold Adams 77
Knister, Raymond 56
Leacock, Stephen (Butler) 2
Lewis, (Percy) Wyndham 2, 9, 104
McCrae, John 12
Montgomery, L(ucy) M(aud) 51
Nelligan, Emile 14
Pickthall, Marjorie L(owry) C(hristie) 21
Roberts, Charles G(eorge) D(ouglas) 8
Scott, Duncan Campbell 6
Service, Robert W(illiam) 15
Seton, Ernest (Evan) Thompson 31
Stringer, Arthur 37
Wetherald, Agnes Ethelwyn 81

CHILEAN

Godoy Alcayaga, Lucila 2
Huidobro Fernandez, Vicente Garcia 31
Prado (Calvo), Pedro 75

CHINESE

Liu, E. 15
Lu Hsun 3
Su Man-shu 24
Wen I-to 28

COLOMBIAN

Rivera, José Eustasio 35

CZECH

Brod, Max 115
Chapek, Karel 6, 37
Freud, Sigmund 52
Hasek, Jaroslav (Matej Frantisek) 4
Kafka, Franz 2, 6, 13, 29, 47, 53, 112
Nezval, Vitezslav 44

DANISH

Brandes, Georg (Morris Cohen) 10
Hansen, Martin A(lfred) 32
Jensen, Johannes V. 41
Nexo, Martin Andersen 43
Pontoppidan, Henrik 29

DUTCH

Bok, Edward W. 101
Couperus, Louis (Marie Anne) 15
Heijermans, Herman 24
Hillesum, Etty 49
van Schendel, Arthur(-Francois-Émile) 56

ENGLISH

Alexander, Samuel 77
Barbellion, W. N. P. 24
Baring, Maurice 8
Baring-Gould, Sabine 88
Beerbohm, (Henry) Max(imilian) 1, 24
Bell, Gertrude (Margaret Lowthian) 67
Belloc, (Joseph) Hilaire (Pierre Sebastien Rene Swanton) 7, 18
Bennett, (Enoch) Arnold 5, 20
Benson, E(dward) F(rederic) 27
Benson, Stella 17
Bentley, E(dmund) C(lerihew) 12
Beresford, J(ohn) D(avys) 81
Besant, Annie (Wood) 9
Blackmore, R(ichard) D(oddridge) 27
Blackwood, Algernon (Henry) 5
Bottomley, Gordon 107
Braddon, Mary Elizabeth 111
Bramah, Ernest 72
Bridges, Robert (Seymour) 1
Brooke, Rupert (Chawner) 2, 7
Buchanan, Robert 107
Burke, Thomas 63
Butler, Samuel 1, 33
Butts, Mary 77
Byron, Robert 67
Caine, Hall 97
Carpenter, Edward 88
Chesterton, G(ilbert) K(eith) 1, 6, 64
Childers, (Robert) Erskine 65
Churchill, Winston (Leonard Spencer) 113
Coleridge, Mary E(lizabeth) 73
Collingwood, R(obin) G(eorge) 67
Conrad, Joseph 1, 6, 13, 25, 43, 57
Coppard, A(lfred) E(dgar) 5
Corelli, Marie 51
Crofts, Freeman Wills 55
Crowley, Aleister 7
Dale, Colin 18

Davies, William Henry 5
Delafield, E. M. 61
de la Mare, Walter (John) 4, 53
Dobson, Austin 79
Doughty, Charles M(ontagu) 27
Douglas, Keith (Castellain) 40
Dowson, Ernest (Christopher) 4
Doyle, Arthur Conan 7
Drinkwater, John 57
Dunsany 2, 59
Eddison, E(ric) R(ucker) 15
Elaine 18
Elizabeth 41
Ellis, (Henry) Havelock 14
Firbank, (Arthur Annesley) Ronald 1
Flecker, (Herman) James Elroy 43
Ford, Ford Madox 1, 15, 39, 57
Freeman, R(ichard) Austin 21
Galsworthy, John 1, 45
Gilbert, W(illiam) S(chwenck) 3
Gill, Eric 85
Gissing, George (Robert) 3, 24, 47
Glyn, Elinor 72
Gosse, Edmund (William) 28
Grahame, Kenneth 64
Granville-Barker, Harley 2
Gray, John (Henry) 19
Gurney, Ivor (Bertie) 33
Haggard, H(enry) Rider 11
Hall, (Marguerite) Radclyffe 12
Hardy, Thomas 4, 10, 18, 32, 48, 53, 72
Henley, William Ernest 8
Hilton, James 21
Hodgson, William Hope 13
Hope, Anthony 83
Housman, A(lfred) E(dward) 1, 10
Housman, Laurence 7
Hudson, W(illiam) H(enry) 29
Hulme, T(homas) E(rnest) 21
Hunt, Violet 53
Jacobs, W(illiam) W(ymark) 22
James, Montague (Rhodes) 6
Jerome, Jerome K(lapka) 23
Johnson, Lionel (Pigot) 19
Kaye-Smith, Sheila 20
Keynes, John Maynard 64
Kipling, (Joseph) Rudyard 8, 17
Laski, Harold J(oseph) 79
Lawrence, D(avid) H(erbert Richards) 2, 9, 16, 33, 48, 61, 93
Lawrence, T(homas) E(dward) 18
Lee, Vernon 5
Lee-Hamilton, Eugene (Jacob) 22
Leverson, Ada 18
Lindsay, David 15
Lowndes, Marie Adelaide (Belloc) 12
Lowry, (Clarence) Malcolm 6, 40
Lucas, E(dward) V(errall) 73
Macaulay, (Emilie) Rose 7, 44
MacCarthy, (Charles Otto) Desmond 36
Mackenzie, Compton (Edward Montague) 116
Maitland, Frederic William 65
Manning, Frederic 25
Marsh, Edward 99
McTaggart, John McTaggart Ellis 105
Meredith, George 17, 43
Mew, Charlotte (Mary) 8
Meynell, Alice (Christina Gertrude Thompson) 6
Middleton, Richard (Barham) 56
Milne, A(lan) A(lexander) 6, 88
Moore, G. E. 89
Morrison, Arthur 72
Muggeridge, Thomas (Malcom) 120
Murry, John Middleton 16
Myers, L(eopold) H(amilton) 59
Nightingale, Florence 85
Noyes, Alfred 7
Oppenheim, E(dward) Phillips 45
Owen, Wilfred (Edward Salter) 5, 27
Pankhurst, Emmeline (Goulden) 100

Pinero, Arthur Wing 32
Powys, T(heodore) F(rancis) 9
Quiller-Couch, Arthur (Thomas) 53
Richardson, Dorothy Miller 3
Rolfe, Frederick (William Serafino Austin Lewis Mary) 12
Rosenberg, Isaac 12
Ruskin, John 20
Sabatini, Rafael 47
Saintsbury, George (Edward Bateman) 31
Sapper 44
Sayers, Dorothy L(eigh) 2, 15
Shiel, M(atthew) P(hipps) 8
Sinclair, May 3, 11
Stapledon, (William) Olaf 22
Stead, William Thomas 48
Stephen, Leslie 23
Strachey, (Giles) Lytton 12
Summers, (Alphonsus Joseph-Mary Augustus) Montague 16
Sutro, Alfred 6
Swinburne, Algernon Charles 8, 36
Symons, Arthur 11
Thomas, (Philip) Edward 10
Thompson, Francis (Joseph) 4
Tomlinson, H(enry) M(ajor) 71
Trotter, Wilfred 97
Upward, Allen 85
Van Druten, John (William) 2
Wakefield, Herbert (Russell) 120
Wallace, (Richard Horatio) Edgar 57
Wallas, Graham 91
Walpole, Hugh (Seymour) 5
Ward, Mary Augusta 55
Warung, Price 45
Webb, Mary Gladys (Meredith) 24
Webb, Sidney (James) 22
Welch, (Maurice) Denton 22
Wells, H(erbert) G(eorge) 6, 12, 19
Whitehead, Alfred North 97
Williams, Charles (Walter Stansby) 1, 11
Wodehouse, P(elham) G(renville) 108
Woolf, (Adeline) Virginia 1, 5, 20, 43, 56, 101
Yonge, Charlotte (Mary) 48
Zangwill, Israel 16

ESTONIAN

Talvik, Heiti 87
Tammsaare, A(nton) H(ansen) 27

FINNISH

Leino, Eino 24
Soedergran, Edith (Irene) 31
Westermarck, Edward 87

FRENCH

Alain 41
Apollinaire, Guillaume 3, 8, 51
Arp, Jean 115
Artaud, Antonin (Marie Joseph) 3, 36
Barbusse, Henri 5
Barrès, (Auguste-)Maurice 47
Benda, Julien 60
Bergson, Henri(-Louis) 32
Bernanos, (Paul Louis) Georges 3
Bernhardt, Sarah (Henriette Rosine) 75
Bloy, Léon 22
Bourget, Paul (Charles Joseph) 12
Claudel, Paul (Louis Charles Marie) 2, 10
Cocteau, Jean (Maurice Eugene Clement) 119
Colette, (Sidonie-Gabrielle) 1, 5, 16
Coppee, Francois 25
Crevel, Rene 112
Daumal, Rene 14
Deleuze, Gilles 116
Desnos, Robert 22
Drieu la Rochelle, Pierre(-Eugène) 21
Dujardin, Edouard (Emile Louis) 13
Durkheim, Emile 55

Epstein, Jean 92
Fargue, Leon-Paul 11
Feydeau, Georges (Léon Jules Marie) 22
Gide, André (Paul Guillaume) 5, 12, 36
Giraudoux, Jean(-Hippolyte) 2, 7
Gourmont, Remy(-Marie-Charles) de 17
Halévy, Elie 104
Huysmans, Joris-Karl 7, 69
Jacob, (Cyprien-)Max 6
Jammes, Francis 75
Jarry, Alfred 2, 14
Larbaud, Valery (Nicolas) 9
Léautaud, Paul 83
Leblanc, Maurice (Marie Emile) 49
Leroux, Gaston 25
Lyotard, Jean-François 103
Martin du Gard, Roger 24
Melies, Georges 81
Mirbeau, Octave 55
Mistral, Frédéric 51
Nizan, Paul 40
Péguy, Charles (Pierre) 10
Péret, Benjamin 20
Proust, (Valentin-Louis-George-Eugène-)Marcel 7, 13, 33
Radiguet, Raymond 29
Renard, Jules 17
Rolland, Romain 23
Rostand, Edmond (Eugene Alexis) 6, 37
Roussel, Raymond 20
Saint-Exupéry, Antoine (Jean Baptiste Marie Roger) de 2, 56
Schwob, Marcel (Mayer André) 20
Sorel, Georges 91
Sully Prudhomme, René-François-Armand 31
Teilhard de Chardin, (Marie Joseph) Pierre 9
Valéry, (Ambroise) Paul (Toussaint Jules) 4, 15
Vallette, Marguerite Eymery 67
Verne, Jules (Gabriel) 6, 52
Vian, Boris 9
Weil, Simone (Adolphine) 23
Zola, Émile (Édouard Charles Antoine) 1, 6, 21, 41

GERMAN

Adorno, Theodor W(iesengrund) 111
Andreas-Salome, Lou 56
Arp, Jean 115
Auerbach, Erich 43
Ball, Hugo 104
Barlach, Ernst (Heinrich) 84
Benjamin, Walter 39
Benn, Gottfried 3
Borchert, Wolfgang 5
Brecht, (Eugen) Bertolt (Friedrich) 1, 6, 13, 35
Carossa, Hans 48
Cassirer, Ernst 61
Doeblin, Alfred 13
Einstein, Albert 65
Ewers, Hanns Heinz 12
Feuchtwanger, Lion 3
Frank, Bruno 81
Frisch, Max (Rudolf) 121
George, Stefan (Anton) 2, 14
Goebbels, (Paul) Joseph 68
Haeckel, Ernst Heinrich (Philipp August) 83
Hauptmann, Gerhart (Johann Robert) 4
Heym, Georg (Theodor Franz Arthur) 9
Heyse, Paul (Johann Ludwig von) 8
Hitler, Adolf 53
Horney, Karen (Clementine Theodore Danielsen) 71
Huch, Ricarda (Octavia) 13
Husserl, Edmund (Gustav Albrecht) 100
Kaiser, Georg 9
Klabund 44
Kolmar, Gertrud 40
Lasker-Schueler, Else 57

Liliencron, (Friedrich Adolf Axel) Detlev von **18**
Luxemburg, Rosa **63**
Mann, (Luiz) Heinrich **9**
Mann, (Paul) Thomas **2, 8, 14, 21, 35, 44, 60**
Mannheim, Karl **65**
Michels, Robert **88**
Morgenstern, Christian (Otto Josef Wolfgang) **8**
Neumann, Alfred **100**
Nietzsche, Friedrich (Wilhelm) **10, 18, 55**
Ophuls, Max **79**
Otto, Rudolf **85**
Plumpe, Friedrich Wilhelm **53**
Raabe, Wilhelm (Karl) **45**
Rilke, Rainer Maria **1, 6, 19**
Schwitters, Kurt (Hermann Edward Karl Julius) **95**
Simmel, Georg **64**
Spengler, Oswald (Arnold Gottfried) **25**
Sternheim, (William Adolf) Carl **8**
Sudermann, Hermann **15**
Toller, Ernst **10**
Vaihinger, Hans **71**
von Hartmann, Eduard **96**
Wassermann, (Karl) Jakob **6**
Weber, Max **69**
Wedekind, (Benjamin) Frank(lin) **7**
Wiene, Robert **56**

GHANIAN

Casely-Hayford, J(oseph) E(phraim) **24**

GREEK

Cavafy, C(onstantine) P(eter) **2, 7**
Kazantzakis, Nikos **2, 5, 33**
Palamas, Kostes **5**
Papadiamantis, Alexandros **29**
Sikelianos, Angelos **39**

HAITIAN

Roumain, Jacques (Jean Baptiste) **19**

HUNGARIAN

Ady, Endre **11**
Babits, Mihaly **14**
Csath, Geza **13**
Herzl, Theodor **36**
Horváth, Ödön von **45**
Jozsef, Attila **22**
Karinthy, Frigyes **47**
Mikszath, Kalman **31**
Molnár, Ferenc **20**
Moricz, Zsigmond **33**
Radnóti, Miklós **16**

ICELANDIC

Sigurjonsson, Johann **27**

INDIAN

Chatterji, Saratchandra **13**
Dasgupta, Surendranath **81**
Gandhi, Mohandas Karamchand **59**
Ghose, Aurabinda **63**
Iqbal, Muhammad **28**
Naidu, Sarojini **80**
Premchand **21**
Ramana Maharshi **84**
Tagore, Rabindranath **3, 53**
Vivekananda, Swami **88**

INDONESIAN

Anwar, Chairil **22**

IRANIAN

Hedabayat, Sādeq **21**

IRISH

A.E. **3, 10**
Baker, Jean H. **3, 10**
Cary, (Arthur) Joyce (Lunel) **1, 29**
Gogarty, Oliver St. John **15**
Gregory, Isabella Augusta (Persse) **1**
Harris, Frank **24**
Joyce, James (Augustine Aloysius) **3, 8, 16, 35, 52**
Ledwidge, Francis **23**
Martin, Violet Florence **51**
Moore, George Augustus **7**
O'Grady, Standish (James) **5**
Shaw, George Bernard **3, 9, 21, 45**
Somerville, Edith Oenone **51**
Stephens, James **4**
Synge, (Edmund) J(ohn) M(illington) **6, 37**
Tynan, Katharine **3**
Wilde, Oscar (Fingal O'Flahertie Wills) **1, 8, 23, 41**
Yeats, William Butler **1, 11, 18, 31, 93, 116**

ITALIAN

Alvaro, Corrado **60**
Betti, Ugo **5**
Brancati, Vitaliano **12**
Campana, Dino **20**
Carducci, Giosuè (Alessandro Giuseppe) **32**
Croce, Benedetto **37**
D'Annunzio, Gabriele **6, 40**
Deledda, Grazia (Cosima) **23**
Gentile, Giovanni **96**
Giacosa, Giuseppe **7**
Jovine, Francesco **79**
Levi, Primo **109**
Malaparte, Curzio **52**
Marinetti, Filippo Tommaso **10**
Montessori, Maria **103**
Mosca, Gaetano **75**
Mussolini, Benito (Amilcare Andrea) **96**
Papini, Giovanni **22**
Pareto, Vilfredo **69**
Pascoli, Giovanni **45**
Pavese, Cesare **3**
Pirandello, Luigi **4, 29**
Saba, Umberto **33**
Tozzi, Federigo **31**
Verga, Giovanni (Carmelo) **3**

JAMAICAN

De Lisser, H(erbert) G(eorge) **12**
Garvey, Marcus (Moziah Jr.) **41**
Mais, Roger **8**
Redcam, Tom **25**

JAPANESE

Akutagawa Ryunosuke **16**
Dazai Osamu **11**
Futabatei, Shimei **44**
Hagiwara, Sakutaro **60**
Hayashi, Fumiko **27**
Ishikawa, Takuboku **15**
Kunikida, Doppo **99**
Masaoka, Shiki **18**
Miyamoto, (Chujo) Yuriko **37**
Miyazawa, Kenji **76**
Mizoguchi, Kenji **72**
Mori Ogai **14**
Nagai, Kafu **51**
Nishida, Kitaro **83**
Noguchi, Yone **80**
Santoka, Taneda **72**
Shimazaki Toson **5**
Suzuki, Daisetz Teitaro **109**
Yokomitsu, Riichi **47**
Yosano Akiko **59**

LATVIAN

Berlin, Isaiah **105**
Rainis, Jānis **29**

LEBANESE

Gibran, Kahlil **1, 9**

LESOTHAN

Mofolo, Thomas (Mokopu) **22**

LITHUANIAN

Kreve (Mickevicius), Vincas **27**

MEXICAN

Azuela, Mariano **3**
Gamboa, Federico **36**
Gonzalez Martinez, Enrique **72**
Nervo, (Jose) Amado (Ruiz de) **11**
Reyes, Alfonso **33**
Romero, José Rubén **14**
Villaurrutia, Xavier **80**

NEPALI

Devkota, Laxmiprasad **23**

NEW ZEALANDER

Mander, (Mary) Jane **31**

NICARAGUAN

Darío, Rubén **4**

NORWEGIAN

Bjoernson, Bjoernstjerne (Martinius) **7, 37**
Bojer, Johan **64**
Grieg, (Johan) Nordahl (Brun) **10**
Ibsen, Henrik (Johan) **2, 8, 16, 37, 52**
Kielland, Alexander Lange **5**
Lie, Jonas (Lauritz Idemil) **5**
Obstfelder, Sigbjoern **23**
Skram, Amalie (Bertha) **25**
Undset, Sigrid **3**

PAKISTANI

Iqbal, Muhammad **28**

PERUVIAN

Palma, Ricardo **29**
Vallejo, César (Abraham) **3, 56**

POLISH

Asch, Sholem **3**
Borowski, Tadeusz **9**
Conrad, Joseph **1, 6, 13, 25, 43, 57**
Peretz, Isaac Loeb **16**
Prus, Boleslaw **48**
Przybyszewski, Stanislaw **36**
Reymont, Wladyslaw (Stanislaw) **5**
Schulz, Bruno **5, 51**
Sienkiewicz, Henryk (Adam Alexander Pius) **3**
Singer, Israel Joshua **33**
Witkiewicz, Stanislaw Ignacy **8**

PORTUGUESE

Pessoa, Fernando (António Nogueira) **27**
Sa-Carniero, Mario de **83**

PUERTO RICAN

Hostos (y Bonilla), Eugenio Maria de **24**

ROMANIAN

Bacovia, George **24**
Caragiale, Ion Luca **76**
Rebreanu, Liviu **28**

RUSSIAN

Aldanov, Mark (Alexandrovich) **23**
Andreyev, Leonid (Nikolaevich) **3**
Annensky, Innokenty (Fyodorovich) **14**
Artsybashev, Mikhail (Petrovich) **31**

Babel, Isaak (Emmanuilovich) **2, 13**
Bagritsky, Eduard **60**
Balmont, Konstantin (Dmitriyevich) **11**
Bely, Andrey **7**
Berdyaev, Nikolai (Aleksandrovich) **67**
Bergelson, David **81**
Blok, Alexander (Alexandrovich) **5**
Bryusov, Valery Yakovlevich **10**
Bulgakov, Mikhail (Afanas'evich) **2, 16**
Bulgya, Alexander Alexandrovich **53**
Bunin, Ivan Alexeyevich **6**
Chekhov, Anton (Pavlovich) **3, 10, 31, 55, 96**
Der Nister **56**
Eisenstein, Sergei (Mikhailovich) **57**
Esenin, Sergei (Alexandrovich) **4**
Fadeyev, Alexander **53**
Gladkov, Fyodor (Vasilyevich) **27**
Gumilev, Nikolai (Stepanovich) **60**
Gurdjieff, G(eorgei) I(vanovich) **71**
Guro, Elena **56**
Hippius, Zinaida **9**
Ilf, Ilya **21**
Ivanov, Vyacheslav Ivanovich **33**
Kandinsky, Wassily **92**
Khlebnikov, Velimir **20**
Khodasevich, Vladislav (Felitsianovich) **15**
Klimentov, Andrei Platonovich **14**
Korolenko, Vladimir Galaktionovich **22**
Kropotkin, Peter (Aleksieevich) **36**
Kuprin, Aleksander Ivanovich **5**
Kuzmin, Mikhail **40**
Lenin, V. I. **67**
Mandelstam, Osip (Emilievich) **2, 6**
Mayakovski, Vladimir (Vladimirovich) **4, 18**
Merezhkovsky, Dmitry Sergeyevich **29**
Nabokov, Vladimir (Vladimirovich) **108**
Pavlov, Ivan Petrovich **91**
Petrov, Evgeny **21**
Pilnyak, Boris **23**
Prishvin, Mikhail **75**
Remizov, Aleksei (Mikhailovich) **27**
Rozanov, Vassili **104**
Shestov, Lev **56**
Sologub, Fyodor **9**
Stalin, Joseph **92**
Tolstoy, Alexey Nikolaevich **18**
Tolstoy, Leo (Nikolaevich) **4, 11, 17, 28, 44, 79**
Trotsky, Leon **22**
Tsvetaeva (Efron), Marina (Ivanovna) **7, 35**
Zabolotsky, Nikolai Alekseevich **52**
Zamyatin, Evgeny Ivanovich **8, 37**
Zhdanov, Andrei Alexandrovich **18**
Zoshchenko, Mikhail (Mikhailovich) **15**

SCOTTISH

Barrie, J(ames) M(atthew) **2**
Brown, George Douglas **28**
Buchan, John **41**
Cunninghame Graham, Robert (Gallnigad) Bontine **19**
Davidson, John **24**
Doyle, Arthur Conan **7**
Frazer, J(ames) G(eorge) **32**
Lang, Andrew **16**
MacDonald, George **9, 113**
Muir, Edwin **2, 87**
Murray, James Augustus Henry **117**
Sharp, William **39**
Tey, Josephine **14**

SLOVENIAN

Cankar, Ivan **105**

SOUTH AFRICAN

Bosman, Herman Charles **49**
Campbell, (Ignatius) Roy (Dunnachie) **5**
Mqhayi, S(amuel) E(dward) K(rune Loliwe) **25**
Plaatje, Sol(omon) T(shekisho) **73**
Schreiner, Olive (Emilie Albertina) **9**
Smith, Pauline (Urmson) **25**
Vilakazi, Benedict Wallet **37**

SPANISH

Alas (y Urena), Leopoldo (Enrique Garcia) **29**
Aleixandre, Vicente **113**
Barea, Arturo **14**
Baroja (y Nessi), Pio **8**
Benavente (y Martinez), Jacinto **3**
Blasco Ibáñez, Vicente **12**
Echegaray (y Eizaguirre), Jose (Maria Waldo) **4**
García Lorca, Federico **1, 7, 49**
Jiménez (Mantecón), Juan Ramón **4**
Machado (y Ruiz), Antonio **3**
Martinez Sierra, Gregorio **6**
Martinez Sierra, Maria (de la O'LeJarraga) **6**
Miro (Ferrer), Gabriel (Francisco Victor) **5**
Ortega y Gasset, José **9**
Pereda (y Sanchez de Porrua), Jose Maria de **16**
Pérez Galdós, Benito **27**
Ramoacn y Cajal, Santiago **93**
Salinas (y Serrano), Pedro **17**
Unamuno (y Jugo), Miguel de **2, 9**
Valera y Alcala-Galiano, Juan **10**
Valle-Inclán, Ramón (Maria) del **5**

SWEDISH

Bengtsson, Frans (Gunnar) **48**
Dagerman, Stig (Halvard) **17**
Ekelund, Vilhelm **75**
Heidenstam, (Carl Gustaf) Verner von **5**
Key, Ellen (Karolina Sofia) **65**
Lagerloef, Selma (Ottiliana Lovisa) **4, 36**
Söderberg, Hjalmar **39**
Strindberg, (Johan) August **1, 8, 21, 47**

SWISS

Ramuz, Charles-Ferdinand **33**
Rod, Edouard **52**
Saussure, Ferdinand de **49**
Spitteler, Carl (Friedrich Georg) **12**
Walser, Robert **18**

SYRIAN

Gibran, Kahlil **1, 9**

TURKISH

Sait Faik **23**

UKRAINIAN

Aleichem, Sholom **1, 35**
Bialik, Chaim Nachman **25**

URUGUAYAN

Quiroga, Horacio (Sylvestre) **20**
Sánchez, Florencio **37**

WELSH

Davies, William Henry **5**
Evans, Caradoc **85**
Lewis, Alun **3**
Thomas, Dylan (Marlais) **1, 8, 45, 105**

ISBN 0-7876-5936-3